W9-DJI-198

493

1975
CATHOLIC
ALMANAC

FELICIAN A. FOY, O.F.M.
Editor

Our Sunday Visitor, Inc.
Huntington, Indiana 46750

Acknowledgements: NC News Service for coverage of news and documentary texts; *The Documents of Vatican II*, Walter M. Abbott, S.J., general editor, Herder and Herder, Association Press, New York, 1966, for quotations; *Annuario Pontificio, 1974; The Official Catholic Directory, 1974*, P. J. Kenedy & Sons, New York; The United States Mission Council, 1325 Massachusetts Ave. N.W., Washington, D.C., for U.S. foreign mission compilations and statistics; *1974 Britannica Book of the Year*, copyright 1974 by Encyclopaedia Britannica, Inc., Chicago, for reprinting with permission of statistics on religious population of the world; *Catholic Press Directory 1974; 1974 Directory of Catholic Communications Personnel*, National Catholic Office of Information. Other sources are credited in various entries.

Published with Ecclesiastical Approval

© *Copyright by Our Sunday Visitor, Inc., 1974*

ISBN 0-87973-818-9 Paperbound Edition
ISBN 0-87973-871-5 Clothbound Edition

Library of Congress Catalog Card Number: A43-2500

Published, printed and bound in U.S.A. by
Our Sunday Visitor, Inc.
Huntington, Indiana 46750

Table of Contents

Index

Abortion Payments: As long as the Supreme Court has ruled that abortion is a "constitutional right," Medicaid and any national health insurance program must pay for at least some abortions, according to a spokesman of the Department of Health, Education and Welfare. To do otherwise would be to discriminate against lower income women who could not pay for an abortion themselves, he said, adding that he opposed Congressional efforts to prohibit the use of federal funds to pay for abortions.

OCTOBER 1974 BRIEFS

Draft Rejected

The Synod of Bishops rejected Oct. 22 three-fourths of a 40-page draft document on evangelization, leaving observers in the dark about what final recommendations would be made and what form they would take.

The document, drafted by a dozen synod participants and experts, was drawn from a mass of documentation created during three weeks of meetings. The documentation included over 200 speeches, plus reports of discussion groups on theological themes and pastoral experiences.

Some members of the synod felt that, while the draft touched on areas of current concern, it failed to address clearly specific problems faced by an evangelizing Church under contemporary conditions.

The one section of the document accepted "in substance" attempted to develop "an integral picture of what evangelization consists in," according to one bishop. Included were sections on the Church as the sacrament of salvation, the role of the Holy Spirit in evangelization, Christ as the center of evangelization, conversion and witness of life, and the importance of mass media in the work of evangelization.

But even this section, although approved by a wide majority, could be amended.

Archbishop Bernardin

Archbishop Joseph L. Bernardin of Cincinnati was the only bishop out of more than 200 at the Synod of Bishops to be elected on the first ballot with an absolute majority (103 of 197 votes) to serve on the body's general secretariat for the next three years.

The secretariat of 15 bishops acts as an interim body between assemblies of the synod to complete the business of the past one and to prepare for the next one.

The archbishop, in an address at one of the synodal meetings, said that "ecumenism is in danger today," but that the ecumenical movement must go on. "What is clear," he said, "is that unity cannot be achieved by compromise, that is, by relinquishing what is inseparable from Catholic existence . . . (But) the churches can and must proclaim to the world that, in the midst of our dismaying divisions, we all preach only one name under heaven by which all must be saved."

New Commissions

Pope Paul established two new commissions for the purpose of improving relations between the Church and the two great monotheistic non-Christian religions, Judaism and Islam.

The Commission for Catholic-Jewish Relations and the Commission for Catholic-Islamic Relations were linked, respectively, with the Secretariat for Promoting Christian Unity and the Secretariat for Non-Christians.

Canterbury Statement

Representatives of the Anglican clergy in England voted unanimously to welcome the agreed statement on ministry and ordination drawn up in 1973 by the Anglican-Roman Catholic International Commission of theologians. (See Canterbury Statement.)

Bus Decision

The U.S. Supreme Court upheld by a 7 to 2 vote a lower court ruling that states providing bus service to public school students as a public safety measure are not obliged to provide the same service for nonpublic school students.

A dissent written by Justice Byron White and joined in by Chief Justice Warren Burger contended that the decision may stretch the doctrine of separation of Church and state so far that it violates the First Amendment right of free exercise of religion by withholding public services from people because of their religion.

Violence in Boston

The National Catholic Conference for Interracial Justice decried what it called "the racism, lawlessness and violence of the white people of South Boston," and attacked President Gerald R. Ford for giving "moral support to racism in South Boston and across the country."

In a statement released in Boston, the conference's board of directors said they felt "a special pain and shame because so many people in South Boston share with us the Catholic faith." The conference called on Catholics in the area to support the observance of law and constitutional rights, and to condemn the racial hatred and violence flaring in weeks-long controversy over court-ordered busing of public schools students.

Catholic-Jewish Relations

Archbishop Jean Jadot, apostolic delegate in the United States, told leaders of the American Jewish Committee in New York that the issues of abortion and aid to private schools "should be subjected to a fuller, deeper and more open dialogue." The archbishop said that Catholic-Jewish relations "have recently run into rough water."

He added that some Catholic had the mistaken impression that "on the issues of Israel and Soviet Jewry, Jews have been successful and we have helped them; whereas, in regard to abortion and state aid to private schools, we have not been successful and Jews have opposed us."

President Ford placed a wreath on the tomb of missionary Father Eusebio Kino at Magdalena during his October trip to Mexico.

Archbishop Defended

Prelates of the Catholic, Orthodox and Protestant churches in Damascus, Syria, expressed their support for Archbishop Ilarion Capucci, Melkite-Rite patriarchal vicar for Jerusalem, who was being tried in Israel on charges of gun-running.

In a statement released by the headquarters of the Apostolic Exarchate for Melkite-Rite Catholics in the U.S., the nine clergymen said that the archbishop, as an Arab prelate and the pastor of Palestinian Arabs, was entitled to take a stand against "the illegal Israeli occupation of the West Bank and unlawful policy of occupying it with the aim of Judaizing the Holy City."

Signers of the statement included Melkite-Rite Patriarch Maximos V Hakim of Antioch and Syrian-Rite Archbishop Georges Chelhot of Damascus.

Archbishop Byrne Dies

Coadjutor-Archbishop Leo C. Byrne of St. Paul and Minneapolis died Oct. 21 in St. Paul, apparently of a cardiac arrest. He was found in his room at 8:15 a.m., but a coroner indicated his death had probably occurred between 2 a.m. and 4 a.m.

The 66-year-old archbishop, a native of St. Louis, had been vice president of the National Conference of Catholic Bishops since 1971. He was among the representatives of the U.S. bishops at the 1971 assembly of the Synod of Bishops.

ADDITIONS AND CHANGES

Cardinals (p. 197): Cardinal Ildebrando Antoniutti died Aug. 1, 1974; see page 105.

Diplomats at the Vatican (pp. 214-215): Australia, John Mills McMillan, Ambassador; Kenya, Henry Nzioka Mulli, Ambassador; Malawi, Joe Kachingwe, Ambassador; Portugal, Calvet de Magalhaes, Ambassador.

Episcopal Conferences (pp. 438-440): New Zealand, Bishop John P. Kavanaugh of Dunedin, President.

Canada (pp. 446-451): Hierarchy — Most Rev. Maurice Baudoux, Archbishop of St. Boniface, resigned Sept. 7, 1974. Most Rev. Gerard Couturier, Bishop of Hauterive, resigned Sept. 7, 1974. Rev. Louis de Gonzague Langevin, W.F., was appointed auxiliary bishop of St. Hyacinth, August, 1974.

U.S. Jurisdictions, Hierarchy (pp. 480-488): Diocese — The name of the Wheeling, W.Va., diocese was changed to Wheeling-Charleston, October, 1974.

Hierarchy — Appointments: Portland, Me., Edward C. O'Leary, auxiliary bishop from 1971, was named bishop in October, 1974. Yakima, Wash., Rev. Nicholas E. Walsh was ordained bishop Oct. 28, 1974.

Deaths — Archbishop Leo C. Byrne, coadjutor of St. Paul and Minneapolis, Oct. 21, 1974.

American Missionary Bishops (pp. 488-489): Resignation — Melkite Rite Archbishop Joseph Raya of Acre, Israel (see Index).

Cathedrals (pp. 497-498): Sacred Heart Church, Charleston, W. Va., is the co-cathedral of the Wheeling-Charleston diocese.

National Catholic Conferences (pp. 501-503): Officers: — President scheduled to be elected at November, 1974, meeting to succeed Cardinal John J. Krol on the expiration of his three-year term.

Archbishop Leo C. Byrne, vice-president, died Oct. 21, 1974.

State Catholic Conferences (page 506): Charles M. Phillips, executive director of the Wisconsin Catholic Conference, was elected president of the National Association of State Catholic Conference Directors, August, 1974.

Rev. Michael F. Groden was named acting director of the Massachusetts State Catholic Conference, to succeed Joseph J. Reilly who resigned.

United States Catholic Mission Council (p. 582): Rev. Anthony Bellagamba, I.M.C., was appointed acting director to succeed Bro. Thomas More Page, S.X., who was named executive secretary of the Conference of Major Superiors of Men.

Pontifical Academy of Sciences (pp. 621-622): Sir Hugh Taylor, American member of the Academy, died Apr. 17, 1974; see page 106.

Radio, Television, Theatre (pp. 681-682): The National Theatre Arts Conference ceased operations June 15, 1974.

American Catholic Awards (pp. 689-696): The National Theatre Arts Conference (see above) presented its 1974 and last award to Karamu Play House, Cleveland.

John Courtney Murray Award: Rev. Bernard Lonergan, S.J. (1973); George H. Tavard, A.A. (1974).

Mater et Magistra Award, Mother Teresa (1974).

PUBLICATION HISTORY

The Catholic Almanac originated, remotely, from *St. Anthony's Almanac*, a 64-page annual with calendar, feature and devotional contents, published by the Franciscans of Holy Name Province from 1904 to 1929.

Completely revised and enlarged, the publication was issued under the title, *The Franciscan Almanac*, by *The Franciscan Magazine* from 1931 to 1933 and by St. Anthony's Guild from 1936 to 1971. From 1940 to 1969 its title was *The National Catholic Almanac;* the present title was adopted in 1969. The 1959 to 1971 editions were produced jointly by St. Anthony's Guild and Doubleday & Co., Inc.

The Almanac was acquired in 1971 by Our Sunday Visitor, Inc., Huntington, Ind. 46750, publisher of this 1975 edition.

NOVEMBER 1973

VATICAN

Holiness — Men become saints with the help of Christ and hard work, Pope Paul told a gathering of thousands of persons in St. Peter's Square on All Saints' Day, Nov. 1. Speaking of factors resulting in holiness, he said: "One is freely given, the grace of Christ, the only genuine source of holiness and life. The other is more difficult for us, our personal striving toward moral justice, ascetic observance and evangelical perfection." The Pontiff called holiness the highest value man can know, "a victory over death and a gift for eternal life."

Cemetery Visit — The Holy Father joined large crowds on All Souls' Day, Nov. 2, at Verano, the principal municipal cemetery inside the walls of Rome, to pray with them for their "dear departed." He made the visit to demonstrate his desire to be close to the people of his Diocese of Rome on a day charged with great emotional overtones.

United Europe — A united Europe can be achieved only by "uniting audacity with realism," Pope Paul told Cornelius Berkhouver, president of the private organization called the Parliament of Europe, Nov. 9. The purposes of such union, he indicated, should be to promote cooperation by the various nations for the solution of mutual problems and to make "more equal and more humane . . . the conditions of life for all and everyone, without any discrimination."

Third World Aid — The Pope criticized rich countries for failing to set apart at least one per cent of their national incomes to help developing countries, at a Nov. 16 reception for more than 600 participants in the 17th annual meeting of the United Nations Food and Agriculture Organization. While praising FAO agricultural development programs, he called attention to the fact that aid from wealthy nations to the Third World was diminishing rather than increasing. He also stated that contributions of aid had not yet reached the UN-set quota of one per cent of gross national products.

Religious Life — The vows of poverty, chastity and obedience, together with communal life, are unrenounceable elements of the religious life, Pope Paul told 350 participants in the annual general assembly of the International Union of Religious Superiors General. He called religious institutes "a deep source of hope for the Church," and said that religious living according to essential elements of the Gospel give the world "an irreplaceable witness within the heart of the Church." The Pope decried any tendency to laicize religious life, noting that its "criterion and strength do not lie in social or apostolic activity, however beneficial, but in total consecration to the Lord."

Power of the Media — The potential of the communications media for good and for evil was the theme of an address by the Pope Nov. 17 at a meeting with Italian diocesan directors of social communications. He encouraged the directors to use the media in order "to facilitate the communication of the Gospel message to the modern world."

Serve but Don't Surrender — In one of a series of commentaries on the meaning of Holy Year 1975, the Pope urged a general audience Nov. 21 to appreciate and serve the world but never to surrender to it. A Christian can live in the world and not be overwhelmed by it, he declared, if he establishes rapport with God and his fellowmen and if he is guided by the advice of St. Paul not to conform to the world but, instead, to transform it.

Vocation Crisis — The Holy Father said Nov. 21 that he was hopeful about the outcome of the vocation crisis even though it was "the center of the most urgent preoccupation and concern in the Church." He called on delegates to the International Congress on Plans of Pastoral Action for Vocations (to the priesthood) to "work with faith in God because vocations are the work of God before they are the work of man, and in the young whose generosity today is not less than it was yesterday."

Ukrainian Patriarchate — The Pope assured Ukrainian Catholics Nov. 24 that he was very aware of their problems and had a "sincere desire" to work them out as best he could. He made his remarks against a background of several years of tension generated by Ukrainian demands for a patriarchate of their own headed by Cardinal Josyf Slipyi. Vatican reluctance to establish a patriarchate was based on reasons of history (the Ukrainians had never had a patriarch) and canon law (a patriarch could not function in the Ukraine, where the rite was outlawed by the Soviet government). Members of the Society for a Patriarchal System in the Ukrainian Catholic Church maintained that the Vatican was refusing to establish a patriarchate because such an action would jeopardize political and ecumenical efforts to better relations between the Soviet government, the Russian Orthodox Church and the Vatican.

Energy Crisis — Christians should cooperate fully and patriotically with energy-saving measures during the fuel crisis in Italy, and should also try to help their neighbors in need, Pope Paul told a gathering in St. Peter's Square Nov. 25. "Austerity," he said, "is with us. . . . But let us not lament the sacrifices which now befall us if they do away with our squanderings and excesses." From this "bitter experience" of deprivation, he added, people should "seek new and better principles as a guide to living together."

Reconciliation of Disaffected Catholics — The reconciliation of "those sons of the Church who, without officially breaking with the Church, find themselves in an unusual position in regard to it," was the subject matter of the Pope's address to a general audience Nov. 28. Such persons, he said, "wish to remain in communion with the Church, but they find themselves in an attitude of criticism and contestation." They so disrupt the Church that "they themselves tear up the roots of the vital plant which sustains them." Next, "they appeal to the pluralism of theological interpretations . . . without seeing that they thus construct their own doctrines which are comfortable and easy to adhere to, if not directly contrary to the norms and objectivity of the faith." The Holy Father said that such persons cause him "great sorrow, tempered only by a sentiment of even greater charity for them."

The Pope Also:
• Presided Nov. 5 at a Mass for nine cardinals who died since November, 1972: Fernando Cento, Giuseppe Ferretto, Cesare Zerba, Achille Lienart, Joseph Lefebvre, Benjamin de Arriba Castro, Arcadio Maria Larraona, Rufino Santos, William Heard.
• Told 2,600 Italian soldiers based in Rome that military duty matures young men and grounds them in virtues that help them all through their lives, Nov. 7.
• Assured Adolphe Binagana, Burundi's new ambassador to the Vatican, of the Church's desire to help the thousands of victims of tribal warfare in his country, Nov. 15.
• Called the Shroud of Turin a "precious and pious relic" in comment about a Nov. 23 telecast featuring the linen sheet in which many believe the body of Christ was wrapped for burial after the crucifixion.
• Told President Albert-Bernard Bongo of Gabon that "without freedom, every effort (for the benefit of the people of his country) would be of no avail," Nov. 26.
• Was told Nov. 29 by Owson Paul Gabites, New Zealand's first ambassador to the Vatican, that the "Holy See has done much in the last 25 years or so to restore the damage caused by war and conflict."

Vatican Briefs:
• "Woman as a person, biblical-theological studies on woman in terms of God's plan, women in society and women in the Church," were the four subjects assigned to committees for research by the Commission on The Role of Women in Society and in the Church at the conclusion of its first three-day general meeting, Nov. 17.
• Historian Father Robert Graham, S.J., called the film "Massacre in Rome," which portrayed Pope Pius XII as indifferent to the Nazi massacre of 335 Italians in Rome during World War II, "a total distortion of history."

Light of Hope in Middle East

Pope Paul gave thanks at a general audience Nov. 14 for "a light of hope" shining once more over the Middle East. "Over the horizon of the Middle East, lately darkened by the outbreak of a bloody conflict, there now shines again a light of hope," he said in a statement concerning the Egyptian-Israeli truce announced Nov. 11.

The Pope expressed his appreciation "to those who undertook the (peace) initiative and to those who have cooperated with it in order to reweave with trusting patience the thread of an agreement on a cease-fire . . . so as to open the way to a . . . peace conference." He encouraged those involved in peace-making efforts "to act with long-sighted wisdom and decisive will . . . (for) a definitive and acceptable peaceful solution" to the Arab-Israeli conflict.

DOMESTIC

Abortion, Sterilization Training — The *St. Louis Review* reported early in the month that the federal government, through the Agency for International Development, had granted $840,798 to Washington University's medical school for training foreign doctors in methods of abortion, sterilization and birth prevention. The grant "once again shows the tendency within AID to ignore the value questions that motivate couples regarding family size and the spacing of births," commented Msgr. James T. McHugh, director of the Family Life Division, U.S. Catholic Conference.

Sterilization Practices — A study of sterilization practices published by the Health Research Group, an affiliate of Ralph Nader's Public Citizens, Inc., prompted this statement by Sister Virginia Schwager, director of Health Affairs, U.S. Catholic Conference: "We find regrettable the disclosure that the nationwide upsurge in surgical sterilization is due in no small measure to the lack of information on the part of patients as to the irreversible nature of this operation and its possible adverse physiological and psychological consequences." The study included an analysis of sterilization practices in major U.S. medical centers and focused on the lack of informed consent for sterilization, as well as coercive techniques used to induce patients to submit to it. It was reported that 100,000 men and a comparable number of women sterilized each year were unaware of the irreversible nature of the operation.

Greatest Force in the World — Without the influence of the Catholic Church, "the greatest international, universal force in the world," other international organizations could not function effectively, declared David

A. Morse, special assistant to the director of the UN Development Program, during an interview in Albany, N.Y. Morse based his opinion on the experience of his acquaintance with Popes Pius XII, John XXIII and Paul VI, and his working relations with church personnel and agencies during his 1948 to 1970 tenure as head of the International Labor Organization.

New Jersey School Equipment Auction — More than 60 per cent of the nonpublic schools in New Jersey were successful in bids to retain possession of state-provided educational equipment which the state had been ordered to reclaim. Purchases of the balance by some public school boards, resulting in the loss of equipment by poorer nonpublic schools, as in Jersey City and Blackwood, caused considerable controversy. In other cases, as in Paterson, successful public school bidders made arrangements for resale of the equipment to nonpublic schools.

The statute under which equipment worth $7.5 million had been provided to nonpublic schools was declared unconstitutional in April, 1973, and in July a three-judge federal panel ordered repossession of the equipment by October 31. In lieu of repossession and the expenses it would have entailed, the state instituted public sale of the material by closed bids.

Prisoners of War — Seventeen Catholic, Protestant, Jewish and Orthodox churchmen, in a paid advertisement appearing in the Nov. 7 edition of *The New York Times,* called on governments involved in the Arab-Israeli conflict to "implement without further delay" the prisoner-of-war provisions of the 1949 Geneva Convention — requiring that lists of prisoners be provided by both sides, that all seriously ill prisoners be returned immediately, and that all prisoners be repatriated immediately after the cessation of hostilities.

Women Religious — A task force of 11 nuns and one priest sponsored by the Washington, D.C., ecumenical Center of Concern recommended in a report that women religious as well as men religious and priests be made eligible for appointment as vicars of religious "without discrimination."

Repression in Chile — Father Frederick A. McGuire, C.M., commenting on observations made during a Nov. 4 to 11 visit to Chile, criticized "widespread and systematic repression of human rights" there following the coup which overthrew the government of Salvador Allende in September.

No to Intercommunion Request — The Vatican Secretariat for Promoting Christian Unity rejected a petition for intercommunion by the members of a Catholic and an Episcopal parish in Southbridge, Mass. The petition, made in June and turned down in July, 1973, was made by the pastors and 40 members of the parishes.

No Compromise — For Catholic hospitals, no compromise is possible regarding the issues of abortion, euthanasia or contraceptive sterilization, declared Father Kevin O'Rourke, director of medical-moral affairs for the Catholic Hospital Association, at a meeting with 90 hospital administrators and attorneys in Atlanta. He made the statement at the first of six legal institutes designed to develop ways and means of counteracting challenges posed to Catholic hospitals by the pro-abortion rulings handed down by the U.S. Supreme Court Jan. 22, 1973.

Foot-Dragging on Civil Rights — Father Theodore M. Hesburgh, C.S.C., president of Notre Dame University and former chairman of the U.S. Civil Rights Commission, told a news conference Nov. 14 in Indianapolis that President Nixon's failure to appoint a new commission chairman was evidence of his readiness to let the civil rights movement "die on the vine." He also said that "leadership across the board" — by the White House, Congress, state and local governments — was necessary for revival of the movement. He added, however, that "direction is coming from nobody."

CYO Convention — Approximately 3,100 teenagers and young adults attended sessions of the Nov. 15 to 18 CYO convention in Indianapolis. William S. Fahm, Jr., a Notre Dame University freshman, was elected president of the teenage section. Entertainer Danny Thomas was given the CYO God and Youth Award for his work in founding and supporting the St. Jude Children's Research Hospital in Memphis.

Woodstock College — Officials of the New York and Baltimore provinces of the Jesuits announced that their Woodstock College seminary would be transformed into a Washington, D.C., center of theological reflection. The college, founded in 1869 in Woodstock, Md., was moved to New York City in 1969 and aligned with the Union Theological Seminary and the Jewish Theological Seminary. Its closing as a seminary, announced in January, 1973, was expected in 1974.

No Apartment Living for Priests — Coadjutor Archbishop Leo C. Byrne of St. Paul-Minneapolis rejected an apartment-living plan for priests proposed by the archdiocesan priests' senate. He said the proposed experiment would not be advantageous to the priestly life of those involved, would not serve the general interests of the priesthood, and would be contrary to the welfare and needs of the faithful.

Domestic Briefs:
• Father Joseph B. Collins, S.S., a major figure in the catechetical movement, retired after 31 years of service as director, assistant director and consultant of the National Center of Religious Education — Confraternity of Christian Doctrine.

• An anonymous donor gave $100,000 and pledged $400,000 more over the next five years to keep Aquin High School operating in Cascade, Ia.

• Sister Ardeth Platte was elected Nov. 6 to a seat on the Saginaw, Mich., City Council.

• Bishop Michael J. Begley of Charlotte was elected chairman of the Catholic Committee of Appalachia Nov. 8.

• The National Catholic Rural Life Conference celebrated the 50th anniversary of its founding with jubilee ceremonies in Des Moines.

• National Bible Week was observed Nov. 18 to 25 under the auspices of the ecumenical Laymen's National Bible Committee.

• Bishop James W. Malone of Youngstown was elected president of the ecumenical Ohio Council of Churches Nov. 26.

• Written commitments to daily family prayer were sought from some 6,000 people by Father Patrick Peyton, C.S.C., at a Festival of Prayer rally in St. Louis.

Bishops' Meeting

Internal and external affairs of the Church made up the agenda of the annual meeting of the National Conference of Catholic Bishops and the United States Catholic Conference Nov. 12 to 16 in Washington, D.C.

The bishops issued a pastoral letter on Mary entitled "Behold Your Mother, Woman of Faith." They also agreed that a Vatican directive concerning first confession and first Communion practices required that children be given the opportunity of receiving the sacrament of penance at the same time they make their first Communion. They voted down a motion to ask the Vatican for permission to introduce in-hand reception of Holy Communion in this country, but approved making a request for authorization to establish two new lay ministries — minister of music and catechist.

In other areas, the meeting issued statements on abortion, UN Population Year 1974, penal reform, the crisis in the Middle East, and support for strike and/or boycott action by Farah garment workers and members of the United Farm Workers of America. (See separate article.)

FOREIGN

Schools Taken Over in Chile — By the beginning of the month military authorities in Chile had removed and replaced approximately 35 directors of state high schools and had taken control of two Catholic (Santiago and Valparaiso) and six other universities, in the wake of the coup which toppled the government of former President Salvador Allende.

Bethlehem University — Bethlehem University, organized by a group of Christian Brothers from the United States to serve the higher educational needs of the West Bank Arab community, began its second month of operations with an enrollment of 90 students.

It was hoped that the school, projected as a four-year institution, would plug the brain-drain of students from the area.

Priest Gets 12 Years — Father Patrick Fell, found guilty of having recruited men for a unit of the outlawed Irish Republican Army and of plotting a bombing campaign in Coventry, England, was sentenced Nov. 6 to a prison term of 12 years. The sentencing judge told the 32-year-old assistant pastor: "I believe it would be right to say that some of those in Coventry, who have taken maybe only minor parts in activities of this sort, have been induced to do so because of you. There is a heavy load of guilt on your shoulders, Father Fell, not only for what you have done but for what you caused others to do."

Religious Discrimination — Following a debate in which a Soviet representative, Valeri Loshchinin, attacked the Catholic Church and accused the committee of bias, a United Nations committee failed for the 13th year to agree on a draft declaration against religious discrimination. The proposed declaration was related to Article 18 of the Universal Declaration of Human Rights, proclaiming the right of everyone to freedom of thought, conscience and religion, and freedom to manifest the right in teaching, practice, worship and observance.

Silence about Violence — Cardinal William Conway of Armagh deplored "a cloak of almost total silence" by government officials covering a campaign by extremists "of indiscriminate murder (of more than 150 persons since the beginning of 1972) and destruction against Catholics" in Northern Ireland. He said that the Catholic population "passionately desires peace and an end to all violence," and that "the Protestant population as a whole also detests and abhors these sectarian killings." Yet, he added, the government's concern about the murder campaign "does not appear to be reflected either in official statements or in the promptness or extent of measures taken to combat it."

Anglican Synod — The General Synod of the Church of England voted Nov. 7 for retention of its rules under which a divorced person may not be allowed to remarry in church but may, with the bishop's approval, be readmitted to communion along with the new marriage partner. The synod also voted in support of efforts to influence British investment practices as levers of change in the apartheid policies of South Africa.

Tension in Spain — Six priests, jailed for acts in support of Basque nationalism, burned their belongings Nov. 6 in the yard of their "special" prison at Zamora in protest against detention there rather than with other political prisoners, and went on a hunger strike to dramatize inhumane treatment of such prisoners by the government. Their action triggered anti-government demonstrations in the Basque provinces and an hours-long sit-in Nov. 10 and 11 by more than 100 priests, religious and lay persons at the offices of the papal nuncio in Madrid. Late in the month prelates attending a meeting of the Spanish Bishops' Conference in Madrid were informed that two of their colleagues — Bishops Antonio Anoveros of Bilbao and Antonio Palenzuela of Segovia — had been accused of unpublished charges of slandering and insulting the government.

Mission Reports — Conversions to Catholicism in East Asia declined in recent years, according to reports from bishops in Korea, Japan, Vietnam, Taiwan, Hong Kong and Macao. Among reasons for the decline, they said, were growing materialism and religious indifference, and the still unfulfilled need to adapt religious teaching and practice to the patterns of Asian culture.

Archbishop Duraisamy Lourdusamy, secretary of the Congregation for the Evangelization of Peoples, told members of the Pontifical Association of the Holy Childhood in Pittsburgh that missionary work was progressing satisfactorily. He said: "Last year we took a survey of mission growth in Africa, Asia, Oceania, part of South America and many other countries, covering the past 20 years. Contrary to what we expected, the results were very encouraging, not only in the large growth in numbers but also in the quality of the people and the increasing number of church vocations."

Fides, the Vatican news service on missionary activities, reported that the Catholic Church in mainland China "has been completely swept away, as if by a tidal wave." The *Fides* report reflected the observations of recent visitors to China.

Portuguese Colonialism — Archbishop Emmanuel Milingo of Lusaka, Zambia, urged the Church to take the risk of actively supporting liberation movements against Portuguese colonialism in Mozambique and Angola as controversy continued over the extent and ferocity of atrocities allegedly committed by Portuguese troops in Mozambique in 1971 and 1972. The troops had been engaged for nearly 10 years in action against guerrillas of the Mozambique Liberation Front.

French Bishops — One hundred and 36 bishops and seven superiors of religious orders attended the Nov. 3 to 10 annual plenary meeting of the French Bishops' Conference at Lourdes. In one set of actions, the participants initiated steps for the composition of a document on ministries in the Church. They also heard Cardinal Francois Marty defend the right of bishops to speak out on public issues. He said: "Responsible for a people, the bishop cannot in conscience not speak when he perceives the Gospel clashing with events."

Abortion in England — Approximately 10,000 persons swarmed through the House of Commons in London Nov. 20 to protest before their respective Members of Parliament against abortion-on-demand legislation in effect since 1967.

According to an article in a recent edition of the British *Police College Magazine,* the number of illegal abortions in Great Britain increased rather than decreased after passage of the 1967 Abortion Act. While the number of such abortions was not known, it was reported that more than 500,000 legal abortions had been performed since 1967.

More Missionaries Leave Sabah — Government refusal to issue new work permits forced three more Mill Hill Missionaries — for a total of 34 since March, 1970 — to leave the country during the month. Ten priests and two brothers of the society, along with 12 local priests and 60 sisters, remained to serve the 80,000 Catholics among the country's population of 600,000.

Foreign Briefs:

• The interdenominational Order of Christian Unity said in a letter to Mrs. Margaret Thatcher, British education minister, that there was an increasing movement against Christian education in many state secondary schools, despite the fact that nearly all public opinion polls showed that parents were strongly in favor of it.

• The Union of Major Superiors of France reported that one-third of the candidates for religious life in the country in the previous year had entered contemplative orders. The numbers of contemplatives were reported to be 1,775 men in 39 monasteries and 9,625 nuns in 319 convents.

• Radio July 9, the official station of the Sao Paulo archdiocese, was closed down by Brazilian authorities for what were called "national interests."

• Bishop Franz Hengsbach of Essen, president of Adveniat, reported that the German Catholic aid agency had made grants of $9.5 million for more than 1,600 projects in Latin America during the past year.

Canadian Catholic Conference

The Canadian Catholic Conference of bishops, meeting in Ottawa early in the month, approved plans for changing its organizational structure and operational procedures in order to improve regional as well as national efforts in matters of religious, liturgical, educational and social concern.

The bishops also issued a statement on the formation of conscience and a declaration that children preparing for their first reception of Holy Communion should at the same time be given the opportunity to receive the sacrament of penance. In another action, they set up a committee to study theological principles and pastoral guidelines for the charismatic movement.

(See separate article.)

DECEMBER 1973

VATICAN

Problem of God — Focusing attention on the "problem of God" for the second time in eight days, Pope Paul told a general audience Dec. 12 that many "men walk like blind men, deliberately blind, giving no thought to the existence and importance of the relations" between themselves and God. For some, he said, "the idea of God (is) so new, so grand and so superior to the capacity of human comprehension that the temptation arises to refuse to measure up to it. One prefers to deny it rather than accept the effort to adapt thought to the demands which derive from that idea." He added that "suppression of the 'problem of God' makes a problem of everything."

Canon Law — Pope Paul, in a Dec. 14 address to ecclesiastical judges and canon lawyers, said that the updating of the Code of Canon Law (in progress) is a valid way of giving new vitality to Christian life. The pastoral action of the Church, he declared, "would be rendered ineffective if it were deprived of a firm and wise juridical order.... Charity certainly has the priority; but without justice, which is expressed by laws, charity cannot even exist." The Pontiff put down the idea that laws "represent an arbitrary structure imposed from without" which limits the spiritual character of the biblical message for the true freedom of the sons of God.

Farmers — The Holy Father urged a group of young European farmers Dec. 14 not to be discouraged by "prophets of doom." He said: "Do not let yourselves be discouraged by the prophets of doom over the future of the rural world. (Your) struggle (to save the rural world of Europe and to promote solidarity with farming regions of the Third World) is not simply for new and efficacious structures that will assure the defense of the fields and their survival. This struggle must also be constantly inspired by a search for quality of life. It is not simply a question of having more but, above all, of being more."

Terrorism — "Tragic and detestable events (of terrorist violence) on the ... airfields of Fiumicino and in other countries" were the subject of the Pope's address to a general audience Dec. 19. His reference was to the actions of Arab guerrillas who firebombed a jetliner, killed some 30 persons, hijacked another airplane and took its passengers and crew as hostages Dec. 17 at the Rome airport, later killed another man at Athens and finally surrendered Dec. 19 to authorities in Kuwait.

Panorama of Problems — Problems and other matters of concern in the Church and the world formed the substance of Pope Paul's pre-Christmas address to a consistory of cardinals Dec. 21.

• Church Problems: Two characteristics of

them were movement and difficulty, and all were related somehow to the "germ of protest."

• Holy Year: Its proclamation is an example of the Church's readiness to proclaim her message to the world. "It seems to us that the two points proposed by this program — renewal and reconciliation — can recapitulate the hopes and desires for the life of the Church that we wish to foresee for the closing years of this century...."

• Canonization: The cardinals ratified the Pope's decision to canonize Blessed Teresa de Jesus Jornet Ibars, the Spanish foundress of a congregation of nuns for care of the abandoned poor. (See January News Events.)

More than half of the nearly 4,000-word address dealt with issues of war and peace.

• Middle East: The Pope pledged full cooperation with all negotiations which might "successfully guarantee for all parties concerned a tranquil and secure existence and recognition of their respective rights." He also spoke of his "special preoccupation" with the plight of Palestinian refugees.

• Southeast Asia, Indonesia: "We express the fervent wish that fresh hostilities will not occur in Vietnam. ... We permit ourself to exhort the governments of Saigon and Hanoi to pursue peace negotiations with sincerity, and we likewise express the hope that the people of South Vietnam will be enabled freely to express their desires in elections to be held under the effective control of the United Nations."

• Northern Ireland: While praising "prospects of a positive development" (related to proposals for participation by Catholics in the government), the Pope noted that "there has not been an end to deplorable manifestations of violence." He also noted disturbing situations in Africa and Latin America.

Midnight Mass Homily — In a pastoral homily delivered at Midnight Mass in St. Peter's Basilica, Pope Paul reflected on the birth of Christ, noting: "He came as a baby ... a child ... a worker ... a teacher ... a prophet ... as king of the people of God ... as redeemer to take upon himself all the sins of the world, as a victim in our place, the Lamb of God for mankind. He came for man's life and resurrection, he who is the Alpha and Omega of the universe. He came to make us sons of God.... Let no one think he has celebrated Christmas well unless he has felt himself possessed and almost overcome by this ever new discovery: He has come for me."

The Pope Also:

• Hailed the completion of a new bridge linking Asian and European Turkey across the Bosporus as a symbol of increasing union of the two continents, during a meeting with

Taha Carim, Turkey's new ambassador to the Vatican, Dec. 6.

• Met with a delegation of Russian Orthodox churchmen in Rome as guests of the Secretariat for Promoting Christian Unity, Dec. 13.

• Presided at the funeral of Cardinal Amleto G. Cicognani, former apostolic delegate to the U.S. and secretary of state to John XXIII and Paul VI, Dec. 19. (Another Cardinal, Giuseppe Beltrami, died Dec. 13.)

• Told Ignace Karuhije, Rwanda's new ambassador to the Vatican, that a nation's greatness depends not on its territorial holdings or military power but on the quality of its citizens, Dec. 20.

• Telegraphed his condolences to Francisco Franco, Spanish chief of state, on the assassination of Premier Luis Carrero Blanco, Dec. 21.

• Discussed Middle East peace prospects and concern for the status of Jerusalem with Ethiopian President Haile Selassie, President Gaafar al Nimeiry of Sudan, and representatives of the presidents of Liberia and Zambia, Dec. 22; and with President Habib Bourguiba of Tunisia, Dec. 14.

Mass Adaptations for Children — The Congregation for Divine Worship issued Dec. 20 a "Directory for Masses with Children" designed to initiate youngsters gradually into participation in the Mass. Father Frederick McManus, director of the secretariat of the U.S. Bishops' Committee on the Liturgy, called the 3,500-word document "a thorough attempt . . . to recognize the special needs of Christian children and to remove the principal obstacles to their full sharing in the liturgy."

Vatican Briefs:

• News reports that Pope Paul had been forced to curtail his activities because of a heart condition were denied by the Vatican Press Office Dec. 4.

• The 10-member international Catholic-Jewish Liaison Committee, following a Dec. 4 to 6 meeting in Antwerp, announced plans for a joint study of the moral and spiritual foundations of human rights and religious freedom in their respective religious traditions.

• The Vatican and the World Council of Churches pledged Dec. 7 to continue efforts to do away with "the deep causes of human suffering," in a joint statement marking the 25th anniversary of the UN's Universal Declaration of Human Rights.

Christmas Message

The contrast between secular and Christian humanism was the theme of Pope Paul's Christmas Day message "to the city and the world."

He said that "the humanism of modern culture and sociology . . . has become in some of its typical expressions a cosmic utopia that sets up man as man's god" and dares to affirm "that man is his own absolute cause."

Christian humanism, on the other hand, "recognizes and affirms man's preeminent origin . . . (as) a creature so fine, so noble, so worthy of all our enthusiasm and admiration as to show forth in himself, in his own essential being, 'the image and likeness' of God." Yet, "as he exists, man is not perfect. He is a being essentially in need of restoration (because of sin), of rehabilitation, of fullness, of perfection and of happiness. His is a life which does not suffice to itself; he needs a complement of life, an infinite complement. Exalt man and you will make more evident his deficiency, his incompleteness, his inner need . . . for a Savior."

DOMESTIC

Priests Smeared — Psychologist-author Eugene Kennedy, M.M., disputed the "sensationalism" of an article appearing in the Dec. 3 edition of *Newsweek,* stating it conveyed the impression that the incidence of illicit relationships between priests and women was widespread. Father Kennedy, who was interviewed by *Newsweek* in connection with the subject, said in a letter to the magazine: "I must dissociate myself from the overall impression created by the article on priests' dating. . . . It makes it seem that many American priests are abusing their vow of celibacy and leading sleazy and hypocritical lives. This is not true of men who, according to the extensive research I have conducted, keep their religious promises and try to approach all human relationships with integrity and responsibility."

Death with Dignity — The House of Delegates of the American Medical Association, meeting in Anaheim, Calif., adopted a death-with-dignity resolution providing: "The cessation of the employment of extraordinary means to prolong the life of the body, when there is irrefutable evidence that biological death is imminent, is the decision of the patient, and/or his immediate family." Delegates declared at the same time that mercy killing is contrary to the nature and purposes of the medical profession.

Ending South African Loans — Four of 10 American banks involved in recent loans to the South African government announced they were going to withdraw from existing loan plans or refrain from future loan commitments because they amounted to subsidizing white supremacist policies. The action by the banks followed publication of a report to this effect compiled by the Corporate Information Center of the National Council of Churches, a research agency on corporate investment responsibility. The banks were the Merchants National Bank and Trust Co. of Indianapolis, the City National Bank of Detroit, the Central National Bank of Chicago, and the Wachovia Bank and Trust Co. in North Carolina.

Problems in Puerto Rico — Cardinal Luis

Aponte Martinez and 250 priests, meeting Dec. 7 in San Juan, publicly confessed what they called their responsibility "for the anemia that is devouring" the Church in Puerto Rico. They charged themselves with abuse of their authority, paternalism, despotism and self-seeking.

Title I Aid — Seven national Jewish organizations petitioned the U.S. Supreme Court Dec. 7 to rule in a Missouri school aid case against allowing federally paid teachers to teach even nonreligious subjects on the premises of nonpublic schools. The organizations were the American Jewish Congress, the Anti-Defamation League of B'nai B'rith, the Jewish Labor Committee, the Jewish War Veterans, the National Council of Jewish Women, the Union of American Hebrew Congregations, and the United Synagogue of America.

First Seminary Site To Be Sold — Officials of the Society of St. Sulpice announced Dec. 11 that the site of the first Catholic seminary in the United States — St. Mary's, established in 1791 and closed in 1969 — would be sold to the City of Baltimore.

Our Lady of Charity of Cobre — The newest Marian shrine in the country, designed and built by Cuban refugees, was dedicated in Miami Dec. 2 in ceremonies presided over by Cardinal John J. Krol, president of the National Conference of Catholic Bishops. Archbishop Coleman F. Carroll of Miami said that the shrine, which was named for its patronal counterpart in Cuba, would "be to this area what the Statue of Liberty is to the northeast section of the U.S."

Retirement Checks — The St. Louis Archdiocesan Development Council announced Dec. 17 that Cardinal John Carberry had sent checks totaling $386,400 to 32 religious communities with members teaching in archdiocesan schools. In an accompanying letter, the cardinal said: "We are fully aware of the retirement needs of religious who have served God's people so devotedly over the years, and by this contribution we are trying to show the concern of all people who gave to the Development Fund."

Catholic Character of Notre Dame — A 14-member committee, reporting Dec. 18 on university priorities, said that the University of Notre Dame's "highest and also its most distinctive priority is to understand and to adhere to its evolving Catholic character. . . . To survive without its unique place in the minds of believers, and without its Catholic witnesses in the larger pluralistic society, would be not to survive as Notre Dame."

Juvenile Criminal Code — The first major reform of New Jersey's juvenile code in 40 years was signed into law by Gov. William T. Cahill Dec. 19, providing for the establishment of separate treatment for youths charged with minor offenses and those accused of more serious offenses.

Energy Crisis — The U.S. Catholic Conference urged the federal government Dec. 21 to consider the moral dimensions of the energy crisis and its effects on the poor. "A sound energy policy by the federal government should give highest priority to the moral imperatives of equity and human interdependence," stated Bishop James S. Rausch, general secretary of the conference, in a letter to William E. Simon, federal energy administrator.

Sterilization Law Unconstitutional — An Alabama law allowing state officials to sterilize mental patients was ruled unconstitutional by a three-judge federal court panel in Montgomery. The law "clearly and obviously" violated a patient's constitutional rights, the court said, because it contained "no provision for notice, hearing or any other procedures for safeguard." The suit at issue alleged that 14 persons had been sterilized over the previous 10 years in violation of their constitutional rights.

Domestic Briefs:
• Sister Mary Madonna Crawford of the Sisters of Mercy and Ursuline Sister Amadeus McKevitt were named vicar and associate vicar for religious, respectively, in the Providence diocese and the New York archdiocese.
• The Leadership Conference of Women Religious contributed more than $22,000 for the relief of drought victims in West Africa, announced Catholic Relief Services.
• Herbert W. Mullin was found guilty Dec. 11 of second-degree murder in the slaying of Father Henri Tomei Nov. 2, 1972, in the confessional of the parish church in Los Gatos, Calif.
• Father Daniel Berrigan, S.J., refused to accept the Gandhi Peace Prize after learning that its sponsors were considering withdrawal of its offer because of an anti-Israeli speech he delivered before an Arab audience in Washington, D.C., in October, 1973.

Top Stories of 1973

According to an NC News Service poll of 58 participating editors of Catholic newspapers across the nation, the leading news stories of Catholic interest in 1973 were as follows.

(1) The Jan. 22 decisions of the U.S. Supreme Court against the constitutionality of abortion statutes, and related reactions.

(2) Supreme Court decisions of June 25 against the constitutionality of nonpublic school aid laws and programs in New York and Pennsylvania.

(3) Developments related to a Vatican document made public July 9 which ordered an end to experiments delaying first confession by children until after their first reception of Holy Communion.

(4) Biomedical ethics.

(5) Struggle of the United Farm Workers of

America with the Teamsters and growers of lettuce and grapes in California over contracts and representation rights.

(6) Controversy over summer reruns of two November, 1972, episodes of the Maude TV series regarded as offensive in their treatment of abortion and sterilization.

(7) The Watergate scandal and its convoluted chain of events.

(8) Differences of opinion regarding the practice of in-hand reception of Holy Communion.

(9) The Jan. 27 Vietnam peace agreements, U.S. withdrawal from the war, the release of American prisoners of war, and the continuation of hostilities in Southeast Asia.

(10) Crises in Chile, culminating in overthrow of the Allende regime Sept. 11 and the imposition of rule by a military junta.

Another set of 10 stories of religious interest was selected by the Religion Newswriters Association, an organization for religion writers on daily newspapers, as follows.

(1) Continuing conflict between conservatives and moderates in the Lutheran Church-Missouri Synod.

(2) A continuing trend from social activism to more personal religion.

(3) The refusal of the Episcopal Church's General Convention to approve the ordination of women.

(4) Progress of the charismatic movement.

(5) Key 73, the year-long evangelistic crusade.

(6) Efforts of some parents to rescue their children from communities such as the Children of God.

(7) Vatican reaffirmation of the infallibility of the pope.

(8) Protestant-Catholic contestation in Northern Ireland.

(9) Endorsement by the U.S. Catholic Conference of the United Farm Workers of America boycott of lettuce and grapes, and Catholic support of strikers against the Farah Manufacturing Co.

(10) Return of the United Presbyterian Church in the U.S.A. to the Consultation on Church Union.

FOREIGN

Contraceptive Legislation — The Irish bishops issued a statement early in the month stating their opinion that a proposed bill allowing the importation and sale of contraceptives in the country would do more harm than good. "What the legislators have to decide," they said, "is whether a change in the law would, on balance, do more harm than good, by damaging the character of the society for which they are responsible."

Later in the month the highest court in the Republic ruled in a 4 to 1 decision that an existing law prohibiting the importation and sale of contraceptives was unconstitutional.

Pro-Life Petition — Pro-life groups in Can-

ada, banded together as the Alliance for Life, launched a campaign for a one-million-signature petition demanding that the federal government tighten existing abortion laws in order to protect the lives of the unborn. The petition stated: "We, the undersigned, call upon Parliament to enact legislation providing for the child — conceived but not yet born — the same protection provided for any other person."

Absence of Latin American Laity — Bishop Alfonso Lopez Trujillo of Bogota, in Washington, D.C., for talks with U.S. bishops, said that a general lack of participation by lay persons in church renewal and social action efforts was a major disappointment to him. "In some cases," he declared, "the reason seems to be that the laity is out of touch with the political mainstreams. In other cases, they seem to have been frustrated by early failures."

School Problem in Sri Lanka — The nationalization of denominational schools in 1960 and restrictions imposed by the government on methods of financing such schools that subsequently became private institutions, were reported to be jeopardizing the continuance of religious education.

Torture States — "Torture today is so widespread an instrument of political repression that we can speak of the existence of 'torture states' as a political reality of our times," according to Victor Jokel, director of the British section of Amnesty International, an aid movement for "prisoners of conscience." Jokel said: "In more than 30 countries, as documented in the 'Amnesty International Report on Torture,' torture is systematically applied to extract confessions, elicit information, penalize dissent and deter opposition to repressive governmental policy."

German Synod and Foreign Workers — The 320-member West German Catholic Synod, meeting in Wuerzburg, approved resolutions stating that the human rights of foreign workers should have priority over economic and political considerations, and criticizing a rotation policy which obliged such workers (some 10 per cent of the total labor force) to return to their home countries after working in Germany for certain periods of time.

Conscience — "To follow one's conscience" and to remain a Catholic, one must take into account first and foremost the teaching of the magisterium (the Church's teaching authority), the Canadian bishops said in a "Statement on the Formation of Conscience" released Dec. 12. "For a Catholic, 'to follow one's conscience' is not . . . simply to act as his unguided reason dictates," they said, adding: "When doubt arises due to a conflict of 'my' views and those of the magisterium, the presumption of truth lies on the part of the magisterium."

Conditions in Colombia — A secret document prepared for a meeting of the Colombian Bishops' Conference, reflecting a cross section of views of bishops, priests, religious and lay persons, contained a conclusion that the country was in a pre-revolutionary situation. Other conclusions were: that the hierarchy was out of touch with great national problems, that church teachings were not reaching the people, that an increasing number of priests believed that lack of action by them and other churchmen implied support for a "situation of injustice."

Council of Ireland — Bishop Cahal B. Daly of Ardagh and Clonmacnois praised the recently agreed-upon Council of Ireland designed to link the governments of Northern Ireland and the Republic of Ireland. Bishop William Philbin of Down and Connor called agreement concerning the council "an implicit appeal to everyone to insist that the policies of atrocity and destruction shall have no place in our future." Protestant extremists and members of the outlawed Irish Republican Army denounced the agreement.

Political Prisoners — Sixty priests, seminarians and religious issued a statement in Santo Domingo urging the government of the Dominican Republic to decree general amnesty for political prisoners and the repatriation of all exiled persons.

In a related development, the Bolivian Bishops' Conference asked the government of President Hugo Banzer, in power since August, 1971, to decree a general amnesty for political prisoners and exiles. It was estimated that approximately 350 political prisoners were being held in jails and camps throughout the country.

Chilean Hopes — The reconciliation of supporters of the late President Salvador Allende and partisans of the new government was the theme of the Chilean bishops' Christmas message to the nation. They urged people not to talk in terms of "victors and vanquished," but to "remain hopeful" for "renewed peace."

Human Rights under Martial Law — Dangers to human rights under martial law were stressed in a pastoral letter of the Philippine Bishops' Conference read in many churches on the Sunday before Christmas. It was reported that the Marcos government had detained 22 priests and nuns, among hundreds of others, since the imposition of martial law in September, 1972. The most recent detainee was U.S. Maryknoll Father Edward Gerlock of Binghamton, N.Y.

Interference by Polish Government — Cardinal Stefan Wyszynski said in a Christmas message that Poland's Communist regime "has not abandoned" attempts to block the efforts of the Church, "especially in the field of youth" and education, according to a news report in the Dec. 27 edition of *L'Osservatore Romano.* The news dispatch said the cardinal spoke of new educational proposals of the

government as the "gravest danger for the past 25 years" to the Church in Poland.

Aid Fund Reports — The French Catholic Committee against Hunger and for Development collected $2.8 million during the year, for aid to drought victims in Africa ($500,000), reconstruction projects in Indochina ($200,000) and other development programs ($1.8 million).

German Catholics contributed nearly $12 million for humanitarian projects in Vietnam ($5.5 million) and the drought-stricken Sahelian Zone of Africa ($6.4 million).

Bishop Dominic Conway of Elphin announced late in the month that 70 per cent of more than $1.1 million contributed to the Irish Trocaire fund for developing nations would be allocated to finance special development projects.

Foreign Briefs:

• Fujen Catholic University, originally established in 1925 in Peking, celebrated the 10th anniversary of its reactivation Dec. 8 in Taipei, Taiwan.

• The recent arrest of an undetermined number of priests in Slovakia, Czechoslovakia, was reported from Bratislava.

• Papal Secretary of State Cardinal Jean Villot told a Pan-African meeting on social communications in Ibadan, Nigeria, that it was right in stressing that "a specifically African character must be a dominant element in all media initiatives."

Troubles in Spain

Cardinal Vicente Enrique y Tarancon and the auxiliary bishops of Madrid issued a pastoral letter early in the month urging "the absolute recognition" of human rights in both Spanish "laws and in reality." They made their own the earlier appeal of Cardinal Narciso Jubany Arnau of Barcelona for "legal guarantees of the rights of every man to associate and to meet with legitimate aims, as well as the right to participate effectively in public affairs."

Both appeals belonged to a pattern of events which included:

• A 16-day hunger strike, ended Dec. 11, by six priests serving 12 to 50 year sentences in a special "priests' jail" in Zamoro for participation in Basque separatist activities.

• The assassination of Admiral Luis Carrero Blanco, prime minister of Spain, Dec. 20, for which the Basque separatist organization ETA claimed responsibility.

• The Dec. 20 to 23 trial of 10 men found guilty of "illegal association" with outlawed Workers' Committees.

• A meeting of the Spanish Bishops' Conference concerned with issues involved in continuing tensions in Church-state relations and in efforts by citizens to moderate hard-line government policies restrictive of individual and social freedoms.

JANUARY 1974

VATICAN

No Mafia Mentality — In a New Year's Day address in the southern part of Rome, Pope Paul urged his listeners to reject a "Mafia mentality" that takes justice into its own hands and sets off a chain-reaction of vendetta and counter-vendetta. "Justice achieved in this way," he said, "is a continual injustice."

God the Son Reveals God the Father — Christ's birth revealed not only himself but also the "dazzling, delightful vision of God's fatherhood," Pope Paul told a general audience Jan. 2. He noted that the revelation of the Father "was one of the principal purposes of the Incarnation, one of the aims that dominated the life of Christ . . . this revelation . . . (is) the keystone of all our thought and . . . the beatific font of all our spiritual life."

Parish Is for Everybody — In an address to a group of 80 Dominican priests Jan. 5, the Pope said that "the missionary drive that derives essentially from the universal Church communicates itself to the diocese and overflows into the parish. From that point of view, the parish's pastoral effort must be directed not only toward practicing Catholics but must turn with holy industry toward all those who live in the territory."

Making Christmas Spirit Last — Mary's practice of keeping "in mind all these things, pondering them in her heart," was proposed by Pope Paul as a formula for preserving the Christmas spirit throughout the year. He also commented Jan. 9 before a general audience: "First memory, then awareness, followed by understanding, wonder and, finally, contemplation. Are they not, perhaps, the phases of Our Lady's spiritual life?"

Criticism — Pope Paul, commenting on criticism leveled against the Church and its leaders for failing to hasten the decline of the old order and the arrival of a new "messianic" society, said that such a new order might well be "less just and less stable" than the old. He also told members of the diplomatic corps accredited to the Vatican Jan. 12 that "the search for peace is the pivotal point of the diplomatic mission in international life."

In reference to the criticism, he said: "Faced with criticisms of this kind, the first reflection that comes to our mind is that certain radicalisms are often not only mistaken and unjust because of their partial or one-sided way of judging reality and the responsibilities it imposes, but they are moreover dangerous. They are dangerous because of what they would like to see achieved, and just as dangerous because of what they do not want to see achieved or because of achievements they succeed in preventing." The Pontiff called for the useful expenditure of effort in unspectacular undertakings that "nonetheless represent real progress for humanity."

Kohoutek and Mystery — Pope Paul told a gathering of people in St. Peter's Square Jan. 13 that in observing the Comet Kohoutek he "experienced once again the sense of cosmic mystery, unlimited space, time without end, the incalculable sidereal panorama — its perfect and inexorable movement, its frighteningly profound silence, its phenomena of matter which today is widely explored but which can be said to be still almost unknown." All these phenomena, he said, are stamped with the name of God, their creator.

Concern for Truth — The Pope, addressing the communications committee of the German Bishops' Conference Jan. 16, called Christians to "energetic concern for truth in information, and an undaunted rejection of what is slanted and false." He said it would be "doubly serious if Christians, heedless of their responsibilities and lacking critical sense, should accept and diffuse false information."

Ecumenical Movement — Pope Paul hailed the ecumenical movement Jan. 20 as a "positive solution" of the divisions that scar Christianity, in an address marking the 1974 Week of Prayer for Christian Unity. He told a gathering in St. Peter's Square that "the one faith and universal charity lead us to the authentic sheepfold of Christ, to his Church, founded on Peter, with the keys which the Lord placed in his hands, not so that he would dominate but rather so that he would be the shepherd . . . the servant of the servants of God, the visible and fundamental principle of unity." He said that "this vision of the Church requires of us Catholics a firmness of doctrine . . . even greater humility . . . and greater good will" toward others.

Saint of Our Times — Pope Paul, shortly after the end of ceremonies Jan. 27 for the canonization of St. Teresa of Jesus Jornet y Ibars, called her "truly a Saint of our times and for our times." The Spanish Saint, who lived from 1843 to 1897, founded the Little Sisters of the Abandoned Aged in 1873. At the time of her death, her community of 1,260 members had foundations in Spain, Cuba and Puerto Rico.

Prayer — Speaking for the second week in a row on the subject of the prayer, Pope Paul told a general audience Jan. 30 that Christian life without prayer is like a "blown-out candle." He said: "Prayer is the first dialogue that man can hold with God. Given the existence of a relationship with God . . . the need to express our words to him is born spontaneously at first and then becomes a duty." Despite the aversion of many people to prayer, the Holy Father observed that "there is being reborn in the heart of the present generation a need for, an orientation and sympathetic feeling toward, some form of prayer."

Criticism Criticized — The Pope, in a Jan. 31 speech at an annual meeting with judges of the Roman Rota, rejected a charge by Prof. Pietro D'Avack, dean of ecclesiastical law at the University of Rome, that the marriage laws of the Church are "decrepit, out of date and paradoxically inhuman." He said: "Judgment regarding the worth of the existing canon law on matrimony still merits trusts today, as it interprets and teaches the sacred and fundamental norms for man, matrimony, the family and society, even if, in conformity with the teaching of the recent (Second Vatican) Council, we hope these norms will be formulated in a more complete and modern legislation."

The Pope Also:
• Commemorated the 10th anniversary of his 1964 pilgrimage to the Holy Land by asking prayers for "wise and just solutions" for the Middle East crisis.
• Met with: Lombume Kallymazi, Zaire's new ambassador to the Vatican, Jan. 7; George P. Shultz, U.S. secretary of the treasury, Jan. 18; Pierre Ilboudo, Upper Volta's first ambassador to the Vatican, Jan. 24.
• Approved the elections of Cardinals Luigi Traglia and Carlo Confalonieri as dean and assistant dean, respectively, of the College of Cardinals. They were elected by the cardinal bishops.

Anointing of the Sick — The Congregation for Divine Worship announced Jan. 22 that it had extended the Jan. 1, 1974, date for use of the revised rite for the sacrament of anointing of the sick in order to give episcopal conferences sufficient time for translating Latin texts into vernacular languages.

Vatican Briefs:
• Friendlier relations between the United States and the Soviet Union and China were the outstanding developments of 1973, in the opinion of Federico Alessandrini, head of the Vatican Press Office. He stated this view in an article published in *L'Osservatore della Domenica.*
• Within hours of the signing of the Israel-Egyptian pullback-of-forces agreement Jan. 18, Vatican Radio said that the agreement raised hopes that all the problems troubling the Middle East "can find a solution."
• A note drafted by the Vatican Committee for the Family, for circulation among bishops throughout the world, warned that the 1974 UN World Population Year might prompt some Catholics "to develop concepts that are divergent from those of the teaching authority of the Church," with respect to birth regulation and family life.

Peace Day Message

"Peace Depends on You Too" was the title of Pope Paul's message for the Jan. 1, 1974, World Day of Peace. His wish was "that the new year might let us savor the maintenance of peace in justice and liberty, and see again its restoration where it is still a fiction, or unstable or compromised."

The Pope said in the course of the lengthy message:
• "The idea of peace is already victorious in the thought of all men in posts of responsibility."
• "If the idea of peace effectively wins men's hearts, peace will be safe; indeed, it will save mankind."
• "If public opinion is the element that determines the fate of peoples, the fate of peace also depends on each of us. For each of us forms part of the civic body operating with a democratic system which, in varying forms and degrees, today characterizes the life of the nations organized in a modern manner. This is what we wish to say: Peace is possible if each one of us wants it; if each one of us loves peace, educates and forms his own outlook to peace, defends peace, works for peace. Each one of us must listen in his own conscience to the impelling call: 'Peace depends on you too.' "

DOMESTIC

Church History Neglected — Church history is a neglected science in the nation's seminaries, Msgr. John Tracy Ellis told a meeting of the American Catholic Historical Association Jan. 2 in San Francisco. Reporting findings based on replies from 22 seminaries, he said that 11 required a survey of Church history from the beginning to the present, eight required no such survey, and three others offered only surveys of various periods.

Reconciliation Program — Fred J. Niehaus, vice president of the International Council of Catholic Men, announced Jan. 8 that the council would work over the next two years to promote the 1975 Holy Year theme of reconciliation. Reporting on a recent meeting of the ICCM board in Cologne, Germany, he said the organization's 1974-75 program would emphasize active participation in the Holy Year observance and a rejection of "the spirit and practice of materialism."

Office for Divorced Catholics — Bishop Walter Curtis of Bridgeport announced Jan. 7 that he was going to open a diocesan Office for Pastoral Care of the Separated, Divorced and Remarried. It was believed that the office would be the first of its kind in the country.

Coercion of Family Planning — *The Wall St. Journal* expressed agreement editorially Jan. 10 with a recent statement in which the nation's Catholic diocesan family life directors maintained that married couples should be free from the "coercive influence of government" in family planning. While acknowledging that the government has a legitimate interest in encouraging couples to keep the birth rate in check, the Journal said that a number of suggestions made for doing that "border on the dangerous. . . . We mean (suggestions) that would set up the government with the power to decree family size."

Catholic School Students Have More Hope — Sociologists Father Andrew M. Greeley and William C. McCready stated in the Jan. 11 edition of the *National Catholic Reporter* that Catholics who attended Catholic schools had a greater sense of hope than Catholics who attended other schools. They said their study indicated that the group of "hopefuls . . . faces squarely the problem of evil . . . does not try to cover it over, but still believes good to be stronger than evil." They also stated the opinion that the hopefuls "are . . . more likely to be confident of human survival, to enjoy higher levels of psychological well-being, more satisfying marriage relationships, and to be both less racist and more trusting of others."

Seton Bicentennial Year — Governor Marvin Mandel of Maryland issued a proclamation Jan. 11 declaring 1974 as Seton Bicentennial Year. The proclamation said: "Blessed Elizabeth Ann Seton, the first native-born citizen of the United States to be proclaimed Blessed by the Catholic Church, has brought honor to her country and to this state by her exemplary practice of the virtues proper to her many roles as daughter, wife, mother, religious, educator and ecumenist."

Drop in Church-Going — The Gallup Poll organization attributed the steady drop in American church-going since 1958 "almost entirely" to falling attendance by Catholics (55 per cent in 1973 as compared with 71 per cent in 1964). Overall attendance was reported to be about 40 per cent of the adult population. Attendance rates were said to be 37 per cent of Protestants and 19 per cent of Jews.

Another study, based on data collected in July, 1972, and July, 1973, stated that "among Catholics there has been a decline in weekly or almost weekly attendance from 61 per cent to 48 per cent. The percentage of those never going to church has almost doubled — from 8 per cent to 14 per cent." Also: "The decline is taking place among those between 30 and 49-years-old (13 percentage points) and especially among those over 50 (21 percentage points)." The study, by Father Andrew M. Greeley and William C. McCready, was published in the Nov. 16, 1973, edition of the *National Catholic Reporter.*

Black Secretariat — A black secretariat was established by Archbishop William W. Baum for some 70,000 of the 390,000 Catholics in the Washington archdiocese. Father John Richard, S.S.J., a spokesman for the board, said the secretariat would have an "advocacy role" and would assure a "black presence" in decision-making bodies and structures of the archdiocese. Black secretariats had already been established in Detroit and Pittsburgh.

Employment Data — The Church Project on Equal Employment Opportunity announced plans Jan. 22 to file stockholder resolutions with nine major U.S. corporations, seeking the disclosure of data concerning policy, plans and status of equal employment opportunities for women and members of minority groups. The project was a cooperative venture of six Protestant denominations, a Catholic religious institute (the Graymoor Friars) and the National Council of Churches.

Boys Town Center — Plans for the establishment of a Boys Town Center for the Study of Youth and Development at the Catholic University of America were announced Jan. 22. The function of the center — to be funded at a rate of $450,000 a year for 25 years — would be to study such problems as parental rejection of youngsters, drug addiction among youth, anti-social behavior and learning disabilities.

Support for Lutheran Seminary Faculty — The faculties of St. Louis University's Divinity School and Eden Theological Seminary issued a joint statement Jan. 28 in support of the Rev. John H. Tietjen, the suspended president of Concordia Seminary, and sympathetic faculty members who walked out in protest against his removal and brought the normal activity of the seminary to a halt. Dr. Tietjen was accused of heresy and the others were under various degrees of suspicion because of views regarded as unorthodox by conservative authorities of the church.

Project Equality — With a national budget reduced from $138,000 to $91,000, Project Equality announced reorganization plans and the establishment of a national office in Kansas City, Mo. The Rev. Arthur Waidmann, executive director, said the equal employment efforts of the program would be continued in and through the operations of 11 regional and additional local offices.

The Exorcist — The range of reactions to the film "The Exorcist" — from curiosity to revulsion and morbidity — increased through the month in step with the number of viewers since its release in 20 cities just after Christmas. It was not a documentary film, although its basis was an exorcism performed in 1949 by a Jesuit priest on a 14-year-old boy in a suburb of Washington, D.C. It was called "little more than an expensive horror movie in the escapist entertainment vein," in a review in the "Catholic Film Newsletter" published by the Division of Film and Broadcasting, U.S. Catholic Conference.

Domestic Briefs:

• Auxiliary Bishop Thomas J. Gumbleton of Detroit and the Rev. Dr. Eugene Carson Blake, former general secretary of the World Council of Churches, were elected vice president and president, respectively, of Bread for the World, a newly formed group for combatting world poverty and hunger.

• The Denver archdiocese announced Jan. 23 that it would raise the salaries of sisters in its service from $3,100 to $4,600 in the 1974-75 school year.

• For her "radical commitment to the Gospel," Dorothy Day, founder of the Catholic Worker movement, was presented with the first annual Isaac Hecker Award Jan. 25 by the Paulist Center in Boston.

Right to Life Demonstrations

Rallies and demonstrations in dozens of cities across the country on Jan. 22 marked the first anniversary of U.S. Supreme Court decisions which outlawed legal restrictions on abortion and thereby made abortion on demand a constitutional right. While counter-demonstrators voiced support for the Court, thousands of persons of various faiths signaled not only opposition to the decisions but also continuing commitment to press for a constitutional amendment to protect the right of the unborn to life. The principal event was the National March for Life in Washington, D.C., where many of some 15,000 persons tried to elicit support for pro-life legislation from their Senators and Representatives.

Several days after the anniversary, the Senate subcommittee on constitutional amendments announced that hearings would begin "within the first three weeks of March" on:

• An amendment introduced May 31, 1973, by Sen. James L. Buckley of New York which would outlaw abortion except in cases where the continuation of pregnancy would endanger the life of the mother.

• A proposal made June 29, 1973, by Sen. Jesse A. Helms of North Carolina which would give "equal protection" and "due process of law" to "any human being, from the moment of conception."

Action in the House of Representatives on an amendment proposed by Rep. Lawrence Hogan of Maryland, identical with the Helms measure, remained stalled because of Hogan's lack of success in obtaining the 218 signatures necessary to bring the bill to the floor of the House.

FOREIGN

Resistance to Family Planning — India's Vice President G. S. Pathak reported that government programs for family planning and birth control were meeting considerable resistance throughout the country. The counteractive factors were family traditions related to social and economic conditions, especially in rural areas.

Optimistic about 1974 — Despite gloomy facts and forecasts of economic and political chaos, a number of Catholic commentators in London appeared optimistic about prospects for the Church in 1974. *The Universe*, a national Catholic weekly, reflected their views in the statement: "There are growing signs that the Church in Britain and throughout the world is beginning to regain its confidence after the period of division and conflict following Vatican Two."

Rite for Priestless Parishes — Officials of the northern Italian Diocese of Novara were reported Jan. 11 to be studying a religious rite that could be carried out by lay persons in parishes without priests to celebrate Mass on Sundays and holydays. An episcopal vicar of the diocese, Msgr. Eugenio Lupo, commented that, because of a shortage of priests (resulting in the closing of one-third of the churches), "the laity now is facing new responsibilities for the continuation of religious life."

Uncertainty of Anglican Belief — An Anglican scholar warned Jan. 15 that the Church of England's position in the Christian unity movement had been weakened by the uncertainty of beliefs in the Anglican Communion. Dr. J. I. Packer, associate principal of Trinity College, Bristol, said that the foundations of Anglicanism — the Book of Common Prayer and the 39 Articles — had lost their central place and had been replaced by "woolliness and wildness" in doctrinal thinking in some quarters, including the rank of bishops.

Famine Threat Not Ended — Supplies of food and other materials, provided by Catholic and other agencies of various countries, had helped to prevent a catastrophe in famine-stricken Ethiopia, but the battle against hunger was continuing, according to relief workers there. UN personnel estimated that there was still a deficit of nearly 15,000 tons of grain cereals in the hardest hit provinces of Tigre and Wollo, and said that only long-range development projects could free the people from fear of famine.

Young People Challenged — Archbishop Joseph A. Plourde of Ottawa, in his monthly "Message," challenged young people to take positive action to improve social conditions at odds with Christian standards. "Criticizing, fault-finding and blaming others is easy," he said. "What is really difficult is doing something to improve the situation. . . . As long as you refuse to do something about it by trying to improve yourself and your fellow humans, don't blame the world for the state it's in."

Ireland's Underground Armies — The continued existence of underground armies rather than the issues they exploited were called Ireland's problem by Bishop William Philbin in an address to the Irish Association in Manchester, England. Bishop Philbin, whose diocese included violence-wracked Belfast, said that such armies had become "either the sovereign legitimate authority, the ultimate arbiters of right and wrong, of good and evil, in Ireland, or they are immoral forces and oppressors of liberty usurping the rights of the population."

Christian Education — A lobbying group organized by the interdenominational Order of Christian Unity petitioned the House of Commons for the retention of Christian education in the state schools of England. The petitioners asked that specific Christian instruction be positively assured in all schools for all children whose parents want it, and that students and teachers wishing to specialize in teaching the Christian faith be given more encouragement and guidance in teacher-training colleges.

Polish Priest Harassed — The secretariat of the Polish Bishops' Conference accused government authorities of harassing a priest by confining him to a mental hospital after he said Mass at the request of villagers in a town near Bialystok in northeastern Poland. "We are convinced," the secretariat said in a statement, "the whole situation arose because Father Zabielski celebrated Mass for the local people."

Mexican Bishops' Statement — The Mexican Bishops' Conference criticized both capitalism and Marxism and declared that the Church must defend human rights, in a statement on "The Christian Commitment and Social and Political Options." The bishops said that "Christians must look for better forms of social organization (which) are compatible with faith. A Christian cannot make a choice without regard for the demands of faith." They also said: "Priests as well as the Church must adopt a clear stand in defense of human rights, in the promotion of humanity and in working for the cause of peace and justice with means of the Gospel."

Opposition to Abortion — A Gallup Poll of a sample of 505 men and 580 women indicated that 71 per cent of the public in England were opposed to abortion on demand, and that more men than women were in favor of readily available abortion. Several weeks before release of the poll results late in the month, participants in a memorial service claimed that 170,000 unborn children had been killed in Britain in the previous year. It was estimated that more than 500,000 legalized abortions had been performed since passage of the Abortion Act in 1967.

Ancestors Honored — Catholic observances honoring ancestors on the Chinese New Year Jan. 23 were more widespread than ever before in Taiwan, with participation by Cardinal Paul Yu Pin, Archbishop Stanislaus Lo Kuang of Taipei, several other bishops and priests, and thousands of lay persons. Ceremonies included the offering of flowers, incense and wine before ancestral tablets, and the celebration of a special Mass. Participation in traditional ceremonies, banned for Catholics from 1742 to 1939, had increased greatly in the previous three years.

False Charges — Cardinal Eugenio de Araujo Sales rejected Jan. 26 charges of Communist influence in the Church raised at a congress of the Latin American Anti-Communist Confederation in Rio de Janeiro. He said: "Only to advocate strengthening trade unions, freedom or change of unjust social structures, or respect for human beings and community development, is motive enough for accusations of subservience to Communism."

State of Siege in Bolivia — The government of Bolivian President Hugo Banzer, in its worst crisis since ousting leftist President Jose Torres in 1971, abrogated constitutional law with a state-of-siege decree Jan. 28. Reasons for the action were a runaway economy and a wave of strikes, in addition to alleged activities of guerrillas. The Bolivian Bishops' Conference, in a document issued Jan. 24, blamed government inefficiency and corruption for economic woes of the country.

Religion in Cuba — Churches remain open but religion has to remain "highly personal" for Catholics in Cuba, according to Father Carlos M. Ariz, rector of the Catholic University of Santa Maria la Antigua, Panama City, just returned from a visit to the Castro-controlled island.

Foreign Briefs:

• Lopez Rodo, the last member of Opus Dei in the government of assassinated Premier Luis Carrero Blanco, was passed over in Cabinet appointments made by the newly installed Premier Carlos Arias Navarro of Spain.

• Pilar Diaz Penalver y Colino, the first woman to hold the position, was appointed president of the Spanish Catholic Action organization by the permanent commission of the Spanish Bishops' Conference.

Racism in Africa

Racism and its evil effects in African life were the themes of statements issued by several conferences of bishops.

• The bishops of Kenya, Malawi, Tanzania, Uganda and Zambia found it "offensive to human dignity that racism and colonialism are still permitted to exist on our continent, and we reject any perverted attempts to appeal to Christianity and civilization to justify their continued existence."

• A pastoral message read or distributed in churches in Rhodesia said: "Discrimination based on race must be eliminated, equality of opportunity must be guaranteed, there must be proper parliamentary representation, job reservation (for whites) must go, land reform must be seriously tackled, with more equitable distribution and appropriate contol. . . . Much of the blame (for existing conditions of inequity) rests with the present Rhodesian administration and with those who support its racist policies."

• The bishops of Rwanda and Burundi blamed political upheaval and two years of Hutu-Tutsi strife in their countries on "racism, underdevelopment, and a Christianity not properly understood and deprived of its essential qualities of faith, charity and justice."

FEBRUARY 1974

VATICAN

Tribute to Nuns — "You beloved daughters in Christ are consecrated to the good of the whole Church," Pope Paul told thousands of women religious in St. Peter's Basilica Feb. 2, the feast of the Presentation. "Your vocation," he said, "is in total oblation to the Church, whether your lives are worked out in the secret and crucified life of the cloister or they follow along the innumerable roads of charity which you follow untiringly and in the service of all human needs."

Chance for Reflection — Hard times and tight economics offer Christians an opportunity to reflect more seriously on the meaning of life, Pope Paul said in a Feb. 3 address to persons gathered in St. Peter's Square. He asked: "May not this brief pause of austerity favor a common reflection and give rise to a more solid and positive purpose of harmony, industriousness and social action? Our religious spirit, which fuses sacrifice with love, can help us to seek after the effort needed for a good recovery."

Supernatural Birthday — The real birthday of a Christian is the day of his baptism, Pope Paul said at a general audience Feb. 6. Quoting his encyclical *Ecclesiam Suam* on what it means to be a Christian, he declared: "It is especially important that the baptized person should have a highly conscious esteem of his elevation or, rather, of his rebirth to the most happy reality of being an adopted son of God, to the dignity of being a brother of Christ . . . to the vocation to a new life . . . to follow Christ."

Mexican President — President Luis Echeverria, the first Mexican chief of state ever to visit the Vatican, met with Pope Paul for three-quarters of an hour Feb. 9. The Pontiff told him of the Church's interest in following "all the civil and social undertakings promoted by Mexico and directed at that authentic progress which is (expressed) in the thinking and aspirations of all its citizens."

In the background of the meeting was a long history of government persecution of the Church, especially during the 1920s and 1930s when religious functions were banned, and priests and religious were hunted down and even executed as enemies of the state.

Knowing Jesus — "Knowing Jesus," which is different from being able to define him, is a gradual process, Pope Paul declared before an audience of 6,000 persons Feb. 13. He said: "If indeed we know him, we must add that we do not know him sufficiently. Indeed, that which we know of him does not satisfy our needs . . . but stimulates us . . . to know him better." This knowledge "is gradual" and does not come just with reading the Gospel or a book about Christ. "If this knowledge truly impressed on our soul, it awakens our

desire to . . . deepen it, to verify its significance and its contents."

Willing To Cooperate — The Pope affirmed the Church's willingness to cooperate with the government in promoting the development of the people of Spain, at a first meeting with Gabriel Fernandez de Valderrama y Moreno, that country's new ambassador to the Vatican, Feb. 15.

Rotary Members Praised — Rotary Club members around the world were praised by Pope Paul Feb. 16 for their service to mankind, on the 50th anniversary of the first Italian Rotary Club in Milan. He also called on them to pass on to the young their strong sense of dedication to service.

God's Love the Secret — "The secret of Christianity," Pope Paul said at a general audience Feb. 20, "is the salvific love of God and therefore of Christ who 'loved me and sacrificed himself for me.' . . . We are loved by God. He has first loved us, without our deserving that love but being entirely in need of it."

Discussion with Gromyko — Pope Paul and Soviet Foreign Minister Andrei Gromyko met Feb. 21 for the fourth time since 1965. The subjects of their conversation, according to Vatican press spokesman Federico Alessandrini, were "the major problems regarding peace in the world."

Priests and Their Ministry — In a pre-Lenten address to priests of Rome, the Holy Father stated that "the ministry of the Church . . . must be intense . . . if it wishes to be efficacious, diligent, strong, enduring and full of that pastoral sense which Jesus radically fills with the inherent spirit of sacrifice." Among other counsels, he urged the priests to practice the virtue of obedience; warned that "our charitable and social interest should not work to the detriment of our proper religious activity, neither in personal nor community life"; and called for positive effort to counteract "the spirit of contestation" in the Church which "has become almost an epidemic and a form of anti-Church feeling . . . addressed neither to truth nor charity."

Liturgy in Lent — The Holy Father advised thousands of persons at an Ash Wednesday audience to observe Lent with intelligent use of the liturgy, which "rises not only like an incomparable work of art because of its variety of themes divine and human, but offers . . . to the faithful the possibility of participating in a marvelous and complex celebration." He added: "This celebration recalls the perennial history of the ineffable dialogue between God and man."

Right to Life — Pope Paul told an international group of scientists Feb. 27 that "the

Church recognizes . . . man's inalienable right to live, from the first moment of his existence — a right which no human can set aside, a right which applies also to his fellow men and, above all, to his family, and the conditions necessary for a truly human life." He also said: "The Church . . . puts the problems of life in the light of a faith that reveals the full sense of man on the path of a long experience of an assent to life."

The Pope Also:

• Told some 300 European and African participants in a conference of parliamentarians that rich and poor nations alike can no longer afford "closed, self-sufficient national economies," Feb. 1.

• Defended the validity of the Lateran pacts between the Vatican and Italy, which settled the Roman Question, on Feb. 10, the 35th anniversary of the death of Pius XI who negotiated the agreements.

• In a cable sent Feb. 20 to foreign ministers of 23 Latin American nations and U.S. Secretary of State Henry Kissinger, meeting in Mexico City Feb. 19 to 23, said he was pleased to know that they were studying proposals to convert part of the defense budget of each nation "to works of a social and economic nature." (The Pope had made such proposals at a press conference Dec. 4, 1964, in Bombay and in his 1967 encyclical *Populorum Progressio* ("Development of Peoples").

Penance, Reconciliation — The Vatican made public Feb. 7 the 121-page Latin text of a document containing new rites for the sacrament of penance or reconciliation. (See separate entry.)

Problems of Rome — Despite criticism of the Church for lack of sufficient concern for the poor, Vatican officials reacted favorably to a convention of some 4,000 persons held Feb. 12 to 15 under the auspices of Cardinal Ugo Poletti, the Pope's vicar for the Diocese of Rome. The convention was praised for what the Catholic daily *Avvenire* called its "total frankness and full freedom of expression." Cardinal Poletti told journalists that the diocese "was searching for elements of cohesion, unity and collaboration within itself in order to bring to the City of Rome a witness of truth, charity and justice, since men of this city hunger and thirst for these supernatural virtues."

U.S. Marriage Court Rules — Six U.S. bishops, meeting with Pope Paul Feb. 23, appealed for an extension beyond July 1, 1974, of 23 special procedural norms in effect since 1970 in marriage tribunals in this country. The chief merit of the norms was the way in which they expedited the handling of cases concerning the validity or invalidity of marriages.

Vatican Briefs:

• Agreement to continue negotiations for better Church-state relations was reached in Warsaw by representatives of the Polish government and papal diplomat Archbishop Agostino Casaroli, according to a joint communique published Feb. 7.

• A Vatican Radio editorial called Alexander Solzhenitsyn a "grand writer of international fame" while reporting that he "was arrested (Feb. 12, in Moscow) for having informed the world of the repressive measures of a regime and who . . . has been expelled from his country" (Feb. 13, to West Germany).

• In a pre-trial hearing Feb. 12, a Roman criminal court agreed to hear a defamation case brought by the niece of Pope Pius XII against an American writer and the producer and director of the film "Massacre in Rome."

Cardinal Mindszenty

Pope Paul, in a letter dated Jan. 30 and released Feb. 5, relieved Cardinal Jozsef Mindszenty of his title as archbishop of Esztergom, thus severing completely his connection with the principal see of Hungary which he had held for 25 years in prison and exile. A communique from the Vatican said the "Holy Father, after considering the pastoral problems of the Archdiocese of Esztergom and after an ample exchange of correspondence," had decided "to declare the aforementioned diocese vacant." At the same time, he appointed an apostolic administrator for the archdiocese.

Cardinal Mindszenty made it clear in a statement Feb. 7 that the decision resulting in his removal was made by the Pope and that he had not volunteered to resign. He objected to the action because, he said, it left unchanged the subjection of the Church in Hungary to substantial government control.

DOMESTIC

Smallest Population Growth — The rate of growth of the U.S. population in 1973 — 0.8 per cent, to 210,740,000 from 209,123,000 — was the lowest annual rate since 1938, according to figures released by the Census Bureau late in January. The increase included births, newly arrived immigrants and servicemen returning from overseas. The National Center for Health Statistics estimated that the 1973 birth rate — 15 for every 1,000 persons — was the lowest in the nation's history.

Sterilization — Thomas Poteat, secretary of the South Carolina Department of Social Services, announced a committee decision to go "on record as flatfootedly opposed to involuntary sterilization" in the state, no matter what "fail-safe methods" might be proposed by the U.S. Department of Health, Education and Welfare for regulating sterilization of persons incapable of free, informed consent. "Morally, ethically and otherwise we are absolutely opposed to involuntary sterilization, and we will not allow it," he declared. Concern over the practice was heightened during the summer of 1973 with the disclosure that doctors working in a county hospital in Aiken refused to deliver the babies of 18 Medicaid patients until they agreed to sterilization procedures.

Conscience Clauses — The Catholic Hospital Association announced Feb. 4 that 39 states had adopted conscience clauses providing general civil and criminal immunity to hospitals, physicians and employes refusing to take part in abortion procedures for moral, ethical or religious reasons.

Ecumenism and Charismatic Renewal — These were called the two most important current movements in the Church by Cardinal Leo J. Suenens of Belgium in an address at a seminar for Episcopalian bishops at Trinity Institute, New York City. Speaking of the same subjects again Feb. 6 at a gathering of North Texas clergy and lay persons in Dallas, he said:

• Charismatic renewal (which he would rather have called renewal in the Spirit) is essentially an invitation to discerning faith, to seeing the presence and action of the Spirit of God, and "how close he is to us in daily life."

• "All in all, we are going forward (in the ecumenical movement), following the lead of the Spirit of God bringing us together more and more every day," and feeling something of the impatience of God for unity.

Parish Priest Most Important — The involvement of priests in special ministries is "all to the good," but the parish priest will continue to play the most important role in pastoral ministry, Archbishop Joseph L. Bernardin of Cincinnati told a meeting of the Houston Serra Club Feb. 7. He said: "While all ministries should be pastorally oriented in the sense that they ultimately serve the needs of people, the parish priest somehow deals more directly with the problems and frustrations, the hopes and the aspirations of the people who are struggling day by day to live in accordance with the Gospel mandates."

Sin — Psychiatrist Karl Menninger, founder of the Menninger Clinic, Topeka, Kan., and author of *Whatever Became of Sin?*, said in Monterey, Calif., that sin definitely still does exist and that anyone who recognizes its existence has a responsibility to do something about it. His definitions of sin were "the uncontrolled propensity for self-destructiveness" and "not caring what happens."

Human Rights in Brazil and Chile — The Administrative Board of the U.S. Catholic Conference protested violations of human rights in Brazil and Chile, and urged the U.S. government to consider halting financial aid to the two countries unless they changed their policies. Two statements, issued after a meeting Feb. 13, marked the board's first criticism of right-wing governments in Latin America, according to Father Frederick McGuire, C.M., director of the Division for Latin America, USCC.

Priest Will Run — Father Eugene J. Boyle of San Francisco announced Feb. 14 that he would run for a seat in the California legislature even though Archbishop Joseph T. McGucken had refused permission for him to do so. He said he was standing for election because of his concern as a priest for the poor. In refusing permission the archbishop said: "In conscience I cannot agree that the time and circumstances demand an exception to the general norm (against priests running for public office), in effect a declaration that we lack competent laymen to assume the role which is properly theirs." Father Boyle remained in good standing although his authorization to preach from the pulpit was withdrawn because of his political commitment to speak on partisan issues.

New Maturity on TV? — The *Catholic Film Newsletter* questioned in its Feb. 15 edition whether the insertion of previously taboo themes into tired television formats justified the claim of "new maturity." The publication said: "To dignify such shows with arguments about creative freedom, contemporary relevance or maturity is nonsense. The fact is such material, injected into escapist entertainment formats, does not satisfy the mature viewer," does not elucidate complex questions, and may do harm to the young and the immature.

Population Problem — Father Robert L. Faricy, S.J., writing in the February edition of *Homiletic and Pastoral Review*, said that two basic concerns of the Church relevant to the world population problem were for the intrinsic value of human life and for the quality of life — especially the life of poor people and developing nations. Any policy that contradicts either the value of life or any nation's cultural heritage must be condemned, declared the theology professor of Rome's Gregorian University.

Seminary in Exile — Responding to the ouster of 450 students and nearly 50 faculty members from the Lutheran Concordia Seminary, St. Louis University and Eden Theological Seminary (of the United Church of Christ) inaugurated a Joint Project for Theological Education to enable the seminarians to complete the academic year ending May 22. The two schools said in a joint statement that their action was intended for the welfare of the students and "in no way involves a judgment about the internal affairs of the Lutheran Church-Missouri Synod or the controversies which are at present taking place within the Synod." The Rev. Jacob A. O. Preuss, president of the Synod, accused the schools of contributing to the break-up of Concordia Seminary.

Integrity in Government — Formation of a Religious Committee for Integrity in Government was announced Feb. 22 in Washington, D.C. Catholic sponsors of the interdenominational committee included Auxiliary Bishop

John J. Dougherty of Newark, Bishop Carroll T. Dozier of Memphis, and Msgr. John J. Egan, chairman of the Catholic Committee on Urban Ministry.

Domestic Briefs:

• The Catholic Medical Mission Board reported 1973 shipments of 990 tons of medical supplies with a wholesale value of approximately $6.3 million to 2,772 medical missions around the world.

• William Atkinson, a quadriplegic as the result of an accident causing the loss of natural movement of his arms and legs, was ordained to the priesthood by Cardinal John J. Krol in Upper Darby, Pa.

• Francisco de Jesus Schuck, secretary of justice, stated in San Juan that the position of the Puerto Rican government "has been firm and clear, and we do not favor the legalization of abortion in Puerto Rico."

• Mother M. Viola, superior general of the Sisters of the Third Order of St. Francis, Syracuse, N.Y., disclosed that the Congregation for the Causes of Saints had agreed to consider the beatification cause of Mother Marianne Kopp. She was the American nun who succeeded Father Damien DeVeuster as spiritual leader of the Molokai leper colony in Hawaii.

• Catholic Relief Services reported that more than 16 million pounds of usable clothing, blankets, bedding and footwear, valued at $25 million, had been collected for needy persons in its 1973 Thanksgiving campaign.

• The Catholic Daughters of America awarded some $40,000 in grants to a variety of programs in this country and abroad. Aided were campus ministry, foreign health missions and St. Jude's Hospital in Memphis.

• La Concepcion Hospital, San Juan, Puerto Rico, celebrated the 450th anniversary of its founding in 1524.

Farah Strike Ends

A 21-month strike of the Farah Manufacturing Co. by the Amalgamated Clothing Workers of America was settled Feb. 24 with voluntary agreement by the firm to abide by the choice of 63 per cent of its employes and to recognize the union as their bargaining agent. In the course of the strike the work force dropped from 10,400 to just over 6,000, the company was forced to close plants in three Texas cities, and sales losses through the first half of 1973 amounted to some $20 million.

The strike and a related boycott had the interdenominational support of many church groups. Its outstanding proponent was Bishop Sidney M. Metzger of El Paso. Such support "made the difference" in bringing about the settlement, according to Father Donald Bauer, a union organizer.

FOREIGN

Arrests in Brazil — The information office of the Sao Paulo archdiocese reported that dozens of persons working for church-related organizations were arrested there and in Rio de Janeiro early in the month. The arrests came in the wake of accusations by the Ministry of Education that the Catholic Church was spreading "Communist ideas" and that its Basic Education Movement was infiltrated by Communists. The charges were denied by the information office.

Religious Face Social Injustice — "What we are trying to do is to find a way to incarnate our religious vocation into the realities of our people, but without jeopardizing our primary duty of being witnesses to the Gospel," said a spokesman of the Jan. 27 to Feb. 2 meeting of the Latin American Confederation of Religious in San Jose, Costa Rica. The central emphasis of a document discussed at the meeting, according to Father Carlos Palmes, confederation president, was "high politics, that is, ideology and human rights, such as justice, freedom and dignity, and what a religious can do for the total man, body and soul." The assembly was attended by delegates from religious institutes in 26 countries.

Search in Lithuania — Secret police in Lithuania were engaged in a massive search of homes, offices and churches in an effort to find dissidents responsible for illegal publications and protest actions, according to accounts in the *Chronicle of the Lithuanian Catholic Church.* The underground newspaper reported numerous cases of alleged religious repression and violations of civil rights, and indicated that a loose organization of underground groups had developed in the country.

Arms Race — The Australian bishops at their semiannual meeting expressed regret that the international arms race was continuing at the expense of development programs and called on all governments and citizens of countries with nuclear weapons to bring it to an end. "The world's resources are needed for more basic and urgent tasks than developing skills and weapons for destruction," they said.

Doubt about Missionaries in Rhodesia — The future role of foreign missionaries in Rhodesia came under question following refusal by the Ian Smith government to permit eight Swiss priests to work in the Gwelo diocese. Reasons given for the refusal were that missionaries there tended to influence Africans against the government, that the diocesan newspaper promoted disloyalty among the people, and that some missionaries had been guilty of immoral behavior.

Mexican Education Law — The Mexican Congress overrode objections of the bishops' conference of the country in approving a new education law establishing state control over private schools and all educational systems, and barring religious organizations from intervening "in any form" in education of "any type or degree." Passage of the law marked a change in years-long tolerance of Catholic schools by the government despite the anti-religious thrust of Article 3 of the federal constitution.

Freedom in Vietnam — The Bishops' Conference of Vietnam appealed to the North Vietnamese government to grant its citizens freedom to practice their religion and to the South Vietnamese regime to "accentuate the liberalization of political activities." In a statement issued at the end of their four-day annual plenary assembly in Saigon, they urged "the two governments of South and North Vietnam to stop outright all warlike activity and, moved by a sentiment of patriotic affection, to cease all campaigns of reciprocal disparagement and hate."

Imprimatur — Cardinal Francois Marty of Paris, writing in his archdiocesan bulletin, reminded Catholics of the obligation to seek the approval of church authorities for books on theological subjects. He wrote: "Theological research must be done in the Church. The Christian community has a right to have the bishop assume effectively his duty of guarding and promoting the faith. It is a good thing for the theologian himself to be re-questioned in season and out of season in order to manifest the coherence of his writing with the authentic doctrine of the Church given by tradition. That is precisely the present function of the *Imprimatur*" (permission of the bishop to "let it be published").

Peoples' Peace Prize — Brazilian Archbishop Helder Camara, widely acclaimed for his efforts to aid the poor and promote works of human development on an international scale, was awarded the $250,000 Peoples' Peace Prize Feb. 10 in Oslo, Norway. The prize — financed by collections in Scandinavia, Germany, The Netherlands, Belgium and Italy — was initiated by groups in Norway dissatisfied with the choice of recipients of the 1973 Nobel Peace Prize, U.S. Secretary of State Henry Kissinger and North Vietnamese peace negotiator Le Duc Tho.

Third World Aid — Some 500,000 Britons were signatories of a nationwide petition to Parliament seeking improved aid to the Third World of developing nations. The petition, sponsored by Catholic and other organizations, called for improved trading opportunities for developing countries in the European Common Market and for acceptance by the British government of the UN-set target of 0.7 per cent of the gross national product as official development assistance.

Schismatic Church — Cardinal Avelar Brandao Vilela of Sao Salvador called on the Brazilian press to use caution and discretion in reporting affairs of the schismatic Catholic Apostolic Roman Church. Faulty reporting and popular misunderstanding over the years had resulted in confusion among the people regarding the true identity of the church and

its lack of unity with the Catholic Church. The schismatic body, established in 1945, had a membership estimated to range from 100,000 to two million persons.

French Sisterhoods — A survey of French sisterhoods from 1969 to 1973 disclosed:

• The number of nuns fell more than eight per cent, from 109,900 to 100,700. Noncontemplative congregations were the biggest losers, of 7,900 sisters because of deaths and an annual average of 353 departures.

• The number of novices in noncontemplative congregations declined from 1,399 to 519.

• One thousand small communities of sisters were started during the period which marked the closing of 1,435 convents.

Bishop Arrested — Bishop Antonio Anoveros and his vicar general were reported Feb. 28 to be under virtual house arrest in Bilbao. It was also reported that the Spanish government was trying to take legal action against the bishop because of a sermon in which he called for more freedom for the Basques in the northern part of the country.

Foreign Briefs:

• Catholic Relief Services reported Feb. 8 that approximately 300,000 refugees in Cambodia were being aided by its programs, especially through the operation of agricultural self-help projects.

• The Dominican Republic's "instant divorce industry" for foreigners, mostly from the U.S., was reported to have produced some $3.5 million for the country. It was estimated that nearly 8,000 divorces had been decreed by various courts since June 20, 1971.

• Father Mario Pais de Oliveira, a critic of Portuguese military policy in Africa, was sentenced to a month in jail or a $90 fine for "inciting public disobedience."

• The World Council of Churches announced Feb. 27 that it was distributing $450,000 to 29 organizations engaged in efforts to combat racism, mostly in Africa. The amount was the largest for a single year since the first such donations were made in 1970.

New Sexual Culture

The bishops of Lombardy and Veneto, Italy, issued a pastoral letter concerning positive and negative aspects of "a new sexual culture."

They acknowledged such positive aspects as "a better understanding of the values of sexuality, a personalistic concept of love, (a change in) the role of women in society, the rediscovery of the dignity of married couples, and the educational and pastoral function of the family."

On the negative side, they scored widespread diffusion of pornography and "morally unworthy films," support for "unlimited eroticism in sexual anarchy, and facile and uncritical conformity to a permissive morality."

MARCH 1974

VATICAN

Sacrifice for Others — In a lenten message published Mar. 2 in *L'Osservatore Romano,* Pope Paul appealed to Christians to make personal sacrifices and to contribute to the assistance of persons in need of the basic necessities of life. He said: "If we are to share together in the Body of the Lord, we must sincerely desire that no one should lack what is necessary, even though this should involve us in some personal sacrifice."

Not Seriously III — An attack of influenza forced the Pope to limit his participation in a retreat Mar. 3 to 9. A "slight indisposition" reported Mar. 26 caused incidental curtailment of a few activities.

Pius XII Praised — Pope Paul paid tribute to Pius XII, with whom he had been closely associated, in a brief address Mar. 10. He called him "a strong and loving man in the defense of justice and peace (who) . . . always dared to do, in concrete and difficult circumstances, whatever was in his power to prevent inhuman and unjust acts." The tribute was interpreted as a reply to charges by the author of *Massacre in Rome* and his movie-producer associates that Pius XII had failed to take action to stop the execution of more than 300 persons in Rome by Nazis in March, 1944.

Illusion of Consumerism — "A sober, simple, modest life-style must characterize the Christian life," Pope Paul declared in an address telecast Mar. 10 in Canada. He scored "a widespread illusion (of a society of affluent consumers) that the possession of economic goods and the enjoyment of the pleasures they obtain can answer human aspirations." He asserted: "First of all, we must restructure within our spirit the (Christian) scale of values."

Neither Contraception nor Abortion — Responsible parenthood does not include recourse to contraception or abortion, stated the Holy Father Mar. 13 before the Committee on the Family. "In fact," he said, "there is no question of turning the procreative act aside from its purpose, still less of taking life away from the human being that has been conceived." The Pope spoke at the conclusion of the committee's second general assembly since its establishment in January, 1973.

Prodigals Need Their Father — People today, like the prodigal son in the Gospel parable, can find happiness by becoming aware of the sadness within themselves and returning to God their Father, Pope Paul told a general audience Mar. 13. He called the parable "dramatic and stupendous," and added: "This act of personal, solitary and courageous reflection lies at the root of recovering a genuine and reinvigorating life for man."

Scripture Scholars and Their Work — Speaking of the work of scriptural scholars at a meeting with the Pontifical Biblical Commission Mar. 14, Pope Paul said: "Without a clear biblical foundation, moral theology risks drying itself up in philosophical theorizing and becoming a stranger to man . . . wounded by sin but saved in Christ." He also said: "The biblical scholar is called to render a similar service to the ecumenical and missionary task of the Church." The Pontiff called the Bible "the privileged terrain of encounter with churches and ecclesial communities in imperfect communion with the Catholic Church."

Pastoral Strategy — The Church must develop a "pastoral strategy" for preaching the Gospel in a world characterized "by the absence of God," Pope Paul told members of the Secretariat for Non-Believers Mar. 15. He said the secretariat's work "opens up new fields that up to now have been almost unexplored" by the Church in trying to make contact "with those areas of today's world that are most distant and resistant to the Church."

Eastern Canon Law — The Pope joined patriarchs and other Eastern Rite officials Mar. 18 for the opening of a plenary assembly of the Pontifical Commission for the Revision of the Code of Canon Law of Eastern Rite Churches.

Sin and God's Mercy — Sin is real and can kill despite the world's attempt to erase its "name and reality" from everyday discussion, Pope Paul told 7,000 persons at a general audience Mar. 20. He said: "The consequence of sin is death. This is the truth, this is the lot of man who knowingly and willingly detaches himself from the highest and only source of life, which is God. But there is another truth which follows. Another lot is reserved for man . . . the mercy of God. The mercy of God rescues man from the misery of sin."

Beatification of Liborius Wagner — The Holy Father presided Mar. 24 at ceremonies for the beatification of Liborius Wagner, a German priest and convert from Lutheranism who was martyred Dec. 9, 1631, at the age of 38. The Pope said that Blessed Liborius, who was put to death because he refused to renounce Catholicism, was a "witness, a martyr . . . and encouragement for reconciliation (among Christians) . . . not an excuse for polemics and recriminations."

Population Control — Pope Paul warned Mar. 28 against "a great temptation" to slow down population growth by "radical measures that are often in contrast with the laws implanted by God in man's nature" and that "fall short of due respect for the dignity of human life and man's just liberty." The "radical measures," although not named, were pinpointed as contraception, abortion and policies harmful to family life and prejudicial to human liberties.

The message of the Pope, who was suffering from a "slight indisposition," was presented by Cardinal Jean Villot, secretary of state, to UN Population Year 1974 officials Rafael Salas and Antonio Carillo-Flores.

The Pope Also:

• Prayed that Europe might be defended from inner rivalries threatening its unity, Mar. 17.

• Told a group of parents of Israeli soldiers who were still prisoners of war that he hoped an exchange of prisoners would soon take place as a peace gesture in the troubled Middle East, Mar. 20.

• Met privately Mar. 25 with Prince Rainier III of Monaco and his family; Father Theodore M. Hesburgh, C.S.C., president of the University of Notre Dame, and French biblical scholar Father Pierre Benoit, O.P.

Commission on Women — The Commission for the Role of Women in the Church and Society, established by Pope Paul in mid-1973, concluded a six-day plenary assembly Mar. 3. On Mar. 4 Vatican Radio announced that the life of the 25-member commission was being extended to at least January, 1976.

Pontifical Secrecy — Vatican press officer Federico Alessandrini released the text of a new instruction on pontifical secrecy at a press conference Mar. 14. The document, which was substantially the same as one issued in 1968, covered classifiable material, persons bound to secrecy (mostly personnel of the Roman Curia and other church officials), the nature of the secrecy obligation and sanctions for violations (including suspension and discharge from office), and a secrecy oath. Alessandrini said the basic reason for pontifical secrecy, the tightest that can be imposed, is the "imperative requirement of the common good of the Church, as well as of dignity and personal honor." Subject to secrecy for these reasons were various categories of pontifical documents and Vatican information concerning church affairs and personnel.

Vatican Briefs:

• An authoritative note in the Mar. 4-5 edition of *L'Osservatore Romano* said that the Vatican had refrained from taking a public stand on efforts of the Spanish government to expel Bishop Antonio Anoveros of Bilbao in hopes that the interested parties might "reach a satisfactory solution of the grave dispute."

• The Congregation for Religious disclosed that it had sent to major superiors of religious institutes in January a directive that they should provide properly for the spiritual, moral, social and economic well-being of those who leave religious life.

• Diplomat Archbishop Agostino Casaroli flew to Cuba Mar. 27 at the invitation of the bishops there.

Missions

"Self-styled theologians" and others who seek to "snuff out the Church's missionary zeal" were the targets of an article by Cardinal Agnelo Rossi in the Mar. 28 edition of *L'Osservatore Romano*.

The prefect of the Congregation for the Evangelization of Peoples decried lopsided emphasis on local church concerns and preference for dialogue, social liberation and human development efforts over works of evangelization. He called "incredible" the advocacy of such positions "in an epoch which has seen the Second Vatican Council solemnly and unequivocally confirm the primary mission of the entire Church to evangelize," and "when two-thirds of mankind still does not know Our Lord Jesus Christ."

DOMESTIC

Thomas Aquinas Anniversary — Father Robert Henle, S.J., president of Georgetown University, predicted "another great revival of Thomistic study," in a Washington, D.C., address commemorating the 700th anniversary of the death of St. Thomas Aquinas. He made the prediction during a Feb. 28 to Mar. 3 convention of the American Catholic Philosophical Association.

The Papacy — A "renewed papacy" might well become a focus of unity for all Christians, was one of the key lines in a statement issued Mar. 4 by the U.S. National Lutheran-Catholic Dialogue group of theologians sponsored by the Bishops' Committee on Ecumenical and Interreligious Affairs and the U.S.A. National Committee of the Lutheran World Federation.

Schools Not Havens — Catholic schools "must not become havens for those trying to escape integrated public schools," according to a policy statement on admission practices issued by Archbishop Thomas J. McDonough of Louisville. The statement, like another one released by the Boston archdiocese during the month, was intended to counteract efforts by some parents to transfer students from public to Catholic schools in order to evade court-ordered desegregation of public schools in three Kentucky districts.

Right to Life Amendment Hearings — Four cardinals — John J. Krol, John P. Cody, Timothy Manning and Humberto S. Medeiros — testified Mar. 7 before a Senate subcommittee considering constitutional amendments that would protect the life of the unborn. They spoke in support of such an amendment but did not endorse versions authored by Sen. James L. Buckley of New York and Sen. Jesse Helms of North Carolina.

Baby Death Probe — Prosecutor Gary Flakne of Hennepin County acknowledged Mar. 11 that his office was investigating reports that two babies who survived abortion procedures were denied medical treatment and allowed to die Oct. 5 and 9, 1973, at the University of Minnesota Hospitals. The acknowledgment was made following publication of a copyrighted story about the incidents in *The Catholic Bulletin*, the newspaper of the St. Paul-Minneapolis archdiocese.

Funds for Latin America — The Division for Latin America, U.S. Catholic Conference, collected the record amount of $1,558,371 in 1973 for funding 103 projects in Latin America. The types of programs and fund allocations were: pastoral, $827,290; evangelization, $154,430; human development, $99,510; research, $46,000; education, $44,014. The sum of $254,000 was granted for support of the general secretariat and departments and activities of the Latin American Bishops' Conference.

Critics Blasted — "Third parties," neither bishops nor competent theologians, who are "assuming a role reserved to the official teaching authority of the Church" in judging the orthodoxy of professional theologians and biblical scholars, were severely criticized by Bishop James S. Rausch in a Mar. 14 speech in Washington, D.C. His remarks were apparently prompted by a request from the executive board of the Catholic Biblical Association urging bishops to repudiate attacks on biblical scholars in certain conservative Catholic publications.

Political Prisoners in South Vietnam — The Committee on Social Development and World Peace, U.S. Catholic Conference, urged the U.S. government to bring influence to bear on the South Vietnamese to allow international inspection of prisons and to release civilian political prisoners. A committee statement said that "persistent evidence of detention, torture and ill treatment of civilian political prisoners" in both North and South Vietnam is "one of the most distressing aftermaths of the war in Indochina."

Boys Town Worth — The net worth of Father Flanagan's Boys Town increased during the past year by nearly $9 million, raising the total to $226,622,709.77. Accounting for most of the increase was $13.66 million in contributions to the institution's endowment fund. Following disclosures of its worth by the Sun Newspapers of Omaha in 1972, the home began to develop and implement plans for expanding its facilities and services to youth.

Notre Dame Policy — Faculty member Dr. Joseph Scott challenged Notre Dame University's policy with respect to the hiring of black professors (seven were on the staff) and the admission of students from minority groups (less than three per cent were black). He raised the questions at a Mar. 21 to 22 civil rights conference held on the campus to mark the 20th anniversary of Brown vs. the Board of Education, the 1954 decision of the U.S. Supreme Court which outlawed segregation in the nation's public schools.

Death with Dignity — Dr. Arthur Dyck of Harvard University told participants in the New England Conference of the Catholic Hospital Association Mar. 26 that lessening of legal restraint on abortion had created a climate of acceptance for infanticide and euthanasia. One supportive piece of evidence was a "Death with Dignity" bill awaiting action in the Florida legislature for the sixth time since 1968.

Death Penalty — Lopsided votes in both houses of the legislature overrode a gubernatorial veto to make Pennsylvania the 23rd state to reinstate the death penalty for specified major crimes since June 29, 1972. The Pennsylvania Catholic Conference had urged the legislators to explore every possible alternative before taking action.

Farah Support — Bishop Edward A. McCarthy of Phoenix issued a statement Mar. 29 asking support of the Farah Manufacturing Co. following termination of its labor dispute with the Amalgamated Clothing Workers of America. After noting his earlier criticism of the firm, he said: "I would recommend that buyers seriously consider purchasing Farah clothing products in order that the company and its workers might prosper and be an example that will lead to a wider acceptance of the ideals of social justice." Several similar statements were published by other supporters of the workers.

Domestic Briefs:

• Charging that some fraternal organizations in the Boston area had "racial and prejudicial attitudes," Cardinal Humberto S. Medeiros said Mar. 1 "there is no place for Catholics and Christians in organizations which violate the equal dignity of persons."

• Georgetown University issued a commemorative magazine honoring Father Patrick F. Healy, who was installed as its president in 1874; he was the first black president of a predominantly white university in the U.S.

• Bishop John L. Morkovsky lost the sight of his left eye Mar. 8 when two gunmen pistol-whipped him during a robbery in his home in Houston.

• Msgr. James F. Rigney, rector of St. Patrick's Cathedral, New York City, was named an honorary canon of the Episcopal Cathedral of St. John the Divine.

• Mary Pat Siczek was appointed Mar. 18 co-director of the St. Thomas Aquinas Center, the Catholic parish at Purdue University, West Lafayette, Ind.

• Honored: Cardinal John J. Krol as "American Prelate of the Year," by the Polish-American Congress; Archbishop Ignatius J. Strecker as the "Outstanding Kansan for 1973," by the Kansas State Society of Washington, D.C.; Cardinal John J. Carberry for his work in promoting devotion to the Blessed Virgin Mary, by the Blue Army of Our Lady of Fatima.

NFPC Convention

Between 175 and 200 representatives of 130 priests' councils throughout the country attended the Mar. 17 to 21 convention of the House of Delegates of the National Federation of Priests' Councils in San Francisco. Delegates passed a wide variety of resolutions on:

• Pastoral programs: possible administration of the sacrament of anointing of the sick for alcoholics and drug addicts; more democratic procedures for the selection of bishop candidates; better distribution of the clergy; care for divorced persons; vocational recruitment.

• Social concerns: impeachment of President Nixon; halting the $50 billion Bl bomber program; moral responsibility of corporate investment practices; prison reform; needs of the rural poor; unconditional amnesty for all war resisters. Homosexuality was the subject of debate and resolutions (for study, against discrimination) during the meeting.

President Reid C. Mayo was reelected president of the federation for another two years.

FOREIGN

Swiss Synod and Theologians — For the second time in two years, the Swiss national synod appealed to the country's bishops to ask the Vatican for broader legal rights for theologians threatened with censorship for views alleged to be contrary to the teaching of the Church. The 131 delegates also adopted a resolution calling on theologians and all other Catholics to be aware of appropriate responsibility with respect to the proper interpretation of doctrines of faith.

Immigrants in France — The Commission for Migration of the French Bishops' Conference asked Catholics early in the month to work for a solution to "the exploitation of immigrant workers" in the country. Involved issues, they said, were: causes of migration; personal relations, housing, employment and segregation of immigrants; legal protection of their rights; educational opportunities for their children and respect for their culture; political self-expression; recognition of their cultural expressions of religious faith.

Population and Economic Development — The control of world population is directly related to the economic development of people and is doomed to failure if reliance is placed on contraceptive education in underdeveloped countries, according to Dr. Reg Gallop, head of the food science department of Manitoba University, Canada. Interviewed by *The Catholic Register* of Toronto, he said the only solution to population control lies in providing the Third World with the minimum essentials for human dignity, development and peace.

Consortium Meeting — Three hundred and 50 sisters from 10 countries took part in the Feb. 23 to Mar. 4 international meeting of the Consortium Perfectae Caritatis in Rome. Cardinal Jean Danielou, S.J., at a press conference Mar. 24, called "secularism, a false idea of freedom and a misunderstanding of renewal," a significant factor in the contemporary crisis in religious life.

Anglican Independence of Parliament — According to a delayed Mar. 5 report, the General Synod of the Church of England voted overwhelmingly Feb. 20 to give final approval to a measure that would make it rather than Parliament the final arbiter in questions concerning doctrine and worship. The measure, which required approval of the law-making body, would end well over 300 years of parliamentary control over the Church.

Diplomatic Relations Not Wanted — Speaking for his fellow bishops Mar. 6, Archbishop Carlos Quintero Arce of Hermosillo said they did not want diplomatic relations established between the Vatican and the Mexican government. The bishops wished to avoid possibly compromising effects of such relations.

Anti-Abortion Petition — The Alliance for Life officially launched Mar. 8 a campaign to collect one million signatures for a petition asking the Canadian Parliament to provide legal protection for the lives of the unborn. Some pro-life groups charged that 1969 amendments to the Criminal Code, permitting abortion to save a mother's life or health, were not being strictly enforced and that, as a consequence, the country had almost de facto abortion on demand.

In Ontario, under new government regulations approved in February and published this month, 16-year-old girls had the right to legal abortion without parental consent.

Sahelian Drought Aid — The Canadian Catholic Organization for Development and Peace made a second allocation, of $205,000, for emergency relief and medium and long-term development programs in the drought-stricken Sahelian region of Africa — Chad, Mali, Mauretania, Niger, Senegal, Upper Volta and Ethiopia. The total value of relief funds from the organization amounted to $400,000.

Anglican Primate Resigns — Archbishop Michael Ramsey of Canterbury, 69, spiritual head of the Church of England since 1961, announced Mar. 11 that he would resign from the see Nov. 15, his 70th birthday.

Priest Shortages — Priest shortages, caused by a variety of factors, were reported from several countries.

• The Nigerian Bishops' Conference appealed to the government to issue entry permits to foreign priests because a clergy shortage had reached "alarming proportions" in the country. No permits had been issued for the past three years.

• Three U.S. Maryknoll Missioners and eight other foreign priests, accused of interfering in politics, were ordered out of Guatemala by the military government of Gen. Carlos Arana Osorio.

• A lack of priests, brothers and nuns was "acutely felt all over the country," the bishops of Sudan said in a letter published at the conclusion of their annual meeting in Khartoum.

Cardinal Mindszenty Removal — German bishops, following a meeting in Stuttgart, said in a statement that they "are convinced that only a justified pastoral concern for men had led the Pope to take the sorrowful step (of removing Cardinal Mindszenty from his office as Archbishop of Ezstergom and Primate of Hungary). In any case, it is untenable to affirm that the Pope and the Vatican misunderstood the value and the necessity of the witness to the faith and of opposing, even at the risk of martyrdom, atheism and violence. Together with the Pope, the German bishops are convinced that between the ideology of atheistic Communism and the Gospel no compromise is possible."

Violence in Argentina — Cardinal Antonio Caggiano of Buenos Aires strongly criticized violence and terrorism which continued "to grow and to deteriorate public peace everywhere" in Argentina. He called on all Christians to oppose terrorist groups and to follow democratic procedures for achieving social justice and solving political problems.

Portuguese African Territories — While some 10 years of warfare continued between the Mozambique Liberation Front (Frelimo) and Portuguese troops, the bishops declared in a pastoral letter: "We are anxious to see peace in Mozambique, but peace can only be built on justice which puts aside all racial discrimination, hate and vengeance so that we can live as brothers."

The Portuguese government announced in the middle of the month the dismissal of two generals — Francesco de Costa Gomes, chairman of the Joint Chiefs of Staff, and his assistant, Antonio de Spinola. The dismissals climaxed a crisis touched off by a book written by the latter in which he said that military victory by Portuguese forces over guerrillas in Mozambique, Angola and Guinea-Bissau was impossible.

St. Patrick's Day Killings — The killing of eight persons over the St. Patrick's Day weekend in Northern Ireland brought pleas for an end to violence from Cardinal William Conway of Armagh and Anglican Archbishop Alan Buchanan.

Danger Only from Within — The greatest threat to the survival of Catholic schools in Ontario was not bigotry or the honest opposition of persons with a different philosophy, but from within — from the possible failure of Catholic educators to fulfill their responsibilities in religious education. So stated Bishop G. Emmett Carter of London at the 31st annual convention of the Ontario English Catholic Teachers' Association in Toronto.

Stand-Off in Spain — "I only tried to unite the two parties of a dispute," said Bishop Antonio Anoveros of Bilbao late in the month concerning a homily he approved for delivery in churches of his diocese in February. The results were: temporary house arrest for him for allegedly threatening the "national unity of Spain"; a demand by the government for his removal from the diocese and departure from the country; strong support for him from the Spanish Bishops' Conference, in a statement of Mar. 9; and, by the end of March, deterrence of the government from translating its stand against the bishop into a disruption of relations with the Church.

Foreign Briefs:

• The seventh centennial of the death of St. Thomas Aquinas was commemorated Mar. 7 to 9 with seven conferences and related activities at the University of Teheran.

• Archbishop Octaviano Marquez Toriz of Pueblo started a program of home building (of 200 dwellings) and social services for victims of the 1973 earthquake in nearby Quecholac. Meanwhile, the director of the Mexican government's effort to help the people confessed failure in the task of reconstruction.

• The Roman Catholic and Anglican dioceses of Hong Kong signed an agreement Mar. 15 recognizing the validity of baptisms conferred by priests or ministers of either church.

• A survey by the Ghana Bishops' Conference indicated that laymen were strongly opposed to any plan that would permit them to distribute Holy Communion as extraordinary ministers of the Eucharist.

• The Colombian Ministry of War announced Mar. 23 that Father Domingo Lain Sanz, who had joined guerrilla forces, was killed Feb. 20 in a clash with government troops in Antioquia.

Church on Side of Poor

Participants in a regional workshop sponsored by the Bishops' Institute for Social Action in Manila declared that the Church in Southeast Asia must be on the side of the poor even if this stance involved the risk of alienation from the wealthy and influential.

They said: "Opting to be with the poor involves risk: the risk of conflict with vested interests or 'establishments,' religious, economic, social and political. It also involves, for leaders of the Church especially, loss of security. . . . For it means taking the unfamiliar course of looking for guidelines of policy and action . . . in a discernment of the historical process taking place among our own people."

The declaration asked pastors not to sever contact with better-off groups but to influence them "to share our concern that the poor be enabled to participate in the decisions that vitally affect them."

APRIL 1974

VATICAN

Confessional Remains — Pope Paul, after a week's confinement because of mild illness, told a general audience Apr. 3 that he felt he should "make clear and rectify some inexact reports that have been made about the new rite of the sacrament of penance, such as the reported abolition of the confessional. The confessional, as a protective screen between the confessor and the penitent to guarantee the absolute confidence of the conversation imposed on and reserved to them, clearly must remain." The new ritual, published in February, provided for retention of the confessional while leaving to bishops the decision to permit alternative settings for confession.

Evangelization — In an address to the council of the Synod of Bishops Apr. 5, the Pope said: "The Church exists to announce the Gospel of Jesus, the Son of God. . . . The Church's very own function is summarized and defined by evangelization." This was the principal topic to be discussed during the Synod assembly scheduled to start Sept. 27 at the Vatican.

Ovulation Research — In an Apr. 5 message to a Rome meeting of gynecologists and other medical experts, Pope Paul hailed efforts to develop practical ways and means of determining the time of ovulation. His message echoed a statement from his 1968 encyclical, *Humanae Vitae:* "We wish to encourage men of science who can considerably advance the welfare of marriage and the family . . . if they labor to explain more thoroughly conditions favoring a proper regulation of births" by natural rather than artificial means.

Youth — The Holy Father urged a throng of young Italian Catholics on Palm Sunday to be proud of their faith and ready to defend the Church from "unjust criticism." He said: "You bear witness to Christ if and because you live like Christians," and added that witness "involves some positive act of loyalty to Christ" and demands courage. . . . We must not be ashamed and run away when showing ourselves to be Christians causes others to despise us, or in some way endangers our reputation or interests. . . . Be faithful and humble, and you will be strong, and you will be able to bear good and positive witness to your Christian and Catholic belief."

Gap between Haves and Have-Nots — In a 1,400-word message to an extraordinary session of the UN General Assembly, Pope Paul said that failure to close the gap between rich and underdeveloped countries could lead to "despair . . . on the part of the poor and powerless . . . that will spur them on to aggressive search for methods — other than international cooperation — to gain what they consider to be their economic rights." The theme of the Pope's message was the need for and the moral demand on developed nations to aid poorer nations for the sake of justice and world peace. The General Assembly began deliberations Apr. 9 concerning the availability of and trade in raw materials, and the manner in which both affect the development of poor nations.

Peace in Troubled Areas — Pope Paul, during a general audience Apr. 10, urged governments and ordinary citizens to work for peace in Vietnam and Northern Ireland: "We encourage the sincere efforts of so many, those in government, social communications or ordinary citizens, who strive for joyful concord in the world."

Christians and Moslems against Materialism — Pope Paul expressed hope that Christians and Moslems might join forces in combating materialism in the world, in a personal message to King Faisal of Saudi Arabia. The message was delivered to the monarch Apr. 12 by Cardinal Sergio Pignedoli, president of the Vatican Secretariat for Non-Christians.

Easter Message — Pope Paul in his Easter message called on people to renounce the pleasure-seeking "false gospel of life" and to live instead by the gospel of the cross, which he called "the law of duty, service, sorrow, love and sacrifice, and . . . the wise and true interpretation of human life." The Holy Father delivered the message during a Mass celebrated on the steps of St. Peter's Basilica before a throng of some 200,000.

Baptism and Its Effects — Christ has transmitted to Christians the effects of his life, suffering and death through the sacraments, "and especially in . . . baptism," declared the Pope at a general audience Apr. 17. Calling attention to "the most extraordinary fact of our participation in the divine life as transmitted by baptism," he said: "If we are Christians, we are a new humanity. There is in us something original that did not exist before in earthly and human phenomenology; that is, the grace of God. It makes us new men, in our way of thinking, of acting, in our style of life and especially in brotherly charity. If we are truly companions of Christ, we must be brothers to other men and we must wish to do good and to show charity toward our brothers, above all to those within our ecclesial society." He concluded, saying: "Easter will not have come and gone for us in vain if it has rekindled within us the awareness of our baptism."

St. Thomas Aquinas Centenary — St. Thomas Aquinas "still speaks to us as the voice of a living teacher" with validity and relevance, the Pope told 1,300 participants in an eight-day international congress marking the 700th anniversary of his death. The Pope emphasized in his talk Apr. 20 "the art of thinking well." He said: "We must pay heed to logic . . . the rigorous and honest use of intelligence in seeking the truth of things and of life." Without it, he added, "we fear a dearth of authentic philosophy capable of sustaining human thought." He called the study of Thomistic writings "an elementary but providential introduction to that intellectual scaling of the heights, whether philosophical or theological, which demands respect for the laws of thought."

Blessed Frances Schervier — Pope Paul paid tribute Apr. 28 to Sister Maria Franziska Schervier during beatification ceremonies in St. Peter's Basilica, calling her a woman who did everything "as if God was always with her." The foundress of the Franciscan Sisters of the Poor was born in Aachen, Germany, in 1819, visited communities of the institute in the U.S. in 1863 and 1868, and died in 1876.

The Pope Also:

• Sent a message of condolence to the people of France on the death Apr. 2 of President Georges Pompidou.

• Sent financial assistance to victims of recent floods in Brazil.

• Telegraphed his "deepest sorrow" to the people of Czechoslovakia at the death Apr. 6 of Cardinal Stepan Trochta, 69, of Litomerice, a "defender of the faith and a most worthy citizen of his nation."

• Met with two new ambassadors to the Vatican: Hector Riesle of Chile, Apr. 6, and Hyun joon Shin of South Korea, Apr. 8.

• Told radio and television executives from several nations Apr. 8 that Holy Year 1975 responds to a deep human need, and urged them to give it "a large place in your broadcasts."

• Expressed his sympathy to the families of 18 victims of an Arab terrorist attack on the Israeli village of Qiryat Shemona.

Vatican Briefs:

• Archbishop Agostino Casaroli, secretary of the Council for the Public Affairs of the Church, said of an Apr. 4 visit with Premier Fidel Castro of Cuba: "My visit, although it did not have formally the character of an official one, offered . . . the possibility of a serious exchange of views on the most responsible levels."

• Roman Catholic and Coptic Orthodox representatives of a mixed commission announced in a communique released Apr. 10 agreement on the necessity and value of deeper theological investigation of their Christian beliefs.

• The Vatican Library opened an Apr. 19 to Dec. 20 exhibition of original manuscripts of Sts. Thomas Aquinas and Bonaventure in commemoration of the seventh centenaries of their deaths.

• *The Holy See and the Victims of War, January 1941-December 1942* was published. A major part of the 807-page volume dealt with the Vatican's opposition to anti-Semitic laws and the first deportations of Jews from Germany and Nazi-dominated countries.

Holy Land Catholics

Pope Paul, in an apostolic exhortation released at a press conference Apr. 5, appealed to Catholics throughout the world to help support the "living witness" of some 110,000 Catholics in Israel, Jordan and adjoining occupied territories.

Practically, he asked:

• that special prayers be offered "for our brethren of the Church in the Holy Land";

• that an annual collection be taken up and "used for the upkeep not only of the Holy Places but, above all, of those pastoral, charitable, educational and social works which the Church supports in the Holy Land for the welfare of the Christian brethren and the local communities."

The document disavowed any political significance, although it appeared that the problems of Arab Christians were its central concern.

In comment on the Pope's exhortation, Msgr. John G. Nolan, president of the Pontifical Mission for Palestine, said: "He didn't deal in generalities. He came right to the point and asked Catholics to help support Christians in the Holy Land, and not just help preserve the stone shrines."

DOMESTIC

Moral Short-Sightedness — Emphasis on "efficiency, expediency, immediate satisfaction and personal self-fulfillment" has caused people to lose sight of ultimate moral demands, declared Archbishop Joseph L. Bernardin of Cincinnati at a consultation on the decline of public morality. This "moral shortsightedness" has become "the basic ethical problem of our times," he told participants in the meeting held at Indiana University.

The Rosary — Pope Paul's apostolic exhortation on devotion to Mary, made public Mar. 22, will end "the eclipse that enveloped Mary" for some years and will spur new interest in the Rosary, stated Father Patrick Peyton, C.S.C., national director of the Family Rosary Crusade. Speaking in Albany, N.Y., Apr. 4, he said: "The Rosary is now revealed in a brilliant light for what it is . . . a Gospel prayer, a prologue and epilogue of the Eucharistic Sacrifice, the Mass, and one of the greatest and most effective prayers for the family."

Boys Town Research — Archbishop Daniel E. Sheehan of Omaha announced that Stanford University would join the Catholic University of America in the $25.5 million, long-term research program of youth development funded by Boys Town in January.

Aid to Poorest Countries — The U.S. Catholic Conference appealed Apr. 5 to Congress to approve a $1.5 billion contribution over a four-year period to the International Development Agency of the World Bank for aid to the poorest countries in the world.

Opinions about Abortion — The most significant aspect of the latest Gallup survey of opinion on abortion was the consistency of its findings with those gathered before the Jan. 22, 1973, Supreme Court decision legalizing abortion during the first three months of pregnancy. In December, 1972, the pro and con percentages were 46 and 45; in the latest survey, they were 47 and 44. It seemed that advocates of a permissive attitude toward abortion had not been able to swing the American public over to their side even with the support of the Supreme Court ruling.

Busing in Boston — Cardinal Humberto Medeiros announced his strong support of Massachusetts' 1965 Racial Imbalance Act providing for the busing of more than 5,000 Boston-area students in September, 1974. Against a background of demonstrations against the law, he said he opposed attempts to "either repeal or weaken" the statute "because it is right — because it calls upon our citizens to collaborate for the common good of all."

Tornado Victims Aided — Aid for persons and places devastated by tornadoes in 16 dioceses of 11 states, mostly in the Midwest, was being supplied by the National Conference of Catholic Charities, the Christian Appalachian Project, numerous dioceses and a disaster committee of the U.S. Catholic Conference. Twisters killed 300 persons early in the month.

Offensive Comic Book — Republican Senator Richard Schweiker of Pennsylvania protested the use of Agency for International Development funds to circulate 10,000 copies of an offensive comic book endorsing artificial contraception. *Los Supermachos,* distributed in Panama, pictured the Virgin Mary on the cover with the caption, "Little Virgin, you who conceived without sinning, help me to sin without conceiving."

Project FORWARD — Four bishops and heads of several national Catholic organizations joined other religious leaders in sponsorship of Project FORWARD '76, designed to deepen popular awareness of the nation's religious heritage during the 1976 celebration of the 200th anniversary of the Declaration of Independence. The project was under the auspices of the Interchurch Center, New York City.

Mass-Like Service Forces Resignation — Ursuline Sister Gloria Fitzgerald was asked to, and did, resign her post as a campus minister after celebrating a Mass-like service Mar. 15 for nine persons at Boston University's Newman Center. Father Robert W. Bullock, Boston archdiocesan director for campus ministry, said that the resignation would have been "demanded if a similar

Mass ritual was performed by any unordained person, man or woman."

Spanish-Language Liturgical Center — Bishop Walter W. Curtis, chairman of the Liturgy Committee of the National Conference of Catholic Bishops, announced Apr. 22 that the Mexican-American Cultural Center in San Antonio had been designated as a center of research in Spanish-language liturgy.

Student Aid — By a vote of 352,815 to 260,889, Louisianans approved a new state constitution permitting several forms of aid — free textbooks, instructional materials, bus rides, lunches — to nonpublic as well as public school students. The new constitution was to go into effect at midnight Dec. 31, 1974.

Reverse Discrimination — The U.S. Supreme Court declined on technical grounds Apr. 22 to rule on the constitutionality of "reverse discrimination" against Marco DeFunis, a white law student, who was denied admission to the 1971 freshman class of the University of Washington even though he had scored higher on qualification tests than a number of black students. Five of the Justices said that the Court could not consider the substantive issue presented by the case. The reason was that DeFunis, who was admitted to the university under court order, would complete his studies at the end of the current term regardless of any decision reached on the merits of his case.

UFWA Boycott — Cesar Chavez and some 500 workers were intensifying efforts to spread boycott action across the country against the purchase of grapes and lettuce not bearing the label of the United Farm Workers of America. Their purpose was to pressure owners into signing new labor contracts with them. They claimed that their earlier three-year agreements with many growers had been replaced with "sweetheart" Teamster contracts in the summer of 1973.

CPA Convention — Two hundred and 50 delegates attended the Apr. 24 to 26 convention of the Catholic Press Association in Denver. The main concerns of participants were the "vital function" of the Catholic press in disseminating information and interpretation of religious news, and practical problems of publication management. The convention met jointly with the predominantly Protestant Associated Church Press.

Bearings Suspends Operations — Malcolm Pennington, chairman of the board of directors, announced Apr. 26 that Bearings for Re-Establishment was suspending operations begun in 1966 to assist former clergymen and religious to make the transition to secular life. Diminished need for its services was the reason.

Conscience Clause Covers All Indiana Hospitals — The conscience clause of the 1973 Indiana abortion law gives public, tax-supported hospitals, as well as private hospitals, the right to refuse to perform abortions, according to State Attorney General Theodore L. Sendak.

Solidarity Day — Protest against the continuation of anti-Semitism in the Soviet Union was the purpose of an Apr. 28 Solidarity Day observance at the United Nations sponsored by the National Interreligious Task Force on Soviet Jewry. "This (practice of the Soviet government) is an ethical genocide, not in body this time, but in mind and soul," declared Father Edward Flannery, executive secretary of the U.S. bishops' Secretariat for Catholic-Jewish Relations.

Domestic Briefs:

• The Knights of Columbus in New Jersey pledged Apr. 11 financial and recruiting aid for the 15 Birthright centers in the state.

• Named to various offices during the month were: Msgr. Charles Fahey, director of Catholic Charities for the Syracuse diocese, to the Federal Council on the Aging; Father James W. Moore, S.J., director of admissions at St. Joseph's College, Philadelphia, (elected) president of the Catholic College Coordinating Council of admissions directors; Gerald Dill, the first layman to be superintendent of schools for the Lafayette, La., diocese; Father Edward Hamel of Chicago, to the national chaplain team of the Christian Family Movement;

• Honored were: Bennet Bolton, with the 1973 national Sigma Delta Chi Award for distinguished public service in radio journalism; the Division of Creative Services, U.S. Catholic Conference, with three awards for excellence from the Religious Public Relations Council; Dominican Sister Rose Thering, with the first Leonard C. Yaseen Interreligious Award from the American Jewish Committee; the Anglican-Roman Catholic International Commission, with the Christian Unity Award from the Graymoor Friars.

NCEA Convention

Some 10,000 persons attended and participated in some manner in the 71st annual convention of the National Catholic Educational Association Apr. 15 to 18 in Cleveland. The theme of the meeting was "To Teach as Jesus Did: Message, Community, Service."

The service aspect received the most emphasis. Archbishop Joseph L. Bernardin of Cincinnati struck this note in a homily during the Mass which opened the convention. He said: "Our responsibility is not only to teach the Gospel to students within our Catholic schools, but also to Catholics in public schools, to Catholics who have not yet entered school, to Catholics who long ago finished school, to those who may never enter school, and — beyond that — to those who do not claim membership in our Church."

Father C. Albert Koob, O.Praem., whose seven years as president were to end with his resignation in June, was awarded the NCEA National Merit Award for his "outstanding contribution to Catholic education in America."

FOREIGN

Priest's Death and Socialism — The death of guerrilla Father Domingo Lain Feb. 20 in a clash with government troops — like the similar death of Father Camilo Torres in 1966 — "has become another seed in the process toward socialism" in Colombia, declared Father Rene Garcia in Bogota. Father Garcia was the only priest active in ministry left among members of the dwindling Golconda movement of social-activist priests.

Population Year Statement — "There must be respect for life and reverence for sex. There must be firm support for marriage and family life, which are prerequisites of a healthy society." So declared the bishops of England and Wales in an early April statement of moral guidelines on UN Population Year 1974. The bishops said that poor nations and persons should not be compelled or subjected to undue pressure to use methods of family planning in conflict "with their religious beliefs and social customs."

Church Freedom Urged in Spain — The bishops' National Committee for the Holy Year called on "the leaders of Spanish society" to give the Church "unconditional freedom to enable it to develop its evangelizing mission." The committee's statement was issued two months after the Church-state confrontation caused by the house arrest of Bishop Antonio Anoveros of Bilbao.

Nuns and Priests in Czechoslovakia — According to reports received in Vienna, nuns working in hospitals for the incurably ill in Czechoslovakia had to wear civilian dress if they joined their communities after 1968. The relatively few priests licensed to function were under orders to renew their licenses and under scrutiny for "loyalty to the state."

Mass in Old Barracks — Cardinal Stefan Wyszynski celebrated Easter Sunday Mass Apr. 14 in a suburb of Warsaw at a converted army barracks that had served as a temporary church for 20 years. His choice of the site was interpreted as a protest gesture against the government's refusal to permit the building of new churches.

In an earlier development, the Polish Bishops' Conference announced at the end of a meeting in March that it approved of Vatican negotiations for the improvement of Church-state relations. At the same time, the bishops recalled Pope Paul's pledge that "no decision is to be taken without the participation of the Polish episcopate."

Missionaries Expelled from Mozambique — Vatican Radio reported Apr. 16 that the Vatican was following "with particular and extraordinary attention" events in the Portuguese territories of Angola and Mozambique, following the expulsion of 11 missionaries and the police-assisted "evacuation" of a bishop from Mozambique during Holy Week.

Swedish Business in South Africa — Swedish firms doing business in South Africa were assuming no more social responsibility for black workers there than other foreign companies, according to a two-year study sponsored by the Swedish Council of Churches. The council said it would demand legislative changes affecting the companies if they failed to act for the benefit of black workers over the next two years.

Population Control in Mexico — The "responsible parenthood program started in Mexico with many promises of respect for the conscience of couples is in danger of becoming a campaign of contraceptive propaganda." In a statement authorized by his fellow bishops, Bishop Alfonso Toriz Cabian said: "The public powers go beyond their authority when they use moral pressure . . . in their efforts to establish contraceptive practices among the people."

The Whole Question of Life — The right-to-life movement deals with the whole question of life, of man made in the image of his Creator, declared British author Malcolm Muggeridge during a press conference in London, Canada. He said, in part: "It is my firm and profound conviction that, when the story of the decline of our civilization is written, a very essential part of that story will be the moment when it became overt policy of our Western societies that erotic satisfaction, pleasure, could be envisaged and accepted without reference to its purpose, which is procreation, or its condition, which is abiding love."

Papal Envoy in Taipei — The Apr. 21 appearance in Taipei of the papal envoy to China, after an absence of nearly 30 months, dispelled speculation that the Vatican was planning to downgrade its representation to Nationalist China. The speculation had been triggered by Archbishop Edward Cassidy's departure from Taiwan late in 1971 at about the same time that Taiwan lost its seat in the United Nations to Red China.

Hummel Copyrights — The Supreme Court of West Germany ruled late in the month that the Franciscan Sisters of Siessen were the sole legitimate owners of all copyrights to the artwork of Sister Mary Innocentia Hummel, creator of the world-famous Hummel figurines. The decision had the effect of nullifying licenses issued by the nun's mother and brother for the reproduction of her work. Sister Hummel died in 1946.

New Government and Hopes in Portugal — In a statement emanating from an Apr. 23 to 26 meeting at Fatima, the bishops of Portugal said they hoped that the new military government would "contribute to the betterment of Portuguese society with justice, reconciliation and mutual respect." The new regime, es-

tablished by coup Apr. 25, replaced the government of Premier Marcelo Caetano. It was headed by Gen. Antonio de Spinola, a leader in protest against fruitless, years-long military campaigns against independence forces in Mozambique and other Portuguese territories in Africa.

Atheism Irish Style — This was the title of an article written by Father Michael P. Gallagher, S.J., and published in *The Furrow* magazine. He said the "slow death of Irish Catholicism" may already have begun.

Dialogue with Asian Religions — More than 40 bishops attending the Apr. 22 to 27 first plenary assembly of the Federation of Asian Bishops' Conferences in Taipei, Taiwan, agreed on the need for increased dialogue with the great religions of Asia. The theme of the assembly was "Evangelization in Modern-Day Asia."

Foreign Briefs:
• Swiss theologian Father Stephanus Pfuertner, O.P., announced he was leaving the priesthood and the Dominican Order. He had been asked by the Congregation for the Doctrine of the Faith in 1972 to make a public retraction of his "theses on sexual ethics."
• The Lutheran University of Uppsala, Sweden, announced it would award an honorary doctorate for the first time to a Catholic, scriptural scholar Father Raymond E. Brown, S.S.
• The Sovereign Military Order of Malta, an earlier contributor of $46,000 to the UN Children's Fund, offered additional funds Apr. 11 for the support of treatment programs for children with leprosy.

Bishops and Junta in Chile

In a statement reflecting "the thoughts of the majority of the (28) Chilean bishops," the nation's hierarchy condemned the repressive tactics, economic measures and educational policies of the military government in control since the downfall of the Allende regime Sept. 11, 1973.

Items of concern cited in the strongly worded document, made public Apr. 24, were:
• "a climate of insecurity and fear";
• "unemployment and firings for arbitrary or ideological reasons";
• "arbitrary arrests and long imprisonments";
• "interrogations with physical and moral pressures, limited possibilities of legal defense, unequal sentences . . ., restrictions of the right to appeal";
• "lack of participation by parents and the community" in the structure and orientation of the educational system.

The bishops, especially Cardinal Raul Silva Henriquez of Santiago, were under attack from the left for allegedly going along with the military government, and from the right for alleged support of the previous Marxist regime of Salvador Allende.

MAY 1974

VATICAN

Work — The Christian attitude toward work was the theme of an address by the Holy Father on the feast of St. Joseph the Worker, May 1. He said: "Work, . . . viewed only as activity for the possession of and domination over temporal well-being, needs a complementary, indispensable element — the authentic element of the spirit, of faith, of being a gift of supernatural life. The ancient formula of St. Benedict, "Pray and work," is "an always modern formula of Christian life."

Vocations — In a World Vocations Day message May 5, Pope Paul said that "human respect" was probably "the most serious practical and psychological obstacle" blocking response to Christ's call to the priesthood or religious life. Other obstacles were the question, "Is it worth it?", and human imperfection in the Church.

Latin Hymns — The Vatican disclosed May 6 that at Easter time the Pope had sent bishops throughout the world a booklet of Gregorian chants in the hope that they would encourage the use of Latin hymns in some parts of the liturgy. An accompanying letter called attention to his wish that all Catholics "should know some Latin chants for the Mass; for example, the Gloria, Credo, Sanctus, Pater Noster and Agnus Dei." Liturgists commented that such use of Latin hymns would be in line with liturgical directives of the Second Vatican Council.

Alcoholism — Pope Paul commended spiritually oriented efforts to combat alcoholism in a May 11 address to members of the Calix Society, a 25-year-old adjunct of Alcoholics Anonymous. He said: "We are even more pleased when efforts, like your own (to overcome alcoholism), take into account supernatural reality and admit the impact that must come from Christian principles and from the exercise of the Catholic faith."

Divorce Law — Pope Paul voiced "surprise and sorrow at the outcome of the referendum of May 12 and 13 that retained a three-year-old divorce law in Italy despite strong opposition from him and the bishops. He told an audience of newlyweds May 15 that "this is a cause of surprise and sorrow because the rightful solidarity of many members of the Church's community was lacking in support of the just and good position on the indissolubility of marriage." Nineteen million voters cast ballots for retention of the law, by a three-to-two margin.

Missions — Pope Paul told about 50 national directors of mission aid societies that their responsibility was not just to raise funds and supply material assistance for missions but "principally to keep alive the missionary spirit in the people of God." Speaking at a special audience May 17, the last day of a four-day meeting of the general assembly of the Pontifical Missionary Works, he said that aid societies should "sensitize the faithful more and more concerning their precise responsibilities toward the world still to be evangelized."

St. Thomas Aquinas Index — The Pope said that a massive new index of the works of St. Thomas would help the intellectual world in rediscovering solid reference points it lost when it "wrenched itself from the valid methods of logic" and "from the very matrices of Christian thought." He made the remark May 19 on receiving the first five volumes of the index.

Discrimination — The Holy Father told members of the UN Special Committee on Apartheid May 22 that the Church had unhesitatingly and repeatedly called for the end of all discrimination, whether "in law or in fact." In support of this claim, he cited 11 different papal statements on the subject.

Resurrection of Christ — Pope Paul, noting at a May 22 general audience that some theologians had recently called into question "the historical and physical reality" of Christ's resurrection from the dead, declared flatly that Catholic teaching "allows no doubts about this event. Jesus Christ is truly risen. After his death — a true death — he, by divine power, really returned to life, soul and body, but in a new state, as 'heavenly man.' "

Nursing — In an address to participants in a Catholic nursing congress May 24, Pope Paul said they were continuously in contact with "sacred realities" involving "a child who is to be born or old people, victims of accidents or the sick, the physically or mentally handicapped." The congress was the tenth held by the International Catholic Committee of Nurses and Medical-Social Assistants.

Communications Day — In carrying out their duty to spread the Gospel, Christians are "conditioned by the particular circumstances of each period in history. Thus it must in our time be carried out by means of the instruments of social communications." So stated Pope Paul in a message marking May 26 as World Communications Day. The theme of the day was "Social Communications and Evangelization in Today's World."

Doctors Are Ambassadors — Pope Paul told a convention of the International Federation of Catholic Doctors that "doctors are the principal protectors of the weak. . . . They are like ambassadors sent to them to offer all the relief which God has placed at the disposition of his creatures." In a letter addressed to the May 26 to 29 meeting in Barcelona, the Pontiff said that the Christian faith stresses the "respect due the dignity of the sick person and holds high a hierarchy of values which the world, in its race toward technical progress, runs the risk of forgetting."

State of Grace — "It is necessary, always, to be in the state of grace," Pope Paul said during a general audience May 29. He called this state "the friendship of God. . . . It is the presence of God, a new, living, joyous presence; the presence of the Holy Spirit who is love, who is joy, who is consolation, who is help, who is light, who is strength and courage and life. It is the living God who comes to dwell within us." Persons in the state of grace are open to the movement of the Holy Spirit, who "can make of us and out of our natural weakness a person who is a witness, a hero, a martyr, a saint, that is, the true follower of Christ."

The Pope Also:
• Received the thanks of Rear Admiral Jeremiah A. Denton, Jr., an eight-year prisoner of war in North Vietnam, for his efforts in behalf of American POWs, May 6.
• Broadcast a public appeal to the abductors of Italian Judge Mario Sossi to return him immediately "to his anguished and innocent family," May 8.
• Condemned May 17 bombings that took at least 30 lives in Dublin, and deplored retaliatory strikes by Israeli aircraft against Palestinian refugee camps and villages in Lebanon.
• Urged American priests attending Rome's Institute for the Continuing Education of the Clergy "to continue on, united in spirit and ideals, toward the great goal of Christian renewal," May 22.
• Met Jose Luis de Cossio y Ruiz de Somocurcio, Peru's new ambassador to Vatican City, May 30.

Diplomatic Relations with Cuba — Full diplomatic relations with Cuba were restored with the appointment of Bishop Cesare Zacchi, announced May 24, to the post of apostolic nuncio. He had been charge d'affaires in the Havana nunciature since 1961, when the Vatican withdrew the nuncio from the country in response to Fidel Castro's harassment of the Church. The resumption of full relations followed conversation in March between Castro and Archbishop Agostino Casaroli, secretary of the Council for the Public Affairs of the Church.

Caritas Internationalis — The worldwide federation of national Catholic charities organizations reported May 31 that it had provided $25.38 million worth of emergency goods and funds from November, 1973, to April, 1974. The U.S. share of the total, from Catholic Relief Services, amounted to $12.8 million.

Vatican Briefs:
• Twenty new Swiss Guards pledged to defend the Pope with their lives at an oath-taking ceremony May 6, the 447th anniversary of the day on which 147 members of the corps died in defense of Clement VII during the sack of Rome.

• The Congregation for the Doctrine of the Faith authorized U.S. bishops to permit priests who had undergone or were undergoing treatment for alcoholism to receive the Eucharist under the form of bread alone in concelebrated Masses and to use unfermented grape juice instead of wine in Masses celebrated alone. Similar authorization had already been granted to bishops in several other countries.

Holy Year 1975 Proclaimed

Official announcement of Holy Year 1975 was made with the solemn proclamation May 23 of the papal bull *Apostolorum Limina* ("The Memorials of the Apostles"). The document stated that the observance, oriented to spiritual renewal and reconciliation, would begin and end with the opening and closing of the holy doors in Rome's four major basilicas Dec. 24, 1974 and 1975. The document listed a number of major purposes of the Holy Year and indicated the conditions for gaining special indulgences and related spiritual benefits.

Pope Paul said he hoped that during the Holy Year "pilgrims to the tombs of the Apostles Peter and Paul and to the memorials of the other martyrs will come more easily into contact with the ancient sources of the Church's faith and life, in order to be converted by repentance, strengthened in charity and united more closely with their brethren, by the grace of God."

(For excerpts from the bull, see separate entry.)

DOMESTIC

Church Noise in Puerto Rico — Gov. Rafael Hernandez Colon signed into law three bills protecting churches in Puerto Rico against prosecution for violating laws on noise pollution. The statutes were enacted following a freedom-of-religion controversy in which the island's supreme court declared that noisy rites of a Pentecostal church in San Juan were public disturbances.

Catholic School Losses Small — 1973-74 declines in the number of Catholic elementary schools (down 211) and secondary schools (down 54) and their enrollments (elementary, down 160,000; secondary, down 16,000) were the smallest in seven years, according to an annual data summary published May 3 by the National Catholic Educational Association.

Bishop Protests — Bishop Joseph M. Breitenbeck resigned May 3 as honorary chairman of the board of trustees of Aquinas College, Grand Rapids, in protest against the college's decision to grant an honorary degree to Rep. Shirley Chisholm of New York. He said he could not acquiesce "in the granting by a Catholic college of an honorary degree to a person who has taken so clear and so emphatic a public pro-abortion position" as Rep. Chisholm.

Evangelization — "Evangelization in the

Modern World"·was the theme of the Apr. 29 to May 3 Inter-American Bishops' Meeting in Miami. The 24 prelates said in a statement: "In the process of evangelization, two extremes must be avoided: Either preaching a purely theoretical, abstract message removed from the lives of people, or reducing the Gospel to a political tool or movement."

Surrender the Canal Zone — Archbishop Marcos McGrath said in a May 3 Vatican Radio interview that the bishops of Panama planned to release new documents in support of the government's demand that the United States surrender control of the Panama Canal Zone to the Panamanians. The essential demand, he said, was for "the final transfer to Panama of the administration of our country's most vital and precious area, the isthmus."

Churches Rank Third — Churches and religious organization ranked third in esteem — behind the U.S. military establishment, colleges and universities — among 15 public and private institutions in the country, according to a poll of 1,444 persons conducted by the University of Michigan's Institute for Social Research.

Family Planning in Puerto Rico — Members of the John XXIII Social Center in San Juan charged that the Puerto Rican government's $5 million population control program was a "conspiracy" to attain zero population growth. They said also that the declared voluntary nature of the program was a fiction.

Black Secretariat — Announcement was made May 9 of Archbishop William W. Baum's approval of the constitution for a permanent Secretariat for Black Catholics, to facilitate their full participation in activities of the Washington archdiocese.

In a related development John Guillory, president of the National Black Lay Catholic Caucus, told a regional meeting of the organization May 22 that black Catholics were "committed to the black community and to change for a better life."

Scouts for Vocations — Nearly 200 delegates to the 23rd biennial conference of the National Catholic Committee on Scouting, meeting in Seattle, approved May 16 a proposal to place extra emphasis on the promotion of vocations to the priesthood and religious life in the movement and program.

Christian Support for Israel — An American Jewish Committee study found that demonstrations by Christians of support and concern for Israel were more widespread in the U.S. during the October, 1973, war than they had been during the six-day war in 1967. The report, authored by Mrs. Judith Banki, noted that "statements issued and endorsed by local and regional Christian leadership, and by denominational leaders speaking out as individuals, identified more directly with Israel than the statements issued by their national or denominational headquarters."

Farm Labor Law in California — Against the background of conflict between the United Farm Workers of America and the Teamsters, Msgr. Roger M. Mahony of Fresno called on the state legislature May 21 to pass a law which would "bring peace and justice" to California's farm labor scene. He stated three principles for such legislation: guarantees for the workers to establish really representative unions; the right of farm workers to select their union without outside interference; the right of workers to make decisions concerning union representation through secret-ballot elections.

Income Maintenance — Catholic social agencies should take an "advocacy stance" on a national policy of income maintenance for the poor, stated Father Joseph Sullivan, president of the board of directors of the National Conference of Catholic Charities, at a regional meeting of the conference in Omaha.

Bread for the World — This new organization, dedicated to fighting world hunger, appealed May 23 to U.S. Christians to abstain from meat three days a week as a way of aiding nations with food shortages. It was estimated that a reduction in meat consumption by Americans could result in an increase of grain reserves.

Homosexual Bill Defeated — Opposition by the New York archdiocese was cited by politicians as a major factor in the May 23 defeat, by a City Council vote of 22 to 19, of Intro 2, a bill which would have barred discrimination in housing, jobs or public accommodations on the basis of "sexual orientation." Msgr. Eugene Clark, a spokesman for Cardinal Terence Cooke, said that the archdiocese had feared the bill "might have caused forced relationships between influential homosexuals and youngsters in their formative years." The bill, first introduced Jan. 6, 1971, had been defeated four times before this last decision. Similar legislation was in effect in 11 cities.

Divorces Increasing — National divorce totals more than doubled from 1962 to 1973, and the upward trend was continuing in 1974, according to the most recent "Monthly Vital Statistics Report" released by the National Center for Health Statistics. Totals rose from 413,000 in 1962 to 708,000 in 1970, an increase of 71 percent. Provisional statistics for subsequent years showed that the upsurge was continuing, with about 913,000 divorces reported for 1973.

The Jesuit and the President — Father John J. McLaughlin, S.J., became a subject of publicity during the month because of his defense of President Nixon's moral leadership, his apologia for the President's use of objectionable language in transcribed Watergate conversations, and his criticism of views expressed by his superior, Father Richard T. Cleary, S.J., about his position and style of life as a White House speech writer. Father Cleary stated for the record that Father McLaughlin was and remained a Jesuit in good standing.

Domestic Briefs:

• Retirements: Sister Margaret Claydon, president of Trinity College, Washington, D.C., since 1959, to take effect in 1975; William R. Consedine, for 18 years director of the Legal Department and General Counsel of the U.S. Catholic Conference.

• Honored: Father Boniface L. Wittenbrink, O.M.I., with the Kiwanis International Radio Award for work as executive director of The Talking Book for the Blind and the Physically Handicapped, May 8; John J. Barden, with the first Presidential Award of the National Catholic Educational Association for 50 years of teaching at St. Joseph's Collegiate Institute, Buffalo, N.Y., May 13; Arthur Levitt, comptroller of the State of New York, with the John LaFarge Memorial Award of the N.Y. Catholic Interracial Council for support of aid programs for minorities and the disadvantaged, May 23.

• Results of the Iowa Basic Skills Test indicated that students in the "largest black Catholic school in the U.S." — Holy Angels, Chicago — were functioning on an academic level above the national average.

Catholic, Other Statistics

Statistics released May 9 by the *Official Catholic Directory, 1974,* indicated a slight increase in the U.S. Catholic population between Jan. 1, 1973, and Jan. 1, 1974. The increase amounted to 5,011, raising the former total from 48,460,427 to 48,465,438. The Catholic percentage of the general population declined three-quarters of a point, from 23.67 to 22.95. There was a general decline in all major statistical categories. (See separate entries for statistical tables.)

In other statistical reports:

• 223 religious bodies in the U.S. reported a total membership of 131,424,564 in 1972, according to the *1974 Yearbook of American and Canadian Churches,* published May 5 by the National Council of Churches. The major categories were: Protestants, 71,648,000; Roman Catholics, 48,460,000; Jewish congregations, 6,115,000; Eastern churches, 3,739,000. Gain and loss, respectively, were reflected in the membership figures of conservative-evangelical and mainline Protestant bodies. Canadian churches had 13,811,179 members.

• A study of church membership in 1971 reported the highest percentages of church affiliation in New England (60.4 per cent) and the West North Central area (59.4 per cent). Only 37 per cent of the population in Washington, Oregon and California were reported

to be church members. The study was conducted by the Glenmary Research Center, the Lutheran Church-Missouri Synod and the National Council of Churches.

FOREIGN

No Application for British Church Council Membership — English and Welsh bishops announced a joint decision May 1 that the Catholic Church would not apply for full membership in the British Council of Churches "at the present time." They said they felt that "they must at all times be completely free to declare the full teachings of the Catholic Church without reserve. They are of the opinion that full membership in the British Council of Churches might at the present time make this task more difficult and lead to misunderstanding within the Catholic community." The bishops added, however, that they favored collaboration with the council.

Constitutionality in Bolivia — The Justice and Peace Commission of the Bolivian Bishops' Conference declared in a May Day statement that President Hugo Banzer's call for a "political truce" and "social peace" could be accomplished only through an end to political persecution, amnesty for political prisoners and exiles, and a "speedy return to constitutionality."

Stay Out of Politics — The bishops of Portugal, in a pastoral letter issued May 5 shortly after the military takeover of the government, told priests and religious to leave political and military activities to lay persons.

Communists vs. the Cardinal — Delayed reports from Vienna disclosed that Communist authorities in Czechoslovakia had made many efforts to hamper the funeral of Cardinal Stepan Trochta of Litomerice. They tried to conceal his death from the public, interfered with attendance at the funeral and banned any services outside of Litomerice. One report said that the cardinal succumbed to a cerebral hemorrhage Apr. 6 following harassment by a district official named Dlabal.

Hungarian Refusals — Hungarian officials were reported May 10 to be continuing their refusal to carry on negotiations over special permits for persons wanting to go to Rome for Holy Year celebrations in 1975. They were also continuing to refuse permission for religion classes in church buildings or rectories in major population centers.

Population Control in Mexico — Interior Minister Mario Moya Palencia said that the Mexican government would neither impose birth control policies on the people nor accept the imposition of international population policies on the country. The bishops had expressed fears earlier that a responsible parenthood program was in danger of becoming "a campaign of contraceptive propaganda."

Priest Killed in Argentina — Father Carlos Mujica, 44, a member of the Third World

Movement of progressive priests, was shot to death on the steps of a Buenos Aires church where he had just celebrated Mass. His death, one of more than 30 resulting from left-right conflict in the Peronist movement, was charged to the radical Montoneros, against whom the priests' movement had announced its alignment with President Juan Peron.

New Head of Anglican Communion — Archbishop Donald Coggan of York was named by Queen Elizabeth May 14 to succeed retiring Archbishop Michael Ramsey as Archbishop of Canterbury and leader of the worldwide, 64-million-member Anglican communion.

Abortion Suggested — Catholic education leaders sharply criticized May 16 a decision by the Toronto Board of Education to begin distribution to pregnant high school students of a handbook listing abortion as an alternative to bearing a child.

Brazilian Indian Policy Opposed — Six bishops and a number of missionaries in the Amazonia region issued a 28-page statement saying that they did not "want to be instruments of the Brazilian capitalist system" among Indians there, or supporters of "gigantic farm interests and explorers searching for mineral wealth." The thrust of the statement was against parties and forces that would exploit the Indians and threaten the integrity of their culture.

Priest Freed — The 10-year jail sentence — on charges of "subversion" — which Father Francois Jentel had begun serving May 28, 1973, was overturned by Brazil's highest military court. The 50-year-old priest, a veteran of 19 years of missionary work in the Brazilian interior, had been arrested and sentenced after defending the land rights of poor parishioners against the encroachments of a cattle and lumber company. He returned to France shortly after remission of the sentence.

Clarification of Canterbury Statement Wanted — The bishops of England and Wales, following a recent meeting, requested clarification of two points in the Canterbury Statement on ministry and ordination published Dec. 13, 1973, by the Anglican-Roman Catholic International Commission of theologians. The points were:

• "differences of interpretation of the statement published by members of the commission";

• "understanding of the role of the ordained minister as a sacrificing priest."

Respect for Life Federation — Representatives of groups of anti-abortion physicians from nine countries, meeting in Noordwijkerhout, The Netherlands, announced May 24 the organization of a World Federation for Respect for Life. The physicians, said to represent some 60,000 doctors, said in a statement that they supported the right to life of each individual — "an unconditional and fundamental right, independent of the stage of growth (therefore existing from the time of conception), of mental, physical or material conditions, or of the evolution of society."

Church Music Criticized — Much of the music in current use in churches "would be laughed off the concert platform," according to Colin Mawby, master of music at the Westminster Cathedral. Writing in *The Times* of London late in the month, he said that the quality and performance of music "must be of sufficient stature to be worthy in human terms of the worship of Almighty God." One factor affecting both in the Catholic Church, he said, was the foolishness of attempting to replace the Church's unique musical heritage within 10 years.

Foreign Briefs:

• Honored: The Anglican-Roman Catholic International Commission of theologians, with the Christian Unity Award of the Franciscan Friars of the Atonement, May 3; Archbishop Philip Pocock of Toronto, with an honorary doctorate of divinity from the Anglican Trinity College for his support in "the successful development of the Toronto (ecumenical) School of Theology," May 9; Father Joseph Lecuyer, theologian and superior general of the Congregation of the Holy Spirit, with the Order of Knight of the French Legion of Honor for his studies on episcopal collegiality, May 29.

• Sie Cheou, the first Chinese ambassador to the Vatican, was received into the Church shortly before his death Apr. 22 in Taipei.

• The Spanish press published reports that Father Jose Maria Lopez of Granada, a chaplain of the Blue Division of Spanish volunteers on the Russian front during World War II, was still a prisoner in a camp in Siberia.

• Father Maurilio Sacchi, O.F.M., was welcomed May 28 in Jerusalem as the new head of the Custody of the Holy Land with responsibility for some 40 parishes, pastoral, charitable and other ministries, and care for the Holy Places.

• African countries with the largest numbers of major seminarians in Rome were: Nigeria, 690; Tanzania, 490; Zaire, 437; Uganda, 375; Kenya, 199; Ghana, 118; Malagasy Republic, 110.

Catastrophic Vocations Decline

Bishop Lucien Bardonne of Chalons, speaking at a press conference in Paris early in the month, called the decline in vocations to the priesthood in France catastrophic.

He cited figures showing diminishing numbers of ordinations — 345 (1969), 284 (1970), 237 (1971), 193 (1972), 219 (1973); and of entries into major seminaries — 470 (1969), 402 (1970), 265 (1971), 243 (1972), 151 (1973). The number of priests in the country dropped from 40,994 in 1967 to 36,294 in 1970. It was estimated that there would be a further drop to 31,820 in 1975.

JUNE 1974

VATICAN

Enthusiasm vs. Doubt and Criticism — Pope Paul spoke June 2 in praise of "very many living members of the Church who live the joyful and generous enthusiasm" of their Christian profession. He also said: "We would like Pentecost to bring its spirit of truth, charity and unity into the hearts of those many who are still Catholics and still call themselves Catholics but who are drooping and sad. They vegetate in doubt and in silly criticism. They have acquired the unhappy taste of contradicting Mother Church. They delude themselves that they live the Church's charisms while isolating themselves from her indispensable organism, her hierarchy and her community. And they allow themselves secularist and even pagan concessions under the pretext of approaching the world, which then devours them."

Violence in Ireland — In a Pentecost letter to Cardinal William Conway of Armagh, the Pope said: "We continue to follow with growing anxiety and concern the protraction of an intolerable situation which, far from improving through a general effort to bring about reconciliation, has in fact been aggravated by a tragic increase of blind and unspeakable acts of violence (in north and southern sectors of the country), acts which have claimed so many victims (more than 1,040 since August, 1969) and thrown so many families into mourning."

Love the Church — The Holy Father called the Church "a phenomenon of beauty in history and in the life of humanity" during a general audience June 5. Decrying abrasive criticism of the Church, he urged his listeners to look for its beauty despite the human imperfections which hide it. He said: "Jesus so loved the Church that he gave his life for it. What about us? We, rather than criticizing it, speaking evil of it, deserting it, and being unfaithful to and weary of it, must love it."

Marriage Court Procedure — The Pope authorized the continuing use of 23 special procedural norms in U.S. marriage tribunals "until the new order of matrimonial court procedure is promulgated for the Latin Church." Announcement of the decision was made June 8 by Cardinal John J. Krol. The norms, in provisional effect since July, 1970, expedited tribunal decisions in 1973 in an estimated 8,500 cases concerning the validity of marriage. (See separate entry.)

Catholic Education — In a June 8 address to participants in the ninth congress of the International Office of Catholic Education, Pope Paul said that "Catholic education today renders services so special that everybody can see — and especially Christians — that its disappearance would be an immense loss." He encouraged the educators "to strive so that Catholic schools may be seen as places of encounter for those who want to bear witness to Christian values in all education."

Neuropsychiatry — Pope Paul called on French and Italian specialists in nervous diseases June 10 to maintain complete respect for the human person in their practice. He said: "You know better than we do that this powerful therapy ... might turn against its purpose and diminish man in disturbing the exercise of his intelligence and his will. Nor must man become an object of experimentation."

Youthfulness of the Church — The Pope told a general audience June 12 that the Church "is young because it has a soul ... the grace of God ... the Holy Spirit, who breathes within the Church and keeps it living, ardent and capable — and this is a miracle — of rejuvenating itself." Referring to criticism of the Church, a subject mentioned in several recent addresses, the Pontiff said: "The Church is not a post-Christian phenomenon, but I would say that it is still at its beginning. The Church can prove itself in still more complete forms, still more beautiful forms, and ... still more holy forms than those which it has shown in the past."

The Eucharist — Pope Paul celebrated Mass June 13 before a throng of more than 10,000 persons at a parish church in a working-class district of Rome. In his sermon he called the Eucharist the central point of Christian faith. "The Eucharist is a mystery of a presence willed by love ... In this extraordinary manner Jesus has multiplied himself so that he is available to each of us." The Eucharist "is a call addressed most particularly to those who suffer and labor most, to those who are poor and cry, to those who are alone and without help, to those who are poor and innocent."

Be Builders of the Church — Unity within the Church was the theme of an appeal made by the Pope June 16 to a throng of people in St. Peter's Square. He said: "We must all seek to form ourselves according to an authentic 'sense of the Church' ... And all must seek to be builders, not demolition crews, of the Church."

Christian Life Is Happy — To live a Christian life is to live a happy life — if one knows what Christianity is all about — Pope Paul told a general audience June 19. He put down the opinion that the pursuit of self-satisfaction, unchecked by the demands of God's law, makes for a happy life. He said: "Truly we must form in ourselves the dominating concept that the Christian life is happy. We are speaking of the authentic Christian life ... in the ... sense which has been given to us by love — that is, by the action of the Holy Spirit in our souls. Let us remember this well: He who lives in the grace of God thereby possesses a font of happiness which no exterior evil, nor even interior depression, can dry up or extinguish. The Christian vocation is an invitation to happiness."

Advice to Deacons — Addressing himself June 26 to American deacons soon to be ordained to the priesthood, Pope Paul advised: "We urge you . . . to renew the commitment of your lives to Jesus Christ . . . and to guard this consecration with Christian and priestly discipline. By means of a strong faith and that persevering discipline which is an expression of real love, your lives will indeed be filled with deep joy. In this way — and only in this way — will you accomplish something great and something lasting."

Grace and the Cross — "The coming of the Holy Spirit does not take the cross from the human condition," Pope Paul said at a general audience June 26. "Let it suffice to propose this reply for the consolation of those who are experiencing the ineffable good fortune of grace and the no less mysterious good fortune of suffering. Not only can the two experiences coexist, but they are compatible — they can be coordinated in a plan of goodness and of salvation, a plan whose wisdom and harmony the Lord will one day, we hope, unveil to us."

Mass Stipends — Pope Paul reaffirmed the Church's traditional practice of allowing offerings or stipends for the celebration of Mass, in a document entitled *Firma in Traditione.* The document, which was made public June 27 and had an effective date of July 1, had no significant effect on practices in the United States.

The Pope Also:

• Celebrated Mass in ceremonies commemorating the 11th anniversary of the death of Pope John XXIII, June 3.

• Told the Italian Bishops' Conference of his bitter disappointment at the outcome of the May referendum which approved divorce legislation in the country, June 8.

• Met with Maria Estela Martinez de Peron, vice president of Argentina, June 19.

Vatican Briefs:

• Representatives of the Secretariat for Promoting Christian Unity and the World Council of Churches reported they were working on a document on future ecumenical activity to be presented at the fifth general assembly of the WCC in 1975.

• The formation of seminarians for the celibate priesthood was the subject of an 80-page document sent to bishops throughout the world by the Congregation for Catholic Education. Cardinal Gabriel Garrone, prefect of the congregation, said in a covering letter that the purpose of the document was to set forth "anew and in a way more suited to men of our time the fundamental reasons (and preparation for) sacred celibacy."

• In an editorial denunciation of the bombing of the British House of Commons, *L'Osservatore Romano* lamented "the senseless devastation of such an august and worthy seat of the history of the English people, of their free institutions and of their historical and cultural tradition which is centered in the House of Commons."

• Plans for participation in the UN International Women's Year in 1975 were discussed at a plenary meeting of the Council for the Laity June 25.

Papal Concerns

In a wide-ranging talk to a group of cardinals assembled June 22 to mark the 11th anniversaries of his election and coronation, Pope Paul summarized many matters of concern to him in the Church and the world at large. Key topics were unity in the Church, observance of Holy Year 1975, peace, and care for persons suffering from violence and hunger.

Domestic

Prayers at Commencement — U.S. District Court Judge Robert Merhige, Jr., ruled June 7 in Richmond, Va., that prayers could be part of a public high school graduation ceremony. He handed down the decision in a suit filed by the American Civil Liberties Union on behalf of three graduating students who contended that an invocation and benediction scheduled for their June 10 graduation ceremony would violate court prohibitions against prayer in public schools.

Death-with-Dignity Bill — For the sixth year in a row, the Florida legislature voted down a death-with-dignity bill which had been called "the first step toward euthanasia" by Thomas A. Horkan, executive director of the Florida Catholic Conference.

Unconditional Amnesty — In a statement released early in the month, Bishop James S. Rausch, secretary general of the National Conference of Catholic Bishops, urged that "the nation now give serious consideration to broad, unconditional amnesty" for those who, for reasons of conscience, resisted military service during the Vietnam war. Evidence for the need of such a step toward reconciliation, he said, "is most apparent in the lives of Americans who were directly affected by the war in Vietnam, especially those young men whose consciences led them to resist military service and who now find themselves ostracized and alienated from our society."

Catholic Health Assembly — Abortion, the high cost of health care and euthanasia were three of the subjects on the agenda of the third annual Catholic Health Assembly of 1,500 health administrators meeting in Atlanta.

• Abortion: The only way to restore protection to the unborn "is through an amendment to the United States Constitution," stated Dr. John T. Noonan, Jr., professor of law at the University of California.

• Health Care Cost: Sister Margaret Brennan, I.H.M., referred to "truly shocking figures that can be marshalled to show that we are well down on the list of Western developed countries in the matter of medical help we give all our citizens." In view of the high cost of medical care, she said, "it seems clear that only a comprehensive national system can supply it."

• Euthanasia: "All reasonable efforts should be made to sustain human life, but there are certain circumstances in which certain means (extraordinary) need not be used, even if by their omission the person is allowed to die." So stated Dr. Warren T. Reich, senior research scholar of the Kennedy Institute, Center for Bioethics. He added: "The ethic of sustaining life is always a judgment on the treatment, on a particular means of sustaining life," while active euthanasia is a decisive act against the life of that person.

Migrant Ministry The Brownsville diocese announced that six priests, eight seminarians and 10 sisters would spend part of the summer on the road and in camps ministering to migrant workers in a six-state area. Bishop John J. Fitzpatrick said: "The migrants from the (Rio Grande) valley still belong to the Diocese of Brownsville . . . We feel responsible for them while they are working in the fields of the North."

Minnesota Hospital Personnel Cleared — A Hennepin County grand jury unanimously cleared staff members of the University of Minnesota Hospitals of any possible criminal conduct in three abortion cases. It had been alleged that three aborted fetuses capable of survival outside the womb were allowed to die without medical attention. The allegations were made by persons quoted in reports published in *The Catholic Bulletin* of St. Paul-Minneapolis in March.

Eucharistic Congress in Philadelphia — Cardinal John J. Krol announced June 12 that Pope Paul had approved the celebration of the 41st International Eucharistic Congress in Philadelphia in 1976.

Theological Convention — Father Richard P. McBrien, outgoing president of the Catholic Theological Society of America, told participants in the organization's June 10 to 13 convention in Chicago that theology "is a discipline in the service of the Church," to which it offers "vigorous and independent criticism." The two new chief officers of the society were Brother Luke Salm, F.S.C., of Manhattan College, president, and Father Avery Dulles, S.J., of the Catholic University of America, vice president.

Cardinal Mindszenty — The leader of the Church and personal symbol of resistance to Communism in Hungary for 29 years said at a press conference in San Diego June 18 that he did not "think Rome had anything to gain" by his removal in February from the primatial see of Esztergom. He observed that the Church was still being persecuted in Hungary, that between 1,500 and 2,000 priests

were barred from pastoral ministry, and that "the administrative level of the Church is controlled by the Party."

Charismatics — Approximately 25,000 persons took part in the 1974 International Conference on Charismatic Renewal June 14 to 16 on the campus of the University of Notre Dame, South Bend, Ind. The most dramatic event of the weekend was a four and one-half hour service during which an undisclosed number of persons claimed they experienced physical, psychological, spiritual or inner healing. Some observers had reservations about the emotionally charged atmosphere of the service.

Pro-Life Conventions — Two organizations committed to action in defense of unborn life held conventions during the month, the National Right to Life Committee in Washington, D.C., and Birthright International in Chicago.

Holocaust Symposium — Some 1,200 persons attended the first interdenominational symposium designed to explore Christian responsibility for the slaughter of six million Jews by the Nazis. The four-day meeting in New York City was sponsored by 22 religious groups.

Urban Ethnic Affairs — More than 200 priests from parishes across the country voted at a Cleveland meeting to establish a Catholic Conference on Urban Ethnic Affairs, for the purpose of forming a "network of ethnic church leadership, both religious and lay, who will be supportive of one another in rebuilding ethnic communities in the fabric of American society."

State of the Church — The National Conference of Catholic Bishops released June 24 a state-of-the-Church paper prepared for the fall assembly of the Synod of Bishops. In its "Review of the Principal Trends in the Life of the Catholic Church in the United States," the conference said that "the pertinent issue now is whether Catholics in the United States are more powerfully formed and influenced by the Church or by secular society." (For text, see separate entry.)

Mother Teresa — Mother Teresa of Calcutta, foundress of the Missionaries of Charity to the poorest of the poor, took part in Philadelphia's mile-long candlelight "Pilgrimage of Hope" June 16. The pilgrimage was a major interfaith event in the archdiocesan observance of the Holy Year. Mother Teresa, as on other occasions of a current tour of U.S. cities, spoke of love and service for the poor.

Men Religious Superiors — One hundred and 29 of the 256 members of the Conference of Major Superiors of Men attended a June 16 to 20 annual meeting in Chicago and approved resolutions upholding the right of brothers to be religious superiors and supporting the human rights of political prisoners in Chile. They also elected black Father

Joseph Francis, S.V.D., president for the next two years. The convention theme was "The American Religious as Evangelizer."

Domestic Briefs:

• Four hundred persons attended the 10th annual Wanderer Forum June 14 to 16 in St. Paul, Minn.

• The appointment of Eugene Krasicky, assistant attorney general of Michigan, as general counsel of the U.S. Catholic Conference was announced June 18.

• Readers of *The Tidings*, the Los Angeles archdiocesan newspaper, donated more than $80,000 for the relief of people in four famine-stricken dioceses in the Sahelian region of Africa.

Student Aid Decision

In an 8-to-1 decision handed down June 17, the U.S. Supreme Court ruled in Wheeler v. Barrera that parochial school students must share in federal funds for educationally deprived students on a comparable basis with public school students under the federal Elementary and Secondary Education Act.

At issue in the case was the contention of parents of parochial school students in Kansas City, Mo., that the state was in violation of ESEA because no state-paid teachers were being assigned to work with disadvantaged children on the premises of parochial schools during regular school hours. The state argued that such services were violative of its constitution.

The Supreme Court found that services provided eligible parochial school students in Missouri were "plainly inferior, both qualitatively and quantitatively," to those given public school pupils. It added that comparable but not necessarily identical programs would have to be offered parochial school students, leaving to state officials decisions regarding which of numerous forms of comparable programs should be chosen.

(For additional coverage of the decision, see Wheeler v. Barrera.)

FOREIGN

Eucharistic Statement — Catholic and Anglican theologians in Scotland issued a joint statement of agreement on the Eucharist that was more explicit in some areas than the 1971 "Windsor Statement" on the same subject authored by the Anglican-Roman Catholic International Commission of theologians. In one passage the Scots said that Article 31 of the Anglican 39 Articles of belief — condemning the "sacrifice of Masses" as "blasphemous fables and dangerous deceits" — represented a rejection of something that was never part of authentic Catholic doctrine.

Capitalism and Marxism Rejected — In a statement dated May 15 but not released until early this month, the regional Catalonian Bishops' Conference was highly critical of capitalism and Marxism. The eight bishops of northeastern Spain said: "Neither liberal capitalism, to whose principles the majority of the members of our present society subscribe, nor Marxism, which wants to make inroads among our Christians, fulfills nor can fulfill in an acceptable manner (the goal of) integral Christian liberation." They warned that the Church demands that "any choice of an (ideological) system or political party . . . cannot be treason against the Gospel."

Chilean Cardinal Backed — Some 230 priests and several thousand lay Catholics attended a Mass June 4 in Santiago to signify their support of Cardinal Raul Silva and other bishops under fire from rightists for their criticism of repression and torture in Chile since the military took control of the government in September, 1973. There were no signs of let-up in tensions generated by the policies of the military and the efforts of churchmen to stand for human rights and bring about the reconciliation of opposing factions in the aftermath of the Allende regime.

Protect Art and Religious Objects — The bishops of Italy called for cataloguing all important works of art and other valuable objects housed in the country's churches, monasteries and convents, in an attempt to halt the increasing flow of church goods and property into antique stores, open-air markets and private collections.

IRA Repudiated, Agents of the Devil — Cardinal John Heenan of Westminster, asked about the Church's position with respect to the Irish Republican Army, said: "Bishops are constantly asked to make statements on Northern Ireland, but they have already made clear their abhorrence of the extremists in all parties. It would be unprofitable to issue a fresh pronouncement at each tragic development in the Irish situation."

Bishop Edward Daly of Londonderry, in a related statement late in the month, called the IRA "agents of the devil." He said that they "and their various satellite organizations should not be assisted politically, financially or otherwise until they proclaim a total and permanent cease-fire in this community."

Faith Crisis of Foreign Students — Loss of faith because of loss of contact with the Church was reported to be a problem in England. One indication of this was a statement by Father Anthony Grimshaw, Salford diocesan director for the Overseas Mission of the Church. He said: "We have complaints from many African bishops that the fruits of the missionary labor, and the fruits of their own labors with the indigenous people, are being lost in England. This is very apparent in London with the Catholic students coming from Africa and just losing their faith. They lapse into secularism."

Admit Tongans — Bishop Patrick Finau of Tonga urged abandonment of the "historical anachronism of the white Australian policy" which barred Tongans from permanent immigration and severely limited even temporary residence in the country. He made the plea in discussions with government officials about ways and means of relieving the hardships of the 80,000 inhabitants of the 150 islands of the Kingdom of Tonga.

Remove Bishop from Rhodesia — Members of the Chichester Club in Salisbury asked Pope Paul to remove Bishop Donal Lamont of Umtali from Rhodesia and Africa because of what they said were untruthful statements made by him May 30 at a press conference in New York. The bishop was reported to have said that blacks in Rhodesia were living under a reign of terror comparable to that experienced by the Jews in Nazi Germany, that human rights were grossly violated in the country and that no one seemed to care.

Police in the Cathedral — Archbishop Jose Mendez Asensio condemned local police for forcibly expelling from the Pamplona cathedral a group of workers meeting there to demand better wages and the reinstatement of some fired strikers. He called the action a violation of the concordat between Spain and the government. Several days after the May 31 incident, a second meeting was held in the cathedral without police interference.

Soviet Catholics — Some of the 120,000 Catholics in the Soviet Republics of Armenia and Georgia were participating in Armenian Orthodox services because of a lack of Roman Catholic priests and churches in the Soviet Union, according to a June 20 newscast by Vatican Radio. Pilgrimages to three shrines in particular, the report said, "climaxed with the celebration of the Liturgy by Orthodox priests and, almost always, with the administration of baptism and confirmation."

Islam No Threat to Christians — Sheik Abdul Aziz Issa, Egyptian minister for religious affairs, told 80 American newsmen early in the month in Cairo that the new relationship between Arab states and the emerging nations of Africa presented no danger for Christian and Jewish minorities. "Islam literally means two things — submission to the divine will and peace," he said. "The true Moslem must believe in the morality and the ethics of Judaism and Christianity. Adherence to Islam is, in fact, a guarantee against persecution."

Population Control in Bolivia — In a statement issued after its annual meeting, the Bolivian Bishops' Conference denounced a government population control program, saying that "birth control is not a national necessity." The conference also scored "the pressures of the centers of world economic power on the underdeveloped countries to lure them into birth control policies."

"Righteous Gentile" — Officials of Israel's Memorial to the Holocaust, the shrine of Yad Vashem, conferred the honor of "Righteous Gentile" on Father Rufino Niccacci, O.F.M., who helped save 300 Jews from persecution by the Nazis during World War II by hiding them in an Italian monastery.

University of Bethlehem — Cardinal Paul Philippe, prefect of the Congregation for Oriental Churches, officiated at ceremonies marking the end of the first academic year of the University of Bethlehem. The school, started in October, 1973, and staffed by three American Christian Brothers and 15 Arab professors, was the first Arabic university in Israel.

Education for the Poor — It was reported late in the month that the all-India chapter of the Jesuits had unanimously agreed to shift their educational emphasis from the rich to the poor.

Foreign Briefs:

• An organization called The Ten Million was set up in London to aid the estimated 10 million people lacking decent housing in Great Britain. One of the founding agencies was the Catholic Housing Aid Society.

• Radio May 13th became the third diocesan radio station closed down by the Brazilian government without explanation since November, 1973. Dozens of commercial stations had also been put off the air. One hundred and 16 diocesan stations were reported throughout the country.

• A committee of the French Bishops' Conference joined the Protestant Federation of France in criticism of the nation's new series of nuclear tests in the Pacific. The tests were called biologically dangerous, surely insane, and of no help in ending the menace of the nuclear arms race.

• The board of directors of the International Catholic Press Union announced final plans for the 10th Catholic World Congress of the Press to be held Nov. 18 to 22 in Buenos Aires.

New World Wants Gospel

"I believe that a new world is being born. I am convinced that it seeks God, that it wants to welcome the Message (of the Gospel), on condition that we do not require that it be expressed in the customs, the philosophies, the mentalities, the human norms that are those of another age."

So stated Cardinal Francois Marty at a three-day plenary assembly of the French Bishops' Conference whose agenda centered on problems of youth and their relationship to the faith.

Earlier the bishops had suggested that the 1974 assembly of the Synod of Bishops concentrate on the "evangelization of the world of the young." The reasons, they said, were "because the young will tomorrow be the most numerous of mankind, because they are the bearers of the future, because they pose in a very radical manner the question of faith in Jesus Christ in this new context."

JULY 1974

VATICAN

Critical Moral Judgment — Christians, living in a society which has become radically secularized and emptied of spiritual values, have a major duty to exercise their "critical moral judgment." So stated Pope Paul at a general audience July 3. He said: "One cannot live blindly or be guided passively or even slavishly by dominant public opinion which has not been put to the test of a critical and responsible reflection." He said he trusted that "no aware Christian would betray his baptismal commitment, that no faithful Christian would be unfaithful to the cross of Christ, by virtue of which true salvation comes to us."

Meeting with Kissinger — Pope Paul met privately and unofficially with U.S. Secretary of State Henry A. Kissinger for an hour-and-10-minute discussion of matters of mutual concern. Vatican press officer Federico Alessandrini, in a verbal briefing on the July 6 meeting, told the press that they "amply discussed the major problems of peace in the world, with particular reference to the Middle East and the (recent) Moscow conversations between President Nixon and the Soviet leaders."

Christ Is the Way — The Pope, speaking July 7 to a throng of persons in St. Peter's Square, said he saw two "contrary expressions" in the faces of young people. "We see an expression of great energy, a will to live and to conquer, a need for certainty and fullness. . . . We see another expression of uncertainty, of skepticism, of disappointment. Why live? Whom to live for? Into what values, toward what ideals, should this energy be channelled?" Addressing himself to young people, he said: "You are suffering from the decadence of modern times, from the futility of the goals proposed for your energies, from the emptiness of the hedonism that would substitute itself within you for strength, beauty, love, true happiness . . . We want to assure you . . . that the way (of life) is Christ."

Arthritis Attack — An attack of arthritis in his right knee, called simple in nature but painful by the Vatican press office, forced Pope Paul to cancel his usual weekly general audience July 10. In a talk prepared for the audience and published later, the Pope emphasized the need for unity in the Church and took issue with those who contest the doctrinal authority of the Church.

Discover Rome — Go out and discover Rome, the Holy Father told thousands of pilgrims and tourists in St. Peter's Square July 14. He said: "Rome is not only history, not only art, not only a type of civilization; Rome is mystery. It is this because the transcendental destiny of humanity has here its key, has here its secret, which derives from the fact

that it is the custodian of the tombs of the Apostles Peter and Paul, and of so many other martyrs and saints. It is here that the precedent of unity and of Catholicism is silently but brightly affirmed in that ancient, but ever young, divine-human institution at the service of the world, which is the Catholic Church."

Beware of Secularism — Pope Paul warned a general audience July 17 to beware of the dangers of atheist-inspired secularism in the everyday affairs of the world. The gravest temptation of this age, he said, is "to limit our pleasure to the 'horizonal' sphere . . . to neglect, to forget and finally to negate the 'vertical' sphere — that is, to fix our interest on the visible, experimental, temporal, human area while abdicating our vocation to the invisible, inexpressible, eternal and superhuman kingdom of God. . . . Modern atheism has its most seductive and most dangerous roots in this option, which is exclusively positive in regard to the things of this world and radically negative toward religious and specifically Christian matters." He urged Christians never to lose their deep and real sense of good and evil, or to withdraw from the discipline of the cross which has to guide their pilgrim steps on this earth toward salvation.

Cyprus Conflict — Pope Paul expressed his fear July 21 that hostilities between Greeks and Turks on Cyprus might spark another conflagration in a world already torn by war and guerrilla campaigns. He said: "We can only feel great bitterness and great fear over this. Where there is suffering, there our heart cannot be untouched. We wish to join our wishes with those who love justice and peace so that any new blow to international order and the internal order of peoples may be averted."

World Mission Day — In a 2,500-word message released July 31, the Pope declared that the observance of World Mission Day Oct. 20 would be related to the Holy Year themes of renewal and reconciliation. "Evangelization," he wrote, "as an act which makes Christ known to peoples, aiming at renewing and reconciling them with him and in him, means to extend the area and the degree of knowledge and of acceptance of his person and of his message. It means to broaden the area of reconciliation in justice and love." The Pontiff also said: "The formation of an authentic missionary conscience must be based upon a radical spiritual renewal. Before preaching the Gospel, one must first live it. The first missionary action lies in the life of a Christian or a community."

Beauties of Nature — Eleven days after arriving at Castel Gandolfo for a working vacation, Pope Paul told tourists July 28 to "take advantage of the summer holidays by returning to the vision, the knowledge, the contemplation of that immense, stupendous, authoritative book which is nature."

Christian Freedom — Addressing a general audience July 31, the Pope said: "Christian freedom has a regenerating power, it keeps us on the right path — optimistic, skillful and intelligent in performing good deeds beyond our own interests. It strips us of the bonds of egotism, fear and narrow-mindedness, and permits our free personality to spread itself in social feeling and activity. Men are no longer a pressing mass of strangers or of competitors or of enemies, but an attractive crowd of people who look like us, our associates, our brothers — for whom it is a duty and an honor to offer love and service."

The Pope Also:
• Conveyed his sympathy, "with profound sorrow," to Maria Estela Martinez de Peron, widow of President Juan Peron of Argentina who died July 1.
• Paused on his way to Castel Gandolfo to visit 90-year-old Cardinal Alberto di Jorio, July 17.
• At Castel Gandolfo, welcomed infirm American and Italian priests on pilgrimage to Lourdes, July 24.

Vatican Briefs:
• "Permanent working contacts" with the Polish government, with a view toward normalization of Church-state relations, were announced by the Vatican July 5.
• The president and vice-president of the Swiss Bishops' Conference declared that "public opinion has been informed inexactly and one-sidedly" concerning an investigation of the writings of theologian Father Hans Kung by the Congregation for the Doctrine of the Faith. Most news reports about the investigation were from Father Kung, who charged that the congregation was acting in the manner of a high-handed inquisitorial tribunal.
• Vatican Radio reported that "during the days of July 11 to 17 the Spanish Minister for Foreign Affairs, Pedro Cortina, had talks with the Secretary of the Council for the Public Affairs of the Church, (Archbishop) Agostino Casaroli, over the updating of the (1953) concordat now existing between the Holy See and Spain. All matters of interest to the two parties were studied in depth, thus reaching basic terms capable of being drawn up within the framework of a new concordat."
• Cardinal Sergio Pignedoli, president of the Secretariat for Non-Christians, was touring Japan for meetings with religious leaders there.

Conscience Needs Guidance

The teaching of the Church on liberty, obedience and conscience are valid and contemporary, not anachronistic and outdated, Pope Paul declared during a general audience July 24. Of conscience, he said:

"Conscience does not create its moral

norm but must accept a norm and apply it . . . Conscience is not an inner eye which sees; it is not in itself the light which gives sight; it is not the thing which we must do. For conscience can command only insofar as it obeys (norms) . . . Conscience has need of guidance which transcends it . . . from natural teaching, if this is sufficient, or else from the faith and the teaching authority of the Church which propounds it, when reason is insufficient."

DOMESTIC

No AID Funds for Abortion — In line with federal legislation enacted in the fall of 1973, the Agency for International Development issued a policy banning the use of foreign aid funds to pay for abortions as a method of family planning, or to coerce or motivate any person to practice abortion.

Third World Problems — Problems of the Third World of developing nations should be of interest to Americans because of the military, economic and moral considerations such problems have for this nation, according to Father J. Bryan Hehir, head of the Division of Justice and Peace, U.S. Catholic Conference. Writing in the July/August edition of the *New Catholic World,* he said, summarily: If the gap between the standard of living in the developing nations and the already developed nations continues to widen, the Third World could become a military threat because its poor standard of living could breed frustration leading to violence and military action.

Campus Ministry — The Lilly Foundation of Indianapolis announced July 3 that it had allocated a grant of $1.57 million to fund the organization and first two years of operation of the National Institute for Campus Ministries, an agency for Catholic, Protestant and Jewish clergy and other persons ministering to stud3nts and faculty on church-related and non-sectarian college and university campuses.

No Pro-Life Planks — A July 8 report on recent state conventions of three major political parties in Minnesota disclosed that none of them had adopted a pro-life stance. In Indiana, both Republicans and Democrats had earlier voted down planks endorsing pro-life amendments to the U.S. Constitution.

Works for the Poor — Mother Teresa of Calcutta urged persons working with her spirit in the service of the poor not to "drift from humble works." Speaking with members of the Co-Workers of Mother Teresa in Winona, Minn., early in the month, she said: "Many people would like to do big things; few are willing to do the small things."

Priests Returning — Father Kenneth J. Pierre, director of the Consultation Services Center of the St. Paul and Minneapolis archdiocese, reported that 10 to 15 per cent of priests taking leaves of absence eventually return to the ministry. He also said that the number of those returning was on the increase.

Less Frequent Confession — Seventy-three per cent of more than 2,000 respondents to a survey conducted by *The Pilot* of Boston said they were going to confession less often than they did 10 years earlier; eight per cent indicated they were receiving the sacrament more often. Ninety per cent indicated that they continued to make traditional distinctions between mortal and venial sins.

Cursillo Encounter — Approximately 500 leaders from nearly 100 dioceses attended the second week-long National Encounter of the Cursillo movement at Findlay College, Ohio. "Evangelization of Environments" was the theme of the meeting. Its purpose, according to national coordinator Gerald Hughes, was to "take the movement into the environments in which we live, work and socialize."

Operation Resident — The Catholic Church Extension Society reported July 10 its sponsorship of Operation Resident, a project designed to recruit retired priests for ministry in priest-poor areas of the home missions. "Operation Resident has been set up to help both the retired priest and the mission," stated Father Joseph A. Cusack, Extension president. "The retired priest can use this work to make the best use of his time, experience and talents. And in many cases his presence can make the difference between a living and a dying mission."

Support for UFWA — Members of the National Conference of Major Superiors of Men, at a July 12 press conference in Salinas, Calif. reaffirmed support for the Cesar Chavez-led United Farm Workers of America in their struggle with grape and lettuce growers and the Teamsters for labor contracts and worker representation rights.

Test-Tube Babies — Moral theologian Father Bernard Haering, C.SS.R., voiced great shock at news that three babies conceived in test tubes had been born in Europe following extensive experimentation with fertilized eggs. Calling such experimentation a form of manipulation of human life, he said the procedure was in a field where scientists should not act without advice from ethical thinkers. He also questioned the value of information derived from such experimentation, "if we destroy respect for human life in the process."

Easter Holidays Unconstitutional — Scheduling school holidays around the Easter weekend was ruled unconstitutional because it had the "direct and immediate effect of advancing religion" and was a form of discrimination against non-Christian students. The ruling 2as made by U.S. District Judge C. Clyde Atkins in a suit brought against the Dade County, Fla., public school system.

Black Bishop — The appointment of Josephite Father Eugene A. Marino to be the first black auxiliary bishop of Washington (and the fourth black bishop in U.S. history) was praised July 18 by the National Office for Black Catholics.

In another area, the NOBC called a Supreme Court decision limiting the circumstances in which busing could be used for racial integration in schools "a serious derailment of whatever progress has been made toward the equality of all citizens in this country." The 5-to-4 decision was handed up in a case involving busing from mostly black schools in Detroit to mostly white schools in suburban counties.

No Change in Rosary — The traditional format of the Rosary is not to be changed when it is said publicly, stated Cardinal John J. Krol in a letter to the National Conference of Catholic Bishops. He issued the warning, he said, because "in recent months there have been a number of requests for permission to experiment with the format of the Rosary." One of the experiments suggested four instead of five decades, and five instead of three sets of mysteries.

Xerox Population Booklet — The Xerox Corp. agreed July 24 to withdraw from distribution a booklet on population control after the Catholic League for Religious and Civil Rights threatened legal action for alleged anti-Catholic statements in the publication. The contents of the booklet contrasted sharply with what a Xerox statement claimed was no intention to defame the Pope or to attack the Church for its stand on birth control.

Millions Lost — The Reno diocese and the LaSalette Fathers lost millions of dollars in an investment plan — worth as much as $25 million at one time — that failed, according to a copyrighted story in a late July edition of the *National Catholic Reporter*. Informed sources agreed that no fraud was involved in the case. It was also reported that refinancing was making it possible for the principals to repay creditors.

Natural Family Planning — A contract for up to $115,600 to finance the development of a training curriculum for instructors of natural family planning methods in government-sponsored clinics was finalized July 29 by the U.S. Department of Health, Education and Welfare and the Human Life Foundation.

Episcopalian Women Priests — Eleven women were ordained to the Episcopalian priesthood by four retired bishops July 30 in Philadelphia. Bishop John M. Allin, presiding prelate of the 3.1 million-member church, said the ordaining bishops "have exceeded their authority, and have not acted for the whole church. . . . Accordingly, the ordinations are irregular and may be found invalid."

Domestic Briefs:

• Sister Joan Doyle, president of the Sisters of Charity of the Blessed Virgin Mary, became the first Catholic woman to offer the opening invocation at a session of the U.S. Senate, July 17.

• The information office of the St. Cloud diocese reported that more than 500,000 calls had been made in six years to "Dial a Saint," a daily recorded spiritual message service.

• Survey findings disclosed that the Knights of Columbus gave more than $9 million to charitable and benevolent causes in 1973.

• Father Thomas Smith, O.P., 67, died July 29 in a fire set by an arsonist at the rectory of St. Vincent Ferrer Church, New York City.

• The Council for Financial Aid to Education reported that Notre Dame University received more voluntary financial support — $3.49 million — during 1973 than any other U.S. Catholic university.

National Health Insurance

Representatives of three Catholic organizations urged swift Congressional passage of a universal national health insurance plan July 2, in testimony before the House Ways and Means Committee. Among their proposals were:

• A plan to cover all U.S. citizens, resident aliens and aliens admitted for employment, without any premium payments by them.

• A phase-out of "separate tiers of care" for the poor and elderly, Medicare and Medicaid, and inclusion of these services in a national plan.

• Financing of the plan through a combination of federal revenues, taxes on employer pay rolls and on the self-employed — but not on income from federal assistance, Social Security payments or other such sources.

Those testifying were Sister Virginia Schwager, director of the Division of Health Affairs, U.S. Catholic Conference; Msgr. Lawrence Corcoran, executive director of the National Conference of Catholic Charities; and Sister Mary Maurita Sengelaub, president of the Catholic Hospital Association.

FOREIGN

Peron Dies — Juan Domingo Peron, 78, died July 1, some nine months after being elected to the presidency of Argentina Sept. 23, 1973. During his earlier presidency, from 1946 to 1955, he had initial support from churchmen but lost it — and was excommunicated — because of dictatorial measures and violence antagonistic to the Church and its teachings. His excommunication was lifted in 1963, during a period of exile in Spain. His return to power in 1973 was marked by conflict among opposed factions of his supporters. At the time of his death, there were signs that he was more amenable than previously to cooperation with the Church. He was succeeded in office by his wife, the former Maria Estela Martinez, a political novice.

Self-Supporting Church in Taiwan — The bishops of Taiwan, at the end of an annual meeting in Taipei, called on Catholics to make their Church self-supporting. "Self-support is a necessary stage in the full development of a local church," they said. "The true significance of self-support is that Catholics have a consciousness of participating in the work of the Church, undertake their responsibilities, and make the Church a truly Chinese Church."

Rhodesian Clergy Subversive? — The opinion of an African Methodist bishop offered no support to the claim of a visiting Scottish priest, Father Robert Stuart, that there were subversive elements among the Rhodesian clergy. Father Stuart, speaking in Salisbury before a highly conservative group of Catholic lay persons, strongly criticized Bishop Donal Lamont of Umtali and cast doubt on the credibility of statements issued by the bishops' conference in opposition to the racial policies of the government. Methodist Bishop Abel Muzorewa, however, praised Bishop Lamont — and others like him, by implication — for speaking out "boldly and courageously" for blacks in the white-dominated country.

Catholics in Hungary — "The Catholic people of Hungary are being trained for godlessness," declared Cardinal Joszef Mindszenty on his arrival in Stuttgart, West Germany, after a two-month visit to the United States. He said: "I see nothing that would seem to be profitable for the people of Hungary as a result of my removal from the See of Esztergom (in February). As a matter of fact, conditions for the Church in my homeland are as critical as ever. Nearly 2,000 priests . . . are kept from functioning as such. Even in Esztergom, no religious instruction of the young is allowed. There is no possibility even of a gentlemen's agreement with Hungary's present rulers who practice godlessness and inhumanity."

Pro-Life Petition — Seventy-five pro-life groups in Canada reported the tabulation of more than 350,000 names since December, 1973, in their bid for a one-million-signature petition for tig]tening abortion laws to protect the lives of the unborn. Dr. L. L. de Veber, president of the Alliance for Life, said July 9 that "preliminary results give us a very hopeful indication we will reach our objective."

More Restricted Sunday — The bishops of Ontario, Canada, informed the provincial government that they favored "a more restricted" rather than "a more open Sunday." They said: "What we are against is over-extension of commercial activity, a proliferation of commercial outlets that tend to change the character of the day, the tendency to reduce Sunday to just one other day in the week."

Concerns of Spanish Bishops — Items on the agenda of the 20th general assembly of the Spanish Bishops' Conference included control over religious broadcasts, public morality, the lay apostolate, foreign missions and economic conditions of the clergy. One report said that Catholic Action was in a state of crisis because of the disappearance of specialized organizations and the nominal-only status of others; membership was far below the 500,000 to a million mark reported by 1960.

Appointment of Anglican Bishops — The general synod of the Church of England, meeting in York, voted 270 to 70 in favor of leaving the final appointment of bishops to the Crown while eliminating the role of the prime minister in the process. The synod declared its support of "the principle that the decisive voice in the appointment of diocesan bishops should be that of the church."

Population Year and Conference — In London, the Catholic Institute for International Relations predicted that World Population Year and the World Population Conference in Bucharest in August would be failures unless rich countries would change their attitudes and strategies for coping with population problems. The institute said: "If the World Population Conference concentrates on this issue to the exclusion of the role and responsibility of the rich countries in regard to their disproportionate absorption and consumption of the world's resources, then a crucial opportunity to put the population problem into its full context will have been wasted."

Vocation Sense Lacking — Cardinal John J. Wright, addressing 1,000 persons at the 40th annual convention of Serra International in London, declared July 14 that the major cause of the crisis in religious vocations was a "genuine decline in the sense of vocation itself." He said: "There is an eclipse of awareness that every life involves a special call under the providence of God and a stewardship in which each individual is answerable to God."

No Sale of Contraceptives — By a vote of 75 to 61, the Irish parliament rejected a government bill that would have legalized the sale of contraceptives to married couples. The bill had been proposed following a December, 1973, decision of the Irish Supreme Court that an existing law forbidding the importation of contraceptives was unconstitutional. As a result of the vote in parliament, contraceptives could be imported without control but could not be sold.

Bishop Arrested — Bishop Daniel Tji Haksoun of Wonju was arrested for the second time by Korean Central Intelligence agents July 23 in Seoul. In a "Statement of Conscience," he condemned the "violence, intimidation and fraud" of President Park Chung hee's one-man rule of the country. He described the regime as one that "stifles inalienable fundamental rights and basic human dignity through emergency decrees by only one man." At month's end the bishop was being held for trial at some future date.

Catholic Schools in Brazil — The Brazilian Bishops' Conference published a document supporting the continued existence of Catholic schools and criticizing attempts by the government to make education a state monopoly. Bishop Ivo Lorscheiter, secretary general, said the statement was intended to counteract two "negative tendencies": the approach of liberals in the Church who maintained that Catholics should get into the state system instead of maintaining their own schools; and the approach of the government toward a monopoly of education.

Lord Chancellorship — Queen Elizabeth II gave royal assent to an act approved by the House of Lords providing that a Catholic might become lord chancellor of Great Britain. The office was banned to Catholics since the 16th century. St. Thomas More, who was martyred under Henry VIII, was the first layman and the last Catholic to hold the office.

Foreign Briefs:
- Archbishop Helder Camara of Recife and Olinda, with a portion of his $175,000 People's Peace Prize, purchased two plantations in northeastern Brazil for operation as farmer cooperatives.
- Father John Traugett, M.M., was appointed national chaplain of the Young Christian Workers' organization in Taiwan.
- Fourteen women were ordained to the Methodist ministry in western England.
- Douglas J. Roche, former editor of the *Western Catholic Reporter,* was reelected to the Canadian parliament.
- Boniface Perdjert became the first aborigine to be ordained a permanent deacon in Australia.
- The United Nations Fund for Population Activities announced it would provide a $40 million grant over the next five years to aid India's efforts to control its population rate.
- Father Philip McNamara was awarded Cambodia's medal of the Commander of Sowathara for his work since March, 1973, in directing operations of Catholic Relief Services in the country.

Lausanne Covenant

Some 2,400 invited participants and 1,300 observers took part in the Intrrnational Congress on World Evangelization July 16 to 25 in Lausanne, Switzerland. In a document named for the place of the congress, the evangelicals stated:
- "Evangelism itself is the proclamation of the historical, biblical Christ as Savior and Lord, with a view to persuading people to come to him personally and so be reconciled to God."
- "Reconciliation with man is not reconciliation with God, nor is social action evangelism, nor is political liberation salvation; nevertheless we affirm that evangelism and sociopolitical involvement are both part of our Christian duty."

AUGUST 1974

VATICAN

Media for Evangelization — "There must be an absolute conviction among Christians of the urgent need and duty to utilize to the full the rich promise of the media in order to communicate truth and love to mankind." So stated a letter sent on Pope Paul's behalf to the Aug. 1 to 3 meeting in Tokyo of the Pan-Asian Bishops' Commission on Social Communications. The message also said: "The Church's apostolate of utilizing the mass media takes on . . . an exceptional importance in the modern world. It does so because it is a necessary and effective way of promoting evangelization and of rendering service; and evangelization and service have complete priority by reason of Christ's will."

Novelty and Progress — "In contemporary history," Pope Paul declared Aug. 7 in an address to a general audience, "what is new is progress . . . And it is always judged the winner in the psychological estimate of the young even when, for example, in certain degraded artistic forms and licentious manners, what is new is no longer authentic progress but rather obvious regression." While observing that many people desire progress without any reference to the past, he said that Christian tradition, which the Church continues to transmit, is "a resource and a living commitment" capable of developing growth "in the knowledge of God."

New Abbot — The Pope appointed Father Giuseppe Turbessi, O.S.B., apostolic administrator of the Monastery of St. Paul's Outside the Walls to replace the stormy Father Giovanni Fronzoni. Father Fronzoni resigned the post in 1973 and was forbidden in April, 1974, to celebrate Mass publicly or administer the sacraments, on the grounds that he had "taken positions clearly in conflict with the Church's doctrine" on birth control and other matters. He was subsequently released from his monastic vows at his own request.

Is Christian Life Easy? — There are three answers to the question, the Holy Father told a general audience Aug. 14. It should be easy, he said, because the "Christian life (is) our salvation, and salvation (is) the immense and freely given gift of God the Father, through Christ the Redeemer, in the Holy Spirit. And does not this gift itself include the grace to correspond to the conditions which are required for salvation, that is, faith and good works?" On the other hand, Christian life is not always easy when one recalls that "the human condition . . ., because of original sin, is not normal. It is not whole or perfect . . . and inhibits the moral and spiritual formation of the good, just and pious person." The secret of Christian life according to the Gospel, he said, is this: "It can be easy if duty coincides with love . . . The Christian life, if it is not always easy, can always be happy."

Statistics Not Enough — On the eve of the United Nations World Population Conference, the Pope warned Aug. 18 against attempts to deal with population problems on an exclusively statistical basis, which he described as "basically materialistic." Such an approach, he said, "could prevail with very grave consequences, if every other aspect of the problem were not taken into account by the conference." (See separate article.)

Meaning of Christian — The meaning of the name of Christian and of Christianity itself was the theme of Pope Paul's address before a general audience Aug. 21. He said: "Christian is the name given a man, an action, a philosophical system which refers to original principles of the Gospel and the customs which the Gospel inspired and generated. Christian denotes certain values which give life a fullness, a dignity, an inviolability worthy of being held sacred." He said that the name of Christian "must not be coarsely exploited . . . It cannot symbolize an opinion, an ideology, a supposition. It must be equated with life . . . The name of Christian stamps a seal, a style, a form on human existence."

Counteracting Bad News — "It seems to me we all need a bit of encouragement to counteract the news in the newspapers," Pope Paul told visitors to Castel Gandolfo Aug. 25. "If the daily press were a mirror of our society," he said, "we should indeed be discouraged and demoralized by this sorry and distorted picture of the world in which we live." However, "we must strengthen our spirits as mature men so as not to fall into pessimism or the madness of desperation. We must, first, be personally faithful in professing and promoting truth . . . Secondly, we must be on the lookout for good, which fortunately is much more widespread than evil. We must love our society all the more, no matter how difficult it may seem to share a peaceful coexistence. Thirdly, we must not fall into a 'who cares' attitude and into skepticism. Rather, we must believe in Providence and invoke it humbly and with confidence."

Pluralism — Pope Paul, before a general audience Aug. 28, cautioned that the term "pluralism" can have two meanings when applied to the Catholic Church but that only one of them is acceptable. The acceptable meaning is that Catholic "doctrine preserves a sincere and deep unity of content" while having "an enormous wealth of meaning for all tongues, for all periods of history, for every age and level of human life." He called unacceptable the equation of pluralism with "free examination," which he said had "pulverized the unity of the faith in a countless number of useless or arbitrary personal opinions." Acceptance of such a meaning, he said, "would be retreating into a confusion of tongues." The Pope asked: "What unity of the Church can be brought about without unity of the faith?"

The Pope Also:

• Sent messages of sympathy on the death of eight Canadian servicemen of the UN Middle East peace force who died when their aircraft was shot down in error over Syria Aug. 9.

• Assured President Gerald R. Ford of "prayerful good wishes" and blessings for "all the beloved American people," Aug. 10.

• Branded as "criminal and homicidal" the bombing of a Rome-Munich express train which took a toll of 12 lives, Aug. 11.

• Marked the feast of the Assumption with Mass in the parish church of Castel Gandolfo, where he spoke of his prayers for peace in Cyprus, Aug. 15.

• Welcomed the Stamford, Conn., High School Chorus, Aug. 25.

• Recalled his visit to Australia in 1970 and praised efforts of that nation to promote world peace when he received the credentials of John M. McMillan, the new Australian ambassador to the Vatican, Aug. 27.

Vatican Briefs:

• Long-time Vatican diplomat Cardinal Umberto Mozzoni left Rome Aug. 6 for Mozambique and Angola to investigate problems of the Church in both places. The colonies were poised on the edge of independence following the collapse of the former Portuguese government in April. Before that time, a bishop and at least 20 missionaries had been expelled because of their criticism of Portugal's colonial government.

• The text of a working document, containing points of departure for discussion, was circulated among delegates to the fourth assembly of the Synod of Bishops scheduled to meet near the end of September at the Vatican. (See separate article.)

• The sentencing of South Korean Bishop Daniel Tji Hak Soun to 15 years' imprisonment for contributing money to an allegedly subversive student organization gave "rise to deep sorrow," stated a Vatican Radio commentator Aug. 13.

• Raul Roa Garcia, foreign minister of Cuba, met Aug. 14 with Archbishop Agostino Casaroli, secretary of the Council for the Public Affairs of the Church, to review differences between church authorities and the Castro government. Unresolved matters included the entry of needed foreign priests into Cuba, questions concerning Catholic education, and the restoration of church property seized by the government since 1959.

Population Policies

Vatican Radio maintained in a broadcast Aug. 9 that governments acting to reduce birth rates should do so "within the framework of a policy geared toward the truly integral good of all citizens in justice, without harming the rights and dignity of parents and without insisting on the use of means contrary to the morality and the moral and religious convictions of citizens."

The commentator also said that many developmental problems of nations stem from "international relations, political and economic systems, and from life-styles which hamper the free and sensible use of potentially available resources."

DOMESTIC

Chaplain Wounded — Volunteer hostage Father Joseph J. O'Brien, O.M.I., chaplain at Huntsville State Prison, Tex., was wounded during an 11-day seige that ended in a shootout Aug. 3 with the death of two other hostages and two convicts.

Political Issues — The Pennsylvania Catholic Conference submitted to the state Democratic and Republican parties early in the month a list of 10 issues which, "because of their human and moral dimensions," it felt should be considered by them in planning and adopting their 1974 platforms. The issues concerned the aging, civil rights, educational freedom, farm laborers, fiscal responsibility, health care, the dignity of human life, prison reform, the preservation of family life, pornography and obscenity.

Other Catholic organizations, and Bishop Edward A. McCarthy of Phoenix, were reported making similar representations to candidates for public office.

Lutheran Church Membership — Membership in 14 Lutheran Church bodies in the U.S. and Canada declined by 44,279 to 9,005,213 in 1973, reported the Lutheran Council in the United States. The loss was the smallest in hhree years.

Chaplain Killed — Father Jarman B. Casey, 38, a chaplain at the South Carolina Central Correctional Institute, was found dead in his apartment in Columbia, S.C., Aug. 3. Arrested and charged with murder was Francis Lewis Franklin, a parolee who had been befriended by the priest and was staying at his apartment.

Preaching — A "Manifesto on Evangelization" issued Aug. 8 by the Word of God Institute called preaching the key to evangelization, and called for greater emphasis on this ministry in the training of priests and deacons. The institute pointed out that proclaiming the Gospel is the chief mission of the Church, and said that preaching "is the central, indispensable and constitutive ministry of the Church and the primary duty of priests."

Nixon Resigns, Ford Takes Office — President Richard M. Nixon, admitting mistakes in his handling of the Watergate coverup, announced his decision to resign the presidency Aug. 8. He made the announcement several days after the House Judiciary Committee voted in favor of proceedings for impeachment on three counts and it became evident that such proceedings would be instituted in the House of Representatives. His resignation became effective the following day, a few minutes before Vice President Gerald R. Ford was sworn into office as the 38th President of the United States.

Sad Search — Archbishop Jean Jadot, apostolic delegate to the U.S., told 2,000 delegates at the convention of Retreats International in Buffalo that it is sad that thousands "are seeking truth and freedom through transcendental meditation, zen and yoga." He added: "For these practices, although honorable, do not lead to Christ. And he alone is our hope and freedom."

CRS Report — "Narrowing the Gap" was the title of a 338-page report released Aug. 13 by Catholic Relief Services on 1,362 relief and development projects in 80 nations as of June 30, 1973.

Men Religious Critical — The Conference of Major Superiors of Men declared in a study paper that men religious were becoming more critical of U.S. culture than in the past, and were beginning to realize that their "religious commitment and vows are of great value because of their counter-cultural testimony." The paper said: "U.S. male religious are now more selective in deciding which of the goals of the 'Secular City' are worthy to pursue. The uncritical enthusiasm of the 1960's for death-of-God theology, situation ethics, sensitivity and T-group training has engendered skepticism for faddist or technical solutions, and a much more reflective approach to apostolic involvement." The title of the study paper was "Awareness: The Experience of U.S. Religious Men."

Textbook Loan Ruled Unconstitutional — The School Office of the St. Louis archdiocese was engaged during the month in efforts to soften the impact of a July 30 ruling by the Missouri Supreme Court against the constitutionality of the state's 1972 Free Textbook Law under which books were loaned to nonpublic school students. An earlier ruling by St. Louis County Circuit Judge Orville Richardson had upheld the law under the state constitution.

Books and Buses — Gov. Brendan T. Byrne of New Jersey signed into law Aug. 7 a $3.9 million bill providing textbook loans for students in nonpublic schools.

The Iowa State School Budget Review Committee approved Aug. 16 the allocation of nearly $2 million to public school districts for the purchase of new buses to transport nonpublic school students to school.

Women's Ordinations Invalid — The House of Bishops of the Episcopal Church in the U.S., n324meeting Aug. 14 and 15 in Chicago, declared the conviction — by a vote of 128 to 9 with 10 abstentions — that the ordinations of 11 women to the priesthood July 29 were invalid and that the ordaining bishops acted wrongly.

Christ the King Seminary To Move — Christ the King Seminary, conducted by the Franciscans of the New York-based Holy Name Province and associated with St. Bonaventure University, Allegany, N.Y., for 118 years, was scheduled to relocate in September in the East Aurora, N.Y., facilities of Buffalo's St. John Vianney Seminary. It was announced that Christ the King would continue to operate as a seminary for students of the Buffalo diocese and other dioceses.

Religious Education at Princeton — An agreement marking "a new milestone of cooperation" in religious education was reached during the month by the Trenton diocese and Princeton Theological Seminary. The seminary announced it would open various courses to Catholics and would expand its program to teach Catholic doctrine, perspectives and structures. The seminary said it would appoint Dr. Lawrence Losoncy to the faculty as a visiting lecturer and supervisor of Catholic students.

New Pro-Life Unit — Several prominent right-to-life advocates split from the National Right to Life Committee to form a new group called American Citizens Concerned for Life. The decision to form the new group, announced Aug. 21, "was prompted by a desire to have a vehicle that would concentrate on state organizations and alternatives to abortion as well as the enactment of an amendment" to the U.S. Constitution. The Rev. Warren Schaller, Jr., was president and executive director of the new organization.

Christian Affirmation of Life — The Catholic Hospital Association announced Aug. 23 the publication of the "Christian Affirmation of Life," a document for persons concerned about their medical treatment when near death. Sister Mary Maurita, president of the association, said the affirmation was designed to meet the needs of Christians wishing to state in writing the desire to be informed of and prepared for imminent death, and to avoid unnecessary treatment, suffering and prolongation of life.

Women's Rights — Groups of Catholic women in New York City and Cincinnati marked Women's Rights Day, Aug. 26, by posting proclamations supporting the Equal Rights Amendment on the doors of two cathedrals.

National Hymnal — The criteria for selecting any hymn to be included in a national hymnal, according to Father Patrick Collins of Peoria, are: Is it good music? Does it fit the liturgy? Is it actually suitable for the people who are gathered to worship at this time and place? Father Collins was the executive director of a 30-member committee at work on the compilation of the hymnal.

No Farm Worker Elections Law — The California legislature adjourned without approving a bill that would have permitted secret ballot elections by farm workers for selecting the union of their choice. The measure, supported by the United Farm Workers of America and the state AFL-CIO, was opposed by the Teamsters Union and grower representatives. Its defeat was attributed to the fact that it did not prohibit secondary boycotts, a major weapon in hhe UFWA struggle against the growers.

Domestic Briefs:

• Conventions and conferences included those of: 2,200 West Coast participants in the Catholic Charismatic Renewal movement, Aug. 2 to 4, in San Diego; the National Black Lay Catholic Caucus, in Baltimore; the National Black Sisters' Conference, attended by 40 sisters, in Atlanta.

• Honored: The Miami archdiocese by the Organization of Seminaries of Latin America, for operating its major seminary on a bilingual and bicultural basis to meet the needs of its Spanish-speaking population; Miami's oldest Catholic church, Gesu, designated as a national historic site by the U.S. Department of the Interior; the Christian Brothers' College of Santa Fe by the New Mexico legislature on the 100th anniversary of its incorporation.

• Father John R. Waterman, C.SS.R., 61, of Schenectady, N.Y., was named deputy director of Veteran Administration chaplains.

Controversial Baptism

Father Joseph O'Rourke, S.J., of New York baptized Nathaniel Morreale on the steps of Immaculate Conception Church, Marlboro, Mass., Aug. 20, despite the local pastor's earlier refusal to allow the baptism and against orders from his superiors not to administer the sacrament.

The pastor, Msgr. Francis Meehan, after discussions with the child's mother, deferred the baptism Aug. 11, on the grounds that he did not have sufficient cause to believe the child would be raised as a Catholic because of his mother's public support of pro-abortionist William Baird. His decision was backed by authorities of the archdiocese.

A public appeal by Mrs. Morreale and Baird for a priest to baptize the child brought Father O'Rourke from New York for a circus-like performance. He was dismissed from the Jesuit order in September.

FOREIGN

Opus Dei Ordinations — Forty-four members of Opus Dei were ordained to the priesthood Aug. 4 in Barcelona. Priest membership in the secular institute amounted to two per cent of approximately 56,000 in 80 countries.

No Elections in Chile — Gen. Augusto Pinochet, chief of state, declared that the military government would not be merely transitional and ruled out a call for elections because it would bring back "dirty politics . . . chaos

and . . . revolution." The issue of an early return to democratic processes was at the core of tense relations between the government and the Christian Democrats.

In another development, the Human Rights Commission of the Organization of American States, after 12 days of on-the-spot investigations recommended measures to safeguard the fundamental rights of political prisoners in Chile. Gen. Pinochet subsequently declared that ill treatment and torture of prisoners were prohibited, and that the government had punished members of the armed forces for violating the ban.

In-Hand Reception of Communion — Cardinal Paulo Evaristo Arns of Sao Paulo, Brazil, ordered the start Aug. 8 of in-hand reception of Holy Communion in the archdiocese. The purpose of the order and practice was to limit the spread of infection during an epidemic of meningitis which claimed 305 lives in Sao Paulo in July.

34 Spanish Priests Resign Posts — Thirty-four priests of the Zaragoza archdiocese resigned their posts Aug. 5 in protest against the dismissal of Father Wilberto Delso from his parish by Archbishop Pedro Cantero Cuadrado for "attitudes, ideas and words" unsuitable to a priest. The priests who resigned were considered to be liberals. Archbishop Cantero was a member of parliament.

Brutality in Rhodesia — Eleven leaders of the Catholic, Anglican and Methodist churches in Rhodesia circulated a document alleging 10 cases of brutality by government security personnel against black African tribesmen.

Earlier in the month, methodist Bishop Abel Muzorewa called the July 30 election victory of the ruling Rhodesian Front a panic vote for the supremacy of 271,000 whites over six million blacks in the country.

15 Years for Korean Bishop — A military court in Seoul found Bishop Daniel Tji Hak Soun of Won Ju vuilty of inciting rebellion against the government of President Park Chung Hee — by making a contribution of money to an allegedly subversive student organization — and sentenced him to 15 years in prison. By Aug. 13, a total of 55 persons had been convicted for aiding the National Democratic Student League.

Euthanasia — Informed Catholic opinion in the United Kingdom was convinced that legislation to permit euthanasia could be introduced in England in the next decade, according to Dr. T. P. Linehan, master of the Guild of Catholic Doctors. Behind the opinion was reasoning connected with and analogous to the development of favorable views regarding abortion following passage of the Abortion Act in England in 1967.

The World Federation of Doctors Who Respect Human Life, founded in May, 1974, reported that since July more than 3,000 British doctors had signed a modern form of the

Hippocratic oath emphasizing the sacredness of human life.

World Council of Churches — The Central Committee of the World Council of Churches, meeting Aug. 11 to 18 in West Berlin, resolved to include its controversial five-year Program to Combat Racism among its permanent programs. The program was under criticism from several quarters because of the manner in which, it was charged, it involved the WCC in politically oriented and underground guerrilla movements, especially in Africa. The Rev. Dr. Philip A. Potter, general secretary of the council, complained at the meeting that press reports of the program had created a "distorted image of the WCC." He said that no one "has ever been able to prove that . . . money (supplied by the WCC) is used for anything other than that for which it was destined" — the humanitarian activities of organizations opposed to racial oppression.

Gun-Running Charge against Archbishop — Israeli police arrested Melkite-Rite Archbishop Ilarion Capucci Aug. 15 on suspicion of smuggling weapons into Israel from Lebanon for use by Arab guerrillas. The prelate was suspected of acting as a liaison man and gunrunner between Al Fatah in Lebanon and members of the organization in the West Bank territory occupied by Israel. Jewish newspapers were reported to be taking his guilt for granted. Many Christians and Moslems, not discounting the possibility that the charge and supporting evidence might have been trumped up, were skeptical.

Church-State Relations in Brazil — Conflicting assessments of Church-state relations were voiced by two prelates during the month. Cardinal Eugenio de Araujo Sales of Rio de Janeiro said there were no conflicts between the Church and the state. Cardinal Paulo Evaristo Arns declared that dialogue with the government "is still encountering problems." One point at issue was the freedom of the Church to initiate and carry out works for the social and economic development of the people.

UN World Population Conference — In a statement referring to the United Nations World Population Conference which opened in Bucharest Aug. 19 (see separate entry), the bishops of the Dominican Republic rejected any attempt by developed countries to impose population controls on underdeveloped nations. They branded any such attempt as an "inadmissible new form of colonialism." The bishops also said: Individual and collective sins, "wrong values and unjust social, economic and political structures . . ." are the causes of the population situation and its perpetuation. The only solution, therefore, is in changing values, attitudes and structures. "Anything else will only constitute partial solutions and deceptions, und will ultimately bring failure."

Radio School Graduates — The Jesuit-run Santa Maria radio school in La Vega, the Dominican Republic, graduated 4,749 peasants on their completion of requirements for primary and intermediate education diplomas. They were the most recent of some 15,000 students to complete education cmurses conducted by the diocesan-owned station. The education program, like the first of its kind inaugurated several years earlier in Colombia, combined radio lectures with mail courses and direct contact of students with some 400 teachers.

Priests Jailed — Vatican Radio reported Aug. 29 that courts in the Soviet Ukraine and in Czechoslovakia had jailed priests for violating restrictions on religious freedom. The Lvov newspaper *Lwowskaya Pravda* of Aug. 20 was quoted as authority for a report that Ukrainian Father Bernard Mitskevicg was jailed for "drawing villagers to church, repairing the church, organizing group excursions . . . exhortinv parents to bring their children to church, organizing prayer groups for youth, and distributing crucifixes and other religious objects." The Center for East European Studies reported a sentence of solitary confinement passed Jan. 22, 1974, by a Czech court on Father Jozef Gazda, who was accussd of givinv catechetical lessons to his nephews and some of their friends.

Foreign Briefs:
- The Malagasy Bishops' Conference announced a decision not to organize a Holy Year 1975 pilgrimage to Rome because a costly pilgrimage "would be like an insult to this country which is struggling against poverty."
- Benjamin Mendoza y Amor, who tried to stab Pope Paul during his visit to Manila in 1970, was deported to Bolivia by Philippine authorities.
- Father William Masterson, S.J., of Brooklyn was named to receive a 1975 Magsaysay Award for his work in cural leadership training in the Philippines.
- The bishops of England and Wales were given permission to allow the celebration of the traditional Latin Mass at funerals.

Popular Religion, Marian Devotion

The deeply religious elements of popular religion in Latin America and the desirability of integrating them into the traditional liturgy were the subject of growing interest, reported Father Joaquin Alliende Uco, director of the pastoral department of the Chilean Bishops' Conference.

He said that personnel working with the Latin American Bishops' Council were in agreement that popular religion, coupled with authentic Marian devotion, must be primary elements of a genuine Latin American approach to pastoral problems.

In the past church authorities had been wary of superstition in folk religion and celebrations connected with it.

SEPTEMBER 1974

VATICAN

Something Missing — Something is missing "in the grand and marvelous mechanism of our refined and fragile civilization" which favors armaments and "certain immoral and inhuman programs to reduce the birth rate." So stated Pope Paul Sept. 1. The missing factors, he said, are "the fear of God, a religious concept of life, the operative presence of the Gospel in the dynamics of human kind's history, and the faith."

A Little More — The Holy Father called on Catholics Sept. 4 to "do a little more" for the Church's updating begun by Pope John XXIII. He urged them not to give "punctilious priority to the letter of certain outward religious observances, above the basic spirit, principles and virtues of Christianity."

Make Voice of Church Heard — Pope Paul told nine of his permanent observers or delegates with international agencies that the Church works in such organizations for "the universal, common good." He said Sept. 4 that their "serious and delicate task" is to make the Church's voice heard in these influential bodies.

Peace Depends on Everybody — "Peace must depend not only on the good will of religious and national leaders, but must be anchored firmly and securely in the hearts of all men," declared Pope Paul in an address to 40 Japanese delegates to the recently concluded Aug. 28 to Sept. 3 World Conference of Religions at Louvain University, Belgium. He said that an emphasis common to all religions "is on the need to liberate the things of the spirit, and to give help to our fellow men. May this liberation be truly a liberation from war and hate."

Media and the Holy Year — "In the hands of men dedicated to peace and love among men, how powerful these two great media, radio and television, can be in promoting the objectives of the Holy Year, reconciliation and renewal." This was the theme of a papal message to a meeting of the International Catholic Association for Radio and Television near Dublin, Ireland.

Defense of Life — Declaring Sept. 7 that the Church must "defend human life without fail," Pope Paul reaffirmed the Church's opposition to artificial birth control, abortion and sterilization. Addressing himself to some 1,500 participants in two international assemblies of pharmacists, he said: "We invite men of science to orient their studies and their developments in favor of a healthy regulation of human procreation."

Faith Will Overcome — "Faith is the first requirement to overcome the present difficulties" besetting the Church, the Pope said at a general audience Sept. 11. He lamented in particular that "now there are some sons (of the Church), who have sworn love and fidelity, who are leaving. There are not a few almost deserted seminaries and religious families who find new candidates only with difficulty. And there are the faithful who do not fear to be unfaithful." The greater proportion of evils being experienced by the Church "afflict, weaken and enfeeble it from within," he said.

Work for Well-Being — Deploring two recent days of violence in Rome over housing shortages, the Pope called on civil authorities Sept. 15 to work "to produce for needy persons that human well-being which comes from justice and which is the basis for peace."

Thomas Has Answers — Pope Paul, during a five-hour visit by car and helicopter to places connected with the life and death of St. Thomas Aquinas Sept. 14, said that the writings of the saint offer a real answer to modern anxieties. The answer is "trust in the truth of Catholic religious thought."

Strong Men Needed — Today the Church "needs strong men," Pope Paul declared Sept. 18 during his last public audience at Castel Gandolfo before returning to the Vatican. Observing that surveys showed "human weaknesses, spiritual debility and vileness in the Church and elsewhere," he said that strong men are needed to confront the "fashionable temptations in the world today which would abolish discipline and give free rein to license under the guise of liberty." "By definition," he said, "a Christian, especially if marked by the sacrament of confirmation, must be a strong man."

Bishop's Power for Service — Pope Paul, while concelebrating Mass Sept. 22 with 77 American bishops, said in a homily that their episcopal authority was a "power of service" for the good of the community. He urged them to adopt a "true Gospel figure" of "provident and strong" goodness, and an "inexhaustible spirit of sacrifice." Most of the bishops were in Rome to make their periodic *ad limina* visit and report to the Pope, and to take part in a month-long theological study program at the North American College.

St. Bonaventure's Message — The Pope, speaking Sept. 24 at a congress marking the seventh centenary of the death of St. Bonaventure, said his message was "an invitation to regain his authenticity and attain his full development." He said: "The spiritual journey that St. Bonaventure puts before us is not a solitary one, nor one that has as its goal a distant and unknown horizon. It is a journey with the Son of God . . . toward God within ourselves, in whom he has been pleased to take up his abode."

Fidelity Needed — Echoing the theme of his last public statement at Castel Gandolfo, Pope Paul said Sept. 25 at his first general audience after returning to the Vatican: "The great failure of so many modern Christians is . . . the lack of fidelity to graces received in baptism, or successively in other sacraments, and to solemn and salutary duties assumed toward God, toward Christ, toward the Church in celebration of a pact, an alliance, a communion of supernatural life. . . . On the other hand, it is a great gain to have held faithfully to these duties which give sense, virtue and merit to Christian life."

Music and Evangelization — The unique status of sacred music in the liturgy and evangelization was noted in a letter sent Sept. 26 in Pope Paul's name by Cardinal Jean Villot to the president of the Italian Association of Santa Cecilia. The letter said: "It is the wish of the Supreme Pontiff that public celebrations should not take place without some minimum of song, and that every church should resound with music which elevates those present closer to God, satisfies their innermost aspirations, and strengthens their communion in faith and in love."

The Pope Also:
• Probably discussed the arrest of Archbishop Ilarion Capucci, on a charge of gunrunning in Israel, with Melkite-Rite Patriarch Maximos V Hakim, Sept. 11.
• Received an Indian headdress from four Ottawas following a general audience, Sept 11.
• Returned to the Vatican by helicopter from his summer residence at Castel Gandolfo, Sept. 18.
• Received the thanks of Turks and Greeks alike for the visit of a papal mission to embattled Cyprus.
• Called on Dominicans attending a general chapter of their order to devote themselves to a life of poverty, of community rooted in the Eucharist and prayer, and of "study of the truth," Sept. 21.
• Received new ambassadors to the Vatican: Joe Kachingwe of Malawi, Sept. 7; Henry Nzioka Mulli of Kenya, Sept. 10; Gerard Amanrich of France, Sept. 26.
• Met privately with Cesar Chavez, head of the United Farm Workers of America, Sept. 25.

Vatican Briefs:
• The clearest lesson for the Church to draw from the World Population Conference in Bucharest, Rumania, Aug. 19 to 30, is that education in family life must be intensified, according to Vatican delegate Bishop Edouard Gagnon. "The family," he said, "remained at the center of all debates and controversies."
• Vatican security guards, the former Pontifical Gendarmes, were once again carrying sidearms on duty.
• The Pontifical Commission for Justice and Peace called on the 1974 assembly of the Synod of Bishops Sept. 18 to "reaffirm the need to work for peace and justice within the

perspective of evangelization and as an integral part of it."
• A delegation from the Vatican Secretariat for Non-Christians returned to Rome after a week of meetings with the Council for Islamic Affairs in Egypt. Cardinal Sergio Pignedoli said the delegation discussed "the religious situation of youth in the Moslem and Christian world, and the influence of religious faith on social life and peace."

Synod '74

Pope Paul formally opened the fourth assembly of the Synod of Bishops Sept. 27 with a declaration that preaching God's word goes hand in hand with work for the progress of people.

Comments by dozens of the 200-odd participants during the opening days made it clear that bishops in all parts of the world regarded the commitment and activity of lay persons as essential to evangelization. Other themes were the need for sensitivity to local cultures on the part of the universal Church, the development of smaller ecclesial communities, and the aspirations and potentialities of youth.

DOMESTIC

Pluralism Hurting Church — Undisciplined pluralism, on the rise since the Second Vatican Council, is seriously compromising unity in the Church. So declared Dr. James Hitchcock, professor of history at St. Louis University, at the second international assembly of *Consortium Perfectae Caritatis* in Pasadena, Calif. He said: "There are developing within the Catholic Church such wide theological differences that it becomes doubtful in many cases whether . . . unity (in essentials) still exists. . . . No institution and no community can tolerate unlimited pluralism, else it ceases to be a community and ceases to be a unified institution."

Food Policy — The Executive Committee of the U.S. Catholic Conference called on the Ford administration to present a "broadly conceived and just policy" to the UN World Food Conference to be held Nov. 5 to 16 in Rome. The committee said the policy should include a permanent international food reserve, more short-term emergency relief, and technical assistance for developing nations to increase their production of food.

UFWA Boycott Goes International — George Meany, president of the AFL-CIO, said in a Sept. 9 speech in Washington, D.C., that trade unions in other nations had been asked to support the boycott of table grapes and head lettuce called for by the Chavez-led United Farm Workers of America. He said the boycott in this country had been "heartening," but added that "we must take the boycott message overseas."

Pennsylvania Abortion Law — The legislature made the Abortion Control Act state law

Sept. 10 by overriding the veto of Gov. Milton J. Shapp. The act provided:

• That a wife obtain the consent of her husband for an abortion unless the procedure is necessary to save her life.

• That parental consent is necessary for unmarried woman under the age of 18.

• That physicians determine the viability of a fetus in later stages of pregnancy — when an abortion can be performed only to save the mother's life and when efforts must be made to save the child's life.

No Most-Favored Status — The Soviet Union should not be given "most-favored-nation" treatment by the U.S., declared Bishop James S. Rausch, general secretary of the U.S. Catholic Conference, in a letter to members of the Senate. He praised attempts at detente, but argued that granting such status "would be most inappropriate" in the light of Soviet restrictions on human rights and freedoms.

Boston Busing — The opening of public schools in Boston was marred by controversies, student boycotts and violence. Disturbances related to implementation of a court-ordered plan for racial balance in the schools continued for some weeks.

Bicentennial — The U.S. Bishops' Bicentennial Committee announced Sept. 11 the scheduling of six regional hearings in 1975 to develop the agenda of a national conference on the theme of the 1976 celebration, "Liberty and Justice for All."

President Ford Criticized — President Gerald R. Ford was criticized on two counts by Democratic Representative Father Robert Drinan, S.J. He called his absolute pardon Sept. 8 of former President Nixon "constitutionally and morally wrong," and said that his defense of CIA activity to "destabilize" the government of former President Salvador Allende in Chile was "appalling."

Civil Rights — Three challenges to the civil rights movement were "deep-rooted discrimination," "loss of support . . . by groups which once were a major part of the movement" (e.g., labor unions and Jewish civil rights organizations), and "growing political opposition." So declared Father Theodore M. Hesburgh, C.S.C., president of Notre Dame University and former chairman of the U.S. Commission on Civil Rights, in an article published in *The Nation*.

In a related development William Taylor, director of the Center for National Policy Review at the Catholic University of America, said: "A pattern of faithlessness to legal duty on the part of government officials who have sworn to uphold the law" marked the record of the Department of Health, Education and Welfare in dealing with school segregation in the North.

Signs of Hope — Apostolic Delegate Archbishop Jean Jadot, speaking Sept. 18 in Chicago, said he saw abundant "signs and causes of hopefulness in the present situation of the Church, especially in the United States." Among the signs were:

• "a renewal of Christian responsibility;

• "an increased sense of community and fellowship;

• "expanded information and education, leading to a broader view of reality;

• "a growing movement toward interiorization, toward the development of what one is rather than the accumulation of what one has."

Project Equality — The national board of 10-year-old Project Equality voted to begin issuing performance ratings of some 3,500 business organizations committed to giving fair employment opportunities to women and members of minority groups.

Father Feeney Reconciled — Bishop Bernard J. Flanagan of Worcester confirmed rumors Sept. 26 that Father Leonard Feeney, S.J., had been personally accepted back into the Church two years earlier by Pope Paul VI. He also announced that 29 of his followers, called Slaves of the Immaculate Heart of Mary, had been reconciled with the Church in the spring of 1974. Father Feeney was excommunicated in 1953 because of his interpretation, and related actions, of the doctrine, "Outside the Church there is no salvation."

Money Problems — The Pauline Fathers in Doylestown, Pa., announced Sept. 27 that Bishop George Guilfoyle of Camden and Father Paul Boyle, C.P., had been appointed by the Vatican to investigate ways and means of solving the financial problems of the National Shrine of Our Lady of Czestochowa. The shrine had a debt of approximately $4.2 million.

Episcopal Bishops Charged — The four bishops who participated in the ordination of 11 women to the priesthood in Philadelphia in July were formally charged with failing to receive proper recommendations for ordination from the appropriate committee of each woman's home diocese and of acting without the approval of the bishop of Pennsylvania. The charges were lodged by four bishops in the Midwest.

Rockefeller Nomination — The nomination of Nelson Rockefeller for the vice presidency was opposed in Senate hearings late in the month by objectors to his pro-abortion legislative record and his handling of the Attica State Prison revolt while he was governor of New York.

Domestic Briefs:

• Jerald terHorst, White House press secretary, told reporters Sept. 3 that Father John J. McLaughlin's job as a presidential speech writer would be abolished. terHorst himself resigned his job about a week later in protest against President Ford's pardon of former President Nixon.

• Sister Anna Marie Kane was installed

Sept. 16 as an assistant chaplain at Holy Cross College, Worcester, Mass.

• John Riccardo, national chairman, announced Sept. 17 that Robert G. Fanelli of Greenwich, Conn., had been named associate chairman for the 34th annual interfaith National Bible Week Nov. 24 to Dec. 1, 1974.

• Sister Clare Dunn, after winning the Democratic nomination to the Arizona House of Representatives from District 3, said she was running for office because "decent, concerned legislators have been too few and too powerless to do much."

• Steven Landregan, editor of the *Texas Catholic*, was elected to chair the 60-member Advisory Council of the U.S. Bishops.

• Thirteen Lutheran and 10 Catholic theologians resumed their mutual study of papal infallibility in four days of discussion, Sept. 19 to 22, in Princeton, N.J. The meeting was the 19th in a series that began in 1965.

• Honored during the month were: Atonement Father Daniel Egan, the "Junkie Priest," with the 1974 Good Samaritan Award of the National Catholic Development Conference for his work with women drug addicts; Father Joseph B. Collins, S.S., director of the National Center of Religious Education — Confraternity of Christian Doctrine from 1942 to 1968, with the St. Thomas Aquinas Catechetics Award of the Dominican Fathers.

• A Spanish-Speaking Catholic Commission was set up by the bishops of Illinois, Indiana, Michigan, Ohio and Wisconsin. Rogelio Manrique, director of the Latin American Pastoral Center in Detroit, was elected executive director.

Masonic Membership

Cardinal John J. Krol released the text of a letter Sept. 18 from the Congregation for the Doctrine of the Faith which stated that Catholic laymen may join Masonic lodges that do not plot against the Church. The letter from Cardinal Franjo Seper, prefect of the congregation, said in part:

"In considering particular cases, it must be remembered that penal law is always subject to strict interpretation. Therefore, one may safely teach and apply the opinion of those authors who hold that Canon 2335 refers only to those Catholics who join associations which plot against the Church."

Most U.S. lodges, and others, were not considered of this type.

The letter also said: "Clerics, religious and members of secular institutes are still forbidden in every case to join any Masonic association."

(See Glossary entry, Freemasons.)

FOREIGN

End Repression in Chile — In a letter to Gen. Augusto Pinochet, Chilean chief of state, the leaders of four major religious bodies appealed for amnesty for political prisoners, lifting the "state of internal war," and review by civilian courts of sentences imposed by military courts. They also asked for "mitigation of the consequences of political struggles we have known and suffered," an apparent reference to continuing repression.

In other developments:

• Regulations issued by the regime on religious meetings during the Chilean celebration of the Holy Year until Dec. 31, 1974, banned political discussions, elections or any other "not specifically religious" activities.

• With one or two exceptions, the bishops stayed away from official celebrations for the first anniversary of the coup that toppled the regime of Salvador Allende Sept. 11, 1973.

• Father Robert L. Plasker of Portland, Ore., superior of the Holy Cross Fathers in the country, was summarily expelled Sept. 17 for undisclosed reasons.

End Martial Law — The bishops of the Philippines called on President Ferdinand E. Marcos early in the month to end martial law, restore civil liberties and end the "climate of fear" in the country. The appeal was presented to the government a week after soldiers raided a Jesuit house in a Manila suburb and arrested 21 persons, including Father Jose Blanco, assistant director of the Jesuit Institute of Social Order.

Food Program Contributions — Dr. Francisco Aquino, executive director of the World Food Program, welcomed Saudi Arabia's $50 million cash pledge for 1975-76 as "the biggest cash contribution in the program's history and the second largest received so far in total value for the next two-year period." The largest total pledge was that of the U.S., for $140 million in cash and commodities.

Cuban Sanctions — Exiled Cuban Bishop Eduardo Boza Masvidal, in a statement issued in Caracas, Venezuela, said that sanctions imposed on Cuba in 1964 should not be lifted — as suggested by Colombia, Costa Rica and Venezuela — for economic reasons or because the Castro regime was no longer "exporting revolution." He said that "the question of a whole nation being oppressed inside Cuba seems to matter little to most leaders." Bishops inside Cuba, however, had asked for the end of the economic embargo because it was causing suffering to the poor.

Harassment in Poland — Cardinal Karol Wojtyla of Cracow confirmed that Polish authorities had demolished a building in a catechetical center and had blocked a pilgrimage marking the anniversary of the death of Blessed Maximilian Kolbe.

Interest in Role of Women — The general assembly of the World Union of Catholic Women's Organizations received Sept. 14 a letter from Cardinal Jean Villot expressing Pope Paul's interest in the role of women in the contemporary world. The letter said: "The Supreme Pontiff wishes to express the confidence he has in the work of the Dar-es-Salaam (Tanzania) assembly in furthering this at a time when women are called upon to exercise new responsibilities in the multiple domains to which he referred recently" in the apostolic exhortation *Marialis Cultus*. (See separate entry.)

Priests' Congress — Some 400 priests took part in a World Congress on the Priesthood in Paray-Le-Monial, France. The congress, which ended Sept. 19, marked the 300th anniversary of the apparition of the Sacred Heart to St. Margaret Mary Alacoque. Pope Paul said in a message to the congress that a priest is called to "sacrifice himself continually for the salvation of men."

Countries with Abortion — Mother Teresa of Calcutta, in an address to a group of nursing home instructors near Stockholm, said: "Sweden and the other industrialized countries have a high standard of technology. But there are people here crying for someone to care for them. It is a sign of great poverty that abortion is performed in so many countries."

Archbishop on Trial — The trial of Archbishop Ilarion Capucci, Melkite-Rite patriarchal vicar, opened Sept. 20 after the court rejected a challenge to its competence. The prelate was charged with illegal contact with enemies of Israel, carrying arms from Lebanon into Jerusalem, and distributing arms to dissident Palestinians on the West Bank. In challenging the court the archbishop's counsel claimed that the place of the trial, East Jerusalem, was not part of Israel; that the archbishop, as a leader of his Church, was exempt from a state trial according to traditional law; and that he, as a holder of Vatican diplomatic passport, had diplomatic immunity from trial.

Sacred Music — Sacred music has all but disappeared from the training of seminarians, declared Msgr. Richard J. Schuler of St. Paul, Minn., in an address before the sixth International Church Music Conference in Salzburg, Austria. In sketching the problem, he said: "It is useless to speak of a course of study for music in the seminary until its professors are convinced of the fundamental truths of the Roman Catholic faith. . . . Because of a widespread denial of the sacred, liturgy and music no longer deal with the relationship between man and God, but rather that of man to man or even to oneself. When man, in a sense, assumes the place of God in the liturgy, then the need for the sacred ceases. . . . What ails music in the service of worship" is symptomatic of "a churning, seething, boiling ferment of error and disbelief. . . . There must be an affirmation of the sacred, and this must begin in the seminaries."

Vocations Up and Down — The Information Center on Religious Vocations in Freiburg reported that the number of aspirants to the priesthood in Germany increased 18 per cent in 1973 after a decade-long decrease of about 15 per cent. Factors related to the increase, according to students, were "personal relationships between priests and the young," and "a truly Christian family environment."

In Spain, however, Archbishop Angel Suguia of Santiago de Compostela said there has been a two-thirds decrease in the number of major seminarians, from 8,021 in 1963-64 to 2,500 in 1973-74.

CCC Meeting — The Canadian Catholic Conference convened Sept. 16 to 20 in Quebec to discuss the topics of evangelization and the nation's catechetical program, and to celebrate the 300th anniversary of the founding of the diocese.

Aid to Honduras — Catholic Relief Services rushed emergency aid to victims of Hurricane Fifi, the worst in Honduran history. Kenneth Brown, CRS representative in Tegucigalpa, was authorized to draw upon supplies in Nicaragua, El Salvador and Guatemala for flood-stricken communities in the northern part of the country. It was estimated that perhaps 400,000 persons were affected by floods in Central America and that at least 5,000 had perished in Honduras.

Foreign Briefs:

• Father Pedro Arrupe, S.J., superior general, told an international meeting of Jesuits in Loyola, Spain, that obedience to church authority is the cornerstone of the Society of Jesus. He said that Jesuits "cannot bypass the authority of the Church or, much less, oppose it, since it is the work of their mission to serve the Church." He denied rumors that the society was contemplating basic changes in its rule.

• The International Atomic Energy Agency, meeting in Vienna, was told Sept. 16 by Dr. Herman J. Abs, chief of the Vatican delegation, that mounting stocks of nuclear weapons and the abuse of existing nuclear pacts could lead to a world holocaust.

• In a statement on world population problems, the bishops of Brazil said that the major thrust of any policy "must be directed at the rational distribution of human and economic resources in order to bring about a better balance" between have and have-not peoples.

Archbishop Resigns

Melkite-Rite Archbishop Joseph Raya of Acre resigned his see and left Israel for Canada Sept. 20. He claimed that the Vatican and Melkite-Rite Patriarch Maximos V Hakim had interfered with his policy and administration of the diocese.

While agreeing that the Vatican was making efforts to keep Christians in the Holy Land, he asserted that the purpose of this policy was "to keep the shrines alive," a policy which he said subordinated people to shrines.

His relentless campaign to have Christians returned to villages evacuated and destroyed by government order had alarmed Israeli authorities.

OCTOBER 1974

VATICAN

Personal Witness — Pope Paul urged the Council of the Laity and thousands of persons present at a general audience Oct. 2 to give personal witness to the faith. He said: "Contemporary man listens more willingly to witnesses than to teachers; or, if he listens to teachers, it is because they are witnesses. Indeed, he finds an instinctive repulsion toward all that is mystification, facade, compromise. In this context can be understood the importance of a life which rings truly of the Gospel."

Panorama of the Church — The Synod of Bishops offered observers a worldwide panorama of the Church thriving in some places, suffering from "infidelity" in others, and even "suffocated" in still others, Pope Paul said Oct. 7. The synod's proceedings showed to the world the "marvelous and laboriously won conquests of Christian civilization," he observed. But they also "oblige us to call attention to the fact that still today the greatest part of mankind awaits the evangelical message. . . . It could almost be said that evangelization is still in its beginnings."

Action Needed — Pope Paul told a general audience Oct. 9 that the Church's greatest need is for action. He said: "The Church has need of action, whether understood in the subjective sense of inner activity, thought, reflection, prayer, contemplation; or action interpreted in the sense of exterior activity, of Catholic action, of good works, of interest in the well-being of one's neighbor, of intervention in matters of social welfare. . . . We accept this formulation. We make it our own program. Now is the time to act, to be doing. A Church that remains willingly inert will not be a true Church. It will not be a living Church. . . . The action that we now consider and which we wish to adopt is not just any kind of action, an activity with no other end than itself or of a kind and scope outside the moral norm. We speak of moral action, conforming to upright reason and the eternal law of God."

Briefs from the Synod of Bishops:

Mixed Record: In an overview of pastoral tendencies in the Church since 1971, Brazilian Archbishop Aloisio Lorscheider reported that the interior renewal proposed by the Second Vatican Council was being accomplished less effectively than exterior changes of structure and procedure. He said there had been signs of vigor and strength since 1971 in such areas as concern for social justice, the growth of community life and a new spirit in seminaries. He observed, however, that there was an "urgent and immediate need" to study the essence of Christianity for meeting problems arising from a "demand for pluralistic options." He also cited a need for the improvement of coordination between the Vatican and local churches.

Protest: Cardinal Josyf Slipyi, major archbishop of Lvov and a long-time prisoner in the Soviet Union, called on the synod "to raise its voice in loud protest" against religious persecution in Russia and elsewhere.

Liberation: Bishops from Asia and Latin America strongly endorsed efforts for the achievement of full human liberation as a viatal part of preaching the Gospel. Cardinal Stephen Kim of Seoul, Korea, claimed that the Church is often more concerned with maintaining churches and schools than in helping oppressed people exercise or defend fundamental human rights. On the other hand, Cardinal William Conway of Armagh, Northern Ireland, expressed the view of various European bishops that focus should be kept on the transcendent message of Christianity, especially in the world of developed nations.

Hungary: Archbishop Jozsef Ijjas of Kalocsa reported that the Church in Hungary had been given permission by the government to teach catechetics to children twice a week.

Defense of Oppressed: The need for the Church to move openly to the defense of the persecuted and oppressed was stressed by Brazilian Archbishop Helder Camara of Olinda and Recife. He declared that Christians who regard Christianity as a passive belief have put Karl Marx in the right "by giving the oppressed, both of the poor and the rich countries, an opiate for the people."

Confusion: A number of bishops spoke Oct. 8 of difficulties over contemporary confusion in theology and of the need for clear doctrinal statements by the teaching authority of the Church.

The synod marked its halfway point Oct. 11 with the conclusion of discussion on experiences in evangelization.

(See also two separate articles on the Synod of Bishops.)

DOMESTIC

Respect Life — A month-long Respect Life Program was scheduled to begin Oct. 6 in parishes acorss the nation. Its themes concerned the unborn, euthanasia, the mentally retarded, the aging and poor, food needs, health care, reforms in the justice and correctional systems, amnesty and gun control. The program, in its third year, was sponsored by the Committee for Pro-Life Activities of the National Conference of Catholic Bishops.

St. Anthony Dining Room — The St. Anthony Dining Room in the tenderloin district of San Francisco marked the 25th anniversary of its founding Oct. 4 with the serving of its 12-millionth free meal to the needy. The dining room, operated by the Franciscans of St.

Boniface Church, served a balanced hot meal to an average of 1,800 persons a day, Monday through Friday.

Released Time — A trend toward having public school students released for entire days of religious education was reported developing in the St. Paul and Minneapolis archdiocese. The trend was given impetus by an opinion of Minnesota Attorney General Warren Spannaus stating that public school students may be released from classes for whole days to attend religious instruction programs instead of for the usual periods of three hours a week. The ruling spurred the development of a wide range of "block" released time programs giving public school students time for day-long retreats, community service projects and intensive religious studies. Such programs were said to be involving more than 3,500 students in about 20 parishes.

Fifi Aid — Nationwide Catholic response to emergency aid appeals for victims of Hurricane Fifi in Honduras and elsewhere in Central America was reported to be mounting above $1.5 million. Catholic Relief Services said that tons of food, clothing, blankets and medical supplies were being shipped to flood-stricken areas by sea and air transport.

NCC Amnesty Unit — The National Council of Churches reported setting up a special agency — Ministries/Vietnam Generation — to provide counseling and other assistance to those affected by President Gerald R. Ford's amnesty-clemency program.

In a related development, delegates to the 60th annual meeting of the National Conference of Catholic Charities in Boston passed a resolution in favor of unconditional amnesty for war resisters. The delegates also called on Catholic charity organizations to make jobs available to draft resisters agreeing to perform the alternative service required by the Ford program.

Contracts in Spanish — A law requiring Spanish language contracts upon a customer's request from any business conducting sales in Spanish was signed into law by Governor Ronald Reagan of California. The law also required merchants to notify customers of the availability of such agreements.

"Chico and the Man" — Mexican Americans in Los Angeles charged that NBC-TV's "Chico and the Man" was making them the subject of ridicule. They charged that the show was reenforcing demeaning stereotypes and raising further barriers to opportunities for Mexican Americans.

N.J. Conscience Clause — A bill allowing medical personnel and hospitals to refuse participation in abortion procedures was signed into law by Governor Brendan T. Byrne.

Pro-Life Amendments Useless — Four law professors testifying before a Senate subcommittee agreed that two proposed pro-life amendments under consideration would not reverse the effect of Supreme Court decisions

striking down most state restrictions against abortion. The amendments would define the fetus as a person under the protection of the Fourteenth Amendment. If made effective, the professors said, the amendments would only establish a conflict of rights between the mother and the fetus. And the Supreme Court, they added, had already ruled that the rights of the mother have priority over those of the fetus.

Lutheran Seminary Head Fired — The Rev. Dr. John Tietjen, the suspended president of Concordia Seminary in St. Louis, announced that he had been fired by the Lutheran institution's board of control. He said the board had found him guilty of 10 charges ranging from heresy to maladministration of the seminary. He called his dismissal a charade but no surprise. Dr. Tietjen was a focal figure in liberal-conservative controversy in the Lutheran Church-Missouri Synod.

Butz Criticized — A number of persons and organizations concerned with the world food crisis called for the removal of Secretary of Agriculture Earl Butz as head of the American delegation to the UN World Food Conference scheduled to meet Nov. 5 to 16 in Rome. Butz had already been the target of criticism because of his hard-line, free-market approach to the food situation in favoring the interests of agribusiness over the needs of consumers.

Pastoral Letter on Violence — Cardinal Humberto Medeiros issued a pastoral letter in which he called for effective efforts to end weeks of violence connected with court-ordered busing of students to Boston public schools. Ending violence, he said, "is not merely the task of public officials, educators and enforcement officers. There is a role for every citizen, old and young, white and black; Christian, Jew or Muslim. All of us are involved; all of us must assume our portion of the burden."

Not Much Effect on Corporations — Four years of effort by church groups had little, if any, effect on the social-responsibility policies and practices of corporations. So stated the September issue of *The Corporate Examiner,* a monthly newsletter published by the Interfaith Center for Corporate Responsibility in New York. The letter said:

"Certainly business knows that the church is there looking over its massive multinational shoulder. It has disclosed information that most likely would never have been made public if the churches hadn't pushed. In many instances it has changed its advertising and public relations goals from product information to total corporate image change or even promotion of its political philosophy.

"But basically the business community remains blind and deaf to the growing dimensions of human awareness around the world that are reshaping the personal meaning of life and calling for social harmony with nature. The commercial philosophy that continues to pander growth, expansion, exploitation, and profit in an age demanding redistribution, equalization and conservation approaches the obscene if not the immoral."

(See separate article, Morality of Corporate Investments.)

Black Vocation Director — The National Office for Black Catholics announced the appointment of Father Kenneth C. Stewart at its national vocational director. Father Stewart, who said he considered himself a "national initiator of vocations in the black Catholic Church," intended to act as a contact man with diocesan and religious vocational recruiters, to coordinate workshops, talk to interested groups, and act as liaison between the NOBC and special interest groups for vocational recruitment.

Departure Ceremony — Plans were announced in Boston for a Mission Sunday departure ceremony for five priests of the Missionary Society of St. James in Latin America. Mission crosses were to be given the priests by Cardinal Humberto Medeiros on the eve of their departure for Lima, Peru.

FOREIGN

Force for Human Rights — The "one effective force for human rights" in Chile appeared to be the inter-church peace committee led by Cardinal Raul Silva of Santiago, declared Anglican Archbishop Michael Ramsey of Canterbury on returning from a 17-day visit to Latin America. He said that the "organization, especially if it has full backing from the Vatican and from the churches generally, really has a chance of influencing the situation in a regime professedly made up of Roman Catholics."

Korean Protests — Christian resistance to the repressive policies of South Korean President Park Chung Hee increased sharply in September as Protestants joined Catholics in prayer vigils and protest demonstrations throughout the country.

Support for *Humanae Vitae* — The bishops of Australia restated their support of Pope Paul's encyclical condemning artificial birth control. They said, however, that priests should show understanding toward Catholics who find its teaching hard to accept. A Catholic who, with good conscience, finds himself at variance with the teaching in the encyclical "would certainly not have cut himself off from the Church," they declared.

Archbishop Mediator — Coadjutor Archbishop Hugo Polanco of Santo Domingo served as a mediator between government officials and guerrillas holding seven hostages at the Venezuelan consulate in Santo Domingo. The hostages were set free after days of detention and their captors were permitted to leave the country.

View on Red China — Most participants in an ecumenical colloquium at Louvain, Belgium, on "Christian Faith and the Chinese Experience" agreed that the People's Republic of China, despite serious flaws, possessed many good qualities. Almost no one disputed Red China's achievements in education, the emancipation of women, and ethics of the sharing of material goods. There was less agreement, however, on the acceptability of the means used by the Chinese Communists. The six-day meeting, sponsored by Pro Mundi Vita, an international Catholic center for information and research in Brussels, and the Lutheran World Federation was attended by about 100 theologians, China scholars and church administrators from 22 countries.

Responsible Parenthood Program — Two Mexican prelates charged that a government-sponsored responsible parenthood program was having the effect of increasing contraception and abortion among Catholics.

Bishop Alfonso Toriz of Queretaro said he had received reports from several parishes about "contraception being forced" upon women attending government clinics for other services.

He said the Church acknowledged the right of governments to seek solutions to problems of overpopulation and resources, "as long as the dignity of the human person is given safeguards." He recalled statements by Mexican President Luis Echeverria that a family program launched two years earlier to curb population was to be voluntary. "We agree with the principle, but I am afraid it is not being followed in practice," he declared.

Cardinal Jose Salazar of Guadalajara reminded Catholic couples that the Church considers provoking abortion "a mortal sin of homicide." "The value of human life is well above material comforts," he said in countering publicity given trends toward relaxed abortion laws in Mexico and other countries.

Choice in Education — Findings of a public opinion survey conducted in May and June indicated that 87 per cent of the French people favored the possibility of choosing between public and private education.

Chesterton Review — Announced in Saskatoon, Canada, was the start of publication in November of the first journal devoted entirely to the study of Catholic essayist and author G. K. Chesterton. Basilian Father J. Ian Boyd, a teacher at St. Thomas More College, was named editor of *The Chesterton Review*. A press release on the review noted that interest in Chesterton extended far beyond Catholic circles, and that even Marxists were interested in his criticism of modern capitalism. Among Chesterton's more popular works were the Father Brown detective stories. A more significant work was a study of St. Thomas Aquinas hailed by philosopher Etienne Gilson as "without exception the best book ever written on St. Thomas."

DEATHS OCTOBER 1, 1973, TO OCTOBER 1, 1974

Abrams, Gen. Creighton W., 59, Sept. 4, Washington, D.C.; commander of U.S. armed forces in Vietnam, 1968-72; had served as tank commander in World War II; convert to Catholicism, 1970.

Antoniutti, Cardinal Ildebrando, 75, Aug. 1, in an automobile accident near Bologna, Italy; veteran papal diplomat; member of College of Cardinals since 1962; prefect of Sacred Congregation for Religious and Secular Institutes, 1963-73, when he retired.

Armstrong, James E., 71, Jan. 16, South Bend, Ind.; executive secretary of Notre Dame University Alumni Association, 1926-67; founding editor of *Notre Dame Magazine.*

Beltrami, Cardinal Giuseppe, 84, Dec. 13, 1973, Rome, Italy; veteran papal diplomat; member of College of Cardinals since 1967.

Briefs, Dr. Goetz A., 85, May 16, Rome, Italy; retired professor of economics, Georgetown University; author of more than 25 books; born in Germany, he came to U.S. in 1934 when he fled the Nazis.

Bucko, Archbishop Ivan, 82, Sept. 21, Rome, Italy; apostolic visitor *emeritus* for Byzantine-Rite Ukrainians in Western Europe; served as apostolic visitor for 26 years to an estimated half-million Ukrainian refugees and 300 Ukrainian priests who moved to western European countries after World War II.

Caffery, Jefferson, 87, Apr. 13, Lafayette, La.; U.S. diplomat; served 44 years in posts in South America, Europe and the Middle East; ranked as dean of U.S. diplomatic corps before his retirement in 1955.

Cannon, Jimmy, 63, Dec. 5, 1973, New York, N.Y.; sportswriter, syndicated columnist.

Cassels, Louis, 52, Jan. 23, Aiken, S.C.; senior editor and religion columnist for United Press International; an Episcopalian.

Caviedes, Rev. Ivan, between Dec. 13-16, 1973, Osorno, Chile, while attempting to climb Osorno Volcano; an experienced mountain climber, he was the first priest to reach survivors of the Uruguayan plane crash in October, 1972.

Cicognani, Cardinal Amleto, 90, Dec. 17, 1973, Vatican City; dean of College of Cardinals and papal Secretary of State, 1961-69; had served as apostolic delegate to the U.S. for 25 years before his elevation to the cardinalate in 1958.

Clarke, Austin, 77, Mar. 20, Dublin, Ire.; Irish poet, playwright.

Collins, Bishop Thomas P., M.M., 58, Dec. 7, 1973, Maryknoll, N.Y.; Maryknoll missioner in Bolivia for 31 years; vicar apostolic of Pando, Bolivia, 1961-69, when he retired.

Corbetta, Roger H., 77, May 26, New York, N.Y.; leader in the construction industry.

Crean, Robert, 50, May 6, New Rochelle, N.Y.; television playwright; works included

"The Defenders," winner of a 1964 Emmy Award, and "Prejudice USA," a dramatization of anti-Semitism, one of the plays he wrote for The Catholic Hour.

Daley, Arthur, 69, Jan. 3, New York, N.Y.; sports columnist for *The New York Times;* Pulitzer prize winner, 1956.

Danielou, Cardinal Jean, 69, May 20, Paris, France; Jesuit theologian; staunch defender of papal infallibility; supporter of ecumenism; member of College of Cardinals since 1969.

Dempsey, Bishop Michael, 55, Jan. 8, Chicago, Ill.; auxiliary bishop of Chicago from 1968; first national director of the U.S. bishops' Campaign for Human Development; known as the "Ghetto Bishop" because of his work with poor.

Doremus, Charles L., 92, May 7, South Bend, Ind.; senior member of Holy Cross Congregation in U.S.; a member of Notre Dame University community from 1903.

Dupont, Rev. Gerald, S.S.E., 61, Feb. 11, Winooski Park, Vt.; president of St. Michael's College, Winooski Park, 1958-69; proponent of more lay control of Catholic universities and colleges.

Foley, Rev. Joseph R., 58, Jan. 5, New York, N.Y.; Paulist priest; leader in religious music; director of Paulist Choristers for more than 30 years.

Herve, Rev. Francois, M.E.P., 99, Dec., 1973, Motomachi, Hakodata, Japan; French-born missionary in Japan for 76 years.

Hettinga, Bishop Nicholas, M.H.M., 65, Dec. 26, 1973, Islamabad, Pakistan; Dutch-born missionary in Pakistan from 1933; bishop of Rawalpindi from 1947.

Hogan, Frank S., 72, Apr. 2, New York, N.Y.; lawyer; Manhattan district attorney for 32 years.

Jentges, Abbot Damian, O.S.B., 71, Sept. 1, St. Benedict, Ore.; Benedictine; abbot of Mt. Angel Abbey, St. Benedict, from 1950.

Kominek, Cardinal Boleslaw, 70, Mar. 10, Wroclaw (Breslau), Poland; archbishop of Wroclaw from 1972, when agreement was reached concerning former German territories ceded to Poland after World War II; had been apostolic administrator of the area from 1962; member of College of Cardinals from Mar. 5, 1973.

Kurz, Bishop Blaise, O.F.M., 79, Dec. 13, 1973, Waldsassen, Germany; exiled prefect apostolic of Yungchow, China; resided in New York after his exile; patron of Traditionalist Movement in 1960's; retired to native Germany, 1969.

Lane, Bishop Raymond A., M.M., 80, July 31, San Francisco, Calif.; missionary in China, 1925-29, 1932-46; imprisoned by Japanese during World War II; superior general of Maryknoll, 1946-56.

Lunn, Sir Arnold, 86, June 2, London, England; ski expert, author; invented the slalom;

wrote works on skiing and in defense of the Faith; convert to Catholicism.

McDonough, Rev. Thomas, C.SS.R., 70, Nov. 19, 1973, Oconomowoc, Wis.; retired national secretary of the Apostleship of the Sea; port chaplain at New Orleans for 25 years.

McGuigan, Cardinal James, 79, Apr. 9, Toronto, Ont.; archbishop of Toronto, 1934-1971, when he retired; member of College of Cardinals from 1946.

McKeefry, Cardinal Peter, 74, Nov. 18, 1973, Wellington, New Zealand; archbishop of Wellington from 1954; first New Zealand member of College of Cardinals, 1969.

Mojica, Rev. Jose Maria de Guadalupe, 78, Sept. 20, Lima, Peru; Franciscan priest; Mexican film star and opera singer who retired in 1942 after a 29-year career to join the Franciscans.

Nelligan, Bishop Charles, 79, Apr. 1, Windsor, Ont.; bishop of Pembroke, 1937-45; on staff of University of Windsor, 1937-62.

Neuhaeusler, Bishop Johannes, 85, Dec., 1973, Munich, Germany; auxiliary bishop of Munich from 1947; vigorous opponent of Adolph Hitler; prisoner in Nazi concentration camp at Dachau for more than four years; wrote *Kreuz and Hakenkreuz* ("The Cross and the Hooked Cross"), 1946, a documentary on resistance of the Church to the Nazi regime.

Nicola, Joseph D., 38, June 1, Manhasset, N.Y.; Catholic journalist; founder and editor of Catholic Press Features (CPF).

O'Malley, Francis J., 62, May 7, South Bend, Ind.; Notre Dame University English professor for 41 years; started hundreds of graduates on writing careers, including Edwin O'Connor.

O'Shea, Michael, 67, Dec. 4, 1973, Dallas, Tex.; stage, film and television actor.

O'Shaughnessy, Ignatius A., 88, Nov. 21, 1973, Miami, Fla.; oil industry executive and philanthropist; Laetare Medalist, 1953.

Peron (Sosa), Juan Domingo, 79, July 1, Buenos Aires, Argentina; president of Argentina, 1946-55, 1973-74.

Pham-Nang-Tinh, Bishop Joseph, 56, Feb. 11, Buichu, North Vietnam; bishop of Buichu from 1960.

Pierce, Billie, 67, Sept. 29, New Orleans, La.; New Orleans Jazz singer and pianist.

Pompidou, Georges Jean Raymond, 62, Apr. 2, Paris, France; president of France, from 1969; adviser to General De Gaulle during World War II.

Royce, Sister Frances Catherine, 74, Apr. 12, Cincinnati, O.; lawyer, teacher; administrative assistant to Michigan State legislature; married to Representative Arthur Royce of Michigan, 1937 (he died 10 years later); convert to Catholicism, 1952; entered Sisters of Charity.

Schroth, Frank D., 89, June 10, New Milford, Conn.; newspaperman; publisher of the *Brooklyn Eagle,* 1939 to 1955, when it was forced to close after a seven-week strike.

Schulte, Rev. Paul, O.M.I., 78, Jan. 7, Swakopmund, Namibia; German-born missionary in Africa and Northern Canada; founder of the Missionary Vehicle Association (MIVA), which provided more than 10,000 vehicles for missionaries since its foundation; known as the "Flying Priest."

Sealey, Blossom, 82, Apr. 17, New York, N.Y.; vaudeville star; her last public appearance was on the "Ed Sullivan Show" in 1966.

Slachta, Sister Margaret, 89, Jan. 9, Buffalo, N.Y.; first woman elected to Hungarian parliament (1920-22 and 1945-47); founded Society of Sisters of Social Service in Hungary in 1923; came to U.S. in 1950 when increased communist pressure led the order to move its generalate to Buffalo.

Smith, Rev. Callistus, O.F.M., 70, Jan. 3, Paterson, N.J.; Franciscan priest; internationally known canon lawyer; co-author of *A Practical Commentary on the Code of Canon Law.*

Tanaka, Dr. Kotaro, Mar. 2, Tokyo, Japan; internationally known jurist; one of Japan's most eminent Catholics; convert, 1926.

Taylor, Sir Hugh, 84, Apr. 17, Princeton, N.J.; physical chemist; dean of Princeton graduate school, 1945-55, when he retired; former president of Pax Romana; member of Pontifical Academy of Sciences.

Trochta, Cardinal Stepan, 68, Apr. 6, Litomerice, Czechoslovakia; archbishop of Litomerice from 1947; impeded from governing his see, 1949-68; detained in concentration camps at Mauthausen and Dachau during World War II; cardinal *in petto* Apr. 28, 1969, his nomination was made public Mar. 5, 1973.

Van Soosten, Baroness Margaret, 79, May 1, La Jolla, Calif.; philanthropist, opera patron; one of founders of Lily Tulip Cup Company; convert to Catholicism, 1940.

Vath, Msgr. Carl H., 65, Aug. 18, Kranuschel, Germany; president of Caritas Internationalis, the Church's International relief agency, since 1972; earned worldwide recognition for his work with needy; awarded Cross of Merit, 1960, and Great Cross of Merit, 1964, by his native Germany, and Order of Commander of the British Empire by Queen Elizabeth, 1970.

Walsh, Edward, 73, Oct. 24, 1973, New York, N.Y.; journalism professor at Fordham University until his retirement in 1968; consultant to Vatican Radio.

Ward, John J., 75, July 27, Miami, Fla.; newspaperman; editor of *The Pittsburgh Catholic,* 1954-59; founding editor of *The Voice,* Miami archdiocesan paper, 1959-1966, when he retired.

HOLY YEAR BULL: APOSTOLORUM LIMINA

Pope Paul VI formally proclaimed Holy Year 1975 in the bull Apostolorum Limina ("Memorials of the Apostles"), dated May 23, 1974. In it, he stated the renewal and reconciliation themes of the year, sketched the history of Holy Years and the background of Old Testament Years of Jubilee, gave the norms for gaining Jubilee Indulgence, and indicated the special hopes he had for the year.

The following excerpts are from the English translation circulated by the NC Documentary Service, Origins, June 6, 1974 (Vol. 4, No. 2).

Advantage of Pilgrimage to Rome: "The aspirations that the two themes (of renewal and reconciliation) enunciate and the lofty ideals that they express will find a more complete realization in Rome, where pilgrims to the tombs of the Apostles Peter and Paul and to the memorials of the other martyrs will come into more ready contact with the ancient sources of the Church's faith and life, in order to be converted by repentance, strengthened in charity and united more closely with their brethren by the grace of God."

Renewal and Reconciliation Aims

"This renewal and reconciliation pertain in the first place to the interior life, above all because the root of all good and, unfortunately, of all evil, is found in the depths of the heart. It is in the depths of the heart, therefore, that conversion or *metanoia* must take place, that is, a change of direction, of attitude, of option, of one's way of life.

'For the whole world this call to renewal and reconciliation is in harmony with the most sincere aspirations for freedom, justice, unity and peace that we see wherever men become aware of their most serious problems and suffer from the mishaps produced by divisions and fratricidal wars. With the message of the Holy Year, therefore, the Church wishes to indicate to all men of good will the vertical dimension of life that ensures reference of all aspirations and experiences to an absolute and truly universal value, without which it is vain to hope that mankind will once more find a point of unification and a guarantee of true freedom. ... the Church ... wishes to impress on men the need to be converted to God, who alone is necessary, and to imbue all their actions with fear and love of him. For faith in God is the most powerful safeguard of the human conscience and is the solid foundation of those relationships of justice and brotherhood the world yearns for."

Doctrine and Purpose of Indulgences: Following a short summary of doctrine concerning indulgences (see separate entry), the bull said: "In fact, the Church's aim in granting indulgences is not only that of helping the faithful to expiate the punishment they have deserved (because of sin) but also that of stimulating them to carry out works of piety, penance and charity, and in particular works that serve to favor the growth of faith and the common good."

Jubilee Indulgence

"We impart the gift of the plenary indulgence to all the faithful who are properly disposed, and who, after confessing their sins and receiving Holy Communion, pray for the intentions of the supreme pontiff and the college of bishops:

• "(1) If they undertake a sacred pilgrimage to one of the patriarchal basilicas (St. Peter's in the Vatican, St. Paul's Outside-the-Walls, the Lateran Archbasilica of the Most Holy Savior, St. Mary Major), or to some other church or place of the city of Rome designated by the competent authority, and devoutly take part in a liturgical celebration, there, especially the Sacrifice of the Mass, or some exercise of piety (e.g., the Way of the Cross, the Rosary).

• "(2) If they visit, in a group or individually, one of the four patriarchal basilicas and spend some time there in devout recollection concluding with the Our Father, the profession of faith in any approved form and a prayer to the Blessed Virgin Mary.

• "(3) If, being prevented by illness or some other grave reason from going on a pilgrimage to Rome, they unite themselves spiritually with this pilgrimage and offer their prayers and sufferings to God.

• "(4) If, being prevented while in Rome by illness or some other grave reason from taking part in a liturgical celebration or exercise of piety or visit made by their group (ecclesial, family or social, as mentioned in 1 and 2 above), they unite themselves spiritually with the group and offer their prayers and sufferings to God.

• "During the Holy Year, moreover, the other concessions of indulgences remain in force, with the proviso as before that a plenary indulgence can be gained only once a day; however, all indulgences can always be applied to the dead *in modum suffragii*.

"For the same reasons, namely, in order that the faithful be provided with every possible aid to salvation, and to help priests, especially confessors, we proclaim that confessors taking part in the Jubilee pilgrimage may use the faculties they have been given in their own dioceses by the legitimate authority, so that both on the journey and in Rome they may hear the confessions of the faithful accompanying them on the pilgrimage, and also the confessions of others."

Aims Concern Church and World

"We stated above that the following two principal purposes have been established for the Holy Year: spiritual renewal in Christ and reconciliation with God, and we have said that these aims concern not only the interior life of each individual but the whole Church, and also, in a certain sense, the whole of human society. For this reason we earnestly exhort all concerned to consider these proposals, to undertake initiatives and to coordinate programs so that during the Holy Year real progress may be made in the renewal of the Church and also in the pursuit of certain goals very dear to us, in accordance with the farsighted spirit of the Second Vatican Ecumenical Council. Repentance, the purification of the heart and conversion to God, must consequently bring about an increase in the apostolic activities of the Church.

Evangelization: "During the Holy Year, therefore, generous efforts must be made to further evangelization, which is certainly the first of all the activites to be promoted."

Synod of Bishops: The bull noted the connection of the Holy Year with the 1974 assembly of the Synod of Bishops, which was to consider "in the light of faith 'the evangelization of the modern world.' "

Catechetical Instruction: "Devout attention to the word of God together with catechetical instruction given to the faithful of every state and of all ages must lead Christians to purify their way of life and to a higher knowledge of faith; it must dispel doubts, and stimulate the negligent to activate joyfully in their lives the Gospel message; it must impel everyone toward a conscious and fruitful sharing in the sacraments; it must encourage communities and individuals to give witness to the faith by the uprightness and strength of their lives, so that the world may see the reason for the hope that is in us."

Pastoral Ministry: "Now, 10 years after the Second Vatican Council began the great and salutary work of renewal in the fields of the pastoral ministry, the practice of penance and the sacred liturgy, we consider it altogether fitting that this work should be reviewed and furthered."

"We wish to draw particular attention to the need to find a just and proper balance between the differing demands of the pastoral ministry today, a balance similar to that which has been admirably achieved in the sacred liturgy. We refer to the balance between tradition and renewal, between the necessarily religious nature of the Christian apostolate and its effectiveness as a force in all fields of social living, between free and spontaneous activity — which some are accustomed to call charismatic — in this apostolate and fidelity to laws based on the commands

of Christ and of the pastors of the church."

"We wish likewise to draw attention to the ever increasing need to promote the kind of apostolate which, without damaging the Church's necessary and traditional institutions, namely dioceses and parishes, takes special account of particular local circumstances and categories of people. Such an apostolate must ensure that the leaven of the Gospel permeates those forms of modern social living which often differ from traditional forms of ecclesial life. . . . The forms we are thinking of are principally those of workers, members of the academic world and young people.

"It will also be necessary to examine carefully the methods of teaching religion and of preaching the sacred word of God, to insure that they meet the needs of our time."

Works of Justice and Charity: "As is well known, in recent years one of the Church's most pressing concerns has been to disseminate everywhere a message of charity, of social awareness and of peace, and to promote, as far as she can, works of justice and solidarity among all men, in fact, whether individuals, social groups or peoples. We earnestly desire, therefore, that the Holy Year, through the works of charity which it suggests to the faithful and which it asks of them, should be an opportune time for strengthening and supporting the moral consciousness of all the faithful and of that wider community of all men which the message of the church can reach if an earnest effort is made.

"The ancient origins of the Jubilee as seen in the laws and institutions of Israel clearly show that this social dimension is part of its very nature. In fact, as we read in the Book of Leviticus (25:8 ff.), the Jubilee Year, precisely because it was dedicated in a special way to God, involved a new ordering of all things that were recognized as belonging to God: the land, which was allowed to lie fallow and was given back to its former owners; economic goods, insofar as debts were remitted; and, above all, man, whose dignity and freedom were reaffirmed in a special way by the emancipation of slaves. The Year of God, then, was also the year of man, the year of the earth, the year of the poor, and upon this view of the whole of human reality there shone a new light which emanated from the clear recognition of the supreme dominion of God over the whole of creation."

Social Concerns: "In today's world also the problems which most disturb and torment mankind — economic and social questions, the question of ecology and sources of energy, and above all that of the liberation of the oppressed and the uplifting of all men to a new dignity of life — can have light cast on them by the message of the Holy Year.

"We wish, however, to invite all the sons and daughters of the church, and especially the pilgrims coming to Rome, to undertake certain definite tasks. . . . We refer to the carrying out of works of faith and charity for the benefit of our needy brethren in Rome and in other churches of the world. These works will not necessarily be grandiose ones, although such are in no way to be excluded."

Programs for Progress: "Nevertheless, the Church feels that it is necessary to give encouragement also to these larger programs for promoting justice and the progress of peoples. She renews her call to all those who have the power and the duty to build up in the world a more perfect order of social and human relations, urging them not to give up because of the difficulties of the present times, and not to be won over by selfish interests. Once more we make a particularly strongappealon behalf of developing countries, and of peoples still afflicted by hunger and by war. Let special attention be given to the many needs which oppress man today, to the finding of employment by which men can provide for the needs of life, to housing which so many lack, to schools which need much assistance, to social and medical aid, and to the development and safeguarding of decent public moral standards."

Amnesty: "We should like also to express the humble and sincere desire that in this present Holy Year too, in accordance with the tradition of previous Jubilees, the proper authorities of the different nations should consider the possibility of wisely granting an amnesty to prisoners, as a witness to clemency and equity, especially to those who have given sufficient proof of moral and civic rehabilitation, or who may have been caught up in political and social upheavals too immense for them to be held fully responsible."

Vocations to Priesthood and Religious Life: "If there is one spiritual advantage which we especially desire from the celebration of the Holy Year, it is an increase in the number of those who devote their lives to serving the Church, especially priests and religious. . . . There will always be a need for those sacred ministers and witnesses of Christ's gospel who by completely following the Lord show their fellowmen, namely, the men of this and subsequent ages, the way of penance and of holiness."

"Through their priesthood and the activity of their religious life they may bear the joyful message of Christ to the ends of the earth, and all give glory to the heavenly Father."

Christian Unity: "Finally, we wish to proclaim and preach that the reconciliation of Christians is one of the principal aims of the Holy Year. . . . The Jubilee Year, which the Catholic Church has accepted as part of her own custom and tradition, can serve as a most opportune period for spiritual renewal and for the promotion of Christian unity."

"The Year of Grace, in this sense, provides an opportunity for doing special penance for the divisions which exist among Christians; it offers an occasion for renewal in the sense of a heightened experience of holiness of life in Christ; it allows progress toward that hoped-for reconciliation by intensified dialogue and concrete Christian collaboration in the salvation of the world: 'That they also may be one in us, so that the world may believe.' "

Widespread Participation Urged

"We have expressed once more our intentions and our desires concerning the celebration of the Holy Year in this City of Rome. Now we invite our brothers in the episcopate and all the pastors and faithful of the churches throughout the world, of those churches also which are not in full communion with the Roman Church, and indeed all who believe in God, to participate at least spiritually in this feast of grace and redemption, in which Christ offers himself as the teacher of life. Together with the pastors and faithful on pilgrimage to the tombs of the Apostles and the early martyrs, we desire to profess faith in God the almighty and merciful Father and in Jesus Christ our Redeemer."

"We would wish also that through our ministry and that of our brother priests a huge multitude of faithful may come to the sources of salvation. May the Holy Door which we shall open on the night of Christmas Eve be a sure sign of this new approach to Christ, who alone is the way and the door. It will be a sure sign too of the paternal affection with which, filled with love and desiring peace, we open our heart to all."

HOLY YEAR ANNOUNCEMENT AND BACKGROUND

The first announcement of Holy Year 1975 was made by Pope Paul VI May 9, 1973, during a general audience with visitors to the Vatican. He said its purposes would be spiritual renewal and the reconciliation of men with God and each other.

Local Start

A unique feature of the celebration of this Holy Year was a reversal of the traditional manner of observance. Earlier, year-long observances in Rome preceded counterpart celebrations in local churches. This time, the Pope said: "The conditions prescribed for acquiring special spiritual benefits will . . . be anticipated and granted to the local churches so that the whole Church spread throughout the world may be able to profit immediately from this great occasion of renewal and reconciliation. In this way the entire Church will be better able to prepare for the climax and conclusion of the Holy Year which will be celebrated in Rome in the year 1975, and which will give to the traditional pilgrimage to the tombs of the Apostles its traditional meaning for those who are able and wish to make the pilgrimage."

The Holy Father set June 10, 1973, as the starting date of the 18-month-long, local-church phase of the Holy Year.

Observances in the churches, adapted to local conditions, included educational and informational programs, pastoral letters and celebrations geared to the renewal-reconciliation themes, retreats, periods for study and reflection, penitential celebrations, pilgrimages to cathedrals and designated churches to fulfill conditions for gaining the Jubilee Indulgence.

The climactic Roman celebration was scheduled to begin and end on Christmas Eve, 1974 and 1975, with the opening and closing, respectively, of the Holy Doors in the Patriarchal Basilicas of St. Peter, St. John Lateran, St. Paul outside the Walls, and St. Mary Major.

Background

Holy Year observances have biblical counterparts in the Years of Jubilee observed at 50-year intervals by the pre-exilic Israelites — when debts were pardoned and slaves freed (Lv. 25:25-54) — and in sabbatical years observed from the end of the Exile to 70 A.D. — in which debts to fellow Jews were remitted.

The practice of Christians from early times to go on pilgrimage to the Holy Land, the shrines of martyrs and the tombs of the Apostles in Rome influenced the institution of Holy Years. There was also a prevailing belief among the people that every 100th year was a year of "Great Pardon." Accordingly, even before Boniface VIII formally proclaimed the first Holy Year Feb. 22, 1300, scores of thousands of pilgrims were already on the way to or in Rome. One report said that two million pilgrims took part in the observance.

Medieval popes embodied in the observance of Holy Years the practice of good works (reception of the sacraments of penance and the Eucharist, pilgrimages and/or visits to the tombs of the Apostles, and related actions) and spiritual benefits (particularly, special indulgences for the souls in purgatory). These and related practices, with suitable changes for celebrations in local churches, remain staple features of Holy Year observances.

The first three Holy Years were observed in 1300, 1350 and 1390. Subsequent ones were celebrated at 25-year intervals except in 1800 and 1850 when, respectively, the French invasion of Italy and political turmoil made observance impossible. Pope Paul II (1464-1471) set the 25-year timetable. In 1500, Pope Alexander VI prescribed the start and finish ceremonies — the opening and closing of the Holy Doors in the major basilicas on successive Christmas Eves. All but a few of the earlier Holy Years were classified as ordinary. Several, like the one held in 1933 to commemorate the 19th centenary of the death and resurrection of Christ, were in the extraordinary category.

Holy Year 1975 coincides with the 10th anniversary of the closing of the Second Vatican Council. Its themes also coincide with the renewal emphasis which dominated the council, and were related to the main topic — the evangelization of the modern world — on the 1974 agenda of the Synod of Bishops.

HOLY YEAR COMMITTEE

Holy Year planning and work to carry it out — through services of promotion, information and coordination in Rome and through contact with nearly 100 episcopal conferences throughout the world — were and continue to be the responsibility of the Central Committee for Holy Year 1975.

The 34-member committee is headed by Cardinal Maximilien de Furstenberg.

Cardinal Timothy Manning of Los Angeles is chairman of the U.S. Holy Year Committee.

BIBLICAL BACKGROUND OF HOLY YEAR

Following are excerpts from an article, "Holy Year 1975 and Its Origins in the Jewish Jubilee Year," by Marc H. Tannenbaum, director of interreligious affairs of the American Jewish Committee. The article was published in a special edition of the Holy Year Bulletin, Jubilaeum, *in 1974.*

Holy Year 1975, proclaimed by Pope Paul VI for observance by the Catholic faithful as a year of renewal and reconciliation, has been frequently characterized as the *Jubilaeus Christianorum,* the Christian Jubilee Year. That reference is to the Jubilee Year which has its origins in Biblical Judaism, and it may therefore be helpful to understand something of the practice and meaning of the Jubilee Year as it was developed and experienced in about 3,000 years of Jewish history.

Meaning of Jubilee

The word "Jubilee" derives from the Hebrew term *yobel* which means "jubilating," or "exulting." It refers to the sounding of the *shofar* — the ram's horn — on the Day of Atonement announcing the inauguration of the Jubilee Year. (Joshua 6:4 speaks of *Shofrot ha-yoblim,* "trumpets of the ram's horn.") *Yom Kippur,* the Day of Atonement, and the Jubilee had much in common. The central intention of both was a "new birth." The Day of Atonement provided an opportunity to free the person from slavery to sin and enabled him/her to start life anew, at one with God and with one's fellow human beings. (Atonement is understood by the rabbis to be a precondition for at-*one*-ment). The Jubilee had for its aim the emancipation of the individual from the shackles of poverty, and the elimination of the various economic inequalities in the Jewish Commonwealth in accordance with the demands of social justice. Since *Yom Kippur* involved the preparation of the hearts of all members of the community for the self-discipline and sacrifices required for such spiritual rectification, it was deemed by Jewish tradition to be the most appropriate day for inauguration of such a year of communal and inter-personal rectification, especially in the social and economic order.

So important was the law regarding the Jubilee that, like the Decalogue, it was ascribed to the divinely-inspired legislation revealed on Mount Sinai (Leviticus 25:1).

Objectives

What objectives were to be served through the observance of the Jubilee Year? The Bible sets forth four-fold obligations, all of which focus on realizing liberation in the actual life of the people of God as basic pre-conditions, or corollaries, to their spiritual liberation:

• human — liberation of the slaves;
• economic — the moralization of the use of property and material goods;
• ecological — liberation of the land;
• educational — the creation of a spiritual democracy by devoting the Jubilee Year to intensive education of all men, women, children and "resident aliens" in the teachings of the Torah.

After proclaiming the observance of the Sabbatical Year (*Shemittah*), the Bible ordains the Jubilee Year (*Yobel*) in these words: "And you shall number seven sabbaths of years unto you, seven times seven years; and there shall be unto you the days of seven sabbaths of years, even forty and nine years. Then shall you make proclamation with the blast of the horn on the tenth day of the seventh month; in the day of atonement shall you make proclamation with the horn throughout all our land. And you shall hallow the fiftieth year, and proclaim liberty throughout the land unto all the inhabitants thereof: it shall be a jubilee unto you; and you shall return every man unto his possession; and you shall return every man unto his family" (Lev. 25:8 ff.).

History of Jubilee Year

The authoritative *Jewish Encyclopedia* states that "the Jubilee was instituted primarily to keep intact the original allotment of the Holy Land among the (Israelite) tribes, and to discountenance the idea of servitude to men." Evidence for this fact is derived from the knowledge that the Sabbatical Year and the Jubilee were not inaugurated before the Holy Land had been conquered and apportioned among the Israelite tribes and their families. This first Sabbatical Year is said to have occurred twenty-one years after the arrival of the Hebrews in Palestine, and the first

Jubilee thirty-three years later. In post-exile times the Jubilee was entirely ignored, though the strict observance of the Sabbatical Year was insisted upon. In the Diaspora, throughout the centuries following the destruction of the Temple in Jerusalem in 70 A.D., the Sabbatical Year was unevenly observed and was mainly nominal in performance.

The cycle of sacred seasons in Judaism revolves about the systems of Sabbaths — the Sabbath at the end of the week, Pentecost (*Shabuoth*) at the end of seven weeks; the seventh month, *Tishri*, as the sacred month featuring the holy days of *Ros Hashonah* and *Yom Kippur*. The cycle is completed by the Sabbatical Year and by the Jubilee, which came after a "week" of Sabbatical Years.

HOLY YEAR PRAYER

This text is from the 2nd Bulletin of the Holy Year issued by the Central Committee for the Holy Year October, 1973.

Lord God and Father, in the death and resurrection of Jesus Christ your Son you willed to reconcile all mankind to yourself and so to reconcile men with each other in peace. Hear the prayer of your people in this year of grace and salvation. (R)

• Let your spirit of life and holiness renew us in the depths of our being; unite us throughout our life to the risen Christ, for He is our brother and Savior. (R)

• With all Christians we seek to follow the way of the Gospel. Keep us faithful to the teaching of the Church and alive to the needs of our brothers; give us strength to work for reconciliation, unity and peace. (R)

• May those who seek the God they do not yet know discover in You the source of light and hope; may those who work for others find strength in You; may those who know You seek even further and experience the depths of Your love. (R)

• Forgive us our sins, deepen our faith, kindle our hope, and enliven our hearts with love for our brothers. (R)

• May we walk in the footsteps of Christ as Your beloved sons and daughters. (R)

• With the help of Mary our Mother, may Your Church be the sign and sacrament of salvation for all men, that the world may believe in Your love and Your truth. (R)

Father, of your great goodness, hear in the words of your people the prayer of the Spirit, to the praise of your glory and the salvation of men. Through Jesus Christ your Son our Lord, the Way, the Truth and the Life, for ever and ever. (R) Amen.

In prayer with a group, one of these responses (R) can be used: Hear our prayer; Lord, graciously hear us; Lord, have mercy.

In private prayer, responses and the final prayer are omitted. Instead of the latter, the simple conclusion.— Through Christ our Lord. Amen. — is used.

A PILGRIM'S WEEK IN ROME

The Central Committee for Holy Year 1975 published the following article in the Sept. 26, 1974, English edition of L'Osservatore Romano, *listing events of a pilgrim's week in Rome.*

In order to have the Pilgrimage to Rome attain its ultimate educational value and reach the highest aims of the Jubilee, a standard week has been planned during which pilgrims may travel around Rome in seven days or less and join the praying communities in the four Patriarchal Basilicas, in the Catacombs or in other memorials of marytrs and saints.

Pilgrims will gather in the above-named places for liturgical prayer (Holy Mass, Office of the Holy Year, rites of penitence) as well as for spontaneous prayer (meditation on the motives and commitments of the Holy Year, the Way of the Cross, the Rosary, recital or singing of the Our Father, the Creed, or a prayer to Mary). In these ways — through signs of conversion, charity and ecclesial communion — it will be possible to share the gift of the Indulgence. Individual pilgrims, who feel close to their brothers in the communion of the Church, may obtain the Indulgence through the same practices. Sick people may equally benefit from the jubilee gift (of Indulgence) by offering prayers or sufferings in union with the Church.

Weekly Liturgical Celebrations

Every Sunday in the Basilica of St. Peter: Community liturgical celebration, with the possible participation of the Pope.

All Weekdays at 9:30 a.m.: Community celebration with Mass on different themes — in St. Peter's, the Apostolicity of the Church; in the Basilica of St. John Lateran, the Unity of the Church; in the Basilica of St. Mary Major, the Holiness of the Church; in the Basilica of St. Paul outside the Walls, Catholicism and Ecumenism; in the Catacombs, the First Christian Testimony.

Additional celebrations may be held in neighboring churches.

Every afternoon: in St. Peter's, the Office of the Jubilee.

Every Wednesday morning: In St. Peter's or nearby, meetings with the Pope.

Every Friday evening: Way of the Cross in St. Peter's Square.

Periodically: Special liturgies for Eastern-Rite pilgrims.

Penitential rites: Will be held in the Basilicas and in the Catacombs for preparation and integration into the community Eucharistic celebrations, consisting of prayer, readings from the Bible, litanies, and other elements. There will also be provision for sacramental confession in many languages. Special places will be available for confession not only in the aforementioned churches but also in neighborhood churches.

Adoration of the Blessed Sacrament, at: St. Peter's — Chapel of the Sisters of the Child Mary (Via S. Uffizio 21) and St. Monica's (Piazza S. Uffizio); St. John Lateran — Holy Stairs; St. Paul's — lower Church of Regina Angelorum (Via Alessandro Severo 58).

Meetings

During the pilgrimage the faithful may meet their brothers and sisters, united in the profession of faith and participating in the sacraments, for information, experience, hopes and spiritual prospects. Such meetings will be held in parishes, religious communities, ecclesiastical universities, seminaries, schools, institutes and other religious bodies.

There will be meetings of pilgrims and some Roman parish communities in order to create an increasingly active relationship between the Roman Church and local churches for a common experience of universality; to rediscoger and improve the living of one's vocation of service for the Church; to express this function of service by projecting it beyond the Jubilee; to favor reciprocal meetings of different churches with their pilgrim members.

Ecumenical meetings will be arranged during which members of various churches and ecclesial communities will seek in prayer and meditation, in the basic motives of faith and the Christian life, the reasons for the deepest unity and the basis of complete ecclesial communion according to the will of the Lord.

Missions

Attention will be given to the missions for the purpose of increasing the interest of pilgrims and all the faithful in the evangelization efforts of the Church.

Youth Week

Monday, 6:00 to 7:00 p.m.: Prayer in the Chapel of the Little Sisters of Jesus at Tre Fontane.

Tuesday, 3:00 to 6:00 p.m.: International meeting of Christian testimony at the Catacombs of St. Callixtus.

Wednesday morning: Meeting with the Pope at St. Peter's Basilica or nearby, with other pilgrims; 6:00 to 7:00 p.m.; prayer at the Little Sisters of Jesus.

Thursday, 3:00 to 6:00 p.m.: Meeting of Christian testimony at the Catacombs of St. Callixtus; 6:00 to 7:00 p.m.: prayer at the Little Sisters.

Friday evening: Way of the Cross in St. Peter's Square, with other pilgrims; 6:00 to 7:00 p.m.: prayer at the Little Sisters of Jesus.

Saturday, 6:00 p.m.: Youth Mass in the Basilica of St. Cecilia; Rosary in St. Peter's Square, with other pilgrims.

Sunday: community celebration at St. Peter's, with other pilgrims.

Special meetings will be held on topics such as Christian commitment, conversion, reconciliation and apostolic works.

SYNOD OF BISHOPS: FOURTH ASSEMBLY

(For coverage of the nature, constitution and previous three assemblies of the Synod, see separate article, Synod of Bishops.)

Pope Paul formally opened the fourth assembly of the Synod of Bishops Sept. 27, 1974, with a keynote address in which he outlined the task before the 209-member body. He said in part:

"The work of evangelization today must be considered with a broad and modern outlook: in methods, in works, in the organization and formation of the workers of the Gospel. It is a work which you, venerable Brothers, are preparing to carry out in this synod with a great sense of responsibility."

"It is obvious that it will never be possible to have recourse to methods which are in open conflict with the spirit of the Gospel. Neither violence, therefore, nor revolution, nor colonialism in any form will serve as means for the Church's evangelizing action, nor will politics for itself. . . ."

"It will be your task to bring face to face the traditional concept of the work of evangelization and new trends, which seek their justification in the (Second Vatican) Council and the changed conditions of the times. There will certainly be a preferential consideration for the structures and institutions of the Church which have already been tested for centuries. But, without renouncing the past or destroying values which have been acquired, there will be an effort to remain serenely open to everything . . . especially when it is a question of movements that are working in collaboration with the hierarchy . . .

"And finally, keep a healthy optimism and be sustained by a twofold bold confidence on which, as on two wings, your work must soar towards new conquests for the Gospel: confidence in your labors, because you are working for the Church; and confidence, above all, in Christ, who is with you, who is living with you, who is making use of your collaboration and experience in order to extend the kingdom of justice and holiness, love and peace in the world."

The 209 participants in the month-long assembly were delegates from nearly 100 episcopal conferences, representative religious, a limited number of Vatican officials and 21 appointees of Pope Paul. The U.S. delegation consisted of Cardinals John J. Krol, John F. Dearden, John J. Carberry, and Archbishops Joseph L. Bernardin (all elected by the National Conference of Catholic Bishops) and John R. Quinn of Oklahoma City (appointed by the Pope).

The first items on the agenda were a number of reports which included regional reviews of the status of the Church submitted by episcopal conferences and a summary overview of the Church throughout the world. The synod then got down to the specifics of evangelization in theory and practice.

Opening Weeks

(The following report, with adaptations, was written by James C. O'Neill of NC News Service.)

Christ's mandate to his Church, to "preach the Gospel to all nations," is clear but no simple thing to fulfill in the last quarter of the 20th century.

This seemed a fair summation of an early week of speeches and discussions emerging from the fourth Synod of Bishops on the subject of evangelization in the modern world. A total of 88 speakers addressed the synod and another 20 submitted their comments in writing during the first phase of meetings, devoted to exchanging local experiences in preaching the Gospel.

Variety of Problems

The experiences related by the speakers showed a great diversity of situations, attitudes and problems.

North Americans and Europeans seemed most concerned with the failure of the Church to reach their own people, many of them only nominally Catholic or Christian.

Africans and Asians were concerned with problems of cultural identity, the lingering taint of colonialism which makes Christianity a foreign import, and the need to be both independent yet helped by their richer Christian brothers.

It was still too early (Oct. 8) to draw conclusions from the single week of discussions by the 209 participants of the synod. The discussions involving practical experiences represented only one phase of the month-long meeting. During the second week the synod participants were to begin discussion of the theological implications of the command to preach the Gospel.

10 Themes

Following the days of open discussions on the floor of the synod hall, the synod Fathers broke up into a dozen smaller language-groups to thresh out what had been said and to attempt to zero-in on the dominant themes which had begun to emerge.

The language-groups devoted themselves to 10 principal areas of discussion:

• (1) interior life, including contemplation and conversion;

• (2) the local church and its local problems;

• (3) basic communities, the small communities which have grown up since the Second Vatican Council;

• (4) popular religiousness, the sense of religiousness or hunger for religious values being expressed in many different ways in modern times;

• (5) pastoral care of lapsed Catholics, a problem which seems especially severe in North American and European societies;

• (6) dialogue and evangelization, dealing with dialogue with other Christians, non-Christians and non-believers — including atheists and Marxists;

• (7) human liberation and evangelization, which asks the question where does concern for the fully free human person meet and merge with concern for man's need for salvation;

• (8) evangelization of the young, a pressing problem for every part of the Church;

• (9) special groups, involving workers, intellectuals and future political and civil leaders;

• (10) evangelization and the principal rights of the human person, which include religious liberty, the right to freedom of conscience and of civil action.

These 10 themes, which were worked over in the small language groups, were drawn from the hours of early public discussions in the synod hall and were proposed by the synod's general secretariat as "action proposals."

Pope Paul VI was present for almost all of the public discussions. The tone of the discussions was frank and self-critical, with more than one churchman asking if it was not the bishops themselves and the clergy in general who had failed to make the message of Christ attractive to modern man.

Laity, Youth, Pluralism

Speakers touched repeatedly on the need for the laity to become more specifically involved in preaching the Gospel to the modern world which will not listen to the established Church. Youths interested in religious, or at least in non-materialistic, values, and their indifference or even hostility to church structures, was also a note which echoed again and again in the speeches in the hall.

Africans and Asians were insistent on the problems of their local churches which were faced with a crisis of identity, brought on both by the great leap to independence of the last two decades and the continuing identification of Christianity with Western culture and colonialism in the minds of their people. They called for ways and means of making local churches more native by permitting them to adapt teaching, liturgy and other elements of community life to local cultural patterns.

The role of women, and especially of religious women, won a good deal of attention throughout the discussions. The insistence was always that women be given greater recognition and a greater role in the evangelization of the world.

In the second full week of discussions, synod participants turned to theological approaches to solutions of the local and universal problems of evangelization in the modern world.

TRENDS IN THE CATHOLIC CHURCH IN THE UNITED STATES

Following is the text of a paper — "A Review of the Principal Trends in the Life of the Catholic Church in the United States" — prepared by the National Conference of Catholic Bishops with the 1974 assembly of the Synod of Bishops in mind.

In perhaps the most significant passage of the paper, the bishops said: "The emerging question for the Catholic community in the United States may well be whether it will in the future, as in the past, derive its fundamental beliefs and attitudes from the traditional value system of Catholic Christianity, or whether its beliefs and attitudes will be drawn more from the secularistic, humanistic value system of the society around it."

This text was circulated by the NC Documentary Service, Origins, July 4, 1974 (Vol. 4, No. 6). Lead lines have been added.

Malaise in Society and Organized Religion: The word "malaise" is often used to describe the current state of U.S. society in general and, in particular, the condition of organized religion in the United States. Many observers find in both the secular and religious spheres a disturbing degree of polarization, confusion, self-doubt and uncertainty about fundamental values and purposes. The more optimistic view this as the necessary prelude to a new era of committed purposefulness, or, as they might say, the birth pangs of a "new consciousness." The more pessimistic hold that the current situation reflects decadence and portends collapse.

It is not the purpose of this paper to suggest that either of these viewpoints is entirely true or entirely false. If history is any guide, it seems possible that both will be proved right to some extent and wrong to some extent. Both secular society and organized religion are passing through a time of rapid and dramatic change. It is probable that both will be different in significant ways in the future. At the same time, many areas of continuity with the past are likely to remain. The present era of change does not represent a total sloughing off of tradition but rather a winnowing process in which some values and institutions may be discarded but others will be reaffirmed and strengthened.

Problems of Society and Organized Religion Are Related: The problems of secular society in the United States and the problems of organized religion are not identical. At the same time it is impossible to dichotomize the "secular" and "religious," particularly when attempting to reflect on the state of mind of individuals, who themselves do not experience their lives as dichotomized. Certainly many issues in the "secular" sphere have "religious" dimensions, and vice versa. Problems in one area tend to reinforce and aggravate those in the other.

1. Secular Society

Elements of Malaise: Many elements enter into the current malaise of secular society in the United States. Only a few can be mentioned here.

It is obvious that the deep divisions caused by U.S. military involvement in Southeast Asia have not been healed. Fundamental questions of conscience raised by the Vietnam war remain unanswered. Considered in this context, the current political crisis in the United States has occurred at the worst possible moment for the well-being of the nation. With the end of active U.S. military involvement in Southeast Asia the American people stood urgently in need of political leadership which would help them achieve reconciliation and regain consensus. Instead disclosures of wrong-doing by public figures have contributed to divisiveness and, worst of all, to feelings of cynicism and disgust with regard to the entire political process. There is evidence that many Americans simply no longer trust public institutions, and that among these institutions government is trusted least of all.

Selfish Tendencies: One result of the weakening of public consensus has been to reinforce the selfish tendencies of groups and individuals. Deep-seated social problems such as poverty and racism seem little closer to solution than they were a decade ago; worse still, in some sectors talk of poverty is regarded as a bore, and racial separatism is advocated as a positive good. The current energy crisis raises additional questions about American altruism and willingness to sacrifice. There is fear that the burdens of the energy shortage will be shifted to those least able to bear them and least able to raise an effective protest: the poor and lower-income individuals and families. Neo-isolationism, following on the Vietnam war and reinforced by the energy crisis, has caused many Americans to ignore or discount the imperatives of international social justice.

Changes in Moral Values: Radical changes in individual moral values have also occurred in recent years and are continuing to occur. Whether or not it is accurate to speak of a "sexual revolution," it is clear that many people now regard sex primarily as an instrument of individual gratification rather than a means for the expression of mutual love and commitment between husband and wife, fundamentally oriented to the begetting of new life. Changing attitudes toward sex, toward the roles of men and women, and toward relationships among members of different gener-

ations have subjected family life to unusual strain. Divorce is widely accepted and divorce rates are extremely high; it is not far-fetched to suppose that the easy availability and social acceptability of divorce encourage a "divorce mentality." There is now widespread, although by no means universal, acceptance of abortion on grounds of convenience. The right of each woman to exercise control over her body is frequently advanced as a total and self-evident justification for the destruction of unborn life. Similarly self-centered and individualistic attitudes underlie the growing movement for legalized euthanasia. Although "humane" arguments are generally put forward in favor of euthanasia, the reality is that many people now accept the idea that persons whose age, illness or incapacity renders them burdensome, have thereby forfeited the right to life.

Many tend to blame communications media for the deterioration of traditional moral values in American society. To some extent this is unfair, since to a significant degree the media simply reflect what is happening in society. However, it is apparent that the media experience great difficulty — some would say unwillingness — in exercising self-control in their depiction of violence, sexual permissiveness, and the pursuit of materialistic values.

2. The State of Organized Religion

Much of the confusion and uncertainty apparent in American society in general is mirrored, in one way or another, in organized religion. Granted that there are few reliable empirical indicators of religiosity (which makes it difficult if not impossible to generalize about the state of religion considered as a matter of individual experience), the fact remains that the churches as institutions seem in many instances to be ailing.

Faith vs. Secularism: Some describe the current difficulties of organized religion in the United States as a "crisis of faith." Whether or not such a crisis exists only God — literally — can say. Beyond question, however, in the United States at the present time transcendent religious belief finds itself engaged in direct contestation with a secularistic, humanistic worldview which rejects supernatural religion and absolute moral values.

Statistical Declines: The difficulties of organized religion express themselves in such ways as declining membership, declining church attendance, and declining contributions. To be sure, a "church" is not constituted by entries in a ledger. Nevertheless the statistics point to basic problems. The churches themselves are in some cases experiencing a crisis of self-identity. The social activism of the 1960s (identified with such causes as civil rights, anti-poverty efforts, and the anti-war movement) has declined and is regarded as passe in some quarters. At the same time many sectors of organized religion have found nothing to take its place. The quest for religious "relevance" continues, but there is little agreement as to what now constitutes relevance. Religious fads come and go with regularity.

Trend toward Religious Individualism? Simultaneously, however, other phenomena of quite a different sort have begun to appear. Some ultra-conservative, fundamentalist churches report all-time high memberships and financial contributions. Pentecostalism and the Jesus Movement continue to attract adherents. There is strong, although in many instances obviously superficial, interest in Eastern religions and the occult. It is extremely difficult to interpret these phenomena with much certainty; perhaps it does them an injustice to lump them together. Nevertheless one may hypothesize that, to some extent at least, each represents in its own way a reaction against socially oriented religion and a retreat to a more individualistic approach.

Less Public Influence: It is generally recognized that the positive influence of organized religion on public policy and public morality has declined sharply in the United States in recent years. Court decisions interpreting separation of church and state along narrowly absolutist lines have excluded religious observance and, for all practical purposes, religious education from the public schools. Many parents, church leaders and others are justifiably concerned about both the immediate and long range implications of this situation for the religious and moral formation of the young and, therefore, the religious and moral bases of American society in the future. It is perfectly true that perfunctory and *pro forma* religious activities in the classroom are unlikely to accomplish much. The special tragedy is that even the perfunctory and *pro forma* are now regarded as beyond the pale of constitutionality.

3. The State of the Catholic Church

Catholic or Secular Values? It has been customary in recent years to discuss tensions within the Catholic Church in the United States in terms of conflict between "conservatives" and "liberals." It may be, however, that the time has come to cast such discussions in different terms. The emerging question for the Catholic community in the United States may well be whether it will in the future, as in the past, derive its fundamental beliefs and attitudes from the traditional value system of Catholic Christianity, or whether its beliefs and attitudes will be drawn more and more from the secularistic, humanistic value system of the society around it.

Historically, the Catholic community in the United States until recent years lived in a certain isolation from attitudes and values which prevailed in the larger society. This is not to say that Catholics were uninfluenced by the

experience of living within American society — something which would have been both undesirable and impossible to effect. It is to say that the Catholic community was relatively isolated and homogeneous, and that in a host of different ways, ranging from the trivial to the urgently important, the distinctiveness of "Catholic" beliefs, "Catholic" values, and "Catholic" practices was affirmed and reinforced.

Are Catholics Influenced More by the Church or by Secular Society? This state of affairs has changed markedly in the last fifteen years, and with increasing rapidity since the end of Vatican Council II. It is beyond the scope of this paper to discuss the reasons for this change, although no doubt some are to be found in the internal life of the Catholic Church during this period while others are due to social trends and forces at work in secular society. In any case, and leaving aside the question of what has caused the change, the pertinent issue now is whether Catholics in the United States are more powerfully formed and influenced by the Church or by secular society. At the very least, many would say that for a large number of Catholics, the influence of secular society — and all that implies, for good as well as ill — counts more heavily than the influence of the Church.

Problems: Viewed in this light, it comes as no surprise that the Catholic Church in the U.S. has many of the same problems as the rest of organized religion. Polarization and ferment are widespread in the Church, not least in the religious life. The shortage of vocations to the priesthood and religious life remains a serious problem. The reaffirmation of clerical celibacy by the 1971 Synod (of Bishops) has helped reduce confrontation on that issue; yet departures from the active ministry continue at a disturbingly high rate. There is even evidence that weekly Mass attendance has begun to decline significantly among some Catholics. This is particularly striking since very high rates of weekly attendance at religious services have up to now been one of the distinguishing traits of the Catholic community. Evidence of the same tendency — toward assimilation of the values and attitudes dominant in the general society — appears in data indicating that many Catholics are tolerant of abortion in at least some circumstances, reject official Church teaching on means of family limitation, have a divorce rate not markedly different from that of other Americans, and regard most social issues very much as their non-Catholic countrymen do. It would be an exaggeration at the present time to say that such Catholics have rejected the Church. There is no reason to think they have; for the most part they continue to perceive themselves as Catholics. But Catholic beliefs and values no longer occupy the same central place in their lives that they did in the lives of their parents and grandparents — and may have done in their own lives in years gone by. And their attitude toward the magisterium is ambivalent at best.

This is, however, only part of the story of the contemporary Catholic community in the United States. The situation is considerably different for that other segment of the community for whom Catholic beliefs and attitudes do continue to hold a position of centrality.

Influence of Court Decisions: The experience of these Catholics has not been particularly happy in recent years. Increasingly they have found themselves at odds with dominant trends and values in the society in which they live. Their discomfort has reached the point at which it now is described by some as "alienation." Two events of 1973 dramatized and exacerbated such alienation in an especially acute way: the January decisions of the U.S. Supreme Court legalizing abortion on demand and the June decisions of the same court apparently closing off most avenues of new and substantial public assistance to nonpublic schools and nonpublic school children and their parents. The January decisions on abortion were a flat contradiction of traditional Catholic attitudes concerning the right to life of the unborn child, as well as traditional Catholic beliefs concerning the role of law and public policy. The June decisions on educational aid were perceived by many Catholics as a callous repudiation, with some anti-Catholic overtones, of their claim to equitable treatment and full, unimpeded participation in the American educational enterprise.

No Simple Return to the Past: It is extremely risky to attempt to predict the future course of events as far as the Catholic community in the U.S. is concerned. The tendencies noted here have become pronounced only recently and with surprising speed. It is possible that a new change of direction will occur with equal suddenness, but it would be presumptuous to assume that such a change will take place. A simple return to the past seems out of the question in any case.

It would be a mistake, however, to conclude that the current condition of the Church in the United States can be adequately summarized by cataloging problems. The problems described here are real, but they do not exhaust the reality of U.S. Catholicism today.

Spiritual Renewal: Many observers feel that a profound spiritual renewal is now taking place among many American Catholics. Centers and movements for the study and practice of spirituality among priests, religious and laity are springing up in many places. There is a deep and growing interest in prayer. Although comprehensive data are lacking, there is reason to believe that the practice of frequent confession is growing again after several years of decline. Many

young people, as well as their elders, are active participants in charismatic groups. Spiritually-oriented movements for married couples are attracting increasing numbers of husbands and wives. After a period of transition, liturgical reforms are now widely accepted and working well.

The spread of parish and diocesan councils has involved more people than ever before in the exercise of shared responsibility. Many priests and religious, after a period of uncertainty and confusion, manifest renewed and selfless dedication to the mission of the Church. The Holy Year theme of renewal and reconciliation has been welcomed with interest and enthusiasm, and many dioceses and parishes are now involved in Holy Year programs.

Religious Education: There is a strong and healthy interest in the future of religious education, which in recent years has already been much enriched in both Catholic schools and out-of-school programs. Well planend efforts are underway at many levels to develop or strengthen programs in which fidelity to the teaching of the Church is combined with the best in contemporary educational methodology. The bishops have given leadership to the movement by their collective pastoral on Catholic education, *To Teach as Jesus Did* (1972) and the document, *Basic Teachings for Catholic Religious Education* (1973), as well as by their plan for a National Catechetical Directory. There are many new and successful programs for the continuing education of clergy and religious, as well as lay persons. National organizations and dioceses manifest a heightened awareness of the social dimensions of the Church's mission to minority and ethnic groups and a greater sensitivity to such issues as women's rights. Ethical and moral abuses, such as legally sanctioned permissiveness concerning abortion, have helped create a renewed sense of unity among concerned Catholics and have awakened them to their responsibility to be a positive force for good in the nation's life.

In short, the Catholic Church in the United States faces many difficult problems at the present time, but along with the problems there are also signs of underlying strength and vitality. American Catholicism is changing, not collapsing, and, while a period of change is not a time for complacency, neither is it a time for gloom.

4. Conclusion

No Easy Answers: In seeking to influence change positively, the Catholic Church in the United States cannot pretend to have easy or failure-proof answers to the problems outlined here, whether of secular society, organized religion, or the Catholic community. In a sense the message of Christ is the "answer" to them all. But in nearly 2000 years of trying, the Church has not been consistently successful in communicating this message. There is no reason to suppose it will discover a panacea in 1974; yet certain avenues to improved performance are well worth exploring.

Role of Parents: As far as the transmission of values from generation to generation is concerned, the role of parents is crucial. The Church could perform a significant service by increasing its direct assistance to parents who are engaged in this vital task. Supportive efforts by the Church are now more essential than ever, since society at large not only no longer offers such assistance to Catholic parents but in many ways fosters values which directly contradict those they wish to transmit to their children. This calls for strengthening Catholic schools and other educational programs in all ways possible. At the same time, however, it must be recognized that, important as these are, they can only reinforce the parental effort; they cannot substitute for it where it is lacking or deficient, nor do they really constitute "direct assistance" to parents themselves. Serious thought should therefore be given to what forms "direct" assistance to parents might take in the future to help them in the task of transmitting values to their children. Efforts to involve parents directly in the religious and moral education of their children, already underway in many programs, should be fostered, and new means and media should be explored for reaching both parents and children.

The Church and Community: Many of the ills now apparent in secular society (and reflected in one way or another in the religious sphere) are manifestations of an almost atomistic individualism. Yet, paradoxically, to judge from popular literature and rhetoric, the quest for "community" has never been more urgent and widespread. It may be, of course, that many are now seeking community precisely because they have lost it or never experienced it. The Church could play a crucial role of reconciliation in society by speaking movingly to men and women today of the community envisioned and brought into being by Jesus. To do this, however, it must become much more of a loving community — and be perceived as such — than it is now.

Effective Evangelization: Effective evangelization lies at the heart of what is needed now. In order to evangelize effectively in the modern world, the Church must do at least two things. First, it must achieve a clear understanding of what evangelization means in the contemporary context. Second, it needs to assess all means of evangelization now at its disposal (and perhaps some which are not now at its disposal but which potentially could be) in order to determine which can best reach and touch minds and hearts today. The pastoral reflections of the Synod (of Bishops in 1974) can be of inestimable value in responding to these two pressing needs.

DEVELOPMENTS SINCE THE CLOSE OF VATICAN II

Significant developments and changes, affecting many areas of life and practice in the Church, have occurred in the nearly 10 years since the close of the Second Vatican Council Dec. 8, 1965. Some are traceable to conciliar enactments, others are not. Some of the developments are sketched below. (Many are covered more fully under various Almanac headings.)

Biblical Studies: These have been stimulated by the *Constitution on Divine Revelation,* which also clarified the concept of inerrancy in Scripture and restated the thesis that Scripture, tradition and the official teaching authority of the Church, all together, constitute the norm of faith. The constitution furthered the trend, already in progress, toward ecumenical collaboration in biblical studies.

Doctrinal Dimensions: The council did not formulate any new doctrine, and no substantial change has resulted in the official teaching of the Church. The council did, however, open the way to doctrinal dimensions in need of exploration and study.

In the *Dogmatic Constitution on the Church,* for example, the various figures used to describe the Church have stimulated study of its nature not only as a structured institution but also as a sacrament mediating Christ to men; as a community of faith; as a pilgrim passing through the imperfect stages of human histo-

ry to final perfection in a way and time known only to God; as a prophetic and charismatic community in service to men.

Similar impetus has been given to the role of lay persons, particularly women, in the mission of the Church.

Ecumenism: The conciliar decree on this subject has had wide effects. It has brought the Church into mainline contact with all leading ecumenical agencies of other churches, has stimulated a wide variety of action by study groups of theologians, and has affected the lowest parish levels. None of these developments, however, have led to any change of doctrine. There has been a definite improvement in interfaith relations, evidenced by greater understanding. Extreme degrees of what might be called tolerance have deteriorated in some quarters into desire and action for religious unity at any price, but this trend has nothing to recommend it.

Evangelization and Development: The *Pastoral Constitution on the Church in the Modern World* has evoked a new attentiveness to the "signs of the times" as indicators of needed directions of ministry. The same document, along with others related to it, have also occasioned questions concerning the nature of evangelization. The questions have led to some extreme positions. For some theorists, social and developmental work for "humanization," especially among the have-not people of the world, takes priority over proclamation of the Gospel and the establishment of the Christian community. This viewpoint coupled with another — that people who have not heard the Gospel should be left alone in the good faith they have in whatever religion they profess or philosophy they follow — has had the effect of weakening missionary spirit and effort. Such work has been called, in a document from the Synod of Bishops, a constitutive dimension of the Church's ministry. But it does not outrank the priority of proclaiming the Gospel.

Liturgy: Liturgical changes have been the most obvious and sweeping, resulting in various measures of reform in all phases of the worship of the Church but leaving basic sacramental doctrine unaltered. Extremists — by going beyond established norms or refusing to comply with new ones — have hindered the development of reform. Emphasis on the liturgy has been a factor in creating a vacuum of popular devotion. (For detailed coverage of changes, see separate article, Liturgical Developments.)

Priests and Religious: The most obvious observation is that the diocesan priesthood and institutes of men and women religious have lost members at an alarming rate in the post-conciliar years, for a wide variety of personal and institutional reasons. The results, along with the nature and effects of renewal and reform measures affecting training, lifestyle and ministry, have altered the character of many aspects of the priesthood and religious life, some for the better.

Religious Education: A reliable estimate of the status of religious education in general might be drawn from the fact that Pope Paul found it necessary to approve and publish a *General Catechetical Directory* in 1971. A similar estimate of its status in the United States might be drawn from the fact that the bishops have issued two major documents on the subject — *To Teach as Jesus Did,* and *Basic Teachings for Catholic Religious Education* (see separate entry) — and have found it necessary, in addition, to initiate steps leading to publication of a *National Catechetical Directory.*

Shared Responsibility: The top level of shared responsibility is the collegiality of bishops with each other, and with and under the pope. Among its lower level counterparts, with similarities but distinctive differences, are the Synod of Bishops, national and regional conferences of bishops, senates and councils of priests and religious, lay councils, diocesan and parochial pastoral councils. All of these represent new emphasis since Vatican II on efforts to engage wider participation by members of the Church in decision-making and decision-taking, while leaving intact the authority role of bishops and other church officials. Bodies such as these, along with their actions, have altered long-standing patterns for the exercise of authority.

Theology: Theology, as a way of explaining and integrating faith and the experience of faith, has undergone considerable change even though doctrine has not. Some theologians have abandoned or diluted the traditional ontological approach of Thomism in favor of existential and phenomenological theories and methodologies. Much has been said and written to advocate pluralism and unity without uniformity in theology — about the need to theologize in different ways and with terms understandable to people of different cultures. The objective is legitimate. Some efforts to reach for it, however, have caused Pope Paul to warn about the vagaries of kinds of pluralism that jeopardize the integrity of Christian doctrine and morals.

WOMEN IN THE CHURCH

Meetings, statements and study marked the search for women's role in society and the Church during the past year.

In late October, 1973, Pope Paul VI met with Betty Friedan, who is considered the founder of the modern liberation movement for women. He stressed that the Church has always honored women and also said that, despite the recent absorption of women in church roles, the Church was not planning at this time "for a radical" new approach to the problem.

In *Marialis Cultus,* the document on devotion to Mary issued in May, 1974, the Pope called on modern woman to look to Mary as a model: "Mary who, taken into dialogue with God, gives her active and responsible consent not to the solution of a contingent problem, but to that 'event of world importance,' as the Incarnation of the Word has been rightly called. . . . The modern woman will note with pleasant surprise that Mary of Nazareth, while completely devoted to the will of God, was far from being a timidly submissive woman or one whose piety was repellent to others."

Views

The papal Commission on Women, established in May, 1973, to study the role of women in society and the Church, held its first meeting in November, 1973, and several more in 1974. Themes discussed were the role of the human person in the creative plan of God, participation and responsibility of women in the salvific mission of the Church, and the place of women in contemporary society in the light of the Second Vatican Council's *Pastoral Constitution on the Church in the Modern World.* Excluded from the competency of the commission was the topic of ordination of women to the priesthood and other ministries.

For some Catholic women, the only way the Church can prove its seriousness about eliminating discrimination against them is by admitting women to ordination. Outspoken in this view is St. Joan's International Alliance, a society founded in 1911 in Great Britain to fight for woman suffrage and now devoted to achieving equality for women. At its annual meeting Apr. 5 to 7, 1974, in New York, the alliance passed a resolution that all "qualified women expressing the desire for full ordination to the priesthood" should be accepted by Catholic seminaries and given the same financial support from their dioceses as male priesthood candidates.

The Leadership Conference of Women Religious has urged that all church ministries be opened to both men and women, and affirmed the principle that women should have active participation in the church's decision-making bodies. These actions were taken at its 1974 general assembly in Houston, Tex., in August.

Rosemary Goldie, a member of the papal Commission on Women and undersecretary of the Vatican Council for the Laity, expresses a different viewpoint of women's role in the Church. She envisages increased pastoral responsibility for women "by taking advantage of all possibilities offered within the Church after the Second Vatican Council for fuller lay participation." She mentions in particular "ministries of catechists (religious education), of assistance, etc., which are not new for women but which must be developed through a greater recognition of responsibility. There is no question here of a demand, but of a desire to serve for the good of the Church and of human society."

Other women members of the Commission on Women have stated that they "found little or no enthusiasm in their respective countries for an 'ordination' ceremony for women to any of the ministries of the Church."

The Ordination Question

Opinion about the ordination of women in the foreseeable future is very negative. Karl Rahner, in a letter to Rev. Martin Bogdan of the Lutheran Synod of Bavaria, stated that theologically the practice of not ordaining women has "absolutely no binding character, such as dogma, because it is based merely on human and historical reflection that was valid in past ages under cultural and social conditions that are now changing rapidly." He did not expect any early change in the policy, however.

Cardinal John Wright, former bishop of Pittsburgh and prefect of the Congregation of the Clergy, noting that the Church had over 2,000 "solid years" of tradition behind it, has said he does not see "any solid trend" developing which would overturn church tradition in favor of the ordination of women priests.

Development for Fulfillment

The theme of several meetings and statements during 1974 was the development of women in order to enable them to fulfill their duty in the Church and in society.

The general assembly of the World Union of Catholic Women's Organizations, meeting in Dar-es-Salaam, Tanzania, in September, 1974, was assured in a letter from Cardinal Jean Villot of the Pope's interest in its work. Cardinal Villot wrote: "You know with what interest the Holy Father follows your effort and shares your hopes. You will find new proof of his pastoral care . . . in the recent creation of the study commission on the role of women in society and in the Church."

Bishop Leo T. Maher of San Diego, in a pastoral letter entitled "Women in the New World" and issued Aug. 15, stated: "Equality with men is not the focal point of Christian women's needs, but the right to develop to fully human and Christian being, to pursue their vocation to the limit of their capabilities in whatever direction it may led them in the support and recognition of their social community and the Church."

Father Pedro Arrupe, superior general of the Jesuits, addressing the second session of the 1974 World Synod of Bishops in September, said: "There is need for reflection and insistence that women in religion occupy the place they merit by virtue of their dedication and fortitude, and that they be in a position to exercise all the offices and ministries that the Church may entrust to them."

UN International Women's Year

There are indications that most women's groups are looking hopefully to 1975 and the year-long observance of the UN Year of Womanhood. The life of the papal Commission on Women has been extended to 1976 to enable it to follow events of the year. The Leadership Conference of Women Religious resolved at its 1974 national assembly to take a leadership role in celebrating the year as a consciousness-raising event. Rosemary Goldie considers it "a very useful opportunity for the Church . . . to reflect on the participation of women even in ecclesial life."

The 1975 UN International Year of Women has as its theme "Equality, Development and Peace." It coincides, accidentally but perhaps prophetically, with the 1975 Holy Year whose theme is reconciliation and renewal.

Expansion of the roles of women in the Church has led women religious, in particular, into new fields of apostolic engagement. Apostolates of opportunity, as well as the traditional ones, have widened their areas of service to the Church.

MARIALIS CULTUS — DEVOTION TO MARY

Following are excerpts from Pope Paul's apostolic exhortation entitled Marialis Cultus ("Devotion to Mary"), dated Feb. 2 and released for publication Mar. 22, 1974. These excerpts are from the translation published in the Apr. 4 English edition of L'Osservatore Romano.

The contents of this document are related to but different in some respects from the Almanac article, "The Mother of Jesus in Catholic Understanding," and the pastoral letter, "Behold Your Mother, Woman of Faith," issued by the bishops of the United States Nov. 21, 1973.

Nature of Marian Devotion

This type of devotion or cult "takes its origin and effectiveness from Christ, and leads through Christ in the Spirit to the Father. In the sphere of worship this devotion necessarily reflects God's redemptive plan, in which a special form of veneration is appropriate to the singular place which Mary occupies in that plan."

Three Themes: The principal themes of the exhortation concern "the relationship between the sacred liturgy and devotion to the Blessed Virgin, . . . considerations and directives for favoring the development of that devotion, and finally . . . a number of reflections intended to encourage the restoration, in a dynamic and more informed manner, of the recitation of the Rosary. . . ."

Mary in the Liturgy

Marian devotion figures significantly in the liturgy through festive celebrations and seasonal observances. Examples are the Solemnity of the Immaculate Conception (Dec. 8), the seasons of Advent and Christmas, the solemnities of Mary the Mother of God (Jan. 1), the Annunciation of the Lord (Mar. 25), the Assumption (Aug. 15), and a variety of auxiliary feasts. Mary is commemorated also in many passages of the Missal (Sacramentary), the Lectionary and the Liturgy of the Hours, which the exhortation calls "the hinges of the liturgical prayer of the Roman Rite."

Singular Place in Worship: ". . . postconciliar renewal (since the Second Vatican Council) . . . has recognized the singular place that belongs to her (Mary) in Christian worship as the holy Mother of God and the worthy Associate of the Redeemer."

Derivation of Marian Devotion: ". . . the veneration which the universal Church today accords to blessed Mary is a derivation from and an extension and unceasing increase of the devotion that the Church of every age has paid to her, . . . From perennial tradition kept alive by reason of the uninterrupted presence of the Spirit and continual attention to the Word of God, the Church of our time draws motives, arguments and incentives for the veneration that she pays to the Blessed Virgin."

Model of the Church: In "a particular aspect of the relationship between Mary and the liturgy," she is viewed "as a model of the spiritual attitude with which the Church celebrates and lives the divine mysteries." Mary "is recognized as a most excellent exemplar of the Church in the order of faith, charity and perfect union with Christ, that is, of that interior disposition with which the Church, the beloved spouse, closely associated with her Lord, invokes Christ and through him worships the eternal Father."

"Mary is the attentive Virgin, who receives the Word of God with faith. . . ."

"Mary is also the Virgin in prayer" (of praise, in the Magnificat; of petition, at the marriage feast in Cana; in community prayer with the Apostles, at Pentecost)."

"Mary is also the Virgin-Mother" who "brought forth on earth the Father's Son."

"Mary is, finally, the Virgin presenting offerings" (initially, of Jesus to the Father in the Temple; finally and climactically, of Jesus in sacrifice, through union with his offering of himself).

Example for All: "Mary is not only an example for the whole Church in the exercise of divine worship but is also, clearly, a teacher of the spiritual life for individual Christians. The faithful at a very early date (in the history of the Church) began to look to Mary and to imitate her in making their lives an act of worship of God and making their worship a commitment of their lives. . . . Mary is above all the example of that worship that consists in making one's life an offering to God."

Development of Devotion: ". . . the forms in which this devotion is expressed, being subject to the ravages of time, show the need for a renewal that will permit them to substitute elements that are transient, to emphasize the elements that are ever new, and to incorporate the doctrinal data obtained from theological reflection and the proposals of the Church's *Magisterium*. . . . We would like . . . revision (of Marian devotion) to be respectful of wholesome tradition and open to the legitimate requests of the people of our time."

Renewal of Devotion

Trinitarian and Christological Aspects: ". . . exercises of piety directed toward the Virgin Mary should clearly express the Trinitarian and Christological note that is intrinsic and necessary to them. Christian worship in fact is of itself worship offered to the Father and to the Son and to the Holy Spirit, or, as the liturgy puts it, to the Father through Christ in the Spirit. From this point of view worship is rightly extended, though in a substantially different way, first and foremost and in a special manner, to the Mother of the Lord and then to saints, in whom the Church proclaims the Paschal Mystery, for they have suffered with Christ and have been glorified with him. In the Virgin Mary everything is relative to Christ and dependent upon him. . . . genuine Christian piety has never failed to highlight the indissoluble link and essential relationship of the Virgin to the Divine Savior."

"It seems to us useful to add to this mention of the Christological orientation of devotion to the Blessed Virgin a reminder of the fittingness of giving prominence in this devotion to one of the essential facts of the faith: the Person and work of the Holy Spirit. . . . the sanctifying intervention of the Spirit in the Virgin of Nazareth was a culminating moment of the Spirit's action in the history of salvation."

Ecclesial Aspect: "It is also necessary that exercises of piety with which the faithful honor the Mother of the Lord should clearly show the place she occupies in the Church; 'the highest place and the closest to us after Christ.' "

". . . devotion to the Blessed Virgin must explicitly show its intrinsic and ecclesiological content."

Guidelines for Devotion

Biblical Guidelines: ". . . every form of worship should have a biblical imprint. . . . texts of prayers and chants should draw their inspiration and their wording from the Bible, and above all . . . devotion to the Virgin should be imbued with the great themes of the Christian message. This will ensure that . . . the faithful in their turn will be enlightened by the divine word, and be inspired to live their lives in accordance with the precepts of Incarnate Wisdom."

Liturgical Guidelines: In line with the norm stated by the Second Vatican Council in the *Constitution on the Sacred Liturgy,* " '. . . it is necessary that (Marian) devotions . . . should be so arranged as to be in harmony with the sacred liturgy. They should somehow derive their inspiration from it, and because of its preeminence they should orient the Christian people toward it.' "

Two Wrong Attitudes: The exhortation takes exception to "two attitudes which in pastoral practice could nullify the norm of the Second Vatican Council. In the first place there are certain persons concerned with the care of souls who scorn, *a priori,* devotions of piety which, in their correct forms, have been recommended by the *Magisterium,* who leave them aside and in this way create a vacuum which they do not fill. They forget that the Council has said that devotions of piety should harmonize with the liturgy, not be suppressed. Secondly there are those who, without wholesome liturgical and pastoral criteria, mix practices of piety and liturgical

acts in hybrid celebrations. It sometimes happens (for example) that novenas or similar practices of piety are inserted into the very celebration of the Eucharistic Sacrifice. . . . exercises of piety should be harmonized with the liturgy, not merged into it."

Ecumenical Guidelines: "For Catholics, devotion to the Mother of Christ and Mother of Christians is . . . a natural and frequent opportunity for seeking her intercession with her Son in order to obtain the union of all the baptized within a single People of God."

Marian "devotion is an approach to Chirst, the source and center of ecclesiastical communion, in which all who openly confess that he is God and Lord, Savior and sole Mediator, are called to be one, with one another, with Christ and with the Father in the unity of the Holy Spirit."

". . . since it is the same power of the Most High which overshadowed the Virgin of Nazareth and which today is at work within the ecumenical movement and making it fruitful, we wish to express our confidence that devotion to the humble Handmaid of the Lord . . . will become, even if only slowly, not an obstacle but a path and a rallying point for the union of all who believe in Christ."

Anthropological Guidelines: "Devotion to the Blessed Virgin must also pay close attention to certain findings of the human sciences. This will help to eliminate one of the causes of the difficulties experienced in devotion to the Mother of the Lord, namely, the discrepancy existing between some aspects of this devotion and modern anthropological discoveries and the profound changes which have occurred in the psycho-sociological field in which modern man lives and works. The picture of the Blessed Virgin presented in a certain type of devotional literature cannot easily be reconciled with today's life style, especially the way women live today."

Difficulties: "In consequence of these phenomena some people are becoming disenchanted with devotion to the Blessed Virgin and finding it difficult to take as an example Mary of Nazareth because the horizons of her life, so they say, seem rather restricted in comparison with the vast spheres of activity open to mankind today. . . . we wish to take the opportunity of offering our own contribution to . . . solution (of a number of difficulties) by making a few observations."

Example of Acceptance: "First, the Virgin Mary has always been proposed to the faithful by the Church as an example to be imitated not precisely in the type of life she led, and much less for the socio-cultural background in which she lived and which today scarcely exists anywhere. She is held up as an example to the faithful rather for the way in which, in her own particular life, she fully and responsibly accepted the will of God (cf. Lk. 1:38), because she heard the word of God and acted on it and because charity and a spirit of service were the driving force of her actions. She is worthy of imitation because she was the first and the most perfect of Christ's disciples. All of this has a permanent and universal exemplary value."

Faulty Images: "Secondly, we would like to point out that the difficulties alluded to above are closely related to certain aspects of the image of Mary found in popular writings. They are not connected with the Gospel image of Mary nor with the doctrinal data which have been made explicit through a slow and conscientious process of drawing from Revelation. ... When the Church considers the long history of Marian devotion she rejoices at the continuity of the element of cult which it shows, but she does not bind herself to any particular expression of an individual cultural epoch or to the particular anthropological ideas underlying such expressions. The Church understands that certain outward religious expressions, while perfectly valid in themselves, may be less suitable to men and women of different ages and cultures."

Mirror of Contemporary Expectations: "Finally, ... the reading of the divine Scriptures, carried out under the guidance of the Holy Spirit, and with the discoveries of the human sciences and the different situations in the world today being taken into account, will help us to see how Mary can be considered a mirror of the expectations of the men and women of our time. Thus, the modern woman, anxious to participate with decision-making power in the affairs of the community, will contemplate with intimate joy Mary who, taken into dialogue with God, gives her active and responsible consent not to the solution of a contingent problem, but to that "event of world importance," as the Incarnation of the Word has been rightly called. The modern woman will appreciate that Mary's choice of the state of virginity, which in God's plan prepared her for the mystery of the Incarnation, was not a rejection of any of the values of the married state but a courageous choice which she made in order to consecrate herself totally to the love of God. The modern woman will note with pleasant surprise that Mary of Nazareth, while completely devoted to the will of God, was far from being a timidly submissive woman or one whose piety was repellent to others; on the contrary, she was a woman who did not hesitate to proclaim that God vindicates the humble and the oppressed, and removes the powerful people of this world from their privileged positions (cf. Lk. 1:51-53). The modern woman will recognize in Mary, who "stands out among the poor and humble of the Lord," a woman of strength, who experienced poverty and suffering, flight and exile (cf. Mt. 2:13-23). These are situations that cannot escape the attention of those who wish to support, with the Gospel spirit, the liberating energies of man and of society. And Mary will appear not as a mother exclusively concerned with her own divine Son but rather as a woman whose action helped to strengthen the apostolic community's faith in Christ (cf. Jn. 2:1-12) and whose maternal role was extended and became universal on Calvary. These are but examples, but examples which show clearly that the figure of the Blessed Virgin does not disillusion any of the profound expectations of the men and women of our time but offers them the perfect model of the disciple of the Lord: the disciple who builds up the earthly and temporal city while being a diligent pilgrim toward the heavenly and eternal city; the disciple who works for that justice which sets free the oppressed and for that charity which assists the needy; but, above all, the disciple who is the active witness of that love which builds up Christ in people's hearts."

Attitudes

Incorrect Attitudes: "... we consider it opportune to draw attention to certain attitudes of piety which are incorrect. The Second Vatican Council has already authoritatively denounced both the exaggeration of content and form which even falsifies doctrine and likewise the small-mindedness which obscures the figure and mission of Mary. The Council has also denounced certain devotional deviations, such as vain credulity which substitutes reliance on merely external practices for serious commitment. Another deviation is sterile and ephemeral sentimentality, so alien to the spirit of the Gospel that demands persevering and practical action. We reaffirm the Council's reprobation of such attitudes and practices. They are not in harmony with the Catholic faith, and therefore they must have no place in Catholic worship. Careful defense against these errors and deviations will render devotion to the Blessed Virgin more vigorous and more authentic. It will make this devotion solidly based, with the consequence that study of the sources of Revelation and attention to the documents of the *Magisterium* will prevail over the exaggerated search for novelties or extraordinary phenomena. It will ensure that this devotion is objective in its historical setting, and for this reason everything that is obviously legendary or false must be eliminated. It will ensure that this devotion matches its doctrinal content — hence the necessity of avoiding a one-sided presentation of the figure of Mary which, by overstressing one element, compromises the overall picture given by the Gospel. It will make this devotion clear in its motivation; hence every unworthy self-interest is to be carefully banned from the area of what is sacred."

Ultimate Purpose: "Finally, insofar as it may be necessary we would like to repeat that the ultimate purpose of devotion to the Blessed Virgin is to glorify God and to lead

Christians to commit themselves to a life which is in absolute conformity with his will."

Two Devotions

While encouraging the revision of existing forms of devotion in honor of Mary and the development of new ones, the exhortation singles out the Angelus and the Rosary for special attention.

Angelus: Of the Angelus, it says: ". . . it reminds us of the Paschal Mystery in which, recalling the Incarnation of the Son of God, we pray that we may be led 'through his Passion and Cross to the glory of his Resurrection.' These factors ensure that the Angelus, despite the passing of centuries, retains an unaltered value and an intact freshness." (See separate entry, Angelus.)

The Rosary: In one representative passage, the exhortation states: ". . . the Rosary reflects the very way in which the Word of God, mercifully entering into human affairs, brought about the Redemption. The Rosary considers in harmonious succession the principal salvific events accomplished in Christ, from his virginal conception and the mysteries of his childhood to the culminating moments of the Passion — the blessed Passion and the glorious Resurrection — and to the effects of this on the infant Church on the day of Pentecost, and on the Virgin Mary when, at the end of her earthly life, she was assumed body and soul into her heavenly home. It has also been observed that the division of the mysteries of the Rosary into three parts not only adheres strictly to the chronological order of the facts but above all reflects the plan of the original proclamation of the faith. . . ."

The exhortation appeals for renewed devotion to the Rosary by individuals, families and communities. At the same time, there were these admonitions:

". . . it is a mistake to recite the Rosary during the celebration of the liturgy, though unfortunately this practice still persists here and there."

". . . this very worthy devotion should not be propagated in a way that is too one-sided or exclusive. The Rosary is an excellent prayer, but the faithful should feel serenely free in its regard. They should be drawn to its calm recitation by its intrinsic appeal."

(See separate entry, Rosary.)

NEW RITUAL FOR PENANCE

The Congregation for Divine Worship published Feb. 7, 1974, the 121-page Latin text of a new ritual for the sacrament of penance or reconciliation, emphasizing the communal and ecclesial as well as personal aspects of the sacrament.

The following news release, issued by the Vatican on publication of Ordo Paenitentiae, was circulated by the NC Documentary Service, Origins, Feb. 14, 1974 (Vol. 3, No. 34).

For additional information, see separate article under Sacraments.

The Sacred Congregation for Divine Worship is publishing a new book of the liturgical reform, approved by the Holy Father, with the Latin title *Ordo Paenitentiae.*

It bears the date of December 2, 1973, the first Sunday of Advent, and comes into force immediately for the Latin version, while for vernacular languages the date will be laid down by the individual episcopal conferences, after the translations which they approved have been confirmed by the Holy See.

Here, as in the case of the other liturgical books, the new aspect is not to be sought in doctrine but in the pastoral directives and indications for the renewal of the practice of the sacrament.

Parts of the Ordo

The *Ordo* has two parts. The first, the official one, contains a number of doctrinal principles, the pastoral and liturgical norms and the rites for the celebration of the sacrament of penance in its various forms (types). The second, published as an aid for the bishops' conferences and liturgical commissions, gives eight forms of penitential celebrations.

Background of Revision

The volume is the fruit of long and patient work carried out first by the experts and by the bishops of the *Consilium ad Exsequendam Constitutionem de Sacra Liturgia* (Council for Implementing the Constitution on the Sacred Liturgy), and then by the Congregation for Divine Worship in collaboration with the other departments of the Holy See concerned in the matter.

An initial phase of research carried out between 1966 and 1970 studied exhaustively all the material in its doctrinal, historical and liturgical aspects, as well as in relation to the situation and needs of the present day. The first draft of the rites then had to await the pastoral norms on general absolution issued by the Sacred Congregation for the Doctrine of the Faith on June 16, 1972. On this foundation the work entered its second phase, which has led to the determination of the rites now published.

The Title

The title of the book represents a new approach from the pastoral point of view. In fact the sacrament of penance is usually referred to by the term "confession," because of the spread of the "private" celebration of the sacrament and a certain emphasis widely placed on the accusation of sins. This does not convey all the richness of meaning which this sacrament has in the life of the Church.

Consequently the change of terminology in this new revised rite is a better indication of its content. The general title of the volume is *Ordo Paenitentiae,* to designate not only the sacramental rite but also the forms of penitential celebrations which are not concluded with sacramental absolution.

In order to indicate the sacramental liturgical action, the term "reconciliation" has been preferred in the individual chapters of the *Ordo.* This term also shows more clearly that sacramental penance is an encounter of God's action and man's, while the term "penance" puts the accent rather on what is done by man. The term "reconciliation," already used in the primitive Church and later by the Council of Trent, will serve to ensure an understanding of a fundamental aspect for the renewal of penance; that of encounter between a son and his father.

Doctrinal and Pastoral Premises

As in all the liturgical books of the postconciliar reform, the description of the revised rites is preceded by an ample introduction, which outlines their spirit, doctrinal basis and the goals to be achieved for the spiritual life of the faithful.

In the course of the centuries the sacrament of penance has undergone a certain variety of forms and of changes in practice. Historical research and theological reflection are continually progressing in this field.

The *Ordo Paenitentiae* presents in synthesis the solid and secure points of the Church's constant doctrine, within the perspectives opened up by the Second Vatican Council in regard to the spiritual and concrete needs of the faithful. The council recommended that revision of this sacrament should be carried out in such a way that the nature and effects of the sacrament might appear more clearly (cf. *Constitution of the Sacred Liturgy,* No. 72).

Communal Character of Penance

Specifically, in the new rite the communal and ecclesial character of penance is made evident: sin is an offense against God and at the same time against one's brethren; penance is therefore a reconciliation with God and with the Church, which works together for conversion with charity, with example and with prayer (cf. *Dogmatic Constitution on the Church,* No. 11).

It had already been recommended in the council that the reform of the rites of penance should show, over and above the personal aspects, also the communal and social aspect of sin, in such a way as to take away from this sacrament the impression that it is a purely individual matter.

Essential Elements

The constitutive elements of the sacrament are presented in accordance with the traditional teaching: sorrow, confession, reparation and absolution. All are necessary, but their order has not always been the same as above, nor is it now.

Today absolution usually comes before reparation, while originally the contrary was the case. Thus, in unusual cases determined by the bishop for collective absolution, the absolution comes before the individual confession of sins. Thus there emerges the importance, above all else, of the interior dispositions — conversion and sorrow — and of the priest's absolution.

The *Praenotanda* clearly distinguish the case in which the celebration of the sacrament is necessary, that is for grave or "mortal" sins, and the optional and frequent use which is recommended to assist the commitment to continual conversion and to perfecting the grace of baptism.

In regard to the place of penance and the vestments of the minister of penance, the *Ordo* refers all specification to the current law and to the bishops' conferences.

Formula of Absolution

The essential words for the absolution of sins have not been changed, but have been inserted into a new single formula which more clearly expresses that the reconciliation of the penitent is a gift coming from the love of God the Father.

This gift of grace is related to the history of salvation, in which God reconciled the world to himself through the death and resurrection of Christ. The action of the Holy Spirit in the conversion and sanctification of the sinner is underlined.

Finally, the ecclesial aspect of reconciliation, which is brought about by means of the Church, is clearly shown.

The New Rites

The new *Ordo Paenitentiae* sets out three different forms, which make it possible to emphasize more clearly the various aspects of penance and to adapt the celebration to the needs of the faithful.

1. Reconciliation of the Individual Penitent: The form in use at present is adopted, but it is enriched with a number of details. The parts of the celebration are: reception of the penitent and the sign of the cross; an exhortation to trust in God; a *possible* reading of a text of Sacred Scripture; the confession of sins; the manifestation of repentance; the imploring of God's indulgence, through the ministry of the Church, and absolution imparted by the priest; the exaltation of God's mercy, and the dismissal.

Some of these elements are optional, but taken as a whole they tend to give penance a character which is one of liberation and salvation, and not of preoccupation with oneself. Besides the admission of sin, there is the proclamation of the power of God who saves and who makes confession an encounter of joy and peace.

2. Reconciliation of Several Penitents, with Individual Confession and Absolution: In the second type of rite for penance individual confession and absolution are inserted into a communal celebration, in which the faithful listen together to the word of God, admit their sinfulness and invoke the mercy of the Lord. There are three basic parts: liturgy of the word and prayers; individual confession and absolution; thanksgiving and proclamation in common of joy at the reconciliation that has taken place.

As in every sacrament, the communal and personal aspects are thus given due emphasis.

3. Reconciliation of Several Penitents with General Confession and Absolution: The "Pastoral Norms" of the Sacred Congregation for the Doctrine of the Faith on general absolution provided that, in very special circumstances, in order not to deprive the faithful for too long a period of the grace of reconciliation and of the possibility of receiving the Eucharist, general absolution may be given, at the discretion of the bishops, with the individual confession of sins being postponed to a future time. Naturally, for the efficacy of the sacrament of penance there are required the interior dispositions, especially conversion, true repentance (also expressed by some external sign to be determined by the episcopal conferences), the intention to make an indi-vidual confession, the willingness to make up for the offenses committed and the resolve to renew one's life. In order to ensure these dispositions, general absolution, always in the cases provided for in the existing legislation, is normally inserted into a penitential celebration.

Penitential Celebrations

In an appendix, the *Ordo* provides eight forms for penitential celebrations: these are communal celebrations, for the liturgical seasons of Advent and Lent, for various categories of people: children, young people and the sick.

These forms are simply models for encouraging and orienting the creation of other forms better adapted to local needs and the various categories of people. They can serve for preparation for confession and also for deepening and expressing in common the continual commitment to conversion. They are also useful for places where there is no priest, in order to stimulate the faithful to a sense of sin, to conversion and to repentance. In these cases the penitential celebrations can be organized by a deacon, a catechist or by a lay person.

In another appendix there is a catechistic form oriented towards the examination of conscience. This can also be adapted according to circumstances and individuals.

MINISTRY AND ORDINATION: CANTERBURY STATEMENT

The Anglican-Roman Catholic International Commission of theologians released for publication a statement on certain points of agreement regarding ministry and ordination Dec. 13, 1973, with the permission of Pope Paul VI and Archbishop Michael Ramsey of Canterbury.

The commission made it clear that the statement is limited in scope and does not cover such related subjects as authority and primacy in the Anglican orders. It was also noted that this Anglican orders. It was also noted that this document, reflecting the views of the commission, is not an official declaration by either the Roman Catholic Church or the Anglican Communion, and that it does not authorize any change in existing doctrine or discipline. The statement, for discussion in the course of ecumenical dialogue and related developments, is subject to ultimate decision by authorities of the respective churches.

These excerpts are from the text circulated Dec. 20, 1973, by the NC Documentary Service, Origins (Vol. 3, No. 26), with permission of the Anglican-Roman Catholic International Commission.

Common Convictions: The statement "seeks to express our basic agreement in the doctrinal areas that have been the source of controversy between us, in the wider context of our common convictions about the ministry."

"Within the Roman Catholic Church and the Anglican Communion there exists a diversity of forms of ministerial service. Of more specific ways of service, while some are undertaken without particular initiative from official authority, others may receive a mandate from ecclesiastical authorities. The ordained ministry can only be rightly understood within this broader context of various ministries, all of which are the work of one and the same Spirit."

Apostolic Ministry: "In the early church the Apostles exercised a ministry which remains of fundamental significance for the church of all ages. . . . two primary features of the original apostolate are clearly discernible: a special relationship with the historical Christ, and a commission from him to the church and the world. . . . The church is apostolic not only because its faith and life must reflect the witness to Jesus Christ given in the early church by the Apostles, but also because it is charged to continue in the Apostles' commission to communicate to the world what it has received."

Ministry in the New Testament: "Within the New Testament ministerial actions are varied and functions not precisely defined. Explicit emphasis is given to the proclamation of the Word and the preservation of apostolic doctrine, the care of the flock, and the example of Christian living. . . . evidence suggests that with the growth of the church the importance of certain functions led to their being located in specific officers of the community. . . . some form of recognition and authorization is already required in the New Testament period for those who exercise them in the name of Christ. Here we can see elements which will remain at the heart of what today we call ordination."

Ministerial Office: ". . . we believe that the provision (of ministerial office) is part of God's design for his people. . . . The early churches may well have had considerable diversity in the structure of pastoral ministry, though it is clear that some churches were headed by ministers who were called *episcopoi* and *presbyteroi*. . . . the full emergence of the threefold ministry of bishop, presbyter, and deacon required a longer period than the apostolic age. Thereafter this threefold structure became universal in the church."

For Service: "The goal of the ordained ministry is to serve (the) priesthood of all the faithful. . . . This ministry assumes various patterns to meet the varying needs of those whom the church is seeking to serve, and it is the role of the minister to coordinate the activities of the church's fellowship and to promote what is necessary and useful for the church's life and mission."

Oversight: "An essential element in the ordained ministry is its responsibility for 'oversight' *(episcope)*. This responsibility involves fidelity to the apostolic faith, its embodiment in the life of the church today and its transmission to the church of tomorrow. Presbyters are joined with the bishop in his oversight of the church and in the ministry of the Word and the sacraments; they are given authority to preside at the Eucharist and to pronounce absolution. Deacons, although not so empowered, are associated with bishops and presbyters in the ministry of Word and sacrament, and assist in oversight."

Eucharistic Ministry: ". . . because the Eucharist is central in the church's life . . . the essential nature of the Christian ministry, however this may be expressed, is most clearly seen in its celebration. . . ." The ministry of those who are ordained "is not an extension of the common Christian priesthood but belongs to another realm of the gifts of the Spirit. It exists to help the church to be 'a royal priesthood, a holy nation, God's own people, to declare the wonderful deeds of him who called (them) out of darkness into his marvelous light' (1 Pt. 2:9; RSV)."

Ordination: "Ordination denotes entry into this apostolic and God-giving ministry, which serves and signifies the unity of the local churches in themselves and with one another. Every individual act of ordination is therefore an expression of the continuing apostolicity and catholicity of the whole church. . . . those who are ordained are called by Christ in the church and through the church."

"In this sacramental act, the gift of God is bestowed upon the ministers, with the promise of divine grace . . . the ministry of Christ is presented to them . . . and the Spirit seals those whom he has chosen and consecrated. . . . ordination is unrepeatable in both our churches."

Communion of Churches, Apostolic Succession: "Both presbyters and deacons are ordained by the bishop. In the ordination of a presbyter, the presbyters present join the bishop in the laying on of hands, thus signifying the shared nature of the commission entrusted to them. In the ordination of a new bishop, other bishops lay hands on him, as they request the gift of the Spirit for his ministry and receive him into their ministerial fellowship. Because they are entrusted with the oversight of other churches, this participation in his ordination signifies that this new bishop and his church are within the communion of churches. Moreover, because they are representative of their churches in fidelity to the teaching and mission of the Apostles and are members of the episcopal college, their participation also ensures the historical continuity of this church with the apostolic church and of its bishop with the original apostolic ministry. The communion of the churches in mission, faith, and holiness, through time and space, is thus symbolized and maintained in the bishop. Here are comprised the essential features of what is meant in our two traditions by ordination in the apostolic succession."

APOSTOLIC SUCCESSION / A CLARIFICATION

Following are excerpts from a study of holy orders and apostolic succession completed by the Vatican's International Theological Commission. Its contents are related to those of the "Canterbury Statement" (see separate article) issued by the Anglican-Roman Catholic International Commission of theologians.

These excerpts, with lead lines added, are from a translation copyrighted by the Tablet of London and circulated Sept. 19, 1974, by the NC Documentary Service, Origins (Vol. 4, No. 13).

Witness of Scripture and Tradition: Scripture and tradition taken together, pondered upon and authentically interpreted by the magisterium, faithfully transmit to us the teaching of Christ our Lord and Savior, and determine the doctrine which it is the church's mission to proclaim to all peoples and to apply to each generation until the end of the world. It is in this theological perspective — fully in accord with the doctrine of Vatican II — that we have written this document on apostolic succession and evaluated the ministries which exist in churches and communities not yet in full communion with the Catholic Church.

The creeds confess their faith in the apostolicity of the church. That means not simply that the church continues to hold the apostolic faith, but that it is determined to live according to the norms of the primitive church which derived from the first witnesses of Christ and was guided by the Holy Spirit.

Institution by Christ: Christ instituted a ministry for the establishment, animation and maintenance of this (common) priesthood of Christians. This ministry was to be the sign and the instrument by which he would communicate to his people in the course of history the fruits of his life, death and resurrection. The first foundations of this ministry were laid when he called the Twelve, who at the same time represent the New Israel as a whole and, after Easter, will be the privileged eyewitnesses sent out to proclaim the gospel of salvation and the leaders of the new people, "fellow workers with God for the building of his temple" (see 1 Cor. 3:9). This ministry has an essential function to fulfill towards each generation of Christians. It must therefore be transmitted from the apostles by an unbroken line of succession. If one can say that the church as a whole is established upon the foundation of the apostles (Eph. 2:20; Rev. 21:14), one has to add that this apostolicity which is common to the whole church is linked with the ministerial apostolic succession, and that this is an inalienable ecclesial structure at the service of all Christians.

The Apostles and Apostolic Succession in History: The documents of the New Testament show that in the early days of the church and in the lifetime of the apostles there was diversity in the way communities were organized, but also that there was, in the period immediately following, a tendency to assert and strengthen the ministry of teaching and leadership.

Those who directed communities in the lifetime of the apostles or after their death have different names in the New Testament texts: the *presbyteroi-episkopoi* are described as *poimenes, hegoumenoi. proistamenoi, kyberneseis.* In comparison with the rest of the church, the feature of the *presbyteroi-episkopoi* is their apostolic ministry of teaching and governing. Whatever the method by which they are chosen, whether through the authority of the Twelve or Paul or some link with them, they share in the authority of the apostles who were instituted by Christ and who maintain for all time their unique character.

Development: In the course of time this ministry underwent a development. This development happened by internal necessity. It was encouraged by external factors, and above all by the need to maintain unity in communities and to defend them against

errors. When communities were deprived of the actual presence of apostles and yet still wanted to refer to the authority, there had to be some way of continuing to exercise adequately the functions which the apostles had exercised in and in relation to them.

Already in the New Testament texts there are echoes of the transition from the apostolic period to the sub-apostolic age, and one begins to see signs of the development which in the second century led to the stabilization and general recognition of the episcopal ministry. The stages of this development can be glimpsed in the last writings of the Pauline tradition and in other texts linked with the authority of the apostles.

Significance of Succession: The significance of the apostles at the time of the foundation of the earliest Christian communities was held to be essential for the structure of the church and local communities in the thinking of the sub-apostolic period. The principle of the apostolicity of the church elaborated in this reflection led to the recognition of the ministry of teaching and governing as an institution derived from Christ by and through the mediation of the apostles. The church lived in the certain conviction that Jesus, before he left this world sent the Twelve on a universal mission and promised that he would be with them at all times until the end of the world (Mt. 28:18-20).

By the end of the first century the situation was that the apostles or their closest helpers or eventually their successors directed the local colleges of *episkopoi* and *presbyteroi*. By the beginning of the second century the figure of a single bishop who is the head of the communities appears very clearly in the letter of St. Ignatius of Antioch, who further claims that this institution is established "unto the ends of the earth" (*Ad Ephesios,* 3, 2).

Ordination and Succession: During the second century and after the letter of Clement this institution is explicitly acknowledged to carry with it the apostolic succession. Ordination with imposition of hands, already witnessed to in the pastoral epistles, appears in the process of clarification to be an important step in preserving the apostolic tradition and guaranteeing succession in the ministry. The documents of the third century (*Tradition of Hyppolytus*) show that this conviction was arrived at peacefully and was considered to be a necessary institution.

Clement and Irenaeus develop a doctrine on pastoral government and on the word in which they derive the idea of apostolic succession from the unity of the word, the unity of the mission and the unity of the ministry of the church; thus apostolic succession became the permanent ground from which the Catholic Church understood its own nature.

Sacrament of the Effective Presence of Christ: An apostolic succession is that aspect of the nature and life of the church which shows the dependence of our present-day community on Christ through those whom he has sent. The apostolic ministry is, therefore, the sacrament of the effective presence of Christ and of his Spirit in the midst of the people of God, and this view in no way underestimates the immediate influence of Christ and his Spirit on each believer.

The charism of apostolic succession is received in the visible community of the church. It presupposes that someone who is to enter the ministry has the faith of the church. The gift of ministry is granted in an act which is the visible and efficacious symbol of the gift of the Spirit, and this act has as its instrument one or several of those ministers who have themselves entered the apostolic succession.

Transmission through Ordination: Thus the transmission of the apostolic ministry is achieved through ordination, including a rite with a visible sign and the invocation of God (*epiklesis*) to grant to the ordinand the gift of his Holy Spirit and the powers that are needed for the accomplishment of his task. This visible sign, from the New Testament onwards, is the imposition of hands (see *Dogmatic Constitution on the Church*, No. 21: Second Vatican Council). The rite of ordination expresses the truth that what happens to the ordinand does not come from human origin and that the church cannot do what it likes with the gift of the Spirit.

The church is fully aware that its nature is bound up with apostolicity and that the ministry handed on by ordination establishes the one who has been ordained in the apostolic confession of the truth of the Father. The church, therefore, has judged that ordination, given and received in the understanding she herself has of it, is necessary to apostolic succession in the strict sense of the word.

The apostolic succession of the ministry concerns the whole church, but it is not something which derives from the church taken as a whole but rather from Christ to the apostles and from the apostles to all bishops to the end of time.

Non-Catholic Ministries

The preceding sketch of the Catholic understanding of apostolic succession now enables us to give in broad outline an evaluation of non-Catholic ministries. In this context it is indispensable to keep firmly in mind the differences that have existed in the origins and in the subsequent development of these churches and communities, as also their own self-understanding.

Orthodox and Others with Succession: (1) In spite of a difference in their appreciation of the office of Peter, the Catholic Church, the Orthodox Church and the other churches which have retained the reality of apostolic succession, are at one in sharing a basic understanding of the sacramentality of the church which developed from the New Testament and through the Fathers, notably through Irenaeus. These churches hold that the sacramental entry into the ministry comes about through the imposition of hands with the invocation of the Holy Spirit, and that this is the indispensable form for the transmission of the apostolic succession which alone enables the church to remain constant in its doctrine and communion. It is this unanimity concerning the unbroken coherence of scripture, tradition and sacrament which explains why communion between these churches and the Catholic Church has never completely ceased and could today be revived.

Anglicans: (2) Fruitful dialogues have taken place with Anglican communions which have retained the imposition of hands, the interpretation of which has varied. We cannot here anticipate the eventual results of this dialogue which has as its object to inquire how far factors constitutive of unity are included in the maintenance of the imposition of hands and accompanying prayers.

Reformation Churches: (3) The communities which emerged from the 16th century Reformation differ among themselves to such an extent that a description of their relationship to the Catholic Church has to take account of the many individual cases. However, some general lines are beginning to emerge. In general it was a feature of the Reformation to deny the link between scripture and tradition and to advocate the view that scripture alone was normative. Even if later on some sort of place for tradition is recognized, it is never given the same position and dignity as in the ancient church. But since the sacrament of orders is the indispensable sacramental expression of communion in the tradition, the proclamation of *sola scriptura* (*scripture alone as the norm of faith*) led inevitably to an obscuring of the older idea of the church and its priesthood.

Thus through the centuries, the imposition of hands either by men already ordained or by others was often in practice abandoned. Where it did take place, it did not have the same meaning as in the church of tradition. This divergence in the mode of entry into the ministry and its interpretation is only the most noteworthy symptom of the different understanding of church and tradition. There have already been a number of promising contacts which have sought to re-establish links with the tradition, although the break has so far not been successfully overcome.

No Intercommunion: In such circumstances, intercommunion remains impossible for the time being, because sacramental continuity in apostolic succession from the beginning is an indispensable element of ecclesial communion both for the Catholic Church and the Orthodox Churches.

To say this is not to say that the ecclesial

and spiritual qualities of the Protestant ministers and communities are thereby negligible. Their ministers have edified and nourished their communities. By baptism, by the study and the preaching of the word, by their prayer together and celebration of the Last Supper, and by their zeal they have guided men towards faith in the Lord and thus helped them to find the way of salvation. There are thus in such communities elements which certainly belong to the apostolicity of the unique church of Christ.

PAPAL PRIMACY: LUTHERAN-CATHOLIC STATEMENT

The National Lutheran-Catholic Dialogue group of theologians in the United States released for publication Mar. 4, 1974, a joint statement entitled "Papal Primacy/Converging Viewpoints." The 5,000-word statement, the first of its kind produced by such an ecumenical group, deals primarily with papal primacy as a form of ministry serving the unity of Christian churches. Total agreement is not stated in the document; neither is coverage of papal infallibility or possibilities of change in the papal office.

The statement reflects the views of participants in the dialogue which produced it over a period of three years. It has not been given official sanction by either the Lutheran or the Catholic Church, and has no current effect on the doctrine or practice of either body.

These excerpts are from the text circulated Mar. 14, 1974, by the NC Documentary Service, Origins (Vol. 3, No. 38).

The Question of Papal Primacy: "Visible unity in the church has from earliest times been served by several forms of the ministry. Some of these forms, such as that exercised in the ecumenical councils, have not been the subject of major disputes between Catholics and Lutherans. By contrast the role of the papacy has been the subject of intense controversy, which has generated theological disagreements, organizational differences, and psychological antagonisms.

"In discussing the papacy as a form of ministry within the universal church we have limited ourselves to the question of papal primacy. No attempt has been made to enter into the problem of papal infallibility."

". . . we focus on the unifying and ordering function of this ministry (of word and sacrament) in relation to the universal church — on how a particular form of this ministry, i.e., the papacy, has served the unity of the universal church in the past and how it may serve it in the future.

Petrine Function: ". . . we have found it appropriate to speak of a 'Petrine function,' using this term to describe a particular form of ministry exercised by a person, officeholder, or local church with reference to the church as a whole. This Petrine function of the ministry serves to promote or preserve the oneness of the church by symbolizing unity, and by facilitating communication, mutual assistance or correction, and collaboration in the church's mission.

"Such a Petrine function has been exercised in some degree by various office-holders, for example by bishops, patriarchs, and church presidents. However, the single most notable representative of this ministry toward the church universal, both in duration and geographical scope, has been the bishop of Rome.

"The Reformers did not totally reject all aspects of the papal expression of the Petrine function, but rather what they regarded as its abuses. They hoped for a reform of the papacy precisely in order to preserve the unity of the church. . . . They continued to concede to the pope all the legitimate spiritual powers of a bishop in his diocese, in this case, Rome. They even granted the propriety of his exercising a larger jurisdiction by human right over communities that had by their own will placed themselves under him."

Disputed Points: "The disputes (between Catholics and Lutherans over the papacy) have centered, first, on the question whether the papacy is biblically warranted. Rome Catholics have read the New Testament as indicating that Jesus conferred on Peter a unique role of leadership in the whole church for all times and in this sense provided for successors in the Petrine function, the bishops of Rome. In this view, the papacy has remained substantially the same through succeeding centuries, all changes being accidental.

"Lutherans, in contrast, have minimized Peter's role in the early church and denied that this role continued in the church in later periods or that the Roman bishops could be considered his successors in any theologically significant sense.

"Closely linked to this historical question regarding the institution of the papacy by Christ is the theological issue whether the papacy is a matter of divine law *(ius divinum)*. Roman Catholics have affirmed that it is and consequently have viewed it as an essential part of the permanent structure of the Church. Lutherans have held, in opposition to this, that the papacy was established by human law, the will of men, and that its claims to divine right are nothing short of blasphemous."

The pope's "jurisdiction over the universal church is in the words of Vatican I, 'supreme,' 'full,' 'ordinary,' and 'immediate.' This authority is not subject to any higher human jurisdiction, and no pope is absolutely bound by disciplinary decisions of his predecessors. This view of the exercise of papal power has been vehemently repudiated by Lutherans and viewed by them as leading to intolerable ecclesiastical tyranny.

"In the course of our discussions, however, we have been able to gain helpful and clarifying insights regarding these points of controversy."

New Testament Background, Forms of the Papacy: ". . . The question whether Jesus appointed Peter the first pope has shifted in modern scholarship to the question of the extent to which the subsequent use of the images of Peter in reference to the papacy is consistent with the thrust of the New Testament."

"The Catholic members of this consultation see the institution of the papacy as developing from New Testament roots under the guidance of the Spirit. Without denying that God could have ordered the church differently, they believe that the papal form of the unifying ministry is, in fact, God's gracious gift to his people.

"Lutheran theologians, although in the past chiefly critical of the structure and functioning of the papacy, can now recognize many of its positive contributions to the life of the church. Both groups can acknowledge that as the forms of the papacy have been adapted to changing historical settings in the past, it is possible that they will be modified the better to meet the needs of the church in the future.

Possibilities of Change: The statement says that modifications might be made within the pattern of principles of: legitimate diversity, in practices of piety, liturgy, theology, custom and law; collegiality, allowing for participation in decision-making on all levels of the church; and subsidiarity, permitting lower or smaller units of the church to handle affairs within their appropriate capabilities. Another possibility might be "voluntary limitations by the pope of the exercise of his jurisdiction," without prejudice to its full or plenary character.

A Lutheran Imperative: ". . . The one thing necessary, from the Lutheran point of view, is that papal primacy be so structured and interpreted that it clearly serve the gospel and the unity of the church of Christ, and that its exercise of power not subvert Christian freedom."

Points of Agreement: "Our discussions in this dialogue have brought to light a number of agreements, among the most significant of which are:

• "Christ wills for his church a unity which is not only spiritual but must be manifest in the world.

• "Promotion of this unity is incumbent on all believers, especially those who are engaged in the ministry of word and sacrament.

• "The greater the responsibility of a ministerial office, the greater the responsibility to seek the unity of all Christians.

• "A special responsibility for this may be entrusted to one individual minister, under the gospel.

• "Such a responsibility for the universal church cannot be ruled out on the basis of the biblical evidence.

• "The bishop of Rome, whom Roman Catholics regard as entrusted by the will of Christ with this responsibility, and who has exercised his ministry in forms that have changed significantly over the centuries, can in the future function in ways which are better adapted to meet both the universal and regional needs of the church in the complex environment of modern times."

Questions for the Churches: ". . . it is now proper to ask, in the light of the agreement we have been able to reach, that our respective churches take specific actions toward reconciliation.

"Therefore *we ask the Lutheran churches:*

• "If they are prepared to affirm with us that papal primacy, renewed in the light of the gospel, need not be a barrier to reconciliation.

• "If they are able to acknowledge not only the legitimacy of the papal ministry in the service of the Roman Catholic communion but even the possibility and the desirability of the papal ministry, renewed under the gospel and committed to Christian freedom, in a larger communion which would include the Lutheran churches.

• "If they are willing to open discussion regarding the concrete implications of such a primacy to them.

"Likewise, *we ask the Roman Catholic church:*

• "If in the light of our findings, it should not give high priority in its ecumenical concerns to the problem of reconciliation with the Lutheran churches.

• "If it is willing to open discussions on possible structures for reconciliation which would protect the legitimate traditions of the Lutheran communities and respect their spiritual heritage.

• "If it is prepared to envisage the possibility of a reconciliation which would recognize the self-government of Lutheran churches within a communion.

• "If, in the expectation of a foreseeable reconciliation, it is ready to acknowledge the Lutheran dialogue as sister-churches which are already entitled to some measure of ecclesiastical communion."

COMMENT

The convergence of viewpoints said to be indicated in the document above is more apparent than real, in the opinion of some observers. Underlying this view are the facts that the document speaks of at least two different concepts of papacy and primacy, and that there can be no convergence acceptable to the Catholic Church which would jeopardize doctrine concerning papal authority by divine — rather than human — right over the universal Church.

RESPECT FOR LIFE

Catholic observances throughout the United States during October, 1974, emphasized the respect for life which is characteristic of traditional Judaeo-Christian morality. The purpose of the observances, the third of their kind in this country, was to stimulate respect and related action not only on behalf of the unborn but also of the poor, the sick and terminally ill, the handicapped, the elderly, and persons in jail and prison.

The aspect of the observances which caught most attention was their pro-life thrust in seeking ways and means of counteracting legal denial to the unborn of the right to life and the abortion on-demand mentality spawned by decisions of the U.S. Supreme Court.

Court Decisions on Abortion

The U.S. Supreme Court, in a 7 to 2 ruling Jan. 22, 1973, against the constitutionality of abortion laws in Texas (Roe v. Wade) and Georgia (Doe v. Bolton), nullified all criminal abortion statutes in the 50 states except those permitting abortion to save the life of the mother.

The Court ruled:

• During the first three months of pregnancy a woman's right to privacy is paramount. Accordingly, she has an unrestricted right to abortion with the consent and cooperation of a physician.

• In the second trimester, the principle controlling legislation on abortion procedures is the health or welfare of the mother, understood in the widest possible sense.

• In "the stage subsequent to viability," the controlling principles are the State's "interest in the potentiality of human life" and "the preservation of the life or health of the mother." The majority opinion stated: "For the stage subsequent to viability the State, in promoting its interest in the potentiality of human life, may, if it chooses, regulate, and even proscribe, abortion except where necessary, in appropriate medical judgment, for the preservation of the life or health of the mother."

Bishops' Reaction

The Administrative Committee of the National Conference of Catholic Bishops responded to the Court's decision Feb. 13, 1973, in a statement which said, in part:

"We find that this majority opinion of the Court is wrong and is entirely contrary to the fundamental principles of morality. Catholic teaching holds that, regardless of the circumstances of its origin, human life is valuable from conception to death because God is the Creator of each human being, and because mankind has been redeemed by Jesus Christ (cf. *Peace on Earth,* Nos. 9 and 10). No court,

no legislative body, no leader of government, can legitimately assign less value to some human life. Thus, the laws that conform to the opinion of the Court are immoral laws, in opposition to God's plan of creation and to the Divine Law which prohibits the destruction of human life at any point of its existence. Whenever a conflict arises between the law of God and any human law, we are held to follow God's law."

(See Abortion entry in Glossary.)

Other Reactions

Spokesmen of pro-life groups were as vocal in dissent as long-term and short-term proponents of legalized abortion were in agreement with the ruling. Among the latter were the American Civil Liberties Union. Planned Parenthood — World Population, the National Organization of Women, and the National Association for the Repeal of Abortion Laws, a coalition of 75 pro-abortion organizations. Joining them later were a national Religious Coalition for Abortion Rights and a group calling itself Catholics for a Free Choice.

The attitudes of various church bodies on the question were mixed. Definite opposition to the Court's decision, however, was in line with known positions of the Assemblies of God, the Lutheran Church — Missouri Synod, the Mormons, the Evangelical Methodist Church, the Baptist General Convention and the Evangelical Free Church of America. Degrees of ambivalence were evident in the statements of several large Protestant churches. Orthodox Christians and Orthodox Jews were firm in opposition.

Pro-life advocates of many religious persuasions reached the conclusion early in the post-decision period that the constitutional route is the one that has to be pursued for a federal amendment to guarantee to the unborn the status of legal recognition as a person with the right to life. Several versions of such an amendment have been introduced in the Congress. Their intended purposes are not only to prevent death to the unborn but also to safeguard the inviolability of life after birth — especially with respect to the aged, the handicapped, and other persons considered by some to be burdens to society.

Senate Hearings

The first of several hearings on two pro-life amendments were held by the Senate Subcommittee on Constitutional Amendments early in March, 1974. The amendments were those proposed by Republican Sen. Jesse Helms of North Carolina (to outlaw abortion entirely) and by Conservative-Republican Sen. James L. Buckley of New York (to allow abortion only "in an emergency situation when a reasonable medical certainty exists that the continuation of the pregnancy will cause the death of the mother").

Among those giving testimony in favor of a pro-life amendment were Cardinals John J. Krol, John P. Cody, Timothy Manning and Humberto Medeiros. One theme of testimony by them and others was that the findings of science and the American legal tradition indicate that the fetus is a person from the moment of conception and is entitled to the rights of personhood guaranteed by the 14th Amendment to the U.S. Constitution.

Opposite views were voiced by other witnesses during the hearings, which resulted in no legislative action.

Legislative Action

Action on restrictive abortion bills in state legislatures during 1974 was generally unproductive because of adverse court decisions. A new Minnesota statute, for example, providing that abortions could be performed after the 20th week of pregnancy only to save the life of the mother, was enjoined in May by a three-judge federal court in St. Paul.

In New York, however, Governor Malcolm Wilson signed into law June 18 a bill providing that abortions after the 12th week of pregnancy be done in a hospital and requiring the attendance of a second physician — to safeguard the possible survival of the fetus — at all abortions performed after the 20th week.

Conscience Clauses

Conscience clauses — generally granting civil and criminal immunity to health personnel and institutions (with some exceptions) refusing to cooperate in abortion procedures for moral, ethical or religious reasons — or their equivalent have been adopted in 39 states. The Catholic Hospital Association reported that, as of Feb. 4, 1974, states without such clauses or providing doubtful protection of this kind were: Alabama, Arkansas, Kentucky, New Hampshire, New Jersey, Ohio, Oklahoma, Pennsylvania, Texas, Vermont and West Virginia.

Indiana Attorney General Theodore L. Sendak ruled Apr. 29, 1974, that the conscience clause in the state's 1973 abortion law applies to public, tax-supported hospitals as well as to private hospitals. He said the law states: "No individual may be compelled to perform an abortion against his will. No hospital may be required to permit its facilities to be utilized for the performance of abortions."

Court Decisions

In 1974 court decisions related to abortion statutes, two federal appeals courts ruled — in Richmond, Va., Mar. 4, and Boston, Mass., Aug. 7 — that indigent pregnant women are entitled to welfare payments for unborn children under the Aid to Families with Dependent Children section of the So-cial Security Act. The Richmond court did not rule on the question of whether an unborn child has a constitutional right to such aid. The Boston opinion noted that a fetus may be in need "of material and medical assistance as easily as a new-born infant, or any child for that matter," and is therefore eligible for Social Security benefits.

In May the U.S. Supreme Court let stand a lower court ruling that states cannot nullify its 1973 decisions on abortion by legislating that a fetus is a "person" entitled to constitutional protection. The lower court held that Rhode Island's 1973 abortion law was unconstitutional because it said that a fetus becomes a "person" at the moment of conception. Only the Supreme Court can declare who is a "person" under the Constitution, the court said.

Right-to-life organizations and individuals, becoming increasingly aware of the need for political clout and public sentiment in support of a pro-life constitutional amendment, made some direct approaches — in Indiana and Arizona, for example — to candidates seeking public office in the 1974 elections. A number of Catholic publications refused advertising from candidates favoring liberal abortion practices. The short and long term effectiveness of such tactics was hopeful but problematic.

Sterilization, Fetal Research

Two other areas of concern to the pro-life movement are sterilization and fetal research.

Eighteen state legislatures considered sterilization bills during 1974. (Twenty-six states had laws providing for sterilization of the insane, retarded and epileptics, as of Aug. 31, 1973.) Msgr. James T. McHugh, director of the Family Life Division, U.S. Catholic Conference, reported in May that he detected in the related proceedings a developing trend away from concern for human rights and toward a "survival of the fittest" mentality. Many of the bills, he said, were "eugenic in intent" or aimed at cutting state welfare roles.

In Washington, U.S. District Court Judge Gerhard A. Gesell declared in March that existing regulations of the Department of Health, Education and Welfare — allowing sterilization of minors and the mentally incompetent — were illegal and invaded "the basic human right to procreate." He said the regulations sought "to sanction one of the most drastic methods of population control — the involuntary, irreversible sterilization of men and women — without any legislative guidance." He also cited "incontrovertible evidence" that minors and the mentally incompetent had been sterilized with federal funds.

The National Institutes of Health have adopted a policy against providing funds for research on aborted fetuses whose hearts are still beating. Regulations sought from the Department of Health, Education and Welfare during 1974 were destined to check the experimental use of fetuses before or after abortion, even though they were not viable. Experiments have been reported in which fetuses were kept alive artificially for long periods after abortion.

Euthanasia

One of the strongest bids to legalize euthanasia has been made in the Florida legislature. Its latest defeat was registered in 1974 when the state senate declined to act on a "death with dignity" bill presented for the sixth consecutive year.

Dr. Arthur Dyck, professor of population ethics at Harvard University, told a regional conference of the Catholic Hospital Association in Boston in March that the lessening of legal restrictions on abortions was creating a climate of acceptance for infanticide and euthanasia.

Right-to-Life Groups

Despite the opinion in some quarters that right-to-life advocates might just as well have fallen over dead after the Supreme Court decisions of 1973, pro-life organizations have shown remarkable vigor in combatting pro-abortion sentiment and relaxed legal standards.

In the process, however, they have been subject to strong counter-campaigns which have labeled them fanatical, criticized them for sensationalism, scored them as hostile to "rights" of women and privacy, and charged them with attempts to subvert the U.S. Constitution.

One of the least credible of the charges is that they are all Catholic inspired and dominated. Such is not the case. Catholic visibility is high in some sectors of the movement, but it is nowhere nearly as dominant as detractors claim.

Representative organizations with members of all religious and philosophical convictions who are concerned with the right-to-life of the unborn and related issues include the following: the National Right-to-Life Committee, the National Committee for a Human Life Amendment, the Ad Hoc Committee in Defense of Life, National Nurses for Life, the Committee of Ten Million, the American Association of Pro-Life Obstetricians and Gynecologists, Alternatives to Abortion, and various groups with Concerned for Life and Right-to-Life titles.

The Alliance for Life is a Canadian organization.

The unique purpose and operations of Brithright are described below.

Law professors have said that a pro-life amendment would be ineffective because the Supreme Court has already given priority of rights to the mother of the unborn.

BIRTHRIGHT

Birthright is a nondenominational counseling and referral service organization offering pregnant women alternatives to abortion, in line with the motto, "It is the right of every pregnant woman to give birth and the right of every child to be born."

Started by Mrs. Louise Summerhill of Toronto, Canada, in 1968, it has chapters in Canada, in the United States and the United Kingdom. Each of these units, manned by volunteers, operates telephone contact services for women in crises of pregnancy and counsels them in what one spokesman calls the "panic period so that they can solve their problems" and avoid the decision for abortion they really do not want to make. It is believed that Birthright services have been instrumental in saving the lives of several hundred thousand babies in North America.

The executive director of Birthright, U.S.A., is Mrs. D. Cocciolone, 18 Euclid St., Woodbury, N.J. 08096.

Birthright, although it has Catholics among its volunteers and draws some support from Catholic sources, insists on its original independent and nondenominational character. Its operations have been adopted by other pro-life groups. Birthright telephone numbers are listed in scores of local directories.

A number of groups have merged the counseling function of Birthright with activist programs of their own to counteract liberalized abortion legislation and practices. Among them are groups with titles like Pro Life, Right to Life, the Coalition for Life, Citizens for Life, Spanish Right to Life in Miami, and the Human Life Amendment Committee headquartered in Washington, D.C.

HUMAN LIFE FOUNDATION

The Human Life Foundation came into being in 1968 as the bishops of the United States responded to the appeal of Pope Paul VI for the initiation of scientific research to improve methods of child spacing in keeping with the tenets of his encyclical, *Humanae Vitae.* The foundation, with a grant of $800,000 in seed money provided by the bishops, became operational in 1969. A nonprofit, tax-exempt charitable foundation, it is totally independent and self-governing with a board of 12 directors, all of whom are laymen and scientists.

Natural family planning research sponsored and funded by the foundation and carried out in the strictest fashion by independent scientists and institutions has verified the validity and reliability of natural methods — as distinct from chemical and mechanical methods — of birth regulation.

Dr. William A. Lynch is chairman of the foundation's science committee. Lawrence J. Kane is executive director. Offices are located at 1776 K St. N.W., Washington, D.C. 20006.

HUMAN DEVELOPMENT

The Campaign for Human Development was undertaken by the U.S. Catholic Conference in November, 1969, to combat poverty in this country in three significant ways:

• by making people in this country, Catholics in particular, aware of poverty among some 35 million persons through programs of education and public information;

• by raising funds to finance programs designed to attack the root causes of poverty;

• by funding self-help programs begun and implemented by the poor.

The campaign got underway with a collection taken up in parishes throughout the country Nov. 22, 1970. The proceeds, the largest ever received in a single, national Catholic collection, amounted to $8.5 million. Seventy-five percent of the money ($6,262,184.72) was earmarked for allocation to self-help projects by a 40-member national committee; 25 per cent ($2.1 million) remained in dioceses where it was collected for similar allocation by committees on local levels.

More than 1,100 fund requests were reviewed by the national committee in 1971, and grants were awarded to 231 organizations for a wide variety of projects.

The second nationwide collection in support of the campaign, made in the fall of 1971, raised close to $7 million. More than 2,000 requests for funding were filed for review by March, 1972, and by Sept. 12 more than 50 organizations were awarded grants totaling more than $1.5 million. Additional allocations of funds were made later in the year.

CHD headquarters, in announcing its first funding of 1973, reported Oct. 4 that $3.4 million had been awarded to 117 community organizations of the poor in 37 states, the District of Columbia and three U.S. possessions. As of that date, a grand total of nearly $20 million had been allocated to more than 500 self-help projects.

In 1974, approximately 155 projects were approved for funding by Sept. 9. The cumulative total of the allotments was $4,593,050.

Father Lawrence J. McNamara of Kansas City, Mo., is executive director.

Offices are located at 1312 Massachusetts Ave. N.W., Washington, D.C. 20005.

UN WORLD POPULATION CONFERENCE

The portion of the following article starting with the head, "Emphasis on Development," consists of parts of two reports by John Muthig of NC News Service.

The first two-week-long United Nations World Population Conference ended Aug. 30, 1974, with agreement by some 1,250 delegates from 135 nations on a "World Population Plan of Action" for the integration of population policies with policies for economic and social development.

The 108-item document produced by the conference in Bucharest, Rumania, did not set any population-limitation goals in terms of numbers. It suggested, however, that individual nations, through programs formulated by themselves, could substantially reduce the two per cent world population growth rate by 1985.

The "Plan of Action" advocated equality for women in all walks of life, and also appealed to affluent nations to reduce their consumption of natural and other resources for reasons of "international equity."

Two Viewpoints

Before and during the conference, the delegations of the more affluent nations attempted to get the conference to treat population as an issue separate from the issue of human development and to give excessive emphasis to demographic questions. This attempt came to naught when the delegations of the less developed nations, with two-thirds of the world's population, refused to accept any plan for action which failed to place population growth problems in the context of their need for economic and social development.

Population Figures

World population reached one billion in 1830, two billion by 1930, three billion by 1960, and was estimated to be 3.86 billion in 1973. Demographers estimate that, at the current growth rate, that number will be doubled in 35 years. The United Nations estimate for the year 2000 is 6.5 billion.

Emphasis on Development

As far as the United Nations is concerned, development has clearly become the new word for population policy, replacing the old exclusive emphasis on birth control.

That message was delivered by delegates from 135 nations at the UN-sponsored World Population Conference in Bucharest where the world's developing nations snatched the thunder of the mighty nations, which had banked on a campaign to reduce births.

The developing nations were able to alter the conference's major document, the "Plan of Action," and have it say: "Population policies are constituent elements of socio-economic development policies, never substitutes for them."

The conference's heavy emphasis on development rather than on outright birth limitation seemed to stem from two strong sentiments:

• The practical frustrations of nations such as India, which had tried to decrease births, through contraception and sterilization, but failed. In their view, socio-economic improvement was not occurring fast enough.

• From the adamant anger of other emerging lands which viewed birth limitation programs and the whole rationale behind the western nations' population program as a plot by "neo-colonialist" powers to keep the Third World of less developed nations in an exploitable position.

Against Overconsumption

Not only did the Third World succeed in inserting into the "Plan of Action" language concerning positive steps — such as improvement of maternal and child health care, lowering of mortality rates, and heightened status for women — but they also included several digs at the overconsuming developed world.

The way of life of the rich nations, according to the plan, "can produce harmful effects, such as wasteful and excessive consumption, and activities which produce pollution."

Control Suggestions

But actual birth-curbing measures, though played down in the conference document, were not absent from it. The conference adopted as a principle of action that "all couples and individuals have the basic human right to decide freely and responsibly the number and spacing of their children, and to have the information, education and means to do so."

The conference backed away from recommending an ideal family size or from setting hard and fast growth-rate targets for various regions of the world, as some developed nations had advocated. But the plan did "invite" nations to consider adopting their own targets regarding birth rates.

The conference also erased from the draft "Plan of Action" a paragraph which stated that the United Nations accepted 1985 as a target date by which any couple in the world who desire it should have education and information on contraception as well as the means for regulating births.

Vatican View

The Vatican delegation to the conference was the only one of 136 delegations to officially dissociate itself from the "Plan of Action."

Bishop Edouard Gagnon, head of the delegation, told the plenary session that the Holy See took this action because of "persistent ambiguities, the introduction of unfortunate expressions, and the omission of certain essential elements" in the final version of the plan.

He stressed in his speech that the Vatican heartily endorsed sections of the plan that placed population policies within the broader context of "integral human development" and within the "establishment of a new economic order in the spirit of international jus-

tice and equalization of worldwide consumption."

But he said that, unlike sovereign states which could deal with the "Plan of Action" on a selective and practical basis within their own lands, the Holy See could deal with it only on the level of principles and values. Some values in the plan, he explained, were unacceptable, especially several sections dealing with "the family, respect for life and indiscriminate use of birth-preventive means."

"You will all appreciate that here we are dealing with elements about which the Holy See by its very nature can allow no compromise." Bishop Gagnon said. The Holy See "must be faithful to him from whom she receives her mission, and likewise to the whole community to whom she offers her cooperation in a spirit of fraternal service."

The bishop told delegates in the final hours of the conference that the Holy See could not risk a misunderstanding of its position, and therefore could not accept the plan, even on a qualified basis.

Delegation Active

Throughout the conference the Vatican delegation took an active and highly visible role. It was able to have its effect on the final "Plan of Action."

Most notable among Vatican amendments accepted into the plan was a clause stating: "Independently of the realization of economic and social objectives, respect for human life is basic to all human societies."

The delegation fought for language that would protect a couple's right to have more children as well as fewer, and for an affirmation that a woman's choice of the role of wife and mother is not inconsistent with her full integration into a nation's political, cultural, social and economic life. These sentiments, however, were not picked up in the final document.

The delegation also tried to have removed a phrase which said that the world should aim to reduce "illegal abortions." The text called for reduction in fertility, defective births and illegal abortion, and the Vatican argued that illegal abortion was a legal question while the others were medical questions. It asked that "miscarriage" — also a medical problem — be substituted for illegal abortion.

But both attempts failed by a vote of 46 to 11, with 10 abstentions and a number of delegations not present for voting.

No Spiritual Considerations

The Vatican delegation was chagrined that the conference ignored spiritual and human considerations in the plan. At one point, Bishop Gagnon reminded the plenary session that man must not be made a servant of "economic and technological goals." He said the job of the conference was not to protect such goals but to "celebrate life."

AMNESTY

President Gerald R. Ford, in a proclamation and two executive orders signed Sept. 16, 1974, offered conditional amnesty to draft evaders and military deserters who had not been convicted or punished, and clemency to those already convicted or under punishment for draft evasion or desertion from military service.

Amnesty

The conditions of amnesty for evaders and deserters at large were:

• That they turn themselves over to appropriate authorities and apply for amnesty by Jan. 31, 1975.

• That they reaffirm "hereafter (to) bear true faith and allegiance" to the United States.

• That they accept a period of public service work not to exceed 24 months — a term subject to reduction because of mitigating circumstances.

• That they would receive a clemency category discharge on fulfillment of these conditions.

The evasion or desertion for which amnesty was offered must have occurred between Aug. 4, 1964, the date of the Senate's Tonkin Gulf Resolution, and Mar. 28, 1973, when the last U.S. combat personnel left Vietnam.

Estimates of the number of men considered eligible for amnesty under these terms ranged from 28,000 to 50,000. Some 4,500 were thought to be in Canada, and about 400 in Sweden.

The plan required those returning from outside the U.S. to apply for amnesty within 15 days of their return.

Attorney General William B. Saxbe estimated that some 2,500 draft evaders and probably more deserters would apply for amnesty. Early response to the invitation to amnesty and clemency, however, was slow and light.

The presidential proclamation ruled out complete pardon.

It also provided that prosecution under original charges would take place against those failing to apply for amnesty by Jan. 31, 1975, and against those failing to comply with amnesty conditions.

Clemency

President Ford established a nine-member clemency board to deal with the cases of men already convicted or under punishment for draft evasion or desertion from military service during the period mentioned above. He authorized it to review petitions for clemency and to make appropriate recommendations to him on a case-by-case basis.

The President named former Republican Senator Charles E. Goodell of New York chairman of the board. Its members included Father Theodore M. Hesburgh, C.S.C., president of Notre Dame University.

Goodell announced Sept. 16 that the board would first handle the cases of men under detention for draft evasion or desertion.

On the same day, the attorney general ordered the release of such men petitioning for clemency for a 30-day period pending resolution of their cases. Ninety-five were in the first group released. Within a week, 120 were gathered at Camp Atterbury, Ind., to await action by the board.

Favorable action by the board and the President would result in discharge from confinement and the grant of an undesirable discharge from service. This could be converted into a clemency category discharge on the fulfillment of a period of public service work.

Clemency board action was ruled out for evaders or deserters imprisoned for other offenses under the Uniform Code of Military Justice.

Reactions

The Ford plan drew mixed reactions from various quarters.

Veterans' organizations generally opposed it, claiming that it went too far and that its provisions were unfair to those who served, suffered and died in the fulfillment of military obligations, and prejudicial to respect for law and order in general.

Spokesmen for evaders and deserters, saying the plan did not go far enough, described it as a "gross miscarriage of justice" against men who had refused to take part in a war they considered immoral in itself and in its conduct. They charged the country with moral dereliction and called for total and unconditional amnesty for all evaders and deserters.

Unconditional amnesty had also been and was still being called for by others, including some Catholic leaders and organizations.

The Executive Board of the U.S. Catholic Conference "greatly welcomed" the Ford plan, finding it in line with appeals for conditional amnesty — with acceptance of "some form of service to the community" — made by the conference in 1971 and 1973.

The board also observed in a statement issued the day the plan was announced that Pope Paul VI had made a general appeal for amnesty in proclaiming Holy Year 1975. The Pope said he hoped the leaders of nations would "consider the possibility of wisely granting an amnesty to prisoners, as a witness to clemency and equity, especially to those who have given sufficient proof of moral and civic rehabilitation, or may have been caught up in political and social upheavals too immense to be held fully responsible."

The degree of public acceptance of the President's plan was uncertain as initial processing of petitions for amnesty and clemency got underway.

PRISON REFORM

Issues connected with criminal justice and 22 suggested prison reform measures were the subjects of a statement approved by the bishops of the U.S. at their Nov. 12 to 16, 1973, annual meeting in Washington, D.C.

The statement was one of many on the same subject issued in the past several years by individual bishops, the National Federation of Priests' Councils, the Conference of Major Superiors of Men (Religious), numerous organizations of sisters and state Catholic conferences, and other religious and civic associations.

The citations below are from the text circulated by the NC Documentary Service, Origins, Nov. 22, 1973 (Vol. 3, No. 22). Subheads and lead lines have been added.

Background Observations

"Punishment, in order to fulfill its proper purpose, must fit the nature of the crime; it must be considerate of the offender's human dignity; and, it must be tempered by mercy and constantly aimed at reconciliation."

Related Problems: "The injustices and inequities that plague our society affect both the incidence of crime and the administration of correctional institutions. The problems in these institutions are also intimately bound up with the inadequacies of our judicial system. These include unreasonably delayed trials, particularly aggravating when the accused is jailed; the lack both of quality and adequate quantity of legal counsel for the needy; difficulties with bail bonds; and widespread abuses of such useful expedients as plea bargaining."

"Several broad issues of criminal justice are distinct from, but related to, conditions in correctional institutions. One is the general slowness and inadequacy of federal and state judicial procedures. Delays and overloads by themselves raise serious questions of equity, most often adversely affecting the poor. The rights of the accused should be protected before and during trial. Before formal charges are made, adequate evidence should be an absolute requirement. Additional analyses and funding to reorganize the criminal justice system to accord with the best aspirations of all our people should be given urgent priority."

Compensation for Victims: "Recompense for the innocent victims of crime is a sensitive and painful problem. Society must share at least some of the responsibility for compensating innocent victims of crime. When a way is found to pay offenders a fair rate for the work they do in confinement, provisions should be made for regular court-determined payments as at least partial recompense to their victims, or the survivors of the victims of their crimes."

Big Prisons or Community-Based Facilities?

"Whether the penal system of the United States should not seek to deal with all except dangerous offenders outside of penal institutions is a question which merits much attention. . . . There is increasing and strongly convincing evidence that a large center of incarceration should not be the major instrument for dealing with convicted offenders. Bigger, better, more modern buildings are not the answer.

"Smaller, community-based facilities are beginning to prove that they are more appropriate and effective. Half-way houses, work contracts and other alternatives need to be more fully explored."

What Are Prisons For? "When one examines the situation of confined, convicted criminals, one finds an urgent need to clarify precisely what society is seeking to achieve in their incarceration. Is a correctional institution an instrument of punishment whereby a criminal 'does time' in expiation for his misdeeds? Is it a place of custody where a dangerous citizen is detained in order to protect and restore order in society? Is it a means of retribution designed to deter the criminal himself and/or the populace at large from engaging in unlawful behavior? Is a correctional institution ultimately a place for rehabilitation in which a criminal is re-educated or reconciled to a lawful way of life? We feel it is, or ought to be, a composite of all of these, but that preeminently it is a place of rehabilitation.

"Correctional institutions in fact do harm if they do not offer opportunity for rehabilitation. We are unequivocally committed to the view that rehabilitation should be their primary concern."

Failure To Rehabilitate: "There is general agreement among qualified commentators that the correctional institutions of our land have, in most cases, failed in the matter of rehabilitation. . . . It is true, of course, that rehabilitation is not the only purpose of prisons and that their historic purpose has been to incarcerate. However, even the effectiveness of prisons in incarcerating is related to their effectiveness in rehabilitation. Certainly with regard to rehabilitation, they are, in general, not performing acceptably."

"Society has a right to protect itself against lawbreakers and even to exact just and measured retribution, but the limits of what is reasonable and just (in penal conditions and punishment) are far exceeded in too many penal institutions. Abuses cannot be justified on the basis of their effectiveness as deterrents to crime. The disturbing statistics of recidivism demonstrate that our correctional institutions have little deterrent effect. It is necessary in any case to raise serious moral objection to tormenting one man unjustly in order to instruct or caution another."

Rehabilitative Purpose: "Correctional institutions should be institutions of rehabilitation. . . . They are places of custody, but they are never to be only that. They are also instruments of retribution and in a measure strategies for deterrence. These purposes, nevertheless, are to be kept in balance with the need to safeguard the moral order in society while at the same time assisting in the rehabilitation of offending human beings who urgently need society's understanding and care."

Suggestions for Reform

"We offer the following suggestions for reform in the correctional institutions of the United States. . . . Our fundamental purpose remains throughout — to insure protection for all the civil rights of confined offenders in an atmosphere of human compassion conducive to reconciliation and rehabilitation."

"1. Correctional institutions whose residents come mainly from urban centers should usually be located near these centers."

"2. Staffs should be recruited on the basis of ability, training and experience without reference to partisan politics."

Varying Needs: "3. In developing programs and facilities careful consideration to the varying needs of men and women are important. Male residents should be separated from female residents in different facilities; juveniles from adults; first offenders from repeaters; sexual offenders in specialized treatment centers. The emotionally disturbed should be treated in institutions designed for this purpose. The availability of educational training and any other appropriate programs for men and women together should be investigated. Extraordinary efforts should be made to rehabilitate juvenile offenders. Few, if any, offenders should be deprived of access to family and friends."

"4. Discrimination because of race, religion, or national or ethnic background is never tolerable."

Practice of Religion: "5. Free exercise of religion should be guaranteed in every institution. Religious services of various faiths and denominations should be regularly available; chaplains should be welcomed on a continuing or an occasion-by-occasion basis, as needed; and dietary laws should be respected. Residents should be free to consult their chaplains in private and at length. The chaplains should never be constrained to testify before parole boards or to share privileged information with members of the staff. Chaplains should not be required to serve on administrative boards which make decisions about discipline, parole, or probation."

Regulations in Writing: "6. All residents should be given the regulations of the institution in writing. They should be advised of their rights and privileges, their responsibilities and obligations, punishments to which they are subject for infractions of regulations, and established grievance procedures. . . . The regulations should be available not only

to inspectors but also to the general public."

"7. Residents should never be authorized to punish one another. Members of the staff should not inflict any punishments other than those stipulated in the regulations for a particular infraction. . . . Penalties which are of their nature cruel or degrading are to be excluded."

"8. All residents should be afforded protection against all assault, sexual or otherwise, even if this requires a transfer."

Education and Work: "9. At least elementary and secondary education and vocational training that is truly useful in free society should be provided all residents who wish to take advantage of these opportunities."

"10. The work to which a resident is assigned should be — and appear to be — worthwhile and compatible with the dignity of a human being. . . . National standards . . . should be adopted and promulgated regarding compensation for work."

"11. National standards should be adopted and promulgated regarding residents' diets," environmental conditions and the availability of medical and psychiatric care.

No Forced Treatments: "12. A resident should be free to refuse treatments, aimed at social rehabilitation, whose appropriateness can be called into question by reasonable persons in and outside the institution. No penalties of any kind should result from such refusal."

Communications Rights: "13. National standards should be adopted and promulgated regarding the residents' right to send and receive mail, censorship of mail (allowing for necessary inspection), access to printed literature within the institution and from without, and opportunities to listen to the radio and watch television."

"14. Authorities should encourage visiting by residents' relatives, friends and acquaintances. . . . Where feasible, opportunity and facilities for conjugal visits should be provided for married residents and their spouses. . . . Furloughs should be more liberal, when this is prudent, in order to strengthen family life. . . . Work-release programs should be extended as far as feasible. Obviously the above opportunities could be made available only to offenders who exhibit an interest in rehabilitation."

Civil Rights Code: "15. A national committee . . . should be assigned the task of establishing a national code of civil rights for the incarcerated and the development of standardized grievance and due-process procedures as well as a bill of rights clearly defining the extent of duties and limits of obligations of the incarcerated."

"16. National standards should be adopted and promulgated regarding the inspection of correctional institutions."

"17. No resident should be detained simply because employment (outside) is not available. . . . Career counseling, testing, guidance and bonding — where applicable — should be offered all who are preparing to be released."

"18. A resident should be informed of the date beyond which further detention demands another intervention of the court."

Parole: "19. Parole is a vital function, both for the offender and for society. Consideration should be given to shifting the 'burden of proof' by making a parole automatic after a definitely determined period of confinement unless there is sound reason against it."

"20. Congress should investigate the feasibility of extending the Social Security Act (OASDI) coverage to residents of correctional institutions."

"21. After release ex-offenders, upon their resumption of life in society, should have their civil rights completely restored."

Arrest Records: "22. The use and dissemination of arrest records should be strictly controlled. The revelation of arrest records, where there was no conviction, should be forbidden, as should the denial of employment for reason of an arrest without conviction."

Care should be taken to prevent exceptions to the foregoing from degenerating into abuses.

Parole and Jails

The statement cited the parole system as an issue "closely connected with concerns about correctional reform." Also involved are the "conditions in jails for those awaiting trial." Of these the statement said:

"In our nation a man is presumed innocent until proved guilty. Yet after arrest he may spend many months awaiting trial in jail under conditions that can only be described as penal. Usually it is the poor who suffer most under these circumstances (because of inability to secure adequate legal counsel or to pay bail). Deprived of freedom, . . . the accused may well wonder just how much value the legal presumption of innocence really has. . . . If the prisons of our nation need reform, so also do the jails — a great many of which are houses of terror."

The statement urged state Catholic conferences, religious communities, parishes and other Catholic groups to develop programs in support of its 22 suggested measures for prison reform.

PRINCIPLES REGARDING HOMOSEXUALITY

"Principles To Guide Confessors in Questions of Homosexuality" was the title of a booklet published Mar. 1, 1974, by the Committee on Pastoral Research and Practices of the National Conference of Catholic Bishops. The principles upheld the traditional view of the Church that homosexuality is not normal and that homosexual relationships are objectively wrong — although the subjective responsibility of homosexuals for such relations may be conditioned and diminished by compulsion and related factors.

Guidelines

Following is a brief synopsis of the guidelines.

"Genital sexual expression should take place only in marriage. Apart from the intentions of the man and of the woman, sexual intercourse has a two-fold meaning. It is an act of union with the beloved, and it is procreative. Neither meaning may be excluded, although for a variety of reasons the procreative meaning may not be attained. By their nature homosexual acts exclude all possibility of procreation of life. (They) are a grave transgression of the goals of human sexuality and of human personality, and are consequently contrary to the will of God."

"The subjective morality of homosexual acts must be considered under two aspects, the origin of the tendency, and the manner in which the person controls it."

"It can be said safely that man or woman does not will to become homosexual. At a certain point in life the person discovers that he is homosexual and usually suffers a certain

amount of trauma. . . . In every case he discovers an already existing condition."

The guidelines note that this condition (regarded by some psychologists as an arrested state of sexual development) involves varying degrees of compulsion.

Assessing Responsibility

"In assessing the responsibility of the homosexual the confessor must avoid both harshness and permissiveness. It is difficult for the homosexual to remain chaste in his environment, and he may slip into sin for a variety of reasons, including loneliness and compulsive tendencies and the pull of homosexual companions. But, generally, he is responsible for his actions, and the worst thing that a confessor can say is that the homosexual is not responsible for his actions.

"This does not mean that in most cases the homosexual has full freedom of will."

Confessors, with due regard for individuals and particular circumstances, are advised to encourage homosexuals to change their sexual orientation, to live a life of chastity, to encourage the formation of stable friendships, to take necessary measures to prevent them from being occasions of sin, to break off from relationships which are regular occasions of sin.

Counterclaims

The guidelines noted that "some Catholic homosexuals argue that, as long as the person is trying to serve God and neighbor, the fact of his sexual deviation is of no major consequence. . . . To these relatively new arguments the confessor should respond with firmness, showing how erroneous is the idea that each person has the right to variety in sexual expression contingent upon his sexual orientation."

Such claims have been advanced by Dignity, an organization of Catholic homosexuals with a reported membership of 850 to 1,000 in about 20 cities of the United States. There were at least 200 organizations of homosexuals in the U.S. in 1974. One of them was the four-and-one-half-year-old Universal Fellowship of Metropolitan Churches, headquartered in Los Angeles, which was reported to have 43 congregations in 19 states and London, England, and an international membership of 15,000.

Dissenting Views

The basic principles of the guidelines are at variance with those advanced by some theologians.

Father Gregory Baum, writing in the Feb. 15, 1974, edition of *Commonweal,* questioned the validity of the traditional concept that homosexual acts are against the law of nature. He stated his basic position in this way: "The important question . . . is whether homosexuality is open to mutuality. Is the homosexual capable of grounding friendship that enables the partners to grow and become more truly human? This is the crucial question. For the structure of redeemed life is mutuality."

According to Father John O'Neill, S.J., associate professor of moral theology at Woodstock College, New York City, "the most desirable alternative (for a homosexual) is heterosexual adjustment, but this is possible in only a small number of cases." Total sexual abstinence, "when this does not result in a serious breakdown or other serious difficulties," is the next best alternative. If neither of these alternatives is possible, he advises the formation of "a personal relationship based on love" with another person, a relationship which does not exclude physical love. "This arrangement," he says, "is certainly preferable to promiscuity." Father O'Neill's views became known at the first convention of Dignity in September 1973. It was disclosed in January, 1974, that his religious superiors had been asked by the Congregation for the Doctrine of the Faith to conduct an inquiry into this theological stance and pastoral practice among homosexuals.

Another opinion, "proposed by comparatively few theologians, sees human sexuality, homo or hetero, only in terms of the quality of the relationship and not in terms of the sex of the other person involved in their relationship." The opinion was cited but not accepted by Father Charles Curran, a moral theologian at the Catholic University of America.

A report by the Gay Ministry Task Force of the Salvatorian Fathers in Milwaukee, published in March, 1974, called not for moral judgment of homosexuality but for a ministry to overcome what was called religious, cultural, legal and social oppression of homosexuals. The report disclaimed theological orientation, but Father Curran noted: "The rationale of the paper throughout is that there is nothing wrong with homosexual relations per se (in themselves) and that there is no difference between homosexuality and heterosexuality. The entire argument of the paper rests on this theological assumption." Such an assumption, along with its corollaries, is not in line with the pastoral and confessional principles stated by the bishops.

The task force report was published after being rejected as "incomplete" at the March, 1974, convention of the National Federation of Priests' Councils.

Appeals for a special ministry to homosexuals, based on acceptance of homosexuality and its various elements as normal, amount to appeals for a change in theological position by the Church. Father Curran has observed that "the primary reason why the Catholic Church has not had a (specific) ministry for gays has been because of its theological position." That position remains unchanged. The confessional guidelines issued by the NCCB make it clear that such a ministry, like all other forms of pastoral ministry, is subject to control by the moral and sacramental requirements set by the Church.

Civil Rights

Limitations on the range of pastoral ministry to homosexuals, as noted in the foregoing article, do not extend to their civil rights. This was noted by Cardinal John Dearden in a letter addressed to priests of the Detroit archdiocese in August, 1974. While reaffirming the teaching of the Church regarding homosexuality, he called for respect for the "proper civil rights" of homosexuals. He said that "arbitrary discrimination" against them is unwarranted and that they are entitled "to fairness and justice."

Opponents of civil rights legislation for homosexuals argue that such laws — in effect in at least 11 U.S. cities by the summer of 1974 — condone and give respectability to homosexuality as a life-style, involve threats of deviant influence, and endanger the values of sexual responsibility and family stability.

These and other arguments, in addition to the stated opposition of archdiocesan officials and various citizen groups, influenced the action of the New York City Council in voting down a civil rights bill in May, 1974.

The opinions of Catholics on the subject are mixed. They appear, however, to be weighted on the negative side.

While the Church does not regard the condition of homosexuality as sinful, it does so regard acts against nature.

CATHOLIC CHARISMATIC RENEWAL

Approximately 25,000 persons from the United States, Canada and other countries attended the June 14 to 16, 1974, International Conference on Charismatic Renewal in the Catholic Church on the campus of Notre Dame University, South Bend, Ind. (See June News Events.) The number was significant as an indicator of the rapid growth of the movement when compared with the 90 participants in the first such conference held in February, 1967.

Background

The movement originated with a handful of Duquesne University students and faculty members in the 1966-67 academic year and spread from there to Notre Dame, Michigan State University and the University of Michigan, other campuses and cities throughout this country.

Scriptural keys to the renewal are:
• Christ's promise to send the Holy Spirit upon the Apostles;
• the description, in the Acts of the Apostles, of the effects of the coming of the Holy Spirit upon the Apostles on Pentecost;
• St. Paul's explanation, in the Letter to the Romans, of the charismatic gifts (for the good of the Church and persons) the Holy Spirit would bestow on Christians;
• New Testament evidence concerning the effects of charismatic gifts in and through the early Church.

Baptism of the Spirit

The personal key to the renewal is Baptism of the Holy Spirit. This is not a new sacrament but the personally experienced actualization of grace already sacramentally received. It is variously described as "a filling with grace and power first recorded in Scripture when the Holy Spirit descended on the Apostles on the day of Pentecost" (whence the name Pentecostals), and as "the release of the power of the Holy Spirit received in the sacrament of confirmation." Its result, according to Stephen Clark, a leader of the movement, is "a change in our relationships with God such that we begin to experience in our lives all the things which God promised that the Holy Spirit would do for believers."

Other Gifts

Other charisms or gifts are secondary in importance to the Baptism of the Spirit and its effects in daily life. Other gifts might be speaking and interpreting strange tongues, healing, prophecy, the interpretation of events. The gift of tongues, whatever it is, is regarded by leaders of the movement as the least of the gifts. Emphasis on its bizarre features by some, as well as the elitism of some groups, has not helped the reputation of the movement.

Among the movement's strongest points of emphasis are prayer, openness to the Holy Spirit, community experience and the sharing of spiritual gifts.

Prayer Meeting and Purpose

The characteristic form of the renewal is the weekly prayer meeting, a gathering which includes periods of spontaneous prayer, singing, sharing of experience and testimony, fellowship and teaching. Leadership teams usually guide the meetings and other activities associated with the movement, such as programs to help newcomers experience the Baptism of the Spirit and seminars on subjects like personal relationships, prayer, marriage and family life, Christian growth.

The purpose of the movement is to restore the charismatic dimension of Christian life to the position of prominence and influence theologians agree it had in the early Church. Father Edward D. O'Connor, C.S.C., associate professor of theology at Notre Dame, has noted that the nature of the charismatic renewal is the same as that of the biblical and liturgical movements — to restore something to the entire Church, not to remain indefinitely as a special group within the Church. Presumably, the charismatic renewal will cease to exist as a movement when the Church becomes charismatically renewed. Cardinal Leo J. Suenens of Belgium, a speaker at several of the international conferences, has called the charismatic renewal "a current of grace, a 'move' of the Spirit, not a movement. It will disappear as a movement as quickly as possible and enter into the blood and life of the Church."

Participation

The movement's service committee estimated in 1974 that some 600,000 Catholics were or had been participants in prayer groups in the United States and Canada. The renewal's spread was also reported in other countries, particularly Australia, France, Ireland and Mexico. The movement's monthly, *New Covenant,* has subscribers in 90 countries.

A substantial number of predominantly Catholic prayer groups include Protestant participants, a development called a good example of grass-roots ecumenism by several observers.

Participants in conferences and various bishops have appealed for greater interest and involvement in the renewal by bishops and priests. Auxiliary Bishop Joseph McKinney of Grand Rapids, liaison official between the renewal's service committee and the National Conference of Catholic Bishops, estimates that about 90 per cent of the bishops are favorably disposed toward the movement itself but not toward the vagaries of some extremists. Reports in that vein were issued by the conference in 1969 and 1972.

Major services of the charismatic renewal are administered by a seven-man service committee whose operations are reviewed periodically by a 47-member advisory committee.

The address of the Communications Center, Charismatic Renewal Services, is P.O. Box 12, Notre Dame, Ind. 46556. Ann Arbor, Mich. 48107, is the location of _New Covenant_ (P.O. Box 102), the Ecumenical Communications Office (P.O. Box 331) and the International Communications Office (P.O. Box 363).

HOUSE OF PRAYER EXPERIENCE

(Source: Sister Ann E. Chester, I.H.M., HOPE Clearing Center, 70 W. Boston Blvd., Detroit, Mich. 48202: _Exploring Inner Space,_ published by the Center.)

The purpose of the House of Prayer Experience (HOPE) movement is to help active religious and priests and lay persons to acquire a contemporary style of contemplative life for renewal, inner growth and a more joyful personal and communal life in the light of the Gospel.

The starting point of participation in the movement is an extended period, from several weeks to several years, of concentration on intensive prayer with a community — a house of prayer experience. The result sought is the development of a style of prayer and contemplation with a carry-over that integrates and permeates religion and life.

Background

HOPE is essentially a movement of the Spirit, a phase of the "New Pentecost" called for by Pope John XXIII. It was born in the hearts of apostolic religious women who were forced by ever increasing apostolic demands to seek a deeper prayer-life. To meet this need, Father Bernard Haring, C.SS.R., recommended that at least one house of an active congregation have prayer as its essential service, adopting a life-style determined by the needs of prayer rather than by the demands of apostolic work. He took its name from the words of Isaiah, "My house will be called a house of prayer" (Is. 56:7). He first presented this concept at the annual meeting of the Conference of Major Superiors of Women Religious in 1965, offering it as an instrument for renewal in depth.

Early in 1968, the Immaculate Heart of Mary Sisters of Monroe, Mich., organized a clearing center to serve as a focal point for idea exchanges which preceded and led up to a national planning conference in the summer of that year. At the four-day meeting, 156 sisters from 96 congregations in the United States and Canada formulated the rationale of a House of Prayer.

To test the theory, the IHM Sisters sponsored a six-week House of Prayer Experience, called HOPE '69, involving 137 sisters from 19 congregations. Each summer since then an increasing number of these programs, some of them for intercommunity groups, have been sponsored.

Priests of the Detroit archdiocese took part in a Praying-Living-Sharing program in 1970, and similar programs, for Holy Cross Brothers, Carmelites and others, have been conducted since then.

Underlying the movement are the convictions that prayer is necessary to integrate religion and life, and that institutionalized and long-practiced forms of prayer and prayer life are not adequate for religious and priests engaged in apostolic ministries and of lay persons involved in the multiple concerns of life in the world. Hence the emphasis on new forms of prayer, the rejuvenation of traditional forms, and especially the development of a contemplative stance toward life.

Programs

The communities of houses of prayer consist of a relatively stable core of members with an authentic call to a deeper prayer life and of guests who come and go for shorter or longer periods of participation. The stability of the core group, while not a now-and-forever type of commitment, is such as to guarantee continuity in programs and the resources of experienced personnel in conducting them. Experience has shown that the ideal size of a community is relatively small, from seven to nine members; also that, within limits, mixed groups are better than homogeneous ones for realizing the purposes of the movement. The importance of communities bound together by interpersonal relationships of spiritual depth rather than by institutional ties is paramount.

Program elements include the liturgy, meditation, scriptural reading and discussion, shared prayer in the shared life of community, silence and solitude, search for new forms of prayer and for new adaptations of traditional forms — all against the background of existential conditions.

Programs are flexible rather than predetermined, taking shape and finding expression in line with the particular charisms of the participants and their response to the Holy Spirit. In this respect, they differ from conventional retreat exercises and monastic practices.

This flexibility opens the way to particular thrusts with which programs become identified. Thus, some are known for their emphasis on forms of prayer and experience characteristic of charismatic renewal or for the adoption of practices of Eastern spiritual traditions, including yoga and Zen, as an aid to contemplation. Others are identifiable with programs stressing solitude and silence. One of the strongest thrusts is the ministry of prayer, to spread HOPE and to increase participation in its abbreviated (day-long, weekend, etc.) as well as extended programs.

All programs represent efforts to develop prayer and prayer experience in a community of interpersonal relationships which is open to dialogue and involvement with the Church and the world at large.

Representative Houses

Following is a partial list of houses representative of the movement and some of its thrusts. The total number of houses is more than 60.

Visitation House (Immaculate Heart of Mary Sisters), 529 Stewart Rd., Monroe, Mich. 48161; guided retreats, spiritual direction.

Kresge House (intercommunity), 70 W. Boston Blvd., Detroit, Mich. 48202; orientation house, varied ministry of prayer.

Community of HOPE (intercommunity), Xavier Center, Convent Station, N.J. 07961; Pentecostal thrust.

Trinity Center (Missionary Servants of the Most Holy Trinity), 1190 Long Hill Rd., Stirling, N.J. 07980; ecumenical thrust.

House of Peace (Canadian Conference of Religious), R.R. No. 2, Combermere, Ont., Canada.

Eastern Point House of Prayer, Eastern Point Retreat Center, Gloucester, Mass. 01930; Eastern spirituality thrust.

Shalom House, Durwood Glenn, Rt. 2, Box 220, Baraboo, Wis. 53913; contemplative thrust.

Kairos House, Rt. 3, Box 653, Spokane, Wash. 99203; Eastern spirituality.

Interest in the HOPE movement has increased steadily not only in this country but also abroad, as indicated by inquiries received at the Clearing Center from places in England, France, Africa, Australia, New Zealand, India and Korea.

OCCULTISM

Occultism is a term designating theories and practices for the understanding and use of hidden knowledge principles and preternatural forces for the control of human destiny and to serve the varied purposes of its practitioners.

Its nature may be esoteric, but its manifestations are far from hidden. Some of these manifestations in the United States are as follows.

Examples

• Satanism: San Francisco's Church of Satan had a dues-paying membership of 10,000 in the summer of 1971, according to a *Newsweek* report. Its leader, "Black Pope" Anton Szandor La Vey, author of *The Satanic Bible*, was the subject of a cover story in the June 19, 1972, edition of *Time*. Practitioners of Satanism in San Francisco and elsewhere have not diminished in numbers since then. Their avowed purposes are to worship the devil in place of God and to render him whatever services he allegedly inspires. Accounts of their bizarre rituals — and crimes — appear in the media with greater or less frequency.

• Astrology: On public view in hundreds of publications, feature columns of at least two of every three daily newspapers, Zodiac jewelry and paraphernalia — with an estimated 10,000 professional astrologers and some 175,000 dabblers. Their aim is to discern the ways and mysteries of life in the light of controlling heavenly bodies. Their mathematically inclined counterparts seek the same objective in the esoteric realm of numerology.

• Witchcraft: "White" and "black," practiced in hundreds of covens. Father Richard J. Woods, O.P., an instructor in philosophy at Loyola University, Chicago, and student of the occult, estimates that there are a minimum of 80,000 "white" witches in the country. Witches, whatever the color of their persuasion, seek to evoke preternatural powers to influence persons and events by spells, incantations and related rituals. Some, like voodooists, practice the art with ominous intent to harm.

• Divination: Involving the use of things — tea leaves, a crystal ball, Tarot and other cards, ouija boards among them — as the means or vehicles for eliciting information and knowledge that is inaccessible to ordinary intelligence. Fortune tellers are practitioners of the art, along with mediums dealing in spiritism, a form of divination for the evocation and revelation of spirits of the dead.

• Eastern Mysticism: From the oldest forms to one of the newest practiced by perhaps 4,000 full-time, saffron-robed devotees of Hare Krishna — with its aims of liberation from matter, desire, care and worry; of identification with a variety of absolutes; of passive surrender to numberless reincarnations for the sake of ultimate impersonal fulfillment.

• Theosophism, Rosicrucianism and other forms of illuminationism and gnosticism: Pursued in a quest for secret principles or knowledge-keys to the mysteries of life.

Observations

These and other forms of occultism derive from esoteric arts and sciences whose features have remained substantially the same since the days of primitive magic in the remote past.

Like religion — with which they have been compared and for which they have been regarded as counterfeits and substitutes — they have a creed (theory and purpose), a code (of conduct) and a cult (liturgies and rites). Unlike religion — whose objective is to conform persons to the will and ways of God — they are oriented to the control and use of the preternatural for reasons of personal and, to some degree, of social service.

One objection to the occult is that it seeks

to replace the theology of redemption and grace with a radically different "theology" of illumination, through hidden knowledge, and of manipulation, through the mastery of hidden forces and powers. A second objection involves the possibility and/or fact that occult practices imply the attribution to creatures of powers proper to God alone.

Catholic doctrine has no quarrel with the verified experimental findings of parapsychology. The case is different, however, with respect to the presuppositions and practices of the pseudo-theology of the occult.

The rise of occultism in recent years has been called an indictment of the failure of contemporary society and religion to provide and communicate goals, meanings and values adequate to the stated needs and aspirations of persons in a profoundly changed and changing world. It has been described, accordingly, as a melange of countercultural phenomena evidenced by efforts to avoid alienation, a search for spiritual security, the pursuit of ecstasy and release from personal and social tensions. Underlying the phenomena is the noumenal reality of the natural, indeed supernatural, thirst for transcendence, liberation and immortality.

Whatever reasons are assigned, it is certain that the lure of the occult will remain constant throughout human history, and that its lore of theory and practice will continue to absorb the lasting interest of the initiates and the on-again, off-again enthusiasm of faddists, young and old.

Word of Caution

Cardinal Humberto Medeiros of Boston, in a June 13, 1974, pastoral letter entitled "Christ Our Victory," warned young people especially against an "unwholesome fascination" with the occult. He wrote:

"In so many ways they (young people) manifest a genuine concern for the relevant and the authentic, a dissatisfaction with the materialism of this technological age, a quest for the transcendent.

"It is reassuring to see so much potential good here; it is also a source of anxiety to see some of it wasted on ill-conceived pursuits, especially if these involve unwholesome fascination with the occult and pseudo-mystic.

"Dabbling in this area can often be harmful. At best, it is frivolous."

Cardinal Medeiros said he was concerned with those who pay heed too easily to "the Pied Pipers who pass through with preparations as elaborate as their claims, who tickle the ears of their listeners for a while but have nothing of substance to offer that will endure for a lifetime and an eternity beyond."

PRIESTS AND RELIGIOUS RUNNING FOR OFFICE

Questions concerning priests and religious running for public office cropped up again in 1974. Developments occasioning the questions included:

• The third candidacy of two-term Representative Father Robert F. Drinan, S.J., of Massachusetts.

• The refusal of Archbishop Joseph T. McGucken of San Francisco to sanction Father Eugene J. Boyle's run for the California legislature.

• The membership of Father Louis R. Gigante in the New York City Council.

• Announcement by Dominican Sister Mary Anne Guthrie June 3 of her intention to run for a seat in the House of Representatives with the approval of Bishop Carroll Dozier of Memphis.

Father Drinan, sponsor of a defeated impeachment article against Richard M. Nixon for authorizing the bombing of Cambodia, was the first priest elected to the House of Representatives.

Father Boyle believed that his pastoral experience and expertise in work for community development and social justice qualified him for a fruitful ministry in politics.

Father Gigante's skill as a practical politician was beyond question.

Sister Mary Anne Guthrie was representative of her counterparts seeking to expand the ministerial roles of women religious.

Church Law

Church law on the subject of priests running for political office starts with Canon 139 of the Code of Canon Law. It states that priests shall not seek elective office without "the permission of their own Ordinary as well as of the Ordinary of the place where the election is to be held." Accordingly, a diocesan priest should have permission from his local bishop; generally the local bishop will also be the Ordinary of the place of the election. A member of a religious order, in addition, should have the permission of the major superior of his or her institute.

The U.S. bishops, at a semi-annual meeting in April, 1970, in San Francisco, accepted without dissent a committee report which noted that Canon 139 continued in force and that bishops should generally "discourage" priests from running for office.

A document issued by the third assembly of the Synod of Bishops in 1971 said that a priest, for the good of the community, might run for office "in concrete and exceptional circumstances."

This document was quoted by Archbishop McGucken in February, 1974, when he turned down Father Boyle's request for permission to run for the California legislature. "Since political options are by nature contingent and never in an entirely adequate and perennial way interpret the Gospel, the priest, who is the witness of things to come, must keep a certain distance from any political office or involvement."

Noting that the synodal norm allowed exceptions in the absence of competent lay persons to run for office, the archbishop said: "In conscience I cannot agree that the time and circumstances demand an exception to the general norm, in effect a declaration that we lack competent laymen to assume the role which is properly theirs."

Opinions

Such a restrictive ruling was in line with the opinion of the author of an editorial in a May, 1974, issue of *The Catholic Standard and Times* or Philadelphia. He wrote: "Priests, it is apparent from the official documents of the Church, should provide that moral motivation and spiritual guidance which are essential to the formation of effective lay leaders of high principle and undoubted integrity in public life."

MORALITY IN PUBLIC LIFE
Background

Richard M. Nixon resigned the office of President of the United States Aug. 8, 1974. He did so after:

• The Judiciary Committee of the House of Representatives passed three articles calling for impeachment proceedings against him by the Senate. One of the charges was for obstruction of justice in the Watergate cover-up.

• Late disclosure by himself of previously denied implication in the cover-up.

• It became evident that he had suffered a total erosion of political support for his continuance in the Presidency.

Nixon's resignation halted impeachment proceedings but left him open to criminal prosecution on Watergate and other charges. Such prosecution was blocked, however, by the action of President Gerald R. Ford in granting him a total and unconditional pardon Sept. 8, before and in lieu of the start of any legal proceedings against him.

Moral Concern

Morality in the conduct of public officials was the theme and concern of comment by editorial writers and religious leaders on the resignation and pardon of Richard M. Nixon. Following are samples of opinion from Catholic publications and several bishops.

Before Resignation

Gerard R. Sherry, editor-manager of *The Monitor,* San Francisco: "The President of the United States now admits that he knew of the Watergate affair several days after it occurred; that he participated in the cover-up of the unlawful break-in; that he lied to the people of this nation several times when making televised reports on the situation."

There could be "no joy" about a Nixon decision to resign or face impeachment. "We

A more open policy was advocated by the National Federation of Priests' Councils, in an article appearing in the July, 1974, edition of *Priests USA.* The writer said: "Candidly we do not feel that the United States Church has priests in large numbers who are both inclined toward and capable of handling political office. . . . For the almost insignificant number of priests whose bag is politics . . . we want to be on record as recommending, in this particular era and in this particular nation, that U.S. priests be not only permitted but indeed encouraged to give their special talents to their constituency in this holy and wholesome ministry" of elective office.

Summarily, and despite debate, church law continues to state that priests and religious should not run for elective office without the permission of their competent superiors, and that decision regarding exceptional circumstances for permission rests with the superiors.

grieve for him, we grieve for his family and, most importantly, we grieve for the country."

Father Edmond Bliven, editorial page editor of the *Catholic Sentinel,* Portland, Ore.: Saw Nixon as a "latter-day Hamlet, unable to make the decision that appears inevitable." Resignation was necessary because Nixon "has lost his moral authority. He can no longer govern."

After Resignation

National Catholic Reporter, Kansas City, Mo.: "What of Nixon now? A year ago we wrote that impeachment was part of the American system and should not be feared. Prosecution of a former President for alleged criminal acts is also part of that system, and, therefore, should not be feared either. Proposals for immunity appeal to our compassion, but offend our sense of justice."

America, New York, N.Y.: At the very least, "the nature of the crisis that forced Mr. Nixon's resignation from the Presidency must be made officially and unequivocally evident." In the absence of impeachment proceedings and related records, the magazine suggested a Congressional endorsement of the final report of the House Judiciary Committee as a way to "make clear why Mr. Nixon's resignation . . . does represent an important triumph for our constitutional system in a crisis in which it was tested in an unprecedented way."

The Catholic Free Press, Worcester, Mass.: President Nixon was forced to accept the moral judgment of the nation that he was no longer fit to serve as President, no longer able to govern. "Many might scoff at moral judgment, but America rose to the heights these last several weeks. No longer would 'inoperatives' serve, no longer would casual denials obtain, no longer would ordinary people accept whatever was put out by press flacks.

The nation made its moral judgment, and Mr. Nixon was found lacking."

Interreligious Committee of General Secretaries (Bishop James S. Rausch, U.S. Catholic Conference; Dr. Claire Randall, National Council of Churches; Rabbi Henry Siegman, Synagogue Council of America): "The electorate does not want a monarchy or a king. Rather our democratic system of government demands of political officials that they respect citizens' rights to privacy and that they give expression and direction to the finest aspirations in America's traditional ideals. Further, the democratic electorate expects of its political leadership that it encourage widened participation by the public sectors of the nation, such as the churches and synagogues, the media and voluntary associations, in the difficult but essential task of being vigilant against government incursions into that sacred area of individuals' lives where the full range of human rights reside.

"Watergate is not what American political life is all about, any more than was Mylai characteristic of U.S. foreign policy. These were merely aberrations. But these can also be maturing experiences. Integrity, honesty, vision, and a sense of high moral purpose — these are marks of the American political tradition. These are the characteristics Americans are seeking to regain again, now."

Cardinal John J. Krol, president of the National Conference of Catholic Bishops and the U.S. Catholic Conference: "People look for high standards from their leaders, and have every right to demand them. Political life is a difficult profession, but one that must always be based on ethical and moral principles. Thank God, we have a system of government where disclosures of improprieties can be made and appropriate remedies taken. Our history shows we have the resilience to rise above serious crises and tragedies. This sad experience should alert all public office holders to their accountability before God and the people."

After Pardon

Auxiliary Bishop Thomas J. Gumbleton of Detroit: Called the pardon "disheartening, discouraging and a tragic mistake." The reasons that President Ford gave for granting the pardon — basically that former President Nixon had "suffering enough" — were not "sufficient to justify" the pardon. "It recreates a sense of mistrust in government and the whole system."

The Evangelist, Albany, N.Y.: "The pardon of Richard Nixon is legal, irrevocable and in some ways justified. But it raises several questions about the even hand of justice which only further presidential action can resolve. Unconditional amnesty for those who chose out of moral commitment not to fight in Vietnam must surely be considered now. Regarding John Dean and a host of other Watergate conspirators, decisions at which even Solomon would shudder must be made."

The Long Island Catholic, Rockville Centre, N.Y.: "The nation cannot help but be conscious of the fact that Nixon's closest associates could be convicted on the testimony of the Chief Executive in whose name and supposed interests" the Watergate cover-up was carried out.

Noting President Ford's concern for mercy, the paper said that "the glaring inconsistencies of compassion for one man while others still suffer the lash of strict justice can easily offend that other great American instinct for fairness and equality before the law."

MORALITY OF CORPORATE INVESTMENTS

The morality of corporate practices — and, by implication, of participation in them through investment — was the subject of a statement published Sept. 25, 1974, by the Department of Social Development, U.S. Catholic Conference.

A multinational corporation is generally considered to be a company having production and marketing facilities in many countries, enjoying worldwide access to capital, depending on foreign income, and under management with a worldwide point of view.

Multinationals

The statement, entitled "Development-Dependency: The Role of Multinational Corporations," said there was mounting evidence that the concentrated power "of a relatively few multinational corporations and banks inhibits development and deters the process of achieving social justice here and abroad."

The document was a reflection on a charge made by Pope Paul VI in 1971 that "multinational enterprises ... can conduct autonomous strategies which are largely independent of the national political powers and therefore not subject to control from the point of view of the common good."

Time for Questions

The general thrust of the USCC statement was that: "The time is at hand for us not only to question the enormous power wielded by so few people (in management) and institutions (of this kind), but, in a more fundamental way, to question the underlying motivation behind such unbridled power.

"The motivation continually to increase profit (characteristic of multinationals) emerges from values which promote excessive individualism, unnecessary consumption, and disregard for the quality of human life, all of which are contrary to the deepest values of the Judaeo-Christian tradition."

The statement said: "A growing number of

Catholics are beginning to share Pope Paul's concern about the emerging power of multinational corporations. Church people, both here and in the Third World (of developing nations), are becoming increasingly aware that many U.S. domestic and international policies are linked together to serve the interests of these transnational business enterprises."

Latin American Impact

Focusing on the impact of multinationals in the Third World, and particularly in Latin America, the statement observed:

"Realization is growing that so-called economic development and the resultant growth in gross national product does not assure the amelioration of the harsh living conditions of the vast majority of people of the Third World.

"The oppressive conditions of poverty and marginality frequently result from the influx of foreign private capital. The fact that concentrated economic power results in enriching 30 per cent of a population in Latin America at the expense of the other 70 per cent indicts it as a major impediment to world justice."

The statement said it was important to recognize the fact that "multinational business interests, which play such a dominant role in the less developed countries of Latin America, also dominate, to a great extent, our own domestic economy." It pointed to accounts of "tax write-offs, increasing monopoly activity, political lobbying, machinations of the oil industry during the 'energy crisis' " as "grim testimony to the detrimental effect on U.S. citizens of the concentration of economic power."

Inequality in U.S.

The statement noted continuing inequality in the distribution of income in the United States. "The top 20 per cent of wealth holders in the country own over three-fourths of all personal wealth. The top one per cent alone holds between 20 to 30 per cent of all personal wealth and have done so for decades."

In conclusion, the statement declared:

"In the Third World, most people have the daily experience of powerlessness in the face of the relative few who own and control most of the wealth and income, land industry, political and military power. In our country, there is a growing sense among working people as well as minority groups that power belongs only to those few who hold enormous wealth.

"As Catholics we must continue to rediscover our own distinct identity as a religious, prophetic people who stand apart from the powers which possess dominant control in society."

Together with the Church in the Third World, "we are moved to pronounce God's judgment on the side of the powerless life,

whether of the unborn child, of the elderly without care or security, of the overtaxed citizen, or of the poor in the barrios of Latin America."

A Basic Principle

The moral concern behind the USCC statement was prompted by a principle stated by the Second Vatican Council in its *Pastoral Constitution on the Church in the Modern World.*

The council said: "The fundamental purpose of (society's) productivity must not be the mere multiplication of products. It must not be profit or domination. Rather, it must be the service of man, and indeed of the whole man, viewed in terms of his material needs and the demands of his intellectual, moral, spiritual and religious life."

In practice, the principle involves responsibility for participation, by means of investment, in the production, marketing, service and other operations of corporations.

The related broad question is whether individuals or religious bodies can justify such participation in terms of the social dimensions of their commitment to the Gospel.

Options

Some religious bodies have withdrawn investments from firms doing business thought to be at variance with Christian social doctrine. The World Council of Churches, for example, announced in January, 1973, that it had liquidated $1.5 million in holdings in U.S., British, Swiss and Dutch banks doing business in South Africa considered detrimental to the human rights of the black population there.

Other religious organizations, opting to maintain their investments, are seeking to influence policies and practices through the exercise of stockholders' rights and resolutions. This course of action was taken by the Sisters of Loretto early in 1974 when they filed a resolution to obtain a detailed report on U.S. Steel's alleged strip-mining in Appalachia. The Franciscan Friars of the Atonement, in conjunction with other members of an interfaith Church Project on Investments in South Africa, have taken similar action for stockholder resolutions with Texaco, Getty Oil, Exxon, IBM, Bethlehem Steel and other corporations.

Guidelines

The National Federation of Priests' Councils adopted a set of investment guidelines entitled "Exploitation or Liberation: Ethics for Investors," in 1972. The NFPC was also instrumental in setting up the National Catholic Coalition for Responsibile Investment in January, 1973, to provide educational and advisory services concerning church investments.

One set of guidelines, adopted by the St.

Paul and Minneapolis archdiocese in September, 1974, stated that the archdiocese would not invest in companies that make weapons "likely to destroy human life"; that engage in "discrimination, exploitation or abuse of people, their environment, and natural resources"; that provide "significant quantities, products or services which are contrary to the moral teachings of the Church."

The National Conference of Catholic Bishops and the U.S. Catholic Conference reported their standing policy in May, 1974, that "their funds shall not be invested in entities engaged in activities which are contrary to the conferences' policy of concern for human life at every stage of its existence, or whose employment and other operational patterns raise serious questions of social justice. It is also NCCB and USCC policy to vote proxies in a manner consistent with this position."

Religious bodies will find it easier to judge themselves as corporate investors than to estimate their potential to influence corporate policies and operations. Perhaps their moral influence will outweigh their financial impotence as holders of less than one per cent of the total value of corporate holdings in this country.

VATICAN POLICY ON JERUSALEM

Outlines of Vatican policy with respect to Jerusalem, and other aspects of the Holy Land, were sketched by Pope Paul VI in his 1973 Christmas address to the College of Cardinals and in another address to a general audience Apr. 10, 1974.

He told the cardinals: "Jerusalem is the city whose destinies are mysterious and unique, in which there is a convergence of a pluralism of historical and religious rights. A solution touching Jerusalem must take account of the exigencies of the special character of the city, unique in all the world, and the rights and legitimate aspirations of those belonging to the three great monotheistic religions of the Holy Land" (Judaism, Christianity, Islam).

During his Apr. 10 general audience, the Pope called for "an appropriate statute with international guarantees for the Holy City of Jerusalem and a convenient juridical guardianship for the Holy Places."

The Pope's view envisions some form of international statute that would define the boundaries of historic and religious Jerusalem, and spell out the rights of the three different communities there.

Proposals

Related proposals are for:

• An international statute or agreement guaranteeing free access to the city of Jerusalem for all and the rights of Christians and Moslems to keep their homes there. (Christian and Moslem presence has been undermined since 1971 when Israeli authorities began expropriating non-Jewish property and carrying out a kind of urban renewal program almost exclusively for Jews.)

• A statute including "an appropriate protection" for all Holy Places in the Holy Land. (Israel agrees to this, and other nations have no objection.)

• A "just and generous response" to the plight of "hundreds of thousands" of Palestinians "who have been made refugees from their land, reduced to desperate conditions of life, or in some other way frustrated in their legitimate aspiration." (The UN officially lists as refugees 1.5 million Palestinians who have lost their homes since 1948 and have been living in Lebanon, East Jordan, on the west bank of the Jordan River, the Gaza Strip, Syria, Israel and Egypt. Another two million have moved to other places.)

Earlier Vatican policy had been in line with a resolution adopted by the United Nations Nov. 29, 1947. It called for the creation of a separate body, consisting of the city of Jerusalem and its immediate environs, under the control of an international regime. The resolution was never implemented. A trend toward the present Vatican policy became evident in December, 1967.

According to one Vatican diplomat: "The Holy See does not exclude the exercise of sovereignty over the city of Jerusalem by Israel or the Arabs or the Palestinians or by any other responsible group. It would insist, however, that any group would limit the exercise of that sovereignty either by self-control or a control imposed from the outside. The Holy See is willing for the United Nations to define the exercise of sovereignty."

As Things Stand

• Jerusalem remains a problem. Israel, in possession, claims the whole city as Jewish. The Vatican, however, does not acknowledge this exclusive claim. Neither do the United States, France, Italy, Belgium, Spain, Turkey, Greece and Great Britain — all of which maintain double consulates (to Israel and Jordan) in Jerusalem.

• Israeli authorities are in apparent agreement with Vatican policy calling for special status of the Holy Places and guaranteeing access thereto by members of all faiths.

• The Vatican is concerned at the dwindling presence of Christians as a living community in Jerusalem. This concern was reflected in Pope Paul's apostolic exhortation of Apr. 5, 1974, regarding "the increased needs of the Church in the Holy Land." Melkite-Rite Archbishop Joseph Raya, formerly of Acre, described the exodus of Christians from the Holy Land as "a distressing stampede, without hope or joy."

• The Palestinian refugee problem remains unsolved and out of control.

Pope Paul VI

(See additional entries under News Events, Vatican, Pope Paul, titles of documents, topical headings for coverage of 1974 and other events.)

Cardinal Giovanni Montini was elected Pope June 21, 1963, on the fifth or sixth ballot cast by the 79th and largest conclave of cardinals in the history of the Church. Taking the name Paul VI as the 261st successor to St. Peter as Bishop of Rome, he was crowned June 30 in solemn ceremonies in St. Peter's Square.

Early Career

Giovanni Battista Montini was born Sept. 26, 1897, at Concesio, near Brescia, in the foothills of the Italian Alps. He was the second of the three sons of Giorgio Montini and Giuditta Alghisi.

He suffered from ill health during his boyhood and youth and lived mostly at home while pursuing studies for the priesthood at the Cesare Arici Institute and Christ the King Seminary in Brescia. He was ordained in the cathedral there May 29, 1920. After a short period spent in parish work, he continued studies at the Gregorian University, the University of Rome and the academy for Vatican diplomats. He received degrees in civil and canon law, theology and philosophy.

Named as attaché at the nunciature at Warsaw, he served there for less than a year, returning to Rome for reasons of health in 1923. He then became chaplain of the Catholic Students' Club at the University of Rome and, in 1925, national moderator of the Italian Catholic University Federation's publications program. The student organization was suppressed by Mussolini in 1931.

He became a clerk in the Vatican Secretariat of State in 1933 and was appointed undersecretary three years later. He was named substitute secretary of state in 1944 and prosecretary for ordinary affairs in 1952.

During his period of service in the secretariat, he worked closely with Pius XII, who left the office of secretary vacant following the death of Cardinal Maglione in 1944. With a 10-year background of practical experience in Catholic Action and a longer involvement in diplomatic tasks, he is thought to have been influential in supporting the Christian Democratic parties in Europe, in helping to mobilize action against Communists at the polls in Italy in 1948, and in fostering the priest-worker experiment in France after World War II.

He was ordained archbishop of Milan Dec. 12, 1954, and was installed in the See the following Jan. 6. He was the first of 52 cardinals created by John XXIII Dec. 15, 1958, and served in the Roman Curia as a member of the Consistorial Congregation (Congregation of Bishops), the Congregation for Extraordinary Ecclesiastical Affairs (Secretariat of State, Council for the Public Affairs of the Church), and the Congregation of Seminaries and Universities (Congregation for Catholic Education).

In eight and one-half years in Milan he conducted a two-year visitation of the 1,000 churches in the archdiocese, built or renovated 200 churches and chapels, set up a modern system for social services, established a center for study by his priests of pastoral methods suited to contemporary conditions, stimulated Catholic Action, and made direct and effective contact with the people and their conditions of life in the Communist-affected region of northern Italy.

Renewal Commitment

On the day following his election to the papacy, Paul VI announced on Vatican Radio his intention of carrying on with the Church renewal policy and program of his predecessor. Accordingly and in his own way, he has been seeking to move forward and make last what John XXIII, in his unique and charismatic way, stimulated — despite conflicting and obstructive currents of progressivism and conservatism in the Church.

Vatican II

Immediately on his election, Paul announced he would reconvene the Second Vatican Council, which had completed only one session before the death of John XXIII.

He opened the second session Sept. 29, 1963, and at its conclusion Dec. 4 approved the promulgation of the first two conciliar documents, the *Constitution on the Sacred Liturgy* and a *Decree on Media of Social Communication*. Between the second, third and fourth sessions, he ordered that measures be taken by the various conciliar commissions to simplify and streamline the work load and to modify procedures for the smoother and faster conduct of business. At the end of the third session Nov. 21, 1964, by which time the Council had in work all of the items in its wide-ranging agenda, he approved the promulgation of the *Dogmatic Constitution on the Church, a Decree on Ecumenism* and a *Decree on Eastern Catholic Churches*. On Sept. 14, 1965, he opened the fourth and final session by concelebrating Mass with a group of the Council Fathers.

During the last three sessions of the Council, he generally followed the hands-off policy of John XXIII with respect to deliberations and the general conduct of business. Like John, however, who intervened during the first sesssion to prevent fruitless consideration of a draft proposal on revelation which hardly any of the Fathers favored, he took a direct hand in Council affairs on several occasions.

On June 23, 1964, he announced he was reserving to himself for study and decision a number of questions regarding birth control. Assisting him in the study was a mixed commission of some 60 persons including priests, theologians, married men and women, physicians and psychiatrists. Their reports — for and against relaxation of Church teaching and practice on the subject — were submitted to him for decision.

During the third session of the Council, at the request of a large majority of the Council Fathers, he also took under personal advisement a number of questions related to mixed marriages and similar matters.

Several weeks after the fourth session began, he cut off Council discussion of clerical celibacy because of the delicacy of the matter and the emotional manner of its treatment in communications media. His action was hailed by the Fathers of the Council.

Before final action was taken on several documents at the end of the third session, he made 19 changes in the *Decree on Ecumenism* and proclaimed Mary the Mother of the Church in the *Dogmatic Constitution on the Church.*

Another incident worthy of note at the close of the third session was his refusal to order a vote on the proposed *Declaration on Religious Freedom.* A final version of several draftings of the document was proposed for balloting but was withheld by the Council's presiding board. He refused to override their decision, which was in accordance with rules of Council procedure. He stated at the time that the decree would be given first place on the agenda of the fourth session. It was so placed, and was approved.

He brought the Second Vatican Council to a close Dec. 8, 1965. He noted in a final address that the decisive phase of *aggiornamento*-in-action was already underway, and declared a special jubilee of prayer, study and work in the Church for the purpose of realizing in practice the objectives laid down in the 16 documents of the Council. He later extended the period of jubilee from May 29 to Dec. 8, 1966. He also announced at the Council closing that the beatification causes of his predecessors, John XXIII and Pius XII, were being set in motion.

He has implemented enactments of the Council in various documents. The motu proprio *Ecclesiae Sanctae* of Aug. 6, 1966, laid down executive norms for the four decrees on the pastoral office of bishops, the ministry and life of priests, the adaptation and renewal of religious life and the missionary activity of the Church. The motu proprio *Catholicam Christi Ecclesiam* of Jan. 6, 1967, established the Council of the Laity and the Commission for Justice and Peace. The encyclical *The Development of Peoples* represented an effort to implement the *Pastoral Constitution on the Church in the Modern World.* His authorization of activities and publications of the secretariats for interfaith affairs was in line with provisions of the *Decree on Ecumenism.* His approval of the establishment of scores of territorial conferences of bishops, the creation of the Synod of Bishops and the statement of norms in 1967 regarding the reestablishment of the permanent diaconate in the Roman Rite were efforts in pursuit of conciliar objectives regarding the action and composition of the hierarchy in the Church.

Two documents issued in 1966 embodied the thinking and spirit of the Council: the apostolic constitution *Paenitemini* of Feb. 17, a major statement on the revision of penitential discipline; and a decree of Mar. 18, with respect to mixed marriages. In 1967, he issued an apostolic constitution entitled *The Doctrine and Practice of Indulgences* which stated new norms in this area of Church life.

To quicken the spirit of faith in the Church, the Pope ordered observance throughout the world of a Year of Faith from June 29, 1967, to June 29, 1968, and of Holy Year 1975, with preliminaries starting in 1973.

Collegiality

The Second Vatican Council completed the work of the First by spelling out, among other things, the doctrine of collegiality of the bishops. With and under the Pope — as the successors of the Apostles with and under the leadership of Peter — the bishops as a body are the pastors of the Church whose mission, while concentrated in the sphere of their own proper jurisdictions, extends also to care, concern, and collective action with each other and the pope for the good of the universal Church.

On Nov. 21, 1964, when the third session promulgated the *Dogmatic Constitution on the Church,* Pope Paul told the assembled bishops that he intended to associate them more closely with himself in the work of the whole Church, through participation in postconciliar commissions and in other ways.

This led to the establishment of the Synod of Bishops on paper Sept. 15, 1965. The initial meeting of the Synod from Sept. 29 to Oct. 25, 1967, represented the first papal effort in modern times to seek the consultation of bishops gathered in a collegial assembly outside of an ecumenical council. Second and third meetings in 1969 and 1971 dealt with questions concerning collegiality, territorial conferences of bishops, clerical celibacy and problems of world justice and peace.

In a move toward decentralizing and delegating authority, he increased the powers of bishops, in virtue of the motu proprio *De Episcoporum Muneribus* of July 11, 1966. In 1967, he extended the same grants of authority to bishops of the Eastern Rites. Additional faculties have since been given to bishops.

Roman Curia

He started a reorganization of the Roman Curia in 1965 by revising the Sacred Congregation of the Holy Office. He gave the body a new name, the Sacred Congregation for the Doctrine of the Faith, made the orientation of its work more positive, and abolished the Index of Forbidden Books. He issued Aug. 15, 1967, the apostolic constitution *Regimini Ecclesiae Universae,* providing for the overall reorganization of the Curia and for the inclusion of diocesan bishops in its various departments. The constitution was put into effect in 1968.

He established an International Theological Commission in 1969, and reconstituted the Biblical Commission in 1971 and the Commission for the Codification of Oriental Canon Law in 1972.

In addition to reorganizing the Curia, he has given it a greater international complexion than it ever had in previous history.

Cardinals

By elevating 27 prelates to the rank of cardinal on Feb. 22, 1965, he increased the membership of the College of Cardinals to the high total of 103 and made it more representative (43 nations) of the Church throughout the world than it had ever been. Of greater significance than the increased geographical representation, however, was the fact that the new cardinals included three major patriarchs of Eastern Rite. Without prejudice to their patriarchal prerogatives, these prelates, and a fourth patriarch already in the Sacred College, became cardinal bishops.

He further increased the membership of the College to the all-time high total of 118 in 1967. The creation of the new cardinals, which took place in ceremonies held between June 26 and June 29, seemed to answer negatively some speculation that the College might be phased out of existence or its functions diminished. He named additional cardinals in March, 1969 (35), and February, 1973 (30).

In November, 1970, he decreed that, as of Jan. 1, 1971, cardinals 80 years of age and older could not take part in a conclave for the election of a Pope or be active in the administration of Church affairs in the Roman Curia. The decree *(Ingravescentem Aetatem)* immediately affected 25 cardinals.

He also asked for the resignation of active bishops at the age of 75.

Liturgical Renewal

He authorized promulgation of the *Constitution on the Sacred Liturgy* Dec. 8, 1963, and ordered some of its provisions into effect as of Feb. 16, 1964. On Jan. 28, 1964, he announced the formation of a post-conciliar commission with responsibility for continuing work in this field.

Progressive liturgical renewal was the sub-

ject of several documents issued by the Pope during 1967. The principal ones were instructions on sacred music, dated Mar. 5; the adaptations of rites and ceremonies, May 4; and Eucharistic worship, May 25.

In 1968, through the Consilium for Implementing the Constitution on the Sacred Liturgy, approval was given for three new Canons and eight prefaces in the Mass.

A New Order of the Mass, related to revisions of the universal liturgical calendar and the Liturgy of the Hours (revised in 1970) was decreed in 1969, to take the place of the form of Mass ordered and standardized for the Roman Rite by the Council of Trent in the 16th century. Universal adoption of these reforms was delayed pending the preparations of vernacular translations of official texts and for other reasons.

Interfaith Relations

He approved promulgation of the *Decree on Ecumenism* at the conclusion of the third session of the Second Vatican Council, and gave the late Cardinal Augustin Bea, head of the Secretariat for Promoting Christian Unity, and his successor, Cardinal Jan Willebrands, a free hand in relations with members and communities of other Christian churches. To supplement interfaith relations among others, he established a Secretariat for Non-Christians May 19, 1964.

While on pilgrimage to the Holy Land Jan. 4 to 6, 1964, he held two conversations with Orthodox Patriarch Athenagoras I. He was the first Pope since St. Peter to visit the Holy Places and the first Pontiff in more than 500 years to hold conversations with an Orthodox Patriarch.

The prelates met on two more occasions, in Istanbul in July and at the Vatican in October, 1967. The visit of Athenagoras to Rome was the first by a Patriarch of Constantinople since 1451.

Between the two sets of visits, the Pope and Patriarch nullified Dec. 7, 1965, mutual Catholic-Orthodox excommunications imposed in 1054.

Also on the personal contact level, the Pope has met with numerous Orthodox prelates, Anglican Archbishop Michael Ramsey in 1966, leaders of the World Council of Churches and representatives of other religious bodies.

He authorized the initiation in May, 1965, of exploratory talks and steps toward dialogue with the World Council of Churches, and has approved of high-level talks with Anglicans and the Lutheran World Federation.

While on a visit to the Geneva headquarters of the World Council of Churches in June, 1969, he told members of the staff that the Church had great interest in the council but that the time was not yet ripe for a request for Catholic membership.

For all of his interest in ecumenism, he has repeatedly cautioned Catholics engaged in interfaith endeavors to stay within the bounds of sound doctrine. Ecumenism at any price is false, he has stated.

Encyclicals

The first of Paul's encyclicals, *Ecclesiam Suam*, dated Aug. 6, 1964, developed four principal themes related to *aggiornamento* and the aims and purposes of the Second Vatican Council: (1) the awareness the Church has of itself, and the need for this to increase and develop in depth; (2) internal renewal in the Church, and external expression of it; (3) the dialogue the Church must conduct internally among its members and externally with all men; (4) an offer of his services for furthering the cause of peace in the world.

Mense Maio, dated Apr. 29, 1965, urged prayer, especially through the intercession of the Blessed Virgin Mary during the month of May, for the success of the Second Vatican Council and for peace in the world.

Mysterium Fidei, dated Sept. 3, 1965, was a strong statement of traditional doctrine concerning the Holy Eucharist.

Prayer for peace, especially the Rosary during the month of October, was the subject of his fourth encyclical, *Christi Matri Rosarii,* Sept. 15, 1966.

The Development of Peoples was the title and subject of his fifth encyclical, dated Mar. 26, 1967. Wide in concept and definite in practical guidelines, the widely hailed document extended the social doctrine of Pope John's *Peace on Earth* and blueprinted the application to the Third World of the contents of the Second Vatican Council's *Pastoral Constitution on the Church in the Modern World.*

Priestly Celibacy dated June 24, 1967, restated the traditional doctrine and practice of the Latin Church on clerical celibacy. The well-documented and backgrounded encyclical was not received favorably by those who were arguing for change in this discipline.

Of Human Life, dated July 25, 1968, restated traditional doctrine concerning the regulation of birth.

Documents published in 1971, with the significance but not the title of encyclicals, were an apostolic letter to Cardinal Maurice Roy, on social questions; a *Pastoral Instruction: The Media, Public Opinion and Human Progress;* and an apostolic exhortation addressed to religious.

Communism

In his first encyclical, *Ecclesiam Suam,* he said he had no intention of excluding Communists from dialogue with the Church even though such dialogue would probably be incomplete and extremely difficult. In February, 1965, he urged members of an Italian workers' association to maintain contact with their fellow workers, including those with Communist leanings, but not to compromise their fidelity to Christian social principles.

One of the purposes of the Secretariat for Non-Believers, authorized and established Apr. 8, 1965, is to study and initiate relations with Communists and others on the subject of atheism. Since that time, some limited dialogue has taken place but hardly any observable results have been noted. In 1967, he approved release by the secretariat of an introductory document on dialogue of this kind. Detailed guidelines were published in October, 1968.

Negotiations with the Hungarian government, in progress for about two months before Paul's election, led to agreement in September, 1964, with respect to some Vatican freedom in making bishops' appointments and to modification of a loyalty oath expected of the clergy. The negotiations, as anticipated, left many problems unsettled, including the status of Cardinal Mindszenty who remained in seclusion in the American Embassy in Budapest until September, 1971.

Four sets of diplomatic conversations over a two-year period were concluded June 25, 1966, with the signing by Vatican and Yugoslav representatives of an agreement designed to regularize Church-State relations. Full diplomatic relations were established in 1970.

Some measure of agreement was reached with the Polish government in 1972 when Polish bishops were appointed to head four jurisdictions formerly held by German prelates in the Oder-Niesse territory.

Negotiations with Czechoslovakia, underway for several years, have had few results, and the diplomatic doors of other Communist countries have remained closed.

Peace

From the very beginning of his pontificate, he made known his dedication to the cause of world peace.

In 1963, he spoke in favor of negotiations for a nuclear test ban agreement which was finally signed by nearly 100 nations.

At the very beginning of 1964, while in Jerusalem as a pilgrim visiting the Holy Places, he sent 220 peace messages to heads of state and other international leaders. Eleven months later, while attending the 38th International Eucharistic Congress in Bombay, he again appealed for peace and disarmament, and urged nations to spend for useful and humanitarian purposes — to relieve hunger, misery, illness and ignorance — funds and efforts that could be saved through disarmament. He repeated these ideas in his annual Christmas message to the world a few weeks later.

Time and again during 1965, he raised his voice in pleas for peace — in Vietnam, the Congo, the Dominican Republic, India, Pakistan and Kashmir. In February, he told the bishops of Vietnam in a letter that he had initiated confidential approaches for the sake of peace in the divided nation. On another occasion, he decried the use of terrorist guerrilla tactics under any and all circumstances.

In one of many appeals for the outlawing of nuclear weapons, he prayed on the occasion of the 20th anniversary of the atomic bombing of Japan: "May the world never again see a day of misfortune like that of Hiroshima."

To plead, "No more war; never again war," was the simple and uncomplicated — yet extremely complex — purpose of his visit to the United Nations headquarters Oct. 4, 1965.

With the quickening of the tempo of war in Vietnam from the end of 1965, he escalated his efforts for peace. In many addresses, he pleaded for a Christmas truce, for negotiations and disarmament, and for the humane treatment of prisoners. In the fall of 1966, he sent a special delegation to Vietnam for conversations with the bishops of the country and, probably, for fact-finding purposes. Peace was the subject of many private talks, especially with persons like UN Ambassador Arthur Goldberg, US Ambassador to Vietnam Henry Cabot Lodge, and Soviet Foreign Minister Andrei Gromyko.

In July, 1966, it was reported that a fundraising campaign begun the previous December in response to a papal appeal had collected almost $7.5 million for the relief of famine, particularly in India and Pakistan.

Throughout 1967, he missed no opportunity to appeal and to offer his services for peace-making in Vietnam, but without results. He made similar appeals to prevent, and then to stop, the Israeli-Arab conflict which erupted during the first week of June and continued sporadically thereafter. The most he could do was to mobilize Vatican relief forces to assist refugees.

Beginning in July, he made peace overtures to leaders of opposing factions in Nigeria where bloody tribal and political warfare took a terrible toll of life.

In 1968 and 1969, strife in these areas continued to preoccupy the Pope. He offered the Vatican as a site for Vietnam peace talks, and coupled pleas for peace in Nigeria-Biafra with appeals for stepped-up relief measures there. In August, 1968, with most other world leaders, he decried the Soviet invasion and occupation of Czechoslovakia.

The war in Indochina and Arab-Israeli hostility were subjects of frequent comment in talks from 1971 to 1973. He made several appeals in 1971 for the cessation of civil war in East Pakistan and called for international action to relieve the pressing needs of the millions of refugees in India.

He added Northern Ireland to his litany of prayers and appeals for peace as conflict continued there from 1971 to 1973.

Pilgrimages

While John XXIII was the first Pope to venture outside the Vatican since 1870, Paul VI is the first Pontiff to travel outside of Italy since Pius VII was forced to do so by Napoleon more than 150 years ago.

Paul traveled to the Holy Land as a pilgrim to the Holy Places and to meet Ecumenical Patriarch Athenagoras I from Jan. 4 to 6, 1964.

He went to Bombay, Dec. 2 to 5, 1964, to take part in the 38th International Eucharistic Congress.

He spent nearly 14 hours in New York Oct. 4, 1965, appearing as a pilgrim to plead for peace before representatives of 116 countries at the United Nations.

In December, 1966, he made a short pilgrimage of sympathy so he could be with the people of the Florentine area of Italy which was devastated by a flood of catastrophic proportions.

To pray at the Marian shrine as a pilgrim of peace was the purpose of his one-day flying pilgrimage to Fatima, Portugal May 13, 1967.

On July 25, 1967, he flew to Turkey to see Patriarch Athenagoras I of Constantinople and to visit the ancient city of Ephesus, the locale of the house where, according to an old tradition, the Blessed Virgin Mary lived toward the end of her life, and the place of meeting of the ecumenical council which ratified her title, Mother of God *(Theotokos)*, in 431. The purposes of the pilgrimage were plainly ecumenical and Marian.

On the sixth of his journeys outside Italy, he made a three-day flying visit to take part in the 39th International Eucharistic Congress in Bogota, Colombia, in August, 1968.

He made two visits in 1969: to Geneva, where he delivered addresses at the headquarters of the International Labor Organization and the World Council of Churches, in June; and to Kampala, to honor the martyrs of Uganda, July 31 to Aug. 2.

His ninth trip, Apr. 24, 1970, was a one-day visit to Sardinia, where he joined the islanders for a celebration in honor of their patroness, Our Lady of Bonaria.

The 10th, also in 1970, was the most extensive of all his trips with stops in Teheran, Nov. 26; Manila, the Philippines, Nov. 27 to 29; Samoa, Nov. 29; Sydney, Australia, Nov. 30 to Dec. 3; Djakarta, Indonesia, Dec. 3 and 4; Hong Kong, Dec. 4; Colombo, Ceylon, Dec. 4; and cyclone-ravaged Pakistan. Rome departure and return dates were Nov. 26 and Dec. 5. An attempt was made on the Pope's life in Manila.

He visited Udine, Italy, Sept. 16, 1972, to take part in a Eucharistic congress there. En route, he stopped in Venice.

Visits outside the Vatican since that time have been generally limited to Castel Gandolfo and the environs of Rome.

Dates and Events in Church History

First Century

Early 30's: First Christian Pentecost: gathering together of the Christian community, outpouring of the Holy Spirit, preaching of St. Peter to Jews in Jerusalem, baptism and aggregation of some 3,000 persons to the Christian community.

St. Stephen, deacon, was stoned to death at Jerusalem; he is venerated as the first Christian martyr.

34-64/67: St. Paul, formerly Saul the persecutor of Christians, was converted, baptized and joined to the college of Apostles. After three major missionary journeys, he was martyred in 64 or 67 at Rome.

39: The Gentile Cornelius and his family were baptized by St. Peter.

42: Persecution of Christians in Palestine broke out during the rule of Herod Agrippa; St. James the Greater, the first Apostle to die, was beheaded in 44; St. Peter was imprisoned for a short time; many Christians fled to Antioch and elsewhere.

At Antioch, the followers of Christ were first called Christians.

49: Christians at Rome, who were considered members of a Jewish sect, were adversely affected by a decree of Claudius which forbade Jewish worship there.

51: The Council of Jerusalem, in which all the Apostles participated under the presidency of St. Peter, decreed that circumcision, dietary regulations, and various other prescriptions of Mosaic Law were not obligatory for Gentile converts to the Christian community. The decree was issued in opposition to Judaizers who contended that observance of the Mosaic Law in its entirety was necessary for salvation.

64: Persecution under Nero: The emperor, accusing Christians of starting a fire which destroyed half of Rome, inaugurated the era of major Roman persecutions.

64/65: Martyrdom of St. Peter at Rome during the Neronian persecution. He established his see and spent his last years there after preaching in and around Jerusalem, establishing a see at Antioch, and presiding at the Council of Jerusalem.

70: Destruction of Jerusalem by Titus.

88-97: Pontificate of St. Clement I, third successor of St. Peter as bishop of Rome, one of the Apostolic Fathers. The *First Epistle of Clement to the Corinthians*, with which he has been identified, was addressed by the Church of Rome to the Church at Corinth, the scene of irregularities and divisions in the Christian community.

95: Domitian persecuted Christians, principally at Rome.

c. 100: Death of St. John, Apostle and Evangelist, marking the end of the Age of the Apostles and the first generation of the Church.

Second Century

c. 107: St. Ignatius of Antioch was martyred at Rome. He was the first writer to use the expression, "the Catholic Church."

112: Rescript to Pliny. Emperor Trajan instructed Pliny, governor of Bithynia, not to search out Christians but to punish them if they were publicly denounced and refused to do homage to the Roman gods. The rescript set a pattern of discretionary leniency for Roman magistrates in dealing with Christians.

117-138: Persecution under Hadrian. Many *Acts of Martyrs* date from this period.

c. 125: Spread of Gnosticism.

c. 155: St. Polycarp, bishop of Smyrna and disciple of St. John the Evangelist, was martyred.

c. 156: Beginning of Montanism.

161-180: Reign of Marcus Aurelius. His persecution, launched in the wake of natural disasters, was more violent than those of his predecessors.

165: St. Justin, an important early Christian writer, was martyred at Rome.

c. 180: St. Irenaeus, bishop of Lyons and one of the great early theologians, wrote *Adversus Haereses*. He stated that the teaching and tradition of the Roman See was the standard for belief.

196: Easter Controversy.

The *Didache*, written in the second century, was an important record of Christian belief, practice and government in the first century.

Latin was introduced in the West as a liturgical language.

The Catechetical School of Alexandria, founded about the middle of the century, increased in importance.

Third Century

202: Persecution under Septimius Severus, who wanted to establish one common religion in the Empire.

206: Tertullian, a convert since 197 and the first great ecclesiastical writer in Latin, joined the heretical Montanists. He died in 230.

215: Death of Clement of Alexandria, teacher of Origen and a founding father of the School of Alexandria.

217-235: St. Hippolytus, the first antipope. He was reconciled to the Church while in prison during persecution in 235.

232-254: Origen established the School of Caesarea after being deposed in 231 as head of the School of Alexandria; he died in 254. A scholar and voluminous writer, he was one of the founders of systematic theology and exerted wide influence for many years.

c. 242: Manichaeism originated in Persia.

249-251: Persecution under Decius. Many of those who denied the faith *(lapsi)* sought readmission to the Church at the end of the persecution in 251. Pope St. Cornelius had correspondence with St. Cyprian on the subject and ordered that *lapsi* were to be readmitted after suitable penance.

250-300: Neo-Platonism of Plotinus and Porphyry gained followers.

251: Novatian, an antipope, was condemned at Rome.

256: Pope St. Stephen I upheld the validity of baptism administered by heretics, in the Rebaptism Controversy.

257: Persecution under Valerian, who attempted to destroy the Church as a social structure.

258: St. Cyprian, bishop of Carthage, was martyred.

c. 260: St. Lucian founded the exegetical School of Antioch.

Pope St. Dionysius condemned teachings of Sabellius and the Marcionites.

St. Paul of Thebes became a hermit.

261: Gallienus issued an edict of toleration which ended general persecution for nearly 40 years.

c. 266: Sabellianism was condemned and Paul of Samosata deposed.

292: Diocletian divided the Roman Empire into East and West. The division emphasized political, cultural and other differences between the two parts of the Empire and influenced the Church in the East and West. The prestige of Rome began to decline.

Fourth Century

303: Persecution broke out under Diocletian. It ended in the West in 306 but continued for 10 years in the East; it was particularly violent in 304.

305: St. Anthony of Heracles established a foundation for hermits near the Red Sea in Egypt.

c. 306: The first local legislation on clerical celibacy was enacted by a council held at Elvira, Spain; bishops, priests, deacons and other ministers were forbidden to have wives.

310: St. Hilarion established a foundation for hermits in Palestine.

311: An edict of toleration issued by Galerius at the urging of Constantine and Licinius officially ended persecution in the West; some persecution continued in the East.

313: The *Edict of Milan* issued by Constantine and Licinius recognized Christianity as a lawful religion and the legal freedom of all religions in the Roman Empire.

314: The Council of Arles condemned Donatism in Africa and declared that baptism by heretics was valid.

318: St. Pachomius established the first foundation of the cenobitic (common) life, as compared with the solitary life of hermits in Upper Egypt.

325: The Ecumenical Council of Nicaea (I),

first of its kind in the history of the Church, condemned Arianism; see separate entry.

326: Discovery of the True Cross on which Christ was crucified.

337: Baptism and death of Constantine.

c. 342: Beginning of a 40-year persecution in Persia.

343-344: A local Council of Sardica reaffirmed doctrine formulated by Nicaea I and declared that bishops had the right of appeal to the pope as the highest authority in the Church.

361-363: Julian the Apostate waged an unsuccessful campaign against the Church in an attempt to restore paganism as the religion of the Empire.

c. 365: Persecution under Valens in the East.

c. 376: Beginning of the barbarian invasion in the West.

379: Death of St. Basil, the Father of Monasticism in the East. His writings contributed greatly to the development of rules for the religious life.

381: The Ecumenical Council of Constantinople (I); see separate entry.

382: The *Decree of Pope St. Damasus* listed the Canon of Sacred Scripture.

382-c. 406: St. Jerome translated the Old and New Testaments into Latin. His work is called the Vulgate Version of the Bible.

396: St. Augustine became bishop of Hippo in North Africa.

397: A local Council of Carthage published the Canon of Sacred Scripture.

Fifth Century

410: Visigoths sacked Rome.

411: Donatism was condemned by a council at Carthage.

430: St. Augustine, bishop of Hippo for 35 years, died. He was a strong defender of orthodox doctrine against Manichaeism, Donatism and Pelagianism. The depth and range of his writings made him a dominant influence in Christian thought for many centuries.

431: The Ecumenical Council of Ephesus; see separate entry.

432: St. Patrick arrived in Ireland. By the time of his death in 461 most of the country had been converted, monasteries founded and the hierarchy established.

438: The *Theodosian Code*, a compilation of decrees for the Empire, was issued by Theodosius II. It had great influence on subsequent civil and ecclesiastical law.

449: The Robber Council of Ephesus, which did not have ecclesiastical sanction, declared itself in favor of the opinions of Eutyches who contended that Christ had only one nature.

451: The Ecumenical Council of Chalcedon; see separate entry.

452: Pope St. Leo the Great persuaded Attila the Hun to spare Rome.

455: Vandals sacked Rome. The decline of

imperial Rome dates approximately from this time.

484: Patriarch Acacius of Constantinople was excommunicated for signing the *Henoticon,* a unity law published by Emperor Zeno in 482 to end the turmoil associated with the Monophysite heresy. The document capitulated to the heresy. The excommunication triggered a 35-year-long schism.

494: Pope St. Gelasius I declared in a letter to Emperor Anastasius that the pope had power and authority over the emperor in spiritual matters.

496: Clovis, King of the Franks, was converted and became the defender of Christianity in the West. The Franks became a Catholic people.

Sixth Century

520 and later: Irish monasteries flourished as centers for spiritual life, missionary training and scholarly activity.

529: The Second Council of Orange condemned Semi-Pelagianism.

c. 529: St. Benedict founded the Monte Cassino Abbey. Some years before his death in 543 he wrote a monastic rule which exercised tremendous influence on the form and style of religious life. He is called the Father of Monasticism in the West.

533: John II became the first pope to change his name. The practice did not become general until the time of Sergius IV (1009).

533-534: Emperor Justinian promulgated the *Corpus Juris Civilis* for the Roman world. Like the *Theodosian Code,* it influenced subsequent civil and ecclesiastical law.

c. 545: Death of Dionysius Exiguus who was the first to date history from the birth of Christ, a practice which resulted in use of the B.C. and A.D. abbreviations. His calculations were at least four years late.

553: The Ecumenical Council of Constantinople (II); see separate entry.

585: St. Columban founded an influential monastic school at Luxeuil. He died in 615.

589: The most important of several councils of Toledo was held. The Visigoths renounced Arianism, and St. Leander began the organization of the Church in Spain.

590-604: Pontificate of Pope St. Gregory I the Great. He set the form and style of the papacy which prevailed throughout the Middle Ages; exerted great influence on doctrine and liturgy; was strong in support of monastic discipline and clerical celibacy; authored writings on many subjects. Gregorian Chant is named in his honor.

596: Pope St. Gregory I the Great sent St. Augustine of Canterbury and 40 monks to do missionary work in England.

597: St. Columba died. He founded an important monastery at Iona, established schools and did notable missionary work in Scotland.

By the end of the century, monasteries of nuns were common; Western monasticism was flourishing; monasticism in the East, under the influence of Monophysitism and other factors, was losing its vigor.

Seventh Century

613: St. Columban established the influential Monastery of Bobbio in northern Italy.

622: The Hegira (flight) of Mohammed from Mecca to Medina signalled the beginning of Islam which, by the end of the century, claimed almost all of the southern Mediterranean area.

629: Emperor Heraclius recovered the True Cross from the Persians.

649: A Lateran Council condemned two erroneous formulas *(Ecthesis* and *Type)* issued by emperors Heraclius and Constans II as means of reconciling Monophysites with the Church.

664: Actions of the Synod of Whitby advanced the adoption of Roman usages in England, especially regarding the date for the observance of Easter. (See Easter Controversy.)

680-681: The Ecumenical Council of Constantinople (III); see separate entry.

692: Trullan Synod. Eastern-Church discipline on clerical celibacy was settled, permitting marriage before ordination to the diaconate and continuation in marriage afterwards, but prohibiting marriage following the death of the wife thereafter. Anti-Roman canons contributed to East-West alienation.

During the century, the monastic influence of Ireland and England increased in Western Europe; schools and learning declined; regulations regarding clerical celibacy became more strict in the East.

Eighth Century

711: Moslems began the conquest of Spain.

726: Emperor Leo III, the Isaurian, launched a campaign against the veneration of sacred images and relics; called Iconoclasm (image-breaking), it caused turmoil in the East until about 843.

731: Pope Gregory II and a synod at Rome condemned Iconoclasm, with a declaration that the veneration of sacred images was in accord with Catholic tradition.

Venerable Bede issued his *Ecclesiastical History of the English People.*

732: Charles Martel defeated the Moslems at Poitiers, halting farther advance by them in the West.

744: The Monastery of Fulda was established by St. Sturm, a disciple of St. Boniface.

754: A council of more than 300 Byzantine bishops endorsed Iconoclast errors. This council and its actions were condemned by the Lateran Synod of 769.

Stephen II (III) crowned Pepin ruler of the Franks. Pepin twice invaded Italy, in 754 and 756, to defend the pope against the Lombards. His land grants to the papacy, called the Donation of Pepin, were later extended by Charlemagne (773) and formed part of the States of the Church.

c. 755: St. Boniface (Winfrid) was martyred. He was called the Apostle of Germany for his missionary work and organization of the hierarchy there.

781: Alcuin was chosen by Charlemagne to organize a Palace School, which became a center of intellectual leadership.

787: The Ecumenical Council of Nicaea (II); see separate entry.

792: A council at Ratisbon condemned Adoptionism.

The famous *Book of Kells* ("The Great Gospel of Columcille") dates from the early eighth or late seventh century.

Ninth Century

800: Charlemagne was crowned Emperor by Pope Leo III on Christmas Day.

Egbert became king of West Saxons. He unified England and strengthened the See of Canterbury.

813: Emperor Leo V, the Armenian, revived Iconoclasm, which persisted until about 843.

814: Charlemagne died.

843: The Treaty of Verdun split the Frankish kingdom among Charlemagne's three grandsons.

844: A Eucharistic controversy involving the writings of Paschasius Radbertus, Ratramnus and Rabanus Maurus occasioned the development of terminology regarding the doctrine of the Real Presence.

846: The Moslems invaded Italy and attacked Rome.

847-852: Period of composition of the *False Decretals,* a collection of forged documents attributed to popes from St. Clement (88-97) to Gregory II (715-731). The *Decretals,* which strongly supported the autonomy and rights of bishops, were suspect for a long time before being repudiated entirely about 1628.

848: The Council of Mainz condemned Gottschalk for heretical teaching regarding predestination. He was also condemned by the Council of Quierzy in 853.

857: Photius displaced Ignatius as patriarch of Constantinople. This marked the beginning of the Photian Schism, a confused state of East-West relations which has not yet been cleared up by historical research. Photius, a man of exceptional ability, died in 891.

865: St. Ansgar, Apostle of Scandinavia, died.

868: Sts. Cyril (d. 869) and Methodius (d. 885) were consecrated bishops. The Apostles of the Slavs devised an alphabet and translated the Gospels and liturgy into the Slavonic language.

869: The Ecumenical Council of Constantinople (IV); see separate entry.

871-c. 900: Reign of Alfred the Great, the only English king ever anointed by a pope at Rome.

Tenth Century

910: William, Duke of Aquitaine, founded the Benedictine Abbey of Cluny, which became a center of monastic and ecclesiastical reform.

915: Pope John X played a leading role in the expulsion of Saracens from central and southern Italy.

955: St. Olga, of the Russian royal family, was baptized.

962: Otto I, the Great, crowned by Pope John XII, revived Charlemagne's kingdom, which became the Holy Roman Empire.

966: Mieszko, first of a royal line in Poland, was baptized; he brought Latin Christianity to Poland.

989: Vladimir, ruler of Russia, was baptized. Russia was subsequently Christianized by Greek missionaries.

993: John XV was the first pope to decree the official canonization of a saint (Ulrich) for the universal Church.

997: St. Stephen became ruler of Hungary. He assisted in organizing the hierarchy and establishing Latin Christianity in that country.

999-1003: Pontificate of Sylvester II (Gerbert of Aquitaine), a Benedictine monk and the first French pope.

Eleventh Century

1009: Beginning of lasting East-West schism in the Church, marked by dropping of the name of Pope Sergius IV from the Byzantine diptychs (the listing of persons prayed for during the liturgy). The deletion was made by Patriarch Sergius II of Constantinople.

1012: St. Romuald founded the Camaldolese Hermits.

1025: The Council of Arras, and other councils later, condemned the Cathari (Neo-Manichaeans, Albigenses).

1027: The Council of Elne proclaimed the Truce of God as a means of stemming violence. The truce involved armistice periods of varying length, which were later extended.

1038: St. John Gualbert founded the Vallombrosians.

1043-1059: Constantinople patriarchate of Michael Cerularius, the key figure in a controversy concerning the primacy of the papacy. His and the Byzantine synod's refusal to acknowledge this primacy in 1054 widened and hardened the East-West schism in the Church.

1047: Pope Clement II died. He was the only pope ever buried in Germany.

1049-54: Pontificate of St. Leo IX, who inaugurated a movement of papal, diocesan, monastic and clerical reform.

1055: Condemnation of the Eucharistic doctrine of Berengarius.

1059: A Lateran Council issued new legislation regarding papal elections. Voting power was entrusted to the Roman cardinals.

1066: Death of St. Edward the Confessor, King of England from 1042 and restorer of Westminster Abbey.

Defeat, at Hastings, of Harold by William I, who subsequently exerted strong influence on the life style of the Church in England.

1073-1085: Pontificate of St. Gregory VII (Hildebrand). A strong pope, he carried forward programs of clerical and general ecclesiastical reform and struggled against Henry IV and other rulers to end the evils of lay investiture. He introduced the Latin liturgy in Spain and set definite dates for the observance of ember days.

1077: Henry IV, excommunicated and suspended from the exercise of imperial powers by Gregory VII, sought absolution from the Pope at Canossa. Henry later repudiated this action and in 1084 forced Gregory to leave Rome.

1079: The Council of Rome condemned Eucharistic errors of Berengarius, who retracted.

1084: St. Bruno founded the Carthusians.

1097-1099: The first of several Crusades undertaken between this time and 1265. Recovery of the Holy Places and gaining free access to them for Christians were the original purposes, but these were diverted to less worthy objectives in various ways. Results included: a Latin Kingdom of Jerusalem, 1099-1187; a military and political misadventure in the form of a Latin Empire of Constantinople, 1204-1261; acquisition, by treaties, of visiting rights for Christians in the Holy Land. East-West economic and cultural relationships increased during the period. In the religious sphere, actions of the Crusaders had the effect of increasing the alienation of the East from the West.

1098: St. Robert founded the Cistercians.

Twelfth Century

1108: Beginnings of the influential Abbey and School of St. Victor.

1115: St. Bernard established the Abbey of Clairvaux and inaugurated the Cistercian Reform.

1118: Christian forces captured Saragossa, Spain; the beginning of the Moslem decline in that country.

1121: St. Norbert established the original monastery of the Praemonstratensians near Laon, France.

1122: The Concordat of Worms (Pactum Callixtinum) was formulated and approved by Pope Callistus II and Emperor Henry V to settle controversy concerning the investiture of prelates. The concordat provided that the emperor could invest prelates with symbols of temporal authority but had no right to invest them with spiritual authority, which came from the Church alone, and that the emperor was not to interfere in papal elections. This was the first concordat in history.

1123: The Ecumenical Council of the Lateran (I), the first of its kind in the West; see separate entry.

1139: The Ecumenical Council of the Lateran (II); see separate entry.

1140: St. Bernard met Abelard in debate at the Council of Sens. Abelard, whose rationalism in theology was condemned for the first time in 1121, died in 1142 at Cluny.

1148: The Synod of Rheims enacted strict disciplinary decrees for communities of women religious.

1152: The Synod of Kells reorganized the Church in Ireland.

1160: Gratian, whose *Decretum* became a basic text of Canon Law, died.

Peter Lombard, compiler of the *Four Books of Sentences,* a standard theology text for nearly 200 years, died.

1170: St. Thomas Becket, archbishop of Canterbury, who clashed with Henry II over Church-state relations, was murdered in his cathedral.

1171: Pope Alexander III reserved the process of canonization of saints to the Holy See.

1179: The Ecumenical Council of the Lateran (III); see separate entry.

1184: Waldenses and other heretics were excommunicated by Pope Lucius III.

Thirteenth Century

1198-1216: Pontificate of Innocent III, during which the papacy reached its medieval peak of authority, influence and prestige in the Church and in relations with civil rulers.

1208: Innocent III called for a crusade, the first in Christendom itself, against the Albigensians.

1209: Verbal approval was given by Innocent III to a rule of life for the Order of Friars Minor, started by St. Francis of Assisi.

1212: The Second Order of Franciscans, the Poor Clares, was founded.

1215: The Ecumenical Council of the Lateran (IV); see separate entry.

1216: Formal papal approval was given to a rule of life for the Order of Preachers, started by St. Dominic.

The Portiuncula Indulgence was granted by the Holy See at the request of St. Francis of Assisi.

1221: The Third Order of St. Francis for lay persons was founded.

1226: Death of St. Francis of Assisi.

1245: The Ecumenical Council of Lyons (I); see separate entry.

1247: Preliminary approval was given by the Holy See to a Carmelite rule of life.

1270: St. Louis IX, king of France, died. Beginning of papal decline.

1274: The Ecumenical Council of Lyons (II); see separate entry.

Death of St. Thomas Aquinas, Doctor of the Church, of lasting influence; see separate entry.

1280: Pope Nicholas III, who made the *Breviary* the official prayer book for clergy of the Roman Church, died.

1281: The excommunication of Michael Palaeologus by Pope Martin IV ruptured the union effected with the Eastern Church in 1274.

Fourteenth Century

1302: Pope Boniface VIII issued the bull *Unam Sanctam,* concerning the unity of the Church and the temporal power of princes, against the background of a struggle with Philip IV of France; it was the most famous medieval document on the subject.

1308-1378: For a period of approximately 70 years, seven popes resided at Avignon because of unsettled conditions in Rome and other reasons; see separate entry.

1311-1312: The Ecumenical Council of Vienne; see separate entry.

1321: Dante Alighieri died a year after completing the *Divine Comedy.*

1324: Marsilius of Padua completed *Defensor Pacis,* a work condemned by Pope John XXII as heretical because of its denial of papal primacy and the hierarchical structure of the Church, and for other reasons. It was a charter for conciliarism.

1337-1453: Period of the Hundred Years' War, a dynastic struggle between France and England.

1338: Four years after the death of Pope John XXII, who had opposed Louis IV of Bavaria in a years-long controversy, electoral princes declared at the Diet of Rhense that the emperor did not need papal confirmation of his title and right to rule. Charles IV later (1356) said the same thing in a *Golden Bull,* eliminating papal rights in the election of emperors.

1347-1350: The Black Death swept across Europe, killing perhaps one-fourth to one-third of the total population; an estimated 40 per cent of the clergy succumbed.

1374: Petrarch, poet and humanist, died.

1378: Return of the papacy from Avignon to Rome.

Beginning of the Western Schism; see separate entry.

Fifteenth Century

1409: The Council of Pisa, without canonical authority, tried to end the Western Schism but succeeded only in complicating it by electing a third claimant to the papacy; see Western Schism.

1414-1418: The Ecumenical Council of Constance ended the Western Schism; see separate entry.

1431: St. Joan of Arc was burned at the stake.

1431-1449: The Council of Basle, which began with convocation by Pope Martin V in 1431, turned into an anti-papal forum of conciliarists seeking to subject the primacy and authority of the pope to the overriding authority of an assembly of bishops. It was not an ecumenical council.

1438: The Pragmatic Sanction of Bourges was enacted by Charles VIII and the French parliament to curtail papal authority over the Church in France, in the spirit of conciliarism. It found expression in Gallicanism and had effects lasting at least until the French Revolution.

1438-1443: The Ecumenical Council of Florence affirmed the primacy of the pope in opposition to conciliarism and effected a measure of union with separated Eastern Christians; see separate entry.

1453: The fall of Constantinople to the Turks.

c. 1456: Gutenberg issued the first edition of the Bible printed from movable type, at Mainz, Germany.

1476: Pope Sixtus IV ordered observance of the feast of the Immaculate Conception on Dec. 8 throughout the Church.

1492: Columbus discovered the Americas.

1493: Pope Alexander VI issued a *Bull of Demarcation* which determined spheres of influence for the Spanish and Portuguese in the Americas.

The Renaissance, a humanistic movement which originated in Italy in the 14th century, spread to France, Germany, the Low Countries and England. A transitional period between the medieval world and the modern secular world, it introduced profound changes which affected literature and the other arts, general culture, politics and religion.

Sixteenth Century

1512-1517: The Ecumenical Council of the Lateran (V); see separate entry.

1517: Martin Luther signalled the beginning of the Reformation by posting 95 theses at Wittenberg. Subsequently, he broke completely from doctrinal orthodoxy in discourses and three published works (1519 and 1520); was excommunicated on more than 40 charges of heresy (1521); remained the dominant figure in the Reformation in Germany until his death in 1546.

1519: Zwingli triggered the Reformation in Zurich and became its leading proponent there until his death in combat in 1531.

1524: Luther's encouragement of German princes in putting down the two-year Peasants' Revolt gained political support for his cause.

1528: The Order of Friars Minor Capuchin was approved as an autonomous division of the Franciscan Order; like the Jesuits, the Capuchins became leaders in the Counter-Reformation.

1530: The *Augsburg Confession* of Lutheran faith was issued; it was later supplemented by the *Smalcald Articles* approved in 1537.

1533: Henry VIII divorced Catherine of Aragon, married Anne Boleyn, was excommunicated. In 1534 he decreed the Act of Supremacy, making the sovereign the head of the Church in England, under which Sts. John Fisher and Thomas More were executed in 1535. Despite his rejection of papal primacy and actions against monastic life in England, he generally maintained doctrinal orthodoxy until his death in 1547.

1536: John Calvin, leader of the Reformation in Switzerland until his death in 1564, issued the first edition of *Institutes of the Christian Religion,* which became the classical text of Reformed (non-Lutheran) theology.

1540: The constitutions of the Society of Jesus (Jesuits), founded by St. Ignatius of Loyola, were approved.

1541: Start of the 11-year career of St. Francis Xavier as a missionary to the East Indies and Japan.

1545-1563: The Ecumenical Council of Trent formulated statements of Catholic doctrine under attack by the Reformers and mobilized the Counter-Reformation; see separate entry.

1549: The first *Book of Common Prayer* was issued by Edward VI. Revised editions were published in 1552, 1559 and 1662.

1553: Start of the five-year reign of Mary Tudor who tried to counteract actions of Henry VIII against the Roman Church.

1555: Enactment of the Peace of Augsburg, an arrangement of religious territorialism rather than toleration, which recognized the existence of Catholicism and Lutheranism in the German Empire and provided that citizens should adopt the religion of their respective rulers.

1558: Beginning of the reign of Elizabeth I, during which the Church of England took on its definitive form.

1559: Establishment of the hierarchy of the Church of England, with the consecration of Matthew Parker as archbishop of Canterbury.

1563: The first text of the *39 Articles* of the Church of England was issued. Also enacted were a new Act of Supremacy and Oath of Succession to the English throne.

1570: Elizabeth I was excommunicated. Penal measures against Catholics subsequently became more severe.

1571: Defeat of the Turkish armada at Lepanto staved off the invasion of Eastern Europe.

1577: The *Formula of Concord,* the classical statement of Lutheran faith, was issued; it was, generally, a Lutheran counterpart of the canons of the Council of Trent. In 1580, along with other formulas of doctrine, it was included in the *Book of Concord.*

1582: The Gregorian Calendar, named for Pope Gregory XIII, was put into effect and was eventually adopted in most countries: England delayed adoption until 1752.

Seventeenth Century

1605: The Gunpowder Plot, an attempt by Catholic fanatics to blow up James I of England and the houses of Parliament, resulted in an anti-Catholic Oath of Allegiance; the Oath was condemned by Pope Paul V in 1606.

1610: Death of Matteo Ricci, outstanding Jesuit missionary to China, pioneer in cultural relations between China and Europe.

Founding of the first community of Visitation Nuns by Sts. Francis de Sales and Jane de Chantal.

1611: Founding of the Oratorians.

1613: Catholics were banned from Scandinavia.

1625: Founding of the Congregation of the Mission (Vincentians) by St. Vincent de Paul. He founded the Sisters of Charity in 1633.

1642: Death of Galileo, scientist, who was censured by the Congregation of the Holy Office for supporting the Copernican theory of the sun-centered planetary system.

Founding of the Sulpicians by Jacques Olier.

1643: Start of publication of the Bollandist *Acta Sanctorum,* a critical work on lives of the saints.

1648: Provisions in the Peace of Westphalia, ending the Thirty Years' War, extended terms of the Peace of Augsburg (1555) to Calvinists and gave equality to Catholics and Protestants in the 300 states of the Holy Roman Empire.

1649: Oliver Cromwell invaded Ireland and began a severe persecution of the Church there.

1653: Pope Innocent X condemned five propositions of Jansenism, a complex theory which distorted doctrine concerning the relations between divine grace and human freedom. Jansenism was also a rigoristic movement which seriously disturbed the Church in France, the Low Countries and Italy in this and the 18th century.

1673: The Test Act in England barred from public office Catholics who would not deny the doctrine of transubstantiation and receive Communion in the Church of England.

1678: Many English Catholics suffered death as a consequence of the Popish Plot, a false allegation by Titus Oates that Catholics planned to assassinate Charles I, land a French army in the country, burn London, and turn over the government to the Jesuits.

1682: The four articles of the *Gallican Declaration,* drawn up by Bossuet, asserted political and ecclesiastical immunities of France from papal control. The articles, which rejected the primacy of the pope, were condemned in 1690.

1689: The Toleration Act granted a measure of freedom of worship to other English dissenters but not to Catholics.

This century is called the age of Enlightenment or Reason because of the predominating rational and scientific approach of its leading philosophers, scientists and writers with respect to religion, ethics and natural law. This approach downgraded the fact and significance of revealed religion. Also characteristic of the Enlightenment were subjectivism, secularism and optimism regarding human perfectibility.

Eighteenth Century

1704: Chinese Rites—involving the Christian adaptation of elements of Confucianism, veneration of ancestors and Chinese terminology in religion — were condemned by Clement XI. An earlier ban was issued in 1645; a later one, in 1742.

1720: The Passionists were founded by St. Paul of the Cross.

1724: Persecution in China.

1732: The Redemptorists were founded by St. Alphonsus Liguori.

1738: Freemasonry was condemned by Clement XII and Catholics were forbidden to join, under penalty of excommunication; the prohibition was repeated by Benedict XIV in 1751 and by later popes.

1760's: Josephinism, a theory and system of state control of the Church, was initiated in Austria; it remained in force until about 1850.

1764: Febronianism, an unorthodox theory and practice regarding the constitution of the Church and relations between Church and state, was condemned for the first of several times. Proposed by an auxiliary bishop of Trier using the pseudonym Justinus Febronius, it had the effects of minimizing the office of the pope and supporting national churches under state control.

1773: Clement XIV issued a brief of suppression against the Jesuits, following their expulsion from Portugal in 1759, from France in 1764 and from Spain in 1767. Political intrigue and unsubstantiated accusations were principal factors in these developments. The ban, which crippled the Society, contained no condemnation of the Jesuit constitutions, particular Jesuits or Jesuit teaching. The Society was restored in 1814.

1778: Catholics in England were relieved of some civil disabilities dating back to the time of Henry VIII, by an act which permitted them to acquire, own and inherit property. Additional liberties were restored by the Roman Catholic Relief Act of 1791 and subsequent enactments of Parliament.

1789: Religious freedom in the United States was guaranteed under the First Amendment to the Constitution.

Beginning of the French Revolution which resulted in: the secularization of church property and the Civil Constitution of the Clergy in 1790; the persecution of priests, religious and lay persons loyal to papal authority; invasion of the Papal States by Napoleon in 1796; renewal of persecution from 1797-1799; attempts to dechristianize France and es-

tablish a new religion; the occupation of Rome by French troops and the forced removal of Pius VI to France in 1798.

Nineteenth Century

1809: Pius VII was made a captive by Napoleon and deported to France where he remained in exile until 1814. During this time he refused to cooperate with Napoleon who sought to bring the Church in France under his own control.

The turbulence in church-state relations in France at the beginning of the century recurred in connection with the Bourbon Restoration, the July Revolution, the second and third Republics, the Second Empire and the Dreyfus case.

1814: The Society of Jesus, suppressed since 1773, was restored.

1817: Reestablishment of the Congregation for the Propagation of the Faith (Propaganda) by Pius VII was an important factor in increasing missionary activity during the century.

1820: Years-long persecution, during which thousands died for the faith, ended in China. Thereafter, communication with the West remained cut off until about 1834. Vigorous missionary work got underway in 1842.

1822: The Pontifical Society for the Propagation of the Faith, inaugurated in France by Pauline Jaricot for the support of missionary activity, was established.

1829: The Catholic Emancipation Act relieved Catholics in England and Ireland of most of the civil disabilities to which they had been subject from the time of Henry VIII.

1832: Gregory XVI, in the encyclical *Mirari Vos,* condemned indifferentism, one of the many ideologies at odds with Christian doctrine which were proposed during the century.

1833: Start of the Oxford Movement which affected the Church of England and resulted in some notable conversions, including that of John Henry Newman in 1845, to the Catholic Church.

Frederick Ozanam founded the Society of St. Vincent de Paul in France. The society, whose objective was works of charity, became worldwide.

1848: The *Communist Manifesto,* a revolutionary document symptomatic of socioeconomic crisis, was issued.

1850: The hierarchy was reestablished in England and Nicholas Wiseman made the first archbishop of Westminster. He was succeeded in 1865 by Henry Manning, an Oxford convert and proponent of the rights of labor.

1853: The Catholic hierarchy was reestablished in Holland.

1854: Pius IX proclaimed the dogma of the Immaculate Conception in the bull *Ineffabilis Deus.*

1858: The Blessed Virgin Mary appeared to

St. Bernadette at Lourdes, France; see separate entry.

1864: Pius IX issued the encyclical *Quanta Cura* and the *Syllabus of Errors* in condemnation of some 80 propositions derived from the scientific mentality and rationalism of the century. The subjects in question had deep ramifications in many areas of thought and human endeavor; in religion, they explicitly and/or implicitly rejected divine revelation and the supernatural order.

1867: The first volume of *Das Kapital* was published. Together with the Communist First International, formed in the same year, it had great influence on the subsequent development of Communism and Socialism.

1869: The Anglican Church was disestablished in Ireland.

1869-1870: The First Vatican Council; see separate entry.

1870-1871: Victor Emmanuel II of Sardinia, crowned king of Italy after defeating Austrian and papal forces, marched into Rome in 1870 and expropriated the Papal States after a plebiscite in which Catholics, at the order of Pius IX, did not vote. In 1871, Pius IX refused to accept a Law of Guarantees. Confiscation of church property and hindrance of ecclesiastical administration by the regime followed.

1871: The German Empire, a confederation of 26 states, was formed. Government policy launched a Kulturkampf whose May Laws of 1873 were designed to annul papal jurisdiction in Prussia and other states and to place the Church under imperial control. Resistance to the enactments and the persecution they legalized forced the government to modify its anti-Church policy by 1887.

1878: Beginning of the pontificate of Leo XIII, who was pope until his death in 1903. Leo is best known for the encyclical *Rerum Novarum*, which greatly influenced the course of Christian social thought and the labor movement. His other accomplishments included promotion of a revival of Scholastic philosophy and the impetus he gave to scriptural studies.

1881: The first International Eucharistic Congress was held in Lille, France.

Alexander II of Russia died. His policies of Russification — as well as those of his two predecessors and a successor during the century — caused great suffering to Catholics, Jews and Protestants in Poland, Lithuania, the Ukraine and Bessarabia.

1882: Charles Darwin died. His theory of evolution by natural selection, one of several scientific highlights of the century, had extensive repercussions in the faith-and-science controversy.

1889: The Catholic University of America was founded in Washington, D.C.

1893: The US apostolic delegation was set up in Washington, D. C.

Twentieth Century

1901: Restrictive measures in France forced the Jesuits, Benedictines, Carmelites and other religious orders to leave the country. Subsequently, 14,000 schools were suppressed; religious orders and congregations were expelled; the concordat was renounced in 1905; church property was confiscated in 1906. For some years the Holy See, refusing to comply with government demands for the control of bishops' appointments, left some ecclesiastical offices vacant.

1903: Start of the 11-year pontificate of St. Pius X. He initiated the codification of canon law, 1904; removed the ban against participation by Catholics in Italian national elections, 1905; issued decrees calling upon the faithful to receive Holy Communion frequently and daily, and stating that children should begin receiving the Eucharist at the age of seven, 1905 and 1910, respectively; ordered the establishment of the Confraternity of Christian Doctrine in all parishes throughout the world, 1905; condemned Modernism in the decree *Lamentabili* and the encyclical *Pascendi*, 1907.

1908: The United States and England, long under the jurisdiction of the Congregation for the Propagation of the Faith as mission territories, were removed from its control and placed under the common law of the Church.

1910: Laws of separation were enacted in Portugal, marking a point of departure in church-state relations.

1911: The Catholic Foreign Mission Society of America — Maryknoll, the first US-founded society of its type — was established.

1914: Start of World War I, which lasted until 1918.

Start of the eight-year pontificate of Benedict XV. Much of his pontificate was devoted to seeking ways and means of minimizing the material and spiritual havoc of World War I. In 1917 he offered his services as a mediator to the belligerent nations, but his pleas for settlement of the conflict went unheeded.

1917: The Blessed Virgin Mary appeared to three children at Fatima, Portugal; see separate entry.

A new constitution, embodying repressive laws against the Church, was enacted in Mexico. Its implementation resulted in persecution in the 1920's and 1930's.

Bolsheviks seized power in Russia and set up a Communist dictatorship. The event marked the rise of Communism in Russian and world affairs. One of its immediate, and lasting, results was persecution of the Church, Jews and other segments of the population.

1918: The *Code of Canon Law*, in preparation for more than 10 years, went into effect in the Western Church.

1919: Benedict XV stimulated missionary work through the decree *Maximum Illud*, in which he urged the recruiting and training of native clergy in places where the Church was not firmly established.

1922: Beginning of the 17-year pontificate of Pius XI. He subscribed to the Lateran Treaty, 1929, which settled the Roman Question created by the confiscation of the Papal States in 1871; issued the encyclical *Casti Connubii*, 1930, an authoritative statement on Christian marriage; resisted the efforts of Benito Mussolini to control Catholic Action and the Church, in the encyclical *Non Abbiamo Bisogno*, 1931; opposed various Fascist policies; issued the encyclicals *Quadragesimo Anno*, 1931, developing the social doctrine of Leo XIII's *Rerum Novarum*, and *Divini Redemptoris*, 1937, calling for social justice and condemning atheistic Communism; condemned anti-Semitism, 1937.

Ireland was partitioned. All but two of the predominantly Catholic counties were included in the southern part of the country, which eventually attained the status of an independent republic in 1949.

1926: The Catholic Relief Act repealed virtually all legal disabilities of Catholics in England.

1931: Leftists proclaimed Spain a republic and proceeded to disestablish the Church, confiscate church property, deny salaries to the clergy, expel the Jesuits and ban teaching of the Catholic faith. These actions were preludes to the civil war of 1936-1939.

1933: Emergence of Adolf Hitler to power in Germany. By 1935 two of his aims were clear, the elimination of the Jews and control of a single national church. Persecution decimated the Jews over a period of years. The Church was subject to repressive measures, which Pius XI protested futilely in the encyclical *Mit Brennender Sorge* in 1937.

1936: A three-year civil war broke out in Spain between the leftist Loyalists and forces led by Francisco Franco. The Loyalists were defeated and one-man, one-party rule was established. A number of priests, religious and lay persons fell victims to Loyalist persecution.

1939: Start of World War II, which lasted until 1945.

Start of the 19-year pontificate of Pius XII; see separate entry.

1940: Start of a decade of Communist conquest in more than 13 countries, resulting in conditions of persecution for a minimum of 60 million Catholics as well as members of other faiths; see various countries.

Persecution diminished in Mexico through non-enforcement of anti-religious laws still on record.

1950: Pius XII proclaimed the dogma of the Assumption of the Blessed Virgin Mary.

1954: St. Pius X was canonized.

1957: The Communist regime of China attempted to start a national schismatic church.

1958: Beginning of the five-year pontificate of John XXIII; see separate entry.

1962: The Second Vatican Council began the first of four sessions; see separate entry.

1963: Paul VI began his pontificate; see separate entry.

HERESIES

Heresy is the formal and obstinate denial or doubt by a baptized person, who remains a nominal Christian, of any truth which must be believed as a matter of divine and Catholic faith. Formal heresy involves deliberate resistance to the authority of God who communicates revelation through Scripture and tradition and the teaching authority of the Church. Obstinate refusal to accept the infallible teaching of the Church constitutes the canonical crime of heresy.

Formal heretics automatically incur the penalty of excommunication (Canon 1325 of the Code of Canon Law). Material heretics are those who, in good faith and without formal obstinacy, do not accept articles or matters of divine and Catholic faith.

Heresies have been significant not only as disruptions of unity of faith but also as occasions for the clarification and development of doctrine.

Heresies from the beginning of the Church to the 13th century are listed below.

Judaizers: Early converts who claimed that members of the Church had to observe all the requirements of Mosaic Law as well as the obligations of Christian faith. This view was condemned by the Council of Jerusalem held in 51 under the presidency of St. Peter (Acts 15:28).

Gnosticism: A combination of elements of Platonic philosophy and Eastern mystery religions which claimed that its secret knowledge-principle gave its adherents a deeper insight into Christian doctrine than divine revelation and faith. One Gnostic thesis denied the divinity of Christ; others denied the reality of his humanity, calling it mere appearance (**Docetism, Phantasiasm**).

Modalism: A general term covering propositions (**Monarchianism, Patripassianism, Sabellianism**) that the Father, Son and Holy Spirit are not really distinct divine Persons but are only three different modes of being and self-manifestation of the one God. Various forms of Modalism, which appeared in the East in the second century and spread westward, were all condemned.

Marcionism: A Gnostic creation named for its author, who claimed there was total opposition and no connection at all between the Old Testament and the New Testament, between the God of the Jews and the God of the Christians; and that the canon of Scripture consisted only of portions of Luke's Gospel and 10 Epistles of Paul. Marcion was excommunicated in 144 at Rome, and his tenets were condemned again by a Roman council about 260. The heresy was checked at Rome by 200 but persisted for several centuries in the East and had some adherents as late as the Middle Ages.

Montanism: A form of extremism preached about 170 by Montanus of Phrygia, Asia Minor. Its principal tenets were: an imminent second coming of Christ, denial of the divine nature of the Church and its power to forgive sin, excessively rigorous morality. Condemned by Pope St. Zephyrinus (199-217). Tertullian was one of its victims.

Novatianism: A heresy of excessive rigorism named for its author, a priest of Rome and antipope. Its principal tenet was that persons who fell away from the Church under persecution and/or those guilty of serious sin after baptism could not be absolved and readmitted to communion with the Church. The heresy, condemned by a Roman synod in 251, slowly subsided in the West and died in the East by the end of the seventh century.

Subordinationism, Adoptionism: Christological errors and logical antecedents of Arianism. The key tenet was that Christ, while the most excellent of creatures, was subordinate to God whose Son he was by adoption rather than by nature. First proposed at Rome late in the second century, it was condemned by Pope St. Victor in 190 and again in the following century, in 785 by Pope Adrian I, in 794 by a Council of Frankfurt, and in 1177 by Pope Alexander III.

Arianism: Denial of the divinity of Christ, the most devastating of the early heresies, authored by Arius of Alexandria and condemned by the Council of Nicaea I in 325. Arians and several kinds of **Semi-Arians** propagandized their tenets widely, raised havoc in the Church for several centuries, and established their own hierarchies and churches.

Macedonianism: Denial of the divinity of the Holy Spirit, who was said to be a creature of the Son. Condemned by the Council of Constantinople I in 381. Macedonians were also called **Pneumatomachists,** enemies of the Spirit; and **Marathonians,** after the name of one of their leaders, a bishop of Nicomedia.

Nestorianism: Denial of the real unity of divine and human natures in the single divine Person of Christ, proposed by Nestorius, patriarch of Constantinople. He also held that Mary could not be called the Mother of God *(Theotokos);* that is, of the Second Person of the Trinity made Man. Condemned by the councils of Ephesus in 431 and Chalcedon in 451.

Monophysitism: Denial of Christ's human nature; also called **Eutychianism,** after the name of one of its leading advocates. Condemned by the Council of Chalcedon in 451.

Monothelitism: Denial of the human will of Christ. Severus of Antioch and Sergius, patriarch of Constantinople, were leading advocates of the heresy, which was condemned by the Council of Constantinople III in 681.

Priscillianism: A fourth century amalgamation of elements from various sources — Sabellianism, Arianism, Docetism, Pantheism, belief in the diabolical nature of marriage, corruption of Scripture. Condemned by a Council of Braga in 563 on 17 different counts.

Donatism: A development of the error at the heart of the third century **Rebaptism Controversy** (baptism conferred by heretics is invalid because persons deprived of grace are incapable of being ministers of grace to others). Followers of Donatus the Great asserted throughout the fourth century that sacraments administered by sinners were invalid. Condemnation of the heresy is traced to Pope St. Stephen I (254-257) and the principle that sacraments have their efficacy from Christ, not from their human ministers.

Pelagianism: Denial of the supernatural order of things, proposed by Pelagius (360-420), a Breton monk. Proceeding from the assumption that Adam had a natural right to supernatural life, the theory held that man could attain salvation through the efforts of his own free will and natural powers. The theory involved errors concerning the nature of original sin, the meaning of grace and other matters. St. Augustine opposed the heresy, which was condemned by the Council of Ephesus in 431. **Semi-Pelagianism** was condemned by a Council of Orange in 529.

Iconoclasm: An image-breaking campaign which resulted from an edict issued by Eastern Emperor Leo the Isaurian in 726, that the veneration of images, pictures and relics was idolatrous. The theoretical basis of the heresy was the Monophysite error which denied the humanity of Christ. It was denounced several times before its condemnation by the Council of Nicaea II in 787.

Berengarian Heresy: Denial of the Real Presence of Christ under the appearances of bread and wine, the first clear-cut Eucharistic heresy; proposed by Berengarius of Tours (c. 1000-1088). Condemned by various synods and finally by a council held at Rome in 1079.

Waldensianism: Claimed by Peter Waldo, a merchant of Lyons, to be a return to pure Christianity, the heresy rejected the hierarchical structure of the Church, the sacramental system and other doctrines. Its adherents were excommunicated in 1184 and their tenets were condemned several times thereafter.

Albigensianism, Catharism: Related errors based on the old **Manichaean** assumption that two supreme principles of good and evil were operative in creation and life, and that the supreme objective of human endeavor was liberation from evil (matter). The heresy denied the humanity of Christ, the sacramental system and the authority of the Church (and state), and endorsed a moral code which threatened seriously the fabric of social life in southern France and northern Italy in the 12th and 13th centuries. Condemned by councils of the Lateran III and Lateran IV in 1179 and 1215.

ECUMENICAL COUNCILS

An ecumenical council is an assembly of the college of bishops, with and under the presidency of the pope, which has supreme authority over the Church in matters pertaining to faith, morals, worship and discipline.

The Second Vatican Council stated: "The supreme authority with which this college (of bishops) is empowered over the whole Church is exercised in a solemn way through an ecumenical council. A council is never ecumenical unless it is confirmed or at least accepted as such by the successor of Peter. It is the prerogative of the Roman Pontiff to convoke these councils, to preside over them, and to confirm them" *(Dogmatic Constitution on the Church*, No. 22).

Pope Presides

The pope is the head of an ecumenical council; he presides over it either personally or through legates. Conciliar decrees and other actions have binding force only when confirmed and promulgated by him. If a pope dies during a council, it is suspended until reconvened by another pope. An ecumenical council is not superior to a pope; hence, there is no appeal from a pope to a council.

Collectively, the bishops with the pope represent the whole Church. They do this not as democratic representatives of their faithful in a kind of church parliament, but as the successors of the Apostles with divinely given authority, care and responsibility over the whole Church.

Council participants with a deliberative vote are: cardinals; residential patriarchs, primates, archbishops and bishops, even if they are not yet consecrated; abbots and certain other prelates, an abbot primate, abbot superiors of monastic congregations and heads of exempt clerical religious; titular bishops, on invitation. Experts in theology and canon law may be given a consultative vote. Others, including lay persons, may address a council or observe its actions, but may not vote.

Basic legislation concerning ecumenical councils is contained in Canons 222-229 of the Code of Canon Law. Basic doctrinal considerations were stated by the Second Vatican Council in the *Dogmatic Constitution on the Church*.

Background

Ecumenical councils had their prototype in the Council of Jerusalem in 51, at which the Apostles under the leadership of St. Peter decided that converts to the Christian faith were not obliged to observe all the prescriptions of Old Testament law (Acts 15). As early as the second century, bishops got together in regional meetings, synods or councils to take common action for the doctrinal and pastoral good of their communities of faithful. The ex-

pansion of such limited assemblies to ecumenical councils was a logical and historical evolution, given the nature and needs of the Church.

Emperors were active in summoning or convoking the first eight councils, especially the first five and the eighth. Among reasons for intervention of this kind were the facts that the emperors regarded themselves as guardians of the faith; that the settlement of religious controversies, which had repercussions in political and social turmoil, served the cause of peace in the state; and that the emperors had at their disposal ways and means of facilitating gatherings of bishops. Imperial actions, however, did not account for the formally ecumenical nature of the councils.

Some councils were attended by relatively few bishops, and the ecumenical character of several was open to question for a time. However, confirmation and de facto recognition of their actions by popes and subsequent councils established them as ecumenical.

Role in History

The councils have played a highly significant role in the history of the Church by witnessing to and defining truths of revelation, by shaping forms of worship and discipline, and by promoting measures for the ever-necessary reform and renewal of Catholic life. In general, they have represented attempts of the Church to mobilize itself in times of crisis for self-preservation, self-purification and growth.

The first eight ecumenical councils were held in the East; the other 13, in the West. The majority of separated Eastern Churches — e.g., the Orthodox — recognize the ecumenical character of the first seven councils, which formulated a great deal of basic doctrine. Nestorians, however, acknowledge only the first two councils; the Monophysite Armenians, Syrians, and Copts acknowledge the first three.

The 21 Councils

The 21 ecumenical councils in the history of the Church are listed below, with indication of their names or titles (taken from the names of the places where they were held); the dates; the reigning and/or approving popes; the emperors who were instrumental in convoking the eight councils in the East; the number of bishops who attended, when available; the number of sessions; the most significant actions.

1. Nicaea I, 325: St. Sylvester I (Emperor Constantine I); attended by approximately 300 bishops; sessions held between May 20 or June 19 to near the end of August. Condemned Arianism, which denied the divinity of Christ; contributed to formulation of the Nicene Creed; fixed the date of Easter; passed regulations concerning clerical discipline; adopted the civil division of the Empire as the model for the organization of the Church.

2. Constantinople I, 381: St. Damasus I (Emperor Theodosius I); attended by approximately 150 bishops; sessions held from May to July. Condemned various brands of Arianism, and Macedonianism which denied the divinity of the Holy Spirit; contributed to formulation of the Nicene Creed; approved a canon which made the bishop of Constantinople the ranking prelate in the East, with primacy next to that of the pope. Doubt about the ecumenical character of this council was resolved by the ratification of its acts by popes and the Council of Chalcedon.

3. Ephesus, 431: St. Celestine I (Emperor Theodosius II); attended by 150 to 200 bishops; five sessions held between June 22 and July 17. Condemned Nestorianism, which denied the real unity of the divine and human natures in the Person of Christ; defined *Theotokos* ("Bearer of God") as the title of Mary, Mother of the Son of God made Man; condemned Pelagianism, which reduced the supernatural to the natural order of things.

4. Chalcedon, 451: St. Leo I (Emperor Marcian); attended by approximately 600 bishops; 17 sessions held between Oct. 8 and Nov. 1. Condemned: Monophysitism, also called Eutychianism, which denied the humanity of Christ by holding that he had only one, the divine, nature; and the Monophysite Robber Synod of Ephesus, of 449.

5. Constantinople II, 553: Vigilius (Emperor Justinian I); attended by 165 bishops; eight sessions held between May 5 and June 2. Condemned the *Three Chapters,* Nestorian-tainted writings of Theodore of Mopsuestia, Theodoret of Cyprus and Ibas of Edessa.

6. Constantinople III, 680-681; St. Agatho, St. Leo II (Emperor Constantine IV); attended by approximately 170 bishops; 16 sessions held between Nov. 7, 680, and Sept. 16, 681. Condemned Monothelitism, which held that there was only one will, the divine, in Christ; censured Pope Honorius I for a letter to Sergius, bishop of Constantinople, in which he made an ambiguous but not infallible statement about the unity of will and/or operation in Christ. Constantinople III is also called the Trullan Council because its sessions were held in the domed hall, Trullos, of the imperial palace.

7. Nicaea II, 787: Adrian I (Empress Irene); attended by approximately 300 bishops; eight sessions held between Sept. 24 and Oct. 23. Condemned: Iconoclasm, which held that the use of images was idolatry; and Adoptionism, which claimed that Christ was not the Son of God by nature but only by adoption. This was the last council regarded as ecumenical by Orthodox Churches.

8. Constantinople IV, 869-870: Adrian II (Emperor Basil I); attended by 102 bishops; six sessions held between Oct. 5, 869, and Feb. 28, 870. Condemned Iconoclasm; condemned and deposed Photius as patriarch of Constantinople; restored Ignatius to the patriarchate. This was the last ecumenical council held in the East. It was first called ecumenical by canonists toward the end of the 11th century.

9. Lateran I, 1123: Callistus II; attended by approximately 300 bishops; sessions held between Mar. 18 and Apr. 6. Endorsed provisions of the Concordat of Worms concerning the investiture of prelates: approved reform measures in 25 canons.

10. Lateran II, 1139: Innocent II; attended by 900 to 1,000 bishops and abbots; three sessions held in April. Adopted measures against a schism organized by antipope Anacletus; approved 30 disciplinary measures and canons, one of which stated that holy orders is an invalidating impediment to marriage.

11. Lateran III, 1179: Alexander III; attended by at least 300 bishops; three sessions held between Mar. 5 and 19. Enacted measures against the Waldenses and Albigensians; approved reform decrees in 27 canons; provided that popes be elected by two-thirds vote of the cardinals.

12. Lateran IV, 1215: Innocent III; sessions held between Nov. 11 and 30. Ordered annual confession and Communion; defined and made first official use of the term "transubstantiation"; adopted measures to counteract the Cathari and Albigensians; approved 70 canons.

13. Lyons I, 1245: Innocent IV; attended by approximately 150 bishops; three sessions held between June 28 and July 17. Confirmed the deposition of Emperor Frederick II; approved 22 canons.

14. Lyons II, 1274: Gregory X; attended by approximately 500 bishops; six sessions held between May 7 and July 17. Accomplished a temporary reunion of separated Eastern Churches with the Roman Church; issued regulations concerning conclaves for papal elections; approved 31 canons.

15. Vienne, 1311-1312: Clement V; attended by 132 bishops; three sessions held between Oct. 16, 1311, and May 6, 1312. Suppressed the Knights Templar; enacted a number of reform decrees.

16. Constance, 1414-1418: Gregory XII, Martin V; attended by nearly 200 bishops, plus other prelates and many experts; 45 sessions held between Nov. 5, 1414, and Apr. 22, 1418. Took successful action to end the Western Schism; rejected the teachings of Wycliff; condemned Hus as a heretic. One decree, passed in the earlier stages of the council, asserted the superiority of an ecumenical council over the pope; this was later rejected.

17. Florence (also called Basel-Ferrara-Florence), 1438-1445: Eugene IV; attended by many Latin-Rite and Eastern-Rite bishops; preliminary sessions were held at Basel and Ferrara before definitive work was accomplished at Florence. Reaffirmed the primacy of the pope against the claims of Conciliarists that an ecumenical council is superior to the pope; formulated and approved decrees of union — with the Greeks, July 6, 1439; with the Armenians, Nov. 22, 1439; with the Jacobites, Feb. 4, 1442. These decrees failed to gain general or lasting acceptance in the East.

18. Lateran V, 1512-1517: Julius II, Leo X; 12 sessions held between May 3, 1512, and Mar. 16, 1517. Stated the relation and position of the pope with respect to an ecumenical council; acted to counteract the Pragmatic Sanction of Bourges and exaggerated claims of liberty by the French Church; condemned erroneous teachings concerning the nature of the human soul; stated doctrine concerning indulgences. The council reflected concern for abuses in the Church and the need for reforms but failed to take decisive action in the years immediately preceding the Reformation.

19. Trent, 1545-1563: Paul III, Julius III, Pius IV; 25 sessions held between Dec. 13, 1545, and Dec. 4, 1563. Issued a great number of decrees concerning doctrinal matters opposed by the Reformers, and mobilized the Counter-Reformation. Definitions covered the rule of faith, the nature of justification, grace, faith, original sin and its effects, the seven sacraments, the sacrificial nature of the Mass, the veneration of saints, use of sacred images, belief in purgatory, the doctrine of indulgences, the jurisdiction of the pope over the whole Church. Initiated many reforms for renewal in the liturgy and general discipline in the Church, the promotion of religious instruction, the education of the clergy through the foundation of seminaries, etc. Trent ranks with Vatican II as the greatest ecumenical council held in the West.

20. Vatican I, 1869-1870: Pius IX; attended by approximately 800 bishops and other prelates; four public sessions and 89 general meetings held between Dec. 8, 1869, and July 7, 1870. Defined papal primacy and infallibility in a dogmatic constitution on the Church; covered natural religion, revelation, faith, and the relations between faith and reason in a dogmatic constitution on the Catholic faith. The council suspended sessions Sept. 1 and was adjourned Oct. 20, 1870.

Vatican II

The Second Vatican Council, which was forecast by Pope John XXIII Jan. 25, 1959, was held in four sessions in St. Peter's Basilica.

Pope John convoked it and opened the first session, which ran from Sept. 11 to Dec. 8, 1962. Following John's death June 3, 1963, Pope Paul VI reconvened the council for the other three sessions which ran from Sept. 29 to Dec. 4, 1963; Sept. 14 to Nov. 21, 1964; Sept. 14 to Dec. 8, 1965.

A total of 2,860 Fathers participated in council proceedings, and attendance at meetings varied between 2,000 and 2,500. For various reasons, including the denial of exit from Communist-dominated countries, 274 Fathers could not attend.

The council formulated and promulgated 16 documents — two dogmatic and two pastoral constitutions, nine decrees and three declarations — all of which reflect its basic pastoral orientation toward renewal and reform in the Church. Given below are the Latin and English titles of the documents and their dates of promulgation.

• *Lumen Gentium* (Dogmatic Constitution on the Church), Nov. 21, 1964.

• *Dei Verbum* (Dogmatic Constitution on Divine Revelation), Nov. 18, 1965.

• *Sacrosanctum Concilium* (Constitution on the Sacred Liturgy), Dec. 4, 1963.

• *Gaudium et Spes* (Pastoral Constitution on the Church in the Modern World), Dec. 7, 1965.

• *Christus Dominus* (Decree on the Bishops' Pastoral Office in the Church), Oct. 28, 1965.

• *Ad Gentes* (Decree on the Church's Missionary Activity), Dec. 7, 1965.

• *Unitatis Redintegratio* (Decree on Ecumenism), Nov. 21, 1964.

• *Orientalium Ecclesiarum* (Decree on Eastern Catholic Churches), Nov. 21, 1964.

• *Presbyterorum Ordinis* (Decree on the Ministry and Life of Priests), Dec. 7, 1965.

• *Optatam Totius* (Decree on Priestly Formation), Oct. 28, 1965.

• *Perfectae Caritatis* (Decree on the Appropriate Renewal of the Religious Life), Oct. 28, 1965.

• *Apostolicam Actuositatem* (Decree on the Apostolate of the Laity), Nov. 18, 1965.

• *Inter Mirifica* (Decree on the Instruments of Social Communication), Dec. 4, 1963.

• *Dignitatis Humanae* (Declaration on Religious Freedom), Dec. 7, 1965.

• *Nostra Aetate* (Declaration on the Relationship of the Church to Non-Christian Religions), Oct. 28, 1965.

• *Gravissimum Educationis* (Declaration on Christian Education), Oct. 28, 1965.

The key documents were the four constitutions, which set the ideological basis for all the others. To date, the documents with the most visible effects are those on the liturgy, the Church, the Church in the world, ecumenism, the renewal of religious life, the life and ministry of priests, the lay apostolate.

The main business of the council was to explore and make explicit dimensions of doctrine and Christian life requiring emphasis for the full development of the Church and the better accomplishment of its mission in the contemporary world.

These purposes moved Pope Paul to proclaim the Year of Faith observance of 1967 and 1968, and more recently to issue the call for observance of a Holy Year in 1975. The spiritual effects of such observances are essential to true renewal of the Church.

Popes

LIST OF POPES

(Source: *Annuario Pontificio.*)

Information includes the name of the pope, in many cases his name before becoming pope, his birthplace or country of origin, the date of accession to the papacy, and the date of the end of reign which, in all but a few cases, was the date of death. Double dates indicate times of election and coronation.

St. Peter (Simon Bar-Jona): Bethsaida in Galilee; d. c. 67.

St. Linus: Tuscany; 67-76.

St. Anacletus (Cletus): Rome; 76-88.

St. Clement: Rome; 88-97.

St. Evaristus: Greece; 97-105.

St. Alexander I: Rome; 105-115.

St. Sixtus I: Rome; 115-125.

St. Telesphorus: Greece; 125-136.

St. Hyginus: Greece; 136-140.

St. Pius I: Aquileia; 140-155.

St. Anicetus: Syria; 155-166.

St. Soter: Campania; 166-175.

St. Eleutherius: Nicopolis in Epirus; 175-189.

Up to the time of St. Eleutherius, the years indicated for the beginning and end of pontificates are not absolutely certain. Also, up to the middle of the 11th century, there are some doubts about the exact days and months given in chronological tables.

St. Victor I: Africa; 189-199.

St. Zephyrinus: Rome; 199-217.

St. Callistus I: Rome; 217-222.

St. Urban I: Rome; 222-230.

St. Pontian: Rome; July 21, 230, to Sept. 28, 235.

St. Anterus: Greece; Nov. 21, 235, to Jan. 3, 236.

St. Fabian: Rome; Jan. 10, 236, to Jan. 20, 250.

St. Cornelius: Rome; Mar., 251, to June, 253.

St. Lucius I: Rome; June 25, 253, to Mar. 5, 254.

St. Stephen I: Rome; May 12, 254, to Aug. 2, 257.

St. Sixtus II: Greece; Aug. 30, 257, to Aug. 6, 258.

St. Dionysius: July 22, 259, to Dec. 26, 268.

St. Felix I: Rome; Jan. 5, 269, to Dec. 30, 274.

St. Eutychian: Luni; Jan. 4, 275, to Dec. 7, 283.

St. Caius: Dalmatia; Dec. 17, 283, to Apr. 22, 296.

St. Marcellinus: Rome; June 30, 296, to Oct. 25, 304.

St. Marcellus I: Rome; May 27, 308, or June 26, 308, to Jan. 16, 309.

St. Eusebius: Greece; Apr. 18, 309 or 310, to Aug. 17, 309 or 310.

St. Melchiades (Miltiades): Africa; July 2, 311, to Jan. 11, 314.

St. Sylvester I: Rome; Jan. 31, 314, to Dec. 31, 335. (Most of the popes before St. Sylvester I were martyrs.)

St. Marcus: Rome; Jan. 18, 336, to Oct. 7, 336.

St. Julius I: Rome; Feb. 6, 337, to Apr. 12, 352.

Liberius: Rome; May 17, 352, to Sept. 24, 366.

St. Damasus I: Spain; Oct. 1, 366, to Dec. 11, 384.

St. Siricius: Rome; Dec. 15, or 22 or 29, 384, to Nov. 26, 399.

St. Anastasius I: Rome; Nov. 27, 399, to Dec. 19, 401.

St. Innocent I: Albano; Dec. 22, 401, to Mar. 12, 417.

St. Zozimus: Greece; Mar. 18, 417, to Dec. 26, 418.

St. Boniface I: Rome; Dec. 28 or 29, 418, to Sept. 4, 422.

St. Celestine I: Campania; Sept. 10, 422, to July 27, 432.

St. Sixtus III: Rome; July 31, 432, to Aug. 19, 440.

St. Leo I (the Great): Tuscany; Sept. 29, 440, to Nov. 10, 461.

St. Hilary: Sardinia; Nov. 19, 461, to Feb. 29, 468.

St. Simplicius: Tivoli; Mar. 3, 468, to Mar. 10, 483.

St. Felix III (II): Rome; Mar. 13, 483, to Mar. 1, 492.

He should be called Felix II, and his successors of the same name should be numbered accordingly. The discrepancy in the numerical designation of popes named Felix was caused by the erroneous insertion in some lists of the name of St. Felix of Rome, a martyr.

St. Gelasius I: Africa; Mar. 1, 492, to Nov. 21, 496.

Anastasius II: Rome; Nov. 24, 496, to Nov. 19, 498.

St. Symmachus: Sardinia; Nov. 22, 498, to July 19, 514.

St. Hormisdas: Frosinone; July 20, 514, to Aug. 6, 523.

St. John I, Martyr: Tuscany; Aug. 13, 523, to May 18, 526.

St. Felix IV (III): Samnium; July 12, 526, to Sept. 22, 530.

Boniface II: Rome; Sept. 22, 530, to Oct. 17, 532.

John II: Rome; Jan. 2, 533, to May 8, 535.

John II was the first pope to change his name. His given name was Mercury.

St. Agapitus I: Rome; May 13, 535, to Apr. 22, 536.

St. Silverius, Martyr: Campania; June 1 or 8, 536, to Nov. 11, 537 (d. Dec. 2, 537).

St. Silverius was violently deposed in March, 537, and abdicated Nov. 11, 537. His successor, Vigilius, was not recognized as pope by all the Roman clergy until his abdication.

Vigilius: Rome; Mar. 29, 537, to June 7, 555.

Pelagius I: Rome; Apr. 16, 556, to Mar. 4, 561.

John III: Rome; July 17, 561, to July 13, 574.

Benedict I: Rome; June 2, 575, to July 30, 579.

Pelagius II: Rome; Nov. 26, 579, to Feb. 7, 590.

St. Gregory I (the Great): Rome; Sept. 3, 590, to Mar. 12, 604.

Sabinian: Blera in Tuscany; Sept. 13, 604, to Feb. 22, 606.

Boniface III: Rome; Feb. 19, 607, to Nov. 12, 607.

St. Boniface IV: Abruzzi; Aug. 25, 608, to May 8, 615.

St. Deusdedit (Adeodatus I): Rome; Oct. 19, 615, to Nov. 8, 618.

Boniface V: Naples; Dec. 23, 619, to Oct. 25, 625.

Honorius I: Campania; Oct. 27, 625, to Oct. 12, 638.

Severinus: Rome; May 28, 640, to Aug. 2, 640.

John IV: Dalmatia; Dec. 24, 640, to Oct. 12, 642.

Theodore I: Greece; Nov. 24, 642, to May 14, 649.

St. Martin I, Martyr: Todi; July, 649, to Sept. 16, 655 (in exile from June 17, 653).

St. Eugene I: Rome; Aug. 10, 654, to June 2, 657.

St. Eugene I was elected during the exile of St. Martin I, who is believed to have endorsed him as pope.

St. Vitalian: Segni; July 30, 657, to Jan. 27, 672.

Adeodatus II: Rome; Apr. 11, 672, to June 17, 676.

Donus: Rome; Nov. 2, 676, to Apr. 11, 678.

St. Agatho: Sicily; June 27, 678, to Jan. 10, 681.

St. Leo II: Sicily; Aug. 17, 682, to July 3, 683.

St. Benedict II: Rome; June 26, 684, to May 8, 685.

John V: Syria; July 23, 685, to Aug. 2, 686.

Conon: birthplace unknown; Oct. 21, 686, to Sept. 21, 687.

St. Sergius I: Syria; Dec. 15, 687, to Sept. 8, 701.

John VI: Greece; Oct. 30, 701, to Jan. 11, 705.

John VII: Greece; Mar. 1, 705, to Oct. 18, 707.

Sisinnius: Syria; Jan. 15, 708, to Feb. 4, 708.

Constantine: Syria; Mar. 25, 708, to Apr. 9, 715.

St. Gregory II: Rome; May 19, 715, to Feb. 11, 731.

St. Gregory III: Syria; Mar. 18, 731, to Nov., 741.

St. Zachary: Greece; Dec. 10, 741, to Mar. 22, 752.

Stephen II (III): Rome; Mar. 26, 752, to Apr. 26, 757.

After the death of St. Zachary, a Roman priest named Stephen was elected but died (four days later) before his consecration as bishop of Rome, which would have marked the beginning of his pontificate. Another Stephen was elected to succeed Zachary as Stephen II. (The first pope with this name was St. Stephen I, 254-57.) The ordinal III appears in parentheses after the name of Stephen II because the name of the earlier elected but deceased priest was included in some lists. Other Stephens have double numbers.

St. Paul I: Rome; Apr. (May 29), 757, to June 28, 767.

Stephen III (IV): Sicily; Aug. 1 (7), 768, to Jan. 24, 772.

Adrian I: Rome; Feb. 1 (9), 772, to Dec. 25, 795.

St. Leo III: Rome; Dec. 26 (27), 795, to June 12, 816.

Stephen IV (V): Rome; June 22, 816, to Jan. 24, 817.

St. Paschal I: Rome; Jan. 25, 817, to Feb. 11, 824.

Eugene II: Rome; Feb. (May), 824, to Aug., 827.

Valentine: Rome; Aug. 827, to Sept., 827.

Gregory IV: Rome; 827, to Jan., 844.

Sergius II: Rome; Jan., 844 to Jan. 27, 847.

St. Leo IV: Rome; Jan. (Apr. 10), 847, to July 17, 855.

Benedict III: Rome; July (Sept. 29), 855, to Apr. 17, 858.

St. Nicholas I (the Great): Rome; Apr. 24, 858, to Nov. 13, 867.

Adrian II: Rome; Dec. 14, 867, to Dec. 14, 872.

John VIII: Rome; Dec. 14, 872, to Dec. 16, 882.

Marinus I: Gallese; Dec. 16, 882, to May 15, 884.

St. Adrian III: Rome; May 17, 884, to Sept., 885. Cult confirmed June 2, 1891.

Stephen V (VI): Rome; Sept., 885, to Sept. 14, 891.

Formosus: Portus; Oct. 6, 891, to Apr. 4, 896.

Boniface VI: Rome; Apr., 896, to Apr., 896.

Stephen VI (VII): Rome; May, 896, to Aug., 897.

Romanus: Gallese; Aug., 897, to Nov., 897.

Theodore II: Rome; Dec., 897, to Dec., 897.

John IX: Tivoli; Jan., 898, to Jan., 900.

Benedict IV: Rome; Jan. (Feb.), 900, to July, 903.

Leo V: Ardea; July, 903, to Sept., 903.

Sergius III: Rome; Jan. 29, 904, to Apr. 14, 911.

Anastasius III: Rome; Apr., 911, to June, 913.

Landus: Sabina; July, 913, to Feb., 914.

John X: Tossignano (Imola); Mar., 914, to May, 928.

Leo VI: Rome; May, 928, to Dec., 928.

Stephen VII (VIII): Rome; Dec., 928, to Feb., 931.

John XI: Rome; Feb. (Mar.), 931, to Dec., 935.

Leo VII: Rome; Jan. 3, 936, to July 13, 939.

Stephen VIII (IX): Rome; July 14, 939, to Oct., 942.

Marinus II: Rome; Oct. 30, 942, to May, 946.

Agapitus II: Rome; May 10, 946, to Dec., 955.

John XII (Octavius): Tusculum; Dec. 16, 955, to May 14, 964 (date of his death).

Leo VIII: Rome; Dec. 4 (6), 963, to Mar. 1, 965.

Benedict V: Rome; May 22, 964, to July 4, 966.

Confusion exists concerning the legitimacy of claims to the pontificate by Leo VIII and Benedict V. John XII was deposed Dec. 4, 963, by a Roman council. If this deposition was invalid, Leo was an antipope. If the deposition of John was valid, Leo was the legitimate pope and Benedict was an antipope.

John XIII: Rome; Oct. 1, 965, to Sept. 6, 972.

Benedict VI: Rome; Jan. 19, 973, to June, 974.

Benedict VII: Rome; Oct. 974, to July 10, 983.

John XIV (Peter Campenora): Pavia; Dec., 983, to Aug. 20, 984.

John XV: Rome; Aug., 985, to Mar., 996.

Gregory V (Bruno of Carinthia): Saxony; May 3, 996, to Feb. 18, 999.

Sylvester II (Gerbert): Auvergne; Apr. 2, 999, to May 12, 1003.

John XVII (Siccone): Rome; June, 1003, to Dec., 1003.

John XVIII (Phasianus): Rome; Jan., 1004, to July, 1009.

Sergius IV (Peter): Rome; July 31, 1009, to May 12, 1012.

The custom of changing one's name on election to the papacy is generally considered to date from the time of Sergius IV. Before his time, several popes had changed their names. After his time, this became a regular practice, with few exceptions; e.g., Adrian VI and Marcellus II.

Benedict VIII (Theophylactus): Tusculum; May 18, 1012, to Apr. 9, 1024.

John XIX (Romanus): Tusculum; Apr. (May), 1024, to 1032.

Benedict IX (Theophylactus): Tusculum; 1032, to 1044.

Sylvester III (John): Rome; Jan. 20, 1045, to Feb. 10, 1045.

Sylvester III was an antipope if the forcible removal of Benedict IX in 1044 was not legitimate.

Benedict IX (second time): Apr. 10, 1045, to May 1, 1045.

Gregory VI (John Gratian): Rome; May 5, 1045, to Dec. 20, 1046.

Clement II (Suitger, Lord of Morsleben and Hornburg): Saxony; Dec. 24 (25), 1046, to Oct. 9, 1047.

If the resignation of Benedict IX in 1045 and his removal at the December, 1046, synod were not legitimate, Gregory VI and Clement II were antipopes.

Benedict IX (third time): Nov. 8, 1047, to July 17, 1048 (d. c. 1055).

Damasus II (Poppo): Bavaria; July 17, 1048, to Aug. 9, 1048.

St. Leo IX (Bruno): Alsace; Feb. 12, 1049, to Apr. 19, 1054.

Victor II (Gebhard): Swabia; Apr. 16, 1055, to July 28, 1057.

Stephen IX (X) (Frederick): Lorraine; Aug. 3, 1057, to Mar. 29, 1058.

Nicholas II (Gerard): Burgundy; Jan. 24, 1059, to July 27, 1061.

Alexander II (Anselmo da Baggio): Milan; Oct. 1, 1061, to Apr. 21, 1073.

St. Gregory VII (Hildebrand): Tuscany; Apr. 22 (June 30), 1073, to May 25, 1085.

Bl. Victor III (Dauferius; Desiderius): Benevento; May 24, 1086, to Sept. 16, 1087. Cult confirmed July 23, 1887.

Bl. Urban II (Otto di Lagery): France; Mar. 12, 1088, to July 29, 1099. Cult confirmed July 14, 1881.

Paschal II (Raniero): Ravenna; Aug. 13 (14), 1099, to Jan. 21, 1118.

Gelasius II (Giovanni Caetani): Gaeta; Jan. 24 (Mar. 10), 1118, to Jan. 28, 1119.

Callistus II (Guido of Burgundy): Burgundy; Feb. 2 (9), 1119, to Dec. 13, 1124.

Honorius II (Lamberto): Fiagnano (Imola); Dec. 15 (21), 1124, to Feb. 13, 1130.

Innocent II (Gregorio Papareschi): Rome; Feb. 14 (23), 1130, to Sept. 24, 1143.

Celestine II (Guido): Citta di Castello; Sept. 26 (Oct. 3), 1143, to Mar. 8, 1144.

Lucius II (Gerardo Caccianemici): Bologna: Mar. 12, 1144, to Feb. 15, 1145.

Bl. Eugene III (Bernardo Paganelli di Montemagno): Pisa; Feb. 15 (18), 1145, to July 8, 1153. Cult confirmed Oct. 3, 1872.

Anastasius IV (Corrado): Rome; July 12, 1153, to Dec, 3, 1154.

Adrian IV (Nicholas Breakspear): England; Dec. 4 (5), 1154, to Sept. 1, 1159.

Alexander III (Rolando Bandinelli): Siena; Sept. 7 (20), 1159, to Aug. 30, 1181.

Lucius III (Ubaldo Allucingoli): Lucca; Sept. 1 (6), 1181, to Sept. 25, 1185.

Urban III (Uberto Crivelli): Milan; Nov. 25 (Dec. 1), 1185, to Oct. 20, 1187.

Gregory VIII (Alberto de Morra): Benevento; Oct. 21 (25), 1187, to Dec. 17, 1187.

Clement III (Paolo Scolari): Rome; Dec. 19 (20), 1187, to Mar., 1191.

Celestine III (Giacinto Bobone): Rome; Mar. 30 (Apr. 14), 1191, to Jan. 8, 1198.

Innocent III (Lotario dei Conti di Segni); Anagni; Jan. 8 (Feb. 22), 1198, to July 16, 1216.

Honorius III (Cencio Savelli): Rome; July 18 (24), 1216, to Mar. 18, 1227.

Gregory IX (Ugolino, Count of Segni): Anagni; Mar. 19 (21), 1227, to Aug. 22, 1241.

Celestine IV (Goffredo Castiglioni): Milan; Oct. 25 (28), 1241, to Nov. 10, 1241.

Innocent IV (Sinibaldo Fieschi): Genoa; June 25 (28), 1243, to Dec. 7, 1254.

Alexander IV (Rinaldo, Count of Segni): Anagni; Dec. 12 (20), 1254, to May 25, 1261.

Urban IV (Jacques Pantaléon): Troyes; Aug. 29 (Sept. 4), 1261, to Oct. 2, 1264.

Clement IV (Guy Foulques or Guido le Gros): France; Feb. 5 (15), 1265, to Nov. 29, 1268.

Bl. Gregory X (Teobaldo Visconti): Piacenza; Sept. 1, 1271 (Mar. 27, 1272), to Jan. 10, 1276. Cult confirmed Sept. 12, 1713.

Bl. Innocent V (Peter of Tarentaise): Savoy; Jan. 21 (Feb. 22), 1276, to June 22, 1276. Cult confirmed Mar. 13, 1898.

Adrian V (Ottobono Fieschi): Genoa: July 11, 1276, to Aug. 18, 1276.

John XXI (Petrus Juliani or Petrus Hispanus): Portugal; Sept. 8 (20), 1276, to May 20, 1277.

Elimination was made of the name of John XX in an effort to rectify the numerical designation of popes named John. The error dates back to the time of John XV.

Nicholas III (Giovanni Gaetano Orsini): Rome; Nov. 25 (Dec. 26), 1277, to Aug. 22, 1280.

Martin IV (Simon de Brie): France; Feb. 22 (Mar. 23), 1281, to Mar. 28, 1285.

The names of Marinus I (882-84) and Marinus II (942-46) were construed as Martin. In view of these two pontificates and the earlier reign of St. Martin I (649-55), this pope was called Martin IV.

Honorius IV (Giacomo Savelli): Rome; Apr. 2 (May 20), 1285, to Apr. 3, 1287.

Nicholas IV (Girolamo Masci): Ascoli; Feb. 22, 1288, to Apr. 4, 1292.

St. Celestine V (Pietro del Murrone): Isernia; July 5 (Aug. 29), 1294, to Dec. 13, 1294; d. 1296. Canonized May 5, 1313.

Boniface VIII (Benedetto Caetani): Anagni; Dec. 24, 1294 (Jan. 23, 1295), to Oct. 11, 1303.

Bl. Benedict XI (Niccolo Boccasini): Treviso; Oct. 22 (27), 1303, to July 7, 1304. Cult confirmed Apr. 24, 1736.

Clement V (Bertrand de Got): France; June 5 (Nov. 14), 1305, to Apr. 20, 1314. (First of Avignon popes.)

John XXII (Jacques d'Euse): Cahors; Aug. 7 (Sept. 5), 1316, to Dec. 4, 1334.

Benedict XII (Jacques Fournier): France; Dec. 20, 1334 (Jan. 8, 1335), to Apr. 25, 1342.

Clement VI (Pierre Roger): France; May 7 (19), 1342, to Dec. 6, 1352.

Innocent VI (Etienne Aubert): France; Dec. 18 (30), 1352, to Sept. 12, 1362.

Bl. Urban V (Guillaume de Grimoard): France; Sept. 28 (Nov. 6), 1362, to Dec. 19, 1370. Cult confirmed Mar. 10, 1870.

Gregory XI (Pierre Roger de Beaufort): France; Dec. 30, 1370 (Jan. 5, 1371), to Mar. 26, 1378. (Last of Avignon popes.)

Urban VI (Bartolomeo Prignano): Naples; Apr. 8 (18), 1378, to Oct. 15, 1389.

Boniface IX (Pietro Tomacelli): Naples; Nov. 2 (9), 1389, to Oct. 1, 1404.

Innocent VII (Cosma Migliorati): Sulmona; Oct. 17 (Nov. 11), 1404, to Nov. 6, 1406.

Gregory XII (Angelo Correr): Venice; Nov. 30 (Dec. 19), 1406, to July 4, 1415, when he voluntarily resigned from the papacy to permit the election of his successor. He died Oct. 18, 1417. (See The Western Schism.)

Martin V (Oddone Colonna): Rome; Nov. 11 (21), 1417, to Feb. 20, 1431.

Eugene IV (Gabriele Condulmer): Venice; Mar. 3 (11), 1431, to Feb. 23, 1447.

Nicholas V (Tommaso Parentucelli): Sarzana; Mar. 6 (19), 1447, to Mar. 24, 1455.

Callistus III (Alfonso Borgia): Jativa (Va-

lencia); Apr. 8 (20), 1455, to Aug. 6, 1458.

Pius II (Enea Silvio Piccolomini): Siena; Aug. 19 (Sept. 3), 1458, to Aug. 15, 1464.

Paul II (Pietro Barbo): Venice; Aug. 30 (Sept. 16), 1464, to July 26, 1471.

Sixtus IV (Francesco della Rovere): Savona; Aug. 9 (25), 1471, to Aug. 12, 1484.

Innocent VIII (Giovanni Battista Cibo): Genoa; Aug. 29 (Sept. 12), 1484, to July 25, 1492.

Alexander VI (Rodrigo Borgia): Jativa (Valencia); Aug. 11 (26), 1492, to Aug. 18, 1503.

Pius III (Francesco Todeschini-Piccolomini): Siena; Sept. 22 (Oct. 1, 8), 1503, to Oct. 18, 1503.

Julius II (Giuliano della Rovere): Savona; Oct. 31 (Nov. 26), 1503, to Feb. 21, 1513.

Leo X (Giovanni de' Medici): Florence; Mar. 9 (19), 1513, to Dec. 1, 1521.

Adrian VI (Adrian Florensz): Utrecht; Jan. 9 (Aug. 31), 1522, to Sept. 14, 1523.

Clement VII (Giulio de' Medici): Florence; Nov. 19 (26), 1523, to Sept. 25, 1534.

Paul III (Alessandro Farnese): Rome; Oct. 13 (Nov. 3), 1534, to Nov. 10, 1549.

Julius III (Giovanni Maria Ciocchi del Monte): Rome; Feb. 7 (22), 1550, to Mar. 23, 1555.

Marcellus II (Marcello Cervini): Montepulciano; Apr. 9 (10), 1555, to May 1, 1555.

Paul IV (Gian Pietro Carafa): Naples; May 23 (26), 1555, to Aug. 18, 1559.

Pius IV (Giovan Angelo de' Medici): Milan; Dec. 25, 1559 (Jan. 6, 1560), to Dec. 9, 1565.

St. Pius V (Antonio-Michele Ghislieri): Bosco (Alexandria); Jan. 7 (17), 1566, to May 1, 1572. Canonized May 22, 1712.

Gregory XIII (Ugo Buoncompagni): Bologna; May 13 (25), 1572, to Apr. 10, 1585.

Sixtus V (Felice Peretti): Grottammare (Ripatransone); Apr. 24 (May 1), 1585, to Aug. 27, 1590.

Urban VII (Giovanni Battista Castagna): Rome; Sept. 15, 1590, to Sept. 27, 1590.

Gregory XIV (Niccolo Sfondrati): Cremona; Dec. 5 (8), 1590, to Oct. 16, 1591.

Innocent IX (Giovanni Antonio Facchinetti): Bologna; Oct. 29 (Nov. 3), 1591, to Dec. 30, 1591.

Clement VIII (Ippolito Aldobrandini): Florence; Jan. 30 (Feb. 9), 1592, to Mar. 3, 1605.

Leo XI (Alessandro de' Medici): Florence; Apr. 1 (10), 1605, to Apr. 27, 1605.

Paul V (Camillo Borghese): Rome; May 16 (29), 1605, to Jan. 28, 1621.

Gregory XV (Alessandro Ludovisi): Bologna; Feb. 9 (14), 1621, to July 8, 1623.

Urban VIII (Maffeo Barberini): Florence; Aug. 6 (Sept. 29), 1623, to July 29, 1644.

Innocent X (Giovanni Battista Pamfili): Rome; Sept. 15 (Oct. 4), 1644, to Jan. 7, 1655.

Alexander VII (Fabio Chigi): Siena; Apr. 7 (18), 1655, to May 22, 1667.

Clement IX (Giulio Rospigliosi): Pistoia;

June 20 (26), 1667, to Dec. 9, 1669.

Clement X (Emilio Altieri): Rome; Apr. 29 (May 11), 1670, to July 22, 1676.

Bl. Innocent XI (Benedetto Odescalchi): Como; Sept. 21 (Oct. 4), 1676, to Aug. 12, 1689.

Alexander VIII (Pietro Ottoboni): Venice; Oct. 6 (16), 1689, to Feb. 1, 1691.

Innocent XII (Antonio Pignatelli): Spinazzola; July 12 (15), 1691, to Sept. 27, 1700.

Clement XI (Giovanni Francesco Albani): Urbino; Nov. 23, 30 (Dec. 8), 1700, to Mar. 19, 1721.

Innocent XIII (Michelangelo dei Conti): Rome; May 8 (18), 1721, to Mar. 7, 1724.

Benedict XIII (Pietro Francesco — Vincenzo Maria — Orsini): Gravina (Bari); May 29 (June 4), 1724, to Feb. 21, 1730.

Clement XII (Lorenzo Corsini): Florence; July 12 (16), 1730, to Feb. 6, 1740.

Benedict XIV (Prospero Lambertini): Bologna; Aug. 17 (22), 1740, to May 3, 1758.

Clement XIII (Carlo Rezzonico): Venice; July 6 (16), 1758, to Feb. 2, 1769.

Clement XIV (Giovanni Vincenzo Antonio — Lorenzo — Ganganelli): Rimini; May 19, 28 (June 4), 1769, to Sept. 22, 1774.

Pius VI (Giovanni Angelo Braschi): Cesena; Feb. 15 (22), 1775, to Aug. 29, 1799.

Pius VII (Barnaba — Gregorio — Chiaramonti): Cesena; Mar. 14 (21), 1800, to Aug. 20, 1823.

Leo XII (Annibale della Genga): Genga (Fabriano); Sept. 28 (Oct. 5), 1823, to Feb. 10, 1829.

Pius VIII (Francesco Saverio Castiglioni): Cingoli; Mar. 31 (Apr. 5), 1829, to Nov. 30, 1830.

Gregory XVI (Bartolomeo Alberto — Mauro — Cappellari): Belluno; Feb. 2 (6), 1831, to June 1, 1846.

Pius IX (Giovanni M. Mastai Ferretti): Senigallia; June 16 (21), 1846, to Feb. 7, 1878.

Leo XIII (Gioacchino Pecci): Carpineto (Anagni); Feb. 20 (Mar. 3), 1878, to July 20, 1903.

St. Pius X (Giuseppe Sarto): Riese (Treviso); Aug. 4 (9), 1903, to Aug. 20, 1914. Canonized May 29, 1954.

Benedict XV (Giacomo della Chiesa): Genoa; Sept. 3 (6), 1914, to Jan. 22, 1922.

Pius XI (Achille Ratti): Desio (Milan); Feb. 6 (12), 1922, to Feb. 10, 1939.

Pius XII (Eugenio Pacelli): Rome; Mar. 2 (12), 1939, to Oct. 9, 1958.

John XXIII (Angelo Giuseppe Roncalli): Sotto il Monte (Bergamo); Oct. 28 (Nov. 4). 1958 to June 3, 1963.

Paul VI (Giovanni Battista Montini): Concessio (Brescia); June 21 (June 30), 1963 to —.

(See additional entries under 20th Century Popes and Pope Paul VI.)

Pope Paul announced early in 1973 that a study was underway of proposals for including representative bishops as well as eligible cardinals in procedures for the election of a pope.

ANTIPOPES

(Source: *Annuario Pontificio*.)

This list of men who claimed or exercised the papal office in an uncanonical manner includes names, birthplaces and dates of alleged reigns.

St. Hippolytus: Rome; 217-235; was reconciled before his death.

Novatian: Rome; 251.

Felix II: Rome; 355 to Nov. 22, 365.

Ursinus: 366-367.

Eulalius: Dec. 27 or 29, 418, to 419.

Lawrence: 498; 501-505.

Dioscorus: Alexandria; Sept. 22, 530, to Oct. 14, 530.

Theodore: ended alleged reign, 687.

Paschal: ended alleged reign, 687.

Constantine: Nepi; June 28 (July 5), 767, to 769.

Philip: July 31, 768; retired to his monastery on the same day.

John: ended alleged reign, Jan., 844.

Anastasius: Aug., 855, to Sept., 855; d. 880.

Christopher: Rome; July or Sept., 903, to Jan., 904.

Boniface VII: Rome; June, 974, to July, 974; Aug., 984, to July, 985.

John XVI: Rossano; Apr., 997, to Feb., 998.

Gregory: ended alleged reign, 1012.

Benedict X: Rome; Apr. 5, 1058, to Jan. 24, 1059.

Honorius II: Verona; Oct. 28, 1061, to 1072.

Clement III: Parma; June 25, 1080 (Mar. 24, 1084), to Sept. 8, 1100.

Theodoric: ended alleged reign, 1100; d. 1102.

Albert: ended alleged reign, 1102.

Sylvester IV: Rome; Nov. 18, 1105, to 1111.

Gregory VIII: France; Mar. 8, 1118, to 1121.

Celestine II: Rome; ended alleged reign, Dec., 1124.

Anacletus II: Rome; Feb. 14 (23), 1130, to Jan. 25, 1138.

Victor IV: Mar., 1138, to May 29, 1138; submitted to Pope Innocent II.

Victor IV: Montecelio; Sept. 7 (Oct. 4), 1159, to Apr. 20, 1164; he did not recognize his predecessor (Victor IV, above).

Paschal III: Apr. 22 (26), 1164, to Sept. 20, 1168.

Callistus III: Arezzo; Sept., 1168, to Aug. 29, 1178; submitted to Pope Alexander III.

Innocent III: Sezze; Sept. 29, 1179, to 1180.

Nicholas V: Corvaro (Rieti); May 12 (22), 1328, to Aug. 25, 1330; d. Oct. 16, 1333.

Four antipopes of the Western Schism:

Clement VII: Sept. 20 (Oct. 31), 1378, to Sept. 16, 1394.

Benedict XIII: Aragon; Sept. 28 (Oct. 11), 1394, to May 23, 1423.

Alexander V: Crete; June 26 (July 7), 1409, to May 3, 1410.

John XXIII: Naples; May 17 (25), 1410, to May 29, 1415.

Felix V: Savoy; Nov. 5, 1439 (July 24, 1440), to April 7, 1449; d. 1451.

Avignon Papacy

Avignon was the residence of a series of French popes from Clement V to Gregory XI (1309-77). Prominent in the period were power struggles over the mixed interests of Church and state with the rulers of France (Philip IV, John II), Bavaria (Lewis IV), England (Edward III); factionalism of French and Italian churchmen; political as well as ecclesiastical turmoil in Italy, a factor of significance in prolonging the stay of popes in Avignon. Despite some positive achievements, the Avignon papacy was a prologue to the Western Schism which began in 1378.

Western Schism

The Western Schism was a confused state of affairs which divided Christendom into two and then three papal obediences from 1378 to 1417.

It occurred some 50 years after Marsilius theorized that a general (not ecumenical) council of bishops and other persons was superior to a pope and nearly 30 years before the Council of Florence stated definitively that no kind of council had such authority.

It was a period of disaster preceding the even more disastrous period of the Reformation.

Urban VI, following transfer to Rome of the 70-year papal residence at Avignon, was elected pope Apr. 8, 1378, and reigned until his death in 1389. He was succeeded by Boniface IX (1389-1404), Innocent VII (1404-1406) and Gregory XII (1406-1415). These four are considered the legitimate popes of the period.

Some of the cardinals who chose Urban pope, dissatisfied with his conduct of the office, declared that his election was invalid. They proceeded to elect Clement VII, who claimed the papacy from 1378 to 1394. He was succeeded by Benedict XIII.

Prelates seeking to end the state of divided papal loyalties convoked the Council of Pisa which, without authority, found Gregory XII and Benedict XIII, in absentia, guilty on 30-odd charges of schism and heresy, deposed them, and elected a third claimant to the papacy, Alexander V (1409-1410). He was succeeded by John XXIII (1410-1415).

The schism was ended by the Council of Constance (1414-1418). This council, although originally called into session in an irregular manner, acquired authority after being convoked by Gregory XII in 1415. In its early irregular phase, it deposed John XXIII whose election to the papacy was uncanonical anyway. After being formally convoked, it accepted the abdication of Gregory in 1415 and dismissed the claims of Benedict XIII two years later, thus clearing the way for the election of Matin V on Nov. 11, 1417. The Council of Constance also rejected the theories of John Wycliff and condemned John Hus as a heretic.

20th CENTURY POPES

Leo XIII

Leo XIII (Gioacchino Vincenzo Pecci) was born May 2, 1810, in Carpineto, Italy. Although all but three years of his life and pontificate were of the 19th century, his influence extended well into the 20th century.

He was educated at the Jesuit college in Viterbo, the Roman College, the Academy of Noble Ecclesiastics, and the University of the Sapienza. He was ordained to the priesthood in 1837.

He served as an apostolic delegate to two States of the Church, Benevento from 1838 to 1841 and Perugia in 1841 and 1842. Ordained titular archbishop of Damietta, he was papal nuncio to Belgium from January, 1843, until May, 1846; in the post, he had controversial relations with the government over education issues and acquired his first significant experience of industrialized society.

He was archbishop of Perugia from 1846 to 1878. He became a cardinal in 1853 and chamberlain of the Roman Curia in 1877. He was elected to the papacy Feb. 20, 1878. He died July 20, 1903.

Canonizations: He canonized 18 saints and beatified a group of English martyrs.

Church Administration: He established 300 new dioceses and vicariates; restored the hierarchy in Scotland, set up an English, as contrasted with the Portuguese, hierarchy in India; approved the action of the Congregation for the Propagation of the Faith in reorganizing missions in China.

Encyclicals: He issued 50 encyclicals, on subjects ranging from devotional to social. In the former category were *Annum Sacrum,* on the Sacred Heart, in 1899, and nine letters on Mary and the Rosary.

Interfaith Relations: He was unsuccessful in unity overtures made to Orthodox and Slavic Churches. He declared Anglican orders invalid in the apostolic bull *Apostolicae Curae* Sept. 13, 1896.

International Relations: Leo was frustrated in seeking solutions to the Roman Question arising from the seizure of church lands by the Kingdom of Italy in 1870. He also faced anticlerical situations in Belgium and France and in the Kulturkampf policies of Bismarck in Germany.

Social Questions: Much of Leo's influence stemmed from social doctrine stated in numerous encyclicals, concerning liberalism, liberty, the divine origin of authority; socialism, in *Quod Apostolici Muneris,* 1878; the Christian concept of the family, in *Arcanum,* 1880; socialism and economic liberalism, relations between capital and labor, in *Rerum Novarum,* 1891. Two of his social encyclicals were against the African slave trade.

Studies: In the encyclical *Aeterni Patris* of Aug. 4, 1879, he ordered a renewal of philosophical and theological studies in seminaries along scholastic, and especially Thomistic, lines, to counteract influential trends of liberalism and Modernism. He issued guidelines for biblical exegesis in *Providentissimus Deus* Nov. 18, 1893, and established the Pontifical Biblical Commission in 1902.

In other actions affecting scholarship and study, he opened the Vatican Archives to scholars in 1883 and established the Vatican Observatory.

United States: He authorized establishment of the apostolic delegation in Washington, D.C. Jan. 24, 1893. He refused to issue a condemnation of the Knights of Labor. With a document entitled *Testem Benevolentiae,* he eased resolution of questions concerning what was called an American heresy in 1899.

St. Pius X

St. Pius X (Giuseppe Melchiorre Sarto) was born in 1835 in Riese, Italy.

Educated at the college of Castelfranco and the seminary at Padua, he was ordained to the priesthood Sept. 18, 1858. He served as a curate in Trombolo for nine years before beginning an eight-year pastorate at Salzano. He was chancellor of the Treviso diocese from November, 1875, and bishop of Mantua from 1884 until 1893. He was cardinal-patriarch of Venice from that year until his election to the papacy by the conclave held from July 31 to Aug. 4, 1903.

Aims: Pius' principal objectives as pope were "to restore all things in Christ, in order that Christ may be all and in all," and "to teach (and defend) Christian truth and law."

Canonizations, Encyclicals: He canonized four saints and issued 16 encyclicals. One of the encyclicals was issued in commemoration of the 50th anniversary of the proclamation of the dogma of the Immaculate Conception of Mary.

Catechetics: He introduced a whole new era of religious instruction and formation with the encyclical *Acerbo Nimis* of Apr. 15, 1905, in which he called for vigor in establishing and conducting parochial programs of the Confraternity of Christian Doctrine.

Catholic Action: He outlined the role of official Catholic Action in two encyclicals in 1905 and 1906. Favoring organized action by Catholics themselves, he had serious reservations about interconfessional collaboration.

He stoutly maintained claims to papal rights in the anticlerical climate of Italy. He authorized bishops to relax prohibitions against participation by Catholics in some Italian elections.

Church Administration: With the motu proprio *Arduum Sane* of Mar. 19, 1904, he inaugurated the work which resulted in the Code of Canon Law; the code was completed in 1917 and went into effect in the following year. He reorganized and strengthened the Roman Curia with the apostolic constitution *Sapienti Consilio* of June 29, 1908. While promoting the expansion of missionary work, he removed from the jurisdiction of the Congregation for the Propagation of the Faith the Church in the United States, Canada, Newfoundland, England, Ireland, Holland and Luxembourg.

International Relations: He ended traditional prerogatives of Catholic governments with respect to papal elections, in 1904. He opposed anti-Church and anticlerical actions in several countries: Bolivia in 1905, because of anti-religious legislation; France in 1906, for its 1901 action in annulling its concordat with the Holy See, and for the 1905 Law of Separation by which it decreed separation of Church and state, ordered the confiscation of church property, and blocked religious education and the activities of religious orders; Portugal in 1911, for the separation of Church and state and repressive measures which resulted in persecution later.

In 1912 he called on the bishops of Brazil to work for the improvement of conditions among Indians.

Liturgy: "The Pope of the Eucharist," he strongly recommended the frequent reception of Holy Communion in a decree dated Dec. 20, 1905; in another decree, *Quam Singulari,* of Aug. 8, 1910, he called for the early reception of the sacrament by children. He initiated measures for liturgical reform with new norms for sacred music and the start of work on revision of the *Breviary* for recitation of the Divine Office.

Modernism: Pius was a vigorous opponent of "the synthesis of all heresies," which threatened the integrity of doctrine through its influence in philosophy, theology and biblical exegesis. In opposition, he condemned 65 of its propositions as erroneous in the decree *Lamentabili* July 3, 1907; issued the encyclical *Pascendi* in the same vein Sept. 8, 1907; backed both of these with censures; and published the Oath against Modernism in September, 1910, to be taken by all the clergy. Ecclesiastical studies suffered to some extent from these actions, necessary as they were at the time.

Pius followed the lead of Leo XIII in promoting the study of scholastic philosophy. He established the Pontifical Biblical Institute May 7, 1909.

His death, Aug. 20, 1914, was hastened by the outbreak of World War I. He was beatified in 1951 and canonized May 29, 1954. His feast is observed Aug. 21.

Benedict XV

Benedict XV (Giacomo della Chiesa) was born Nov. 21, 1854, in Pegli, Italy.

He was educated at the Royal University of Genoa and Gregorian University in Rome. He was ordained to the priesthood Dec. 21, 1878.

He served in the papal diplomatic corps from 1882 to 1907; as secretary to the nuncio to Spain from 1882 to 1887, as secretary to the papal secretary of state from 1887, and as undersecretary from 1901.

He was ordained archbishop of Bologna Dec. 22, 1907, and spent four years completing a pastoral visitation there. He was made a cardinal just three months before being elected to the papacy Sept. 3, 1914, He died Jan. 22, 1922. Two key efforts of his pontificate were for peace and the relief of human suffering caused by World War I.

Canonizations: Benedict canonized three saints; one of them was Joan of Arc.

Canon Law: He published the Code of Canon Law, developed by the commission set up by St. Pius X, June 28, 1917; it went into effect the following year.

Curia: He made great changes in the personnel of the Curia. He established the Congregation for the Oriental Churches May 1, 1917, and founded the Pontifical Oriental Institute in Rome later in the year.

Encyclicals: He issued 12 encyclicals. Peace was the theme of three of them. In another, published two years after the cessation of hostilities, he wrote about child victims of the war. He followed the lead of Leo XIII in *Spiritus Paraclitus*, Sept. 15, 1920, on biblical studies.

International Relations: He was largely frustrated on the international level because of the events and attitudes of the war period, but the number of diplomats accredited to the Vatican nearly doubled, from 14 to 26, between the time of his accession to the papacy and his death.

Peace Efforts: Benedict's stance in the war was one of absolute impartiality but not of disinterested neutrality. Because he would not take sides, he was suspected by both sides and the seven-point peace plan he offered to all belligerents Aug. 1, 1917, was turned down. The points of the plan were: recognition of the moral force of right; disarmament; acceptance of arbitration in cases of dispute; guarantee of freedom of the seas; renunciation of war indemnities; evacuation and restoration of occupied territories; examination of territorial claims in dispute.

Relief Efforts: Benedict assumed personal charge of Vatican relief efforts during the war. He set up an international missing persons bureau for contacts between prisoners and their families, but was forced to close it because of the suspicion of warring nations that it was a front for espionage operations. He persuaded the Swiss government to admit into the country military victims of tuberculosis.

Roman Question: Benedict arranged a meeting of Benito Mussolini and the papal secretary of state, which marked the first step toward final settlement of the question in 1929.

Pius XI

Pius XI (Ambrogio Damiano Achille Ratti) was born May 31, 1857, in Desio, Italy.

Educated at seminaries in Seviso and Milan, and at the Lombard College, Gregorian University and Academy of St. Thomas in Rome, he was ordained to the priesthood in 1879.

He taught at the major seminary of Milan from 1882 to 1888. Appointed to the staff of the Ambrosian Library in 1888, he remained there until 1911, acquiring a reputation for publishing works on palaeography and serving as director from 1907 to 1911. He then moved to the Vatican Library, of which he was prefect from 1914 to 1918. In 1919, he was named apostolic visitor to Poland in April, nuncio in June, and was made titular archbishop of Lepanto Oct. 28. He was made archbishop of Milan and cardinal June 13, 1921, before being elected to the papacy Feb. 6, 1922. He died Feb. 10, 1939.

Aim: The objective of his pontificate, as stated in the encyclical *Ubi Arcano*, Dec. 23, 1922, was to establish the reign and peace of Christ in society.

Canonizations: He canonized 34 saints, including the Jesuit Martyrs of North America, and conferred the title of Doctor of the Church on Sts. Peter Canisius, John of the Cross, Robert Bellarmine and Albertus Magnus.

Eastern Churches: He called for better understanding of the Eastern Churches in the encyclical *Rerum Orientalium* of Sept. 8, 1928, and developed facilities for the training of Eastern-Rite priests. He inaugurated steps for the codification of Eastern-Church law in 1929. In 1935 he made Syrian Patriarch Tappouni a cardinal.

Encyclicals: His first encyclical, *Ubi Arcano*, in addition to stating the aims of his pontificate, blueprinted Catholic Action and called for its development throughout the Church. In *Quas Primas*, Dec. 11, 1925, he established the feast of Christ the King for universal observance. Subjects of some of his other encyclicals were: Christian education, in *Divini Illius Magistri*, Dec. 31, 1929; Christian marriage, in *Casti Connubii*, Dec. 30, 1930; social conditions and pressure for social change in line with the teaching in *Rerum Novarum*, in *Quadragesimo Anno*, May 15, 1931; atheistic Communism, in *Divini Redemptoris*, Mar. 19, 1937; the priesthood, in *Ad Catholici Sacerdotii*, Dec. 20, 1935.

Missions: Following the lead of Benedict XV, Pius called for the training of native clergy in the pattern of their own respective cultures, and promoted missionary developments in various ways. He ordained six native bishops for China in 1926, one for Japan in 1927, and others for regions of Asia, China and India in 1933. He placed the first 40 mission dioceses under native bishops, saw the number of native priests increase from about 2,600 to more than 7,000 and the number of Catholics in missionary areas more than double from nine million.

In the apostolic constitution *Deus Scientiarum Dominus* of May 24, 1931, he ordered the introduction of missiology into theology courses.

Interfaith Relations: Pius was negative to the ecumenical movement among Protestants but approved the Malines Conversations, 1921 to 1926, between Anglicans and Catholics.

International Relations: Relations with the Mussolini government deteriorated from 1931 on, as indicated in the encyclical *Non Abbiamo Bisogno,* when the regime took steps to curb liberties and activities of the Church; they turned critical in 1938 with the emergence of racist policies. Relations deteriorated also in Germany from 1933 on, resulting finally in condemnation of the Nazis in the encyclical *Mit Brennender Sorge,* March, 1937. Pius sparked a revival of the Church in France by encouraging Catholics to work within the democratic framework of the Republic rather than foment trouble over restoration of a monarchy. Pius was powerless before the civil war which erupted in Spain in July, 1936; sporadic persecution and repression by the Calles regime in Mexico; and systematic persecution of the Church in the Soviet Union. Many of the 10 concordats and two agreements reached with European countries after World War I became casualties of World War II.

Roman Question: Pius negotiated for two and one-half years with the Italian government to settle the Roman Question by means of the Lateran Agreement of 1929. The agreement provided independent status for the State of Vatican City; made Catholicism the official religion of Italy, with pastoral and educational freedom and state recognition of Catholic marriages, religious orders and societies; and provided a financial payment to the Vatican for expropriation of the former States of the Church.

Pius XII

Pius XII (Eugenio Maria Giovanni Pacelli) was born Mar. 2, 1876, in Rome.

Educated at the Gregorian University and the Lateran University, in Rome, he was ordained to the priesthood Apr. 2, 1899.

He entered the Vatican diplomatic service in 1901, worked on the codification of canon law, and was appointed secretary of the Congregation for Ecclesiastical Affairs in 1914. Three years later he was ordained titular archbishop of Sardis and made apostolic nuncio to Bavaria. He was nuncio to Germany from 1920 to 1929, when he was made a cardinal, and took office as papal secretary of state in the following year. His diplomatic negotiations resulted in concordats between the Vatican and Bavaria (1924), Prussia (1929), Baden (1932), Austria and the German Republic (1933). He took part in negotiations which led to settlement of the Roman Question in 1929.

He was elected to the papacy Mar. 2, 1939. He died Oct. 9, 1958, at Castel Gandolfo after the 12th longest pontificate in history.

Canonizations: He canonized 33 saints, including Mother Frances X. Cabrini, the first US citizen-Saint.

Cardinals: He raised 56 prelates to the rank of cardinal in two consistories held in 1946 and 1953. There were 57 cardinals at the time of his death.

Church Organization and Missions: He increased the number of dioceses from 1,696 to 2,048. He established native hierarchies in China (1946), Burma (1955), and parts of Africa, and extended the native structure of the Church in India. He ordained the first black bishop for Africa.

Communism: In addition to opposing and condemning Communism on numerous occasions, he decreed in 1949 the penalty of excommunication for all Catholics holding formal and willing allegiance to the Communist Party and its policies. During his reign the Church was persecuted in some 15 countries which fell under Communist domination.

Doctrine and Liturgy: He proclaimed the dogma of the Assumption of the Blessed Virgin Mary Nov. 1, 1950 (apostolic constitution, *Munificentissimus Deus*).

In various encyclicals and other enactments, he provided background for the *aggiornamento* introduced by his successor, John XXIII: by his formulations of doctrine and practice regarding the Mystical Body of Christ, the liturgy, sacred music and biblical studies; by the revision of the Rites of Holy Week; by initiation of the work which led to the calendar-missal-breviary reform ordered into effect Jan. 1, 1961; by the first of several modifications of the Eucharistic fast; by extending the time of Mass to the evening. He instituted the feasts of Mary, Queen, and of St. Joseph the Worker, and clarified teaching concerning devotion to the Sacred Heart.

His 41 encyclicals and nearly 1,000 public addresses made Pius one of the greatest teaching popes. His concern in all his communications was to deal with specific points at issue and/or to bring Christian principles to bear on contemporary world problems.

Peace Efforts: Before the start of World War II, he tried unsuccessfully to get the contending nations — Germany and Poland, France and Italy — to settle their differences peaceably. During the war, he offered his services to mediate the widened conflict, spoke out against the horrors of war and the suffering it caused, mobilized relief work for its victims, proposed a five-point program for peace in Christmas messages from 1939 to 1942, and secured a generally open status for the city of Rome. After the war, he endorsed the principles and intent of the United Nations and continued efforts for peace.

United States: Pius appointed more than 200 of the 265 American bishops resident in the US and abroad in 1958, erected 27 dioceses in this country, and raised seven dioceses to archiepiscopal rank.

John XXIII

John XXIII (Angelo Roncalli) was born Nov. 25, 1881, at Sotte il Monte, Italy.

He was educated at the seminary of the Bergamo diocese and the Pontifical Seminary in Rome, where he was ordained to the priesthood Aug. 10, 1904.

He spent the first nine or 10 years of his priesthood as secretary to the bishop of Bergamo and as an instructor in the seminary there. He served as a medic and chaplain in the Italian army during World War I. Afterwards, he resumed duties in his own diocese until he was called to Rome in 1921 for work with the Society for the Propagation of the Faith.

He began diplomatic service in 1925 as titular archbishop of Areopolis and apostolic visitor to Bulgaria. A succession of offices followed: apostolic delegate to Bulgaria (1931-1935); titular archbishop of Mesembria, apostolic delegate to Turkey and Greece, administrator of the Latin vicariate apostolic of Istanbul (1935-1944); apostolic nuncio to France (1944-1953). On these missions, he was engaged in delicate negotiations involving Roman, Eastern-Rite and Orthodox relations; the needs of people suffering from the consequences of World War II; and unsettling suspicions arising from wartime conditions.

He was made a cardinal Jan. 12, 1953, and three days later was appointed patriarch of Venice, the position he held until his election to the papacy Oct. 28, 1958. He died of stomach cancer June 3, 1963.

John was a strong and vigorous pope whose influence far outmeasured both his age and the shortness of his time in the papacy.

Second Vatican Council: John announced Jan. 25, 1959, his intention of convoking the 21st ecumenical council in history to renew life in the Church, to reform its structures and institutions, and to explore ways and means of promoting unity among Christians. Through the council, which completed its work two and one-half years after his death, he ushered in a new era in the history of the Church.

Canon Law: He established a commission Mar. 28, 1963, for revision of the Code of Canon Law. The work of this commission, still underway, will greatly influence the future course of Catholic life and the conduct of ecclesiastical affairs.

Canonizations: He canonized 10 saints. He also beatified Mother Elizabeth Ann Seton, the first native of the US ever so honored. He named St. Lawrence of Brindisi a Doctor of the Church.

Cardinals: He created 52 cardinals in five consistories, raising membership of the College of Cardinals above the traditional number of 70; at one time in 1962, the membership was 87. He made the college more international in representation than it had ever been, appointing the first cardinals from the Philippines, Japan and Africa. He ordered episcopal ordination for all cardinals. He relieved the suburban bishops of Rome of ordinary jurisdiction over their dioceses so they might devote all their time to business of the Roman Curia.

Eastern Rites: He made all Eastern-Rite patriarchs members of the Congregation for the Oriental Churches.

Ecumenism: He assigned to the Second Vatican Council the task of finding ways and means of promoting unity among Christians. He established the Vatican Secretariat for Promoting Christian Unity June 5, 1960. He showed his desire for more cordial relations with the Orthodox by sending personal representatives to visit Patriarch Athenagoras I June 27, 1961; approved a mission of five delegates to the General Assembly of the World Council of Churches which met in New Delhi, India, in November, 1961; removed a number of pejorative references to Jews in the Roman-Rite liturgy for Good Friday.

Encyclicals: Of the eight encyclicals he issued, the two outstanding ones were *Mater et Magistra* ("Christianity and Social Progress"), in which he recapitulated, updated and extended the social doctrine stated earlier by Leo XIII and Pius XI; and *Pacem in Terris* ("Peace on Earth"), the first encyclical ever addressed to all men of good will as well as to Catholics, on the natural-law principles of peace.

Liturgy: In forwarding liturgical reforms already begun by Pius XII, he ordered a calendar-missal-breviary reform into effect Jan. 1, 1961. He authorized the use of vernacular languages in the administration of the sacraments and approved giving Holy Communion to the sick in afternoon hours. He selected the liturgy as the first topic of major discussion by the Second Vatican Council.

Missions: He issued an encyclical on the missionary activity of the Church; established native hierarchies in Indonesia, Vietnam and Korea; and called on North American superiors of religious institutes to have one-tenth of their members assigned to work in Latin America by 1971.

Peace: John spoke and used his moral influence for peace in 1961 when tension developed over Berlin, in 1962 during the Algerian revolt from France, and later the same year in the Cuban missile crisis. His efforts were singled out for honor by the Balzan Peace Foundation. In 1963, he was posthumously awarded the US Presidential Medal of Freedom.

CANONIZATIONS BY LEO XIII AND HIS SUCCESSORS

Canonization is an infallible declaration by the pope that a person who suffered martyrdom and/or practiced Christian virtue to a heroic degree is in glory with God in heaven and is worthy of public honor by the universal Church and of imitation by the faithful.

Leo XIII
(1878-1903)

1881: Clare of Montefalco, virgin (d. 1308); John Baptist de Rossi, priest (1698-1764); Lawrence of Brindisi, doctor (d. 1619); Benedict J. Labre (1748-1783).

1888: Seven Holy Founders of the Servite Order; Peter Claver, priest (1581-1654); John Berchmans (1599-1621); Alphonsus Rodriguez, lay brother (1531-1617).

1897: Anthony M. Zaccaria, founder of Barnabites (1502-1539); Peter Fourier, cofounder of Augustinian Canonesses of Our Lady (1565-1640).

1900: John Baptist de La Salle, founder of Christian Brothers (1651-1719); Rita of Cascia (1381-1457).

St. Pius X
(1903-1914)

1904: Alexander Sauli, bishop (1534-1593); Gerard Majella, lay brother (1725-1755).

1909: Joseph Oriol, priest (1650-1702); Clement M. Hofbauer, priest (1751-1820).

Benedict XV
(1914-1922)

1920: Gabriel of the Sorrowful Mother (1838-1862); Margaret Mary Alacoque, virgin (1647-1690); Joan of Arc, virgin (1412-1431).

Pius XI
(1922-1939)

1925: Therese of Lisieux, virgin (1873-1897); Peter Canisius, doctor (1521-1597); Mary Magdalen Postel, foundress of Sisterhood of Christian Schools (1756-1846); Mary Magdalen Sophie Barat, foundress of Society of the Sacred Heart (1779-1865); John Eudes, founder of Eudist Fathers (1601-1680); John Baptist Vianney (Curé of Ars), priest (1786-1859).

1930: Lucy Filippini, virgin (1672-1732); Catherine Thomas, virgin (1533-1574); Jesuit North American Martyrs (see Index); Robert Bellarmine, bishop-doctor (1542-1621); Theophilus of Corte, priest (1676-1740).

1931: Albert the Great, bishop-doctor (1206-1280) (equivalent canonization).

1933: Andrew Fournet, priest (1752-1834); Bernadette Soubirous, virgin (1844-1879).

1934: Joan Antida Thouret, foundress of Sisters of Charity of St. Joan Antida (1765-1826); Mary Michaeli, foundress of Institute of Handmaids of the Blessed Sacrament (1809-1865); Louise de Marillac, foundress of Sisters of Charity (1591-1660); Joseph Benedict Cottolengo, priest (1786-1842); Pompi-

lius M. Pirotti, priest (1710-1756); Teresa Margaret Redi, virgin (1747-1770); John Bosco, founder of Salesians (1815-1888); Conrad of Parzham, lay brother (1818-1894).

1935: John Fisher, bishop-martyr (1469-1535); Thomas More, martyr (1478-1535).

1938: Andrew Bobola, martyr (1592-1657); John Leonardi, founder of Clerics Regular of the Mother of God (c. 1550-1609); Salvatore of Horta, lay brother (1520-1567).

Pius XII
(1939-1958)

1940: Gemma Galgani, virgin (1878-1903); Mary Euphrasia Pelletier, foundress of Good Shepherd Sisters (1796-1868).

1943: Margaret of Hungary, virgin (d. 1270) (equivalent canonization).

1946: Frances Xavier Cabrini, foundress of Missionary Sisters of the Sacred Heart (1850-1917).

1947: Nicholas of Flue, hermit (1417-1487); John of Britto, martyr (1647-1693); Bernard Realini, priest (1530-1616); Joseph Cafasso, priest (1811-1860); Michael Garicoits, founder of Auxiliary Priests of the Sacred Heart (1797-1863); Jeanne Elizabeth des Ages, cofoundress of Daughters of the Cross (1773-1838); Louis Marie Grignon de Montfort, founder of Montfort Fathers (1673-1716); Catherine Laboure, virgin (1806-1876).

1949: Jeanne de Lestonnac, foundress of Religious of Notre Dame of Bordeaux (1556-1640); Maria Josepha Rossello, foundress of Daughters of Our Lady of Pity (1811-1880).

1950: Emily de Rodat, foundress of Congregation of the Holy Family of Villefranche (1787-1852); Anthony Mary Claret, bishop, founder of Claretians (1807-1870); Bartolomea Capitanio (1807-1833) and Vincenza Gerosa (1784-1847), foundresses of Sisters of Charity of Lovere; Jeanne de Valois, foundress of Annonciades of Bourges (1461-1504); Vincenzo M. Strambi, bishop (1745-1824); Maria Goretti, virgin-martyr (1890-1902); Mariana Paredes of Jesus, virgin (1618-1645).

1951: Maria Domenica Mazzarello, cofoundress of Daughters of Our Lady Help of Christians (1837-1881); Emilie de Vialar, foundress of Sisters of St. Joseph "of the Apparition" (1797-1856); Anthony M. Gianelli, bishop (1789-1846); Ignatius of Laconi, lay brother (1701-1781); Francis Xavier Bianchi, priest (1743-1815).

1954: Pius X, pope (1835-1914); Dominic Savio (1842-1857); Maria Crocifissa di Rosa, foundress of Handmaids of Charity of Brescia (1813-1855); Peter Chanel, priest-martyr (1803-1841); Gaspar del Bufalo, founder of Missioners of the Most Precious Blood (1786-1837); Joseph M. Pignatelli, priest (1737-1811).

1958: Herman Joseph, O. Praem., priest (1150-1241) (equivalent canonization).

John XXIII
(1958-1963)

1959: Joaquina de Vedruna de Mas, foundress of Carmelite Sisters of Charity (1783-1854); Charles of Sezze, lay brother (1613-1670).

1960: Gregory Barbarigo, bishop (1625-1697) (equivalent canonization); John de Ribera, bishop (1532-1611).

1961: Bertilla Boscardin, virgin (1888-1922).

1962: Martin de Porres, lay brother (1569-1639); Peter Julian Eymard, founder of Blessed Sacrament Fathers (1811-1868); Anthony Pucci, priest (1819-1892); Francis Mary of Camporosso, lay brother (1804-1866).

1963: Vincent Pallotti, founder of Pallotine Fathers (1795-1850).

Paul VI
(1963-   )

1964: Twenty-two Martyrs of Uganda.

1967: Benilde, lay brother (1805-1862).

1969: Julia Billiart, foundress of Sisters of Notre Dame de Namur (1751-1816).

1970: Maria Della Dolorato Torres Acosta, foundress of Servants Sisters of Mary (1826-1887); Leonard Murialdo, priest, founder of Congregation of St. Joseph (1828-1890); Therese Couderc, foundress of Congregation of Our Lady of the Cenacle (1805-1885); John of Avila, preacher and spiritual director (1499-1569); Sts. Nicholas Tavelic, Deodatus of Aquitaine, Peter of Narbonne and Stephen of Cuneo, martyrs (d. 1391); Forty English and Welsh Martyrs (d. 16th cent.).

1974: Teresa of Jesus Journet Ibars, foundress of Little Sisters of Abandoned Aged (1843-1897).

English and Welsh Martyrs

Forty Martyrs of England and Wales, victims of persecution from 1535 to 1671, were canonized by Pope Paul Oct. 25, 1970.

The martyrs were prosecuted and executed as traitors for refusal to comply with laws enacted by Henry VIII and Elizabeth I regarding supremacy (the sovereign was proclaimed the highest authority of the Church in England, acknowledgment of papal primacy was forbidden), succession and the prohibition of native-born to study for the priesthood abroad and return to England for practice of the ministry.

John Houghton, prior of the London Charterhouse, was the first of his group to die (1535) for opposing Henry's Acts of Supremacy and Succession. Cuthbert Mayne (d. 1577) was the protomartyr of the English seminary at Douay. Margaret Clitherow (d. 1586) and Swithun Wells (d. 1591) were executed for sheltering priests. Richard Gwyn (d. 1584), poet, was the protomartyr of Wales.

Others in the group were:

John Almond, Edmund Arrowsmith, Ambrose Barlow, John Boste, Alexander Briant, Edmund Campion, Philip Evans, Thomas Garnet, Edmund Gennings;

Philip Howard, John Jones, John Kemble, Luke Kirby, Robert Lawrence, David Lewis, Ann Line, John Lloyd;

Henry Morse, Nicholas Owen, John Paine, Polydore Plasden, John Plessington, Richard Reynolds, John Riggby, John Roberts;

Alban Roe, Ralph Serwin, Robert Southwell, John Southworth, John Stone, John Wall, Henry Walpole, Margaret Ward, Augustine Webster and Eustace White.

ENCYCLICALS ISSUED BY LEO XIII AND HIS SUCCESSORS

An encyclical letter is a pastoral letter addressed by a pope to the whole Church. In general, it concerns matters of doctrine, morals or discipline. Its formal title consists of the first few words of the official text. A few encyclicals, notably *Pacem in Terris* by John XXIII and *Ecclesiam Suam* by Paul VI, have been addressed to "all men of good will" as well as to bishops and the faithful in communion with the Church.

An encyclical epistle, which is like an encyclical letter in many respects, is addressed to part of the Church, that is, to the bishops and faithful of a particular country or area. Its contents may concern other than doctrinal, moral or disciplinary matters of universal significance; for example, the commemoration of historical events, conditions in a particular country.

The authority of encyclicals was stated by Pius XII in the encyclical *Humani Generis* Aug. 12, 1950.

"Nor must it be thought that what is contained in encyclical letters does not of itself demand assent, on the pretext that the popes do not exercise in them the supreme power of their teaching authority. Rather, such teachings belong to the ordinary magisterium, of which it is true to say: 'He who hears you, hears me' (Lk. 10:16); for the most part, too, what is expounded and inculcated in encyclical letters already appertains to Catholic doctrine for other reasons. But if the supreme pontiffs in their official documents purposely pass judgment on a matter debated until then, it is obvious to all that the matter, according to the mind and will of the same pontiffs, cannot be considered any longer a question open for discussion among theologians."

The following list contains the titles and indicates the subject matter of encyclical letters and epistles. The latter are generally distinguishable by the limited scope of their titles or contents.

Leo XIII
(1878-1903)

1878: Inscrutabili Dei Consilio (Evils of Society), Apr. 21.

Quod Apostolici Muneris (Socialism, Communism, Nihilism), Dec. 28.

1879: Aeterni Patris (Scholastic Philosophy, Especially of Thomas Aquinas), Aug. 4.

1880: Arcanum (Christian Marriage), Feb. 10.

Grande Munus (Sts. Cyril and Methodius), Sept. 30.

Sancta Dei Civitas (Three French Societies), Dec. 3.

1881: Diuturnum (Origin of Civil Power), June 29.

1882: Etsi Nos (Conditions in Italy), Feb. 15.

Auspicato Concessum (Third Order of St. Francis), Sept. 17.

Cum Multa (Conditions in Spain), Dec. 8.

1883: Supremi Apostolatus Officio (The Rosary), Sept. 1.

1884: Nobilissima Gallorum Gens (Religious Question in France), Feb. 8.

Humanum Genus (Freemasonry), Apr. 20.

Superiore Anno (Recitation of the Rosary), Aug. 30.

1885: Immortale Dei (The Christian Constitution of States), Nov. 1.

Quod Auctoritate (Proclamation of Extraordinary Jubilee Year), Dec. 22.

1886: Quod Multum (Liberty of the Church in Hungary), Aug. 22.

Pergrata Nobis (Needs of the Church in Portugal), Sept. 14.

1888: Libertas (Human Liberty), June 20.

Paterna Caritas (Recalling the Dissenting Armenians), July 25.

Quam Aerumnosa (Italian Immigrants in America), Dec. 10.

1889: Quamquam Pluries (Patronage of St. Joseph and the Blessed Virgin Mary), Aug. 15.

1890: Sapientiae Christianae (Chief Duties of Christian Citizens), Jan. 10.

Ab Apostoli (To the Clergy and People of Italy), Oct. 15.

1891: Rerum Novarum (Condition of the Working Classes), May 15.

Octobri Mense (The Rosary), Sept. 22.

1892: Au Milieu des Sollicitudes (Church and State in France), Feb. 16.

Magnae Dei Matris (The Rosary), Sept. 8.

1893: Ad Extremas (Seminaries in the East Indies), June 24.

Constanti Hungarorum (Conditions of the Church in Hungary), Sept. 2.

Laetitiae Sanctae (The Rosary), Sept. 8.

Providentissimus Deus (Study of Holy Scripture), Nov. 18.

1894: Caritatis (Conditions in Poland), Mar. 19.

Iucunda Semper Expectatione (The Rosary), Sept. 8.

Christi Nomen (Society for the Propagation of the Faith), Dec. 24.

1895: Adiutricem (The Rosary), Sept. 5.

1896: Satis Cognitum (Church Unity), June 29.

Fidentum Piumque Animum (The Rosary), Sept. 20.

1897: Divinum Illud Munus (The Holy Spirit, doctrine and devotion), May 9.

Militantis Ecclesiae (Third Centenary of the Death of St. Peter Canisius), Aug. 1.

Augustissimae Virginis (The Rosary), Sept. 12.

Affari Vos (The Manitoba School Question), Dec. 8.

1898: Caritatis Studium (The Magisterium of the Church in Scotland), July 25.

Spesse Volte (Catholic Action in Italy) Aug. 5.

1899: Annum Sacrum (Consecration of Mankind to the Sacred Heart), May 25.

Depuis le Jour (Ecclesiastical Education in France), Sept. 8.

1900: Tametsi Futura Prospicientibus (Jesus Christ, Our Redeemer), Nov. 1.

1901: Graves de Communi Re (Christian Democracy), Jan. 18.

1902: Mirae Caritatis (The Most Holy Eucharist), May 28.

Fin dal Principio (Education of the Clergy in Italy), Dec. 8.

Saint Pius X
(1903-1914)

1903: E Supremi (Restoration of All Things in Christ), Oct. 4.

1904: Ad Diem Illum Laetissimum (Jubilee of the Immaculate Conception), Feb. 2.

Iucunda Sane (Thirteenth Centenary of the Death of St. Gregory the Great), Mar. 12.

1905: Acerbo Nimis (Teaching of Christian Doctrine), Apr. 15.

Il Fermo Proposito (Catholic Action in Italy), June 11.

1906: Vehementer Nos (French Separation Law), Feb. 11.

Tribus Circiter (Condemnation of the Mariavites), Apr. 5.

Pieni l'Animo (Clergy in Italy), July 28.

Gravissimo Officio Munere (Forbidding Associations Cultuelles), Aug. 10.

1907: Une Fois Encore (Separation of Church and State in France), Jan. 6.

Pascendi Dominici Gregis (Modernism), Sept. 8.

1909: Communium Rerum (Eighth Centenary of the Death of St. Anselm), Apr. 21.

1910: Editae Saepe (Third Centenary of the Death of St. Charles Borromeo), May 26.

1911: Iamdudum (Separation Law in Portugal), May 24.

1912: Lacrimabili Statu (Indians of South America), June 7.

Singulari Quadam (Labor Organizations in Germany), Sept. 24.

Benedict XV
(1914-1922)

1914: Ad Beatissimi Apostolorum (Appeal for Peace), Nov. 1.

1917: Humani Generis Redemptionem (Preaching), June 15.

1918: Quod Iam Diu (Peace Congress, Paris), Dec. 1.

1919: In Hac Tanta (Twelfth Centenary of St. Boniface), May 14.

Paterno Iam Diu (Christian Charity of the Children of Central Europe), Nov. 24.

1920: Pacem, Dei Munus Pulcherrimum (Peace and Christian Reconciliation), May 23.

Spiritus Paraclitus (Holy Scripture), Sept. 15.

Principi Apostolorum Petro (St. Ephrem the Syrian, declared Doctor), Oct. 5.

Annus Iam Plenus (Child War Victims), Dec. 1.

1921: Sacra Propediem (Seventh Centenary of the Third Order of St. Francis), Jan. 6.

In Praeclara Summorum (Sixth Centenary of Dante's Death), Apr. 30.

Fausto Appetente Die (Seventh Centenary of the Death of St. Dominic), June 29.

Pius XI
(1922-1939)

1922: Ubi Arcano Dei Consilio (Peace of Christ in the Kingdom of Christ), Dec. 23.

1923: Rerum Omnium Perturbationem (Third Centenary of the Death of St. Francis de Sales), Jan. 26.

Studiorum Ducem (Sixth Centenary of the Canonization of St. Thomas Aquinas), June 29.

Ecclesiam Dei (Third Centenary of the Death of St. Josaphat, Archbishop of Polotsk), Nov. 12.

1924: Maximam Gravissimamque (French Diocesan Associations), Jan. 18.

1925: Quas Primas (Feast of Christ the King), Dec. 11.

1926: Rerum Ecclesiae (Catholic Missions), Feb. 28.

Rite Expiatis (Seventh Centenary of the Death of St. Francis of Assisi), Apr. 30.

Iniquis Afflictisque (Persecution of the Church in Mexico), Nov. 18.

1928: Mortalium Animos (Promotion of True Religious Unity), Jan. 6.

Miserentissimus Redemptor (Reparation Due the Sacred Heart), May 8.

Rerum Orientalium (Reunion with the Eastern Churches), Sept. 8.

1929: Mens Nostra (Promotion of Spiritual Exercises), Dec. 20.

Quinquagesimo Ante (Sacerdotal Jubilee), Dec. 23.

Divini Illius Magistri (Rappresentanti in Terra) (Christian Education of Youth), Dec. 31.

1930: Ad Salutem (Fifteenth Centenary of the Death of St. Augustine), Apr. 20.

Casti Connubii (Christian Marriage), Dec. 31.

1931: Quadragesimo Anno (Social Reconstruction), May 15.

Non Abbiamo Bisogno (Catholic Action), June 29.

Nova Impendet (Economic Crisis, Unemployment, Armaments), Oct. 2.

Lux Veritatis (Fifteenth Centenary of the Council of Ephesus), Dec. 25.

1932: Caritate Christi Compulsi (Sacred Heart and World Distress), May 3.

Acerba Animi (Persecution of the Church in Mexico), Sept. 29.

1933: Dilectissima Nobis (Conditions in Spain), June 3.

1935: Ad Catholici Sacerdotii (Catholic Priesthood), Dec. 20.

1936: Vigilanti Cura (Clean Motion Pictures), June 29.

1937: Mit Brennender Sorge (Church in Germany), Mar. 14.

Divini Redemptoris (Atheistic Communism), Mar. 19.

Firmissimam Constantiam (Nos Es Muy Conocida) (Conditions in Mexico), Mar. 28.

Ingravescentibus Malis (The Rosary) Sept. 29.

Pius XII
(1939-1958)

1939: Summi Pontificatus (Function of the State in Modern World), Oct. 20.

Sertum Laetitiae (To the Church in the United States), Nov. 1.

1940: Saeculo Exeunte Octavo (Missions), June 13.

1943: Mystici Corporis Christi (Mystical Body), June 29.

Divino Afflante Spiritu (Biblical Studies), Sept. 30.

1944: Orientalis Ecclesiae Decus (Fifteenth Centenary of the Death of St. Cyril of Alexandria), Apr. 9.

1945: Communium Interpretes Dolorum (Appeal for Prayers), Apr. 15.

Orientales Omnes Ecclesias (Anniversary of the Ruthenian Reunion), Dec. 23.

1946: Quemadmodum (Call for Intensified Aid to Youth), Jan. 6.

Deiparae Virginis Mariae (Proposing to the Bishops the Question of the Definition of the Dogma of the Assumption), May 1.

1947: Fulgens Radiatur (Fourteenth Centenary of the Death of St. Benedict), Mar. 21.

Mediator Dei (Sacred Liturgy), Nov. 20.

Optatissima Pax (Peace and Social Disorders), Dec. 18.

1948: Auspicia Quaedam (Prayer to Blessed Virgin Mary for Peace), May 1.

In Multiplicibus Curis (Crisis in Palestine), Oct. 24.

1949: Redemptoris Nostri (Internationalization of Jerusalem), Apr. 15.

1950: Anni Sacri (Holy Year Call for Public Prayer), Mar. 12.

Summi Maeroris (Renewed Holy Year Call for Public Prayer), July 19.

Humani Generis (Warnings against Attempts to Distort Catholic Truths), Aug. 12.

Mirabile Illud (Call for Renewed Crusade of Prayers for Peace), Dec. 6.

1951: Evangelii Praecones (Call for Greater Missionary Effort), June 2.

Sempiternus Rex (Fifteenth Centenary of the Council of Chalcedon), Sept. 8.

Ingruentium Malorum (Recitation of the Rosary), Sept. 15.

1952: Orientales Ecclesias (Communist Persecution of the Church; Call for Prayers for the Persecuted), Dec. 15.

1953: Doctor Mellifluus (Eighth Centenary of Death of St. Bernard), May 24.

Fulgens Corona (Call for Catholics to Observe Marian Year), Sept. 8.

1954: Sacra Virginitas (Preeminence of Evangelical Chastity), Mar. 25.

Ecclesiae Fastos (Commemoration of St. Boniface), June 5.

Ad Sinarum Gentem (The Church in China), Oct. 7.

Ad Caeli Reginam (Feast of Queenship of Mary), Oct. 11.

1955: Musicae Sacrae (Sacred Music), Dec. 25.

1956: Haurietis Aquas (The Sacred Heart), May 15.

Luctuosissimi Eventus (Prayers for Hungary), Oct. 28.

Laetamur Admodum (Middle East Crisis), Nov. 1.

Datis Nuperrime (Prayers for Peace), Nov. 5.

1957: Fidei Donum (Missionary Effort, especially in Africa), Apr. 21.

Invicti Athletae Christi (Third Centenary of Death of St. Andrew Bobola), May 16.

Le Pelerinage de Lourdes (Centenary of Lourdes Apparitions), July 2.

Miranda Prorsus (Radio, TV and Motion Pictures), Sept. 8.

1958: Ad Apostolorum Principis (Critical Situation of the Church in China), June 29.

Meminisse Juvat (Prayers for Peace and the Persecuted Church), July 14.

John XXIII
(1958-1963)

1959: Ad Petri Cathedram (Appeal to Separated Christians to Reunite with Church), June 29.

Sacerdotii Nostri Primordia (Centenary of the Cure of Ars), Aug. 1.

Grata Recordatio (Rosary), Sept. 26.

Princeps Pastorum (Missions), Nov. 28.

1961: Mater et Magistra (Christianity and Social Progress), May 15.

Aeterna Dei Sapientia (Fifteenth Centenary of the Death of St. Leo the Great), Nov. 11.

1962: Paenitentiam Agere (Appeal for Works of Penance for Success of the Second Vatican Council), July 1.

1963: Pacem in Terris (Peace on Earth), Apr. 11.

Paul VI
(1963-)

1964: Ecclesiam Suam (Second Vatican Council Themes), Aug. 6.

1965: Mense Maio (Prayer for Success of Vatican II, Peace), Apr. 29.

Mysterium Fidei (The Eucharist), Sept. 3.

1966: Christi Matri Rosarii (The Rosary), Sept. 15.

1967: Populorum Progressio (Development of Peoples), Mar. 26.

Sacerdotalis Caelibatus (Priestly Celibacy), June 24.

1968: Humanae Vitae (Birth Control), July 25.

COMMUNISM

The substantive principles of modern Communism, a theory and system of economics and social organization, were stated about the middle of the 19th century by Karl Marx, author of *The Communist Manisfesto* and, with Friedrich Engels, *Das Kapital.*

The elements of Communist ideology include: radical materialism; dialectical determinism; the inevitability of class struggle, which is to be furthered, for the ultimate establishment of a worldwide classless society; common ownership of productive and other goods; the subordination of all persons and institutions to the dictatorship of the collectivity; denial of the rights, dignity and liberty of persons; militant atheism and hostility to religion; utilitarian morality.

Communism in theory and practice has been the subject of many papal documents and statements. Pius IX condemned it in 1846. Leo XIII dealt with it at length in the encyclicals *Quod Apostolici Muneris* in 1878 and *Rerum Novarum* in 1891. Pius XI wrote on the same subject in the encyclicals *Quadragesimo Anno* in 1931 and *Divini Redemptoris* in 1937.

Pius XII, besides writing and speaking about Communism on many occasions, authorized the June 13, 1949, decree of the Congregation of the Holy Office which contained these as well as other provisions: Catholics are forbidden to join the Communist Party; Catholics who knowingly and willingly profess the doctrines of Communism, or defend its principles, or spread its errors are automatically excommunicated. Catholics who join the Communist Party under the force of hard circumstances (as in Iron Curtain countries, for the sake of work needed to support their families) but do not subscribe to its ideology, are not excommunicated.

Hierarchy of the Catholic Church

ORGANIZATION AND GOVERNMENT

As a structured society, the Catholic Church is organized and governed along lines corresponding mainly to the jurisdictions of the pope and bishops.

The pope is the supreme head of the Church. He has primacy of jurisdiction as well as honor over the entire Church.

Bishops, in union with and in subordination to the pope, are the successors of the Apostles for care of the Church and for the continuation of Christ's mission in the world. They serve the people of their own dioceses, or local churches, with ordinary authority and jurisdiction. They also share, with the pope and each other, in common concern and effort for the general welfare of the whole Church.

Bishops of exceptional status are Eastern Rite patriarchs who, subject only to the pope, are heads of the faithful belonging to their rites throughout the world.

Subject to the Holy Father and directly responsible to him for the exercise of their ministry of service to people in various jurisdictions or divisions of the Church throughout the world are: resident archbishops and metropolitans (heads of archdioceses), resident bishops (heads of dioceses), vicars and prefects apostolic (heads of vicariates apostolic and prefectures apostolic), certain abbots and prelates, apostolic administrators. Each of these, within his respective territory and according to the provisions of canon law, has ordinary jurisdiction over pastors (who are responsible for the administration of parishes), priests, religious and lay persons.

Also subject to the Holy Father are titular archbishops and bishops (who have delegated jurisdiction), religious orders and congregations of pontifical right, pontifical institutes and faculties, papal nuncios and apostolic delegates.

Assisting the pope and acting in his name in the central government and administration of the Church are cardinals and other officials of the Roman Curia.

THE HIERARCHY

The ministerial hierarchy is the orderly arrangement of the ranks and orders of the clergy to provide for the spiritual care of the faithful, the government of the Church, and the accomplishment of the Church's total mission in the world. Persons belong to this hierarchy by virtue of ordination and canonical mission.

The term hierarchy is also used to designate an entire body or group of bishops; for example, the hierarchy of the Church, the hierarchy of the United States.

Hierarchy of Order: Consists of the pope, bishops, priests and deacons, by divine law. Their purpose, for which they are ordained to holy orders, is to carry out the sacramental and pastoral ministry of the Church.

Hierarchy of Jurisdiction: Consists of the pope and bishops by divine law, and other church officials by ecclesiastical institution and mandate, who have authority to govern and direct the faithful for spiritual ends.

Prelates: Clerics with the authority of public office in the Church — i. e., the authority of jurisdiction in the external forum. They are: the pope, patriarchs, residential archbishops and bishops, certain abbots and prelates, vicars and prefects apostolic, vicars general, certain superiors in clerical exempt religious communities. Titular archbishops and bishops without ordinary jurisdiction are not prelates in the strict sense of the term; neither are pastors, who have very limited jurisdiction in the external forum.

The Pope

His Holiness the Pope is the Bishop of Rome, the Vicar of Jesus Christ, the successor of St. Peter, Prince of the Apostles, the Supreme Pontiff who has the primacy of jurisdiction and not merely of honor over the universal Church, the Patriarch of the West, the Primate of Italy, the Archbishop and Metropolitan of the Roman Province, the Sovereign of the State of Vatican City.

Cardinals
(See Index)

Patriarchs

Patriarch, a term which had its origin in the Eastern Church, is the title of a bishop who, second only to the pope, has the highest rank in the hierarchy of jurisdiction. He is the incumbent of one of the sees listed below. Subject only to the pope, an Eastern-Rite patriarch is the head of the faithful belonging to his rite throughout the world. The patriarchal sees are so called because of their special status and dignity in the history of the Church.

The Council of Nicaea (325) recognized three patriarchs — the bishops of Alexandria and Antioch in the East, and of Rome in the West. The First Council of Constantinople (381) added the bishop of Constantinople to the list of patriarchs and gave him rank second only to that of the pope, the bishop of Rome and patriarch of the West; this action was seconded by the Council of Chalcedon (451) and was given full recognition by the Fourth Lateran Council (1215). The Council of Chalcedon also acknowledged patriarchal rights of the bishop of Jerusalem. Since 451, the major patriarchates have been listed in this order of precedence: Rome, Constantinople, Alexandria, Antioch and Jerusalem.

Eastern Rite patriarchs are as follows: one of Alexandria, for the Copts; three of Antioch, one each for the Syrians, Maronites and Melkites (the latter also has the personal title of Melkite patriarch of Alexandria and of Jerusalem). The patriarch of Babylonia, for the Chaldeans, and the patriarch of Sis, or Cilicia, for the Armenians, should be called, more properly, *Katholikos* — that is, a prelate delegated for a universality of causes. These patriarchs are elected by bishops of their rites: they receive approval and the pallium, symbolic of their office, from the pope.

Latin Rite patriarchates were established for Antioch, Jerusalem, Alexandria and Constantinople during the Crusades; afterwards, they became patriarchates in name only. Jerusalem, however, was reconstituted as a patriarchate by Pius IX, in virtue of the bull *Nulla Celebrior* of July 23, 1847. In 1964, the Latin titular patriarchates of Constantinople, Alexandria and Antioch. long a bone of contention in relations with Eastern Rites, were abolished.

As of July 20, 1974, the patriarchs in the Church were:

Paul VI, Bishop of Rome, Pope, Patriarch of the West; Cardinal Stephanos I Sidarouss, C.M., of Alexandria, for the Copts; Ignace Antoine Hayek, of Antioch, for the Syrians; Maximos V Hakim, of Antioch, for the Melkites (he atso has the titles of Alexandria and Jerusalem for the Melkites); Cardinal Paul Meouchi, of Antioch, for the Maronites; Giacomo Beltritti, of Jerusalem, for the Latin Rite; Paul II Cheikho, of Babylon, for the Chaldeans; Ignace Pierre XVI Batanian, of Cilicia, for the Armenians.

The titular patriarchs (in name only) of the Latin Rite were: Jose Vieira Alvernaz, of the East Indies; Cardinal Antonio Ribeiro, of Lisbon; Cardinal Albino Luciani, of Venice. The patriarchate of the West Indies has been vacant since 1963.

Archbishops, Metropolitans

Archbishop: A bishop with the title of an archdiocese.

Metropolitan Archbishop: Head of the principal see, an archdiocese, in an ecclesiastical province consisting of several dioceses. He has the full powers of bishop in his own archdiocese and limited supervisory jurisdiction and influence over the other (suffragan) dioceses in the province.

Titular Archbishop: Has the title of an archdiocese which formerly existed in fact but now exists in title only. He does not have ordinary jurisdiction over an archdiocese.

Archbishop ad personam: A title of personal honor and distinction granted to some bishops. They do not have ordinary jurisdiction over an archdiocese.

Primate: A title given to the ranking prelate of some countries or regions.

Bishops

Residential Bishop: A bishop in charge of a diocese.

Titular Bishops: Have the titles of dioceses which formerly existed in fact but now exist in title only. They have delegated authority of jurisdiction, by grant in line with their assignments, rather than the ordinary jurisdiction of office which belongs to a residential bishop. An auxiliary bishop (titular) is an assistant to a residential bishop. A coadjutor bishop (titular) is an assistant bishop of higher status; some coadjutors have the right of succession to residential sees.

Episcopal Vicar: An assistant, who may or may not be a bishop, appointed by a residential bishop as his deputy for a certain part of a diocese, a determined type of apostolic work, or the faithful of a certain rite.

Eparch, Exarch: Titles of bishops of Eastern-Rite churches.

Nomination of Bishops: Nominees for episcopal ordination are selected in several ways. Final appointment in all cases is subject to decision by the pope.

In the US, bishops periodically submit the names of candidates to the archbishop of their province. The names are then considered at a meeting of the bishops of the province, and those receiving a favorable vote are forwarded to the apostolic delegate for transmission to the Holy See. Bishops are free to seek the counsel of priests, religious and lay persons with respect to nominees.

Eastern-Rite churches have their own procedures and synodal regulations for nominating and making final selection of candidates for episcopal ordination.

In some countries where concordat or other special arrangements are in effect, civil governments have specified privileges to express approval or disapproval of candidates for the episcopacy.

Ad Limina Visit: Residential bishops and military vicars are obliged to make a periodic *ad limina* visit ("to the threshold" of the Apostles) to the tombs of Sts. Peter and Paul, have audience with the Holy Father and present a written report of conditions in their dioceses or military jurisdictions. European bishops are required to make the visit every five years. The visits may be made every 10 years by bishops of dioceses on other continents, but a report must be submitted every five years.

Other Prelates

Some prelates and abbots, formerly called *nullius*, have jurisdiction over territories (abbacies, prefectures, prelatures) not under the authority of diocesan bishops.

Vicar Apostolic: Usually a titular bishop who has ordinary jurisdiction over a mission territory. A vicar apostolic could also serve as the administrator of a vacant diocese or a diocese whose bishop is impeded from the exercise of his office.

Prefect Apostolic: A prelate with ordinary jurisdiction over a mission territory.

Apostolic Administrator: Usually a bishop appointed to administer an ecclesiastical jurisdiction temporarily. Administrators of lesser rank are also appointed for special and more restricted supervisory duties.

Vicar General: A bishop's deputy for the administration of a diocese. Such a vicar does not have to be a bishop.

Honorary Prelates

Honorary prelates belonging to the Pontifical Household are: Apostolic Prothonotaries, Honorary Prelates of His Holiness, and Chaplains of His Holiness. Their title is Reverend Monsignor.

SYNOD OF BISHOPS

The Synod of Bishops was chartered by Pope Paul Sept. 15, 1965, in a document he issued on his own initiative under the title, *Apostolica Sollicitudo.* According to the document:

• The purposes of the Synod are: "to encourage close union and valued assistance between the Sovereign Pontiff and the bishops of the entire world; to insure that direct and real information is provided on questions and situations touching upon the internal action of the Church and its necessary activity in the world of today; to facilitate agreement on essential points of doctrine and on methods of procedure in the life of the Church."

• The Synod is a central ecclesiastical institution, permanent by nature.

• The Synod is directly and immediately subject to the Pope, who has authority to assign its agenda, to call it into session, and to give its members deliberative as well as advisory authority.

• In addition to a limited number of ex officio members and a few heads of male religious institutes, the majority of the members are elective by and representative of national or regional episcopal conferences. The Pope reserved the right to appoint the general secretary, special secretaries and no more than 15 per cent of the total membership.

The secretary general is Bishop Ladislaw Rubin of Poland. Cardinal John J. Krol, president of the U.S. bishops' conference, is one of the 15 members of the Synod's advisory council.

First Meeting, 1967

The Synod met for the first time from Sept. 29 to Oct. 29, 1967, in Vatican City. Its objectives, as stated by Pope Paul, were "the preservation and strengthening of the Catholic faith, its integrity, its force, its development, its doctrinal and historical coherence."

One result of synodal deliberations was a recommendation to the Pope to establish an international commission of theologians to assist the Congregation for the Doctrine of the Faith and to broaden approaches to theological research. The commission was subsequently set up by Pope Paul in 1969.

In other actions, the Synod called for the formulation of a Code of Canon Law more pastoral than the one in force since 1918 and more in touch with the mentality, aspirations and needs of people in contemporary circumstances; favored the view that episcopal conferences should have major control over seminaries in their respective areas; suggested some changes in pastoral procedures with respect to mixed marriages, which were authorized in 1970; gave general approval to the New Order of the Mass which was promulgated and put into effect in 1969.

The first meeting of the Synod had 197 participants: 135 representatives of more than 90 episcopal conferences, 13 representatives of Eastern-Rite churches, 13 cardinals of the Roman Curia, 10 representatives of the Union of Superiors General of Religious, 25 members and a secretary general appointed by Pope Paul.

Extraordinary Session

The second Synod of Bishops, meeting in extraordinary session Oct. 11 to 28, 1969, opened the door to wider participation by the bishops with the Pope and each other in the government of the Church.

The business assigned to the meeting by Pope Paul was to seek and examine ways and means of putting into practice the principle of collegiality which figured largely in declarations of the Second Vatican Council on the Church and the pastoral office of bishops.

Accordingly, proceedings were oriented to three main points: (1) the nature and implications of collegiality; (2) the relationships of bishops and their conferences to the Pope; (3) the relationships of bishops and their conferences to each other. The end results were three proposals approved by the bishops and the Pope, and five times that number approved and placed under advisement by the Pope. All proposals pointed in the direction of more cooperative action by all the bishops with the Pope in the conduct of Church affairs.

The three proposals which were approved and moved for action provided for regular meetings of the Synod at two-year intervals, (later extended to three years), staff organization and operations of the general secretariat in the interim between meetings, and openness of the synodal agenda to suggestions by bishops.

The second meeting had 146 participants: 93 presidents of episcopal conferences — 22 from Europe, 14 from Asia, 29 from Africa, 24 from the Americas, four from Oceania; 13

representatives of Eastern-Rite Churches — six patriarchs, one major archbishop, six metropolitans; three religious, elected by the Union of Superiors General; 19 officials from the various departments of the Roman Curia; secretary general Bishop Ladislaw Rubin, and 17 appointees of Pope Paul.

Between the second and third meetings of the Synod, an advisory council of 15 members (12 elected, three appointed by the Pope) was formed to provide the secretariat with adequate staff for carrying on liaison with episcopal conferences and for drawing up the agenda of synodal meetings. The council, at its first meeting May 12 to 15, 1970, followed the lead of the second assembly by opening the agenda of the 1971 meeting to the suggestions of bishops from all over the world.

Synod '71

The ministerial priesthood and justice in the world were the principal topics of discussion at the third and longest meeting, the Second General Assembly of the Synod, Sept. 30 to Nov. 6, 1971.

Advisory reports on these subjects, compiled from views expressed by the bishops before and during the synodal sessions, were presented to Pope Paul at the end of the meeting. He authorized publication of the reports and said, in a letter made public Dec. 9, that he accepted conclusions reached by the bishops, which "conform to the current norms" of church teaching.

The Priesthood

In its report on the priesthood, the Synod described difficulties experienced by priests, stated traditional doctrinal principles on the priesthood, and drew from these principles a set of guidelines for priestly life and ministry in the mission of Christ and the Church, and in the communion of the Church.

The report emphasized the primary and permanent dedication of priests in the Church to the ministry of word, sacrament and pastoral service as a full-time occupation.

The synodal Fathers — with 168 votes in favor without reservations, 21 votes in favor with reservations, and 10 votes against — supported the existing discipline of clerical celibacy. They favored leaving to the discretion of the Pope decisions regarding the ordination of already married men in special circumstances. They did not consider the question of permitting already ordained priests to marry. The majority voted against permitting priests who had left the ministry to resume priestly duties, although they said such priests could serve the Church in other ways and should be treated in a just and fraternal manner.

Justice in the World

In connection with "the mission of the People of God to further justice in the world," a synodal report reviewed a wide range of existing injustices; cited the social-justice imperatives of the Gospel; called for the practice of justice throughout the Church and for greater efforts in education and ecumenical collaboration for justice; and outlined an eight-point program for international action.

Behind the Synod's recommendations were the convictions:

• "The Church . . . has a proper and specific responsibility which is identified with her mission of giving witness before the world of the need for love and justice contained in the Gospel message, a witness to be carried out in church institutions themselves and in the lives of Christians."

• "Action on behalf of justice and participation in the transformation of the world fully appear to us as a constitutive dimension of the preaching of the Gospel; or, in other words, of the Church's mission for the redemption of the human race and its liberation from every oppressive situation."

• "The present situation of the world, seen in the light of faith, calls us back to the very essence of the Christian message, creating in us a deep awareness of its true meaning and of its urgent demands. The mission of preaching the Gospel dictates at the present time that we should dedicate ourselves to the liberation of man even in his present existence in this world. For, unless the Christian message of love and justice shows its effectiveness through action in the cause of justice in the world, it will only with difficulty gain credibility with the men of our times."

The assembly had 210 participants: six patriarchs, one major archbishop, seven Eastern-Rite metropolitans (one of whom was listed also as a representative of an episcopal conference), 142 elected representatives of 94 episcopal conferences, 10 men religious elected by the Union of Major Superiors, 19 cardinals of the Roman Curia, and 26 papal appointees — the general secretary, 22 bishops and three priests. Ten delegates were from the United States. American Fathers John F. Cronin and Barnabas Ahern, C.P., were among 23 priests designated by Pope Paul to attend the session.

Synod '74

Pope Paul announced Feb. 19, 1973, that the fourth session, to be held in the fall of 1974, would concern itself with "Evangelization of the Modern World."

According to the draft of a preliminary working paper circulated among bishops' conferences early in the summer of 1973, evangelization was called "the activity whereby the Church proclaims the Gospel so that faith may be aroused, may unfold and may grow." Such an umbrella type of definition appeared to open the agenda of the session to numerous topics related to evangelization in mission territories, its relation to

works for human development there and elsewhere, its intensification among the faithful in places where the Church is established, and ways and means of effective evangelization.
(See separate entry under Special Reports.)

ROMAN CURIA

The Roman Curia consists of the Secretariat of State, the Sacred Council for the Public Affairs of the Church, ten congregations, three tribunals, three secretariats, and a complex of commissions, councils and offices which administer church affairs at the highest level.

Background

The Curia evolved gradually from advisory assemblies or synods of the Roman clergy with whose assistance the popes directed church affairs during the first 11 centuries. Its original office was the Apostolic Chancery, dating from the fourth century. The antecedents of its permanently functioning agencies and offices were special commissions of cardinals and prelates. Its establishment in a form resembling what it is now dates from the second half of the 16th century.

Pope Paul VI gave the following short account of the background of the Curia in the apostolic constitution *Regimini Ecclesiae Universae* ("For the Government of the Universal Church"), dated Aug. 15, 1967.

"The Roman Pontiffs, successors to Blessed Peter, have striven to provide for the government of the Universal Church by making use of experts to advise and assist them.

"In this connection, we should remember both the Presbyterium of the City of Rome and the College of Cardinals of the Holy Roman Church which in the course of centuries evolved from it. Then, little by little, as we know, out of that office (Apostolic Chancery) which was set up in the fourth century to transmit papal documents, many offices developed; to these was added the Auditorium, which was a well-developed tribunal in the 13th century and which was more thoroughly organized by John XXII (1316-1334).

"With an increase in the volume of things to be dealt with, bodies or commissions of cardinals selected to treat of specific questions began to be more efficiently organized in the 16th century, from which eventually arose the congregations of the Roman Curia. It is to the credit of our predecessor Sixtus V that, in the constitution *Immensa Aeterni Dei* of Jan. 22, 1588, he arranged the sacred councils in an orderly manner and wisely described the structure of the Roman Curia.

"With the progress of time, however, it happened that some of them became obsolete, others had to be added, and others had to be restructured. This is the work our predecessor St. Pius X set out to do with the consti-

tution *Sapienti Consilio* of June 29, 1908. Its provisions, a lasting testimony to that wise and ingenious pastor of the Church, were with a few changes incorporated into the Code of Canon Law" (Canons 242-264).

Reorganization

Pope Paul initiated a four-year reorganization study in 1963 which resulted in the constitution *Regimini Ecclesiae Universae*. The document was published Aug. 18, 1967, and went into full effect in March, 1968.

While the study was underway, the Pope took preliminary steps toward curial reorganization by reorienting and changing the title of the Sacred Congregation of the Holy Office (to the Sacred Congregation for the Doctrine of the Faith) and by appointing a number of non-Italians to key curial positions.

The stated purposes of the reorganization were to increase the efficiency of the Curia and to make it more responsive to the needs and concerns of the Universal Church. The pursuit of these objectives involved various modifications.

Curial Departments

• The Office of the Pope, including the Papal Secretariat or Secretariat of State and the Council for the Public Affairs of the Church.

• Ten congregations, instead of twelve as formerly. The functions of the Sacred Congregation of Ceremonies were transferred to the Prefecture of the Pontifical Household; the duties of the Sacred Congregation for Extraordinary Ecclesiastical Affairs were taken over by the Sacred Council for the Public Affairs of the Church; the Sacred Congregation of the Basilica of St. Peter was reduced in rank. In 1969, the Sacred Congregation of Rites was phased out of existence and its functions were assigned to the Sacred Congregation for the Causes of Saints and the Sacred Congregation for Divine Worship.

• Three secretariats, the Council for the Laity and the Pontifical Commission on Justice and Peace.

• Three tribunals.

• Six offices, including the former Apostolic Chancery (abolished in 1973) and Apostolic Chamber, and the newly constituted Prefecture of Economic Affairs, Prefecture of the Pontifical Household, Administration of the Patrimony of the Apostolic See, and Central Statistics Office. Functions of the former Apostolic Datary and the Secretariats of State, of Briefs to Princes, and of Latin Letters were transferred to the Secretariat of State.

Operational Procedures

• The papal secretary or secretary of state has authority to take initiative in coordinating and expediting business through meetings and other cooperative procedures.

• Officials of departments have five-year terms of office, which may be renewed. Resignation is automatic on the death of a pope. The five-year terms of consultors are renewable.

• Diocesan bishops as well as full-time curial personnel have membership in curial departments, in accordance with provisions of the decree *Pro Comperto Sane* of Aug. 6, 1967. Seven diocesan bishops hold five-year membership in each congregation, with full rights to participation in the more important plenary assemblies scheduled once a year. They are also entitled to take part in routine meetings whenever they are in Rome. Three general superiors of male religious institutes hold similar membership in the Sacred Congregation for Religious and Secular Institutes.

• Lay persons are eligible to serve as consultors to curial departments.

• Close liaison with episcopal conferences is required. They should be given prior notice of forthcoming curial decrees affecting them in any special way.

• In line with customary procedure, matters in which the competence of two or more departments is involved are handled on a cooperative basis, with mutual consultation and decision.

• Although Latin remains the official language of the Curia, communication in any of the widely known modern languages is acceptable.

• Informational and financial services are centralized in the Central Statistics Office and the Prefecture of Economic Affairs, respectively.

• Heads of curial departments are required to notify the pope before conducting any serious or extraordinary business.

• Authority to act and decide on many matters belongs to departmental officials in virtue of delegation from the pope. Some matters, however, have to be referred to the pope for final decision.

Internationalization

The international complexion of personnel in the Roman Curia changed considerably during the decade from 1961 to 1970. The number of non-Italians increased from 570 to more than 1,400, a rise of 145 per cent, while the number of Italians increased from 750 to 850, a rise of only 14 per cent.

In 1974, heads of the 22 departments of the Roman Curia (all cardinals except one) were from the following countries: Italy, 6 (Baggio, Raimondi, Paupini, Staffa, Pignedoli, Vagnozzi); France, 4 (Villot, head of four departments, Philippe, Garrone, Martin); one each from Australia (Knox, head of two congregations), Austria (Koenig), Brazil (Rossi), Netherlands (Willebrands), Poland (Most Rev. Msgr. Boleslaus Filipiak), Spain, United States, Yugoslavia.

DEPARTMENTS OF THE CURIA

Secretariat of State

The Secretariat of State provides the pope with the closest possible assistance in the care of the Universal Church and in dealings with all departments of the Curia.

The cardinal secretary is the key coordinator of curial operations. He has authority to call meetings of the prefects of all departments for expediting the conduct of business, for consultation and intercommunication. He handles: any and all matters entrusted to him by the pope, and ordinary matters which are not within the competence of other departments; some relations with bishops; relations with representatives of the Holy See, civil governments and their representatives, without prejudice to the competence of the Council for the Public Affairs of the Church.

The cardinal secretary has been likened to a prime minister or head of government because of the significant role he plays in coordinating curial operations at the highest level.

The secretariat has two offices for preparing and writing letters for the pope (functions formerly performed by the Secretariat of Briefs to Princes and the Secretariat of Latin Letters), and a Central Statistics Office.

It also handles work formerly done by the Apostolic Datary (the dating and countersigning of papal documents, and the management of church benefices), and the Apostolic Chancery, abolished in 1973 (care of the pope's leaden seal and the Fisherman's Ring).

It has supervisory duties over the Commission for the Instruments of Social Communication, two Vatican publications, *Acta Apostolicae Sedis* and *Annuario Pontificio*, and the Vatican Personnel Office.

The Prefecture of Vatican City is answerable to the secretary of state.

OFFICIALS: Cardinal Jean Villot, secretary of state, Most Rev. Giovanni Benelli, substitute secretary and secretary of the Cifra.

Council for Public Affairs

The Council for the Public Affairs of the Church handles diplomatic and other relations with civil governments. With the Secretariat of State, it supervises matters concerning nunciatures and apostolic delegations. It also has supervision of the Pontifical Commission for Russia.

OFFICIALS: Cardinal Jean Villot, prefect, secretary of state; Most Rev. Agostino Casaroli, secretary.

BACKGROUND: Originated by Pius VI in 1793 as the Congregation for Extraordinary Affairs from the Kingdom of the Gauls; given wider scope by Pius VII, July 19, 1814; formerly called the Sacred Congregation for Extraordinary Ecclesiastical Affairs.

CONGREGATIONS

Doctrine of the Faith

The function of the Sacred Congregation for the Doctrine of the Faith is to safeguard the doctrine of faith and morals.

Accordingly, it examines doctrinal questions; promotes studies thereon; evaluates theological opinions and, when necessary and after prior consultation with concerned bishops, reproves those regarded as opposed to principles of the faith; examines books on doctrinal matters and can reprove such works, if the contents so warrant, after giving authors the opportunity to defend themselves.

It examines matters pertaining to the Privilege of Faith (Petrine Privilege) in marriage cases, and safeguards the dignity of the sacrament of penance.

It has working relations with the Pontifical Biblical Commission.

In 1969, Pope Paul set up a Theological Commission (see separate entry) as an adjunct to the congregation, to provide it with the advisory services of additional experts in theology and allied disciplines.

OFFICIALS: Cardinal Franjo Seper, prefect; Most Rev. Jerome Hamer, O.P., secretary.

BACKGROUND: At the beginning of the 13th century, legates of Innocent III were commissioned as the Holy Office of the Inquisition to combat heresy; the same task was entrusted to the Dominican Order by Gregory IX in 1231 and to the Friars Minor by Innocent IV from 1243 to 1254. On July 21, 1542 (apostolic constitution *Licet),* Paul III instituted a permanent congregation of cardinals with supreme and universal competence over matters concerning heretics and those suspected of heresy. Pius IV, St. Pius V and Sixtus V further defined the work of the Congregation. St. Pius X changed its name to the Congregation of the Holy Office.

Paul VI, in virtue of the motu proprio *Integrae Servandae* of Dec. 7, 1965, began reorganization of the Curia with this body, to which he gave the new title, Sacred Congregation for the Doctrine of the Faith. Its orientation is not merely negative, in the condemnation of error, but positive, in the promotion of orthodox doctrine. The right of appeal, judicial representation, and the consultation of their proper regional conference of bishops, are assured to persons accused of unorthodox doctrine. The office for the censorship of books and the Roman Index of Prohibited Books were abolished.

Oriental Churches

The Sacred Congregation for the Oriental Churches has competence in matters concerning the persons and discipline of Eastern Rite Churches. It has jurisdiction over territories in which the majority of Christians belong to Oriental Rites (i. e., Egypt, the Sinai Peninsula, Eritrea, Northern Ethiopia, Southern Albania, Bulgaria, Cyprus, Greece, Iran, Iraq, Lebanon, Palestine, Syria, Jordan, Turkey, Afghanistan, the part of Thrace subject to Turkey); also, over minority communities of Orientals no matter where they live.

To assure adequate and equal representation, it has as many offices as there are rites of Oriental Churches in communion with the Holy See.

It is under mandate to consult with the Secretariat for Promoting Christian Unity on questions concerning separated Oriental Churches, and with the Secretariat for Non-Christians, especially in relations with Moslems.

It has a special commission on the liturgy and an Oriental Church Information Service.

OFFICIALS: Cardinal Paul Philippe, O.P., prefect; Most Rev. Mario Brini, secretary.

Members include all Eastern Rite patriarchs and the president of the Secretariat for Promoting Christian Unity. Consultors include the secretary of the same secretariat.

BACKGROUND: Special congregations for the affairs of the Greek and other Oriental Churches were founded long before this body was created by Pius IX Jan. 6, 1862 (apostolic constitution *Romani Pontifices),* and united with the Sacred Congregation for the Propagation of the Faith. The congregation was made autonomous by Benedict XV May 1, 1917 (motu proprio *Dei Providentis),* and given wider authority by Pius XI Mar. 25, 1938 (motu proprio *Sancta Dei Ecclesia).* John XXIII appointed six patriarchs, five of Eastern Rites and one of the Roman Rite, to the congregation and gave them the same rights as cardinals belonging to the body, in March, 1963. Paul VI named representatives of all Eastern-Rite bodies to serve as consultors of the rongregation, in November, 1963.

Bishops

The Sacred Congregation for Bishops, formerly called the Sacred Consistorial Congregation, has functions related in one way or another to bishops and the jurisdictions in which they serve.

Its concerns are: the establishment and changing of dioceses, provinces, military vicariates and other jurisdictions; providing for the naming of bishops and other prelates; studying things concerning the persons, work and pastoral activity of bishops; providing for the care of bishops when they leave office; receiving and studying reports on the conditions of dioceses; general supervision of the holding and recognition of particular councils and conferences of bishops; publishing and circulating pastoral norms and guidelines through conferences of bishops.

It supervises the Pontifical Commission for

Latin America and the Pontifical Commission for Migration and Tourism.

OFFICIALS: Cardinal Sebastiano Baggio, prefect; Most Rev. Ernesto Civardi, secretary.

Ex officio members are the prefects of the Council for the Public Affairs of the Church, and of the Congregations for the Doctrine of the Faith, for the Clergy, and for Catholic Education. The substitute secretaries and undersecretaries of these curial departments are ex officio consultors.

BACKGROUND: Established by Sixtus V Jan. 22, 1588 (apostolic constitution *Immensa*); given an extension of powers by St. Pius X June 20, 1908, and Pius XII Aug. 1, 1952 (apostolic constitution *Exsul Familia*).

Discipline of the Sacraments

The Sacred Congregation for the Discipline of the Sacraments supervises the discipline of the seven sacraments, without prejudice to the competencies of the Sacred Congregation for the Doctrine of the Faith and other curial departments.

It issues decrees regarding the discipline of the sacraments and the celebration of Mass, and has the power of decision regarding the fact of non-consummation in marriage and concerning questions about the obligations and validity of holy orders.

OFFICIALS: Cardinal James R. Knox, prefect; Most Rev. Antonio Innocenti, secretary.

BACKGROUND: The congregation was instituted by St. Pius X June 29, 1908 (apostolic constitution *Sapienti Consilio*).

Divine Worship

The Sacred Congregation for Divine Worship has general competence over the ritual and pastoral aspects of divine worship in the Roman and other Latin Rites. These matters were formerly handled by the Congregation of Rites.

The congregation has three offices.

One office deals with divine worship from the ritual or pastoral point of view and supervises the updating and publication of liturgical books. A second office handles relations with regional episcopal conferences and is responsible for decisions on liturgical adaptations proposed by such conferences. The third office has liaison duties with national liturgical commissions.

OFFICIALS: Cardinal James R. Knox, prefect; Most Rev. Annibale Bugnini, C.M., secretary.

BACKGROUND: The functions and title of the congregation were determined by Paul VI May 8, 1969 (apostolic constitution *Sacra Rituum Congregatio*). Formerly, its duties were performed by the Congregation of Rites, which was established by Sixtus V in 1588 and affected by legislation of Pius XI in 1930.

In 1970 the congregation took over the functions of the Consilium for Implementing the Second Vatican Council's *Constitution on the Sacred Liturgy*, an auxiliary body established in 1964.

Causes of Saints

The Sacred Congregation for the Causes of Saints handles all matters connected with beatification and canonization procedures, and the preservation of relics. These affairs were formerly under the supervision of the Congregation of Rites.

The congregation carries on its work through three sections or offices.

One section is a juridical office with supervisory responsibility over procedures and examinations conducted to determine the holiness of prospective saints. It includes a medical commission for the study of miracles attributed to the intercession of candidates for sainthood.

A second section, headed by the promoter general of the faith, who is popularly called the "Devil's Advocate," serves the purpose of establishing beyond reasonable doubt the evidence of holiness advanced in support of beatification and canonization causes.

Research and evaluation of documentary evidence figuring in canonization causes are the functions of the historic-hagiographical section.

OFFICIALS: Cardinal Luigi Raimondi, prefect; Most Rev. Giuseppe Casoria, secretary.

BACKGROUND: The functions and title of this congregation were determined by Paul VI May 8, 1969 (apostolic constitution *Sacra Rituum Congregatio*). Formerly, its duties were carried out by the Congregation of Rites, which was established by Sixtus V in 1588 and affected by legislation of Pius XI in 1930.

Clergy

The Sacred Congregation for the Clergy, formerly called the Sacred Congregation of the Council, handles matters concerning the persons, work and pastoral ministry of clerics who exercise their apostolate in a diocese. Such clerics are diocesan deacons and priests, and religious who are engaged in ordinary parochial ministry in a diocese.

It carries on its work through three offices.

One office promotes the spiritual growth and formation as well as the professional competence of priests by encouraging the establishment and operation of pastoral institutes and other study opportunities; oversees the general discipline of the clergy, the establishment and conduct of pastoral councils and senates of priests, and resolves controversies among clerics; has a mandate to draw up a set of general principles to direct a better distribution of priests for pastoral service.

A second office, in view of its primary concern for preaching of the word of God, encourages effective apostolic programs and methods, with special emphasis on catechetical and other forms of religious training and formation for the faithful.

A third office has supervisory responsibility over church property and the temporalities of priestly life; among its functions are efforts to provide for the support of the clergy through suitable salary scales, pensions, security and health insurance programs, and other measures.

OFFICIALS: Cardinal John J. Wright, prefect; Most Rev. Maximino Romero de Lema, secretary.

BACKGROUND: Established by Pius IV Aug. 2, 1564 (apostolic constitution *Alias Nos*), under the title, Sacred Congregation of the Cardinals Interpreters of the Council of Trent; affected by legislation of Gregory XIII and Sixtus V.

Religious and Secular Institutes

The extension of the title of this congregation, which was formerly known as the Sacred Congregation of Religious or for the Affairs of Religious, indicates its dual competence over institutes of religious, together with societies of the common life without vows, and secular institutes.

One section deals with the affairs of all religious institutes and societies of the common life, and their members. It has authority in matters related to the establishment, general direction and suppression of institutes; general discipline in line with their rules and constitutions; the movement toward renewal and adaptation of institutes in contemporary circumstances; the setting up and encouragement of councils and conferences of major religious superiors for intercommunication and other purposes.

A second section has the same competence over the affairs and members of secular institutes as the first has over religious.

OFFICIALS: Cardinal Arturo Tabera Araoz, prefect; Most. Rev. Augustine Mayer, O.S.B., secretary.

BACKGROUND: Founded by Sixtus V May 27, 1586, with the title, Sacred Congregation for Consultations of Regulars (apostolic constitution *Romanus Pontifex*); confirmed by the apostolic constitution *Immensa* Jan. 22, 1588; made part of the Congregation for Consultations of Bishops and other Prelates in 1601; made autonomous by St. Pius X in 1908.

Catholic Education

The Sacred Congregation for Catholic Education, formerly known as the Sacred Congregation of Seminaries and Universities, has supervisory competence over institutions and works of Catholic education.

It carries on its work through three offices. One office handles matters connected with the direction, discipline and temporal administration of seminaries, and with the education of diocesan clergy, religious and members of secular institutes.

A second office oversees Catholic universities, faculties of study and other institutions of higher learning inasmuch as they depend on the authority of the Church; encourages cooperation and mutual assistance among Catholic institutions, and the establishment of Catholic hospices and centers on campuses of non-Catholic institutions.

A third office is concerned in various ways with all Catholic schools below the college-university level, with general questions concerning education and studies, and with the cooperation of conferences of bishops and civil authorities in educational matters.

The congregation supervises Pontifical Works for Priestly Vocations.

OFFICIALS: Cardinal Gabriel Garrone, prefect; Most Rev. Joseph Schroeffer, secretary.

BACKGROUND: The title and functions of the congregation were defined by Benedict XV Nov. 4, 1915; Pius XI, in 1931 and 1932, and Pius XII, in 1941 and 1949, extended its functions. Its work had previously been carried on by two other congregations erected by Sixtus V in 1588 and Leo XII in 1824.

Evangelization of Peoples
Propagation of the Faith

This congregation, which has alternative titles, directs and coordinates missionary work throughout the world.

Accordingly, it has competence over those matters which concern all the missions established for the spread of Christ's kingdom. These include: fostering missionary vocations; providing for the training of missionaries in seminaries; assigning missionaries to fields of work; establishing ecclesiastical jurisdictions and proposing candidates to serve them as bishops and in other capacities; encouraging the recruitment and development of indigenous clergy; mobilizing spiritual and financial support for missionary activity.

In general, the varied competence of the congregation extends to most persons and affairs of the Church in areas classified as mission territories.

To promote missionary cooperation, the congregation has a Supreme Council for the Direction of Pontifical Missionary Works. Subject to this council are the general councils of the Missionary Union of the Clergy, the Society for the Propagation of the Faith, the Society of St. Peter the Apostle for Native Clergy, the Society of the Holy Childhood, and the *Fides* news agency.

OFFICIALS: Cardinal Agnelo Rossi, prefect; Most Revs. Bernardin Gantin and Duraisamy S. Lourdusamy, secretaries.

The heads of the Secretariats for Promoting Christian Unity, for Non-Christians, and for Non-Believers are ex officio members of the congregation.

BACKGROUND: Originated as a commission of cardinals by Gregory XIII and modified by Clement VIII to promote the reconciliation of separated Eastern Christians; erected as a stable congregation by Gregory XV June 22, 1622 (apostolic constitution *Inscrutabili*).

TRIBUNALS
Sacred Apostolic Penitentiary

This tribunal has jurisdiction for the internal forum only (sacramental and non-sacramental). It issues decisions on questions of conscience; grants absolutions, dispensations, commutations, sanations and condonations; has charge of non-doctrinal matters pertaining to indulgences.

OFFICIALS: Cardinal Giuseppe Paupini, major penitentiary; Msgr. Giovanni Sessolo, regent.

BACKGROUND: Origin dates back to the 12th century; affected by the legislation of many popes; radically reorganized by St. Pius V in 1569; jurisdiction limited to the internal forum by St. Pius X; Benedict XV annexed the Office of Indulgences to it Mar. 25, 1917.

Apostolic Signatura

The principal concerns of this supreme court of the Church are to resolve questions concerning juridical procedure and to supervise the observance of laws and rights at the highest level. It decides the jurisdictional competence of lower courts and has jurisdiction in cases involving personnel and decisions of the Rota. It is the supreme court of the State of Vatican City.

OFFICIALS: Cardinal Dino Staffa, prefect; Most Rev. Aurelio Sabattani, secretary.

BACKGROUND: A permanent office of the Signatura has existed since the time of Eugene IV in the 15th century; affected by the legislation of many popes; reorganized by St. Pius X in 1908 and made the supreme tribunal of the Church.

Sacred Roman Rota

The Rota is the ordinary court of appeal for cases appealed to the Holy See. It is best known for its competence and decisions in cases concerning the validity of marriage.

OFFICIAL: Most Rev. Boleslaus Filipiak, dean.

BACKGROUND: Originated in the Apostolic Chancery; affected by the legislation of many popes; reorganized by St. Pius X in 1908 and further revised by Pius XI in 1934.

SECRETARIATS
Christian Unity

Promoting unity among Christians is the function and competence of this secretariat.

Accordingly, it handles relations with members of other ecclesial communities; deals with the correct interpretation and execution of the principles of ecumenism; initiates or promotes Catholic ecumenical groups and coordinates on national and international levels the efforts of those promoting Christian unity; undertakes dialogue regarding ecumenical questions and activities with churches and ecclesial communities separated from the Apostolic See; sends Catholic observer-representatives to Christian gatherings, and invites to Catholic gatherings observers of other churches; orders into execution conciliar decrees dealing with ecumenical affairs.

It has competence in the religious aspects of matters pertaining to the Jews.

It has two offices, for the West and for the East. Each office is under the immediate direction of a delegate.

The prefects of the Congregation for the Oriental Churches and of the Congregation for the Evangelization of Peoples are ex officio members of the secretariat. Consultors include the secretaries of these two departments.

OFFICIALS: Cardinal Jan Willebrands, president; Rev. Charles Moeller, secretary.

BACKGROUND: Established by John XXIII June 5, 1960, as a preparatory secretariat of the Second Vatican Council; raised to commission status during the first session of the council in the fall of 1962; this status confirmed Jan. 3, 1966.

For Non-Christians

This secretariat is concerned with persons who are not Christians but profess some kind of religious faith. Its function is to promote studies and dialogue for the purpose of increasing mutual understanding and respect between Christians and non-Christians.

It has a special office for handling relations with Moslems.

The prefect of the Congregation for the Evangelization of Peoples is an ex officio member of the secretariat.

OFFICIALS: Cardinal Sergio Pignedoli, president; Msgr. Pietro Rossano, secretary.

BACKGROUND: Established by Paul VI May 19, 1964.

For Non-Believers

This secretariat studies the background and philosophy of atheism, and initiates and carries on dialogue with non-believers.

OFFICIALS: Cardinal Franz Koenig, president; Most Rev. Antonio Mauro, vice-president; Rev. Vincenzo Miano, S.D.B., secretary.

BACKGROUND: Established by Paul VI Apr. 9, 1965.

Representatives of the secretariat have recently been engaged in conversations with religious leaders in the East.

COUNCILS, COMMISSIONS

Council of the Laity: Instituted by Paul VI Jan. 6, 1967, to promote the development of the lay apostolate as a service agency for: coordinating apostolic works, establishing liaison between lay persons and the hierarchy, compiling doctrinal studies on the role of lay persons in pastoral activity, establishing and maintaining a documentation center; Cardinal Maurice Roy, president.

Commission on Justice and Peace: Instituted by Paul VI Jan. 6, 1967, to develop awareness among the People of God of their mission to promote the progress of poor nations, to encourage international social justice, to help underdeveloped nations work for their own improvement, to seek ways and means of establishing peace in the world; Cardinal Maurice Roy, president.

Revision of the Code of Canon Law: Instituted by John XXIII Mar. 28, 1963, to replace a former commission dating from 1917; Cardinal Pericle Felici, president.

Revision of the Code of Oriental Canon Law: Reconstituted by Paul VI in 1972 to replace a former commission dating from July 17, 1935, "to prepare . . . the reform of the Code of Oriental Canon Law, both in the sections already published by . . . four motu proprios" (1,950 canons concerning marriage; processes; religious, church property and terminology; Eastern Rites and persons), "and in the remaining sections which have been completed but not published" (the balance of a total of 2,666 canons); Cardinal Joseph Parecattil, president.

Interpretation of the Decrees of the Second Vatican Council: Cardinal Pericle Felici, president.

Social Communication: Instituted on an experimental basis by Pius XII in 1948; reorganized three times in the 1950's; made permanent commission by John XXIII Feb. 22, 1959; name changed to present title Apr. 11, 1964; authorized to implement the *Decree on the Instruments of Social Communication* promulgated by the Second Vatican Council; under supervision of the Secretariat of State and the Council for the Public Affairs of the Church; Most Rev. Andre-Marie Deskur, president; Most Rev. Martin J. O'Connor, president emeritus.

Latin America: Instituted by Pius XII Apr. 19, 1958; placed under supervision of the Congregation for Bishops July, 1969; Cardinal Sebastiano Baggio, president.

Migration and Tourism: Instituted by Paul VI Mar. 19, 1970, for pastoral assistance to migrants, nomads, tourists, sea and air travelers; placed under the general supervision and direction of the Congregation for Bishops; Cardinal Sebastiano Baggio, president.

Cor Unum: Instituted by Paul VI July 15, 1971, to provide informational and coordinating services for Catholic aid and human development organizations and projects on a worldwide scale; Cardinal Jean Villot, president.

Theological Commission: Instituted by Paul VI Apr. 11, 1969, as an advisory adjunct of no more than 30 theologians to the Congregation for the Doctrine of the Faith; Cardinal Franjo Seper, president.

Biblical Commission: Instituted by Leo XIII Oct. 30, 1902; completely restructured by Paul VI June 27, 1971; Cardinal Franjo Seper, president.

Abbey of St. Jerome for the Revision and Emendation of the Vulgate: Instituted by Pius XI June 15, 1933, to replace an earlier commission established by St. Pius X; Rev. Vincent Truijen, superior.

Revision of the New Vulgate: Instituted by Paul VI in 1965 to augment the work of the Abbey of St. Jerome; Most Rev. Edward Schick, president.

Sacred Archeology: Instituted by Pius IX Jan. 6, 1852; Most Rev. Gennaro Verolino, president.

Historical Sciences: Instituted by Pius XII Apr. 7, 1954, as a continuation of a commission dating from 1883; Msgr. Michael Maccarrone, president.

Ecclesiastical Archives of Italy: Instituted by Pius XII Apr. 5, 1955; Msgr. Martino Giusti, president.

Sacred Art in Italy: Instituted by Pius XI Sept. 1, 1924; Most Rev. Giovanni Fallani, president.

Sanctuaries of Pompei and Loreto: Originated by Leo XIII; under supervision of the Congregation for the Clergy; Cardinal Umberto Mozzoni, president.

Russia: Instituted by Pius XI Apr. 6, 1930, to handle all ecclesiastical affairs of the country; placed under supervision of the Congregation for Extraordinary Ecclesiastical Affairs (now the Council for the Public Affairs of the Church) in 1934, with jurisdiction limited to clergy and faithful of the Roman Rite; under supervision of the Council for the Public Affairs of the Church; Most Rev. Agostino Casaroli, president.

State of Vatican City: Cardinal Jean Villot, president.

Protection of the Historical and Artistic Monuments of the Holy See: Instituted by Pius XI in 1923, reorganized by Paul VI in 1963; Most Rev. Giovanni Fallani, president.

Preservation of the Faith, Erection of New Churches in Rome: Instituted by Pius XI Aug. 5, 1930, to replace a commission dating from 1902; Cardinal Ugo Poletti, president.

Works of Religion: Instituted by Pius XII June 27, 1942, to bank and administer funds for works of religion; replaced an earlier administration established by Leo XIII in 1887; Most Rev. Paul C. Marcinkus, president.

Family: Instituted by Paul VI Jan. 11, 1973, for pastoral research and supportive effort with respect to the spiritual, moral and social needs of the family. The president of the committee representative of bishops, priests and lay persons is the Most Rev. Edouard Gagnon.

Commission on Role of Women

Pope Paul carried out a recommendation of the 1971 assembly of the Synod of Bishops by establishing May 3, 1973, an ad hoc Study Commission on the Role of Women in Society and the Church. Appointed to membership were 15 women (including two nuns and American Deborah Cheloman, a 20-year-old college student), seven priests and three laymen; Titular Archbishop Enrico Bartoletti was named president.

OFFICES
Prefecture of Economic Affairs

The Prefecture of the Economic Affairs of the Holy See is a financial office which coordinates and supervises administration of the temporalities of the Holy See.

OFFICIALS: Cardinal Egidio Vagnozzi, president; Msgr. Giovanni Angelo Abbo, secretary.

BACKGROUND: Established by Paul VI Aug. 15, 1967.

Apostolic Chamber

This office administers the temporal goods and rights of the Holy See between the death of one pope and the election of another, in accordance with special laws.

OFFICIALS: Cardinal Jean Villot, chamberlain of the Holy Roman Church; Most Rev. Vittorio Bartoccetti, vice-chamberlain.

BACKGROUND: Originated in the 11th century; reorganized by Pius XI in 1934.

Administration of Patrimony

The Administration of the Patrimony of the Apostolic See handles the estate of the Apostolic See under the direction of papal delegates acting with ordinary or extraordinary authorization.

OFFICIALS: Cardinal Jean Villot, president: Most Rev. Giuseppe Caprio, secretary.

BACKGROUND: Some of its functions date back to 1878; established by Paul VI Aug. 15, 1967.

Prefecture of Pontifical Household

This office oversees the papal chapel — which is at the service of the pope in his capacity as spiritual head of the Church — and the pontifical family — which is at the service of the pope as a sovereign. It arranges papal audiences, has charge of preparing non-liturgical elements of papal ceremonies, makes all necessary arrangements for papal visits and trips outside the Vatican, and settles questions of protocol connected with papal audiences and other formalities.

OFFICIALS: Most Rev. Jacques Martin, prefect; Msgr. Dino Monduzzi, regent.

BACKGROUND: Established by Paul VI Aug. 15, 1967, under the title, Prefecture of the Apostolic Palace; it supplanted the Sacred Congregation for Ceremonies founded by Sixtus V Jan. 22, 1588. The office was updated and reorganized under the present title by Paul VI, Mar. 28, 1968.

Central Statistics Office

The functions of this service office are to compile, systematize and analyze information on the status and condition of the Church and the needs of its pastoral ministry, from the parish level on up to the top.

The office is one of the organs of the Secretariat of State.

OFFICIAL: Francesco Norese.

BACKGROUND: Established by Paul VI Aug. 15, 1967.

Eleemosynary Office

This office distributes alms and aid to the aged, sick, handicapped and other persons in need.

OFFICIAL: Most Rev. Antonio M. Travia.

BACKGROUND: The office originated as a charitable office in the time of Bl. Gregory X (1271-1276).

Vatican II Archives

The function of the office is preservation of the acts and other documents of the Second Vatican Council.

OFFICIAL: Cardinal Pericle Felici.

Personnel

This office was set up by Paul VI May 9, 1971, to handle personnel relations in the offices and other agencies of the Vatican.

OFFICIAL: Msgr. Michele Buro.

THEOLOGICAL COMMISSION

Establishment of a Theological Commission as an adjunct to the Congregation for the Doctrine of the Faith was announced by Pope Paul Apr. 28, 1969. The move had been recommended by the Second Vatican Council and was proposed by the Synod of Bishops in 1967.

The purpose of the commission is to provide the Doctrinal Congregation with the consultative and advisory services of theologians and scriptural and liturgical experts representative of various schools of thought. The international membership is restricted to 30.

Membership

The commission is headed by Cardinal Franjo Seper, prefect of the Doctrinal Congregation. Its members, all of whom were appointed by the Pope, are: Bishops Carlo Colombo, president of the Institute Giuseppe Toniolo (Italy); Tharcisse Tshibangu, auxiliary of Kinshasa (Zaire), and Ignace Abdo Khalife, auxiliary of the Patriarchate of Antioch for the Maronites (Lebanon), and Fathers:

Barnabas Ahern, C.P. (US); Juan Alfaro, S.J. (Spain); Catalino Arevelo, S.J. (Philippines); Hans Urs von Balthasar (Switzerland); Louis Bouyer, C.O. (France); Walter Burghardt, S.J. (US); Carlo Caffaro (Italy); Raniero Cantalamessa (Italy); Ives Congar, O.P. (France); Philippe Delhaye (Belgium); Wilhelm Ernst (East Germany); Olegario Gonzalez de Cardedal (Spain); Edouard Hamel, S.J. (Canada); Boguslav Inlender (Poland); Bonaventure Kloppenburg, O.F.M. (Brazil); Marie-Joseph Le Guillou, O.P. (France); Karl Lehmann (Germany); J. F. Lescrauwaet, Miss. S.C. (Holland); John Mahoney, S.J. (Great Britain); Gustave Martelet, S.J. (France);Jorge Medina (Chile); Vincent Mulago (Zaire);

Joseph Ratzinger (Germany); Georges Saber, Maronite Monk (Lebanon); Heinrich Schurmann (East Germany); Otto Semmelroth, S.J. (Germany); Anto Strle (Yugoslavia); Jean-Marie Tillard, O.P. (Canada); Cipriano Vagaggini, O.S.B. (Italy); Jan Walgrave, O.P. (Belgium).

Msgr. Philippe Delhaye of Belgium is executive secretary.

These members were appointed to a five-year term by Pope Paul VI, Aug. 1, 1974.

Meetings

The commission met for the first time Oct. 6 to 8, 1969, for organizational purposes and the assignment of subcommissions to studies on the priesthood, the theology of hope, unity of faith and pluralism in theology, the criteria of moral knowledge, and collegiality.

Twenty-six members attending the second meeting, Oct. 5 to 10, 1970, discussed reports on the priestly ministry and collegiality.

By early 1971, the commission had prepared the basis of a feasible working paper on the priesthood for the Synod of Bishops, which met for the third time in the fall. At its own meeting, held at about the same time, the commission went over some of the ground covered in synodal discussions and planned the continuation of its own work.

Pluralism in theology — concerning different ways of treating, presenting and expressing in practice the unity of faith — was the main subject under consideration at the fourth general assembly Oct. 5 to 11, 1972.

The October, 1973, meeting, attended by 21 members, completed work on a statement concerning apostolic succession and ordination to holy orders. The necessary sacramental sign of both, the statement said, is the imposition of hands by successors of the Apostles acting in accord with the intention of the Church.

COLLEGE OF CARDINALS

Cardinals are chosen by the pope to serve as his principal assistants and advisers in the central administration of church affairs. Collectively, they form the Sacred College of Cardinals.

The college evolved gradually from synods of Roman clergy with whose assistance popes directed church affairs in the first 11 centuries. The first cardinals, in about the sixth century, were priests of the leading churches of Rome who were assigned liturgical, advisory and administrative duties with the Holy See, and the regional deacons of Rome.

For all cardinals except Eastern patriarchs, membership in the college involves aggregation to the clergy of Rome. This aggregation is signified by the assignment to each cardinal, except the patriarchs, of a special or titular church in Rome.

History of the College

The Sacred College of Cardinals was not constituted in its present form and categories of membership until the 12th century, although before that time the pope had a body of advisers selected from among the bishops of dioceses neighboring Rome, priests and deacons of Rome. The college was given definite form in 1150, and in 1179 the selection of cardinals was reserved exclusively to the pope. Sixtus V fixed the number at 70, in 1586. John XXIII raised the number to 79 in 1959, to 85 in 1960 and to 87 in 1962. Paul VI increased membership to 118 in 1967, to 134 (plus two *in petto*) in 1969 and to 145 in 1973.

In 1567 the title of cardinal was reserved to members of the college; previously it had been used by priests attached to parish churches of Rome and by the leading clergy of other notable churches. The Code of Canon Law promulgated in 1918 decreed that all cardinals must be priests. Previously there had been lay cardinals (e.g., Cardinal Giacomo Antonelli, d. 1876, Secretary of State to Pius IX). John XXIII provided in the motu proprio *Cum Gravissima* Apr. 15, 1962, that all cardinals would henceforth be bishops.

Pope Paul VI placed age limits on the functions of cardinals in the apostolic letter *Ingravescentem Aetatem*, dated Nov. 21, 1970, and effective as of Jan. 1, 1971. At 80, they cease to be members of curial departments and offices, and become ineligible to take part in papal elections. They retain membership in the College of Cardinals, however, with relevant rights and privileges.

Three Categories

The three categories of members of the college are cardinal bishops, cardinal priests and cardinal deacons.

Cardinal bishops include the six titular bishops of the suburban sees of Rome and two Eastern patriarchs.

First in rank are the titular bishops of the suburban sees, neighboring Rome: Ostia, Palestrina, Porto and Santa Rufina, Albano, Velletri, Frascati, Sabina and Poggio Mirteto. The dean of the college holds the title of the See of Ostia as well as his other suburban see. These cardinal bishops are engaged in full-time service in the central administration of church affairs in departments of the Roman Curia.

Four Eastern patriarchs, two of whom have since died, were made cardinal bishops by Paul VI in virtue of the motu proprio *Ad Purpuratorum Patrum* Feb. 11, 1965. Full recognition was given to their position as the heads of ancient liturgies and of sees of apostolic origin. Because of their patriarchal dignity and titles, which antedated the dignity and titles of cardinals, they were not aggregated to the Roman clergy and were not, like other cardinals, given title to Roman churches. The patriarchs were assigned rank among the cardinals in order of seniority, following the suburban titleholders. Patriarchs, at their request, were not included among the 30 new cardinals inducted into the college in 1973.

Cardinal priests, who were formerly in charge of leading churches in Rome, are bishops whose dioceses are outside Rome.

Cardinal deacons, who were formerly chosen according to regional divisions of Rome, are titular bishops assigned to full-time service in the Roman Curia.

The officers of the college are the dean and sub-dean, a chamberlain and a secretary. The dean and sub-dean are elected by the cardinal bishops, in accordance with a decree issued by Paul VI Feb. 26, 1965.

The dean of the college is Cardinal Luigi Traglia.

Selection and Duties

Cardinals are selected by the pope and are inducted into the college in a three-step process. Their nomination is announced and approved at a meeting (secret consistory) attended only by the pope and cardinals who are already members of the college; word of their election and confirmation is then communicated to the cardinals designate by means of a document called a *biglietto*. In successive and more public ceremonies, they receive the cardinalatial red biretta and ring, and concelebrate Mass with the pope and their fellow cardinals.

Cardinals under the age of 80: elect the pope when the Holy See becomes vacant (the maximum number of cardinal electors was limited to 120 by Paul VI Mar. 5, 1973); are major administrators of church affairs, serving in one or more departments of the Roman Curia. All cardinals enjoy a number of special rights and privileges. Their title, while symbolic of high honor, does not signify any extension of the powers of holy orders. They are called princes of the Church.

A **cardinal in petto** is one whose selection has been made by the pope but whose name has not been disclosed; he has no title, rights or duties until such disclosure is made, at which time he takes precedence from the time of the secret selection.

BIOGRAPHIES OF CARDINALS

Biographies of the cardinals, as of May 20, 1974, are given below in alphabetical order. For historical notes, order of seniority and geographical distribution of cardinals, see separate entries.

Alfrink, Bernard Jan: b. July 5, 1900, Nijkerk, Netherlands; ord. priest Aug. 15, 1924; professor of Sacred Scripture at Utrecht major seminary, 1933; consultor to Pontifical Biblical Commission, Rome, 1944; professor at Catholic University of Nijmegen, 1945; ord. titular archbishop of Tiana and coadjutor archbishop of Utrecht, July 17, 1951; archbishop of Utrecht, Oct. 31, 1955; cardinal Mar. 28, 1960; titular church, St. Joachim. Archbishop of Utrecht, military vicar for Netherlands, member of:
Congregations: Catholic Education, Evangelization of Peoples;
Commission: Revision of Code of Canon Law.

Antonelli, Ferdinando Giuseppe, O.F.M.: b. July 14, 1896, Subbiano, Italy; solemnly professed in Order of Friars Minor, Apr. 7, 1914; ord. priest July 25, 1922; taught church history, 1928-32, and Christian archeology, 1932-65, at Antonianum; rector magnificus of Antonianum, 1937-43, 1953-59; definitor general of Friars Minor, 1939-45; held various offices in Roman Curia; secretary of Congregation of Rites, 1965-69, and Congregation for Causes of Saints, 1969-73; ord. titular archbishop of Idicra, Mar. 19, 1966; cardinal Mar. 5, 1973; deacon, San Sebastian (on the Palatine). Member of:
Congregation: Religious and Secular Institutes.

Antoniutti, Ildebrando: b. Aug. 3, 1898, Nimis, Italy; ord. priest Dec. 5, 1920; served in Vatican diplomatic missions in China and Portugal, 1927-36; apostolic delegate to Albania, 1936-37; ord. titular archbishop of Synnada in Phrygia, June 29, 1936; charge d'affaires in Spain, 1937-38; apostolic delegate to Canada, 1938-53; nuncio to Spain, 1953-62; cardinal Mar. 19, 1962; entered order of cardinal bishops as titular bishop of Velletri Sept. 13, 1973. Chamberlain of the College of Cardinals, member of:
Council for Public Affairs of Church;
Congregations: Oriental Churches, Bishops, Clergy, Evangelization of Peoples;
Commission: Revision of Code of Canon Law.

Aponte Martinez, Luis: b. Aug. 4, 1922, Lajas, Puerto Rico; ord. priest Apr. 10, 1950; parish priest at Ponce; ord. titular bishop of Lares and auxiliary of Ponce, Oct. 12, 1960;

bishop of Ponce, 1963-64; archbishop of San Juan, Nov. 4, 1964; cardinal Mar. 5, 1973; titular church, St. Mary Mother of Providence (in Monteverde). Archbishop of San Juan, president of Puerto Rican Episcopal Conference, member of:
Congregation: Causes of Saints.

Arns, Paulo Evaristo, O.F.M.: b. Sept. 14, 1921, Forquilhinha, Brazil; ord. priest Nov. 30, 1945; held various teaching posts; director of *Sponsa Christi,* monthly review for religious, and of the Franciscan publication center in Brazil; ord. titular bishop of Respetta and auxiliary of Sao Paulo, July 3, 1966; archbishop of Sao Paulo, Oct. 22, 1970; cardinal Mar. 5, 1973; titular church, St. Anthony of Padua (in Via Tuscolana). Archbishop of Sao Paulo, member of:
Secretariat: Non-Believers.

Baggio, Sebastiano: b. May 16, 1913, Rosa, Italy; ord. priest Dec. 21, 1935; ord. titular archbishop of Ephesus, July 26, 1953; served in Vatican diplomatic corps, 1953-69; nuncio to Chile, apostolic delegate to Canada, nuncio to Brazil; cardinal Apr. 28, 1969; titular church, St. Sebastian (delle Catacombe); Archbishop of Cagliari; 1969-73. Prefect of Sacred Congregation for Bishops, 1973, member of:
Council for Public Affairs of Church;
Congregations: Divine Worship, Doctrine of the Faith, Catholic Education, Evangelization of Peoples;
Commissions: Revision of Code of Canon Law, Latin America (President), Migration and Tourism (President), Sanctuaries of Pompei and Loreto;
Office: Patrimony of Holy See.

Barbieri, Antonio Maria, O.F.M. Cap.: b. Oct. 12, 1892, Montevideo, Uruguay; ord. priest Dec. 17, 1921; ord. titular archbishop of Macra and coadjutor archbishop of Montevideo, Nov. 8, 1936; founder of Catholic Action movement, major seminary in Uruguay; archbishop of Montevideo, Nov. 20, 1940; cardinal Dec. 15, 1958; titular church, St. Chrysogonus. Archbishop of Montevideo.

Bengsch, Alfred: b. Sept. 10, 1921, Berlin, Germany; called for military service while in seminary at Fulda, gravely wounded at Normandy and prisoner of Americans, 1944; resumed his studies after the war; ord. priest Apr. 2, 1950; member of faculty of seminaries at Erfurt and Neuzelle; ord. titular bishop of Tubia and auxiliary bishop of Berlin, June 11, 1959; bishop of Berlin, Aug. 16, 1961; received personal title of archbishop, Jan. 14, 1962; cardinal June 26, 1967; titular church, St. Philip Neri (in Eurosia). Archbishop of Berlin, member of:
Congregations: Religious and Secular Institutes, Divine Worship;
Commission: Revision of Code of Canon Law.

Bertoli, Paolo: b. Feb. 1, 1908, Poggio Garfagnana, Italy; ord. priest Aug. 15, 1930; ord. titular archbishop of Nicomedia May 11, 1952; served in Vatican diplomatic corps, 1952-69; apostolic delegate to Turkey, nuncio to Colombia, Lebanon and France; cardinal Apr. 28, 1969; titular church, St. Jerome. Prefect of Congregation for Causes of Saints, 1969-73. Member of:
Council for Public Affairs of Church;
Congregations: Bishops, Oriental Churches, Divine Worship, Evangelization of Peoples;
Tribunal: Apostolic Signatura.
Commission: Revision of Code of Canon Law.

Biayenda, Emile: b. 1927 at Mpangala, Congo; ord. priest Oct. 26, 1958; national chaplain of Legion of Mary; under house arrest for several months in 1964; studied in France for three years; ord. titular archbishop of Garba and coadjutor of Brazzaville, May 17, 1970; archbishop of Brazzaville, June 14, 1971; cardinal Mar. 5, 1973; titular church, San Mark (in "Agro Laurentino"). Archbishop of Brazzaville, president of Congo Episcopal Conference, member of:
Congregation: Clergy.

Brandao Vilela, Avelar: b. June 13, 1912, Vicosa, Brazil; ord. priest Oct. 27, 1935; professor and spiritual director at diocesan seminary at Aracaju; ord. bishop of Petrolina, Oct. 27, 1946; archbishop of Teresina, Nov. 5, 1955; established 20 social centers and a radio station; introduced agrarian reform of church properties; erected the Institute of Catechetics: Archbishop of Sao Salvador da Bahia, Mar. 25, 1971; presdent of CELAM, 1967-72; co-president of Medellin Conference, 1968; cardinal Mar. 5, 1973; titular church, Sts. Boniface and Alexius. Archbishop of Sao Salvador da Bahia, member of:
Congregations: Clergy, Causes of Saints.

Bueno y Monreal, Jose Maria: b. Sept. 11, 1904, Zaragoza, Spain; ord. priest Mar. 19, 1927; ord. bishop of Jaca, Mar. 19, 1946; bishop of Vitoria, May 13, 1950; titular archbishop of Antioch in Pisidia and coadjutor archbishop of Seville, Oct. 27, 1954; archbishop of Seville, Apr. 8, 1957; cardinal Dec. 15, 1958; titular church, Sts. Vitus, Modestus and Crescentia. Archbishop of Seville, member of:
Congregations: Religious and Secular Institutes, Causes of Saints.

Caggiano, Antonio: b. Jan. 30, 1889, Coronda, Argentina; ord. priest Mar. 23, 1912; general ecclesiastical counselor of Argentine Catholic Action, 1931; military vicar, 1933; ord. bishop of Rosario, Mar. 17, 1935; cardinal Feb. 18, 1946; titular church, St. Lawrence (in Panisperna). Archbishop of Buenos Aires, Aug. 15, 1959, ordinary for Eastern Rite Catholics in Argentina without ordinaries of their own rites, military vicar of Argentina, member of:
Congregation: Causes of Saints;

Commission: Revision of Code of Canon Law.

Carberry, John J.: b. July 31, 1904, Brooklyn, N. Y.; ord. priest July 28, 1929; ord. titular bishop of Elis and coadjutor bishop of Lafayette, Ind., July 25, 1956; bishop of Lafayette, Nov. 20, 1957; bishop of Columbus, Jan. 16, 1965; archbishop of St. Louis, Feb. 17, 1968; cardinal Apr. 28, 1969; titular church, St. John the Beptist (de Rossi). Archbishop of St. Louis, member of:

Congregations: Bishops, Evangelization of Peoples.

Carpino, Francesco: b. May 18, 1905, Palazzolo Acreide, Italy; ord. priest Aug. 14, 1927; ord. titular archbishop of Nicomedia and coadjutor archbishop of Monreale, Apr. 8, 1951; archbishop of Monreale, 1951-61; titular archbishop of Sardica, Jan. 19, 1961; assessor of Sacred Consistorial Congregation, 1961; pro-prefect of Sacred Congregation of the Council, Apr. 7, 1967; cardinal June 26, 1967; titular church, St. Mary Auxiliatrix; archbishop of Palermo, 1967-70. Former archbishop of Palermo, referendary of the Congregation of Bishops, 1970, and member of:

Congregations: Bishops, Clergy.

Casariego, Mario, C.R.S.: b. Feb. 13, 1909, Figueras de Castropol, Spain; ord. priest July 19, 1936; ord. titular bishop of Pudenziana and auxiliary bishop of Guatemala, Dec. 27, 1958; coadjutor archbishop of Guatemala, Sept. 22, 1963; archbishop of Guatemala, Dec. 12, 1964; cardinal Apr. 28, 1969; titular church, St. Mary in Aquira. Archbishop of Guatemala, member of:

Congregations: Bishops, Causes of Saints.

Cerejeira, Manuel Goncalves: b. Nov. 29, 1888, Lousado,Portugal;ord. priest Apr. 1, 1911; ord. titular archbishop of Mytilene and auxiliary archbishop of Lisbon, June 17, 1928; patriarch of Lisbon, 1929-71; cardinal Dec. 16, 1929; titular church, Sts. Marcellus and Peter. Former patriarch of Lisbon.

Cody, John P.: b. Dec. 24, 1907, St. Louis, Mo.; ord. priest Dec. 8, 1931, Rome, Italy; served in Rome, 1932-38; ord. titular bishop of Apollonia and auxiliary bishop of St. Louis, July 2, 1947; coadjutor bishop of St. Joseph, Mo., Jan. 27, 1954; apostolic administrator of St. Joseph, May 9, 1955; coadjutor bishop of Kansas City-St. Joseph, Aug. 29, 1956; bishop of Kansas City-St. Joseph, 1956-61; titular archbishop of Bostra and coadjutor archbishop of New Orleans, Aug. 10, 1961; apostolic administrator of New Orleans, June 1, 1962; archbishop of New Orleans, Nov. 8, 1964; archbishop of Chicago, June 14, 1965; cardinal June 26, 1967; titular church, St. Cecilia. Archbishop of Chicago, member of:

Congregations: Clergy, Evangelization of Peoples, Divine Worship;

Office: Prefecture of Economic Affairs.

Colombo, Giovanni: b. Dec. 6, 1902, Caronno, Italy; ord. priest May 29, 1926; rector of Milan Seminary, 1953; ord. titular bishop of Filippopoli and auxiliary bishop of Milan, Dec. 7, 1960; archbishop of Milan, Aug. 10, 1963; cardinal Feb. 22, 1965; titular church, Sts. Sylvester and Martin (in Montibus). Archbishop of Milan, member of:

Congregations: Discipline of Sacraments, Catholic Education;

Commission: Revision of Code of Canon Law.

Concha, Luis: b. Nov. 7, 1891, Bogota, Colombia; ord. priest Oct. 28, 1916; ord. bishop of Manizales, Nov. 30, 1935; first archbishop of Manizales, May 10, 1954; archbishop of Bogota, 1959-72; cardinal Jan. 16, 1961; titular church, St. Mary (Nuova). Former archbishop of Bogota, military vicar of Colombia.

Confalonieri, Carlo: b. July 25, 1893, Seveso, Italy; ord. priest Mar. 18, 1916; private secretary to Pius XI for 17 years, to Pius XII for two years; ord. archbishop of L'Aquila, May 4, 1941; transferred to titular archbishopric of Nicopoli al Nesto, Feb. 22, 1950; cardinal Dec. 15, 1958; entered order of cardinal bishops as titular bishop of Palestrina, Mar. 14, 1972); prefect of Sacred Congregation for Bishops, 1967-73. Archpriest of Patriarchal Liberian Basilica, sub-dean of College of Cardinals (1974), member of:

Commission: Institute for Works of Religion.

Conway, William: b. Jan. 22, 1913, Belfast, Ireland; ord. priest June 20, 1937; ord. titular bishop of Neve and auxiliary bishop of Armagh, July 27, 1958; archbishop of Armagh and primate of all Ireland, Sept. 9, 1963; cardinal Feb. 22, 1965; titular church, St. Patrick. Archbishop of Armagh, member of:

Congregations: Bishops, Clergy, Evangelization of Peoples, Divine Worship, Catholic Education;

Commission: Revision of Code of Canon Law.

Cooke, Terence J.: b. Mar. 1, 1921, New York, N. Y.; ord. priest Dec. 1, 1945; ord. titular bishop of Summa and auxiliary bishop of New York, Dec. 13, 1965; archbishop of New York, Mar. 2, 1968; military vicar for the US; cardinal Apr. 28, 1969; titular church, Sts. John and Paul. Archbishop of New York, member of:

Congregations: Bishops, Oriental Churches;

Commission: Migration and Tourism.

Cooray, Thomas B., O. M. I.: b. Dec. 28, 1901, Periyamulla Negombo, Ceylon; ord. priest June 23, 1929; ord. titular archbishop of Preslavo, Ma. 7, 1946; coadjutor archbishop of Colombo, Ceylon, 1946-47; succeeded as archbishop of Colombo, July 26, 1947; cardinal Feb. 22, 1965; titular church, Sts. Nereus and Achilleus. Archbishop of Colombo, Ceylon (Sri Lanka), member of:

Commission: Revision of Code of Canon Law.

Cordeiro, Joseph: b. Jan. 19, 1918, Bombay, India; ord. priest Aug. 24, 1946; served in educational and other diocesan posts at Karachi, Pakistan; ord. archbishop of Karachi, Aug. 24, 1958, the first native-born prelate in that see; cardinal Mar. 5, 1973; titular church, St. Andrew Apostle ("de Hortis"). Archbishop of Karachi, member of council of general secretariat of Synod of Bishops and member of:
  Congregation: Evangelization of Peoples.
  Da Costa Nunes, Jose: b. Mar. 15, 1880, Azores; ord. priest July 26, 1903; ord. bishop Nov. 20, 1921; bishop of Macao, 1921-40; archbishop of Goa, primate of the East and patriarch of the East Indies, 1940-53; titular archbishop of Odessus with personal title of patriarch, Dec. 16, 1953; vice-camerlengo of the Holy Roman Church, 1953-62; cardinal Mar. 19, 1962; titular church, St. Prisca.
  Darmojuwono, Justin: b. Nov. 2, 1914, Godean, Indonesia; ord. priest May 25, 1947; ord. archbishop of Semarang, Apr. 6, 1964; cardinal June 26, 1967; titular church, Most Holy Names of Jesus and Mary. Archbishop of Semarang, military vicar of Indonesia, member of:
  Secretariat: Non-Christians.
  De Araujo Sales, Eugenio: b. Nov. 8, 1920, Acari, Brazil; ord. priest Nov. 21, 1943; ord. titular bishop of Tibica and auxiliary bishop of Natal, Aug. 15, 1954; archbishop of Sao Salvador, 1968-71; cardinal Apr. 28, 1969; titular church, St. Gregory VII. Archbishop of Rio de Janeiro (1971), member of:
  Congregation: Clergy;
  Commission: Social Communications.
  Dearden, John F.: b. Oct. 15, 1907, Valley Falls, R. I.; ord, priest Dec. 8, 1932; ord. titular bishop of Sarepta and coadjutor bishop of Pittsburgh, May 18, 1948; bishop of Pittsburgh, Dec. 22, 1950; archbishop of Detroit, Dec. 18, 1958; first president of the National Conference of Catholic Bishops and the United States Catholic Conference, 1966-71; cardinal Apr. 28, 1969; titular church, St. Pius X (alla Balduina). Archbishop of Detroit, member of:
  Congregations: Discipline of the Sacraments, Divine Worship;
  Secretariat: Non-Christians.
  De Furstenberg, Maximilien: b. Oct. 23, 1904, Heerlen, Netherlands; ord. priest Aug. 9, 1931; ord. titular archbishop of Palto and apostolic delegate to Japan, Apr. 25, 1949; internuncio, 1952, when Japan established diplomatic relations with the Vatican; apostolic delegate to Australia, New Zealand and Oceania, Feb. 11, 1960; nuncio to Portugal, 1962-67; cardinal June 26, 1967; titular church, Most Sacred Heart of Jesus (a Castro Pretorio); prefect of the Congregation for the Oriental Churches, 1969-73. Grand Master of Equestrian Order of Holy Sepulchre of Jerusalem, member of:
  Council for Public Affairs of Church;

Congregations: Bishops, Religious and Secular Institutes, Evangelization of Peoples;
  Commissions: Revision of Code of Canon Law, Revision of Oriental Code of Canon Law, Interpretation of Decrees of Vatican II, State of Vatican City, Institute for Works of Religion.
  di Jorio, Alberto: b. July 18, 1884, Rome, Italy; ord. priest Apr. 18, 1908; regent of College of Cardinals, 1948; secretary of the 1958 conclave; cardinal Dec. 15, 1958; titular church, St. Pudentiana; ord. titular archbishop of Castra Nova, Apr. 19, 1962.
  Doepfner, Julius: b. Aug. 26, 1913, Hausen, Germany; ord. priest Oct. 29, 1939; ord. bishop of Wuerzburg, Oct. 14, 1948; bishop of Berlin, Jan. 15, 1957; cardinal Dec. 15, 1958; titular church, St. Mary (della Scala). Archbishop of Munich and Freising (1961), member of:
  Congregations: Oriental Churches, Clergy, Catholic Education, Evangelization of Peoples;
  Commission: Revision of Code of Canon Law.
  Duval, Leon-Etienne: b. Nov. 9, 1903, Chenex, France; ord. priest Dec. 18, 1926; ord. bishop of Constantine, Algeria, Feb. 11, 1947; archbishop of Algiers, Feb. 3, 1954; cardinal Feb. 22, 1965; titular church, St. Balbina. Archbishop of Algiers, member of:
  Congregations: Discipline of Sacraments, Evangelization of Peoples;
  Secretariat: Non-Christians;
  Commissions: Revision of Code of Canon Law, Pontifical Council *Cor Unum.*
  Enrique y Tarancon, Vicente: b. May 14, 1907, Burriana, Spain; ord. priest Nov. 1, 1929; ord. bishop of Solsona, Mar. 24, 1946; bishop of Oviedo, Apr. 12, 1964; archbishop of Toledo, 1969-71; cardinal Apr. 28, 1969; titular church, St. John Chrysostom. Archbishop of Madrid (1971), member of:
  Congregations: Bishops, Divine Worship;
  Commission: Revision of Code of Canon Law.
  Felici, Pericle: b. Aug. 1, 1911, Segni, Italy; ord. priest Oct. 28, 1933; rector of Pontifical Roman Seminary for Legal Studies, 1938-48; judge of Roman Rota, 1947; served on antepreparatory commissions of the Second Vatican Council; ord. titular archbishop of Samosata, Oct. 28, 1960; secretary-general of the Second Vatican Council; accompanied Pope Paul VI on his trip to the UN, Oct. 4, 1965; cardinal June 26, 1967; deacon, St. Apollinare. Member of:
  Council for Public Affairs of Church;
  Congregations: Doctrine of Faith, Bishops, Discipline of Sacraments, Divine Worship, Causes of Saints;
  Office: Administration of Patrimony of Holy See;
  Commissions: Revision of Code of Canon Law (President), Revision of Oriental Code

of Canon Law, Interpretation of Decrees of Vatican II (President).

Feltin, Maurice: b. May 15, 1883, Delle, France; ord. priest July 3, 1909; ord. bishop of Troyes, Mar. 11, 1928; archbishop of Sens, Aug. 16, 1932; archbishop of Bordeaux, Dec. 16, 1935; archbishop of Paris, 1949-66; cardinal Jan. 12, 1953; titular church, St. Mary (della Pace). Former archbishop of Paris.

Flahiff, George B., C.S.B.: b. Oct. 26, 1905, Paris, Ont., Canada; ord. priest Aug. 17, 1930; professor of medieval history at the University of Toronto and Pontifical Institute of Medieval Studies in Toronto, 1934-54; superior general of Basilian Fathers, 1954; ord. archbishop of Winnipeg, May 31, 1961; president of Canadian Conference of Bishops, 1963-65; cardinal Apr. 28, 1969; titular church, St. Mary della Salute (Primavalle). Archbishop of Winnipeg, member of:
Congregations: Religious and Secular Institutes, Catholic Education.

Florit, Ermenegildo: b. July 5, 1901, Fagagna, Italy; ord. priest Apr. 11, 1925; taught Sacred Scripture at Lateran University from 1929; pro-rector of Lateran University and Institute of Civil and Canon Law, 1951-54; ord. titular archbishop of Hieropolis and coadjutor archbishop of Florence, Sept. 12, 1954; archbishop of Florence, Mar. 19, 1962; cardinal Feb. 22, 1965; titular church, Queen of the Apostles. Archbishop of Florence, member of:
Congregation: Causes of Saints;
Commission: Revision of Code of Canon Law.

Forni, Efrem: b. Jan. 10, 1889, Milan, Italy; ord. priest July 6, 1913; served in Vatican diplomatic service in Portugal and France, 1921-37; ord. titular archbishop of Darnis, Feb. 20, 1938; nuncio to Ecuador, 1937-53; nuncio to Belgium, 1953-62; cardinal Mar. 19, 1962; titular church, Holy Cross in Jerusalem. Member of:
Council for Public Affairs of Church;
Congregations: Bishops, Causes of Saints.

Freeman, James D.: b. Nov. 19, 1907, Sydney, Australia; ord. priest July 13, 1940; ord. titular bishop of Ermopoli minore and auxiliary of Sydney, Jan. 27, 1957; bishop of Armidale, 1968-71; archbishop of Sydney, July 9, 1971; cardinal Mar. 5, 1973; titular church, St. Mary Queen of Peace. Archbishop of Sydney, member of:
Secretariat: Non-Christians.

Frings, Josef: b. Feb. 6, 1887, Neuss, Germany; ord. priest Aug. 10, 1910; ord. archbishop June 21, 1942; archbishop of Cologne, 1942-69; cardinal Feb. 18, 1946; titular church, St. John (a Porta Latina). Former archbishop of Cologne, member of:
Congregation: Religious and Secular Institutes.

Garrone, Gabriel: b. Oct. 12, 1901, Aix-les-Bains, France; ord. priest Apr. 11, 1925; captain during World War II, cited for brav-

ery, taken prisoner; rector of major seminary of Chambery, 1947; ord. titular archbishop of Lemno and coadjutor of Toulouse, June 24, 1947; archbishop of Toulouse, 1956-66; prefect of Congregation of Seminaries and Universities, Mar. 24, 1966; cardinal June 26, 1967; titular church, St. Sabina. Prefect of Congregation for Catholic Education, grand chancellor of the Pontifical Gregorian University, member of:
Congregations: Doctrine of Faith, Oriental Churches. Bishops, Evangelization of Peoples, Causes of Saints;
Commission: Revision of Code of Canon Law.

Gilroy, Norman Thomas: b. Jan. 22, 1896, Sydney, Australia; ord. priest Dec. 24, 1923; ord. bishop of Port Augusta, Mar. 17, 1935; titular archbishop of Cipsela and coadjutor archbishop of Sydney, July 1, 1937; archbishop of Sydney, 1940-71; cardinal Feb. 18, 1946; titular church, Four Crowned Martyrs. Former archbishop of Sydney, member of:
Commission: Revision of Code of Canon Law.

Gonzalez Martin, Marcelo: b. Jan. 16, 1918, Villanubla, Spain; ord. priest June 29, 1941; taught theology and sociology at Valladolid diocesan seminary; founded organization for construction of houses for poor; ord. bishop of Astorga, Mar. 5, 1961; titular archbishop of Case Mediane and coadjutor of Barcelona, Feb. 21, 1966; archbishop of Barcelona, 1967-71; archbishop of Toledo, Dec. 3, 1971; cardinal Mar. 5, 1973; titular church, Sant'Augustine. Archbishop of Toledo, member of:
Congregation: Evangelization of Peoples.

Gouyon, Paul: b. Oct. 24, 1910, Bordeaux, France; ord. priest Mar. 13, 1937; ord. bishop of Bayonne, Oct. 7, 1957; titular archbishop of Pessinonte and coadjutor archbishop of Rennes, Sept. 6, 1963; archbishop of Rennes, Sept. 4, 1964; cardinal Apr. 28, 1969; titular church, the Nativity (Via Gallia). Archbishop of Rennes, member of:
Secretariat: Non-Believers;
Commission: Social Communications.

Gracias, Valerian: b. Oct. 23, 1900, Karachi, Pakistan; ord. priest Oct. 3, 1926; ord. titular bishop of Thennesus and auxiliary bishop of Bombay, June 29, 1946; archbishop of Bombay, Dec. 1, 1950; cardinal Jan. 12, 1953; titular church, St. Mary (in Via Lata). Archbishop of Bombay, member of:
Congregations: Discipline of Sacraments, Divine Worship;
Secretariat: Non-Christians;
Commission: Revision of Code of Canon Law.

Grano, Carlo: b. Oct. 14, 1887, Rome, Italy; ord. priest July 14, 1912; master of pontifical ceremonies for 26 years; ord. titular archbishop of Thessalonica, Dec. 27, 1958, by Pope John XXIII; nuncio to Italy, 1958-67;

cardinal June 26, 1967; titular church, St. Marcellus. Member of:
Council for Public Affairs of Church;
Congregation: Causes of Saints.

Gray, Gordon J.: b. Aug. 10, 1910, Edinburgh, Scotland; ord. priest June 15, 1935; ord. archbishop of Saint Andrews and Edinburgh, Sept. 21, 1951; chairman of International Committee for English in the Liturgy; cardinal Apr. 28, 1969; titular church, St. Clare. Archbishop of Saint Andrews and Edinburgh, member of:
Congregations: Evangelization of Peoples, Divine Worship;
Commission: Social Communications.

Guerri, Sergio: b. Dec. 25, 1905, Tarquinia, Italy; ord. priest Mar. 30, 1929; ord. titular archbishop of Trevi, Apr. 27, 1969; cardinal Apr. 28, 1969; deacon, Holy Name of Mary. Pro-president of Pontifical Commission for State of Vatican City, member of:
Congregations: Oriental Churches, Evangelization of Peoples;
Commission: Social Communications.

Guyot, Louis J.: b. July 7, 1905, Bordeaux, France; ord. priest June 29, 1932; held various offices in Bordeaux diocese; ord. titular bishop of Helenopolis and coadjutor of Constance, May 4, 1949; bishop of Constance, 1950-66; archbishop of Toulouse, Apr. 28, 1966; invested with Legion of Honor by French government; cardinal Mar. 5, 1973; titular church, Saint Agnes Outside the Walls. Archbishop of Toulouse, member of:
Congregation: Clergy.

Heenan, John: b. Jan. 26, 1905, Ilford, England; ord. priest July 6, 1930; ord. bishop of Leeds, Mar. 12, 1951; archbishop of Liverpool, May 2, 1957; archbishop of Westminster, Sept. 2, 1963; cardinal Feb. 22, 1965; titular church, St. Sylvester (in Capite). Archbishop of Westminster, member of:
Congregation: Bishops;
Commission: Revision of Canon Law.

Hoeffner, Joseph: b. Dec. 24, 1906, Horhausen, Germany; ord. priest Oct. 30, 1932; ord. bishop of Munster, Sept. 14, 1962; titular archbishop of Aquileia and coadjutor archbishop of Cologne, Jan. 6, 1969; archbishop of Cologne, Feb. 24, 1969; cardinal Apr. 28, 1969; titular church, St. Andrew of the Valley. Archbishop of Cologne, member of:
Congregations: Religious and Secular Institutes, Catholic Education;
Secretariat: Non-Believers;
Office: Prefecture of Economic Affairs.

Jaeger, Lorenz: b. Sept. 23, 1892, Halle an der Saale, Germany; ord. priest Apr. 1, 1922; chaplain German army, 1939-41; active in ecumenical movement (Una Sancta): ord. archbishop of Paderborn, Oct. 19, 1941 (resigned June 30, 1973); cardinal Feb. 22, 1965; titular church, St. Leo I. Former archbishop of Paderborn.

Journet, Charles: b. Jan. 26, 1891, Geneva, Switzerland; ord. priest July 15, 1917; professor of Dogmatic Theology at diocesan seminary at Fribourg, 1924; ord. titular archbishop of Fornos Minore, Feb. 20, 1965; cardinal Feb. 22, 1965; titular church, St. Mary (in Portico).

Jubany Arnau, Narciso: b. Aug. 12, 1913, Santa Coloma de Farnes, Spain; ord. priest July 30, 1939; professor of law at Barcelona seminary; served on ecclesiastical tribunal; ord. titular bishop of Ortosia and auxiliary of Barcelona, Jan. 22, 1956; bishop of Gerona, 1964-71; archbishop of Barcelona, 1971; cardinal Mar. 5, 1973; titular church, San Lorenzo (in Damaso). Archbishop of Barcelona, member of:
Congregation: Divine Worship;
Commission: Revision of Code of Canon Law.

Kim, Stephan Sou Hwan: b. May 8, 1922, Tae Gu, Korea; ord. priest Oct. 27, 1947; ord. bishop of Masan, May 31, 1966; archbishop of Seoul, Apr. 9, 1968; cardinal Apr. 28, 1969; titular church, St. Felix of Cantalice (Centocelle). Archbishop of Seoul, member of:
Congregation: Evangelization of Peoples;
Secretariat: Non-Christians;
Commission: Interpretation of Decrees of Vatican II.

Knox, James R.: b. Mar. 2, 1914, Bayswater, Australia; ord. priest Dec. 22, 1941 at Rome; forced to remain in Rome because of World War II; chaplain and later vice rector of Pontifical Urban University; secretary of apostolic delegation in Japan; ord. titular archbishop of Melitene, Nov. 8, 1953; apostolic delegate to British Africa, 1953-57; internuncio to India and apostolic delegate to Burma and Ceylon (Sri Lanka), 1957-67; archbishop of Melbourne, Australia, 1967-74; cardinal Mar. 5, 1973; titular church, Santa Maria (in Vallicella). Prefect of Sacred Congregations for Discipline of Sacraments and Divine Worship, member of:
Congregation: Evangelization of Peoples.

Koenig, Franz: b. Aug. 3, 1905, Rabenstein, Lower Austria; ord. priest Oct. 28, 1933; ord. titular bishop of Livias and coadjutor bishop of Sankt Poelten, Aug. 31, 1952; archbishop of Vienna, May 10, 1956; cardinal Dec. 15, 1958; titular church, St. Eusebius. Archbishop of Vienna, ordinary for faithful of Byzantine Rite living in Austria, president of Secretariat for Non-Believers, member of:
Congregation: Evangelization of Peoples;
Commission: Revision of Code of Canon Law.

Krol, John J.: b. Oct. 26, 1910, Cleveland, Ohio; ord. priest Feb. 20, 1937; ord. titular bishop of Cadi and auxiliary bishop of Cleveland, Sept. 2, 1953; archbishop of Philadelphia, Feb. 11, 1961, installed Mar. 22, 1961; vice-president NCCB/USCC, 1966-72; cardinal June 26, 1967; titular church, St. Mary (della Merced) and St. Adrian Martyr. Archbishop of Philadelphia, president NCCB/USCC, 1972- , member of:

Congregations: Doctrine of the Faith, Oriental Churches;

Commissions: Revision of Code of Canon Law, Social Communications.

Landazuri Ricketts, Juan, O. F. M: b. Dec. 19, 1913, Arequipa, Peru; entered Franciscans, 1933; ord. priest Apr. 16, 1939; ord. titular archbishop of Roina and coadjutor archbishop of Lima, Aug. 24, 1952; archbishop of Lima, May 2, 1955; cardinal Mar. 19, 1962; titular church, St. Mary (in Aracoeli). Archbishop of Lima, member of:

Congregations: Discipline of Sacraments, Clergy, Causes of Saints, Religious and Secular Institutes;

Commission: Revision of Code of Canon Law.

Leger, Paul Emile, S.S.: b. Apr. 26, 1904, Valleyfield, Quebec, Canada; ord. priest May 25, 1929; rector Canadian College, Rome, 1947; ord. archbishop of Montreal, Apr. 26, 1950; cardinal Jan. 12, 1953; titular church, St. Mary (of the Angels); resigned as archbishop of Montreal in 1967 to become missionary to lepers. Member of:

Congregations: Discipline of Sacraments, Causes of Saints, Evangelization of Peoples;

Commissions: Revision of Code of Canon Law, Migration and Tourism.

Lercaro, Giacomo: b. Oct. 28, 1891, Quinto al Mare, Italy; ord. priest July 25, 1914; ord. archbishop of Ravenna, Mar. 19, 1947; archbishop of Bologna, 1952-68; cardinal Jan. 12, 1953; titular church, St. Mary (in Traspontina). Former archbishop of Bologna.

Luciani, Albino: b. Oct. 17, 1912, Forno di Canale, Italy; ord. priest July 7, 1935; taught dogmatic and moral theology at Gregorian Seminary at Belluno; ord. bishop of Vittorio Veneto, Dec. 27, 1958; patriarch of Venice, Dec. 15, 1969; cardinal Mar. 5, 1973; titular church, San Marco (at Piazza Venezia). Patriarch of Venice, member of:

Congregation: Divine Worship.

McCann, Owen: b. June 29, 1907, Woodstock, South Africa; ord. priest Dec. 21, 1935; ord. titular bishop of Stettorio and vicar apostolic of Cape Town, May 18, 1950; first archbishop of Cape Town, Jan. 11, 1951; opponent of apartheid policy; cardinal Feb. 22, 1965; titular church, St. Praxedes. Archbishop of Cape Town, member of:

Congregations: Evangelization of Peoples, Causes of Saints.

McIntyre, James Francis: b. June 25, 1886, New York, N. Y.; ord. priest May 21, 1921; ord. titular bishop of Cirene and auxiliary bishop of New York, Jan. 8, 1941; titular archbishop of Palto and coadjutor archbishop of New York, July 20, 1946; archbishop of Los Angeles, 1948-70; cardinal Jan. 12, 1953; titular church, St. Anastasia. Former archbishop of Los Angeles.

Malula, Joseph: b. Dec. 12, 1917, Kinshasa, Zaire; ord. priest June 9, 1946; ord. titular bishop of Attanaso and auxiliary bishop of Kinshasa, Sept. 20, 1959; archbishop of Kinshasa. July 7, 1964; cardinal Apr. 28, 1969; titular church, the Protomartyrs (via Aurelia Antica). Archbishop of Kinshasa, member of:

Congregations: Evangelization of Peoples, Divine Worship;

Secretariat: Non-Christians.

Manning, Timothy: b. Nov. 15, 1909, Ballingeary, Ireland; completed studies for the priesthood at St. Patrick's Seminary, Menlo Park, Calif.; ord. priest June 16, 1934; became American citizen Jan. 14, 1944; ord. titular bishop of Lesvi and auxiliary of Los Angeles, Oct. 15, 1946; first bishop of Fresno, 1967-69; titular archbishop of Capri and coadjutor of Los Angeles, May 26, 1969; archbishop of Los Angeles, Jan. 21, 1970; cardinal Mar. 5, 1973; titular church, Santa Lucia. Archbishop of Los Angeles, member of:

Congregation: Religious and Secular Institutes.

Marella, Paolo: b. Jan. 25, 1895, Rome, Italy; ord. priest Feb. 23, 1918; aide in Congregation for Propagation of the Faith; on staff of apostolic delegation, Washington, D. C., 1923-33; ord. titular archbishop of Doclea, Oct. 29, 1933; apostolic delegate to Japan, 1933-48, to Australia, New Zealand and Oceania, 1948-53; nuncio to France, 1953-59; cardinal Dec. 14, 1959; entered order of cardinal bishops as titular bishop of Porto and Santa Rufina, Mar. 14, 1972; president of Secretariat for Non-Christians, 1967-73. Archpriest of St. Peter's Basilica, member of:

Council for Public Affairs of Church;

Congregations: Bishops, Evangelization of Peoples;

Tribunal: Apostolic Signatura;

Commissions: Revision of Code of Canon Law, Sacred Art in Italy (Honorary President).

Martin, Joseph: b. Aug. 9. 1891, Orleans, France; ord. priest Dec. 18, 1920; chief military chaplain of French Army's 35th Division, 1939-40; ord. bishop of Le Puy-en-Velay, Apr. 2, 1940; archbishop of Rouen, 1948-68; cardinal Feb. 22, 1965; titular church, St. Teresa, Virgin. Former archbishop of Rouen.

Marty, Francois: b. May 18, 1904, Pachins, France; ord. priest June 28, 1930; ord. bishop of Saint-Flour, May 1, 1952; titular archbishop of Emesa and coadjutor archbishop of Rheims, Dec. 14, 1959; archbishop of Rheims, May 9, 1960; archbishop of Paris, Mar. 26, 1968; cardinal Apr. 28, 1969; titular church, St. Louis of France. Archbishop of Paris, ordinary for Eastern Rite Catholics in France without ordinaries of their own rites, member of:

Congregations: Oriental Churches, Clergy, Divine Worship;

Commission: Revision of Code of Canon Law.

Maurer, Jose Clemente, C.SS.R.: b. Mar. 13, 1900, Puttlingen, Germany; ord. priest

Sept. 19, 1925; assigned to Bolivian missions, 1926; became a Bolivian citizen; ord. titular bishop of Cea and auxiliary bishop of La Paz, Apr. 16, 1950; archbishop of Sucre, Oct. 27, 1951; cardinal June 26, 1967; titular church, Most Holy Redeemer and St. Alphonsus. Archbishop of Sucre.

Medeiros, Humberto: b. Oct. 6, 1915, Arrifes, S. Miguel, Azores; came to U.S. at age of 15; became American citizen, 1940; ord. priest June 15, 1946; ord. bishop of Brownsville, Tex., June 9, 1966; archbishop of Boston, 1970; cardinal Mar. 5, 1973; titular church, Santa Susanna. Archbishop of Boston, member of:
Congregation: Catholic Education.

Meouchi, Paul Peter: b. Apr. 1, 1894, Djezzine, Lebanon; ord. priest Dec. 7, 1917; served in US Maronite parishes, 1920-34, became naturalized American but relinquished citizenship, 1934; ord archbishop of Tyr of Maronites, Dec. 8, 1934; patriarch of Antioch of the Maronites, May 25, 1955; cardinal Feb. 22, 1965. Patriarch of Antioch for the Maronites, member of:
Congregation: Oriental Churches;
Commissions: Revision of Code of Canon Law, Revision of Oriental Canon Law.

Mindszenty, Jozsef: b. Mar. 29, 1892, Csehimindszent, Hungary; ord. priest June 12, 1915; ord. bishop of Veszprem, Mar. 25, 1944; archbishop of Esztergom and primate of Hungary, Oct. 2, 1945; cardinal Feb. 18, 1946; titular church, St. Stephen (al Monte Celio). He was sentenced to life imprisonment by Communistic Hungarian government Feb. 8, 1949; lived in refuge in US Embassy, Budapest, Nov. 1956-Oct. 1971. Archbishop of Esztergom and primate of Hungary, 1945 (impeded from 1949)-1974.

Miranda y Gomez, Miguel Dario: b. Dec. 19, 1895, Leon, Mexico; ord. priest Oct. 28, 1918; ord. bishop of Tulancingo, Dec. 8, 1937; titular archbishop of Selimbra and coadjutor archbishop of Mexico City, 1955; archbishop of Mexico City, June 28, 1956; president of the Latin American Bishops' Council (CELAM), 1960; cardinal Apr. 28, 1969; titular church, St. Mary of Guadalupe (Montemario). Archbishop of Mexico City, member of:
Congregation: Discipline of Sacraments;
Commission: Revision of Canon Law.

Motta, Carlos Carmelo de Vasconcellos: b. July 16, 1890, Bom Jesus do Amparos, Brazil; ord. priest June 29, 1918; ord. titular bishop of Algiza and auxiliary bishop of Diamantina, Oct. 30, 1932; archbishop of Sao Luis do Maranhao, Dec. 19, 1935; archbishop of Sao Paulo del Brasile, 1944-64; cardinal Feb. 18, 1946; titular church, St. Pancratius. Archbishop of Aparecida (1964).

Mozzoni, Umberto: b. June 29, 1904, Buenos Aires, Argentina; holds Italian citizenship; ord. priest Aug. 14, 1927; professor of theology and canon law at Macerata semi-nary, Italy; served on Vatican diplomatic staff at Ottawa, London and Lisbon; ord. titular archbishop of Side, Dec. 5, 1954; nuncio to Bolivia, 1954-58, Argentina, 1958-69, Brazil, 1969-73; cardinal Mar. 5, 1973; deacon, St. Eugene. Member of:
Congregations: Oriental Churches, Religious and Secular Institutes, Causes of Saints;
Tribunal: Apostolic Signatura.

Munoz Duque, Anibal: b. Oct. 3, 1908, Santa Rosa de Osos, Colombia; ord. priest Nov. 19, 1933; ord. bishop of Soccoro y San Gil, May 23, 1951; bishop of Bucaramango, 1952-59; bishop of Nueva Pamplona, 1959-68; titular archbishop of Cariana and coadjutor archbishop of Bogota, 1968; archbishop of Bogota, July 29, 1972; cardinal Mar. 5, 1973; titular church, St. Bartholomew. Archbishop of Bogota, military vicar, member of:
Congregation: Discipline of Sacraments.

Munoz Vega, Paolo, S. J.: b. May 23, 1903, Mira, Ecuador; ord. priest July 25, 1933; ord. titular bishop of Ceramo and auxiliary bishop of Quito, Mar. 19, 1964; archbishop of Quito, June 23, 1967; cardinal Apr. 28, 1969; titular church, St. Robert Bellarmine. Archbishop of Quito, member of:
Congregations: Religious and Secular Institutes, Catholic Education.

Nasalli Rocca di Corneliano, Mario: b. Aug. 12, 1903, Piacenza, Italy; ord. priest Apr. 9, 1927; ord. titular archbishop of Anzio, Apr. 20, 1969; cardinal Apr. 28, 1969; deacon, St. John the Baptist. Member of:
Congregations: Discipline of Sacraments, Causes of Saints;
Secretariat: Non-Believers.

O'Boyle, Patrick A.: b. July 18, 1896, Scranton, Pa.; ord. priest May 21, 1921; executive director of War Relief Services, NCWC, 1943; ord. archbishop of Washington, Jan. 14, 1948 (retired, 1973); cardinal June 26, 1967; titular church, St. Nicholas (in Carcere). Former archbishop of Washington.

Oddi, Silvio: b. Nov. 14, 1910, Morfasso, Italy; ord. priest May 21, 1933; ord. titular archbishop of Mesembria, Sept. 27, 1953; served in Vatican diplomatic corps, 1953-69; apostolic delegate to Jerusalem, Palestine, Jordan and Cyprus, internuncio to the United Arab Republic, and nuncio to Belgium and Luxembourg; cardinal Apr. 28, 1969; deacon, St. Agatha of the Goths, president of the Commission for Sanctuaries of Pompei and Loreto, member of:
Council for Public Affairs of Church;
Congregations: Bishops, Clergy, Oriental Churches, Causes of Saints.

Ottaviani, Alfredo: b. Oct. 29, 1890, Rome, Italy; ord. priest Mar. 18, 1916; undersecretary of Congregation for Extraordinary Ecclesiastical Affairs, 1928; substitute secretary of state, 1929; assessor of Sacred Congregation of the Holy Office, 1935-52; prefect of Congregation of Holy Office (now Doctrine of Faith), 1952-68; cardinal Jan. 12, 1953;

ord. titular archbishop of Berrea, Apr. 19, 1962; titular church, St. Mary (in Dominica). Prefect emeritus of the Congregation for the Doctrine of the Faith, member of:
Council for Public Affairs of Church;
Congregations: Doctrine of Faith, Bishops; Commission: Revision of Code of Canon Law.

Otunga, Maurice: b. January, 1923, Chebukwa, Kenya; son of pagan tribal chief; baptized 1935, at age of 12; ord. priest Oct. 3, 1950, at Rome; taught at Kisumu major seminary for three years; attaché in apostolic delegation at Mombasa, 1953-56; ord. titular bishop of Tacape and auxiliary of Kisumu, Feb. 25, 1957; bishop of Kisii, 1960-69; titular archbishop of Bomarzo and coadjutor of Nairobi, Nov. 15, 1969; archbishop of Nairobi, Oct. 24, 1971; cardinal Mar. 5, 1973; titular church, St. Gregory Barbarigo. Archbishop of Nairobi, member of:
Congregation: Discipline of Sacraments.

Palazzini, Pietro: b. May 19, 1912, Piobbico, Pesaro, Italy; ord. priest Dec. 6, 1934; assistant vice-rector of Pontifical Major Roman Seminary and vice-rector and bursar of Pontifical Roman Seminary for Juridical Studies; professor of moral theology at Lateran University; held various offices in Roman Curia; secretary of Congregation of Council (now Clergy), 1958-73; ord. titular archbishop of Caesarea in Cappadocia, Sept. 21, 1962; author of numerous works on moral theology and law; cardinal Mar. 5, 1973; deacon, St. Peter Damian. Member of:
Congregations: Discipline of Sacraments, Oriental Churches;
Tribunal: Apostolic Signatura;
Commissions: Revision of Code of Canon Law, Interpretation of Decrees of Vatican II.

Pappalardo, Salvatore: b. Sept. 23, 1918, Villafranca Sicula, Sicily; ord. priest Apr. 12, 1941; entered diplomatic service of secretariat of state, 1947; ord. titular archbishop of Miletus, Jan. 16, 1966; pro-nuncio in Indonesia, 1959-69; president of Pontifical Ecclesiastical Academy, 1969-70; archbishop of Palermo, Oct. 17, 1970; cardinal Mar. 5, 1973; titular church, St. Mary Odigitria of the Sicilians. Archbishop of Palermo, member of:
Congregation: Oriental Churches.

Parecattil, Joseph: b. Apr. 1, 1912, Kidangoor, India; ord. priest Aug. 24, 1939; ord. titular bishop of Aretusa for Syrians and auxiliary bishop of Ernakulam, Nov. 30, 1953; archbishop of Ernakulam (Chaldean-Malabar Rite), July 20, 1956; vice-president of the Indian Bishops' Conference, 1966; appointed one of seven members of Pope Paul VI's advisory council for Eastern Rite churches, 1968; cardinal Apr. 28, 1969; titular church, Our Lady Queen of Peace. Archbishop of Ernakulam of the Chaldean-Malabar Rite, member of:
Congregation: Oriental Churches;
Commissions: Revision of Code of Canon

Law, Revision of Oriental Code of Canon Law (President).

Parente, Pietro: b. Feb. 16, 1891, Casalnuovo, Italy; ord. priest Mar. 18, 1916; director of Arhiepiscopal Seminary at Naples, 1916-26; rector of Pontifical Urban College of Propagation of the Faith, 1934-38; Consultor of the Congregations of the Holy Office, Council, Propagation of the Faith, and Seminaries and Universities; ord. archbishop of Perugia, Oct. 23, 1955; titular archbishop of Tolemaide di Tebaide, Oct. 23, 1959; assessor of Congregation of Holy Office (now Doctrinal Congregation), 1959; cardinal June 26, 1967; titular church, St. Lawrence (in Lucina).

Paupini, Giuseppe: b. Feb. 25, 1907, Mondavio, Italy; ord. priest Mar. 19, 1930; ord. titular archbishop of Sebastopolis in Abasgia, Feb. 26, 1956; served in Vatican diplomatic corps, 1956-69; internuncio to Iran, 1956-57; nuncio to Guatemala and El Salvador, 1957-58, nuncio to Colombia, 1959-69; cardinal Apr. 28, 1969; deacon, All Saints Church. Major penitentiary 1973, member of:
Council for Public Affairs of Church;
Congregations: Bishops, Causes of Saints;
Commission: State of Vatican City.

Pellegrino, Michele: b. Apr. 25, 1903, Centallo, Italy; ord. priest Sept. 19, 1925; ord. archbishop of Turin, Oct. 17, 1965; cardinal June 26, 1967; titular church, Most Holy Name of Jesus. Archbishop of Turin, member of:
Congregations: Clergy, Divine Worship, Catholic Education.

Philippe, Paul, O.P.: b. Apr. 16, 1905, Paris, France; entered Dominican Order, 1926; ord. priest July 6, 1932; professor at Angelicum, Rome, from 1935; founded Institute of Spirituality for masters of novices at Angelicum, 1950, and school for mistresses of novices, 1953; apostolic visitor of various religious institutes, 1951-56; commissary of the Holy Office, 1955; consultor of various pontifical commissions and congregations from 1958; secretary of Congregation for Religious, 1959; ord. titular archbishop of Heracleopolis Magna, Sept. 21, 1962; secretary of Congregation for Doctrine of Faith, 1967-73; cardinal Mar. 5, 1973; deacon, St. Pius V. Prefect of Congregation for Oriental Churches, 1973, member of:
Congregations: Religious and Secular Institutes, Evangelization of peoples;
Secretariat: Christian Unity;
Commissions: Revision of Code of Canon Law, Revision of Oriental Code of Canon Law.

Pignedoli, Sergio: b. June 4, 1910, Felina, Italy; ord. priest Apr. 1, 1933; chaplain in Italian navy during World War II; secretary general for organization of 1950 Holy Year; ord. titular archbishop of Iconium, Feb. 11, 1951; nuncio in Bolivia, 1950-54, and Venezuela, 1954-55; auxiliary to Cardinal Montini (now Paul VI) at Milan, 1955-60; apostolic delegate to Central-West Africa, 1960-64, and Canada, 1964-67; secretary of Congregation for Evangelization of Peoples, 1967-73; sent on special mission to Vietnam, 1966; cardinal Mar. 5, 1973; deacon, San Giorgio. President of Secretariat for Non-Christians, 1973, member of:

Congregations: Catholic Education, Evangelization of Peoples, Causes of Saints; Secretariat: Christian Unity.

Poletti, Ugo: b. Apr. 19, 1914, Omegna, Italy; ord. priest June 29, 1938; served in various diocesan offices at Novara; ord. titular bishop of Medeli and auxiliary of Novaro, Sept. 14, 1958; president of Pontifical Mission Aid Society for Italy, 1964-67; archbishop of Spoleto, 1967-69; titular archbishop of Cittanova, 1969; served as second viceregent of Rome, 1969-72; pro-vicar general of Rome, 1972, following the sudden death of Cardinal Dell'Acqua; cardinal Mar. 5, 1973; titular church, Sts. Ambrose and Charles. Vicar general of Rome, 1973, archpriest of Patriarchal Lateran Basilica, 1973, member of:

Congregation: Clergy.

Poma, Antonio: b. June 12, 1910, Villanterio, Italy; ord. priest Apr. 15, 1933; ord. titular bishop of Tagaste and auxiliary bishop of Mantova, Dec. 9, 1951; bishop of Mantova, Sept. 8, 1954; titular archbishop of Gerpiniano and coadjutor archbishop of Bologna, July 16, 1967; archbishop of Bologna, Feb. 12, 1968; cardinal Apr. 28, 1969; titular church, St. Luke (al Prenestino). Archbishop of Bologna, member of:

Congregations: Clergy, Catholic Education.

Primatesta, Raul Francisco: b. Apr. 14, 1919, Capilla del Senor, Argentina; ord. priest Oct. 25, 1942, at Rome; taught at minor and major seminaries of La Plata; contributed to several theology reviews; ord. titular bishop of Tanais and auxiliary of La Plata, Aug. 15, 1957; bishop of San Rafael, 1961-65; archbishop of Cordoba, Feb. 16, 1965; cardinal Mar. 5, 1973; titular church, St. Mary Sorrowful Virgin. Archbishop of Cordoba, member of:

Congregations: Catholic Education, Religious and Secular Institutes.

Quintero, Jose Humberto: b. Sept. 22, 1902, Mucuchies, Venezuela; ord. priest Aug. 22, 1926; ord. titular archbishop of Acrida and coadjutor archbishop of Merida, Dec. 6, 1953; archbishop of Caracas Aug. 31, 1960; cardinal Jan. 16, 1961; titular church, Sts. Andrew and Gregory (al Monte Celio). Archbishop of Caracas, member of:

Congregation: Causes of Saints; Secretariat: Christian Unity.

Raimondi, Luigi: b. Oct. 25, 1912, Acqui-Lussito, Italy; ord. priest June 6, 1936; entered diplomatic service of Holy See, 1938; secretary of nunciature at Guatemala, 1938-42; auditor of apostolic delegation in U.S.,

1942-49; consultor and charge d'affaires of internunciature in India, 1949-53; ord. titular archbishop of Tarsus, Jan. 31, 1954; nuncio to Haiti, 1954-67; apostolic delegate to U.S., 1967-73; cardinal, Mar. 5, 1973; deacon, Sts. Biagio and Carlo. Prefect of the Sacred Congregation for Causes of Saints, member of:

Congregation: Evangelization of Peoples.

Rakotomalala, Jerome: b. July 15, 1914, Sainte Marie, Madagascar; ord. priest July 31, 1943; ord. archbishop of Tananarive, May 8, 1960; cardinal Apr. 28, 1969; titular church, St. Mary the Consoler (Casalbertone). Archbishop of Tananarive, member of;

Congregation: Evangelization of Peoples; Secretariat: Non-Christians.

Renard, Alelandre C.: b. June 7, 1906, Avelin, France; ord. priest July 12, 1931; ord. bishop of Versailles, October 19, 1953; archbishop of Lyons, May 28, 1967; cardinal June 26, 1967; titular church, St. Francis of Paola (ad Montes). Archbishop of Lyons, member of:

Congregations: Religious and Secular Institutes, Evangelization of Peoples.

Ribeiro, Antonio: b. May 21, 1928, Gandarela di Basta, Portugal; ord. priest July 5, 1953; professor of fundamental theology at major seminary at Braga; ord. titular bishop of Tigillava and auxiliary of Braga, Sept. 17, 1967; patriarch of Lisbon, May 10, 1971; cardinal Mar. 5, 1973; titular church, St. Anthony of Padua (in Rome). Patriarch of Lisbon, military vicar member of:

Congregation: Catholic Education; Commission: Social Communications.

Roberti, Francesco: b. July 7, 1889, Pergola, Italy; ord. priest Aug. 3, 1913; professor of Canon Law at Apollinare, 1918-38; held offices in several Roman Congregations; cardinal Dec. 15, 1958; ord. titular archbishop of Colonnata, Apr. 19, 1962; titular church, Twelve Apostles; Prefect emeritus of Apostolic Signatura.

Rosales, Julio: b. Sept. 18, 1906, Calbayog, Philippines; ord. priest June 2, 1929; ord. bishop of Tagbilaran, Sept. 21, 1946; archbishop of Cebu, Dec. 17, 1949; cardinal Apr. 28, 1969; titular church, Sacred Heart of Jesus (a Vitinia). Archbishop of Cebu, member of:

Congregations: Clergy, Catholic Education; Secretariat: Non-Christians.

Rossi, Agnelo: b. May 4, 1913, Joaquim Egidio, Brazil; ord. priest Mar. 27, 1937; ord. bishop of Barra do Pirai, Apr. 15, 1956; archbishop of Ribeirao Preto, 1962-64; archbishop of Sao Paulo del Brazil, 1964-70; cardinal Feb. 22, 1965; titular church, Mother of God. Prefect of Congregation for Evangelization of Peoples, member of:

Council for Public Affairs of Church; Congregations: Clergy, Doctrine of Faith, Bishops, Oriental Churches, Causes of Saints, Religious and Secular Institutes, Catholic Education;

Secretariats: Christian Unity, Non-Christians;

Commissions: Revision of Code of Canon Law, Revision of Oriental Code of Canon Law, Institute for Works of Religion.

Roy, Maurice: b. Jan. 25, 1905, Quebec, Canada; ord. priest June 12, 1927; chief of chaplains of Canadian Armed Forces during World War II; ord. bishop of Trois Rivieres, May 1, 1946; military vicar, June 8, 1946; archbishop of Quebec, June 2, 1947; primate of Canada, Jan. 25, 1956; cardinal Feb. 22, 1965; titular church, Our Lady of the Most Holy Sacrament and the Holy Canadian Martyrs. Archbishop of Quebec, primate of Canada, military vicar of Canada, member of:

Congregations: Clergy, Catholic Education;

Council of Laity (President), Commission on Justice and Peace (President);

Commission: Revision of Code of Canon Law.

Rugambwa, Laurean: b. July 12, 1912, Bukongo, Tanzania; ord. priest Dec. 12, 1943; ord. titular bishop of Febiano and vicar apostolic of Lower Kagera, Feb. 10, 1952; bishop of Rutabo, Mar. 25, 1953; cardinal Mar. 28, 1960; titular church, St. Francis (a Ripa); bishop of Bukoba, 1960-68. Archbishop of Dar-es-Salaam, 1968, member of:

Congregations: Divine Worship, Causes of Saints;

Commission: Revision of Code of Canon Law.

Salazar Lopez, Jose: b. Jan. 12, 1910, Ameca, Mexico; ord. priest May 26, 1934, in Rome; instrumental in building of new seminary at Guadalajara, the largest in Mexico; vice-rector and later rector of seminary; ord. titular bishop of Prusiade and coadjutor bishop of Zamora, Aug. 20, 1961; bishop of Zamora, 1967-70; archbishop of Guadalajara, Feb. 21, 1970; cardinal Mar. 5, 1973; titular church, Santa Emerentia. Archbishop of Guadalajara, member of:

Congregation: Divine Worship.

Samore, Antonio: b. Dec. 4, 1905, Bardi, Italy; ord. priest June 10, 1928; served in apostolic nunciatures at Lithuania and Switzerland; worked in Vatican Secretariat of State during World War II; assigned to apostolic delegation in Washington, D.C., 1947; nuncio to Colombia, 1950; ord. titular archbishop of Tirnovo, Apr. 16, 1950; secretary of Congregation of Extraordinary Ecclesiastical Affairs, 1953-67; cardinal June 26, 1967; titular church, St. Mary (sopra Minerva); prefect of Congregation for Discipline of Sacraments, 1968-74. Librarian and archivist of Holy Roman Church, 1974, member of:

Council for Public Affairs of Church;

Congregations: Oriental Churches, Bishops, Evangelization of Peoples, Divine Worship;

Tribunal: Apostolic Signatura;

Commissions: Revision of Code of Canon Law, Revision of Oriental Code of Canon Law.

Scherer, Alfred Vicente: b. Feb. 5, 1903, Bom Principio, Brazil; ord. priest Apr. 3, 1926; ord. archbishop of Porto Alegre, Feb. 23, 1947; cardinal Apr. 28, 1969; titular church, Our Lady of La Salette. Archbishop of Porto Alegre, Brazil, member of:

Congregations: Bishops, Evangelization of Peoples.

Seper, Franjo: b. Oct. 2, 1905, Osijek, Yugoslavia; ord. priest Oct. 26, 1930; secretary of Cardinal Stepinac, 1934-41; rector of Zagreb's major seminary, 1941-51; ord. titular archbishop of Filippopoli and coadjutor archbishop of Zagreb, Sept. 21, 1954; archbishop of Zagreb, 1960-69; cardinal Feb. 22, 1965; titular church, Sts. Peter and Paul (in Via Ostia). Prefect of Congregation for Doctrine of the Faith, member of:

Council for Public Affairs of Church;

Congregations: Bishops, Discipline of Sacraments, Clergy, Catholic Education;

Office: Administration of Patrimony of Holy See;

Commissions: Biblical (President), Theological (President), Revision of Code, Interpretation of Decrees of Vatican II.

Shehan, Lawrence J.: b. Dec. 18, 1898, Baltimore, Md.; ord. priest Dec. 23, 1922; ord. titular bishop of Lidda and auxiliary bishop of Baltimore and Washington, Dec. 12, 1945; bishop of Bridgeport, 1953-61; titular archbishop of Nicopolis ad Nestum and coadjutor archbishop of Baltimore, July 10, 1961; archbishop of Baltimore, 1961-74; cardinal Feb. 22, 1965; titular church, St. Clement. Former archbishop of Baltimore, member of:

Commission: Revision of Code of Canon Law.

Sidarouss, Stephanos I, C.M.: b. Feb. 22, 1904, Cairo, Egypt; ord. priest July 2, 1939; ord. titular bishop of Sais, Jan. 25, 1948; auxiliary to the patriarch of Alexandria for the Copts, 1948-58; patriarch of Alexandria, May 10, 1958; cardinal Feb. 22, 1965. Patriarch of Alexandria for the Copts, member of:

Congregation: Oriental Churches;

Commissions: Revision of Code of Canon Law, Revision of Code of Oriental Canon Law.

Silva Henriquez, Raul, S.D.B.: b. Sept. 27, 1907, Talca, Chile; ord. priest July 3, 1938; ord. bishop of Valparaiso, Nov. 29, 1959; archbishop of Santiago de Chile, Mar. 14, 1961; cardinal Mar. 19, 1962; titular church, St. Bernard (alle Terme). Archbishop of Santiago de Chile, member of:

Congregations: Clergy, Divine Worship, Catholic Education;

Commission: Revision of Code of Canon Law.

Siri, Giuseppe: b. May 20, 1906, Genoa, Italy; ord. priest Sept. 22, 1928; ord. titular bishop of Liviade and auxiliary bishop of

Genoa, May 7, 1944; archbishop of Genoa, May 14, 1946; cardinal Jan. 12, 1953; titular church, St. Mary (della Vittoria). Archbishop of Genoa, member of:
Congregations: Discipline of Sacraments, Clergy, Catholic Education;
Commission: Revision of Code of Canon Law.

Slipyi or Slipyj, Josyf (Kobernyckyj-Dyckowskyj): b. Feb. 17, 1892, Zazdrist in the Ukraine; ord. priest Sept. 30, 1917; ord. titular archbishop of Serre, Dec. 22, 1939; coadjutor archbishop of Lwow for the Ukrainians, 1939-44; archbishop of Lwow, Nov. 1, 1944; imprisoned 1945-63 for unspecified crimes; released by Soviets and allowed to go to Rome in February, 1963; named major archbishop by Paul VI, 1963; cardinal Feb. 22, 1965; titular church, St. Athanasius. Archbishop of Lwow (not permitted to exercise his office; he resides in Vatican City), major archbishop of the Ukraine.

Staffa, Dino: b. Aug. 14, 1906, Santa Maria in Fabriago, Italy; ord. priest May 25, 1929; judge of Roman Rota, 1944; secretary of Congregation of Seminaries and Universities, 1958-67; ord. titular archbishop of Caesarea in Palestina, Oct. 28, 1960; cardinal June 26, 1967; titular church, Sacred Heart of Christ the King;. Prefect of Apostolic Signatura, member of:
Congregations: Oriental Churches, Discipline of Sacraments;
Commission: Revision of Code of Canon Law.

Suenens, Leo Josef: b. July 16, 1904, Brussels, Belgium; ord. priest Sept. 4, 1927; ord. titular bishop of Isinda, Dec. 16, 1945; auxiliary bishop of Mechelen, 1945-61; archbishop of Mechelen-Brussels, 1961; cardinal Mar. 19, 1962; titular church, St. Peter in Chains. Archbishop of Mechelen-Brussels, military vicar for Belgium; member of:
Congregations: Evangelization of Peoples, Causes of Saints;
Commission: Revision of Canon Law.

Tabera Araoz, Arturo, C.M.F.: b. Oct. 29, 1903, Barco de Avila, Spain; ord. priest Dec. 22, 1928; ord. titular bishop of Lirbe and apostolic administrator of Barbastro, May 5, 1946; bishop of Barbastro, Feb. 2, 1950; bishop of Albacete, May 13, 1950; archbishop of Pamplona, 1968-71; cardinal Apr. 28, 1969; titular church, St. Peter (in Montorio); prefect of Sacred Congregation for Divine Worship, 1971-73. Former archbishop of Pamplona, prefect of Sacred Congregation for Religious and Secular Institutes, 1974, member of:
Congregations: Causes of Saints, Discipline of Sacraments;
Tribunal: Apostolic Signatura;
Commissions: Revision of Code of Canon Law; Interpretation of Decrees of Vatican II;
Office: Administration of Patrimony of Holy See.

Taguchi, Paul Yoshigoro: b. July 20, 1902, Shittsu, Japan; studied at Rome; ord. priest Dec. 22, 1928; returned to Japan, 1931; worked in publications; apostolic administrator of Diocese of Osaka, Nov. 30, 1940; ord. bishop of Osaka, Dec. 14, 1941; first archbishop of Osaka, July 24, 1969, when see was raised to metropolitan rank; cardinal Mar. 5, 1973; titular church, Santa Maria (in Via). Archbishop of Osaka, president of Japanese Episcopal Conference, member of:
Secretariat: Non-Christians.

Taofinu'u, Pio, S.M.: b. Dec. 9, 1923, Falealupo, W. Samoa; ord. priest Dec. 8, 1954; joined Society of Mary, 1955; ord. bishop of Apia, May 29, 1968, the first Polynesian bishop; cardinal Mar. 5, 1973; titular church, Sant' Onofrio (on the Janiculum). Bishop of Apia, member of:
Congregation: Causes of Saints.

Traglia, Luigi: b. Apr. 3, 1895, Albano Laziale, Italy; ord. priest Aug. 10, 1917; clerk of Congregation for Propagation of the Faith, 1927; judge of Roman Rota, 1936; ord. titular archbishop of Cesarea of Palestine and viceregent of Rome, Jan. 6, 1937; cardinal Mar. 28, 1960; chancellor of Holy Roman Church, 1967-73; titular bishop of suburban see of Albano, Mar. 14, 1972, when he entered order of cardinal bishops, and Ostia, 1974, when he was elected dean of the College of the Cardinals. Dean of College of Cardinals, member of:
Congregations: Oriental Churches, Bishops, Discipline of Sacraments, Evangelization of Peoples, Causes of Saints;
Tribunal: Apostolic Signatura;
Commission: State of Vatican City.

Ursi, Corrado: b. July 26, 1908, Andria, Italy; ord. priest July 25, 1931; vice-rector and later rector of the Pontifical Regional Seminary of Molfetta, 1931-51; ord. bishop of Nardo, Sept. 30, 1951; archbishop of Acerenza, Nov. 30, 1961; archbishop of Naples, May 23, 1966; cardinal June 26, 1967; titular church, St. Callistus. Archbishop of Naples, member of:
Congregation: Catholic Education.

Vagnozzi, Egidio: b. Feb. 2, 1906, Rome, Italy; ord. priest Dec. 22, 1928; served in US apostolic delegation; ord. titular archbishop of Mira, May 22, 1949; apostolic delegate to the Philippines, 1949; first nuncio to Philippines, 1951; apostolic delegate to the US, 1958-67; cardinal June 26, 1967; titular church, St. Joseph. President of Prefecture of Economic Affairs of Holy See, member of:
Council for Public Affairs of Church;
Congregations: Bishops, Oriental Churches;
Tribunal: Apostolic Signatura;
Office: Economic Affairs of the Holy See.

Villot, Jean: b. Oct. 11, 1905, Saint-Amant-Tallende, France; ord. priest Apr. 19, 1930; ord. titular bishop of Vinda and auxiliary bishop of Paris, Oct. 12, 1954; titular archbishop of Bosphorus and coadjutor archbishop of Lyons, Dec. 17, 1959; archbishop of Lyons, 1965-67; cardinal Feb. 22, 1965; titular church, Most Holy Trinity (in Monte Pincio). Secretary of State (1969), prefect of Council for Public Affairs of the Church, chamberlain of the Holy Roman Church, member of:

Congregations: Doctrine of Faith, Bishops, Evangelization of Peoples, Causes of Saints;

Office: Administration of Patrimony of Holy See (President);

Commissions: Revision of Code of Canon Law, Revision of Oriental Code of Canon Law, Pontifical Council *Cor Unum* (President), Institute for Works of Religion, State of Vatican City (President).

Violardo, Giacomo: b. May 10, 1898, Govone, Italy; ord. priest June 29, 1923; ord. titular archbishop of Satafi, Mar. 19, 1966; secretary of Congregation for Discipline of the Sacraments, 1966-69; cardinal Apr. 28, 1969; deacon, St. Eustachius. Member of:

Congregations: Discipline of Sacraments, Oriental Churches;

Tribunal: Apostolic Signatura;

Office: Prefecture of Economic Affairs of Holy See;

Commissions: Revision of Code of Canon Law, Interpretation of Decrees of Vatican II, State of Vatican City.

Volk, Hermann: b. Dec. 27, 1903, Steinheim, Germany; ord. priest Apr. 2, 1927; professor of dogmatic theology at University of Muenster; ord. bishop of Mainz, June 5, 1962; cardinal Mar. 5, 1973; titular church, Saints Fabian and Venazio (at Villa Fiorelli). Bishop of Mainz, member of:

Congregations: Doctrine of Faith, Discipline of Sacraments;

Secretariat: Christian Unity.

Willebrands, Jan: b. Sept. 4, 1909, Bovenkarspel, Netherlands; ord. priest May 26, 1934; ord. titular bishop of Mauriana, June 28, 1964; secretary of Secretariat for Christian Unity, 1960-69; cardinal Apr. 28, 1969; deacon, Sts. Cosmas and Damian. President of Secretariat for Christian Unity (1969), member of:

Congregations: Doctrine of Faith, Discipline of Sacraments, Oriental Churches, Catholic Education, Evangelization of Peoples, Divine Worship;

Commission: Revision of Code of Canon Law.

Wojtyla, Karol: b. May 18, 1920, Wadowice, Poland; ord. priest Nov. 1, 1946; served on faculties of Catholic University of Lublin and University of Cracow; ord. titular bishop of Ombi and auxiliary bishop of Cracow, Sept. 28, 1958; archbishop of Cracow, Jan. 13, 1964; cardinal June 26, 1967; titular church, St. Caesarius (in Palatio). Archbishop of Cracow, member of:

Congregations: Clergy, Divine Worship, Catholic Education.

Wright, John J.: b. July 18, 1909; Dorchester, Mass.; ord. priest Dec. 8, 1935; ord. titular bishop of Egee and auxiliary bishop of Boston, June 30, 1947; bishop of Worcester, Jan. 28, 1950; bishop of Pittsburgh, 1959-69; cardinal Apr. 28, 1969; titular church, Jesus the Divine Teacher. Prefect of Congregation for the Clergy (1969), member of:

Council for Public Affairs of Church;

Congregations: Doctrine of Faith, Bishops, Catholic Education, Evangelization of Peoples;

Commissions: Revision of Code of Canon Law, State of Vatican City, Sanctuaries of Pompei and Loreto.

Wyszynski, Stefan: b. Aug. 3, 1901, Zuzela, Poland; ord. priest Aug. 3, 1924; ord. bishop of Lublin, May 12, 1946; archbishop of Gniezno and Warsaw, Nov. 12, 1948; cardinal Jan. 12, 1953; titular church, St. Mary (in Trastavere). He was "deposed" by Polish government in fall of 1953, recognized, 1956. Archbishop of Gniezno and Warsaw, primate of Poland, member of:

Congregation: Oriental Churches;

Commission: Revision of Canon Law.

Yu Pin, Paul: b. Apr. 13, 1901, Lan-si Sien, China; ord. priest Dec. 22, 1928; professor of Chinese literature and philosophy at Rome, 1929-36; returned to China, 1936; ord. titular bishop of Sozusa di Palestina and vicar apostolic of Nanking, Sept. 20, 1936; archbishop of Nanking, Apr. 11, 1946; cardinal Apr. 28, 1969; titular church, Jesus the Divine Worker. Archbishop of Nanking (in exile; residing in Taiwan), member of:

Congregations: Evangelization of Peoples, Catholic Education;

Secretariat: Non-Christians.

Zoungrana, Paul: b. Sept. 3, 1917, Ouagadougou, Upper Volta; ord. priest May 2, 1942; ord. archbishop of Ougadougou at St. Peter's Basilica by John XXIII, May 8, 1960; cardinal Feb. 22, 1965; titular church, St. Camillus de Lellis. Archbishop of Ougadougou, member of:

Congregations: Religious and Secular Institutes, Evangelization of Peoples.

BONAVENTURE CENTENARY

Commemoration of the seventh centenary of the death of St. Bonaventure of Bagnoregio in 1974 recalled the career of a theologian and mystic, a Doctor of the Church, a bishop and cardinal, a strong defender of the Gospel life-style of St. Francis of Assisi, a religious whose stature earned him the title of second founder of the Franciscan Order.

St. Banaventure entered the Order of Friars Minor in 1243, studied and presided over the studies of his confreres at the University of Paris, served as minister general of his order from 1257 to 1273, and died a year later while participating in the Second Council of Lyons which attempted to reunite the Eastern and Western Churches.

CATEGORIES OF CARDINALS

(As of Aug. 1, 1974.)
Information below includes categories of cardinals and dates of consistories at which they were created. Seniority or precedence, except in the case of cardinal bishops, usually depends on order of elevation.

One of these cardinals was named by Pius XI (consistory of Dec. 16, 1929); 13 by Pius XII (consistories of Feb. 18, 1946, and Jan. 12, 1953); 18 by John XXIII (consistories of Dec. 15, 1958, Dec. 14, 1959, Mar. 28, 1960, Jan. 16, 1961, and Mar. 19, 1962); 98 by Paul VI (consistories of Feb. 22, 1965, June 26, 1967, Apr. 28, 1969, and Mar. 5, 1973).

Order of Bishops

Bishops of Suburban Sees: Luigi Traglia, Dean (Mar. 28, 1960); Carlo Confalonieri (Dec. 15, 1958); Paolo Marella (Dec. 14, 1959).

Eastern Rite Patriarchs: Paul Peter Meouchi, Stephanos I Sidarouss, C.M. (Feb. 22, 1965).

Order of Priests

1929 (Dec. 16): Manuel Goncalves Cerejeira.

1946 (Feb. 18): Carlos Carmelo de Vasconcellos Motta, Norman Gilroy, Joseph Frings, Jozsef Mindszenty, Antonio Caggiano.

1953 (Jan. 12): Maurice Feltin, Giuseppe Siri, James McIntyre, Giacomo Lercaro, Stefan Wyszynski, Paul Emile Leger, S.S., Valerian Gracias, Alfredo Ottaviani.

1958 (Dec. 15): Antonio Maria Barbieri, Jose M. Bueno y Monreal, Franziskus Koenig, Julius Doepfner, Alberto di Jorio, Francesco Roberti.

1960 (Mar. 28): Bernard Jan Alfrink, Laurean Rugambwa.

1961 (Jan. 16): Jose Humberto Quintero, Luis Concha.

1962 (Mar. 19): Jose da Costa Nunes, Efrem Forni, Juan Landazuri Ricketts, O.F.M., Raul Silva Henriquez, S.D.B., Leo Josef Suenens.

1965 (Feb. 22): Josyf Slipyi, Lorenz Jaeger, Thomas B. Cooray, Maurice Roy, Joseph M. Martin, Owen McCann, Leon-Etienne Duval, Ermenegildo Florit, Franjo Seper, John C. Heenan, Jean Villot, Paul Zoungrana, Lawrence J. Shehan, Agnelo Rossi, Giovanni Colombo, William Conway, Charles Journet.

1967 (June 26): Gabriel Garrone, Patrick O'Boyle, Egidio Vagnozzi, Maximilien de Furstenberg, Antonio Samore, Francesco Carpino, Jose Clemente Maurer, C.SS.R., Pietro Parente, Carlo Grano, Dino Staffa, John J. Krol, John P. Cody, Corrado Ursi, Alfred Bengsch, Justin Darmojuwono, Karol Wojtyla, Michele Pellegrino, Alexandre Renard.

1969 (Apr. 28): Paul Yu Pin, Alfredo Vicente Scherer, Julio Rosales, Gordon J. Gray, Paolo Bertoli, Sebastiano Baggio, Miguel Dario Miranda y Gomez, Joseph Parecattil, John F. Dearden, Francois Marty;

Jerome Rakotomalala, George Flahiff, Paul Gouyon, Mario Casariego, Vicente Enrique y Tarancon, Joseph Malula, Pablo Muñoz Vega, S.J., Antonio Poma;

John J. Carberry, Terence J. Cooke, Stephan Sou Hwan Kim, Arturo Tabera Araoz, C.M.F., Eugenio de Araujo Sales, Joseph Hoeffner, John J. Wright.

1973 (Mar. 5): Albino Luciani, Antonio Ribeiro, James Robert Knox, Avelar Brandao Vilela, Joseph Cordeiro, Anibal Muñoz Duque, Luis Aponte Martinez, Raul Francisco Primatesta, Salvatore Pappalardo, Marcelo Gonzalez Martin, Louis Jean Guyot, Ugo Poletti, Timothy Manning, Paul Yoshigoro Taguchi, Maurice Otunga, Jose Salazar Lopez, Emile Biayenda, Humberto S. Medeiros, Paulo Evaristo Arns, James Darcy Freeman, Narciso Jubany Arnau, Hermann Volk, Pio Taofinu'u.

Order of Deacons

1967 (June 26): Pericle Felici.

1969 (Apr. 28): Silvio Oddi, Giuseppe Paupini, Giacomo Violardo, Jan Willebrands, Mario Nasalli Rocca di Corneliano, Sergio Guerri.

1973 (Mar. 5): Sergio Pignedoli, Luigi Raimondi, Umberto Mozzoni, Paul Philippe, Pietro Palazzini, Fernando Giuseppe Antonelli.

Ineligible To Vote

As of July 20, 1974, 23 cardinals were ineligible to take part in a papal election in line with the apostolic letter *Ingravescentem Aetatem* effective Jan. 1, 1971, which limited the functions of cardinals after completion of their 80th year.

Cardinals affected were: Barbieri, Caggiano, Cerejeira, Concha, Confalonieri, Da Costa Nunes, Di Jorio, Feltin, Forni, Frings, Grano, Jaeger, Journet, Lercaro, McIntyre, Martin, Meouchi, Mindszenty, Motta, Ottaviani, Parente, Roberti, Slipyi.

DISTRIBUTION OF CARDINALS

As of Aug. 1, 1974, there were 130 cardinals from approximately 50 countries or areas. Listed below are areas, countries, number and last names.

Europe — 73

Italy (36): Antonelli, Baggio, Bertoli, Carpino, Colombo, Confalonieri, Di Jorio, Felici, Florit, Forni, Grano, Guerri, Lercaro, Luciani, Marella, Mozzoni, Nasalli Rocca di Corneliano, Oddi, Ottaviani, Palazzini, Pappalardo, Parente, Paupini, Pellegrino, Pignedoli, Poletti, Poma, Raimondi, Roberti, Samore, Siri, Staffa, Traglia, Ursi, Vagnozzi, Violardo.

France (9): Feltin, Garrone, Gouyon, Guyot, Martin, Marty, Philippe, Renard, Villot.

Germany (6): Bengsch, Doepfner, Frings, Jaeger, Hoeffner, Volk.

Spain (5): Bueno y Monreal, Enrique y Tarancon, Gonzalez Martin, Jubany Arnau, Tabera Araoz, C.M.F.

Netherlands (3): Alfrink, De Furstenberg, Willebrands.

Portugal (3); Da Costa Nunes (Azores), Goncalves Cerejeira, Ribeiro.

Poland (2): Wyszynski, Wojtyla.

One from each of the following countries: Austria, Koenig; Belgium, Suenens; England, Heenan; Hungary, Mindszenty; Ireland, Conway; Scotland, Gray; Switzerland, Journet; Ukraine (now in USSR), Slipyi; Yugoslavia, Seper.

Asia — 10

India (2): Gracias, Parecattil.

One from each of the following countries: China, Yu Pin; Indonesia, Darmojuwono; Japan, Taguchi; Korea, Kim; Lebanon, Meouchi; Pakistan, Cordeiro; Philippines, Rosales; Sri Lanka, Cooray.

Oceania — 4

Australia, (3): Gilroy, Freeman, Knox; Pacific Islands (Western Samoa), Taofinu'u.

Africa — 9

One from each of the following countries: Algeria, Duval; Congo, Biayenda; Egypt (United Arab Republic), Sidarouss; Kenya, Otunga; Malagasy Republic, Rakotomalala; South Africa, McCann; Tanzania, Rugambwa; Upper Volta, Zoungrana; Zaire, Malula.

North America — 17

United States (11): Carberry, Cody, Cooke, Dearden, Krol, McIntyre, Manning, Medeiros, O'Boyle, Shehan, Wright.

Canada (3): Flahiff, Leger, Roy.

Mexico (2): Miranda y Gomez, Salazar Lopez.

Puerto Rico (1): Aponte Martinez.

Central and South America — 17

Brazil (6): Arns, Brandao Vilela, De Araujo Sales, Motta, Rossi, Scherer.

Argentina (2): Caggiano, Primatesta.

Colombia (2): Concha, Munoz Duque.

One from each of the following countries: Bolivia, Maurer; Chile, Silva Henriquez; Ecuador, Munoz Vega, S.J.; Guatemala, Casariego (b. Spain); Peru, Landazuri Ricketts; Uruguay, Barbieri; Venezuela, Quintero.

Cardinals of U.S.

As of July 20, 1974, U.S. cardinals, years of elevation and sees:

James McIntyre, 1953, Los Angeles (retired 1970); Lawrence J. Shehan, 1965, Baltimore (retired 1974); Patrick A. O'Boyle, 1967, Washington (retired 1973); John J. Krol, 1967, Philadelphia; John P. Cody, 1967, Chicago; John F. Dearden, 1969, Detroit; John J. Carberry, 1969, St. Louis; Terence J. Cooke, 1969, New York; John J. Wright, 1969, prefect of the Congregation for the Clergy; Timothy Manning, 1973, Los Angeles; Humberto S. Medeiros, 1973, Boston.

Deceased cardinals of the United States. Data: years of elevation, sees, years of birth and death.

John McCloskey, 1875, New York, 1810-1885; James Gibbons, 1886, Baltimore, 1834-1921; John Farley, 1911, New York, 1842-1918; William O'Connell, 1911, Boston, 1859-1944; Dennis Dougherty, 1921, Philadelphia, 1865-1951; Patrick Hayes, 1924, New York, 1867-1938; George Mundelein, 1924, Chicago, 1872-1939; John Glennon, 1946, St. Louis, 1862-1946; Edward Mooney, 1946, Detroit, 1882-1958;

Francis Spellman, 1946, New York, 1889-1967; Samuel Stritch, 1946, Chicago, 1887-1958; John O'Hara, C.S.C., 1958, Philadelphia, 1888-1960; Albert Meyer, 1959, Chicago, 1903-1965; Aloysius Muench, 1959, Fargo (and papal nuncio), 1889-1962; Joseph Ritter, 1961, St. Louis, 1892-1967; Francis Brennan, 1967, official of Roman Curia, 1894-1968; Richard Cushing, 1958, Boston, 1895-1970.

REPRESENTATIVES OF THE HOLY SEE

Papal representatives and their functions were the subject of a document entitled *Sollicitudo Omnium Ecclesiarum* which Pope Paul issued on his own initiative under the date of June 24, 1969.

Delegates and Nuncios

Papal representatives "receive from the Roman Pontiff the charge of representing him in a fixed way in the various nations or regions of the world.

"When their legation is only to local churches, they are known as apostolic delegates. When to this legation, of a religious and ecclesial nature, there is added diplomatic legation to states and governments, they receive the title of nuncio, pro-nuncio, and internuncio."

[An apostolic nuncio has the diplomatic rank of ambassador extraordinary and plenipotentiary. Traditionally, because the Vatican diplomatic service has the longest uninterrupted history in the world, a nuncio has precedence among diplomats in the country to which he is accredited and serves as dean of the diplomatic corps on state occasions. Since 1965 pro-nuncios, also of ambassadorial rank, have been assigned to countries in which this prerogative is not recognized.]

(Other representatives, who are covered in the Almanac article, Vatican Representatives to International Organizations, are clerics and lay persons "who form . . . part of a pontifical mission attached to international organizations or take part in conferences and congresses." They are variously called delegates or observers.)

"The primary and specific purpose of the mission of a papal representative is to render ever closer and more operative the ties that bind the Apostolic See and the local churches.

"The ordinary function of a pontifical representative is to keep the Holy See regularly and objectively informed about the conditions of the ecclesial community to which he has been sent, and about what may affect the life of the Church and the good of souls.

"On the one hand, he makes known to the Holy See the thinking of the bishops, clergy, religious and faithful of the territory where he carries out his mandate, and forwards to Rome their proposals and their requests; on the other hand, he makes himself the interpreter, with those concerned, of the acts, documents, information and instructions emanating from the Holy See."

Service and Liaison

Representatives, while carrying out their general and special duties, are bound to respect the autonomy of local churches and bishops. Their service and liaison responsibilities include the following:

• **Nomination of Bishops:** To play a key role in compiling, with the advice of ecclesiastics and lay persons, and submitting lists of names of likely candidates to the Holy See with their own recommendations.

• **Bishops:** To aid and counsel local bishops without interfering in the affairs of their jurisdictions.

• **Episcopal Conferences:** To maintain close relations with them and to assist them in every possible way. (Papal representatives do not belong to these conferences.)

• **Religious Communities of Pontifical Rank:** To advise and assist major superiors for the purpose of promoting and consolidating conferences of men and women religious and to coordinate their apostolic activities.

• **Church-State Relations:** The thrust in this area is toward the development of sound relations with civil governments and collaboration in work for peace and the total good of the whole human family.

The mission of a papal representative begins with appointment and assignment by the pope and continues until termination of his mandate. He acts "under the guidance and according to the instructions of the cardinal secretary of state and prefect of the Council for the Public Affairs of the Church, to whom he is directly responsible for the execution of the mandate entrusted to him by the Supreme Pontiff." Normally, representatives are required to retire at the age of 75.

The Pope said clearly in the document that it was a response to demands made during the Second Vatican Council for clarification of the whole system of papal representation to local churches and governments throughout the world.

At the same time, but without any statement to that effect, the document appeared to be a response to criticism voiced in some quarters about the validity and desirability of this system. It was variously charged that the system interfered with administration in local churches; that it deprived local churches of reasonable independence; that it made the conduct of local church affairs dependent on the opinion of a foreigner in a country; that it violated the principle of subsidiarity; that it reflected an erroneous image of the pope as a would-be political sovereign. Refutation of all these charges was implicit in the broad introduction and specific articles of the document.

NUNCIOS AND DELEGATES

(Sources: *Annuario Pontificio, L'Osservatore Romano,* NC News Service.)

Data, as of July 15, 1974: country, rank of legation (corresponding to rank of legate unless otherwise noted), name of legate (archbishop unless otherwise noted) as available.

Delegate for Papal Representatives: Archbishop Domenico Enrici, former apostolic delegate to Great Britain, was appointed in July, 1973, to the newly created post of Delegate for Papal Representatives, to coordinate papal diplomatic efforts throughout the world. The office entails responsibility for "following more closely through timely visits the activities of papal representatives . . . and encouraging their rapport with the central offices" of the Secretariat of State and the Council for the Public Affairs of the Church.

Africa, North (Libya, Morocco): Algiers, Algeria, Apostolic Delegation; Sante Portalupi.

Africa, South (Botswana, Rhodesia, South Africa, Namibia, Ngwane): Pretoria, Apostolic Delegation; Alfredo Poledrino.

Algeria: Algiers, Nunciature, Sante Portalupi, Pro-Nuncio.

Argentina: Buenos Aires, Nunciature; Pio Laghi.

Australia: North Sydney, Nunciature; Gino Paro, Pro-Nuncio (also Apostolic Delegate to Papua-New Guinea).

Austria: Vienna, Nunciature; Opilio Rossi.

Bangladesh: Dacca, Nunciature; Edward Cassidy, Pro-Nuncio (also Pro-Nuncio to China-Taiwan).

Belgium: Brussels, Nunciature; Igino Cardinale.

Bolivia: La Paz, Nunciature; Giuseppe Laigueglia.

Brazil: Brasilia, Nunciature; Carmine Rocco.

Burundi: Bujumbura, Nunciature.

Cameroon: Yaounde, Nunciature; Luciano Storero, Pro-Nuncio.

Canada: Ottawa, Nunciature; Guido Del Mestri, Pro-Nuncio.

Central African Republic: Bangui, Nunciature; Mario Tagliaferri, Pro-Nuncio (also Apostolic Delegate to Chad and Congo-Brazzaville).

Chile: Santiago, Nunciature; Sotero Sanz Villalba.

China: Taipei (Taiwan), Nunciature; Edward Cassidy, Pro-Nuncio.

Colombia: Bogota, Nunciature; Angelo Palmas.

Costa Rica: San Jose, Nunciature; Angelo Pedroni.

Cuba: Havana Nunciature; Cesare Zacchi.

Cyprus: Nicosia, Nunciature; William A. Carew, Pro-Nuncio (resides in Jerusalem).

Dahomey: Cotonou, Nunciature; Bruno Wustenberg, Pro-Nuncio (resides in Abidjan, Ivory Coast).

Dominican Republic: Santo Domingo, Nunciature; Giovanni Gravelli (also Apostolic Delegate to Puerto Rico).

Ecuador: Quito, Nunciature; Luigi Accogli.

Egypt: Cairo, Nunciature; Achille Glorieux, Pro-Nuncio.

El Salvador: San Salvador, Nunciature; Emanuele Gerada.

Equatorial Guinea: Santa Isabel, Apostolic Delegation; Luciano Storero (resides in Yaounde, Cameroon).

Ethiopia: Addis Ababa, Nunciature; Raymond Etteldorf, Pro-Nuncio.

Finland: Helsinki, Nunciature; Josip Zabkar, Pro-Nuncio (resides in Copenhagen).

France: Paris, Nunciature; Egano Righi Lambertini.

Gabon Republic: Libreville, Nunciature; Luciano Storero, Pro-Nuncio (resides in Yaounde, Cameroon).

Germany: Bonn, Nunciature; Corrado Bafile.

Ghana: Accra, Apostolic Delegation; Girolamo Prigione (resides in Lagos, Nigeria).

Great Britain: London, Apostolic Delegation; Bruno Heim (also Apostolic Delegate to Gibraltar).

Guatemala: Guatemala City, Nunciature; Emanuele Gerada.

Guinea: Conakry, Apostolic Delegation; Bruno Wustenberg (resides in Abidjan, Ivory Coast).

Haiti: Port-au-Prince, Nunciature; Luigi Barbarito (Apostolic Delegate also for region in Antilles Episcopal Conference.)

Honduras: Tegucigalpa, Nunciature; Gabriel Montalvo.

India: New Delhi, Nunciature; John Gordon, Pro-Nuncio (also Apostolic Delegate to Burma).

Indonesia: Jakarta, Nunciature; Vincenzo Farano, Pro-Nuncio.

Iran: Teheran, Nunciature; Ernesto Gallina, Pro-Nuncio.

Iraq: Baghdad, Nunciature; Jean Rupp, Pro-Nuncio.

Ireland: Dublin, Nunciature; Gaetano Alibrandi.

Italy: Rome, Nunciature; Romolo Carboni.

Ivory Coast: Abidjan, Nunciature ;Bruno Wustenberg, Pro-Nuncio (He is also Pro-Nuncio to Dahomey and Apostolic Delegate to Guinea and Togo.).

Japan: Tokyo, Nunciature; Ippolito Rotoli, Pro-Nuncio.

Jerusalem, Palestine, Jordan, Israel: Jerusalem, Apostolic Delegation; William A Carew.

Kenya: Nairobi, Nunciature; Pierluigi Sartorelli, Pro-Nuncio (also Apostolic Delegate to Seychelles Is.).

Korea: Seoul, Nunciature; Luigi Dossena, Pro-Nuncio.

Kuwait: Al Kuwait, Nunciature; Alfredo Bruniera, Pro-Nuncio (resides in Beirut, Lebanon).

Laos, Malaysia and Singapore: Bangkok, Apostolic Delegation; Giovanni Moretti (resides in Bangkok).

Lebanon: Beirut, Nunciature; Alfredo Bruniera.

Lesotho: Maseru, Nunciature; Alfredo Poledrino, Pro-Nuncio (resides in Pretoria, S. Africa).

Liberia: Monrovia, Nunciature; Francis Carroll, S.M.A., Pro-Nuncio (also Apostolic Delegate for Sierra Leone and Gambia).

Luxembourg: Nunciature; Igino Cardinale (resides in Brussels, Belgium).

Malagasy Republic: Tananarive, Nunciature; Michele Cecchini, Pro-Nuncio (also Apostolic Delegate to Reunion).

Malawi: Zomba, Nunciature; Luciano Angeloni, Pro-Nuncio (resides in Zambia).

Mali: Bamako, Apostolic Delegation; Giovanni Mariani (resides in Dakar, Senegal).

Malta: La Valletta, Nunciature; Edoardo Pecoraio.

Mauritania: Nouakchott, Apostolic Delegation; Giovanni Mariani (resides in Dakar, Senegal).

Mauritius: Port Louis, Nunciature; Michele Cecchini, Pro-Nuncio (resides in Tananarive, Malagasy Republic).

Mexico: Mexico City, Apostolic Delegation; Mario Pio Gaspari.

Netherlands: The Hague, Nunciature; Angelo Felici, Pro-Nuncio.

New Zealand: Wellington, Nunciature; Angelo Acerbi, Pro-Nuncio (also Apostolic Delegate to Pacific Islands).

Nicaragua: Managua, Nunciature; Gabriel Montalvo.

Niger: Niamey, Nunciature; Giovanni Mariani, Pro-Nuncio (resides in Dakar, Senegal).

Nigeria: Lagos, Apostolic Delegation; Girolamo Prigione.

Pakistan: Islamabad, Nunciature; Joseph Uhac, Pro-Nuncio.

Panama: Panama, Nunciature; Edoardo Rovida.

Paraguay: Asuncion, Nunciature; Joseph Mees.

Peru: Lima, Nunciature; Carlo Furno.

Philippines: Manila, Nunciature; Bruno Torpigliani.

Portugal: Lisbon, Nunciature; Giuseppe Sensi.

Red Sea Region (Somalia, Afars and Issas, part of Arabian Peninsula): Apostolic Delegation; Ubaldo Calabresi (resides in Khartoum, Sudan).

Rwanda: Kigali, Nunciature.

Scandinavia (Denmark, Sweden, Norway, Iceland): Copenhagen, Denmark, Apostolic Delegation; Josip Zabkar.

Senegal: Dakar, Nunciature; Giovanni Mariani, Pro-Nuncio. (He is also Pro-Nuncio to Niger and Upper Volta and Apostolic, Delegate to Mali and Mauritania.)

Spain: Madrid, Nunciature; Luigi Dadaglio.

Sri Lanka: Colombo, Apostolic Delegation; Carlo Curis.

Sudan: Khartuom, Nunciature; Ubaldo Calabresi, Pro-Nuncio.

Switzerland: Bern, Nunciature; Ambrogio Marchioni.

Syria (Syrian Arab Republic): Damascus, Nunciature; Amelio Poggi, Pro-Nuncio.

Tanzania: Dar-es-Salaam, Nunciature; Franco Brambilla, Pro-Nuncio.

Thailand: Bangkok, Nunciature; Giovanni Moretti, Pro-Nuncio.

Togo: Lome, Apostolic Delegation, Bruno Wustenberg (resides in Abidjan, Ivory Coast).

Tunisia: Tunis, Nunciature; Sante Portalupi, Pro-Nuncio (resides in Algiers, Algeria).

Turkey: Ankara, Nunciature; Salvatore Asta, Pro-Nuncio.

Uganda: Kampala, Nunciature; Luigi Bellotti, Pro-Nuncio.

United States of America: Washington, D.C., Apostolic Delegation; Jean Jadot.

Upper Volta: Ouagadougou, Nunciature; Giovanni Mariani, Pro-Nuncio (resides in Dakar, Senegal).

Uruguay: Montevideo, Nunciature; Augustine Sepinski, O.F.M.

Venezuela: Caracas, Nunciature; Antonio del Giudice.

Vietnam and Khmer Republic: Saigon, Apostolic Delegation; Henri Lemaitre.

Yugoslavia: Belgrade, Nunciature; Mario Cagna, Pro-Nuncio.

Zaire: Kinshasa, Nunciature; Lorenzo Antonetti.

Zambia: Lusaka, Nunciature; Luciano Angeloni, Pro-Nuncio.

Unilateral severance of relations with hostile regimes is against Vatican policy.

Apostolic Delegate to U.S.

The representative of the Pope to the Catholic Church in the United States is Archbishop Jean Jadot, apostolic delegate. He was born Nov. 23, 1909, in Brussels, Belgium; was ordained to the priesthood Feb. 11, 1934; was appointed titular bishop of Zuri Feb. 23, 1968; received episcopal ordination May 1, 1968; was apostolic delegate for Laos, Malaysia and Singapore (1968-71); held the additional post of pro-nuncio in Thailand (1969-71); was pro-nuncio apostolic in Cameroon and Gabon, and apostolic delegate for Equatorial Guinea (1971-73); was named apostolic delegate to the United States in 1973; is the first non-Italian to hold the post.

The US Apostolic Delegation was established Jan. 21, 1893. It is located at 3339 Massachusetts Ave. N.W., Washington, D.C. 20008.

Archbishop Jadot's predecessors were Archbishops: Francesco Satolli (1893-1896), Sebastiano Martinelli, O.S.O. (1896-1902), Diomede Falconio, O.F.M. (1902-1911), Giovanni Bonzano (1911-1922), Pietro Fumasoni-Biondi (1922-1933), Amleto Cicognani (1933-1958), Egidio Vagnozzi (1958-1967) and Luigi Raimondi (1967-1973).

Amleto Cicognani, for 25 years apostolic delegate to the US, became a cardinal in 1958 and served as papal secretary of state from 1961 to 1969.

DIPLOMATS AT VATICAN

(Sources: *Annuario Pontificio, L'Osservatore Romano,* NC News Service. As of July 15, 1974.)

Algeria: Raouf Boudjakdji, Ambassador.

Argentina: Ambassador.

Australia: Lloyd O. Thomson, Ambassador.

Austria: Hans Reichmann, Ambassador.

Bangladesh: Ambassador.

Belgium: Werner de Merode, Ambassador.

Bolivia: Eduardo Zabalago Canelas, Ambassador.

Brazil: Antonio B. L. Castello Branco, Ambassador.

Burundi: Virgile Binagana, Ambassador.

Cameroon: Ambassador.

Canada: Paul Tremblay, Ambassador.

Central African Republic: Ambassador.

Chile: Ettore Riesle, Ambassador.

China (Taiwan): Chen Chih-Mai, Ambassador.

Colombia: Antonio Rocha, Ambassador.

Costa Rica: Julian Zamora Dobles, Ambassador.

Cuba: Luis Amado-Blanco, Ambassador.

Cyprus: Polys Modinos, Ambassador.

Dahomey: Virgile-Octave Tevoedjre, Ambassador.

Dominican Republic: Alvaro Lograno Batlle, Ambassador.

Ecuador: Ambassador.

Egypt: Salah Edine Mohamed Wasfy, Ambassador.

El Salvador: Gustavo A. Guerrero, Ambassador.

Ethiopia: Abate Agede, Ambassador.

Finland: Jussi Makinen, Ambassador.

France: Rene Brouillet, Ambassador.

Gabon: Ambassador.

Germany: Alexander Böker, Ambassador.

Great Britain: Desmond John Chetwode Crawley, Minister.

Guatemala: Luis Valladares y Aycinena, Ambassador.

Haiti: Francois Guillaume, Ambassador.

Honduras: Carlos Lopez Contreras, Ambassador.

India: Arjan Singh, Ambassador.

Indonesia: Soebagio Surjaningrat, Ambassador.

Iran: Mehdi Vakil, Ambassador.

Iraq: Hassan Mustafa Al-Nakib, Ambassador.

Ireland: Thomas V. Commins, Ambassador.

Italy: Gian Franco Pompei, Ambassador.

Ivory Coast: Joseph Amichia, Ambassador.

Japan: Toshio Yoshioka, Ambassador.

Kenya: Ambassador.

Korea: Hyun Joon Shin, Ambassador.

Kuwait: Faisal Al Saleh al Mutawa, Ambassador.

Lebanon: Nagib Dahdah, Ambassador.

Lesotho: Ambassador.

Liberia: Reide Wiles, Ambassador.

Lithuania: Stasys Lozoraitis, Jr., first secretary.

Luxembourg: Emile Colling, Ambassador.

Malagasy Republic: Ambassador.

Malawi: Ambassador.

Malta: Paolo Farrugia, Ambassador.

Mauritius: Leckraz Teelock, Ambassador.

Monaco: Cesar Charles Solamito, Minister.

Netherlands: Baron Sweder Godfried van Voorst tot Voorst, Ambassador.

New Zealand: Paul Gabites, Ambassador.

Nicaragua: Enrique Fernando Sanchez Salinas, Ambassador.

Niger: Ibra Kabo, Ambassador.

Order of Malta: Count Stanislaus Pecci, Minister.

Pakistan: Mohammad Yousuf, Ambassador.

Panama: Arturo Morgan Morales, Ambassador.

Paraguay: Miguel T. Romero, Ambassador.

Peru: Jose Luis Cossio y Ruiz De Somocurcio, Ambassador.

Philippines: Ambassador.

Portugal: Eduardo Brazao, Ambassador.

Rwanda: Ignace Karuhije, Ambassador.

San Marino: Minister.

Senegal: Henry Rene Dodds, Ambassador.

Spain: Gabriel Fernandez de Valderrame y Moreno, Ambassador.

Sudan: Salal-el-Din Osman Hashim, Ambassador.

Syria (Arab Republic): Sami al-Droubi, Ambassador.

Tanzania: Daniel Narcis Mtonga Mloka, Ambassador.

Thailand: Sangkadis Diskul, Ambassador.

Tunisia: Abdemalek Bergaoui, Ambassador.

Turkey: Taha Carim, Ambassador.

Uganda: Ambassador.

Upper Volta: Pierre Ilboudo, Ambassador.

Uruguay: Venancio Flores, Ambassador.

Venezuela: Francesco Romero Lobo, Ambassador.

Yugoslavia: Stane Kolman, Ambassador.

Zaire: Lombume Mujwan Kallymazi, Ambassador.

Zambia: Amock Israel Phiri, Ambassador.

U.S. — Vatican Relations

Official relations for trade and diplomatic purposes were maintained by the United States and the Papal States while the latter had the character of and acted like other sovereign powers in the international community.

Consular relations developed in the wake of an announcement, made by the papal nuncio in Paris to the American mission there Dec. 15, 1784, that the Papal States had agreed to open several Mediterranean ports to US shipping.

US consular representation in the Papal States began with the appointment of John B. Sartori, a native of Rome, in June, 1797. Sartori's successors as consuls were:Felix Cicognani, also a Roman, and Americans George W. Greene, Nicholas Browne, William C. Sanders, Daniel LeRoy, Horatio V. Glentworth, W.J. Stillman, Edwin C. Cushman, David M. Armstrong.

Consular officials of the Papal States who served in the US were: Count Ferdinand Lucchesi, 1826 to 1829, who resided in Washington; John B. Sartori, 1829 to 1841, who resided in Trenton, N.J.; Daniel J. Desmond, 1841 to 1850, who resided in Philadelphia; Louis B. Binsse, 1850 to 1895, who resided in New York.

US recognition of the consul of the Papal States did not cease when the states were absorbed into the Kingdom of Italy in 1871, despite pressure from Baron Blanc, the Italian minister. Binsse held the title until his death Mar. 28, 1895. No one was appointed to succeed him.

The US Senate approved a recommendation, made by President James K. Polk in December, 1847, for the establishment of a diplomatic post in the Papal States. Jacob L. Martin, the first charge d'affaires, arrived in Rome Aug. 2, 1848, and presented his credentials to Pius IX Aug. 19. Martin, who died within a month, was succeeded by Lewis Cass, Jr. Cass became minister resident in

1854 and served in that capacity until his retirement in 1858.

John P. Stockton, who later became a US Senator from New Jersey, was minister resident from 1858 to 1861. Rufus King was named to succeed him but, instead, accepted a commission as a brigadier general in the Army. Alexander W. Randall of Wisconsin took the appointment. He was succeeded in August, 1862, by Richard M. Blatchford who served until the following year. King was again nominated minister resident and served in that capacity until 1867 when the ministry was ended because of objections from some quarters in the US and failure to appropriate funds for its continuation.

Myron C. Taylor, appointed in 1939, was Pres. Franklin D. Roosevelt's personal representative to Pope Pius XII. Henry Cabot Lodge, appointed iin 1970, was Pres. Richard M. Nixon's personal representative to Pope Paul VI. Neither man had diplomatic status or rank.

VATICAN CITY

The State of Vatican City (Stato della Citta del Vaticano) is the territorial seat of the papacy. The smallest sovereign state in the world, it is situated within the city of Rome, embraces an area of 108.7 acres, and includes within its limits the Vatican Palace, museums, art galleries, gardens, libraries, radio station, post office, bank, astronomical observatory, offices, apartments, service facilities, St. Peter's Basilica, and neighboring buildings between the Basilica and Viale Vaticano.

The extraterritorial rights of Vatican City extend to more than 10 buildings in Rome, including the major basilicas and office buildings of various congregations of the Roman Curia, and to the **Villa of Castel Gandolfo** 15 miles southeast of the City of Rome. Castel Gandolfo is the summer residence of the Holy Father.

The government of Vatican City is in the hands of the reigning pope, who has full executive, legislative and judicial power. The administration of affairs, however, is handled by the Pontifical Commission for the State of Vatican City. The legal system is based on Canon Law; in cases where this code does not obtain, the laws of the City of Rome apply. The City is an absolutely neutral state and enjoys all the rights and privileges of a sovereign power. The Secretariat of State (Papal Secretariat) maintains diplomatic relations with other nations. The citizens of Vatican City, and they alone, owe allegiance to the pope as a temporal head of state.

Cardinals of the Roman Curia residing outside Vatican City enjoy the privileges of extraterritoriality.

The normal population is approximately 1,000. While the greater percentage is made up of priests and religious, there are several hundred lay persons living in Vatican City.

They are housed in their own apartments in the City and are engaged in secretarial, domestic, trade and service occupations. About 3,000 persons are employed by the Vatican.

Services of honor and order are performed by the Swiss Guards, who have been charged with responsibility for the personal safety of popes since 1506. Additional police and ceremonial functions are under the supervision of a special office. These functions were formerly handled by the Papal Gendarmes, the Palatine Guard of Honor, and the Guard of Honor of the Pope (Pontifical Noble Guard) which Pope Paul disbanded Sept. 14, 1970.

The **Basilica of St. Peter,** built between 1506 and 1626, is the largest church in Christendom and the site of most papal ceremonies. The pope's own patriarchal basilica, however, is **St. John Lateran,** whose origins date back to 324.

St. Ann's is the parish church of Vatican City.

The **Vatican Library,** one of five in the City, has among its holdings 70,000 manuscripts, 770,000 printed books, and 7,500 incunabula.

The independent temporal power of the pope, which is limited to the confines of Vatican City and small areas outside, was for many centuries more extensive than it is now. As late as the nineteenth century, the pope ruled 16,000 square miles of Papal States across the middle of Italy, with a population of over 3,000,000. In 1870 forces of the Kingdom of Italy occupied these lands which, with the exception of the small areas surrounding the Vatican and Lateran in Rome and the Villa of Castel Gandolfo, became part of the Kingdom of Italy by the Italian law of May 13, 1871.

The **Roman Question,** occasioned by this seizure and the voluntary confinement of the pope to the limited papal lands, was finally settled with ratification of the Lateran Agreement on June 7, 1929, by the Italian government and Vatican City and provided a financial indemnity for the former Papal States, which became recognized as part of Italy. The Lateran Agreement became Article 7 of the Italian Constitution on Mar. 26, 1947.

Papal Flag

The papal flag consists of two equal vertical stripes of yellow and white, charged with the insignia of the papacy on the white stripe — a triple crown or tiara over two crossed keys, one of gold and one of silver, tied with a red cord and two tassels. The divisions of the crown represent the teaching, sanctifying and ruling offices of the pope. The keys symbolize his jurisdictional authority.

The papal flag is a national flag inasmuch as it is the standard of the Supreme Pontiff as the sovereign of the state of Vatican City. It is also universally accepted by the faithful as a symbol of the supreme spiritual authority of the Holy Father.

In a Catholic church, the papal flag is displayed on a staff on the left side of the sanctuary (facing the congregation), and the American flag is displayed on the right.

Vatican Radio

The declared purpose of Vatican Radio Station HVJ is "that the voice of the Supreme Pastor may be heard throughout the world by means of the ether waves, for the glory of Christ and the salvation of souls." Designed by Guglielmo Marconi, the inventor of radio, and supervised by him until his death, the station was inaugurated by Pope Pius XI in 1931.

Vatican Radio operates on international wave lengths, transmits programs in more than 32 languages, and serves as a channel of communication between the Vatican, church officials and listeners in general in many parts of the world. The station broadcasts about 470 programs a week throughout the world.

The staff of 200 broadcasters and technicians includes 29 Jesuits and is directed by Father Robert Tucci, S.J. Headquarters are located in Vatican City. Studios and offices are at Palazzo Pio, Piazza Pia, 3. The transmitters are situated at Santa Maria di Galeria, a 200-acre site 16 miles from Rome.

1974 Vatican Stamps

The Vatican Philatelic Office had six issues of stamps scheduled for 1974. Four of the six were released by early summer.

• Air mail stamp of 2500 lire, issued Feb. 21, 1974.

• Series commemorating the centenary of the Universal Postal Union, issued April 23 in two values (50 and 90 lire) on two subjects.

• Series dedicated to works entered for the international art competition for students, organized by the Holy See in 1972 on the subject, "The Bible, the Book of Books." Issued April 23 in five values (15, 25, 50, 90 and 100 lire) on five subjects.

• Series commemorating the seventh centenary of the death of St. Thomas Aquinas, issued June 18 in three values (50, 90 and 220 lire). When joined together, the three stamps form a tryptich representing "The School of St. Thomas."

• Series commemorating the seventh centenary of the death of St. Bonaventure.

• Series commemorating the Holy Year.

The St. Bonaventure series, issued in three values (40, 90 and 220 lire) Sept. 26, had three subjects: a view of *Civita,* the medieval quarter of the saint's native town of Bagnoregio; the "Tree of Life" inspired by a work of the 13th century; and a portrayal of the saint as reproduced in the Church of St. Francis at Montefalco.

Papal Audiences

General audiences are scheduled weekly, on Wednesday at noon.

In Vatican City, they are held in the Audience Hall on the south side of St. Peter's Basilica. The hall, which was opened in 1971, has a seating capacity of 6,800 and a total capacity of 12,000.

From about the middle of July to the middle of September, they are held in a smaller hall at Castel Gandolfo, where the pope spends a working vacation.

General audiences last from about 60 to 90 minutes, during which the pope gives a talk and his blessing. A résumé of the talk, which is usually in Italian, is given in several languages.

Arrangements for papal audiences are handled by an office of the Prefecture of the Apostolic Household.

American visitors can obtain passes for general audiences by applying to the Bishops' Office for United States Visitors to the Vatican, on the Via dell'Umilita in downtown Rome. The director of the office is Father John J. Bagley of Worcester, Mass.

Private and group audiences are reserved for dignitaries of various categories and for special occasions.

Publications

Acta Apostolicae Sedis: The only "official commentary" of the Holy See, was established in 1908 for the publication of activities of the Holy See, laws, decrees and acts of congregations and tribunals of the Roman Curia. The first edition was published in January, 1909.

St. Pius X made *AAS* an official organ in 1908. Laws promulgated for the Church ordinarily take effect three months after the date of their publication in this commentary.

The publication, mostly in Latin and Italian, is printed by the Vatican Polyglot Press.

The immediate predecessor of this organ was *Acta Sanctae Sedis,* founded in 1865 and given official status by the Congregation for the Propagation of the Faith in 1904.

Annuario Pontificio: The yearbook of the Holy See. It is edited by the Vatican Secretariat of State and is printed in Italian, with some portions in other languages, by the Vatican Polyglot Press. It covers the worldwide organization of the Church, lists members of the hierarchy, and includes a wide range of statistical information.

The publication of a statistical yearbook of the Holy See dates back to 1716, when a volume called *Notizie* appeared. Publication under the present title began in 1860, was suspended in 1870, and resumed again in 1872 under the title *Catholic Hierarchy.* This volume was printed privately at first, but has been issued by the Vatican Press since 1885. The title *Annuario Pontificio* was restored in 1912, and the yearbook was called an "official publication" until 1924.

L'Osservatore Romano: The daily newspaper of the Holy See. It began publication July

1, 1861, as an independent enterprise under the ownership and direction of four Catholic laymen headed by Marcantonio Pacelli, vice minister of the interior under Pope Pius IX and a grandfather of the late Pius XII. Leo XIII bought the publication in 1890, making it the "pope's" own newspaper.

The only official material in *L'Osservatore Romano* is that which appears under the heading, "Nostre Informazioni." This includes notices of appointments by the Holy See, the texts of papal encyclicals and addresses by the Holy Father and others, various types of documents, accounts of decisions and rulings of administrative bodies, and similar items. Additional material includes news and comment on developments in the Church and the world. Italian is the language most used.

The bulk of the contents of each edition is determined by a "well defined policy in line with the teaching and the attitudes of the Church . . . which the editorial staff follows with full and direct responsibility," according to Federico Alessandrini, Vatican press officer.

The editorial board is directed by Raimondo Manzini. A staff of about 15 reporters covers Rome news sources. A corps of correspondents provides foreign coverage.

A weekly roundup edition in English was inaugurated in 1968. Other weekly editions are printed in French, Spanish, Portuguese and German.

Vatican Press Office: The establishment of a single Vatican Press Office was announced Feb. 29, 1968, to replace service agencies formerly operated by *L'Osservatore Romano* and an office created for press coverage of the Second Vatican Council. Prof. Federico Alessandrini is the director.

Vatican Polyglot Press: The official printing plant of the Vatican.

The Vatican press was conceived by Marcellus II and Pius IV but was actually founded by Sixtus V on Apr. 27, 1587, to print the Vulgate and the writings of the Fathers of the Church and other authors. A Polyglot Press was established in 1626 by the Congregation for the Propagation of the Faith to serve the needs of the Oriental Church. St. Pius X merged both presses under this title.

The plant has facilities for the printing of a wide variety of material in about 30 languages.

Activities of the Holy See: An annual documentary volume covering the activities of the pope — his daily work, general and special audiences, discourses and messages on special occasions, visits outside the Vatican, missionary and charitable endeavors, meetings with diplomats, heads of state and others — and activities of the congregations, commissions, tribunals and offices of the Roman Curia.

Statistical Yearbook of the Church: Issued by the Central Statistics Office of the Church, it contains principal data concerning the presence and work of the Church in the world. The first issue was published in 1972 under the title *Collection of Statistical Tables, 1969.* It is printed in corresponding columns of Italian and Latin. Some of the introductory material is printed in other languages.

VATICAN REPRESENTATIVES

(Sources: *Annuario Pontifico;* NC News Service.)

The Vatican has representatives to a number of quasi-governmental and international organizations.

Governmental Organizations: United Nations (Msgr. Giovanni Cheli, permanent observer); UN Office in Geneva (Msgr. Silvio Luoni, permanent observer); International Atomic Energy Agency (Dr. Hermann Abs, Msgr. Orlano Quilici, delegates); UN Organization for Industrial Development (Msgr. Orlano Quilici, delegate); UN Food and Agriculture Organization (Most Rev. Agostino Ferrari-Toniolo, permanent observer); UN Educational, Scientific and Cultural Organization (Msgr. Luigi Conti, permanent observer);

Council of Europe (Abp. Igino Cardinale, special minister with function of permanent observer); International Institute for the Unification of Private Law (Prof. Pio Ciprotti, delegate); International Committee of Medicine and Pharmacy (Msgr. Victor Heylen); International Union of Official Organizations of Tourism (Rev. Giovanni Arrighi, O.P.); International Geographic Union (Prof. Gastone Imbrighi);

Universal Postal Union; International Telecommunications Union; International Council on Grain; International Union for the Protection of Literary and Artistic Works; International Union for the Protection of Industrial Property.

Additional quasi-governmental and international organizations of influence in which the Vatican has representation and voice are the following:

International Committee of Historical Sciences (Msgr. Michele Maccarrone); International Committee of Paleography (Msgr. Jose Ruysschaert); International Committee of the History of Art (Dr. Deocletio Redig de Campos); International Committee of Anthropolical and Ethnological Sciences;

International Committee for the Neutrality of Medicine (Rev. Michel Riquet, S.J., permanent observer); International Center of Study for the Preservation and Restoration of Cultural Goods (Dr. Deocletio Redig de Campos); International Institute of Administrative Sciences; International Technical Committee for Prevention and Extinction of Fires; World Medical Association.

Doctrine of the Catholic Church

Following are excerpts from the first two chapters of the *Dogmatic Constitution on the Church* promulgated by the Second Vatican Council. They describe the relation of the Catholic Church to the Kingdom of God, the nature and foundation of the Church, the People of God, the necessity of membership and participation in the Church for salvation.

Additional subjects in the constitution are treated in other Almanac entries.

I. MYSTERY OF THE CHURCH

". . . By her relationship with Christ, the Church is a kind of sacrament or sign of intimate union with God, and of the unity of all mankind . . ." (No. 1).

". . . He (the eternal Father) planned to assemble in the holy Church all those who would believe in Christ. Already from the beginning of the world the foreshadowing of the Church took place. She was prepared for in a remarkable way throughout the history of the people of Israel and by means of the Old Covenant. Established in the present era of time, the Church was made manifest by the outpouring of the Spirit. At the end of time she will achieve her glorious fulfillment. Then . . . all just men from the time of Adam, 'from Abel, the just one, to the last of the elect,' will be gathered together with the Father in the universal Church" (No. 2).

"When the work which the Father had given the Son to do on earth (cf. Jn. 17:4) was accomplished, the Holy Spirit was sent on the day of Pentecost in order that He might forever sanctify the Church, and thus all believers would have access to the Father through Christ in the one Spirit (cf. Eph. 2:18). . . .

"The Spirit dwells in the Church and in the hearts of the faithful as in a temple (cf. 1 Cor. 3:16; 6:19). . . . The Spirit guides the Church into the fullness of truth (cf. Jn. 16:13) and gives her a unity of fellowship and service. He furnishes and directs her with various gifts, both hierarchical and charismatic, and adorns her with the fruits of His grace (cf. Eph. 4:11-12; 1 Cor. 12:4; Gal. 5:22). By the power of the gospel He makes the Church grow, perpetually renews her, and leads her to perfect union with her Spouse. . . ." (No. 4).

Foundation of the Church

"The mystery of the holy Church is manifest in her very foundation, for the Lord Jesus inaugurated her by preaching the good news, that is, the coming of God's Kingdom, which, for centuries, had been promised in the Scriptures. . . . In Christ's word, in His works, and in His presence this kingdom reveals itself to men. . . .

"The miracles of Jesus also confirm that the kingdom has already arrived on earth. . . .

"Before all things, however, the kingdom is clearly visible in the very person of Christ, Son of God and Son of Man. . . .

"When Jesus rose up again after suffering death on the cross for mankind, He manifested that He had been appointed Lord, Messiah, and Priest forever (cf. Acts 2:36; Hb. 5:6; 7:17-21), and He poured out on His disciples the Spirit promised by the Father (cf. Acts 2:33). The Church, consequently, equipped with the gifts of her Founder and faithfully guarding His precepts . . . receives the mission to proclaim and to establish among all peoples the kingdom of Christ and of God. She becomes on earth the initial budding forth of that kingdom. While she slowly grows, the Church strains toward the consummation of the kingdom and, with all her strength, hopes and desires to be united in glory with her King" (No. 5).

Figures of the Church

"In the Old Testament the revelation of the kingdom had often been conveyed by figures of speech. In the same way the inner nature of the Church was now to be made known to us through various images. . . .

". . . The Church is a sheepfold . . . a flock . . . a tract of land to be cultivated, the field of God . . . His choice vineyard . . . the true Vine is Christ . . . the edifice of God . . . the house of God . . . the holy temple (whose members are) . . . living stones . . . this Holy City . . . a bride . . . 'our Mother' . . . the spotless spouse of the spotless Lamb . . . an exile. . ." (No. 6).

"In the human nature which He united to Himself, the Son of God redeemed man and transformed him into a new creation (cf. Gal. 6:15; 2 Cor. 5:17) by overcoming death through His own death and resurrection. By communicating His Spirit to His brothers, called together from all peoples, Christ made them mystically into His own body.

"In that body, the life of Christ is poured into the believers, who, through the sacraments, are united in a hidden and real way to Christ who suffered and was glorified. Through baptism we are formed in the likeness of Christ. . . .

"Truly partaking of the body of the Lord in the breaking of the Eucharistic bread, we are taken up into communion with Him and with one another . . ." (No. 7).

One Body in Christ

"As all the members of the human body, though they are many, form one body, so also are the faithful in Christ (cf. 1 Cor. 12:12). Also, in the building up of Christ's body there is a flourishing variety of members and functions. There is only one Spirit who . . . distributes His different gifts for the welfare of the Church (cf. 1 Cor. 12:1-11). Among these gifts stands out the grace given to the apostles. To their authority, the Spirit Himself subjected even those who were endowed with charisms (cf. 1 Cor. 14). . . .

"The head of this body is Christ . . ." (No. 7).

Mystical Body of Christ

"Christ, the one Mediator, established and ceaselessly sustains here on earth His holy Church, the community of faith, hope, and charity, as a visible structure. Through her He communicates truth and grace to all. But the society furnished with hierarchical agencies and the Mystical Body of Christ are not to be considered as two realities, nor are the visible assembly and the spiritual community, nor the earthly Church and the Church enriched with heavenly things. Rather they form one interlocked reality which is comprised of a divine and a human element. For this reason . . . this reality is compared to the mystery of the incarnate Word. Just as the assumed nature inseparably united to the divine Word serves Him as a living instrument of salvation, so, in a similar way, does the communal structure of the Church serve Christ's Spirit, who vivifies it by way of building up the body (cf. Eph. 4:16).

"This is the unique Church of Christ which in the Creed we avow as one, holy, catholic, and apostolic. After His Resurrection our Savior handed her over to Peter to be shepherded (Jn. 21:17), commissioning him and the other apostles to propagate and govern her (cf. Mt. 28:18, ff.). Her He erected for all ages as 'the pillar and mainstay of the truth' (1 Tm. 3:15). This Church, constituted and organized in the world as a society, subsists in the Catholic Church, which is governed by the successor of Peter and by the bishops in union with that successor, although many elements of sanctification and of truth can be found outside of her visible structure. These elements, however, as gifts properly belonging to the Church of Christ, possess an inner dynamism toward Catholic unity.

". . . the Church, embracing sinners in her bosom, is at the same time holy and always in need of being purified, and incessantly pursues the path of penance and renewal.

"The Church, 'like a pilgrim in a foreign land, presses forward . . .' announcing the cross and death of the Lord until He comes (cf. 1 Cor. 11:26) . . ." (No. 8).

II. THE PEOPLE OF GOD

"At all times and among every people, God has given welcome to whosoever fears Him and does what is right (cf. Acts 10:35). It has pleased God, however, to make men holy and save them not merely as individuals without

any mutual bonds, but by making them into a single people, a people which acknowledges Him in truth and serves Him in holiness. He therefore chose the race of Israel as a people unto Himself. With it He set up a covenant. Step by step He taught this people by manifesting in its history both Himself and the decree of His will, and by making it holy unto Himself. All these things, however, were done by way of preparation and as a figure of that new and perfect covenant which was to be ratified in Christ. . . .

". . . Christ instituted this new covenant, that is to say, the new testament, in His blood (cf. 1 Cor. 11:25), by calling together a people made up of Jew and Gentile, making them one, not according to the flesh but in the Spirit.

"This was to be the new People of God . . . reborn . . . through the Word of the living God (cf. 1 Pt. 1:23) . . . from water and the Holy Spirit (cf. Jn. 3:5-6) . . . 'a chosen race, a royal priesthood, a holy nation, a purchased people. . . . You who in times past were not a people, but are now the people of God' (1 Pt. 2:9-10).

"That messianic people has for its head Christ. . . . Its law is the new commandment to love as Christ loved us (cf. Jn. 13:34). Its goal is the kingdom of God, which has been begun by God Himself on earth, and which is to be further extended until it is brought to perfection by Him at the end of time. . . .

". . . This messianic people, although it does not actually include all men, and may more than once look like a small flock, is nonetheless a lasting and sure seed of unity, hope, and salvation for the whole human race. Established by Christ as a fellowship of life, charity, and truth, it is also used by Him as an instrument for the redemption of all, and is sent forth into the whole world as the light of the world and the salt of the earth (cf. Mt. 5:13-16).

"Israel according to the flesh . . . was already called the Church of God (2 Ezr. 13:1; cf. Nm. 20:4; Dt. 23:1, ff.). Likewise the new Israel . . . is also called the Church of Christ (cf. Mt. 16:18). For He has bought it for Himself with His blood (cf. Acts 20:28), has filled it with His Spirit, and provided it with those means which befit it as a visible and social unity. God has gathered together as one all those who in faith look upon Jesus as the author of salvation and the source of unity and peace, and has established them as the Church, that for each and all she may be the visible sacrament of this saving unity . . ." (No. 9)

Priesthood

". . . The baptized, by regeneration and the anointing of the Holy Spirit, are consecrated into . . . a holy priesthood. . . ."

(All members of the Church participate in

the priesthood of Christ, through the common priesthood of the faithful. See Priesthood of the Laity.)

"Though they differ from one another in essence and not only in degree, the common priesthood of the faithful and the ministerial or hierarchical priesthood are nonetheless interrelated. Each of them in its own special way is a participation in the one priesthood of Christ . . ." (No. 10).

"It is through the sacraments and the exercise of the virtues that the sacred nature and organic structure of the priestly community is brought into operation . . ." (No. 11). (See Role of the Sacraments.)

Prophetic Office

"The holy People of God shares also in Christ's prophetic office. It spreads abroad a living witness to Him, especially by means of a life of faith and charity and by offering to God a sacrifice of praise. . . . The body of the faithful as a whole, anointed as they are by the Holy One (cf. Jn. 2:20, 27), cannot err in matters of belief. Thanks to a supernatural sense of faith which characterizes the People as a whole, it manifests this unerring quality when, 'from the bishops down to the last member of the laity,' it shows universal agreement in matters of faith and morals.

". . . God's People accepts not the word of men but the very Word of God (cf. 1 Thes. 2:13). It clings without fail to the faith once delivered to the saints (cf. Jude 3), penetrates it more deeply by accurate insights, and applies it more thoroughly to life. All this it does under the lead of a sacred teaching authority to which it loyally defers.

"It is not only through the sacraments and Church ministries that the same Holy Spirit sanctifies and leads the People of God. . . . He distributes special graces among the faithful of every rank. By these gifts He makes them fit and ready to undertake the various tasks or offices advantageous for the renewal and upbuilding of the Church. . . . These charismatic gifts . . . are to be received with thanksgiving and consolation, for they are exceedingly suitable and useful for the needs of the Church.

". . . Judgment as to their genuineness and proper use belongs to those who preside over the Church, and to whose special competence it belongs . . . to test all things and hold fast to that which is good (cf. 1 Thes. 5:12; 19-21)" (No. 12).

All Are Called

"All men are called to belong to the new People of God. Wherefore this People, while remaining one and unique, is to be spread throughout the whole world and must exist in all ages, so that the purpose of God's will may be fulfilled. In the beginning God made human nature one. After His children were scattered, He decreed that they should at length be united again (cf. Jn. 11:52). It was for this reason that God sent His Son . . . that He might be Teacher, King, and Priest of all, the Head of the new and universal people of the sons of God. For this God finally sent His Son's Spirit as Lord and Lifegiver. He it is who, on behalf of the whole Church and each and every one of those who believe, is the principle of their coming together and remaining together in the teaching of the apostles and in fellowship, in the breaking of bread and in prayers (cf. Acts 2:42)" (No. 13).

One People of God

"It follows that among all the nations of earth there is but one People of God, which takes its citizens from every race, making them citizens of a kingdom which is of a heavenly and not an earthly nature. For all the faithful scattered throughout the world are in communion with each other in the Holy Spirit. . . . the Church or People of God . . . foster(s) and take(s) to herself, insofar as they are good, the ability, resources and customs of each people. Taking them to herself she purifies, strengthens, and ennobles them . . . This characteristic of universality which adorns the People of God is a gift from the Lord Himself. By reason of it, the Catholic Church strives energetically and constantly to bring all humanity with all its riches back to Christ its Head in the unity of His Spirit.

"In virtue of this catholicity each individual part of the Church contributes through its special gifts to the good of the other parts and of the whole Church. Thus through the common sharing of gifts . . . the whole and each of the parts receive increase. . . .

"All men are called to be part of this catholic unity of the People of God. . . . And there belong to it or are related to it in various ways, the Catholic faithful as well as all who believe in Christ, and indeed the whole of mankind. For all men are called to salvation by the grace of God" (No. 13).

The Catholic Church

"This sacred Synod turns its attention first to the Catholic faithful. Basing itself upon sacred Scripture and tradition, it teaches that the Church . . . is necessary for salvation. For Christ, made present to us in His Body, which is the Church, is the one Mediator and the unique Way of salvation. In explicit terms He Himself affirmed the necessity of faith and baptism (cf. Mk. 16:16; Jn. 3:5) and thereby affirmed also the necessity of the Church, for through baptism as through a door men enter the Church. Whosoever, therefore, knowing that the Catholic Church was made necessary by God through Jesus Christ, would refuse to enter her or to remain in her could not be saved.

"They are fully incorporated into the society of the Church who, possessing the Spirit of Christ, accept her entire system and all the means of salvation given to her, and through union with her visible structure are joined to Christ, who rules her through the Supreme Pontiff and the bishops. This joining is effected by the bonds of professed faith, of the sacraments, of ecclesiastical government, and of communion. He is not saved, however, who, though he is part of the body of the Church, does not persevere in charity. He remains indeed in the bosom of the Church, but . . . only in a 'bodily' manner and not 'in his heart.' . . .

"Catechumens who, moved by the Holy Spirit, seek with explicit intention to be incorporated into the Church are by that very intention joined to her. . . . Mother Church already embraces them as her own" (No. 14).

Other Christians, The Unbaptized

"The Church recognizes that in many ways she is linked with those who, being baptized, are honored with the name of Christian, though they do not profess the faith in its entirety or do not preserve unity of communion with the successor of Peter. . . .

" . . . We can say that in some real way they are joined with us in the Holy Spirit, for to them also He gives His gifts and graces, and is thereby operative among them with His sanctifying power . . ." (No. 15).

"Finally, those who have not yet received the gospel are related in various ways to the People of God. In the first place there is the people to whom the covenants and the promises were given and from whom Christ was born according to the flesh (cf. Rom. 9:4-5). On account of their fathers, this people remains 'most dear to God, for God does not repent of the gifts He makes nor of the calls He issues (cf. Rom. 11:28-29).

"But the plan of salvation also includes those who acknowledge the Creator. In the first place among these are the Moslems. . . . Nor is God Himself far distant from those who in shadows and images seek the unknown God. . . .

"Those also can attain to everlasting salvation who through no fault of their own do not know the gospel of Christ or His Church, yet sincerely seek God and, moved by grace, strive by their deeds to do His will as it is known to them through the dictates of conscience. Nor does divine Providence deny the help necessary for salvation to those who, without blame on their part, have not yet arrived at an explicit knowledge of God, but who strive to live a good life, thanks to His grace. Whatever goodness or truth is found among them is looked upon by the Church as a preparation for the Gospel. She regards such qualities as given by Him who enlightens all men so that they may finally have life . . ." (No. 16).

THE POPE, TEACHING AUTHORITY, COLLEGIALITY

The Roman Pontiff — the successor of St. Peter as the Vicar of Christ and head of the Church on earth — has full and supreme authority over the universal Church in matters pertaining to faith and morals (teaching authority), discipline and government (jurisdictional authority).

The primacy of the pope is real and supreme power. It is not merely a prerogative of honor — that is, of his being regarded as the first among equals. Neither does primacy imply that the pope is just the presiding officer of the collective body of bishops. The pope is the head of the Church.

Catholic belief in the primacy of the pope was stated in detail in the dogmatic constitution on the Church, *Pastor Aeternus,* approved in 1870 by the fourth session of the First Vatican Council. Some elaboration of the doctrine was made in the *Dogmatic Constitution on the Church* which was approved and promulgated by the Second Vatican Council Nov. 21, 1964. The entire body of teaching on the subject is based on Scripture and tradition and the centuries-long experience of the Church.

Infallibility

The essential points of doctrine concerning infallibility in the Church and the infallibility of the pope were stated by the Second Vatican

Council in the *Dogmatic Constitution on the Church,* as follows:

"This infallibility with which the divine Redeemer willed his Church to be endowed in defining a doctrine of faith and morals extends as far as extends the deposit of divine revelation, which must be religiously guarded and faithfully expounded. This is the infallibility which the Roman Pontiff, the head of the college of bishops, enjoys in virtue of his office, when, as the supreme shepherd and teacher of all the faithful, who confirms his brethren in their faith (cf. Lk. 22:32), he proclaims by a definitive act some doctrine of faith or morals. Therefore his definitions, of themselves, and not from the consent of the Church, are justly styled irreformable, for they are pronounced with the assistance of the Holy Spirit, an assistance promised to him in blessed Peter. Therefore they need no approval of others, nor do they allow an appeal to any other judgment. For then the Roman Pontiff is not pronouncing judgment as a private person. Rather, as the supreme teacher of the universal Church, as one in whom the charism of the infallibility of the Church herself is individually present, he is expounding or defending a doctrine of Catholic faith.

"The infallibility promised to the Church resides also in the body of bishops when that body exercises supreme teaching authority with the successor of Peter. To the resultant definitions the assent of the Church can never be wanting, on account of the activity of that same Holy Spirit, whereby the whole flock of Christ is preserved and progresses in unity of faith.

"But when either the Roman Pontiff or the body of bishops together with him defines a judgment, they pronounce it in accord with revelation itself. All are obliged to maintain and be ruled by this revelation, which, as written or preserved by tradition, is transmitted in its entirety through the legitimate succession of bishops and especially through the care of the Roman Pontiff himself.

"Under the guiding light of the Spirit of truth, revelation is thus religiously preserved and faithfully expounded in the Church. The Roman Pontiff and the bishops, in view of their office and of the importance of the matter, strive painstakingly and by appropriate means to inquire properly into that revelation and to give apt expression to its contents. But they do not allow that there could be any new public revelation pertaining to the divine deposit of faith" (No. 25).

Authentic Teaching

The pope rarely speaks *ex cathedra* — that is, "from the chair" of St. Peter, for the purpose of making an infallible pronouncement. More often and in various ways he states authentic teaching in line with Scripture, tradition, the living experience of the Church, and the whole analogy of faith. Of such teaching, the Second Vatican Council said in its *Dogmatic Constitution on the Church* (No. 25):

". . . Religious submission of will and of mind must be shown in a special way to the authentic teaching authority of the Roman Pontiff, even when he is not speaking *ex cathedra*. That is, it must be shown in such a way that his supreme magisterium is acknowledged with reverence, the judgments made by him are sincerely adhered to, according to his manifest mind and will. His mind and will in the matter may be known chiefly either from the character of the documents, from his frequent repetition of the same doctrine, or from his manner of speaking."

With respect to bishops, the constitution said: "They are authentic teachers, that is, teachers endowed with the authority of Christ, who preach to the people committed to them the faith they must believe and put into practice. By the light of the Holy Spirit, they make that faith clear, bringing forth from the treasury of revelation new things and old (cf. Mt. 13:52), making faith bear fruit and vigilantly warding off any errors which threaten their flock (cf. Tm. 4:1-4).

"Bishops, teaching in communion with the Roman Pontiff, are to be respected by all as witnesses to divine and Catholic truth. In matters of faith and morals, the bishops speak in the name of Christ and the faithful are to accept their teaching and adhere to it with a religious assent of soul."

Magisterium—Teaching Authority

Responsibility for teaching doctrine and judging orthodoxy belongs to the official teaching authority of the Church.

This authority is personalized in the pope, the successor of St. Peter as head of the Church, and in the bishops together and in union with the pope, as it was originally committed to Peter and to the whole college of Apostles under his leadership. They are the official teachers of the Church.

Others have auxiliary relationships with the magisterium: theologians, in the study and clarification of doctrine; teachers — priests, religious, lay persons — who cooperate with the pope and bishops in spreading knowledge of religious truth; the faithful, who by their sense of faith and personal witness contribute to the development of doctrine and the establishment of its relevance to life in the Church and the world.

The magisterium, Pope Paul noted in an address at a general audience Jan. 11, 1967, "is a subordinate and faithful echo and secure interpreter of the divine word." It does not reveal new truths, "nor is it superior to Sacred Scripture." Its competence extends to the limits of divine revelation manifested in Scripture and tradition and the living experience of the Church, with respect to matters of faith and morals and related subjects.

Official teaching in these areas is infallible when it is formally defined, for belief and acceptance by all members of the Church, by the pope, acting in the capacity of supreme shepherd of the flock of Christ; and when doctrine is proposed and taught with moral unanimity of bishops with the pope in a solemn collegial manner as in an ecumenical council, and/or in the ordinary course of events. Even when not infallibly defined, official teaching in the areas of faith and morals is authoritative and requires religious assent.

The teachings of the magisterium have been documented in creeds, formulas of faith, decrees and enactments of ecumenical and particular councils, various kinds of doctrinal statements, and other teaching instruments. They have also been incorporated into the liturgy, with the result that the law of prayer is said to be a law of belief.

Collegiality

The bishops of the Church, in union with the pope, have supreme teaching and pastoral authority over the whole Church in addition to the authority of office they have for their own dioceses.

This collegial authority is exercised in a solemn manner in an ecumenical council and can be exercised in other ways as well, "provided that the head of the college calls them to collegiate action, or at least so approves or freely accepts the united action of the dispersed bishops, that it is made a true collegiate act."

This doctrine is grounded on the fact that: "Just as, by the Lord's will, St. Peter and the other apostles constituted one apostolic college, so in a similar way the Roman Pontiff as the successor of Peter, and the bishops as the successors of the apostles are joined together."

Doctrine on collegiality was stated by the Second Vatican Council in the *Dogmatic Constitution on the Church* (Nos. 22 and 23).

REVELATION

Following are excerpts from the *Constitution on Revelation* promulgated by the Second Vatican Council. They describe the nature and process of divine revelation, inspiration and interpretation of Scripture, the Old and New Testaments, and the role of Scripture in the life of the Church.

I. Revelation Itself

". . . God chose to reveal Himself and to make known to us the hidden purpose of His will (cf. Eph. 1:9) by which through Christ, the Word made flesh, man has access to the Father in the Holy Spirit and comes to share in the divine nature (cf. Eph. 2:18; 2 Pt. 1:4). Through this revelation, therefore, the invisible God (cf. Col. 1:15; 1 Tm. 1:17) . . . speaks to men as friends (cf. Ex. 33:11; Jn. 15:14-15) and lives among them (cf. Bar. 3:38) so that He may invite and take them into fellowship with Himself. This plan of revelation is realized by deeds and words having an inner unity: the deeds wrought by God in the history of salvation manifest and confirm the teaching and realities signified by the words, while the words proclaim the deeds and clarify the mystery contained in them. By this revelation then, the deepest truth about God and the salvation of man is made clear to us in Christ, who is the Mediator and at the same time the fullness of all revelation" (No. 2).

"God . . . from the start manifested Himself to our first parents. Then after their fall His promise of redemption aroused in them the hope of being saved (cf. Gn. 3:15), and from that time on He ceaselessly kept the human race in His care, in order to give eternal life to those who perseveringly do good in search of salvation (cf. Rom. 2:6-7). . . . He called Abraham in order to make of him a great nation (cf. Gn. 12:2). Through the patriarchs, and after them through Moses and the prophets, He taught this nation to acknowledge Himself as the one living and true God . . . and to wait for the Savior promised by Him. In this manner He prepared the way for the gospel down through the centuries" (No. 3).

Revelation in Christ

"Then, after speaking in many places and varied ways through the prophets, God 'last of all in these days has spoken to us by His Son' (Hb. 1:1-2). . . . Jesus perfected revelation by fulfilling it through His whole work of making Himself present and manifesting Himself: through His words and deeds, His signs and wonders, but especially through His death and glorious resurrection from the dead and final sending of the spirit of truth. Moreover, He confirmed with divine testimony what revelation proclaimed: that God is with us to free us from the darkness of sin and death, and to raise us up to life eternal.

"The Christian dispensation, therefore, as the new and definitive covenant, will never pass away, and we now await no further new public revelation before the glorious manifestation of our Lord Jesus Christ (cf. 1 Tm. 6:14; Ti. 2:13)" (No. 4).

II. Transmission of Revelation

". . . God has seen to it that what He had revealed for the salvation of all nations would abide perpetually in its full integrity and be handed on to all generations. Therefore Christ the Lord, in whom the full revelation of the supreme God is brought to completion (cf. 2 Cor. 1:20; 3:16; 4:6), commissioned the apostles to preach to all men that gospel which is the source of all saving truth and moral teaching, and thus to impart to them divine gifts. This gospel had been promised in former times through the prophets, and Christ Himself fulfilled it and promulgated it with His own lips. This commission was faithfully fulfilled by the apostles who, by their oral preaching, by example, and by ordinances, handed on what they had received from . . . Christ . . . or what they had learned through the prompting of the Holy Spirit. The commission was fulfilled, too, by those apostles and apostolic men who under the inspiration of the same Holy Spirit committed the message of salvation to writing" (No. 7).

Tradition

"But in order to keep the gospel forever whole and alive within the Church, the apostles left bishops as their successors, 'handing over their own teaching role' to them. This sacred tradition, therefore, and sacred Scripture of both the Old and the New Testament are like a mirror in which the pilgrim Church on earth looks at God . . ." (No. 7).

". . . The apostolic preaching, which is expressed in a special way in the inspired books, was to be preserved by a continuous succession of preachers until the end of time. Therefore the apostles, handing on what they themselves had received, warn the faithful to hold fast to the traditions which they have learned. . . . Now what was handed on by the apostles includes everything which contributes to the holiness of life, and the increase in faith of the People of God; and so the Church, in her teaching, life, and worship, perpetuates and hands on to all generations all that she herself is, all that she believes" (No. 8).

Development of Doctrine

"This tradition which comes from the apostles develops in the Church with the help of the Holy Spirit. For there is a growth in the understanding of the realities and the words which have been handed down. This happens through the contemplation and study made by believers . . . through the intimate understanding of spiritual things they experience, and through the preaching of those who have received through episcopal succession the sure gift of truth. For, as the centuries succeed one another, the Church constantly moves forward toward the fullness of divine truth until the words of God reach their complete fulfillment in her.

"The words of the holy Fathers witness to the living presence of this tradition, whose wealth is poured into the practice and life of the believing and praying Church. Through the same tradition the Church's full canon of the sacred books is known, and the sacred writings themselves are more profoundly understood and unceasingly made active in her; . . . and the Holy Spirit, through whom the living voice of the gospel resounds in the Church, and through her, in the world, leads unto all truth those who believe and makes the word of Christ dwell abundantly in them (cf. Col. 3:16)" (No. 8).

Tradition and Scripture

"Hence there exist a close connection and communication between sacred tradition and sacred Scripture. For both of them, flowing from the same divine wellspring, in a certain way merge into a unity and tend toward the same end. For sacred Scripture is the word of God inasmuch as it is consigned to writing under the inspiration of the divine Spirit. To the successors of the apostles, sacred tradition hands on in its full purity God's word, which was entrusted to the apostles by Christ the Lord and the Holy Spirit. Thus, led by the light of the Spirit of truth, these successors can in their preaching preserve this word of God faithfully, explain it, and make it more widely known. Consequently, it is not from sacred Scripture alone that the Church draws her certainty about everything which has been revealed. Therefore both sacred tradition and sacred Scripture are to be accepted and venerated with the same sense of devotion and reverence" (No. 9).

"Sacred tradition and sacred Scripture form one sacred deposit of the word of God, which is committed to the Church" (No. 10).

Teaching Authority of Church

"The task of authentically interpreting the word of God, whether written or handed on, has been entrusted exclusively to the living teaching office of the Church, whose authority is exercised in the name of Jesus Christ. This teaching office is not above the word of God, but serves it, teaching only what has been handed on . . . it draws from this one deposit of faith everything which it presents for belief as divinely revealed.

"It is clear, therefore, that sacred tradition, sacred Scripture, and the teaching authority of the Church . . . are so linked and joined together that one cannot stand without the others, and that all together and each in its own way under the action of the one Holy Spirit contribute effectively to the salvation of souls" (No. 10).

III. Inspiration, Interpretation

"Those . . . revealed realities . . . contained and presented in sacred Scripture have been committed to writing under the inspiration of the Holy Spirit. Holy Mother Church, relying on the belief of the apostles, holds that the books of both the Old and New Testament in their entirety, with all their parts, are sacred and canonical because, having been written under the inspiration of the Holy Spirit (cf. Jn. 20:31; 2 Tm. 3:16; 2 Pt. 1:19-21; 3:15-16) they have God as their author and have been handed on as such to the Church herself. In composing the sacred books, God chose men and while employed by Him they made use of their powers and abilities, so that with Him acting in them and through them, they, as true authors, consigned to writing everything and only those things which He wanted" (No. 11).

Inerrancy

"Therefore, since everything asserted by the inspired authors or sacred writers must be held to be asserted by the Holy Spirit, it follows that the books of Scripture must be acknowledged as teaching firmly, faithfully, and without error that truth which God wanted put into the sacred writings for the sake of our salvation. Therefore 'all Scripture is inspired by God and useful for teaching, for reproving, for correcting, for instruction in justice; that the man of God may be perfect, equipped for every good work' (2 Tm. 3:16-17)" (No. 11).

Literary Forms

"However, since God speaks in sacred Scripture through men in human fashion, the interpreter of sacred Scripture, in order to see clearly what God wanted to communicate to us, should carefully investigate what meaning the sacred writers really intended, and what God wanted to manifest by means of their words.

". . . The interpreter must investigate what meaning the sacred writer intended to express and actually expressed in particular circumstances as he used contemporary literary forms in accordance with the situation of his own time and culture. For the correct understanding of what the sacred author wanted to assert, due attention must be paid to the customary and characteristic styles of perceiving, speaking, and narrating which prevailed at the time of the sacred writer, and to the customs men normally followed at that period in their everyday dealings with one another" (No. 12).

Analogy of Faith

". . . No less serious attention must be given to the content and unity of the whole of Scripture, if the meaning of the sacred texts is to be correctly brought to light. The living tradition of the whole Church must be taken into account along with the harmony which exists between elements of the faith. . . . all of what has been said about the way of interpreting Scripture is subject finally to the judgment of the Church, which carries out the divine commission and ministry of guarding and interpreting the word of God" (No. 12).

IV. The Old Testament

"In carefully planning and preparing the salvation of the whole human race, the God of supreme love, by a special dispensation, chose for Himself a people to whom He might entrust His promises. First He entered into a covenant with Abraham (cf. Gn. 15:18) and, through Moses, with the people of Israel (cf. Ex. 24:8). To this people which He had acquired for Himself, He so manifested Himself through words and deeds as the one true and living God that Israel came to know by experience the ways of God with men. . . . The plan of salvation, foretold by the sacred authors, recounted and explained by them, is found as the true word of God in the books of the Old Testament: these books, therefore, written under divine inspiration, remain permanently valuable . . ." (No. 14).

Principal Purpose

"The principal purpose to which the plan of the Old Covenant was directed was to prepare for the coming both of Christ, the universal Redeemer, and of the messianic kingdom. . . . Now the books of the Old Testament, in accordance with the state of mankind before the time of salvation established by Christ, reveal to all men the knowledge of God and of man and the ways in which God . . . deals with men. These books . . . show us true divine pedagogy . . ." (No. 15).

". . . The books of the Old Testament with all their parts, caught up into the proclamation of the gospel, acquire and show forth their full meaning in the New Testament (cf. Mt. 5:17; Lk. 24:27; Rom. 16:25-26; 2 Cor. 3:14-16) and in turn shed light on it and explain it" (No. 16).

V. The New Testament

"The word of God . . . is set forth and shows its power in a most excellent way in the writings of the New Testament. For when the fullness of time arrived (cf. Gal. 4:4), the Word was made flesh and dwelt among us in the fullness of grace and truth (cf. Jn. 1:14). Christ established the Kingdom of God on earth, manifested His Father and Himself by deeds and words, and completed His work by His death, resurrection, and glorious ascension and by the sending of the Holy Spirit. Having been lifted up from the earth, He draws all men to Himself (cf. Jn. 12:32). . . . This mystery had not been manifested to other generations as it was now revealed to His holy apostles and prophets in the Holy Spirit (cf. Eph. 3:4-6), so that they might preach the Gospel, stir up faith in Jesus, Christ and Lord, and gather the Church together. To these realities, the writings of the New Testament stand as a perpetual and divine witness" (No. 17).

The Gospels and Other Writings

". . . The Gospels have a special preeminence . . . for they are the principal witness of the life and teaching of the incarnate Word, our Savior.

"The Church has always and everywhere held and continues to hold that the four Gospels are of apostolic origin. For what the apostles preached . . . afterwards they themselves and apostolic men, under the inspiration of the divine Spirit, handed on to us in writing: the foundation of faith, namely, the fourfold Gospel, according to Matthew, Mark, Luke, and John" (No. 18).

". . . The four Gospels, . . . whose historical character the Church unhesitatingly asserts, faithfully hand on what Jesus Christ, while living among men, really did and taught for their eternal salvation until the day He was taken up into heaven (see Acts 1:1-2). Indeed, after the ascension of the Lord the apostles handed on to their hearers what He had said and done. . . . The sacred authors wrote the four Gospels, selecting some things from the many which had been handed on by word of mouth or in writing, reducing some of them to a synthesis, explicating some things in view of the situation of their churches, and preserving the form of proclamation but always in such fashion that they told us the honest truth about Jesus. For their intention in writing was that . . . we might know 'the truth' concerning those matters about which we have been instructed (cf. Lk. 1:2-4)" (No. 19).

"Besides the four Gospels, the canon of the New Testament also contains the Epistles of St. Paul and other apostolic writings, composed under the inspiration of the Holy Spirit. In these writings . . . those matters which concern Christ the Lord are confirmed, His true teaching is more and more fully stated, the saving power of the divine work of Christ is preached, the story is told of the beginnings of the Church and her marvelous growth, and her glorious fulfillment is foretold" (No. 20).

VI. Scripture in Church Life

"The Church has always venerated the divine Scriptures just as she venerates the body of the Lord. . . . She has always regarded the Scriptures together with sacred tradition as the supreme rule of faith, and will ever do so. For, inspired by God and committed once and for all to writing, they impart the word of God Himself without change, and make the voice of the Holy Spirit resound in the words of the prophets and apostles. Therefore, like the Christian religion itself, all the preaching of the Church must be nourished and ruled by sacred Scripture . . ." (No. 21).

"Easy access to sacred Scripture should be provided for all the Christian faithful. That is why the Church from the very beginning accepted as her own that very ancient Greek translation of the Old Testament which is named after seventy men (the Septuagint); and she has always given a place of honor to other translations, Eastern and Latin, especially the one known as the Vulgate. But since the word of God should be available at all times, the Church with maternal concern sees to it that suitable and correct translations are made into different languages, especially from the original texts of the sacred books. And if, given the opportunity and the approval of Church authority, these translations are produced in cooperation with the separated brethren as well, all Christians will be able to use them" (No. 22).

Biblical Studies, Theology

The constitution encouraged the development and progress of biblical studies "under the watchful care of the sacred teaching office of the Church." (Such studies have made great progress in recent years.)

It noted also: "Sacred theology rests on the written word of God, together with sacred tradition, as its primary and perpetual foundation," and that "the study of the sacred page is, as it were, the soul of sacred theology" (Nos. 23, 24).

PONTIFICAL BIBLICAL COMMISSION

The Pontifical Biblical Commission, which has been instrumental in directing the course of Catholic biblical scholarship, was established by Leo XIII Oct. 30, 1902, with the apostolic letter *Vigilantiae*, at a time when biblical studies were open to great promise as well as to the threat of Modernism.

The commission was ordered to promote biblical studies; to safeguard the correct interpretation of Scripture, in the pattern of the rule of faith and against the background of sound scholarship; to state positions which had to be held by Catholics on biblical questions; to indicate questions requiring further study and/or those which were open to the judgment of competent scholars. The commission was also authorized to set up standards for biblical studies and to grant degrees in Sacred Scripture.

The commission issued 23 decrees or decisions between 1905 and 1953; letters on the scientific study of the Bible (1941) and the Pentateuch (1948); instructions on teaching Scripture in seminaries (1950), biblical associations (1955), and the historical truth of the Gospels (1964).

Pope St. Pius X stated the authority of decisions of the commission in the letter *Illibatae*, which he issued June 29, 1910, on his own initiative:

"All are bound in conscience to submit to the decisions of the Pontifical Biblical Commission pertaining to doctrine, whether already issued or to be issued in the future, in the same way as to the decrees of the Sacred Congregations (of the Roman Curia) approved by the Pontiff; nor can they avoid the stigma both of disobedience and temerity or be free from grave sin who by any spoken or written words impugn these decisions."

Decisions of the commission regarding points of doctrine are not infallible of themselves. They require religious assent, however, so long as there is no positive evidence that they are wrong. They do not close the door to continuing investigation and study.

The commission was reorganized July 8, 1971, in line with directives issued by Paul VI on his own initiative.

Fifteen new norms changed its structure from a virtually independent office of cardinals aided by lifetime consultors into a group of 20 biblical scholars with five-year terms (renewable) linked with the Congregation for the Doctrine of the Faith. Functionally, however, it remains the same.

The commission:

• receives questions and study topics referred to it by a variety of sources, from the pope to Catholic universities and biblical associations;

• is required to meet in plenary session at least once a year and to submit conclusions reached in such meetings to the pope and the Congregation for the Doctrine of the Faith;

• is under directive to promote relationships with non-Catholic as well as Catholic institutes of biblical studies;

• is to be consulted before any new norms on biblical matters are issued;

• retains its authorization to confer academic degrees in biblical studies.

THE BIBLE

The Catholic canon of the Old Testament consists of:

• The Pentateuch, the first five books: Genesis (Gn.), Exodus (Ex.), Leviticus (Lv.), Numbers (Nm.), Deuteronomy (Dt.).

• Historical Books: Joshua (Jos.), Judges (Jgs.), Ruth (Ru.), 1 and 2 Samuel (Sm.), 1 and 2 Kings (Kgs.), 1 and 2 Chronicles (Chr.), Ezra (Ezr.), Nehemiah (Neh.), Tobit (Tb.), Judith (Jdt.), Esther (Est.), 1 and 2 Maccabees (Mc.),

• Wisdom Books: Job (Jb.), Psalms (Ps.), Proverbs (Prv.), Ecclesiastes (Eccl.), Song of Songs (Song), Wisdom (Wis.), Sirach (Sir.).

• The Prophets: Isaiah (Is.), Jeremiah (Jer.), Lamentations (Lam.), Baruch (Bar.), Ezechiel (Ez.), Daniel (Dn.), Hosea (Hos.), Joel (Jl.), Amos (Am.), Obadiah (Ob.), Jonah (Jon.), Micah (Mi.), Nahum (Na.), Habakkuk (Hb.), Zephaniah (Zep.), Haggai (Hg.), Zechariah (Zec.), Malachi (Mal.).

The Catholic canon of the New Testament consists of:

• The Gospels of Matthew (Mt.), Mark (Mk.), Luke (Lk.), John (Jn.)
• The Acts of the Apostles (Acts).
• The Pauline Letters — Romans (Rom.), 1 and 2 Corinthians (Cor.), Galatians (Gal.), Ephesians (Eph.), Philippians (Phil.), Colossians (Col.), 1 and 2 Thessalonians (Thes.), 1 and 2 Timothy (Tm.), Titus (Ti.), Philemon (Phlm.), Hebrews (Heb.); the Catholic Letters — James (Jas.), 1 and 2 Peter (Pt.), 1, 2 and 3 John (Jn.), Jude (Jude).
• Revelation (Rv.).

Catholic and Other Canons

The Catholic canon of the Old Testament was determined by the tradition of the Church. It was firm by the fifth century, despite some questioning by scholars, and was stated by the African councils of Hippo in 393 and Carthage in 397 and 419, by Innocent I in 405, and by the Council of Florence in 1441. It was defined by the Council of Trent in the dogmatic decree *De Canonicis Scripturis,* Apr. 8, 1546.

The Jews, although they generally accepted 22 or 24 books as sacred in the first century A.D., did not have a definite canon of sacred writings until late in the second or early in the third century. This canon was fixed by the consensus of rabbinical schools.

The canon of the Hebrew Masoretic Text, which is accepted by modern Jews, consists of 24 books, as follows:

• The Law: Genesis, Exodus, Leviticus, Numbers, Deuteronomy.
• The Prophets: earlier prophets — Joshua, Judges, Samuel, Kings; later prophets — Isaiah, Jeremiah, Ezekiel, and 12 others in one book (Hosea, Joel, Amos, Obadiah, Jonah, Micah, Nahum, Habakkuk, Zephaniah, Haggai, Zechariah, Malachi).

• The Writings: Psalms, Job, Proverbs, Ruth, Song of Songs, Ecclesiastes, Lamentations, Esther, Daniel, Ezra-Nehemiah, Chronicles.

This canon does not include a number of books in the Alexandrian collection of sacred writings — viz., 1 and 2 Maccabees, Tobit, Judith, Sirach, Wisdom, Baruch, and portions of Esther and Daniel (chapters 13 and 14). These additional books and passages, contained in the Septuagint version of the Old Testament and called deuterocanonical, are in the Catholic canon.

These books and passages, called deuterocanonical in terminology coined by Sixtus of Siena (1520-1569), were under discussion for some time until questions about their canonicity were settled. Books admitted into the canon with little or no debate were called protocanonical. The canonical status of both categories of books is the same in the Catholic Bible.

The Protestant canon, in an arrangement of 39 books, is the same as the Hebrew canon.

The Old Testament canon has not been definitely settled by the Orthodox. Since the time of the Reformation, however, they have given some preference to the Protestant canon.

The New Testament canon was firm by the end of the fourth century. By the end of the second century all of the New Testament books were generally known and most of them were acknowledged as inspired. The Muratorian Fragment, dating from about 200, listed most of the books recognized in later decrees as canonical. Prior to the end of the fourth century, however, there were controversies over the inspired character of several books — viz., the Letter to the Hebrews, James, Jude, 2 Peter, 2 and 3 John, and Revelation. Controversy over these books ended in the fourth century, and the canon stated by the councils of Hippo and Carthage and reaffirmed by Innocent I in 405 was solemnly defined by the Council of Trent (1545-63).

Although Martin Luther eliminated the aforementioned books from his New Testament canon, they were reinstated by his followers by the year 1700. Anglicans and Calvinists always retained them.

The Greek and Russian Orthodox have the same New Testament canon as the Catholic Church. Some variations exist among other separated Eastern churches.

Languages of the Bible

Hebrew, Aramaic and Greek are the original languages of the Bible. Most of the Old Testament books were written in Hebrew. Portions of Daniel, Ezra, Jeremiah, Esther, and probably the books of Tobit and Judith were written in Aramaic. The Book of Wisdom, 2 Maccabees and all the books of the New Testament were written in Greek.

Manuscripts and Versions

The original writings of the inspired authors have been lost. The Bible has been transmitted through ancient copies called manuscripts and through translations or versions.

Authoritative Greek manuscripts include the Sinaitic and Vatican manuscripts of the fourth century and the Alexandrine and Parisian of the fifth century A. D.

The Septuagint and Vulgate translations are in a class by themselves.

The Septuagint version, a Greek translation of the Old Testament, was begun about 250 and completed about 100 B. C. The work of several Jewish translators at Alexandria, it differed from the Hebrew Bible in the arrangement of books and included several, later called deuterocanonical, which were not acknowledged as sacred by the community at Jerusalem.

The Vulgate was a Latin version of the Old and New Testaments produced from the original languages by St. Jerome from about 383 to 404. It became the most widely used Latin text for centuries and was regarded as basic long before the Council of Trent designated it as authentic and suitable for use in public reading, controversy, preaching and teaching. Because of its authoritative character, it became the basis for many translations into other languages.

Hebrew and Aramaic manuscripts of great antiquity and value have figured more significantly than before in recent scriptural work by Catholic scholars, especially since their use was strongly encouraged, if not mandated, in 1943 by Pius XII in the encyclical _Divino Afflante Spiritu._

The English translation of the Bible in general use among Catholics until recent years was the _Douay-Rheims,_ so called because of the places where it was prepared and published, the New Testament at Rheims in 1582 and the Old Testament at Douay in 1609. The translation was made from the Vulgate text. As revised and issued by Bishop Richard Challoner in 1749 and 1750, it became the standard Catholic English version for about 200 years.

A revision of the Challoner New Testament, made on the basis of the Vulgate text by scholars of the Catholic Biblical Association of America, was published in 1941 in the United States under the sponsorship of the Episcopal Committee of the Confraternity of Christian Doctrine.

New American Bible

A new translation of the entire Bible, the first ever made directly into English from the original languages under Catholic auspices, was projected in 1944 and completed in the fall of 1970 with publication of the _New American Bible._ The Episcopal Committee of the Confraternity of Christian Doctrine sponsored the NAB. The translators were members of the Catholic Biblical Association of America and several fellow scholars of other faiths. The typical edition was produced by St. Anthony Guild Press, Paterson, N. J.

Old Testament portions of the NAB were published in separate volumes before undergoing final revision and being bound in one cover. Genesis and Psalms were issued in 1948 and 1950; Genesis to Ruth, in 1952; Job to Sirach, in 1955; the Prophets, in 1961; Samuel to the Maccabees, in 1969. The new translation of the New Testament was issued for the first time in 1970.

Versions of the Bible approved for use in the Catholic liturgy are the _Douay-Rheims,_ the _New American Bible, A New Translation from the Latin Vulgate_ by Ronald A. Knox, the Catholic edition of the _Revised Standard Version,_ and the _Jerusalem Bible._

The _Jerusalem Bible_ is an English translation of a French version based on the original languages. It was published by Doubleday & Co., Inc., which is also working toward completion of the _Anchor Bible._

The Protestant counterpart of the _Douay-Rheims Bible_ was the _King James Bible,_ called the _Authorized Version_ in England. Originally published in 1611, it was in general use for more than three centuries. Its modern revisions include the _English Revised Version,_ published between 1881 and 1885; the _American Revised Version,_ 1901, and revisions of the New Testament (1946) and the Old Testament (1952) published in 1957 in the United States as the _Revised Standard Version._

The latest revision, a translation in the language of the present day made from Greek and Hebrew sources, is the _New English Bible,_ published Mar. 16, 1970. Its New Testament portion was originally published in 1961.

Biblical Federation

In November, 1966, Pope Paul commissioned the Secretariat for Promoting Christian Unity to start work for the widest possible distribution of the Bible and to coordinate endeavors toward the production of Catholic-Protestant Bibles in all languages.

The World Catholic Federation for the Biblical Apostolate, established in 1969, sponsors a program designed to create greater awareness among Catholics of the Bible and its use in everyday life. Cardinal Franz Koenig, president of the federation since its inception, agreed to serve in the post for another six years at a four-day plenary meeting of 20 delegates from member organizations early in May, 1972. The meeting was held in Vienna.

The U. S. Center for the Catholic Biblical Apostolate, under the direction of Father Stephen Hartdegen, O.F.M., is related to the Division of Religious Education, U. S. Catholic Conference. Address: 1312 Massachusetts Ave. N. W., Washington, D.C. 20005.

APOCRYPHA

Apocrypha are books which have some resemblance to the canonical books in subject matter and title but which have not been recognized as canonical by the Church. They are characterized by a false claim to divine authority; extravagant accounts of events and miracles alleged to be supplemental revelation; material favoring heresy (especially in "New Testament" apocrypha); minimal, if any, historical value.

Among examples of this type of literature itemized by J. McKenzie, S.J., in *Dictionary of the Bible* are: *the Books of Adam and Eve, Martyrdom of Isaiah, Testament of the Patriarchs, Assumption of Moses, Sibylline Oracles; Gospel of James, Gospel of Thomas, Arabic Gospel of the Infancy, History of Joseph the Carpenter; Acts of John, Acts of Paul, Acts of Peter, Acts of Andrew,* and numerous epistles.

Books of this type are called pseudepigrapha by Protestants. They regard the deuterocanonical books in the Catholic canon of Scripture as apocrypha.

DEAD SEA SCROLLS

The Qumran Scrolls, popularly called the Dead Sea Scrolls, are a collection of manuscripts, all but one of them in Hebrew, found between 1947 and 1956 in caves in the Desert of Juda west of the Dead Sea.

Among the findings were a complete text of Isaiah dating from the second century, B.C., more or less extensive fragments of other Old Testament texts (including the deuterocanonical Tobit), and a commentary on Habakkuk. Until the discovery of these materials, the oldest known Hebrew manuscripts were from the 10th century, A.D.

Also found were messianic and apocalyptic texts, and other writings describing the beliefs and practices of the Essenes, a rigoristic Jewish sect.

The scrolls, dating from about the first century before and after Christ, are important sources of information about Hebrew literature, Jewish history during the period between the Old and New Testaments, and the history of Old Testament texts. They established the fact that the Hebrew text of the Old Testament was fixed before the beginning of the Christian era and have had definite effects in recent critical studies and translations of the Old Testament. Together with other scrolls found at Masada, they are still the subject of intensive study.

A theory was proposed in 1972 by Father Jose O'Callaghan, a Spanish papyrologist, that a scrap of one of the scrolls might be a fragment of St. Mark's Gospel dating from about the year 50. Father Pierre Benoit, O. P., discounted the hypothesis, stating that it was based on an erroneous analysis of a photocopy of the scrap in question.

BOOKS OF THE BIBLE

Old Testament
(Dates are before Christ.)

Pentateuch

The Pentateuch is the collective title of the first five books of the Bible. Substantially, they identify the Israelites as Yahweh's Chosen People, cover their history from Egypt to the threshold of the Promised Land, contain the Mosaic Law and Covenant, and disclose the promise of salvation to come. Principal themes concern the divine promise of salvation, Yahweh's fidelity, and the Covenant. Work on the composition of the Pentateuch was completed in the sixth century.

Genesis: The book of origins, according to its title in the Septuagint. In two parts, covers: religious prehistory, including accounts of the origin of the world and man, the original state of innocence and the fall, the promise of salvation, patriarchs before and after the Deluge, the Tower of Babel narrative, genealogies (first 11 chapters); the covenant with Abraham and patriarchal history from Abraham to Joseph (balance of the 50 chapters). Significant are the themes of Yahweh's universal sovereignty and mercy.

Exodus: Named with the Greek word for departure, is a religious epic which describes the oppression of the 12 tribes in Egypt and their departure, liberation or passover therefrom under the leadership of Moses; Yahweh's establishment of the Covenant with them, making them his Chosen People, through the mediation of Moses at Mt. Sinai; instructions concerning the tabernacle, the sanctuary and Ark of the Covenant; the institution of the priesthood. The book is significant because of its theology of liberation and redemption. In Christian interpretation, the Exodus is a figure of baptism.

Leviticus: Mainly legislative in theme and purpose, contains laws regarding sacrifices, ceremonies of ordination and the priesthood of Aaron, legal purity, the holiness code, atonement, the redemption of offerings, and other subjects. Summarily, Levitical laws provided directives for all aspects of religious observance and for the manner in which the Israelites were to conduct themselves with respect to Yahweh and each other. Leviticus was the liturgical handbook of the priesthood.

Numbers: Taking its name from censuses recounted at the beginning and near the end, is a continuation of Exodus. It combines narrative of the Israelites' desert pilgrimage from Sinai to the border of Canaan with laws related to and expansive of those in Leviticus.

Deuteronomy: The concluding book of the Pentateuch, recapitulates, in the form of a testament of Moses, the Law and much of the desert history of the Israelites; enjoins fidelity to the Law as the key to good or bad fortune for the people; gives an account of the commissioning of Joshua as the successor of Moses. Notable themes concern the election of Israel by Yahweh, observance of the Law, prohibitions against the worship of foreign gods, worship of and confidence in Yahweh, the power of Yahweh in nature. The Deuteronomic Code or motif, embodying all of these elements, was the norm for interpreting Israelite history.

Joshua, Judges, Ruth

Joshua: Records the fulfillment of Yahweh's promise to the Israelites in their conquest, occupation and division of Canaan under the leadership of Joshua. It also contains an account of the return of Transjordanian Israelites and of a renewal of the Covenant. It was redacted in final form probably in the sixth century or later.

Judges: Records the actions of charismatic leaders, called judges, of the tribes of Israel between the death of Joshua and the time of Samuel, and a crisis of idolatry among the people. The basic themes are sin and punishment, repentance and deliverance; its purpose was in line with the Deuteronomic motif, that the fortunes of the Israelites were related to their observance or non-observance of the Law and the Covenant. It was redacted in final form probably in the sixth century.

Ruth: Named for the Gentile (Moabite) woman who, through marriage with Boaz, became an Israelite and an ancestress of David (her son, Obed, became his grandfather). Themes are filial piety, faith and trust in Yahweh, the universality of messianic salvation. Dates ranging from c. 950 to the seventh century have been assigned to the origin of the book, whose author is unknown.

Historical Books

These books, while they contain a great deal of factual material, are unique in their preoccupation with interpreting it, in the Deuteronomic manner, in primary relation to the Covenant on which the nation of Israel was founded and in accordance with which community and personal life were judged.

The books are: Samuel 1 and 2, from the end of Judges (c. 1020) to the end of David's reign (c. 961); Kings 1 and 2, from the last days of David to the start of the Babylonian Exile and the destruction of the Temple (587); Chronicles 1 and 2, from the reign of Saul (c. 1020-1000) to the return of the people from the Exile (538); Ezra and Nehemiah, covering the reorganization of the Jewish community after the Exile (458-397); Maccabees 1 and 2, recounting the struggle against attempted suppression of Judaism (168-142).

Three of the books listed below — Tobit, Judith and Esther — are categorized as religious novels.

Samuel 1 and 2: A single work in concept and contents, containing episodic history of the last two Judges, Eli and Samuel, the establishment and rule of the monarchy under Saul and David, and the political consequences of David's rule. The royal messianic dynasty of David was the subject of Nathan's Oracle in 2 Sm. 7. They were edited in final form probably late in the seventh century or during the Exile.

Kings 1 and 2: Cover the last days of David and the career of Solomon, including the building of the Temple and the history of the kingdom during his reign; stories of the prophets Elija and Elisha; the history of the divided kingdom to the fall of Israel in the North (721) and the fall of Judah in the South (587), the destruction of Jerusalem and the Temple. They reflect the Deuteronomic motif in attributing the downfall of the people to corruption of belief and practice in public and private life. They were completed probably in the sixth century.

Chronicles 1 and 2: A collection of historical traditions interpreted in such a way as to present an ideal picture of one people governed by divine law and united in one Temple worship of the one true God. Contents include genealogical tables from Adam to David, the careers of David and Solomon, coverage of the kingdom of Judah to the Exile, and the decree of Cyrus permitting the return of the people and rebuilding of Jerusalem. Both are related to and were written about 400 by the same author, the Chronicler, who composed Ezra and Nehemiah.

Ezra and Nehemiah: A running account of the return of the people to their homeland after the Exile and of practical efforts, under the leadership of Ezra and Nehemiah, to restore and reorganize the religious and political community on the basis of Israelite traditions, divine worship and observance of the Law. Events of great significance were the building of the second Temple, the building of a wall around Jerusalem, and the proclamation of the Law by Ezra. This restored community was the start of Judaism. Both are related to and were written about 400 by the same author, the Chronicler, who composed Chronicles 1 and 2.

Tobit: Written in the literary form of a novel and having greater resemblance to wisdom than to historical literature, narrates the personal history of Tobit, a devout and charitable Jew in exile, and persons connected with him, viz., his son Tobiah, his kinsman Raguel, and Raguel's daughter Sarah. Its purpose was to teach people how to be good Jews. One of its principal themes is patience under trial, with trust in divine Providence which is symbolized by the presence and action of the angel Raphael. It was written about 200.

Judith: Recounts, in the literary form of a historical novel or romance, the preservation of the Israelites from conquest and ruin through the action of Judith. The essential themes are trust in God for deliverance from danger and emphasis on observance of the Law. It was written probably during the Maccabean period.

Esther: Relates, in the literary form of a historical novel or romance, the manner in which Jews in Persia were saved from annihilation through the central role played by Esther, the Jewish wife of Ahasuerus; a fact commemorated by the Jewish feast of Purim. Like Judith, it has trust in divine Providence as its theme and indicates that God's saving will is sometimes realized by persons acting in unlikely ways. Its origin and date are uncertain; it may have been written about 200 near the beginning of the period of strong Hellenistic influence on the Jews.

Maccabees 1 and 2: While related to some extent because of common subject matter, are quite different from each other.

The first book recounts the background and events of the 40-year (175-135) struggle for religious and political freedom led by Judas Maccabeus and his brothers against the Hellenist Seleucid kings and some Hellenophiles among the Jews. Victory was symbolized by the rededication of the Temple. Against the background of opposition between Jews and Gentiles, the author equated the survival of belief in the one true God with survival of the Jewish people, thus identifying religion with patriotism. It was written probably by a Palestinian Jew after 104.

The second book supplements the first to some extent, covering and giving a theological interpretation to events from 180 to 162. It explains the feast of the Dedication of the Temple, a key event in the survival of Judaism which is commemorated in the feast of Hanukkah; stresses the primacy of God's action in the struggle for survival; and indicates belief in an afterlife and the resurrection of the body. It was written probably by a Jew of Alexandria after 120.

Wisdom Books

With the exceptions of Psalms and the Song of Songs, the titles listed under this heading are called wisdom books because their purpose was to formulate the fruits of human experience in the context of meditation on sacred Scripture and to present them as an aid toward understanding the problems of life. Hebrew wisdom literature was distinctive from pagan literature of the same type, but it had limitations; these were overcome in the New Testament, which added the dimensions of the New Covenant to those of the Old. Solomon was regarded as the archtype of the wise man.

Job: A dramatic, didactic poem consisting mainly of several dialogues between Job and his friends concerning the mystery involved in the coexistence of the just God, evil, and the suffering of the just. It describes an innocent man's experience of suffering and conveys the truth that faith in and submission to God rather than complete understanding, which is impossible, make the experience bearable; also, that the justice of God cannot be defended by affirming that it is realized in this world. Of uncertain authorship, it was written probably between the fifth and third centuries.

Psalms: A collection of 150 religious songs or lyrics reflecting Israelite belief and piety dating from the time of the monarchy to the post-Exilic period, a span of well over 500 years. The psalms, which are a compendium of Old Testament theology, were used in the temple liturgy and were of several types suitable for the king, hymns, lamentations, expressions of confidence and thanksgiving, prophecy, historical meditation and reflection, and the statement of wisdom. About one-half of them are attributed to David; many, by unknown authors, date from the early post-Exilic period.

Proverbs: The oldest book of the wisdom type in the Bible, consisting of collections of sayings attributed to Solomon and other persons regarding a wide variety of subjects including wisdom and its nature, rules of conduct, duties with respect to one's neighbor, the conduct of daily affairs. It reveals many details of Jewish life. Its nucleus dates from the period before the Exile, but no definite date can be assigned for its final compilation.

Ecclesiastes: A treatise about many subjects whose unifying theme is the vanity of strictly human efforts and accomplishments with respect to the achievement of lasting happiness; the only things which are not vain are fear of the Lord and observance of his commandments. The pessimistic tone of the book is due to the absence of a concept of afterlife. It was written by an unknown author about 250.

Song of Songs: A collection of erotic lyrics reflecting various themes, including the celebration of fidelity and love between man and woman. According to one interpretation, the book is a parable of the love of Yahweh for Israel. It was written by an unknown author after the Exile.

Wisdom: Deals with many subjects including the reward of justice; praise of wisdom, a gift of Yahweh proceeding from belief in him and the practice of his Law; the part played by him in the history of his people, especially in their liberation from Egypt; the folly and shame of idolatry. Its contents are taken from the whole sacred literature of the Jews and represent a distillation of its wisdom based on the law, beliefs and traditions of Israel. Contains the first Old Testament affirmation of an afterlife with God. The last book of the Old Testament to be written, it was probably composed about 50 years before Christ by an unknown author to confirm the faith of the Jewish community in Alexandria.

Sirach: Resembling Proverbs, is a collection of sayings handed on by a grandfather to his grandson. It contains a variety of moral instruction and eulogies of patriarchs and other figures in Israelite history. Its moral maxims apply to individuals, the family and community, relations with God, friendship, education, wealth, the Law, divine worship. Its theme is that true wisdom consists in the Law. (It was formerly called Ecclesiasticus, the Church Book, because of its extensive use by the Church for moral instruction.) It was written in Hebrew between 200 and 175, during a period of strong Hellenistic influence, and was translated into Greek after 132.

The Prophets

These books and the prophecies they contain "express judgments of the people's moral conduct, on the basis of the Mosaic alliance between God and Israel. They teach sublime truths and lofty morals. They contain exhortations, threats, announcements of punishment, promises of deliverance. . . . In the affairs of men, their prime concern is the interests of God, especially in what pertains to the Chosen People through whom the Messiah is to come; hence their denunciations of idolatry and of that externalism in worship which exclude the interior spirit of religion. They are concerned also with the universal nature of the moral law, with personal responsibility, with the person and office of the Messiah, and with the conduct of foreign nations" (*The Holy Bible*, Prophetic Books, CCD Edition, 1961; Preface). There are four major (Isaiah, Jeremiah, Ezekiel, Daniel) and 12 minor prophets (distinguished by the length of books), Lamentations and Baruch. Earlier prophets, mentioned in historical books, include Samuel, Gad, Nathan, Elijah and Elisha.

Before the Exile, prophets were the intermediaries through whom God communicated revelation to the people. Afterwards, prophecy lapsed and the written word of the Law served this purpose.

Isaiah: Named for the greatest of the prophets whose career spanned the reigns of three Hebrew kings from 742 to the beginning of the seventh century, in a period of moral breakdown in Judah and threats of invasion by foreign enemies. It is an anthology of poems and oracles credited to him and a number of followers deeply influenced by him. Of special importance are the prophecies concerning Immanuel (6 to 12), including the prophecy of the virgin birth (7:14). Chapters 40 to 55, called Deutero-Isaiah, are attributed to an anonymous poet toward the end of the Exile; this portion contains the Songs of the Servant. The concluding part of the book (56-66) contains oracles by later disciples. One of many themes in Isaiah concerned the saving mission of the remnant of Israel in the divine plan of salvation. It was edited in its present form by 180.

Jeremiah: Combines history, biography and prophecy in a setting of crisis caused by internal and external factors, viz., idolatry and general infidelity to the Law among the Israelites and external threats from the Assyrians, Egyptians and Babylonians. Jeremiah prophesied the promise of a new covenant as well as the destruction of Jerusalem and the Temple. His career began in 626 and ended some years after the beginning of the Exile. The book, the longest in the Bible, was edited in final form after the Exile.

Lamentations: A collection of five laments or elegies over the fall of Jerusalem and the fate of the people in Exile, written by an unknown eyewitness not long after 587. They convey the message that Yahweh struck the people because of their sins and reflect confidence in his love and power to restore his converted people.

Baruch: Against the background of the already begun Exile, it consists of an introduction and several parts: an exile's prayer of confession and petition for forgiveness and the restoration of Israel; a poem praising wisdom and the Law of Moses; a lament in which Jerusalem, personified, bewails the fate of her people and consoles them with the hope of blessings to come; and a polemic against idolatry. Although ascribed to Baruch, Jeremiah's secretary, it was written by several authors probably in the second century.

Ezekiel: Named for the priest-prophet who prophesied in Babylon from 593 to 571, during the first phase of the Exile. To prepare his fellow early exiles for the impending fall of Jerusalem, he reproached the Israelites for past sins and predicted woes to come upon them. After the destruction of the city, the burden of his message was hope and promise of restoration. Ezekiel had great influence on the religion of Israel after the Exile. The book, which contains the substance of his teaching, had a number of authors and editors.

Daniel: The protagonist is a fictional young Jew, taken early to Babylon where he lived until 537, who figured in a series of edifying stories. The stories, which originated from Israelite tradition, recount the trials and triumphs of Daniel and his three companions, and other episodes including those concerning Susannah, Bel, and the Dragon. The book is more apocalyptic than prophetic: it envisions Israel in glory to come and conveys the message that men of faith can resist temptation and overcome adversity. It states the prophetic themes of right conduct, divine control of men and events, and the final triumph of the kingdom. It was written by an unknown author in the 160's to give moral support to Jews during the persecutions of the Maccabean period.

Hosea: Consists of a prophetic parallel between Hosea's marriage and Yahweh's relations with his people. As the prophet was married to a faithless wife whom he would not give up, Yahweh was bound in Covenant with an idolatrous and unjust Israel whom he would not desert but would chastise for purification. Hosea belonged to the Northern Kingdom of Israel and began his career about the middle of the eighth century. He inaugurated the tradition of describing Yahweh's relation to Israel in terms of marriage.

Joel: Is apocalyptic and eschatological regarding divine judgment, the Day of the Lord, which is symbolized by a ravaging invasion of locusts, the judgment of the nations in the Valley of Josaphat, and the outpouring of the Spirit in the messianic era to come. Its message is that God will vindicate and save Israel, in view of the prayer and repentance of the people, and will punish their enemies. It was composed after the period of Nehemiah.

Amos: Consists of an indictment against foreign enemies of Israel; a strong denunciation of the people of Israel, whose infidelity, idolatry and injustice made them subject to divine judgment and punishment; and a messianic oracle regarding Israel's restoration. Amos prophesied in the Northern Kingdom of Israel, at Bethel, in the first half of the eighth century; chronologically, he was the first of the canonical prophets.

Obadiah: A 21-verse prophecy, the shortest and one of the sternest in the Bible, against the Edomites, invaders of southern Judah and enemies of those returning from the Exile to their homeland. It was redacted in final form no later than the end of the fourth century.

Jonah: A parable of divine mercy with the theme that Yahweh wills the salvation of all, not just a few, men who respond to his call. Its protagonist is a disobedient prophet; forced by circumstances beyond his control to preach penance among Gentiles, he is highly successful in his mission but baffled by the divine concern for those who do not belong to the Chosen People. It was written after the Exile.

Micah: Attacks the injustice and corruption of priests, false prophets, officials and people; announces judgment and punishment to come; foretells the restoration of Israel; refers to the saving remnant of Israel. Micah was a contemporary of Isaiah.

Nahum: Dating from about 613, concerns the destruction of Nineveh in 612 and the overthrow of the Assyrian Empire by the Babylonians.

Habakkuk: Dating from about 605-597, concerns sufferings to be inflicted by oppressors on the people of Judah because of their infidelity to the Lord. It also sounds a note of confidence in the Lord, the Savior, and declares that the just will not perish.

Zephaniah: Exercising his ministry in the second half of the seventh century, during a time of widespread idolatry, superstition and religious degradation, he prophesied impending judgment and punishment for Jerusalem and its people. He prophesied too that a holy remnant of the people (Anawim, mentioned also by Amos) would be spared. Zephaniah was a forerunner of Jeremiah.

Haggai: One of the first prophets after the Exile, Haggai in 520 encouraged the returning exiles to reestablish their community and to complete the second Temple (dedicated in 515), for which he envisioned greater glory, in a messianic sense, than that enjoyed by the original Temple of Solomon.

Zechariah: A contemporary of Haggai, he prophesied in the same vein. A second part of the book, called Deutero-Zechariah and composed by one or more unknown authors, relates a vision of the coming of the Prince of Peace, the Messiah of the Poor.

Malachi: Written by an anonymous author, presents a picture of life in the post-Exilic community between 516 and the initiation of reforms by Ezra and Nehemiah about 432. Blame for the troubles of the community is placed mainly on priests for failure to carry out ritual worship and to instruct the people in the proper manner; other factors were religious indifference and the influence of doubters who were scandalized at the prosperity of the wicked. The vision of a universal sacrifice to be offered to Yahweh (1:11) is interpreted in Christian theology as a prophecy of the sacrifice of the Mass. Malachi was the last of the minor prophets.

OLD TESTAMENT DATES

c. 1800 — c. 1600: Period of the patriarchs (Abraham, Isaac, Jacob).
c. 1600: Israelites in Egypt.
c. 1250: Exodus of Israelites from Egypt.
c. 1210: Entrance of Israelites into Canaan.
c. 1210 — c. 1020: Period of the Judges.
c. 1020 — c. 1000: Reign of Saul, first king.
c. 1000 — c. 961: Reign of David.
c. 961 — 922: Reign of Solomon. Temple built during his reign.
922: Division of the Kingdom into Israel (North) and Judah (South).
721: Conquest of Israel by Assyrians.
587-538: Conquest of Judah by Babylonians. Babylonian Captivity and Exile. Destruction of Jerusalem and the Temple, 587. Captivity ended with the return of exiles, following the decree of Cyrus permitting the rebuilding of Jerusalem.
515: Dedication of the Second Temple.
458-397: Restoration and reform of the Jewish religious and political community; building of the Jerusalem wall, 439. Leaders in the movement were Ezra and Nehemiah.
168-142: Period of the Maccabees; war against Syrians.
142: Independence granted to Jews by Demetrius II of Syria.
135-37: Period of the Hasmonean dynasty.
63: Beginning of Roman rule.
37-4: Period of Herod the Great.

New Testament Books

Gospels

The term Gospel is derived from the Anglo-Saxon *god-spell* and the Greek *euangelion,* meaning good news, good tidings. In Christian use, it means the good news of salvation proclaimed by Christ and the Church, and handed on in written form in the Gospels of Matthew, Mark, Luke and John.

The initial proclamation of the coming of the kingdom of God was made by Jesus in and through his Person, teachings and actions, and especially through his Passion, death and resurrection. This proclamation became the center of Christian faith and the core of the oral Gospel tradition with which the Church spread the good news by apostolic preaching over some 30 years before it was committed to writing by the Evangelists.

According to an Instruction issued by the Pontifical Commission for Biblical Studies Apr. 21, 1964:

• The sacred writers selected from the material at their disposal (the oral Gospel tradition, some written collections of sayings and deeds of Jesus, eyewitness accounts) those things which were particularly suitable to the various conditions (liturgical, catechetical, missionary) of the faithful and the aims they had in mind, and they narrated these things in such a way as to correspond with those circumstances and their aims.

• The life and teaching of Jesus were not simply reported in a biographical manner for the purpose of preserving their memory but were "preached" so as to offer the Church the basis of doctrine concerning faith and morals.

• In their works, the Evangelists presented the true sayings of Jesus and the events of his life in the light of the better understanding they had following their enlightenment by the Holy Spirit. They did not transform Christ into a "mythical" Person, nor did they distort his teaching.

Passion narratives are the core of all the Gospels, covering the suffering, death and resurrection of Jesus as central events in bringing about and establishing the New Covenant. Leading up to them are accounts of the mission of John the Baptizer and the ministry of Jesus, especially in Galilee and finally in Jerusalem before the Passion. The infancy of Jesus is covered by Luke and Matthew with narratives inspired by Old Testament citations appropriate to the birth of the Messiah.

Matthew, Mark and Luke, while different in various respects, have so many similarities that they are called Synoptic; their relationships are the subject of the Synoptic Problem.

Matthew: Written in the 70's or 80's for Jewish Christians, with clear reference to Jewish background and identification of Jesus as the divine Messiah, the fulfillment of the Old Testament. Distinctive are the use of Old Testament citations regarding the Person, activity and teaching of Jesus, and the presentation of doctrine in sermons and discourses. The canonical Matthew was written in Greek, with dependence on Mark.

Mark: The first of the Gospels, dating from about 65. Written for Gentile Christians, it is noted for the realism and wealth of concrete details with which it reveals Jesus as Son of God and Savior more by his actions and miracles than by his discourses. Theologically, it is less refined than the other Gospels.

Luke: Written in the 70's or 80's for Gentile Christians. It is noted for the universality of its address, the insight it provides into the Christian way of life, the place it gives to women, the manner in which it emphasizes Jesus' friendship with sinners and compassion for the suffering.

John: Written sometime in the 90's, is the most sublime and theological of the Gospels, and is different from the Synoptics in plan and treatment. Combining accounts of signs with longer discourses and reflections, it progressively reveals the Person and mission of Jesus — as Word, Way, Truth, Life, Light — in line with the purpose, "to help you believe that Jesus is the Messiah, the Son of God, so that through this faith you may have life in his name" (Jn. 20:31). There are questions about the authorship but no doubt about the Johannine tradition behind the Gospel.

Acts of the Apostles

Acts of the Apostles: Written by Luke in the 70's or 80's as a supplement to his Gospel. It describes the origin and spread of Christian communities through the action of the Holy Spirit from the resurrection of Christ to the time of Paul's first Roman imprisonment.

Letters (Epistles)

These letters, the first documents of the New Testament, were written in response to existential needs of the early Christian communities for doctrinal and moral instruction, disciplinary action, practical advice, and exhortation to true Christian living.

Pauline Letters

These letters, which comprise approximately one-fourth of the New Testament, are primary and monumental sources of the development of Christian theology. Several of them may not have had Paul as their actual author, but evidence of the Pauline tradition behind them is strong. The letters to the Colossians, Philippians, Ephesians and Philemon have been called the "Captivity Letters" because of a tradition that they were written while Paul was under house arrest in Rome from 61 to 63.

Romans: Written in the late 50's from

Corinth on the central significance of Christ and faith in him for salvation, and the relationship of Christianity to Judaism; the condition of mankind without Christ; justification and the Christian life; duties of Christians.

Corinthians 1: Written near the beginning of 57 from Ephesus to counteract factionalism and disorders, it covers community dissensions, moral irregularities, marriage and celibacy, conduct at religious gatherings, the Eucharist, spiritual gifts (charisms) and their function in the Church, charity, the resurrection of the body.

Corinthians 2: Written later in the same year as 1 Cor., concerning Paul's defense of his apostolic life and ministry, and an appeal for a collection to aid poor Christians in Jerusalem.

Galatians: Written probably between 54 and 57 (perhaps earlier, according to some scholars) to counteract Judaizing opinions and efforts to undermine his authority, it asserts the divine origin of Paul's authority and doctrine, states that justification is not through Mosaic Law but through faith in Christ, insists on the practice of evangelical virtues, especially charity.

Ephesians: Written probably between 61 and 63, or perhaps in the 70's, mainly on the Church as the Mystical Body of Christ.

Philippians: Written between 61 and 63 primarily to thank the Philippians for their kindness to him while he was under house arrest in Rome.

Colossians: Written while he was under house arrest in Rome from 61 to 63 to counteract the influence of self-appointed teachers who were watering down doctrine concerning Christ. It includes two highly important Christological passages, a warning against false teachers, and an instruction on the ideal Christian life.

Thessalonians 1 and 2: Written within a short time of each other probably in 51 from Corinth, mainly on doctrine concerning the Parousia, the second coming of Christ.

Timothy 1 and 2, Titus: Written between 65 and 67, or perhaps in the 70's, giving pastoral counsels to Timothy and Titus who were in charge of churches in Ephesus and Crete, respectively. 1 Tm. emphasizes pastoral responsibility for preserving unity of doctrine; 2 Tm. describes Paul's imprisonment in Rome.

Philemon: A private letter written between 61 and 63 to a wealthy Colossian concerning a slave, Onesimus, who had escaped from him; Paul appealed for kind treatment of the man.

Hebrews: Dating from some time between the mid-60's and the 80's, a complex theological treatise on Christology, the priesthood and sacrifice of Christ, the New Covenant, and the pattern for Christian living. Critical opinion is divided as to whether it was addressed to Judaeo or Gentile Christians.

Catholic Letters, Revelation

These seven letters have been called "catholic" because it was thought for some time, not altogether correctly, that they were not addressed to particular communities.

James: Written sometime between the mid-60's and the 80's (although datable before 62 according to some scholars) in the spirit of Hebrew wisdom literature and the moralism of Tobit. An exhortation to practical Christian living, it is also noteworthy for the doctrine it states on good works and its citation regarding anointing of the sick.

Peter 1 and 2: The first letter may have been written in the mid-60's; the second dates from 100 to 125. Addressed to Christians in Asia Minor, both are exhortations to perseverance in the life of faith despite trials and difficulties arising from pagan influences, isolation from other Christians, and false teaching.

John 1: Written sometime in the 90's and addressed to Asian churches, its message is that God is made known to us in the Son and that fellowship with the Father is attained by living in the light, justice and love of the Son.

John 2: Written sometime in the 90's and addressed to a church in Asia, it commends the people for standing firm in the faith and urges them to perseverance.

John 3: Written sometime in the 90's, it appears to represent an effort to settle a jurisdictional dispute in one of the churches.

Jude: Written sometime between the 70's and 90's, it is a brief treatise against erroneous teachings and practices opposed to law, authority and true Christian freedom.

Revelation: Written in the 90's along the lines of Johannine thought, it is a symbolic and apocalyptic treatment of things to come combined with warning but hope and assurance to the Church regarding the coming of the Lord in glory.

BIBLICAL AUTHORSHIP

Some books of the Bible were not written by the authors to whom they have been traditionally attributed; New Testament examples are the Gospels of Matthew and John, Hebrews, 1 and 2 Timothy, Titus, James, Jude.

This fact, which has never been the subject of dogmatic definition by the Church, does not militate against the canonicity of the books, since canonicity concerns the theological matter of inspiration rather than the historical question of human authorship.

Questions concerning authorship are explained in various ways: (1) according to an old custom whereby literary works of importance were sometimes attributed to famous persons so they would get a reading; (2) authorship, by a disciple or school of disciples, of works derived from the doctrine of a master; (3) authorship by persons writing in the spirit and tradition of a master.

GOSPEL PASSAGES

Discourses

The Sermon on the Mount is probably the best known of the many Gospel discourses.

Vindication of his authority (Jn. 2:18-22).

Spiritual rebirth, origin of his teaching, purpose of his coming, judgment on unbelievers; with Nicodemus (Jn. 3:1-21).

Of himself, his mission, everlasting life through him; with a Samaritan woman (Jn. 4:7-30).

Defense of his disciples for not fasting, for plucking corn on the Sabbath (Mt. 9:14-17, 12:1-8; Mk. 2:18-28; Lk. 5:33-39, 6:1-5).

Defense of himself for healing a man with a withered hand on the Sabbath (Mt. 12:9-13; Mk. 3:15; Lk. 6:6-10).

Sermon on the Mount (Mt. 5:1 to 7:29; Lk. 6:20-49).

Testimony concerning John the Baptist (Mt. 11:17-19; Lk. 7:24-35, 16:16).

Instructions for the apostolate (Mt. 10: 5-42; Mk. 6:8-13; Lk. 9:3-6, 10:1-12).

The bread of life (Jn. 6:22-72).

Defense of his claim to divinity (Jn. 5:19-47).

Defense of his disciples against Pharisees (Mt. 15:1-20; Mk. 7:1-23).

Promise of primacy to Peter (Mt. 16:13-20).

Predictions of the Passion and Resurrection (Mt. 16:21-23, 17:21-22, 20:17-19; Mk. 8:31-33, 9:29-31, 10:32-34; Lk. 9:22, 9:44-45, 18:31-34).

Doctrine of the cross (Mt. 16:24-28; Mk. 8:34-39; Lk. 9:23-27).

Scandal (Mt. 18:5-9; Mk. 9:41-49; Lk. 17:1-2).

Fraternal correction (Mt. 18:15-17, 21-22; Lk. 17:3-4).

Conversation with Martha and Mary (Lk. 10:38-42).

The adulteress (Jn. 8:3-11).

Efficacy of prayer (Mt. 7:7-11; Lk. 11:9-13).

Defense of his authority (Mt. 21:23-27; Mk. 11:27-33; Lk. 20:1-8).

Tribute to Caesar (Mt. 22:15-22; Mk. 12:13-17; Lk. 20:20-26).

The great commandment (Mt. 23:34-40; Mk. 12:28-34).

Destruction of Jerusalem and the Temple (Mt. 24:1-3, 15-22, 32-35; Mk. 13:1-20, 28-31; Lk. 21:5-6, 20-24, 29-33).

End of the world and coming of the Son of Man (Mt. 24:4-14, 23-31, 36-51 to 25:1-3; Mk. 13:21-27, 32-37; Lk. 21:7-19, 25-28, 34-36).

Last judgment (Mt. 25:31-46).

Discourses at the Last Supper (Mt. 26:20-29; Mk. 14:17-25; Lk. 22:14-38; Jn. 13:2 to 17:26).

Conferring of primacy on Peter (Jn. 21:15-17).

Commission of the Apostles to teach and baptize (Mt. 28:16-20; Mk. 16:15-18).

Parables

Essential to understanding a parable is identification of its points of reference and application to life.

The sower (Mt. 13:1-23; Mk. 4:1-20; Lk. 8:4-15).

The weeds (Mt. 13:24-30, 36-43).

The mustard seed (Mt. 13:31-32; Mk. 4:30-32; Lk. 13:18-19).

The leaven (Mt. 13:33; Lk. 12:20-21).

The treasure (Mt. 13:44).

The pearl (Mt. 13:45-46).

The net (Mt. 13:47-50).

The seed (Mk. 4:26-29).

The house built on rock (Mt. 7:24-27; Lk. 6:47-49).

The two debtors (Lk. 7:41-48).

The unmerciful servant (Mt. 18:21-35).

The good Samaritan (Lk. 10:25-37).

The importunate friend (Lk. 11:5-8).

The rich fool (Lk. 12:16-21).

A barren fig tree (Lk. 13:6-9).

The last seat (Lk. 14:7-11).

The lost sheep (Mt. 18:10-14; Lk. 15:1-7).

The lost coin (Lk. 15:8-10).

The prodigal son (Lk. 15:11-32).

The unjust steward (Lk. 16:1-13).

The rich man (Dives) and Lazarus (Lk. 16:19-31).

The godless judge (Lk. 18:1-8).

The Pharisee and the tax collector. (Lk. 18:9-14).

The laborers in the vineyard (Mt. 20:1-16).

The gold pieces (Lk. 19:11-27).

The two sons (Mt. 21:28-32).

The vine-dressers (Mt. 21:33-46; Mk. 12:1-12; Lk. 20:9-19).

The marriage feast (Mt. 22:1-10; Lk. 14:7-24).

The wedding garment (Mt. 22:11-14).

The great supper (Lk. 14:15-24).

The ten virgins (Mt. 25:1-13).

The talents (Mt. 25:14-30).

Similitudes and Allegories

"Physician, cure yourself" (Lk. 4:23).

The savor of salt (Mt. 5:13; Mk. 9:49; Lk. 14:34-35).

The lamp under a bushel basket (Mt. 5:14-15; Mk. 4:21; Lk. 8:16-18, 11:33-36).

The city on a mountain (Mt. 5:14).

The opponent (Mt. 5:25-26; Lk. 12:58-59).

The lamp of the body (Mt. 6:22-23; Lk. 11:33-36).

The two masters (Mt. 6:24; Lk. 16:13).

A son's request (Mt. 7:9-11; Lk. 11:11-13).

The tree and its fruit (Mt. 7:15-20, 12:33-37; Lk. 6:43-45).

The physician and the sick (Mt. 9:12-13; Mk. 2:17; Lk. 5:31-32).

The bridegroom and the wedding guests (Mt. 9:14-15; Mk. 2:18-20; Lk. 5:33-35).

A patch of raw cloth on an old garment (Mt. 9:16; Mk. 2:21; Lk. 5:36).

New wine in old wineskins (Mt. 9:17; Mk. 2:22; Lk. 5:37-38).

Secrets to be uncovered (Mt. 10:26-27; Mk. 4:22; Lk. 8:17, 12:2-3).

The servant not above the master (Mt. 10:24-25; Lk. 6:40).

The stubborn children (Mt. 11:16-19; Lk. 7:31-35).

The divided kingdom (Mt. 12:25-26; Mk. 3:23-26; Lk. 11:17-18).

The unclean spirit (Mt. 12:43-45; Lk. 11:24-26).

The wise scribe (Mt. 13:52).

The defilement of man (Mt. 15:10-20; Mk. 7:14-23).

Blind guides of blind men (Lk. 6:39; Mt. 15:14).

The children's bread (Mt. 15:26-27; Mk. 7:27-28).

Building a tower (Lk. 14:28-30).

Preparation for war (Lk. 14:31-33).

The watchful servants (Lk. 12:35-38; Mk. 13:34).

Faithful and unfaithful servants (Mt. 24:45-51; Lk. 12:42-48).

The unprofitable servant (Lk. 17:7-10).

The body and the vultures (Mt. 24:28; Lk. 17:37).

The thief (Mt. 24:43-44; Lk. 12:39-40).

The fig tree and the branches (Mt. 24:32-33; Mk. 13:28-29; Lk. 21:29-31).

The good Shepherd (Jn. 10:1-18).

The vine and the branches (Jn. 15:1-17).

Miracles

Changing of water into wine at the marriage feast (Jn. 2:1-11).

Cure of an official's son (Jn. 4:46-54).

Miraculous draft of fishes (Lk. 5:1-11).

The cure of a man possessed by the devil (Mk. 1:23-28; Lk, 4:33-37).

Cure of the fever of Peter's mother-in-law (Mt. 8:14-15; Mk. 1:29-31; Lk. 4:38-39).

Healing of many sick and diseased (Mt. 8:16-17; Mk. 1:32-34; Lk. 4:40-41).

Cure of a leper (Mt. 8:1-4; Mk. 1:40-45; Lk. 5:12-14).

Christ escapes from a mob (Lk. 4:28-30).

Cure of a paralytic (Mt. 9:1-8; Mk. 2:1-12; Lk. 5:18-26).

Cure of a sick man (Jn. 5:1-9).

Cure of a man with a withered hand (Mt. 12:9-13; Mk. 3:1-5; Lk. 6:6-10).

Healing of many sick and diseased (Lk. 6:18-19).

Cure of a centurion's servant (Mt. 8:5-13; Lk. 7:1-10).

Raising to life of a widow's son (Lk. 7:11-17).

Cure of a blind and mute possessed man (Mt. 12:22-37).

Calming of a storm (Mt. 8:23-27; Mk. 4:36-40; Lk. 8:22-25).

Exorcism of unclean spirits (Mt. 8:28-34; Mk. 5:1-15; Lk. 8:26-35).

Cure of a woman with a hemorrhage (Mt. 9:20-22; Mk. 5:25-34; Lk. 8:43-48).

Raising to life of Jairus' daughter (Mt. 9:18-19, 23-26; Mk. 5:20-24, 35-43; Lk. 8:41-42, 49-56).

Cure of two blind men (Mt. 9:27-31).

Exorcism of a mute possessed man (Mt. 9:32-34).

Feeding of over 5,000 with five loaves and two fishes (Mt. 14:13-21; Mk. 6:31-44; Lk. 9:12-17; Jn. 6:1-15).

Walking on the water (Mt. 14:22-33; Mk. 6:45-52; Jn. 6:16-21).

The exorcism of a Canaanite woman's daughter (Mt. 15:21-28; Mk. 7:24-30).

Cure of a deaf mute (Mk. 7:31-37).

Healing of many sick (Mt. 15:29-31).

Feeding of about 4,000 with seven loaves and a few fishes (Mt. 15:32-38; Mk. 8:1-9).

Cure of a blind man (Mk. 8:22-26).

Transfiguration (Mt. 17:1-9; Mk. 9:1-8; Lk. 9:28-36).

Exorcism of a possessed boy (Mt. 17:14-20; Mk. 9:13-28; Lk. 9:37-43).

Temple tax (Mt. 17:23-26).

Escape from his enemies (Jn. 8:59).

Cure of a man born blind (Jn. 9:1-41).

Exorcism of a possessed man (Lk. 11:14-26).

Cure of a crippled woman (Lk. 13:10-17).

Cure of a man afflicted with dropsy (Lk. 14:1-6).

Cure of 10 lepers (Lk. 17:12-19).

Raising of Lazarus to life (Jn. 11:1-44).

Cure of Bartimeus and another blind beggar (Mt. 20:29-34; Mk. 10:46-52; Lk. 18:35-43).

Withering of a barren fig tree (Mt. 21:18-19; Mk. 11:12-14).

Cure of many sick (Mt. 21:14).

Healing of a soldier's ear in the Garden (Mt. 26:51-52; Mk. 14:47; Lk. 22:49-51; Jn. 18:10-11).

Resurrection (Mt. 28:1-10; Mk. 16:1-14; Lk. 24:1-43; Jn. 20:1-20).

Miraculous draft of fishes after the Resurrection (Jn. 21:1-14).

The Ascension (Mk. 16:19; Lk. 24:50-51).

THE FIFTH GOSPEL

Gino Concetti, writing in the Mar. 21, 1974, English edition of *L'Osservatore Romano,* said:

"The geographical and historical setting of Palestine bears a quite special witness (to Christ). It has been said that the Holy Land is itself a gospel, the fifth gospel. The judgment is not an exaggerated one. Everything in Palestine speaks of Christ, his announcement by the prophets, his birth, his life, his miracles, his passion, his death and his resurrection. Those places that Christians have venerated, since the beginning, as sacred because sanctified by the Savior, are still able today, 2,000 years later, to re-echo his voice and his message. . . .

"The Holy Land, like the Bible, is a patrimony of faith. . . . Direct knowledge of the theatre of the history of salvation will strengthen faith in Christ and facilitate the reunification of peoples."

INTERPRETATION OF THE BIBLE

According to the *Constitution on Revelation* issued by the Second Vatican Council, "the interpreter of Sacred Scripture, in order to see clearly what God wanted to communicate to us, should carefully investigate what meaning the sacred writers really intended, and what God wanted to manifest by means of their words" (No. 12).

Hermeneutics, Exegesis

This careful investigation proceeds in accordance with the rules of hermeneutics, the normative science of biblical interpretation and explanation. Hermeneutics in practice is called exegesis.

The principles of hermeneutics are derived from various disciplines and many factors which have to be considered in explaining the Bible and its parts. These include: the original languages and languages of translation of the sacred texts, through philology and linguistics; the quality of texts, through textual criticism; literary forms and genres, through literary and form criticism; cultural, historical, geographical and other conditions which influenced the writers, through related studies; facts and truths of salvation history; the truths and analogy of faith.

Distinctive to biblical hermeneutics, which differs in important respects from literary interpretation in general, is the premise that the Bible, though written by human authors, is the work of divine inspiration in which God reveals his plan for the salvation of men through historical events and persons, and especially through the Person and mission of Christ.

Textual, Form Criticism

Textual criticism is the study of biblical texts, which have been transmitted in copies several times removed from the original manuscripts, for the purpose of establishing the real state of the original texts. This purpose is served by comparison of existing copies; by application to the texts of the disciplines of philology and linguistics; by examination of related works of antiquity; by study of biblical citations in works of the Fathers of the Church and other authors; and by other means of literary study.

Since about 1920, the sayings of Christ have been a particular object of New Testament study, the purpose being to analyze the forms of expression used by the Evangelists in order to ascertain the words actually spoken by him.

Literary Criticism

Literary criticism aims to determine the origin and kinds of literary composition, called forms or genres, employed by the inspired authors. Such determinations are necessary for decision regarding the nature and purpose and, consequently, the meaning of biblical passages. Underlying these studies is the principle that the manner of writing was conditioned by the intention of the authors, the meaning they wanted to convey, and the then-contemporary literary style, mode or medium best adapted to carry their message — e.g., true history, quasi-historical narrative, poems, prayers, hymns, psalms, aphorisms, allegories, discourses. Understanding these media is necessary for the valid interpretation of their message.

Literal Sense

The key to all valid interpretation is the literal sense of biblical passages. Regarding this matter and the relevance to it of the studies and procedures described above, Pius XII wrote the following in the encyclical *Divino Afflante Spiritu.*

"What the literal sense of a passage is, is not always as obvious in the speeches and writings of ancient authors of the East as it is in the works of our own time. For what they wished to express is not to be determined by the rules of grammar and philology alone nor solely by the context; the interpreter must, as it were, go back wholly in spirit to those remote centuries of the East and with the aid of history, archeology, ethnology, and other sciences accurately determine what modes of writing, so to speak, the authors of that ancient period would be likely to use and in fact did use. . . . In explaining the Sacred Scripture and in demonstrating and proving its immunity from all error (the Catholic interpreter) should make a prudent use of this means, determine to what extent the manner of expression or literary mode adopted by the sacred writer may lead to a correct and genuine interpretation; and let him be convinced that this part of his office cannot be neglected without serious detriment to Catholic exegesis."

The literal sense of the Bible is the meaning in the mind of and intended by the inspired writer of a book or passage of the Bible. This is determined by the application to texts of the rules of hermeneutics. It is not to be confused with word-for-word literalism.

Typical Sense

The typical sense is the meaning which a passage has not only in itself but also in reference to something else of which it is a type or foreshadowing. A clear example is the account of the Exodus of the Israelites: in its literal sense, it narrates the liberation of the Israelites from death and oppression in Egypt; in its typical sense, it foreshadowed the liberation of men from sin through the redemptive death and resurrection of Christ. The typical sense of this and other passages emerged in the working out of God's plan of salvation history. It did not have to be in the mind of the author of the original passage.

Accommodated Senses

Accommodated, allegorical and consequent senses are figurative and adaptive meanings given to books and passages of the Bible for moral and other purposes. Such interpretations involve the danger of stretching the literal sense beyond proper proportions. Hermeneutical principles require that interpretations like these respect the integrity of the literal sense of the passages in question.

In the Catholic view, the final word on questions of biblical interpretation belongs to the teaching authority of the Church. In other views, generally derived from basic principles stated by Martin Luther, John Calvin and other Reformers, the primacy belongs to individual judgment acting in response to the inner testimony of the Holy Spirit, the edifying nature of biblical subject matter, the sublimity and simplicity of the message of salvation, the intensity with which Christ is proclaimed.

Biblical Studies

The first center for biblical studies, in some strict sense of the term, was the School of Alexandria, founded in the latter half of the second century. It was noted for allegorical exegesis. Literal interpretation was a hallmark of the School of Antioch.

St. Jerome, who produced the Vulgate, and St. Augustine, author of numerous commentaries, were the most important figures in biblical studies during the patristic period. By the time of the latter's death, the Old and New Testament canons had been stabilized. For some centuries afterwards, there was little or no progress in scriptural studies, although collections were made of scriptural excerpts from the writings of the Fathers of the Church, and the systematic reading of Scripture became established as a feature of monastic life.

Advances were made in the 12th and 13th centuries with the introduction of new principles and methods of scriptural analysis stemming from renewed interest in Hebraic studies and the application of dialectics.

By the time of the Reformation, the Bible had become the first book set in movable type, and more than 100 vernacular editions were in use throughout Europe.

The Council of Trent

In the wake of the Reformation, the Council of Trent formally defined the Canon of the Bible; it also reasserted the authoritative role of tradition and the teaching authority of the Church as well as Scripture with respect to the rule of faith. In the heated atmosphere of the 16th and 17th centuries, the Bible was turned into a polemical weapon; Protestants used it to defend their doctrines, and Catholics countered with citations in support of the dogmas of the Church. One result of this state of affairs was a lack of substantial progress in biblical studies during the period.

Toward the end of the 17th century, Louis Cappel, a Protestant, introduced a methodology for textual criticism, and Richard Simon, a Catholic, inaugurated modern literary and historical criticism. Their work was poorly regarded, however, and went into eclipse until about the beginning of the 19th century. It was then taken over by men whose work threatened to destroy the credibility of not only the Bible but Christianity itself.

Rationalists, and later Modernists, denied the reality of the supernatural and doctrine concerning inspiration of the Bible, which they generally regarded as a strictly human production expressive of the religious sense and experience of mankind. In their hands, the tools of positive critical research became weapons for biblical subversion. The defensive Catholic reaction to their work had the temporary effect of alienating scholars of the Church from solid advances in archeology, philology, history, textual and literary criticism.

Catholic Developments

Major influences in bringing about a change in Catholic attitude toward use of these disciplines in biblical studies were two papal encyclicals and two institutes of special study, the Ecole Biblique, founded in Jerusalem in 1890, and the Pontifical Biblical Institute established in Rome in 1909. The encyclical *Providentissimus Deus,* issued by Leo XIII in 1893, marked an important breakthrough; in addition to defending the concept of divine inspiration and the formal inspiration of the Scriptures, it encouraged the study of allied and ancillary sciences and techniques for a more fruitful understanding of the sacred writings. The encyclical *Divino Afflante Spiritu,* 50 years later, gave encouragement for the use of various forms of criticism as tools of biblical research. The documents encouraged the work of scholars and stimulated wide communication of the fruits of their study.

Great changes in the climate and direction of biblical studies have occurred in recent years. One of them has been an increase in cooperative effort among Catholic, Protestant, Orthodox and Jewish scholars. Their common investigation of the Dead Sea Scrolls is well known. More recently productive was the collaboration in England of Catholics and Protestants in turning out a Catholic edition of the Revised Standard Version of the Bible.

The development and results of biblical studies in this century have directly and significantly affected all phases of the contemporary renewal movement in the Church. Their influence on theology, liturgy, catechetics, and preaching indicate the importance of their function in the life of the Church.

APOSTLES AND EVANGELISTS

The Apostles were the men selected, trained and commissioned by Christ to preach the Gospel, to baptize, to establish, direct and care for his Church as servants of God and stewards of his mysteries. They were the first bishops of the Church.

St. Matthew's Gospel lists the Apostles in this order: Peter, Andrew, James the Greater, John, Philip, Bartholomew, Thomas, Matthew, James the Less, Jude, Simon and Judas Iscariot. Matthias was elected to fill the place of Judas. Paul became an Apostle by a special call from Christ. Barnabas was called an Apostle.

Two of the Evangelists, John and Matthew, were Apostles. The other two, Luke and Mark, were closely associated with the apostolic college.

Andrew: Born in Bethsaida, brother of Peter, disciple of John the Baptist, a fisherman, the first Apostle called; according to legend, preached the Gospel in Northern Greece, Epirus and Scythia, and was martyred at Patras about 70; in art, is represented with an x-shaped cross, called St. Andrew's Cross; feast, Nov. 30; is honored as the patron of Russia and Scotland.

Barnabas: Originally called Joseph but named Barnabas by the Apostles, among whom he is ranked because of his collaboration with Paul; a Jew of the Diaspora, born on Cyprus; a cousin of Mark and member of the Christian community at Jerusalem, influenced the Apostles to accept Paul, with whom he became a pioneer missionary outside Palestine and Syria, to Antioch, Cyprus and southern Asia Minor; legend says he was martyred on Cyprus during the Neronian persecution; feast, June 11.

Bartholomew (Nathaniel): A friend of Philip; according to various traditions, preached the Gospel in Ethiopia, India, Persia, and Armenia where he was martyred by being flayed and beheaded; in art, is depicted holding a knife, an instrument of his death; feast, Aug. 24 in the Roman Rite, Aug. 25 in the Byzantine Rite.

James the Greater: A Galilean, son of Zebedee, brother of John (with whom he was called a "son of thunder"), a fisherman; with Peter and John, witnessed the raising of Jairus' daughter to life, the transfiguration, the agony of Jesus in the Garden of Gethsemani; first of the Apostles to die, by the sword in 44 during the rule of Herod Agrippa; there is doubt about a journey legend says he made to Spain and also about the authenticity of relics said to be his at Santiago de Compostela; in art, is depicted carrying a pilgrim's bell; feast, July 25 in the Roman Rite, Apr. 30 in the Byzantine Rite.

James the Less: Son of Alphaeus, called "Less" because he was younger in age or shorter in stature than James the Greater; one of the "catholic" epistles bears his name; was stoned to death in 62 or thrown from the top of the temple in Jerusalem and clubbed to death in 66; in art, is depicted with a club or heavy staff; feast, May 3 in the Roman Rite, Oct. 9 in the Byzantine Rite.

John: A Galilean, son of Zebedee, brother of James the Greater (with whom he was called a "son of thunder"), a fisherman, probably a disciple of John the Baptist, one of the Evangelists, called the "beloved disciple"; with Peter and James the Greater, witnessed the raising of Jairus' daughter to life, the transfiguration, the agony of Jesus in the Garden of Gethsemani; Mary was commended to his special care by Christ; the fourth Gospel, three "catholic" Epistles and Revelation bear his name; according to various accounts, lived at Ephesus in Asia Minor for some time and died a natural death about 100; in art, is represented by an eagle, symbolic of the sublimity of the contents of his Gospel; feast, Dec. 27 in the Roman Rite, May 8 in the Byzantine Rite.

Jude Thaddeus: One of the "catholic" epistles, the shortest, bears his name; various traditions say he preached the Gospel in Mesopotamia, Persia and elsewhere, and was martyred; in art, is depicted with a halberd, instrument of his death; feast, Oct. 28 in the Roman Rite, June 19 in the Byzantine Rite.

Luke: A Greek convert to the Christian community, called "our most dear physician" by Paul, of whom he was a missionary companion; author of the third Gospel and Acts of the Apostles; the place — Achaia, Bithynia, Egypt — and circumstances of his death are not certain; in art, is depicted as a man, a writer, or an ox (because his Gospel starts at the scene of Temple sacrifice); feast, Oct. 18.

Mark: A cousin of Barnabas and member of the first Christian community at Jerusalem; a missionary companion of Paul and Barnabas, then of Peter; author of the Gospel which bears his name; according to legend, founded the Church at Alexandria, was bishop there and was martyred in the streets of the city; in art, is depicted with his Gospel and a winged lion, symbolic of the voice of John the Baptist crying in the wilderness, at the beginning of his Gospel; feast, Apr. 25.

Matthew: A Galilean, called Levi by Luke and John and the son of Alphaeus by Mark, a tax collector, one of the Evangelists; according to various accounts, preached the Gospel in Judea, Ethiopia, Persia and Parthia, and was martyred; in art, is depicted with a spear, the instrument of his death, and as a winged man in his role as Evangelist; feast, Sept. 21 in the Roman Rite, Nov. 16 in the Byzantine Rite.

Matthias: A disciple of Jesus whom the faithful 11 Apostles chose to replace Judas before the Resurrection; uncertain traditions report that he preached the Gospel in Palestine, Cappadocia or Ethiopia; in art, is represented with a cross and a halberd, the instruments of his death as a martyr; feast, May 14 in the Roman Rite, Aug. 9 in the Byzantine Rite.

Paul: Born at Tarsus, of the tribe of Benjamin, a Roman citizen; participated in the persecution of Christians until the time of his miraculous conversion on the way to Damascus; called by Christ, who revealed himself to him in a special way; became the Apostle of the Gentiles, among whom he did most of his preaching in the course of three major missionary journeys through areas north of Palestine, Cyprus, Asia Minor and Greece; 14 epistles bear his name; two years of imprisonment at Rome, following initial arrest in Jerusalem and confinement at Caesarea, ended with martyrdom, by beheading, outside the walls of the city in 64 or 67 during the Neronian persecution; in art, is depicted in various ways with St. Peter, with a sword, in the scene of his conversion; feasts, June 29, Jan. 25 (Roman Rite).

Peter: Simon, son of Jona, born in Bethsaida, brother of Andrew, a fisherman; called Cephas or Peter by Christ who made him the chief of the Apostles and head of the Church as his vicar; named first in the listings of Apostles in the Synoptic Gospels and the Acts of the Apostles; with James the Greater and John, witnessed the raising of Jairus' daughter to life, the transfiguration, the agony of Jesus in the Garden of Gethsemani; was the first to preach the Gospel in and around Jerusalem and was the leader of the first Christian community there; established a local Church in Antioch; presided over the Council of Jerusalem in 51; wrote two "catholic" epistles to the Christians in Asia Minor; established his see in Rome where he spent his last years and was martyred by crucifixion in 64 or 65 during the Neronian persecution; in art, is depicted carrying two keys, symbolic of his primacy in the Church; feasts, June 29, Feb. 22 (Roman Rite).

Philip: Born in Bethsaida; according to legend, preached the Gospel in Phrygia where he suffered martyrdom by crucifixion; feast, May 3 in the Roman Rite, Nov. 14 in the Byzantine Rite.

Simon: Called the Cananean or the Zealot; according to legend, preached in various places in the Near East and suffered martyrdom by being sawed in two; in art, is depicted with a saw, the instrument of his death, or a book, symbolic of his zeal for the Law; feast, Oct. 28 in the Roman Rite, May 10 in the Byzantine Rite.

Thomas (Didymus): Notable for his initial incredulity regarding the Resurrection and his subsequent forthright confession of the divinity of Christ risen from the dead; according to legend, preached the Gospel in places from the Caspian Sea to the Persian Gulf and eventually reached India where he was martyred near Madras; Thomas Christians trace their origin to him; in art, is depicted kneeling before the risen Christ, or with a carpenter's rule and square; feast, July 3 in the Roman Rite, Oct. 6 in the Byzantine Rite.

JUDAS

The Gospels record only a few facts about Judas, the Apostle who betrayed Christ.

The only non-Galilean among the Apostles, he was from Carioth, a town in southern Juda. He was keeper of the purse in the apostolic band. He was called a petty thief by John. He voiced dismay at the waste of money, which he said might have been spent for the poor, in connection with the anointing incident at Bethany. He took the initiative in arranging the betrayal of Christ. Afterwards, he confessed that he had betrayed an innocent man and cast into the Temple the money he had received for that action. Of his death, Matthew says that he hanged himself; the Acts of the Apostles states that he swelled up and burst open; both reports deal more with the meaning than the manner of his death — the misery of the death of a sinner.

The consensus of speculation over the reason why Judas acted as he did in betraying Christ focuses on disillusionment and unwillingness to accept the concept of a suffering Messiah and personal suffering of his own as an Apostle.

APOSTOLIC FATHERS, FATHERS, DOCTORS OF THE CHURCH

The writers listed below, were outstanding and authoritative witnesses to authentic Christian belief and practice, and played significant roles in giving them expression.

Apostolic Fathers

The Apostolic Fathers were Christian writers of the first and second centuries who are known or believed to have had personal relations with the Apostles, and whose writings echo genuine apostolic teaching.

Chief in importance are: St. Clement (d.c. 97), bishop of Rome and third successor of St. Peter in the papacy; St. Ignatius (50-c. 107), bishop of Antioch and second successor of St. Peter in that see, reputed to be a disciple of St. John; St. Polycarp (69-155), bishop of Smyrna and a disciple of St. John. The authors of the *Didache* and the *Epistle of Barnabas* are also numbered among the Apostolic Fathers.

Other early ecclesiastical writers included: St. Justin, martyr (100-165), of Asia Minor and Rome, a layman and apologist; St. Irenaeus (130-202), bishop of Lyons, who opposed Gnosticism; and St. Cyprian (210-258), bishop of Carthage, who opposed Novatianism.

Fathers and Doctors

The Fathers of the Church were theologians and writers of the first eight centuries who were outstanding for sanctity and learning. They were such authoritative witnesses to the belief and teaching of the Church that their unanimous acceptance of doctrines as divinely revealed has been regarded as evidence that such doctrines were so received by the Church in line with apostolic tradition and Sacred Scripture. Their unanimous rejection of doctrines branded them as heretical. Their writings, however, were not necessarily free of error in all respects.

The greatest of these Fathers were: Sts. Ambrose, Augustine, Jerome and Gregory the Great in the West; Sts. John Chrysostom, Basil the Great, Gregory of Nazianzen and Athanasius in the East.

The Doctors of the Church were ecclesiastical writers of eminent learning and sanctity who have been given this title because of the great advantage the Church has derived from their work. These writings, however, were not necessarily free of error in all respects.

Albert the Great, St. (c. 1200-1280): Born in Swabia, Germany; Dominican; bishop of Regensburg (1260-1262); wrote extensively on logic, natural sciences, ethics, metaphysics, Scripture, systematic theology; contributed to development of Scholasticism; teacher of St. Thomas Aquinas; canonized and proclaimed doctor, 1931; named patron of natural scientists, 1941; called Doctor Universalis, Doctor Expertus; feast, Nov. 15.

Alphonsus Liguori, St. (1696-1787): Born near Naples, Italy; bishop of Agatha of the Goths (1762-1775); founder of the Redemptorists; in addition to his principal work, *Theologiae Moralis,* wrote on prayer, the spiritual life, and doctrinal subjects in response to controversy; canonized, 1839; proclaimed doctor, 1871; named patron of confessors and moralists, 1950; feast, Aug. 1.

Ambrose, St. (c. 340-397): Born in Treves, Germany; bishop of Milan (374-397); one of the strongest opponents of Arianism in the West; his homilies and other writings — on faith, the Holy Spirit, the Incarnation, the sacraments and other subjects — were pastoral and practical; influenced the development of a liturgy at Milan which was named for him; Father and Doctor of the Church; feast, Dec. 7.

Anselm, St. (1033-1109): Born in Aosta, Piedmont, Italy; Benedictine; archbishop of Canterbury (1093-1109); in addition to his principal work, *Cur Deus Homo,* on the atonement and reconciliation of man with God through Christ, wrote about the existence and attributes of God and defended the *Filioque* explanation of the procession of the Holy Spirit from the Father and the Son; canonized, 1494; proclaimed doctor, 1720; called Father of Scholasticism; feast, Apr. 21.

Anthony of Padua, St. (1195-1231): Born in Lisbon, Portugal; first theologian of the Franciscan Order; preacher; canonized, 1232; proclaimed doctor, 1946; called Evangelical Doctor; feast, June 13.

Athanasius, St. (c. 297-373): Born in Alexandria, Egypt; bishop of Alexandria (328-373); participant in the Council of Nicaea I while still a deacon; dominant opponent of Arians whose errors regarding Christ he refuted in *Apology against the Arians, Discourses against the Arians,* and other works; Father and Doctor of the Church; called Father of Orthodoxy; feast, May 2.

Augustine, St. (354-430): Born in Tagaste, North Africa; bishop of Hippo (395-430) after conversion from Manichaeism; works include the autobiographical and mystical *Confessions, City of God,* treatises on the Trinity, grace, passages of the Bible, and doctrines called into question and denied by Manichaeans, Pelagians and Donatists; had strong and lasting influence on Christian theology and philosophy; Father and Doctor of the Church; called Doctor of Grace; feast, Aug. 28.

Basil the Great, St. (c. 329-379): Born in Caesarea, Cappadocia, Asia Minor; bishop of Caesarea (370-379); wrote three books *Contra Eunomium* in refutation of Arian errors, a treatise on the Holy Spirit, many homilies, and several rules for monastic life, on which he had lasting influence; Father and Doctor of the Church; called Father of Monasticism in the East; feast, Jan. 2.

Bede the Venerable, St. (c. 673-735): Born in Northumberland, England; Benedictine; in addition to his principal work, *Ecclesiastical History of the English Nation* (covering the period 597-731), wrote scriptural commentaries; regarded as probably the most learned man in Western Europe of his time; called Father of English History; feast, May 25.

Bernard of Clairvaux, St. (c. 1090-1153): Born near Dijon, France; abbot; monastic reformer, called the second founder of the Cistercian Order; mystical theologian with great influence on devotional life; opponent of the rationalism brought forward by Abelard and others; canonized, 1174; proclaimed doctor, 1830; called Mellifluous Doctor because of his eloquence; feast, Aug. 20.

Bonaventure, St. (c. 1217-1274): Born near Viterbo, Italy; Franciscan; bishop of Albano (1273-1274); cardinal; wrote *Itinerarium Mentis in Deum, De Reductione Artium ad Theologiam, Breviloquium,* scriptural commentaries, additional mystical works affecting devotional life, and a life of St. Francis of Assisi; canonized, 1482; proclaimed doctor, 1588; called Seraphic Doctor; feast, July 15.

Catherine of Siena, St. (c. 1347-1380): Born in Siena, Italy; member of the Third Order of St. Dominic; mystic; authored a long series of letters, mainly concerning spiritual instruction and encouragement, to associates, and

Dialogue, a spiritual testament in four treatises; was active in support of a crusade against the Turks and efforts to end war between papal forces and the Florentine allies; had great influence in inducing Gregory XI to return himself and the Curia to Rome in 1376, to end the Avignon period of the papacy; canonized, 1461; proclaimed the second woman doctor, Oct. 4, 1970; feast, Apr. 29.

Cyril of Alexandria, St. (c. 376-444): Born in Egypt; bishop of Alexandria (412-444); wrote treatises on the Trinity, the Incarnation and other subjects, mostly in refutation of Nestorian errors; made key contributions to the development of Christology; presided at the Council of Ephesus, 431; proclaimed doctor, 1882; feast, June 27.

Cyril of Jerusalem, St. (c. 315-387): Bishop of Jerusalem (350-387); vigorous opponent of Arianism; principal work, *Catecheses,* a pre-baptismal explanation of the creed of Jerusalem; proclaimed doctor, 1882; feast, Mar. 18.

Ephraem, St. (c. 306-373): Born in Nisibis, Mesopotamia; counteracted the spread of Gnostic and Arian errors with poems and hymns of his own composition; wrote also on the Eucharist and Mary; proclaimed doctor, 1920; called Deacon of Edessa and Harp of the Holy Spirit; feast, June 9.

Francis de Sales, St. (1567-1622): Born in Savoy; bishop of Geneva (1602-1622); spiritual writer with strong influence on devotional life through treatises such as *Introduction to a Devout Life,* and *The Love of God;* canonized, 1665; proclaimed doctor, 1877; patron of Catholic writers and the Catholic press; feast, Jan. 24.

Gregory Nazianzen, St. (c. 330-c. 390): Born in Arianzus, Cappadocia, Asia Minor; bishop of Constantinople (381-390); vigorous opponent of Arianism; in addition to five theological discourses on the Nicene Creed and the Trinity for which he is best known, wrote letters and poetry; Father and Doctor of the Church; called the Christian Demosthenes because of his eloquence and, in the Eastern Church, The Theologian; feast, Jan. 2.

Gregory I, the Great, St. (c. 540-604): Born in Rome; pope (590-604): wrote many scriptural commentaries, a compendium of theology in the *Book of Morals* based on Job, *Dialogues* concerning the lives of saints, the immortality of the soul, death, purgatory, heaven and hell, and 14 books of letters; enforced papal supremacy and established the position of the pope vis-a-vis the emperor; worked for clerical and monastic reform and the observance of clerical celibacy; Father and Doctor of the Church; feast, Sept. 3.

Hilary of Poitiers, St. (c. 315-368): Born in Poitiers, France; bishop of Poitiers (c. 353-368); wrote *De Synodis,* with the Arian controversy in mind, and *De Trinitate,* the first lengthy study of the doctrine in Latin; introduced Eastern theology to the West; con-

tributed to the development of hymnology; proclaimed doctor, 1851; called the Athanasius of the West because of his vigorous defense of the divinity of Christ against Arians; feast, Jan. 13.

Isidore of Seville, St. (c. 560-636): Born in Cartagena, Spain; bishop of Seville (c. 600-636); in addition to his principal work, *Etymologiae,* an encyclopedia of the knowledge of his day, wrote on theological and historical subjects; regarded as the most learned man of his time; proclaimed doctor, 1722; feast, Apr. 4.

Jerome, St. (c. 343-420): Born in Stridon, Dalmatia; translated the Old Testament from Hebrew into Latin and revised the existing Latin translation of the New Testament to produce the Vulgate version of the Bible; wrote scriptural commentaries and treatises on matters of controversy; regarded as Father and Doctor of the Church from the eighth century; called Father of Biblical Science; feast, Sept. 30.

John Chrysostom, St. (c. 347-407): Born in Antioch, Asia Minor; archbishop of Constantinople (398-407); wrote homilies, scriptural commentaries and letters of wide influence in addition to a classical treatise on the priesthood; proclaimed doctor by the Council of Chalcedon, 451; called the greatest of the Greek Fathers; named patron of preachers, 1909; called golden-mouthed because of his eloquence; feast, Sept. 13.

John Damascene, St. (c. 675-c. 749): Born in Damascus, Syria; monk; wrote *Fountain of Wisdom,* a three-part work including a history of heresies and an exposition of the Christian faith, three *Discourses against the Iconoclasts,* homilies on Mary, biblical commentaries and treatises on moral subjects; proclaimed doctor, 1890; called Golden Speaker because of his eloquence; feast, Dec. 4.

John of the Cross, St. (1542-1591): Born in Old Castile, Spain; Carmelite; founder of Discalced Carmelites; one of the greatest mystical theologians, wrote *The Ascent of Mt. Carmel — The Dark Night, The Spiritual Canticle, The Living Flame of Love;* canonized, 1726; proclaimed doctor, 1926; called Doctor of Mystical Theology; feast, Dec. 14.

Lawrence of Brindisi, St. (1559-1619): Born in Brindisi, Italy; Franciscan (Capuchin); vigorous preacher of strong influence in the post-Reformation period; 15 tomes of collected works include scriptural commentaries, sermons, homilies and doctrinal writings; canonized, 1881; proclaimed doctor, 1959; feast, July 21.

Leo I, the Great, St. (c. 400-461): Born in Tuscany, Italy; pope (440-461); wrote the *Tome of Leo,* to explain doctrine concerning the two natures and one Person of Christ, against the background of the Nestorian and Monophysite heresies; other works included sermons, letters, and writings against the errors of Manichaeism and Pelagianism; was instrumental in dissuading Attila from sacking Rome in 452; proclaimed doctor, 1574; feast, Nov. 10.

Peter Canisius, St. (1521-1597): Born in Nijmegen, Holland; Jesuit; wrote popular expositions of the Catholic faith in several catechisms which were widely circulated in 20 editions in his lifetime alone; was one of the moving figures in the Counter-Reformation period, especially in southern and western Germany; canonized and proclaimed doctor, 1925; feast, Dec. 21.

Peter Chrysologus, St. (c. 400-450): Born in Imola, Italy; served as archbishop of Ravenna (c. 433-450); his sermons and writings, many of which were designed to counteract Monophysitism, were pastoral and practical; proclaimed doctor, 1729; feast, July 30.

Peter Damian, St. (1007-1072): Born in Ravenna, Italy; Benedictine; cardinal; his writings and sermons, many of which concerned ecclesiastical and clerical reform, were pastoral and practical; proclaimed doctor, 1828; feast, Feb. 21.

Robert Bellarmine, St. (1542-1621): Born in Tuscany, Italy; Jesuit; archbishop of Capua (1602-1605); wrote *Controversies,* a three-volume exposition of doctrine under attack during and after the Reformation, two catechisms and the spiritual work, *The Art of Dying Well,* was an authority on ecclesiology

and Church-state relations; canonized, 1930; proclaimed doctor, 1931; feast, Sept. 17.

Theresa of Avila, St. (1515-1582): Born in Avila, Spain; entered the Carmelite Order, 1535; in the early 1560's, initiated a primitive Carmelite, discalced-Alcantarine reform which greatly influenced men and women religious, especially in Spain; wrote extensively on spiritual and mystical subjects; principal works included her *Autobiography, Way of Perfection, The Interior Castle, Meditations on the Canticle, The Foundations, Visitation of the Discalced Nuns;* canonized, 1614; proclaimed first woman doctor, Sept. 27, 1970; feast, Oct. 15.

Thomas Aquinas, St. (1225-1274): Born near Naples, Italy; Dominican; teacher and writer on virtually the whole range of philosophy and theology; principal works were *Summa contra Gentiles,* a manual and systematic defense of Christian doctrine, and *Summa Theologiae,* a new (at that time) exposition of theology on philosophical principles; canonized, 1323; proclaimed doctor, 1567; called Doctor Communis, Doctor Angelicus, the Great Synthesizer because of the way in which he related faith and reason, theology and philosophy (especially that of Aristotle), and systematized the presentation of Christian doctrine; named patron of Catholic schools and education, 1880; feast, Jan. 28.

CREEDS

Creeds are formal and official statements of Christian doctrine. As summaries of the principal truths of faith, they are standards of orthodoxy and are useful for instructional purposes, for actual profession of the faith, and for expression of the faith in the liturgy.

The classical creeds are the Apostles' Creed and the Creed of Nicaea-Constantinople. Two others are the Athanasian Creed and the Creed of Pius IV.

Apostles' Creed

Text: I believe in God, the Father almighty, Creator of heaven and earth.

And in Jesus Christ, his only Son, our Lord; who was conceived by the Holy Spirit, born of the Virgin Mary, suffered under Pontius Pilate, was crucified, died, and was buried. He descended into hell; the third day he arose again from the dead; he ascended into heaven, sits at the right hand of God, the Father almighty; from thence he shall come to judge the living and the dead.

I believe in the Holy Spirit, the holy Catholic Church, the communion of saints, the forgiveness of sins, the resurrection of the body, and life everlasting. Amen.

Background: The Apostles' Creed reflects the teaching of the Apostles but is not of apostolic origin. It probably originated in the second century as a rudimentary formula of faith professed by catechumens before the reception of baptism. Baptismal creeds in

fourth-century use at Rome and elsewhere in the West closely resembled the present text, which was quoted in a handbook of Christian doctrine written between 710 and 724. This text was in wide use throughout the West by the ninth century. The Apostles' Creed is common to all Christian confessional churches in the West, but is not used in Eastern Churches.

Nicene Creed

The following translation of the Latin text of the creed was prepared by the International Committee on English in the Liturgy.

Text: We believe in one God, the Father, the Almighty, maker of heaven and earth, of all that is seen and unseen.

We believe in one Lord, Jesus Christ, the only Son of God, eternally begotten of the Father, God from God, Light from Light, true God from true God, begotten, not made, one in Being with the Father. Through him all things were made. For us men and for our salvation he came down from heaven: by the power of the Holy Spirit he was born of the Virgin Mary, and became man. For our sake he was crucified under Pontius Pilate; he suffered, died, and was buried. On the third day he rose again in fulfillment of the Scriptures; he ascended into heaven and is seated at the right hand of the Father. He will come again in glory to judge the living and the dead, and his kingdom will have no end.

We believe in the Holy Spirit, the Lord, the giver of life, who proceeds from the Father and the Son. With the Father and the Son he is worshiped and glorified. He has spoken through the prophets.

We believe in one holy catholic and apostolic Church. We acknowledge one baptism for the forgiveness of sins. We look for the resurrection of the dead, and the life of the world to come. Amen.

Background: The Nicene Creed (Creed of Nicaea-Constantinople) consists of elements of doctrine contained in an early baptismal creed of Jerusalem and enactments of the Council of Nicaea (325) and the Council of Constantinople (381). Its strong trinitarian content reflects the doctrinal errors, especially of Arianism, it served to counteract. Theologically, it is much more sophisticated than the Apostles' Creed. Since late in the fifth century, the Nicene Creed has been the only creed in liturgical use in the Eastern Churches. The Western Church adopted it for liturgical use by the end of the eighth century.

The Athanasian Creed

The Athanasian Creed, which has a unique structure, is a two-part summary of doctrine concerning the Trinity and the Incarnation-Redemption bracketed at the beginning and end with the statement that belief in the cited truths is necessary for salvation; it also contains a number of anathemas or condemnatory clauses regarding doctrinal errors. Although attributed to St. Athanasius, it was probably written after his death, between 381 and 428, and may have been authored by St. Ambrose. It is not accepted in the East; in the West, it has place in the liturgy of some other Christian churches as well as in the Roman-Rite Liturgy of the Hours and for the Solemnity of the Holy Trinity.

Creed of Pius IV

The Creed of Pius IV, also called the Profession of Faith of the Council of Trent, was promulgated in the bull *Injunctum Nobis,* Nov. 13, 1564. It is a summary of doctrine defined by the council concerning: Scripture and tradition, original sin and justification, the Mass and sacraments, veneration of the saints, indulgences, the primacy of the See of Rome. It was slightly modified in 1887 to include doctrinal formulations of the First Vatican Council.

REDDITIO OF CREED

The "giving back," by profession, of a baptismal creed by candidates for baptism to a bishop or his representative was one of the immediate preliminaries to reception of the sacrament at the conclusion of the catechumenate in the early Church.

The interrogation concerning truths of faith in the present baptismal rite is reminiscent of this ancient practice.

MORAL OBLIGATIONS

The basic norm of Christian morality is life in Christ. This involves, among other things, the observance of the Ten Commandments, their fulfillment in the twofold law of love of God and neighbor, the implications of the Sermon on the Mount and the whole New Testament, and membership in the Church established by Christ.

The Ten Commandments

The Ten Commandments, the Decalogue, were given by God through Moses to his Chosen People for the guidance of their moral conduct in accord with the demands of the Covenant he established with them as a divine gift. Their observance was essential to participation in the Covenant and the order of salvation based on it.

In the traditional Catholic enumeration and according to Dt. 5:6-21, the Commandments are:

1. "I, the Lord, am your God . . . You shall not have other gods besides me. You shall not carve idols. . . ."
2. "You shall not take the name of the Lord, your God, in vain. . . ."
3. "Take care to keep holy the Sabbath day. . . ."
4. "Honor your father and your mother. . . ."
5. "You shall not kill."
6. "You shall not commit adultery."
7. "You shall not steal."
8. "You shall not bear dishonest witness against your neighbor."
9. "You shall not covet your neighbor's wife."
10. "You shall not desire your neighbor's house or field, nor his male or female slave, nor his ox or ass, nor anything that belongs to him" (summarily, his goods).

Another version of the Commandments, substantially the same, is given in Ex. 20:1-17.

The traditional enumeration of the Commandments in Protestant usage differs from the above. Thus: two commandments are made of the first, as above; the third and fourth are equivalent to the second and third, as above, and so on; and the 10th includes the ninth and 10th, as above.

Love of God and Neighbor

The first three of the commandments deal directly with man's relations with God, viz.: acknowledgment of one true God and the rejection of false gods and idols; honor due to God and his name; observance of the Sabbath as the Lord's day.

The rest cover interpersonal relationships, viz.: the obedience due to parents and, logically, to other persons in authority, and the obligations of parents to children and of persons in authority to those under their care; respect for life and physical integrity; fidelity in marriage, and chastity; justice and rights; truth; internal respect for faithfulness in marriage, chastity, and the goods of others.

Perfection in Christian Life

The moral obligations of the Ten Commandments are complemented by others flowing from the twofold law of love, the whole substance and pattern of Christ's teaching, and everything implied in full and active membership and participation in the community of salvation formed by Christ in his Church. Some of these matters are covered in other sections of the Almanac under appropriate headings.

Precepts of the Church

The precepts of the Church of Roman Rite oblige Catholics to:

1. Assist at Mass on Sundays and holy days of obligation. (Also, to desist from unnecessary servile work on these days.)

2. Fast and abstain on the days appointed. (The fasting obligation binds persons from the 21st until the 59th birthday; the days of fast are Ash Wednesday and Good Friday. The abstinence obligation binds from the 14th birthday on these days, and is recommended for all Fridays in Lent; it may be obligatory in some dioceses.) These regulations, which have been modified in recent years, are penitential in purpose but do not exhaust obligations of penance. Other ways of doing penance are left to personal option.

3. Confess their sins at least once a year.

4. Receive Holy Communion during the Easter time. (In the U.S., the Easter time extends from the First Sunday of Lent to Trinity Sunday.)

5. Contribute to the support of the Church.

6. Observe the laws of the Church concerning marriage.

SOCIAL DOCTRINE

Since the end of the last century, Catholic social doctrine has been formulated in a progressive manner in a number of authoritative documents. Outstanding examples are the encyclicals: *Rerum Novarum,* issued by Leo XIII in 1891; *Quadragesimo Anno,* by Pius XI in 1931; *Mater et Magistra* ("Christianity and Social Progress") and *Pacem in Terris* ("Peace on Earth"), by John XXIII in 1961 and 1963, respectively; and *Populorum Progressio* ("Development of Peoples"), by Paul VI in 1967. Pius XII, among other accomplishments of ideological importance in the social field, made a distinctive contribution with his formulation of a plan for world peace and order in Christmas messages from 1939 to 1941, and in other documents.

These documents represent the most serious attempts in modern times to systematize the social implications of the Gospel and the rest of divine revelation as well as the socially relevant writings of the Fathers and Doctors of the Church. Their contents are theological penetrations into social life, with particular reference to human rights, the needs of the poor and those in underdeveloped countries, and humane conditions of life, freedom, justice and peace. In some respects, they read like juridical documents; underneath, however, they are Gospel-oriented and pastoral in intention.

Nature of the Doctrine

Pope John, writing in *Christianity and Social Progress,* made the following statement about the nature and scope of the doctrine stated in the encyclicals in particular and related writings in general.

"What the Catholic Church teaches and declares regarding the social life and relationships of men is beyond question for all time valid.

"The cardinal point of this teaching is that individual men are necessarily the foundation, cause, and end of all social institutions . . . insofar as they are social by nature, and raised to an order of existence that transcends and subdues nature.

"Beginning with this very basic principle whereby the dignity of the human person is affirmed and defended, Holy Church — especially during the last century and with the assistance of learned priests and laymen, specialists in the field — has arrived at clear social teachings whereby the mutual relationships of men are ordered. Taking general norms into account, these principles are in accord with the nature of things and the changed conditions of man's social life, or with the special genius of our day. Moreover, these norms can be approved by all."

The Church in the World

Even more Gospel-oriented and pastoral in a distinctive way is the *Pastoral Constitution on the Church in the Modern World* promulgated by the Second Vatican Council in 1965.

Its purpose was to search out the signs of God's presence and meaning in and through the events of this time in human history. Accordingly, it dealt with the situation of men in present circumstances of profound change, challenge and crisis on all levels of life.

The first part of the constitution developed the theme of the Church and man's calling, and focused attention on the dignity of the human person, the problem of atheism, the community of mankind, man's activity throughout the world, and the serving and saving role of the Church in the world. This portion of the document, it has been said, represents the first presentation by the Church in an official text of an organized Christian view of man and society.

The second part of the document considered several problems of special urgency: fostering the nobility of marriage and the family (see Marriage Doctrine), the proper development of culture, socio-economic life, the life of the political community, the fostering of peace (see Peace and War), and the promotion of a community of nations.

In conclusion, the constitution called for action to implement doctrine regarding the role and work of the Church for the total good of mankind.

Following are a number of key excerpts from the ideological heart of the constitution.

One Human Family and Community: "God, who has fatherly concern for everyone, has willed that all men should constitute one family and treat one another in a spirit of brotherhood. . . .

"For this reason, love for God and neighbor is the first and greatest commandment. Sacred Scripture . . . teaches us that the love of God cannot be separated from love of neighbor. . . . To men growing daily more dependent on one another, and to a world becoming more unified every day, this truth proves to be of paramount importance . . ." (No. 24).

Human Person Is Central: "Man's social nature makes it evident that the progress of the human person and the advance of society itself hinge on each other. For the beginning, the subject and the goal of all social institutions is and must be the human person, which for its part and by its very nature stands completely in need of social life. This social life is not something added on to man. Hence, through his dealings with others, through reciprocal duties, and through fraternal dialogue he develops all his gifts and is able to rise to his destiny."

Influence of Social Circumstances: "But if by this social life the human person is greatly aided in responding to his destiny, even in its religious dimensions, it cannot be denied that men are often diverted from doing good and spurred toward evil by the social circumstances in which they live and are immersed from their birth. To be sure the disturbances which so frequently occur in the social order result in part from the natural tensions of economic, political, and social forms. But at a deeper level they flow from man's pride and selfishness, which contaminate even the social sphere. When the structure of affairs is flawed by the consequences of sin, man, already born with a bent toward evil, finds there new inducements to sin, which cannot be overcome without strenuous efforts and the assistance of grace" (No. 25).

"Every social group must take account of the needs and legitimate aspirations of other groups, and even of the general welfare of the entire human family."

Human Necessities: "At the same time however, there is a growing awareness of the exalted dignity proper to the human person, since he stands above all things, and his rights and duties are universal and inviolable. Therefore, there must be made available to all men everything necessary for leading a life truly human, such as food, clothing, and shelter; the right to choose a state of life freely and to found a family, the right to education, to employment, to a good reputation, to respect, to appropriate information, to activity in accord with the upright norm of one's own conscience, to protection of privacy and to rightful freedom in matters religious too.

"Hence, the social order and its development must unceasingly work to the benefit of the human person if the disposition of affairs is to be subordinate to the personal realm and not contrariwise, as the Lord indicated when He said that the Sabbath was made for man, and not man for the Sabbath."

Improvement of Social Order: "This social order requires constant improvement. It must be founded on truth, built on justice, and animated by love; in freedom it should grow every day toward a more humane balance. An improvement in attitudes and widespread changes in society will have to take place if these objectives are to be gained.

"God's Spirit, who with a marvelous providence directs the unfolding of time and renews the face of the earth, is not absent from this development. The ferment of the gospel, too, has aroused and continues to arouse in man's heart the irresistible requirements of his dignity" (No. 26).

Regard for Neighbor as Another Self: "Coming down to practical and particularly urgent consequences, this Council lays stress on reverence for man; everyone must consider his every neighbor without exception as another self, taking into account first of all his life and the means necessary to living it with dignity. . . .

"In our times a special obligation binds us to make ourselves the neighbor of absolutely every person, and of actively helping him when he comes across our path. . . ."

Inhuman Evils: ". . . Whatever is opposed to life itself, such as any type of murder, genocide, abortion, euthanasia, or willful self-destruction, whatever violates the integrity of the human person, such as mutilation, torments inflicted on body or mind, attempts to coerce the will itself; whatever insults human dignity, such as subhuman living conditions, arbitrary imprisonment, deportation, slavery, prostitution, the selling of women and children; as well as disgraceful working conditions, where men are treated as mere tools for profit, rather than as free and responsible persons; all these things and others of their like are infamies indeed. They poison human society, but they do more harm to those who practice them than those who suffer from the injury. Moreover, they are a supreme dishonor to the Creator" (No. 27).

Respect for Those Who Are Different: "Respect and love ought to be extended also to those who think or act differently than we do in social, political, and religious matters. In fact, the more deeply we come to understand their ways of thinking through such courtesy and love, the more easily will we be able to enter into dialogue with them."

Distinction between Error and Person in Error: "This love and good will,, to be sure, must in no way render us indifferent to truth and goodness. Indeed love itself impels the disciples of Christ to speak the saving truth to all men. But it is necessary to distinguish between error, which always merits repudiation, and the person in error, who never loses the dignity of being a person, even when he is flawed by false or inadequate religious notions. God alone is the judge and searcher of hearts; for that reason He forbids us to make judgments about the internal guilt of anyone.

"The teaching of Christ even requires that we forgive injuries, and extends the law of love to include every enemy . . ." (No. 28).

Men Are Equal but Different: "Since all men possess a rational soul and are created in God's likeness, since they have the same nature and origin, have been redeemed by Christ, and enjoy the same divine calling and destiny, the basic equality of all must receive increasingly greater recognition.

"True, all men are not alike from the point of view of varying physical power and the diversity of intellectual and moral resources. Nevertheless, with respect to the fundamental rights of the person, every type of discrimination, whether social or cultural, whether based on sex, race, color, social condition, language, or religion, is to be overcome and eradicated as contrary to God's intent. . . ."

Humane Conditions for All: ". . . Although rightful differences exist between men, the equal dignity of persons demands that a more humane and just condition of life be brought about. For excessive economic and social differences between the members of the one human family and population groups cause scandal, and militate against social justice, equity, the dignity of the human person, as well as social and international peace.

"Human institutions, both private and public, must labor to minister to the dignity and purpose of man. At the same time let them put up a stubborn fight against any kind of slavery, whether social or political, and safeguard the basic rights of man under every political system. Indeed human institutions themselves must be accommodated by degrees to the highest of all realities, spiritual ones, even though, meanwhile, a long enough time will be required before they arrive at the desired goal" (No. 29).

"Profound and rapid changes make it particularly urgent that no one, ignoring the trend of events or drugged by laziness, content himself with a merely individualistic morality. It grows increasingly true that the obligations of justice and love are fulfilled only if each person, contributing to the common good, according to his own abilities and the needs of others, also promotes and assists the public and private institutions dedicated to bettering the conditions of human life."

Social Necessities Are Prime Duties: "Let everyone consider it his sacred obligation to count social necessities among the primary duties of modern man, and to pay heed to them. For the more unified the world becomes, the more plainly do the offices of men extend beyond particular groups and spread by degrees to the whole world. But this challenge cannot be met unless individual men and their associations cultivate in themselves the moral and social virtues, and promote them in society. Thus, with the needed help of divine grace, men who are truly new and artisans of a new humanity can be forthcoming" (No. 30).

"In order for individual men to discharge with greater exactness the obligations of their conscience toward themselves and the various groups to which they belong, they must be carefully educated to a higher degree of culture through the use of the immense resources available today to the human race. . . ."

Living Conditions and Freedom: ". . . A man can scarcely arrive at the needed sense of responsibility unless his living conditions allow him to become conscious of his dignity, and to rise to his destiny by spending himself for God and for others. But human freedom is often crippled when a man falls into extreme poverty, just as it withers when he indulges in too many of life's comforts and imprisons himself in a kind of splendid isolation. Freedom acquires new strength, by contrast, when a man consents to the unavoidable requirements of social life, takes on the manifold demands of human partnership, and commits himself to the service of the human community.

"Hence, the will to play one's role in common endeavors should be everywhere encouraged . . ." (No. 31).

Communitarian Character of Life: "God did not create man for life in isolation, but for the formation of social unity. So also 'it has pleased God to make men holy and save them not merely as individuals, without any mutual bonds, but by making them into a single people, a people which acknowledges Him in truth and serves Him in holiness' (*Dogmatic Constitution on the Church*, No. 9). So from the beginning of salvation history He has chosen men not just as individuals but as members of a certain community. Revealing His mind to them, God called these chosen ones 'His people' (Ex. 3:7-12), and, furthermore, made a covenant with them on Sinai.

"This communitarian character is developed and consummated in the work of Jesus Christ. For the very Word made flesh willed to share in the human fellowship. He was present at the wedding of Cana, visited the house of Zacchaeus, ate with publicans and sinners. He revealed the love of the Father and the sublime vocation of man in terms of the most common of social realities and by making use of the speech and the imagery of plain everyday life. Willingly obeying the laws of His country, He sanctified those human ties, especially family ones, from which social relationships arise. He chose to lead the life proper to an artisan of His time and place.

"In His preaching He clearly taught the sons of God to treat one another as brothers. In His prayers He pleaded that all His disciples might be 'one.' Indeed, as the Redeemer of all, He offered Himself for all even to the point of death. . . . He commanded His apostles to preach to all peoples the gospel message so that the human race might become the Family of God, in which the fullness of the Law would be love."

The Community Founded by Christ: "As the first-born of many brethren and through the gift of His Spirit, He founded after His death and resurrection a new brotherly community composed of all those who receive Him in faith and in love. This he did through His Body, which is the Church. There everyone, as members one of the other, would render mutual service according to the different gifts bestowed on each.

"This solidarity must be constantly increased until that day on which it will be brought to perfection. Then, saved by grace, men will offer flawless glory to God as a family beloved of God and of Christ their Brother" (No. 32).

PEACE AND WAR

The following excerpts, stating principles and objectives of social doctrine concerning peace and war, are from the *Pastoral Constitution on the Church in the Modern World* (Nos. 77 to 82) promulgated by the Second Vatican Council.

Call to Peace: ". . . This Council fervently desires to summon Christians to cooperate with all men in making secure among themselves a peace based on justice and love, and in setting up agencies of peace. This Christians should do with the help of Christ, the Author of peace" (No. 77).

Conditions for Peace: "Peace is not merely the absence of war. Nor can it be reduced solely to the maintenance of a balance of power between enemies. Nor is it brought about by dictatorship. Instead, it is rightly and appropriately called 'an enterprise of justice' (Is. 32:7). Peace results from that harmony built into human society by its divine Founder, and actualized by men as they thirst after ever greater justice.

"The common good of men is in its basic sense determined by the eternal law. Still the concrete demands of this common good are constantly changing as time goes on. Hence peace is never attained once and for all, but

must be built up ceaselessly. Moreover, since the human will is unsteady and wounded by sin, the achievement of peace requires that everyone constantly master his passions and that lawful authority keep vigilant.

"But such is not enough. This peace cannot be obtained on earth unless personal values are safeguarded and men freely and trustingly share with one another the riches of their inner spirits and their talents. A firm determination to respect other men and peoples and their dignity, as well as the studied practice of brotherhood, are absolutely necessary for the establishment of peace. Hence peace is likewise the fruit of love, which goes beyond what justice can provide."

Renunciation of Violence: ". . . We cannot fail to praise those who renounce the use of violence in the vindication of their rights and who resort to methods of defense which are otherwise available to weaker parties too, provided that this can be done without injury to the rights and duties of others or of the community itself . . ." (No. 78).

Mass Extermination: ". . . The Council wishes to recall first of all the permanent binding force of universal natural law and its all-embracing principles. Man's conscience itself gives ever more emphatic voice to these principles. Therefore, actions which deliberately conflict with these same principles, as well as orders commanding such actions, are criminal. Blind obedience cannot excuse those who yield to them. Among such must first be counted those actions designed for the methodical extermination of an entire people, nation, or ethnic minority. These actions must be vehemently condemned as horrendous crimes. The courage of those who openly and fearlessly resist men who issue such commands merits supreme commendation."

International Agreements: "On the subject of war, quite a large number of nations have subscribed to various international agreements aimed at making military activity and its consequences less inhuman. Such are conventions concerning the handling of wounded or captured soldiers, and various similar agreements. Agreements of this sort must be honored. They should be improved upon."

Conscientious Objectors: ". . . It seems right that laws make humane provisions for the case of those who for reasons of conscience refuse to bear arms, provided, however, that they accept some other form of service to the human community."

Legitimate Defense: "Certainly, war has not been rooted out of human affairs. As long as the danger of war remains and there is no competent and sufficiently powerful authority at the international level, governments cannot be denied the right to legitimate defense once every means of peaceful settlement has been exhausted. Therefore, government authorities and others who share public responsibility have the duty to protect the welfare of the people entrusted to their care and to conduct such grave matters soberly.

"But it is one thing to undertake military action for the just defense of the people, and something else again to seek the subjugation of other nations. Nor does the possession of war potential make every military or political use of it lawful. Neither does the mere fact that war has unhappily begun mean that all is fair between the warring parties."

Nature of Military Service: "Those who are pledged to the service of their country as members of its armed forces should regard themselves as agents of security and freedom on behalf of their people. As long as they fulfill this role properly, they are making a genuine contribution to the establishment of peace" (No. 79).

Total War Condemned: ". . . This most holy Synod makes its own the condemnations of total war already pronounced by recent Popes, and issues the following declaration:

"Any act of war aimed indiscriminately at the destruction of entire cities or of extensive areas along with their population is a crime against God and man himself. It merits unequivocal and unhesitating condemnation.

"The unique hazard of modern warfare consists in this: it provides those who possess modern scientific weapons with a kind of occasion for perpetrating just such abominations. Moreover, through a certain inexorable chain of events, it can urge men on to the most atrocious decisions. That such in fact may never happen in the future, the bishops of the whole world, in unity assembled, beg all men, especially government officials and military leaders, to give unremitting thought to the awesome responsibility which is theirs before God and the entire human race" (No. 80).

Retaliation and Deterrence: "Scientific weapons, to be sure, are not amassed solely for use in war. The defensive strength of any nation is considered to be dependent upon its capacity for immediate retaliation against an adversary. Hence this accumulation of arms, which increases each year, also serves, in a way heretofore unknown, as a deterrent to possible enemy attack. Many regard this state of affairs as the most effective way by which peace of a sort can be maintained between nations at the present time."

Arms Race: "Whatever be the case with this method of deterrence, men should be convinced that the arms race in which so many countries are engaged is not a safe way to preserve a steady peace. Nor is the so-called balance resulting from this race a sure and authentic peace. Rather than being eliminated thereby, the causes of war threaten to grow gradually stronger.

"While extravagant sums are being spent for the furnishing of ever new weapons, an adequate remedy cannot be provided for the multiple miseries afflicting the whole modern world. Disagreements between nations are not really and radically healed. On the contrary other parts of the world are infected with them. New approaches initiated by reformed attitudes must be adopted to remove this trap and to restore genuine peace by emancipating the world from its crushing anxiety.

"Therefore, it must be said again: the arms race is an utterly treacherous trap for humanity, and one which injures the poor to an intolerable degree. It is much to be feared that, if this race persists, it will eventually spawn all the lethal ruin whose path it is now making ready . . ." (No. 81).

Outlaw War: "It is our clear duty, then, to strain every muscle as we work for the time when all war can be completely outlawed by international consent. This goal undoubtedly requires the establishment of some universal public authority acknowledged as such by all, and endowed with effective power to safeguard, on the behalf of all, security, regard for justice, and respect for rights."

Multilateral and Controlled Disarmament: "But before this hoped-for authority can be set up, the highest existing international centers must devote themselves vigorously to the pursuit of better means for obtaining common security. Peace must be born of mutual trust between nations rather than imposed on them through fear of one another's weapons. Hence everyone must labor to put an end at last to the arms race, and to make a true beginning of disarmament, not indeed a unilateral disarmament, but one proceeding at an equal pace according to agreement, and backed up by authentic and workable safeguards.

"In the meantime, efforts which have already been made and are still under way to eliminate the danger of war are not to be underrated. On the contrary, support should be given to the good will of the very many leaders who work hard to do away with war, which they abominate. . . ."

Public Opinion: ". . . Men should take heed not to entrust themselves only to the efforts of others, while remaining careless about their own attitudes. For government officials, who must simultaneously guarantee the good of their own people and promote the universal good, depend on public opinion and feeling to the greatest possible extent. It does them no good to work at building peace so long as feelings of hostility, contempt, and distrust, as well as racial hatred and unbending ideologies, continue to divide men and place them in opposing camps.

"Hence arises a surpassing need for renewed education of attitudes and for new inspiration in the area of public opinion. Those who are dedicated to the work of education . . . should regard as their most weighty task the effort to instruct all in fresh sentiments of peace" (No. 82).

The nature and purpose of the liturgy, along with norms for its revision, were the subject matter of the *Constitution on the Sacred Liturgy* promulgated by the Second Vatican Council. The principles and guidelines stated in this document, the first issued by the Council, are summarized here and/or are incorporated in other Almanac entries on liturgical subjects.

Nature and Purpose of Liturgy

"It is through the liturgy, especially the divine Eucharistic Sacrifice, that 'the work of our redemption is exercised.' The liturgy is thus the outstanding means by which the faithful can express in their lives, and manifest to others, the mystery of Christ and the real nature of the true Church . . ." (No. 2).

"The liturgy is considered as an exercise of the priestly office of Jesus Christ. In the Liturgy the sanctification of man is manifested by signs perceptible to the senses, and is effected in a way which is proper to each of these signs; in the liturgy full public worship is performed by the Mystical Body of Jesus Christ, that is, by the Head and His members.

"From this it follows that every liturgical celebration, because it is an action of Christ the priest and of His Body the Church, is a sacred action surpassing all others. No other action of the Church can match its claim to efficacy, nor equal the degree of it" (No. 7).

"The liturgy is the summit toward which the activity of the Church is directed; at the same time it is the fountain from which all her power flows. For the goal of apostolic works is that all who are made sons of God by faith and baptism should come together to praise God in the midst of His Church, to take part in her sacrifice, and to eat the Lord's supper.

". . . From the liturgy, therefore, and especially from the Eucharist, as from a fountain, grace is channeled into us; and the sanctification of men in Christ and the glorification of God, to which all other activities of the Church are directed as toward their goal, are most powerfully achieved" (No. 10).

Full Participation

"Mother Church earnestly desires that all the faithful be led to that full, conscious, and active participation in liturgical celebrations which is demanded by the very nature of the liturgy. Such participation by the Christian people as 'a chosen race, a royal priesthood, a holy nation, a purchased people' (1 Pt. 2:9; cf. 2:4-5), is their right and duty by reason of their baptism.

"In the restoration and promotion of the sacred liturgy, this full and active participation by all the people is to be considered before all else; for it is the primary and indispensable source from which the faithful are to derive the true Christian spirit . . ." (No. 14).

"In order that the Christian people may more securely derive an abundance of graces from the sacred liturgy, holy Mother Church desires to undertake with great care a general restoration of the liturgy itself. For the liturgy is made up of unchangeable elements divinely instituted, and elements subject to change. The latter not only may but ought to be changed with the passing of time if features have by chance crept in which are less harmonious with the intimate nature of the liturgy, or if existing elements have grown less functional.

"In this restoration, both texts and rites should be drawn up so that they express more clearly the holy things which they signify. Christian people, as far as possible, should be able to understand them with ease and to take part in them fully, actively, and as befits a community . . ." (No. 21).

Norms

Norms regarding the reforms concern the greater use of Scripture; emphasis on the importance of the sermon or homily on biblical and liturgical subjects; use of vernacular languages for prayers of the Mass and for administration of the sacraments; provision for adaptation of rites to cultural patterns.

Approval for reforms of various kinds — in liturgical texts, rites, etc — depends on the Holy See, regional conferences of bishops and individual bishops, according to provisions of law. No priest has authority to initiate reforms on his own. Reforms may not be introduced just for the sake of innovation, and any that are introduced in the light of present-day circumstances should embody sound tradition.

To assure the desired effect of liturgical reforms, training and instruction are necessary for the clergy, religious and the laity. The functions of diocesan and regional commissions for liturgy, music and art are to set standards and provide leadership for instruction and practical programs in their respective fields.

Most of the constitution's provisions regarding liturgical reforms have to do with the Roman Rite. The document clearly respects the equal dignity of all rites, leaving to the Eastern Churches control over their ancient liturgies.

For coverage of the **Mystery of the Eucharist,** see The Mass; **Other Sacraments,** see separate entry.

Sacramentals

Sacramentals, instituted by the Church, "are sacred signs which bear a resemblance to the sacraments: they signify effects, particularly of a spiritual kind, which are obtained through the Church's intercession. By them men are disposed to receive the chief effect of the sacraments, and various occasions in life are rendered holy" (No. 60).

"Thus, for well-disposed members of the faithful, the liturgy of the sacraments and sacramentals sanctifies almost every event in their lives; they are given access to the stream of divine grace which flows from the paschal mystery of the passion, death, and resurrection of Christ, the fountain from which all sacraments and sacramentals draw their power. There is hardly any proper use of material things which cannot thus be directed toward the sanctification of men and the praise of God" (No. 61). Some common sacramentals are priestly blessings, blessed palm, candles, holy water, medals, scapulars, prayers and ceremonies of the Roman Ritual.

Liturgy of the Hours

The Liturgy of the Hours (Divine Office) is the public prayer of the Church for praising God and sanctifying the day. Its daily celebration is required as a sacred obligation by men in holy orders and by men and women religious who have professed solemn vows. Its celebration by others is highly commended and is to be encouraged in the community of the faithful.

"By tradition going back to early Christian times, the Divine Office is arranged so that the whole course of the day and night is made holy by the praises of God. Therefore, when this wonderful song of praise is worthily rendered by priests and others who are deputed for this purpose by Church ordinance, or by the faithful praying together with the priest in an approved form, then it is truly the voice of the bride addressing her bridegroom; it is the very prayer which Christ Himself, together with His body, addresses to the Father" (No. 84).

"Hence all who perform this service are not only fulfilling a duty of the Church, but also are sharing in the greatest honor accorded to Christ's spouse, for by offering these praises to God they are standing before God's throne in the name of the Church their Mother" (No. 85).

The revised Liturgy of the Hours — its background, contents, scope and purposes — was described by Pope Paul in the apostolic constitution *Canticum Laudis,* dated Nov. 1, 1970. It consists of:

• Lauds and Vespers, the morning and evening prayers called "the hinges" of the Office;

• Matins, to be said at any time of the day, which retains the form of a nocturnal vigil service and is called the Office of Readings;

• Terce, Sext, None, any one of which may be chosen for prayer at an appropriate time of the day (9 a.m., 12 noon, 3 p.m.);

• Compline, a night prayer.

The hour of Prime was suppressed.

In the new Office, the hours are shorter than they had been, with greater textual variety, meditation aids, and provision for intervals of silence and meditation. The psalms are distributed over a four-week period instead of a week; some psalms, entirely or in part, are not included. Additional canticles from the Old and New Testaments are assigned for Lauds and Vespers, respectively. Additional scriptural texts have been added and variously arranged for greater internal unity, correspondence to readings at Mass, and relevance to events and themes of salvation history. Readings include some of the best material from the Fathers of the Church and other authors and improved selections on the lives of saints.

The book used for recitation of the Office is the **Breviary.**

The official English translation of the Latin text of the revised Roman Breviary has not yet been completed. An interim substitute embodying its major elements, *Prayer of Christians,* was published in 1971 by the U.S. Federation of Diocesan Liturgical Commissions in conjunction with the Catholic Book Publishing Co.

For coverage of the **Liturgical Year,** see Church Calendar.

Sacred Music

"The musical tradition of the universal Church is a treasure of immeasurable value, greater even than that of any other art. The main reason for this pre-eminence is that, as sacred melody united to words, it forms a necessary or integral part of the solemn liturgy.

". . . Sacred music increases in holiness to the degree that it is intimately linked with liturgical action, winningly expresses prayerfulness, promotes solidarity, and enriches sacred rites with heightened solemnity. The Church indeed approves of all forms of true art, and admits them into divine worship when they show appropriate qualities" (No. 112).

The constitution decreed:

• Vernacular languages for the people's parts of the liturgy, as well as Latin, may be used.

• Participation in sacred song by the whole body of the faithful, and not just by choirs, is to be encouraged and brought about.

• Provisions should be made for proper musical training for clergy, religious and lay persons.

• While Gregorian Chant has a unique dignity and relationship to the Latin liturgy, other kinds of music are acceptable.

• Native musical traditions should be used, especially in mission areas.

• Various instruments compatible with the dignity of worship may be used.

Gregorian Chant: A form and style of chant called Gregorian was the basis and most highly regarded standard of liturgical music for centuries. It originated probably during the formative period of the Roman liturgy and developed in conjunction with Gallican and other forms of chant. Gregory the Great's connection with it is not clear, although it is known that he had great concern for and interest in church music. The earliest extant written versions of Gregorian chant date from the ninth century. A thousand years later, the Benedictines of Solesmes, France, initiated a revival of chant which gave impetus to the modern liturgical movement.

Sacred Art and Furnishings

"Very rightly the fine arts are considered to rank among the noblest expressions of human genius. This judgment applies especially to religious art and to its highest achievement, which is sacred art. By their very nature both of the latter are related to God's boundless beauty, for this is the reality which these human efforts are trying to express in some way. To the extent that these works aim exclusively at turning men's thoughts to God persuasively and devoutly, they are dedicated to God and to the cause of His greater honor and glory" (No. 122).

The objective of sacred art is "that all things set apart for use in divine worship should be truly worthy, becoming, and beautiful, signs and symbols of heavenly realities. . . . The Church has . . . always reserved to herself the right to pass judgment upon the arts, deciding which of the works of artists are in accordance with faith, piety, and cherished traditional laws, and thereby suited to sacred purposes.

". . . Sacred furnishings should worthily and beautifully serve the dignity of worship . . ." (No. 122).

According to the constitution:

• Contemporary art, as well as that of the past, shall "be given free scope in the Church, provided that it adorns the sacred buildings and holy rites with due honor and reverence . . ." (No. 123).

• Noble beauty, not sumptuous display, should be sought in art, sacred vestments and ornaments.

• "Let bishops carefully exclude from the house of god and from other sacred places those works of artists which are repugnant to faith, morals, and Christian piety, and which offend true religious sense either by their distortion of forms or by lack of artistic worth, by mediocrity or by pretense.

• "When churches are to be built, let great care be taken that they be suitable for the celebration of liturgical services and for the active participation of the faithful" (No. 124).

• "The practice of placing sacred images in churches so that they may be venerated by the faithful is to be firmly maintained. Nevertheless, their number should be moderate and their relative location should reflect right order. Otherwise they may create confusion among the Christian people and promote a faulty sense of devotion" (No. 125).

• Artists should be trained and inspired in the spirit and for the purposes of the liturgy.

• The norms of sacred art should be revised. "These laws refer especially to the worthy and well-planned construction of sacred buildings, the shape and construction of altars, the nobility, location, and security of the Eucharistic tabernacle, the suitability and dignity of the baptistery, the proper use of sacred images, embellishments, and vestments . . ." (No. 128).

RITES

A rite is the manner in which liturgical worship is carried out. It includes the forms and ceremonial observances of liturgical worship.

Different rites have evolved in the course of Church history, giving to liturgical worship forms and usages peculiar and proper to the nature of worship itself and to the culture of the faithful in various circumstances of time and place. Thus, there has been development since apostolic times in prayers and ceremonies of the Mass, the administration of the sacraments, requirements for celebration of the Divine Office. Practices within the patriarchates of Antioch, Rome, Alexandria and Constantinople were the principal sources of the rites in present use.

Eastern Rites, described elsewhere in the Almanac, are proper to Eastern Catholic Churches.

The **Roman** or **Latin Rite,** described in this section, prevails in the Western Church. It was derived from Roman practices and the use of Latin as an official language from the third century onward. Other rites in limited use in the Western Church have been the Ambrosian, the Mozarabic, the Lyonnais, the Braga, and rites peculiar to some religious orders like the Dominicans, Carmelites and Carthusians.

The revision of rites in progress since the Second Vatican Council is meant to renew them, not to eliminate the rites of particular churches or to reduce all rites to uniformity.

RECONCILIATION TEXTS

Texts for a Week of Reconciliation during the Holy Year are included in a directory prepared by the Congregation for Divine Worship. The themes and days are: "Hope of the World and the Kingdom of God" (Sunday or Monday), "The Word Made Flesh" (Monday or Tuesday), "Be Converted and Believe" (Wednesday), "Through Death to Life" (Thursday), "Reconciliation" (Friday), "The Church United in the Holy Spirit" (Saturday), "The Mystery of Unity" (Sunday).

MASS, EUCHARISTIC SACRIFICE AND BANQUET

Declarations of Vatican II

The Second Vatican Council made the following declarations, among others, with respect to the Mass.

"At the Last Supper, on the night when He was betrayed, our Savior instituted the Eucharistic Sacrifice of His Body and Blood. He did this in order to perpetuate the sacrifice of the Cross throughout the centuries until He should come again, and so to entrust to His beloved spouse, the Church, a memorial of His death and resurrection: a sacrament of love, a sign of unity, a bond of charity, a paschal banquet in which Christ is consumed, the mind is filled with grace, and a pledge of future glory is given to us" (*Constitution on the Sacred Liturgy*, No. 47).

". . . As often as the sacrifice of the cross in which 'Christ, our passover, has been sacrificed' (1 Cor. 5:7) is celebrated on an altar, the work of our redemption is carried on. At the same time, in the sacrament of the Eucharistic bread the unity of all believers who form one body in Christ (cf. 1 Cor. 10:17) is both expressed and brought about. All men are called to this union with Christ . . ." (*Dogmatic Constitution on the Church*. No. 3).

". . . The ministerial priest, by the sacred power he enjoys, molds and rules the priestly people. Acting in the person of Christ, he brings about the Eucharistic Sacrifice, and offers it to God in the name of all the people. For their part, the faithful join in the offering of the Eucharist by virtue of their royal priesthood . . ." (*Ibid.*, No. 10).

Declarations of Trent

Among its decrees on the Holy Eucharist, the Council of Trent stated the following points of doctrine on the Mass.

1. There is in the Catholic Church a true Sacrifice, the Mass instituted by Jesus Christ. It is the Sacrifice of His Body and Blood, Soul and Divinity, Himself, under the appearances of bread and wine.

2. This Sacrifice is identical with the Sacrifice of the Cross, inasmuch as Christ is the Priest and Victim in both. A difference lies in the manner of offering, which was bloody upon the Cross and is bloodless on the altar.

3. The Mass is a propitiatory Sacrifice, atoning for sins of the living and dead for whom it is offered.

4. The efficacy of the Mass is derived from the Sacrifice of the Cross, whose super-abundant merits it applies to men.

5. Although the Mass is offered to God alone, it may be celebrated in honor and memory of the saints.

6. Christ instituted the Mass at the Last Supper.

7. Christ ordained the Apostles priests, giving them power and the command to consecrate His Body and Blood to perpetuate and renew the Sacrifice.

ORDER OF MASS

The Mass consists of two principal divisions called the **Liturgy of the Word,** which features the proclamation of the Word of God, and the **Eucharistic Liturgy,** which focuses on the central act of sacrifice in the Consecration and on the Eucharistic Banquet in Holy Communion. (Formerly, these divisions were called, respectively, the **Mass of the Catechumens** and the **Mass of the Faithful.**) In addition to these principal divisions, there are ancillary introductory and concluding rites.

The following description covers the Mass as celebrated with participation by the people. This Order of the Mass was approved by Pope Paul VI in the apostolic constitution *Missale Romanum* dated Apr. 3, 1969, and promulgated in a decree issued Apr. 6, 1969, by the Congregation for Divine Worship. The assigned effective date was Nov. 30, 1969.

Introductory Rites

Entrance: The introductory rites begin with the singing or recitation of the Introit or an equivalent entrance song while the priest approaches the altar, kisses it, and goes to the place where he will be seated. The Introit consists of one or more scriptural verses stating the theme of the mystery, season or feast commemorated in the Mass.

Greeting: The priest and people make the Sign of the Cross together. The priest then greets them in one of several alternative ways and they reply in a corresponding manner.

Introductory Remarks: At this point, the priest or another of the ministers may introduce the theme of the Mass.

Penitential Rite: The priest and people together acknowledge their sins as a preliminary step toward worthy celebration of the sacred mysteries. This rite includes a brief examination of conscience, a general confession of sin and plea for divine mercy in one of three ways, and a prayer of absolution by the priest. The *Kyrie, eleison* ("Lord, have mercy") is then said if it was not included in one of the foregoing pleas for divine mercy.

Glory to God: A doxology, a hymn of praise to God, sung or said on festive occasions.

Opening Prayer: A prayer of petition offered by the priest on behalf of the worshipping community.

I. Liturgy of the Word

Readings: The featured elements of this liturgy are several readings of passages from the Bible. If three readings are in order, the first is usually from the Old Testament, the second from the New Testament (Epistles, Acts, Revelation), and the third from one of the Gospels; the final reading is always a selection from a Gospel. The first reading(s) is concluded with the formula, "This is the Word of the Lord," to which the people respond, "Thanks be to God." The Gospel reading is concluded with the formula, "This is the Gospel of the Lord," to which the people respond, "Praise to you, Lord Jesus Christ," Between the readings, psalm verses and a Gospel acclamation are sung or said.

Homily: Sermon on a scriptural or liturgical subject; ideally, it should be related to the liturgical service in progress.

Creed: The Nicene profession of faith, by priest and people, on certain occasions.

Prayer of the Faithful: Litany-type prayers of petition, with participation by the people. Called general intercessions, they concern needs of the Church, the salvation of the world, public authorities, persons in need, the local community.

II. Eucharistic Liturgy

Offertory Song: Scriptural verses related to the theme of the Mass, or a suitable hymn, sung or said while things are prepared at the altar for the Eucharistic Liturgy and while the offerings of bread and wine are brought to the altar.

Offertory Procession: Presentation to the priest of the gifts of bread and wine, principally, by participating members of the congregation.

Offering of the Gifts: Consists of the prayers and ceremonies with which the priest offers bread and wine as the elements of the sacrifice to take place during the Eucharistic Prayer and of the Lord's Supper to be shared in Holy Communion. If singing takes place during the offering, the priest can say the prayers and carry out the action silently; if there is no singing, he says the prayers aloud and the people, after each offering, respond with the words, "Blessed be God forever."

Washing of Hands: After offering the bread and wine, the priest cleanses his fingers with water in a brief ceremony of purification.

Pray, Brethren: Prayer that the sacrifice to take place will be acceptable to God. The first part of the prayer is said by the priest; the second, by the people.

Prayer over the Gifts: A prayer of petition offered by the priest on behalf of the worshiping community.

Eucharistic Prayer

Preface: A hymn of praise, introducing the Eucharistic Prayer or Canon, sung or said by the priest following responses by the people. The Order of the Mass contains a variety of prefaces, for use on different occasions.

Holy, Holy, Holy; Blessed Is He: Divine praises sung or said by the priest and people.

Canon: The Eucharistic Prayer of the Mass whose central portion is the Consecration, when the essential act of sacrificial offering

takes place with the changing of bread and wine into the Body and Blood of Christ. The prayers of the Canon, which are said by the celebrant only, commemorate principal mysteries of salvation history and include petitions for the Church, the living and dead, and remembrances of saints. There are four Eucharistic Prayers, for use on various occasions and at the option of the priest.

Doxology: A formula of divine praise sung or said by the priest while he holds aloft the chalice containing the consecrated wine in one hand and the paten containing the consecrated host in the other.

Communion Rite

Lord's Prayer: Sung or said by the priest and people.

Prayer for Deliverance from evil: Called an **embolism** because it is a development of the final petition of the Lord's Prayer; said by the priest. It concludes with a memorial of the return of the Lord to which the people respond, "For the kingdom, the power, and the glory are yours, now and forever."

Prayer for Peace: Said by the priest, with corresponding responses by the people. The priest can, in accord with local custom, bid the people to exchange a greeting of peace with each other.

Lamb of God: A prayer for divine mercy sung or said while the priest breaks the consecrated host and places a piece of it into the consecrated wine in the chalice.

Communion: The priest, after saying a preparatory prayer, administers Holy Communion to himself and then to the people, thus completing the sacrifice-banquet of the Mass. (This completion is realized even if the celebrant alone receives the Eucharist.) On giving the Eucharist to the people, the priest says, "The Body of Christ," to each recipient; the customary response is "Amen." If the Eucharist is administered under the forms of bread and wine, the priest says, "The Body and Blood of Christ."

Communion Song: Scriptural verses or a suitable hymn sung or said during the distribution of Holy Communion. After Holy Communion is received, some moments may be spent in silent meditation or in the chanting of a psalm or hymn of praise.

Prayer after Communion: A prayer of petition offered by the priest on behalf of the worshipping community.

Concluding Rite

Announcements: Brief announcements to the people are in order at this time.

Dismissal: Consists of a final greeting by the priest, a blessing, and a formula of dismissal. This rite is omitted if another liturgical action immediately follows the Mass; e.g., a procession, the blessing of the body during a funeral rite.

Some parts of the Mass are changeable

with the liturgical season or feast, and are called the **proper** of the Mass. Other parts are said to be **common** because they always remain the same.

Additional Mass Notes

Catholics are seriously obliged to attend Mass in a worthy manner on Sundays and holy days of obligation. Failure to do so without a proportionately serious reason is gravely wrong.

It is the custom for priests to celebrate Mass daily whenever possible. To satisfy the needs of the faithful on Sundays and holy days of obligation, they are authorized to say Mass twice (**bination**) or even three times (**trination**). Bination is also permissible on weekdays. On Christmas and All Souls' Day every priest may say three Masses. Mass may be celebrated in the morning, afternoon or evening.

The **fruits of the Mass,** which in itself is of infinite value, are: **general,** for all the faithful; **special (ministerial),** for the intentions or persons specifically intended by the celebrant; **most special (personal),** for the celebrant himself. On Sundays and certain other days pastors are obliged to offer Mass for their parishioners. If a priest accepts a stipend or offering for a Mass, he is obliged in justice to apply the Mass for the designated intention. Mass may be applied for the living and the dead, or for any good intention.

Mass can be celebrated in several ways: e.g., with people present, without their presence (privately), with two or more priests as co-celebrants (concelebration), with greater or less solemnity.

Some of the various types of Masses are: **for the dead** (Funeral Mass or Mass of Christian Burial, Mass for the Dead — formerly called Requiem Mass); **nuptial,** for married couples, with or after the wedding ceremony; **votive,** to honor a Person of the Trinity, a saint, or for some special intention; **conventual,** the community Mass in houses of solemnly professed religious. A **red Mass** is a Votive Mass of the Holy Spirit, celebrated for members of the legal profession that they might exercise prudence and equity in their official capacities. **Gregorian Masses** are a series of 30 Masses celebrated on 30 consecutive days for a deceased person.

The only day of the year on which Mass is not celebrated is Good Friday. In its place, there is a **Solemn Liturgical Action.**

Places, Altars for Mass

The ordinary place for celebrating the Eucharist is a church or other sacred place, at a permanent or movable altar.

Outside of a sacred place, Mass may be celebrated in an appropriate place at a suitable table covered with a linen cloth and corporal. An **altar stone** containing the relics of saints, which was formerly prescribed, is not required by regulations in effect since the promulgation Apr. 6, 1969, of *Institutio Generalis Missalis Romani.*

A **permanent altar** should have a table of stone, be consecrated, and have enclosed within it relics of some saints.

A **movable altar** may be made of any solid and suitable material. If made of stone and consecrated, it should have enclosed within it relics of some saints; if blessed rather than consecrated, the enclosure of relics is not required.

LITURGICAL VESTMENTS

In the early years of the Church, vestments worn by the ministers at liturgical functions were the same as the garments in ordinary popular use. They became distinctive when their form was not altered to correspond with later variations in popular style. Liturgical vestments are symbolic of the sacred ministry and add appropriate decorum to divine worship.

Mass Vestments

Alb: A body-length tunic of white fabric; a vestment common to all ministers of divine worship.

Amice: A rectangular piece of white cloth worn about the neck, tucked into the collar and falling over the shoulders; worn under the alb.

Chasuble: Originally, a large mantle or cloak covering the body, it is the outer vestment of a priest celebrating Mass or carrying out other sacred actions connected with the Mass.

Cincture: A cord which serves the purpose of a belt, holding the alb close to the body.

Dalmatic: The outer vestment worn by a deacon in place of a chasuble.

Stole: A long, band-like vestment worn about the neck and falling to about the knees. (A stole is used for other functions also.)

The material, form and ornamentation of the aforementioned and other vestments are subject to variation and adaptation, according to norms and decisions of the Holy See and concerned conferences of bishops. The overriding norm is that they should be appropriate for use in divine worship. The customary ornamented vestments are the chasuble, dalmatic and stole.

The minimal vestments required for a priest celebrating Mass are the alb, stole and chasuble.

Liturgical Colors

The colors of outer vestments vary with liturgical seasons, feasts and other circumstances. The colors and their use are:

Green: For the season of the year.

Purple: For Advent and Lent; may also be used in Masses for the dead.

Red: For the Sunday of the Passion, the Wednesday of Holy Week, Good Friday,

Pentecost; feasts of the Passion of Our Lord, the Apostles and Evangelists, martyrs.

Rose: May be used in place of purple on the Third Sunday of Advent (Gaudete Sunday) and the Fourth Sunday of Lent (Laetare Sunday).

White: For Christmastide and Eastertide; feasts and commemorations of Our Lord, except those of the Passion; feasts and commemorations of the Blessed Virgin Mary, angels, saints who are not martyrs, All Saints (Nov. 1), St. John the Baptist (June 24), St. John the Evangelist (Dec. 27), the Chair of St. Peter (Feb. 22), the Conversion of St. Paul (Jan. 25). White may generally be substituted for other colors, and can be used for funeral and other Masses for the dead.

On more solemn occasions, better than ordinary vestments may be used, even though their color (e.g., gold) does not match the requirements of the day.

Considerable freedom is permitted in the choice of colors of vestments worn for votive Masses.

Other Vestments

Cappa Magna: Flowing vestment with a train, worn by bishops and cardinals.

Cassock: A full-length, close-fitting robe worn by priests and other clerics under liturgical vestments and in ordinary use; usually black for priests, purple for bishops and other prelates, red for cardinals, white for the pope. In place of a cassock, priests belonging to religious institutes wear the habit proper to their institute.

Cope: A mantle-like vestment open in front and fastened across the chest; worn by sacred ministers in processions and other ceremonies, as prescribed by appropriate directives.

Gremial: A rectangular veil of silk or linen placed over the knees of a bishop when he is seated during various episcopal ceremonies.

Habit: The ordinary garb of members of religious institutes, analogous to the cassock of diocesan priests; the form of habits varies from institute to institute.

Humeral Veil: A rectangular vestment worn about the shoulders by a deacon. or priest in Eucharistic processions and for other prescribed liturgical ceremonies.

Mitre: A headdress worn at some liturgical functions by bishops, abbots and, in certain cases, other ecclesiastics.

Pallium: A circular band of white wool about two inches wide, with front and back pendants, marked with six crosses, worn about the neck by some major prelates. Symbolic of the fullness of the episcopal office, it is given by the pope on request to patriarchs, primates, archbishops and, rarely, bishops. The pallium is made from the wool of lambs blessed by the pope on the feast of St. Agnes (Jan. 21).

Rochet: A knee-length, white linen-lace

garment of prelates worn under outer vestments.

Surplice: A loose, flowing vestment of white fabric with wide sleeves. For some functions, it is interchangeable with an alb.

Zucchetto: A skullcap worn by bishops and other prelates.

SACRED VESSELS, LINENS

Vessels

Chalice and Paten: The principal sacred vessels required for the celebration of Mass are the **chalice** (cup) and **paten** (plate) in which wine and bread, respectively, are offered, consecrated and consumed. Both should be made of solid and noble material which is not easily breakable or corruptible. Gold coating is required of the interior parts of sacred vessels subject to rust. The cup of a chalice should be made of non-absorbent material.

Vessels for containing consecrated hosts (see below) can be made of material other than solid and noble metal — e. g., ivory, more durable woods — provided the substitute material is locally regarded as noble or rather precious and is suitable for sacred use.

Sacred vessels should be blessed or consecrated, according to prescribed requirements.

Vessels, in addition to the paten, for containing consecrated hosts are:

Ciborium: Used to hold hosts for distribution to the faithful and for reservation in the tabernacle.

Luna, Lunula, Lunette: A small receptacle which holds the sacred host in an upright position in the monstrance.

Monstrance, Ostensorium: A portable receptable so made that the sacred host, when enclosed therein, may be clearly seen, as at Benediction or during extended exposition of the Blessed Sacrament.

Pyx: A watch-shaped vessel used in carrying the Eucharist to the sick.

Linens

Altar Cloth: A white cloth, usually of linen, covering the table of an altar. One cloth is sufficient. Three were used according to former requirements.

Burse: A square, stiff flat case, open at one end, in which the folded corporal is placed; the outside is covered with material of the same kind and color as the outer vestments of the celebrant.

Corporal: A square piece of white linen spread on the altar cloth, on which rest the vessels holding the Sacred Species — the consecrated host(s) and wine — during the Eucharistic Liturgy. The corporal is similarly used whenever the Blessed Sacrament is removed from the tabernacle; e. g., during Benediction the vessel containing the Blessed Sacrament rests on a corporal.

Finger Towel: A white rectangular napkin used by the priest to dry his fingers after cleansing them following the offering of gifts at Mass.

Pall: A square piece of stiff material, usually covered with linen, used to cover the chalice at Mass.

Purificator: A white rectangular napkin used for cleansing sacred vessels after the reception of Communion at Mass.

Veil: The chalice intended for use at Mass is covered with a veil made of the same material as the outer vestments of the celebrant.

THE CHURCH BUILDING

A church is a building set aside and dedicated for purposes of divine worship, the place of assembly for a worshiping community.

A Catholic church is the ordinary place in which the faithful assemble for participation in the Eucharistic Liturgy and other forms of divine worship.

In the early years of Christianity, the first places of assembly for the Eucharistic Liturgy were private homes (Acts 2:46; Rom. 16:5; 1 Cor. 16:5; Col. 4:15) and, sometimes, catacombs. Church building began in the latter half of the second century during lulls in persecution and became widespread after enactment of the Edict of Milan in 313, when it finally became possible for the Church to emerge completely from the underground. The oldest and basic norms regarding church buildings date from about that time.

The essential principle underlying all norms for church building was reformulated by the Second Vatican Council, as follows: "When churches are to be built, let great care be taken that they be suitable for the celebration of liturgical services and for the active participation of the faithful" *(Constitution on the Sacred Liturgy*, No. 124).

This principle was subsequently elaborated in detail by the Congregation for Divine Worship in a document entitled *Institutio Generalis Missalis Romani,* which was approved by Paul VI Apr. 3 and promulgated by a decree of the congregation dated Apr. 6, 1969. Coverage of the following items reflects the norms stated in Chapter V of this document.

Sanctuary: The part of the church where the altar of sacrifice is located, the place where the ministers of the liturgy lead the people in prayer, proclaim the word of God and celebrate the Eucharist. It is set off from the body of the church by a distinctive structural feature — e. g., elevation above the main floor — or by ornamentation. (The traditional **communion rail,** which has been removed in recent years in many churches, served this purpose of demarcation.) The customary location of the sanctuary is at the front of the church; it may, however, be centrally located.

Altar: The main altar of sacrifice and table of the Lord is the focal feature of the sanctuary and entire church. It stands by itself, so that the ministers can move about it freely, and is so situated that they face the people during the liturgical action. In addition to this main altar, there may also be others; in new churches, these are situated in side chapels or alcoves removed to some degree from the body of the church.

Adornment of the Altar: The altar table is covered with a suitable linen cloth. Required candelabra and a cross are placed upon or near the altar in plain sight of the people and are so arranged that they do not obscure their view of the liturgical action.

Seats of the Ministers: The seat of the celebrant, corresponding with his role as the presiding minister of the assembly, is best located behind the altar and facing the people; it is raised a bit above the level of the altar but must not have the appearance of a throne. The seats of other ministers are also located in the sanctuary.

Ambo, Pulpit: The stand at which scriptural lessons and psalm responses are read, the word of God preached, and the prayer of the faithful offered. It is so placed that the ministers can be easily seen and heard by the people.

Places for the People: Seats and kneeling benches (**pews**) and other accommodations for the people are so arranged that they can participate in the most appropriate way in the liturgical action and have freedom of movement for the reception of Holy Communion. Reserved seats are out of order.

Place for the Choir: Where it is located depends on the most suitable arrangement for maintaining the unity of the choir with the congregation and for providing its members maximum opportunity for carrying out their proper function and participating fully in the Mass.

Tabernacle: The best place for reserving the Blessed Sacrament is in a chapel suitable for the private devotion of the people. If this is not possible, reservation should be at a side altar or other appropriately adorned place. In either case, the Blessed Sacrament should be kept in a tabernacle, i. e., a safe-like, secure receptacle.

Statues: Images of the Lord, the Blessed Virgin Mary and the saints are legitimately proposed for the veneration of the faithful in churches. Their number and arrangement, however, should be ordered in such a way that they do not distract the people from the central celebration of the Eucharistic Liturgy. There should be only one statue of one and the same saint in a church.

General Adornment and Arrangement of Churches: Churches should be so adorned and fitted out that they serve the direct requirements of divine worship and the needs and reasonable convenience of the people.

Other Items

Ambry: A box containing the holy oils, attached to the wall of the sanctuary in some churches.

Baptistery: The place for administering baptism. Some churches have baptisteries adjoining or near the entrance, a position symbolizing the fact that persons are initiated in the Church and incorporated in Christ through this sacrament. Contemporary liturgical practice favors placement of the baptistery near the sanctuary and altar, or the use of a portable font in the same position, to emphasize the relationship of baptism to the Eucharist, the celebration in sacrifice and banquet of the death and resurrection of Christ.

Candles: Used more for symbolical than illuminative purposes, they represent Christ, the light and life of grace, at liturgical func-

tions. They are made of beeswax.

Confessional: A booth-like structure for the hearing of confessions, with separate compartments for the priest and penitents and a grating or screen between them. The use of confessionals became general in the Roman Rite after the Council of Trent.

Crucifix: A cross bearing the figure of the body of Christ, representative of the Sacrifice of the Cross.

Cruets: Vessels containing the wine and water used at Mass. They are placed on a credence table in the sanctuary.

Holy Water Fonts: Receptacles containing holy water, usually at church entrances, for the use of the faithful.

Sanctuary Lamp: A lamp which is kept burning continuously before a tabernacle in which the Blessed Sacrament is reserved, as a sign of the Real Presence of Christ.

LITURGICAL DEVELOPMENTS

The principal developments covered in this article are enactments of the Holy See and actions related to their implementation in the United States.

Modern Movement

Origins of the modern movement for renewal in the liturgy date back to the 19th century. The key contributing factor was a revival of liturgical and scriptural studies. Of special significance was the work of the Benedictine monks of Solesmes, France, who aroused great interest in the liturgy through the restoration of Gregorian Chant. St. Pius X approved their work in a motu proprio of 1903 and gave additional encouragement to liturgical study and development.

St. Pius X did more than any other single pope to promote early first Communion and the practice of frequent Communion, started the research behind a revised Breviary, and appointed a group to investigate possible revisions in the Mass.

The movement attracted some attention in the 1920's and 30's but made little progress.

Significant pioneering developments in the US during the 20's, however, were the establishment of the Liturgical Press, the beginning of publication of *Orate Fratres* (now *Worship*), and the inauguration of the League of the Divine Office by the Benedictines at St. John's Abbey, Collegeville, Minn. Later events of influence were the establishment of the Pius X School of Liturgical Music at Manhattanville College of the Sacred Heart and the organization of a summer school of liturgical music at Mary Manse College by the Gregorian Institute of America. The turning point toward real renewal was reached during and after World War II.

Pius XII gave it impetus and direction, principally through the background teaching in his encyclicals on the *Mystical Body* (1943),

Sacred Liturgy (1947), and the *Discipline of Sacred Music* (1955), and by means of specific measures affecting the liturgy itself. His work was continued during the pontificates of John XXIII and Paul VI. The Second Vatican Council, in virtue of its *Constitution on the Sacred Liturgy*, inaugurated changes of the greatest significance.

Before and After Vatican II

The most significant liturgical changes made in the years immediately preceding the Second Vatican Council were the following:

(1) Revision of the Rites of Holy Week, for universal observance from 1956.

(2) Modification of the Eucharistic fast and permission for afternoon and evening Mass, in effect from 1953 and extended in 1957.

(3) The Dialogue Mass, introduced in 1958.

(4) Use of popular languages in administration of the sacraments.

(5) Calendar-missal-breviary reform, in effect from Jan. 1, 1961.

(6) Seven-step administration of baptism for adults, approved in 1962.

The *Constitution on the Sacred Liturgy* approved (2,174 to 4) and promulgated by the Second Vatican Council Dec. 4, 1963, marked the beginning of a profound renewal in the Church's corporate worship. Implementation of some of its measures was ordered by Paul VI Jan. 25, 1964, in the motu proprio *Sacram Liturgiam*. On Feb. 29, a special commission, the Consilium for Implementing the Constitution on the Sacred Liturgy, was formed to supervise the execution of the entire program of liturgical reform. Implementation of the program on local and regional levels was left to bishops acting through their own liturgical commissions and in concert with their fellow bishops in national conferences.

Liturgical reform in the United States has

been carried out under the direction of the Liturgy Committee, National Conference of Catholic Bishops. Its secretariat, established early in 1965, is located at 1312 Massachusetts Ave. N.W., Washington, D.C. 20005.

Stages of Development

Liturgical development after the Second Vatican Council proceeded in several stages. It started with the formulation of guidelines and directives, and with the translation into vernacular languages of virtually unchanged Latin ritual texts. Then came structural changes in the Mass, the sacraments, the calendar, the Divine Office and other phases of the liturgy. These revisions were just about completed with the publication of a new order for the sacrament of penance in February, 1974. A continuing phase of development, in progress from the beginning, involves efforts to deepen the liturgical sense of the faithful, to increase their participation in worship and to relate it to full Christian life.

Texts and Translations

The master texts of all documents on liturgical reform were in Latin. Effective dates of their implementation depended on the completion and approval of appropriate translations into vernacular languages. English translations were made by the International Committee for English in the Liturgy.

The principal features of liturgical changes and the effective dates of their introduction in the United States are covered below under topical headings. (For expanded coverage of various items, especially the sacraments, see additional entries.)

The Mass

A new Order of the Mass, supplanting the one authorized by the Council of Trent in the 16th century, was introduced in the U.S. Mar. 22, 1970. It had been approved by Paul VI in the apostolic constitution *Missale Romanum*, dated Apr. 3, 1969.

Preliminary and related to it were the following developments.

Mass in English: Introduced Nov. 29, 1964. In the same year, Psalm 42 was eliminated from the prayers at the foot of the altar.

Incidental Changes: The last Gospel (prologue of John) and vernacular prayers following Mass were eliminated Mar. 7, 1965. At the same time, provision was made for the celebrant to say aloud some prayers formerly said silently.

Rubrics: An instruction entitled *Tres Abhinc Annos*, dated May 4 and effective June 29, 1967, simplified directives for the celebration of Mass, approved the practice of saying the canon aloud, altered the Communion and dismissal rites, permitted purple instead of black vestments in Masses for the dead, discontinued wearing of the maniple, and ap-

proved in principle the use of vernacular languages for the canon, ordination rites, and lessons of the Divine Office when read in choir.

Canons or Eucharistic Prayers: Three additional Eucharistic prayers authorized May 23, 1968, were approved for use in vernacular translation the following Aug. 15. They have the same basic structure as the traditional Roman Canon, whose use in English was introduced Oct. 22, 1967.

The customary Roman Canon, which dates at least from the beginning of the fifth century and has remained substantially unchanged since the seventh century, is the first in the order of listing of the Eucharistic prayers. It can be used at any time, but is the one of choice for most Sundays, some special feasts like Easter and Pentecost, and for feasts of the Apostles and other saints who are commemorated in the canon. Any preface can be used with it.

The second Eucharistic prayer, the shortest and simplest of all, is best suited for use on weekdays and various special circumstances. It has a preface of its own, but others may be used with it. This canon bears a close resemblance to the one framed by St. Hippolytus about 215.

The third Eucharistic prayer is suitable for use on Sundays and feasts as an alternative to the Roman Canon. It can be used with any preface and has a special formula for remembrance of the dead.

The fourth Eucharistic prayer, the most sophisticated of them all, presents a broad synthesis of salvation history. Based on the Eastern tradition of Antioch, it is best suited for use at Masses attended by persons versed in Sacred Scripture. It has an unchangeable preface.

Lectionary: A new compilation of scriptural readings and psalm responsories for Mass was introduced Mar. 22, 1970. The *Lectionary* contains a three-year cycle of readings for Sundays and solemn feasts, a two-year weekday cycle, and a one-year cycle for the feasts of saints, in addition to readings for a great variety of Masses, ritual Masses and Masses for various needs. There are also responsorial psalms to follow the first readings, and gospel or alleluia versicles to follow the second readings.

Sacramentary (Missal): The Vatican Polyglot Press began distribution in June, 1970, of the Latin text of a new *Roman Missal*, the first revision published in 400 years. The English translation was authorized for optional use beginning July 1, 1974; the mandatory date for use was Dec. 1, 1974.

The missal is the celebrant's book of prayers and sacramental formulas and does not include the readings of the Mass, such as the Gospel and the Epistle. It contains the texts of entrance songs, prefaces and other prayers of the Mass. The number of prefaces is four times greater than it had been. There are 10 commons (or sets of Mass prayers) of martyrs, two of doctors of the Church, and a dozen for saints or groups of saints of various kinds, such as religious, educators and mothers of families. There are Masses during which certain sacraments are administered and others for religious profession, the Church, the pope, priests, Christian unity, the evangelization of nations, persecuted Christians, and other intentions.

Mass for Special Groups: Reasons and norms for the celebration of Mass at special gatherings of the faithful were the subject of an instruction issued May 15, 1969. Two years earlier, the U.S. Bishops' Liturgy Committee went on record in support of the celebration of Mass in private homes.

Sunday Mass on Saturday: The Congregation for the Clergy, under date of Jan. 10, 1970, granted the request that the faithful, where bishops consider it pastorally necessary or useful, may satisfy the precept of participating in Mass in the late afternoon or evening hours of Saturdays and the days before holy days of obligation.

Trination: The Congregation for the Sacraments, under date of Jan. 20, 1970, granted to all U.S. bishops the authority to permit priests to celebrate Mass three times on Saturdays and days preceding holy days of obligation, on condition that the first and second Masses are celebrated for weddings and/or funerals and the third Mass is celebrated in the evening so that the precept (of participating in Mass) will be satisfied by the faithful.

Mass in Latin: According to a notice issued by the Congregation for Divine Worship June 1, 1971: (1) Bishops may permit the celebration of Mass in Latin for mixed-language groups. (2) Priests may celebrate Mass in Latin when people are not present. (3) The approved revised Order of the Mass is to be used in Latin as well as vernacular languages. (4) By way of exception, bishops may permit older and handicapped priests to use the Council of Trent's Order of the Mass in private celebration of the holy Sacrifice.

Inter-Ritual Concelebration: The Apostolic Delegation in Washington, D.C., announced in June, 1971, that it had received authorization to permit priests of Roman and Eastern rites to celebrate Mass together in the rite of the host church. It was understood that the inter-ritual concelebrations would always be "a manifestation of the unity of the Church and of communion among particular churches."

Ordo of the Sung Mass: In a decree dated June 24 and made public Aug. 24, 1972, the Congregation for Divine Worship issued a new *Ordo of the Sung Mass* — containing Gregorian chants in Latin — to replace the *Graduale Romanum.*

Mass for Children: Late in 1973, the Congregation for Divine Worship issued special guidelines for children's Masses, providing accommodations to the mentality and spiritual growth of pre-adolescents while retaining the principal parts and structures of the Mass. The *Directory for Masses with Children* was approved by Paul VI Oct. 22 and was dated Nov. 1, 1973.

Sacraments

The general use of English in administration of the sacraments was approved for the U.S. Sept. 14, 1964. Structural changes of the rites were subsequently made and introduced in the U.S. as follows.

Anointing of the Sick: Revised rites, covering also administration of the Eucharist to sick persons, were approved Nov. 30,. 1972, and published Jan. 18, 1973. The effective date for use of the English prayer formula was Dec. 1, 1974.

Baptism: New rites for the baptism of infants, approved Mar. 19, 1969, were introduced June 1, 1970.

Christian Initiation of Adults: Revised rites were issued Jan. 6, 1972, for the Christian initiation of adults — affecting preparation for and reception of baptism, the Eucharist and confirmation; also, the reception of already baptized adults into the Church. These rites, which were introduced in the U.S. on the completion of English translation, nullified a seven-step baptismal process approved in 1962.

Confirmation: Revised rites, issued Aug. 15, 1971, became mandatory in the U.S. Jan. 1, 1973.

Eucharist: Several enactments concerning the Eucharist have been issued since 1966 when permission was given for the superiors of convents to administer Holy Communion in the absence of priests. Paul VI issued an instruction on *Worship of the Eucharistic Mystery* May 25, 1967, and another on the manner of administering Holy Communion May 20, 1969. Limited permission for lay persons to serve as extraordinary ministers of the Eucharist was given in 1971 and extended in 1972. Also in 1972, instructions were issued regarding administration of the Eucharist to other Christians, and in particular circumstances.

Holy Orders: Revised ordination rites for deacons, priests and bishops, validated by prior experimental use, were approved in 1970. The sacrament of holy orders underwent further revision in 1972 with the elimination of the Church-instituted orders of porter, reader, exorcist, acolyte and subdeacon, and of the tonsure ceremony symbolic of entrance into the clerical state. The former minor orders of reader and acolyte were changed from orders to ministries.

Matrimony: New rites, issued Mar. 19, 1969, were introduced June 1, 1970. Minor revisions had been made in 1964 in conjunc-

Sacraments

The sacraments are actions of Christ and his Church which signify grace, cause it in the act of signifying it, and confer it upon persons properly disposed to receive it. They perpetuate the redemptive activity of Christ, making it present and effective. They infallibly communicate the fruit of that activity — namely, grace — to responsive persons with faith. Sacramental actions consist of the union of sensible signs (matter of the sacraments) with the words of the minister (form of the sacraments).

Christ instituted the sacraments: three of them — baptism, Holy Eucharist, penance — directly; the other four — confirmation, holy orders, anointing of the sick, matrimony — through the Church.

Christ is the principal priest or minister of every sacrament; human agents — an ordained priest, baptized persons contracting marriage with each other, any person conferring emergency baptism in a proper manner — are secondary ministers. Sacraments have efficacy from Christ, not from the personal dispositions of their human ministers.

Each sacrament confers sanctifying grace for the special purpose of the sacrament; this is, accordingly, called sacramental grace. It involves a right to actual graces corresponding to the purposes of the respective sacraments.

While sacraments infallibly produce the grace they signify, recipients benefit from them in proportion to their personal dispositions. One of these is the intention to receive sacraments as sacred signs of God's saving and grace-giving action. The state of grace is also necessary for fruitful reception of the Holy Eucharist, confirmation, matrimony, holy orders and anointing of the sick. Baptism is the sacrament in which grace is given in the first instance and original sin is remitted. Penance is the secondary sacrament of reconciliation, in which persons guilty of serious sin after baptism are reconciled with God and the Church, and in which persons already in the state of grace are strengthened in that state.

Role of Sacraments

The Second Vatican Council prefaced a description of the role of the sacraments with the following statement concerning participation by all the faithful in the priesthood of Christ and the exercise of that priesthood by receiving the sacraments (*Dogmatic Constitution on the Church*, Nos. 10 and 11).

". . . The baptized by regeneration and the anointing of the Holy Spirit, are consecrated into a spiritual house and a holy priesthood. Thus through all those works befitting Christian men they can offer spiritual sacrifice and proclaim the power of Him who

has called them out of darkness into His marvelous light (cf. 1 Pt. 2:4-10). . . ."

"Though they differ from one another in essence and not only in degree, the common priesthood of the faithful and the ministerial or hierarchical priesthood (of those ordained to holy orders) are nonetheless interrelated. Each of them in its own special way is a participation in the one priesthood of Christ. The ministerial priest, by the sacred power he enjoys, molds and rules the priestly people. Acting in the person of Christ, he brings about the Eucharistic Sacrifice, and offers it to God in the name of all the people. For their part, the faithful join in the offering of the Eucharist by virtue of their royal priesthood. They likewise exercise that priesthood by receiving the sacraments, by prayer and thanksgiving, by the witness of a holy life, and by self-denial and active charity."

"It is through the sacraments and the exercise of the virtues that the sacred nature and organic structure of the priestly community is brought into operation."

Baptism: "Incorporated into the Church through baptism, the faithful are consecrated by the baptismal character to the exercise of the cult of the Christian religion. Reborn as sons of God, they must confess before men the faith which they have received from God through the Church."

Confirmation: "Bound more intimately to the Church by the sacrament of confirmation, they are endowed by the Holy Spirit with special strength. Hence they are more strictly obliged to spread and defend the faith both by word and by deed as true witnesses of Christ."

Eucharist: "Taking part in the Eucharistic Sacrifice, which is the fount and apex of the whole Christian life, they offer the divine Victim to God, and offer themselves along with It. Thus, both by the act of oblation and through holy Communion, all perform their proper part in this liturgical service, not, indeed, all in the same way but each in that way which is appropriate to himself. Strengthened anew at the holy table by the Body of Christ, they manifest in a practical way that unity of God's People which is suitably signified and wondrously brought about by this most awesome sacrament."

Penance: "Those who approach the sacrament of penance obtain pardon from the mercy of God for offenses committed against Him. They are at the same time reconciled with the Church, which they have wounded by their sins, and which by charity, example, and prayer seeks their conversion."

Anointing of the Sick: "By the sacred anointing of the sick and the prayer of her priests, the whole Church commends those who are ill to the suffering and glorified Lord, asking that He may lighten their suffering and save them (cf. Jas. 5:14-16). She exhorts them, moreover, to contribute to the welfare of the whole People of God by associating themselves freely with the passion and death of Christ (cf. Rom. 8:17; Col. 1:24; 2 Tm. 2:11-12; 1 Pt. 4:13)."

Holy Orders: "Those of the faithful who are consecrated by holy orders are appointed to feed the Church in Christ's name with the Word and the grace of God."

Matrimony: "Christian spouses, in virtue of the sacrament of matrimony, signify and partake of the mystery of that unity and fruitful love which exists between Christ and His Church (cf. Eph. 5:32). The spouses thereby help each other to attain to holiness in their married life and by the rearing and education of their children. And so, in their state and way of life, they have their own special gift among the People of God (cf. 1 Cor. 7:7).

"For from the wedlock of Christians there comes the family, in which new citizens of human society are born. By the grace of the Holy Spirit received in baptism these are made children of God, thus perpetuating the People of God through the centuries. The family is, so to speak, the domestic Church. In it parents should, by their word and example, be the first preachers of the faith to their children. They should encourage them in the vocation which is proper to each of them, fostering with special care any religious vocation.

"Fortified by so many and such powerful means of salvation, all the faithful, whatever their condition or state, are called by the Lord, each in his own way, to that perfect holiness whereby the Father Himself is perfect."

Baptism

Baptism is the sacrament of spiritual regeneration by which a person is incorporated in Christ and made a member of His Mystical Body, given grace, and cleansed of original sin. Actual sins and the punishment due for them are remitted also if the person baptized was guilty of such sins (e.g., in the case of a person baptized after reaching the age of reason). The theological virtues of faith, hope and charity are given with grace. The sacrament confers a character on the soul and can be received only once. Baptism has been called a sacrament of the dead because its purpose is to confer sanctifying grace on persons who do not have it.

The matter is the pouring of water. The form is: "I baptize you in the name of the Father and of the Son and of the Holy Spirit."

The minister of solemn baptism is a priest or deacon, but in case of emergency anyone, including a non-Catholic, can validly baptize. The minister pours water on the forehead of the person being baptized and says the words of the form while the water is flowing. The

water used in solemn baptism is blessed during the rite.

The Church recognizes as valid baptism by **immersion, aspersion** (sprinkling of the water), or **infusion** (pouring of the water). In the Western Church, i.e., Roman Rite, the method of infusion is prescribed. The Church recognizes as valid baptisms properly performed by non-Catholic ministers. The baptism of infants has always been considered valid and the general practice of infant baptism was well established by the fifth century. Baptism is conferred conditionally when there is doubt about the validity of a previous baptism or the dispositions of the person.

Baptism is necessary for salvation. If a person cannot receive the baptism of water described above, this can be supplied by baptism of blood (martyrdom suffered for the Catholic faith or some Christian virtue) or by baptism of desire (perfect contrition joined with at least the implicit intention of doing whatever God wills that men should do for salvation).

A sponsor is required for the person being baptized. (See Godparents, below).

A person must be validly baptized before he can receive any of the other sacraments.

Christian Initiation of Infants: Infants should be solemnly baptized as soon after birth as conveniently possible. In danger of death, anyone may baptize an infant. If the child survives, the ceremonies of solemn baptism should be supplied.

The sacrament is ordinarily conferred by a priest or deacon of the parents' parish.

Only Catholics, in their 14th year or older, may be **godparents** or sponsors. Only one is required. Two, one of each sex, are permitted. A non-Catholic cannot be a godparent for a Catholic child, but may serve as a witness to the baptism. A Catholic may not be a godparent for a child baptized in a non-Catholic religion, but may be a witness.

The role of godparents in baptismal ceremonies is secondary to the role of the parents. They serve as representatives of the community of faith and with the parents request baptism for the child and perform other ritual functions. Their function after baptism is to serve as proxies for the parents if the parents should be unable or fail to provide for the religious training of the child.

At baptism every child should be given a name with Christian significance, usually the name of a saint, to symbolize newness of life in Christ.

Christian Initiation of Adults: According to the *Ordo Initiationis Christianae Adultorum* ("Rite of the Christian Initiation of Adults") issued by the Congregation for Divine Worship under date of Jan. 6, 1972, adults are prepared for baptism and reception into the Church in several stages:

• An initial period of inquiry, instruction and evangelization.

• The catechumenate, a period of formal instruction and progressive formation in and familiarity with Christian life. It starts with a statement of purpose and includes a rite in which the catechumen is signed with the cross, blessings, exorcisms, and introduction into church for celebration of the word of God.

• Immediate preparation, called a period of purification and enlightenment, from the beginning of Lent to reception of the sacraments of initiation — baptism, confirmation, Holy Eucharist — at Easter. The period is marked by scrutinies, formal giving of the creed and the Lord's Prayer, the choice of a Christian name, and a final statement of intention.

• A final phase whose objective is greater familiarity with Christian life in the Church through observances of the Easter season and association with the community of the faithful.

The priest who baptizes a catechumen can also administer the sacrament of confirmation.

A sponsor is required for the person being baptized.

The *Ordo* also provides a simple rite of initiation for adults in danger of death and for cases in which all stages of the initiation process are not necessary, and guidelines for: (1) the preparation of adults for the sacraments of confirmation and Holy Eucharist in cases where they have been baptized but have not received further formation in the Christian life; (2) for the formation and initiation of children of catechetical age.

The Church recognizes the right of anyone over the age of seven to request baptism and to receive the sacrament after completing a course of instruction and giving evidence of good will. Practically, in the case of minors in a non-Catholic family or environment, the Church accepts them when other circumstances favor their ability to practice the faith — e.g., well-disposed family situation, the presence of another or several Catholics in the family. Those who are not in such favorable circumstances are prudently advised to defer reception of the sacrament until they attain the maturity necessary for independent practice of the faith.

Reception of Baptized Christians: Procedure for the reception of already baptized Christians into full communion with the Catholic Church is distinguished from the catechumenate, since they have received some Christian formation. Instruction and formation are provided as necessary, however; and conditional baptism is administered if there is reasonable doubt about the validity of the person's previous baptism.

In the rite of reception, the person is invited to join the community of the Church in professing the Nicene Creed and is asked to state:

"I believe and profess all that the holy Catholic Church believes, teaches, and proclaims as revealed by God." The priest places his hand on the head of the person, states the formula of admission to full communion, confirms (in the absence of a bishop), gives a sign of peace, and administers Holy Communion during a Eucharistic Liturgy.

Confirmation

Confirmation is the sacrament by which a baptized person, through anointing with chrism and the imposition of hands, is endowed with the gifts and special strength of the Holy Spirit for mature Christian living. The sacrament, which completes the Christian initiation begun wth baptism, confers a character on the soul and can be received only once.

According to the apostolic constitution *Divinae Consortium Naturae* dated Aug. 15, 1971, in conjunction with the *Ordo Confirmationis* ("Rite of Confirmation"): "The sacrament of confirmation is conferred through the anointing with chrism on the forehead, which is done by the imposition of the hand (matter of the sacrament), and through the words: 'N . . . . , receive the seal of the Holy Spirit, the Gift of the Father' " (form of the sacrament).

The ordinary minister of confirmation in the Roman Rite is a bishop. Priests may be delegated for the purpose. A pastor can confirm a parishioner in danger of death, and a priest can confirm in ceremonies of Christian initiation.

Ideally, the sacrament is conferred during the Eucharistic Liturgy. Elements of the rite include renewal of the promises of baptism, which confirmation ratifies and completes, and the laying on of hands — by symbolic elevation over the heads of those being confirmed — by the confirming bishop and priests participating in the ceremony.

"The entire rite," according to the *Ordo;* "has a twofold meaning. The laying of hands upon the candidates, done by the bishop and the concelebrating priests, expresses the biblical gesture by which the gift of the Holy Spirit is invoked. . . . The anointing with chrism and the accompanying words clearly signify the effect of the Holy Spirit. Signed with the perfumed oil by the bishop's hand, the baptized person receives the indelible character, the seal of the Lord, together with the Spirit who is given and who conforms the person more perfectly to Christ and gives him the grace of spreading the Lord's presence among men."

A sponsor is required for the person being confirmed. This can be one of the baptismal sponsors or another person. Parents can serve as sponsors for their own children.

In the Roman Rite, it has been customary for children to receive confirmation within a reasonable time after first Communion and confession. There is a developing trend, however, to defer confirmation until later when its significance for mature Christian living becomes more evident. In the Eastern Rites, confirmation is administered at the same time as baptism.

The Holy Eucharist

The Holy Eucharist is a sacrifice (see The Mass) and the sacrament in which Christ is present and is received under the appearances of bread and wine.

The matter is bread of wheat, unleavened in the Roman Rite and leavened in the Eastern Rites, and wine of grape. The form consists of the words of consecration said by the priest at Mass: "This is my body. . . . This is the cup of my blood" (according to the traditional usage of the Roman Rite).

Only a priest can consecrate bread and wine so they become the body and blood of Christ. After consecration, however, the Eucharist can be administered by deacons and, for various reasons, by religious and lay persons.

Priests celebrating Mass receive the Eucharist under the appearances of bread and wine. In the Roman Rite, others usually receive under the appearances of bread only, i.e., the consecrated host; in some circumstances, however, they may receive under the appearances of both bread and wine. In Eastern-Rite practice, the faithful generally receive a piece of consecrated leavened bread which has been dipped into consecrated wine (i.e., by intinction).

Conditions for receiving the Eucharist, commonly called **Holy Communion**, are the state of grace, the right intention, and observance of the Eucharistic fast.

The faithful of Roman Rite are required by a precept of the Church to receive the Eucharist at least once a year, during the Easter time (in the US, from the First Sunday of Lent to Trinity Sunday, inclusive).

(See Eucharistic Fast, Mass, Transubstantiation, Viaticum.)

First Communion and Confession: Children are to be prepared for and given opportunity for receiving both sacraments on reaching the age of discretion, at which time they become subject to general norms concerning confession and Communion. This, together with a stated preference for first confession before first Communion, was the central theme of a document published July 9, 1973, by the Congregation for the Discipline of the Sacraments and the Congregation for the Clergy, with the approval of Pope Paul VI.

What the document prescribed was the observance of practices ordered by St. Pius X in the decree *Quam Singulari* of Aug. 8, 1910. Its purpose was to counteract pastoral and catechetical experiments virtually denying children the opportunity of receiving both sacra-

ments at the same time. Termination of such experiments was ordered by the end of the 1972-73 school year.

At the time the document was issued, two- or three-year experiments of this kind — routinely deferring reception of the sacrament of penance until after the first reception of Holy Communion — were in effect in more than half of the dioceses of the U.S.

One reason stated in support of such experiments was the view that children are not capable of serious sin at the age of seven or eight, when Communion is generally received for the first time, and therefore prior reception of the sacrament of penance is not necessary. Another reason was the purpose of making the distinctive nature of the two sacraments clearer to children.

The Vatican view reflected convictions that the principle and practice of devotional reception of penance are as valid for children as they are for adults, and that sound catechetical programs can avoid misconceptions about the two sacraments.

Holy Communion under the Forms of Bread and Wine (by separate taking of the consecrated bread and wine or by intinction, the reception of the host dipped in the wine): Such reception is permitted under conditions stated in instructions issued by the Congregation for Divine Worship (May 25, 1967; June 29, 1970), the *General Instruction on the Roman Missal* (No. 242), and directives of bishops' conferences and individual bishops.

Accordingly, Communion can be administered in this way to: persons being baptized, received into communion with the Church, confirmed, receiving anointing of the sick; couples at their wedding or jubilee; religious at profession or renewal of profession; lay persons receiving an ecclesiastical assignment (e.g., lay missionaries); participants at concelebrated Masses, retreats, pastoral commission meetings; on other special occasions.

Holy Communion Twice a Day: The reception of Holy Communion at Mass a second time on the same day is permitted in accord with provisions of the "Instruction on Facilitating Communion in Particular Circumstances" *(Immensae Caritatis)* approved by Pope Paul VI Jan. 20 and published by the Congregation for Divine Worship Mar. 29, 1973.

The occasions are: Sunday Mass on Saturday evening or a holy day Mass the previous evening; a second Mass on Christmas or Easter, following reception at midnight Mass or the Mass of the Easter Vigil; the evening Mass of Holy Thursday, following reception at the earlier Mass of Chrism; Masses in which baptism, confirmation, holy orders, matrimony, anointing of the sick, first Communion, Viaticum are administered; some Masses for the dead (e.g., of Christian burial, first anniversary); special occasions — consecration of a church or altar, religious profession, conferring an ecclesiastical assignment (e.g., to lay missionaries), feast of Corpus Christi, parochial visitation, canonical visitation or special meetings of religious, Eucharistic and other congresses, pilgrimages, preaching missions; other occasions designated by the local bishop.

Holy Communion and Eucharistic Devotion outside of Mass: These were the subjects of an instruction *(De Sacra Communione et de Cultu Mysterii Eucharistici extra Missam)* dated June 21 and made public Oct. 18, 1973, by the Congregation for Divine Worship.

Holy Communion can be given outside of Mass to persons unable for a reasonable cause to receive it during Mass on a given day. The ceremonial rite is modeled on the structure of the Mass, consisting of a penitential act, a scriptural reading, the Lord's Prayer, a sign or gesture of peace, giving of the Eucharist, prayer and final blessing. Viaticum and Communion to the sick can be given by extraordinary ministers (authorized lay persons) with appropriate rites.

Forms of devotion outside of Mass are exposition of the Blessed Sacrament (by men or women religious, especially, or lay persons in the absence of a priest; but only a priest can give the blessing), processions and congresses with appropriate rites.

Intercommunion: Church policy on intercommunion was stated in an "Instruction on the Admission of Other Christians to the Eucharist," dated June 1 and made public July 8, 1972, against the background of the *Decree on Ecumenism* approved by the Second Vatican Council, and the *Directory on Ecumenism* issued by the Secretariat for Promoting Christian Unity in 1967.

Basic principles related to intercommunion are:

• "There is an indissoluble link between the mystery of the Church and the mystery of the Eucharist, or between ecclesial and Eucharistic communion; the celebration of the Eucharist of itself signifies the fullness of profession of faith and ecclesial communion" (1972 Instruction).

• "Eucharistic communion practiced by those who are not in full ecclesial communion with each other cannot be the expression of that full unity which the Eucharist of its nature signifies and which in this case does not exist; for this reason such communion cannot be regarded as a means to be used to lead to full ecclesial communion" (1972 Instruction).

• The question of reciprocity "arises only with those churches which have preserved the substance of the Eucharist, the sacrament of orders and apostolic succession" (1967 Directory).

• "A Catholic cannot ask for the Eucharist except from a minister who has been validly ordained" (1967 Directory).

The policy distinguishes between separated Eastern Christians and other Christians.

With Separated Eastern Christians (e.g., Orthodox): These may be given the Eucharist (as well as penance and anointing of the sick) at their request. Catholics may receive these same sacraments from priests of separated Eastern churches if they experience genuine spiritual necessity, seek spiritual benefit, and access to a Catholic priest is morally or physically impossible. This policy (of reciprocity) derives from the facts that the separated Eastern churches have apostolic succession through their bishops, valid priests, and sacramental beliefs and practices in accord with those of the Catholic Church.

With Other Christians (e.g., members of Reformation-related churches, others): Admission to the Eucharist in the Catholic Church, according to the *Directory on Ecumenism,* "is confined to particular cases of those Christians who have a faith in the sacrament in conformity with that of the Church, who experience a serious spiritual need for the Eucharistic sustenance, who for a prolonged period are unable to have recourse to a minister of their own community and who ask for the sacrament of their own accord; all this provided that they have proper dispositions and lead lives worthy of a Christian." The spiritual need is defined as "a need for an increase in spiritual life and a need for a deeper involvement in the mystery of the Church and of its unity."

Circumstances under which Communion may be given to other properly disposed Christians are danger of death, imprisonment, persecution, grave spiritual necessity coupled with no chance of recourse to a minister of their own community. Judgment regarding these and other special circumstances rests with the local bishop.

Catholics cannot ask for the Eucharist from ministers of other Christian churches who have not been validly ordained to the priesthood.

Penance

Penance is the sacrament by which sins committed after baptism are forgiven and a person is reconciled with God and the Church.

A revised ritual for the sacrament — *Ordo Paenitentiae,* published by the Congregation of Divine Worship Feb. 7, 1974 — reiterates standard doctrine concerning the sacrament; emphasizes the social (communal and ecclesial) aspects of sin and conversion, with due regard for personal aspects and individual reception of the sacrament; prescribes three forms for celebration of the sacrament; and presents models for community penitential services.

The Latin version of the ritual, dated Dec. 2, 1973, is already in force. Provision was made for other versions to become effective on appropriate approval of translations by episcopal conferences and the Congregation for Divine Worship.

The basic elements of the sacrament are sorrow for sin because of a supernatural motive, confession (of previously unconfessed mortal or grave sins, required; of venial sins also, but not of necessity), and reparation (by means of prayer or other act enjoined by the confessor), all of which comprise the matter of the sacrament; and absolution, which is the form of the sacrament.

The traditional words of absolution remain unchanged at the conclusion of this formula: "God, the Father of mercies, has reconciled the world to himself through the death and resurrection of his Son and has poured forth the Holy Spirit for the forgiveness of sins. May he grant you pardon and peace through the ministry of the Church. And I absolve you from your sins in the name of the Father, and of the Son, and of the Holy Spirit."

The minister of the sacrament is an authorized priest — i.e., one who, besides having the power of orders to forgive sins, also has faculties of jurisdiction granted by an ecclesiastical superior and/or by canon law.

The sacrament can be celebrated in three ways.

• For individuals: The traditional manner remains acceptable but is enriched with additional elements including: reception of the penitent and making of the Sign of the Cross; an exhortation by the confessor to trust in God; a possible reading from Scripture; confession of sins; manifestation of repentance; petition for God's forgiveness through the ministry of the Church and the absolution of the priest; praise of God's mercy, and dismissal in peace. Some of these elements are optional.

• For several penitents, in the course of a community celebration including a liturgy of the Word of God and prayers, individual confession and absolution, and an act of thanksgiving.

• For several penitents, in the course of a community celebration, with general confession and general absolution. This method is reserved for special circumstances in which it is morally or physically impossible for persons to confess and be absolved individually, and in view of their need for reconciliation and reception of the Eucharist. Penitents are required to confess at their next individual confession any grave sins absolved in such a general celebration of the sacrament.

Communal celebrations of the sacrament are not held in connection with Mass.

The place of individual confession, as determined by episcopal conferences in accordance with given norms, can be the traditional confessional or another appropriate setting.

The sacrament is necessary, by the institution of Christ, for the reconciliation of persons guilty of grave sins committed after baptism.

A precept of the Church obliges the faithful guilty of grave sin to confess at least once a year.

The Church favors more frequent reception of the sacrament not only for the reconciliation of persons guilty of serious sins but also for reasons of devotion. Devotional confession — in which venial sins or previously forgiven sins are confessed — serves the purpose of confirming persons in penance and conversion.

Penitential Celebrations: Communal penitential celebrations are designed to emphasize the social dimensions of Christian life — the community aspects and significance of penance and reconciliation.

Elements of such celebrations are community prayer, hymns and songs, scriptural and other readings, examination of conscience, general confession and expression of sorrow for sin, acts of penance and reconciliation, and a form of non-sacramental absolution resembling the one in the penitential rite of the Mass.

If the sacrament is celebrated during the service, there must be individual confession and absolution of sin.

(See Absolution, Confession, Confessional, Confessor, Contrition, Faculties, Forgiveness of Sin, Power of the Keys, Seal of Confession, Sin.)

Anointing of the Sick

This sacrament, promulgated by St. James the Apostle (Jas. 5:13-15), is administered to persons who are dangerously ill. By the anointing with blessed oil and the prayer of a priest, the sacrament confers on the person comforting grace; the remission of venial sins and inculpably unconfessed mortal sins, together with at least some of the temporal punishment due for sins; and, sometimes, results in an improved state of health.

The matter of this sacrament is the anointing with blessed oil (of the sick — olive oil, or vegetable oil if necessary) of the forehead and hands; in cases of necessity, a single anointing of another portion of the body suffices. The form is: "Through this holy anointing and his most loving mercy, may the Lord assist you by the grace of the Holy Spirit so that, when you have been freed from your sins, he may save you and in his goodness raise you up."

Anointing of the sick, formerly called extreme unction, may be received more than once, e.g., in new or continuing stages of serious illness. Ideally, the sacrament should be administered while the recipient is conscious and in conjunction with the sacraments of penance and the Eucharist. It may be administered conditionally even after apparent death.

The sacrament can be administered during a communal celebration in some circumstances, as in a home for the aged.

Pope Paul VI authorized a revision of the

rite for administration of the sacrament in the apostolic constitution *Sacram Unctionem Infirmorum* ("Sacred Anointing of the Sick") which was approved Nov. 30, 1972, and made public Jan. 18, 1973. He ordered the new rite into effect as of Jan. 1, 1974. The Latin version of the new rite went into effect Jan. 1, 1974. The provisional English version became effective in the U.S. Dec. 1, 1974.

Matrimony

Coverage of the sacrament of matrimony is given in the articles, Marriage Doctrine of Vatican II, Marriage Laws of the Church, Mixed Marriage Guidelines.

Holy Orders

Holy orders is the sacrament by which spiritual power and grace are given to enable an ordained minister to consecrate the Eucharist, forgive sins, perform other pastoral and ecclesiastical functions, and form the community of the People of God. Holy orders confers a character on the soul and can be received only once. The minister of the sacrament is a bishop.

Holy orders, like matrimony but in a different way, is a social sacrament. As the Second Vatican Council declared in the *Dogmatic Constitution on the Church:*

"For the nurturing and constant growth of the People of God, Christ the Lord instituted in His Church a variety of ministries, which work for the good of the whole body. For those ministers who are endowed with sacred power are servants of their brethren, so that all who are of the People of God, and therefore enjoy a true Christian dignity, can work toward a common goal freely and in an orderly way, and arrive at salvation" (No. 18).

"With their helpers, the priests and deacons, bishops have . . . taken up the service of the community, presiding in place of God over the flock whose shepherds they are, as teachers of doctrine, priests of sacred worship, and officers of good order" (No. 20).

The fullness of the priesthood belongs to those who have received the order of **bishop.** Bishops, in hierarchical union with the pope and their fellow bishops, are the successors of the apostles as pastors of the Church: they have individual responsibility for the care of the local churches they serve and collegial responsibility for the care of the universal Church (see Collegiality). In the ordination or consecration of bishops, the essential form is the imposition of hands by the consecrator(s) and the assigned prayer in the preface of the rite of ordination.

A **priest** is an ordained minister with the power to celebrate Mass, administer the sacraments, preach and teach the word of God, impart blessings, and perform additional pastoral functions, according to the mandate of his ecclesiastical superior.

Concerning priests, the Second Vatican Council stated in the *Dogmatic Constitution on the Church* (No. 28):

". . . The divinely established ecclesiastical ministry is exercised on different levels by those who from antiquity have been called bishops, priests, and deacons. Although priests do not possess the highest degree of the priesthood, and although they are dependent on the bishops in the exercise of their power, they are nevertheless united with the bishops in sacerdotal dignity. By the power of the sacrament of orders, and in the image of Christ the eternal High Priest (Hb. 5:1-10; 7:24; 9:11-28), they are consecrated to preach the gospel, shepherd the faithful, and celebrate divine worship as true priests of the New Testament. . . .

"Priests, prudent cooperators with the episcopal order as well as its aides and instruments, are called to serve the People of God. They constitute one priesthood with their bishop, although that priesthood is comprised of different functions. . . ."

In the ordination of a priest of Roman Rite, the essential matter is the imposition of hands on the heads of those being ordained by the ordaining bishop. The essential form is the accompanying prayer in the preface of the ordination ceremony. Other elements in the rite are the presentation of the implements of sacrifice — the chalice containing wine and the paten containing a host — with accompanying prayers.

Regarding the order of **deacon,** the *Dogmatic Constitution on the Church* (No. 29) stated:

"At a lower level of the hierarchy are deacons, upon whom hands are imposed 'not unto the priesthood, but unto a ministry of service.' For strengthened by sacramental grace, in communion with the bishop and his group of priests, they serve the People of God in the ministry of the liturgy, of the word, and of charity. It is the duty of the deacon, to the extent that he has been authorized by competent authority, to administer baptism solemnly, to be custodian and dispenser of the Eucharist, to assist at and bless marriages in the name of the Church, to bring Viaticum to the dying, to read the sacred Scripture to the faithful, to instruct and exhort the people, to preside at the worship and prayer of the faithful, to administer sacramentals, and to officiate at funeral and burial services. (Deacons are) dedicated to duties of charity and administration. . . ."

". . . The diaconate can in the future be restored as a proper and permanent rank of the hierarchy. It pertains to the competent territorial bodies of bishops, of one kind or another, to decide, with the approval of the Supreme Pontiff, whether and where it is opportune for such deacons to be appointed for the care of souls. With the consent of the Roman Pontiff, this diaconate will be able to be conferred upon men of more mature age, even upon those living in the married state. It may also be conferred upon suitable young men. For them, however, the law of celibacy must remain intact" (No. 29).

The Apostles ordained the first seven deacons (Acts 6:1-6): Stephen, Philip, Prochorus, Nicanor, Timon, Parmenas, Nicholas.

Other Ministries: The Church later assigned ministerial duties to men in several other orders, as:

Subdeacon, with specific duties in liturgical worship, especially at Mass. The order, whose first extant mention dates from about the middle of the third century, was regarded as minor until the 13th century; afterwards, it was called a major order in the West but not in the East.

Acolyte, to serve in minor capacities in liturgical worship; a function now performed by Mass servers.

Exorcist, to perform services of exorcism for expelling evil spirits; a function which came to be reserved to specially delegated priests.

Lector, to read scriptural and other passages during liturgical worship; a function now generally performed by lay persons.

Porter, to guard the entrance to an assembly of Christians and to ward off undesirables who tried to gain admittance; an order of early origin and utility but of present insignificance.

Long after it became evident that these positions and functions had fallen into general disuse or did not require clerical ordination, the Holy See started a revision of the orders in 1971. By an indult of Oct. 5, the bishops of the United States were permitted to omit ordaining porters and exorcists. Another indult, dated three days later, permitted the use of revised rites for ordaining acolytes and lectors, and authorized the use of a service celebrating admission to the clerical state in place of the ceremony of tonsure which had previously served this purpose.

To complete the revision, Pope Paul VI abolished Sept. 14, 1972, the orders of porter, exorcist and subdeacon; decreed that laymen, as well as candidates for the diaconate and priesthood, can be installed (rather than ordained) in the ministries (rather than orders) of acolyte and lector; reconfirmed the suppression of tonsure and its replacement with a service of dedication to God and the Church; and stated that a man enters the clerical state on ordination to the diaconate.

There were no doctrinal obstacles to the Pope's action, because the abolished orders had been instituted by the Church for functional purposes and were not considered to be parts of the sacrament of holy orders.

PERMANENT DIACONATE

Authorization for restoration of the permanent diaconate in the Roman Rite — making it possible for men to become deacons without being required to become priests — was promulgated by Pope Paul VI June 27, 1967, in a document entitled *Sacrum Diaconatus Ordinem* ("Sacred Order of the Diaconate").

The Pope's action implemented the desire expressed by the Second Vatican Council for reestablishment of the diaconate as an independent order in its own right not only to supply ministers for carrying on the work of the Church but also to complete the hierarchical structure of the Church of Roman Rite.

Permanent deacons have been traditional in the Eastern Church. The Western Church, however, which followed the practice of conferring the diaconate only as a sacred order preliminary to the priesthood, did not have them for centuries.

The Pope's document, issued on his own initiative, provided:

• Qualified unmarried men 25 years of age or older may be ordained permanent deacons. They cannot marry after ordination.

• Qualified married men 35 years of age or older may be ordained permanent deacons. The consent of the wife of a prospective deacon is required. A married deacon cannot remarry after the death of his wife.

• Preparation for the diaconate includes a two- or three-year course of study and formation.

• Candidates who are not religious must be affiliated with a diocese.

• Deacons will practice their ministry under the direction of a bishop and the priests with whom they will be associated. (For functions, see the description of deacon, under Holy Orders.)

Restoration of the permanent diaconate in the United States was approved by the Holy See in October, 1968. Shortly afterwards the US Bishops established a committee of the same name, which is chaired by Archbishop Daniel E. Sheehan. The committee operates through a secretariat, of which Msgr. Ernest J. Fiedler is executive director. Its offices are located at 1312 Massachusetts Ave. N. W., Washington, D.C. 20005.

Present Status

The bishops' secretariat reported in June, 1974, that more than 500 permanent deacons had been ordained in the U.S.; that 60 dioceses had deacons ordained or candidates in training, and 60 more were either preparing training programs or were interested in doing so; that a total of 1,100 candidates were in training.

Functions

Deacons have various functions, depending on the nature of their assignments. Liturgically, they can officiate at baptisms, and weddings, can preach and distribute Holy Communion. Some are engaged in religious education work. All are intended to carry out works of charity and pastoral service of one kind or another.

The majority of permanent deacons, 92 percent of whom are married, continue in their secular work. Their ministry of service is developing in three dimensions: of liturgy, of the word, and of charity. Depending on the individual deacon's abilities and preference, he is assigned by his bishop to either a parochial ministry or to one particular field of service. The latter is the most challenging ministry to develop. Deacons are now active in a variety of ministries including those to prison inmates and their families, the sick in hospitals, nursing homes and homes for the aged, alienated youth, the elderly and the poor, and in various areas of legal service to the indigent, of education and campus ministry. A few have been assigned as pastors of multi-county, rural parishes. The unlimited possibilities for diaconal ministry are under realistic assessment, diocese by diocese.

Training Programs

There were 53 training centers for deacons as of June, 1974. The first four were established in 1969.

Continuing efforts are made to recruit Spanish-speaking, black and other minority candidates in training programs. Of the permanent deacons ordained up to June, 1974, 77 per cent were Anglos, 9 per cent were black, and 13 per cent were Spanish-speaking.

Training programs of spiritual, doctrinal and pastoral formation are generally based on *Permanent Deacons in the United States: Guidelines on Their Formation and Ministry,* published by the Bishops' Committee on the Permanent Diaconate in September, 1971.

Permanent diaconate training programs and their directors, as of June, 1974, were as follows. The listing is alphabetical, by diocese.

Agana: Rev. William D. D'Arcy, P.O. Box 125, Agana, Guam 96910.

Albany: Rev. William Ryan, 40 N. Main Ave., Albany, N.Y. 12203.

Altoona-Johnstown: The Chancery, Logan Blvd., Hollidaysburg, Pa. 16648.

Amarillo: Rev. James C. Gursynaski, P.O. Box 5644, Amarillo, Tex. 79607.

Arlington: Rev. Msgr. Richard J. Burke, 101 N. Thomas St., Arlington, Va. 22203.

Atlanta: Rev. Joseph A. Sanches, 756 W. Peachtree, N.W., Atlanta, Ga. 30308.

Baltimore: Anthony S. Maranto, 5404 Hamlet Ave., Baltimore, Md. 21214.

Baton Rouge: Rev. Leo Guillot, P.O. Box 290, Port Allen, La. 70767.

Birmingham: Rev. Frank J. Mujscolino, P.O. Box 2086, Birmingham, Ala., 35201.

Boston: Rev. William C. Burckhart, 345 Waverly St., Belmont, Mass. 02178.

Brooklyn: Rev. John H. O'Brien (director, Spanish-Speaking Apostolate) and Auxiliary Bishop John J. Snyder (vicar general), 75 Greene Ave., Brooklyn, N.Y. 11238.

Burlington: Rev. John A. Guischard, P.O. Box 902, Burlington, Vt. 05401.

Camden: Rev. Donald D. Velozo, 128 N. Broad St., Swedesboro, N.J. 08058.

Caroline and Marshall Islands (Vicariate Apostolic): Rev. Allen Cameron, S.J., Catholic Mission, Truk, P.O. Box 250, U.S. Trust Territory Pacific 96942.

Charleston: Rev. Thomas Duffy, 119 Broad St., Charleston, S.C. 29401.

Cheyenne: Rev. Carl Beavers, P.O. Box 1117, Florington, Wyo. 82240.

Chicago: Rev. John D. Ring, 1307 S. Wabash Ave., Chicago, Ill. 60605.

Cincinnati: Rev. John Rea, Mt. St. Mary Seminary, 5440 Moeller Ave., Cincinnati, O. 45212.

Cleveland: Rev. Robert F. Pfeiffer, 1227 Ansel Rd., Cleveland, O. 44108.

Dallas: Rev. Msgr. Robert C. Rehkemper, P.O. Box 19507, Dallas, Tex. 75219.

Denver: Rev. Leo R. Horrigan, 938 Bannock St., Denver, Colo. 80204.

Des Moines: Rev. Duane J. Weiland, P.O. Box 1816, Des Moines, Ia. 50306.

Detroit: Rev. Gary M. Tierney, 1234 Washington Blvd., Detroit, Mich. 48226; also: Rev. Anthony Kosnik, Orchard Lake Seminary, Orchard Lake, Mich. 48034.

El Paso: Rev. John F. Peters, P.O. Box 17548, El Paso, Tex., 79917.

Fairbanks: Rev. John Hinsvark, Chefornak, Alaska 99561.

Fort Wayne-South Bend: Kevin M. Ranaghan, 1035 N. St. Peter, South Bend, Ind. 46617.

Gallup: Rev. Pius Winter, O.F.M., 415 Green Ave., Gallup, N.M. 87301.

Galveston-Houston: Rev. Milam E. Kleas, 10726 Bessemer St., Houston, Tex. 77034; also: Rev. Warren Dicharry, C.M., 9845 Memorial Dr., Houston, Tex. 77024.

Grand Rapids: Rev. Michael A. Danner, The Christopher House, 2001 Robinson Rd., S.E., Grand Rapids, Mich. 49506.

Green Bay: Rev. Thomas Allen, Sacred Heart Center for Christian Formation, Oneida, Wis. 54155.

Harrisburg: Rev. David T. McAndrew, 610 Church St., Harrisburg, Pa. 17108.

Hartford: Rev. Joseph P. Donahue, 467 Bloomfield Ave., Bloomfield, Conn. 06002.

Helena: Rev. Gary Reller, 530 N. Ewing St., Helena, Mont. 59601.

Joliet: Rev. Arno Dennerlein, 710 W. Marian St., Joliet, Ill. 60436.

Kansas City-St. Joseph: Rev. Patrick Rush, P.O. Box 1037, Kansas City, Mo. 64141.

Los Angeles: Rev. Peter Healy, Catholic Information Center, 809 S. Flower St., Los Angeles, Calif. 90017.

Louisville: Rev. Nick Rice, 2000 Norris Pl., Louisville, Ky. 40205.

Melkite Apostolic Exarchate: Most Rev. Joseph Tawil, 19 Dartmouth St., West Newton, Mass. 02165.

Memphis: Rev. Patrick J. Lynch, 1325 Jefferson Ave., Memphis, Tenn. 38104.

Milwaukee: Rev. Paul Esser, 3257 S. Lake Dr., Milwaukee, Wis. 53207.

Nashville: Rev. James K. Mallett, 2500 Citico Ave., Nashville, Tenn. 37404.

Natchez-Jackson: Rev. Henry Shelton, 2225 Boling St., Jackson, Miss. 39205.

Newark: Rev. Msgr. Richard M. McGuinness, 221 W. Market St., Newark, N.J. 07103.

New Orleans: Rev. John C. Favarola, 2901 S. Carrollton Ave., New Orleans, La. 70118.

New York: Rev. Msgr. Austin Vaughan, St. Joseph Seminary, Dunwoodie, Yonkers, N.Y. 10704.

Oakland: Rev. Jerrold F. Kennedy, 2900 Lakeshore Ave., Oakland, Calif. 94610; also: Rev. James Schexnayder, 25580 Campus Dr., Hayward, Calif. 94542.

Oklahoma City: Rev. Henry P. Robertson, 2706 S. Shartel St., Oklahoma City, Okla. 94847.

Omaha: Rev. Patrick McCaslin, 5316 N. 14th Ave., Omaha, Nebr. 68110.

Paterson: Rev. Kenneth E. Lasch, 24 DeGrasse St., Paterson, N.J. 07505.

Peoria: Rev. J. Thomas Henseler, 904 E. Lake Ave., Peoria Heights, Ill. 61614.

Phoenix: Rev. Bill O'Brien, O. Carm., 400 E. Monroe St., Phoenix, Ariz. 85004.

Pittsburgh: Rev. George E. Saladna, 2900 Noblestown Rd., Pittsburgh, Pa. 15205.

Providence: Rev. John E. Tavares, Seminary College, Warwick, R.I. 02889.

Rapid City: Rev. Laurence Welsh, P.O. Box 752, Rapid City, S.D. 57701.

Richmond: Rev. Edward J. Bobinchock and Rev. N. Robert Quirin, 807 Cathedral Pl., Richmond, Va. 23220.

Rockford: Rev. Lawrence M. Urbaniak, Rural Rt. 2, Box 214-A, Rockford, Ill. 61102.

Saginaw: Rev. Richard Van Mullekom, 2555 Wieneke Rd., Saginaw, Mich. 48603.

St. Cloud: Rev. Kieran Nolan, O.S.B., St. John's University, Collegeville, Minn. 56321.

St. Louis: Rev. Clarence Deddens, 4445 Lindell Blvd., St. Louis, Mo. 63108.

St. Paul-Minneapolis: Rev. Michael J. O'Connell, 226 Summit Ave., St. Paul, Minn. 55102.

Salt Lake City: Rev. Terence E. Moore, 1327 E. Second St., Salt Lake City, Utah. 84102.

San Antonio: Rev. Alton Rudolph, 2600 W. Woodlawn Ave., San Antonio, Tex. 78284.

San Diego: Rev. Henry F. Fawcett, 5961 Linda Vista Rd., San Diego, Calif. 92110.

San Francisco: Rev. Anthony E. McGuire, 4609 Alum Rock Ave., San Jose, Calif. 95127.

Santa Fe: Rev. Spencer Stopa, 9101 La Barranca N.E., Albuquerque, N.M. 87111.

Seattle: Rev. Michael G. Ryan, 907 Terry Ave., Seattle, Wash. 97104.

Toledo: Rev. Cleo Schmenk, 1933 Speilbusch Ave., Toledo, O. 43624.

Trenton: Rev. James P. McManimon, 230 Genesee St., Trenton, N.J. 08611.

Tulsa: Rev. James White, P.O. Box 36, Poteau, Okla. 74953.

Washington/Richmond: Rev. Robert Kearns, S.S.J., Josephite Training Center, 1200 Varnum St., N.E., Washington, D.C. 20017.

Wheeling: Rev. Joseph W. Debias, P.O. Box 230, Wheeling, W. Va. 26003.

Youngstown: Rev. David Rhodes, 144 W. Wood St., Youngstown, O. 44503.

TEAM MINISTRY

This is a form of ministry intended to share responsibility among priests in a given assignment. Experiments with it have multiplied since late in the 1960's.

Boston archdiocesan guidelines call team ministry "an arrangement whereby one associate pastor is recommended by the others (and subsequently appointed by the bishop) to be the pastor." The guidelines also say that "all priests that staff the parish (should) have a deliberative vote in all parish affairs," and that "the parish council should be considered a part of the team ministry."

NFPC

The National Federation of Priests' Councils was organized by 233 delegates from 127 priests' organizations at a charter meeting held in Chicago May 20 and 21, 1968.

Its stated purposes are to:

• give priests' councils, official or unofficial, a representative voice in matters of concern to the Church and with respect to problems facing the nation, including racism and poverty;

• improve communications among priests all over the country;

• coordinate programs of research and make recommendations to priests, bishops and others on specific matters;

• cooperate with lay persons, religious and bishops in meeting the contemporary needs of the Church.

The NFPC has a membership of 131 senates, councils and associations, including several provinces of men religious and PADRES, a national priests' group concerned with the needs of the Spanish-speaking. The NFPC publication is *Priests/USA*, a monthly.

The president is Father Reid C. Mayo of Burlington, Vt.

Headquarters are located at 1307 S. Wabash Ave., Chicago, Ill. 60605.

MARRIAGE DOCTRINE

The following excerpts, stating key points of doctrine on marriage, are from the *Pastoral Constitution on the Church in the Modern World* (Nos. 48 to 51) promulgated by the Second Vatican Council.

Conjugal Covenant

"The intimate partnership of married life and love has been established by the Creator and qualified by His laws. It is rooted in the conjugal covenant of irrevocable personal consent. . . .

". . . God Himself is the author of matrimony, endowed as it is with various benefits and purposes. All of these have a very decisive bearing on the continuation of the human race, on the personal development and eternal destiny of the individual members of a family, and on the dignity, stability, peace, and prosperity of the family itself and of human society as a whole. By their very nature, the institution of matrimony itself and conjugal love are ordained for the procreation and education of children, and find in them their ultimate crown.

"Thus a man and a woman . . . render mutual help and service to each other through an intimate union of their persons and of their actions. Through this union they experience the meaning of their oneness and attain to it with growing perfection day by day. As a mutual gift of two persons, this intimate union, as well as the good of the children, imposes total fidelity on the spouses and argues for an unbreakable oneness between them" (No. 48).

Sacrament of Matrimony

"Christ the Lord abundantly blessed this many-faceted love. . . . The Savior of men and the Spouse of the Church comes into the lives of married Christians through the sacrament of matrimony. He abides with them thereafter so that, just as He loved the Church and handed Himself over on her behalf, the spouses may love each other with perpetual fidelity through mutual self-bestowal.

". . . Graced with the dignity and office of fatherhood and motherhood, parents will energetically acquit themselves of a duty which devolves primarily on them, namely education, and especially religious education.

". . . The Christian family, which springs from marriage as a reflection of the loving covenant uniting Christ with the Church, and as a participation in that covenant, will manifest to all men the Savior's living presence in the world, and the genuine nature of the Church . . ." (No. 48).

Conjugal Love

"The biblical Word of God several times urges the betrothed and the married to nourish and develop their wedlock by pure conjugal love and undivided affection. . . .

"This love is an eminently human one since it is directed from one person to another through an affection of the will. It involves the good of the whole person. Therefore it can enrich the expressions of body and mind with a unique dignity, ennobling these expressions as special ingredients and signs of the friendship distinctive of marriage. This love the Lord has judged worthy of special gifts, healing, perfecting, and exalting gifts of grace and of charity.

"Such love, merging the human with the divine, leads the spouses to a free and mutual gift of themselves, a gift proving itself by gentle affection and by deed. Such love pervades the whole of their lives. Indeed, by its generous activity it grows better and grows greater. Therefore it far excels mere erotic inclination, which, selfishly pursued, soon enough fades wretchedly away.

"This love is uniquely expressed and perfected through the marital act. The actions within marriage by which the couple are united intimately and chastely are noble and worthy ones. Expressed in a manner which is truly human, these actions signify and promote that mutual self-giving by which spouses enrich each other with a joyful and a thankful will.

"Sealed by mutual faithfulness and hallowed above all by Christ's sacrament, this love remains steadfastly true in body and in mind, in bright days or dark. It will never be profaned by adultery or divorce. Firmly established by the Lord, the unity of marriage will radiate from the equal personal dignity of wife and husband, a dignity acknowledged by mutual and total love.

"The steady fulfillment of the duties of this Christian vocation demands notable virtue. For this reason, strengthened by grace for holiness of life, the couple will painstakingly cultivate and pray for constancy of love, largeheartedness, and the spirit of sacrifice . . ." (No. 49).

Fruitfulness of Marriage

"Marriage and conjugal love are by their nature ordained toward the begetting and educating of children. Children are really the supreme gift of marriage and contribute very substantially to the welfare of their parents. . . . God Himself . . . wished to share with man a certain special participation in His own creative work. Thus He blessed male and female, saying: 'Increase and multiply' (Gn. 1:28).

"Hence, while not making the other purposes of matrimony of less account, the true practice of conjugal love, and the whole meaning of the family life which results from it, have this aim: that the couple be ready with stout hearts to cooperate with the love of the

Creator and the Savior, who through them
will enlarge and enrich His own family day by
day.

"Parents should regard as their proper mission the task of transmitting human life and
educating those to whom it has been transmitted. They should realize that they are
thereby cooperators with the love of God the
Creator, and are, so to speak, the interpreters
of that love. Thus they will fulfill their task
with human and Christian responsibility . . ." (No. 50).

Norms of Judgment

"They will thoughtfully take into account
both their own welfare and that of their children, those already born and those which
may be foreseen. For this accounting they will
reckon with both the material and the spiritual conditions of the times as well as of their
state in life. Finally, they will consult the interests of the family group, of temporal society, and of the Church herself.

"The parents themselves should ultimately
make this judgment in the sight of God. But
in their manner of acting, spouses should be
aware that they cannot proceed arbitrarily.
They must always be governed according to a
conscience dutifully conformed to the divine
law itself, and should be submissive toward
the Church's teaching office, which authentically interprets that law in the light of the gospel. That divine law reveals and protects the
integral meaning of conjugal love, and impels
it toward a truly human fulfillment. . . .

"Marriage to be sure is not instituted solely
for procreation. Rather, its very nature as an
unbreakable compact between persons, and
the welfare of the children, both demand that
the mutual love of the spouses, too, be embodied in a rightly ordered manner, that it
grow and ripen. Therefore, marriage persists
as a whole manner and communion of life,
and maintains its value and indissolubility,
even when offspring are lacking — despite,
rather often, the very intense desire of the
couple" (No. 50).

Love and Life

"This Council realizes that certain modern
conditions often keep couples from arranging
their married lives harmoniously, and that
they find themselves in circumstances where
at least temporarily the size of their families
should not be increased. As a result, the faithful exercise of love and the full intimacy of
their lives are hard to maintain. But where the
intimacy of married life is broken off, it is not
rare for its faithfulness to be imperiled and its
quality of fruitfulness ruined. For then the
upbringing of the children and the courage to
accept new ones are both endangered.

"To these problems there are those who
presume to offer dishonorable solutions. Indeed, they do not recoil from the taking of
life. But the Church issues the reminder that a

true contradiction cannot exist between the
divine laws pertaining to the transmission of
life and those pertaining to the fostering of
authentic conjugal love.

"For God, the Lord of Life, has conferred
on men the surpassing ministry of safeguarding life — a ministry which must be fulfilled
in a manner which is worthy of men. Therefore from the moment of its conception life
must be guarded with the greatest care, while
abortion and infanticide are unspeakable
crimes. The sexual characteristics of man and
the human faculty of reproduction wonder-
fully exceed the dispositions of lower forms of
life. Hence the acts themselves which are
proper to conjugal love and which are exercised in accord with genuine human dignity
must be honored with great reverence" (No.
51).

Church Teaching

"Therefore when there is question of har-
monizing conjugal love with the responsible
transmission of life, the moral aspect of any
procedure does not depend solely on the sincere intentions or on an evaluation of motives. It must be determined by objective
standards. These, based on the nature of the
human person and his acts, preserve the full
sense of mutual self-giving and human procreation in the context of true love. Such a
goal cannot be achieved unless the virtue of
conjugal chastity is sincerely practiced. Relying on these principles, sons of the Church
may not undertake methods of regulating
procreation which are found blameworthy by
the teaching authority of the Church in its unfolding of the divine law.

"Everyone should be persuaded that
human life and the task of transmitting it are
not realities bound up with this world alone.
Hence they cannot be measured or perceived
only in terms of it, but always have a bearing
on the eternal destiny of men" (No. 51).

Humanae Vitae

Marriage doctrine and morality were the
subjects of the encyclical *Humanae Vitae* ("Of
Human Life") issued by Pope Paul July 29,
1968. Following are a number of key excerpts
from the document, which was framed in the
pattern of traditional teaching and statements
by the Second Vatican Council.

". . . each and every marriage act ('quilibet
matrimonii usus') must remain open to the
transmission of life" (No. 11).

"Indeed, by its intimate structure, the conjugal act, while most closely uniting husband
and wife, capacitates them for the generation
of new lives, according to laws inscribed in
the very being of man and of woman. By safeguarding both these essential aspects, the uni-
tive and the procreative, the conjugal act preserves in its fullness the sense of true mutual
love and its ordination toward man's most
high calling to parenthood" (No. 12).

"It is, in fact, justly observed that a conjugal act imposed upon one's partner without regard for his or her condition and lawful desires is not a true act of love, and therefore denies an exigency of right moral order in the relationships between husband and wife. Hence, one who reflects well must also recognize that a reciprocal act of love which jeopardizes the responsibility to transmit life — which God the Creator, according to particular laws, inserted therein — is in contradiction with the design constitutive of marriage and with the will of the Author of life. To use this divine gift, destroying, even if only partially, its meaning and its purpose, is to contradict the nature both of man and of woman and of their most intimate relationship, and therefore it is to contradict also the plan of God and His will" (No. 13).

Forbidden Actions: ". . . the direct interruption of the generative process already begun, and, above all, directly willed and procured abortion, even if for therapeutic reasons, are to be absolutely excluded as licit means of regulating birth.

"Equally to be excluded . . . is direct sterilization, whether perpetual or temporary, whether of the man or of the woman. Similarly excluded is every action which, either in anticipation of the conjugal act, or in its accomplishment, or in the development of its natural consequences, proposes, whether as an end or as a means, to render procreation impossible.

Inadmissible Principles: "To justify conjugal acts made intentionally infecund, one cannot invoke as valid reasons the lesser evil, or the fact that such acts would constitute a whole together with the fecund acts already performed or to follow later and hence would share in one and the same moral goodness. In truth, if it is sometimes licit to tolerate a lesser evil in order to avoid a greater evil or to promote a greater good, it is not licit, even for the gravest reasons, to do evil so that good may follow therefrom; that is, to make into the object of a positive act of the will something which is intrinsically disorder, and hence unworthy of the human person, even when the intention is to safeguard or promote individual, family or social well-being.

"Consequently, it is an error to think that a conjugal act which is deliberately made infecund, and so is intrinsically dishonest, could be made honest and right by the ensemble of a fecund conjugal life" (No. 14).

Rhythm: "If, then, there are serious motives to space out births, which derive from the physical or psychological conditions of husband and wife, or from external conditions, the Church teaches that it is then licit to take into account the natural rhythms immanent in the generative functions, for the use of marriage in the infecund periods only, and in this way to regulate birth without offending" earlier stated principles (No. 16).

Authoritative Teaching: Pope Paul called the foregoing teaching authoritative, although not infallible. He left it open for further study. As a practical norm to be followed, however, he said it involved the binding force of religious assent.

With pastoral concern, the Pope said: "We do not at all intend to hide the sometimes serious difficulties inherent in the life of Christian married persons; for them, as for everyone else, 'the gate is narrow and the way is hard that leads to life.' But the hope of that life must illuminate their way, as with courage they strive to live with wisdom, justice and piety in this present time, knowing that the figure of this world passes away.

"Let married couples, then, face up to the efforts needed, supported by the faith and hope which 'do not disappoint . . . because God's love has been poured into our hearts through the Holy Spirit, who has been given to us.' Let them implore divine assistance by persevering prayer; above all, let them draw from the source of grace and charity in the Eucharist. And, if sin should still keep its hold over them, let them not be discouraged but rather have recourse with humble perseverance to the mercy of God, which is poured forth in the sacrament of penance" (No. 25).

Reactions: Exception was taken to the binding force of the encyclical — notably by the bishops of Belgium, Austria and France, and many theologians — for several reasons: rights of conscience; questions concerning the natural-law concept underlying the encyclical; the thesis of totality; the proposition that contraception may in some cases be the lesser of two evils. All agreed, however, that conscientious objection to the encyclical could not be taken without serious reasons and reflection.

Pope Paul, since publication of the encyclical, has not moved to alter its contents or to mitigate its binding force.

MARRIAGE LAWS

The Catholic Church, in line with the belief that it was established and commissioned by Christ to provide and administer the means of salvation to men, claims jurisdiction over its members in matters pertaining to marriage, which is a sacrament. The purpose of its laws in this area is to safeguard the validity and lawfulness of marriage.

Catholics are bound by all marriage laws of the Church. Non-Catholics, whether baptized or not, are not considered bound by these ecclesiastical laws except in cases of marriage with a Catholic. Certain natural laws, in the Catholic view, bind all men and women, irrespective of their religious beliefs; accordingly, marriage is prohibited before the time of puberty, without knowledge and free mutual consent, in the case of an already existing valid marriage bond, in the case of antecedent and perpetual impotence.

Formalities

These include, in addition to arrangements for the time and place of the marriage ceremony, doctrinal and moral instruction concerning marriage and the recording of data which verifies in documentary form the eligibility and freedom of the persons to marry. Records of this kind, which are confidential, are preserved in the archives of the church where the marriage takes place.

Premarital instructions are the subject matter of Pre-Cana Conferences.

Mixed Marriages

Pastoral experience, which the Catholic Church shares with other religious bodies, confirms the fact that marriages of persons of different beliefs involve special problems related to the continuing religious practice of the concerned persons and to the religious education and formation of their children.

Pastoral measures to minimize these problems include instruction of a non-Catholic party in essentials of the Catholic faith for purposes of understanding. Desirably, some instruction should also be given the Catholic party regarding his or her partner's beliefs.

The Catholic party to a mixed marriage is required to declare his (her) intention of continuing practice of the Catholic faith and to promise to do all in his power to share his faith with children born of the marriage by having them baptized and raised as Catholics. No declarations or promises are required of the non-Catholic party, but he (she) must be informed of the declaration and promise made by the Catholic.

Notice of the Catholic's declaration and promise is an essential part of the application made to a bishop for dispensation from the impediment of mixed religion or disparity of worship (see below).

Mixed marriages may take place with a Nuptial Mass.

A non-Catholic minister may not only attend a marriage but may also address, pray with and give his blessing to the couple following the marriage ceremony.

If a dispensation from the canonical form of marriage is granted by a bishop, a non-Catholic minister can officiate at a mixed marriage.

Banns

The banns are public announcements made in their parish churches, usually on three successive Sundays, of the names of persons who intend to marry. Persons who know of reasons in church law why a proposed marriage should not take place, are obliged to make them known to the pastor.

Marital Consent

The exchange of consent to the marriage contract, which is essential for valid marriage, must be rational, free, true and mutual.

Matrimonial consent can be invalidated by an essential defect, substantial error, the strong influence of force and fear, the presence of a condition or intention against the nature of marriage.

Form of Marriage

A Catholic is required, for validity and lawfulness, to contract marriage — with another Catholic or with a non-Catholic — in the presence of a competent priest or deacon and two witnesses.

There are two exceptions to this law. A Roman Rite Catholic (since Mar. 25, 1967) or an Eastern Rite Catholic (since Nov. 21, 1964) can contract marriage validly in the presence of a priest of a separated Eastern Rite Church, provided other requirements of law are complied with. With permission of the competent Roman-Rite or Eastern-Rite bishop, this form of marriage is lawful, as well as valid. (See Eastern Rite Laws, below.)

With these two exceptions, and aside from cases covered by special permission, the Church does not regard as valid any marriages involving Catholics which take place before non-Catholic ministers of religion or civil officials. (See Mixed Marriage Guidelines.)

An excommunication formerly in force against Catholics who celebrated marriage before a non-Catholic minister was abrogated in a decree issued by the Sacred Congregation for the Doctrine of the Faith on Mar. 18, 1966.

The ordinary place of marriage is the parish of the bride, of the Catholic party in case of a mixed marriage, or of an Eastern Rite groom.

Church law regarding the form of marriage does not affect non-Catholics in marriages among themselves. The Church recognizes as valid the marriages of non-Catholics before ministers of religion and civil officials, unless they are rendered null and void on other grounds.

Impediments

Impediments to marriage are factors which render a marriage unlawful or invalid.

Prohibitory Impediments, which make a marriage unlawful but do not affect validity:

• simple vows of virginity, perpetual chastity, celibacy, to enter a religious order or to receive sacred orders;

• difference of religion, which obtains when one party is a Catholic and the other is a baptized non-Catholic.

The impediment of legal relationship is not in force in the US.

Diriment Impediments, which make a marriage invalid as well as unlawful:

• age, which obtains before completion of the 14th year for a woman and the 16th year for a man;

• impotency, if it is antecedent to the marriage and permanent (this differs from sterility, which is not an impediment);

• the bond of an existing valid marriage;

• disparity of worship, which obtains when one party is a Catholic and the other party is unbaptized;

• sacred orders;

• religious profession of the solemn vow of chastity;

• abduction, which impedes the freedom of the person abducted;

• crime, variously involving elements of adultery, promise or attempt to marry, conspiracy to murder a husband or wife;

• blood relationship in the direct line (father-daughter, mother-son, etc.) and within the third degree of the collateral line (brother-sister, first and second cousins);

• affinity, or relationship resulting from a valid marriage, in any degree of the direct line and within the second degree of the collateral line;

• spiritual relationship arising through baptism — between a godchild and godparent, between the person baptized and the one who performed the baptism;

• public honesty, arising from an invalid marriage or from public or notorious concubinage; it renders either party incapable of marrying relatives of the other in the first and second degrees of the direct line.

Dispensations from Impediments: Persons hindered by impediments either may not or cannot marry unless they are dispensed therefrom in view of reasons recognized in canon law. Local bishops can dispense from the impediments most often encountered (e.g., difference of religion, disparity of worship) as well as others.

Decision regarding some dispensations is reserved to the Holy See.

Separation

A valid and consummated marriage of baptized persons cannot be dissolved by any human authority or any cause other than the death of one of the persons.

In other circumstances:

• 1. A valid but unconsummated marriage of baptized persons, or of a baptized and an unbaptized person, can be dissolved:

a. by the solemn religious profession of one of the persons, made with permission of the pope. In such a case, the bond is dissolved at the time of profession, and the other person is free to marry again;

b. by dispensation from the pope, requested for a grave reason by one or both of the persons. If the dispensation is granted, both persons are free to marry again.

Dispensations in these cases are granted for reasons connected with the spiritual welfare of the concerned persons.

• 2. A legitimate marriage, even consummated, of unbaptized persons can be dis-

solved in favor of one of them who subsequently receives the sacrament of baptism. This is the Pauline Privilege, so called because it was promulgated by St. Paul (1 Cor. 7:12-15) as a means of protecting the faith of converts. Requisites for granting the privilege are:

a. marriage prior to the baptism of either person;

b. reception of baptism by one person;

c. refusal of the unbaptized person to live in peace with the baptized person and without interfering with his or her freedom to practice the Christian faith. The privilege does not apply if the unbaptized person agrees to these conditions.

• 3. A legitimate and consummated marriage of a baptized and an unbaptized person can be dissolved by the pope in virtue of the Privilege of Faith, also called the Petrine Privilege.

Civil Divorce: Because of the unity and the indissolubility of marriage, the Church denies that civil divorce can break the bond of a valid marriage, whether the marriage involves two Catholics, a Catholic and a non-Catholic, or non-Catholics with each other.

In view of serious circumstances of marital distress, the Church permits an innocent and aggrieved party, whether wife or husband, to seek and obtain a civil divorce for the purpose of acquiring title and right to the civil effects of divorce, such as separate habitation and maintenance, and the custody of children. Permission for this kind of action should be obtained from proper church authority. The divorce, if obtained, does not break the bond of a valid marriage.

Under other circumstances — as would obtain if a marriage was invalid (see Decree of Nullity, below) — civil divorce is permitted for civil effects and as a civil ratification of the fact that the marriage bond really does not exist.

In the United States, according to a decree of the Third Plenary Council of Baltimore, the penalty of excommunication is automatically incurred by persons who attempt to contract marriage after having obtained a divorce from a valid marriage.

Decree of Nullity, sometimes improperly called an annulment. This is a decision by a competent church authority — e.g., a bishop, a diocesan marriage tribunal, the Sacred Roman Rota — that an apparently valid marriage was actually invalid from the beginning because of the unknown or concealed existence, from the beginning, of a diriment impediment, an essential defect in consent, radical incapability for marriage, or a condition placed by one or both of the parties against the very nature of marriage.

Eastern Rite Laws

Marriage laws of the Eastern Church differ in several respects from the legislation of the Roman Rite. The regulations in effect since

May 2, 1949, were contained in the motu proprio *Crebre Allatae* issued by Pius XII the previous February.

According to both the Roman Code of Canon Law and the Oriental Code, marriages between Roman Rite Catholics and Eastern Rite Catholics ordinarily take place in the rite of the groom and have canonical effects in that rite.

Regarding the form for the celebration of marriages between Eastern Catholics and baptized Eastern non-Catholics, the Second Vatican Council declared:

"By way of preventing invalid marriages between Eastern Catholics and baptized Eastern non-Catholics, and in the interests of the permanence and sanctity of marriage and of domestic harmony, this sacred Synod decrees that the canonical 'form' for the celebration of such marriages obliges only for lawfulness. For their validity, the presence of a sacred minister suffices, as long as the other requirements of law are honored" *(Decree on Eastern Catholic Churches,* No. 18).

Marriages taking place in this manner are lawful, as well as valid, with permission of a competent Eastern Rite bishop.

The Rota

The Sacred Roman Rota is the ordinary court of appeal for marriage, and some other cases, which are appealed to the Holy See from lower church courts. Appeals are made to the Rota if decisions by diocesan and archdiocesan courts fail to settle the matter in dispute.

MIXED MARRIAGES

Following are excerpts from a statement, *Implementation of the Apostolic Letter on Mixed Marriages,* approved by the National Conference of Catholic Bishops Nov. 16, 1970, and effective in the US since Jan. 1, 1971. The text of the statement was circulated by NC News Service. The text of the letter on which the statement was based, *Matrimonia Mixta,* was issued by Pope Paul VI Mar. 31, 1970; it appeared in the 1971 edition of the Almanac, pp. 278-81.

Aim of Church

Within marriage the Church seeks always to uphold the strength and stability of marital union and the family which flows from it.

As the Apostolic Letter observes, the "perfect union of mind and full communion of life" to which married couples aspire can be more readily achieved when both partners share the same Catholic belief and life. For this reason, the Church greatly desires that Catholics marry Catholics and generally discourages mixed marriages.

Yet, recognizing that mixed marriages do occur, the Church, upholding the principles of Divine Law, makes special arrangements for them. And, recognizing that these

marriages do at times encounter special difficulties, the Church wishes to see that special help and support are extended to the couples concerned.

Pastoral Concern

The Apostolic Letter stresses the importance of individualized support for diverse situations. It recognizes that ". . . the canonical discipline on mixed marriages cannot be uniform and must be adapted . . ." and "the pastoral care to be given to the married people and children of marriage" must also be adapted "according to the distinct circumstances of the married couple and the differing degrees of their ecclesiastical communion." Consequently, pastors, in exercising their ministry in behalf of marriages that unite Catholics and others will do so with zealous concern and respect for the couples involved. They should have an active and positive regard for the holy state in which such couples are united.

In such marriages, the conscientious devotion of the Catholic to the Catholic Church is to be safeguarded, and the conscience of the other partner is to be respected. This is in keeping with the principle of religious liberty. (Cf. *Declaration on Religious Freedom,* No. 30.)

Values in Marriage

The sacred character of all valid marriages, including those which the Church does not consider as sacramental, is recognized.

The broad areas of agreement which unite Christians and Jews in their appreciation of the religious character of marriage should be kept significantly in mind. (Cf. *Joint Statement on Marriage and Family Life in the United States,* issued by the United States Catholic Conference, the National Council of the Churches of Christ, and the Synagogue Council of America, June 8, 1966.)

In this context, it should be clearly noted that, while Catholics are required to observe the Catholic form of marriage for validity, unless dispensed by their bishop, the Catholic Church recognizes the reality of marriages contracted validly among those who are not Christians and among those Christians separated from us.

Sacramental Marriage

In addition to the sacred character of all valid marriages, still more must be said of marriages between a Catholic and another baptized Christian. According to our Catholic tradition, we believe such marriages to be truly sacramental. The Apostolic Letter states that there exists between the persons united in them a special "communion of spiritual benefits." These spiritual bonds in which couples are united are grounded in the "true though imperfect, communion" which exists between the Catholic Church and all who believe in

Christ and are properly baptized (cf. *Decree on Ecumenism,* No. 3). Along with us, such persons are honored by the title of Christian and are rightly regarded as brothers in the Lord. In marriages which unite Catholics and other baptized Christians, the couple should be encouraged to recognize in practical ways what they share together in the life of grace, in faith, hope and charity along with other interior gifts of the Holy Spirit, and that in service to the same Lord they await the salvation which He promised to those who would be His followers.

Difficulties

A number of the particular difficulties faced by Catholics and other Christians in mixed marriages result from the division among Christians. However successful these marriages may be, they do not erase the pain of that wider division. Yet this division need not weaken these marriages; and, given proper understanding, they may lead to a deep spiritual unity between the spouses.

Joint Pastoral Care

In order to aid these couples to come to this deep understanding of their married life together, when possible, their Catholic and other Christian pastors should jointly do all that they can to prepare them for marriage and to support them and their families with all the aids their ministry can provide.

The pastors of the different Christian communities can best bring the couple to a keen awareness of all that they have in common as Christians as well as to a proper appreciation of the gravity of the differences that yet remain between their churches.

In their homes, these couples should be encouraged in practical ways to develop a common life of prayer, calling upon the many elements of spirituality which they share as a common Christian heritage and expressing their own common faith in the Lord, together asking Him to help them grow in their love for each other, to bless their families with the graces they need, and to keep them always mindful of the needs of others. The example of parents united in prayer is especially important for the children whom God may give them. In regard to public worship together in each other's churches, pastors may explain to the couple the provisions made for this by the Holy See in the *Ecumenical Directory.*

Religious Education

Beyond this, parents have the right and the responsibility to provide for the religious education of their children. This right is clearly taught by Vatican II: "Since the family is a society in its own original right, it has the right freely to live its own domestic religious life under the guidance of parents. Parents, moreover, have the right to determine, in accordance with their own religious beliefs, the kind of religious education that their children are to receive" *(Declaration on Religious Freedom,* No. 5).

It is evident that in preparing for a mixed marriage, the couple will have to reach decisions and make specific choices in order to fulfill successfully the responsibility that is theirs toward their children in this respect. It is to be hoped for their own sake that in this matter the couple may reach a common mind.

If this issue is not resolved before marriage, the couple, as sad experience has shown, find a severe strain in their marital life that can subject them to well-meaning but tension-building pressures from relatives on both sides.

If this issue cannot be resolved, there is a serious question whether the couple should marry.

In reaching a concrete decision concerning the baptism and religious education of children, both partners should remember that neither thereby abdicates the fundamental responsibility of parents to see that their children are instilled with deep and abiding religious values.

In this the Catholic partner is seriously bound to act in accord with his faith which recognizes that: "This is the unique Church of Christ which in the Creed we avow as one, holy, catholic and apostolic. After His Resurrection our Savior handed her over to Peter to be shepherded (Jn. 21:17), commissioning him and the other apostles to propagate and govern her (cf. Mt. 28:18, ff.). Her He erected for all ages as 'the pillar and mainstay of the truth,' (1 Tm. 3:15). This Church, constituted and organized in the world as a society, subsists in the Catholic Church, which is governed by the successor of Peter and by the bishops in union with that successor, although many elements of sanctification and of truth can be found outside of her visible structure. These elements, however, as gifts properly belonging to the Church of Christ, possess an inner dynamism toward Catholic unity" *(Dogmatic Constitution on the Church,* No. 8). This faith is the source of a serious obligation in conscience on the part of the Catholic, whose conscience in this regard must be respected.

Norms

Pastoral Responsibility: In every diocese, there shall be appropriate informational programs to explain both the reasons for restrictions upon mixed marriages and the positive spiritual values to be sought in such marriages when permitted. This is particularly important if the non-Catholic is a Christian believer and the unity of married and family life is ultimately based upon the baptism of both wife and husband. If possible, all such programs should be undertaken . . . in conjunction with non-Catholic authorities.

In addition to the customary marriage

preparation programs, it is the serious duty of each one in the pastoral ministry, according to his own responsibility, office or assignment, to undertake:

(a) the spiritual and catechetical preparation, especially in regard to the "ends and essential properties of marriage (which) are not to be excluded by either party" (cf. *Matrimonia Mixta,* No. 6), on a direct and individual basis, of couples who seek to enter a mixed marriage, and

(b) continued concern and assistance to the wife and husband in mixed marriages and to their children, so that married and family life may be supported in unity, respect for conscience, and common spiritual benefit.

In the assistance which he gives in preparation for marriage between a Catholic and a non-Catholic, and his continued efforts to help all married couples and families, the priest should endeavor to be in contact and to cooperate with the minister or religious counselor of the non-Catholic.

Promise: The declaration and promise by the Catholic, necessary for dispensation from the impediment to a mixed marriage (either mixed religion or disparity of worship), shall be made in the following words or their substantial equivalent:

"I reaffirm my faith in Jesus Christ and, with God's help, intend to continue living that faith in the Catholic Church.

"I promise to do all in my power to share the faith I have received with our children by having them baptized and reared as Catholics."

The declaration and promise are made in the presence of a priest or deacon either orally or in writing as the Catholic prefers.

The form of the declaration and promise is not altered in the case of the marriage of a Catholic with another baptized Christian, but the priest should draw the attention of the Catholic to the communion of spiritual benefits in such a Christian marriage. The promise and declaration should be made in the light of the "certain, though imperfect, communion" of the non-Catholic with the Catholic Church because of his belief in Christ and baptism (cf. *Decree on Ecumenism,* No. 3).

Informing the Non-Catholic: At an opportune time before marriage, and preferably as part of the usual premarital instruction, the non-Catholic must be informed of the promises and of the responsibility of the Catholic. No precise manner or occasion of informing the non-Catholic is prescribed. It may be done by the priest, deacon or the Catholic party. No formal statement of the non-Catholic is required. But the mutual understanding of this question beforehand should prevent possible disharmony that might otherwise arise during married life.

The priest who submits the request for dispensation from the impediment to a mixed marriage shall certify that the declaration and promise have been made by the Catholic and that the non-Catholic has been informed of this requirement. This is done in the following or similar words:

"The required promise and declaration have been made by the Catholic in my presence. The non-Catholic has been informed of this requirement so that it is certain that he (she) is aware of the promise and obligation on the part of the Catholic."

The promise of the Catholic must be sincerely made, and is to be presumed to be sincerely made. If, however, the priest has reason to doubt the sincerity of the promise made by the Catholic, he may not recommend the request for the dispensation and should submit the matter to the local Ordinary.

Form, Ceremony of Marriage: Where there are serious difficulties in observing the Catholic canonical form in a mixed marriage, the local Ordinary of the Catholic party or of the place where the marriage is to occur may dispense the Catholic from the observance of the form for a just pastoral cause. An exhaustive list is impossible, but the following are the types of reasons: to achieve family harmony or to avoid family alienation, to obtain parental agreement to the marriage, to recognize the significant claims of relationship or special friendship with a non-Catholic minister, to permit the marriage in a church that has particular importance to the non-Catholic. If the Ordinary of the Catholic party grants a dispensation for a marriage which is to take place in another diocese, the Ordinary of that diocese should be informed beforehand.

Ordinarily this dispensation from the canonical form is granted in view of the proposed celebration of a religious marriage service. In some exceptional circumstances (e.g., certain Catholic-Jewish marriages) it may be necessary that the dispensation be granted so that a civil ceremony may be performed. In any case, a public form that is civilly recognized for the celebration of marriage is required.

It is not permitted to have two religious marriage services or to have a single service in which both the Catholic marriage ritual and a non-Catholic marriage ritual are celebrated jointly or successively (cf. *Matrimonia Mixta,* No. 13).

With the permission of the local Ordinary and the consent of the appropriate authority of the other church or community, a non-Catholic minister may be invited to participate in the Catholic marriage service by giving additional prayers, blessings, or words of greeting or exhortation. If the marriage is not part of the Eucharistic celebration, the minister may also be invited to read a lesson and/or to preach (cf. *Directory on Ecumenism* Part I, No. 56).

In the case where there has been a dispensation from the Catholic canonical form and the priest has been invited to participate in the non-Catholic marriage service, with the permission of the local Ordinary and the consent of the appropriate authority of the other church or communion, he may do so by giving additional prayers, blessings, or words of greeting and exhortation. If the marriage service is not part of the Lord's Supper or the principal liturgical service of the Word, the priest, if invited, may also read a lesson and/or preach (cf. *Ibid*).

To the extent that Eucharistic sharing is not permitted by the general discipline of the Church, this is to be considered when plans are being made to have the mixed marriage at Mass or not.

Place of Marriage: The ordinary place of marriage is in the parish church or other sacred place. For serious reasons, the local Ordinary may permit the celebration of a mixed marriage, when there has been no dispensation from the canonical form and the Catholic marriage service is to be celebrated, outside a Catholic church or chapel, providing there is no scandal involved and proper delegation is granted (for example, where there is no Catholic church in the area, etc.).

If there has been a dispensation from canonical form, ordinarily the marriage service is celebrated in a non-Catholic church.

PROCEDURAL RULES

Pope Paul VI promulgated, June 11, 1971, a set of 13 rules designed to speed up the handling of cases in which the validity of marriage is questioned. Norms given in the document, which was issued by the Pope on his own initiative and became effective Oct.31, concern "the constitution of ecclesiastical tribunals and . . . the judicial process which will expedite the matrimonial process itself."

The norms do not affect the reasons for the validity or invalidity of marriages, but only the way in which cases of this kind are handled in church courts.

Marriage Judgments

An article on the foregoing norms, appearing in the July 1, 1971, English edition of *L'Osservatore Romano,* noted: The judgments the Church "expresses with marriage sentences are of a spiritual nature, aimed at establishing the original nullity of marriage, at restoring spiritual order where disorder had been created owing to an invalid celebration" (of marriage).

"The Church does not . . . declare a validly contracted bond to be dissolved. . . . A bond that has never been contracted and is only apparently existent cannot be a source of sacramental grace for a Catholic until it is validated. . . . If, for objective reasons (of a serious type), she (the Church) makes modifications in the procedure that accompanies these processes (of investigating and judging cases), this in no way challenges the principle of the in-

dissolubility of marriage or alters the structure or essence of the process." The process "aims at the spiritual good of the spouses."

U. S. Norms

Twenty-three experimental norms — drawn up by the Canon Law Society of America, approved by the National Conference of Catholic Bishops and the Holy See, and in effect since July, 1970 — were broader in some respects than those decreed by Pope Paul. Among other things, they provided for: one-priest tribunals for specific periods of time instead of just for individual cases; dispensation by the NCCB from the need for review of first decisions regarding the validity or invalidity of a marriage; circumstances affecting the competence of tribunals. Continuing use of the experimental procedural norms was authorized by Paul VI in a letter dated May 22 and announced June 8, 1974 — "until the new order of matrimonial court procedure is promulgated for the Latin Church" in connection with the on-going revision of the Code of Canon Law. Termination of their use had been scheduled for June 30, 1974, following an original authorization for one year and an extension for three more years.

Cases of Non-Consummation

Pope Paul VI promulgated May 31, 1972, norms designed to speed up the handling of cases involving questions about the validity of marriages entered legally but never consummated sexually. The regulations which went into effect July 1, granted local bishops powers previously reserved to the Holy See.

Accordingly local bishops can initiate procedures in cases of this type; testimony and documents are acceptable in any modern language and on tape; physical proof of non-consummation can be omitted if the bishop is satisfied with the statements of the parties and/or witnesses; the number of witnesses is left to the discretion of the bishop.

ERRONEOUS OPINIONS

In a letter whose contents became known in August, 1973, the Congregation for the Doctrine of the Faith advised bishops that erroneous opinions concerning the indissolubility of marriage were being circulated "in books, Catholic newspapers, and even in seminaries and Catholic schools; and also, in practice, in some ecclesiastical tribunals."

"These opinions," the letter said, "are being used . . . to justify abuses . . . contrary to the present discipline governing the admission to the sacraments of persons who live in irregular (matrimonial) unions."

Norms state that the sacraments may be administered to separated or divorced persons who have not remarried; to those who have received a declaration of nullity regarding the previous marriage; and to those who, although remarried, are living in a brother-sister relationship of sexual continence.

The Church Calendar

The calendar of the Roman Church consists of an arrangement throughout the year of a series of liturgical seasons and feasts of saints for purposes of divine worship.

The purposes of this calendar were outlined in the *Constitution on the Sacred Liturgy* (Nos. 102-105) promulgated by the Second Vatican Council.

"Within the cycle of a year . . . (the Church) unfolds the whole mystery of Christ, not only from His incarnation and birth until His ascension, but also as reflected in the day of Pentecost, and the expectation of a blessed, hoped-for return of the Lord.

"Recalling thus the mysteries of redemption, the Church opens to the faithful the riches of her Lord's powers and merits, so that these are in some way made present at all times, and the faithful are enabled to lay hold of them and become filled with saving grace" (No. 102).

"In celebrating this annual cycle of Christ's mysteries, holy Church honors with special love the Blessed Mary, Mother of God . . ." (No. 103).

"The Church has also included in the annual cycle days devoted to the memory of the martyrs and the other saints. . . . (who) sing God's perfect praise in heaven and offer prayers for us. By celebrating the passage of these saints from earth to heaven the Church proclaims the paschal mystery as achieved in the saints who have suffered and been glorified with Christ; she proposes them to the faithful as examples who draw all to the Father through Christ, and through their merits she pleads for God's favors" (No. 104).

". . . In the various seasons of the year and according to her traditional discipline, the Church completes the formation of the faithful by means of pious practices for soul and body, by instruction, prayer, and works of penance and mercy. . ." (No. 105).

THE REVISED CALENDAR

Pope Paul announced May 9, 1969, his approval of a reorganization of the liturgical year and calendar for the Roman Rite, in implementation of a directive from the Second Vatican Council in 1964. He made the announcement in a document issued on his own initiative and entitled *Paschalis Mysterii.*

The purpose of the action, the Pope said, was "no other . . . than to permit the faithful to communicate in a more intense way, through faith, hope and love, in 'the whole mystery of Christ which . . . unfolds within the cycle of a year.' "

The motu proprio was dated Feb. 14, 1969. The new calendar was promulgated a month later by a decree of the Congregation for Divine Worship and went into effect Jan. 1, 1970, with provisional modifications. Full implementation of all its parts was delayed in 1970 and 1971, pending the completion of work on related liturgical texts. The US bishops ordered the whole new calendar into effect for 1972.

The revised calendar, whose principal architect was Father Pierre Jounel, professor of liturgy at the Catholic University of Paris, involved some restructuring of the liturgical cycles and changes affecting the feasts of saints.

The Seasons

Advent: The liturgical year begins with the First Sunday of Advent, which introduces a season of four weeks or slightly less duration with the theme of expectation of the coming of Christ. During the first two weeks, the final coming of Christ as Lord and Judge at the end of the world is the focus of attention. From Dec. 17 to 24, the emphasis shifts to anticipation of the celebration of his Nativity on the feast of Christmas.

Advent has four Sundays. Since the 10th century, the first Sunday has marked the beginning of the liturgical year in the Western Church. In the Middle Ages, a kind of pre-Christmas fast was in vogue during the season.

Christmastide: Christmastide opens with the feast of the Nativity, Dec. 25, and lasts until the Sunday after Epiphany. The Holy Family is commemorated on the Sunday within the Christmas octave. Jan. 1 — formerly called the Octave Day of the Nativity and, before that, the feast of the Circumcision of Jesus — has the title of Solemnity of Mary the Mother of God. The Epiphany, scheduled for Jan. 6 in the universal calendar, is celebrated in the US on a Sunday between Jan. 2 and 8. The Baptism of the Lord, observed on the Sunday following Epiphany, marks the end of Christmastide.

The period between the end of Christmastide and the beginning of Lent belongs to the Season-through-the-Year. Of variable length, the pre-Lenten phase of this season includes what were formerly called the Sundays after Epiphany and the suppressed Sundays of Septuagesima, Sexagesima and Quinquagesima.

Lent: The penitential season of Lent begins on Ash Wednesday, which occurs between Feb. 4 and Mar. 11, depending on the date of Easter, and lasts until Easter. It has six Sundays and 40 weekdays. The climactic last week is called Holy Week. The last three days (Holy Thursday, Good Friday and Holy Saturday) are called the Paschal Triduum.

The origin of Lenten observances dates back to the fourth century or earlier.

Eastertide: Eastertide, whose theme is resurrection from sin to the life of grace, lasts for 50 days, from Easter to Pentecost. Easter, the first Sunday following the vernal equinox, occurs between Mar. 22 and Apr. 25. The terminal phase of Eastertide, between the feast of the Ascension of the Lord and Pentecost, stresses anticipation of the coming and action of the Holy Spirit.

Season-through-the-Year: The Season-through-the-Year includes not only the period between the end of Christmastide and the beginning of Lent, as noted above, but also all Sundays after Pentecost to the last Sunday of the liturgical year, which is celebrated as the feast of Christ the King. The number of Sundays before Lent and after Pentecost varies, depending on the date of the key feast of Easter. The overall purpose of the season is to elaborate the themes of salvation history.

The various liturgical seasons are characterized in part by the scriptural readings and Mass prayers assigned to each of them. During Advent, for example, the readings are messianic; during Eastertide, from the Acts of the Apostles, chronicling the Resurrection and the original proclamation of Christ by the Apostles, and from the Gospel of John; during Lent, baptismal and penitential passages. Mass prayers reflect the meaning and purpose of the various seasons.

Feasts of Saints

The feasts of saints are celebrated concurrently with the liturgical seasons and feasts of our Lord. Their purpose always has been to illustrate the paschal mysteries as reflected in the lives of saints, to honor them as heroes of holiness, and to appeal for their intercession. For various reasons, however, the number and variety of feasts distracted attention to some degree from the central mysteries of redemption and the universality of holiness in the Church. To remedy these defects, Pope Paul ordered a number of significant changes affecting the feasts of saints.

In line with revised regulations, some feasts were either abolished or relegated to observance in particular places by local option for one of two reasons: (1) lack of sufficient historical evidence for observance of the feasts; (2) lack of universal significance. More than 40 feasts were eliminated; 92 were made optional for particular places, e.g., the diocese or country in which a saint was martyred; more than 60 were ordered for observance throughout the Roman Rite.

Commenting on the elimination of some feasts, *L'Osservatore Della Domenica,* the Vatican City weekly, said: "Generally, the removal of a name from the calendar does not mean passing judgment on the nonexistence (of a saint) or lack of holiness. Many (saints) have been removed (from the calendar) because all that remains certain about them is their name, and this would say too little to the faithful in comparison with many others.

Other feasts were removed because they lacked universal significance."

Traditional feasts of our Lord have been retained, except for those of the Holy Name and the Precious Blood which were suppressed.

Most feasts of Blessed Mary the Virgin have been retained. Universal observance obtains for the feasts of the Assumption, Immaculate Conception, Birth, Annunciation (of Our Lord), Presentation of the Lord, Visitation, Our Lady of Sorrows, Our Lady of the Rosary, Presentation, Queenship. Local option governs celebration of the memorials of Our Lady of Lourdes, Our Lady of Mt. Carmel, Dedication of (the Basilica of) St. Mary Major, the Immaculate Heart.

St. Joseph, Husband of Mary, is honored universally on Mar. 19 and by local option on another date (feast of St. Joseph the Worker, which may be observed May 1).

The archangels — Michael, Raphael and Gabriel — are honored with a common feast, Sept. 29, instead of with three separate feasts as before. The feast of the Guardian Angels, Oct. 2, stands.

The traditional feasts of the Apostles and Evangelists have been retained, with several date changes. Sts. Peter and Paul, who are honored with a common feast June 29, each has an additional feast on Feb. 22 (Chair of St. Peter) and Jan. 25 (Conversion of St. Paul).

Other saints, as noted above, are honored on universal and optional feasts throughout the year.

The universality of holiness in the Church is reflected in the distribution of feasts among saints of different periods and locations. Sixty-four saints are of the first 10 centuries, 79 of the last 10 centuries. Most represented are the fourth century (25 saints), the 12th (12), the 16th (17), and the 17th (17). Geographically, there are 126 feasts of European saints, 14 of Asians, eight of Africans, four of Americans, and one of a saint of Oceania.

The feast of a saint, as a general rule, is observed on the day of his death *(dies natalis,* day of birth to glory with God in heaven). Exceptions to this rule include the feasts of St. John the Baptist, who is honored on the day of his birth; Sts. Basil the Great and Gregory Nazianzen, and the brother Saints, Cyril and Methodius, who are commemorated in joint feasts.

Application of this general rule in the revised calendar resulted in date changes of some feasts.

Sundays and Feast Days

Sunday is the original Christian feast day because of the unusually significant events of salvation history which took place and are commemorated on the first day of the week — viz., the Resurrection of Christ, the key event of his life and the fundamental fact of

Christianity; and the descent of the Holy Spirit upon the Apostles on Pentecost, the birthday of the Church. The transfer of observance of the Lord's Day from the Sabbath to Sunday was made in apostolic times. The Mass and Liturgy of the Hours (Divine Office) of each Sunday reflect the themes and set the tones of the various liturgical seasons.

Categories of feasts according to dignity and manner of observance are: solemnity (highest, corresponding to former first-class feasts); feast (corresponding to former second-class feasts); memorial (corresponding to former third-class feasts); optional memorial (observable by local choice). Feasts of the first three categories are observed universally in the Roman Rite.

Fixed feasts are those which are regularly celebrated on the same calendar day each year.

Movable feasts are those which are not observed on the same calendar day each year. Examples of these are Easter (the first Sunday after the first full moon following the vernal equinox), Ascension (40 days after Easter), Pentecost (50 days after Easter), Trinity Sunday (first after Pentecost), Christ the King (last Sunday of the liturgical year).

Holy Days of Obligation

Holy days of obligation are special feasts on which Catholics who have reached the age of reason are seriously obliged, as on Sundays, to assist at Mass and to avoid unnecessary servile work. Serious reasons excuse from the observance of either or both of these obligations.

By enactment of the Third Plenary Council of Baltimore, and with the approval of the Holy See, the holy days of obligation observed in the United States are: Christmas, the Nativity of Jesus, Dec. 25; Solemnity of Mary the Mother of God, Jan. 1; Ascension of the Lord; Assumption of Blessed Mary the Virgin, Aug. 15; All Saints' Day, Nov. 1; Immaculate Conception of Blessed Mary the Virgin, Dec. 8.

In addition to these, there are four other holy days of obligation prescribed in the general law of the Church which are not so observed in the US: Epiphany; St. Joseph, Mar. 19; Corpus Christi; Sts. Peter and Paul, June 29.

Ferial, Ember, Rogation Days

Ferial days are weekdays on which no proper feast or vigil is celebrated in the Mass or Liturgy of the Hours (Divine Office). On such days, the Mass may be that of the preceding Sunday, which expresses the liturgical spirit of the season, an optional memorial, a votive Mass, or a Mass for the dead. Ferial days of Advent and Lent are in a special category of their own.

Aside from feast-day considerations, Monday through Friday are called ferial days, and are consecutively numbered from two to six. The first day of the week is Sunday or the Lord's Day, and the seventh is called the Sabbath.

Ember days originated at Rome about the fifth century, probably as Christian replacements for seasonal festivals of agrarian cults. They were observances of penance, thanksgiving, and petition for divine blessing on the various seasons; they also were occasions of special prayer for clergy to be ordained. These days were observed four times a year: on the Wednesday, Friday and Saturday following the Third Sunday of Advent, the First Sunday of Lent, Pentecost, and the third Sunday of September. In line with the calendar reform of 1969, decision with respect to the observance of ember days rests with the National Conference of Catholic Bishops.

Rogation days originated in France about the fifth century. They were penitential in character and also occasions of prayer for a bountiful harvest and protection against evil. Minor days of rogation were observed on the three days before the feast of the Ascension; Apr. 25 was a day of major rogation. In line with the calendar reform of 1969, decision with respect to the observance of rogation days rests with the National Conference of Catholic Bishops.

Days of Abstinence and Fast

The apostolic constitution *Paenitemini,* in effect since Feb. 23, 1966, authorized the substitution of other works of penance for the customary and common observances of abstinence and fast on various days of the year.

In this country, in line with provisions of the constitution and a 1974 decision of the National Conference of Catholic Bishops, Ash Wednesday and Good Friday are days of fast and abstinence, and all Fridays of Lent are days of abstinence.

The obligation to abstain from meat binds Catholics 14 years of age and older. The obligation to fast, limiting oneself to one full meal and two lighter meals in the course of a day, binds Catholics from the ages of 21 to 59.

BYZANTINE CALENDAR

The Byzantine-Rite calendar has many distinctive features of its own, although it shares common elements with the Roman-Rite calendar—e.g., general purpose, commemoration of the mysteries of faith and of the saints, identical dates for some feasts. Among the distinctive things are the following.

The liturgical year begins on Sept. 1, the **Day of Indiction,** in contrast with the Latin or Roman start on the First Sunday of Advent late in November or early in December. The Advent season begins on Dec. 10.

Cycles of the Year

As in the Roman usage, the dating of feasts follows the Gregorian Calendar. Formerly, until well into this century, the Julian Calendar was used. (The Julian Calendar, which is now about 13 days late, is still used by some Eastern-Rite Churches.)

The year has several cycles, which include proper seasons, the feasts of saints, and series of New Testament readings. All of these elements of worship are contained in liturgical books of the rite.

The ecclesiastical calendar, called the **Menologion,** explains the nature of feasts, other observances and matters pertaining to the liturgy for each day of the year. In some cases, its contents include the lives of saints and the history and meaning of feasts.

The Divine Liturgy (Mass) and Divine Office for the proper of the saints, fixed feasts, and the Christmas season are contained in the **Menaion.** The **Triodion** covers the pre-Lenten season of preparation for Easter; Lent begins two days before the Ash Wednesday observance of the Roman Rite. The **Pentecostarion** contains the liturgical services from Easter to the Sunday of All Saints, the first after Pentecost. The **Evangelion** and **Apostolos** are books in which the Gospels, and Acts of the Apostles and the Epistles, respectively, are arranged according to the order of their reading in the Divine Liturgy and Divine Office throughout the year.

The cyclic progression of liturgical music throughout the year, in successive and repetitive periods of eight weeks, is governed by the **Oktoechos,** the Book of Eight Tones.

Sunday Names

Many Sundays are named after the subject of the Gospel read in the Mass of the day or after the name of a feast falling on the day — e.g., Sunday of the Publican and Pharisee, of the Prodigal Son, of the Samaritan Woman, of St. Thomas the Apostle, of the Fore-Fathers (Old Testament Patriarchs). Other Sundays are named in the same manner as in the Roman calendar — e.g., numbered Sundays of Lent and after Pentecost.

Holy Days, Abstinence, Fast

The calendar lists about 28 holy days. Many of the major holy days coincide with those of the Roman calendar, but the feast of the Immaculate Conception is observed on Dec. 9 instead of Dec. 8, and the feast of All Saints falls on the Sunday after Pentecost rather than on Nov. 1. Instead of a single All Souls' Day, there are five All Souls' Saturdays.

According to regulations in effect in the Byzantine-Rite (Ruthenian) Dioceses of Passaic and Pittsburgh, holy days are obligatory, solemn and simple, and attendance at the Divine Liturgy is required on five obligatory days — the feasts of the Epiphany, the Ascension, Sts. Peter and Paul, the Assumption of the Blessed Virgin Mary, and Christmas. Although attendance at the liturgy is not obliga-

tory on 15 solemn and seven simple holy days, it is recommended.

Lent

The first day of Lent — the Monday before Ash Wednesday of the Roman Rite — and Good Friday are days of strict abstinence for persons between the ages of 21 and 59. No meat, eggs, or dairy products may be eaten on these days.

All persons over the age of 14 must abstain from meat on Fridays during Lent, Holy Saturday, and the vigils of the feasts of Christmas and Epiphany; abstinence is urged, but is not obligatory, on Wednesdays of Lent. The abstinence obligation is not in force on certain "free" or "privileged" Fridays.

Synaxis

An observance without a counterpart in the Roman calendar is the synaxis. This is a commemoration, on the day following a feast, of persons involved with the occasion for the feast — e.g., Sept. 9, the day following the feast of the Nativity of the Blessed Virgin Mary, is the Synaxis of Joachim and Anna, her parents.

CALENDAR NOTES

Scriptural Readings

The texts of scriptural readings for Mass on Sundays, holy days and some other days are indicated under the respective dates. The first (A) cycle of readings in the Lectionary is prescribed for the 1975 liturgical year; the second (B) cycle is prescribed for the 1976 liturgical year which begins with the first Sunday of Advent, Nov. 30, 1975.

Weekday cycles of readings are the first and second, respectively, for liturgical years 1975 and 1976.

Holiday Masses

Liturgical experiments in recent years have led to the development of votive Masses for national holidays, like those introduced in the US for Thanksgiving Day in 1969 and July 4 in 1972. This development is in line with a custom whereby "from the earliest times the Church has crowned many non-Christian feasts with Christian fulfillment by instituting its own liturgical festivals" to coincide with them.

Labor Day, in lieu of a special votive Mass, may be observed with celebration of the Mass of St. Joseph the Worker.

Monthly Prayer Intentions

General and mission intentions recommended by Pope Paul to the prayers of the Apostles of Prayer are given under each month of the 1975 calendar.

JANUARY 1975

1—**Wed. Solemnity of Mary, Mother of God. Holy day of obligation.** (Nm. 6:22-27; Gal. 4:4-7; Lk. 2:16-21.)

2—Thurs. Sts. Basil the Great and Gregory Nazianzen, bishops-doctors; memorial.

3—Fri. Weekday.

4—Sat. Bl. Elizabeth Ann Seton; memorial (in U.S.).

5—**Sun. Epiphany of the Lord** (in U.S.); **solemnity.** (Is. 60:1-6; Eph. 3:2-3a, 5-6; Mt. 2:1-12.) [Bl. John Neumann, bishop; memorial in U.S.]

6—Mon. Weekday.

7—Tues. Weekday. St. Raymond of Penyafort, priest; optional memorial.

8—Wed. Weekday.

9—Thurs. Weekday.

10—Fri. Weekday.

11—Sat. Weekday.

12—**Sun. Baptism of the Lord; feast.** (Is. 42:1-4, 6-7; Acts 10:34-38; Mt. 3:13-17.)

13—Mon. Weekday. St. Hilary, bishop-doctor; optional memorial.

14—Tues. Wed. Weekday.

15—Wed. Weekday.

16—Thurs. Weekday.

17—Fri. St. Anthony, abbot; memorial.

18—Sat. Weekday.

19—**Second Sunday of the Year.** (Is. 49:3, 5-6; 1 Cor. 1:1-3; Jn. 1:29-34.)

20—Mon. Weekday. St. Fabian, pope-martyr, or St. Sebastian, martyr; optional memorials.

21—Tues. St. Agnes, virgin-martyr; memorial.

22—Wed. Weekday. St. Vincent, deacon-martyr; optional memorial.

23—Thurs. Weekday.

24—Fri. St. Francis de Sales, bishop-doctor; memorial.

25—Sat. Conversion of St. Paul, apostle; feast.

26—**Third Sunday of the Year.** (Is. 8:23b to 9:3; 1 Cor. 1:10-13, 17; Mt. 4:12-23.) [Sts. Timothy and Titus, bishops; memorial.]

27—Mon. Weekday. St. Angela Merici, virgin; optional memorial.

28—Tues. St. Thomas Aquinas, priest-doctor; memorial.

29—Wed. Weekday.

30—Thurs. Weekday.

31—Fri. St. John Bosco, priest; memorial.

GENERAL PRAYER INTENTION: For Christian unity through conversion of hearts. That, through sincere conversion of hearts, genuine ecumenism may be effectively promoted.

MISSION PRAYER INTENTION: For growth in unity of faith, despite differing cultures. That youthful churches, which have to plant the Gospel in their countries' cultural forms, may rightly express the universaltiy of the Christian message.

FEBRUARY 1975

1—Sat. Weekday.

2—**Sun. Presentation of the Lord; feast.** (Mal. 3:1-4; Heb. 2:14-18; Lk. 2:22-40 or Lk. 2:22-32.)

3—Mon. (Fourth Week of the Year.) Weekday. St. Blase, bishop-martyr, or St. Ansgar, bishop; optional memorials.

4—Tues. Weekday.

5—Wed. St. Agatha, virgin-martyr; memorial.

6—Thurs. Sts. Paul Miki and companions, martyrs; memorial.

7—Fri. Weekday.

8—Sat. Weekday. St. Jerome Emiliani; optional memorial.

9—**Fifth Sunday of the Year.** (Is. 58:7-10; 1 Cor. 2:1-5; Mt. 5:13-16.)

10—Mon. St. Scholastica, virgin; memorial.

11—Tues. Weekday. Our Lady of Lourdes; optional memorial.

12—Ash Wednesday. Beginning of Lent. *Fast and abstinence.*

13—Thurs. Weekday of Lent.

14—Fri. Weekday of Lent. *Abstinence.* [Sts. Cyril, monk, and Methodius, bishop; memorial.]

15—Sat. Weekday of Lent.

16—**First Sunday of Lent.** (Gn. 2:7-9, 3:1-7; Rom. 5:12-19; Mt. 4:1-11.)

17—Mon. Weekday of Lent. [Seven Holy Founders of the Servite Order; optional memorial.]

18—Tues. Weekday of Lent.

19—Wed. Weekday of Lent.

20—Thurs. Weekday of Lent.

21—Fri. Weekday of Lent. *Abstinence.* [St. Peter Damian, bishop-doctor; optional memorial.]

22—Sat. Chair of St. Peter; feast. Weekday of Lent.

23—**Second Sunday of Lent.** (Gn. 12:1-4a; 2 Tm. 1:8b-10; Mt. 17:1-9.) [St. Polycarp, bishop-martyr; memorial.]

24—Mon. Weekday of Lent.

25—Tues. Weekday of Lent.

26—Wed. Weekday of Lent.

27—Thurs. Weekday of Lent.

28—Fri. Weekday of Lent. *Abstinence.*

GENERAL PRAYER INTENTION: For reconciliation with God and our neighbors. That a spirit of true reconciliation with God and among men may be strongly fostered.

MISSION PRAYER INTENTION: For reconciliation among poor and rich as a result of Holy Year 1975. That the Year of Jubilee may awaken a sense of reconciliation among poor and rich countries, and may promote mutual recognition and cooperation for the benefit of all. This intention has the purpose of increasing awareness of international interdependence and of the obligations of "have" to "have-not" nations of the Third World.

MARCH 1975

1—Sat. Weekday of Lent.
2—**Third Sunday of Lent.** (Ex. 17:3-7; Rom. 5:1-2, 5-8; Jn. 4:5-42.)
3—Mon. Weekday of Lent.
4—Tues. Weekday of Lent. [St. Casimir, optional memorial.]
5—Wed. Weekday of Lent.
6—Thurs. Weekday of Lent.
7—Fri. Weekday of Lent. *Abstinence.* [Sts. Perpetua and Felicity, martyrs; memorial.]
8—Sat. Weekday of Lent. [St. John of God, religious; optional memorial.]
9—**Fourth Sunday of Lent.** (1 Sm. 16:1b, 6-7, 10-13a; Eph. 5:8-14; Jn. 9:1-41.) [St. Frances of Rome, religious; optional memorial.]
10—Mon. Weekday of Lent.
11—Tues. Weekday of Lent.
12—Wed. Weekday of Lent.
13—Thurs. Weekday of Lent.
14—Fri. Weekday of Lent. *Abstinence.*
15—Sat. Weekday of Lent.
16—**Fifth Sunday of Lent.** (Ez. 37:12-14; Rom. 8:8-11; Jn. 11:1-45.)
17—Mon. Weekday of Lent. [St. Patrick, bishop; optional memorial.]
18—Tues. Weekday of Lent. [St. Cyril of Jerusalem, bishop-doctor; optional memorial.]
19—Wed. St. Joseph; solemnity. Weekday of Lent.
20—Thurs. Weekday of Lent.
21—Fri. Weekday of Lent. *Abstinence.*
22—Sat. Weekday of Lent.
23—**Sunday of the Passion (Palm Sunday).** (Procession — Mt. 21:1-11. Mass — Is. 50:4-7; Phil. 2:6-11; Mt. 26:14 to 27:66.) [St. Turibius, bishop; optional memorial.]
24—Monday of Holy Week.
25—Tuesday of Holy Week.
26—Wednesday of Holy Week.
27—Thursday of Holy Week. Holy Thursday. The Paschal Triduum begins with the evening Mass of the Supper of the Lord.
28—Friday of the Passion of the Lord. Good Friday. *Fast and abstinence.*
29—Holy Saturday. The Easter Vigil.
30—**Easter Sunday; solemnity.** (Acts 10:34a, 37-43; Col. 3:1-4 or 1 Cor. 5:6b-8; Jn. 20:1-9 or Mt. 28:1-10 or (evening) Lk. 24:13-35.)
31—Easter Monday.

GENERAL PRAYER INTENTION: For the promotion of dialogue between Christian faith and the human sciences in Catholic universities.

MISSION PRAYER INTENTION: For theological reflection on the Church's mission. That theological meditation on the mission of the Church may strengthen zeal for evangelization.

APRIL 1975

1—Easter Tuesday.
2—Easter Wednesday. [St. Francis of Paola, hermit; optional memorial.]
3—Easter Thursday.
4—Easter Friday. [St. Isidore of Seville, bishop-doctor; optional memorial.]
5—Easter Saturday. [St. Vincent Ferrer, priest; optional memorial.]
6—**Second Sunday of Easter.** (Acts 2:42-47; 1 Pt. 1:3-9; Jn. 20:19-31.)
7—Mon. Annunciation of the Lord; solemnity (transferred from Mar. 25). [St. John Baptist de la Salle, priest; memorial.]
8—Tues. Weekday.
9—Wed. Weekday.
10—Thurs. Weekday.
11—Fri. Weekday. St. Stanislaus, bishop-martyr; optional memorial.
12—Sat. Weekday.
13—**Third Sunday of Easter.** (Acts 2:14, 22-28; 1 Pt. 1:17-21; Lk. 24:13-35.) [St. Martin I, pope-martyr; optional memorial.]
14—Mon. Weekday.
15—Tues. Weekday.
16—Wed. Weekday.
17—Thurs. Weekday.
18—Fri. Weekday.
19—Sat. Weekday.
20—**Fourth Sunday of Easter.** (Acts 2:14a, 36-41; 1 Pt. 2:20b-25; Jn. 10:1-10.)
21—Mon. Weekday. St. Anselm, bishop-doctor; optional memorial.
22—Tues. Weekday.
23—Wed. Weekday. St. George, martyr; optional memorial.
24—Thurs. Weekday. St. Fidelis of Sigmaringen, priest-martyr; optional memorial.
25—Fri. St. Mark, evangelist; feast.
26—Sat. Weekday.
27—**Fifth Sunday of Easter.** (Acts 6:1-7; 1 Pt. 2:4-9; Jn. 14:1-12.)
28—Mon. Weekday. St. Peter Chanel, priest-martyr; optional memorial.
29—Tues. St. Catherine of Siena, virgin-doctor; memorial.
30—Wed. Weekday. St. Pius V, pope; optional memorial.

GENERAL PRAYER INTENTION: For the promotion of Holy Year goals by the media. That the media of social communications may faithfully and efficaciously contribute to attainment of the noble goals of the Holy Year.

MISSION PRAYER INTENTION: For media cooperation in promoting the Holy Year. That the media may help to prepare the hearts of one and all to receive the gift of Holy Year indulgences fruitfully.

One of Pope Paul's strongest appeals in support of these intentions was made during a meeting with an international group of radio and television executives in April, 1974.

MAY 1975

1—Thurs. Weekday. St. Joseph, Worker; optional memorial.

2—Fri. St. Athanasius, bishop-doctor; memorial.

3—Sat. Sts. Philip and James, apostles; feast.

4—**Sixth Sunday of Easter** (Acts 8:5-8, 14-17; 1 Pt. 3:15-18; Jn. 14:15-21.)

5—Mon. Weekday.

6—Tues. Weekday.

7—Wed. Weekday.

8—**Thurs. Ascension of the Lord; solemnity. Holy day of obligation.** (Acts 1:1-11; Eph. 1:17-23; Mt. 28:16-20.)

9—Fri. Weekday.

10—Sat. Weekday.

11—**Seventh Sunday of Easter.** (Acts 1:12-14; 1 Pt. 4:13-16; Jn. 17:1-11a.)

12—Mon. Weekday. Sts. Nereus and Achilleus, martyrs, or St. Pancras, martyr; optional memorials.

13—Tues. Weekday.

14—Wed. St. Matthias, apostle; feast.

15—Thurs. Weekday. St. Isidore the Farmer; optional memorial (in U.S.).

16—Fri. Weekday.

17—Sat. Weekday.

18—**Sun. Pentecost; solemnity.** (Acts 2:1-11; 1 Cor. 12:3b-7, 12-13; Jn. 20:19-23.) [St. John I, pope-martyr; optional memorial.]

19—Mon. (Seventh Week of the Year.) Weekday.

20—Tues. Weekday. St. Bernardine of Siena, priest; optional memorial.

21—Wed. Weekday.

22—Thurs. Weekday.

23—Fri. Weekday.

24—Sat. Weekday.

25—**Sun. Holy Trinity; solemnity.** (Ex. 34:4b-6, 8-9; 2 Cor. 13:11-13; Jn. 3:16-18.) [St. Bede the Venerable, priest-doctor, or St. Gregory VII, pope, or St. Mary Magdalene de Pazzi, virgin; optional memorials.]

26—Mon. (Eighth Week of the Year.) St. Philip Neri, priest; memorial.

27—Tues. Weekday. St. Augustine of Canterbury, bishop; optional memorial.

28—Wed. Weekday.

29—Thurs. Weekday.

30—Fri. Weekday.

31—Sat. Visitation of Blessed Mary the Virgin; feast.

GENERAL PRAYER INTENTION: For spiritual progress through devotion to the Mother of God. That we may generously cultivate devotion to Mary and seek her intercession for the spiritual fruitfulness of the Holy Year.

MISSION PRAYER INTENTION: For cooperation among the peoples of Africa and Asia in pursuit of friendly and fraternal reconciliation.

JUNE 1975

1—**Sun. Corpus Christi (in U.S.); solemnity.** (Dt. 8:2-3, 14b-16a; 1 Cor. 10:16-17; Jn. 6:51-58.) [St. Justin, martyr; memorial.]

2—Mon. (Ninth Week of the Year.) Weekday. Sts. Marcellinus and Peter, martyrs; optional memorials.

3—Tues. Sts. Charles Lwanga and companions, martyrs; memorial.

4—Wed. Weekday.

5—Thurs. St. Boniface, bishop-martyr; memorial.

6—Fri. Sacred Heart of Jesus; solemnity. (Dt. 7:6-11; 1 Jn. 4:7-16; Mt. 11:25-30.) [St. Norbert, bishop; optional memorial.]

7—Sat. Weekday. Immaculate Heart of Mary; optional memorial.

8—**Tenth Sunday of the Year.** (Hos. 6:3-6; Rom. 4:18-25; Mt. 9:9-13.)

9—Mon. Weekday. St. Ephraem, deacon-doctor; optional memorial.

10—Tues. Weekday.

11—Wed. St. Barnabas, apostle; memorial.

12—Thurs. Weekday.

13—Fri. St. Anthony of Padua, priest-doctor; memorial.

14—Sat. Weekday.

15—**Eleventh Sunday of the Year.** (Ex. 19:2-6a; Rom. 5:6-11; Mt. 9:36 to 10:8.)

16—Mon. Weekday.

17—Tues. Weekday.

18—Wed. Weekday.

19—Thurs. Weekday. St. Romuald, abbot; optional memorial.

20—Fri. Weekday.

21—Sat. St. Aloysius Gonzaga, religious; memorial.

22—**Twelfth Sunday of the Year.** (Jer. 20:10-13; Rom. 5:12-15; Mt. 10:26-33.) [St. Paulinus of Nola, bishop, or Sts. John Fisher, bishop-martyr, and Thomas More, martyr; optional memorials.]

23—Mon. Weekday.

24—Tues. Birth of St. John the Baptist; solemnity. (Acts 12:1-11; 2 Tm. 4:6-8, 17-18; Mt. 16:13-19.)

25—Wed. Weekday.

26—Thurs. Weekday.

27—Fri. Weekday. St. Cyril of Alexandria, bishop-doctor; optional memorial.

28—Sat. St. Irenaeus, bishop-martyr; memorial.

29—**Sun. Sts. Peter and Paul, apostles; solemnity.** (Acts 12:1-11; 2 Tm. 4:6-8, 17-18; Mt. 16:13-19.)

30—Mon. (Thirteenth Week of the Year.) Weekday. First Martyrs of the Roman Church; optional memorial.

GENERAL PRAYER INTENTION: For renewed devotion to the Heart of Jesus in 1975.

MISSION PRAYER INTENTION: For the formation of priests and religious in accordance with the doctrinal norms of the Church.

JULY 1975

1—Tues. Weekday.
2—Wed. Weekday.
3—Thurs. St. Thomas, apostle; feast.
4—Fri. Weekday. St. Elizabeth of Portugal; optional memorial.
5—Sat. Weekday. St. Anthony Mary Zaccaria, priest; optional memorial.
6—**Fourteenth Sunday of the Year.** (Zec. 9:9-10; Rom. 8:9, 11-13; Mt. 11:25-30.) [St. Maria Goretti, virgin-martyr; optional memorial.]
7—Mon. Weekday.
8—Tues. Weekday.
9—Wed. Weekday.
10—Thurs. Weekday.
11—Fri. St. Benedict, abbot; memorial.
12—Sat. Weekday.
13—**Fifteenth Sunday of the Year.** (Is. 55:10-11; Rom. 8:18-23; Mt. 13:1-23.) [St. Henry; optional memorial.]
14—Mon. Weekday. St. Camillus de Lellis, priest; optional memorial.
15—Tues. St. Bonaventure, bishop-doctor; memorial.
16—Wed. Weekday. Our Lady of Mt. Carmel; optional memorial.
17—Thurs. Weekday.
18—Fri. Weekday.
19—Sat. Weekday.
20—**Sixteenth Sunday of the Year.** (Wis. 12:13, 16-19; Rom. 8:26-27; Mt. 13:24-43.)
21—Mon. Weekday. St. Lawrence of Brindisi, priest-doctor; optional memorial.
22—Tues. St. Mary Magdalene; memorial.
23—Wed. Weekday. St. Bridget of Sweden, religious; optional memorial.
24—Thurs. Weekday.
25—Fri. St. James the Greater, apostle; feast.
26—Sat. Sts. Joachim and Ann, parents of Mary; memorial.
27—**Seventeenth Sunday of the Year.** (1 Kgs. 3:5, 7-12; Rom. 8:28-30; Mt. 13:44-52.)
28—Mon. Weekday.
29—Tues. St. Martha; memorial.
30—Wed. Weekday. St. Peter Chrysologus, bishop-doctor; optional memorial.
31—Thurs. St. Ignatius of Loyola, priest; memorial.

GENERAL PRAYER INTENTION: For social renewal through personal renewal. That the spiritual renewal of individuals may become a source of social renewal. This intention reflects a basic theme of Catholic social doctrine — that the condition for reform of social structures, institutions and processes is the reform of members of society according to Gospel-inspired principles of justice and charity.
MISSION PRAYER INTENTION: For social justice for migrants in cities of Asia and Africa. That social problems affecting them may be solved in a proper manner.

AUGUST 1975

1—Fri. St. Alphonsus Liguori, bishop-doctor; memorial.
2—Sat. Weekday. St. Eusebius of Vercelli, bishop; optional memorial.
3—**Eighteenth Sunday of the Year.** (Is. 55:1-3; Rom. 8:35, 37-39; Mt. 14:13-21.)
4—Mon. St. John Mary Vianney, Curé of Ars, priest; memorial.
5—Tues. Weekday. Dedication of St. Mary Major Basilica; optional memorial.
6—Wed. Transfiguration of the Lord; feast.
7—Thurs. Weekday. Sts. Sixtus II, pope, and companions, martyrs, or St. Cajetan, priest; optional memorials.
8—Fri. St. Dominic, priest; memorial.
9—Sat. Weekday.
10—**Nineteenth Sunday of the Year.** (1 Kgs. 19:9a; 11-13a; Rom. 9:1-5; Mt. 14:22-33.) [St. Lawrence, deacon-martyr; feast.]
11—Mon. St. Clare, virgin; memorial.
12—Tues. Weekday.
13—Wed. Weekday. Sts. Pontian, pope, and Hippolytus, priest, martyrs; optional memorial.
14—Thurs. Weekday.
15—**Fri. Assumption of Blessed Mary the Virgin; solemnity. Holy day of obligation.** (Rv. 11:19a and 12:1-6a, 10ab; 1 Cor. 15:20-26; Lk. 1:39-56.)
16—Sat. Weekday. St. Stephen of Hungary; optional memorial.
17—**Twentieth Sunday of the Year.** (Is. 56:1, 6-7; Rom. 11:13-15, 29-32; Mt. 15:21-28.)
18—Mon. Weekday.
19—Tues. Weekday. St. John Eudes, priest; optional memorial.
20—Wed. St. Bernard of Clairvaux, abbot-doctor; memorial.
21—Thurs. St. Pius X, pope; memorial.
22—Fri. Queenship of Blessed Mary the Virgin; memorial.
23—Sat. Weekday. St. Rose of Lima, virgin; optional memorial.
24—**Twenty-First Sunday of the Year.** (Is. 22:19-23; Rom. 11:33-36; Mt. 16:13-20.) [St. Bartholomew, apostle; feast.]
25—Mon. Weekday. St. Louis, or St. Joseph Calasanz, priest; optional memorials.
26—Tues. Weekday.
27—Wed. St. Monica; memorial.
28—Thurs. St. Augustine, bishop-doctor; memorial.
29—Fri. Beheading of St. John the Baptist; memorial.
30—Sat. Weekday.
31—**Twenty-Second Sunday of the Year.** (Jer. 20:7-9; Rom. 12:1-2; Mt. 16:21-27.)

GENERAL PRAYER INTENTION: For a greater receptivity to the Holy Spirit.
MISSION PRAYER INTENTION: For the success of the work of the Pontifical Mission Union in arousing missionary spirit and vocations.

SEPTEMBER 1975

1—Mon. Weekday.
2—Tues. Weekday.
3—Wed. St. Gregory the Great, pope-doctor; memorial.
4—Thurs. Weekday.
5—Fri. Weekday.
6—Sat. Weekday.
7—**Twenty-Third Sunday of the Year.** (Ez. 33:7-9; Rom. 13:8-10; Mt. 18:15-20.)
8—Mon. Birth of Blessed Mary the Virgin; feast.
9—Tues. St. Peter Claver, priest; memorial (in U.S.).
10—Wed. Weekday.
11—Thurs. Weekday.
12—Fri. Weekday.
13—Sat. St. John Chrysostom, bishop-doctor; memorial.
14—**Sun. Triumph of the Cross; feast.** (Nm. 21:4-9; Phil. 2:6-11; Jn. 3:13-17.)
15—Mon. (Twenty-Fourth Week of the Year.) Our Lady of Sorrows; memorial.
16—Tues. Sts. Cornelius, pope, and Cyprian, bishop, martyrs; memorial.
17—Wed. Weekday. St. Robert Bellarmine, bishop-doctor; optional memorial.
18—Thurs. Weekday.
19—Fri. Weekday. St. Januarius, bishop-martyr; optional memorial.
20—Sat. Weekday.
21—**Twenty-Fifth Sunday of the Year.** (Is. 55:6-9; Phil. 1:20c-24, 27a; Mt. 20:1-16a.) [St. Matthew, apostle; feast.]
22—Mon. Weekday.
23—Tues. Weekday.
24—Wed. Weekday.
25—Thurs. Weekday.
26—Fri. Weekday. Sts. Cosmas and Damian, martyrs; optional memorial.
27—Sat. St. Vincent de Paul, priest; memorial.
28—**Twenty-Sixth Sunday of the Year.** (Ez. 18:25-28; Phil. 2:1-11; Mt. 21:28-32.) [St. Wenceslaus, martyr; optional memorial.]
29—Mon. Sts. Michael, Gabriel and Raphael, archangels; feast.
30—Tues. St. Jerome, priest-doctor; memorial.

GENERAL PRAYER INTENTION: For more rapid implementation of the decrees of the Second Vatican Council. That the religious movement of the Holy Year may efficaciously serve this purpose. The renewal-reconciliation theme of the Holy Year matches the thrust of all the enactments of Vatican II in the direction of individual and institutional reform in the Church.

MISSION PRAYER INTENTION: For updating by priests, religious and lay persons of their missionary techniques. That they may adapt themselves — theologically and with new methods and approaches — to the conditions of pastoral ministry in contemporary society.

OCTOBER 1975

1—Wed. St. Therese of the Child Jesus, virgin; memorial.
2—Thurs. Guardian Angels; memorial.
3—Fri. Weekday.
4—Sat. St. Francis of Assisi; memorial.
5—**Twenty-Seventh Sunday of the Year.** (Is. 5:1-7; Phil. 4:6-9; Mt. 21:33-43.)
6—Mon. Weekday. St. Bruno, priest; optional memorial.
7—Tues. Our Lady of the Rosary; memorial.
8—Wed. Weekday.
9—Thurs. Weekday. Sts. Denis, bishop, and companions, martyrs, or St. John Leonard, priest; optional memorials.
10—Fri. Weekday.
11—Sat. Weekday.
12—**Twenty-Eighth Sunday of the Year.** (Is. 25:6-10a; Phil. 4:12-14, 19-20; Mt. 22:1-14.)
13—Mon. Weekday.
14—Tues. Weekday. St. Callistus I, pope-martyr; optional memorial.
15—Wed. St. Teresa of Avila, virgin-doctor; memorial.
16—Thurs. Weekday. St. Hedwig, religious, or St. Margaret Mary Alacoque, virgin; optional memorials.
17—Fri. St. Ignatius of Antioch, bishop-martyr; memorial.
18—Sat. St. Luke, evangelist; feast.
19—**Twenty-Ninth Sunday of the Year.** (Is. 45:1, 4-6; 1 Thes. 1:1-5b; Mt. 22:15-21.) [Sts. Isaac Jogues, John de Brebeuf, priests, and companions, martyrs, memorial (in U.S.); or St. Paul of the Cross, optional memorial.]
20—Mon. Weekday.
21—Tues. Weekday.
22—Wed. Weekday.
23—Thurs. Weekday. St. John of Capistrano, priest; optional memorial.
24—Fri. Weekday. St. Anthony Mary Claret, bishop; optional memorial.
25—Sat. Weekday.
26—**Thirtieth Sunday of the Year.** (Ex. 22:20-26; 1 Thes. 1:5c-10; Mt. 22:34-40.)
27—Mon. Weekday.
28—Tues. Sts. Simon and Jude, apostles; feast.
29—Wed. Weekday.
30—Thurs. Weekday.
31—Fri. Weekday.

GENERAL PRAYER INTENTION: For a deeper realization of the power of prayer. That the Holy Year may shed light upon the power and effectiveness of prayer.

MISSION PRAYER INTENTION: For family prayer as a safeguard for the Christian faith. That common family prayer may foster and safeguard the Christian faith in youthful churches. Such prayer is a powerful inspiration and support for families as well as the churches.

NOVEMBER 1975

1—**Sat. All Saints; solemnity. Holy day of obligation.** (Rv. 7:2-4, 9-14; 1 Jn. 3:1-3; Mt. 5:1-12a.)

2—**Sun. Commemoration of All the Faithful Departed** (All Souls' Day). Three Masses proper.

3—Mon. (Thirty-First Week of the Year.) St. Martin de Porres, religious; optional memorial.

4—Tues. St. Charles Borromeo, bishop; optional memorial.

5—Wed. Weekday.

6—Thurs. Weekday.

7—Fri. Weekday.

8—Sat. Weekday.

9—**Sun. Dedication of St. John Lateran Basilica;** feast.

10—Mon. (Thirty-Second Week of the Year.) St. Leo the Great, pope-doctor; memorial.

11—Tues. St. Martin of Tours, bishop; memorial.

12—Wed. St. Josaphat, bishop-martyr; memorial.

13—Thurs. St. Frances X. Cabrini, virgin; memorial (in U.S.).

14—Fri. Weekday.

15—Sat. Weekday. St. Albert the Great, bishop-doctor; optional memorial.

16—**Thirty-Third Sunday of the Year.** (Prv. 31:10-13, 19-20, 30-31; 1 Thes. 5:1-6; Mt. 25:14-30.) [St. Margaret of Scotland, or St. Gertrude, virgin; optional memorials.]

17—Mon. St. Elizabeth of Hungary, religious; memorial.

18—Tues. Weekday. Dedication of Basilicas of Sts. Peter and Paul; optional memorial.

19—Wed. Weekday.

20—Thurs. Weekday.

21—Fri. Presentation of Blessed Mary the Virgin; memorial.

22—Sat. St. Cecilia, virgin-martyr; memorial.

23—**Sun. Christ the King; solemnity.** (Ez. 34:11-12, 15-17; 1 Cor. 15:20-26, 28; Mt. 25:31-46.) [St. Clement I, pope-martyr, or St. Columban, abbot; optional memorials.]

24—Mon. (Thirty-Fourth and Last Week of the Year.) Weekday.

25—Tues. Weekday.

26—Wed. Weekday.

27—Thurs. Thanksgiving Day Votive Mass (in U.S.). Weekday.

28—Fri. Weekday.

29—Sat. Weekday.

30—**First Sunday of Advent.** (Is. 63:16b-17, 19b and 64:2b-7; 1 Cor. 1:3-9; Mk. 13:33-37.) [St. Andrew, apostle; feast.]

PRAYER INTENTIONS: For response to God's love through service, religious and lay vocations.

DECEMBER 1975

1—Mon. Weekday.

2—Tues. Weekday.

3—Wed. St. Francis Xavier, priest; memorial.

4—Thurs. Weekday. St. John Damascene, priest-doctor; optional memorial.

5—Fri. Weekday.

6—Sat. Weekday. St. Nicholas, bishop; optional memorial.

7—**Second Sunday of Advent.** (Is. 40:1-5, 9-11; 2 Pt. 3:8-14; Mk. 1:1-18.) [St. Ambrose, bishop-doctor; memorial.]

8—**Mon. Immaculate Conception of Blessed Mary the Virgin; solemnity. Holy day of obligation.** (Gn. 3:9-15, 20; Eph. 1:3-6, 11-12; Lk. 1:26-38.)

9—Tues. Weekday.

10—Wed. Weekday.

11—Thurs. Weekday. St. Damasus I, pope; optional memorial.

12—Fri. Our Lady of Guadalupe; memorial (in U.S.). Weekday. St. Jane Frances de Chantal, religious; optional memorial.

13—Sat. St. Lucy, virgin-martyr; memorial.

14—**Third Sunday of Advent.** (Is. 61:1-2a, 10-11; 1 Thes. 5:16-24; Jn. 1:6-8, 19-28.) [St. John of the Cross, priest-doctor; memorial.]

15—Mon. Weekday of Advent.

16—Tues. Weekday of Advent.

17—Wed. Weekday of Advent.

18—Thurs. Weekday of Advent.

19—Fri. Weekday of Advent.

20—Sat. Weekday of Advent.

21—**Fourth Sunday of Advent.** (2 Sm. 7:1-5, 8b-11, 16; Rom. 16:25-27; Lk. 1:26-38.) [St. Peter Canisius, priest-doctor; optional memorial.]

22—Mon. Weekday of Advent.

23—Tues. Weekday of Advent. [St. John of Kanty, priest; optional memorial.]

24—Wed. Weekday of Advent.

25—**Thurs. Christmas. Birth of the Lord; solemnity.** (Midnight — Is. 9:1-6; Ti. 2:11-14; Lk. 2:1-14. Dawn — Is. 62:11-12; Ti. 3:4-7; Lk. 2:15-20. During the day — Is. 52:7-10; Heb. 1:1-6; Jn. 1:1-18.)

26—Fri. St. Stephen, first martyr; feast.

27—Sat. St. John, apostle-evangelist; feast.

28—**Sun. Holy Family; feast.** (Sir. 3:2-6, 12-14; Col. 3:12-21; Lk. 2:22-40.) [Holy Innocents, martyrs; feast.]

29—Mon. Fifth Day of Christmas Octave. St. Thomas Becket, bishop-martyr; optional memorial.

30—Tues. Sixth Day of Christmas Octave.

31—Wed. Seventh Day of Christmas Octave. St. Sylvester I, pope; optional memorial.

PRAYER INTENTIONS: For peace in hearts and society, and for the pastoral care of students and workers from mission lands.

TABLE OF MOVABLE FEASTS

Year	Ash Wednesday	Easter	Ascension	Pentecost	Weeks of Season-through-Year				First Sunday of Advent
					Before Lent		After Pent.		
					Week	Ends	Week	Begins	
1975	Feb. 12	Mar. 30	May 8	May 18	5	Feb. 11	7	May 19	Nov. 30
1976	Mar. 3	Apr. 18	May 27	June 6	8	Mar. 2	10	June 7	Nov. 28
1977	Feb. 23	Apr. 10	May 19	May 29	7	Feb. 22	9	May 30	Nov. 27
1978	Feb. 8	Mar. 26	May 4	May 14	5	Feb. 7	6	May 15	Dec. 3
1979	Feb. 28	Apr. 15	May 24	June 3	8	Feb. 27	9	June 4	Dec. 2
1980	Feb. 20	Apr. 6	May 15	May 25	6	Feb. 19	8	May 26	Nov. 30
1981	Mar. 4	Apr. 19	May 28	June 7	8	Mar. 3	10	June 8	Nov. 29
1982	Feb. 24	Apr. 11	May 20	May 30	7	Feb. 23	9	May 31	Nov. 28
1983	Feb. 16	Apr. 3	May 12	May 22	6	Feb. 15	8	May 23	Nov. 27
1984	Mar. 7	Apr. 22	May 31	June 10	9	Mar. 6	10	June 11	Dec. 2
1985	Feb. 20	Apr. 7	May 16	May 26	6	Feb. 19	8	May 27	Dec. 1
1986	Feb. 12	Mar. 30	May 8	May 18	5	Feb. 11	7	May 19	Nov. 30
1987	Mar. 4	Apr. 19	May 28	June 7	9	Mar. 3	10	June 8	Nov. 29
1988	Feb. 17	Apr. 3	May 12	May 22	6	Feb. 16	8	May 23	Nov. 27
1989	Feb. 8	Mar. 26	May 4	May 14	5	Feb. 7	6	May 15	Dec. 3
1990	Feb. 28	Apr. 15	May 24	June 3	8	Feb. 27	9	June 4	Dec. 2
1991	Feb. 13	Mar. 31	May 9	May 19	5	Feb. 12	7	May 20	Dec. 1
1992	Mar. 4	Apr. 19	May 28	June 7	9	Mar. 3	10	June 8	Nov. 29
1993	Feb. 24	Apr. 11	May 20	May 30	7	Feb. 23	9	May 31	Nov. 28
1994	Feb. 16	Apr. 3	May 12	May 22	6	Feb. 15	8	May 23	Nov. 27
1995	Mar. 1	Apr. 16	May 25	June 4	8	Feb. 28	9	June 5	Dec. 3
1996	Feb. 21	Apr. 7	May 16	May 26	7	Feb. 20	8	May 27	Dec. 1
1997	Feb. 12	Mar. 30	May 8	May 18	5	Feb. 11	7	May 19	Nov. 30
1998	Feb. 25	Apr. 12	May 21	May 31	7	Feb. 24	9	June 1	Nov. 29
1999	Feb. 17	Apr. 4	May 13	May 23	6	Feb. 16	8	May 24	Nov. 28
2000	Mar. 8	Apr. 23	June 1	June 11	9	Mar. 7	10	June 12	Dec. 3
2001	Feb. 28	Apr. 15	May 24	June 3	7	Feb. 27	9	June 4	Dec. 2
2002	Feb. 13	Mar. 31	May 9	May 19	5	Feb. 12	7	May 20	Dec. 1
2003	Mar. 5	Apr. 20	May 29	June 8	8	Mar. 4	10	June 9	Nov. 30
2004	Feb. 25	Apr. 11	May 20	May 30	7	Feb. 24	9	May 31	Nov. 28

Season through Year

Weeks between the end of Christmastide and the beginning of Lent, and from the day after Pentecost to the last Sunday of the liturgical year, belong to the Season-through-the-Year. The table indicates the number and terminal date of the week ending the first part, and the number and starting date of the week beginning the second part, of this season. In some years, a week of this season is eliminated because of calendar conditions.

Date of Easter

The Second Vatican Council's *Constitution on the Sacred Liturgy* said there would be no objection "if the feast of Easter were assigned to a particular Sunday of the Gregorian calendar, provided that those whom it may concern, especially the brethren who are not in communion with the Apostolic See, give their assent." Agreement has not yet been reached, although the late Ecumenical Patriarch Athenagoras I proposed that Easter be celebrated each year on the second Sunday of April. Calendar expert Father Pierre Jounel made this comment on the subject: "There is no change in the new liturgical calendar concerning fixing the date of Easter. . . . It seems there is no way of arriving at a universal agreement on this point for many years, especially until the general council of the Orthodox Church puts the problem on its agenda."

HOLY DAYS AND OTHER FEASTS

The following list includes the six holy days of obligation observed in the United States and additional observances of devotional and historical significance. The dignity or rank of observances is indicated by the terms: **solemnity** (highest in rank, the equivalent of former first class feasts): **feast** (equivalent to former second class feasts); **memorial** (equivalent to former third class feasts, for universal observance); **optional memorial** (for celebration by choice).

All Saints, Nov. 1, holy day of obligation, solemnity. Commemorates all the blessed in heaven, and is intended particularly to honor the blessed who have no special feasts. The background of the feast dates to the fourth century when groups of martyrs, and later other saints, were honored on a common day in various places. In 609 or 610, the Pantheon, a pagan temple at Rome, was consecrated as a Christian church for the honor of Our Lady and the martyrs (later all saints). In 835, Gregory IV fixed Nov. 1 as the date of observance.

All Souls, Commemoration of the Faithful Departed, Nov. 2 (transferable to Nov. 3). The dead were prayed for from the earliest days of Christianity. By the sixth century it was customary in Benedictine monasteries to hold a commemoration of deceased members of the order at Pentecost. A common commemoration of all the faithful departed on the day after All Saints was instituted in 998 by St. Odilo, of the Abbey of Cluny, and an observance of this kind was generally adopted throughout the Church. In 1915, Benedict XV granted priests throughout the world permission to celebrate three Masses for this commemoration. He also granted a special indulgence for the occasion.

Annunciation of the Lord (formerly, Annunciation of the Blessed Virgin Mary), Mar. 25, solemnity. A feast of the Incarnation which commemorates the announcement by the Archangel Gabriel to the Virgin Mary that she was to become the Mother of Christ (Lk. 1:26-38), and the miraculous conception of Christ by her. The feast was instituted about 430 in the East. The Roman observance dates from the seventh century, when celebration was said to be universal.

Ascension of the Lord, movable observance held 40 days after Easter, holy day of obligation, solemnity. Commemorates the Ascension of Christ into heaven 40 days after his Resurrection from the dead (Mk. 16:19; Lk. 24:51; Acts 1:2). The feast recalls the completion of Christ's mission on earth for the salvation of men and his entry into heaven with glorified human nature. The Ascension is a pledge of the final perfection of all who achieve salvation. Documentary evidence of the feast dates from early in the fifth century, but it was observed long before that time in connection with Pentecost and Easter.

Ash Wednesday, movable observance, six and one-half weeks before Easter. It was set as the first day of Lent by St. Gregory the Great (590-604) with the extension of an earlier and shorter penitential season to a total period including 40 weekdays of fasting before Easter. Ashes, symbolic of penance, are blessed and distributed among the faithful during the day. They are used to mark the forehead with the Sign of the Cross, with the reminder: "Remember, man, that you are dust, and unto dust you shall return," or: "Repent, and believe the Good News."

Assumption Aug. 15, holy day of obligation, solemnity. Commemorates the taking into heaven of Mary, soul and body, at the end of her life on earth, a truth of faith that was proclaimed a dogma by Pius XII on Nov. 1, 1950. One of the oldest and most solemn feasts of Mary, it has a history dating back to at least the seventh century when its celebration was already established at Jerusalem and Rome.

Baptism of the Lord, movable, celebrated on the Sunday after Epiphany, feast. Recalls the baptism of Christ by John the Baptist (Mk. 1:9-11), an event associated with the liturgy of the Epiphany. This baptism was the occasion for Christ's manifestation of Himself at the beginning of his public life.

Birth of Mary, Sept. 8, feast. This is a very old feast which originated in the East and found place in the Roman liturgy in the seventh century.

Candlemas Day, Feb. 2. See Presentation of the Lord.

Chair of Peter, Feb. 22, feast. Commemorates establishment of the see of Antioch by Peter. The feast, which has been in the Roman calendar since 336, is a liturgical expression of belief in the episcopacy and hierarchy of the Church.

Christmas, Birth of Our Lord Jesus Christ, Dec. 25, holy day of obligation, solemnity. Commemorates the birth of Christ (Lk. 2:1-20). This event was originally commemorated in the East on the feast of Epiphany or Theophany. The Christmas feast itself originated in the West; by 354 it was certainly kept on Dec. 25. This date may have been set for the observance to offset pagan ceremonies held at about the same time to commemorate the birth of the sun at the winter solstice. Priests may celebrate three Masses on Christmas Day. Christmastide begins with this feast and continues until the Sunday after Epiphany.

Christ the King, movable, celebrated on the last Sunday of the liturgical year, solemnity. Commemorates the royal prerogatives of Christ and is equivalent to a declaration of his rights to the homage, service and fidelity of men in all phases of individual and social life. Pius XI instituted the feast Dec. 11, 1925.

Corpus Christi, movable observance held in the US on the Sunday following Trinity Sunday, solemnity. Commemorates the institution of the Holy Eucharist (Mt. 26:26-28). The feast originated at Liege in 1246 and was extended throughout the Church in the West by Urban IV in 1264. St. Thomas Aquinas composed the Office for the feast.

Dedication of St. John Lateran, Nov. 9, feast. Commemorates the first public consecration of a church, that of the Basilica of the Most Holy Savior by Pope St. Sylvester Nov. 9, 324. The church, as well as the Lateran Palace, was the gift of Emperor Constantine. Since the 12th century it has been known as St. John Lateran, in honor of John the Baptist after whom the adjoining baptistery was named. It was rebuilt by Innocent X (1644-55), reconsecrated by Benedict XIII in 1726, and enlarged by Leo XIII (1878-1903). This basilica is regarded as the church of highest dignity in Rome and throughout the Roman Rite.

Dedication of St. Mary Major, Aug. 5, optional memorial. Commemorates the rebuilding and dedication by Sixtus III (432-40) of a church in honor of Blessed Mary the Virgin. This is the Basilica of St. Mary Major on the Esquiline Hill in Rome. An earlier building was erected during the pontificate of Liberius (352-66); according to legend, it was located on a site covered by a miraculous fall of snow seen by a nobleman favored with a vision of Mary.

Easter, movable celebration held on the first Sunday after the full moon following the vernal equinox (between Mar. 22 and Apr. 25), solemnity with an octave. Commemorates the Resurrection of Christ from the dead (Mk. 16:1-7). The observance of this mystery, kept since the first days of the Church, extends throughout the Easter season which lasts until the feast of Pentecost, a period of 50 days. Every Sunday in the year is regarded as a "little" Easter. The date of Easter determines the dates of movable feasts, such as Ascension and Pentecost, and the number of Sundays after Epiphany and Pentecost.

Easter Vigil (Holy Saturday), day before Easter. Ceremonies are all related to the Resurrection and renewal-in-grace theme of Easter: blessing of the new fire and Paschal Candle, reading of prophecies, blessing of water and the baptismal font, the baptism of converts and renewal of baptismal vows by the faithful, the Litany of the Saints, and the celebration of Mass. The vigil ceremonies are held after sundown, preferably at a time that makes possible the celebration of Mass at midnight.

Epiphany of Our Lord, Jan. 6 or (in the US) a Sunday between Jan. 2 and 8, solemnity. Commemorates the manifestations of the divinity of Christ. It is one of the oldest Christian feasts, with an Eastern origin traceable to the beginning of the third century and antedating the Western feast of Christmas. Originally, it commemorated the manifestations of Christ's divinity — or Theophany — in his birth, the homage of the Magi, and baptism by John the Baptist. Later, the first two of these commemorations were transferred to Christmas when the Eastern Church adopted that feast between 380 and 430. The central feature of the Eastern observance now is the manifestation or declaration of Christ's divinity in his baptism and at the beginning of his public life. The Epiphany was adopted by the Western Church during the same period in which the Eastern Church accepted Christmas. In the Roman Rite, commemoration is made in the Mass of the homage of the wise men from the East (Mt. 2:1-12).

Good Friday, the Friday before Easter, privileged feria of Holy Week. Liturgical elements of the observance are commemoration of the Passion and Death of Christ in the reading of the Passion (according to John), special prayers for the Church and people of all ranks, the veneration of the Cross, and a Communion service. The Solemn Liturgical Action takes place between noon and 9 p.m. This is the only day in the year on which the Eucharistic Liturgy is not celebrated in the Roman Rite.

Guardian Angels, Oct. 2, memorial. Commemorates the angels who protect men from spiritual and physical dangers and assist them in doing good. A feast in their honor celebrated in Spain in the 16th century was extended to the whole Church by Paul V in 1608. In 1670, Clement X set Oct. 2 as the date of observance. Earlier, guardian angels were honored liturgically in conjunction with the feast of St. Michael.

Holy Family, movable observance on the Sunday after Christmas, feast. Commemorates the Holy Family of Jesus, Mary and Joseph as the model of domestic society, holiness and virtue. The devotional background of the feast was very strong in the 17th century. In the 18th century, in prayers composed for a special Mass, a Canadian bishop likened the Christian family to the Holy Family. Leo XIII consecrated families to the Holy Family. In 1921, Benedict XV extended the Divine Office and Mass of the feast to the whole Church.

Holy Innocents, Dec. 28, feast. Commemorates the infants who suffered death at the hands of Herod's soldiers seeking to kill the child Jesus (Mt. 2:13-18). A feast in their honor has been observed since the fifth century.

Holy Thursday, the Thursday before Easter, privileged feria of Holy Week. Commemorates the institution of the Holy Eucharist (which is later celebrated on the special feast of Corpus Christi) and other events of the Last Supper. Ceremonies include the celebration of a principal Mass between 4 and

9 p.m., the washing of feet in imitation of the act of Christ who washed the feet of the Apostles at the Last Supper, the stripping of the altar at the conclusion of Mass. There is also a procession of the Blessed Sacrament to a special place of reposition where It is reserved for veneration by the faithful until the Solemn Liturgical Action on Good Friday. At a special Mass of Chrism, bishops bless oils (of catechumens, chrism, of the sick) for use during the year.

Immaculate Conception, Dec. 8, holy day of obligation, solemnity. Commemorates the fact that Mary, in view of her calling to be the Mother of Christ and in virtue of his merits, was preserved from the first moment of her conception from original sin and was filled with grace from the very beginning of her life. She was the only person so preserved from original sin. The present form of the feast dates from Dec. 8, 1854, when Pius IX defined the dogma of the Immaculate Conception. An earlier feast of the Conception, which testified to long-existing belief in this truth, was observed in the East by the eighth century, in Ireland in the ninth, and subsequently in European countries. In 1846, Mary was proclaimed patroness of the US under this title.

Immaculate Heart of Mary, Saturday following the second Sunday after Pentecost, optional memorial. On May 4, 1944, Pius XII ordered this feast observed throughout the Church in order to obtain Mary's intercession for "peace among nations, freedom for the Church, the conversion of sinners, the love of purity and the practice of virtue." Two years earlier, he consecrated the entire human race to Mary under this title. Devotion to Mary under the title of her Most Pure Heart originated during the Middle Ages. It was given great impetus in the 17th century by the preaching of St. John Eudes, who was the first to celebrate a Mass and Divine Office of Mary under this title. A feast, celebrated in various places and on different dates, was authorized in 1799.

Joachim and Ann, July 26, memorial. Commemorates the parents of Mary. A joint feast, celebrated Sept. 9, originated in the East near the end of the sixth century. Devotion to Ann, introduced in the eighth century at Rome, became widespread in Europe in the 14th century; her feast was extended throughout the Latin Church in 1584. A feast of Joachim was introduced in the West in the 15th century.

John the Baptist, Birth, June 24, solemnity. The precursor of Christ, whose cousin he was, was commemorated universally in the liturgy by the fourth century. He is the only saint, except the Blessed Virgin Mary, whose birthday is observed as a feast. Another feast, on Aug. 29, commemorates his passion and death at the order of Herod (Mk. 6:14-29).

Joseph, Mar. 19, solemnity. Joseph is honored as the husband of the Blessed Virgin Mary, the patron and protector of the universal Church and workman. Devotion to him already existed in the eighth century in the East, and in the 11th in the West. Various feasts were celebrated before the 15th century when Mar. 19 was fixed for his commemoration; this feast was extended to the whole Church in 1621 by Gregory XV. In 1955, Pius XII instituted the feast of St. Joseph the Workman for observance May 1; this feast, which may be celebrated by local option, supplanted the Solemnity or Patronage of St. Joseph formerly observed on the third Wednesday after Easter. St. Joseph was proclaimed protector and patron of the universal Church in 1870 by Pius IX.

Michael, Gabriel and Raphael, Archangels, Sept. 29, feast. A feast bearing the title of Dedication of St. Michael the Archangel formerly commemorated on this date the consecration in 530 of a church near Rome in honor of Michael, the first angel given a liturgical feast. For a while, this feast was combined with a commemoration of the Guardian Angels. The separate feasts of Gabriel (Mar. 24) and Raphael (Oct. 24) were suppressed by the calendar reform of 1969 and this joint feast of the three archangels was instituted.

Octave of Christmas, Jan. 1. See Solemnity of Mary, Mother of God.

Our Lady of Sorrows, Sept. 15, memorial. Recalls the sorrows experienced by Mary in her association with Christ: the prophecy of Simeon (Lk. 2:34-35), the flight into Egypt (Mt. 2:13-21), the three-day separation from Jesus (Lk. 2:41-50), and four incidents connected with the Passion: her meeting with Christ on the way to Calvary, the crucifixion, the removal of Christ's body from the cross, and his burial (Mt. 27:31-61; Mk. 15:20-47; Lk. 23:26-56; Jn. 19:17-42). A Mass and Divine Office of the feast were celebrated by the Servites, especially, in the 17th century, and in 1817 Pius VII extended the observance to the whole Church.

Our Lady of the Rosary, Oct. 7, memorial. Commemorates the Virgin Mary through recall of the mysteries of the Rosary which recapitulate events in her life and the life of Christ. The feast was instituted to commemorate a Christian victory over invading Mohammedan forces at Lepanto on Oct. 7, 1571, and was extended throughout the Church by Clement XI in 1716.

Passion (Palm) Sunday, the Sunday before Easter. Recalls the triumphal entry of Christ into Jerusalem at the beginning of the last week of his life (Mt. 21:1-9). A procession and other ceremonies commemorating this event were held in Jerusalem from very early Christian times and were adopted in Rome by the ninth century, when the blessing of palm for the occasion was introduced. Full liturgical observance includes the blessing of palm and a procession before the principal Mass of the day. The Passion, by Matthew, Mark or Luke, is read during the Mass.

Pentecost, also called **Whitsunday,** movable celebration held 50 days after Easter, solemnity. Commemorates the descent of the Holy Spirit upon the Apostles, the preaching of Peter and the other Apostles to Jews in Jerusalem, the baptism and aggregation of some 3,000 persons to the Christian community (Acts 2:1-41). It is regarded as the birthday of the Catholic Church. The original observance of the feast antedated the earliest documentary evidence from the third century.

Peter and Paul, June 29, solemnity. Commemorates the dual martyrdom of Peter by crucifixion and Paul by beheading during the Neronian persecution. This joint commemoration of the two greatest Apostles dates at least from 258 at Rome.

Presentation of the Lord (formerly called Purification of the Blessed Virgin Mary, also Candlemas), Feb. 2, feast. Commemorates the presentation of Jesus in the Temple — according to prescriptions of Mosaic Law (Lv. 12:2-8; Ex. 13:2; Lk. 2:22-32) — and the purification of Mary 40 days after his birth. In the East, where the feast antedated fourth century testimony regarding its existence, it was observed primarily as a feast of Our Lord; in the West, where it was adopted later, it was regarded more as a feast of Mary until the calendar reform of 1969. Its date was set for Feb. 2 after the celebration of Christmas was fixed for Dec. 25, late in the fourth century. The blessing of candles, probably in commemoration of Christ who was the Light to enlighten the Gentiles, became common about the 11th century and gave the feast the secondary name of Candlemas.

Queenship of Mary, Aug. 22, memorial. Commemorates the high dignity of Mary as Queen of heaven, angels and men. Universal observance of the memorial was ordered by Pius XII in the encyclical *Ad Caeli Reginam* Oct. 11, 1954, near the close of a Marian Year observed in connection with the centenary of the proclamation of the dogma of the Immaculate Conception and four years after the proclamation of the dogma of the Assumption. The original date of the memorial was May 31.

Resurrection. See Easter.

Sacred Heart of Jesus, movable observance held on the Friday after Corpus Christi, solemnity. The object of the devotion is the divine Person of Christ, whose heart is the symbol of his love for men — for whom he accomplished the work of Redemption. The Mass and Office now used on the feast were prescribed by Pius XI in 1929. Devotion to the Sacred Heart was introduced into the liturgy in the 17th century through the efforts of St. John Eudes who composed an Office and Mass for the feast. It was furthered as the result of the revelations of St. Margaret Mary

Alacoque after 1675 and by the work of Claude de la Colombiere, S.J. In 1765, Clement XIII approved a Mass and Office for the feast, and in 1856 Pius IX extended the observance throughout the Roman Rite.

Solemnity of Mary, Mother of God, Jan. 1, holy day of obligation, solemnity. The calendar reform of 1969, in accord with Eastern tradition, reinstated the Marian character of this commemoration on the octave day of Christmas. The former feast of the Circumcision, dating at least from the first half of the sixth century, marked the initiation of Jesus (Lk. 02:21) in Judaism and by analogy focused attention on the initiation of persons in the Christian religion and their incorporation in Christ through baptism. The feast of the Solemnity supplants the former feast of Maternity of Mary observed on Oct. 11.

Transfiguration of the Lord, Aug. 6, feast. Commemorates the revelation of his divinity by Christ to Peter, James and John on Mt. Tabor (Mt. 17:1-9). The feast, which is very old, was extended throughout the universal Church in 1457 by Callistus III.

Trinity, Most Holy, movable observance held on the Sunday after Pentecost, solemnity. Commemorates the most sublime mystery of the Christian faith, i.e., that there are Three Divine Persons — Father, Son and Holy Spirit — in one God (Mt. 28:18-20). A votive Mass of the Most Holy Trinity dates from the seventh century; an Office was composed in the 10th century; in 1334, John XXII extended the feast to the universal Church.

Triumph of the Cross, Sept. 14, feast. Commemorates the finding of the cross on which Christ was crucified, in 326 through the efforts of St. Helena, mother of Constantine; the consecration of the Basilica of the Holy Sepulchre nearly 10 years later: and the recovery in 628 or 629 by Emperor Heraclius of a major portion of the cross which had been removed by the Persians from its place of veneration at Jerusalem. The feast originated in Jerusalem and spread through the East before being adopted in the West. General adoption followed the building at Rome of the Basilica of the Holy Cross "in Jerusalem," so called because it was the place of enshrinement of a major portion of the cross of crucifixion.

Visitation, May 31, feast. Commemorates Mary's visit to her cousin Elizabeth after the Annunciation and before the birth of John the Baptist, the precursor of Christ (Lk. 1:39-47). The feast had a medieval origin and was observed in the Franciscan Order before being extended throughout the Church by Urban VI in 1389. It is one of the feasts of the Incarnation and is notable for its recall of the Magnificat, one of the few New Testament canticles, which acknowledges the unique gifts of God to Mary because of her role in the redemptive work of Christ. The canticle is recited at Vespers in the Liturgy of the Hours.

SAINTS

Biographical sketches of additional saints are under other Almanac titles. See Index.

An asterisk with a feast date indicates that a memorial or feast is observed according to the revised Roman-Rite calendar.

Adjutor, St. (d. 1131): Norman knight; fought in First Crusade; monk-recluse after his return; legendary accounts of incidents on journey to Crusade probably account for his patronage of yachtsmen; Apr. 30.

Agatha, St. (d. c. 250): Sicilian virgin-martyr; her intercession credited in Sicily with stopping eruptions of Mt. Etna; patron of nurses; Feb. 5*.

Agnes, St. (d. c. 304): Roman virgin-martyr; martyred at age of 10 or 12; patron of young girls; Jan. 21*.

Aloysius Gonzaga, St. (1568-1591): Italian Jesuit; died while nursing plague-stricken; canonized 1726; patron of youth; June 21*.

Amand, St. (d. c. 676): Apostle of Belgium; b. France; established monasteries throughout Belgium; Feb. 6.

Andre Grasset de Saint Sauveur, Bl. (1758-1792): Canadian priest; martyred in France, Sept. 2, 1792, during the Revolution; one of a group called the Martyrs of Paris who were beatified in 1926.

Andrew Corsini, St. (1302-1373): Italian Carmelite; bishop of Fiesoli; mediator between quarrelsome Italian states; canonized 1629; Feb. 4.

Andrew Fournet, St. (1752-1834): French priest; co-founder with St. Jeanne Elizabeth des Anges of the Congregation of Daughters of the Cross; canonized 1933; May 13.

Angela Merici, St. (1474-1540): Italian nun; foundress of Institute of St. Ursula, 1535, the first teaching order of nuns in the Church; canonized 1807; Jan. 27*.

Anne Mary Javouhey, Bl. (1779-1851): French virgin; foundress of Institute of St. Joseph of Cluny, 1812; beatified 1950; July 15.

Ansgar, St. (801-865): Bishop, Benedictine monk; b. near Amiens; missionary in Denmark, Sweden, Norway and Northern Germany; apostle of Denmark; Feb. 3*.

Anthony Abbot, St. (c. 251-c. 354): Egyptian hermit; patriarch of all monks; established communities for hermits which became models for monastic life, especially in the East; friend and supporter of St. Athanasius in the latter's struggle with the Arians; Jan. 17*.

Anthony Mary Claret, St. (1807-1870): Spanish priest; founder of Missionary Sons of the Immaculate Heart of Mary (Claretians), 1849; archbishop of Santiago, Cuba, 1851-57; canonized 1950; Oct. 24*.

Anthony Mary Zaccaria, St. (1502-1539): Italian priest; founder of Barnabites (Clerks Regular of St. Paul), 1530; canonized 1897; July 5*.

Apollonia, St. (d. 249): Deaconess of Alexandria; martyred during persecution of Decius; her patronage of dentists probably rests on tradition that her teeth were broken by pincers by her persecutors; Feb. 9.

Augustine of Canterbury, St. (d. 604 or 605): Italian missionary; apostle of the English; sent by Pope Gregory I with 40 monks to evangelize England; arrived there 597; first archbishop of Canterbury; May 27*.

Benedict of Nursia, St. (c. 480-547): Abbot; founder of monasticism in Western Europe; established monastery at Monte Cassino; proclaimed patron of Europe by Paul VI in 1964; July 11*.

Benedict the Black (il Moro), St. (1526-1589): Sicilian Franciscan; born a slave; joined Franciscans as lay brother; appointed guardian and novice master; canonized 1807; Apr. 4.

Bernadette Soubirous, St. (1844-1879): French peasant girl favored with series of visions of Blessed Virgin Mary at Lourdes (see Lourdes Apparitions); joined Institute of Sisters of Notre Dame at Nevers, 1866; canonized 1933; Apr. 16.

Bernard of Menthon, St. (d. 1081): Italian priest; founded Alpine hospices near the two passes named for him; patron of mountaineers; May 28.

Bernardine of Siena, St. (1380-1444): Italian Franciscan; noted preacher and missioner; spread of devotion to Holy Name is attributed to him; represented in art holding to his breast the monogram IHS; canonized 1450; May 20*.

Blase, St. (d. c. 316): Armenian bishop; martyr; the blessing of throats on his feast day derives from tradition that he miraculously saved the life of a boy who had half-swallowed a fish bone; Feb. 3*.

Boniface (Winfrid), St. (d. 754): English Benedictine; bishop, martyr; apostle of Germany; established monastery at Fulda which became center of German missionary work; archbishop of Mainz; martyred near Dukkum in Holland; June 5*.

Brendan, St. (c. 489-583): Irish abbot; founded monasteries; his patronage of sailors probably rests on tradition that he made a seven-year voyage in search of a fabled paradise; called Brendan the Navigator; May 16.

Bridget (Brigid), St. (c. 450-525): Irish nun; founded nunnery at Kildare, the first erected on Irish soil; patron, with Sts. Patrick and Columba, of Ireland; Feb. 1.

Bridget (Birgitta), St. (c. 1303-1373): Swedish mystic; widow; foundress of Order of Our Savior (Brigittines); canonized 1391; wrote *Revelationes*, accounts of her visions; patroness of Sweden; July 23*.

Bruno, St. (1030-1101): German monk; founded Carthusians, 1084, in France; Oct. 6*.

Cabrini, Mother: See Index.

Cajetan of Thiene, St. (1480-1547): Italian lawyer; religious reformer; a founder of Oratory of Divine Love, forerunner of the Theatines; canonized 1671; Aug. 7*.

Callistus I, St. (d. 222): Pope, 217-222; martyr; condemned Sabellianism and other heresies; advocated a policy of mercy toward repentant sinners; Oct. 14*.

Camillus de Lellis, St. (1550-1614): Italian priest; founder of Camillians (Ministers of the Sick); canonized 1746; patron of the sick and of nurses; July 14*.

Casimir, St. (1458-1484): Polish prince; grand duke of Lithuania; noted for his piety; buried at cathedral in Vilna, Lithuania; canonized 1521; patron of Poland and Lithuania; Mar. 4*.

Cassian, St. (d. 298): Roman martyr; an official court stenographer who declared himself a Christian; patron of stenographers; Dec. 3.

Catherine Laboure, St. (1806-1876): French nun; favored with series of visions; first Miraculous Medal (see Index) struck as the result of one of the visions; canonized 1947; Dec. 31.

Catherine of Bologna, St. (1413-1463): Italian Poor Clare; mystic, writer, artist; canonized 1712; patron of artists; Mar. 9.

Cecilia, St. (2nd-3rd century): Roman virgin-martyr; traditional patron of musicians; Nov. 22*.

Charles Borromeo, St. (1538-1584): Italian cardinal; nephew of Pope Pius IV; cardinal bishop of Milan; influential figure in Church reform in Italy; promoted education of clergy; canonized 1610; Nov. 4*.

Charles Lwanga and Companions, Sts. (d. 1886 and 1887): Martyrs of Uganda; pages of King Mwanga of Uganda; Charles Lwanga and 12 companions were martyred near Rubaga, June 3, 1886; the other nine were martyred between May 26, 1886, and Jan. 27, 1887; canonized 1964; first martyrs of black Africa; June 3*.

Christopher, St. (3rd cent.): Early Christian martyr inscribed in Roman calendar about 1550; feast relegated to particular calendars because of legendary nature of accounts of his life; traditional patron of travelers; July 25.

Clare, St. (1194-1253): Foundress of Poor Clares; b. at Assisi; later joined in religious life by her sisters Agnes and Beatrice, and her mother Ortolana; canonized 1255; patroness of television; Aug. 11*.

Clement I, St. (d. c. 100): Pope, 88-97; third successor of St. Peter; wrote important letter to Church in Corinth settling disputes there; venerated as a martyr; Nov. 23*.

Columba, St. (521-597): Irish monk; founded monasteries in Ireland; missionary in Scotland; established monastery at Iona which became the center for conversion of Picts, Scots, and Northern English; Scotland's most famous saint; June 9.

Columban, St. (545-615): Irish monk; scholar; founded monasteries in England and Brittany (famous abbey of Luxeuil), forced into exile because of his criticism of Frankish court; spent last years in northern Italy where he founded abbey at Bobbio; Nov. 23*.

Contardo Ferrini, Bl. (1859-1902): Italian Franciscan tertiary; model of the Catholic professor; beatified 1947; patron of universities; Oct. 17.

Cornelius, St. (d. 253): Pope, 251-253; promoted a policy of mercy with respect to readmission of repentant Christians who had fallen away during the persecution of Decius *(lapsi)*; banished from Rome during persecution of Gallus; regarded as a martyr; Sept. 16 (with Cyprian)*.

Cosmas and Damian, Sts. (d. c. 303): Arabian twin brothers; physicians who were martyred during Diocletian persecution; patrons of physicians; Sept. 26*.

Crispin and Crispinian, Sts. (3rd cent.): Early Christian martyrs; said to have met their deaths in Gaul; patrons of shoemakers, a trade they pursued; Oct. 25.

Cyprian, St. (d. 258): Early ecclesiastical writer; b. Africa; bishop of Carthage, 249-258; supported Pope St. Cornelius concerning the readmission of Christians who had apostasized in time of persecution; erred in his teaching that baptism administered by heretics and schismatics was invalid; wrote *De Unitate;* Sept. 16 (with St. Cornelius).*

Cyril and Methodius, Sts.: Greek missionaries; brothers venerated as apostles of the Slavs; Cyril (d. 869) and Methodius (d. 885) began their missionary work in Moravia in 863; developed a Slavonic alphabet; eventually their use of the vernacular in the liturgy was approved; Feb. 14*.

Damasus I, St. (d. 384): Pope, 366-384; opposed Arians and Apollinarians; commissioned St. Jerome to work on Bible translation; developed Roman liturgy; Dec. 11*.

Damian, St.: See Cosmas and Damian, Sts.

David, St. (5th-6th cent.): Welsh monk; founded monastery at Menevia; patron saint of Wales; Mar. 1.

Denis and Companions, Sts. (d. 3rd cent.): Denis, bishop of Paris, and two companions identified by early writers as Rusticus, a priest, and Eleutherius, a deacon; martyred near Paris; Denis is popularly regarded as apostle of France; Oct. 9*.

Dismas, St. (1st cent.): Name given to repentant thief (Good Thief) to whom Jesus promised salvation; regarded as patron of prisoners; Mar. 25.

Dominic, St. (Dominic de Guzman) (1170-1221): Spanish priest; founder of Dominican Order (Friars Preachers), 1215; preached against the Albigensian heresy; a contemporary of St. Francis of Assisi; canonized 1234; Aug. 8*.

Dominic Savio, St. (1842-1857): Italian youth; pupil of St. John Bosco; died before his 15th birthday; canonized 1954; patron of choir boys; Mar. 9.

Dunstan, St. (c. 910-988): English monk; archbishop of Canterbury; initiated reforms in religious life; royal counselor to several kings; considered one of greatest Anglo-Saxon saints; patron of armorers, goldsmiths, locksmiths, jewelers; May 17.

Dymphna, St. (dates uncertain): Nothing certain known of her life; presumably she was an Irish maiden whose relics were discovered at Gheel near Antwerp, Belgium, in the 13th century; since that time many cases of mental illness and epilepsy have been cured at her shrine; patron of those suffering from mental illness; May 15.

Edmund Campion, St. (1540-1581): English Jesuit; convert 1573; martyred at Tyburn; canonized 1970, one of the Forty English and Welsh Martyrs; Dec. 1.

Elizabeth Bayley Seton, Bl. (1774-1821): American foundress; convert, 1905; founded Sisters of Charity in the US; beatified 1963, the first American-born blessed; Jan. 4 (US)*.

Elizabeth of Hungary, St. (1207-1231): Queen; became Franciscan tertiary after death of her husband in 1227; devoted life to poor and destitute; a patron of the Third Order of St. Francis; Nov. 17*.

Elizabeth of Portugal, St. (1271-1336): Queen of Portugal; b. Spain; retired to Poor Clare convent as a tertiary after the death of her husband; July 4*.

Erasmus, St. (d. 303): Life surrounded by legend; martyred during Diocletian persecution; patron of sailors; June 2.

Ethelbert, St. (552-676): King of Kent; baptized by St. Augustine 597; issued legal code; furthered spread of Christianity; Feb. 24.

Euphrasia Pelletier, St. (1796-1868): French nun; founded Sisters of the Good Shepherd at Angers, 1829; canonized 1940; Apr. 24.

Eusebius of Vercelli, St. (283-370): Italian bishop; exiled from his see for a time because of his opposition to Arianism; considered a martyr because of sufferings he endured; Aug. 2*.

Fabian, St. (d. 250): Pope, 236-250; martyred under Decius; Jan. 20*.

Felicity, St.: See Perpetua and Felicity, Sts.

Ferdinand III, St. (1198-1252): King of Castile and Leon; waged successful crusade against Mohammedans in Spain; founded university at Salamanca; canonized 1671; May 30.

Fiacre, St. (d. c. 670): Irish hermit; patron of gardeners; Aug. 30.

Fidelis of Sigmaringen, St. (Mark Rey) (1577-1622): German Capuchin; lawyer before he joined the Capuchins; missionary to Swiss Protestants; stabbed to death by peasants who were told he was agent of Austrian emperor; Apr. 24*.

Frances of Rome, St. (1384-1440): Italian model for housewives and widows; happily married for 40 years; after death of her husband in 1436 joined community of Benedictine Oblates she had founded; canonized 1608; patron of motorists; Mar. 9*.

Frances Xavier Cabrini, St. (Mother Cabrini) (1850-1917): American foundress; b. Italy; foundress of Missionary Sisters of the Sacred Heart, 1877; settled in the US 1889; became an American citizen at Seattle 1909; worked among Italian immigrants; canonized 1946, the first American citizen so honored; Nov. 13 (US)*.

Francis Borgia, St. (1510-1572): Spanish Jesuit; joined Jesuits after death of his wife in 1546; became general of the Order, 1565; Oct. 10.

Francis of Assisi, St. (Giovanni di Bernardone) (1182-1226): Founder of the Franciscans, 1209; received stigmata 1224; canonized 1228; one of best known and best loved saints; patron of Catholic Action and of Italy; Oct. 4*.

Francis of Paola, St. (1416-1507): Italian hermit; founder of Minim Friars; Apr. 2*.

Francis Xavier, St. (1506-1552): Spanish Jesuit; missionary to Far East; canonized 1602; patron of foreign missions; considered one of greatest Christian missionaries; Dec. 3*.

Gabriel of the Sorrowful Mother, St. (Francis Possenti) (1838-1862): Italian Passionist; died while a scholastic; canonized 1920; Feb. 27.

Genesius, St. (d. c. 300): Roman actor; according to legend, was converted while performing a burlesque of Christian baptism and was subsequently martyred; patron of actors.

Genevieve, St. (422-500): French nun; a patroness and protectress of Paris; events of her life not authenticated; Jan. 3.

George, St. (d. c. 300): Martyr, probably during Diocletian persecution in Palestine; all other incidents of his life, including story of the dragon, are legendary; patron of England; Apr. 23*.

Gerard Majella, St. (1725-1755): Italian Redemptorist lay brother; noted for supernatural occurrences in his life including bilocation and reading of consciences; canonized 1904; patron of mothers; Oct. 16.

Gertrude, St. (1256-1302): German mystic; writer; helped spread devotion to the Sacred Heart; Nov. 16*.

Gregory VII (Hildebrand), St. (1020?-1085): Pope, 1075-1085; Benedictine monk; adviser to several popes; as pope, strengthened interior life of Church and fought against lay investiture; driven from Rome by Henry IV; died in exile; May 25*.

Gregory the Illuminator, St. (257-332): Martyr; bishop; apostle and patron saint of Armenia; helped free Armenia from the Persians; Sept. 30.

Hedwig, St. (1174-1243): Moravian noblewoman; married duke of Silesia, head of Polish royal family; fostered religious life in country; canonized 1266; Oct. 16*.

Helena, St. (250-330): Empress; mother of Constantine the Great; associated with discovery of the True Cross; Aug. 18.

Henry, St. (972-1024): Bavarian emperor; cooperated with Benedictine abbeys in restoration of ecclesiastical and social discipline; canonized 1146; July 13*.

Hippolytus, St. (d. c. 236): Roman priest; opposed Pope St. Callistus I in his teaching about the readmission of Christians who had apostasized during time of persecution; elected antipope; reconciled before his martyrdom; important ecclesiastical writer; Aug. 13*.

Hubert, St. (d. 727): Bishop; his patronage of hunters is based on legend that he was converted while hunting; Nov. 3.

Hugh of Cluny (the Great), St. (1024-1109): Abbot of Benedictine foundation at Cluny; supported popes in efforts to reform ecclesiastical abuses; canonized 1120; Apr. 29.

Ignatius of Antioch, St. (d. c. 107): Early ecclesiastical writer; martyr; bishop of Antioch in Syria for 40 years; Oct. 17*.

Ignatius of Loyola, St. (1491-1556): Spanish soldier; renounced military career after recovering from wounds received at siege of Pampeluna (Pamplona) in 1521; founded Society of Jesus (Jesuits), 1534, at Paris; canonized 1622; author *The Book of Spiritual Exercises;* July 31*.

Irenaeus of Lyons, St. (130-202): Early ecclesiastical writer; opposed Gnosticism; bishop of Lyons; traditionally regarded as a martyr; June 28*.

Isidore the Farmer, St. (d. 1170): Spanish layman; farmer; canonized 1622; patron of farmers; Oct. 25 (US)*.

Jane Frances de Chantal, St. (1572-1641): French widow; foundress, under guidance of St. Francis de Sales, of Order of the Visitation; canonized 1767; Dec. 12*.

Januarius (Gennaro), St. (d. 304): Bishop of Benevento; martyred during Diocletian persecution; fame rests on liquefaction of some of his blood preserved in a phial at Naples, an unexplained phenomenon which has occurred regularly about 18 times each year for over 400 years; Sept. 19*.

Jerome Emiliani, St. (1481-1537): Venetian priest; founded Somascan Fathers, 1532, for care of orphans; canonized 1767; patron of orphans and abandoned children; Feb. 8*.

Joan of Arc, St. (1412-1431): French heroine, called The Maid of Orleans, La Pucelle; led French army against English invaders; captured by Burgundians, turned over to ecclesiastical court on charge of heresy, found guilty and burned at the stake; her innocence was declared in 1456; canonized 1920; patroness of France; May 30.

John I, St. (d. 526): Pope, 523-526; martyr; May 18*.

John Baptist de la Salle, St. (1651-1719): French priest; founder of Brothers of the Christian Schools, 1680; canonized 1900; Apr. 7*.

John Berchmans, St. (1599-1621): Belgian Jesuit scholastic; patron of Mass servers; canonized 1888; Aug. 13.

John Bosco, St. (1815-1888): Italian priest; founded Salesians, 1864, for education of boys and the Daughters of Mary Auxiliatrix for education of girls; canonized 1934; Jan. 31*.

John Capistran, St. (1386-1456): Italian Franciscan; preacher; papal diplomat; canonized 1690; Oct. 23*.

John Eudes, St. (1601-1680): French priest; founder of Sisters of Our Lady of Charity of Refuge, 1642, and Congregation of Jesus-Mary (Eudists), 1643; canonized 1925; Aug. 19*.

John Fisher, St. (1469-1535): English prelate; theologian; martyr; bishop of Rochester, cardinal; refused to recognize validity of Henry VIII's marriage to Anne Boleyn; upheld supremacy of the pope; beheaded for refusing to acknowledge Henry as head of the Church; canonized 1935; June 22 (with St. Thomas More)*.

John Kanty (Cantius), St. (1395-1473): Polish theologian; canonized 1767; Dec. 23*.

John Leonardi, St. (1550-1609): Italian priest; worked among prisoners and the sick; founded Clerics Regular of the Mother of God; canonized 1938; Oct. 9*.

John Nepomucene, St. (1345-1393): Bohemian priest; regarded as a martyr; canonized 1729; patron of Czechoslovakia; May 16.

John Nepomucene Neumann, Bl. (1811-1860): American prelate; b. Bohemia; ordained in New York 1836; missionary among Germans near Niagara Falls before joining Redemptorists, 1840; bishop of Philadelphia, 1852; first bishop in US to prescribe Forty Hours devotion in his diocese; beatified 1963; Jan. 5 (US)*.

John of God, St. (1495-1550): Portuguese founder; his work among the sick poor led to foundation of Brothers Hospitallers of St. John of God, 1540, in Spain; canonized 1690; patron of sick, hospitals, nurses; Mar. 8*.

John Vianney (Cure of Ars), St. (1786-1859): French parish priest; noted confessor, spent 16 to 18 hours a day in confessional; canonized 1925; patron of parish priests; Aug. 4*.

Josaphat Kuncevyc, St. (1584-1623): Basilian monk; b. Poland; archbishop of Polotsk, Lithuania; worked for reunion of separated Easterners; martyred by mob of schismatics; canonized 1867; Nov. 12*.

Joseph Benedict Cottolengo, St. (1786-1842): Italian priest; established Little Houses of Divine Providence (Piccolo Casa) for care of orphans and the sick; canonized 1934; Apr. 30.

Joseph Cafasso, St. (1811-1860): Italian priest; renowned confessor; promoted devotion to Blessed Sacrament; canonized 1947; June 22.

Joseph Calasanz, St. (1556-1648): Spanish priest; founder of Piarists (Order of Pious Schools); canonized 1767; Aug. 25*.

Joseph of Cupertino, St. (1603-1663): Italian Franciscan; noted for remarkable incidents of levitation; canonized 1767; Sept. 18.

Justin Martyr, St. (100-165): Early ecclesiastical writer; *Apologies for the Christian Religion, Dialog with the Jew Tryphon;* martyred at Rome; June 1*.

Ladislaus, Saint (1040-1095): King of Hungary; supported Pope Gregory VII against Henry IV; canonized 1192; June 27.

Lawrence, St. (d. 258): Widely venerated martyr who suffered death, according to a long-standing but unverifiable legend, by being roasted alive on a gridiron; Aug. 10*.

Leonard of Port Maurice, St. (1676-1751): Italian Franciscan; ascetical writer; preached missions throughout Italy; canonized 1867; patron of parish missions; Nov. 26.

Louis IX, St. (1215-1270): King of France, 1226-1270; participated in Sixth Crusade; patron of Third Order of St. Francis; canonized 1297; Aug. 25*.

Louis de Montfort, St. (1673-1716): French priest; founder of Sisters of Divine Wisdom, 1703, and Missionaries of Company of Mary, 1715; wrote *True Devotion to the Blessed Virgin;* canonized 1947; Apr. 28.

Louise de Marillac, St. (1591-1660): French foundress, with St. Vincent de Paul, of the Sisters of Charity; canonized 1934; Mar. 15.

Lucy, St. (d. 304): Sicilian maiden; martyred during Diocletian persecution; one of most widely venerated early virgin-martyrs; patron of Syracuse, Sicily; invoked by those suffering from eye diseases (based on legend that she offered her eyes to a suitor who admired them); Dec. 13*.

Marcellinus and Peter, Sts. (d.c. 304): Early Roman martyrs; June 2*.

Margaret Clitherow, St. (1556-1586): English martyr; convert shortly after her marriage; one of Forty Martyrs of England and Wales; canonized 1970.

Margaret Mary Alacoque, St. (1647-1690): French nun; spread devotion to Sacred Heart in accordance with revelations made to her in 1675 (see Sacred Heart); canonized 1920; Oct. 16*.

Margaret of Scotland, St. (1050-1093): Queen of Scotland; noted for solicitude for the poor and promotion of justice; canonized 1251; Nov. 16*.

Maria Goretti, St. (1890-1902): Italian virgin-martyr; a model of purity; canonized 1950; July 6*.

Mariana Paredes of Jesus, St. (1618-1645): South American recluse; Lily of Quito; canonized, 1950; May 26.

Martha, St. (1st cent.): Sister of Lazarus and Mary of Bethany; Gospel accounts record her concern for homely details; patron of cooks; July 29*.

Martin I, St. (d. 655): Pope, 649; banished from Rome by emperor because of his condemnation of Monothelites; considered a martyr; Apr. 13*.

Martin of Tours, St. (316-397): Bishop of Tours; opposed Arianism and Priscillianism; pioneer of Western monasticism, before St. Benedict; Nov. 11*.

Mary Magdalene, St. (1st cent.): Gospels record her as devoted follower of Christ to whom he appeared after the Resurrection; her identification with Mary of Bethany (sister of Martha and Lazarus) and the woman sinner (Lk 7:36-50) has been questioned; July 22*.

Mary Magdalene de Pazzi, St. (1566-1607): Italian Carmelite nun; recipient of mystical experiences; canonized 1669; May 25*.

Maximilian Kolbe, Bl. (1894-1941): Polish Conventual Franciscan; prisoner at Auschwitz who heroically offered his life in place of a fellow prisoner; beatified 1971.

Methodius, St.: See Index.

Monica, St. (332-387): Mother of St. Augustine; model of a patient mother; her feast is observed in the Roman calendar the day before her son's; Aug. 27*.

Nereus and Achilleus, Sts. (d. c. 100): Early Christian martyrs; soldiers who, according to legend, were baptized by St. Peter; May 12*.

Nicholas of Myra, St. (4th cent.): Bishop of Myra in Asia Minor; one of most popular saints in both East and West; most of the incidents of his life are based on legend; patron of Russia; Dec. 6*.

Nicholas of Tolentino, St. (1245-1365): Italian hermit; famed preacher; canonized 1446; Sept. 10.

Norbert, St. (1080-1134): German bishop; founder of Norbertines or Premonstratensians, 1120; promoted reform of the clergy, devotion to Blessed Sacrament; canonized 1582; June 6*.

Odilia, St. (d. c. 720): Benedictine abbess; according to legend she was born blind, abandoned by her family and adopted by a convent where her sight was miraculously restored; patron of blind; Dec. 13.

Oliver Plunkett, Bl. (1629-1681): Irish martyr; theologian; archbishop of Armagh and primate of Ireland; beatified 1920.

Pancras, St. (d. c. 304): Roman martyr; May 12*.

Paschal Baylon, St. (1540-1592): Spanish Franciscan lay brother; spent life as doorkeeper in various Franciscan friaries; defended doctrine of Real Presence in Blessed Sacrament; canonized 1690; patron of all Eucharistic confraternities and congresses, 1897; May 17.

Patrick, St. (389-461): Famous missionary of Ireland; began missionary work in Ireland about 432; organized the Church there and established it on a lasting foundation; patron of Ireland, with Sts. Bridget and Columba; Mar. 17*.

Paul Miki and Companions, Sts. (d. 1597): Martyrs of Japan; Paul Miki, Jesuit, and twenty-five other priests and laymen were martyred at Nagasaki; canonized 1862, the first canonized martyrs of the Far East; Feb. 6*.

Paul of the Cross, St. (1694-1775): Italian religious; founder of the Passionists; canonized 1867; Oct. 19*.

Paulinus of Nola, St. (d. 451): Bishop of Nola (Spain); writer; June 22*.

Peregrine, St. (1260-1347): Italian Servite; invoked against cancer (he was miraculously cured of cancer of the foot after a vision); canonized 1726; May 1.

Perpetua and Felicity, Sts. (d. 203): Martyrs; Mar. 7*.

Peter Chanel, St. (1803-1841): French Marist; missionary to Oceania, where he was martyred; canonized 1954; Apr. 28*.

Peter Gonzalez, St. (1190-1246): Spanish Dominican; worked among sailors; court chaplain and confessor of King St. Ferdinand of Castile; patron of sailors; Apr. 14.

Peter of Alcantara, St. (1499-1562): Spanish Franciscan; mystic; initiated Franciscan reform; confessor of St. Teresa of Avila; canonized 1669; Oct. 19.

Philip Neri, St. (1515-1595): Italian religious; founded Congregation of the Oratory; considered a second apostle of Rome because of his mission activities there; canonized 1622; May 26*.

Philip of Jesus, St. (1571-1597): Mexican Franciscan; martyred at Nagasaki, Japan; canonized 1862; patron of Mexico City; Feb. 6*.

Pius V, St. (1504-1572): Pope, 1566-1572; enforced decrees of Council of Trent; organized expedition against Turks resulting in victory at Lepanto: canonized 1712; Apr. 30*.

Polycarp, St. (2nd cent.): Bishop of Smyrna; ecclesiastical writer; martyr; Feb. 23*.

Pontian, St. (d. c. 235): Pope, 230-235; exiled to Sardinia by the emperor; regarded as a martyr; Aug. 13 (with Hippolytus)*.

Raymond Nonnatus, St. (d. 1240): Spanish Mercedarian; cardinal; devoted his life to ransoming captives from the Moors; Aug. 31.

Raymond of Penyafort, St. (1175-1275): Spanish Dominican; confessor of Gregory IX; systematized and codified canon law, in effect until 1917; master general of Dominicans, 1238; canonized 1601; Jan. 7*.

Robert Southwell, St. (1561-1595): English Jesuit; poet; martyred at Tyburn; canonized 1970; one of the Forty English and Welsh Martyrs.

Roch, St. (1350-1379): French layman; pilgrim; devoted life to care of plague-stricken; widely venerated; invoked against pestilence; Aug. 17.

Romuald, St. (951-1027): Italian monk; founded Camaldolese Benedictines; June 19*.

Rose of Lima, St. (1586-1617): Peruvian Dominican tertiary; first native-born saint of the New World; canonized 1671; Aug. 23*.

Scholastica, St. (d. c. 559): Sister of St. Benedict; regarded as first nun of the Benedictine Order; Feb. 10*.

Sebastian, St. (3rd cent.): Roman martyr; traditionally pictured as a handsome youth; martyred by being pierced with arrows; patron of athletes; Jan. 20*.

Seven Holy Founders of the Servants of Mary (Buonfiglio Monaldo, Alexis Falconieri, Benedict dell'Antello, Bartholomew Amidei, Ricovero Uguccione, Gerardino Sostegni, John Buonagiunta Monetti): Florentine youths who founded Servites, 1233, in obedience to a vision; canonized 1888; Feb. 17*.

Sixtus II and Companions, Sts. (d. 258): Sixtus, pope 257-258, and four deacons, martyrs; Aug. 7*.

Stanislaus, St. (1030-1079): Polish bishop; martyr; canonized 1253; Apr. 11*.

Stephen, St. (d. c. 33): First Christian martyr; chosen by the Apostles as the first of the seven deacons; stoned to death; Dec. 26*.

Stephen, St. (975-1038): King; apostle of Hungary; welded Magyars into national unity; canonized 1087; Aug. 16*.

Sylvester I, St. (d. 335): Pope 314-335; first ecumenical council held at Nicaea during his pontificate; Dec. 31*.

Tarcisius, St. (d. 3rd cent.): Early martyr; according to tradition, was martyred while carrying the Blessed Sacrament to some Christians in prison; patron of first communicants; Aug. 15.

Therese Couderc, St. (1805-1885): French religious; foundress of the Religious of Our Lady of the Retreat in the Cenacle, 1827; canonized 1970; Sept. 26.

Therese of Lisieux, St. (1873-1897): French Carmelite nun; b. Therese Martin; allowed to enter Carmel at 15, died nine years later of tuberculosis; her "little way" of spiritual perfection became widely known through her spiritual autobiography; despite her obscure life, became one of the most popular saints; canonized 1925; patron of foreign missions; Oct. 1*.

Thomas Becket, St. (1118-1170): English martyr; archbishop of Canterbury; chancellor under Henry II; murdered for upholding rights of the Church; canonized 1173; Dec. 29*.

Thomas More, St. (1478-1535): English martyr; statesman, chancellor under Henry VIII; author of *Utopia;* opposed Henry's divorce, refused to renounce authority of the papacy; beheaded; canonized 1935; June 22 (with St. John Fisher)*.

Timothy, St. (d. c. 97): Bishop of Ephesus; disciple and companion of St. Paul; martyr; Jan. 26*.

Titus, St. (d. c. 96): Bishop; companion of

St. Paul; recipient of one of Paul's epistles; Jan. 26*.

Valentine, St. (d. 269): Priest, physician; martyred at Rome; legendary patron of lovers; Feb. 14.

Vincent, St. (d. 304): Spanish deacon; martyr; Jan. 22*.

Vincent de Paul, St. (1581?-1660): French priest; founder of Congregation of the Mission (Vincentians, Lazarists) and co-founder of Sisters of Charity; declared patron of all charitable organizations and works by Leo XIII; canonized 1737; Sept. 27*.

Vincent Ferrer, St. (1350-1418): Spanish Dominican; famed preacher; Apr. 5*.

Wenceslaus, St. (d. 935): Duke of Bohemia; martyr; patron of Bohemia; Sept. 28*.

Zita, St. (1218-1278): Italian maid; noted for charity to poor; patron of domestics.

SAINTS—PATRONS AND INTERCESSORS

A patron is a saint who is venerated as a special intercessor before God. Most patrons have been so designated as the result of popular devotion and long-standing custom. In many cases, the fact of existing patronal devotion is clear despite historical obscurity regarding its origin. The Church has made official designation of relatively few patrons; in such cases, the dates of designation are given in the list below. The theological background of the patronage of saints includes the dogmas of the Mystical Body of Christ and the Communion of Saints.

Listed below are patron saints of occupations and professions, and saints whose intercession is sought for special needs.

Accountants: St. Matthew.

Actors: St. Genesius.

Advertisers: St. Bernardine of Siena (May 20, 1960).

Alpinists: St. Bernard of Menthon (Aug. 20, 1923).

Altar boys: St. John Berchmans.

Anesthetists: St. Rene Goupil.

Archers: St. Sebastian.

Architects: St. Thomas, Apostle.

Armorers: St. Dunstan.

Art: St. Catherine of Bologna.

Artists: St. Luke, St. Catherine of Bologna.

Astronomers: St. Dominic.

Athletes: St. Sebastian.

Authors: St. Francis de Sales.

Aviators: Our Lady of Loreto (1920), St. Therese of Lisieux, St. Joseph of Cupertino.

Bakers: St. Elizabeth of Hungary, St. Nicholas.

Bankers: St. Matthew.

Barbers: Sts. Cosmas and Damian, St. Louis.

Barren women: St. Anthony of Padua, St. Felicity.

Basket-makers: St. Anthony, Abbot.

Blacksmiths: St. Dunstan.

Blind: St. Odilia, St. Raphael.

Blood banks: St. Januarius.

Bodily ills: Our Lady of Lourdes.

Bookbinders: St. Peter Celestine.

Bookkeepers: St. Matthew.

Booksellers: St. John of God.

Boy Scouts: St. George.

Brewers: St. Augustine of Hippo, St. Luke, St. Nicholas of Myra.

Bricklayers: St. Stephen.

Brides: St. Nicholas of Myra.

Brush makers: St. Anthony, Abbot.

Builders: St. Vincent Ferrer.

Butchers: St. Anthony, Abbot, St. Luke.

Cab drivers: St. Fiacre.

Cabinetmakers: St. Anne.

Cancer patients: St. Peregrine.

Canonists: St. Raymond of Penyafort.

Carpenters: St. Joseph.

Catechists: St. Viator, St. Charles Borromeo, St. Robert Bellarmine.

Catholic Action: St. Francis of Assisi (1916).

Chandlers: St. Ambrose, St. Bernard of Clairvaux.

Charitable societies: St. Vincent de Paul (May 12, 1885).

Children: St. Nicholas of Myra.

Children of Mary: St. Agnes, St. Maria Goretti.

Choir boys: St. Dominic Savio (June 8, 1956), Holy Innocents.

Church: St. Joseph (Dec. 8, 1870).

Clerics: St. Gabriel of the Sorrowful Mother.

Comedians: St. Vitus.

Communications personnel: St. Bernardine.

Confessors: St. Alphonsus Liguori (Apr. 26, 1950), St. John Nepomucene.

Convulsive children: St. Scholastica.

Cooks: St. Lawrence, St. Martha.

Coopers: St. Nicholas of Myra.

Coppersmiths: St. Maurus.

Dairy workers: St. Brigid.

Deaf: St. Francis de Sales.

Dentists: St. Apollonia.

Desperate situations: St. Gregory of Neocaesarea, St. Jude Thaddeus.

Dietitians (in hospitals): St. Martha.

Dyers: Sts. Maurice and Lydia.

Dying: St. Joseph.

Ecologists: St. Francis of Assisi.

Editors: St. John Bosco.

Emigrants: St. Frances Xavier Cabrini, (Sept. 8, 1950).

Epilepsy: St. Vitus.

Engineers: St. Ferdinand III.

Eucharistic congresses and societies: St. Paschal Baylon (Nov. 28, 1897).

Expectant mothers: St. Raymund Nonnatus, St. Gerard Majella.

Eye diseases: St. Lucy.

Falsely accused: St. Raymund Nonnatus.

Farmers: St. George, St. Isidore.

Farriers: St. John Baptist.
Firemen: St. Florian.
Fire prevention: St. Catherine of Siena.
First communicants: St. Tarcisius.
Fishermen: St. Andrew.
Florists: St. Therese of Lisieux.
Forest workers: St. John Gualbert.
Foundlings: Holy Innocents.
Fullers: St. Anastasius the Fuller, St. James the Less.
Funeral directors: St. Joseph of Arimathea, St. Dismas.
Gardeners: St. Adelard, St. Tryphon, St. Fiacre, St. Phocas.
Glassworkers: St. Luke.
Goldsmiths: St. Dunstan, St. Anastasius.
Gravediggers: St. Anthony, Abbot.
Greetings: St. Valentine.
Grocers: St. Michael.
Hairdressers: St. Martin de Porres.
Happy meetings: St. Raphael.
Hatters: St. Severus of Ravenna, St. James the Less.
Haymakers: Sts. Gervase and Protase.
Headache sufferers: St. Teresa of Avila.
Heart patients: St. John of God.
Hospital administrators: St. Basil the Great, St. Frances X. Cabrini.
Hospitals: St. Camillus de Lellis and St. John of God (June 22, 1886), St. Jude Thaddeus.
Housewives: St. Anne.
Hunters: St. Hubert, St. Eustachius.
Infantrymen: St. Maurice.
Innkeepers: St. Amand, St. Martha.
Invalids: St. Roch.
Jewelers: St. Eligius, St. Dunstan.
Journalists: St. Francis de Sales (Apr. 26, 1923).
Jurists: St. John Capistran.
Laborers: St. Isidore, St. James, St. John Bosco.
Lawyers: St. Ivo, St. Genesius, St. Thomas More.
Learning: St. Ambrose.
Librarians: St. Jerome.
Lighthouse keepers: St. Venerius.
Locksmiths: St. Dunstan.
Maids: St. Zita.
Marble workers: St. Clement I.
Mariners: St. Michael, St. Nicholas of Tolentino.
Medical record librarians: St. Raymond of Penyafort.
Medical social workers: St. John Regis.
Medical technicians: St. Albert the Great.
Mentally ill: St. Dymphna.
Merchants: St. Francis of Assisi, St. Nicholas of Myra.
Messengers: St. Gabriel.
Metal workers: St. Eligius.
Millers: St. Arnulph, St. Victor.
Missions, Foreign: St. Francis Xavier (Mar. 25, 1904), St. Therese of Lisieux (Dec. 14, 1927).

Missions, Negro: St. Peter Claver (1896, Leo XIII), St. Benedict the Black.
Missions, Parish: St. Leonard of Port Maurice (Mar. 17, 1923).
Mothers: St. Monica.
Motorcyclists: Our Lady of Grace.
Motorists: St. Christopher, St. Frances of Rome.
Mountaineers: St. Bernard of Menthon.
Musicians: St. Gregory the Great, St. Cecilia, St. Dunstan.
Nail makers: St. Cloud.
Notaries: St. Luke, St. Mark.
Nurses: St. Camillus de Lellis and St. John of God (1930, Pius XI), St. Agatha, St. Raphael.
Nursing and nursing service: St. Elizabeth of Hungary, St. Catherine of Siena.
Orators: St. John Chrysostom (July 8, 1908).
Organ builders: St. Cecilia.
Orphans: St. Jerome Emiliani.
Painters: St. Luke.
Paratroopers: St. Michael.
Pawnbrokers: St. Nicholas.
Pharmacists: Sts. Cosmas and Damian, St. James the Greater.
Pharmacists (in hospitals): St. Gemma Galgani.
Philosophers: St. Justin.
Physicians: St. Pantaleon, Sts. Cosmas and Damian, St. Luke, St. Raphael.
Pilgrims: St. James.
Plasterers: St. Bartholomew.
Poets: St. David, St. Cecilia.
Poison sufferers: St. Benedict.
Policemen: St. Michael.
Poor: St. Lawrence, St. Anthony of Padua.
Poor souls: St. Nicholas of Tolentino.
Porters: St. Christopher.
Possessed: St. Bruno, St. Denis.
Postal employees: St. Gabriel.
Priests: St. Jean-Baptiste Vianney (Apr. 23, 1929).
Printers: St. John of God, St. Augustine of Hippo, St. Genesius.
Prisoners: St. Dismas, St. Joseph Cafasso.
Protector of crops: St. Ansovinus.
Public relations: St. Bernardine of Siena (May 20, 1960).
Public relations (of hospitals): St. Paul, Apostle.
Radiologists: St. Michael (Jan. 15, 1941).
Radio workers: St. Gabriel.
Retreats: St. Ignatius Loyola (July 25, 1922).
Rheumatism: St. James the Greater.
Saddlers: Sts. Crispin and Crispinian.
Sailors: St. Cuthbert, St. Brendan, St. Eulalia, St. Christopher, St. Peter Gonzales, St. Erasmus, St. Nicholas.
Scholars: St. Brigid.
Schools, Catholic: St. Thomas Aquinas (Aug. 4, 1880), St. Joseph Calasanz (Aug. 13, 1948).
Scientists: St. Albert (Aug. 13, 1948).

Sculptors: St. Claude.

Seamen: St. Francis of Paola.

Searchers for lost articles: St. Anthony of Padua.

Secretaries: St. Genesius.

Seminarians: St. Charles Borromeo.

Servants: St. Martha, St. Zita.

Shoemakers: Sts. Crispin and Crispinian.

Sick: St. Michael, St. John of God and St. Camillus de Lellis (June 22, 1886).

Silversmiths: St. Andronicus.

Singers: St. Gregory, St. Cecilia.

Skaters: St. Lidwina.

Skiers: St. Bernard.

Social workers: St. Louise de Marillac (Feb. 12, 1960).

Soldiers: St. Hadrian, St. George, St. Ignatius, St. Sebastian, St. Martin of Tours, St. Joan of Arc.

Speleologists: St. Benedict.

Stenographers: St. Genesius, St. Cassian.

Stonecutters: St. Clement.

Stonemasons: St. Stephen.

Students: St. Thomas Aquinas.

Surgeons: Sts. Cosmas and Damian, St. Luke.

Swordsmiths: St. Maurice.

Tailors: St. Homobonus.

Tanners: Sts. Crispin and Crispinian, St. Simon.

Tax collectors: St. Matthew.

Teachers: St. Gregory the Great, St. John Baptist de la Salle (May 15, 1950).

Telecommunications workers: St. Gabriel (Jan. 12, 1951).

Telegraph/telephone workers: St. Gabriel.

Television: St. Clare of Assisi (Feb. 14, 1958).

Television workers: St. Gabriel.

Tertiaries (Franciscan): St. Louis of France, St. Elizabeth of Hungary.

Theologians: St. Augustine, St. Alphonsus Liguori.

Throat sufferers: St. Blase.

Travelers: St. Anthony of Padua, St. Nicholas of Myra, St. Christopher, St. Raphael.

Travel hostesses: St. Bona (Mar. 2, 1962).

Universities: Blessed Contardo Ferrini.

Vocations: St. Alphonsus.

Watchmen: St. Peter of Alcantara.

Weavers: St. Paul the Hermit, St. Anastasius the Fuller, St. Anastasia.

Wine merchants: St. Amand.

Women in labor: St. Anne.

Women's Army Corps: St. Genevieve.

Workingmen: St. Joseph.

Writers: St. Francis de Sales (Apr. 26, 1923), St. Lucy.

Yachtsmen: St. Adjutor.

Young girls: St. Agnes.

Youth: St. Aloysius Gonzaga (1729, Benedict XIII; 1926, Pius XI), St. John Berchmans, St. Gabriel of the Sorrowful Mother.

Patrons are exemplars of Christian witness as well as intercessors before God.

Patrons of Places

Alsace: St. Odile.

Americas: Our Lady of Guadalupe; St. Rose of Lima.

Argentina: Our Lady of Lujan.

Armenia: St. Gregory Illuminator.

Asia Minor: St. John, Evangelist.

Australia: Our Lady Help of Christians.

Belgium: St. Joseph.

Bohemia: Sts. Wenceslaus, Ludmilla.

Borneo: St. Francis Xavier.

Brazil: Nossa Senhora de Aparecida, Immaculate Conception; St. Peter of Alcantara.

Canada: St. Joseph; St. Anne.

Ceylon (Sri Lanka): St. Lawrence.

Chile: St. James; Our Lady of Mt. Carmel.

China: St. Joseph.

Colombia: St. Peter Claver; St. Louis Bertran.

Corsica: Immaculate Conception.

Czechoslovakia: St. Wenceslaus; St. John Nepomucene; St. Procopius.

Denmark: St. Ansgar; St. Canute.

Dominican Republic: Our Lady of High Grace; St. Dominic.

East Indies: St. Thomas, Apostle.

Ecuador: Sacred Heart.

England: St. George.

Europe: St. Benedict.

Finland: St. Henry.

France: Our Lady of the Assumption; St. Joan of Arc; St. Therese.

Germany: Sts. Boniface, Michael.

Greece: St. Nicholas; St. Andrew.

Holland: St. Willibrord.

Hungary: Blessed Virgin, "Great Lady of Hungary"; St. Stephen, King.

India: Our Lady of Assumption.

Ireland: Sts. Patrick, Brigid and Columba.

Italy: St. Francis of Assisi; St. Catherine of Siena.

Japan: St. Peter Baptist.

Lesotho: Immaculate Heart of Mary.

Lithuania: St. Casimir, Bl. Cunegunda.

Malta: St. Paul; Our Lady of the Assumption.

Mexico: Our Lady of Guadalupe.

Monaco: St. Devota.

Moravia: Sts. Cyril and Methodius.

New Zealand: Our Lady Help of Christians.

Norway: St. Olaf.

Paraguay: Our Lady of Assumption.

Peru: St. Joseph.

Philippines: Sacred Heart of Mary.

Poland: St. Casimir; Bl. Cunegunda; St. Stanislaus of Cracow; Our Lady of Czestochowa.

Portugal: Immaculate Conception; St. Francis Borgia; St. Anthony of Padua; St. Vincent; St. George.

Republic of South Africa: Our Lady of Assumption.

Russia: St. Andrew; St. Nicholas of Myra; St. Therese of Lisieux.

Scandinavia: St. Ansgar.
Scotland: St. Andrew; St. Columba.
Silesia: St. Hedwig.
Slovakia: Our Lady of Sorrows.
South America: St. Rose of Lima.
Spain: St. James; St. Teresa.
Sweden: St. Bridget; St. Eric.
United States: Immaculate Conception.
Uruguay: Our Lady of Lujan.
Wales: St. David.
West Indies: St. Gertrude.

Apostles of Places, Peoples

Alps: St. Bernard of Menthon.
Andalusia (Spain): St. John of Avila.
Antioch: St. Barnabas.
Armenia: St. Gregory the Illuminator; St. Bartholomew.
Austria: St. Severine.
Bavaria: St. Killian.
Brazil: Jose Anchieta.
California: Junipero Serra.
Carinthia (Yugoslavia): St. Virgil.
Colombia: St. Louis Bertran.
Corsica: St. Alexander Sauli.
Crete: St. Titus.
Cyprus: St. Barnabas.
Denmark: St. Ansgar.
England: St. Augustine of Canterbury; St. Gregory the Great.
Ethiopia: St. Frumentius.
Finland: St. Henry.
Florence: St. Andrew Corsini.
France: St. Remigius; St. Martin of Tours; St. Denis.
Friesland (Germany): St. Suitbert; St. Willibrord.
Gaul: St. Irenaeus.
Gentiles: St. Paul.
Georgia (Russia): St. Nino.
Germany: St. Boniface; St. Peter Canisius.
Gothland (Sweden): St. Sigfrid.
Guelderland (Holland): St. Plechelm.
Highlanders (Scotland): St. Columba.
Hungarians (Magyars): St. Stephen, King; St. Gerard; Bl. Astricus.
India: St. Thomas, Apostle.
Indies: St. Francis Xavier.
Ireland: St. Patrick.
Iroquois: Francois Picquit.
Italy: St. Bernardine of Siena.
Japan: St. Francis Xavier.
Malta: St. Paul.
Mexico: The twelve Apostles of Mexico (Franciscans), headed by Fra. Martin de Valencia.
Negro Slaves: St. Peter Claver.
Netherlands: St. Willibrord.
Northumbria (Britain): St. Aidan.
Norway: St. Olaf.
Ottawas (Indians): Fr. Claude Allouez.
Persia: St. Maruthas.
Poland: St. Hyacinth. .
Portugal: St. Christian.
Prussia (Slavs): St. Adalbert; St. Bruno of Querfurt.

Rome: St. Philip Neri.
Rumania: St. Nicetas.
Ruthenia: St. Bruno.
Sardinia: St. Ephesus.
Saxony: St. Willihad.
Scandinavia (North): St. Ansgar.
Scotland: St. Palladius.
Slavs: Sts. Cyril and Methodius, St. Adalbert.
Spain: St. James; Sts. Euphrasius and Felix.
Sweden: St. Ansgar.
Switzerland: St. Andeol.
Tournai (Belgium): St. Eligius, St. Piaton.

Emblems of Saints

St. Agatha: Tongs, veil.
St. Agnes: Lamb.
St. Ambrose: Bees, dove, ox, pen.
St. Andrew: Transverse cross.
St. Anne, Mother of the Blessed Virgin: A door.
St. Anthony, Abbot: Bell, hog.
St. Anthony of Padua: Infant Jesus, bread, book, lily.
St. Augustine of Hippo: Dove, child, shell, pen.
St. Barnabas: Stones, ax, lance.
St. Bartholomew: Knife, flayed and holding his skin.
St. Benedict: Broken cup, raven, bell, crosier, bush.
St. Bernard of Clairvaux: Pen, bees, instruments of Passion.
St. Bernardine of Siena: Tablet or sun inscribed with IHS.
St. Blase: Wax, taper, iron comb.
St. Bonaventure: Communion, ciborium, cardinal's hat.
St. Boniface: Oak, ax, book, fox, scourge, fountain, raven, sword.
St. Bridget of Sweden: Book, pilgrim's staff.
St. Bridget of Kildare: Cross, flame over her head, candle.
St. Catherine of Ricci: Ring, crown, crucifix.
St. Catherine of Siena: Stigmata, cross, ring, lily.
St. Cecilia: Organ.
St. Charles Borromeo: Communion, coat of arms with word *Humilitas*.
St. Christopher: Giant, torrent, tree, Child Jesus on his shoulders.
St. Clare of Assisi: Monstrance.
Sts. Cosmas and Damian: A phial, box of ointment.
St. Cyril of Alexandria: Blessed Virgin holding the Child Jesus, pen.
St. Cyril of Jerusalem: Purse, book.
St. Dominic: Rosary, star.
St. Edmund the Martyr: Arrow, sword.
St. Elizabeth of Hungary: Alms, flowers, bread, the poor, a pitcher.
St. Francis of Assisi: Deer, wolf, birds, fish, skull, the Stigmata.

St. Francis Xavier: Crucifix, bell, vessel, Negro.

St. Genevieve: Bread, keys, herd, candle.

St. George: Dragon.

St. Gertrude: Crown, taper, lily.

Sts. Gervase and Protase: Scourge, club, sword.

St. Gregory I (the Great): Tiara, crosier, dove.

St. Helena: Cross.

St. Hilary: Stick, pen, child.

St. Ignatius Loyola: Communion, chasuble, book, apparition of Our Lord.

St. Isidore: Bees, pen.

St. James the Greater: Pilgrim's staff, shell, key, sword.

St. James the Less: Square rule, halberd, club.

St. Jerome: Lion.

St. John Berchmans: Rule of St. Ignatius, cross, rosary.

St. John Chrysostom: Bees, dove, pen.

St. John of God: Alms, a heart, crown of thorns.

St. John the Baptist: Lamb, head cut off on platter, skin of an animal.

St. John the Evangelist: Eagle, chalice, kettle, armor.

St. Josaphat Kuncevyc: Chalice, crown, winged deacon.

St. Joseph, Spouse of the Blessed Virgin: Infant Jesus, lily, rod, plane, carpenter's square.

St. Jude: Sword, square rule, club.

St. Justin Martyr: Ax, sword.

St. Lawrence: Cross, book of the Gospels, gridiron.

St. Leander of Seville: A pen.

St. Liborius: Pebbles, peacock.

St. Longinus: In arms at foot of the cross.

St. Louis IX of France: Crown of thorns, nails.

St. Lucy: Cord, eyes.

St. Luke: Ox, book, brush, palette.

St. Mark: Lion, book.

St. Martha: Holy water sprinkler, dragon.

St. Mary Magdalene: Alabaster box of ointment.

St. Matilda: Purse, alms.

St. Matthew: Winged man, purse, lance.

St. Matthias: Lance.

St. Maurus: Scales, spade, crutch.

St. Meinrad: Two ravens.

St. Michael: Scales, banner, sword, dragon.

St. Monica: Girdle, tears.

St. Nicholas: Three purses or balls, anchor or boat, child.

St. Patrick: Cross, harp, serpent, baptismal font, demons, shamrock.

St. Paul: Sword, book or scroll.

St. Peter: Keys, boat, cock.

St. Philip, Apostle: Column.

St. Philip Neri: Altar, chasuble, vial.

St. Roch: Angel, dog, bread.

St. Rose of Lima: Crown of thorns, anchor, city.

St. Sebastian: Arrows, crown.

Sts. Sergius and Bacchus: Military garb, palm.

St. Simon: Saw, cross.

St. Simon Stock: Scapular.

St. Teresa of Avila: Heart, arrow, book.

St. Therese of Lisieux: Roses entwining a crucifix.

St. Thomas, Apostle: Lance, ax.

St. Thomas Aquinas: Chalice, monstrance, dove, ox, person trampled under foot.

St. Vincent: Gridiron, boat.

St. Vincent de Paul: Children.

St. Vincent Ferrer: Pulpit, cardinal's hat, trumpet, captives.

THE MOTHER OF JESUS IN CATHOLIC UNDERSTANDING

(This article was written for the Catholic Almanac by the Rev. Eamon R. Carroll, O. Carm., professor in the School of Sacred Theology, Catholic University of America.)

Current Catholic understanding about the Virgin Mary, Mother of Jesus, is based on the place the Second Vatican Council gave to the mystery of Mary. The key statements are found in the *Constitution on the Sacred Liturgy* and in the final chapter of the *Dogmatic Constitution on the Church.*

Considering the liturgy and the way in which the Church unfolds the whole mystery of Christ's life in the course of a year — so that the events of redemption are "in some way made present at all times" — the council said: "In celebrating this annual cycle of Christ's mysteries, holy Church honors with special love the Blessed Mary, Mother of God, who is joined by an inseparable bond to the saving work of her Son. In Mary the Church holds up and admires the most excellent fruit of the redemption; in Mary the

Church joyfully contemplates, as in a spotless model, that which the Church herself wholly desires and aspires to be" (*Constitution on the Sacred Liturgy*, No. 103).

In linking respect for Mary to the liturgical celebration of the mystery of Christ in the Church, the council joined doctrine and devotion. The *Dogmatic Constitution on the Church* took a similar approach, with a follow-through from the place of Mary in the communion of saints in the seventh chapter to treatment in the eighth chapter of "The Blessed Virgin Mary, Mother of God, in the Mystery of Christ and the Church." The seventh chapter recalls Mary's place with the risen Christ, as in the eucharistic prayer: "In union with the whole Church we honor Mary, the ever-virgin Mother of Jesus Christ our Lord and God." The eighth chapter opens and closes with the same liturgical theme, on Mary's place among God's friends, and appeals also to the Church, "knowing Mary's role by experience" (*Ibid.*, No. 52) and "contemplating Mary's hidden holiness" *(Ibid., No. 64)*, in support of "the singular cult of Mary that has always existed in the Church" *(Ibid., No. 66)*.

Mary in the Bible

Recent studies by Protestants and Catholics have traced in the Bible a theological portrait of the Mother of Jesus which emphasizes her faith-commitment to God's will and her Son's saving work. Differences in Catholic and Protestant interpretations of the sense in which Mary is joined to the saving work of Jesus underlie different views regarding Mary as a type of the Church.

Not only the stories of the birth and childhood of Jesus in Matthew and Luke but also John's Gospel illustrate the meaning of Mary with respect to Christ and to the Church. In her "pilgrimage of faith," her earthly association with Jesus "even to the cross," Mary was "a type of the Church — in the order of faith, charity and perfect union with Christ" *(Dogmatic Constitution on the Church, Nos. 58, 63)*.

The opening chapters of Matthew and Luke are complex reflections on Jesus as Messiah and Redeemer, permeated with the sense of fulfillment of the Old Testament. When the Evangelists composed the Gospels, they worked backwards, beginning with the death and resurrection, then taking up the public life, beginning with Jesus' baptism by John the Baptist, and finally adding the stories of his infancy and childhood — the better to bring out the meaning of the Redeemer's mission. The light of the Easter faith shines with particular strength on these opening chapters, the last to be written down.

In harmony with the Gospel sense of fulfillment, the council referred to Mary as "the exalted daughter of Zion in whom the times are fulfilled, after the long waiting for the promise, and the new economy inaugurated when the Son of God takes on human nature from her in order to free men from sin by the mysteries of His flesh" *(Dogmatic Constitution on the Church, No. 55)*. Daughter of Zion in the Old Testament meant the people of Israel. Daughter of her people, Mary of Nazareth fulfills all the longings of Israel for the coming of the Messiah. "She stands out among the Lord's lowly and poor who confidently look for salvation from Him and receive it" *(Ibid., No. 55)*.

Virgin Birth of Christ

Matthew and Luke state the fact of the "virgin birth," that Mary conceived Jesus without a human father — a truth that has formed part of the faith from the earliest creeds to the present teaching and preaching of the Church, in East and West alike.

In her religious and cultural world, it is not likely Mary had previously resolved to remain a virgin; the Old Testament regarded being unmarried as a calamity and childlessness as a disgrace. Mary's question, "How shall this be because I know not man" (Lk. 1:34), is regarded as the inspired reflection of the early Church on the virginal conception of Jesus, comparable to Matthew's account of Joseph's dream-vision (Mt. 1:20). Mary and Joseph accepted as God's will the virginal conception, an unprecedented event that put them both totally at the service of Jesus.

The Gospel offers a comparison between the faith of Abraham — whose son, Isaac, was born of the aged Sara — and Mary's faith in God's power to bring forth the Messiah from her virginal womb. God accomplishes salvation independently of the will of the flesh and of the will of man (Jn. 1:13), though not without a free and loving, if certainly wondering too, acceptance by the humble handmaid of the Lord. God shows his favor when and as he chooses, whether in the barren Sara or in the Virgin Mary, "because nothing shall be impossible with God" (Lk. 1:37 and Gn. 18:14). Jews and Christians honor Abraham as "our father in faith." On Gospel evidence, Mary is "mother in faith, mother of believers."

Mary at Cana and Calvary

John's Gospel pictures Mary at Cana and Calvary, the beginning and end of her Son's public life. In both incidents Jesus addresses her as "woman"; both scenes refer to the "hour" of Jesus' glorification at his death.

Mary's presence at Cana has deeper overtones than her sensitivity to the need for more wine. Jesus' reply to his Mother is an invitation to deepen her faith, to look beyond the failing wine to his messianic career about to begin. The change of water into wine symbolizes the benefits the Savior brings; the marriage feast looks to the "hour" in which the Bridegroom, Christ, will lay down his life in love for his Bride, the Church. Mary is present as the "daughter of Zion" greeting the messianic Bridegroom; she is model of the Church, new People of God, spotless Bride of Christ.

On Calvary Mary stands "by the cross of Jesus," and John records the words of the dying Jesus as he sees her there together with the beloved disciple: "Woman, behold your son. . . . Behold your mother" (Jn. 19:26-27). It is certain that more is meant here than simply our Lord's providing for his Mother's care. The word, "woman," finds an explanation in the Savior's farewell discourse at the Last Supper. To strengthen his followers, Jesus recalled an example from the Bible: "A woman about to give birth has sorrow because her hour has come. But when she has brought forth the child, she no longer remembers the anguish for her joy that a man is born into the world" (Jn. 16:21). Israel's longing for the messianic age was sometimes compared to labor pains. The daughter of Zion had been promised a progeny that would include all races, all nations. The words of Jesus announce the fulfillment of that promise, for Mary on Calvary symbolizes the "woman" who is mother Church, new Israel, new People of God, mother of all, Jew and Gentile.

About Mary's later life, the Scriptures are silent. The last time she appears is in the Acts of the Apostles, at the heart of the band of Apostles praying for the coming of the Holy Spirit at Pentecost. At the overshadowing of the Spirit at the Annunciation, Mary awaited the birth of Jesus; now she awaits again the coming of the Spirit and the birth of Jesus in His Church. (*Dogmatic Constitution on the Church*, No. 59; *Decree on the Missionary Activity of the Church*, No. 4)

Understanding and Veneration

The process of understanding the mystery of Mary that began in Gospel times has continued in the Church. This is true also of Christian veneration for the Mother of Jesus, shown already in the words of the Magnificat — "All generations shall call me blessed," (Lk. 1:48) — and in the incident from Jesus' public life when the praise of an enthusiastic woman from the crowd is repeated on a deeper level by Jesus himself, "Still happier those who hear the word of God and keep it" (Lk. 11:28). For Luke, no one heard the word of God more perfectly than the Mother of Jesus, as in Elizabeth's praise of Mary's faith: "Of all women you are the most blessed . . . blessed is she who believed that the promise made her by the Lord would be fulfilled" (Lk. 1:42- 45).

The New Eve

The oldest title for Mary after the Gospel is "new Eve." Christian authors as early as the mid-second century compared Mary, the obedient virgin who heard the angel's word, to the first Eve, who heeded the evil angel and disobeyed God. The axiom, "Death through Eve, life through Mary," was coined by the time of St. Jerome.

By the fourth century, Christians were holding that Mary remained a virgin all her life. The Gospels speak of "brethren" of Jesus, but leave their identity undecided — whether they were blood brothers and sisters or cousins. Christian experience of the faith solved the question not by scientific study of the Scriptures but by a contemplative awareness that Mary's commitment to Jesus was lifelong in this virginal sense also.

What is at stake here is an early example of "development of doctrine," and Protestant and Catholic positions still differ strongly on the legitimacy of such a "traditional" interpretation, where the Scriptures are not clear or are even silent.

Two other Roman Catholic beliefs about Mary encounter the same Protestant objection of the seeming silence of the Scriptures: the Immaculate Conception (Mary's freedom from original sin) and the Assumption (Mary's being one with the risen Christ in the fullness of her being, body as well as soul). Both doctrines have been solemnly proclaimed as revealed truth in dogmatic definitions, by Pius IX in 1854 and by Pius XII in 1950.

Mother of God

In early Christian times it was usually the need to defend the mystery of Jesus Christ and of Christian life that called forth from the Church clarifications about the Mother of Jesus. In the fourth century the Christian sense of Mary as model of a life of consecrated virginity led to the understanding that she remained always a virgin. At Ephesus in 431, the third ecumenical council defined the title, "Bearer of God" *(Theotokos)* as revealed truth, precisely to defend the truth that the Son of Mary is actually the Son of God, for Jesus is the God-man. To this day, "Mother of God" remains a title that protects the central truth of the Incarnation, even though some Western Christians find difficulty in the popular use of "Mother of God" for Mary in Catholic and Eastern Orthodox traditions. They fear the conciliar title is not well understood by many who use it, that sometimes it is almost pagan in meaning.

Mother in Order of Grace

As Christianity developed, people turned to Mary as a model of holy response to Christ, as the perfect believer in Jesus. The sense of communion between Mary in heaven and the brethren of her Son on earth grew stronger also. This is what is meant by the "intercession of Mary in the communion of saints" — a mysterious bond between those who are already with the risen Christ and their earthly brothers and sisters still on pilgrimage. Mary's association with Jesus on earth continues now with the risen Lord in a further stage beyond the limitations of the present world. As early as St. Augustine (d. 430), Mary was regarded as the "Mother of the members of Christ" — that is, the members of his Body, which is the Church; for, more than anyone else, she cooperated by her love and faith in the birth of the faithful in the Church, fulfilling the advice of Jesus, "Anyone who does the will of God, that person is my brother and sister and mother" (Mk. 3:35).

In this sense Mary has become "our Mother in the order of grace" *(Dogmatic Constitution on the Church*, No. 61), with a maternity not limited to her life of faith and union with Jesus on earth, but with a "saving role" that continues even "to the eternal ful-

fillment of the elect" (*Ibid.,* No. 62). "Inseparably joined to the saving work of Christ," is
the way the *Constitution on the Sacred Liturgy*
states this. What Catholics call Mary's "mediation of grace" is her continuing involvement in God's saving plan.

Early Christian authors, like St. Ambrose
in the fourth century, expressed the view that
Mary was a model to the Church, that her virginal maternity was reflected in the Church's
spiritual maternity of the brethren of Christ.
In the Middle Ages the likenesses between
Mary and the Church were further explored.
As the French Cistercian, Blessed Guerric of
Igney (d. 1157), put it: "Like the Church of
which she is a figure, Mary is Mother of all
those who are born to life." Medieval devotion shifted the emphasis from admiration of
the holiness of the Mother of God to confidence in her role as all-powerful intercessor,
Queen and Mother. Doctrine and devotion to
Mary were in accord with the strong sense of
community between the Church on earth and
the Church triumphant in heaven.

At times devotion to Mary and other saints
took bizarre forms, and there were many
abuses. When the Reformation took place,
calling upon the saints, even St. Mary, for
help was rejected by the Reformers as taking
away from the unique mediatorship of Christ.
Ever since that time, Christians of the West
have differed in their understanding of this
aspect of the communion of saints.

Ecumenical Considerations

The dogmas of the Immaculate Conception
and the Assumption, which remain formida-
ble ecumenical difficulties, are now viewed
less as "special privileges," personal and private to Mary, than as saving events that happened to her for the sake of Christ and his
Church.

Mary was the child of two human parents,
but kept free from original sin. This initial holiness, called the Immaculate Conception,
was entirely God's gift to her and is a sign of
the love Christ has for his Bride, the Church,
which — even though composed of sinners —
is "holy Church."

Mary's Assumption means that she is one
with the risen Christ in body and soul, that is,
in the fullness of her personality. The meaning for the Church is that the Mother of Jesus
is "a sign of sure hope and comfort for the
pilgrim People of God," showing forth the

fullest meaning of being redeemed. Here
again Mary is the "spotless image" of the
Church responding in joy to the invitation of
Christ, himself the "first-fruits from the
dead" and the glorious Bridegroom inviting
his Church to join him at the Father's right
hand. The Church has answered her Lord's
invitation in one of her daughters — Mary assumed into heaven — who is "the image and
beginning of the Church as she is to be perfected in the world to come" (*Dogmatic Constitution on the Church,* No. 68).

Approach of Vatican II

The Second Vatican Council was highly
sensitive to the views and feelings of other
Christians when it spoke about the Mother of
Jesus. Only once, for example, did it use the
difficult term, "Mediatrix," which it explained as strengthening, rather than lessening confidence in Christ, the one Mediator.
More significantly, its biblical approach to
Mary, with a strong accent on her pilgrimage
of faith, is in accord with the pattern of Protestant theology.

Catholics and Protestants, in spite of a
common faith in the Trinity and in Christ, are
still divided about several main doctrinal
issues. In connection with them, the council
noted the necessity of remembering "that in
Catholic teaching there exists an order or 'hierarchy,' of truths, since they vary in their
relationship to the foundation of the Christian faith." (*Decree on Ecumenism,* No. 11).
The council also listed these truths in this
order: the meaning of redemption, the mystery and ministry of the Church, and the role
of Mary in the work of salvation (*Ibid.,* No.
20).

Present indications are that the mystery of
Mary in the setting of the larger mystery of
Christ and the Church will occupy increasing
attention from Catholics, Protestants and Orthodox listening to one another in the Spirit
of Jesus — the same Spirit who inspired
Mary's prophecy: "All generations shall call
me blessed, because he who is mighty has
done great things for me" (Lk. 1:48-49).

Bishops' Pastoral Letter

The foregoing article by Father Eamon
Carroll, O.Carm., was a primary nucleus of
the pastoral letter, "Behold Your Mother,
Woman of Faith," published by the National
Conference of Catholic Bishops in 1973.

APPARITIONS OF THE BLESSED VIRGIN MARY

Only eight of the best known apparitions of
the Blessed Virgin Mary are described briefly
below.

The sites of the following apparitions have
become shrines and centers of pilgrimage.
Miracles of the moral and physical orders
have been reported as occurring at these
places and/or in connection with related
practices of prayer and penance.

Banneux, near Liege, Belgium: Mary appeared eight times between Jan. 15 and Mar.
2, 1933, to an 11-year-old peasant girl,
Mariette Beco, in a garden behind the family
cottage in Banneux, near Liege. She called
herself the Virgin of the Poor, and has since
been venerated as Our Lady of the Poor, the
Sick, and the Indifferent. A small chapel was
built by a spring near the site of the appari-

tions and was blessed Aug. 15, 1933. Approval of devotion to Our Lady of Banneux was given in 1949 by Bishop Louis J. Kerkhofs of Liege, and a statue of that title was solemnly crowned in 1956.

Over 100 sanctuaries are dedicated to the honor of Our Lady of Banneux.

The **International Union of Prayer,** for devotion to the Virgin of the Poor, has approximately two million members.

Beauraing, Belgium: Mary appeared 33 times between Nov. 29, 1932, and Jan. 3, 1933, to five children in the garden of a convent school in Beauraing. A chapel, which became a pilgrimage center, was erected on the spot. Reserved approval of devotion to Our Lady of Beauraing was given Feb. 2, 1943, and final approbation July 2, 1949, by Bishop Charue of Namur.

The **Marian Union of Beauraing,** a prayer association for the conversion of sinners, has thousands of members throughout the world (see Pro Maria Committee).

Fatima, Portugal: Mary appeared six times between May 13 and Oct. 13, 1917, to three children in a field called Cova da Iria near Fatima, north of Lisbon. She recommended frequent recitation of the Rosary; urged works of mortification for the conversion of sinners; called for devotion to herself under the title of her Immaculate Heart; asked that the people of Russia be consecrated to her under this title, and that the faithful make a Communion of reparation on the first Saturday of each month.

The apparitions were declared worthy of belief in October, 1930, after a seven-year canonical investigation, and devotion to Our Lady of Fatima was authorized under the title of Our Lady of the Rosary. In October, 1942, Pius XII consecrated the world to Mary under the title of her Immaculate Heart. Ten years later, in the first apostolic letter addressed directly to the peoples of Russia, he consecrated them in a special manner to Mary.

(See First Saturday Devotion.)

Guadalupe, Mexico: Mary appeared four times in 1531 to an Indian, Juan Diego, on Tepeyac hill outside of Mexico City, and instructed him to tell Bishop Zumarraga of her wish that a church be built there. The bishop complied with the request about two years later after being convinced of the genuineness of the apparition by the evidence of a miraculously painted life-size figure of the Virgin on the mantle of the Indian. The mantle bearing the picture has been preserved and is enshrined in the Basilica of Our Lady of Guadalupe, which has a long history as a center of devotion and pilgrimage in Mexico. The shrine church, originally dedicated in 1709 and subsequently enlarged, has the title of basilica.

Benedict XIV, in a decree issued in 1754, authorized a Mass and Office under the title of Our Lady of Guadalupe for celebration on Dec. 12, and named Mary the patroness of New Spain. Our Lady of Guadalupe was designated patroness of Latin America by St. Pius X in 1910 and patroness of the Americas by Pius XII in 1945.

Knock, Ireland: An apparition of Mary, along with the figures of St. Joseph and St. John the Apostle, was witnessed by at least 15 persons in the evening of Aug. 21, 1879, near the parish church of Knock, County Mayo. A commission appointed by the Bishop of Tuam to investigate the matter reported that testimony confirming the apparition was "trustworthy and satisfactory."

La Salette, France: Mary appeared as a sorrowing and weeping figure Sept. 19, 1846, to two peasant children, Melanie Matthieu, 15, and Maximin Giraud, 11, at La Salette in southern France. The message she confided to them, regarding the necessity of penance, was communicated to Pius IX in 1851 and has since been known at the "secret" of La Salette. Bishop de Bruillard of Grenoble declared in 1851 that the apparition was credible, and devotion to Mary under the title of Our Lady of La Salette was authorized. The devotion has been confirmed by popes since the time of Pius IX, and a Mass and Office with this title were authorized in 1942. The shrine church was given the title of minor basilica in 1879.

Lourdes, France: Mary, identifying herself as the Immaculate Conception, appeared 18 times between Feb. 11 and July 16, 1858, to 14-year-old Bernadette Soubirous at the grotto of Massabielle near Lourdes in southern France. Her message concerned the necessity of prayer and penance for the conversion of men. Mary's request that a chapel be built at the grotto and spring was fulfilled in 1862 after four years of rigid examination established the credibility of the apparitions. Devotion under the title of Our Lady of Lourdes was authorized later, and a Feb. 11 feast commemorating the apparitions was instituted by Leo XIII. St. Pius X extended this feast throughout the Church in 1907.

The Church of Notre Dame was made a basilica in 1870, and the Church of the Rosary was built later. The underground Church of St. Pius X, consecrated Mar. 25, 1958, is the second largest church in the world, with a capacity of 20,000 persons.

Our Lady of the Miraculous Medal, France: Mary appeared three times in 1830 to Catherine Laboure in the chapel of the motherhouse of the Daughters of Charity of St. Vincent de Paul, Rue de Bac, Paris. She commissioned Catherine to have made the medal of the Immaculate Conception, now known as the Miraculous Medal, and to spread devotion to her under this title. In 1832, the medal was struck according to the model revealed to Catherine.

Eastern Catholic Churches

The Eastern Catholic Churches are those which are organized under the major patriarchates of Alexandria, Antioch and Jerusalem (Constantinople, formerly), and the minor patriarchates of Babylon (Iraq) and Cilicia (Turkey).

Origin

The Church had its beginnings in Palestine, whence it spread to other regions of the world. As it spread, certain cities or jurisdictions became key centers of Christian life and missionary endeavor—notably, Jerusalem, Alexandria, Antioch and Constantinople in the East, and Rome in the West — with the result that their practices became diffused throughout their spheres of influence. Various rites originated from these practices which, although rooted in the essentials of Christian faith, were different in significant respects because of their relationships to particular cultural patterns.

Patriarchal Jurisdictions

The main lines of Eastern Church organization and liturgy were drawn before the Roman Empire was separated into Eastern and Western divisions in 292. It was originally co-extensive with the boundaries of the Eastern Empire. Its jurisdictions were those of the patriarchates of Alexandria and Antioch (recognized as such by the Council of Nicaea in 325), and of Jerusalem and Constantinople (given similar recognition by the Council of Chalcedon in 451). These were the major parent bodies of the Eastern Rite Churches which for centuries were identifiable only with limited numbers of nationality and language groups in Eastern Europe, the Middle East and parts of Asia and Africa. Their members are now scattered throughout the world.

Vatican II Decree

The Second Vatican Council, in its *Decree on Eastern Catholic Churches,* stated the following points.

"That Church, Holy and Catholic, which is the Mystical Body of Christ, is made up of the faithful who are organically united in the Holy Spirit through the same faith, the same sacraments, and the same government and who, combining into various groups held together by a hierarchy, form separate Churches or rites. . . . It is the mind of the Catholic Church that each individual Church or rite retain its traditions whole and entire, while adjusting its way of life to the various needs of time and place" (No. 2).

"Such individual Churches, whether of the East or of the West, although they differ somewhat among themselves in what are called rites (that is, in liturgy, ecclesiastical discipline, and spiritual heritage) are, nevertheless, equally entrusted to the pastoral guidance of the Roman Pontiff, the divinely appointed successor of St. Peter in supreme government over the universal Church. They are consequently of equal dignity, so that none of them is superior to the others by reason of rite" (No. 3).

Eastern Heritage: "Each and every Catholic, as also the baptized . . . of every non-Catholic Church or community who enters into the fullness of Catholic communion, should everywhere retain his proper rite, cherish it, and observe it to the best of his ability . . ." (No. 4).

". . . The Churches of the East, as much as those of the West, fully enjoy the right, and are in duty bound, to rule themselves. Each should do so according to its proper and individual procedures . . ." (No. 5).

"All Eastern rite members should know and be convinced that they can and should always preserve their lawful liturgical rites and their established way of life, and that these should not be altered except by way of an appropriate and organic development . . ." (No. 6)

Patriarchs: "The institution of the patriarchate has existed in the Church from the earliest times and was recognized by the first ecumenical Synods.

"By the name Eastern Patriarch is meant the bishop who has jurisdiction over all bishops (including metropolitans), clergy, and people of his own territory or rite, in accordance with the norms of law and without prejudice to the primacy of the Roman Pontiff . . ." (No. 7).

"Though some of the patriarchates of the Eastern Churches are of later origin than others, all are equal in patriarchal dignity. Still the honorary and lawfully established order of precedence among them is to be preserved" (No. 8).

"In keeping with the most ancient tradition of the Church, the Patriarchs of the Eastern Churches are to be accorded exceptional respect, since each presides over his patriarchate as father and head.

"This sacred Synod, therefore, decrees that their rights and privileges should be re-established in accord with the ancient traditions of each Church and the decrees of the ecumenical Synods.

"The rights and privileges in question are those which flourished when East and West were in union, though they should be somewhat adapted to modern conditions.

"The Patriarchs with their synods constitute the superior authority for all affairs of the patriarchate, including the right to establish new eparchies and to nominate bishops of their rite within the territorial bounds of the patriarchate, without prejudice to the inalienable right of the Roman Pontiff to intervene in individual cases" (No. 9).

"What has been said of Patriarchs applies as well, under the norm of law, to major archbishops, who preside over the whole of some individual Church or rite" (No. 10).

Sacraments: "This sacred Ecumenical Synod endorses and lauds the ancient discipline of the sacraments existing in the Eastern Churches, as also the practices connected with their celebration and administration . . ." (No. 12).

"With respect to the minister of holy chrism (confirmation), let that practice be fully restored which existed among Easterners in most ancient times. Priests, therefore, can validly confer this sacrament, provided they use chrism blessed by a Patriarch or bishop" (No. 13).

"In conjunction with baptism or otherwise, all Eastern-Rite priests can confer this sacrament validly on all the faithful of any rite, including the Latin; licitly, however, only if the regulations of both common and particular law are observed. Priests of the Latin rite, to the extent of the faculties they enjoy for administering this sacrament, can confer it also on the faithful of Eastern Churches, without prejudice to rite. They do so licitly if the regulations of both common and particular law are observed" (No. 14).

"The faithful are bound on Sundays and feast days to attend the divine liturgy or, according to the regulations or custom of their own rite, the celebration of the Divine Praises. That the faithful may be able to satisfy their obligation more easily, it is decreed that this obligation can be fulfilled from the Vespers of the vigil to the end of the Sunday or the feast day . . ." (No. 15).

"Because of the everyday intermingling of the communicants of diverse Eastern Churches in the same Eastern region or territory, the faculty for hearing confession, duly and unrestrictedly granted by his proper bishop to a priest of any rite, is applicable to the entire territory of the grantor, also to the places and the faithful belonging to any other rite in the same territory, unless an Ordinary of the place explicitly decides otherwise with respect to the places pertaining to his rite" (No. 16).

". . . This sacred Synod ardently desires that where it has fallen into disuse the office of the permanent diaconate be restored. The legislative authority of each individual church should decide about the subdiaconate and the minor orders . . ." (No. 17).

"By way of preventing invalid marriages between Eastern Catholics and baptized Eastern non-Catholics, and in the interests of the permanence and sanctity of marriage and of domestic harmony, this sacred Synod decrees that the canonical 'form' for the celebration of such marriages obliges only for lawfulness. For their validity, the presence of a sacred minister suffices, as long as the other requirements of law are honored" (No. 18).

Worship: "Henceforth, it will be the exclusive right of an ecumenical Synod or the Apostolic See to establish, transfer, or suppress feast days common to all the Eastern Churches. To establish, transfer, or suppress feast days for any of the individual Churches is within the competence not only of the Apostolic See but also of a patriarchal or archiepiscopal synod, provided due consideration is given to the entire region and to other individual Churches" (No. 19).

"Until such time as all Christians desirably concur on a fixed day for the celebration of Easter, and with a view meantime to promoting unity among the Christians of a given area or nation, it is left to the Patriarchs or supreme authorities of a place to reach a unanimous agreement, after ascertaining the views of all concerned, on a single Sunday for the observance of Easter" (No. 20).

"With respect to rules concerning sacred seasons, individual faithful dwelling outside the area or territory of their own rite may conform completely to the established custom of the place where they live. When members of a family belong to different rites, they are all permitted to observe sacred seasons according to the rules of any one of these rites" (No. 21).

"From ancient times the Divine Praises have been held in high esteem among all Eastern Churches. Eastern clerics and religious should celebrate these Praises as the laws and customs of their own traditions require. To the extent they can, the faithful too should follow the example of their forbears by assisting devoutly at the Divine Praises" (No. 22).

RITES AND FAITHFUL OF EASTERN CHURCHES

(Principal source of statistics: *Annuario Pontificio*. The statistics are for Eastern-Rite jurisdictions only, and do not include Eastern-Rite Catholics under the jurisdiction of Roman-Rite bishops. Some of the figures reported are only approximate. Some of the jurisdictions listed may be inactive because of government suppression.)

The Byzantine, Alexandrian, Antiochene, Armenian and Chaldean are the five principal rites used in their entirety or in modified form by the various Eastern churches. The number of Eastern Catholics throughout the world is approximately 11 million.

Alexandrian Rite

Called the Liturgy of St. Mark, the Alexandrian Rite was modified by the Copts and Melkites, and contains elements of the Byzantine Rite of St. Basil and the liturgies of Sts. Mark, Cyril and Gregory of Nazianzen. The liturgy is substantially that of the Coptic

Church, which is divided into two branches — the Coptic or Egyptian, and the Ethiopian or Abyssinian.

The faithful of this rite are:

COPTS: Returned to Catholic unity about 1741; situated in Egypt, the Near East; liturgical languages are Coptic, Arabic. Jurisdictions (located in Egypt): patriarchate of Alexandria, three dioceses; 107,000.

ETHIOPIANS: Returned to Catholic unity in 1846: situated in Ethiopia, Eritrea, Jerusalem, Somalia; liturgical language is Geez. Jurisdictions (located in Ethiopia): one archdiocese, two dioceses; 90,735.

Antiochene Rite

This is the source of more derived rites than any of the other parent rites. Its origin can be traced to the Eighth Book of the *Apostolic Constitutions* and to the Liturgy of St. James of Jerusalem, which ultimately spread throughout the whole patriarchate and displaced older forms based on the *Apostolic Constitutions*.

The faithful of this rite are:

MALANKARESE: Returned to Catholic unity in 1930; situated in India; liturgical languages are Syrian, Malayalam. Jurisdictions (located in India): one archdiocese, one diocese; 202,602.

MARONITES: United to the Holy See since the time of their founder, St. Maron; have no counterparts among the separated Eastern Christians: situated throughout the world: liturgical languages are Syriac, Arabic. Jurisdictions (located in Lebanon, Cyprus, Egypt, Syria, US, Brazil, Australia): patriarchate of Antioch, one metropolitan, 13 archdioceses and dioceses, one apostolic administration; 1,188,622. Where no special jurisdictions exist, they are under jurisdiction of local Roman-Rite bishops.

SYRIANS: Returned to Catholic unity in 1781; situated in Asia, Africa, the Americas, Australia; liturgical languages are Syriac, Arabic. Jurisdictions (located in Lebanon, Iraq, Egypt, Syria and Turkey): patriarchate of Antioch, eight archdioceses and dioceses; 96,894.

Armenian Rite

Substantially, although using a different language, this is the Greek Liturgy of St. Basil; it is considered an older form of the Byzantine Rite, and incorporates some modifications from the Antiochene Rite.

The faithful of this rite are:

ARMENIANS, exclusively: Returned to Catholic unity during the time of the Crusades; situated in the Near East, Europe, Africa, the Americas, Australasia: liturgical language is Classical Armenian. Jurisdictions (located in Lebanon, Iran, Iraq, Egypt, Syria, Turkey, Poland, France, Greece, Rumania): patriarchate of Cilicia, 8 archdioceses and dioceses, one exarchate, two ordinariates; 375,540.

Byzantine Rite

Based on the Rite of St. James of Jerusalem and the churches of Antioch, and reformed by Sts. Basil and John Chrysostom, the Byzantine Rite is proper to the Church of Constantinople. (The city was called Byzantium before Constantine changed its name; the modern name is Istanbul.) It is now used by the majority of Eastern Catholics and by the Eastern Orthodox Church (which is not in union with Rome). It is, after the Roman, the most widely used rite.

The faithful of this rite are:

ALBANIANS: Returned to Catholic unity about 1628; situated in Albania; liturgical language is Albanian. Jurisdiction (located in Albania): one apostolic administration.

BULGARIANS: Returned to Catholic unity about 1861; situated in Bulgaria; liturgical language is Old Slavonic. Jurisdiction (located in Bulgaria): one apostolic exarchate.

BYELORUSSIANS, also known as WHITE RUSSIANS: Returned to Catholic unity in the 17th century; situated in Europe, the Americas, Australia; liturgical language is Old Slavonic. They have an apostolic visitor residing at Rome.

GEORGIANS: Returned to Catholic unity in 1861; situated in Georgia (Southern Russia), France; liturgical language is Georgian. They have an apostolic administrator.

GREEKS: Returned to Catholic unity in 1829; situated in Greece, Asia Minor, Europe; liturgical language is Greek. Jurisdictions (located in Greece and Turkey): two exarchates; 3,075.

HUNGARIANS: Descendants of Ruthenians who returned to Catholic unity in 1646; situated in Hungary, the rest of Europe, the Americas; liturgical languages are Greek, Hungarian, English. Jurisdictions (located in Hungary): one diocese and one exarchate; 267,924.

ITALO-ALBANIANS: Have never been separated from Rome; situated in Italy, Sicily, the Americas; liturgical languages are Greek, Italo-Albanian. Jurisdictions (located in Italy): two dioceses, one abbacy; 66,788.

MELKITES: Returned to Catholic unity during the time of the Crusades, but definitive reunion did not take place until early in the 18th century; situated in the Middle East, Asia, Africa, Europe, the Americas, Australia; liturgical languages are Greek, Arabic, English, Portuguese, Spanish. Jurisdictions (located in Syria, Lebanon, Jordan, Israel, US, Brazil): patriarchate of Antioch (also has jurisdiction over Melkites in Egypt, Sudan, Jerusalem and Iraq), 15 archdioceses and dioceses and one exarchate; approximately one million.

ROMANIANS: Returned to Catholic unity in 1697; situated in Rumania, the rest of Europe, the Americas; liturgical language is Modern Romanian. Jurisdictions (located in

Rumania): one archdiocese, four dioceses. They have an apostolic visitor in the US.

RUSSIANS: Returned to Catholic unity about 1905; situated in Europe, the Americas, Australia, China; liturgical language is Old Slavonic. Jurisdictions (located in Russia and China): two exarchates.

RUTHENIANS, or CARPATHO-RUSSIANS (Rusins): Returned to Catholic unity in the Union of Brest-Litovek, 1596, and the Union of Uzhorod, Apr. 24, 1646; situated in Hungary, Czechoslovakia, elsewhere in Europe, the Americas, Australia; liturgical languages are Old Slavonic, English. Jurisdictions (located in Russia and the US): one archdiocese, three dioceses.

SLOVAKS: Jurisdiction (located in Czechoslovakia): one diocese (also has jurisdiction over Ruthenians, Ukrainians and Hungarians of country).

UKRAINIANS, or GALICIAN RUTHENIANS: Returned to Catholic unity about 1595; situated in Europe, the Americas, Australasia; liturgical languages are Old Slavonic and Ukrainian. Jurisdictions (located in Russian Galicia, Poland, the US, Canada, England, Australia, Guam, France, Brazil, Argentina): three archdioceses, nine dioceses, six apostolic exarchates; 4,305,985 (some figures date from 1943).

YUGOSLAVS, SERBS and CROATIANS: Returned to Catholic unity in 1611; situated in Yugoslavia, the Americas; liturgical language is Old Slavonic. Jurisdiction (located in Yugoslavia): one diocese (which also has jurisdiction over all Byzantine-Rite faithful in Yugoslavia); 51,250. They are under the jurisdiction of Ruthenian bishops elsewhere.

Chaldean Rite

This rite, listed as separate and distinct by the Sacred Congregation for the Oriental Churches, was derived from the Antiochene Rite.

The faithful of this rite are:

CHALDEANS: Descendants of the Nestorians, returned to Catholic unity in 1692; situated throughout the Middle East, in Europe, Africa, the Americas; liturgical languages are Syriac, Arabic. Jurisdictions (located in Iraq, Iran, Lebanon, Syria, Turkey): patriarchate of Babylonia, 18 archdioceses and dioceses; 289,304. There are patriarchal vicars for Jordan and Egypt.

SYRO-MALABARESE: Descended from the St. Thomas Christians of India; situated mostly in the Malabar region of India; they use a Westernized and Latinized form of the Chaldean Rite in Syriac and Malayalam. Jurisdictions (located in India): two archdioceses, six dioceses, six exarchates; 2,058,907.

St. Thomas Christians are so called because they belong to the local church originally formed by the Apostle.

EASTERN JURISDICTIONS

For centuries Eastern-Rite Catholics were identifiable with a limited number of nationality and language groups in certain countries of the Middle East, Eastern Europe, Asia and Africa. The persecution of religion in the Soviet Union since 1917 and in Iron Curtain countries since World War II, however — in addition to decimating and destroying the Church in those places—has resulted in the emigration of many Eastern-Rite Catholics from their homelands. This forced emigration, together with voluntary emigration, has led to the spread of Eastern Rites and their faithful to many other countries.

Europe

(Ukrainian faithful of the Byzantine Rite in Eastern Europe who have no bishop of their own have an apostolic visitor, Archbishop Miroslav Marusyn.)

ALBANIA: Byzantine Rite, apostolic administration.

AUSTRIA: Byzantine Rite, ordinariate.

BULGARIA: Byzantine Rite (Bulgarians), apostolic exarchate.

CZECHOSLOVAKIA: Byzantine Rite (Slovakians and other Byzantine-Rite Catholics), eparchy.

ENGLAND: Byzantine Rite (Ukrainians), apostolic exarchate.

FRANCE: Byzantine Rite (Ukrainians), apostolic exarchate.

Armenian Rite, apostolic exarchate.

Ordinariate for all other Eastern-Rite Catholics.

GERMANY: Byzantine Rite (Ukrainians), apostolic exarchate.

GREECE: Byzantine Rite, apostolic exarchate.

Armenian Rite, ordinariate.

HUNGARY: Byzantine Rite (Hungarians), eparchy, apostolic exarchate.

ITALY: Byzantine Rite (Italo-Albanians), two eparchies, one abbacy.

POLAND: Byzantine Rite, apostolic exarchate.

Armenian Rite, archeparchy.

RUMANIA: Byzantine Rite (Romanians), metropolitan, four eparchies.

Armenian Rite, ordinariate.

RUSSIA: Byzantine Rite (Russians), apostolic exarchate; (Ruthenians), eparchy; (Ukrainians), major archeparchy, two eparchies.

YUGOSLAVIA: Byzantine Rite (Yugoslav and other Byzantine-Rite Catholics), eparchy.

Asia

CHINA: Byzantine Rite (Russians), apostolic exarchate.

CYPRUS: Antiochene Rite (Maronites), archeparchy.

INDIA: Antiochene Rite (Malankarese), metropolitan see, eparchy.

Chaldean Rite (Syro-Malabarese), two metropolitan sees, six eparchies, six apostolic exarchates.

IRAN: Chaldean Rite (Chaldeans), two metropolitan sees, one archeparchy, one eparchy.

Armenian Rite, eparchy.

IRAQ: Antiochene Rite (Syrians), two archeparchies.

Byzantine Rite (Melkites), patriarchal vicar.

Chaldean Rite (Chaldeans), patriarchate, two metropolitan sees, eight archeparchies and eparchies.

Armenian Rite, archeparchy.

ISRAEL (includes Jerusalem): Antiochene Rite (Syrians), patriarchal vicar.

Byzantine Rite (Melkites), archeparchy, patriarchal vicar.

Chaldean Rite (Chaldeans), patriarchal vicar.

Armenian Rite, patriarchal vicar.

JORDAN: Byzantine Rite (Melkites), archeparchy.

LEBANON: Antiochene Rite (Maronites), patriarchate, one metropolitan see, six archeparchies and eparchies; (Syrians), patriarchate.

Byzantine Rite (Melkites), seven metropolitan and archeparchal sees.

Chaldean Rite (Chaldeans), eparchy.

Armenian Rite, patriarchal, eparchy.

SYRIAN ARAB REPUBLIC: Antiochene Rite (Maronites), one archeparchy, one eparchy, one apostolic administration; (Syrians), four archeparchies.

Byzantine Rite (Melkites), patriarchate, four metropolitan sees, one archeparchy.

Chaldean Rite (Chaldeans), eparchy.

Armenian Rite, archeparchy, eparchy, patriarchal vicariate.

TURKEY (Europe and Asia): Antiochene Rite (Syrians), patriarchal vicar.

Byzantine Rite, apostolic exarchate.

Chaldean Rite (Chaldeans), one archeparchy, one eparchy.

Armenian Rite, patriarchate (patriarch resides in Lebanon), archeparchy.

Oceania

AUSTRALIA: Byzantine Rite (Ukrainians), apostolic exarchate.

Antiochene Rite (Maronites), eparchy.

Africa

EGYPTIAN ARAB REPUBLIC: Alexandrian Rite (Copts), patriarchate, three eparchies.

Antiochene Rite (Maronites), eparchy; (Syrians), eparchy.

Byzantine Rite (Melkites), patriarchal vicar.

Chaldean Rite (Chaldeans), patriarchal vicar.

Armenian Rite, eparchy.

ETHIOPIA: Alexandrian Rite (Ethiopians), metropolitan see, two eparchies.

SUDAN: Byzantine Rite (Melkites), patriarchal vicar.

North America

CANADA: Byzantine Rite (Ukrainians), one metropolitan, four eparchies; (Slovaks), apostolic visitor.

UNITED STATES: Antiochene Rite (Maronites), eparchy.

Byzantine Rite (Ukrainians), one metropolitan see, two eparchies; (Ruthenians), one metropolitan see, two eparchies; (Melkites), apostolic exarchate; (Romanians), apostolic visitor.

Other Eastern-Rite Catholics are under the jurisdiction of local Roman-Rite bishops. (See Eastern-Rite Catholics in the United States.)

South America

ARGENTINA: Byzantine Rite (Ukrainians), apostolic exarchate.

Ordinariate for all other Eastern-Rite Catholics.

BRAZIL: Antiochene Rite (Maronites), eparchy.

Byzantine Rite (Melkites), eparchy; (Ukrainians), eparchy.

Ordinariate for all other Eastern-Rite Catholics.

SYNODS, ASSEMBLIES

These assemblies are collegial bodies which have pastoral authority over members of the Eastern Rite Churches.

Patriarchal Synods: Maronites: Cardinal Paul Pierre Meouchi, patriarch of Antioch of the Maronites.

Melkites: Maximos V Hakim, patriarch of Antioch of the Melkites.

Chaldeans: Paul II Cheikho, patriarch of Babylonia of the Chaldeans.

Copts: Cardinal Stephanos I Sidarouss, C.M., patriarch of Alexandria of the Copts.

Syrians: Ignace Antoine Hayek, patriarch of Antioch of the Syrians.

Armenians: Ignace Pierre XVI Batanian, patriarch of Cilicia of the Armenians.

Assemblies: Assembly of Ordinaries of the United Arab Republic: Cardinal Stephanos I Sidarouss, C.M., patriarch of Alexandria of the Copts.

Assembly of Catholic Patriarchs and Bishops of Lebanon: Cardinal Paul Pierre Meouchi, patriarch of Antioch of the Maronites.

Assembly of Ordinaries of the Syrian Arab Republic: Maximos V Hakim, patriarch of Antioch of the Melkites.

Conference of the Ukrainian Catholic Hierarchy (Feb. 9, 1962): Archbishop Maxim Hermaniuk, Winnipeg.

Malabarese Episcopal Conference: Cardinal Joseph Parecattil, Ernakulam.

Of the collegial bodies listed above, the patriarchal synods have the most authority. In addition to other prerogatives, they have the right to elect bishops and regulate discipline for their respective rites.

EASTERN RITES IN U.S.

(Statistics, from the *Official Catholic Directory, 1974*, are actual membership figures reported by Eastern-Rite jurisdictions. Additional Eastern-Rite Catholics are included in statistics for Roman-Rite dioceses.)

Byzantine Rite

Ukrainians: There are 167,300 in three jurisdictions in the US: the metropolitan see of Philadelphia (1924, metropolitan 1958) and the suffragan sees of Stamford, Conn. (1956), and St. Nicholas of Chicago (1961).

Ruthenians: There are approximately 278,000 in three jurisdictions in the US: the metropolitan see of Munhall (formerly Pittsburgh, est. 1924; metropolitan and transferred to Munhall, 1969) and the suffragan sees of Passaic, N.J. (1963), and Parma, Ohio (1969). Hungarian and Croatian Byzantine Catholics in the US are also under the jurisdiction of Ruthenian-Rite bishops.

Melkites: In 1974, 21,676 (of approximately 55,000) were reported under the jurisdiction of the exarchate established in 1965, with headquarters at Boston, Mass.

Romanians: There are approximately 5,000 in 18 Romanian Catholic Byzantine Rite parishes in the US, each under the jurisdiction of the Roman-Rite bishop of the territory in which it is located: Cleveland diocese (3 parishes), Detroit (2), Erie (2), Los Angeles (1), Gary (2), Pittsburgh (1), Rockford (2), Trenton (2), and Youngstown (3). No separate statistics are available. The Association of Romanian Catholics of America (see Index) was established in 1948 to preserve the identity of Romanian Catholics within the general framework of the Catholic Church in America. It has petitioned the Holy See for a bishop of the rite in the US. In 1972, the Holy See assigned Msgr. Octavian Barlea as an apostolic visitor to Romanians in the US.

Byelorussians: Have one parish in the US — Christ the Redeemer, Chicago, Ill. — and are under the jurisdiction of the local Roman-Rite bishop.

Russians: Have parishes in California (St. Andrew, El Segundo, and Our Lady of Fatima Center, San Francisco); Illinois (Annunciation Reunion Center, Chicago); Massachusetts (Our Lady of Kazan, Boston); New York (St. Michael's Chapel, Pope John XXIII Reunion Center); and Oregon (Our Lady of Tychvin Chapel, Portland). They are under the jurisdiction of local Roman-Rite bishops.

Antiochene Rite

In 1974, 65,541 (of approximately 153,000) Maronites were reported under the jurisdiction of the eparchy of St. Maron of Detroit (established as an exarchate, 1966; eparchy, 1972).

Armenian Rite

Have parishes in California (Queen of Martyrs, Los Angeles); Massachusetts (Holy Cross, Cambridge); Michigan (St. Vartan, Detroit); New Jersey (Sacred Heart, Paterson); New York (Armenian Catholic Community, 343 W. 25th St., New York, N.Y. 10001); and Pennsylvania (St. Mark, Philadelphia). They are the jurisdiction of local Roman-Rite bishops.

Chaldean Rite

Have parishes in California (St. Thomas the Apostle, Turlock); Illinois (St. Ephram, Chicago); and Michigan (Mother of God, Detroit). They are under the jurisdiction of local Roman-Rite bishops.

BYZANTINE DIVINE LITURGY

The Divine Liturgy in all rites is based on the consecration of bread and wine by the narration-reactualization of the actions of Christ at the Last Supper. Aside from this fundamental usage, there are differences between the Roman (Latin) Rite and Eastern Rites, and among the Eastern Rites themselves. Following is a general description of the Byzantine Divine Liturgy which is in widest use in the Eastern-Rite Churches.

In the Byzantine, as in all Eastern Rites, the bread and wine are prepared at the start of the Liturgy. The priest does this in a little niche or at a table in the sanctuary. Taking a round loaf of leavened bread stamped with religious symbols, he cuts out a square host and other particles while reciting verses expressing the symbolism of the action. When the bread and wine are ready, he says a prayer of offering and incenses the oblations, the altar, the icons and the people.

At the altar a litany for all classes of people is sung by the priest. The congregation answers, "Lord, have mercy."

The Little Entrance comes next. In procession, the priest leaves the sanctuary carrying the Book of the Gospels, and then returns. He sings prayers especially selected for the day and the feast. These are followed by the solemn singing of the prayer, "Holy God, Holy Mighty One, Holy Immortal One."

The Epistle follows. The Gospel is sung or read by the priest facing the people at the middle door of the sanctuary.

An interruption after the Liturgy of the Catechumens, formerly an instructional period for those learning the faith, is clearly marked. Catechumens, if present, are dismissed with a prayer. Following this are a prayer and litany for the faithful.

The Great Entrance or solemn Offertory

Procession then takes place. The priest first says a long silent prayer for himself, in preparation for the great act to come. Again he incenses the oblations, the altar, the icons and people. He goes to the table on the gospel side for the veil-covered paten and chalice. When he arrives back at the sanctuary door, he announces the intention of the Mass in the prayer: "May the Lord God remember all of you in his kingdom, now and forever."

After another litany, the congregation recites the Nicene Creed.

Consecration

The most solemn portion of the sacrifice is introduced by the preface, which is very much like the preface of the Roman Rite. At the beginning of the last phrase, the priest raises his voice to introduce the singing of the Sanctus. During the singing he reads the introduction to the words of consecration.

The words of consecration are sung aloud, and the people sing "Amen" to both consecrations. As the priest raises the Sacred Species in solemn offering, he sings: "Thine of Thine Own we offer unto Thee in behalf of all and for all."

A prayer to the Holy Spirit is followed by the commemorations, in which special mention is made of the all-holy, most blessed and glorious Lady, the Mother of God and ever-Virgin Mary. The dead are remembered and then the living.

A final litany for spiritual gifts precedes the Our Father. The Sacred Body and Blood are elevated with the words, "Holy Things for the Holy." The Host is then broken and commingled with the Precious Blood. The priest recites preparatory prayers for Holy Communion, consumes the Sacred Species, and distributes Holy Communion to the people under the forms of both bread and wine. During this time a communion verse is sung by the choir or congregation.

The Liturgy closes quickly after this. The consecrated Species of bread and wine are removed to the side table to be consumed later by the priest. A prayer of thanksgiving is recited, a prayer for all the people is said in front of the icon of Christ, a blessing is invoked upon all, and the people are dismissed.

VESTMENTS, APPURTENANCES

Sticharion: A long white garment of linen or silk with wide sleeves and decorated with embroidery; formerly the vestment for clerics in minor orders, acolytes, lectors, chanters, and subdeacons; symbolic of purity.

Epitrachelion: A stole with ends sewn together, having a loop through which the head is passed; its several crosses symbolize priestly duties.

Zone: A narrow clasped belt made of the same material as the epitrachelion; symbolic of the wisdom of the priest, his strength against enemies of the Church and his willingness to perform holy duties.

Epimanikia: Ornamental cuffs; the right cuff symbolizing strength, the left, patience and good will.

Phelonion: An ample cape, long in the back and sides and cut away in front; symbolic of the higher gifts of the Holy Spirit.

Antimension: A silk or linen cloth laid on the altar for the Liturgy; it may be decorated with a picture of the burial of Christ and the instruments of his passion; the relics of martyrs are sewn into the front border.

Eileton: A linen cloth which corresponds to the Roman-Rite corporal.

Poterion: A chalice or cup which holds the wine and Precious Blood.

Diskos: A shallow plate, which may be elevated on a small stand, corresponding to the Roman-Rite paten.

Asteriskos: Made of two curved bands of gold or silver which cross each other to form a double arch; a star depends from the junction, which forms a cross; it is placed over the diskos holding the consecrated bread and is covered with a veil.

Veils: Three are used, one to cover the poterion, the second to cover the diskos, and the third to cover both.

Spoon: Used in administering Holy Communion by intinction; consecrated leavened bread is dipped into consecrated wine and spooned onto the tongue of the communicant.

Lance: A metal knife used for cutting up the bread to be consecrated during the Liturgy.

BYZANTINE FEATURES

Art: Named for the empire in which it developed, Byzantine art is a unique blend of imperial Roman and classic Hellenic culture with Christian inspiration. The art of the Greek Middle Ages, it reached a peak of development in the 10th or 11th century. Characteristic of its products, particularly in mosaic and painting, are majesty, dignity, refinement and grace. Its sacred paintings, called icons, are reverenced highly in all Eastern Rites.

Church Building: The classical model of Byzantine church architecture is the Church of the Holy Wisdom (Hagia Sophia), built in Constantinople in the first half of the sixth century and still standing. The square structure, extended in some cases in the form of a cross, is topped by a distinctive onion-shaped dome and surmounted by a triple-bar cross. The altar is at the eastern end of building, where the wall bellies out to form an apse. The altar and sanctuary are separated from the body of the church by a fixed or movable screen, the iconostas, to which icons or sacred pictures are attached (see below).

Clergy: The Byzantine Rite has married as well as celibate priests. In places other than the US, where married candidates have not been accepted for ordination since about 1929, men already married can be ordained to the diaconate and priesthood and can continue in marriage after ordination. Celibate deacons and priests cannot marry after ordination; neither can a married priest remarry after the death of his wife. Bishops must be unmarried.

Iconostas: A large screen decorated with sacred pictures or icons which separates the sanctuary from the nave of a church; its equivalent in the Roman Rite, for thus separating the sanctuary from the nave, is an altar rail.

An iconostas has three doors through which the sacred ministers enter the sanctuary during the Divine Liturgy: smaller (north and south) Deacons' Doors and a large central Royal Door.

The Deacons' Doors usually feature the icons of Sts. Gabriel and Michael; the Royal Door, the icons of the Evangelists — Matthew, Mark, Luke and John. To the right and left of the Royal Door are the icons of Christ the Teacher and of the Blessed Virgin Mary with the Infant Jesus. To the extreme right and left are the icons of the patron of the church and St. John the Baptist (or St. Nicholas of Myra).

Immediately above the Royal Door is a picture of the Last Supper. To the right are six icons depicting the major feasts of Christ, and to the left are six icons portraying the major feasts of the Blessed Virgin Mary. Above the picture of the Last Supper is a large icon of Christ the King.

Some icon screens also have pictures of the 12 Apostles and the major Old Testament prophets surmounted by a crucifixion scene.

Liturgical Language: In line with Eastern tradition, Byzantine practice has favored the use of the language of the people in the liturgy. Two great advocates of the practice were Sts. Cyril and Methodius, apostles of the Slavs, who devised the Cyrillic alphabet and pioneered the adoption of Slavonic in the liturgy.

Sacraments: Baptism is administered by immersion, and confirmation is conferred at the same time. The Eucharist is administered by intinction, i.e., by giving the communicant a piece of consecrated leavened bread which has been dipped into the consecrated wine. When giving absolution in the sacrament of penance, the priest holds his stole over the head of the penitent. Distinctive marriage ceremonies include the crowning of the bride and groom. Ceremonies for anointing the sick closely resemble those of the Roman Rite. Holy orders are conferred by a bishop.

Sign of the Cross: Eastern-Rite Catholics have a distinctive way of making it (see entry in the Glossary). The sign of the cross in conjunction with a deep bow, instead of a genuflection, expresses reverence for the presence of Christ in the Blessed Sacrament.

EASTERN-RITE BRIEFS

Ukrainian Patriarchate

Members of the Society for the Promotion of a Patriarchal System in the Ukrainian Catholic Church continued during 1974 to press two demands on the Vatican:

• that Cardinal Josyf Slipyi be raised officially to the rank of patriarch;

• that an autonomous Ukrainian patriarchate (for the largest Eastern-Rite body) be established within the Church with the right to hold its own synods, nominate its own bishops, establish dioceses and administer its internal affairs, in union with the Holy See.

No action was taken by Pope Paul VI in response to these and other demands made by Ukrainians in the United States and Canada.

One reason against establishment of a patriarchate was fear that it might exacerbate the condition of several million Ukrainian Catholics in the Soviet Union. Additional members of the Church were in other countries where agitation for the patriarchate originated.

Two other reasons against a patriarchate were canonical — a patriarch would be prevented by the Soviet Union from complying with church law requiring the exercise of jurisdiction in his home territory, and historical — there never had been a Ukrainian patriarchate.

A supporting argument drawn from the Vatican II *Decree on Eastern Catholic Churches* — equating major archbishops like Cardinal Slipyi with patriarchs — was not strong enough for establishment of a patriarchate under existing conditions.

Developments in the controversy have included actions of the Society for the Promotion of a Patriarchal System for the Ukrainian Catholic Church since 1970, a 1971 letter of Pope Paul against establishment, and meetings of a non-canonical Ukrainian synod since 1971.

The society's choice for patriarch, 82-year-old Cardinal Slipyi, spent 18 years in Soviet prisons and labor camps before being released in 1963.

The society declared, in resolutions passed June 8, 1974, at a convention of 100 delegates in New York, that "the Ukrainian Catholic Church in its native territory is denied legal existence by laws imposed by an alien regime" (which forced its merger with the Russian Orthodox Church after World War II) and "remains undefended by those Vatican authorities who might be expected to provide it with paternal protection."

It was also declared that the existence of the Ukrainian Catholic Church outside the Soviet Union was "being systematically undermined by (Vatican) authorities who consistently attempt to deny its rights . . . limit the jurisdiction of its primate, and reduce its episcopate to virtually suffragan status within a Latin-Rite framework."

Dr. Myroslav Nawrickyj of Philadelphia is president of the society. The mailing address of the society is P.O. Box 11012, Philadelphia, Pa. 19141.

Ukrainian Appointments

It was announced July 2, 1974, that Pope Paul VI had established a new eparchy or diocese for Ukrainian-Rite Catholics at New Westminster, Canada, to be headed by Father Jerome Chimy of the Basilian Order of St. Josaphat, rector of the Ukrainian College in Rome.

Also announced were the appointments of Father Martin Greschuk to be auxiliary bishop of the Ukrainian-Rite Edmonton diocese, and of Msgr. Miroslav Marusyn to be apostolic visitor for Ukrainian Catholics in Western Europe.

Romanians Want Bishop

A resolution to petition the Vatican again for the establishment of an episcopate for Romanian Catholics in the United States was adopted by the 26th annual convention of the Association of Romanian Catholics of America, meeting June 27 to 30, 1974, in East Chicago, Ind. Such an establishment would replace the existing jurisdiction of Roman-Rite bishops over 5,000 Romanians in 18 parishes of nine dioceses.

Other resolutions adopted by the convention concerned the strengthening of existing parishes, the establishment of new ones where warranted, and efforts to attract and encourage young people to more active participation in church affairs.

One of the speakers at the convention was Msgr. Octavian Barlea, apostolic visitor and the highest ranking Romanian churchman in the country.

Patriarchal Electors

UNIREA, the publication of the Association of Romanian Catholics of America, reported in June, 1974, that a large majority of participants in a Melkite synod held in Lebanon several weeks earlier approved a suggestion by Pope Paul VI that all Eastern-Rite patriarchs take part in future papal elections.

Pope Paul, in explaining the suggestion, said: "We ask ourselves whether it would not be good to consider the opportuneness of using the assistance which they (the patriarchs) could give in the election of a Supreme Pontiff."

A strong minority at the synod opposed the suggestion. Their objections were based on the Roman character of the College of Cardinals and on their insistence that, although they were in communion with Rome, they were part of an "Eastern" rather than the "Roman" Church.

SEPARATED EASTERN CHURCHES

Orthodox

Orthodox Churches, the largest and most widespread of the separated Eastern Churches, have much in common with their Eastern Catholic counterparts, including many matters of faith and morals, general discipline, valid orders and sacraments, and liturgy. One important difference is their acceptance of only the first seven ecumenical councils. Another is their rejection of any single supreme head of the Church. They do not acknowledge and hold communion with the pope.

Like their Catholic counterparts, Orthodox Churches are organized in jurisdictions under patriarchs. The patriarchs are the heads of approximately 15 autocephalic and several other autonomous jurisdictions organized along lines of nationality and/or language.

The Ecumenical Patriarch of Constantinople, Dimitrios I, has the primacy of honor among his equal patriarchs but his actual jurisdiction is limited to his own patriarchate. As the spiritual head of worldwide Orthodoxy, he keeps the book of the Holy Canons of the Autocephalous Churches, in which recognized Orthodox Churches are registered, and has the right to call Pan-Orthodox assemblies.

The definitive Orthodox break with Rome dates from 1054.

Top-level relations between the Churches have improved in recent years through the efforts of former Ecumenical Patriarch Athenagoras I, John XXIII, Paul VI and Patriarch Dimitrios I. Pope Paul met with Athenagoras three times before the latter's death in 1972. The most significant action of both spiritual leaders was their mutual nullification of excommunications imposed by the two Churches on each other in 1054.

The largest Orthodox body in the western hemisphere is the Greek Orthodox Archdiocese of North and South America headed by Archbishop Iakovos, with an estimated membership of some 1.5 million. The second largest is the Orthodox Church of America, with approximately 850,000 members; it was given independent status by the Patriarchate of Moscow May 18, 1970, against the will of Athenagoras I who refused to register it in the book of the Holy Canons of Autocephalous Churches. An additional 650,000 or more Orthodox belong to smaller national and language jurisdictions.

Heads of Orthodox jurisdictions in this hemisphere hold membership in the Standing Conference of Canonical Orthodox Bishops in the Americas.

Jurisdictions

The principal jurisdictions of the Greek, Russian and other Orthodox Churches are as follows.

Greek: Patriarchate of Constantinople, with jurisdiction in Turkey, Crete, the Dodecanese, Western Europe, the Americas, Australia; Dimitrios I is Ecumenical Patriarch.

Patriarchate of Alexandria, with jurisdiction in Egypt and the rest of Africa; there is also a native African Orthodox Church in Kenya and Uganda.

Patriarchate of Antioch (Melkites or Syrian Orthodox), with jurisdiction in Syria, Lebanon, Iraq, Australasia, the Americas; Syrian or Arabic, in place of Greek, is the liturgical language.

Patriarchate of Jerusalem, with jurisdiction in Israel and Jordan.

Churches of Greece, Cyprus and Sinai are autocephalic but maintain relations with their fellow Orthodox.

Russian: Patriarchate of Moscow with jurisdiction centered in the Soviet Union.

Other: Patriarchate of Serbia, with jurisdiction in Yugoslavia, Western Europe, the Americas, Australasia.

Patriarchates of Rumania and Bulgaria.

Katholikate of Georgia, the Soviet Union.

Byelorussians and Ukrainian Byzantines.

Churches of Albania, China, Czechoslovakia, Estonia, Finland, Hungary, Japan, Latvia, Lithuania, Poland.

Other minor communities in various places; e.g., Korea, the US, Carpatho-Russia.

The Armenian Apostolic (Oriental Orthodox) Church in America, with US headquarters in Philadelphia, has 35 parishes in North America.

The Division of Archives and Statistics of the Eastern Orthodox World Foundation reported a 1970 estimate of more than 200 million Orthodox Church members throughout the world. Other sources estimate the total to be approximately 125 million.

Nestorians, Monophysites

Unlike the majority of Eastern Christian Churches, several bodies do not acknowledge all of the first seven ecumenical councils. Nestorians acknowledge only the first two councils; they do not accept the doctrinal definition of the Council of Ephesus concerning Mary as the Mother of God. Monophysite Armenians, Syrians, Copts, Ethiopians and Jacobites acknowledge only the first three councils; they do not accept the doctrinal definition of the Council of Chalcedon concerning the two natures in Christ.

The Armenian Church has communicants in the Soviet Union, the Middle and Far East, the Americas.

The Coptic Church has communicants in Egypt and elsewhere.

The Ethiopian or Abyssinian Church has communicants in Africa, the Middle East, the Americas, India.

The Jacobite Church (West Syrians) has communicants in the Middle East, the Americas, India.

Nestorians (Assyrians) are scattered throughout the world.

It is estimated that there are approximately 10 million or more members of these other Eastern Churches throughout the world. For various reasons, a more accurate determination is not possible.

Conference of Orthodox Bishops

The Standing Conference of Canonical Orthodox Bishops in the Americas was established in 1960 to achieve cooperation among the various ethnic churches. Officers of the conference are Archbishop Iakovos, primate of the Greek Orthodox Archdiocese of North and South America, chairman; Bishop John Martin of the Carpatho-Russian Orthodox Greek Catholic Church, vice-chairman; Bishop Andrei Kuschak of the Ukrainian Orthodox, treasurer; Father Robert G. Stephanopoulos, general secretary.

Member churches of the conference are the: Albanian Orthodox Diocese of America (Ecumenical Patriarchate), American Carpatho-Russian Greek Catholic Diocese, Antiochian Orthodox Christian Archdiocese of New York and All North America, Bulgarian Eastern Orthodox Church, Greek Orthodox Archdiocese of North and South America, Orthodox Church of America, Romanian Orthodox Missionary Episcopate in America, Serbian Orthodox Church in the United States of America and Canada, Ukrainian Orthodox Church of America (Ecumenical Patriarchate), Holy Ukrainian Autocephalic Orthodox Church in Exile.

Patriarchs: High-ranking patriarchs of separated Eastern Churches are Ecumenical Orthodox Patriarch Dimitrios I (Papadopoulos) of Constantinople (Istanbul) and Coptic Orthodox Patriarch Shenouda III (Nazeer Gayed) of Alexandria.

EASTERN ECUMENISM

The Second Vatican Council, in the *Decree on Eastern Catholic Churches,* pointed out the special role they have to play "in promoting the unity of all Christians, particularly Easterners." The document also stated in part:

"The Eastern Churches in communion with the Apostolic See of Rome have a special role to play in promoting the unity of all Christians, particularly Easterners, according to the principles of this sacred Synod's *Decree on Ecumenism* first of all by the example of their lives, then by religious fidelity to ancient Eastern traditions, by greater mutual knowledge, by collaboration, and by a brotherly regard for objects and attitudes" (No. 24).

"If any separated Eastern Christian should, under the guidance of grace of the Holy Spirit, join himself to Catholic unity, no more should be required of him than what a simple profession of the Catholic faith demands. A valid priesthood is preserved among Eastern clerics. Hence, upon joining themselves to the unity of the Catholic Church, Eastern clerics are permitted to exercise the orders they possess, in accordance with the regulations established by the competent authority" (No. 25).

"Divine Law forbids any common worship (*communicatio in sacris*) which would damage the unity of the Church, or involve formal acceptance of falsehood or the danger of deviation in the faith, of scandal, or of indifferentism. At the same time, pastoral experience clearly shows that with respect to our Eastern brethren there should and can be taken into consideration various circumstances affecting individuals, wherein the unity of the Church is not jeopardized nor are intolerable risks involved, but in which salvation itself and the spiritual profit of souls are urgently at issue.

"Hence, in view of special circumstances of time, place, and personage, the Catholic Church has often adopted and now adopts a milder policy, offering to all the means of salvation and an example of charity among Christians through participation in the sacraments and in other sacred functions and objects. With these considerations in mind, and 'lest because of the harshness of our judgment we prove an obstacle to those seeking salvation,' and in order to promote closer union with the Eastern Churches separated from us, this sacred Synod lays down the following policy:

"In view of the principles recalled above, Eastern Christians who are separated in good faith from the Catholic Church, if they ask of their own accord and have the right dispositions, may be granted the sacraments of penance, the Eucharist, and the anointing of the sick. Furthermore, Catholics may ask for these same sacraments from those non-Catholic ministers whose Churches possess valid sacraments, as often as necessity or a genuine spiritual benefit recommends such a course of action, and when access to a Catholic priest is physically or morally impossible" (Nos. 26, 27).

"Again, in view of these very same principles, Catholics may for a just cause join with their separated Eastern brethren in sacred functions, things, and places" (No. 28).

"This more lenient policy with regard to common worship involving Catholics and their brethren of the separated Eastern Churches is entrusted to the care and execution of the local Ordinaries so that, by taking counsel among themselves and, if circumstances warrant, after consultation also with the Ordinaries of the separated Churches, they may govern relations between Christians by timely and effective rules and regulations" (No. 29).

ECUMENICAL BRIEFS

Orthodox Guidelines: A 66-page document entitled "Guidelines for Orthodox Churches in Ecumenical Relations" was published in February, 1974, by the Standing Conference of Canonical Orthodox Bishops in the Americas. Among the subjects of guidelines were:

• Marriage: Normally marriage in the Orthodox Church "takes place only between members of that Church." There are, however, occasions in which an Orthodox priest may perform a "mixed marriage," under certain conditions. Clergy of other churches may give a blessing or exhort a couple, but do not actually "assist" or "participate" in the marriage service.

• Baptism: Orthodox Churches accept baptism in the name of the Trinity in another church if "proof of the fact of baptism" can be authenticated.

• Eucharist: "Holy Communion will not be sought by Orthodox Christians outside the Church, nor will it be offered to those who do not yet confess the Orthodox Church as their mother."

• Reciprocity: The "principle of reciprocity" governs preaching in ecumenical situations, meaning that Orthodox priests may preach in non-Orthodox churches and non-Orthodox may speak in Orthodox churches.

Dialogue with Copts: The first meeting of representatives of the Catholic Church and the Coptic Orthodox Church was held Mar. 26 to 30, 1974, in Cairo. The meeting resulted from an agreement reached by Pope Paul VI and Coptic Patriarch Shenouda III in May, 1973, that steps should be taken toward the goal of Christian unity. A joint communique issued after the meeting said:

"During its sessions the commission studied the progress made up to now by theological studies with the double aim of seeing if further steps can be made in understanding Christology and to determine which are the points requiring further clarification and deeper study . . .

"It is possible to take a step forward in presenting the daily faith of our two churches in Jesus Christ, the Son of God."

Orthodox Dialogue: Measuring the progress of Catholic-Orthodox relations was the objective of a week-long colloquium in the spring of 1974 between theologians from the Orthodox Ecumenical Patriarchate, the Vatican's Secretariat for Promoting Christian Unity, and the Pro Oriente Catholic Institute of Austria. A summary statement released at the end of the meeting said that "substantial progress has been made in the last several years." The tone of the statement was optimistic, but no one could predict the when, where and how of eventual union of the churches.

Protestant Churches

Men, Doctrines, Churches of the Reformation

Some of the leading figures, doctrines and churches of the Reformation are covered below. A companion article covers Major Protestant Churches in the United States.

John Wycliff (c. 1320-1384): English priest and scholar who advanced one of the leading Reformation ideas nearly 200 years before Martin Luther — that the Bible alone is the sufficient rule of faith — but had only an indirect influence on the 16th century Reformers. Supporting belief in an inward and practical religion, he denied the divinely commissioned authority of the pope and bishops of the Church; he also denied the Real Presence of Christ in the Holy Eucharist, and wrote against the sacrament of penance and the doctrine of indulgences. Nearly 20 of his propositions were condemned by Gregory XI in 1377; his writings were proscribed more extensively by the Council of Constance in 1415. His influence was strongest in Bohemia and Central Europe.

John Hus (c. 1369-1415): A Bohemian priest and preacher of reform who authored 30 propositions condemned by the Council of Constance. Excommunicated in 1411 or 1412, he was burned at the stake in 1415. His principal errors concerned the nature of the Church and the origin of papal authority. He spread some of the ideas of Wycliff but did not subscribe to his views regarding faith alone as the condition for justification and salvation, the sole sufficiency of Scripture as the rule of faith, the Real Presence of Christ in the Eucharist, and the sacramental system. In 1457 some of his followers founded the Church of the Brotherhood which later became known as the United Brethren or Moravian Church and is considered the earliest independent Protestant body.

Martin Luther (1483-1546): An Augustinian friar, the key figure in the Reformation. In 1517, as a special indulgence was being preached in Germany, and in view of needed reforms within the Church, he published at Wittenberg 95 theses concerning matters of Catholic belief and practice. Leo X condemned 41 statements from Luther's writings in 1520. Luther, refusing to recant, was excommunicated the following year. His teachings strongly influenced subsequent Lutheran theology, although the norm of Lutheran doctrine is not Luther's teaching alone but the Book of Concord (1580), which consists of the three catholic creeds, plus seven particular symbols or confessions of faith, of which only three are by Luther.

Luther's doctrine included the following:

The sin of Adam, which corrupted human nature radically (but not substantially), has affected every aspect of man's being. Although God holds man responsible for his moral actions, unregenerated man cannot by his innate powers, without the help of divine grace, make himself acceptable to God. Justification, understood as the forgiveness of sins, is by grace for Christ's sake through faith. Faith involves not merely intellectual assent but an act of confidence by the will. Good works are indispensably necessary concomitants of faith, but do not merit salvation. Of the sacraments, Luther retained baptism, penance and the Holy Communion as effective vehicles of the grace of the Holy Spirit; he held that in the Holy Communion the consecrated bread and wine are the Body and Blood of Christ. The rule of faith is the divine revelation in the Sacred Scriptures. He rejected purgatory, indulgences and the invocation of the saints, and held that prayers for the dead have no efficacy.

Lutheran tenets not in agreement with Catholic doctrine were condemned by the Council of Trent.

Anabaptism: Originated in Saxony in the first quarter of the 16th century and spread rapidly through southern Germany. Its doctrine included several key Lutheran tenets but was not regarded with favor by Luther, Calvin or Zwingli. Anabaptists believed that baptism is for adults only and that infant baptism is invalid. Their doctrine of the Inner Light, concerning the direct influence of the Holy Spirit on the believer, implied rejection of Catholic doctrine concerning the sacraments and the nature of the Church. Eighteen articles of faith were formulated in 1632 in Holland. Mennonites are Anabaptists.

Ulrich Zwingli (1484-1531): A priest who triggered the Reformation in Switzerland with a series of New Testament lectures in 1519, later disputations and by other actions. He held the Gospel to be the only basis of truth; rejected the Mass (which he suppressed in 1525 at Zurich), penance and other sacraments; denied papal primacy and doctrine concerning purgatory and the invocation of saints; rejected celibacy, monasticism and many traditional practices of piety. His symbolic view of the Eucharist, which was at odds with Catholic doctrine, caused an irreconcilable controversy with Luther and his followers. Zwingli was killed in a battle between the forces of Protestant and Catholic cantons in Switzerland.

John Calvin (1509-1564): French leader of the Reformation in Switzerland, whose key tenet was absolute predestination of some persons to heaven and others to hell. He rejected Catholic doctrine in 1533 after becoming convinced of a personal mission to reform the Church. In 1536 he published the first edition of *Institutes of the Christian Religion,* a systematic exposition of his doctrine which became the classic textbook of Reformed — as distinguished from Lutheran — theology. To Luther's principal theses — regarding Scripture as the sole rule of faith, the radical corruption of human nature, and justification by faith alone — he added absolute predestination, certitude of salvation for the elect, and the incapability of the elect to lose grace. His Eucharistic theory, which failed to mediate the Zwingli-Luther controversy, was at odds with Catholic doctrine. From 1555 until his death Calvin was the virtual dictator of Geneva, the capital of the non-Lutheran Reformation in Europe.

Arminianism: A modification of the rigid predestinationism of Calvin, set forth by Jacob Arminius (1560-1609) and formally stated in the *Remonstrance* of 1610. Arminianism influenced some Calvinist bodies.

Unitarianism: A 16th century doctrine which rejected the Trinity and the divinity of Christ in favor of a uni-personal God. It claimed scriptural support for a long time but became generally rationalistic with respect to "revealed" doctrine as well as in ethics and its world-view. One of its principal early proponents was Faustus Socinus (1539-1604), a leader of the Polish Brethren.

A variety of communions developed in England in the Reformation and post-Reformation periods.

Anglican Communion: This communion, which regards itself as the same apostolic Church as that which was established by early Christians in England, derived not from Reformation influences but from the renunciation of papal jurisdiction by Henry VIII (1491-1547). His Act of Supremacy in 1534 called Christ's Church an assembly of local churches subject to the prince, who was vested with fullness of authority and jurisdiction. In spite of Henry's denial of papal authority, this Act did not reject substantially other principal articles of faith. Notable changes, proposed and adopted for the reformation of the church, took place in the subsequent reigns of James VI and Elizabeth, with re-

spect to such matters as Scripture as the rule of faith, the sacraments, the nature of the Mass, and the constitution of the hierarchy.

The Anglican Communion is called Episcopal because its prelates have the title and function of bishops. (See Anglican Orders.)

Puritans: Extremists who sought church reform along Calvinist lines in severe simplicity. (Use of the term was generally discontinued after 1660.)

Presbyterians: Basically Calvinistic, called Presbyterian because church polity centers around assemblies of presbyters or elders. John Knox (c. 1513-1572) established the church in Scotland.

Congregationalists: Evangelical in spirit and seeking a return to forms of the primitive church, they uphold individual freedom in religious matters, do not require the acceptance of a creed as a condition for communion, and regard each congregation as autonomous. Robert Browne influenced the beginnings of Congregationalism.

Quakers: Their key belief is in internal divine illumination, the inner light of the living Christ, as the only source of truth and inspiration. George Fox (1624-1691) was one of their leaders in England. Called the Society of Friends, the Quakers are noted for their pacificism.

Baptists: So called because of their doctrine concerning baptism. They reject infant baptism and consider only baptism by immersion as valid. Leaders in the formation of the church were John Smyth (d. 1612) in England and Roger Williams (d. 1683) in America.

Methodists: A group who broke away from the Anglican Communion under the leadership of John Wesley (1703-1791), although some Anglican beliefs were retained. Doctrines include the witness of the Spirit to the individual and personal assurance of salvation. Wesleyan Methodists do not subscribe to some of the more rigid Calvinistic tenets held by other Methodists.

Universalism: A product of 18th-century liberal Protestantism in England. The doctrine is not Trinitarian and includes a tenet that all men will ultimately be saved.

MAJOR PROTESTANT CHURCHES IN THE UNITED STATES

There are more than 250 Protestant church bodies in the United States.

The majority of US Protestants belong to the following denominations: Baptist, Methodist, Lutheran, Presbyterian, Protestant Episcopal, the United Church of Christ, the Christian Church (Disciples of Christ), Holiness Sects.

Baptist Churches

(Courtesy of the Rev. Victor Tupitza, Division of Communication, American Baptist Churches in the U.S.A.)

Baptist churches, comprising the largest of all American Protestant denominations, were

first established by John Smyth near the beginning of the 17th century in England. The first Baptist church in America was founded at Providence by Roger Williams in 1639.

Largest of the nearly 30 Baptist bodies in the US are:

The Southern Baptist Convention, 460 James Robertson Parkway, Nashville, Tenn. 37219, with 12.3 million members;

The National Baptist Convention, U.S.A., Inc., 915 Spain St., Baton Rouge, La. 70802, with 6.5 million members;

The National Baptist Convention of America, 1058 Hogan St., Jacksonville, Fla. 32202, with 2.6 million members.

The American Baptist Churches in the U.S.A., Valley Forge, Pa. 19481, with 1.5 million members.

The total number of US Baptists is more than 29 million. The world total is 33 million.

Proper to Baptists is their doctrine on baptism. Called an "ordinance" rather than a sacrament, baptism by immersion is a sign that one has experienced and decided in favor of the salvation offered by Christ. It is administered only to persons who are capable of the experience of faith, which is the sole criterion of salvation and which involves the obligation to a life of virtue. Baptism is not administered to infants.

Baptists do not have a formal creed but generally subscribe to two professions of faith formulated in 1689 and 1832 and are in general agreement with classical Protestant theology regarding Scripture as the sole rule of faith, original sin, justification through faith in Christ, and the nature of the Church. Their local churches are autonomous.

Worship services differ in form from one congregation to another. Usual elements are the reading of Scripture, a sermon, hymns, vocal and silent prayer. The Lord's Supper, called an "ordinance," is celebrated at various intervals.

Methodist Churches

(Courtesy of the Librarian, Commission on Archives and History, and Dr. A. Walz, Statistician.)

Methodism derived from the teaching of John Wesley, an Anglican minister who experienced a new conversion to Christ in 1738. The first self-supporting Methodist congregation was established in London two years later. By the end of the 18th century Methodism was strongly rooted in America.

Methodists, with approximately 14 million members, comprise the second largest Protestant denomination in the US. The United Methodist Church, formed in a merger of the Methodist Church and the Evangelical United Brethren Church in 1968, is the largest of more than 20 bodies, with 10.5 million members; its principal agencies are located in New York, Evanston, Ill., Nashville, Tenn., Washington, D.C., Dayton, O., and Lake Junaluska, N.C. The second largest body, with some 1.5 million communicants, is the African Methodist Episcopal Church; its headquarters are located at 1724 Villa Place, Nashville, Tenn.

Methodism, although it has a base in Calvinistic theology, rejects absolute predestination and maintains that Christ offers grace freely to all men, not just to a select elite. Wesley's distinctive doctrine was the "witness of the Spirit" to the individual soul and personal assurance of salvation. He also emphasized the central themes of conversion and holiness. Methodists are in general agreement with classical Protestant theology regarding

Scripture as the sole rule of faith, original sin, justification through faith in Christ, the nature of the Church, and the sacraments of baptism and the Lord's Supper. Church polity is structured along episcopal, presbyterian and congregational lines. Congregations are free to choose various forms of worship services, which generally follow those in the Book of Common Prayer. Elements of a typical service are readings from Scripture, a sermon, prayers and hymns.

Lutheran Churches

(Courtesy of Erik W. Modean, director of the Lutheran Council News Bureau, 315 Park Ave., South, New York, N. Y. 10010.)

The actual origin of Lutheranism is generally traced to Oct. 31, 1517, when Martin Luther published a list of 95 theses and tacked them to the door of the church at Wittenberg. This act signaled the beginning of the Reformation in Germany. While the Lutheran Reformers did not intend to establish a new denomination, the subsequent excommunication of Luther and his followers completed the shattering of Western religious unity. The separate institutional existence of the Lutheran Church was necessitated in 1530 when, at the Diet of Augsburg, the Holy Roman Emperor, Charles V, rejected the Augsburg Confession of the Lutherans.

During the 17th century, Lutheranism came to this hemisphere chiefly from its strongholds in Northern and Central Europe. Its membership increased greatly as a result of the immigrations of the 19th century. Lutherans now form the third largest Protestant denomination in the United States, with more than 9 million members.

The three largest Lutheran bodies in the US are:

The Lutheran Church in America, 231 Madison Ave., New York, N.Y. 10016, with 3.2 million members. This body was formed June 28, 1962, by consolidation of the American Evangelical Lutheran Church, the Augustana Evangelical Lutheran Church, the Finnish Evangelical Lutheran Church, and the United Lutheran Church in America.

The Lutheran Church-Missouri Synod, 210 N. Broadway, St. Louis, Mo., with 2.8 million members. This body was formed in 1847.

The American Lutheran Church, 422 S. 5th St., Minneapolis, Minn., with 2.5 million members. This body was formed in April, 1960, by a merger of the American Lutheran Church, the Evangelical Lutheran Church, and the United Evangelical Lutheran Church, joined later by the Lutheran Free Church.

These three bodies participate in the Lutheran Council in the U.S.A., a cooperative agency for theological studies and Christian service in missions, welfare, education and related fields. The LC/USA, formed in 1966, is headquartered in New York City.

The normative statement of Lutheran beliefs is found in the *Book of Concord* (1580). All the major Lutheran bodies in this country subscribe to this collection of symbolical documents, which consists of the three ancient Creeds (Apostles', Nicene and Athanasian), the *Augsburg Confession* (1530), the *Apology of the Augsburg Confession* (1531), the *Smalcald Articles* (1536-1538), the *Treatise on the Authority and Primacy of the Pope* (1537), the *Large and Small Catechisms* (1529), and the *Formula of Concord* (1577), plus the Preface to the *Book of Concord*.

That we "receive forgiveness of sins and become righteous before God by grace, for Christ's sake, through faith," is the central article of faith in the Lutheran confessions. Lutherans believe in two sacraments, baptism and the Holy Eucharist, both of which are visible means of grace. Baptism is necessary for salvation (*Augsburg Confession*, II and IX), and through it a person is born again to newness of life. In the Holy Eucharist, the consecrated bread and wine are the Body and the Blood of Christ (*Smalcald Article* 3, Part Two, VI). The sacraments are "signs and testimonies of God's will toward us for the purpose of awakening and strengthening our faith" (*Augsburg Confession*, XIII). Although private confession is not obligatory, it is regarded as highly beneficial (*Apology*, XIII, 4). The formula reads: "According to the command of our Lord Jesus Christ, I forgive you all your sins in the name of the Father and of the Son and of the Holy Ghost" (*Small Catechism*, V. 28). Through the rite of confirmation, which is not regarded as a sacrament, children and baptized converts are admitted to adult membership in the Lutheran Church.

In the United States, church polity is largely congregation-centered, although national bodies, synods and conferences exercise differing degrees of influence and control over member congregations.

Although forms of worship and ceremonial are not wholly uniform, the commonly followed order of the service consists of Introit, Kyrie, Gloria, collect, (Old Testament lesson), epistle, gospel, creed, sermon, offertory, Great Intercession, preface and Sanctus, consecration, Pax Agnus, distribution of Holy Communion, post communion, Benedicamus and blessing, with interspersed hymns. When Holy Communion is not celebrated, a blessing after the Great Intercession ends the service. Matins and Vespers are used occasionally. The historic vestments are worn to a varying extent. Lutherans follow the church year. Music has always occupied a prominent place in Lutheran liturgical worship and successive generations have built up a rich tradition of church music and hymnody.

An assembly held late in the summer of 1973 evidenced a strong wave of conservative pressure and the formulation of related policies regarding classicism and fundamentalism in doctrine, seminary and biblical studies, liturgical practice, and a de-emphasis of trends toward social activism.

Presbyterian Churches

(Courtesy of Gerald W. Gillette, United Presbyterian Church in the U.S.A.; and Office of the General Assembly, Presbyterian Church in the United States.)

Presbyterians are so called because of their type of church government, by presbyters or elders.

Presbyterianism was founded on Reformed (as distinguished from Lutheran) theological positions laid down by John Calvin. Countries in which it acquired early strength and influence were Switzerland, France, Holland, Scotland and England.

Presbyterianism spread widely in this country in the latter part of the 18th century and afterwards. Presently, it has approximately 4.5 million communicants in nine bodies. The largest of these are:

The United Presbyterian Church in the U.S.A., 475 Riverside Drive, New York, N.Y. 10027, with 3 million members. This body was formed May 28, 1958, by a merger of the Presbyterian Church in the U.S.A and the United Presbyterian Church of North America.

The Presbyterian Church in the United States, 341 Ponce de Leon Boulevard N.E., Atlanta, Ga. 30308, with about 950,000 members.

In Presbyterian doctrine, baptism and the Lord's Supper, viewed as seals of the covenant of grace, are regarded as sacraments. Baptism, which is not necessary for salvation, is conferred on infants and adults. The Lord's Supper is celebrated as a covenant of the Sacrifice of Christ.

The Church is twofold, being invisible and also visible; it consists of all of the elect and all those Christians who are united in Christ as their immediate head.

Presbyterians are in general agreement with classical Protestant theology regarding Scripture as the sole rule of faith, original sin, and justification through faith in Christ.

Presbyterian congregations are governed by elders and ministers. On higher levels there are presbyteries, synods and a general assembly with various degrees of authority over local bodies.

Worship services, simple and dignified, include sermons, prayer, reading of the Scriptures and hymns. The Lord's Supper is celebrated at intervals.

Doctrinal developments of the past several years included approval in May, 1967, by the General Assembly of the United Presbyterian Church of a contemporary confession of faith to supplement the historic Westminster Confession. The new confession emphasizes the commitment of the Church and its members to reconciliatory and apostolic works in society.

Protestant Episcopal Church

(Courtesy of Charles M. Guilbert, Executive Officer of the General Convention and Custodian of the Standard Book of Common Prayer.)

The Protestant Episcopal Church, also officially known as the Episcopal Church, regards itself as the same apostolic church as that which was established by early Christians in England. It was established in this country during the Revolutionary period. Its constitution and Prayer Book were adopted at a general convention held in 1789. It has approximately 3.4 million members.

Offices of the US executive council are located at 815 Second Ave., New York, N.Y. 10017.

This church, which belongs to the Anglican Communion, subscribes to the branch theory of the Church of Christ, holding that it consists of the Church of Rome, the Eastern Orthodox Church, and the Anglican Communion, and that the heads of these churches are of equal rank in authority.

There is considerable variety in Protestant Episcopal beliefs and practices. Official statements of belief and practice are found in the Apostles' Creed, the Nicene Creed and the Book of Common Prayer, but interpretation is not uniform. Scripture has primary importance with respect to the rule of faith, and some authority is attached to tradition.

All seven sacraments, veneration of the saints, and a great many other Catholic teachings are accepted by some Episcopalians but contested by others.

An episcopal system of church government prevails, but clergymen of lower rank and lay persons also have an active voice in ecclesiastical affairs. The levels of government are the general convention, the executive council, territorial provinces and dioceses, and local parishes. At the parish level, the congregation has the right to select its own rector or pastor.

Liturgical worship is according to the Book of Common Prayer or authorized experimental forms, but ceremonial practices correspond with the doctrinal positions of the various congregations and range from a ceremony similar to the Roman Mass to services of a less elaborate character.

United Church of Christ

(Courtesy of the Rev. David A. Tillyer, Office of Communication, United Church of Christ.)

The 1,867,810-member United Church of Christ was formed in 1957 by a union of the Congregational Christian and the Evangelical and Reformed Churches. The former was originally established by the Pilgrims and the Puritans of the Massachusetts Bay Colony, while the latter was founded in Pennsylvania in the early 1700's by settlers from Central Europe. The denomination has 6,617 congregations throughout the United States.

Its headquarters are located at 297 Park Ave. South, New York, N.Y. 10010.

Its statement of faith recognizes Jesus Christ as "our crucified and risen Lord (who) shared our common lot, conquering sin and death and reconciling the world to himself." It believes in the life after death, and the fact that God "judges men and nations by his righteous will declared through prophets and apostles."

The United Church further believes that Christ calls its members to share in his baptism "and eat at his table, to join him in his passion and victory." Ideally, according to its Lord's Day Service, Communion is to be celebrated weekly. Like other Calvinistic bodies, it believes that Christ is spiritually present in the sacrament.

The United Church is governed along congregational lines, and each local church is autonomous. However, the pronouncements of its biennial general synod are taken with great seriousness by congregations. Between synods, a 42-member executive council oversees the work of the church.

Christian Church (Disciples of Christ)

(Courtesy of Robert L. Friedly, Executive Director, Office of Communication.)

The Christian Church (Disciples of Christ) originated early in the 1800's from two movements against rigid denominationalism led by Presbyterians Thomas and Alexander Campbell in western Pennsylvania and Barton W. Stone in Kentucky. The two movements developed separately for about 25 years before being merged in 1832.

The church, which identifies itself with the Protestant mainstream, now has approximately 1.3 million members in the US and Canada. The greatest concentration of members in the US is located roughly along the old frontier line, in an arc sweeping from Ohio and Kentucky through the Midwest and down into Oklahoma and Texas.

The general offices of the church are located at 222 South Downey Ave., Box 1986, Indianapolis, Ind. 46206..

The church's persistent concern for Christian unity is based on a conviction expressed in a basic document, *Declaration and Address*, dating from its founding. The document states: "The church of Christ upon earth is essentially, intentionally and constitutionally one."

The Disciples have no official doctrine or dogma. Their worship practices vary widely from more common informal services to what could almost be described as "high church" services. Membership is granted after a simple statement of belief in Jesus Christ and baptism by immersion; many congregations admit un-immersed transfers from other denominations. The Lord's Supper, generally called Communion, is always open to Christians of all persuasions. Laymen routinely preside over the Lord's Supper, which is celebrated each Sunday; they often preach and perform other pastoral functions as well. Distinction between ordained and non-ordained members is blurred somewhat because of the Disciples' emphasis on all members of the church as ministers.

The Christian Church is oriented to congregational government, and has a unique structure in which three levels of polity (general, regional and congregational) operate as equals rather than in a pyramid of authority. At the national or international level, it is governed by a general assembly which has voting representation direct from congregations and regions as well as all ordained clergy.

The Holiness Sects

Perfectionist and Pentecostal churches and sects have a total membership of some two million persons in the US.

These groups do not form a denomination in the strict sense of the term, since they are separate and have their own particular characteristics. Classification under a common heading is possible, however, because they all share the same general spirit and spring from a common origin. John Wesley's teaching on justification is the doctrinal thread common to all of these churches — personal holiness, realized in the life of each individual, is the key to a full Christian life. Hence the name, "Holiness Movement." Its origin is traceable to the revival movement of the 19th century.

The Perfectionist branch of this large group includes such foundations as the Church of the Nazarene, the Church of God (Anderson, Ind.), and the Pilgrim Holiness Church. On the Pentecostal side are the Assemblies of God, the numerous Churches of God, and many bodies with the word Pentecostal in their titles. There are also many other very small cults which are similar in spirit to the larger churches.

Among the fundamental Christian doctrines maintained by Holiness believers are those of the Trinity and the divinity of Christ. They accept baptism. Classical Protestantism is reflected in their beliefs regarding the effect of original sin on human nature, the nature of justification, principles of biblical interpretation, and the rejection of tradition.

Some tenets are limited to the Pentecostal and Perfectionist bodies, such as beliefs in the imminent coming of Christ for the second time and a second baptism of the Holy Spirit in which holiness is acquired. There are many different opinions regarding the nature of this holiness.

The Pentecostals hold that justification and holiness are essentially related to the events that accompanied the descent of the Holy Spirit upon the Apostles at Pentecost. Hence, speaking in tongues and other related phenomena are significant.

WORLD RELIGIOUS POPULATION
(Source: *1974 Britannica Book of the Year.*)

CHRISTIANS, TOTAL: **967,793,450** (North and Central America, 224,933,250; South America, 163,567,000; Europe, 372,425,700; Asia, 87,396,500; Africa, 98,862,000; Oceania, 20,609,000).

Roman Catholic: **551,949,000** (North and Central America, 128,995,500; South America, 157,831,000; Europe, 179,684,000; Asia, 46,456,500; Africa, 34,587,000; Oceania, 4,395,000).

Eastern Orthodox: **91,580,700** (North and Central America, 4,117,000; South America, 54,000; Europe, 67,380,500; Asia, 2,135,000; Africa, 17,410,000; Oceania, 484,000).

Protestant: **324,263,750** (North and Central America, 91,820,750; South America, 5,682,000; Europe, 125,361,000; Asia, 38,805,000; Africa, 46,865,000; Oceania, 15,730,000).

JEWISH: **14,443,925** (North and Central America, 6,344,475; South America, 680,700; Europe, 3,983,750; Asia, 3,064,050; Africa, 297,950; Oceania, 73,000).

MUSLIM: **513,174,500** (North and Central America, 205,000; South America, 185,000; Europe, 4,088,000; Asia, 414,796,000; Africa, 93,328,500; Oceania, 572,000).

ZOROASTRIAN: **181,050** (Asia, 180,600; Africa, 450).

SHINTO: **63,150,000** (North and Central America, 55,000; South America, 90,000; Asia, 63,005,000).

TAOIST: **31,367,700** (North and Central America, 15,000; South America, 12,000; Asia, 31,340,700).

CONFUCIAN: **275,898,865** (North and Central America, 92,165; South America, 90,000; Europe, 40,000; Asia, 275,630,700; Africa, 500; Oceania, 45,500).

BUDDHIST: **223,655,500** (North and Central America, 142,000; South America, 175,000; Europe, 200,000; Asia, 223,136,500; Africa, 2,000).

HINDU: **515,580,500** (North and Central America, 65,000; South America, 470,000; Europe, 300,000; Asia, 513,755,500; Africa, 461,000; Oceania, 529,000).

TOTAL RELIGIOUS POPULATION: **2,605,245,490** (North and Central America, 231,851,890; South America, 165,269,700; Europe, 381,037,450; Asia, 1,612,305,550; Africa, 192,952,400; Oceania, 21,828,500).

TOTAL POPULATION OF WORLD: **3,788,200,000** (North and Central America, 332,000,000; South America, 201,000,000; Europe, 717,000,000; Asia, 2,154,000,000; Africa, 364,000,000; Oceania, 20,200,000).

The modern ecumenical movement, which started about 1910 among Protestants and led to formation of the World Council of Churches in 1948, developed outside the mainstream of Catholic interest for many years. It has now become for Catholics as well one of the great religious facts of our time.

The magna charta of ecumenism for Catholics is a complex of several documents which include, in the first place, the *Decree on Ecumenism* promulgated by the Second Vatican Council Nov. 21, 1964. Other enactments underlying and expanding this decree are the *Dogmatic Constitution on the Church,* the *Decree on Eastern Catholic Churches,* and the *Pastoral Constitution on the Church in the Modern World.*

VATICAN II DECREE

The following excerpts from the *Decree on Ecumenism* cover the broad theological background and principles and indicate the thrust of the Church's commitment to ecumenism.

". . . Men who believe in Christ and have been properly baptized are brought into a certain, though imperfect, communion with the Catholic Church. Undoubtedly, the differences that exist in varying degrees between them and the Catholic Church — whether in doctrine and sometimes in discipline, or concerning the structure of the Church — do indeed create many and sometimes serious obstacles to full ecclesiastical communion. These the ecumenical movement is striving to overcome . . ." (No. 3).

Elements Common to Christians

"Moreover some, even very many, of the most significant elements or endowments which together go to build up and give life to the Church herself can exist outside the visible boundaries of the Catholic Church: the written word of God; the life of grace; faith, hope, and charity, along with other interior gifts of the Holy Spirit and visible elements. All of these, which come from Christ and lead back to Him, belong by right to the one Church of Christ" (No. 3).

[In a later passage, the decree singled out a number of elements which the Catholic Church and other churches have in common but not in complete agreement: confession of Christ as Lord and God and as mediator between God and man; belief in the Trinity; reverence for Scripture as the revealed word of God; baptism and the Lord's Supper; Christian life and worship; faith in action; concern with moral questions.]

"The brethren divided from us also carry out many of the sacred actions of the Christian religion. Undoubtedly, in ways that vary according to the condition of each Church or Community, these actions can truly engender a life of grace, and can be rightly described as capable of providing access to the community of salvation.

"It follows that these separated Churches and Communities, though we believe they suffer from defects already mentioned, have by no means been deprived of significance and importance in the mystery of salvation. For the Spirit of Christ has not refrained from using them as means of salvation which derive their efficacy from the very fullness of grace and truth entrusted to the Catholic Church" (No. 3).

Unity Lacking

"Nevertheless, our separated brethren, whether considered as individuals or as Communities and Churches, are not blessed with that unity which Jesus Christ wished to bestow on all those whom He has regenerated and vivified into one body and newness of life — that unity which the holy Scriptures and the revered tradition of the Church proclaim. For it is through Christ's Catholic Church alone, which is the all-embracing means of salvation, that the fullness of the means of salvation can be obtained. It was to the apostolic college alone, of which Peter is the head, that we believe our Lord entrusted all the blessings of the New Covenant, in order to establish on earth the one Body of Christ into which all those should be fully incorporated who already belong in any way to God's People . . ." (No. 3).

What the Movement Involves

"Today, in many parts of the world, under the inspiring grace of the Holy Spirit, multiple efforts are being expended through prayer, word, and action to attain that fullness of unity which Jesus Christ desires. This sacred Synod, therefore, exhorts all the Catholic faithful to recognize the signs of the times and to participate skillfully in the work of ecumenism.

"The 'ecumenical movement' means those activities and enterprises which, according to various needs of the Church and opportune occasions, are started and organized for the fostering of unity among Christians. These are:

• "First, every effort to eliminate words, judgments, and actions which do not respond to the condition of separated brethren with truth and fairness and so make mutual relations between them more difficult.

• "Then, 'dialogue' between competent experts from different Churches and Communities (scholarly ecumenism). . . .

• "In addition, these Communions cooperate more closely in whatever projects a Christian conscience demands for the common good (social ecumenism).

• "They also come together for common prayer, where this is permitted (spiritual ecumenism).

• "Finally, all are led to examine their own faithfulness to Christ's will for the Church and, wherever necessary, undertake with vigor the task of renewal and reform.

". . . It is evident that the work of preparing and reconciling those individuals who wish for full Catholic communion is of its nature distinct from ecumenical action. But there is no opposition between the two, since both proceed from the wondrous providence of God" (No. 4).

Primary Duty of Catholics

"In ecumenical work, Catholics must assuredly be concerned for their separated brethren, praying for them, keeping them informed about the Church, making the first approaches towards them. But their primary duty is to make an honest and careful appraisal of whatever needs to be renewed and achieved in the Catholic household itself, in order that its life may bear witness more loyally and luminously to the teachings and ordinances which have been handed down from Christ through the apostles.

". . . Every Catholic must . . . aim at Christian perfection (cf. Jas. 1:4; Rom. 12:1-2) and, each according to his station, play his part so that the Church . . . may daily be more purified and renewed, against the day when Christ will present her to Himself in all her glory, without spot or wrinkle (cf. Eph. 5:27).

". . . Catholics must joyfully acknowledge and esteem the truly Christian endowments from our common heritage which are to be found among our separated brethren. . . .

"Nor should we forget that whatever is wrought by the grace of the Holy Spirit in the hearts of our separated brethren can contribute to our own edification. Whatever is truly Christian never conflicts with the genuine interests of the faith; indeed, it can always result in a more ample realization of the very mystery of Christ and the Church . . ." (No. 4).

Participation in Worship

Norms concerning participation by Catholics in the worship of other Christian Churches were sketched in this conciliar decree and elaborated in a number of other documents such as: the *Decree on Eastern Catholic Churches,* promulgated by the Second Vatican Council in 1964; *Interim Guidelines for Prayer in Common,* issued June 18, 1965, by the US Bishops' Committee for Ecumenical and Inter-Religious Affairs; a *Directory on Ecumenism,* published in 1967 by the Vatican Secretariat for Promoting Christian Unity; additional communications from the US Bishops' Committee, and numerous sets of guidelines issued locally by and for dioceses throughout the US.

The norms encourage common prayer services for Christian unity and other intentions. Beyond that, they draw a distinction between separated churches of the Reformation tradition and separated Eastern churches, in view of doctrine and practice the Catholic Church has in common with the latter concerning the apostolic succession of bishops, holy orders, liturgy, and other credal matters.

Full participation by Catholics in official Protestant liturgies is prohibited, because it implies profession of the faith expressed in the liturgy. Intercommunion by Catholics at Protestant liturgies is prohibited. Under certain conditions, Protestants may be given Holy Communion in the Catholic Church (see Intercommunion). A Catholic may stand as a witness, but not as a sponsor, in baptism, and as a witness in the marriage of separated Christians. Similarly, a Protestant may stand as a witness, but not as a sponsor, in a Catholic baptism, and as a witness in the marriage of Catholics.

Separated Eastern Churches

The principal norms regarding liturgical participation with separated Eastern Christians are included under Eastern Ecumenism.

ECUMENICAL AGENCIES

Vatican Secretariat

The top-level agency for Catholic ecumenical efforts is the Vatican Secretariat for Promoting Christian Unity, which originated in 1960 as a preparatory commission for the Second Vatican Council. Its purposes are to provide guidance and, where necessary, coordination for ecumenical endeavor by Catholics, and to establish and maintain relations with representatives of other Christian Churches for ecumenical dialogue and action.

The secretariat, first under the direction of Cardinal Augustin Bea, S. J., and now of Cardinal Jan Willebrands, has established firm working relations with a number of representative agencies of other churches, principally the World Council of Churches and the Lutheran World Federation; has joined the Anglican Communion and the Orthodox in dialogue; and is carrying forward with the World Alliance of Reformed Churches (a Presbyterian alliance) studies regarding the possibilities of future dialogue. In the past several years, staff members and representatives of the secretariat have been involved in one way or another in nearly every significant ecumenical enterprise and meeting held throughout the world, including the Fourth General Assembly of the World Council of Churches and the Tenth Lambeth Conference in 1968.

While the secretariat and its counterparts in other churches have focused primary attention on theological and other related problems of Christian unity, they have also begun, and in increasing measure, to emphasize the responsibilities of the churches for greater unity of witness and effort in areas of humanitarian need.

Bishops' Committee

The US Bishops' Committee for Ecumenical and Interreligious Affairs was established by the American hierarchy in 1964. Its purposes are to maintain relationships with other Christian churches and other religious communities at the national level, to advise and assist dioceses in developing and applying ecumenical policies, and to maintain liaison with corresponding Vatican offices — the Secretariats for Christian Unity, Non-Christian Religions, and Non-Believers.

This standing committee of the National Conference of Catholic Bishops is chaired by Archbishop William W. Baum of Washington. Operationally, the committee is assisted by secretariats headed by the Rev. John F. Hotchkin, secretary for Christian Unity, and the Rev. Edward H. Flannery, secretary for Catholic-Jewish Relations.

The committee co-sponsors several national consultations with other churches and confessional families. These bring together on a regular basis Catholic representatives and their counterparts from the American Baptist Convention, the Christian Church (Disciples of Christ), the Episcopal Church, the Lutheran World Federation (US Committee), the United Methodist Church, the Orthodox Churches, and the Alliance of Reformed Churches (North American area). Reports of consultations conducted under committee auspices are published periodically and are available through the Publications Office of the US Catholic Conference. (See Ecumenical Dialogues.)

The committee has also facilitated regional meetings in conjunction with the Home Mission Board of the Southern Baptist Convention.

The committee relates with the National Council of Churches of Christ, and is sponsoring a joint study committee investigating the possibility of Roman Catholic membership in that body.

Advisory and other services are provided by the committee to ecumenical commissions and agencies in dioceses throughout the country.

Through the Secretariat for Catholic-Jewish Relations, the committee is in contact with several national Jewish agencies and bodies. Issues of mutual interest and shared concern are reviewed for the purpose of furthering deeper understanding between the Catholic and Jewish communities.

Through the Secretariat for Non-Christians, moderated by Archbishop Baum, and the Secretariat for Human Values, moderated by Bishop Mark Hurley, the committee promotes activity in wider areas of dialogue. The

Rev. John F. Hotchkin serves as executive secretary for these secretariats.

Offices of the committee are located at 1312 Massachusetts Ave. N. W., Washington, D. C. 20005.

World Council

The World Council of Churches is a fellowship of churches which acknowledge "Jesus Christ as Lord and Savior." It is a permanent organization providing constituent members — in 1974, 267 churches with some 450 million communicants in 90 countries — with opportunities for meeting, consultation and cooperative action with respect to doctrine, worship, practice, social mission, evangelism and missionary work, and other matters of mutual concern.

The WCC was formally established Aug. 23, 1948, in Amsterdam with ratification of a constitution by 147 communions. This action merged two previously existing movements — Life and Work (social mission), Faith and Order (doctrine) — which had initiated practical steps toward founding a fellowship of Christian churches at meetings held in Oxford, Edinburgh and Utrecht in 1937 and 1938. A third movement for cooperative missionary work, which originated about 1910 and, remotely, led to formation of the WCC, was incorporated into the council in 1971 under the title of the International Missionary Council (World Mission and Evangelism).

Three additional general assemblies of the council have been held since the charter meeting of 1948, in Evanston, Ill. (1954), New Delhi, India (1961), and Uppsala, Sweden (1968).

Between assemblies, the council operates through a central committee which meets every 12 or 18 months, and an executive committee which meets every six months.

The council continues the work of the International Missionary Council, the Commission on Faith and Order, and the Commission on Church and Society. The structure of the council has three program units: Faith and Witness, Justice and Service, Education and Communication.

Liaison between the council and the Vatican has been maintained since 1966 through a joint working group. Roman Catholic membership in the WCC is a question officially on the agenda of this body. The Joint Commission on Society, Development and Peace (SODEPAX) is an agency of the council and the Pontifical Commission for Justice and Peace. Roman Catholics serve individually as full members of the Commission on Faith and Order and in various capacities on other program committees of the council.

WCC headquarters are located in Geneva, Switzerland. The United States Conference for the World Council of Churches at 475 Riverside Drive, New York, N. Y. 10027, provides liaison between the US churches and Geneva. The WCC also maintains fraternal relations with regional, national and local councils of churches throughout the world.

The Rev. Philip A. Potter, a Methodist from the Island of Dominica, West Indies, was elected secretary general of the WCC in August, 1972.

WCC presidents are: Mrs. Dr. Kiyoko Takeda Cho (Japan), His Holiness German (Yugoslavia), Rev. Dr. Hanns Lilje (Germany), Rev. Dr. Ernest A. Payne (United Kingdom), Rev. Dr. John Coventry Smith (USA), Rt. Rev. A. H. Zulu (South Africa).

National Council

The National Council of The Churches of Christ in the USA, the largest ecumenical organization in the United States, is a cooperative federation of 31 Protestant, Orthodox and Anglican church bodies having about 42 million members.

The NCC, established by the churches in 1950, was structured through the merger of 12 separate cooperative agencies. Presently, through three main program divisions and five commissions, the NCC carries on work in behalf of member churches in home and overseas missions, Christian education and communications, disaster relief and rehabilitation, family life, religious broadcast and film-making, regional and local ecumenism, and other areas.

The NCC is governed by a governing board of approximately 350 members appointed by the constituent churches which meets twice a year.

The NCC's annual budget approximates $16 million, about 60 percent of which is devoted to compassionate ministries of aid and relief to victims of disasters and endemic poverty in lands overseas. The work of the NCC is financially supported for the most part by the member churches and their boards and agencies.

Dr. W. Sterling Cary was elected to a three-year term as president in 1972.

NCC headquarters are located at 475 Riverside Drive, New York, N. Y. 10027.

Consultation

The Consultation on Church Union, officially begun in 1962, is a venture of American churches seeking a united church "truly catholic, truly evangelical, and truly reformed." The nine churches engaged in this process, representing 25 million Christians, are the African Methodist Episcopal Church, the African Methodist Episcopal Zion Church, the Christian Church (Disciples of Christ), the Christian Methodist Episcopal Church, the Episcopal Church, the Presbyterian Church in the United States, the United Church of Christ, the United Methodist Church, and the United Presbyterian Church in the U.S.A.

From 1970 to 1973 the member churches studied the first draft of a plan of union for the proposed Church of Christ Uniting. The responses to this plan, on the one hand, gave evidence of an historic consensus on faith, worship, and ministry; on the other hand, they revealed the need for mature involvement in order to discover the structures of a united church. The 11th plenary at Memphis, April, 1973, called for a future agenda involving the congregations more intimately, explored divisive factors such as racism, and affirmed the doctrinal and liturgical rapprochement already achieved. The 12th plenary was scheduled for Nov. 4 to 8, 1974, in Cincinnati.

Two experimental liturgies, "An Order of Worship for The Proclamation of the Word of God and The Celebration of the Lord's Supper With Commentary" (1968) and "An Order for Holy Baptism" (1973), have been developed. A joint commission of Roman Catholic and COCU liturgical scholars is preparing an ecumenical marriage rite.

The general secretary of COCU is the Rev. Gerald F. Moede.

Offices are located at 228 Alexander St., Princeton, N.J. 08540.

ECUMENICAL DIALOGUES

(Source: Secretariat for Ecumenical and Interreligious Affairs, National Conference of Catholic Bishops.)

Following is a list of principal consultations, from Mar. 16, 1965, involving representatives of the US Catholic Bishops' Committee for Ecumenical and Interreligious Affairs and representatives of other Christian Churches, with names of the churches, places and dates of meetings, and the subject matter of discussions.

Baptist Convention, American (Division of Cooperative Christianity): (1) De Witt, Mich., Apr. 3, 1967 — American Baptist and Roman Catholic dialogue; a Baptist view of areas of theological agreement. (2) Green Lake, Wis., Apr. 29, 1968 — Baptism and confirmation; Christian freedom and ecclesiastical authority. (3) Schiller Park, Ill., Apr. 28, 1969 — Nature and communication of grace; Christian freedom and ecclesiastical authority; baptism and confirmation.

(4) Atchison, Kan., Apr. 17, 1970 — Role of the Church, resume of years past and the future; Roman Catholic-American Baptist dialogues; observations concerning bilateral ecumenical conversations and the future course of American Baptist-Roman Catholic conversations.

(5) Detroit, Mich., Apr. 23 to 24, 1971 — Theological perspective on clergy and lay issues and relations; theology of the local church; growth in understanding. (6) Liberty, Mo., Apr. 14 to 15, 1972 — Relationships between Church and State.

Baptists, Southern (Ecumenical Institute, Wake Forest University): (1) Winston-Salem,

N. C., May 8, 1969 — Impact of biblical criticism on Roman Catholicism and contemporary Christianity in general; holy use of the world; creeds and the Faith; liturgy and spontaneity in worship; retreat, revival and monasticism; world view of ecumenism. (2) St. Benedict, La., Feb. 4, 1970 — Liturgy and spontaneity in worship; perspectives on Baptist views on Scripture and tradition; the priesthood of all Christians; authority of the Old Testament; Baptist concepts of the Church; retreat, revival and monasticism. (3) Louisville, Ky., May 13, 1970 — The priesthood of all Christians; the ecumenical tide — a pastoral perspective; the enduring meaning of the Old Testament; retreat, revival and monasticism.

(4) Daytona Beach, Fla., Feb. 1 to 3, 1971 — Issues and answers, prepared by the Interfaith Witness Department of the Southern Baptist Convention. (5) Houston, Tex., Oct. 16 to 18, 1972 — Second regional conference planned in conjunction with the Interfaith Witness Department.

(6) Marriottsville, Md., Feb. 4 to 6, 1974 — Third regional conference, planned in conjunction with the Interfaith and Witness Department, concerning different types of reform and their appropriateness at different levels of church life.

Christian Church, Disciples of Christ (Council on Christian Unity): (1) Indianapolis, Ind., Mar. 16, 1967 — A look at Disciples for Catholics. (2) Kansas City, Mo., Sept. 25, 1967 — Roman Catholic view of the nature of unity being sought; opportunities in the contemporary ecumenical movement. (3) St. Louis, Mo., Apr. 29, 1968 — Eucharistic sharing.

(4) Washington, D. C., Oct. 16, 1968 — Disciple of Christ inquiry regarding the sacramentality of marriage; pastoral reflections on mixed marriage. (5) New York, N. Y., Apr. 25, 1969 — Recognition and reconciliation of ministries; theological presuppositions concerning ministry among the Disciples; role of the priest in the Catholic community.

(6) Columbus, O., Nov. 3 to 5, 1970 — The parish concept in a plan of union (Consultation on Church Union); directions emerging in Catholic parish life. (7) New York, N.Y., June 8 to 10, 1971 — Disciples' theology of baptism; meaning of baptism as liberation, incorporation, empowerment.

(8) Indianapolis, Ind., Mar. 8 to 10, 1972 — Ministry of healing and reconciliation as practiced in the two communities. (9) Madison, Wis., June 26 to 28, 1972 — Review and summary of five years of dialogue; planning for future themes.

(10) Pleasant Hill, Shaker Town, Ky., May 22 to 24, 1973 — The Church in the New Testament.

Episcopal (The Anglican-Roman Catholic Consultation, Joint Commission on Ecumenical Relations): (1) Washington, D.C., June 22, 1965 — Preliminary discussions. (2) Kansas City, Mo., Feb. 2, 1966 — Eucharist as source or expression of community; Eucharist as sign and cause of unity, and the Church as a Eunharistic fellowship.

(3) Providence, R.I., Oct. 10, 1966 — Function of the minister in Eucharistic celebration; minister of the Eucharist. (4) Milwaukee, Wis., May 2, 1967 — Eucharist. (5) Jackson, Miss., Jan. 5, 1968 — Various aspects of the ministerial priesthood and the priesthood of the faithful in Eucharistic celebration; the priest's place and function in the Church's mission of service; the laity in Episcopal Church government.

(6) Liberty, Mo., Dec. 2, 1968 — Directions of the ecumenical movement; episcopal symbol of unity in the Christian community; collegiality; Citizens for Educational Freedom; a layman's view of jurisdictional and cultural factors in division; Church and society in contemporary America.

(7) Boynton Beach, Fla., Dec. 8, 1969 — All in each place; toward the reconciliation of the Roman Catholic Church and Churches of the Anglican Communion; an approach to designing a Roman Catholic-Episcopal parish; preparation of joint statement on the meeting. (8) Green Bay, Wis., June 17, 1970 — Is the (COCU — Consultation on Church Union) plan of union truly Catholic, with special reference to the priest and the episcopacy?; Anglican-Roman Catholic dialogue — achievement and prognostication.

(9) St. Benedict, La., Jan. 26 to 29, 1971 — The primacy of jurisdiction of the Roman Pontiff according to the First Vatican Council; the teaching of the Second Vatican Council concerning the hierarchy of truths; analysis of the ground of "Church Elements: An Ecclesiological Investigation."

(10) Liberty, Mo., June 20 to 23, 1971 — Gift of infallibility; sharing in the teaching authority of the Church; official view of episcopacy in the Episcopal Church in the USA; symposium on Hans Kung's *Infallibility? An Inquiry*; dogma as an ecumenical problem; Revelation and statement in Anglicanism; revised working paper on theological truth, propositions and Christian unity; reflections on the teaching ministry of the Church.

(11) New York, N.Y., Jan 20 to 24, 1972 — Theological truth, propositions and Christian unity; the Protestant Episcopal Church's view of authority, tradition and the Bible; a comment on the Windsor "Statement of Eucharistic Agreement" issued by the International Anglican-Roman Catholic Consultation.

(12) Cincinnati, O., June 12 to 15, 1972 — The notion of *typos* and *typoi* as applied to the forms of the Christian Church; correspondences and differences in the Anglican and Roman Catholic understanding and exercise of teaching authority.

(13) Cincinnati, O., Mar. 18 to 22, 1973 —

Formulation of a preliminary draft on the purpose of the Church. (14) Vicksburg, Miss., Jan. 6 to 10, 1974 — Formulation of a response to the "Canterbury Statement" of the International Anglican-Roman Catholic Consultation on ministry and ordination; discussion and amendment of a draft on the purpose of the Church; other subjects in a continuing dialogue on the mission of the Church.

Lutheran, U.S.A. (National Committee of the Lutheran World Federation): (1) Baltimore, Md., Mar. 16, 1965 — Exploratory discussion. (2) Baltimore, Md., July 6, 1965 — Nicene Creed as dogma of the Church. (3) Chicago, Ill., Feb. 10, 1966 — Baptism, in the context of the New Testament; Lutheran understanding; teaching of the Council of Trent. (4) Washington, D.C., Sept. 22, 1966 — Eucharist as sacrifice, in traditional and contemporary Catholic and Lutheran contexts. (5) New York, N.Y., Apr 7, 1967 — Propitiation and five presentations on various aspects of the Eucharist. (6) St. Louis, Mo.. Sept. 29, 1967 — Eucharist. (7) New York, Mar. 8, 1968 — Intercommunion, with respect to Catholic discipline, Lutheran practice, and theological reflections.

(8) Williamsburg, Va., Sept. 27, 1968 — Ministry; the competent minister of the Eucharist; scriptural foundations of diakonia (ministry of service). (9) San Francisco, Calif., Feb. 21, 1969 — Apostolic succession in the patristic era and in a contemporary view; Lutheran view of the validity of Lutheran orders; Christian priesthood in the light of documents of the Second Vatican Council.

(10) Baltimore, Md., Sept. 26, 1969 — The minister of the Eucharist, according to the Council of Trent; the use of "Church" as applied to Protestant denominations in the documents of Vatican II; Lutheran doctrine of the ministry — Catholic and Reformed; the ordained minister and layman in Lutheranism. (11) St. George, Bermuda, Feb. 19, 1970 — Preparation of joint statement on the ministry.

(12) New York, N.Y., May, 1970. (13) Chicago, Ill., Oct. 30 to Nov. 1, 1970. (14) Miami, Fla., Feb. 19 to 22, 1971 — Peter and the New Testament; the papacy in the late patristic era, Middle Ages, Renaissance; text of the *Dogmatic Constitution on the Church* (Vatican II) with respect to the papacy and infallibility.

(15) Seabury, Conn., Sept. 24 to 27, 1971 — An investigation of the concept of divine right *(jus divinum);* teaching of the First Vatican Council on primacy and infallibility; a Lutheran understanding of what papal primacy in the Church might mean.

(16) New Orleans, La., Feb. 18 to 21, 1972 — Further discussion of the concept of divine right; ecumenical projections concerning the Petrine office; teaching authority in the Lutheran Church. (17) Minneapolis, Minn.,

Sept. 22 to 25, 1972 — Further investigation of the Petrine function; councils and conciliarism.

(18) San Antonio, Tex., Feb. 16 to 19, 1973 — Discussion of work and papers of the Petrine panel concerning ministry and the Church universal, Catholic and Lutheran interpretive statements; work on papal primacy papers. (19) Allentown, Pa., Sept. 21 to 24, 1973 — Work on a joint statement concerning ministry and the Church universal, the concluding session on this topic; selection of infallibility as the next topic for consideration. (20) Marriottsville, Md., Feb. 15 to 17, 1974 — Start of discussion on infallibility; commissioning of 16 future research papers.

Methodist (United Methodist Church): (1) Chicago, Ill., June 28, 1966 — Methodists and Roman Catholics: comments for Catholic-Methodist conversation. (2) Chicago, Ill., Dec. 18, 1966 — Salvation, faith and good works; Catholic Church and faith. (3) Lake Junaluska, N. C., June 28, 1967 — Roman Catholic position regarding the Spirit in the Church; mission of the Holy Spirit, in the light of the Second Vatican Council's *Dogmatic Constitution on the Church* and the writings of John Wesley.

(4) New York, N.Y., Dec. 17, 1967 — Three generations of Church-State argumentation. (5) San Antonio, Tex., Sept. 30, 1968 — Shared convictions about education. (6) Delaware, O., Oct. 9, 1969 — Major Methodist ecumenical documents; an appraisal of some documents of Vatican II; racial confrontation in Roman Catholicism, Methodism and the National Council of Churches. (7) Chicago, Ill., Jan. 30, 1970 — Review and planning.

(8) Washington, D. C., Dec. 16, 1970 — Completion of a statement of shared convictions about education. Task force meetings during 1971. (9) Cincinnati, O., Feb. 25 to 26, 1972 — Ministry in the United Methodist Church and the spirituality of the ordained ministry; problems of ministry. (10) Dec. 13 to 14, 1972 — Further dialogue on the spirituality of the ministry.

(11) Washington, D.C., Mar. 9 to 10, 1973 — Spirituality of the ministry. (12) Washington, D.C., Nov. 1 to 2, 1973 — Start of preparatory work on a consensus statement on spirituality of the ministry.

Orthodox (Standing Conference of Canonical Orthodox Bishops of America): Sept. 9, 1965 — Preliminary discussions. (1) New York, N. Y., Sept. 29, 1966 — Consultation led to appointment of task forces to investigate differences in theological methods, questions of sacramental sharing, possible cooperation in theological education and the formation of seminarians. (2) Worcester, Mass., May 5, 1967 — Theological diversity and unity; intercommunion; common witness in theological education. (3) Maryknoll, N. Y., Dec. 7, 1968 — Eucharist and Church;

indissolubility of marriage; Cooperation in theological education.

(4) Worcester, Mass., Dec. 12, 1969 — Orthodox and Catholic views of the Eucharist and membership in the Church; an agreed statement on the Eucharist. (5) New York, N.Y., May 19, 1970 — New Order of the Mass; membership of schismatics and heretics in the ancient Church; current legislation of the Catholic Church and current practices of the Greek Orthodox Church concerning common worship; current legislation of the Catholic Church concerning mixed marriages; Orthodox view of mixed marriages; an agreed statement on mixed marriages.

(6) Brookline, Mass., Dec. 4, 1970 — Ministers, doctrine and practice of matrimony in Eastern and Western traditions. (7) Barlin Acres, Mass., Nov. 3 to 4, 1971 — Ethical issues relating to marriage; revision of an agreed statement on mixed marriages; the primacy of Rome as seen by the Eastern Church.

(8) New York, N.Y., Dec. 6, 1973 — Study of a draft statement on the sanctity of marriage. (9) Washington, D.C., May 23 to 24, 1974 — Dialogical process; witness of the Church on the American scene; approval of an agreed statement on respect for life; Orthodox and Catholic views of contemporary Orthodoxy and Catholicism.

Presbyterian Reformed (The Roman Catholic-Presbyterian Consultation Group, North American Council of the World Alliance of Reformed Churches): (1) Washington, D.C., July 27, 1965 — Exploratory discussions. (2) Philadelphia, Pa., Nov. 26, 1965 — Role of the Holy Spirit in renewal and reform of the Church. (3) New York, May 12, 1966 — Roman Catholic view of Scripture and tradition; apostolic and ecclesiastical tradition.

(4) Chicago, Ill., Oct. 27, 1966 — Development of doctrine; dialogue, a program of peace, prayer and study for Roman Catholics and Protestants. (5) Collegeville, Minn., Apr. 26, 1967 — Order and ministry in the Reformed tradition; validity of orders; changes in mixed marriage. (6) Lancaster, Pa., Oct. 26, 1967 — Work was begun on a joint statement on ministry. (7) Bristow, Va., May 9, 1968 — Structures and ministries. (8) Allen Park, Mich., Oct. 24, 1968 — Marriage. (9) Charleston, S.C., May 21, 1969 — Validation of ministries and ministry; theological view of marriage.

(10) Macatawa, Mich., Oct. 30, 1969 — Apostles and apostolic succession in the patristic era; report concerning office; divorce and remarriage as understood in the United Presbyterian Church in the USA; the Church and second marriage; recommendations for changes regarding inter-Christian marriages. (11) Morristown, N.J., May 13, 1970 — Joint statements on ministry in the Church and women in Church and society.

(12) Princeton, N.J., Oct. 29 to 30, 1970 — Episcopal/presbyteral polity; episcopacy.

(13) Columbus, O., May 13 to 15, 1971 — Ministry in the Church; man-woman relationships; the future of the Church. (14) Richmond, Va., Oct. 28 to 30, 1971 — Reports finalized on women in the Church and ministry in the Church. (15) Oct. 26 to 29, 1972 — The shape of the unity we seek.

(16) Columbus, O., May 30 to June 2, 1973 — Theological and sociological views of the shape of unity we seek. (17) Columbus, O., Oct. 24 to 27, 1973 — Renewed discussion of the previous topic. (18) Columbus, O., May 8 to 11, 1974 — Further discussion of the previous topic in the light of Scripture, tradition, theology and reflection on the total Christian experience; worship and belief; discussion of plans for publication of a book on progress of the dialogue.

ECUMENICAL BRIEFS

Guidelines: The Vatican Secretariat for Promoting Christian Unity reported late in November, 1973, that final work was in progress on a set of guidelines for ecumenical action on local, regional and national levels. The first comprehensive guidelines, under the title *Directory on Ecumenism,* were issued by the secretariat in 1967. The new ones were expected to reflect ecumenical experience since that time.

Key 73: The year-long ecumenical evangelical venture, while a disappointment in some respects, had positive results in spurring interfaith activity on some local levels.

Moral Issues: "Moral and ethical issues have enormous potential for polarization and divisiveness on local, national and international levels, and this potential may even overshadow that of more strictly doctrinal concerns." So stated Father Arthur F. Gouthro, S.A., director of the Graymoor Ecumenical Institute. "Make no mistake about it," he said, "unless there are serious and consistent attempts at accord and understanding on these issues (e.g., abortion, euthanasia, birth control, divorce) . . . ecumenical progress may be seriously impaired and ecumenism may well be a matter of academics for those who have time for it. . . . Without joint Christian witness in the area of morals, consensus on matters of doctrine will have little effect on the lives of Christian people."

Progress and Problems: Speaking at the Mar. 10-12, 1974, National Workshop for Christian Unity, Archbishop William W. Baum noted these signs of ecumenical progress:

• Publication of agreed statements on the ministry and the papacy by the Anglican-Roman Catholic International Commission of theologians and the Lutheran-Roman Catholic Consultation in the U.S., respectively.

• Prayer is the soul of the ecumenical movement. "If we try to do everything else but fail to do this, the life of the spirit will leave the ecumenical movement."

• "Difficult work" lies ahead in several areas. "Not sufficient thought has been given to the questions of the episcopacy. . . . And what can be said about the extent to which the Church . . . is the efficacious point of contact (in word and sacrament) between God's path and man's vocation?" And: "Another area to which we must turn our attention . . . is the tragic disagreement among Christians concerning the moral demands of the Gospel. Moral issues are too rarely mentioned in our ecumenical dialogues. Yet some agreements are urgently needed in this area, so crucial to the practical life of the faithful."

Archbishop Baum was chairman of the U.S. Bishops' Committee for Ecumenical and Interreligious Affairs.

Spiritual Ecumenism: Father Herbert Ryan, S.J., keynoting the 11th National Workshop on Christian Unity Mar. 10, 1974, in Charleston, S.C., said that the emphasis in ecumenism had shifted from social action to renewed interest in the spiritual life. He said the ecumenical trend in the 1960's "was for Christian outreach, joint social action . . . because this was seen as a means to carry out the social witness of the Gospel message." Observing that strong enthusiasm for social action had diminished, he said ecumenical efforts needed a new thrust because "Christians in America today have started a search for deepening of their inner lives. This search crosses denominational barriers, and the emerging forms that it has taken — prayer groups, discussion and bible groups, charismatic fellowships, religious communes — are already thoroughly ecumenical." He called on workshop participants to take up this new "spiritual challenge" while avoiding the pitfalls of "impious withdrawal" from social action. Father Ryan was a member of the Anglican-Roman Catholic International Commission of theologians.

Statements: Running comment continued during 1974 on three agreed statements published by Catholic, Anglican and Lutheran theologians. The statements reflect the views of participants in the dialogues which produced them. To date, they have not been accepted by the respective churches as statements of doctrine or points of departure for practical changes in discipline.

• The "Windsor Statement" on Eucharistic doctrine, published Dec. 31, 1971, by the Anglican-Roman Catholic International Commission of theologians: Earlier and current comment by ecumenists was generally favorable. Clarification of some points has been requested. The statement does not cover Eucharistic belief in the Anglican Communion in the past nor the vital question of the validity of Anglican orders.

• The "Canterbury Statement" on ministry and ordination, published Dec. 13, 1973, by the same commission. (See separate entry.)

• "Papal Primacy / Converging Viewpoints," published Mar. 4, 1974, by the dialogue group sanctioned by the U.S.A. National Convention of the Lutheran World Federation and the U.S. Bishops' Committee for Ecumenical and Interreligious Affairs. (See sepaate entry.)

Status of Ecumenism: Ecumenism was called one of the most important contemporary movements in the Church by Cardinal Leo J. Suenens of Belgium while attending a seminar for Episcopalian bishops at the Trinity Institute, New York City, in February, 1974. Asked to comment on the view that the ecumenical movement was at a standstill, he said: "This is not my feeling at all. It is true that at the moment there are no such sensational and spectacular events as the meetings a few years ago between Orthodox Patriarch Athenagoras and Pope Paul, or of the visit of (Anglican) Archbishop (Michael) Ramsey of Canterbury to Rome. But I strongly believe the ecumenical movement is going on at different levels."

Week of Prayer: Attendance at observances of the annual Week of Prayer for Christian Unity in January was in decline, after peaking in the wake of the Second Vatican Council. *America* magazine said in an editorial Jan. 26, 1974, that "a consensus appears to exist that greater attention must be given to the pastoral level of interfaith activity." The editorial noted "considerable progress . . . in recent years in the conversations held among theologians from the different denominations," but raised the question: "What kind of a religious response does such theological discussion evoke in the members of the Christian congregations?"

Catholic-WCC Working Group: Proposals to be presented at the fifth world assembly of the World Council of Churches in 1975 were reviewed at a week-long meeting in June, 1974, of joint working group representatives of the Roman Catholic Church and the WCC. The meeting, held in Venice, was the 14th held by the group since its establishment in 1966. Father John Long, S.J., a staff member of the Vatican Secretariat for Promoting Christian Unity, reported that proposals and themes which "look beyond 1975" include new methods for common witness, a deeper evaluation of the nature of Christian unity, a joint study of development and peace, the concept of ecumenical education, and possible study "of the work which has been done up to now by bilateral conversations between the Roman Catholic Church and other churches, such as the Anglicans and the Lutherans." The group also studied reports on the growth of charismatic movements, the functions of lay persons in the mission of the Church, and the new role of women in the Church and world.

CATHOLIC-JEWISH RELATIONS

The Second Vatican Council, in addition to the *Decree on Ecumenism* concerning the movement for unity among Christians, stated the mind of the Church on a similar matter in a *Declaration on the Relationship of the Church to Non-Christian Religions.* This document, as the following excerpts indicate, backgrounds the reasons and directions of the Church's regard for the Jews. (Other portions of the document, not cited here, refer to Hindus, Buddhists and Moslems.)

Spiritual Bond

"As this sacred Synod searches into the mystery of the Church, it recalls the spiritual bond linking the people of the New Covenant with Abraham's stock.

"For the Church of Christ acknowledges that, according to the mystery of God's saving design, the beginnings of her faith and her election are already found among the patriarchs, Moses, and the prophets. She professes that all who believe in Christ, Abraham's sons according to faith (cf. Gal. 3:7), are included in the same patriarch's call, and likewise that the salvation of the Church was mystically foreshadowed by the Chosen People's exodus from the land of bondage.

"The Church, therefore, cannot forget that she received the revelation of the Old Testament through the people with whom God in His inexpressible mercy deigned to establish the Ancient Covenant. Nor can she forget that she draws sustenance from the root of that good olive tree onto which have been grafted the wild olive branches of the Gentiles (cf. Rom.11:17-24). Indeed, the Church believes that by His cross Christ, our Peace, reconciled Jew and Gentile, making them both one in Himself (cf. Eph. 2:14-16).

". . . The Jews still remain most dear to God because of their fathers, for He does not repent of the gifts He makes nor of the calls He issues (cf. Rom. 11:28-29). In company with the prophets and the same Apostle (Paul), the Church awaits that day, known to God alone, on which all peoples will address the Lord in a single voice and 'serve him with one accord' (Zeph. 3:9; Cf. Is. 66:23; Ps. 65:4; Rom. 11:11-32).

"Since the spiritual patrimony common to Christians and Jews is thus so great, this sacred Synod wishes to foster and recommend that mutual understanding and respect which is the fruit above all of biblical and theological studies, and of brotherly dialogues.

No Anti-Semitism

"True, authorities of the Jews and those who followed their lead pressed for the death of Christ (cf. Jn. 19:6); still, what happened in His passion cannot be blamed upon all the Jews then living, without distinction, nor upon the Jews of today. Although the Church is the new People of God, the Jews should not be presented as repudiated or cursed by God, as if such views followed from the holy Scriptures. All should take pains, then, lest in catechetical instruction and in the preaching of God's Word they teach anything out of harmony with the truth of the gospel and the spirit of Christ.

"The Church repudiates all persecutions against any man. Moreover, mindful of her common patrimony with the Jews, and motivated by the gospel's spiritual love and by no political considerations, she deplores the hatred, persecutions, and displays of anti-Semitism directed against the Jews at any time and from any source. . . ." (4).

". . . The Church rejects, as foreign to the mind of Christ, any discrimination against men or harassment of them because of their race, color, condition of life, or religion. . . ." (No. 5).

Bishops' Secretariat

The American hierarchy's first move toward implementation of the Vatican II *Declaration on the Relationship of the Church to Non-Christian Religions* was to establish, in 1965, a Subcommission for Catholic-Jewish Relations in the framework of its Commission for Ecumenical and Interreligious Affairs. This subcommission was reconstituted and given the title of secretariat in September, 1967. Its moderator is Bishop Francis J. Mugavero of Brooklyn. The executive director is Father Edward Flannery. The Secretariat for Catholic-Jewish Relations is located at 1312 Massachusetts Ave. N.W., Washington, D.C. 20005.

According to the key norm of a set of guidelines issued by the secretariat Mar. 16, 1967: "The general aim of all Catholic-Jewish meetings (and relations) is to increase our understanding both of Judaism and the Catholic faith, to eliminate sources of tension and misunderstanding, to initiate dialogue or conversations on different levels, to multiply intergroup meetings between Catholics and Jews, and to promote cooperative social action."

Opinions on Relations

Dr. Gerhard Riegner, in a late 1973 interview in New York, warned Jews that only intensive contacts with Catholics and Protestants on all levels, not withdrawal, could produce continued understanding among Christians for Israel and Jewish causes. He said that such communications "must be a two-way street. We have to explain our problems and seek their assistance, while at the same time listening and understanding their concern."

Dr. Riegner was secretary general of the

World Jewish Congress and a member of the International Jewish Committee for Interreligious Consultations.

Archbishop Jean Jadot, apostolic delegate to the United States, told a New York meeting of the Synagogue Council of America Mar. 26, 1974, that the positions of both Christians and Jews had undergone some "retrenchment," but that this was evidence of a new and "more sober" stage in the development of their dialogue. Some leveling off of initial enthusiasm in the Christian-Jewish dialogue should have been expected but should not discourage anyone, he added.

Past differences between Christians and Jews, the archbishop said, must be faced before meaningful discussions of the present and future can begin.

"To face one's past has a purifying and regenerating effect, and this applies to the historical as well as the personal task. I am aware of the heavy debt that lies on the Christian side in coming to terms with our past alienation. I am confident that Christians will not flinch before it."

The present task of Christians and Jews, Archbishop Jadot declared, is twofold: "We must sustain and advance our dialogue, and at the same time increase our cooperation to contribute to the solution of the grave and pressing problems the world in which we live faces."

JUDAISM

Judaism is the religion of the Old Testament and of contemporary Jews. Divinely revealed and with a patriarchal background (Abraham, Isaac, Jacob), it originated with the Mosaic Covenant, was identified with the Israelites, and achieved distinctive form and character as the religion of The Law from this Covenant and reforms initiated by Ezra and Nehemiah after the Babylonian Exile.

Judaism does not have a formal creed but its principal points of belief are clear. Basic is belief in one transcendent God who reveals himself through The Law, the prophets, the life of his people and events of history. The fatherhood of God involves the brotherhood of men. Religious faith and practice are equated with just living according to The Law. Moral conviction and practice are regarded as more important than precise doctrinal formulation and profession. Formal worship, whose principal act was sacrifice from Canaanite times to 70 A. D., is by prayer, reading and meditating upon the sacred writings, and observance of the Sabbath and festivals.

Judaism has messianic expectations of the complete fulfillment of the Covenant, the coming of God's kingdom, the ingathering of his people, final judgment and retribution for all men. Views differ regarding the manner in which these expectations will be realized— through a person, the community of God's

people, an evolution of historical events, an eschatological act of God himself. Individual salvation expectations also differ, depending on views about the nature of immortality, punishment and reward, and related matters.

The sacred books are the 24 books of the Masoretic Hebrew Text of The Law, the Prophets and the Writings (see The Bible). Together, they contain the basic instruction or norms for just living. In some contexts, the term Law or Torah refers only to the Pentateuch (Genesis, Exodus, Leviticus, Numbers, Deuteronomy); in others, it denotes all the sacred books and/or the whole complex of written and oral tradition.

Also of great authority are two Talmuds which were composed in Palestine and Babylon in the fourth and fifth centuries A.D., respectively. They consist of the Mishna, a compilation of oral laws, and the Gemara, a collection of rabbinical commentary on the Mishna. Midrash are collections of scriptural comments and moral counsels.

Priests were the principal official ministers during the period of sacrificial and temple worship. Rabbis were, and continue to be, teachers and leaders of prayer. The synagogue is the place of community worship. The family and home are focal points of many aspects of Jewish worship and practice.

Of the various categories of Jews, Orthodox are the most conservative in adherence to strict religious traditions. Others — Reformed, Conservative, Reconstructionist — are liberal in comparison with the Orthodox. They favor greater or less modification of religious practices in accommodation to contemporary culture and living conditions.

Principal events in Jewish life include the circumcision of males, according to prescriptions of the Covenant; the bar mitzvah which marks the coming-of-age of boys in Judaism at the age of 13; marriage; and observance of the Sabbath and festivals.

Sabbath and Festivals

Observances of the Sabbath and festivals begin at sundown of the previous calendar day and continue until the following sundown.

Sabbath: Saturday, the weekly day of rest prescribed in the Decalogue.

Booths (Tabernacles): A seven-to-nine-day festival in the month of Tishri (Sept.-Oct.), marked by some Jews with Covenant-renewal and reading of The Law. It originated as an agricultural feast at the end of the harvest and got its name from the temporary shelters used by workers in the fields.

Hanukkah (The Festival of Lights, the Feast of Consecration and of the Maccabees): Commemorates the dedication of the new altar in the Temple at Jerusalem by Judas Maccabeus in 165 B.C. The eight-day festival, during which candles in an eight-branch candelabra are lighted in succession, one each day, occurs near the winter solstice, close to Christmas time.

Passover: A seven-day festival commemorating the liberation of the Israelites from Egypt. The narrative of the Exodus, the Haggadah, is read at ceremonial Seder meals on the first and second days of the festival, which begins on the 14th day of Nisan (Mar.-Apr.).

Pentecost (Feast of Weeks): Observed 50 days after Passover. Some Jews regard it as commemorative of the anniversary of the revelation of The Law to Moses.

Purim: A joyous festival observed on the 14th day of Adar (Feb.-Mar.), commemorating the rescue of the Israelites from massacre by the Persians through the intervention of Esther. The festival is preceded by a day of fasting. A gift- and alms-giving custom became associated with it in medieval times.

Rosh Hashana (Feast of the Trumpets, New Year): Observed on the first day of Tishri (Sept.-Oct.), the festival focuses attention on the day of judgment and is marked with meditation on the ways of life and the ways of death. It is second in importance only to the most solemn observance of Yom Kippur, which is celebrated 10 days later.

Yom Kippur (Day of Atonement): The highest holy day, observed with strict fasting. It occurs 10 days after Rosh Hashana.

ISLAM

Islam is the religion of Mohammed and his followers, called Moslems, Muslims, Mohammedans. Islam, meaning submission to God, originated with Mohammed (570-632), an Arabian, who taught that he had received divine revelation and was the last and greatest of the prophets.

Moslems believe in one God. There were six great prophets—Adam, Noah, Abraham, Moses, Jesus and Mohammed—and Mohammed was the greatest. The creed states: "There is no God but Allah and Mohammed is the prophet of Allah."

The principal duties of Moslems are to: profess the faith by daily recitation of the creed; pray five times a day facing in the direction of the holy city of Mecca; give alms; fast daily from dawn to dusk during the month of Ramadan; make a pilgrimage to Mecca once if possible.

Moslems believe in a final judgment, heaven and hell. Polygamy is practiced. Some dietary regulations are in effect. The weekly day of worship is Friday, and the principal service is at noon in a mosque. Moslems do not have an ordained ministry. The general themes of their prayer are adoration and thanksgiving.

The basis of Islamic belief is the Koran, the created word of God revealed to Mohammed by the angel Gabriel over a period of 20 years. The contents of this sacred book are complemented by the Sunna, a collection of sacred traditions, and reinforced by Ijma, the consensus of Moslems which guarantees them against error in matters of belief and practice. There are several sects of Moslems.

Conciliar Statement

The attitude of the Church toward Islam was stated as follows in the Second Vatican Council's *Declaration on the Relationship of the Church to Non-Christian Religions* (No. 3).

"Upon the Moslems, too, the Church looks with esteem. They adore one God, living and enduring, merciful and all-powerful, Maker of heaven and earth and Speaker to men. They strive to submit wholeheartedly even to His inscrutable decrees, just as did Abraham, with whom the Islamic faith is pleased to associate itself. Though they do not acknowledge Jesus as God, they revere Him as a prophet. They also honor Mary, His virgin mother; at times they call on her, too, with devotion. In addition they await the day of judgment when God will give each man his due after raising him up. Consequently, they prize the moral life, and give worship to God especially through prayer, almsgiving and fasting.

"Although in the course of the centuries many quarrels and hostilities have arisen between Christians and Moslems, this most sacred Synod urges all to forget the past and to strive sincerely for mutual understanding. On behalf of all mankind, let them make common cause of safeguarding and fostering social justice, moral values, peace and freedom."

Dialogue

The purposes of Catholic-Moslem dialogue, which has been rather sketchy, were the subject of joint agreement between Cardinal Paul Marella, president of the Vatican Secretariat for Non-Christians, and a delegation of the Supreme Council of Islamic Affairs, at a Vatican meeting Dec. 16 to 20, 1970.

Their objectives, as stated in a communique, were to:

• hold regular consultations on Moslem-Christian relations, social, cultural and spiritual questions;

• maintain contact through appointed officers and in other ways;

• do everything possible to develop good relations between Christians and Moslems, in order to strengthen the fraternity existing among believers who share respect for all religious values and faith in God;

• continue efforts for justice and peace in the world.

Representatives of the secretariat and the council denounced every type of discrimination in national and international life. They also expressed hope for the success of efforts to establish peace with justice and honor in the Middle East.

NON-REVEALED RELIGIONS

Hinduism: The traditional religion of India with origins dating to about 5,000 B.C. Its history is complex, including original Vedic Hinduism, with a sacred literature (Veda) of hymns, incantations and other elements, and with numerous nature gods; Brahmanism, with emphasis on ceremonialism and its power over the gods; philosophical speculation, reflected in the Upanishads, with development of ideas concerning Karma, reincarnation, Brahman, and the manner of achieving salvation; the cults of Vishnu, Shiva and other deities; reforms in Hinduism and in relation to Islam and Christianity.

The principal tenets of Hinduism are open to various interpretations. Karma is the law of the deed, of sowing and reaping, of retribution. It determines the progress of a person toward liberation from the cycle of rebirths necessary for salvation. Liberation is accomplished in stages, through successive reincarnations which indicate the previous as well as the existing state of a person. The means of liberation are the practice of ceremonialism and asceticism; faith in, devotion to and worship of the gods Vishnu and Shiva in their several incarnations; and/or knowledge attained through disciplined meditation called Yoga. Salvation, according to philosophical Hinduism, consists in absorption in Brahman, the neuter world-soul. Vishnu, the sun-god, and Shiva, the destroyer or generative force of the universe, are the principal popular deities. Ancient belief in nature gods (pantheism) is reflected in sacred respect for some animals. The concept of reincarnation underlies the caste system in Indian society.

There are many sects in Hinduism, which does not have a definite creed. It lends itself easily to syncretism or amalgamation with other beliefs, as evidenced in the 15th century Sikh movement which adopted the monotheism and militancy of Islam. Hindu rituals are various and elaborate, with respect to foods, festivals, pilgrimages, marriage and other life-events.

Buddhism: Originated in the sixth century B.C. in reaction to formalism, pantheism and other trends in Hinduism. The Buddha, the Enlightened One, was Sidartha Gautama, an Indian prince, who sought to explain human suffering and evil and to find a middle way between the extremes of austerity and sensuality.

The four noble truths of Buddhism are: (1) existence involves suffering or pain; (2) suffering comes from craving: (3) craving can be overcome; (4) the way to overcome craving is to follow the "noble eightfold path" of right views, right intention, right speech, right action, right livelihood, right effort, right mindfulness and right concentration.

Karma, the deed-principle of judgment and retribution, and reincarnation are elements of Buddhism. The ultimate objective of life is Nirvana — the absorption of a person in the absolute — which ends the cycles of rebirth.

Buddhism is essentially atheistic and more of a moral philosophy and ethical system than a religion. It has a cultic element in veneration for Buddha. Monasteries, temples and shrines are places of contemplation and ritualistic observance. There are several categories of Buddhist monks and nuns.

Buddhism has many sects. Mahayana Buddhism, with an elaborate ideology, is strong in China, Korea and Japan. Hinayana Buddhism is common in Southeast Asia. Zen Buddhism is highly contemplative. Lamaism in Tibet is a combination of Buddhism and local demonolatry.

Confucianism: An ethical system based on the teachings of Confucius (c. 551-479 B.C.). It is oriented toward the moral perfection of individuals and society, the attainment of the harmony of individual and social life with the harmony of the universe, through conduct governed by the relationships of humanity, justice, ritual and courtesy, wisdom, and fidelity. Originally and basically humanistic, Confucianism was eventually mingled with elements of Chinese religion. It exerted a strong influence on national life in China from 125 to the beginning of the 20th century, despite some periods of decline.

Taoism: Originated in China several centuries before the Christian era and became a fully developed religious system by the fifth century A.D. As a religion of mystery, it developed extreme polytheism, with the Jade Emperor as the highest deity; sought blessings and long life by means of alchemy; fostered superstition and witchcraft; took on organizational and other aspects of Buddhism, with several categories of priests and nuns; exerted strong ethical influence on the lower classes; split into many sects; adopted features from other religions; became the starting point of many secret societies. One of its key tenets — that the way of nature is the guide to human conduct — resulted in a form of quietism opposed to the social concern of Confucianism.

Shinto: The way of the gods, the sum total of the cultic beliefs and practices of the ancestral religion of Japan which originated from nature and ancestor worship. Shinto is pantheistic and has many objects of devotion, the highest being the Ruler of Heaven; is practiced with detailed rituals in public shrines, which are cultic centers; has strong social influence. Sectarian Shinto has about 13 recognized sects and many offshoots. Shinto, with principal concern for this-worldly blessing, has ben affected by Buddhist and Confucian influences.

Eastern cults — with their mysticism and associated disciplines and practices — have recurrent periods of vogue in the West.

Glossary

A

Abbess: The female superior of a monastic community of nuns; e.g., Benedictines, Poor Clares, some others. Elected by members of the community, an abbess has general authority over her community but no sacramental jurisdiction. Earliest evidence of the use of the title, a feminine derivative of the Aramaic *abba* (father), dates from early in the sixth century.

Abbey: See Monastery.

Abbot: The male superior of a monastic community of men religious; e.g., Benedictines, Cistercians, some others. Elected by members of the community, an abbot has ordinary jurisdiction and general authority over his community. He has some episcopal privileges. The title derives from the Aramaic *abba* (father); first given to the spiritual fathers and guides of hermits in Egypt in the fourth century, it was appropriated in the Rule of St. Benedict to the heads of abbeys and monasteries. Eastern-Rite equivalents of an abbot are a *hegumen* and an *archimandrite*.

A regular abbot is the head of an abbey or monastery. An abbot general or archabbot is the head of a congregation consisting of several monasteries. An abbot primate is the head of the modern Benedictine Confederation. A few regular abbots have jurisdiction over the residents and institutions of a district *(abbacy)* which does not belong to any diocese; jurisdiction of this kind is similar to that of a bishop in his diocese. The only abbot of this kind in the US is the abbot of Belmont Abbey, N.C.

Abjuration: Renunciation of apostasy, heresy or schism by a solemn oath.

Ablution: A term derived from Latin, meaning washing or cleansing, and referring to the cleansing of the hands of a priest celebrating Mass, after the offering of gifts; and to the cleansing of the chalice with water and wine after Communion.

Abortion: The expulsion of a nonviable human fetus from the womb of the mother, with moral implications stemming from the humanity of the fetus from the moment of conception and its consequent right to life.

Accidental expulsion, as in cases of miscarriage, is without moral fault.

Direct abortion, in which a fetus is intentionally removed from the womb, constitutes a direct attack on an innocent human being, a violation of the Fifth Commandment. It is punished in church law by the penalty of excommunication, which is automatically incurred by all baptized persons involved; i.e., the consenting mother and necessary physical and/or moral cooperators. Direct abortion is not justifiable for any reason, e.g.: therapeutic, for the physical and/or psychological welfare of the mother; preventive, to avoid the birth of a defective or unwanted child; social, in the interests of family and/or community.

Indirect abortion, which occurs when a fetus is expelled during medical or other treatment of the mother for a reason other than procuring expulsion, is permissible under the principle of double effect for a proportionately serious reason; e.g., when a medical or surgical procedure is necessary to save the life of the mother.

Absolution: The act by which an authorized priest, acting as the agent of Christ and minister of the Church, grants forgiveness of sins in the sacrament of penance. The essential formula of absolution is: "I absolve you from your sins; in the name of the Father, and of the Son, and of the Holy Spirit. Amen."

Priests receive the power to absolve in virtue of their ordination and the right to exercise this power in virtue of faculties of jurisdiction given them by their bishop, their religious superior, or by canon law. The faculties of jurisdiction can be limited or restricted regarding certain sins and penalties or censures.

In cases of necessity, and also in cases of the absence of their own confessors, Eastern and Roman Rite Catholics may ask for and receive sacramental absolution from a priest of a separated Eastern Church. Separated Eastern Christians may similarly ask for and receive sacramental absolution from an Eastern or Roman Rite priest.

Any priest can absolve a person in danger of death; in the absence of a priest with the usual faculties, this includes a laicized priest or a priest under censure.

(See additional entry under Sacraments.)

Absolution, General: (1) Sacramental absolution given without confession of sin, when confession is impossible. Persons so absolved are required to confess, in their next confession, the mortal sins from which they were so absolved.

(2) A blessing of the Church to which a plenary indulgence is attached, given at the hour of death, and at stated times to members of religious institutes and third orders.

Accessory to Another's Sin: One who culpably assists another in the performance of an evil action. This may be done by counsel, command, provocation, consent, praise, flattery, concealment, participation, silence, defense of the evil done.

Adoration: The highest act and purpose of religious worship, which is directed in love and reverence to God alone in acknowledgment of his infinite perfection and goodness, and of his total dominion over creatures. Adoration, which is also called *latria,* consists of internal and external elements, private and social prayer, liturgical acts and ceremonies, and especially sacrifice.

Adultery: (1) Sexual intercourse between a married person and another to whom one is not married; a violation of the obligations of chastity and justice. The Sixth Commandment prohibition against adultery is also regarded as a prohibition against all external sins of a sexual nature.

(2) Any sin of impurity (thought, desire, word, action) involving a married person who is not one's husband or wife has the nature of adultery.

Adventists: Members of several Christian sects whose doctrines are dominated by belief in a more or less imminent second advent or coming of Christ upon earth for a glorious 1,000-year reign of righteousness. This reign, following victory by the forces of good over evil in a final Battle of Armageddon, will begin with the resurrection of the chosen and will end with the resurrection of all other men and the annihilation of the wicked. Thereafter, the just will live forever in a renewed heaven and earth. A sleep of the soul takes place between the time of death and the day of judgment. There is no hell. The Bible, in fundamentalist interpretation, is regarded as the only rule of faith and practice.

About six sects have developed in the course of the Adventist movement which originated with William Miller (1782-1849) in the United States. Miller, on the basis of calculations made from the Book of Daniel, predicted that the second advent of Christ would occur between 1843 and 1844. After the prophecy went unfulfilled, divisions occurred in the movement and the Seventh Day Adventists, whose actual formation dates from 1860, emerged as the largest single body. The observance of Saturday instead of Sunday as the Lord's Day dates from 1844.

Advent Wreath: A wreath of laurel, spruce, or similar foliage with four candles which are lighted successively in the weeks of Advent to symbolize the approaching celebration of the birth of Christ, the Light of the World, at Christmas. The wreath originated among German Protestants.

Agape: A Greek word, meaning love, love feast, designating the meal of fellowship eaten at some gatherings of early Christians. Although held in some places in connection with the Mass, the agape was not part of the Mass, nor was it of universal institution and observance. Legislation against it was passed by the Council of Carthage (397) and other councils because of abuses. It was infrequently observed by the fifth century and disappeared altogether between the sixth and eighth centuries. In recent years, a limited revival has taken place in the course of the liturgical and ecumenical movements.

Age of Reason: (1) The time of life when one begins to distinguish between right and wrong, to understand an obligation and take on moral responsibility; seven years of age is the presumption in church law.

(2) Historically, the 18th century period of Enlightenment in England and France, the age of the Encyclopedists and Deists. According to a basic thesis of the Enlightenment, human experience and reason are the only sources of certain knowledge of truth; consequently, faith and revelation are discounted as valid sources of knowledge, and the reality of supernatural truth is called into doubt and/or denied.

Aggiornamento: An Italian word having the general meaning of bringing up to date, renewal, revitalization, descriptive of the processes of spiritual renewal and institutional reform and change in the Church; fostered by the Second Vatican Council.

Agnosticism: A theory which holds that man cannot have certain knowledge of immaterial reality, especially the existence of God and things pertaining to him. Immanuel Kant, one of the philosophical fathers of agnosticism, stood for the position that God, as well as the human soul, is unknowable on speculative grounds; nevertheless, he found practical imperatives for acknowledging God's existence, a view shared by many agnostics. The First Vatican Council declared that the existence of God and some of his attributes can be known with certainty by human reason, even without divine revelation. The word agnosticism was first used, in the sense given here, by T. H. Huxley in 1869.

Agnus Dei: A Latin phrase, meaning Lamb of God.

(1) A title given to Christ, the Lamb (victim) of the Sacrifice of the New Law (on Calvary and in Mass).

(2) A prayer said at Mass before the reception of Holy Communion.

(3) A sacramental. It is a round paschal-candle fragment blessed by the pope. On one side it bears the impression of a lamb, symbolic of Christ. On the reverse side, there may be any one of a number of impressions; e.g., the figure of a saint, the name and coat of arms of the reigning pope. The *agnus dei* may have originated at Rome in the fifth century. The first definite mention of it dates from about 820.

Alleluia: An exclamation of joy derived from Hebrew, All hail to him who is, praise God. It is used in the liturgy and other prayer on joyful occasions during the church year.

Allocution: A formal type of papal address, as distinguished from an ordinary sermon or statement of views.

Alms: An act, gift or service of compassion, motivated by love of God and neighbor, for the help of persons in need; an obligation of charity, which is measurable by the ability of one person to give assistance and by the degree of another's need. Almsgiving, along with prayer and fasting, is regarded as a work of penance as well as an exercise of charity. (See Corporal and Spiritual Works of Mercy.)

Alpha and Omega: The first and last letters of the Greek alphabet, used to symbolize the eternity of God (Rv. 1:8) and the divinity and eternity of Christ, the beginning and end of all things (Rv. 21:6; 22:13). Use of the letters as a monogram of Christ originated in the fourth century or earlier.

Amen: A Hebrew word meaning truly, it is true. In the Gospels, Christ used the word to add a note of authority to his statements. In other New Testament writings, as in Hebrew usage, it was the concluding word to doxologies. As the concluding word of prayers, it expresses assent to and acceptance of God's will.

Anathema: A Greek word with the root meaning of cursed or separated and the adapted meaning of excommunication, used in church documents, especially the canons of ecumenical councils, for the condemnation of heretical doctrines and of practices opposed to proper discipline.

Anchorite: A kind of hermit living in complete isolation and devoting himself exclusively to exercises of religion and severe penance according to a rule and way of life of his own devising. In early Christian times, anchorites were the forerunners of the monastic life. The closest contemporary approach to the life of an anchorite is that of Carthusian and Camaldolese hermits.

Angels: Purely spiritual beings with intelligence and free will, whose name indicates their mission as ministers of God and ministering spirits to men. They were created before the creation of the visible universe; the devil and bad angels, who were created good, fell from glory through their own fault. In addition to these essentials of defined doctrine, it is held that angels are personal beings; they can intercede for men; fallen angels were banished from God's glory in heaven to hell; bad angels can tempt men to commit sin. The doctrine of guardian angels, although not explicitly defined as a matter of faith, is rooted in long-standing tradition. No authoritative declaration has ever been issued regarding choirs or various categories of angels: according to theorists, there are nine choirs, consisting of seraphim, cherubim, thrones, dominations, principalities, powers, virtues, archangels and angels. In line with scriptural usage, only three angels can be named—Michael, Raphael and Gabriel.

Angelus: A devotion which commemorates the Incarnation of Christ. It consists of three versicles, three Hail Marys and a special prayer, and recalls the announcement to Mary by the Archangel Gabriel that she was chosen to be the Mother of Christ, her acceptance of the divine will, and the Incarnation (Lk. 1:26-38). The Angelus is recited at 6 a.m., noon and 6 p.m. The practice of reciting the Hail Mary in honor of the Incarnation was introduced by the Franciscans in 1263. The *Regina Caeli,* commemorating the joy of

Mary at Christ's Resurrection, replaces the Angelus during the Easter season.

Anger: Passionate displeasure arising from some kind of offense suffered at the hands of another person, frustration or other cause, combined with a tendency to strike back at the cause of the displeasure; a violation of the Fifth Commandment and one of the capital sins if the displeasure is out of proportion to the cause and/or if the retaliation is unjust.

Anglican Orders: Holy orders conferred according to the rite of the Anglican (Episcopal) Church, which Leo XIII declared null and void in the bull *Apostolicae Curae,* Sept. 13, 1896. The orders were declared null because they were conferred according to a rite that was considered substantially defective in form and intent, and because of a break in apostolic succession that occurred when Matthew Parker became head of the Anglican hierarchy in 1559.

In making his declaration, Pope Leo cited earlier arguments against validity made by Julius III in 1553 and 1554 and by Paul IV in 1555. He also noted related directives requiring absolute ordination, according to the Catholic ritual, of convert ministers who had been ordained according to the Anglican Ordinal.

Antichrist: The man of sin, the lawless and wicked antagonist of Christ and the work of God; a mysterious figure of prophecy mentioned in the New Testament. Supported by Satan, submitting to no moral restraints, and armed with tremendous power, Antichrist will set himself up in opposition to God, work false miracles, persecute the People of God, and employ unimaginable means to lead men into error and evil during a period of widespread defection from the Christian faith before the end of time; he will be overcome by Christ. Catholic thinkers have regarded Antichrist as a person, a caricature of Christ, who will lead a final violent struggle against God and His people; they have also applied the title to personal and impersonal forces in history hostile to God and the Church. Official teaching has said little about Antichrist. In 1318, it labeled as partly heretical, senseless, and fanciful the assertions made by the Fraticelli about his coming; in 1415, the Council of Constance condemned the Wycliff thesis that excommunications made by the pope and other prelates were the actions of Antichrist.

Antiphon: (1) A short verse or text, generally from Scripture, recited in the Liturgy of the Hours before and after psalms and canticles.

(2) Any verse sung or recited by one part of a choir or congregation in response to the other part, as in antiphonal or alternate chanting.

Apologetics: The science and art of building and presenting the case for, accounting for, explaining, defending, justifying the reasonableness of the Christian faith, by a wide variety of means including facts of experience, history, science, philosophy. The constant objective of apologetics is preparation for response to God in faith; its ways and means, however, are subject to change in accordance with the various needs of people and different sets of circumstances.

Apostasy: (1) The total and obstinate rejection or abandonment of the Christian faith by a baptized person who continues to call himself a Christian. External manifestation of this rejection constitutes the crime of apostasy, and the person, called an *apostate,* automatically incurs a penalty of excommunication.

(2) Apostasy from orders is the unlawful withdrawal from or rejection of the obligations of the clerical state by a man who has received major orders. The canonical penalty for such apostasy is excommunication.

(3) Apostasy from the religious life occurs when a religious with perpetual vows unlawfully leaves the community with the intention of not returning, or actually remains outside the community for 30 days without permission. The canonical penalty for such apostasy is excommunication.

Apostolate: The ministry or work of an apostle. In Catholic usage, the word is an umbrella-like term covering all kinds and areas of work and endeavor for the service of God and the Church and the good of people. Thus, the apostolate of bishops is to carry on the mission of the Apostles as pastors of the People of God: of priests, to carry out the sacramental and pastoral ministry for which they are ordained; of religious, to follow and do the work of Christ in conformity with the evangelical counsels and their rule of life; of lay persons, as individuals and/or in groups, to give witness to Christ and build up the kingdom of God through practice of their faith, professional competence and the performance of good works in the concrete circumstances of daily life. Apostolic works are not limited to those done within the Church or by specifically Catholic groups, although some apostolates are officially assigned to certain persons or groups and are under the direction of church authorities. Apostolate derives from the commitment and obligation of baptism, confirmation, holy orders, matrimony, the duties of one's state in life, etc.

Archangel: An angel who carries out special missions for God in his dealings with men. Three of them are named in the Bible: Michael, leader of the angelic host and protector of the synagogue; Raphael, guide of Tobiah and healer of his father, who is regarded as the patron of travelers; Gabriel, called the angel of the Incarnation because of his announcement to Mary that she was to be the Mother of Christ.

Archdiocese: An ecclesiastical jurisdiction headed by an archbishop. An archdiocese is usually a metropolitan see, i.e., the principal one of a group of dioceses comprising a province; the other dioceses in the province are suffragan sees.

Archives: Documentary records, and the place where they are kept, of the spiritual and temporal government and affairs of the Church, a diocese, church agencies like the departments of the Roman Curia, bodies like religious institutes, and individual parishes. The collection, cataloguing, preserving, and use of these records are governed by norms stated in canon law and particular regulations. The strictest secrecy is always in effect for confidential records concerning matters of conscience, and documents of this kind are destroyed as soon as circumstances permit.

Archpriest: For some time, before and during the Middle Ages, a priest who took the place of a bishop at liturgical worship. In Europe, the term is sometimes used as an honorary title. It is also an honorary title in Eastern-Rite Churches.

Asceticism: The practice of self-discipline. In the spiritual life, asceticism — by personal prayer, meditation, self-denial, works of mortification, and outgoing interpersonal works — is motivated by love of God and contributes to growth in holiness.

Ashes: Religious significance has been associated with their use as symbolic of penance since Old Testament times. Thus, ashes of palm blessed on the previous Sunday of the Passion are placed on the foreheads of the faithful on Ash Wednesday to remind them to do works of penance, especially during the season of Lent, and that they are dust and unto dust will return. Ashes are a sacramental.

Aspergillum: A vessel or device used for sprinkling holy water. The ordinary type is a metallic rod with a bulbous tip which absorbs the water and discharges it at the motion of the user's hand.

Aspersory: A portable metallic vessel, similar to a pail, for carrying holy water.

Aspiration: Short exclamatory prayer; e.g., My Jesus, mercy.

Atheism: Denial of the existence of God, finding expression in a system of thought (speculative atheism) or a manner of acting (practical atheism) as though there were no God.

The Second Vatican Council, in its *Pastoral Constitution on the Church in the Modern World* (Nos. 19 to 21), noted that a profession of atheism may represent an explicit denial of God, the rejection of a wrong notion of God, an affirmation of man rather than of God, an extreme protest against evil. It said that such a profession might result from acceptance of such propositions as: there is no absolute truth; man can assert nothing, absolutely nothing, about God; everything can be explained by scientific reasoning alone; the whole question of God is devoid of meaning.

The constitution also cited two opinions of

influence in atheistic thought. One of them regards recognition of dependence on God as incompatible with human freedom and independence. The other views belief in God and religion as a kind of opiate which sedates man on earth, reconciling him to the acceptance of suffering, injustice, shortcomings, etc., because of hope for greater things after death, and thereby hindering him from seeking and working for improvement and change for the better here and now.

All of these views, in one way or another, have been involved in the No-God and Death-of-God schools of thought in recent and remote history.

Atonement: The redemptive activity of Christ, who reconciled man with God through his Incarnation and entire life, and especially by his suffering and Resurrection. The word also applies to prayer and good works by which men join themselves with and take part in Christ's work of reconciliation and reparation for sin.

Attributes of God: Perfections of God. God possesses—and is—all the perfections of being, without limitation. Because he is infinite, all of these perfections are one, perfectly united in him. Man, however, because of the limited power of understanding, views these perfections separately, as distinct characteristics—even though they are not actually distinct in God. God is: almighty, eternal, holy, immortal, immense, immutable, incomprehensible, ineffable, infinite, invisible, just, loving, merciful, most high, most wise, omnipotent, omniscient, omnipresent, patient, perfect, provident, supreme, true.

Avarice (Covetousness): A disorderly and unreasonable attachment to and desire for material things; called a capital sin because it involves preoccupation with material things to the neglect of spiritual goods and obligations of justice and charity.

Ave Maria: See Hail Mary.

B

Baldachino: A canopy over an altar.

Beatification: A preliminary step toward canonization of a saint. It begins with an investigation of the candidate's life, writings and heroic practice of virtue, and the certification of at least two miracles worked by God through his intercession. If the findings of the investigation so indicate, the pope decrees that the Servant of God may be called *Blessed* and may be honored locally or in a limited way in the liturgy. Additional procedures lead to canonization (see separate entry).

Beatific Vision: The intuitive, immediate and direct vision and experience of God enjoyed in the light of glory by all the blessed in heaven. The vision is a supernatural mystery.

Beatitude: A literary form of the Old and New Testaments in which blessings are promised to persons for various reasons. Beatitudes are mentioned 26 times in the Psalms, and in other books of the Old Testament. The best known beatitudes — identifying blessedness with participation in the kingdom of God and his righteousness, and descriptive of the qualities of Christian perfection — are those recounted in Mt. 5:3-11 and Lk. 6:20-22.

In Matthew's account, the beatitudes are:

"How blest are the poor in spirit: the reign of God is theirs.

"Blest too are the sorrowing; they shall be consoled.

"(Blest are the lowly; they shall inherit the land.)

"Blest are they who hunger and thirst for holiness; they shall have their fill.

"Blest are they who show mercy; mercy shall be theirs.

"Blest are the single-hearted for they shall see God.

"Blest too are the peacemakers; they shall be called sons of God.

"Blest are those persecuted for holiness' sake; the reign of God is theirs.

"Blest are you when they insult you and persecute you and utter every kind of slander against you because of me."

In Luke's account, the beatitudes are:

"Blest are you poor; the reign of God is yours.

"Blest are you who hunger; you shall be filled.

"Blest are you who are weeping; you shall laugh.

"Blest shall you be when men hate you, when they ostracize you and insult you and proscribe your name as evil because of the Son of Man."

Benediction of the Blessed Sacrament: A short exposition of the Eucharist for adoration by and blessing of the faithful. Devotional practices include the singing of Eucharistic and other hymns, and recitation of the Divine Praises. Benediction, in its present form, dates from about the 15th century and is a form of liturgical worship.

Benedictus: The canticle or hymn uttered by Zechariah at the circumcision of St. John the Baptist (Lk. 1:68-79). It is an expression of praise and thanks to God for sending John as a precursor of the Messiah. The *Benedictus* is recited in the Liturgy of the Hours as part of Lauds.

Bible Service: A devotion consisting essentially of common prayer of a biblical or liturgical character, several readings from Scripture, and a homily on the texts.

Biglietto: A papal document of notification of appointment to the cardinalate.

Biretta: A stiff, square hat with three ridges on top worn by clerics in church and on other occasions.

Blasphemy: Any expression of insult or contempt with respect to God, principally, and to holy persons and things, secondarily; a violation of the honor due to God in the context of the First and Second Commandments.

Blasphemy of the Spirit: Deliberate resistance to the Holy Spirit, called the unforgivable sin (Mt. 12:31) because it makes his saving action impossible. Thus, the only unforgivable sin is the one for which a person will not seek pardon from God.

Blessing: Invocation of God's favor, by official ministers of the Church or by private individuals. Blessings are recounted in the Old and New Testaments, and are common in the Christian tradition. The Church, through its ordained ministers (bishops and priests, especially), invokes divine favor in liturgical blessings; e.g., of the people at Mass, of the gifts to be consecrated at Mass, of persons and things on various occasions. Sacramentals — such as crucifixes, crosses, rosaries, scapulars, medals — are blessed by ministers of the Church for the invocation of God's favor on those who use them in the proper manner. Many types of blessings are listed in the *Roman Ritual.* Private blessings, as well as those of an official kind, are efficacious. Blessings are imparted with the Sign of the Cross and appropriate prayer.

Boat: A small vessel used to hold incense which is to be placed in the censer.

Brief, Apostolic: A papal letter, less formal than a bull, signed for the pope by a secretary and impressed with the seal of the Fisherman's Ring. Simple apostolic letters of this kind are issued for beatifications and with respect to other matters.

Bull, Apostolic: The most solemn form of papal document, beginning with the name and title of the pope (e.g., Paul VI, Servant of the Servants of God), dealing with an important subject, and having attached to it either a leaden seal called a *bulla* or a red ink imprint of the device on the seal. Bulls are known as apostolic letters with the seal. The seal, on one side, has representations of the heads of Sts. Peter and Paul; on the other side, the name of the reigning pope. Bulls are issued to confer the titles of bishops and cardinals, to promulgate canonizations, and for other purposes. A collection of bulls is called a *bullarium.*

Burial, Ecclesiastical: Interment with church rites and in consecrated ground. Catechumens as well as baptized Catholics have a right to ecclesiastical burial. A non-Catholic partner in a mixed marriage may be buried in a Catholic cemetery with the Catholic partner.

C

Calumny: Harming the name and good reputation of a person by lies; a violation of obligations of justice and truth. Restitution is due for calumny.

Calvary: A knoll about 15 feet high just outside the western wall of Jerusalem where Christ was crucified, so called from the Latin *calvaria* (skull) which described its shape.

Canon: A Greek word meaning rule, norm, standard, measure.

(1) The word designates the Canon of Sacred Scripture, which is the list of books recognized by the Church as inspired by the Holy Spirit.

(2) In the sense of regulating norms, the word designates the body or corpus of Canon Law enacted and promulgated by ecclesiastical authority for the orderly administration and government of the Church. The Code of Canon Law now in force in the Roman Church has been in effect since 1918. It consists of 2,414 canons which are divided into five books covering general rules, ecclesiastical persons, sacred things, trials, crimes and punishments. The code is now under review for the purpose of revision. Eastern-Rite Churches have their own canon law.

(3) The term also designates the four canons, (Eucharistic prayers, anaphoras) of the Mass, the core of the liturgy.

(4) Certain dignitaries of the Church have the title of Canon, and some religious are known as Canons.

Canonization: An infallible declaration by the pope that a person, who died as a martyr and/or practiced Christian virtue to a heroic degree, is now in heaven and is worthy of honor and imitation by all the faithful. Such a declaration is preceded by the process of beatification and another detailed investigation concerning the person's reputation for holiness, his writings, and (except in the case of martyrs) miracles ascribed to his intercession after his death. Miracles are not required for martyrs. The pope can dispense from some of the formalities ordinarily required in canonization procedures (equivalent canonization), as Pope John XXIII did in the canonization of St. Gregory Barbarigo on May 26, 1960. A saint is worthy of honor in liturgical worship throughout the universal Church.

From its earliest years the Church has venerated saints. Public official honor always required the approval of the bishop of the place. Martyrs were the first to be honored. St. Martin of Tours, who died in 397, was the first non-martyr venerated as a saint. The first official canonization by a pope for the universal Church was that of St. Ulrich by John XV in 993. Alexander III reserved the process of canonization to the Holy See in 1171. In 1588 Sixtus V established the Sacred Congregation of Rites for the principal purpose of handling causes for beatification and canonization: this function is now the work of the Congregation for the Causes of Saints. The present procedure is outlined in canons 1999-2141 of the Code of Canon Law and in a 1969 enactment by Paul VI.

The essential portion of a canonization decree states:

"For the honor of the holy and undivided Trinity; for the exaltation of the Catholic faith and the increase of Christian life; with the authority of our Lord Jesus Christ, of the blessed Apostles Peter and Paul, and with our own authority; after mature deliberation and with the divine assistance, often implored; with the counsel of many of our brothers.

"We decree and define that (name) is a saint and we inscribe him (her) in the Catalogue of Saints, stating that he (she) shall be venerated in the universal Church with pious devotion.

"In the name of the Father and of the Son and of the Holy Spirit. Amen."

The official listing of saints and blessed is contained in the *Roman Martyrology* and related decrees issued after its last publication. Butler's unofficial *Lives of the Saints* (1956) contains 2,565 entries.

The Church regards all persons in heaven as saints, not just those who have been officially canonized.

(See Beatification, Saints, Canonizations by Leo XIII and His Successors.)

Canticle: A scriptural chant or prayer differing from the psalms. Three of the canticles prescribed for use in the Liturgy of the Hours are: the *Magnificat* (Lk. 1:46-55), the *Benedictus* (Lk. 1:68-79), and the *Nunc Dimittis* (Lk. 2:29-32.)

Capital Punishment: Punishment for crime by means of the death penalty. The political community, which has authority to provide for the common good, has the right to defend itself and its members against unjust aggression and may in extreme cases punish with the death penalty persons found guilty before the law of serious crimes against individuals and a just social order. Such punishment is essentially vindictive. Its value as a crime-deterrent is a matter of perennial debate. The prudential judgment as to whether or not there should be capital punishment belongs to the civic community. The U.S. Supreme Court ruled June 29, 1972, against the constitutionality of existing statutes on capital punishment. Within 14 months of the decision, which had the effect of staying some 600 executions, 17 states enacted new laws designating as capital offenses mass murder, murder of a policeman, fireman or prison guard, and murder while perpetrating rape, kidnapping, arson or hijacking a commercial vehicle.

Capital Sins: Moral faults which, if habitual, give rise to many more sins. They are: pride, covetousness, lust, anger, gluttony, envy, sloth.

The opposite virtues are: humility, liberality, chastity, meekness, temperance, brotherly love, diligence.

Cardinal Virtues: The four principal moral virtues are prudence, justice, temperance and fortitude.

Catacombs: Underground Christian cemeteries in various cities of the Roman Empire and Italy, especially in the vicinity of Rome; the burial sites of many martyrs and other Christians. Developed from aboveground cemeteries, their passageways, burial niches and assembly rooms were dug out of tuffa, a soft clay which hardened into rock-like consistency on drying. The earliest ones date from the third century; in the fourth, they became the scene of memorial services as the veneration of martyrs increased in popularity; in the seventh and eighth centuries, they were plundered by the Lombards and other invaders. The relics of many martyrs were removed to safer places in the ninth century; afterwards, the catacombs fell into neglect and oblivion until interest in them revived in the 16th century. The catacombs have been excavated extensively, yielding considerable information about early Christian symbolism and art, dating from the third century on, and other aspects of Christian life and practice.

Catafalque: A small structure like a bier, used at services for the dead in the absence of the corpse.

Catechism: A summary of Christian doctrine in question and answer form, used for purposes of instruction.

Catechumen: A person preparing, in a program of instruction and spiritual formation, for baptism and reception into the Church.

Cathedra: A Greek word for chair, designating the chair or seat of a bishop in the principal church of his diocese, which is therefore called a cathedral (see separate entry).

Cathedraticum: The tax paid to a bishop by all churches and benefices subject to him for the support of episcopal administration and for works of charity.

Catholic: A Greek word, meaning universal, first used in the title Catholic Church in a letter written by St. Ignatius of Antioch about 107 to the Christians of Smyrna.

Celebret: A Latin word, meaning Let him celebrate, the name of a document issued by a bishop or other superior stating that a priest is in good standing and therefore should be given opportunity to celebrate Mass or perform other priestly functions.

Celibacy: The unmarried state of life, required in the Roman or Latin Church of candidates for holy orders and of men already ordained to holy orders, for the practice of perfect chastity and total dedication to the service of people in the ministry of the Church. Celibacy is enjoined as a condition for ordination by church discipline and law, not by dogmatic necessity.

In the Roman Church, a consensus in favor of celibacy developed in the early centuries while the clergy included both celibates and men who had been married once. The first local legislation on the subject was enacted by a local council held in Elvira, Spain, about 306; it forbade bishops, priests, deacons and other ministers to have wives. Similar enactments were passed by other local councils from that time on, and by the 12th century particular laws regarded marriage by clerics in major orders to be not only unlawful but also null and void. The latter view was translated by the Second Lateran Council in 1139 into what seems to be the first written universal law making holy orders an invalidating impediment to marriage. In 1563 the Council of Trent ruled definitely on the matter and established the discipline still in force in the Roman Church.

Some exceptions to this discipline have been made in recent years. Several married Protestant ministers who became converts and were subsequently ordained to the priesthood have been permitted to continue in marriage. Married men over the age of 35 can be ordained to the permanent diaconate.

Recent agitation for optional rather than mandatory celibacy for priests has diminished, without change in church law.

Eastern Church discipline on celibacy differs from that of the Roman Church. In line with legislation enacted by the Synod of Trullo in 692 and still in force, candidates for holy orders may marry before becoming deacons and may continue in marriage thereafter, but marriage after ordination is forbidden. Eastern-Rite bishops in the US, however, do not ordain married candidates for the priesthood. Eastern-Rite bishops are unmarried.

Cenacle: The room in Jerusalem where Christ ate the Last Supper with his Apostles.

Censer: A metal vessel with a perforated cover and suspended by chains, in which incense is burned. It is used at some Masses, Benediction of the Blessed Sacrament and other liturgical functions.

Censorship of Books: An exercise of vigilance by the Church for safeguarding authentic religious teaching.

Censorship procedure requires that books and other works dealing with matters of faith and morals and related subjects be cleared for doctrinal orthodoxy before publication. This is accomplished by having the works reviewed by officials called censors.

Permission to publish works of a religious character, together with the apparatus of reviewing them beforehand, generally falls under the authority of the bishop of the place where the writer lives or where the works are published.

Clearance for publication is usually indicated by the terms *Nihil obstat* (Nothing stands in the way) issued by the censor and *Imprimatur* (Let it be printed) authorized by the bishop. The occasional equivalent of these formal terms is the statement, Printed with ecclesiastical approval. The clearing of works for publication does not necessarily imply approval of an author's viewpoint or his manner of handling a subject.

Censures: Spiritual penalties inflicted by the Church on baptized persons for committing certain serious sins, which are classified as crimes in canon law, and for being or remaining obstinate therein. Excommunication, suspension and interdict have been the censures in force since the time of Innocent III (1214). Their intended purposes are to deter persons from committing sins which, more seriously and openly than others, threaten the common good of the Church and its members; to punish and correct offenders; and to provide for the making of reparation for harm done to the community of the Church. Censures may be incurred automatically (*ipso facto*) on the commission of certain offenses for which fixed penalties have been laid down in church law (*latae sententiae*); or they may be inflicted by sentence of a judge (*ferendae sententiae*). Obstinacy in crime—also called contumacy, disregard of a penalty, defiance of church authority — is presumed by law in the commission of crimes for which automatic censures are decreed. The presence and degree of contumacy in other cases, for which judicial sentence is required, is subject to determination by a judge. Absolution can be obtained from any censure, provided the person repents and desists from obstinacy. Absolution may be reserved to the pope, the bishop of a place, or the major superior of an exempt clerical religious institute. In danger of death, any priest can absolve from all censures; in other cases, faculties to absolve from reserved censures can be exercised by competent authorities or given to other priests.

Ceremonies, Master of: One who directs the proceedings of a rite or ceremony during the function.

Chamberlain: (1) The Chamberlain of the Holy Roman Church is a cardinal who administers the property and revenues of the Holy See. On the death of the pope he becomes head of the College of Cardinals and summons and directs the conclave until a new pope is elected.

(2) The Chamberlain of the Sacred College of Cardinals has charge of the property and revenues of the College and keeps the record of business transacted in consistories.

(3) The Chamberlain of the Roman Clergy is the president of the secular clergy of Rome.

Chancellor: Notary of a diocese, who draws up written documents in the government of the diocese; takes care of, arranges and indexes diocesan archives, records of dispensations and ecclesiastical trials.

Chancery (1) A branch of church administration that handles written documents used in the government of a diocese.

(2) The administrative office of a diocese, a bishop's office.

Chapel: A building or part of another building used for divine worship; a portion of a church set aside for the celebration of Mass or for some special devotion.

Chaplain: A priest appointed for the pastoral service of any division of the armed forces, religious communities, institutions, various groups of the faithful.

Chaplet: A term, meaning little crown, applied to a rosary or, more commonly, to a small string of beads used for devotional purposes; e.g., the Infant of Prague chaplet.

Chapter: A general meeting of delegates of religious orders for elections and the handling of other important affairs of their communities.

Charisms: Gifts or graces given by God to men for the good of others and the Church. Examples are special gifts for apostolic work, prophecy, healing, discernment of spirits, the life of evangelical poverty, here-and-now witness to faith in various circumstances of life.

The Second Vatican Council made the following statement about charisms in the *Dogmatic Constitution on the Church* (No. 12):

"It is not only through the sacraments and Church ministries that the same Holy Spirit sanctifies and leads the People of God and enriches it with virtues. Allotting His gifts 'to everyone according as he will' (1 Cor. 12:11), He distributes special graces among the faithful of every rank. By these gifts He makes them fit and ready to undertake the various tasks or offices advantageous for the renewal and upbuilding of the Church, according to the words of the Apostle: 'The manifestation of the Spirit is given to everyone for profit' (1 Cor. 12:7). These charismatic gifts, whether they be the most outstanding or the more simple and widely diffused, are to be received with thanksgiving and consolation, for they are exceedingly suitable and useful for the needs of the Church.

"Still, extraordinary gifts are not to be rashly sought after, nor are the fruits of apostolic labor to be presumptuously expected from them. In any case, judgment as to their genuineness and proper use belongs to those who preside over the Church, and to whose special competence it belongs, not indeed to extinguish the Spirit, but to test all things and hold fast to that which is good" (cf. 1 Thes. 5:12; 19-21).

Charity: Love of God above all things for his own sake, and love of one's neighbor as oneself because and as an expression of one's love for God; the greatest of the three theological virtues. The term is sometimes also used to designate sanctifying grace.

Chastity: Properly ordered behavior with respect to sex. In marriage, the exercise of the procreative power is integrated with the norms and purposes of marriage. Outside of marriage, the rule is self-denial of the voluntary exercise and enjoyment of the procreative faculty in thought, word or action.

The vow of chastity, which reinforces the virtue of chastity with the virtue of religion, is an evangelical counsel and one of the three vows professed by religious.

Chirograph or Autograph Letter: A letter written by a pope himself, in his own handwriting.

Christ: The title of Jesus, derived from the Greek translation *Christos* of the Hebrew term *Messiah,* meaning the Anointed of God, the Savior and Deliverer of his people. Christian use of the title is a confession of belief that Jesus is the Savior.

Christianity: The sum total of things related to belief in Christ — the Christian religion, Christian churches, Christians themselves, society based on and expressive of Christian beliefs, culture reflecting Christian values.

Christians: The name first applied about the year 43 to followers of Christ at Antioch, the capital of Syria. It was used by the pagans as a contemptuous term. The word applies to persons who profess belief in the divinity and teachings of Christ and who give witness to him in life.

Christian Science: A religious doctrine consisting of Mary Baker Eddy's interpretation and formulation of the actions and teachings of Christ. Its basic tenets reflect Mrs. Eddy's ideas regarding the reality of spirit and its control and domination of what is not spirit. The basic statement of the doctrine is contained in *Science and Health, with Key to the Scriptures,* which she first published in 1875, nine years after being saved from death and healed on reading the New Testament.

Mary Baker Eddy (1821-1910) established the church in 1879, and in 1892 founded at Boston the First Church of Christ, Scientist, of which all other Christian Science churches are branches. The individual churches are self-governing and self-supporting under the general supervision of a board of directors. Services consist of readings of portions of Scripture and *Science and Health.* One of the church's publications, *The Christian Science Monitor,* has a worldwide reputation as a journal of news and opinion.

Church: (1) See several entries under Church, Catholic. The universal Church is the Church spread throughout the world. The local Church is the Church in a particular locality; e.g., a diocese. Inasmuch as the members of the Church are on earth, in purgatory, or in glory in heaven, the Church is called militant, suffering, or triumphant.

(2) In general, any religious body.

(3) Place of divine worship.

Churching: A rite of thanksgiving in which a blessing is given to women after childbirth. The rite is reminiscent of the Old Testament ceremony of purification (Lv. 12:2-8).

Circumcision: A ceremonial practice symbolic of initiation and participation in the covenant between God and Abraham.

Circumincession: The indwelling of each divine Person of the Holy Trinity in the others.

Clergy: Men ordained to holy orders and assigned to pastoral and other ministries for the service of the people and the Church.

(1) Diocesan or secular clergy are committed to pastoral ministry in parishes and in other capacities in a local church (diocese)

under the direction of their bishop, to whom they are bound by a promise of obedience.

(2) Regular clergy belong to religious institutes (orders, congregations, societies) and are so called because they observe the rule (*regula*, in Latin) of their respective institutes. They are committed to the ways of life and apostolates of their institutes. In ordinary pastoral ministry, they are under the direction of local bishops as well as their own superiors.

Clericalism: A term generally used in a derogatory sense to mean action, influence and interference by the Church and the clergy in matters with which they allegedly should not be concerned. Anticlericalism is a reaction of antipathy, hostility, distrust and opposition to the Church and clergy arising from real and/or alleged faults of the clergy, overextension of the role of the laity, or for other reasons.

Cloister: The enclosure of a convent or monastery, which members of the community may not leave or outsiders enter without due permission. Enclosure is of two kinds: papal, in monasteries of religious with solemn vows; episcopal, in the houses of other religious.

Code: A digest of rules or regulations, such as the Code of Canon Law.

Collegiality: The bishops of the Church, in union with and subordinate to the pope — who has full, supreme and universal power over the Church which he can always exercise independently — have supreme teaching and pastoral authority over the whole Church. In addition to their proper authority of office for the good of the faithful in their respective dioceses or other jurisdictions, the bishops have authority to act for the good of the universal Church. This collegial authority is exercised in a solemn manner in an ecumenical council and can also be exercised in other ways sanctioned by the pope. Doctrine on collegiality was set forth by the Second Vatican Council in the *Dogmatic Constitution on the Church*. (See separate entry.)

By extension, the concept of collegiality is applied to other forms of participation and co-responsibility by members of a community.

Commissariat of the Holy Land: A special jurisdiction within the Order of Friars Minor, whose main purposes are the collecting of alms for support of the Holy Places in Palestine and staffing of the Holy Places and missions in the Middle East with priests and brothers. There are 69 such commissariats in 33 countries. One of them has headquarters at Mt. St. Sepulchre, Washington, D.C. Franciscans have had custody of the Holy Places since 1342.

Communion of Faithful, Saints: The communion of all the People of God — on earth, in heavenly glory, in purgatory — with Christ and each other in faith, grace, prayer and good works.

Concelebration: The liturgical act in which several priests, led by one member of the group, offer Mass together, all consecrating the bread and wine. Concelebration has always been common in churches of Eastern Rite. In the Roman Rite, it was long restricted, taking place only at the ordination of bishops and the ordination of priests. The *Constitution on the Sacred Liturgy* issued by the Second Vatican Council set new norms for concelebration.

Concordat: A Church-state treaty with the force of law concerning matters of mutual concern — e.g., rights of the Church, appointment of bishops, arrangement of ecclesiastical jurisdictions, marriage laws, education. Approximately 150 agreements of this kind have been negotiated since the Concordat of Worms in 1122.

Concupiscence: Any tendency of the sensitive appetite. The term is most frequently used in reference to desires and tendencies for sinful sense pleasure.

Confession: Sacramental confession is the act by which a person tells or confesses his sins to a priest who is authorized to give absolution in the sacrament of penance.

Confessor: (1) A male saint who lived a life of eminent sanctity and heroic virtue, but who did not suffer martyrdom for his faith. The first confessor honored as a saint was Martin of Tours.

(2) A priest who administers the sacrament of penance.

Confraternity: An association whose members practice a particular form of religious devotion and/or are engaged in some kind of apostolic work. When a confraternity reaches the stage where affiliations similar to itself are formed and adopt its rules, it takes the name of archconfraternity.

Conscience: Practical judgment concerning the moral goodness or sinfulness of an action. In the Catholic view, this judgment is made by reference of the action, its attendant circumstances and the intentions of the person to the requirements of divine law as expressed in the Ten Commandments, the summary law of love for God and neighbor, the life and teaching of Christ, and the authoritative teaching and practice of the Church with respect to the total demands of divine Revelation.

A person is obliged: (1) to obey a certain and correct conscience; (2) to obey a certain conscience even if it is inculpably erroneous; (3) not to obey, but to correct, a conscience known to be erroneous or lax; (4) to rectify a scrupulous conscience by following the advice of a confessor and by other measures; (5) to resolve doubts of conscience before acting.

It is legitimate to act for solid and probable reasons when a question of moral responsibility admits of argument (see Probabilism). It is also legitimate to resolve doubts in difficult cases by having recourse to a reflex principle (e.g., by following the manner of acting of a well-informed and well-intentioned group of persons in similar circumstances).

Conscience, Examination of: Self-examination to determine one's spiritual state before God, especially regarding one's sins and faults. It is recommended as a regular practice and is practically necessary in preparing for the sacrament of penance. The *particular examen* is a regular examination to assist in overcoming specific faults and imperfections.

Consecration of a Church: See Dedication of a Church.

Consistory: An assembly of cardinals presided over by the pope. Consistories are secret (pope and cardinals only), semi-public (plus other prelates), and public (plus other attendants).

Constitution: (1) An apostolic or papal constitution is a document in which a pope enacts and promulgates law.

(2) A formal and solemn document issued by an ecumenical council on a doctrinal or pastoral subject, with binding force in the whole Church; e.g., the four constitutions issued by the Second Vatican Council on the Church, liturgy, Revelation, and the Church in the modern world.

(3) The constitutions of religious orders spell out details of and norms drawn from the various rules for the guidance and direction of the life and work of members of each institute.

Consubstantiation: A theory which holds that the Body and Blood of Christ coexist with the substance of bread and wine in the Holy Eucharist. This theory, also called *impanation,* is incompatible with the doctrine of transubstantiation.

Contraception: Anything done by positive interference to prevent sexual intercourse from resulting in conception. Direct contraception is against the order of nature. Indirect contraception — as a secondary effect of medical treatment or other action having a necessary, good, non-contraceptive purpose — is permissible under the principle of the double effect. The practice of rhythm is not contraception because it does not involve positive interference with the order of nature.

Contrition: Sorrow for sin coupled with a purpose of amendment. Contrition arising from a supernatural motive is necessary for the forgiveness of sin.

(1) Perfect contrition is total sorrow for and renunciation of attachment to sin, arising from the motive of pure love of God. Perfect contrition, which implies the intention of doing all God wants done for the forgiveness of sin, is sufficient for the forgiveness of serious sin and the remission of all temporal punishment due for sin. Confession is required before the reception of another sacrament. (The intention to receive the sacrament of penance is implicit — even if unrealized, as

in the case of some persons — in perfect contrition.)

(2) Imperfect contrition or attrition is sorrow arising from a quasi-selfish supernatural motive; e.g., the fear of losing heaven, suffering the pains of hell, etc. Imperfect contrition is sufficient for the forgiveness of serious sin when joined with absolution in confession, and sufficient for the forgiveness of venial sin even outside of confession.

Contumely: Personal insult, reviling a person in his presence by accusation of moral faults, by refusal of recognition or due respect; a violation of obligations of justice and charity.

Corporal Works of Mercy: Feeding the hungry, giving drink to the thirsty, clothing the naked, visiting the imprisoned, sheltering the homeless, visiting the sick, burying the dead.

Councils: Bodies representative of various categories of members of the Church which participate with bishops and other church authorities in making decisions and carrying out action programs for the good of the Church and the accomplishment of its mission to its own members and society in general. Examples are priests' senates or councils, councils of religious and lay persons, parish councils, diocesan pastoral councils.

Councils, Plenary: National councils or councils of the bishops of several ecclesiastical provinces, assembled under the presidency of a papal legate to take action related to the life and mission of the Church in the area under their jurisdiction. The membership of such councils is fixed by canon law; their decrees, when approved by the Holy See, are binding in the territory (see Index, Three Plenary Councils of Baltimore).

Councils, Provincial: Meetings of the bishops of a province. The metropolitan, or ranking archbishop, of an ecclesiastical province convenes and presides over such councils in a manner prescribed by canon law to take action related to the life and mission of the Church in the province. Acts and decrees must be approved by the Holy See before being promulgated. Provincial councils should be held at least once every 20 years.

Counsels, Evangelical: Gospel counsels of perfection, especially voluntary poverty, perfect chastity and obedience, which were recommended by Christ to those who would devote themselves exclusively and completely to the immediate service of God. Religious bind themselves by public vows to observe these counsels in a life of total consecration to God and service to people through various kinds of apostolic works.

Counter-Reformation: The period of approximately 100 years following the Council of Trent, which witnessed a reform within the Church to stimulate genuine Catholic life and to counteract effects of the Reformation.

Covenant: A bond of relationship between

parties pledged to each other. God-initiated covenants in the Old Testament included those with Abraham, Noah, Moses, Levi, David. The Mosaic (Sinai) covenant made Israel God's Chosen People on terms of fidelity to true faith, true worship, and righteous conduct according to the Decalogue. The New Testament covenant, prefigured in the Old Testament, is the bond men have with God through Christ. All men are called to be parties to this perfect and everlasting covenant, which was mediated and ratified by Christ.

Creation: The production by God of something out of nothing. The biblical account of creation is contained in the first two chapters of Genesis.

Creator: God, the supreme, self-existing Being, the absolute and infinite First Cause of all things.

Creature: Everything in the realm of being is a creature, except God.

Cremation: The reduction of a human corpse to ashes by means of fire. Cremation is not in line with Catholic tradition and practice, even though it is not opposed to any article of faith. It can be permitted for serious reasons. The general practice, however, was forbidden in a decree issued May 19, 1886, by the Sacred Congregation of the Holy Office.

This ruling was incorporated in the Code of Canon Law (Canons 1203, 1240), which generally banned the practice of cremation, forbade following orders for cremation, and deprived of the last rites and ecclesiastical burial those who directed that their bodies be cremated and did not retract the directions.

The principal reason behind the prohibition against cremation was the fact that, historically, the practice had represented an attempt to deny the doctrine of the resurrection of the body. It also appeared to be a form of violence against the body which, as the temple of the Holy Spirit during life, should be treated with reverence.

The Congregation for the Doctrine of the Faith, under date of May 8, 1963, circulated among bishops an instruction which upheld the traditional practices of Christian burial but modified anti-cremation legislation. Cremation may be permitted for serious reasons, of a private as well as public nature, provided it does not involve any contempt of the Church or of religion, or any attempt to deny, question, or belittle the doctrine of the resurrection of the body. The person may receive the last rites and be given ecclesiastical burial. A priest may say prayers for the deceased at the crematorium, but full liturgical ceremonies may not take place there.

Crib: A devotional representation of the birth of Jesus. The custom of erecting cribs is generally attributed to St. Francis of Assisi who in 1223 obtained from Pope Honorius III permission to use a crib and figures of the Christ Child, Mary, St. Joseph, and others, to represent the mystery of the Nativity.

Crosier: The bishop's staff, symbolic of his pastoral office, responsibility and authority.

Crypt: An underground or partly underground chamber.

Cura Animarum: A Latin phrase, meaning care of souls, designating the pastoral ministry and responsibility of bishops and priests.

Curia: The personnel and offices through which (1) the pope administers the affairs of the universal Church, the *Roman Curia* (see separate entry), or (2) a bishop the affairs of a diocese, *diocesan curia*. The principal officials of a diocesan curia are the vicar general of the diocese, the chancellor, officials of the diocesan tribunal or court, examiners, consultors, auditors, notaries.

Custos: A religious superior who presides over a number of convents collectively called a custody. In some religious institutes, a custos may be the deputy of a higher superior.

D

Dean: (1) A priest with supervisory responsibility over a section of a diocese known as a deanery. The post-Vatican II counterpart of a dean is an episcopal vicar.

(2) The senior or ranking member of a group.

Dean of the Sacred College: The president of the College of Cardinals (the ranking cardinal bishop). He is elected by the cardinals holding title to the suburban sees of Rome.

Decision: A judgment or pronouncement on a cause or suit, given by a church tribunal or official with judicial authority. A decision has the force of law for concerned parties.

Declaration: (1) An ecclesiastical document which presents an interpretation of an existing law.

(2) A position paper on a specific subject; e.g., the three declarations issued by the Second Vatican Council on religious freedom, non-Christian religions, and Christian education.

Decree: An edict or ordinance issued by a pope and/or by an ecumenical council, with binding force in the whole Church; by a department of the Roman Curia, with binding force for concerned parties; by a territorial body of bishops, with binding force for persons in the area; by individual bishops, with binding force for concerned parties until revocation or the death of the bishop.

Dedication of a Church: The ceremony whereby a church is solemnly set apart for the worship of God. The custom of dedicating churches had an antecedent in Old Testament ceremonies for the dedication of the Temple, as in the times of Solomon and the Maccabees. The earliest extant record of the dedication of a Christian church dates from early in the fourth century, when it was done simply by the celebration of Mass. Other ceremonies developed later. A church can be dedicated by a simple blessing or a solemn consecration. The rite of consecration is performed by a bishop.

Definitors: Members of the governing council of a religious order, each one having a decisive vote equal to the vote of the general or provincial superior.

Deism: A system of natural religion which acknowledges the existence of God but regards him as so transcendent and remote from man and the universe that divine revelation and the supernatural order of things are irrelevant and unacceptable. It developed from rationalistic principles in England in the 17th and 18th centuries, and had Voltaire, Rousseau and the Encyclopedists among its advocates in France.

Despair: Abandonment of hope for salvation arising from the conviction that God will not provide the necessary means for attaining it, that following God's way of life for salvation is impossible, or that one's sins are unforgivable; a serious sin against the Holy Spirit and the theological virtues of hope and faith, involving distrust in the mercy and goodness of God and a denial of the truths that God wills the salvation of all men and provides sufficient grace for it. Real despair is distinguished from unreasonable fear with respect to the difficulties of attaining salvation, from morbid anxiety over the demands of divine justice, and from feelings of despair.

Detachment: Control of affection for creatures by two principles: (1) supreme love and devotion belong to God; (2) love and service of creatures should be an expression of love for God.

Detraction: Revelation of true but hidden faults of a person without sufficient and justifying reason; a violation of requirements of justice and charity, involving the obligation to make restitution when this is possible without doing more harm to the good name of the offended party. In some cases, e.g., to prevent evil, secret faults may and should be disclosed.

Devil: (1) Lucifer, Satan, chief of the fallen angels who sinned and were banished from heaven. Still possessing angelic powers, he can cause such diabolical phenomena as possession and obsession, and can tempt men to sin.

(2) Any fallen angel.

Devil's Advocate: See Promoter of the Faith.

Devotion: (1) Religious fervor, piety; dedication.

(2) The consolation experienced at times during prayer; a reverent manner of praying.

Devotions: Pious practices of members of the Church include not only participation in various acts of the liturgy but also in other acts of worship generally called popular or private devotions. Concerning these, the Second Vatican Council said in the *Constitution on the Sacred Liturgy* (No. 13): "Popular devotions of the Christian people are warmly commended, provided they accord with the laws and norms of the Church. Such is especially the case with devotions called for by the Apostolic See. Devotions proper to the individual churches also have a special dignity. . . . These devotions should be so drawn up that they harmonize with the liturgical seasons, accord with the sacred liturgy, are in some fashion derived from it, and lead the people to it, since the liturgy by its very nature far surpasses any of them."

Devotions of a liturgical type are Benediction of the Blessed Sacrament, recitation of the Little Office of the Blessed Virgin Mary or of Vespers and Compline. Examples of paraliturgical devotion are a Bible Service or Vigil, and the Angelus, Rosary and Stations of the Cross, which have a strong scriptural basis.

Dies Irae: The opening Latin words, Day of Wrath, of a hymn for requiem Masses, written in the 13th century by the Franciscan Thomas of Celano.

Diocese: A fully organized ecclesiastical jurisdiction under the pastoral direction of a bishop as local ordinary.

Discalced: Of Latin derivation and meaning without shoes, the word is applied to religious orders or congregations whose members go barefoot or wear sandals.

Disciple: A term used sometimes in reference to the Apostles but more often to a larger number of followers (70 or 72) of Christ mentioned in Lk. 10:1.

Disciplina Arcani: A Latin phrase, meaning discipline of the secret and referring to a practice of the early Church, especially during the Roman persecutions, to: (1) conceal Christian truths from those who, it was feared, would misinterpret, ridicule and profane the teachings, and persecute Christians for believing them; (2) instruct catechumens in a gradual manner, withholding the teaching of certain doctrines until the catechumens proved themselves of good faith and sufficient understanding.

Dispensation: The relaxation of a law in a particular case. Laws made for the common good sometimes work undue hardship in particular cases. In such cases, where sufficient reasons are present, dispensations may be granted by proper authorities. Bishops, religious superiors and others may dispense from certain laws; the pope can dispense from all ecclesiastical laws. No one has authority to dispense from obligations of the divine law.

Divination: Attempting to foretell future or hidden things by means of things like dreams, necromancy, spiritism, examination of entrails, astrology, augury, omens, palmistry, drawing straws, dice, cards, etc. Practices like these attribute to creatural things a power which belongs to God alone and are violations of the First Commandment.

Divine Praises: Fourteen praises recited or sung at Benediction of the Blessed Sacrament in reparation for sins of sacrilege, blasphemy and profanity. Some of these praises date from the end of the 18th century.

Blessed be God.
Blessed be his holy Name.
Blessed be Jesus Christ, true God and true Man.
Blessed be the Name of Jesus.
Blessed be his most Sacred Heart.
Blessed be his most Precious Blood.
Blessed be Jesus in the most holy Sacrament of the Altar.
Blessed be the Holy Spirit, the Paraclete.
Blessed be the great Mother of God, Mary most holy.
Blessed be her holy and Immaculate Conception.
Blessed be her glorious Assumption.
Blessed be the name of Mary, Virgin and Mother.
Blessed be St. Joseph, her most chaste Spouse.
Blessed be God in his Angels and in his Saints.

Double Effect Principle: Actions sometimes have two effects closely related to each other, one good and the other bad, and a difficult moral question can arise: Is it permissible to place an action from which two such results follow? It is permissible to place the action, if: the action is good in itself and is directly productive of the good effect; the circumstances are good; the intention of the person is good; the reason for placing the action is proportionately serious to the seriousness of the indirect bad effect. For example: Is it morally permissible for a pregnant woman to undergo medical or surgical treatment for a pathological condition if the indirect and secondary effect of the treatment will be the loss of the child? The reply is affirmative, for these reasons: The action, i.e., the treatment, is good in itself, cannot be deferred until a later time without very serious consequences, and is ordered directly to the cure of critically grave pathology. By means of the treatment, the woman intends to save her life, which she has a right to do. The loss of the child is not directly sought as a means for the cure of the mother but results indirectly and in a secondary manner from the placing of the action, i.e., the treatment, which is good in itself.

The double effect principle does not support the principle that the end justifies the means.

Doxology: (1) The lesser doxology, or ascription of glory to the Trinity, is the Glory be to the Father. The first part dates back to the third or fourth century, and came from the form of baptism. The concluding words, As it was in the beginning, etc., are of later origin.

(2) The greater doxology, Glory to God in the highest, begins with the words of angelic praise at the birth of Christ recounted in the Infancy Narrative (Lk. 2:14). It is often recited at Mass. Of early Eastern origin, it is found in the *Apostolic Constitutions* in a form much like the present.

Dulia: A Greek term meaning the veneration or homage, different in nature and degree from that given to God, paid to the saints. It includes honoring the saints and seeking their intercession with God.

Duty: A moral obligation deriving from the binding force of law, the exigencies of one's state in life, and other sources.

E

Easter Controversy: A three-phase controversy over the time for the celebration of Easter.

Some early Christians in the Near East, called Quartodecimans, favored the observance of Easter on the 14th day of Nisan, the spring month of the Hebrew calendar, whenever it occurred. Against this practice, Pope St. Victor I, about 190, ordered a Sunday observance of the feast.

The Council of Nicaea, in line with usages of the Church at Rome and Alexandria, decreed in 325 that Easter should be observed on the first Sunday following the first full moon of spring.

Uniformity of practice in the West was not achieved until several centuries later, when the British Isles, in delayed compliance with measures enacted by the Synod of Whitby in 664, accepted the Roman date of observance.

Unrelated to the controversy is the fact that some Eastern Christians, in accordance with traditional calendar practices, celebrate Easter at a different time than the Roman and Eastern-Rite churches.

Easter Duty: The serious obligation binding Catholics of Roman Rite, by a precept of the Church, to receive Holy Communion during the Easter time; in the US, from the first Sunday of Lent to Trinity Sunday.

Easter Water: Holy water blessed with special ceremonies and distributed on the Easter Vigil; used during Easter Week for blessing the faithful and homes.

Ecclesiology: Study of the nature, constitution, members, mission, functions, etc., of the Church.

Ecstasy: An extraordinary state of mystical experience in which a person is so absorbed in God that the activity of the exterior senses is suspended.

Ecumenism: The movement of Christians and their churches toward the unity willed by Christ. The Second Vatican Council called the movement "those activities and enterprises which, according to various needs of the Church and opportune occasions, are started and organized for the fostering of unity among Christians" (*Decree on Ecumenism*, No. 4). Spiritual ecumenism, i.e., mutual prayer for unity, is the heart of the movement. The movement also involves scholarly and pew-level efforts for the development of mutual understanding and better interfaith relations in general, and collaboration by the churches and their members in the social area.

Elevation: The raising of the host after consecration at Mass for adoration by the faithful. The custom was introduced in the Diocese of Paris about the close of the 12th century to offset an erroneous teaching of the time which held that transubstantiation of the bread did not take place until after the consecration of the wine in the chalice. The elevation of the chalice following the consecration of the wine was introduced in the 15th century.

End Justifies the Means: An unacceptable ethical principle which states that evil means may be used to produce good effects.

Envy: Sadness over another's good fortune because it is considered a loss to oneself or a detraction from one's own excellence; one of the seven capital sins, a violation of the obligations of charity.

Epikeia: A Greek word meaning reasonableness and designating a moral theory and practice, a mild interpretation of the mind of a legislator who is prudently considered not to wish positive law to bind in certain circumstances. Use of the principle is justified in practice when the lawgiver himself cannot be appealed to and when it can be prudently assumed that in particular cases, e.g., because of special hardship, he would not wish the law to be applied in a strict manner. Epikeia may not be applied with respect to acts that are intrinsically wrong or those covered by laws which automatically make them invalid.

Episcopate: (1) The office, dignity and sacramental powers bestowed upon a bishop at his ordination.

(2) The body of bishops collectively.

Equivocation: (1) The use of words, phrases, or gestures having more than one meaning in order to conceal information which a questioner has no strict right to know. It is permissible to equivocate (have a broad mental reservation) in some circumstances.

(2) A lie, i.e., a statement of untruth. Lying is intrinsically wrong. A lie told in joking, evident as such, is not wrong.

Eschatology: Doctrine concerning the last things: death, judgment, heaven and hell, and the final state of perfection of the People and Kingdom of God at the end of time.

Eternity: The interminable, perfect possession of life in its totality without beginning or end; an attribute of God, who has no past or future but always is. Man's existence has a beginning but no end and is, accordingly, called immortal.

Ethics: Moral philosophy, the science of the morality of human acts deriving from natural law, the natural end of man, and the powers of human reason. It includes all the spheres of human activity — personal, social, economic, political, etc. Ethics is distinct from but can be related to moral theology, whose primary principles are drawn from divine Revelation.

Eucharistic Congresses: Public demonstrations of faith in the Holy Eucharist. Combining liturgical services, other public ceremonies, subsidiary meetings, different kinds of instructional and inspirational elements, they are unified by central themes and serve to increase understanding of and devotion to Christ in the Eucharist, and to relate this liturgy of worship and witness to life.

International congresses are planned and held under the auspices of a permanent committee for international Eucharistic congresses. Participants include clergy, religious and lay persons from many countries, and representatives of national and international Catholic organizations. Popes have usually been represented by legates, but Paul VI attended two congresses personally, the 38th at Bombay and the 39th at Bogota.

Forty international congresses were held from 1881 to 1973:

Lille (1881), Avignon (1882), Liege (1883), Freiburg (1885), Toulouse (1886), Paris (1888), Antwerp (1890), Jerusalem (1893), Rheims (1894), Paray-le-Monial (1897), Brussels (1898), Lourdes (1899), Angers (1901), Namur (1902), Angouleme (1904), Rome (1905), Tournai (1906), Metz (1907), London (1908), Cologne (1909), Montreal (1910), Madrid (1911), Vienna (1912), Malta (1913), Lourdes (1914), Rome (1922), Amsterdam (1924), Chicago (1926), Sydney (1928), Carthage (1930), Dublin (1932), Buenos Aires (1934), Manila (1937), Budapest (1938), Barcelona (1952), Rio de Janeiro (1955), Munich, Germany (1960), Bombay, India (1964), Bogota, Colombia (1968), Melbourne, Australia (1973).

Eugenics: The science of heredity and environment for the physical and mental improvement of offspring. Extreme eugenics is untenable in practice because it advocates immoral means, such as compulsory breeding of the select, sterilization of persons said to be unfit, abortion, and unacceptable methods of birth regulation.

Euthanasia: Mercy killing, the direct causing of death by painless means for the purpose of ending human suffering. Euthanasia is murder and is totally illicit, for the natural law forbids the direct taking of one's own life or that of an innocent person.

The use of drugs to relieve suffering in serious cases, even when this results in a shortening of life as an indirect and secondary effect, is permissible under conditions of the double effect principle. It is also permissible for a seriously ill person to refuse to follow — or for other responsible persons to refuse to permit — extraordinary medical procedures even though the refusal might entail shortening of life.

Evolution: Scientific theory concerning the development of the physical universe from unorganized matter (inorganic evolution) and, especially, the development of existing forms of vegetable, animal and human life from earlier and more primitive organisms (organic evolution). Various ideas about evolution were advanced for some centuries before scientific evidence in support of the main-line theory of organic evolution, which has several formulations, was discovered and verified in the second half of the 19th century and afterwards. This evidence — from the findings of comparative anatomy and other sciences — confirmed evolution within species and cleared the way to further investigation of questions regarding the processes of its accomplishment. While a number of such questions remain open with respect to human evolution, a point of doctrine not open to question is the immediate creation of the human soul by God.

For some time, theologians regarded the theory with hostility, considering it to be in opposition to the account of creation in the early chapters of Genesis and subversive of belief in such doctrines as creation, the early state of man in grace, and the fall of man from grace. This state of affairs and the tension it generated led to considerable controversy regarding an alleged conflict between religion and science. Gradually, however, the tension was diminished with the development of biblical studies from the latter part of the 19th century onwards, with clarification of the distinctive features of religious truth and scientific truth, and with the refinement of evolutionary concepts.

So far as the Genesis account of creation is concerned, the Catholic view is that the writer(s) did not write as a scientist but as the communicator of religious truth in a manner adapted to the understanding of the people of his time. He used anthropomorphic language, the figure of days and other literary devices to state the salvation truths of creation, the fall of man from grace, and the promise of redemption. It was beyond the competency and purpose of the writer(s) to describe creation and related events in a scientific manner.

Excommunication: A penalty or censure by which a baptized person is excluded from the communion of the faithful, for committing and remaining obstinate in certain sins specified in canon law and technically called crimes. As by baptism a person is made a member of the Church in which there is a communication of spiritual goods, so by excommunication he is deprived of the same spiritual goods until he repents and receives absolution. Even though excommunicated, a person is still responsible for the normal obligations of a Catholic.

Existentialism: A philosophy with radical concern for the problems of individual existence and identity viewed in particular here-and-now patterns of thought which presuppose irrationality and absurdity in human life and the whole universe. It is preoccupied with questions about freedom, moral decision and responsibility against a background of denial of objective truth and universal norms of conduct; is characterized by prevailing anguish, dread, fear, pessimism, despair; is generally atheistic, although its modern originator, Soren Kierkegaard (d. 1855), and Gabriel Marcel attempted to give it a Christian orientation. Pius XII called it "the new erroneous philosophy which, opposing itself to idealism, immanentism and pragmatism, has assumed the name of existentialism, since it concerns itself only with the existence of individual things and neglects all consideration of their immutable essences" (Encyclical *Humani Generis,* Aug. 12, 1950).

Exorcism: (1) Driving out evil spirits; a rite in which evil spirits are charged and commanded on the authority of God and with the prayer of the Church to depart from a person or to cease causing harm to a person suffering from diabolical possession or obsession. The sacramental is officially administered by a priest delegated for the purpose by the bishop of the place. Elements of the rite include the Litany of Saints; recitation of the Our Father, one or more creeds, and other prayers; specific prayers of exorcism; the reading of Gospel passages, and use of the Sign of the Cross. Private exorcism for the liberation of a person from the strong influence of evil spirits, through prayer and the use of sacramentals like holy water, can be done by anyone.

(2) Exorcisms which do not imply the conditions of either diabolical possession or obsession form part of the ceremony of baptism, and are also included in formulas for various blessings; e.g., of water.

F

Faculties: Grants of jurisdiction, or authority, granted by the law of the Church or superiors (pope, bishop, religious superior) for exercise of the powers of holy orders; e.g., priests are given faculties to hear confessions, officiate at weddings; bishops are given faculties to grant dispensations, etc.

Faith: In religion, faith has several aspects. Catholic doctrine calls faith the assent of the mind to truths revealed by God, the assent being made with the help of grace and by command of the will on account of the authority and trustworthiness of God revealing. The term faith also refers to the truths that are believed (content of faith) and to the way in which a person, in response to Christ, gives witness to and expresses his belief in daily life (living faith).

All of these elements, and more, are included in the following statement:

" 'The obedience of faith' (Rom. 16:26; cf. 1:5; 2 Cor. 10:5-6) must be given to God who reveals, an obedience by which man entrusts his whole self freely to God, offering 'the full submission of intellect and will to God who reveals' (First Vatican Council, *Dogmatic Constitution on the Catholic Faith,* Chap. 3), and freely assenting to the truth revealed by Him. If this faith is to be shown, the grace of God and the interior help of the Holy Spirit must precede and assist, moving the heart and turning it to God, opening the eyes of the mind, and giving 'joy and ease to everyone in assenting to the truth and believing it' " (Second Council of Orange, Canon 7) (Second Vatican Council, *Constitution on Revelation,* No. 5). Faith is necessary for salvation.

Faith, Rule of: The norm or standard of religious belief. The Catholic doctrine is that belief must be professed in the divinely revealed truths in the Bible and tradition as interpreted and proposed by the infallible teaching authority of the Church.

Fast, Eucharistic: Eating and the drinking of any liquids except water are prohibited for one hour before the reception of Holy Communion. Water never breaks the Eucharistic fast, which is prescribed for reasons of reverence and preparation. By way of exception, the period of fasting is 15 minutes for the sick and aged, even though not confined to bed or a home, and those caring for them who wish to receive Communion with them but cannot fast for an hour without inconvenience (Instruction, *Immensae Caritatis,* Congregation for the Discipline of the Sacraments, Jan. 29, 1973).

Those who are ill, even though not confined to bed, may take nonalcoholic beverages and liquid or solid medicine before Holy Communion without any time limit.

Father: A title of priests, who are regarded as spiritual fathers because they are the ordinary ministers of baptism, by which persons are born to supernatural life, and because of their pastoral service to people.

Fear: A mental state caused by the apprehension of present or future danger. Grave fear does not necessarily remove moral responsibility for an act, but may lessen it.

First Friday: A devotion consisting of the reception of Holy Communion on the first Friday of nine consecutive months in honor of the Sacred Heart of Jesus and in reparation for sin. (See Sacred Heart, Promises.)

First Saturday: A devotion tracing its origin to the apparitions of the Blessed Virgin Mary at Fatima in 1917. Those practicing the devotion go to confession and, on the first Saturday of five consecutive months, receive Holy Communion, recite five decades of the Rosary, and meditate on the mysteries for 15 minutes.

Fisherman's Ring: A signet ring engraved with the image of St. Peter fishing from a boat, and encircled with the name of the reigning pope. It is not worn by the pope. It is used to seal briefs, and is destroyed after each pope's death.

Forgiveness of Sin: Catholics believe that sins are forgiven by God through the mediation of Christ in view of the repentance of the sinner and by means of the sacrament of penance. (See Penance.)

Fortitude: Courage to face dangers or hardships for the sake of what is good; one of the four cardinal virtues and one of the seven gifts of the Holy Spirit.

Fortune Telling: Attempting to predict the future or the occult by means of cards, palm reading, etc.; a form of divination, prohibited by the First Commandment.

Forum: The sphere in which ecclesiastical authority or jurisdiction is exercised.

(1) External: Authority is exercised in the external forum to deal with matters affecting the public welfare of the Church and its members. Those who have such authority because of their office (e.g., diocesan bishops) are called ordinaries.

(2) Internal: Authority is exercised in the internal forum to deal with matters affecting the private spiritual good of individuals. The sacramental forum is the sphere in which the sacrament of penance is administered; other exercises of jurisdiction in the internal forum take place in the non-secramental forum.

Franciscan Crown: A seven-decade rosary used to commemorate the seven Joys of the Blessed Virgin: the Annunciation, the Visitation, the Nativity of Our Lord, the Adoration of the Magi, the Finding of the Child Jesus in the Temple, the Apparition of the Risen Christ to his Mother, the Assumption and Coronation of the Blessed Virgin. Introduced in 1422, the Crown originally consisted only of seven Our Fathers and 70 Hail Marys. Two Hail Marys were added to complete the number 72 (thought to be the number of years of Mary's life), and one Our Father, Hail Mary and Glory be to the Father are said for the intention of the pope.

Freedom, Religious: The Second Vatican Council declared that the right to religious freedom in civil society "means that all men are to be immune from coercion on the part of individuals or of social groups and of any human power, in such wise that in matters religious no one is to be forced to act in a manner contrary to his own beliefs. Nor is anyone to be restrained from acting in accordance with his own beliefs, whether privately or publicly, whether alone or in association with others, within due limits" of requirements for the common good. The foundation of this right in civil society is the "very dignity of the human person" (*Declaration on Religious Freedom,* No. 2).

The conciliar statement did not deal with the subject of freedom within the Church. It noted the responsibility of the faithful "carefully to attend to the sacred and certain doctrine of the Church" (No. 14).

Freemasons: A fraternal order which originated in London in 1717 with the formation of the first Grand Lodge of Freemasons. From England, the order spread to Europe and elsewhere. Its original deistic and non-denominational ideology was transformed in Latin countries into a compound of atheism, anticlericalism and irreligion. Since 1877, Grand Orient Freemasonry has been denied recognition by the Scottish and York Rites because of its failure to require belief in God and the immortality of the soul as a condition of membership. In some places, Freemasonry has been regarded as subversive of the state; in Catholic quarters, it has been considered hostile to the Church and its doctrine. In the United States, Freemasonry is generally known as a fraternal and philanthropic order.

Catholics have been forbidden to join the Freemasons, under penalty of excommunication, for serious pastoral reasons. Eight different popes in 17 different pronouncements, and at least six different local councils, condemned Freemasonry. The first condemnation was made by Clement XII in 1738. Eastern Orthodox and many Protestant bodies have also opposed the order.

Present relations between the Catholic Church and Freemasonry in the United States are marked by greater cordiality and mutual understanding than in the past, but the prohibition against Catholic membership still stands.

Free Will: The faculty or capability of making a reasonable choice among several alternatives. Freedom of will underlies the possibility and fact of moral responsibility.

Friar: Term applied to members of mendicant orders to distinguish them from members of monastic orders. (See Mendicants.)

Fruits of the Holy Spirit: Charity, joy, peace, patience, benignity, goodness, longanimity, mildness, faith, modesty, continence, chastity.

G

Gambling: The backing of an issue with a sum of money or other valuables, which is permissible if the object is honest, if the two parties have the free disposal of their stakes without prejudice to the rights of others, if the terms are thoroughly understood by both parties, and if the outcome is not known beforehand. Gambling often falls into disrepute and may be forbidden by civil law, as well as by divine law, because of cheating, fraud and other accompanying evils.

Gehenna: Greek form of a Jewish name, *Gehinnom*, for a valley near Jerusalem, the site of Moloch worship; used as a synonym for hell.

Genuflection: Bending of the knee, a natural sign of adoration or reverence, as when persons genuflect with the right knee in passing before the tabernacle to acknowledge the Eucharistic presence of Christ.

Gethsemani: A Hebrew word meaning oil press, designating the place on the Mount of Olives where Christ prayed and suffered in agony the night before he died.

Gifts of the Holy Spirit: Supernatural habits disposing a person to respond promptly to the inspiration of grace; promised by Christ and communicated through the Holy Spirit, especially in the sacrament of confirmation. They are: wisdom, understanding, counsel, fortitude, knowledge, piety, fear of the Lord.

Gluttony: An unreasonable appetite for food and drink; one of the seven capital sins.

God: The infinitely perfect Supreme Being, uncaused and absolutely self-sufficient, eternal, the Creator and final end of all things. The one God subsists in three equal Persons, the Father and the Son and the Holy Spirit. God, although transcendent and distinct from the universe, is present and active in the world in realization of his plan for the salvation of men, principally through Revelation, the operations of the Holy Spirit, the life and ministry of Christ, and the continuation of Christ's ministry in the Church.

The existence of God is an article of faith, clearly communicated in divine Revelation. Even without this Revelation, however, the Church teaches, in a declaration by the First Vatican Council, that men can acquire certain knowledge of the existence of God and some of his attributes. This can be done on the bases of principles of reason and reflection on human experience.

Non-revealed arguments or demonstrations for the existence of God have been developed from the principle of causality; the contingency of man and the universe; the existence of design, change and movement in the universe; human awareness of moral responsibility; widespread human testimony to the existence of God.

Grace: A free gift of God to men (and angels), grace is a created sharing or participation in the life of God. It is given to men through the merits of Christ and is communicated by the Holy Spirit. It is necessary for salvation. The principal means of grace are the sacraments (especially the Eucharist), prayer and good works.

Sanctifying or habitual grace makes men holy and pleasing to God, adopted children of God, members of Christ, temples of the Holy Spirit, heirs of heaven capable of supernaturally meritorious acts. With grace, God gives men the supernatural virtues and gifts of the Holy Spirit. The sacraments of baptism and penance were instituted to give grace to those who do not have it; the other sacraments, to increase it in those already in the state of grace. The means for growth in holiness, or the increase of grace, are prayer, the sacraments, and good works. Sanctifying grace is lost by the commission of serious sin.

Each sacrament confers sanctifying grace for the special purpose of the sacrament; in this context, grace is called sacramental grace.

Actual grace is a supernatural help of God which enlightens and strengthens a person to do good and to avoid evil. It is not a permanent quality, like sanctifying grace. It is necessary for the performance of supernatural acts. It can be resisted and refused. Persons in the state of serious sin are given actual grace to lead them to repentance.

Grace at Meals: Prayers said before meals, asking a blessing of God, and after meals, giving thanks to God. In addition to traditional prayers for these purposes, many variations suitable for different occasions are possible, at personal option.

H

Habit: (1) A disposition to do things easily, given with grace (and therefore supernatural) and/or acquired by repetition of similar acts.
(2) The garb worn by religious.

Hagiography: Writings or documents about saints and other holy persons.

Hail Mary: A prayer addressed to the Blessed Virgin Mary; also called the *Ave Maria* (Latin equivalent of Hail Mary) and the Angelic Salutation. In three parts, it consists of the words addressed to Mary by the Archangel Gabriel on the occasion of the Annunciation, in the Infancy Narrative (Hail full of grace, the Lord is with you, blessed are you among women.); the words addressed to Mary by her cousin Elizabeth on the occasion of the Visitation (Blessed is the fruit of your womb.); a concluding petition (Holy Mary, Mother of God, pray for us sinners now and at the hour of our death. Amen.). The first two salutations were joined in Eastern Rite formulas by the sixth century, and were similarly used at Rome in the seventh century. Insertion of the name of Jesus at the conclusion of the salutations was probably made by Urban IV about 1262. The present form of the petition was incorporated into the breviary in 1514.

Heaven: The state of those who, having achieved salvation, are in glory with God and enjoy the beatific vision.

The phrase, kingdom of heaven, refers to the order or kingdom of God, grace, salvation.

Hell: The state of punishment of the damned — i.e., those who die in mortal sin, in a condition of self-alienation from God and of opposition to the divine plan of salvation. The punishment of hell begins immediately after death and lasts forever.

Hermit: See Anchorite.

Heroic Act of Charity: The completely unselfish offering to God of one's good works and merits for the benefit of the souls in purgatory rather than for oneself. Thus, a person may offer to God for the souls in purgatory all the good works he performs during life, all the indulgences he gains, and all the prayers and indulgences that will be offered for him after his death. The act is revocable at will,

and is not a vow. Its actual ratification depends on the will of God.

Heterodoxy: False doctrine, teaching or belief; a departure from truth.

Holy See: (1) The diocese of the pope, Rome.
(2) The pope himself and/or the various officials and bodies of the Church's central administration at Vatican City — the Roman Curia — which act in the name and by authority of the pope.

Holy Spirit: God the Holy Spirit, third Person of the Holy Trinity, who proceeds from the Father and the Son and with whom he is equal in every respect; inspirer of the prophets and writers of sacred Scripture; promised by Christ to the Apostles as their advocate and strengthener; appeared in the form of a dove at the baptism of Christ and as tongues of fire at his descent upon the Apostles; soul of the Church and guarantor, by his abiding presence and action, of truth in doctrine; communicator of grace to men, for which reason he is called the sanctifier.

Holy Water: Water blessed by the Church and used as a sacramental, a practice which originated in apostolic times.

Holy Year: A year during which the pope grants the Jubilee Indulgence to all the faithful who fulfill the prescribed conditions (confession, Communion, visits and prayer for the intentions of the pope in the basilicas of St. Peter, St. John Lateran, St. Paul, St. Mary Major). The Holy Year has been proclaimed every 25 years since 1450.

This year of special grace and prayer, which begins and ends with the opening and closing of the holy doors in the major basilicas of Rome on consecutive Christmas Eves, has a historical precedent in the year of jubilee prescribed by God in the Old Testament (Lv. 25:10-15).

Hope: One of the three theological virtues, by which one firmly trusts that God wills his salvation and will give him the means to attain it.

Hosanna: A Hebrew word, meaning O Lord, save, we pray.

Host, The Sacred: The bread under whose appearances Christ is and remains present in a unique manner after the consecration which takes place during Mass. (See Transubstantiation.)

Humility: A virtue which induces a person to evaluate himself at his true worth, to recognize his dependence on God, and to give glory to God for the good he has and can do.

Hyperdulia: The special veneration accorded the Blessed Virgin Mary because of her unique role in the mystery of Redemption, her exceptional gifts of grace from God, and her pre-eminence among the saints. Hyperdulia is not adoration; only God is adored.

Hypnosis: A mental state resembling sleep, induced by suggestion, in which the subject does the bidding of the hypnotist. Hypnotism is permissible under certain conditions: the existence of a serious reason, e.g., for anesthetic or therapeutic purposes, and the competence and integrity of the hypnotist. Hypnotism may not be practiced for the sake of amusement. Experiments indicate that, contrary to popular opinion, hypnotized subjects may be induced to perform immoral acts which, normally, they would not do.

Hypostatic Union: The union of the human and divine natures in the one divine Person of Christ.

I

Icons: Byzantine-style paintings or representations of Christ, the Blessed Virgin and other saints, venerated in the Eastern Churches where they take the place of statues.

Idolatry: Worship of any but the true God; a violation of the First Commandment.

IHS: In Greek, the first three letters of the name of Jesus — Iota, Eta, Sigma.

Immortality: The survival and continuing existence of the human soul after death.

Immunity of the Clergy: Exemption of clerics from military duty and civil service.

Impurity: Unlawful indulgence in sexual pleasure. (See Chastity.)

Incardination: The affiliation of a priest to his diocese. Every secular priest must belong to a certain diocese. Similarly, every priest of a religious community must belong to some jurisdiction of his community; this affiliation, however, is not called incardination.

Incarnation: (1) The coming-into-flesh or taking of human nature by the Second Person of the Trinity. He became human as the Son of Mary, being miraculously conceived by the power of the Holy Spirit, without ceasing to be divine. His divine Person hypostatically unites his divine and human natures.

(2) The supernatural mystery coextensive with Christ from the moment of his human conception and continuing through his life on earth; his sufferings and death; his resurrection from the dead and ascension to glory with the Father; his sending, with the Father, of the Holy Spirit upon the Apostles and the Church; and his unending mediation with the Father for the salvation of men.

Incense: A granulated substance which, when burnt, emits an aromatic smoke. It symbolizes the zeal with which the faithful should be consumed, the good odor of Christian virtue, the ascent of prayer to God.

Incest: Sexual intercourse with relatives by blood or marriage; a sin of impurity and also a grave violation of the natural reverence due to relatives. Other sins of impurity (desire, etc.) concerning relatives have the nature of incest.

Index of Prohibited Books: A list of books which Catholics were formerly forbidden to read, possess or sell, under penalty of excommunication. The books were banned by the Holy See after publication because their treatment of matters of faith and morals and related subjects were judged to be erroneous or serious occasions of doctrinal error. Some books were listed in the Index by name; others were covered under general norms. The Congregation for the Doctrine of the Faith declared June 14, 1966, that the Index and its related penalties of excommunication no longer had the force of law in the Church. Persons are still obliged, however, to take normal precautions against occasions of doctrinal error.

The first *Roman Index of Prohibited Books,* which served the same purposes as earlier lists, was published in 1559 by the Holy Office at the order of Paul IV. The Council of Trent, with the approval of the same pope, authorized another Index in 1564. Seven years later, St. Pius V set up a special Congregation for the Reform of the Index and Correction of Books, and gave it universal jurisdiction. In the course of time, many additions and modifications affecting the Index were made. In 1897, Leo XIII issued complete legislation on the subject, and in 1917 Benedict XV turned over to the Congregation of the Holy Office the function of censoring publications in accordance with the provisions of canon law.

Indifferentism: A theory that any one religion is as true and good — or false — as any other religion, and that it makes no difference, objectively, what religion one professes, if any. The theory is completely subjective, finding its justification entirely in personal choice without reference to or respect for objective validity. It is also self-contradictory, since it regards as equally acceptable — or unacceptable — the beliefs of all religions, which in fact are not only not all the same but are in some cases opposed to each other.

Indulgence: According to *The Doctrine and Practice of Indulgences,* an apostolic constitution issued by Paul VI Jan. 1, 1967, an indulgence is the remission before God of the temporal punishment due for sins already forgiven as far as their guilt is concerned, which a follower of Christ — with the proper dispositions and under certain determined conditions — acquires through the intervention of the Church. The Church grants indulgences in accordance with doctrine concerning the superabundant merits of Christ and the saints, the Power of the Keys, and the sharing of spiritual goods in the Communion of Saints.

An indulgence is partial or plenary, depending on whether it does away with either part or all of the temporal punishment due for sin. Both types of indulgences can always be applied to the dead by way of suffrage; the actual disposition of indulgences applied to the dead rests with God.

(1) Partial indulgence: Properly disposed faithful who perform an action to which a partial indulgence is attached obtain, in addition to the remission of temporal punishment

acquired by the action itself, an equal remission of punishment through the intervention of the Church. (This grant was formerly designated in terms of days and years.) The proper dispositions for gaining a partial indulgence are sorrow for sin and freedom from serious sin, performance of the required good work, and the intention (which can be general or immediate) to gain the indulgence.

In addition to customary prayers and other good works to which partial indulgences are attached, the *Enchiridion Indulgentiarum* published in 1968 included general grants of partial indulgences to the faithful who: (a) with some kind of prayer, raise their minds to God with humble confidence while carrying out their duties and bearing the difficulties of everyday life; (b) motivated by the spirit of faith and compassion, give of themselves or their goods for the service of persons in need; (c) in a spirit of penance, spontaneously refrain from the enjoyment of things which are lawful and pleasing to them.

(2) Plenary indulgence: To gain a plenary indulgence, it is necessary for a person to be free of all attachment to sin, to perform the work to which the indulgence is attached, and to fulfill the three conditions of sacramental confession, Eucharistic Communion, and prayer for the intention of the pope. The three conditions may be fulfilled several days before or after the performance of the prescribed work, but it is fitting that Communion be received and prayers for the intentions of the pope be offered on the same day the work is performed. The condition of praying for the pope's intention is fully satisfied by praying one Our Father and one Hail Mary, and sometimes the Creed, but persons are free to choose other prayers.

Four of the several devotional practices for which a plenary indulgence is granted are: (a) adoration of the Blessed Sacrament for at least one-half hour; (b) devout reading of sacred Scripture for at least one-half hour; (c) the Way of the Cross; (d) recitation of the Marian Rosary in a church or public oratory or in a family group, a religious community or pious association. Only one plenary indulgence can be gained in a single day.

Indult: A favor or privilege granted by competent ecclesiastical authority, giving permission to do something not allowed by the common law of the Church.

Infant Jesus of Prague: An 18-inch-high wooden statue of the Child Jesus which has figured in a form of devotion to the Holy Childhood and Kingship of Christ since the 17th century. Of uncertain origin, the statue was presented by Princess Polixena to the Carmelites of Our Lady of Victory Church, Prague, in 1628.

Infused Virtues: The theological virtues of faith, hope, and charity; principles or capabilities of supernatural action, they are given with sanctifying grace by God rather than ac-

quired by repeated acts of a person. They can be increased by practice; they are lost by contrary acts. Natural-acquired moral virtues, like the cardinal virtues of prudence, justice, temperance, and fortitude, can be considered infused in a person whose state of grace gives them supernatural orientation.

Inquisition: A tribunal for dealing with heretics, authorized by Gregory IX in 1231 to search them out, hear and judge them, sentence them to various forms of punishment, and in some cases to hand them over to civil authorities for punishment. The Inquisition was a creature of its time when crimes against faith, which threatened the good of the Christian community, were regarded also as crimes against the state, and when heretical doctrines of such extremists as the Cathari and Albigensians threatened the very fabric of society. The institution, which was responsible for many excesses, was most active in the second half of the 13th century.

Inquisition, Spanish: An institution peculiar to Spain and the colonies in Spanish America. In 1478, at the urging of King Ferdinand, Pope Sixtus IV approved the establishment of the Inquisition for trying charges of heresy brought against Jewish (Marranos) and Moorish (Moriscos) converts. It acquired jurisdiction over other cases as well, however, and fell into disrepute because of irregularities in its functions, cruelty in its sentences, and the manner in which it served the interests of the Spanish crown more than the accused persons and the good of the Church. Protests by the Holy See failed to curb excesses of the Inquisition, which lingered in Spanish history until early in the 19th century.

I N R I: The first letters of words in the Latin inscription atop the cross on which Christ was crucified: (I)esus (N)azaraenus, (R)ex (J)udaeorum — Jesus of Nazareth, King of the Jews.

Insemination, Artificial: The implanting of human semen by some means other than consummation of natural marital intercourse. In view of the principle that procreation should result only from marital intercourse, donor insemination is not permissible. The use of legitimate artificial means to further the fruitfulness of marital intercourse is permissible.

In Sin: The condition of a person called spiritually dead because he does not possess sanctifying grace, the principle of supernatural life, action and merit. Such grace can be regained through repentance.

Instruction: A document containing doctrinal explanations, directive norms, rules, recommendations, admonitions, issued by the pope, a department of the Roman Curia or other competent authority in the Church. To the extent that they so prescribe, instructions have the force of law.

Intercommunion: The common celebration and reception of the Eucharist by members of different Christian churches; a pivotal issue in ecumenical theory and practice. Catholic participation and intercommunion in the Eucharistic liturgy of another church without a valid priesthood and with a variant Eucharistic belief is out of order. Under certain conditions, other Christians may receive the Eucharist in the Catholic Church (see additional Intercommunion entry). Intercommunion is acceptable to some Protestant churches and unacceptable to others.

Interdict: An ecclesiastical penalty imposed on persons and places for certain violations of church law. If the interdict is personal, the interdicted persons may not take part in certain liturgical services, administer or receive certain sacraments. If the interdict is local, persons may not take part in certain liturgical services, administer or receive certain sacraments in the interdicted places.

Interdict is different from excommunication, and does not involve exclusion of a person from the community of the faithful.

Interregnum: The period of time between the death of one pope and the election of his successor. Another term applied to the period is *Sede vacante,* meaning the See (of Rome) being vacant.

Interregnum procedures follow norms contained in two apostolic constitutions: *Vacantis Apostolicae Sedis,* issued by Pius XII Dec. 8, 1945, and *Summi Pontificis Electione,* issued by John XXIII Sept. 5, 1962.

The main concerns during an interregnum are things connected with the death and burial of the pope, the election of his successor, and the maintenance of ordinary routine for the proper functioning of the Roman Curia.

The chamberlain of the Holy Roman Church takes over the ordinary administration of most Roman affairs. He — or the dean of the College of Cardinals prior to a chamberlain's election by the cardinals — certifies the death of the pope; orders the destruction of the Fisherman's Ring and other personal seals of the pope; and sets in motion the procedures for notifying the world about the pope's death, for funeral preparations, and for summoning the cardinals to a conclave for the election of a new pontiff.

The vicar of Rome exercises ordinary jurisdiction over the diocese.

The congregations, offices and tribunals of the Roman Curia retain ordinary jurisdiction for routine affairs but may not initiate new business during the interregnum.

The secretary of the College of Cardinals replaces the secretary of state and maintains the secretariat in a status quo.

The deceased pope is buried in St. Peter's Basilica within four or five days, following the usual customs for public viewing of the body and the offering of a solemn Mass. Nine consecutive daily Masses are offered for the repose of the pontiff, and the mourning period lasts for an interval of 10 days.

The conclave for the election of a new pope begins no later than 18 days after the death of his predecessor. On the election of the new pope, the interregnum comes to an end. (See Papal Election.)

Intinction: A method of administering Holy Communion under the dual appearances of bread and wine, in which the consecrated host is dipped in the consecrated wine before being given to the communicant. The administering of Holy Communion in this manner, which has been traditional in Eastern-Rite liturgies, was authorized in the Roman Rite for various occasions by the *Constitution on the Sacred Liturgy* promulgated by the Second Vatican Council.

Irenicism: Peace-seeking, conciliation, as opposed to polemics; an important element in ecumenism, provided it furthers pursuit of the Christian unity willed by Christ without degenerating into a peace-at-any-price disregard for religious truth.

Irregularity: An impediment to the lawful reception or exercise of holy orders. The Church instituted irregularities — which include apostasy, heresy, homicide, attempted suicide — out of reverence for the dignity of the sacraments.

Itinerarium: Prayers for a spiritually profitable journey.

J

Jansenism: Opinions developed and proposed by Cornelius Jansenius (1585-1638). He held that: human nature was radically and intrinsically corrupted by original sin; some men are predestined to heaven and others to hell; Christ died only for those predestined to heaven; for those who are predestined, the operations of grace are irresistible. Jansenism also advocated an extremely rigorous code of morals and asceticism. The errors were proscribed by Urban VIII in 1642, by Innocent X in 1653, by Clement XI in 1713, and by other popes. Despite these condemnations, the rigoristic spirit of Jansenism lingered for a long time afterwards, particularly in France.

Jehovah's Witnesses: The Witnesses, together with the Watchtower and Bible Tract Society, trace their beginnings to a Bible class organized by Charles Taze Russell in 1872 at Allegheny, Pa. They take their name from a passage in Isaiah (43:12): " 'You are my witnesses,' says Jehovah." They are generally fundamentalist and revivalist with respect to the Bible, and believe that Christ is God's Son but is inferior to God. They place great emphasis on the Battle of Armageddon (as a decisive confrontation of good and evil) that is depicted vividly in Revelation, believing that God will then destroy the existing system of things and that, with the establishment of Jehovah's Kingdom, a small band of 144,000 spiritual sons of God will go to heaven, rule with Christ, and share in some way their happiness with some others.

Each Witness is considered by the society to be an ordained minister charged with the duty of spreading the message of Jehovah, which is accomplished through publications, house-to-house visitations, and other methods. The Witnesses refuse to salute the flag of any nation, regarding this as a form of idolatry, or to sanction blood transfusions even for the saving of life. There are approximately one million Witnesses in more than 22,000 congregations in some 80 countries. The freedom and activities of Witnesses are restricted in some places.

Jesus: The name of Jesus, meaning Savior in Christian usage, derived from the Aramaic and Hebrew *Yeshua* and *Joshua,* meaning *Yahweh* is salvation.

Jesus Prayer: A form of prayer dating back to the fifth century, "Lord Jesus Christ, Son of God, have mercy on me (a sinner)."

Joys of the Blessed Virgin Mary, Seven: (See Franciscan Crown.)

Judgment: (1) Last or final judgment: Final judgment by Christ, at the end of the world and the general resurrection.

(2) Particular judgment: The judgment that takes place immediately after a person's death, followed by entrance into heaven, hell or purgatory.

Jurisdiction: Right, power, authority to rule. Jurisdiction in the Church is of divine institution; has pastoral service for its purpose; includes legislative, judicial and executive authority; can be exercised only by persons with the power of orders.

(1) Ordinary jurisdiction is attached to ecclesiastical offices by law; the officeholders, called ordinaries, have authority over those who are subject to them.

(2) Delegated jurisdiction is that which is granted to persons rather than attached to offices. Its extent depends on the terms of the delegation.

Justice: One of the four cardinal virtues by which a person gives to others what is due to them as a matter of right. (See Cardinal Virtues.)

Justification: The act by which God makes a person just, and the consequent change in the spiritual status of a person, from sin to grace; the remission of sin and the infusion of sanctifying grace through the merits of Christ and the action of the Holy Spirit.

K

Kerygma: Proclaiming the word of God, in the manner of the Apostles, as here and now effective for salvation. This method of preaching or instruction, centered on Christ and geared to the facts and themes of salvation history, is designed to dispose people to faith in Christ and/or to intensify the experience and practice of that faith in those who have it.

Keys, Power of the: Spiritual authority and jurisdiction in the Church, symbolized by the keys of the kingdom of heaven. Christ promised the keys to St. Peter, as head-to-be of the Church (Mt. 16:19), and commissioned him with full pastoral responsibility to feed his lambs and sheep (Jn. 21:15-17), The pope, as the successor of St. Peter, has this power in a primary and supreme manner. The bishops of the Church also have the power, in union with and subordinate to the pope. Priests share in it through holy orders and the delegation of authority.

Examples of the application of the Power of the Keys are the exercise of teaching and pastoral authority by the pope and bishops, the absolving of sins in the sacrament of penance, the granting of indulgences, the imposing of spiritual penalties on persons who commit certain serious sins.

L

Laicization: (1) The process by which a man ordained to holy orders is relieved of the obligations of orders and the ministry and is returned to the status of a lay person. Applications by diocesan clergy are filed with their bishop and forwarded for processing to the congregation of the Roman Curia authorized to grant the indult of laicization.

(2) The process by which a religious is relieved of the obligations of vows and membership in his or her institute. Applications are filed with the proper religious superior and forwarded for processing to the Congregation for Religious which is authorized to grant the appropriate indult.

Languages of the Church: The first language in church use, for divine worship and the conduct of ecclesiastical affairs, was Aramaic, the language of the first Christians in and around Jerusalem. As the Church spread westward, Greek was adopted and prevailed until the third century when it was supplanted by Latin for official use in the West.

According to traditions established very early in churches of the Eastern Rites, many different languages were adopted for use in divine worship and for the conduct of ecclesiastical affairs. The practice was, and still is, to use the vernacular or a language closely related to the common tongue of the people.

In the Western Church, Latin prevailed as the general official language until the promulgation on Dec. 4, 1963, of the *Constitution on the Sacred Liturgy* by the second session of the Second Vatican Council. Since that time, vernacular languages have come into use in the Mass, administration of the sacraments, and the Liturgy of the Hours. The change was introduced in order to make the prayers and ceremonies of divine worship more informative and meaningful to all. Latin, however, remains the official language for administrative and procedural matters.

Law: An ordinance or rule governing the activity of things.

(1) Natural law: Moral norms corresponding to man's nature by which he orders

his conduct toward God, neighbor, society and himself. This law, which is rooted in human nature, is of divine origin, can be known by the use of reason, and binds all men having the use of reason. The Ten Commandments are declarations and amplifications of natural law. The primary precepts of natural law, to do good and to avoid evil, are universally recognized, despite differences with respect to understanding and application resulting from different philosophies of good and evil.

(2) Divine positive law: That which has been revealed by God. Among its essentials are the twin precepts of love of God and love of neighbor, and the Ten Commandments.

(3) Ecclesiastical law: That which is established by the Church for the spiritual welfare of the faithful and the orderly conduct of ecclesiastical affairs. (See Canon Law.)

(4) Civil law: That which is established by a socio-political community for the common good.

Lector: A reader of scriptural passages and other selections at Mass and other services of worship.

Legitimation: Removal of the status of illegitimacy; e.g., by marriage of the parents.

Liberalism: A multiphased trend of thought and movement favoring liberty, independence and progress in moral, intellectual, religious, social, economic and political life. Traceable to the Renaissance, it developed through the Enlightenment, the rationalism of the 19th century, and modernist- and existentialist-related theories of the 20th century. Evaluations of various kinds of liberalism depend on the validity of their underlying principles. Extremist positions — regarding subjectivism, libertinarianism, naturalist denials of the supernatural, and the alienation of individuals and society from God and the Church were condemned by Gregory XVI in the 1830's, Pius IX in 1864, Leo XIII in 1899, and St. Pius X in 1907. There is, however, nothing objectionable about forms of liberalism patterned according to sound principles of Christian doctrine.

Life in Outer Space: Whether rational life exists on other bodies in the universe besides earth, is a question for scientific investigation to settle. The possibility can be granted, without prejudice to the body of revealed truth.

Limbo: The limbo of the fathers was the state of rest and natural happiness after death enjoyed by the just of pre-Christian times until they were admitted to heaven following the Ascension of Christ. Belief in this matter is stated in the Apostles' Creed. The existence of a limbo for unbaptized persons of infant status — a state of rest and natural happiness — has never been formally defined.

Litany: A prayer in the form of responsive petition; e.g., St. Joseph, pray for us, etc. There are seven litanies approved for liturgical use: Litanies of Loreto (Litany of the Blessed Mother), the Holy Name, All Saints, the Sacred Heart, the Precious Blood, St. Joseph, Litany for the Dying. Others may be used privately.

Little Office of the Blessed Virgin Mary: A shortened version of a Liturgy of the Hours honoring the Blessed Virgin. It dates from about the middle of the eighth century.

Liturgical Languages: (See Languages of the Church.)

Loreto, House of: A Marian shrine in Loreto, Italy, consisting of the home of the Holy Family which, according to an old tradition, was transported in a miraculous manner from Nazareth to Dalmatia and finally to Loreto between 1291 and 1294. Investigations conducted shortly after the appearance of the structure in Loreto revealed that its dimensions matched those of the house of the Holy Family missing from its place of enshrinement in a basilica at Nazareth. Among the many popes who regarded it with high honor was John XXIII, who went there on pilgrimage Oct. 4, 1962. The house of the Holy Family is enshrined in the Basilica of Our Lady.

Lust: A disorderly desire for sexual pleasure; one of the seven capital sins.

M

Magi: In the Infancy Narrative of St. Matthew's Gospel (2:1-12), three wise men from the East whose visit and homage to the Child Jesus at Bethlehem indicated Christ's manifestation of himself to non-Jewish people. The narrative teaches the universality of salvation. The traditional names of the Magi are Caspar, Melchior and Balthasar.

Magnificat: The canticle or hymn uttered by the Virgin Mary after she was greeted by her cousin Elizabeth on the occasion of the Visitation (Lk. 1:46-55). It is an expression of praise, thanksgiving and acknowledgement of the great blessings given by God to Mary, the Mother of the Second Person of the Blessed Trinity made Man.

Martyr: A Greek word, meaning witness, denoting one who voluntarily suffered death for the faith or some Christian virtue.

Martyrology: A catalogue of martyrs and other saints, arranged according to the calendar. The *Roman Martyrology* contains the official list of saints venerated by the Church. Additions to the list are made in beatification and canonization decrees of the Congregation for the Causes of Saints. The Martyrology is being revised to conform with other liturgical books.

Mass for the People: On Sundays and certain feasts throughout the year pastors are required to offer Mass for the faithful committed to their care. If they cannot offer the Mass on these days, they must do so at a later date or provide that another priest offer the Mass.

Master of Novices: The person in charge of the training and formation of candidates for a religious institute during novitiate.

Materialism: Theory which holds that matter is the only reality, and everything in existence is merely a manifestation of matter; there is no such thing as spirit, and the supernatural does not exist. Materialism is incompatible with Christian doctrine.

Meditation: Mental, as distinguished from vocal, prayer, in which thought, affections, and resolutions of the will predominate. There is a meditative element to all forms of prayer, which always involves the raising of the heart and mind to God.

Mendicants: A term derived from Latin and meaning beggars, applied to members of religious orders without property rights; the members, accordingly, worked or begged for their support. The original mendicants were Franciscans and Dominicans in the early 13th century; later, the Carmelites, Augustinians, Servites and others were given the mendicant title and privileges, with respect to exemption from episcopal jurisdiction and wide faculties for preaching and administering the sacrament of penance. The practice of begging is limited at the present time, although it is still allowed with the permission of competent superiors and bishops. Mendicants are supported by free will offerings and income received for spiritual services and other work.

Mercy, Divine: The love and goodness of God, manifested particularly in a time of need.

Merit: In religion, the right to a supernatural reward for good works freely done for a supernatural motive by a person in the state of and with the assistance of grace. The right to such reward is from God, who binds himself to give it. Accordingly, good works, as described above, are meritorious for salvation.

Metempsychosis: Theory of the passage or migration of the human soul after death from one body to another for the purpose of purification from guilt. The theory denies the unity of the soul and human personality, and the doctrine of individual moral responsibility.

Millennium: A thousand-year reign of Christ and the just upon earth before the end of the world. This belief of the Millenarians, Chiliasts, and some sects of modern times is based on an erroneous interpretation of Rv. 20.

Miracles: Observable events or effects in the physical or moral order of things, with reference to salvation, which cannot be explained by the ordinary operation of laws of nature and which, therefore, are attributed to the direct action of God. They make known, in an unusual way, the concern and intervention of God in human affairs for the salvation of men. The most striking examples are the miracles worked by Christ. Numbering about 35, they included his own Resurrection; the raising of three persons to life (Lazarus, the daughter of Jairus, the son of the widow of Naim); the healing of blind, leprous and other persons; nature miracles; and prophecies, or miracles of the intellectual order.

The foregoing notion of miracles, which is based on the concept of a fixed order of nature, was not known by the writers of Sacred Scripture. In the Old Testament, particularly, they called some things miraculous which, according to the definition in contemporary use, may or may not have been miracles. Essentially, however, the occurrences so designated were regarded as exceptional manifestations of God's care and concern for the salvation of his people. The miracles of Christ were miracles in the full sense of the term.

The Church believes it is reasonable to accept miracles as manifestations of divine power for purposes of salvation. God, who created the laws of nature, is their master; hence, without disturbing the ordinary course of things, he can — and has in the course of history before and after Christ — occasionally set aside these laws and has also produced effects beyond their power of operation. The Church does not call miraculous anything which does not admit of easy explanation; on the contrary, miracles are admitted only when the events have a bearing on the order of grace and every possible natural explanation has been tried and found wanting.

(The transubstantiation — i.e., the conversion of the whole substance of bread and wine, their sensible appearances alone remaining, into the Body and Blood of Christ in the act of Consecration at Mass — is not an observable event. Traditionally, however, it has been called a miracle.)

Missal: A liturgical book of Roman Rite also called the *Sacramentary,* containing the celebrant's prayers of the Mass, along with general instructions and ceremonial directives. The Latin text of the new *Roman Missal,* replacing the one authorized by the Council of Trent in the 16th century, was published by the Vatican Polyglot Press in 1970. Its use in English was made mandatory in the U.S. from Dec. 1, 1974. Readings and scriptural responsories formerly in the missal are contained in the *Lectionary.*

Missiology: Study of the missionary nature, constitution and activity of the Church in all aspects: theological reasons for missionary activity, laws and instructions of the Holy See, history of the missions, social and cultural background, methods, norms for carrying on missionary work.

Mission: (1) Strictly, it means being sent to perform a certain work, such as the mission of Christ to redeem mankind, the mission of the Apostles and the Church and its members to perpetuate the prophetic, priestly and royal mission of Christ.

(2) A place where: the Gospel has not been proclaimed; the Church has not been firmly established; the Church, although established, is weak.

(3) An ecclesiastical territory with the sim-

plest kind of canonical organization, under the jurisdiction of the Congregation for the Evangelization of Peoples.

(4) A church or chapel without a resident priest.

(5) A special course of sermons and spiritual exercises conducted in parishes for the purpose of renewing and deepening the spiritual life of the faithful and for the conversion of lapsed Catholics.

Modernism: The "synthesis of all heresies," which appeared near the beginning of the 20th century. It undermines the objective validity of religious beliefs and practices which, it contends, are products of the subconscious developed by mankind under the stimulus of a religious sense. It holds that the existence of a personal God cannot be demonstrated, the Bible is not inspired, Christ is not divine, nor did he establish the Church or institute the sacraments. A special danger lies in modernism, which is still influential, because it uses Catholic terms with perverted meanings. St. Pius X condemned 65 propositions of modernism in 1907 in the decree *Lamentabili* and issued the encyclical *Pascendi* to explain and analyze its errors.

Monastery: The dwelling place, as well as the community thereof, of monks belonging to the Benedictine and Benedictine-related orders like the Cistercians and Carthusians; also, the Augustinians and Canons Regular. Distinctive of monasteries are: their separation from the world; the papal enclosure or strict cloister; the permanence or stability of attachment characteristic of their members; autonomous government in accordance with a monastic rule, like that of St. Benedict in the West or of St. Basil in the East; the special dedication of its members to the community celebration of the liturgy as well as to work that is suitable to the surrounding area and the needs of its people. Monastic superiors of men have such titles as abbot and prior; of women, abbess and prioress. In most essentials, an abbey is the same as a monastery.

Monk: A member of a monastic order — e.g., the Benedictines, the Benedictine-related Cistercians and Carthusians, and the Basilians, who bind themselves by religious profession to stable attachment to a monastery, the contemplative life and the work of their community. In popular use, the title is wrongly applied to many men religious who really are not monks.

Monotheism: Belief in and worship of one God.

Morality: Conformity or difformity of behavior to standards of right conduct. (See Commandments of God, Precepts of the Church, Conscience, Law.)

Moral Re-Armament: The title, since 1938, of a movement initiated by Frank Buchman, a Lutheran minister with wide experience in evangelistic preaching and work in the US and abroad; also called Buchmanism, after him, and the Oxford Group Movement, because of the membership of Oxford University students in the First Christian Century Fellowship organized by Buchman in England in the late 1920's. MRA aspires to reform the world through propagation of and witness to the four absolutes of honesty, disinterestedness, purity and love.

Mormons: Members of the Church of Jesus Christ of Latter-Day Saints. The church was established by Joseph Smith (1805-1844) at Fayette, N.Y., three years after he said he had received from an angel golden tablets containing the *Book of the Prophet Mormon*. This book, the Bible, *Doctrine and Covenants,* and *The Pearl of Great Price,* are the basic doctrinal texts of the church. Characteristic of the Mormons are strong belief in the revelations of their leaders, among whom was Brigham Young; a strong community of religious-secular concern; a dual secular and spiritual priesthood, and vigorous missionary activity. The headquarters of the church are located at Salt Lake City, Utah, where the Mormons first settled in 1847.

Mortification: Acts of self-discipline, including prayer, hardship, austerities and penances undertaken for the sake of progress in virtue.

Motu Proprio: A Latin phrase designating a document issued by a pope on his own initiative. Documents of this kind often concern administrative matters.

Mysteries of Faith: Supernatural truths whose existence cannot be known without revelation by God and whose intrinsic truth, while not contrary to reason, can never be wholly understood even after revelation. These mysteries are above reason, not against reason. Among them are the divine mysteries of the Trinity, Incarnation and Eucharist.

Some mysteries — e.g., concerning God's attributes — can be known by reason without revelation, although they cannot be fully understood.

N

Necromancy: Supposed communication with the dead; a form of divination.

Non-Expedit: A Latin expression. It is not expedient (fitting, proper), used to state a prohibition or refusal of permission.

Novena: A term designating public or private devotional practices over a period of nine consecutive days; or, by extension, over a period of nine weeks, in which one day a week is set aside for the devotions.

Novice: A person preparing, in a formal period of trial and formation called the *novitiate,* for membership in a religious institute. The novitiate lasts more than a year and ends with the profession of temporary vows or other temporary commitment to the religious life. Current norms require a total 12-month period of seclusion for novices; to this is added other periods of time spent in apostolic work for the sake of experience. A novice, while acquiring experience of the religious life, is not bound by the obligations of professed members of the institute, is free to leave at any time, and may be discharged at the discretion of competent superiors. The immediate superior of a novice is a master or mistress of novices.

Nun (1) Strictly, a member of a religious order of women with solemn vows (moniales).

(2) In general, all women religious, even those in simple vows who are more properly called sisters.

Nunc Dimittis: The canticle or hymn of Simeon when he saw Christ at the Temple on the occasion of his presentation (Lk. 2:29-32). It is an expression of joy and thanksgiving for the blessing of having lived to see the Messiah. It is one of the canticles prescribed in the Liturgy of the Hours.

O

Oath: Calling upon God to witness the truth of a statement. Violating an oath, e.g., by perjury in court, or taking an oath without sufficient reason, is a violation of the honor due to God.

Obedience: Submission to one in authority. General obligations of obedience fall under the Fourth Commandment. The vow of obedience professed by religious is one of the evangelical counsels.

Obsession, Diabolical: The extraordinary state of one who is seriously molested by evil spirits in an external manner. Obsession is more than just temptation.

Occultism: Practices involving ceremonies, rituals, chants, incantations, other cult-related activities intended to affect the course of nature, the lives of practitioners and others, through esoteric powers of magic, diabolical or other forces; one of many forms of superstition.

Octave: A period of eight days given over to the celebration of a major feast such as Easter.

Oils, Holy: The oils consecrated by bishops on Holy Thursday or another suitable day, and by priests under certain conditions for use in certain sacraments and consecrations.

(1) The oil of catechumens (olive or vegetable oil), used at baptism and the ordination of priests.

(2) Chrism (olive or vegetable oil mixed with balm), used at baptism, in confirmation, at the ordination of a bishop, in the consecration of churches, altars, altarstones, chalices, patens, and in the blessing of bells.

(3) Oil of the sick (olive or vegetable oil) used in anointing the sick.

Old Catholics: Several sects, including (1) the Church of Utrecht which severed relations with Rome in 1724; (2) the National Polish Church in the US, which had its origin near the end of the 19th century; (3) the Yugoslav Old Catholic Church; (4) especially, a denomination founded by German priests and lay persons who broke away from union with Rome following the First Vatican Council in 1870. The doctrinal reason for the break was strong objection to the dogma of papal infallibility.

The formation of this Old Catholic Church began in 1870 at a public meeting held in Nuremberg under the leadership of A. Dollinger; four years later, episcopal succession was established with the valid consecration of a German bishop by a prelate of the Church of Utrecht. Old Catholics accept the first seven ecumenical councils and doctrine formulated before 1054, but reject communion with the pope and a number of Roman Catholic doctrines and practices. Since 1932, they have had full intercommunion with the Anglican Church. The Roman Church recognizes the validity of Old Catholic orders and other sacraments.

Oratory: A chapel.

Ordinariate: An ecclesiastical jurisdiction for special purposes and people. Examples are the military ordinariate of the US, for service personnel, and Eastern-Rite ordinariates in places where Eastern-Rite dioceses do not exist.

Ordinary: One who has the jurisdiction of an office: the pope, diocesan bishops, vicars general, prelates of missionary territories, vicars apostolic, prefects apostolic, vicars capitular during the vacancy of a see, superiors general, abbots primate and other major superiors of men religious.

Ordination: The consecration of sacred ministers for divine worship and the service of men in things pertaining to God. The power of ordination comes from Christ and the Church, and must be conferred by a minister capable of communicating it.

Organ Transplants: The transplanting of organs from one person to another is permissible for serious reasons provided it is done with the consent of the concerned parties and does not result in the death or essential mutilation of the donor. Advances in methods and technology have increased the range of transplant possibilities in recent years. Despite such progress, unresolved problems have slowed the pace of some transplant practice, especially with respect to the heart. The first successful heart transplant was performed Dec. 3, 1967, on Louis Washkansky, 56, by a team headed by Dr. Christian Barnard in Cape Town, South Africa.

Original Sin: The sin of Adam (Gn. 2:8—3:24), personal to him and passed on to all men as a state of privation of grace. Despite this privation and the related wounding of human nature and weakening of natural powers, original sin leaves unchanged all that man himself is by nature. The scriptural basis of the doctrine was stated especially by St. Paul in 1 Cor. 15:21, ff., and Romans 5:12-21.

Original sin is remitted by baptism and incorporation in Christ, through whom grace is given to persons.

O Salutaris Hostia: The first three Latin words, O Saving Victim, of a Benediction hymn.

Oxford Movement: A movement in the Church of England from 1833 to about 1845 which had for its objective a threefold defense of the church as a divine institution, the apostolic succession of its bishops, and the Book of Common Prayer as the rule of faith. The movement took its name from Oxford University and involved a number of intellectuals who authored a series of influential *Tracts for Our Times*. Some of its leading figures — e.g., F. W. Faber, John Henry Newman and Henry Edward Manning — became converts to the Catholic Church. In the Church of England, the movement affected the liturgy, historical and theological scholarship, the status of the ministry, and other areas of ecclesiastical life.

P

Paganism: A term referring to non-revealed religions, i.e., religions other than Christianity, Judaism and Mohammedanism.

Palms: Blessed palms are a sacramental. They are blessed and distributed on the Sunday of the Passion in commemoration of the triumphant entrance of Christ into Jerusalem. Ashes of the burnt palms are used on Ash Wednesday.

Pange Lingua: First Latin words, Sing, my tongue, of a hymn in honor of the Holy Eucharist, used particularly on Holy Thursday and in Eucharistic processions.

Pantheism: Theory that all things are part of God, divine, in the sense that God realizes himself as the ultimate reality of matter or spirit through being and/or becoming all things that have been, are, and will be. The theory leads to hopeless confusion of the Creator and the created realm of being, identifies evil with good, and involves many inherent contradictions.

Papal Election: The Roman Pontiff is elected by the cardinals in secret conclave, being chosen by a two-thirds majority vote (if the number present and voting is exactly divisible by three) or by a two-thirds, plus one, majority (if the number is not exactly divisible by three). This procedure, a modification of former voting methods, was decreed by John XXIII in the apostolic letter *Summi Pontificis Electio*, Sept. 5, 1962.

The conclave, which is held in a sealed-off area of the Vatican Palace, may begin on the 15th day after the death of a pope and must begin no later than the 18th day. Cardinals under the age of 80 are eligible to attend and vote. "The number of cardinals entitled to participate must not exceed 120," Pope Paul VI decreed in an allocution Mar. 5, 1973.

Voting takes place in the Sistine Chapel where four secret ballots are cast each day, two in the morning and two in the afternoon. Voting continues until one of the candidates receives the required majority.

The candidate so elected is asked by the dean of the College of Cardinals whether he accepts the office of the papacy. He becomes pope immediately on giving an affirmative reply. The subsequent coronation is only a ceremonial recognition of the fact that he is the pope. In a ceremony called *adoratio*, the cardinals signify their obedience to the new pontiff in the Sistine Chapel before public announcement of his name is made from the main balcony of the Vatican. The fact of election is first signaled to the outside world by means of white smoke.

The pope is elected for life. If he should resign, which he may do, a new pope is elected. Any male Catholic may be elected, even one who is not a priest. If a layman were elected and accepted the office, he would be ordained as a priest and bishop. If a priest were chosen he would be ordained as a bishop.

Paraclete: A title of the Holy Spirit meaning, in Greek, Advocate, Consoler.

Parental Duties: All duties related to the obligation of parents to provide for the welfare of their children. These obligations fall under the Fourth Commandment.

Parish: A community of the faithful served by a pastor charged with responsibility for providing them with full pastoral service. Most parishes are territorial, embracing all of the faithful in a certain area of a diocese; some are personal or national, for certain classes of people, without strict regard for their places of residence.

Parousia: The coming, or saving presence, of Christ which will mark the completion of salvation history and the coming to perfection of God's kingdom at the end of the world.

Paschal Candle: A large candle, symbolic of the risen Christ, blessed and lighted on the Easter Vigil and placed at the Gospel side of the altar until Ascension Day. It is ornamented with five large grains of incense, representing the wounds of Christ, inserted in the form of a cross; the Greek letters Alpha and Omega, symbolizing Christ the beginning and end of all things, at the top and bottom of the shaft of the cross; and the figures of the current year of salvation in the quadrants formed by the cross.

Paschal Precept: The church law requiring the faithful to receive Holy Communion during the Easter time.

Passion of Christ: Sufferings of Christ, recorded in the four Gospels.

Pastor: An ordained minister charged with responsibility for the doctrinal, sacramental and related service of people committed to his care; e.g., a bishop for the people in his diocese, a priest for the people of his parish.

Pater Noster: The initial Latin words, Our Father, of the Lord's Prayer.

Peace, Sign of: A gesture of greeting — e.g., a handshake — exchanged by the ministers and participants at Mass.

Pectoral Cross: A cross worn on a chain about the neck and over the breast by bishops and abbots as a mark of their office.

Penance or Penitence: (1) The spiritual change or conversion of mind and heart by which a person turns away from sin, and all that it implies, toward God, through a personal renewal under the influence of the Holy Spirit. In the apostolic constitution *Paenitemini*, Pope Paul VI called it "a religious, personal act which has as its aim love and surrender to God." Penance involves sorrow and contrition for sin, together with other internal and external acts of atonement. It serves the purposes of reestablishing in one's life the order of God's love and commandments, and of making satisfaction to God for sin. A divine precept states the necessity of penance for salvation: "Unless you do penance, you shall all likewise perish" (Lk. 13:3) . . . "Be converted and believe in the Gospel" (Mk. 1:15).

In the penitential discipline of the Church, the various works of penance have been classified under the headings of prayer (interior), fasting and almsgiving (exterior). The Church has established minimum requirements for the common and social observance of the divine precept by Catholics — e.g., by requiring them to fast and/or abstain on certain days of the year. These observances, however, do not exhaust all the demands of the divine precept, whose fulfillment is a matter of personal responsibility; nor do they have any real value unless they proceed from the internal spirit and purpose of penance.

Related to works of penance for sins actually committed are works of mortification. The purpose of the latter is to develop — through prayer, fasting, renunciations and similar actions — self-control and detachment from things which could otherwise become occasions of sin.

(2) Penance is a virtue disposing a person to turn to God in sorrow for sin and to carry out works of amendment and atonement.

(3) The sacrament of penance and sacramental penance.

Perjury: Taking a false oath, lying under oath, a violation of the honor due to God.

Persecution, Religious: A campaign waged against a church or other religious body by persons and governments intent on its destruction. The best known campaigns of this type against the Christian Church were the Roman persecutions which occurred intermittently from about 54 to the promulgation of the Edict of Milan in 313, The most extensive persecutions took place during the reigns of Nero, the first major Roman persecutor, Domitian, Trajan, Marcus Aurelius, and Diocletian. Besides the Roman persecutions, the Catholic Church has been subject to many others, including those of the 20th century in Communist-controlled countries.

Peter's Pence: A collection made each year among Catholics for the maintenance of the pope and his works of charity. It was originally a tax of a penny on each house, and was collected on St. Peter's day, whence the name. It originated in England in the eighth century.

Petition: One of the four purposes of prayer. In prayers of petition, persons ask of God the blessings they and others need.

Pharisees: Influential class among the Jews, referred to in the Gospels, noted for their self-righteousness, legalism, strict interpretation of the Law; acceptance of the traditions of the elders as well as the Law of Moses, and beliefs regarding angels and spirits, the resurrection of the dead and judgment. Most of them were laymen, and they were closely allied with the Scribes; their opposite numbers were the Sadducees. The Pharisaic and rabbinical traditions had a lasting influence on Judaism following the destruction of Jerusalem in 70 A.D.

Pious Fund: Property and money originally accumulated by the Jesuits to finance their missionary work in Lower California. When the Jesuits were expelled from the territory in 1767, the fund was appropriated by the Spanish Crown and used to support Dominican and Franciscan missionary work in Upper and Lower California. In 1842 the Mexican government took over administration of the fund, incorporated most of the revenue into the national treasury, and agreed to pay the Church interest of six per cent a year on the capital so incorporated. From 1848 to 1967 the fund was the subject of lengthy negotiations between the US and Mexican governments because of the latter's failure to make payments as agreed. A lump-sum settlement was made in 1967 with payment by Mexico to the US government of more than $700,000, to be turned over to the Archdiocese of San Francisco.

Polytheism: Belief in and worship of many gods or divinities, especially prevalent in pre-Christian religions.

Poor Box: Alms-box; found in churches from the earliest days of Christianity.

Pope Joan: Alleged name of a woman falsely said to have been pope from 855-858, the years of the reign of Benedict III. The myth was not heard of before the 13th century.

Portiuncula: (1) Meaning little portion (of land), the Portiuncula was the chapel of Our Lady of the Angels near Assisi, Italy, which the Benedictines gave to St. Francis early in the 13th century. He repaired the chapel and made it the first church of the Franciscan Order. It is now enshrined in the Basilica of St. Mary of the Angels in Assisi.

(2) The Portiuncula Indulgence, or Pardon of Assisi, was authorized by Honorius III.

Originally, it could be gained for the souls in purgatory only in the chapel of Our Lady of the Angels; by later concessions, it could be gained also in other Franciscan and parish churches. According to legislation now in force, the Portiuncula Indulgence can be gained once on the day of Aug. 2, or on the following Sunday with permission of the bishop of the place. The conditions are, in addition to freedom from attachment to sin: reception of the sacraments of penance and the Eucharist on or near the day; a visit to a parish church on the day, during which the Our Father and Creed are offered for the intentions of the pope.

Possession, Diabolical: The extraordinary state of a person who is tormented from within by evil spirits who exercise strong influence over his powers of mind and body.

Postulant: One of several names used to designate a candidate for membership in a religious institute during the period before novitiate.

Poverty: (1) The quality or state of being poor, in actual destitution and need, or being poor in spirit. In the latter sense, poverty means the state of mind and disposition of persons who regard material things in proper perspective as gifts of God for the support of life and its reasonable enrichment, and for the service of others in need. It means freedom from unreasonable attachment to material things as ends in themselves, even though they may be possessed in small or large measure.

(2) One of the evangelical counsels professed by religious as a vow. It involves the voluntary renunciation of rights of ownership and of independent use and disposal of material goods (solemn vow); or, the right of independent use and disposal, but not of the radical right of ownership (simple vow). Religious institutes provide their members with necessary and useful goods and services from common resources. The manner in which goods are received and/or handled by religious is determined by poverty of spirit and the rule and constitutions of their institute. Practice of the vow of poverty is undergoing some change in the contemporary renewal in religious life.

Pragmatism: Theory that the truth of ideas, concepts and values depends on their utility or capacity to serve a useful purpose rather than on their conformity with objective standards; also called utilitarianism.

Prayer: The raising of the mind and heart to God in adoration, thanksgiving, reparation and petition. Prayer, which is always mental because it involves thought and love of God, may be vocal, meditative, private and personal, social, and official. The official prayer of the Church as a worshiping community is called the liturgy.

Precepts: Commands or orders given to individuals or communities in particular cases;

they establish law for concerned parties. Preceptive documents are issued by the pope, departments of the Roman Curia and other competent authority in the Church.

Presence of God: A devotional practice of increasing one's awareness of the presence and action of God in daily life.

Presumption: A violation of the theological virtue of hope, by which a person striving for salvation either relies too much on his own capabilities or expects God to do things which he cannot do, in keeping with his divine attributes, or does not will to do, according to his divine plan. Presumption is the opposite of despair.

Preternatural Gifts: Exceptional gifts, beyond the exigencies and powers of human nature, enjoyed by Adam in the state of original justice: immunity from suffering and death, superior knowledge, integrity or perfect control of the passions. These gifts were lost as the result of original sin; their loss, however, implied no impairment of the integrity of human nature.

Pride: Unreasonable self-esteem; one of the seven capital sins.

Pric-Dieu: A French phrase, meaning pray God, designating a kneeler or bench suitable for kneeling while at prayer.

Priesthood of the Laity: Lay persons share in the priesthood of Christ in virtue of the sacraments of baptism and confirmation. They are not only joined with Christ for a life of union with him but are also deputed by him for participation in his mission, now carried on by the Church, of worship, teaching, witness and apostolic works. St. Peter called Christians "a royal priesthood" (1 Pt. 2:9) in this connection. St. Thomas Aquinas declared: "The sacramental characters (of baptism and confirmation) are nothing else than certain sharings of the priesthood of Christ, derived from Christ himself."

The priesthood of the laity differs from the official ministerial priesthood of ordained priests and bishops — who have the power of holy orders for celebrating the Eucharist, administering the other sacraments, and providing pastoral care. The ministerial priesthood, by divine commission, serves the universal priesthood. (See Role of Sacraments.)

Primary Option: The life-choice of a person for or against God which shapes the basic orientation of moral conduct.

Prior: A superior or an assistant to an abbot in a monastery.

Privilege: A favor, an exemption from the obligation of a law. Privileges of various kinds, with respect to ecclesiastical laws, are granted by the pope, departments of the Roman Curia and other competent authority in the Church.

Probabilism: A moral system for use in cases of conscience which involve the obligation of doubtful laws. There is a general principle that a doubtful law does not bind. Probabilism, therefore, teaches that it is permissible to follow an opinion favoring liberty, provided the opinion is certainly and solidly probable. Probabilism may not be invoked when there is question of: a certain law or the certain obligation of a law; the certain right of another party; the validity of an action; something which is necessary for salvation.

Pro-Cathedral: A church used as a cathedral.

Promoter of the Faith: An official of the Congregation for the Causes of Saints, whose role in beatification and canonization procedures is to establish beyond reasonable doubt the validity of evidence regarding the holiness of prospective saints and miracles attributed to their intercession.

Prophecies of St. Malachy: These so-called prophecies, listing the designations of 102 popes and 10 antipopes, bear the name they have because they have been falsely attributed to St. Malachy, bishop of Armagh, who died in 1148. Actually, they are forgeries by an unknown author and came to light only in the last decade of the 16th century.

The first 75 prophecies cover the 65 popes and 10 antipopes from Celestine II (1143-1144) to Gregory XIV (1590-91), and are exact with respect to names, coats of arms, birthplaces, and other identifying characteristics. This portion of the work, far from being prophetic, is the result of historical knowledge or hindsight. The 37 designations following that of Gregory are vague, fanciful, and subject to wide interpretation. According to the prophecies, Paul VI, the Flower of Flowers, will have only four successors before the end of the world.

Prophecy: (1) The communication of divine revelation by inspired intermediaries, called prophets, between God and his people. Old Testament prophecy was unique in its origin and because of its ethical and religious content, which included disclosure of the saving will of Yahweh for the people, moral censures and warnings of divine punishment because of sin and violations of the Law and Covenant, in the form of promises, admonitions, reproaches and threats. Although Moses and other earlier figures are called prophets, the period of prophecy is generally dated from the early years of the monarchy to about 100 years after the Babylonian Exile. From that time on the written Law and its interpreters supplanted the prophets as guides of the people. Old Testament prophets are cited in the New Testament, with awareness that God spoke through them and that some of their oracles were fulfilled in Christ. John the Baptist is the outstanding prophetic figure in the New Testament. Christ never claimed the title of prophet for himself, although some people thought he was one. There were prophets in the early Church, and St. Paul mentioned the charism of prophecy in 1 Cor. 14:1-5. Prophecy disappeared after New Testament times.

Revelation is classified as the prophetic book of the New Testament.

(2) In contemporary non-scriptural usage, the term is applied to the witness given by persons to the relevance of their beliefs in everyday life and action.

Province: (1) A territory comprising one archdiocese called the metropolitan see and one or more dioceses called suffragan sees. The head of the archdiocese, an archbishop, has metropolitan rights and responsibilities over the province.

(2) A division of a religious order under the jurisdiction of a provincial superior.

Prudence: Practical wisdom and judgment regarding the choice and use of the best ways and means of doing good; one of the four cardinal virtues.

Punishment Due for Sin: The punishment which is a consequence of sin. It is of two kinds:

(1) Eternal punishment is the punishment of hell, to which one becomes subject by the commission of mortal sin. Such punishment is remitted when mortal sin is forgiven.

(2) Temporal punishment is a consequence of venial sin and/or forgiven mortal sin; it is not everlasting and may be remitted in this life by means of penance. Temporal punishment unremitted during this life is remitted by suffering in purgatory.

Purgatory: The state or condition in which those who have died in the state of grace, but with some attachment to sin, suffer for a time before they are admitted to the glory and happiness of heaven. In this state and period of passive suffering, they are purified of unrepented venial sins, satisfy the demands of divine justice for temporal punishment due for sins, and are thus converted to a state of worthiness of the beatific vision.

R

Racism: A theory which holds that any one or several of the different races of the human family are inherently superior or inferior to any one or several of the others. The teaching denies the essential unity of the human race, the equality and dignity of all men because of their common possession of the same human nature, and the participation of all men in the divine plan of redemption. It is radically opposed to the virtue of justice and the precept of love of neighbor. Differences of superiority and inferiority which do exist are the result of accidental factors operating in a wide variety of circumstances, and are in no way due to essential defects in any one or several of the branches of the one human race. The theory of racism, together with practices related to it, is incompatible with Christian doctrine.

Rash Judgment: Attributing faults to another without sufficient reason; a violation of the obligations of justice and charity.

Rationalism: A theory which makes the mind the measure and arbiter of all things, including religious truth. A product of the Enlightenment, it rejects the supernatural, divine revelation, and authoritative teaching by any church.

Recollection: Meditation, attitude of concentration or awareness of spiritual matters and things pertaining to salvation and the accomplishment of God's will.

Relativism: Theory which holds that all truth, including religious truth, is relative, i.e., not absolute, certain or unchanging; a product of agnosticism, indifferentism, and an unwarranted extension of the notion of truth in positive science. Relativism is based on the tenet that certain knowledge of any and all truth is impossible. Therefore, no religion, philosophy or science can be said to possess the real truth; consequently, all religions, philosophies and sciences may be considered to have as much or as little of truth as any of the others.

Relics: The physical remains and effects of saints, which are considered worthy of veneration inasmuch as they are representative of persons in glory with God. First class relics are parts of the bodies of saints, and instruments of their penance and death; second class relics are objects which had some contact with their persons. Catholic doctrine proscribes the view that relics are not worthy of veneration. In line with norms laid down by the Council of Trent and subsequent enactments, discipline concerning relics is subject to control by the Congregation for the Causes of Saints.

Religion: The adoration and service of God as expressed in divine worship and in daily life. Religion is concerned with all of the relations existing between God and man, and between man and man because of the central significance of God. Objectively considered, religion consists of a body of truth which is believed, a code of morality for the guidance of conduct, and a form of divine worship. Subjectively, it is man's total response, theoretically and practically, to the demands of faith; it is living faith, personal engagement, self-commitment to God. Thus, by creed, code and cult, a person orders and directs his life in reference to God and, through what the love and service of God implies, to his fellow men and all things.

Reliquary: A vessel for the preservation and exposition of a relic; sometimes made like a small monstrance.

Reparation: The making of amends to God for sin committed; one of the four ends of prayer and the purpose of penance.

Rescript: A written reply by an ecclesiastical superior regarding a question or request; its provisions bind concerned parties only. Papal dispensations are issued in the form of rescripts.

Reserved Case: A sin or censure, absolution from which is reserved to religious superiors, bishops, the pope, or confessors having special faculties. Reservations are made because of the serious nature and social effects of certain sins and censures.

Restitution: An act of reparation for an injury done to another. The injury may be caused by taking and/or retaining what belongs to another or by damaging either the property or reputation of another. The intention of making restitution, usually in kind, is required as a condition for the forgiveness of sins of injustice, even though actual restitution is not possible.

Ring: In the Church a ring is worn as part of the insignia of bishops, abbots, et al.; by sisters to denote their consecration to God and the Church. The wedding ring symbolizes the love and union of husband and wife.

Ritual: A book of prayers and ceremonies used in the administration of the sacraments and other ceremonial functions. In the Roman Rite, the standard book of this kind is the Roman Ritual. Revisions have been made — e.g., in the rites of baptism — since the Second Vatican Council.

Rogito: The official notarial act or document testifying to the burial of a pope.

Rosary: A form of mental and vocal prayer centered on mysteries or events in the lives of Jesus and Mary. Its essential elements are meditation on the mysteries and the recitation of a number of decades of Hail Marys, each beginning with the Lord's Prayer. Introductory prayers may include the Apostles' Creed, an initial Our Father, three Hail Marys and a Glory be to the Father; each decade is customarily concluded with a Glory be to the Father; at the end, it is customary to say the Hail, Holy Queen and a prayer from the liturgy for the feast of the Blessed Virgin Mary of the Rosary.

The **Mysteries of the Rosary,** which are the subject of meditation, are: (1) Joyful — the Annunciation to Mary that she was to be the Mother of Christ, her visit to Elizabeth, the birth of Jesus, the presentation of Jesus in the Temple, the finding of Jesus in the Temple. (2) Sorrowful — Christ's agony in the Garden of Gethsemani, scourging at the pillar, crowning with thorns, carrying of the Cross to Calvary, and crucifixion. (3) Glorious — the Resurrection and Ascension of Christ, the descent of the Holy Spirit upon the Apostles, Mary's Assumption into heaven and her crowning as Queen of angels and men.

The complete Rosary, called the Dominican Rosary, consists of 15 decades. In customary practice, only five decades are usually said at one time. Rosary beads are used to aid in counting the prayers without distraction.

The Rosary originated through the coalescence of popular devotions to Jesus and Mary from the 12th century onward. Its present form dates from about the 15th century. Carthusians contributed greatly toward its development; Dominicans have been its greatest promoters.

S

Sabbath: The seventh day of the week, observed by Jews and Sabbatarians as the day for rest and religious observance.

Sacramentary: One of the first liturgical books, containing the celebrant's part of the Mass and rites for administration of the sacraments. The earliest book of this kind, the Leonine Sacramentary, dates from the middle or end of the sixth century.

The sacramentary, incorporating most of the contents of the *Roman Missal,* was reintroduced in the Roman Rite following the promulgation of the *Constitution on the Sacred Liturgy* by the Second Vatican Council.

Sacrarium: A basin with a drain leading directly into the ground; standard equipment of a sacristy.

Sacred Heart, Enthronement: An acknowledgment of the sovereignty of Jesus Christ over the Christian family, expressed by the installation of an image or picture of the Sacred Heart in a place of honor in the home, accompanied by an act of consecration.

Sacred Heart, Promises: Twelve promises to persons having devotion to the Sacred Heart of Jesus, which were communicated by Christ to St. Margaret Mary Alacoque in a private revelation in 1675: (1) I will give them all the graces necessary in their state in life. (2) I will establish peace in their homes. (3) I will comfort them in all their afflictions. (4) I will be their secure refuge during life and, above all, in death. (5) I will bestow abundant blessing upon all their undertakings. (6) Sinners shall find in my Heart the source and the infinite ocean of mercy. (7) By devotion to my Heart tepid souls shall grow fervent. (8) Fervent souls shall quickly mount to high perfection. (9) I will bless every place where a picture of my Heart shall be set up and honored. (10) I will give to priests the gift of touching the most hardened hearts. (11) Those who promote this devotion shall have their names written in my Heart, never to be blotted out. (12) I will grant the grace of final penitence to those who communicate (receive Holy Communion) on the first Friday of nine consecutive months.

Sacrilege: Violation of and irreverence toward a person, place or thing that is sacred because of public dedication to God; a sin against the virtue of religion. Personal sacrilege is violence of some kind against a cleric or religious, or a violation of chastity with a cleric or religious. Local sacrilege is the desecration of sacred places. Real sacrilege is irreverence with respect to sacred things, such as the sacraments and sacred vessels.

Sacristy: A utility room where vestments, church furnishings and sacred vessels are kept and where the clergy vest for sacred functions.

Sadducees: The predominantly priestly party among the Jews in the time of Christ, noted for extreme conservatism, acceptance only of the Law of Moses, and rejection of the traditions of the elders. Their opposite numbers were the Pharisees.

Saints, Cult of: The veneration, called dulia, of holy persons who have died and are in glory with God in heaven; it includes honoring them and petitioning them for their intercession with God. Liturgical veneration is given only to saints officially recognized by the Church; private veneration may be given to anyone thought to be in heaven. The veneration of saints is essentially different from the adoration given to God alone; by its very nature, however, it terminates in the worship of God.

According to the Second Vatican Council's *Dogmatic Constitution on the Church* (No. 50): "It is supremely fitting . . . that we love those friends and fellow heirs of Jesus Christ, who are also our brothers and extraordinary benefactors, that we render due thanks to God for them and 'suppliantly invoke them and have recourse to their prayers, their power and help in obtaining benefits from God through His Son, Jesus Christ, our Lord, who is our sole Redeemer and Savior.' For by its very nature every genuine testimony of love which we show to those in heaven tends toward and terminates in Christ, who is the 'crown of all saints.' Through Him it tends toward and terminates in God, who is wonderful in His saints and is magnified in them."

Salvation: The liberation of men from sin and its effects, reconciliation with God in and through Christ, the attainment of union with God forever in the glory of heaven as the supreme purpose of life and as the God-given reward for fulfillment of his will on earth. Salvation-in-process begins and continues in this life through union with Christ in faith professed and in action; its final term is union with God and the whole community of the saved in the ultimate perfection of God's kingdom. The Church teaches that: God wills the salvation of all men; men are saved in and through Christ; membership in the Church established by Christ, known and understood as the community of salvation, is necessary for salvation; men with this knowledge and understanding who deliberately reject this Church, cannot be saved. In the context of Catholic belief, the Catholic Church is the Church founded by Christ. (See below, Salvation outside the Church.)

Salvation History: The facts and the record of God's relations with men, in the past, present and future, for the purpose of leading them to live in accordance with his will for the eventual attainment after death of salvation, or everlasting happiness with him in heaven.

The essentials of salvation history are: God's love for all men and will for their salvation; his intervention and action in the world to express this love and bring about their salvation; the revelation he made of himself and the covenant he established with the Israelites in the Old Testament; the perfecting of this revelation and the new covenant of grace through Christ in the New Testament; the continuing action-for-salvation carried on in and through the Mystical Body of Christ, the Church; the communication of saving grace to men through the merits of Christ and the operations of the Holy Spirit in the here-and-now circumstances of daily life and with the cooperation of men themselves.

Salvation outside the Church: The Second Vatican Council covered this subject summarily in the following manner: "Those also can attain to everlasting salvation who through no fault of their own do not know the gospel of Christ or His Church, yet sincerely seek God and, moved by grace, strive by their deeds to do His will as it is known to them through the dictates of conscience. Nor does divine Providence deny the help necessary for salvation to those who, without blame on their part, have not yet arrived at an explicit knowledge of God, but who strive to live a good life, thanks to His grace. Whatever good or truth is found among them is looked upon by the Church as a preparation for the gospel. She regards such qualities as given by Him who enlightens all men so that they may finally have life" *(Dogmatic Constitution on the Church,* No. 16).

Satanism: Worship of the devil, a blasphemous inversion of the order of worship which is due to God alone.

Scandal: Conduct which is the occasion of sin to another person.

Scapular: (1) A part of the habit of some religious orders like the Benedictines and Dominicans; a nearly shoulder-wide strip of cloth worn over the tunic and reaching almost to the feet in front and behind. Originally a kind of apron, it came to symbolize the cross and yoke of Christ.

(2) Scapulars worn by lay persons as a sign of association with religious orders and for devotional purposes are an adaptation of monastic scapulars. Approved by the Church as sacramentals, they consist of two small squares of woolen cloth joined by strings and are worn about the neck. They are given for wearing in a ceremony of investiture or enrollment. There are nearly 20 scapulars for devotional use: the five principal ones are generally understood to include those of Our Lady of Mt. Carmel (the brown Carmelite Scapular), the Holy Trinity, Our Lady of the Seven Dolors, the Passion, the Immaculate Conception.

Scapular Medal: A medallion with a representation of the Sacred Heart on one side and of the Blessed Virgin Mary on the other. Authorized by St. Pius X in 1910, it may be worn or carried in place of a scapular by persons already invested with a scapular.

Scapular Promise: According to a legend of the Carmelite Order, the Blessed Virgin Mary appeared to St. Simon Stock in 1251 at Cambridge and declared that wearers of the brown Carmelite Scapular would be saved from hell and taken to heaven by her on the first Saturday after death. The validity of the legend has never been the subject of official decision by the Church. Essentially, it expresses belief in the intercession of Mary and the efficacy of sacramentals in the context of truly Christian life.

Schism: Derived from a Greek word meaning separation, the term designates formal and obstinate refusal by a baptized person, called a *schismatic,* to be in communion with the pope and the Church. The canonical penalty is excommunication. One of the most disastrous schisms in history resulted in the definitive separation of the Church in the East from union with Rome about 1054.

Scholasticism: The term usually applied to the Catholic theology and philosophy which developed in the Middle Ages.

Scribes: Hebrew intellectuals noted for their knowledge of the Law of Moses, influential from the time of the Exile to about 70 A.D. Many of them were Pharisees. They were the antecedents of rabbis and their traditions, as well as those of the Pharisees, had a lasting influence on Judaism following the destruction of Jerusalem in 70 A.D.

Scruple: A morbid, unreasonable fear and anxiety that one's actions are sinful when they are not, or more seriously sinful than they actually are. Compulsive scrupulosity is quite different from the transient scrupulosity of persons of tender or highly sensitive conscience, or of persons with faulty moral judgment.

Seal of Confession: The obligation of secrecy which must be observed regarding knowledge of things learned in connection with the confession of sin in the sacrament of penance. The seal covers matters whose revelation would make the sacrament burdensome. Confessors are prohibited, under penalty of excommunication, from making any direct revelation of confessional matter; this prohibition holds, outside of confession, even with respect to the person who made the confession unless the person releases the priest from the obligation. Persons other than confessors are obliged to maintain secrecy, but not under penalty of excommunication. General, non-specific discussion of confessional matter does not violate the seal.

Secularism: A school of thought, a spirit and manner of action which ignores and/or repudiates the validity or influence of supernatural religion with respect to individual and social life. In describing secularism in their annual statement in 1947, the bishops of the United States said in part: " . . . There are many men — and their number is daily increasing — who in practice live their lives without recognizing that this is God's world.

For the most part they do not deny God. On formal occasions they may even mention his name. Not all of them would subscribe to the statement that all moral values derive from merely human conventions. But they fail to bring an awareness of their responsibility to God into their thought and action as individuals and members of society. This, in essence, is what we mean by secularism."

See: Another name for diocese or archdiocese.

Seminary: A house of study and formation for men, called seminarians, preparing for the priesthood. Traditional seminaries date from the Council of Trent in the middle of the 16th century; before that time, candidates for the priesthood were variously trained in monastic schools, universities under church auspices, and in less formal ways. At the present time, seminaries are undergoing considerable change for the improvement of academic and formation programs and procedures.

Sermon on the Mount: A compilation of sayings of Our Lord in the form of an extended discourse in Matthew's Gospel (5:1 to 7:27) and, in a shorter discourse, in Luke (6:17-49). The passage in Matthew, called the "Constitution of the New Law," summarizes the living spirit of believers in Christ and members of the kingdom of God. Beginning with the Beatitudes and including the Lord's Prayer, it covers the perfect justice of the New Law, the fulfillment of the Old Law in the New Law of Christ, and the integrity of internal attitude and external conduct with respect to love of God and neighbor, justice, chastity, truth, trust and confidence in God.

Servile Work: Work that is mainly physical and done for the sake of material purposes, in distinction from so-called liberal and artistic work which, although involving physical effort, is of a mental and intellectual nature. Commonly classified as servile are such works as farming, manufacturing, commercial operations, mining, etc. Liberal works are those like studying, teaching, designing, writing, typing, etc. The classification of work as servile or otherwise depends in part on custom and cultural interpretation. The reception of pay for work has nothing to do with its classification. Servile work is prohibited on Sundays and holy days of obligation unless there is sound reason for it.

Seven Last Words of Christ: Words of Christ on the Cross. (1) "Father, forgive them; for they do not know what they are doing." (2) To the penitent thief: "I assure you: today you will be with me in Paradise." (3) To Mary and his Apostle John: "Woman, there is your son . . . There is your mother." (4) "My God, my God, why have you forsaken me?" (5) "I am thirsty." (6) "Now it is finished." (7) "Father, into your hands I commend my spirit."

Shrine, Crowned: A shrine approved by the Holy See as a place of pilgrimage. The approval permits public devotion at the shrine and implies that at least one miracle has resulted from devotion at the shrine. Among the best known crowned shrines are those of the Virgin Mary at Lourdes and Fatima.

Shroud of Turin: A strip of brownish linen cloth, 14 feet, three inches in length and three feet, seven inches in width, bearing the front and back imprint of a human body. A tradition dating from the seventh century, which has not been verified beyond doubt, claims that the shroud is the fine linen in which the body of Christ was wrapped for burial. The early history of the shroud is obscure. It was enshrined at Lirey, France, in 1354 and was transferred in 1578 to Turin, Italy, where it has been kept in the cathedral down to the present time. Scientific investigation, which began in 1898, seems to indicate that the markings on the shroud are those of a human body.

Sick Calls: When a person is confined at home by illness or other cause and is unable to go to church for reception of the sacraments, a parish priest should be informed and arrangements made for him to visit the person at home. Such visitations are common in pastoral practice, both for special needs and for providing persons with regular opportunities for receiving the sacraments.

Prepared for the visit should be: a conveniently placed table covered with a white cloth; on it should be a crucifix, two lighted candles, a glass with water, a spoon and napkin.

The priest, carrying the Blessed Sacrament, should be escorted to and from the sick person by someone carrying a lighted candle. Members of the household should be present when the sick person receives Holy Communion and/or anointing of the sick.

Sign of the Cross: A sign, ceremonial gesture or movement in the form of a cross by which a person confesses faith in the Holy Trinity and Christ, and intercedes for the blessing of himself, other persons, and things. In Roman-Rite practice, a person making the sign touches the fingers of the right hand to his forehead, below the breast, left shoulder and right shoulder while saying: "In the name of the Father, and of the Son, and of the Holy Spirit." The sign is also made with the thumb on the forehead, the lips, and the breast. For the blessing of persons and objects, a large sign of the cross is made by movement of the right hand. In Eastern-Rite practice, the sign is made with the thumb and first two fingers of the right hand joined together and touching the forehead, below the breast, the right shoulder and the left shoulder; the formula generally used is the doxology, "O Holy God, O Holy Strong One, O Immortal One." The Eastern manner of making the sign was general until the first half of the 13th century; by the 17th century, Western practice involved the whole right hand and the reversal of direction from shoulder to shoulder.

Signs of the Times: Contemporary events, trends and features in culture and society, the needs and aspirations of people, all the factors that form the context in and through which the Church has to carry on its saving mission. The Second Vatican Council spoke on numerous occasions about these signs and the relationship between them and a kind of manifestation of God's will, positive or negative, and about subjecting them to judgment and action corresponding to the demands of divine revelation through Scripture, Christ, and the experience, tradition and teaching authority of the Church.

Simony: The deliberate intention and act of selling and/or buying spiritual goods or material things so connected with the spiritual that they cannot be separated therefrom; a violation of the virtue of religion, and a sacrilege, because it wrongfully puts a material price on spiritual things, which cannot be either sold or bought. In church law, actual sale or purchase is subject to censure in some cases. The term is derived from the name of Simon Magus, who attempted to buy from Sts. Peter and John the power to confirm people in the Holy Spirit (Acts 8:4-24).

Sin: (1) Actual sin is rejection of God manifested by free and deliberate violation of his law by thought, word or action. (a) Mortal sin — involving serious matter, sufficient reflection and full consent — results in total alienation from God, making a person dead to sanctifying grace, incapable of performing meritorious supernatural acts and subject to everlasting punishment. (b) Venial sin — involving less serious matter, reflection and consent — does not have such serious consequences.

(2) Original sin is the sin of Adam, with consequences for all men. (See separate entries.)

Sins against the Holy Spirit: Despair of salvation, presumption of God's mercy, impugning the known truths of faith, envy at another's spiritual good, obstinacy in sin, final impenitence. Those guilty of such sins stubbornly resist the influence of grace and, as long as they do so, cannot be forgiven.

Sins, Occasions of: Circumstances (persons, places, things, etc.) which easily lead to sin. There is an obligation to avoid voluntary proximate occasions of sin, and to take precautions against the dangers of unavoidable occasions.

Sins That Cry to Heaven for Vengeance: Willful murder, sins against nature, oppression of the poor, widows and orphans, defrauding laborers of their wages.

Sister: Any woman religious, in popular speech; strictly, the title applies only to women religious belonging to institutes whose members never professed solemn vows. Most of the institutes whose members are properly called sisters were established during and since the 19th century. Women

religious with solemn vows, or belonging to institutes whose members formerly professed solemn vows, are properly called nuns.

Sisterhood: A generic term referring to the whole institution of the life of women religious in the Church, or to a particular institute of women religious.

Situation Ethics: A subjective, individualistic ethical theory which denies the binding force of ethical principles as universal laws and preceptive norms of moral conduct, and proposes that morality is determined only by situational conditions and considerations and the intention of the person. In an instruction issued on the subject in May, 1956, the Congregation for the Holy Office said:

"It ignores the principles of objective ethics. This 'New Morality,' it is claimed, is not only the equal of objective morality, but is superior to it.

"The authors who follow this system state that the ultimate determining norm for activity is not the objective order as determined by the natural law and known with certainty from this law. It is instead some internal judgment and illumination of the mind of every individual by which the mind comes to know what is to be done in a concrete situation.

"This ultimate decision of man is, therefore, not the application of the objective law to a particular case after the particular circumstances of a 'situation' have been considered and weighed according to the rules of prudence, as the more important authors of objective ethics teach; but it is, according to them, immediate, internal illumination and judgment.

"With regard to its objective truth and correctness, this judgment, at least in many things, is not ultimately measured, is not to be measured or is not measurable by any objective norm found outside man and independent of his subjective persuasion, but it is fully sufficient in itself. . . .

"Much that is stated in this system of 'Situation Ethics' is contrary to the truth of reality and to the dictate of sound reason. It gives evidence of relativism and modernism, and deviates far from the Catholic teaching handed down through the ages."

Slander: Attributing to a person faults which he does not have; a violation of the obligations of justice and charity, for which restitution is due.

Sloth: One of the seven capital sins; spiritual laziness, involving distaste and disgust for spiritual things; spiritual boredom, which saps the vigor of spiritual life. Physical laziness is a counterpart of spiritual sloth.

Sorcery: A kind of black magic in which evil is invoked by means of diabolical intervention; a violation of the virtue of religion.

Soteriology: The division of theology which treats of the mission and work of Christ as Redeemer.

Species, Sacred: The appearances of bread

and wine (color, taste, smell, etc.) which remain after the substance has been changed at the Consecration of the Mass into the Body and Blood of Christ. (See Transubstantiation.)

Spiritism: Attempts to communicate with spirits and departed souls by means of seances, table tapping, ouija boards, and other methods; a violation of the virtue of religion. Spiritualistic practices are noted for fakery.

Spiritual Works of Mercy: Works of spiritual assistance, motivated by love of God and neighbor, to persons in need: counseling the doubtful, instructing the ignorant, admonishing sinners, comforting the afflicted, forgiving offenses, bearing wrongs patiently, praying for the living and the dead.

Stational Churches, Days: Churches, especially in Rome, where the clergy and lay people were accustomed to gather with their bishop on certain days for the celebration of the liturgy. The 25 early titular or parish churches of Rome, plus other churches, each had their turn as the site of divine worship in practices which may have started in the third century. The observances were rather well developed toward the latter part of the fourth century, and by the fifth they included a Mass concelebrated by the pope and attendant priests. On some occasions, the stational liturgy was preceded by a procession from another church called a collecta. There were 42 Roman stational churches in the eighth century, and 89 stational services were scheduled annually in connection with the liturgical seasons. Stational observances fell into disuse toward the end of the Middle Ages. Some revival was begun by John XXIII in 1959 and continued by Paul VI.

Stations of the Cross: A series of meditations on the sufferings of Christ: his condemnation to death and taking up of the Cross; the first fall on the way to Calvary; meeting his Mother; being assisted by Simon of Cyrene, and by Veronica who wiped his face; the second fall; meeting the women of Jerusalem; the third fall; being stripped and nailed to the Cross; his death; the removal of his body from the Cross and his burial. Depictions of these scenes are mounted in most churches, chapels and in some other places, beneath small crosses.

A person making the Way of the Cross passes before these Stations, or stopping points, pausing at each for meditation. If the Stations are made by a group of people, only the leader has to pass from Station to Station. Prayer for the intentions of the pope is required for gaining the indulgence granted for the Stations.

Those unable to make the Stations in the ordinary manner, because they are impeded from visiting a church or other place where the Stations are, can still practice the devotion by meditating on the sufferings of Christ;

praying the Our Father, Hail Mary and Glory for each Station and five times in commemoration of the wounds of Christ; and praying for the intentions of the pope. This practice has involved the use of a Stations Crucifix.

A recent development in this devotion is toward greater awareness of the relation of the Passion to the Resurrection-Ascension; this trend, in some circles, has led to the erection of a 15th—unofficial—station. The concept amounts to an extension of the whole customary thrust of the devotion.

The Stations originated, remotely, from the practice of Holy Land pilgrims who visited the actual scenes of incidents in the Passion of Christ. Representations elsewhere of at least some of these scenes were known as early as the fifth century. Later, the Stations evolved in connection with and as a consequence of strong devotion to the Passion in the 12th and 13th centuries. Franciscans, who were given custody of the Holy Places in 1342, promoted the devotion widely; one of them, St. Leonard of Port Maurice, became known as the greatest preacher of the Way of the Cross in the 18th century. The general features of the devotion were fixed by Clement XII in 1731.

Statutes: Virtually the same as decrees (see separate entry), they almost always designate laws of a particular council or synod rather than pontifical laws.

Stigmata: Marks of the wounds suffered by Christ in his crucifixion, in hands and feet by nails, and side by the piercing of a lance. Some persons, called stigmatists, have been reported as recipients or sufferers of marks like these. The Church, however, has never issued any infallible declaration about their possession by anyone, even in the case of St. Francis of Assisi whose stigmata seem to be the best substantiated and may be commemorated in the Roman-Rite liturgy. Ninety percent of some 300 reputed stigmatists have been women. Judgment regarding the presence, significance, and manner of causation of stigmata would depend, among other things, on irrefutable experimental evidence.

Stipend, Mass: An offering given to a priest for applying the fruits of the Mass according to the intention of the donor. The offering is a contribution to the support of the priest. The disposition of the fruits of the sacrifice, in line with doctrine concerning the Mass in particular and prayer in general, is subject to the will of God. In the early Christian centuries, when Mass was not offered for the intentions of particular persons, the participants made offerings of bread and wine for the sacrifice and their own Holy Communion, and of other things useful for the support of the clergy and the poor. Some offerings may have been made as early as the fourth century for the celebration of Mass for particular intentions, and there are indications of the existence of this practice from the sixth century when private Masses began to be offered. The earliest certain proof of stipend practice, however, dates from the eighth century. By the 11th century, along with private Mass, it was established custom.

Stole Fee: An offering given on certain occasions; e.g., at a baptism, wedding, funeral, for the support of the clergy who administer the sacraments and perform other sacred rites.

Stoup: A vessel used to contain holy water.

Suffragan See: Any diocese, except the archdiocese, within a province.

Suicide: The taking of one's own life; a violation of God's dominion over human life. Ecclesiastical burial is denied to persons who deliberately commit suicide while in full possession of their faculties; it is permitted in cases of doubt.

Supererogation: Good and virtuous actions which go beyond the obligations of duty and the requirements enjoined by God's law as necessary for salvation. Examples of these works are the profession and observance of the evangelical counsels of poverty, chastity, and obedience, and efforts to practice charity to the highest degree.

Supernatural: Above the natural; that which exceeds and is not due or owed to the essence, exigencies, requirements, powers and merits of created nature. While man has no claim on supernatural things and does not need them in order to exist and act on a natural level, he does need them in order to exist and act in the higher order or economy of grace established by God for his salvation. God has freely given to man certain things which are beyond the powers and rights of his human nature. Examples of the supernatural are: grace, a kind of participation by man in the divine life, by which man becomes capable of performing acts meritorious for salvation; divine revelation by which God manifests himself to man and makes known truth that is inaccessible to human reason alone; faith, by which man believes divine truth because of the authority of God who reveals it through Sacred Scripture and tradition and the teaching of his Church.

Superstition: A violation of the virtue of religion, by which God is worshipped in an unworthy manner or creatures are given honor which belongs to God alone. False, vain, or futile worship involves elements which are incompatible with the honor and respect due to God, such as error, deception, and bizarre practices. Examples are: false and exaggerated devotions, chain prayers and allegedly unfailing prayers, the mixing of unbecoming practices in worship. The second kind of superstition attributes to persons and things powers and honor which belong to God alone. Examples are: idolatry, divination, magic, spiritism, necromancy.

Suspension: A penalty by which a cleric is forbidden to exercise some or all of his powers of orders and jurisdiction, or to accept the financial support of his benefices.

Swearing: Taking an oath; calling upon God to witness the truth of a statement; a legitimate thing to do for serious reasons and under proper circumstances, as in a court of law. To swear without sufficient reason is to dishonor God's name; to swear falsely in a court of law is perjury.

Swedenborgianism: A doctrine developed in and from the writings of Emmanuel Swedenborg (1688-1772), who claimed that during a number of visions he had in 1745 Christ taught him the spiritual sense of Sacred Scripture and commissioned him to communicate it to others. He held that, just as Christianity succeeded Judaism, so his teaching supplemented Christianity. He rejected belief in the Trinity, original sin, the Resurrection, and all the sacraments except baptism and the Eucharist. His followers are members of the Church of the New Jerusalem or of the New Church.

Syllabus, The: (1) When not qualified, the term refers to the list of 80 errors accompanying Pope Pius IX's encyclical *Quanta Cura,* issued in 1864.

(2) The *Syllabus* of St. Pius X in the decree *Lamentabili,* issued by the Holy Office July 4, 1907, condemning 65 heretical propositions of modernism. This schedule of errors was followed shortly by that pope's encyclical *Pascendi,* the principal ecclesiastical document against modernism, issued Sept. 8, 1907.

Synod, Diocesan: Meeting of representative persons of a diocese — priests, religious, lay persons — with the bishop, called by him for the purpose of considering and taking action on matters affecting the life and mission of the Church in the diocese. Persons taking part in a synod have consultative status; the bishop alone is the legislator, with power to authorize synodal decrees. According to canon law, every diocese should have a synod every 10 years.

T

Te Deum: The opening Latin words, Thee, God, of a hymn of praise and thanksgiving prescribed for use in the Office of Readings (Matins of the Liturgy of the Hours) on many Sundays, solemnities and feasts.

Temperance: Moderation, one of the four cardinal virtues.

Temptation: Any enticement to sin, from any source: the strivings of one's own faculties, the action of the devil, other persons, circumstances of life, etc. Temptation itself is not sin. Temptation can be avoided and overcome with the use of prudence and the help of grace.

Thanksgiving: An expression of gratitude to God for his goodness and the blessings he grants; one of the four ends of prayer.

Theism: A philosophy which admits the existence of God and the possibility of divine revelation; it is generally monotheistic and acknowledges God as transcendent and also active in the world. Because it is a philosophy rather than a system of theology derived from revelation, it does not include specifically Christian doctrines, like those concerning the Trinity, the Incarnation and Redemption.

Theological Virtues: The virtues which have God for their direct object: faith, or belief in God's infallible teaching; hope, or confidence in divine assistance; charity, or love of God. They are given to a person with grace in the first instance, through baptism and incorporation in Christ.

Theology: Knowledge of God and religion, deriving from and based on the data of divine Revelation, organized and systematized according to some kind of scientific method. It involves systematic study and presentation of the truths of divine Revelation in Sacred Scripture, tradition, and Church teaching.

The Second Vatican Council made the following declaration about theology and its relation to divine Revelation: "Sacred theology rests on the written word of God, together with sacred tradition, as its primary and perpetual foundation. By scrutinizing in the light of faith all truth stored up in the mystery of Christ, theology is most powerfully strengthened and constantly rejuvenated by that word. For the sacred Scriptures contain the word of God and, since they are inspired, really are the word of God; and so the study of the sacred page is, as it were, the soul of sacred theology" *(Constitution on Revelation.* No. 24).

Theology has been divided under various subject headings. Some of the major fields have been: dogma, moral, pastoral, ascetics (the practice of virtue and means of attaining holiness and perfection), mysticism (higher states of religious experience). Other subject headings include ecumenism (Christian unity, interfaith relations), ecclesiology (the nature and constitution of the Church), Mariology (doctrine concerning the Blessed Virgin Mary), the sacraments, etc.

Tithing: Contribution of a portion of one's income, originally one-tenth, for purposes of religion and charity. The practice is mentioned 46 times in the Bible. In early Christian times, tithing was adopted in continuance of Old Testament practices of the Jewish people, and the earliest positive church legislation on the subject was enacted in 567. Catholics are bound in conscience to contribute to the support of their church, but the manner in which they do so is not fixed by law. Tithing, which amounts to a pledged contribution of a portion of one's income, has aroused new attention in recent years in the United States.

Titular Sees: Dioceses where the Church once flourished but which later were overrun by pagans or Moslems and now exist only in name or title. Bishops without a territorial or residential diocese of their own; e.g., auxiliary bishops, are given titular sees.

Transfinalization, Transignification: Terms coined to express the sign value of consecrated bread and wine with respect to the presence and action of Christ in the Eucharistic sacrifice and the spiritually vivifying purpose of the Eucharistic banquet in Holy Communion. The theory behind the terms has strong undertones of existential and "sign" philosophy, and has been criticized for its openness to interpretations at variance with the doctrine of transubstantiation and the abiding presence of Christ under the appearances of bread and wine after the sacrifice of the Mass and Communion have been completed. The terms, if used as substitutes for transubstantiation, are unacceptable; if they presuppose transubstantiation, they are acceptable as clarifications of its meaning.

Transubstantiation; "The way Christ is made present in this sacrament (Holy Eucharist) is none other than by the change of the whole substance of the bread into his Body, and of the whole substance of the wine into his Blood (in the Consecration at Mass) . . . this unique and wonderful change the Catholic Church rightly calls transubstantiation" (encyclical *Mysterium Fidei* of Paul VI, Sept. 3, 1965). The first official use of the term was made by the Fourth Council of the Lateran in 1215. Authoritative teaching on the subject was issued by the Council of Trent.

Treasury of the Church: The superabundant merits of Christ and the saints from which the Church draws to confer spiritual benefits, such as indulgences.

Triduum: A three-day series of public or private devotions.

U-Z

Usury: Excessive interest charged for the loan and use of money; a violation of justice.

Veronica: A word resulting from the combination of a Latin word for true, *vera,* and a Greek word for image, *eikon,* designating a likeness of the face of Christ or the name of a woman said to have given him a cloth on which he caused an imprint of his face to appear. The veneration at Rome of a likeness depicted on cloth dates from about the end of the 10th century; it figured in a popular devotion during the Middle Ages, and in the Holy Face devotion practiced since the 19th century. A faint, undiscernible likeness said to be of this kind is preserved in St. Peter's Basilica. The origin of the likeness is uncertain and the identity of the woman is unknown. Before the 14th century, there were no known artistic representations of an incident concerning a woman who wiped the face of Christ with a piece of cloth while He was carrying the Cross to Calvary.

Viaticum: Holy Communion given to those in danger of death. The word, derived from Latin, means provision for a journey through death to life hereafter.

Vicar General: A prelate appointed by a bishop to help him, as a deputy, in the administration of his diocese. Because of his office, he has the same jurisdictional authority as the bishop except in cases reserved to the bishop by himself or by church law.

Virginity: Observance of perpetual sexual abstinence. The state of virginity, which is embraced for the love of God by religious with a public vow or by others with a private vow, was singled out for high praise by Christ (Mt. 19:10-12) and has always been so regarded by the Church. In the encyclical *Sacra Virginitas,* Pius XII stated: "Holy virginity and that perfect chastity which is consecrated to the service of God is without doubt among the most perfect treasures which the founder of the Church has left in heritage to the society which he established."

Paul VI approved in 1970 a rite in which women can consecrate their virginity "to Christ and their brethren" without becoming members of a religious institute. The *Ordo Consecrationis Virginum,* a revision of a rite promulgated by Clement VII in 1596, is traceable to the Roman liturgy of about 500.

Virtue: A habit or established capability for performing good actions. Virtues are *natural* (acquired and increased by repeating good acts) and/or *supernatural* (given with grace by God).

Vocation: A call to a way of life. Generally, the term applies to the common call of all men, from God, to holiness and salvation. Specifically, it refers to particular states of life, each called a vocation, in which response is made to this universal call; viz., marriage, the religious life and/or priesthood, the single state freely chosen or accepted for the accomplishment of God's will. The term also applies to the various occupations in which persons make a living. The Church supports the freedom of each individual in choosing a particular vocation, and reserves the right to pass on the acceptability of candidates for the priesthood and religious life. Signs or indicators of particular vocations are many, including a person's talents and interests, circumstances and obligations, invitations of grace and willingness to respond thereto.

Vow: A promise made to God with sufficient knowledge and freedom, which has as its object a moral good that is possible and better than its voluntary omission. A person who professes a vow binds himself by the virtue of religion to fulfill his promise. The best known examples of vows are those of poverty, chastity and obedience professed by religious (see Evangelical Counsels, individual entries).

Public vows are made before a competent person, acting as an agent of the Church, who accepts the profession in the name of the Church, thereby giving public recognition to the person's dedication and consecration to God and divine worship. Vows of this kind are either solemn, rendering all contrary acts invalid as well as unlawful; or simple, rendering contrary acts unlawful. Solemn vows are for life; simple vows are for a definite period of time or for life. Vows professed without public recognition by the Church are called private vows. The Church, which has authority to accept and give public recognition to vows, also has authority to dispense persons from their obligations for serious reasons.

Week of Prayer for Christian Unity: Eight days of prayer, from Jan. 18 to 25, for the union of all men in the Church established by Christ. On the initiative of Father Paul James Francis, S.A., of Graymoor, N.Y., it originated in 1908 as the Chair of Unity Octave. In recent years, its observance on an interfaith basis has increased greatly.

Witness, Christian: Practical testimony or evidence given by Christians of their faith in all circumstances of life — by prayer and general conduct, through good example and good works, etc.; being and acting in accordance with Christian belief; actual practice of the Christian faith.

Zucchetto: A skullcap worn by bishops and other prelates.

Apparitions Denied

Garabandal: Claims of Vatican support for alleged apparitions of the Blessed Virgin Mary to four young girls at Garabandal, Spain, were denied May 10, 1969, by the Congregation for the Doctrine of the Faith. The congregation, stating that investigation and decision on the matter rested with authorities in the Diocese of Santander, said that it stood by the "official note" authorized by Bishop Vicente Puchol Montiz Aug. 17, 1965. The note said there had been no apparitions of the Blessed Virgin, St. Michael the Archangel or other saints. (It had been reported that the first of several appearances occurred June 18, 1961.) It also said that there was no message of private revelation. (One was reported Oct. 18, 1961.) Summarily, the note stated that all reported incidents were explainable on a natural basis.

Necedah: Reporting in February, 1971, a special commission of the La Crosse diocese agreed with the conclusions of a 1950-1955 investigation that alleged revelations and visions of a woman in Necedah, Wis., were not of supernatural origin. The events were connected with the local Shrine of the Queen of the Holy Rosary, Mediatrix of Peace. The commission recommended that religious worship at the shrine be prohibited.

The authenticity of religious devotion and experience is behind the Church's concern over apparitions and similiar phenomena. To approve of them without adequate investigation and ruling out natural means of explanation would be to foster superstition. The Church admits the credibility of apparitions only with the support of evidence of supernatural origin.

Biographies of Catholics

(In addition to the biographical entries below, others are listed in the Index.)

A

Abelard, Peter (1079-1142); French philosopher, theologian; contributed to scholastic method although he had nominalistic tendencies.

Achillini, Alessandro (1463-1512): Italian physicist, astronomer; inaugurated reaction against Ptolemaic astronomy.

Adam, Karl (1876-1966): German theologian, writer; *Spirit of Catholicism.*

Adenauer, Konrad (1876-1967): German statesman; chancellor of West Germany, 1949-63.

Africanus, Sextus Julius (3rd cent.): Christian historian; wrote history of world from creation to 221 A.D.

Agreda, Mary of (1602-1665): Spanish Poor Clare, mystical writer; *Mystical City of God and the Divine History of the Virgin Mother of God.*

Alan of Walsingham (died 1364): English monk, architect.

Alarcon, Pedro Antonio de (1833-1891): Spanish writer, statesman.

Alberione, Giacomo (1884-1971): Italian priest; founder of Pauline Fathers and Daughters of St. Paul for work in communications field.

Albert or Albrecht (died 1229): Founder and 6first bishop of Riga, apostle of Livonia.

Albornoz, Gil Alvarez Carillo de (1310-1367): Spanish cardinal, general, statesman; negotiated return of the papal states, 1354; his *Egidian Constitutions* for them prevailed until 1816; archbishop of Toledo.

Alcuin, Albinus (735-804): English scholar; abbot of Tours; educator among Franks.

Alexander of Hales (1180-1245): English theologian, philosopher; first Franciscan teacher at Paris; called Doctor Irrefragabilis.

Alfred the Great (849-899): First Saxon king of England; noted for wise laws, spread of religion and learning.

Allen, Frances (1784-1819): American religious; daughter of Ethan Allen; convert, 1807; professed vows in community of Hospital Sisters at Hotel-Dieu, Montreal, 1810.

Allers, Rudolf (1883-1963): Austrian-born psychologist; d. Maryland; taught at Catholic University of America, 1938-48, and Georgetown University, 1948-63.

Allori, Alessandro (1535-1607) and his son **Cristofano** (1577-1621): Italian painters, Florentine school.

Amiot, Jean Marie (1718-1793): French Jesuit, missionary to China, author.

Ammen, Daniel (1820-1898): American naval officer in Civil War; author.

Ampere, Andre Marie (1775-1836): French physicist; pioneer in electrodynamics; term ampere named for him.

Anderson, William H. (1799-1875): American mathematician and astronomer; on US expedition to Dead Sea, 1848; convert, 1849.

Angelico, Fra (Giovanni da Fiesole) (1387-1455): Italian Dominican painter of religious subjects.

Anglin, Timothy (1822-1896): Canadian journalist and legislator. Father of **Margaret Mary Anglin** (1876-1958): actress, Laetare medalist.

Animuccia, Giovanni (1500?-1571): Italian composer of sacred music.

Apponyi, Albert, Count (1846-1933): Hungarian statesman, parliamentary leader for 40 years; head of Hungary's peace delegation in Paris, 1920.

Argenlieu, Georges Thierry d' (1889-1964): French admiral, Carmelite priest; naval officer in World War I; entered Carmelites, 1920, and ordained priest (Father Louis of the Trinity); recalled to active duty during World War II, fought with Free French; governor general of Indo-China after the war; returned to monastery, 1947.

Arnold, Thomas (1823-1900): English educator; convert, 1856.

Avery, Martha (Moore) (1851-1929): American Socialist, political economist, author; convert, 1903; a founder of the Catholic Truth Guild, 1917.

B

Bacon, Roger (1214-1294): English Franciscan, philosopher, experimental scientist; considered optical and astronomical laws, possibilities of scientific invention, gunpowder.

Baegert, Johann Jacob (1717-1777): Jesuit missionary, ethnographer; author of works on Lower California.

Balboa, Vasco Nunez de (1475-1517): Spanish adventurer; discovered Pacific Ocean, 1513.

Baldwin, Charles Sears (1867-1935): American educator, author; convert, 1934.

Baldwin, Geoffrey P. (1892-1951): American military officer in World Wars I and II; convert, 1937; chief of CARE in Italy.

Banim, John (1798-1842) and **Michael** (1796-1874): First national novelists of Ireland; John called the Scott of Ireland.

Barber, Virgil (1787-1847): American Jesuit; prominent New England Episcopal minister before his conversion, 1816, with his wife and five children; all eventually entered religious life; ordained 1822; established first Catholic church and school in New Hampshire at Claremont. His father **Daniel** (1756-1834) was also an Episcopal minister before he followed the rest of his family into the Church in 1818; wrote *Catholic Worships and Piety Explained.*

Barbour, John (1316?-1395): Scottish poet, author of the epic romance, *The Bruce.*

Baring, Maurice (1874-1945): English poet, novelist, critic, author of works on Russia; convert, 1909.

Barry, John (1745-1803): American naval officer, b. Ireland; naval hero in Revolution.

Bartholomeus Anglicus (13th cent.): English Franciscan, author of a medieval encyclopedia of science.

Bartolommeo, Fra (1475-1517): Florentine Dominican, religious painter.

Bayley, James Roosevelt (1814-1877): American prelate; convert, 1842; ordained priest, 1844; bishop of Newark, N. J. 1853-72; archbishop of Baltimore 1872-77.

Bayma, Joseph (1816-1892): Italian Jesuit, mathematician, scientist; author of *Molecular Mechanics.*

Bazin, Rene (1853-1932): French novelist, biographer, travel writer; member of French Academy.

Bea, Augustin (1881-1968): German Jesuit, cardinal, Biblical scholar, leader in Christian reunion movement.

Beardsley, Aubrey Vincent (1872-1898): British illustrator; convert, 1895.

Beaton (Bethune), David (1494-1546): Scottish prelate, statesman; cardinal archbishop of St. Andrews; chancellor of Scotland; opposed efforts of Henry VIII to separate Scotland from loyalty to Holy See.

Beauregard, Pierre (1818-1893): American Confederate general; graduate of West Point; superintendent of West Point for five days; resigned to serve with Confederate Army.

Beccaria, Giovanni Battista (1716-1781): Italian physicist; early researcher in electricity.

Becquerel, Antoine Cesar (1788-1878): French physicist, electrochemist; invented the constant cell, a differential galvanometer, an electric thermometer.

Becquerel, Antoine Henri (1852-1908): French physicist; discoverer of radioactivity in uranium; shared 1903 Nobel Prize in physics with the Curies.

Beethoven, Ludwig van (1770-1827): German composer; works include symphonies, concertos and sonatas.

Behaim, Martin (1459-1507): German geographer; constructed a terrestrial globe, 1492.

Bellini, Gentile (1429-1507) and **Giovanni** (1430-1516): Venetian painters.

Belloc, Hilaire (1870-1953): English journalist, essayist, poet, novelist, historian, biographer, critic, apologist.

Benson, Robert Hugh (1871-1914): English author of historical fiction, other works; Anglican clergyman before conversion, 1903; ordained to priesthood, 1904.

Benson, William Shepherd (1855-1932): American naval officer; first chief of naval operations, 1915-19; convert.

Bentley, John Francis (1839-1902): English architect; promoted Gothic revival in England; designed Cathedral of Westminster.

Berengario da Carpi, Jacopo (1470-1530): Italian anatomist; a founder of modern science of anatomy.

Bernanos, Georges (1888-1948): French journalist, novelist; works concerned principally with struggle of the soul against evil.

Bernard, Claude (1813-1878): French physiologist; studied the glycogenic function of the liver, sympathetic nervous system.

Bernini, Giovanni Lorenzo (1598-1680): Italian sculptor of wide influence; architect of St. Peter's.

Bertrand, Louis (1866-1941): French novelist, biographer.

Beschi, Costanzo Giuseppe (1680-1746): Italian Jesuit missionary; famous for linguistic and literary work in the Tamil language.

Besse, Jean Martial Leon (1861-1920): Benedictine monk, historian.

Bianchini, Francesco (1662-1729): Italian astronomer; secretary, under Clement XI, of papal commission for calendar reform.

Bickerstaffe-Drew, Francis (1858-1928): English author (under pseudonym of **John Ayscough**); convert, priest.

Bielski, Marcin (1495-1575): Polish historian, poet.

Bienville, Sieur de (1680-1768); French explorer, governor of Louisiana colony.

Biggs, Richard Keys (1886-1962): American concert organist, composer, choir master; convert.

Billuart, Charles Rene (1685-1757): Belgian Dominican theologian, preacher.

Binet, Jacques Philippe Marie (1786-1856): French mathematician, astronomer; Binet's theorem.

Biondo, Flavio (1388-1463): Italian historian, archaeologist.

Biot, Jean Baptiste (1774-1862): French physicist; studied polarization of light; Biot's law.

Blondel, Maurice (1861-1949): French philosopher; works include *L'Action, La Pensée.*

Blowick, John (1889-1972): Irish priest; founder with Bishop Edward Galvin of the Society of St. Columban, 1916.

Bloy, Leon (1846-1917): French writer, social reformer.

Boccaccio, Giovanni (1313-1375): Italian author; known as father of Italian prose; *Decameron.*

Boethius, Anicius Manlius (480?-524?): Roman statesman and philosopher;; author of *The Consolation of Philosophy.*

Boileau-Despreaux, Nicolas (1636-1711): French poet, satirist, critic.

Bolland, John van (1596-1665): Flemish Jesuit; editor of *Acta Sanctorum,* continued by Bollandists.

Bolzano, Bernard (1781-1848): Bohemian mathematician; formulated theory of functions.

Bona, Giovanni (1609-1674): Italian cardinal, author of liturgical encyclopedia.

Bonaparte, Charles J. (1851-1921): American cabinet official; secretary of navy 1905-06; attorney general, 1906-09.

Bordone, Paris (1500-1571): Venetian painter, pupil of Titian.

Borrus, Christopher (1583-1632): Oceanic geographer.

Boscovich, Ruggiero Giuseppe (1711-1787); Italian Jesuit, astronomer, physicist; offered a molecular theory of matter.

Bosio, Antonio (1575-1629): Italian archaeologist, called Columbus of the Catacombs.

Bossuet, Jacques Benigne (1627-1704): French prelate; pulpit orator, author.

Botticelli, Sandro (1444-1510): Florentine painter.

Bourdaloue, Louis (1632-1704): French Jesuit; pulpit orator.

Bourgeois, Louis (1819-1878): French archaeologist; presented and developed problem of the eoliths, 1863.

Bracton, Henry de (died 1268): English jurist; author of treatise *On the Laws and Customs of England*.

Braille, Louis (1809-1852): Blind French teacher of the blind; inventor of Braille system of raised-point printing.

Bramante, Donato (1444-1514): Italian architect; made plan for reconstruction of St. Peter's.

Branly, Edouard (1846-1940): French physicist; discovered coherer, making wireless telegraphy possible.

Brennan, Francis J. (1894-1968): American cardinal, Roman Curia official; ordained priest, 1920; professor at St. Charles Seminary, Overbrook, Pa., 1920-40; judge, 1940-59, and dean, 1959-67, of the Sacred Roman Rota; ord. bishop June 25, 1967; cardinal, June 26, 1967.

Brentano, Klemens (1778-1842): German poet; rejoined Catholic Church, 1818; recorded revelations of Anne Catherine Emmerich.

Breuil, Henri (1877-1961): French priest, archaeologist; authority on prehistoric art.

Broun, Heywood Campbell (1888-1939): American journalist, author; convert, 1939.

Browne, Charles Farrar (pseud. Artemus Ward) (1834-1867): American humorist, journalist, lecturer.

Brownson, Orestes Augustus (1803-1876): American scholar, essayist, philosopher, controversialist; was successively a Presbyterian, Universalist minister and Unitarian minister before his conversion, 1844.

Bruckner, Anton (1824-1896): Austrian composer and organist.

Brumidi, Constantini (1805-1880): American painter, b. Italy; became naturalized citizen; noted for his frescoes in Capitol at Washington, D.C.

Brunelleschi, Filippo (1377-1466): Italian architect; called founder of Renaissance architecture; established theory of perspective.

Brunetiere, Ferdinand (1849-1906): French critic, editor, professor of literature; convert.

Buck, Edward Eugene (Gene) (1885-1957): American popular song lyricist, producer; president of American Society of Composers, Authors and Publishers (ASCAP), 1924-41.

Budenz, Louis (1891-1972): American journalist; prominent member of American Communist Party, 1935 to 1945, when he was received back into the Church; major witness in the McCarthy hearings in the 1950's.

Bullitt, William C. (1891-1967): American diplomat; first ambassador to Russia; convert shortly before his death.

Burke, John (1859-1937): American jurist, politician; governor of North Dakota, 1907-21; treasurer of US, 1913-21; judge, 1924, and later chief justice of North Dakota supreme court. Represents North Dakota in Statuary Hall.

Burke, Thomas Nicholas (1830-1882): Irish Dominican preacher.

Burnand, Sir Francis Crowley (1836-1917): English playwright; editor of *Punch* (1880-1906), and English *Catholic Who's Who*; convert, 1857.

Burnett, Peter Hardemann (1807-1895): American jurist, politician; judge of Oregon supreme court, first governor of California, member of California supreme court; convert, 1846.

Butler, Alban (1711-1773): English author; *Lives of the Saints*.

Butler, Pierce (1866-1939): American attorney, jurist; associate justice United States Supreme Court, 1923-39.

Byrd, William (1540?-1623): English organist, composer; founder of English Madrigal School.

C

Cabeza de Vaca, Alvar Nunez (1490-1557): Spanish explorer; colonial governor in Paraguay.

Cabot, John (1450-1498): Italian navigator; discovered mainland of North America, June 24, 1497.

Cabral, Pedro Alvarez de (1460-1526): Portuguese navigator; discovered Brazil, which he named Vera Cruz.

Caedmon (died 670): First great English Christian poet; lay brother at monastery in Whitby.

Caius (Kees, Keys, Kay, Key), John (1510-1573): English physician; one of first to introduce publicly the practice of dissection into England, 1573.

Cajetan, Tommaso De Vio (1469-1534): Italian cardinal, philosopher, theologian.

Caldani, Leopold Marco Antonio (1725-1813): Italian anatomist, physiologist; furthered anatomical studies on function of spinal cord.

Calderon de La Barca, Pedro (1600-1681): Spanish priest, dramatist; author of over 200 works.

Calvert, Cecil (1605-1675): English proprietor; second Lord Baltimore; responsible for enactment of religious toleration in Maryland colony.

Calvert, George (1580-1632): English proprietor; first Lord Baltimore; held important posts under James I; was granted territory of Baltimore colony but died before grant of charter; convert, 1625.

Camel (Kamel), George Joseph (1661-1706): Moravian Jesuit missionary, botanist; studied plants and natural history of Philippines.

Camoes, Luiz Vaz de (1524-1580): Portuguese poet, dramatist.

Campbell, James (1812-1893): American jurist, cabinet official; US postmaster general, 1853-57.

Cano, Melchior (1509-1560): Spanish Dominican, theologian; called father of fundamental theology.

Canova, Antonio (1757-1822): Italian sculptor of the modern classic school.

Canute (II) the Great (994?-1035): King of Denmark, England, Norway.

Cardano, Girolamo (1501-1576): Italian physician, mathematician; solved cubic equation named after him.

Cardijn, Joseph (1882-1967): Belgian cardinal, founder of the Young Christian Workers; cardinal, 1965.

Carey, Mathew (1760-1839): American publisher, economist and author, b. Ireland; first extensive US Catholic publisher.

Carnoy, Jean Baptiste (1836-1899): Belgian priest, founder of the science of cytology.

Carpini, Giovanni di Piano (c. 1180-1252): Italian Franciscan, companion of St. Francis; missionary in Germany; papal envoy to Great Khan of the Mongols, 1246; wrote *Liber Tartarorum* recounting in detail the life and customs of the Mongols.

Carrel, Alexis (1873-1944): French surgeon, biologist; developed surgical techniques, experimented on transplantation of organs; author; member Pontifical Academy of Sciences; Nobel Prize for physiology and medicine, 1912.

Carroll, Charles (1737-1832): American statesman; member of Continental Congress, 1776-78; signer of Declaration of Independence; member Maryland Congress and first US Senate, 1789-92. Represents Maryland in Statuary Hall.

Carroll, Daniel (1730-1796): American patriot; brother of Archbishop John Carroll; delegate to Continental Congress, 1780-84, Constitutional Convention, 1787; congressman from Maryland, 1789-91.

Carroll, John (1735-1815): American prelate; ordained priest, 1761; first bishop of the hierarchy of the US (bishop, 1789-1808, and archbishop, 1808-15 of Baltimore); also apostolic administrator of Louisiana and Two Floridas, 1805-15; founder of Georgetown University, 1791.

Carson, Christopher (Kit) (1809-1868): American trapper, scout, Indian agent.

Cartier, Jacques (1491-c. 1557): French explorer of coasts of Labrador and Newfoundland; ascended the St. Lawrence to Montreal.

Caruso, Enrico (1873-1921): Italian operatic tenor.

Cassini, Jean Dominique (1625-1712): French astronomer; first director of Paris observatory; made important discoveries regarding Saturn, parallax of sun.

Cassiodorus, Flavius Aurelius (c. 490-c. 580): Roman statesman, writer, founder of monasteries.

Castelli, Benedetto (c. 1572-1644): Italian Benedictine, mathematician, physicist; authority on hydraulics.

Cauchy, Augustin Louis (1789-1857): French mathematician; did research in calculus, developed wave theory in optics.

Cavalieri, Francesco Bonaventura (1598-1647): Italian religious, mathematician; originated method of indivisibles; forerunner of integral calculus.

Caxton, William (1422-1491): First English printer.

Cellini, Benvenuto (1500-1571): Italian sculptor; worker in gold and bronze.

Cervantes Saavedra, Miguel de (1547-1616): Spanish novelist; *Don Quixote.*

Cesalpino, Andrea (1519-1603): Italian botanist, physician; important contributor to work on plant morphology, physiology; anticipated Linnaean system of classification.

Cezanne, Paul (1839-1906): French painter; a leader of postimpressionism.

Challoner, Richard (1691-1781): English bishop; re-edited Douay Bible.

Champlain, Samuel de (1567-1635): French explorer; Father of New France, founder of Quebec; discovered Lake Champlain.

Champollion, Jean Francois (1790-1832): French Egyptologist; discovered through the Rosetta Stone a system for deciphering hieroglyphics.

Chandler, Joseph Ripley (1792-1880): American journalist, congressman; Grand Master of Free Masons before conversion, 1849; US minister to Naples during administration of Buchanan; US congressman from Pennsylvania, 1849-55.

Charlemagne (742-814): King of the Franks, Emperor of the West, founder of Holy Roman Empire; promoted spread of Christianity, learning; defender of the papacy.

Charles Martel (c. 689-741): Duke of Austrasia, son of Pepin; halted Saracen advance on western Europe at Battle of Tours (732), and thereafter was called Martel *(The Hammer);* grandfather of Charlemagne.

Chateaubriand, Francois Rene de (1768-1848): French author; influential in history of Romantic Movement.

Chaucer, Geoffrey (1340-1400): Father of English poetry; *Canterbury Tales.*

Chauliac, Guy de (1300-1370): French surgeon; gave authoritative description of bubonic plague, Black Death of 14th century.

Chavez, Dennis (1888-1962): American legislator; member New Mexico State legislature, 1920-30; US congressman, 1931-35; US senator, 1935-62. Represents New Mexico in Statuary Hall.

Cherubini, Maria Luigi (1760-1842): Italian composer of ecclesiastical and operatic works.

Chesterton, Gilbert K. (1874-1936); English essayist, poet, novelist, biographer, journalist; Prince of Paradox; convert, 1922.

Chevreul, Michel Eugene (1786-1889): French chemist; did research in animal fats; discovered margarine, oleine, stearine.

Cimabue, Giovanni (Cenni di Pepo) (1240-1302): Florentine painter; religious subjects.

Claudel, Paul (1868-1955): French author, diplomat; elected to French Academy, 1946.

Clavius, Christopher (1537-1612): Jesuit astronomer, mathematician; introduced decimal point.

Clerke, Agnes Mary (1842-1907): Irish astronomer.

Coady, Moses Michael (1882-1959): Canadian priest, educator; organizer of cooperatives among Canadian fishermen, known as Antigonish movement.

Cobo, Bernabe (1582-1657): Spanish Jesuit, naturalist; author of *History of the New World*, on Latin America.

Cody, Col. William F. (Buffalo Bill) (1846-1917): American Pony Express rider, army guide and scout, hunter, Indian fighter; entered Church just before death.

Collins, Michael (1890-1922): Irish revolutionary leader and soldier.

Colombo, Matteo Realdo (1516-1559): Italian anatomist; discovered pulmonary circulation.

Columbus, Christopher (1451-1506): Genoese explorer; discovered the Americas in 1492.

Connell, Francis J. (1888-1967): American Redemptorist priest, moral theologian, author.

Connelly, Mother Cornelia (1809-1879): American-born foundress; married to Pierce Connelly, an Episcopalian minister; her conversion, 1835, was followed three months later by her husband's; granted permanent separation by Rome and entered convent so her husband could become a priest; sent to England at request of Cardinal Wiseman and founded Society of the Holy Child Jesus, 1846; her husband renounced the priesthood, 1849; his legal attempt to force her to return to married life was unsuccessful.

Constantine the Great (c. 280-337): Roman emperor; granted liberty of worship to Christians by Edict of Milan, 313; established Constantinople as capital of the Eastern Empire.

Copernicus, Nicolaus (1473-1543): Polish astronomer; founder of modern astronomy; taught the revolution of planets around the sun and the rotation of the earth on its axis.

Coppee, Francois (1842-1908): French poet, dramatist, novelist; member of French Academy, 1884.

Cordoba, Francisco Fernandez de (d. 1518?): Spanish explorer; discovered Yucatan, 1517.

Corneille, Pierre (1606-1684): French dramatist; great influence on French tragedy, *Le Cid*.

Corot, Jean Baptiste Camille (1796-1875): French landscape artist.

Correggio, Antonio Allegri (1494-1534): Lombard painter; noted for mastery of light and shade; religious subjects.

Cortez, Hernando (1485-1547): Spanish explorer, soldier; conquered Mexico.

Cory, Herbert Ellsworth (1883-1947): American educator, social scientist, author; convert, 1933.

Coulomb, Charles Augustine (1736-1806): French physicist; investigated electricity and magnetism; stated coulomb's law; the coulomb named for him.

Couperin, Francois (1668-1733): French composer; first great composer for the harpsichord.

Cousin, Jean (1490-1560), and his son **Jean** (1522-1590): French painters, workers in stained glass.

Crashaw, Richard (1613-1649): English poet of metaphysical school; convert, 1646.

Crawford, Francis Marion (1854-1909): American novelist, b. Italy; convert, 1880.

Credi, Lorenz di (1459-1537): Florentine painter; religious subjects.

Creighton, John (1831-1907) and his brother **Edward** (1802-1874): American philanthropists; benefactors of Creighton University; in 1861 took part in laying first telegraph line linking California to rest of the nation.

Cushing, Richard J. (1895-1970): American cardinal; ordained priest, 1921; auxiliary bishop of Boston, 1939-44; archbishop of Boston, 1944-70; cardinal, 1958; founded Missionary Society of St. James the Apostle to recruit diocesan priests for Latin American missions; promoted charitable works especially among exceptional children.

D

Dablon, Claude (1619-1697): French Jesuit missionary in America; superior of Canadian missions.

Daly, Thomas A. (1871-1948): American journalist and poet.

Damien, Father (Joseph de Veuster) (1840-1889): Belgian missionary; joined Picpus Fathers, 1860; from 1873 to his death, devoted his life to caring for lepers on Molokai, in Hawaiian Islands; contracted the disease three years before his death. Represents Hawaii in National Statuary Hall.

Daniel-Rops, Henri (pseud. of Henri Jules Petiot) (1901-1965): French writer on Church history and other subjects; member of French Academy.

Dante Alighieri (1265-1321): Florentine

poet; *Divina Commedia, Vita Nuova, De Monarchia.*

Daumer, Georg Friedrich (1800-1875): German writer; anti-Christian works until conversion, 1858; author of *Meine Konversion.*

Davenport, Sir William (1606-1668): English poet and dramatist.

Dawson, Christopher (1889-1970): English author and scholar; convert from Anglicanism, 1914; principal themes of his works are cultural history and the philosophy of religion.

DeGaulle, Charles Andre Joseph Marie (1890-1970): French general, statesman; leader of French forces in World War II; interim president of France, 1945-46; president of Fifth Republic, 1959-69.

Delacroix, Ferdinand Victor Eugene (1799-1863): French painter; romantic school.

Delaroche, Paul (1797-1856): French painter, of the Eclectic school; portrait and historical subjects.

DeRossi, Giovanni Battista (1822-1894): Italian archaeologist; aroused interest in Christian antiquities.

Descartes, Rene (1596-1650): French scientist and philosopher; founder of analytic geometry.

De Soto, Hernando (1500-1542): Spanish explorer; discovered lower course of Mississippi River, 1541.

De Vaux, Roland (1903-1971): French Dominican; biblical archaeologist and exegete; head of Ecole Biblique, Jerusalem; headed international team of scholars who edited Dead Sea Scrolls.

Devlin, Joseph (1872-1934): Irish politician.

Dias, Bartholomew (1450-1500): Portuguese navigator; discovered Cape of Good Hope, 1488.

Dimnet, Ernest (1869-1954): French priest, lecturer, writer.

Dior, Christian (1905-1957): French fashion designer.

Divisch, Wénceslaus (religious name, **Procopius**) (1698-1765): Moravian Premonstratensian monk; erected a lightning rod in 1754, before Franklin's work was known.

Dolci, Carlo (1616-1686): Florentine painter; religious and portrait subjects.

Donatello or **Donato di Niccolo di Betto Bardi** (1386-1466): Italian sculptor; called the founder of modern sculpture.

Dongon, Thomas (1634-1715): Colonial governor of New York, 1682-88; b. Ireland.

Donizetti, Gaetano (1797-1848): Italian operatic composer.

Dooley, Thomas A. (1927-1961): American physician; co-founder of MEDICO, organized to establish medical services in underdeveloped countries; author.

Doria, Andrea (1468-1560): Genoese admiral, statesman; Father of Peace, Liberator of Genoa.

Drexel, Mary Katherine (1858-1955): American missionary; foundress of Sisters of the Blessed Sacrament for Indians and Colored People, 1891.

Drum, Hugh A. (1879-1951): American army officer in World Wars I and II.

Dryden, John (1631-1700): English poet, playwright; poet laureate, 1670; convert, 1686.

Duffy, Sir Charles Gavan (1816-1903): Irish nationalist, political leader in Australia after he emigrated there (1856), author.

Dulong, Pierre Louis (1785-1838): French chemist, physicist; author with Petit of formula determining the specific heat of solids.

Dumas, Jean Baptiste (1800-1884); French chemist; did important research on vapor densities.

Dunne, Peter Finley (1867-1936): American humorist, journalist; creator of Irish philosophical character "Mr. Dooley."

Duns Scotus, John (1256-1308): Scottish scholastic theologian; Franciscan; advanced best theological arguments for doctrine of the Immaculate Conception; known as Doctor Subtilis.

Durer, Albrecht (1471-1528): German painter of Renaissance school, engraver, wood-cut artist; called the inventor of etching.

Durkin, Martin P. (1894-1955): American union leader, cabinet official; secretary of labor, 1953.

Dutton, Ira (Brother Joseph) (1843-1931): American missionary; convert, 1883; assisted Father Damien in work among lepers at Molokai, served there for 42 years, beginning in 1886.

Dwight, Thomas (1843-1911): American surgeon, anatomist; taught anatomy at Harvard and Maine medical schools; convert, 1855.

E

Eck, Johann (1486-1543): German theologian; outstanding opponent of Luther.

Eckhel, Joseph Hilarius (1737-1798): Austrian Jesuit; founder of the scientific numismatics of classical antiquity.

Eichendorff, Joseph von (1788-1857): German lyric poet, novelist, critic.

Elgar, Edward (1857-1934): English composer. *Pomp and Circumstance.*

Emmerich, Anne Catherine (1774-1824): German Augustinian nun, mystic; her visions were recorded by the poet Klemens Brentano.

Endlicher, Stephen (1804-1849): Hungarian botanist, linguist; elaborated a system of classifying plants.

England, John (1786-1842): American prelate, b. Ireland, bishop of Charleston, S. C., 1820-42; founded *United States Catholic Miscellany,* the first US Catholic weekly newspaper; opponent of trusteeism.

Epee, Charles Michel de L' (1712-1789): French priest; developed a sign alphabet for deaf-mutes.

Erasmus, Desiderius (1466-1536): Dutch scholar, Renaissance leader.

Estaing, Jean Baptiste d' (1729-1794): French naval commander; aided Americans during Revolution.

Eustachius, Bartolommeo (1524-1574): Italian anatomist; Eustachian tube, valve, named for him.

Ewing, J. Franklin (1905-1968): American Jesuit priest, anthropologist, missiologist, author.

Ewing, Thomas (1789-1871): American lawyer; US senator from Ohio, 1831-37, 1850-51; secretary of the treasury, 1841; secretary of the interior, 1849-50; convert, 1871.

Eyck, Hubert Van (1366-1426) and his brother **Jan** (1370-1440): Painters, founders of Flemish school; developed process of oil painting; religious and portrait subjects.

F

Faber, Frederick William (1814-1863): British author of spiritual works, hymns; convert, 1845; priest.

Fabre, Jean Henri (1823-1915): French entomologist and author.

Fabricius, Hieronymus (Fabricius ab Aquapendente) (1537-1619): Italian anatomist, surgeon; described valvular system of the veins; teacher of Harvey.

Fallopio, Gabriello (1523-1562): Italian anatomist; discovered Fallopian tubes.

Farley, John (1842-1918): American cardinal, b. Ireland; came to US 1864; ordained priest, 1870; vicar general, 1891, auxiliary, 1895, and archbishop, 1902-18, of New York; cardinal, 1911.

Faye, Herve Auguste Etienne Albans (1814-1902): French astronomer; discovered comet named for him; invented zenithal collimator.

Fenelon, Francois de Salignac de la Mothe (1651-1715): French prelate, writer; archbishop of Cambrai.

Ferrari, Ludovico (1522-1565): Italian mathematician; discovered method of resolving equations of the fourth degree.

Fink, Francis A. (1907-1971): American editor, publisher; associated with *Our Sunday Visitor* from 1930 until his death; president of the Catholic Press Association, 1950-52; recipient of CPA Award in 1971 for his contribution to the Catholic press in the US and Canada.

Fischer, Max (1893-1954): European and American journalist, b. Germany; teacher, author; convert, while a student.

Fitzgibbon, Catherine (Sister Irene) (1823-1896): American religious, b. England; joined Sisters of Charity, 1850; founder and director of Foundling Hospital in New York City, 1869.

FitzSimons, Thomas (1741-1811): American merchant and congressman, b. Ireland; signer of the Constitution; member of first Congress of US.

Fizeau, Armand Hippolyte Louis (1819-1896): French physicist; experimentally determined velocity of light.

Flanagan, Edward Joseph (1886-1948): American priest, b. Ireland; founder of Boys' Town, Nebraska, 1917.

Floyd, John P. (1807-1863): American politician, cabinet official, military leader; governor of Virginia, 1850-53; secretary of war, 1857-61; brigadier general of Confederate Army, 1861; convert, about 1852.

Foch, Ferdinand (1851-1929): French soldier; supreme commander of Allied forces, 1918; led 1918 offensive to victory.

Ford, Francis X. (1892-1952): American Maryknoll missioner; sent to China, 1918; bishop of Kaying, 1935; imprisoned by communists in 1950; he died as a result of his treatment.

Fortunatus of Brescia (1701-1754); Italian Franciscan, pioneer morphologist.

Fortunatus, Venantius Honorius Clementianus (530-610): Latin poet; bishop of Poitiers; wrote the hymn *Vexilla Regis.*

Foster, John G. (1823-1874): American army officer; served with Union army in Civil War; convert, 1861.

Foucauld, Charles Eugene de (1858-1916): French hermit; army officer and explorer in Africa before joining Trappists, 1890; set up hermitage in Sahara among Moslem tribes; killed by desert tribesmen revolting against French; produced studies of Tuareg language and literature.

Foucault, Jean Bernard Leon (1819-1868): French physicist; experimented on light and heat; invented gyroscope, 1852; discovered Foucault electric current.

Fowler, Gene (1891-1960): American journalist, playwright, author.

Francis of Vitoria (1480-1546): Spanish Dominican, theologian; a founder of international law.

Franck, Cesar Auguste (1822-1890): Belgian-French composer; pioneer of modern French instrumental school.

Frassen, Claudius (1620-1711): French Franciscan theologian; author of *Scotus Academicus,* a presentation of the theology of Duns Scotus.

Fraunhofer, Joseph von (1787-1826): Bavarian physicist, optician; discovered Fraunhofer lines; initiated spectrum analysis, the basis of spectrography.

Frechette, Louis Honore (1839-1908): Canadian journalist, poet, prose writer.

Freppel, Charles Emile (1827-1891): French prelate, pulpit orator; bishop of Angers; leader of clerical party; founder of Catholic University of the West (Angers), 1875.

Fresnel, Augustin Jean (1788-1827): French physicist; contributor to science of optics, wave theory of light; introduced compound lenses for lighthouse use.

Froissart, Jean (1337-1410): French historian.

Frontenac, Louis de Buade, Count (1620-1698): French soldier, colonial governor of New France; encouraged explorations of Joliet, La Salle, others.

G

Gagarin, Ivan Sergeevich (1814-1882): Russian diplomat, writer; convert, 1843; joined Jesuits.

Galilei, Galileo (1564-1642): Italian astronomer, physicist; discovered moon shines with reflected light, observed milky way, four satellites of Jupiter, phases of Venus, sunspots; discovered laws of projectiles, principles of virtual velocities, gave exposition of principles of flotation. Summoned before Inquisition on two occasions for his defense of the Copernican system, an action which at the time was considered irreconcilable with implications of Christian faith.

Galvani, Luigi (1737-1798): Italian physician, physicist; experimented to determine electrical forces involved in muscular movements; founder of galvanism.

Galvin, Edward J. (1882-1956): Irish bishop, missionary in China; co-founder with Father John Blowick of the Columban Fathers, 1916; held under house arrest for three years following Communist takeover of China in 1949; expelled, 1952.

Gama, Vasco da (1469?-1524): Portuguese explorer; discovered new sea route to India.

Garcia, Moreno Gabriel (1821-1875): Ecuadorian journalist, patriot, president of Ecuador; assassinated.

Garrigou-Lagrange, Reginald (1877-1964): French Dominican theologian, philosopher, author of works in all fields of theology; teacher at the University of St. Thomas (Angelicum), Rome, 1909-58; consultor to congregations of the Roman Curia.

Gasquet, Francis Aidan (1846-1929): English Benedictine, cardinal; head of commission for revision of the Vulgate; historian.

Gassendi, Pierre (1592-1655): French philosopher, called Bacon of France; advocate of empirical method.

Gaston, William (1778-1844): American jurist; first student at Georgetown University; North Carolina congressman, judge, member of North Carolina supreme court; responsible for repeal of law which disenfranchised Catholics in his native state, 1835.

Gay-Lussac, Joseph Louis (1778-1850): French chemist, physicist; conducted important research on gases; improved methods of organic analysis.

Geoffrey of Monmouth (1100-1154): English bishop, chronicler; influential in development of national romance in English literature.

Ghiberti, Lorenzo di Cione di Ser Buonaccorso (1378-1455): Florentine painter, sculptor, goldsmith.

Ghirlandajo, Domenico (Domenico de Tommaso Bigordi) (1449-1498): Florentine painter, mosaic and fresco artist; teacher of Michelangelo.

Gibbons, Floyd (1887-1939): American journalist, war correspondent.

Gibbons, James (1834-1921): American cardinal; ordained priest, 1861; vicar apostolic of North Carolina, 1868-72; bishop of Richmond, 1872-77; archbishop of Baltimore 1877-1921; cardinal, 1886; patriot, controversialist, writer; Apostolic Delegate to Third Plenary Council of Baltimore; championed rights of labor.

Gibson, Hugh S. (1883-1954): American diplomat; minister to Poland, ambassador to Belgium, 1927-33, 1937-38, and Brazil; director, Intergovernmental Committee for European Migration; convert, 1938.

Gigli, Beniamino (1890-1957): Italian operatic tenor.

Gill, Eric (1882-1940): English sculptor, engraver, author; convert, 1913.

Gillis, James Martin (1876-1957): American Paulist priest, author, editor, radio orator; editor of the *Catholic World* for 26 years.

Gilmore, Patrick (1829-1892): American bandmaster and composer, b. Ireland.

Giocondo de Verona (1433-1515): Italian Franciscan architect, engineer, antiquarian; architect of St. Peter's.

Gioja, Flavio (14th c.): Italian mariner; contributed to improvement of compass.

Giorgione, Giorgio (1478-1511): Painter of Venetian school.

Giotto di Bondone (1276-1337): Florentine painter, architect, sculptor, fresco artist.

Glennon, John (1862-1946): American cardinal, b. Ireland; ordained priest, 1884; coadjutor bishop of Kansas City, Mo., 1896-1903; archbishop of St. Louis, 1903-46; cardinal, 1946.

Gluck, Christoph Willibald (1714-1787): German operatic composer.

Gobban, Saer (560-645): Irish ecclesiastical architect.

Godfrey of Bouillon (1061-1100): French crusader, duke of Lower Lorraine; elected ruler of Jerusalem after its capture in 1099; defender of the Holy Sepulchre.

Goldstein, David (1870-1958): American apologist, b. England; convert, 1905; pioneer of street preaching and Catholic Evidence Guild work; organized the Catholic Truth Guild of Boston, 1917; author.

Goodyear, William Henry (1846-1923): American author, museum curator in New York and Brooklyn, historian; convert, 1880.

Gordon, Andrew (1712-1751): Scottish Benedictine monk; first to use a cylinder of glass to produce frictional electricity; invented electrical chimes.

Gorres, Joseph von (1776-1848): German journalist, literateur.

Gounod, Charles Francois (1818-1893): French composer of operatic and Church music.

Gower, John (1325-1408): English poet.

Goya y Lucientes, Francisco Jose de (1746-1828): Spanish painter, etcher, lithographer; greatest painter of Spanish national customs.

Greco, El (Kyriakos Theotokopoulos) (1548-1614 or 1625): Greek-born painter of Castillian school.

Gregory of Valencia (1550-1603): Spanish Jesuit, moral theologian; works on usury and lawful rates of interest.

Grijalva, Juan de (1489-1527): Spanish explorer; completed exploration of Yucatan, discovering Mexico.

Grimaldi, Francesco Maria (1618-1663): Italian Jesuit, physicist; discovered diffraction of light.

Guardini, Romano (1885-1968): German priest (b. Italy), theologian, philosopher, author; *The Lord.*

Guido d'Arezzo (995-1050): Benedictine monk, musical theorist; reformer of musical notation.

Guilday, Peter (1884-1947): American priest; leading authority on Church history in US, founder of *Catholic Historical Review.*

Guiney, Louise Imogen (1861-1920): American poet and essayist.

Gurian, Waldemar (1902-1954): American educator and author, b. Russia; convert from Judaism.

Gutenberg, Johann (1400-1468): German printer, inventor of printing from movable type; first to print the Bible, 1452.

H

Haldeman, Samuel Stehman (Felix Aqo, pseud.) (1812-1880): American educator, author; convert, 1843; founder of National Academy of Sciences.

Hannegan, Robert E. (1903-1949): American cabinet official, politician; US postmaster general, 1945-47.

Hardee, William J. (1817-1873): American Confederate general; graduate West Point, 1838; author of *Rifle and Light Infantry Tactics,* used as army textbook at that time.

Harland, Henry (1861-1905): American novelist; used pseudonym **Sidney Luska** in earlier works; convert, 1897.

Harris, Joel Chandler (1848-1908): American journalist, author; creator of Uncle Remus; convert two weeks before his death.

Hassard, John Rose Greene (1836-1888): American journalist, author; convert, 1851; first editor of the *Catholic World.*

Hauy, Rene Just (1743-1822): French priest, mineralogist; a founder of the science of crystallography.

Hawks, Edward F. (1878-1955): American priest, author, b. South Wales; Anglican clergyman before conversion, 1908; ordained priest, 1911.

Haydn, Franz Joseph (1732-1809): Austrian composer; earliest master of symphony and quartet; composer of Austrian national anthem.

Hayes, Carlton J. H. (1882-1964): American historian, educator, diplomat, author; *Political and Social History of Modern Europe;* convert, 1904.

Hayes, Patrick J. (1867-1938): American cardinal; ordained priest, 1892; auxiliary of New York, 1914; ordinary of the armed forces, 1917; archbishop of New York, 1919-

38; cardinal, 1924; one of founders of National Catholic Welfare Council.

Healy, George (1813-1894): American portrait painter.

Hebert, Louis Philippe (1850-1917): Canadian sculptor; member of Royal Canadian Academy, 1883.

Hecker, Isaac Thomas (1819-1888): American priest, founder of the Congregation of St. Paul (Paulists); convert, 1844; joined Redemptorists and ordained priest, 1849; founded Paulists 1858 with several companions; first superior, 1858-88; founder of the *Catholic World.*

Heis, Eduard (1806-1877): German astronomer; first ascertained the point of departure of meteors; drew chart of 5,421 stars, with first authentic map of milky way.

Helmont, Jan Baptista van (1577-1644): Flemish physician, chemist; introduced chemical methods in biological studies; introduced word "gas" to designate aeriform fluids.

Hengler, Lawrence (1806-1858): German priest; inventor of horizontal pendulum used in seismographs.

Hennepin, Louis (1640-1701): Belgian Franciscan, explorer; first European to see, describe and depict Niagara Falls; explored Great Lakes region, upper Mississippi.

Henry the Navigator (1394-1460): Portuguese prince; discovered Azores, Madeira, Cape Verde Islands; traced African coast as far as Sierra Leone.

Herdtrich, Christian Wolfgang (1625-1684): Austrian Jesuit missionary; probably wrote first Chinese-Latin dictionary.

Herrera, Francisco de, the Elder (1576-1656): Spanish painter; a founder of the National School of Spain.

Heude, Pierre (1836-1902): French Jesuit missionary, zoologist; authority on land mollusks of China.

Hewit, Augustine Francis (1820-1897); American priest; Congregationalist, Episcopalian minister before conversion, 1846; ordained priest, 1847; assisted Isaac Hecker in founding Paulists.

Heywood, John (1497-1580): English poet, dramatist.

Hill, John Austin (Speakman) (1779-1828): American Dominican, b. England; after conversion joined Dominicans and was ordained priest at Rome; missionary in Ohio.

Holbein, Hans, the Younger (1497-1543): German portrait and historical painter; woodcut artist.

Holland, John Philip (1840-1914): American inventor, b. Ireland; settled at Paterson, N.J.; inventor of first practical submarine.

Hopkins, Gerard Manley (1844-1889): English Jesuit, poet; convert, 1866.

Horner, William Edmonds (1793-1853): American surgeon, anatomist, author; convert, 1839; discovered tensor tarsi, now called Horner's muscle, 1824.

Hubbard, Bernard R. (1889-1962): American Jesuit explorer; called The Glacier Priest; convert, joined Jesuits, 1908; Alaskan explorer; head of Santa Clara Univ. department of geology.

Hugh of St. Victor (1096-1141): Theologian, philosopher, mystic; a founder of scholasticism.

Hughes, John J. (1797-1864): American prelate, b. Ireland; arrived US, 1817; ordained priest, 1826; coadjutor (1837), bishop (1842) and first archbishop (1850-64) of New York; vigorous defender of Catholicism against Know-Nothings and Native Americans; abolished trusteeism; established Catholic school system in his archdiocese; laid cornerstone of St. Patrick's Cathedral (1858).

Hunton, George K. (1888-1967): American lawyer, editor; pioneer in Catholic field for interracial justice.

Hunyady, Janos (1387-1456): Hungarian defender of Christendom against the Turks; assisted at crucial defense of Belgrade, 1456.

Huysmans, Joris Karl (1848-1907): French novelist; convert 1895; Benedictine Oblate.

I

Ingres, Jean (1780-1867): Leading French classical painter; historical subjects.

Innocent III (1161-1216): Pope, 1198-1216; encouraged fourth crusade, promoted efforts against the Albigensians; convoked and presided at the Fourth Lateran Council, 1215; strenuously asserted supremacy of the Church over the state.

Ireland, John (1838-1918): American prelate, b. Ireland; arrived US, 1849; ordained priest, 1861; chaplain in Union army, 1862-63; bishop (1884) and first archbishop (1888-1918) of St. Paul; helped found Catholic University of America (1889); outspoken opponent of national churches.

Ives, Levi Silliman (1797-1867): American Episcopal bishop; convert, 1852; founder of New York Catholic Protectory.

J

Jacopone da Todi (1230-1306): Italian Franciscan poet; *Stabat Mater.*

Jaricot, Pauline (1799-1862): French charitable worker; founded Society for the Propagation of the Faith, 1822, to raise funds for foreign missions.

Jimenez, Juan Ramon (1881-1958): Spanish lyric poet; awarded Nobel Prize for literature, 1956.

John of Austria, Don (1547-1578): Spanish general; commander of fleet that defeated Turks at Lepanto, 1571.

Joliet, Louis (1645-1700): French Canadian explorer of Mississippi with Marquette, 1673.

Jones, Inigo (1573-1652): English architect; designer of stage sets for Ben Jonson and others; introduced Palladian type of architecture in England.

Jorgensen, Johannes (1866-1956): Danish writer; convert, 1896; author of *St. Francis of Assisi.*

Judge, Thomas A. (1868-1933): American

priest; founder of Missionary Servants of the Most Blessed Trinity (sisters), 1927, and the Missionary Servants of the Most Holy Trinity (priests and brothers).

Jugan, Jeanne (1792-1879): French foundress; established Little Sisters of the Poor, 1839, to care for aged poor.

Jussieu, Bernard de (1699-1777): French botanist; introduced a natural system for classification of plants.

Justinian I (483-565): Eastern Roman emperor; issued *Corpus Juris Civilis,* code of Roman law.

K

Katona, Stephen (1732-1811): Hungarian Jesuit, historian; author of 40-volume history of Hungary.

Kaye-Smith, Sheila (1887-1956): English author; convert 1929.

Kelly, William (1811-1888): American ironmaster; invented converter for the making of steel; now known as Bessemer's process after Englishman who patented a similar process.

Kenna, John E. (1848-1893): American legislator; private in Confederate Army; US congressman, 1876-80; US senator, 1883-93. Represents West Virginia in Statuary Hall.

Kennedy, John F. (1917-1963): Thirty-fifth president of the United States and first Catholic to hold that office; elected to Congress, 1946, 1948, 1950; to the Senate, 1952, 1958; to the presidency of the US, 1960; assassinated Nov. 22, 1963, at Dallas, Tex.; author; *Why England Slept, Profiles in Courage.*

Kennedy, Joseph P. (1888-1969): American businessman, diplomat; father of John and Robert Kennedy.

Kennedy, Robert F. (1925-1968): American politician, brother of President John F. Kennedy; cabinet official; attorney with justice department, 1951-52; US attorney general, 1961-65; US senator from New York, 1965-68; assassinated while campaigning for Democratic presidential nomination.

Keyes, Edward Lawrence (1843-1924): American physician; convert.

Keyes, Frances Parkinson (1885-1970): American author of popular novels and other works; wrote more than 50 books; convert, 1939.

Kilmer, Alfred Joyce (1886-1918): American poet; convert, 1913, with his wife; killed in action in World War I; works include *Trees and Other Poems.* His wife **Aline Murray Kilmer** (1888-1941): Lecturer, poet; wrote several books of collected verse.

Kir, Felix-Adrien (1876-1968): French priest, politician; mayor of Dijon from 1940.

Kircher, Athanasius (1601-1680): German Jesuit, archaeologist; inventor of magic lantern; stated germ theory of disease.

Knox, Ronald A. (1888-1957): English priest, author; convert, ordained, 1919; translated Vulgate Bible into English.

Kodaly, Zoltan (1882-1967): Hungarian composer; authority on folk music.

Konarski, Stanislaus (1700-1773): Polish priest, educator, author; influential in development of modern Polish literature.

Kosciusko, Tadeusz (1746-1817): Polish patriot; served in Continental Army in American Revolution; headed Polish rebellion, 1794, became dictator; died in Switzerland.

Kreisler, Fritz (1873-1962): American violinist and composer, b. Austria; became US citizen, 1943; convert, 1947.

L

La Bruyere, Jean de (1645-1696): French critic and moralist.

Lacordaire, Jean Baptiste Henri (1802-1861): French Dominican, pulpit orator; member of French Academy.

Laennec, Rene Theophile Hyacinthe (1781-1826): French physician; introduced auscultation, invented stethoscope.

La Farge, John (1835-1910): American artist and author.

La Farge, John (1880-1963): American Jesuit priest, son of artist John La Farge; scholar, author, editor of *America*, 1944-1948; leader in interracial work, a founder and director of the Catholic Interracial Council of New York City, and of the National Catholic Rural Life Conference; author of *The Manner Is Ordinary, The Catholic Viewpoint on Race Relations, An American Amen.*

La Fontaine, Jean de (1621-1695): French poet, known as a fabulist.

Lainez, Diego (1512-1565): Spanish theologian; second general of the Society of Jesus; made important contribution to work of Council of Trent.

Lamarck, Jean Baptiste de Monet, Chevalier de (1744-1829): French botanist, zoologist; originator of evolutionary theory called Lamarckism; divided animals into vertebrates and invertebrates.

Langton, Stephen (d. 1228): English prelate, cardinal archbishop of Canterbury; led English barons against King John; first of the subscribing witnesses to the Magna Charta.

Laplace, Pierre Simon (1749-1827): French astronomer, mathematician; proposed the nebular hypothesis.

LaSalle, Rene Robert Cavelier, Sieur de (1643-1687): French explorer; discovered Ohio River, explored Mississippi River valley.

Lasso, Orlando di (1532-1594): Belgian composer of over 2,000 works.

Lathrop, Rose Hawthorne (Mother Alphonsa) (1851-1926): American foundress, author; daughter of Nathaniel Hawthorne; convert, 1891, with her husband, **George Parsons Lathrop** (1851-1898): founded Dominican Congregation of St. Rose of Lima (Servants of Relief for Incurable Cancer) after her husband's death; established home at Hawthorne, N.Y.

Latreille, Pierre Andre (1762-1833): French entomologist; classified insects and crustaceans.

Laurier, Sir Wilfrid (1841-1919): Canadian statesman; prime minister, 1896-1911.

Lavigerie, Charles Martial Allemand (1825-1892): French prelate; archbishop of Algiers, 1867; cardinal, 1882; leader in abolition of slavery; founded White Fathers, 1874, for mission work in Africa.

Lavoisier, Antoine Laurent (1743-1794): French chemist; called father of modern chemistry.

Le Fort, Gertrud von (1876-1971): German poet and novelist; convert, 1925; works include *The Veil of Veronica* and *The Song on the Scaffold*, which was the source for the opera *Dialogue of the Carmelites.*

Lehar, Ferenc or **Franz** (1870-1948): Hungarian composer of operettas, orchestral works.

Lemaitre, Jules (1853-1914): French writer, literary and dramatic critic.

Lemcke, Henry (1796-1882): American Benedictine, b. Germany; Lutheran preacher; convert, 1824; ordained priest, 1826; came to US as missionary, 1834; instrumental in bringing first Benedictines to the US; joined Benedictines, 1852.

L'Enfant, Pierre Charles (1754-1825): French engineer; drew up plans for national capital, Washington, D.C.

Leo XIII (1810-1903): Pope, 1878-1903; scholar, statesman, Latinist; author of many encyclicals (see Index).

Leverrier, Urbain Jean Joseph (1811-1877): French astronomer; calculated presence of Neptune; founded the International Meteorological Institute.

Linacre, Thomas (1460-1524): English physician, humanist; assisted in founding of College of Physicians.

Lingard, John (1771-1851): English priest, author of historical works on England.

Linton, Moses L. (1808-1878): American physician; convert, 1844; president of first US Conference of St. Vincent de Paul Society, 1845; organized first medical monthly in US, *The St. Louis Medical and Surgical Journal,* 1848.

Lippi, Fra Filippo (1406-1469): Florentine painter; religious subjects.

Liszt, Franz von (1811-1886): Hungarian piano virtuoso, composer.

Locke, Jesse A. (1859-1952): American educator; Protestant Episcopal minister; convert, 1893.

Lombard, Peter (1100-1160): Italian theologian; bishop of Paris; author of *Sententiarum Libri Quatuor,* a synthesis of theology which exerted wide influence.

Longstreet, James (1821-1904): American army officer; graduate of West Point; resigned commission to serve with Confederate forces; convert, 1877.

Lord, Daniel (1888-1955): American Jesuit; popular writer; associated with editorial staff of *Queen's Work* from 1913 until his death; wrote hundreds of pamphlets; his books include *Played by Ear,* his autobiography.

Lorraine, Claude de (1600-1682): French painter; landscape subjects.

Louis the Great (1326-1382): King of Hungary, 1342-1382, and Poland, 1370-1382.

Loviner, John Forest (1896-1970): American Franciscan priest; founder and director of St. Anthony's Guild; publisher of catechetical materials for the Confraternity of Christian Doctrine; key figure in production of the *New American Bible.*

Lugo, John de (1583-1660): Spanish Jesuit, cardinal, theologian.

M

Mabillon, Jean (1632-1707): French Benedictine, father of science of paleography; author of *Acta Sanctorum Ordinis S. Benedicti.*

McCarran, Patrick A. (1876-1954): American jurist, legislator; chief justice Nevada supreme court, 1917-18; US senator, 1932-54; sponsored Internal Security (McCarran) Act, 1950; co-sponsor of McCarran-Walter Immigration and Nationality Act, 1952. Represents Nevada in Statuary Hall.

McCarthy, Joseph R. (1908-1957): American politician; senator from Wisconsin, 1946 until his death; controversial investigator of Communism in US.

McClellan, William Hildrup (1874-1951): American educator, author; Episcopalian minister; convert, 1908; ordained Jesuit priest, 1918.

McCloskey, John (1810-1885): First American cardinal; ordained priest, 1834; coadjutor bishop of New York 1844-47; first bishop of Albany, 1847-64; archbishop of New York, 1864-85, cardinal, 1875.

McCormick, Anne O'Hare (1882-1954): American journalist, b. England of American parents; awarded Pulitzer prize (1937) for European correspondence.

McGivney, Michael Joseph (1852-1890): American priest; founder of Knights of Columbus, 1882.

McGranery, James P. (1895-1963): American congressman, cabinet official; US attorney general, 1952-53.

McGrath, J. Howard (1903-1966): American politician, cabinet official; governor of Rhode Island, 1940-46; US senator; 1946; US attorney general, 1949-52.

McKay, Claude (1890-1948): American Negro poet and novelist, b. Jamaica, B.W.I.; came to US, 1912; author of *A Long Way from Home* (1937), his autobiography; convert, 1944.

McKenna, Joseph (1843-1926): American jurist, cabinet official; US congressman from California, 1885-92; US circuit judge, 1892-97; US attorney general 1897-98; associate justice US Supreme Court, 1898-1925.

McLoughlin, John (1784-1857): Pioneer settler of Oregon, b. Canada; fur trader, physician; encouraged settlement of Oregon Territory; became American citizen; called Father of Oregon. Represents Oregon in National Statuary Hall.

MacMahon, Marie Edme Patrice Maurice de (1808-1893): Marshal of France, 1859, and president, 1873-1897; military leader in Crimean War, Franco-Prussian War, other campaigns.

McQuaid, Bernard J. (1823-1909): American prelate; ordained priest, 1848; helped found Seton Hall College; chaplain in Civil War; first bishop of Rochester, N.Y., 1868-1909; voted against definition of papal infallibility at Vatican I; promoter of Catholic schools.

Madeleva, Sister M. (Mary Evaline Wolf) (1887-1964): American educator, poet; joined Holy Cross Sisters, 1908.

Magellan, Ferdinand (1480-1521): Portuguese navigator; led expedition which first circumnavigated globe; discovered Strait of Magellan, Ladrones, Philippines, where he was slain.

Magsaysay, Ramon (1907-1957): Philippine statesman; crushed the Communist (Huk) Rebellion in 1948-53; third president of the Philippine Republic.

Mahler, Gustav (1880-1911): Bohemian composer and conductor; convert, 1897.

Malherbe, Francois de (1555-1628): French poet; influenced exact usage of language.

Mallinckrodt, Hermann von (1821-1874); German leader of Center Party against Kulturkampf.

Mallory, Stephen Russell (1813-1873): American Confederate political leader, b. Trinidad; US senator from Florida, 1851-1861; resigned when Florida seceded; naval secretary of the Confederacy.

Malory, Sir Thomas (d. 1470): English author of the *Morte d'Arthur.*

Malpighi, Marcello (1628-1694): Italian anatomist; called father of microscopic anatomy.

Malus, Etienne Louis (1775-1812): French engineer, physicist; discovered polarization of light, invented polariscope.

Mangan, James C. (1803-1849): Irish poet.

Manning, Henry Edward (1808-1892): English cardinal, author; convert, 1851.

Mansard, Nicolas Francois (1598-1666): French architect.

Mantegna, Andrea (1431-1506): Italian painter, muralist, engraver; leader of Paduan school.

Manutius, Aldus (1450-1515): Italian scholar, printer, publisher; founded Aldine press.

Manzoni, Alessandro (1785-1873): Italian poet, novelist; *I Promessi Sposi.*

Marconi, Guglielmo (1874-1937): Italian engineer, inventor; outstanding contributor to development of wireless telegraphy, radio; Nobel Prize for physics, 1909.

Mariotte, Edme (1620-1684): French physicist; researcher in hydrodynamics.

Martini, Giambattista (1706-1784): Italian Franciscan, composer of Church music, theorist and teacher.

Masaccio, Tommaso (1401-1428): Italian painter; fresco artist of Florentine school; influenced advance to Renaissance painting; called father of modern art.

Massillon, Jean Baptiste (1663-1742): French preacher; bishop of Clermont.

Matthias Corvinus (Hunyady) (1440-1490): One of Hungary's greatest kings, 1458-1490; repelled Turks, fought against Bohemians, Frederick III; patron of arts, literature; introduced Golden Age in Hungary; founded library.

Mauriac, Francois (1885-1970): French writer; awarded Nobel Prize for literature, 1952; works include the novels *The Desert of Love, The Viper's Triangle*.

Mauro, Fra (d. c. 1459): Italian Camaldolese monk, cosmographer; Fra Mauro Highlands, named for him by 17th century astronomers, was the landing site of Apollo 14.

Maxmilian I, the Great (1573-1651): Duke and elector of Bavaria; opposed Protestant cause; founded Catholic League, 1609.

Mazarin, Jules (1602-1661): French cardinal, statesman; prime minister of France under Louis XIII and Louis XIV; concluded Thirty Years' War by the Treaty of Westphalia; strengthened France as a European power.

Meagher, Thomas F. (1823-1867): American politician and soldier, b. Ireland; came to US, 1852; joined Union forces in Civil War; became brigadier general of Irish Brigade organized by him; territorial secretary of Montana, 1865.

Mendel, Gregor Johann (1822-1884): Austrian Augustinian monk, botanist; formulated Mendelian laws of heredity.

Mercier, Desire Joseph (1851-1926): Belgian prelate, philosopher; cardinal archbishop of Malines; promoter of neo-scholastic philosophy; leader against demands of German invaders in 1914; restored Louvain University after World War I; in 1924 began Malines Conversations, an attempt to unify the Anglican and Roman churches.

Mersenne, Marin (1588-1648): French mathematician.

Merton, Thomas (Father M. Louis) (1915-1968): American Trappist priest and author, b. France; convert, 1939; works include *The Seven Storey Mountain* (his autobiography), *Waters of Siloe*, *Conjectures of a Guilty Bystander*, and articles in opposition to nuclear war.

Mestrovic, Ivan (1883-1962): Yugoslav sculptor; religious and mythological subjects, Slav folklore, portrait busts; works include *Pieta* at Notre Dame Univ., where he was a professor from 1955-62.

Metternich, Klemens Wenzel Nepomuk Lothar von (1773-1859): Austrian statesman and diplomat.

Meynell, Alice Thompson (1847-1922): English poet, essayist, leader in Catholic literary revival in England; convert. Her husband, **Wilfrid Meynell** (1852-1948): Journalist, publisher, biographer; he and his wife discovered

Francis Thompson; convert.

Mezzofanti, Giuseppe (1774-1849): Italian cardinal, linguist, custodian-in-chief of Vatican Library.

Michelangelo Buonarroti (1475-1564): Italian architect, sculptor, painter, poet; outstanding figure of the Renaissance.

Mikolajczyk, Stanislaus (1901-1967): Polish politician; leader of Polish Peasant party in exile; settled in US, 1947.

Miller, Nathan L. (1868-1953): American politician; governor of New York; convert shortly before death.

Millet, Jean Francois (1814-1875): French painter; landscape and religious subjects.

Minton, Sherman (1890-1965): American jurist; US senator, 1935-40; associate justice US Supreme Court, 1949-56; convert, 1961.

Mistral, Gabriela (pen name of Lucila Godoy de Alcayaga) (1889-1957): Chilean poet; Nobel Prize for literature, 1945.

Mitchell, James P. (1902-1964): American cabinet official; labor relations expert; US secretary of labor, 1953-61.

Mitchell, John (1870-1919): American labor leader; president of United Mine Workers; convert, 1907.

Mohler, Johann Adam (1796-1838): German theologian.

Mohr, Josef (1792-1848): Austrian priest, poet; *Silent Night*.

Molina, Luis de (1535-1600): Spanish Jesuit, theologian; author of *Concordia*, expounding a system for the reconciliation of grace and free will, called Molinism.

Mondino (dim. for Raimondo) dei Luicci (1275-c. 1327): Italian anatomist.

Monge, Gaspard (1746-1818): French mathematician; called founder of descriptive geometry.

Montcalm, Marquis Louis Joseph de (1712-1759): French marshal, military commander in Canada; fatally wounded in Battle of Quebec.

Montessori, Maria (1870-1952): Italian physician, educator; originator of Montessori method for education of children.

Monteux, Pierre (1875-1964): American conductor, b. France; US citizen, 1942; led most of the world's greatest orchestras.

Moon, Parker Thomas (1892-1936): American historian, educator, author, editor; convert, 1914.

Moore, Thomas (1779-1852): National lyricist of Ireland.

Moore, Thomas Verner (1877-1969): American priest, psychiatrist, educator, author; joined Carthusians in 1947 — had earlier been a Paulist and Benedictine.

Morgagni, Giovanni Battista (1682-1771): Italian physician; founder of anatomical pathology.

Morley, Sylvanus Griswold (1883-1948): American archeologist; convert.

Moylan, Stephen (1734-1811): American patriot, b. Ireland; immigrated to US 1768;

joined Continental Army, 1775; aide-de-camp and secretary to General Washington, 1776; leader of cavalry division.

Mozart, J. C. Wolfgang Amadeus (1756-1791): Austrian composer of more than 600 works in a wide range of forms.

Muench, Aloysius J. (1889-1962): American cardinal; ordained priest, 1913; bishop of Fargo, 1935-59; apostolic visitator and liaison representative between US military government and German hierarchy, 1946; nuncio to Germany, 1951-59; cardinal, 1959.

Muller, Johann (1436-1476): German mathematician, astronomer; assisted in calendar reform.

Muller, Johannes Peter (1801-1858): German physiologist, comparative anatomist.

Murillo, Bartolome Esteban (1617-1682): Spanish artist of the Andalusian school; master of color contrast; religious subjects.

Murphy, Frank (1890-1949): American jurist, cabinet official; mayor of Detroit, 1930-33; US high commissioner to the Philippines, 1935-36; governor of Michigan, 1936-38; US attorney general 1939-40; associate justice of US Supreme Court, 1940-49.

Murphy, John Benjamin (1857-1916): American surgeon; inventor of Murphy button; Laetare Medalist, 1902.

Murray, John C. (1904-1967): American Jesuit priest, educator, theologian, ecumenist, international expert on Church-state relations, author.

Murray, Philip (1886-1952): American labor leader, b. Scotland.

N

Nathan, George Jean (1882-1958): American dramatic critic, editor, author; founder with H. L. Mencken of *The American Mercury*; convert, 1957.

Nelaton, Auguste (1807-1873): French surgeon; inventor of Nelaton probe.

Newman, John Henry (1801-1890): English cardinal, theologian; leader of Oxford Movement; convert, 1845; ordained to priesthood, 1847; founded Oratorians in England; master of prose style; author of historical and apologetical works, poems, novels.

Nicholas of Lyra (1270-1340): Franciscan biblical scholar.

Nieuland, Julius Arthur (1878-1936): American priest of Congregation of Holy Cross, b. Belgium; chemist, botanist; Notre Dame scientist, contributed to invention of Lewisite gas; discovered method for producing synthetic rubber.

Niza, Marcos de (d. 1558); Franciscan missionary, explored parts of Arizona and New Mexico, 1539; accompanied Coronado's expedition.

Nobili, Leopoldo (1784-1835): Italian physicist, inventor of the thermopile.

Noll, John F. (1875-1956): American prelate, author, editor; ordained priest, 1898; bishop of Fort Wayne, Ind., 1925-56; founder and editor of weekly newspaper *Our Sunday Visitor,* 1912; wrote *Father Smith Instructs Jackson,* other books and pamphlets.

Nollet, Jean-Antoine (1700-1770): French priest, physicist; researcher in electricity; invented an electroscope.

Noyes, Alfred (1880-1958): English poet; convert, 1927.

O

O'Callahan, Joseph (1906-1964): American Jesuit priest; Navy chaplain in World War II; awarded the Congressional Medal of Honor, for action aboard the carrier Franklin on Mar. 19, 1945.

Ocampo, Sebastian (1466-1521): Spanish explorer; circumnavigated Cuba, proved its insular character.

O'Connell, Daniel (1775-1847): Irish statesman, nationalist leader; known as the Liberator; responsible for Catholic emancipation, 1829.

O'Connor, (Mary) Flannery (1925-1964): American novelist and short-story writer.

O'Dwyer, Joseph (1841-1898): American physician; developed method of aiding breathing to prevent asphyxia in diphtheria.

Oertel, Abraham (1527-1598): Flemish geographer; publisher of an atlas.

O'Hara, Edwin Vincent (1881-1956): American prelate; ordained priest, 1905; bishop of Great Falls, Mont. 1930-39; bishop of Kansas City, Mo., 1939-56; title of archbishop, 1954; leader in catechetical work in the US; founder of National Catholic Rural Life Conference.

O'Higgins, Bernardo (1778-1842): Chilean soldier, statesman; Liberator of Chile.

Olaf (II) Haraldsson, Saint (995-1030): King of Norway, 1016-1028; attempted conversion of his country; killed in battle; patron of Norway; canonized, 1164.

Orellana, Francisco de (1500-1546): Spanish navigator, explored the Amazon River.

Origen (185-254): Theologian and writer, head of catechetical schools at Alexandria, Caesarea; author of biblical, theological works.

Orosius, Paul (380?-?): Spanish priest; author of book of universal history.

Oursler, Fulton (1893-1952): American author, editor, lecturer; convert 1943; works include *The Greatest Story Ever Told* and *The Greatest Book Ever Written.*

Ozanam, Frederic (1813-1853): French historian; a founder of St. Vincent de Paul Society. (See Index.)

Ozanam, Jacques (1640-1717): French mathematician.

P

Pacioli, Luca (1450?-1520?): Italian Franciscan, mathematician; author of first description of double-entry bookkeeping.

Paderewski, Ignace (1860-1941): Polish pianist, conductor, composer; first premier of Poland after World War I.

Palestrina, Giovanni Pierluigi da (1526-1594): Italian composer of Church music in medieval moods; noted for polyphonic style.

Palladio, Andrea (1518-1580): Italian architect; controlling influence of 17th-century architecture called Palladian.

Palmer, Gretta (1905-1953): American journalist, author; convert, 1946.

Papini, Giovanni (1881-1956): Italian writer; convert, 1918; author of *Life of Christ*.

Pare, Ambroise (1517-1590): French surgeon; called father of modern surgery; introduced artery ligature.

Paris, Bruno Paulin Gaston (1839-1903): French philologist, author.

Parsch, Pius (1884-1954): Austrian Augustinian, theologian, Scripture scholar, liturgist.

Parsons, Wilfrid (1887-1958): American Jesuit priest, editor, author, educator; editor-in-chief of *America*, 1925-36.

Pascal, Blaise (1623-1662): French philosopher, scientist; demonstrated that a column of air has weight; author of *Pensees*.

Pasteur, Louis (1822-1895): French chemist; developed a vaccine against hydrophobia; founded Pasteur Institute; father of bacteriology.

Pastor, Ludwig von (1854-1928): German historian; *The History of the Popes from the Beginning of the Middle Ages*.

Patmore, Coventry (1823-1896): English poet; convert, 1864.

Pazmany, Peter (1570-1637): Hungarian Jesuit, cardinal; leader of Counter Reformation; translated Bible into Hungarian; called founder of modern Hungarian literature.

Peguy, Charles Pierre (1873-1914): French poet and writer; outstanding Catholic defender of Dreyfus; founded the journal *Cahiers de la Quinzaine*; works include *The Mystery of the Charity of Joan of Arc* and religious meditations.

Pelouze, Theophile Jules (1807-1867): French chemist; developed production of guncotton, nitrocellulose.

Pepin the Short (714-768): King of the Franks, son of Charles Martel, father of Charlemagne; first Frank crowned with religious ceremonies; defeated Lombards and restored central Italy to the Holy See.

Perosi, Lorenzo (1872-1956): Italian priest, composer.

Perugino, Il (Pietro Vannucci) (1446-1523): Italian painter; leader of Umbrian school; teacher of Raphael; religious subjects.

Petau (Petavius), Denys (1583-1652): French Jesuit, theologian; called father of the history of dogma.

Petrarch (Francesco Petrarca) (1304-1374): Italian poet.

Piazzi Giuseppe (1746-1826): Italian monk, astronomer; discovered Ceres, first known asteroid.

Picard, Jean (1620-1682): French astronomer; accurately measured degree of a meridian.

Pinturicchio, Bernardino di Betto di Biagio (1454-1513): Italian painter of the Umbrian school; historical and religious subjects.

Pio, Padre (Francesco Forgione) (1887-1968): Italian Capuchin priest; reputed stigmatist.

Pire, Dominique Georges (1910-1969): Belgian priest; awarded Nobel Peace Prize in 1958 for work for displaced persons.

Pisano, Andrea (1270-1348) and his son **Nino** (1315-1368); Italian sculptors.

Pisano, Nicolo (1225-1278): Italian sculptor; works among greatest of Romanesque style. His son, **Giovanni** (1240-1320): Sculptor, architect.

Pitra, Jean Baptiste Francois (1812-1889): French Benedictine, cardinal, scholar.

Pizarro, Francisco (1470-1541): Spanish explorer, conqueror of Peru.

Plumier, Charles (1646-1704): French botanical explorer of Antilles, Central America.

Pole, Reginald (1500-1558): English prelate, cardinal archbishop of Canterbury; opposed divorce of Henry VIII; papal legate, participant in Council of Trent.

Polo, Marco (1245-1324): Early traveler to China, b. Venice; *Book of Marco Polo*.

Ponce de Leon (1460-1521): Spanish explorer; discovered Florida.

Pope, Alexander (1688-1744): English poet; master of the rimed couplet.

Pouget, Jean Francois Albert du, Marquis de Nadaillac, (1817-1904): French anthropologist; authority on cave drawings.

Poussin, Nicolas (1594-1665): French painter; historical and landscape subjects.

Price, Thomas Frederick (1860-1919): American missionary; co-founder with Bishop Walsh of the Catholic Foreign Mission Society of America (Maryknoll Fathers); called the Tar Heel Apostle.

Pro, Miguel (1891-1927): Mexican Jesuit; fled Mexico during 1914 Revolution; returned to Mexico, 1926, after his ordination in Belgium; arrested, 1927, and shot to death by police in Mexico City.

Prohaszka, Ottokar (1858-1927): Hungarian bishop; preacher, author.

Provancher, Leon Abel (1820-1892): Canadian priest, naturalist; called father of natural history in Canada.

Puccini, Giacomo (1858-1924): Italian operatic composer.

Pugin, Augustus Welby Northmore (1812-1852): English architect.

Pulaski, Casimir (1748-1779): Polish patriot, fought in American Revolution; called Father of the American Cavalry; fatally wounded at Savannah.

Puvis de Chavannes, Pierre (1824-1898): French muralist.

Q

Quinlan, Thomas (1896-1970): Irish Columban missionary bishop; served in China, 1920-34; prefect apostolic of Chun Cheon, Korea, 1934; interned by Japanese during World War II; imprisoned by North Koreans, 1950-53.

Quinones, Francis (1482-1540): Spanish

Franciscan, cardinal, liturgist; worked on revision of breviary.

R

Racine, Jean Baptiste (1639-1699): French dramatic poet.

Rameau, Jean-Philippe (1683-1764): French organist, music theorist, operatic composer.

Randall, James Ryder (1839-1908): American journalist, poet, song writer; *Maryland, My Maryland.*

Raphael Santi (1483-1520): Italian painter of religious, portrait, other subjects; architect of St. Peter's; among greatest of Renaissance painters.

Reeve, Arthur Benjamin (1882-1936): American educator, author; convert, 1926.

Regnault, Henri Victor (1810-1878): French chemist, physicist; authority in thermometry.

Reiffenstuel, Anaclete (Johann Georg) (1641-1703): German Franciscan, theologian, canonist.

Reinhold, Hans (1897-1968): American pioneer in liturgical movement, b. Germany; came to US, 1936; naturalized citizen.

Reni, Guido (1575-1642): Italian painter of the Eclectic school; religious and other subjects.

Repplier, Agnes (1858-1950): American author, essayist.

Reymont, Wladislaw (1867-1925): Polish novelist; awarded Nobel Prize for literature in 1924 for *The Peasants.*

Ribera, Jose (1588-1652): Spanish painter of Neapolitan school, etcher; religious subjects.

Ricci, Matteo (1552-1610): Italian Jesuit missionary in India and China; introduced Christianity in China; author.

Riccioli, Giovanni Battista (1598-1671): Italian Jesuit, astronomer; introduced some lunar nomenclature in use today.

Richelieu, Armand Jean du Plessis, Duc de (1585-1642): French cardinal, statesman; founder of the French Academy, 1634.

Ritter, Joseph E. (1892-1967): American cardinal; ordained priest, 1917; auxiliary bishop, 1933, bishop, 1934, and first archbishop, 1944, of Indianapolis; archbishop of St. Louis, 1946-67; cardinal, 1961; ordered desegregation of St. Louis archdiocesan schools, 1957; was outspoken US progressive bishop at Vatican II; first Mass in vernacular in US offered in his diocese.

Robbia, Luca della (1400-1482): Florentine sculptor; developed a glaze for terra cotta ware (Robbia work).

Robinson, William Callyhan (1834-1911): American jurist, author; Episcopalian minister; convert, 1863.

Rochambeau, Jean Baptiste Donatien de Vimeur, Conte de (1725-1807): French general; led French forces sent to aid Americans in Revolution.

Rockne, Knute Kenneth (1888-1931): American football player and coach, b. Norway; immigrated to US, 1893; football coach at Notre Dame University, 1918-31; convert, 1925.

Rodzinski, Artur (1894-1958): American symphony conductor, b. Yugoslavia; became US citizen, 1933.

Rosecrans, William Starke (1819-1898): American army officer; graduate of West Point; army commander during the Civil War; Federal official; convert, 1845.

Rossini, Gioacchino Antonio (1792-1868): Italian operatic composer and innovator in orchestration.

Roualt, Georges (1871-1958): French painter of modern school; convert.

Rubens, Peter Paul (1577-1640): Flemish painter; great colorist, landscape, portrait, historical, religious subjects.

Rubruck, William (1220-1293): French Franciscan missionary and traveler in the East, especially China.

Ruth, George Herman (Babe) (1894-1948): American baseball player and record holder; convert, 1906.

Ruysbroeck, John, Bl. (1293-1381): Flemish mystical theologian; beatified, 1908.

Ryan, Abram J. (1838-1886): American priest, poet; called Poet of the Confederacy.

S

San Gallo, Giuliano Giamberti da (1445-1516); his brother, **Antonio da San Gallo, the Elder** (1455-1534); their nephew, **Antonio da San Gallo, the Younger** (1483-1546): Italian architects.

San Martin, Jose de (1778-1850): South American soldier, statesman; defeated Spanish in Argentina, established independence of Chile, proclaimed independence and called Protector of Peru.

Santorini, Giovanni Domenico (1681-1737): Italian physician, anatomist; discovered emissary veins leading out of sinuses, risory muscles, fissures in external ear.

Sarbiewki, Mathias Casimir (1595-1640): Polish Jesuit, poet; called the Horace of Poland.

Sarto, Andrea del (1486-1531): Florentine painter; great colorist, master of light and shade; religious subjects.

Savage, (Charles) Courtenay (1890-1946): American playwright, author; convert, 1937.

Scanderbeg (George Castriota) (c. 1403-1468): Albanian national hero; leader in Albanian independence movement against Turks.

Scarlatti, Alessandro (1659-1725): Italian operatic composer; called founder of modern opera.

Scheiner, Christoph (1579-1650): German Jesuit, astronomer; made independent discovery of sunspots.

Schlegel, Friedrich von (1772-1829): German Romantic poet, essayist, novelist; convert, 1803.

Schmid, Christoph von (1768-1854): German educator, pioneer writer of children's books.

Schmidt, Wilhelm (1868-1954): German Divine Word priest, ethnologist and historian of religions.

Schubert, Franz Peter (1797-1828): Austrian composer of symphonic and other orchestral works.

Schuman, Robert (1886-1963): French statesman; leader of the Popular Republican Party; Premier of France twice (November, 1947-July, 1948; Aug. 31-Sept. 9, 1948); major figure in post-World War II efforts at European unity; author of Schuman Plan for pooling French and German coal and steel production, a forerunner of the Common Market.

Schuyler, Philippa (1932-1967): American pianist, news correspondent.

Searle, George Mary (1839-1918): American priest and astronomer, b. England of American parents; came to US, 1840; convert, 1866; joined Paulists, 1868; ordained, 1871; director of Vatican Observatory, 1898.

Schwann, Theodor (1810-1882): German anatomist, physiologist; founder of cell theory.

Schwarz, Berthold (13th or 14th c.): German Franciscan; called inventor of gunpowder.

Secchi, Angelo (1818-1878): Italian Jesuit, astronomer; professor at Georgetown University; did spectroscopic work on sun, stars, classification of stars; invented meteorograph.

Segura y Saenz, Pedro (1880-1957): Spanish cardinal, primate of Spain; outspoken critic of Nazism, Fascism and Franco regime.

Seidl, Johann Gabriel (1804-1875): Austrian journalist, poet; author of words for Austrian national anthem.

Semmelweis, Ignaz Philipp (1818-1865): Hungarian physician; pioneer of antiseptic treatment in obstetrics.

Semmes, Raphael (1809-1877): American naval officer, lawyer; commander in US Navy; resigned, 1861, to enter Confederate Navy; commanded the Sumter and the Alabama, commerce destroyers.

Sienkiewicz, Henryk (1846-1916): Polish novelist; awarded Nobel Prize for literature in 1905.

Shea, Sir Ambrose (1815-1905): Canadian political leader.

Shea, John Dawson Gilmary (1824-1892): American historian, author; *History of the Catholic Church in the United States.*

Sheridan, Philip H. (1831-1888): American army officer; graduate of West Point; general cavalry commander during the Civil War.

Shevchenko, Taras (1814-1861): Ukrainian poet, nationalist.

Shields, James (1806-1879): American soldier and statesman, b. Ireland; arrived US, 1823, settled in Kaskaskia. Ill.; army officer, politician; general in Mexican War; governor of Oregon Territory, 1849; US senator from Illinois, 1849-55, from Minnesota, 1858-59; moved to California, 1859; brigadier general in Civil War, resigned commission, 1863; moved to Missouri; US senator from Missouri, 1879. Represents Illinois in Statuary Hall.

Shipman, Andrew Jackson (1857-1915): American lawyer, author; convert, 1876; authority on Church law.

Sitwell, Edith (1887-1964): English poet, critic, novelist; convert, 1955.

Skinner, Henrietta Channing Dana (1857-1928): American author; convert, 1878.

Smith, Alfred Emanuel (1873-1944): American politician; governor of New York; Democratic presidential candidate, 1928, the first Catholic ever nominated.

Smith, Ignatius (1886-1957): American Dominican priest, orator, teacher, retreat master.

Smith, Matthew (1891-1960): American priest, editor; founder of Register chain of newspapers.

Sobieski, John III (1624-1696): Polish king, soldier; rescued Vienna from Turks, caused their expulsion from Poland and Hungary.

Spalding, John Lancaster (1840-1916): American prelate; nephew of Martin Spalding, below; author of books on religion, philosophy and social issues; advocate of Catholic parochial school system; served on President Roosevelt's Anthracite Coal Strike Commission, 1902; first bishop of Peoria, 1876-1908, when he resigned because of ill health.

Spalding, Martin J. (1810-1872): American prelate; bishop of Louisville, 1848-64; archbishop of Baltimore, 1864-72; author of numerous books; helped establish American College of Louvain; advocate of a North American College in Rome and an American Catholic university.

Spallanzani, Lazzaro (1729-1799): Italian naturalist; experimenter on digestion, other functions; disproved theory of spontaneous generation.

Spearman, Frank Hamilton (1859-1937): American author; convert, 1884; Laetare Medalist, 1935.

Spellman, Francis J. (1889-1967): American cardinal; ordained priest, 1916; served in papal secretariat of state, 1925-32; auxiliary of Boston, 1932; archbishop of New York, 1939-67; cardinal, 1946; military vicar of US; author.

Starr, Eliza Allen (1824-1901): American educator, author; convert, 1856; first woman Laetare Medalist, 1885.

Stensen, Niels (Steno, Nicolaus) 1638-1687): Danish bishop, anatomist; discovered excretory duct of parotid glands, convert, 1667.

Stoddard, Charles Warren (1843-1909): American journalist, poet, author; convert, 1867.

Stoddard, John Lawson (1850-1931): American author, lecturer; convert, 1922.

Stone, James Kent (Fr. Fidelis, C.P.) (1840-1921): American missionary priest, author; Episcopalian minister, 1866; convert, 1869; ordained priest, 1872.

Storer, Horatio Robinson (1830-1922): American physician, medical professor, author; convert, 1897.

Stoss, Veit (1440-1533): German sculptor; master wood-carver.

Stradivari, Antonio (1644-1737): Italian violin maker.

Stritch, Samuel (1887-1958): American cardinal; ordained priest, 1910; bishop of Toledo, 1921-30; archbishop of Milwaukee, 1930-39; archbishop of Chicago, 1939-58; cardinal, 1946; first American appointed to the Roman Curia, died before he could take up his post as pro-prefect of the Sacred Congregation for the Propagation of the Faith.

Sturzo, Luigi (1871-1959): Italian priest-statesman.

Suarez, Francisco (1548-1617): Spanish Jesuit, theologian; considered a founder of international law; author of many works; *Doctor Eximius.*

T

Tabb, John Banister (1845-1909): American poet, served in Confederate navy, convert, 1872; ordained priest, 1884.

Taggart, Marion Ames (1866-1945): American author, convert, 1880.

Takamine, Jokichi (1854-1922): Japanese-American chemist; developed Takadiastase, isolated adrenalin; convert.

Talbot, Matthew (1856-1925): Irish layman noted for his sanctity; a reformed alcoholic, is considered a model for those with this condition; his cause for beatification is under consideration.

Taney, Roger Brooke (1777-1864): American jurist, cabinet official; US attorney general, 1831-33; secretary of the treasury, 1833-34; chief justice United States Supreme Court, 1836-64; associated with the Dred Scott decision, 1857.

Tasso, Torquato (1544-1595): Italian poet.

Teilhard de Chardin, Pierre (1881-1955): French Jesuit; paleontologist and explorer.

Tekakwitha, Kateri (1656-1680): American Indian maiden; Lily of the Mohawks; instructed by Jesuit missionaries and baptized at age of 20; her cause for beatification is under consideration.

Thayer, John (1755-1815): American priest; Protestant chaplain during Revolutionary War; convert, 1783; first native New England priest; missionary in Kentucky; author.

Thomas, Charles Louis Ambrose (1811-1896): Alsatian composer of operatic and other works.

Thomas a Kempis (1380-1471): Dutch Augustinian, considered author of the *Imitation of Christ.*

Thomas of Celano (1200-1255): Italian Franciscan; biographer of St. Francis of Assisi.

Thompson, Francis (1859-1907): English poet; *The Hound of Heaven.*

Tieffentaller, Joseph (1710-1785): Jesuit missionary, geographer.

Tintoretto, Jacopo Robusti (1518-1594): Italian painter of Venetian school; religious and portrait subjects.

Tisserant, Eugene (1884-1972): French cardinal, scholar; librarian and archivist of the Vatican; headed Congregation for the Eastern Churches for more than 20 years; dean of the College of Cardinals, 1951-72; specialist in Oriental languages; member of the French Academy.

Titian or **Tiziano Vecelli** (1477-1576): Italian painter, greatest of the Venetian school; frescoes in wide range of subjects; portraits.

Tobin, Maurice J. (1901-1953): American politician, cabinet official; mayor of Boston, 1937, 1941; governor of Massachusetts, 1944; US secretary of labor, 1949-53.

Tocqueville, Alexis Charles de (1805-1859): French writer, statesman; *La Democratie en Amerique.*

Torricelli, Evangelista (1608-1647): Italian mathematician, physicist; improved telescope, invented barometer.

Toscanelli, Paolo dal Pozzo (1397-1482): Italian physician, geographer; probably aided Columbus.

Toscanini, Arturo (1867-1957): Italian operatic and symphony conductor.

Tulasne, Louis Rene (1815-1885): French botanist; called founder of modern mycology.

U

Undset, Sigrid (1882-1949): Norwegian novelist; Nobel Prize for literature, 1928; *Kristen Lavransdatter;* convert, 1924

V

Valentine, Basil (born 1394): Benedictine monk; founder of analytical chemistry.

Vandyke (Van Dyck), Sir Anthony (1599-1641): Flemish associate of Rubens, English court painter; religious and portrait subjects.

Vasari, Giorgio (1511-1574): Italian painter, architect; founder of modern art history and criticism.

Vasquez, Gabriel (1551-1604): Spanish Jesuit, theologian.

Vega, Lope Felix de (Vega) Carpio (1562-1635): Spanish priest, dramatic poet; founder of Spanish national drama.

Velasquez, Diego Rodriguez de Silva y (1599-1660): Spanish painter; master of naturalism; historical, portrait, religious and other subjects.

Verdi, Giuseppe (1813-1901): Italian composer of operatic and other works.

Verne, Jules (1828-1905): French writer; scientific fiction.

Vernier, Pierre (1580-1637): French mathematician; formulated vernier scale for accurate linear and angular magnitude.

Veronese, Paolo (1528-1588): Italian painter of Venetian school; Painter of Pageants; religious frescoes and paintings.

Verrazano, Giovanni da (1485-1528): Italian navigator; explored coast of North America for Francis I of France; claimed by his countrymen to be discoverer of Hudson River.

Verrocchio, Andrea del (1435-1488): Florentine sculptor and painter of Tuscan school.

Vesalius, Andreas (1514-1564): Belgian anatomist; founder of modern anatomy.

Vespucci, Amerigo (1451-1512): Italian navigator; called discoverer of mainland of America, named after him.

Vico, Francesco de (1805-1848): Italian Jesuit, astronomer; discovered six comets.

Viete (Vieta), Francois, Seigneur de La Bigottiere (1540-1603): French mathematician; founder of modern algebra, which he applied to geometry and trigonometry.

Vignola, Giacomo Barozzi da (1507-1573): Italian architect; architectural theorist.

Vincent of Beauvais (1190-1264): French Dominican; author of comprehensive scientific encyclopedia.

Vinci, Leonardo da (1452-1519): Florentine painter, sculptor, architect, engineer, scientist; paintings mainly of religious subjects; founder of science of hydraulics, researcher in meteorology, anatomy, mathematics.

Vladimir, Saint (956-1015): First Christian ruler of Russia.

Volta, Alessandro, Count (1754-1827): Italian physicist; early researcher in electricity; the volt named for him.

Vorosmarty, Michael (1800-1855): Hungarian poet; his lyric poem "Szozat" became a national anthem.

W-Z

Wagner, Robert F. (1877-1953): American public official and judge, b. Nastatten Hessen, Germany; US senator, 1926-49; sponsor of Wagner National Labor Relations Act; convert, 1946.

Waldseemuller, Martin (1470-1518): German cartographer; made first modern atlas; first to use the name America.

Walker, Frank C. (1886-1959): American politician, cabinet official; US postmaster general, 1940-45.

Walsh, James Joseph (1865-1942): American physician, author; *The Thirteenth, the Greatest of Centuries.*

Walsh, William Thomas (1891-1949): American historian.

Walworth, Clarence Augustus (1820-1900): American priest; convert, 1845; ordained, 1848; assisted Isaac Hecker in founding the Paulists, whom he left because of illness; author.

Warren, Leonard (1911-1960): American opera star; convert from Judaism 1942; baritone of Metropolitan Opera.

Wattson, Lewis Thomas (Father James Francis Paul) (1863-1940): American founder; as Episcopalian presbyter, founded Friars of the Atonement, 1899; inaugurated Chair of Unity Octave, 1908; founded St. Christopher's Inn, Garrison, N.Y.; convert with members of his community, 1909; ordained priest, 1910.

Waugh, Evelyn (1903-1966): English writer; convert, 1930.

Weber, Karl Maria von (1786-1826): German composer of operatic and other works; a founder of German opera.

Weigel, Gustave (1900-1964): American Jesuit priest, theologian, author; pioneer in Catholic-Protestant dialogue; consultor of the Vatican Secretariat for Promoting Christian Unity.

White, Edward Douglass (1845-1921): American jurist; US senator, 1891-94; associate justice US Supreme Court, 1894-1910; chief justice, 1910-21; wrote decisions for more than 700 of the 4,000 cases decided during his time on the Court. Represents Louisiana in Statuary Hall.

White, Helen C. (1896-1967): American educator, author.

Wilde, Oscar (1856-1900): Irish poet; dramatist; reconciled to the Church before his death in France.

William of Ockham (Occam) (1300-1349): English Franciscan; philosopher, logician; author of the philosophical axiom, "beings are not to be multiplied without necessity."

William the Conqueror (1027-1087): Duke of Normandy; invaded England, 1066, defeated Harold at Hastings, crowned King of England.

Williams, Michael (1877-1950): American journalist and author, b. Halifax, Nova Scotia; founded *Commonweal*, 1924.

Winckelmann, Johann Joachim (1717-1768): German art historian, classical archaeologist; convert, 1754.

Windle, Sir Bertram (1858-1929): English scientist; professor at Toronto University, Canada, from 1919; author of works intended to explain relations between scientific progress and Church teaching.

Windthorst, Ludwig (1812-1891): German statesman, leader of Center Party.

Wiseman, Nicholas Patrick (1802-1865): English cardinal, archbishop of Westminster; influenced Catholic revival, encouraged Oxford Movement.

Wynne, Robert J. (1851-1922): American cabinet official; US postmaster general, 1904-05.

Ximenez (Jimenez) de Cisneros, Francisco (1437-1517): Spanish Franciscan, cardinal, statesman.

Yoshida, Shigeru (1878-1967): Japanese statesman; prime minister of Japan, 1946-54; convert shortly before his death.

Zrinyi, Nicholas, Count (1620-1664): Hungarian general, poet; author of first Hungarian epic, *The Fall of Szigets.*

Zurbaran, Francisco de (1598-1664): Spanish painter; religious subjects.

MISSIONARIES TO THE AMERICAS

Allouez, Claude Jean (1622-1689): French Jesuit; missionary in Canada and midwestern US; preached to 20 different tribes of Indians and baptized over 10,000; vicar general of Northwest.

Altham, John (1589-1640): English Jesuit; missionary among Indians in Maryland.

Anchieta, Jose (1534-1597): Portuguese Jesuit; missionary in Brazil; writer.

Andreis, Felix de (1778-1820): Italian Vincentian; missionary and educator in western US.

Aparicio, Bl. Sebastian (1502-1600): Franciscan brother, born Spain; settled in Mexico, c. 1533; worked as road builder and farmer before becoming Franciscan at about the age of 70; beatified, 1787.

Badin, Stephen T. (1768-1853): French missioner; came to US, 1792, when Sulpician seminary in Paris was closed; ordained, 1793, Baltimore, the first priest ordained in US; missionary in Kentucky, Ohio and Michigan; bought land on which Notre Dame University now stands; buried on its campus.

Baraga, Frederic (1797-1868): Slovenian missionary bishop in US; studied at Ljubljana and Vienna, ordained, 1823; came to US, 1830; missionary to Indians of Upper Michigan; first bishop of Marquette, 1857-1868; wrote Chippewa grammar, dictionary, prayer book and other works.

Bertran, St. Louis (1526-1581): Spanish Dominican; missionary in Colombia and Caribbean, 1562-69; canonized, 1671.

Bourgeoys, Bl. Marguerite (1620-1700): French foundress, missionary; settled in Canada, 1653; founded Congregation of Notre Dame de Montreal, 1658; beatified, 1950.

Brebeuf, St. John de (1593-1649): French Jesuit; missionary among Huron Indians in Canada; martyred by Iroquois, Mar. 16, 1649; canonized, 1930; one of Jesuit North American martyrs.

Cancer de Barbastro, Louis (1500-1549): Spanish Dominican; began missionary work in Middle America, 1533; killed at Tampa Bay, Fla.

Castillo, Bl. John de (1596-1628): Spanish Jesuit; worked in Paraguay Indian mission settlements (reductions); martyred; beatified, 1934.

Catala, Magin (1761-1830): Spanish Franciscan; worked in California mission of Santa Clara for 36 years.

Chabanel, St. Noel (1613-1649): French Jesuit; missionary among Huron Indians in Canada; murdered by renegade Huron, Dec. 8, 1649; canonized, 1930; one of Jesuit North American martyrs.

Chaumonot, Pierre Joseph (1611-1693): French Jesuit; missionary among Indians in Canada.

Claver, St. Peter (1581-1654): Spanish Jesuit; missionary among Negroes of South America and West Indies; canonized, 1888; patron of Catholic missions among Negroes.

Daniel, St. Anthony (1601-1648): French Jesuit; missionary among Huron Indians in Canada; martyred by Iroquois, July 4, 1648; canonized, 1930; one of Jesuit North American martyrs.

De Smet, Pierre Jean (1801-1873): Belgian-born Jesuit; missionary among Indians of northwestern US; served as intermediary between Indians and US government; wrote on Indian culture.

Duchesne, Bl. Rose Philippine (1769-1852): French nun; educator and missionary in the US; established first convent of the Society of the Sacred Heart in the US, at St. Charles, Mo. (later Florissant); founded schools for girls; did missionary work among Indians; beatified, 1940.

Farmer, Ferdinand (family name, Steinmeyer) (1720-1786): German Jesuit; missionary in Philadelphia, where he died; one of the first missionaries in New Jersey.

Flaget, Benedict J. (1763-1850): French Sulpician bishop; came to US, 1792; missionary and educator in US; first bishop of Bardstown, Ky. (now Louisville), 1810-32; 1833-50.

Gallitzin, Demetrius (1770-1840): Russian prince, born The Hague; convert, 1787; ordained priest at Baltimore, 1795; frontier missionary, known as Father Smith; Gallitzin, Pa., named for him.

Garnier, St. Charles (c. 1606-1649): French Jesuit; missionary among Hurons in Canada; martyred by Iroquois, Dec. 7, 1649; canonized, 1930; one of Jesuit North American martyrs.

Gibault, Pierre (1737-1804): Canadian missionary in Illinois and Indiana; aided in securing states of Ohio, Indiana, Illinois, Michigan and Wisconsin for the Americans during Revolution.

Gonzalez, Bl. Roch (1576-1628): Paraguayan Jesuit; worked in Paraguay Indian mission settlements (reductions); martyred; beatified, 1934.

Goupil, St. Rene (1607-1642): French Jesuit brother; missionary companion of St. Isaac Jogues among the Hurons; martyred, Sept. 29, 1642; canonized, 1930; one of Jesuit North American martyrs.

Gravier, Jacques (1651-1708): French Jesuit; missionary among Indians of Canada and midwestern US.

Jogues, St. Isaac (1607-1646): French Jesuit; missionary among Indians in Canada; martyred near present site of Auriesville, N.Y., by Mohawks, Oct. 18, 1646; canonized, 1930; one of Jesuit North American martyrs.

Kino, Eusebio (1645-1711): Italian Jesuit; missionary and explorer in US; arrived Southwest, 1681; established 25 Indian missions, took part in 14 exploring expeditions in northern Mexico, Arizona and southern California; helped develop livestock raising and farming in the area. He was selected in 1965 to represent Arizona in Statuary Hall.

Lalande, St. John (d. 1646): French Jesuit brother; martyred by Mohawks at Auriesville, N. Y., Oct. 19, 1646; canonized, 1930; one of Jesuit North American martyrs.

Lalemant, St. Gabriel (1610-1649): French Jesuit; missionary among the Hurons in Canada; martyred by the Iroquois, Mar. 17, 1649; canonized, 1930; one of Jesuit North American martyrs.

Lamy, Jean Baptiste (1814-1888): French prelate; came to US, 1839; missionary in Ohio and Kentucky; bishop in Southwest from 1850; first bishop (later archbishop) of Santa Fe, 1850-1885. He was nominated in 1951 to represent New Mexico in Statuary Hall.

Las Casas, Bartolome (1474-1566): Spanish Dominican; missionary in Haiti, Jamaica and Venezuela; reformer of abuses against Indians and Negroes; bishop of Chalapas, Mexico, 1544-47; historian.

Manogue, Patrick (1831-1895): Missionary bishop in US, b. Ireland; migrated to US; miner in California; studied for priesthood at St. Mary's of the Lake, Chicago, and St. Sulpice, Paris; ordained, 1861; missionary among Indians of California and Nevada; coadjutor bishop, 1881-84, and bishop, 1884-86, of Grass Valley; first bishop of Sacramento, 1886-1895, when see was transferred there.

Margil, Antonio (1657-1726): Spanish Franciscan; missionary in Middle America; apostle of Guatemala; established missions in Texas.

Marie de l'Incarnation, Ven. (1599-1672): French Ursuline nun; arrived in Canada, 1639; first superior of Ursulines in Quebec; missionary to Indians; writer.

Marquette, Jacques (1637-1675): French Jesuit; missionary and explorer in America; sent to New France, 1666; began missionary work among Ottawa Indians on Lake Superior, 1668; accompanied Joliet down the Mississippi to mouth of the Arkansas, 1673, and returned to Lake Michigan by way of Illinois River; made a second trip over the same route; his diary and map are of historical significance. He was selected in 1895 to represent Wisconsin in Statuary Hall.

Massias, Bl. John de (1585-1645); Dominican brother, a native of Spain; entered Dominican Friary at Lima, Peru, 1622; served as doorkeeper until his death; beatified, 1837.

Mazzuchelli, Samuel C. (1806-1864): Italian Dominican; missionary in midwestern US; called Builder of the West; writer.

Membre, Zenobius (1645-1687): French Franciscan; missionary among Indians of Illinois; accompanied LaSalle expedition down the Mississippi (1681-1682) and Louisiana colonizing expedition (1684) which landed in Texas; murdered by Indians.

Mogrovejo, St. Toribio Alfonso de (1538-1606): Spanish archbishop of Lima, Peru, c. 1580-1606; canonized 1726.

Nerinckx, Charles (1761-1824): Belgian priest; missionary in Kentucky; founded Sisters of Loretto at the Foot of the Cross.

Nobrega, Manoel (1517-1570): Portuguese Jesuit; leader of first Jesuit missionaries to Brazil, 1549.

Padilla, Juan de (d. 1542): Spanish Franciscan; missionary among Indians of Mexico and southwestern US; killed by Indians in Kansas; protomartyr of the US.

Palou, Francisco (c. 1722-1789): Spanish Franciscan; accompanied Junipero Serra to Mexico, 1749; founded Mission Dolores in San Francisco; wrote history of the Franciscans in California.

Peter of Ghent (d. 1572): Belgian Franciscan brother; missionary in Mexico for 49 years.

Porres, St. Martin de (1569-1639): Peruvian Dominican oblate; his father was a Spanish soldier and his mother a Negro freedwoman from Panama; called wonder worker of Peru; beatified, 1837; canonized, 1962.

Quiroga, Vasco de (1470-1565): Spanish missionary in Mexico; founded hospitals; bishop of Michoacan, 1537.

Ravalli, Antonio (1811-1884): Italian Jesuit; missionary in far-western United States, mostly Montana, for 40 years.

Raymbaut, Charles (1602-1643): French Jesuit; missionary among Indians of Canada and northern US.

Richard, Gabriel (1767-1832): French Sulpician; missionary in Illinois and Michigan; a founder of University of Michigan; elected delegate to Congress from Michigan, 1823; first priest to hold seat in the House of Representatives.

Rodriguez, Bl. Alonso (1598-1628): Spanish Jesuit; missionary in Paraguay; martyred; beatified, 1934.

Rosati, Joseph (1789-1843): Italian Vincentian; missionary bishop in US (vicar apostolic of Mississippi and Alabama, 1822; coadjutor of Louisiana and the Two Floridas, 1823-26; administrator of New Orleans, 1826-29; first bishop of St. Louis, 1826-1843).

Sahagun, Bernardino de (c. 1500-1590): Spanish Franciscan; missionary in Mexico for over 60 years; expert on Aztec archaeology.

Seelos, Francis X. (1819-1867): Redemptorist missionary, born Bavaria; ordained, 1844, at Baltimore; missionary in Pittsburgh and New Orleans.

Serra, Junipero (1713-1784): Spanish Franciscan, b. Majorca; missionary in America; arrived Mexico, 1749, where he did missionary work for 20 years; began work in Upper California in 1769 and established nine of the 21 Franciscan missions along the Pacific coast; baptized some 6,000 Indians and confirmed almost 5,000; a cultural pioneer of California. Represents California in Statuary Hall.

Seghers, Charles J. (1839-1886): Belgian missionary bishop in North America; Apostle of Alaska; archbishop of Oregon City (now Portland), 1880-1884; murdered by berserk companion while on missionary journey.

Solanus, St. Francis (1549-1610): Spanish Franciscan; missionary in Paraguay, Argentina and Peru; Wonder Worker of the New World; canonized, 1726.

Sorin, Edward F. (1814-1893): French priest; member of Congregation of Holy Cross; sent to US in 1841; founder and first president of the University of Notre Dame; missionary in Indiana and Michigan.

Todadilla, Anthony de (1704-1746): Spanish Capuchin; missionary to Indians of Venezuela; killed by Motilones.

Twelve Apostles of Mexico (early 16th century): Franciscan priests; arrived in Mexico, 1524: Fathers Martin de Valencia (leader), Francisco de Soto, Martin de la Coruna, Juan Suares, Antonio de Ciudad Rodrigo, Toribio de Benevente, Garcia de Cisneros, Luis de Fuensalida, Juuan de Ribas, Francisco Ximenes; Brothers Andres de Coroboda, Juan de Palos.

Valdivia, Luis de (1561-1641): Spanish Jesuit; defender of Indians in Peru and Chile.

Vasques de Espinosa, Antonio (early 17th century): Spanish Carmelite; missionary and explorer in Mexico, Panama and western coast of South America.

Vieira, Antonio (1608-1687): Portuguese Jesuit; preacher; missionary in Peru and Chile; protector of Indians against exploitation by slave owners and traders; considered foremost prose writer of 17th-century Portugal.

White, Andrew (1579-1656): English Jesuit; missionary among Indians in Maryland.

Wimmer, Boniface (1809-1887): German Benedictine; missionary among German immigrants in the US.

Youville, Bl. Marie Marguerite d' (1701-1771): Canadian widow; foundress of Sisters of Charity (Grey Nuns), 1738, at Montreal: beatified, 1959.

Zumarraga, Juan de (1468-1548): Spanish Franciscan; missionary; first bishop of Mexico; introduced first printing press in New World, published first book in America, a catechism for Aztec Indians; extended missions in Mexico and Central America; vigorous opponent of exploitation of Indians; approved of devotions at Guadalupe; leading figure in early church history in Mexico.

Bicentennial Observance

Cardinal John F. Dearden, in a letter addressed to bishops throughout the country early in the summer of 1974, called for the development of grassroots participation in a church celebration of the nation's bicentennial in 1976.

The title of the celebration will be "Liberty and Justice for All: An American Catholic Bicentennial Observance." Its central purpose will be "to elicit from the Catholic community an expression of the meaning of 'Liberty and Justice for All.'"

Cardinal Dearden, chairman of the U.S. Bishops' Bicentennial Committee, said the committee felt that "a critically important witness to the religious and cultural heritage (of the country) can be made through this effort."

To that end, he said: "The . . . committee will invite Catholic individuals, groups, associations and institutions throughout country to reflect upon the concept of liberty and justice for all as it relates today to entities which many Americans value in a unique way. These include the family, the neighborhood, one's ethnic or racial roots, the individual person, the nation, the Church, and the world community itself."

One of the highlights of the observance will be a week-long national conference in October, 1976, tentatively in Detroit.

FRANCISCAN MISSIONS OF UPPER CALIFORNIA

The 21 Franciscan missions of Upper California were established during the 54-year period from 1769 to 1822. Located along the old El Camino Real, or King's Highway, they extended from San Diego to San Francisco and were the centers of Indian civilization, Christianity and industry in the early history of the state.

Fray Junipero Serra was the great pioneer of the missions of Upper California. He and his successor as superior of the work, Fray Fermin Lasuen, each directed the establishment of nine missions. One hundred and 46 priests of the Order of Friars Minor, most of them Spaniards, labored in the region from 1769 to 1845; 67 of them died at their posts, two as martyrs. The regular time of mission service was 10 years.

The missions were secularized by the Mexican government in the 1830's but were subsequently restored to the Church by the US government. They are now variously used as the sites of parish churches, a university, houses of study and museums.

The names of the missions and the order of their establishment were as follows:

San Diego de Alcala, San Carlos Borromeo (El Carmelo), San Antonio de Padua, San Gabriel Arcangel, San Luis Obispo de Tolosa, San Francisco de Asis (Dolores), San Juan Capistrano;

Santa Clara de Asis, San Buenaventura, Santa Barbara, La Purisima Concepcion de Maria Santisima, Santa Cruz, Nuestra Senora de la Soledad, San Jose de Guadalupe;

San Juan Bautista, San Miguel Arcangel, San Fernando Rey de Espana, San Luis Rey de Francia, Santa Ines, San Rafael Arcangel, San Francisco Solano de Sonoma (Sonoma).

The Church in Countries Throughout the World

(Principal source for statistics: *Annuario Pontificio, 1974.* Other sources are noted in the text. See Index for additional entries on 1974 events in various countries.)

Abbreviation code: archd., — archdiocese; dioc. — diocese; ap. ex. — apostolic exarchate; prel. — prelature; abb. — abbacy; v.a. — vicariate apostolic; p.a. — prefecture apostolic; a.a. — apostolic administration; card. — cardinal; abp., — archbishop; nat. — native; bp. — bishop; priests (dioc. — diocesan or secular priests; rel. — those belonging to religious orders); sem. — seminarians; p.d. — permanent deacibsl n, rel. — men religious (include brothers and priests belonging to religious orders); w. rel. — women religious; sch. — schools; inst. — charitable institutes; Caths. — Catholic population; tot. pop. — total population.

Afars and Issas (formerly French Somaliland): French territory in east Africa, on the Gulf of Aden; capital, Djibouti. Christianity in the area, formerly part of Ethiopia, antedated but was overcome by the Arab invasion of 1200. Modern evangelization, begun in the latter part of the 19th century, had meager results. The hierarchy was established in 1955. The territory has an apostolic delegate (to the Red Sea Region).

Dioc., 1; bp., 1; parishes, 5; priests, 12 (5 dioc., 7 rel.); sem., 1; m. rel., 20; w. rel., 39; sch., 7; inst., 4; Caths., 12,000 (9.5%); tot. pop., 125,000.

Afghanistan: Republic in south-central Asia; capital, Kabul. Christianity antedated Moslem conquest in the seventh century but was overcome by it. All inhabitants are subject to the law of Islam. Christian missionaries are prohibited. The few Catholics in the country are foreign embassy and technical personnel. Population (UN est., 1972), 17,880,000..

Albania: Communist people's republic in the Balkans, bordering the Adriatic Sea; capital, Tirana. Christianity was introduced before the middle of the fourth century. The Byzantine Church became Orthodox following the schism of 1054. The Orthodox Church now existing is under government control. The Latin (Roman) Church, which prevailed in the north, has been practically wiped out by persecution since 1945, with the expulsion of Italian missionaries; a number of death and prison sentences and other repressive measures against bishops, priests, religious and lay persons; the closing of Catholic schools and a seminary; the cutting of lines of communication with the Holy See. In 1967, the government proclaimed itself the first atheist state in the world.

Archd., 2; dioc., 3; abb., 1; a.a. 1; bp., 3. No statistics are available. The Catholic population was estimated at 143,500 in 1969 by the CSMC *"World Mission Map"; tot. pop. (1971 est.), 2,230,000.*

Algeria: Republic in northwest Africa: capital, Algiers. Christianity, introduced at an early date, succumbed to Vandal devastation in the fifth century and Moslem conquest in 709, but survived for centuries in small communities into the 12th century. Missionary work was unsuccessful except in service to traders, military personnel and captives along the coast. Church organization was established after the French gained control of the territory in the 1830's. A large number of Catholics were among the estimated million Europeans who left the country after it secured independence from France July 5, 1962. Islam is the state religion. Algeria maintains diplomatic relations with Vatican City.

Archd., 1; dioc., 3; card., 1; bp., 3; parishes, 92; priests, 329 (149 dioc., 180 rel.); sem., 1; p.d., 1; m. rel., 229; w. rel., 1,067; sch., 147; inst., 85; Caths., 65,500 (.4%); tot. pop. (UN est., 1972), 15,270,000.

Andorra: Autonomous principality in the Pyrenees, under the rule of co-princes — the French head of state and the bishop of Urgel, Spain; capital, Andorra la Vella. Christianity was introduced at an early date. Catholicism is the state religion. The principality is under the ecclesiastical jurisdiction of the Spanish diocese of Urgel.

Total pop., 23,000 (almost entirely Catholic).

Angola: Portuguese territory in west Africa; capital, Luanda. Evangelization by Catholic missionaries, dating from about 1570, reached high points in the 17th and 18th centuries.

Archd., 1; dioc., 7; abp., 1; bp., 6; parishes, 130; priests, 536 (204 dioc., 332 rel.); sem., 171; m. rel., 482; w. rel., 891; sch., 1,502; inst., 274; Caths., 2,667,210 (45.2%); tot. pop., 5,891,724.

Antigua: Self-governing state in Caribbean; capital, St. John's.

Dioc., 1; bp., 1; parishes, 11; priests, 12 (1 dioc., 11 rel.); m. rel., 17; w. rel., 10; sch., 7; Caths., 9,456; tot. pop., 130,907. (Figures are for diocese of St. John's, Antigua, and include the islands of Antigua, Barbuda, Saint Kitts, Nevis, Anguilla, Montserrat, Redonda, Sombrero.)

Arabian Peninsula: Includes Saudi Arabia, Peoples Republic of Yemen, Yemen Arab Republic, Oman, Bahrein, Qatar, United Arab Emirates. Christianity, introduced in various parts of the peninsula in early Christian centuries, succumbed to Islam in the seventh century. The native population is entirely Moslem. The only Christians are foreigners. The peninsula has an apostolic delegate (to the Red Sea Region).

V.a., 1; parishes, 11; priests, 17 (1 dioc., 16

rel.); m. rel., 14; w. rel., 36; sch., 15; Caths., 8,620; tot. pop., 12,357,800. (Statistics are for the vicariate apostolic of Arabia which includes most of the Arabian Peninsula; the vicariate is located in Aden, Peoples Republic of Yemen.)

Argentina: Republic in southeast South America, bordering on the Atlantic; capital, Buenos Aires. Priests were with the Magellan exploration party and the first Mass in the country was celebrated Apr. 1, 1519. Missionary work began in the 1530's, diocesan organization in the late 1540's, and effective evangelization about 1570. Independence from Spain was proclaimed in 1816. Since its establishment in the country, the Church has been influenced by Spanish cultural and institutional forces, antagonistic liberalism, government interference and opposition; the latter reached a climax during the last five years of the first presidency of Juan Peron (1946-1955). Catholicism is the state religion. Argentina maintains diplomatic relations with Vatican City.

Archd., 12; dioc., 39; prel., 2; ap. ex., 1; ord., 1; card., 2; abp., 10; bp., 51; parishes, 1,873; priests, 5,236 (2,468 dioc., 2,768 rel.); sem., 306; p.d., 1; m. rel., 4,167; w. rel., 12,536; sch., 2,477; inst., 560; Caths., 22,062,214; (90.9%); tot. pop., 24,246,179.

Australia: Commonwealth, member of the British Commonwealth, island continent southeast of Asia; capital, Canberra. The first Catholics in the country were Irish under penal sentence, 1795-1804; the first public Mass was celebrated May 15, 1803. Official organization of the Church dates from 1820. Australia established diplomatic relations with Vatican City in 1973.

Archd., 7; dioc., 20; abb., 1; mission "sui juris," 1; ap. ex., 1; card., 3; abp., 6; bp., 31; parishes, 1,392; priests, 3,756 (2,338 dioc., 1,418 rel.); sem., 512; p.d., 3; m. rel., 4,071; w. rel., 13,220; sch., 1,949; inst., 268; Caths., 3,155,253 (24%); tot. pop. (Gov. est., 1973), 13,020,300.

Austria: Republic in central Europe; capital, Vienna. Christianity was introduced by the end of the third century, strengthened considerably by conversion of the Bavarians from about 600, and firmly established in the second half of the eighth century. Catholicism survived and grew stronger as the principal religion in the country in the post-Reformation period, but suffered from Josephinism in the 18th century. Although liberated from much government harassment in the aftermath of the Revolution of 1848, it came under pressure again some 20 years later in the Kulturkampf. During this time the Church became involved with a developing social movement. The Church faced strong opposition from Socialists after World War I and suffered persecution from 1938 to 1945 during the Nazi regime. Some Church-state matters are regulated by a concordat original-

ly concluded in 1934. Austria maintains diplomatic relations with Vatican City.

Archd., 2; dioc., 7; abb., 1; ord., 1; card., 1; abp., 2; bp., 12; parishes, 2,958; priests, 6,105 (3,635 dioc., 2,470 rel.); sem., 692; p.d., 46; m. rel., 3,515; w. rel., 13,581; sch., 314; inst. 764; Caths., 6,718,038 (90%); tot. pop., 7,454,892.

Azores: North Atlantic island group 750 miles west of Portugal, of which it is part. Christianity was introduced in the second quarter of the 15th century.

Bahamas: Independent (July 10, 1973) island group in the British Commonwealth, consisting of some 700 (30 inhabited) small islands southeast of Florida and north of Cuba; capital, Nassau. On Oct. 12, 1492, Columbus landed on one of these islands, where the first Mass was celebrated in the New World. Organization of the Catholic Church in the Bahamas dates from about the middle of the 19th century.

Dioc., 1; bp., 1; parishes, 29; priests, 44 (11 dioc., 33 rel.); sem., 3; m. rel., 39; w. rel., 77; sch., 18; inst., 5; Caths., 36,040; tot. pop., 176,000.

Bahrein: See Arabian Peninsula.

Balearic Islands: Spanish province consisting of an island group in the western Mediterranean. Statistics are included in those for Spain.

Bangladesh: Formerly the eastern portion of Pakistan. Officially constituted as a separate nation Dec. 16, 1971; capital, Dacca. Islam is the principal religion; freedom of religion is granted. There were Jesuit, Dominican and Augustinian missionaries in the area in the 16th century. A vicariate apostolic (of Bengali) was established in 1834; the hierarchy was erected in 1950. Bangladesh established diplomatic relations with Vatican City in 1972.

Archd., 1; dioc., 3; abp., 1 (nat.); bp., 3 (nat.); parishes, 59; priests, 133 (34 dioc., 99 rel.); sem., 29; m. rel., 165; w. rel., 362; sch., 189; inst., 67; Caths., 120,473 (.1%); tot. pop. (1973 est.), 75,000,000.

Barbados: Parliamentary democracy in the British Commonwealth (independent since 1966), easternmost of the Caribbean islands; capital, Bridgetown. About 70 per cent of the people are Anglicans.

Dioc., 1; bp., 1; parishes, 10; priests, 18 (2 dioc., 16 rel.); sem., 1; m. rel., 28; w. rel., 68; sch., 15; inst., 2; Caths., 24,115; tot. pop., 330,000. (Statistics are for the Bridgetown-Kingston diocese which includes the island of St. Vincent.)

Belgium: Constitutional monarchy in northwestern Europe; capital, Brussels. Christianity was introduced about the first quarter of the fourth century and major evangelization was completed about 730. During the rest of the medieval period the Church had firm diocesan and parochial organization, generally vigorous monastic life, and influential monastic and cathedral schools. Lutherans and Calvinists made some gains during the Reformation period but there was a strong Catholic restoration in the first half of the 17th century, when the country was under Spanish rule. Jansenism disturbed the Church from about 1640 into the 18th century. Josephinism, imposed by an Austrian regime, hampered the Church late in the same century. Repressive and persecutory measures were enforced during the Napoleonic conquest. Freedom came with separation of Church and state in the wake of the Revolution of 1830, which ended the reign of William I. Thereafter, the Church encountered serious problems with philosophical liberalism and political socialism. Catholics have long been engaged in strong educational, social and political movements. Except for one five-year period (1880-1884), Belgium has maintained diplomatic relations with Vatican City since 1835.

Archd., 1; dioc., 7; card., 1; abp., 1; bp., 13; parishes, 3,234; priests, 13,697 (9,278 dioc., 4,419 rel.); sem., 470; p.d., 73; m. rel., 5,516; w. rel., 29,484; sch., 5,484; inst., 902; Caths., 8,816,221 (90.9%); tot. pop. (1973 est.), 9,693,000.

Belize (formerly British Honduras): Self-governing colony in Central America; capital, Belmopan. Its history has points in common with Guatemala, where evangelization began in the 16th century.

Dioc., 1; bp., 1; parishes, 12; priests, 38 (10 dioc., 28 rel.); sem., 5; p.d., 1; Caths., 78,150 (61%); tot. pop., 127,000.

Bermuda: British colony, consisting of 360 islands (20 of them inhabited) nearly 600 miles east of Cape Hatteras; capital, Hamilton. Catholics were not permitted until about 1800. Occasional pastoral care was provided the few Catholics there by visiting priests during the 19th century. Early in the 1900's priests from Halifax began serving the area. A prefecture apostolic was set up in 1953. The first bishop assumed jurisdiction in 1956. The only Catholic school in Bermuda was the first to admit black students, in 1961.

Dioc., 1; bp., 1; parishes, 7; priests, 10 (1 dioc., 9 rel.); m. rel., 9; w. rel., 16; sch., 2; Caths., 8,832 (16.6%); tot. pop., 53,000.

Bhutan: Constitutional monarchy in the Himalayas, northeast of India; capital, Thimphu. Most of the population are Buddhists. Ecclesiastical jurisdiction is under the archdiocese of Shillong-Gauhati, India.

Pop. (1973 est.), 1,150.000.

Bolivia: Republic in central South America; capital, Sucre; seat of government, La Paz. Catholicism, the official religion, was introduced in the 1530's and the first bishopric was established in 1552. Effective evangelization among the Indians, slow to start, reached high points in the middle of the 18th and the beginning of the 19th centuries and was resumed about 1840. Independence from Spain

was proclaimed in 1825, at the end of a campaign that started in 1809. The republic inherited the Spanish right of nominating candidates for bishoprics. Church-state relations are regulated by a 1951 concordat with the Holy See. Bolivia maintains diplomatic relations with Vatican City.

Archd., 2; dioc., 5; prel., 3; v.a., 6; card., 1; abp., 1; bp., 20; parishes, 339; priests, 812 (243 dioc., 569 rel.); sem., 49; m. rel., 797; w. rel., 1,278; sch., 403; inst., 219; Caths., 4,780,603 (93.8%); tot. pop., 5,092,605.

Botswana: Republic (independent since 1966) in southern Africa, member of the British Commonwealth; capital, Gaborone. Botswana has an apostolic delegate (to South Africa).

Dioc., 1; bp., 1; parishes, 15; priests, 26 (2 dioc., 24 rel.); sem., 1; m. rel., 26; w. rel., 37; sch., 11; inst., 2; Caths., 21,009 (3%); tot. pop. 690,000.

Brazil: Republic in northeast South America; capital, Brasilia. One of several priests with the discovery party celebrated the first Mass in the country Apr. 26, 1500. Evangelization began some years later and the first diocese was erected in 1551. During the colonial period, which lasted until 1822, evangelization made some notable progress—especially in the Amazon region between 1680 and 1750—but was seriously hindered by government policy and the attitude of colonists regarding Amazon Indians the missionaries tried to protect from exploitation and slavery. The Jesuits were suppressed in 1782 and other missionaries expelled as well. Liberal anti-Church influence grew in strength. The government gave minimal support but exercised maximum control over the Church. After the proclamation of independence from Portugal in 1822 and throughout the regency, government control was tightened and the Church suffered greatly from dissident actions of ecclesiastical brotherhoods, Masonic anti-clericalism and general decline in religious life. Church and state were separated by the constitution of 1891, proclaimed two years after the end of the empire. The Church carried into the 20th century a load of inherited liabilities and problems amid increasingly difficult political, economic and social conditions affecting the majority of the population. A number of bishops, priests, religious and lay persons have been active in movements for social and religious reform. Brazil maintains diplomatic relations with Vatican City.

Archd., 32; dioc., 138; prel., 41; abb., 2; ord., 1; card., 6; abp., 30; bp., 198; parishes, 5,669; priests, 12,943 (5,124 dioc., 7,819 rel.); sem., 939; p.d., 146; m. rel., 10,927; w. rel., 35,984; sch., 4,317; inst., 3,302; Caths. (est.), 88,963,271 (88.8%); tot. pop. (Govt. est.), 100,000,000.

Brunei: State under British protection, on the northern coast of Borneo; capital, Brunei. Statistics are included in those for Malaysia.

Bulgaria: People's republic in southeastern Europe on the eastern part of the Balkan peninsula; capital, Sofia. Christianity was introduced before 343 but disappeared with the migration of Slavs into the territory. The baptism of Boris I about 865 ushered in a new period of Christianity which soon became involved in switches of loyalty between Constantinople and Rome. Through it all the Byzantine, and later Orthodox, element remained stronger and survived under the rule of Ottoman Turks into the 19th century. The few modern Latin Catholics in the country are traceable to 17th century converts from heresy. The Byzantines are products of a reunion movement of the 19th century. In 1947 the constitution of the new republic decreed the separation of Church and state. Catholic schools and institutions were abolished and foreign religious banished in 1948. A year later the apostolic delegate was expelled. Bishop Eugene Bosilkoff was condemned to death (his fate is still unknown) and Ivan Romanoff, the vicar apostolic of Plovdiv, died in prison in 1952. Roman and Bulgarian Rite vicars apostolic were permitted to attend the Second Vatican Council from 1962 to 1965. All church activity is under surveillance and/or control by the government, which professes to be atheistic. Pastoral and related activities are strictly limited. Most of the population is Orthodox.

Dioc., 1; v.a., 1; ap. ex., 1; bp., 2 (includes Bishop Bosilkoff, see above); tot. pop. (UN est., 1972), 8,580,000. No recent Catholic statistics are available. In 1969, the estimated Catholic population was 50,000.

Burma: Union of Burma, a republic in southeast Asia, on the Bay of Bengal; capital, Rangoon. Christianity was introduced about 1500. Small-scale evangelization had limited results from the middle of the 16th century until the 1850's when effective organization of the Church began. The hierarchy was established in 1955. Buddhism was declared the state religion in 1961, although all other religions are respected. In 1965, church schools were nationalized. In 1966, all foreign missionaries who had entered the country after 1948 for the first time were forced to leave when the government refused to renew their work permits. Despite these setbacks, the Church has shown some progress in recent years. Burma has an apostolic delegate (pronuncio to India).

Archd., 2; dioc., 6; abp., 2 (nat.); bp., 6 (3 nat.); parishes, 120; priests, 161 (115 dioc., 46 rel.); sem., 79; p.d., 19; m. rel., 132; w. rel., 569; sch., 227; inst., 160; Caths., 275,993 (.9%); tot. pop., 28,900,000.

Burundi: Republic since 1966, near the equator in east-central Africa; capital, Bujumbura. The first permanent Catholic mission station was established late in the 19th century. Large numbers of persons were received into the Church following the ordina-

tion of the first Burundi priests in 1925. The first native bishop was appointed in 1959. Most education takes place in schools under Catholic auspices. During the past several years, the country has been torn by tribal warfare between the Tutsis, the ruling minority, and the Hutus. Burundi maintains diplomatic relations with Vatican City.

Archd., 1; dioc., 5; abp., 1 (nat.); bp., 5 (nat.); parishes, 175; priests, 433 (160 dioc., 273 rel.); sem., 58; m. rel., 416; w. rel., 615; sch., 875; inst., 67; Caths., 1,950,929 (57%); tot. pop. (1972 est.), 3,400,000.

Cambodia: See Khmer Republic.

Cameroon: Republic in west Africa, bordering on the Gulf of Guinea; capital, Yaounde. Effective evangelization began in the 1890's, although Catholics had been in the country long before that time. In the 40-year period from 1920 to 1960, the number of Catholics increased from 60,000 to 700,000. The first native priests were ordained in 1935. Twenty years later the first native bishops were ordained and the hierarchy established. In 1971 Bishop Albert Ndongmo of Nkongsamba was sentenced to death after being convicted of plotting to overthrow the government; the sentence was later commuted to life imprisonment. Bishop Ndongmo resigned his see in March, 1973; his subsequent whereabouts and condition have not been reported. Cameroon maintains diplomatic relations with Vatican City.

Archd., 1; dioc., 12; abp., 1 (nat.); bp., 13 (7 nat.); parishes, 212; priests, 736 (236 dioc., 500 rel.); sem., 251; p.d., 11; m. rel., 777; w. rel., 1,090; sch., 1,094; inst.,215; Caths., 1,461,135 (24.3%); tot. pop. (1972 est.); 6,000,000.

Canada: Independent federation in the British Commonwealth, comprising the northern half of North America; capital, Ottawa. (See The Church in Canada.)

Archd., 18; dioc., 49; abb., 1; card., 3; abp., 16; bp., 55; parishes, 4,227; priests, 13,580 (8,082 dioc., 5,498 rel.); sem., 630; p.d., 25; m. rel., 11,045; w. rel., 44,317; sch., 2,498; inst., 409; Caths., 9,975,000 (46.2%); tot. pop., 21,550,000. Catholic and total population statistics are from the 1971 Canadian census; figures were released in 1974. The Catholic Church was the only major religious body with an increased percentage since the 1961 census — from 45.7% to 46.2%.

Canary Islands: Two Spanish provinces, consisting of seven islands, off the northwest coast of Africa. Evangelization began about 1400. Almost all of the one million inhabitants are Catholics. Statistics are included in those for Spain.

Cape Verde Islands: Portuguese overseas territory, consisting of 14 islands 300 miles west of Senegal. Evangelization began some years before establishment of the first diocese in the islands in 1532.

Dioc., 1; bp., 1; parishes, 30; priests, 50 (15

dioc., 35 rel.); sem., 10; m. rel., 38; w. rel., 30; sch., 53; inst., 3; Caths., 259,500 (96%); tot. pop., 270,000.

Caroline and Marshall Islands: US trust territory in the southwest Pacific. Effective evangelization began in the late 1880's.

V.a., 1; bp., 1; parishes, 11; priests, 35 (1 dioc., 34 rel.); sem., 9; m. rel., 47; w. rel., 44; sch., 14; Caths., 39,235 (41%); tot. pop., 95,227. Statistics are from The Official Catholic Directory, 1974.

Central African Republic: Republic (independent since 1960) in central Africa; capital, Bangui. Effective evangelization dates from 1894. The region was organized as a mission territory in 1909. The first native priest was ordained in 1938. The hierarchy was organized in 1955. The Central African Republic maintains diplomatic relations with Vatican City.

Archd., 1; dioc., 4; abp., 1; bp., 3; parishes, 67; priests, 198 (33 dioc., 165 rel.); sem., 20; m. rel., 219; w. rel., 285; sch., 17; inst., 25; Caths., 286,659 (13.3%); tot. pop., 2,145,044.

Ceuta: Spanish possession (city) on the northern tip of Africa, south of Gibraltar. Statistics are included in those for Spain.

Ceylon: See Sri Lanka, Republic of.

Chad: Republic (independent since 1960) in north-central Africa, member of the French Community; capital, N'Djamena (Fort Lamy). Evangelization began in 1929, leading to firm organization in 1947 and establishment of the hierarchy in 1955. Chad has an apostolic delegate (pro-nuncio, Central African Republic).

Archd., 1; dioc., 3; abp., 1; bp., 3; parishes, 41; priests, 165 (27 dioc., 138 rel.); sem., 8; m. rel., 178; w. rel., 109; sch., 47; inst., 30; Caths., 186,271 (4.9%); tot. pop. (est.), 3,800,000.

Chile: Republic on the southwestern coast of South America; capital, Santiago. Priests were with the Spanish conquistadores on their entrance into the territory early in the 16th century. The first parish was established in 1547 and the first bishopric in 1561. Overall organization of the Church took place later in the century. By 1650 most of the peaceful Indians in the central and northern areas were evangelized. Missionary work was more difficult in the southern region. Church activity was hampered during the campaign for independence, 1810 to 1818, and through the first years of the new government, to 1830. Later gains were made, into this century, but hindering factors were shortages of native clergy and religious and attempts by the government to control church administration through the patronage system in force while the country was under Spanish control. Separation of Church and state were decreed in the constitution of 1925. Church-state relations were strained during the regime of Marxist president Salvator Allende Gossens (1970-73). He was overthrown in a bloody

coup and was reported to have committed suicide Sept. 11, 1973. Conditions remained unsettled under the military government which assumed control after the coup. In April, 1974, the Chilean bishops issued a pastoral letter urging reconciliation in the country and criticizing government policies which were serious obstacles to it. Chile maintains diplomatic relations with Vatican City.

Archd., 5; dioc., 14; prel., 3; v.a., 2; card., 1; abp., 3; bp., 21; parishes, 849; priests, 2,206 (913 dioc., 1,293 rel.); sem., 111; p.d., 51; m. rel., 2,058; w. rel., 8,462; sch., 807; inst., 282; Caths., 8,789,333 (87.6%); tot. pop., 10,022,805.

China *(This article concerns mainland China which has been under Communist control since 1949):* People's Republic in eastern part of Asia; capital, Peking. Christianity was introduced by Nestorians who had some influence on part of the area from 635 to 845 and again from the 11th century until 1368. John of Monte Corvino started a Franciscan mission in 1294; he was ordained an archbishop about 1307. Missionary activity involving more priests increased for a while thereafter but the Franciscan mission ended in 1368. The Jesuit Matteo Ricci initiated a remarkable period of activity in the 1580's. By 1700 the number of Catholics was reported to be 300,000. The Chinese Rites controversy, concerning the adaptation of rituals and other matters to Chinese traditions and practices, ran throughout the 17th century, ending in a negative decision by mission authorities in Rome. Bl. Francis de Capillas, the protomartyr of China, was killed in 1648. Persecution, a feature of Chinese history as recurrent as changes in dynasties, occurred several times in the 18th century and resulted in the departure of most missionaries from the country. The Chinese door swung open again in the 1840's and progress in evangelization increased with an extension of legal and social tolerance. At the turn of the 20th century, however, the Boxer Rebellion took one or the other kind of toll among an estimated 30,000 victims. Missionary work in the 1900's reached a new high in every respect before the disaster of persecution initiated by Communists before and especially since they established the republic in 1949. The Reds began a savage persecution as soon as they came into power. Among its results were the expulsion of over 5,000 foreign missionaries, 510 of whom were American priests, brothers and nuns; the arrest, imprisonment and harassment of all members of the native religious, clergy and hierarchy; the forced closing of 3,932 schools, 216 hospitals, 781 dispensaries, 254 orphanages, 29 printing presses and 55 periodicals; denial of the free exercise of religion to all the faithful; the detention of hundreds of priests, religious and lay persons in jail and their employment in slave labor;

the proscription of the Legion of Mary and other Catholic Action groups for "counterrevolutionary activities" and "crimes against the new China"; complete outlawing of missionary work and pastoral activity. The government formally established a Patriotic Association of Chinese Catholics in July, 1957. Relatively few priests and lay persons joined the organization, which was condemned by Pius XII in 1958. The government formed the nucleus of what it hoped might become the hierarchy of a schismatic Chinese church by "electing" 26 bishops and having them consecrated validly but illicitly between Apr. 13, 1958, and Nov. 15, 1959, without the permission or approval of the Holy See. By Jan. 21, 1962, a total of 42 bishops were consecrated in this manner. In March, 1960, Bishop James E. Walsh, M.M., the last American missionary in China, was sentenced and placed in custody for a period of 20 years. He was released in the summer of 1970.

Archd., 20; dioc., 93; p.a., 29. No Catholic statistics are available. In 1949 there were between 3,500,000-4,000,000 Catholics, about .7 per cent of the total population; the 1969 "CSMC World Mission Map" estimated 3,200,000 Catholics, .5 per cent of the population. The latter figure is only an estimate; there is no way of knowing the actual situation. Tot. pop. (UN est., 1972), 800,720.000.

Colombia: Republic in northwest South America, with Atlantic and Pacific borders; capital, Bogota. Evangelization began in 1508. The first two dioceses were established in 1534. Vigorous development of the Church was reported by the middle of the 17th century despite obstacles posed by the multiplicity of Indian languages, government interference through patronage rights and otherwise, rivalry among religious orders and the small number of native priests among the predominantly Spanish clergy. Some persecution, including the confiscation of property, followed in the wake of the proclamation of independence from Spain in 1819. The Church was affected in many ways by the political and civil unrest of the nation through the 19th century and into the 20th. Various aspects of Churchstate relations are regulated by a concordat with the Vatican signed in July, 1973. The new concordat replaced one which had been in effect with some modifications since 1887. Colombia maintains diplomatic relations with Vatican City.

Archd., 9; dioc., 31; prel., 2; v.a., 9; p.a., 7; card., 2; parishes, 1,847; priests, 5,227 (3,053 dioc., 2,174 rel.); sem., 738; p.d., 4; m. rel., 3,505; w. rel., 17,804; sch., 3,652; inst., 1,166; Caths., 24,174,141 (96%); tot. pop., 25,048,659.(Catholic and total population, figures from the Annuario Pontificio, are higher than those from other sources which report an estimated total population of 23,000,000. The number of Catholics remains between 95 and 96 per cent of the total.)

Congo Republic: Republic in west central Africa, member of the French Community; capital, Brazzaville. Small-scale missionary work with little effect preceded modern evangelization dating from the 1880's. The work of the Church has been affected by political instability, Communist influence, tribalism and hostility to foreigners. The hierarchy was established in 1955. Congo has an apostolic delegate (pro-nuncio, Central African Republic).

Archd., 1; dioc., 2; card., 1 (nat.); bp., 2 (1 nat); parishes, 44; priests, 150 (36 dioc., 114 rel.); sem., 27; p.d., 1; m. rel., 128; w. rel., 84; inst., 8; Caths., 437,867 (44%); tot. pop. (UN est., 1972), 980,000.

Cook Islands: Self-governing territory of New Zealand, an archipelago of small islands in Oceania. Evangelization by Protestant missionaries started in 1821, resulting in a predominantly Protestant population. The first Catholic missionary work began in 1894. The hierarchy was established in 1966.

Dioc., 1; bp., 1; parishes, 11; priests, 11 (rel.); m. rel., 11; w. rel., 16; sch., 2; Caths., 3,056; tot. pop., 26,217.

Costa Rica: Republic in Central America; capital, San Jose. Evangelization began about 1520 and proceeded by degrees to real development and organization of the Church in the 17th and 18th centuries. The republic became independent in 1838. Twelve years later church jurisdiction also became independent with the establishment of a bishopric in the present capital. Costa Rica maintains diplomatic relations with Vatican City.

Archd., 1; dioc., 3; v.a., 1; abp., 1; bp., 5; parishes, 129; priests, 357 (240 dioc., 117 rel.); sem., 61; m. rel., 170; w. rel., 887; sch., 57; inst., 32; Caths., 1,751,665 (95%); tot. pop. 1,838,183.

Cuba: Republic under Communist dictatorship, south of Florida; capital, Havana. Effective evangelization began about 1514, leading eventually to the predominance of Catholicism on the island. Native vocations to the priesthood and religious life were unusually numerous in the 18th century but declined in the 19th. The island became independent of Spain in 1902 following the Spanish-American War. Fidel Castro took control of the government Jan. 1, 1959. In 1961, after Cuba was officially declared a socialist state, the University of Villanueva was closed, 350 Catholic schools were nationalized and 136 priests expelled. A greater number of foreign priests and religious had already left the country. Freedom of worship and religious instruction are limited to church premises and no social action is permitted the Church, which survives under surveillance. Cuba maintains diplomatic relations with Vatican City.

Archd., 2; dioc., 4; abp., 2; bp., 7; parishes, 228; priests, 195 (89 dioc., 106 rel.); sem., 49;

m. rel., 144; w. rel., 217; inst., 6; Caths., 4,587,041 (52%); tot. pop. 8,809,093.

Cyprus: Republic in the eastern Mediterranean; capital, Nicosia. Christianity was preached on the island in apostolic times and has a continuous history from the fourth century. Latin and Eastern rites were established but the latter prevailed and became Orthodox after the schism of 1054. Roman and Orthodox Christians have suffered under many governments, particularly during the period of Turkish dominion from late in the 16th to late in the 19th centuries, and from differences between the 80 per cent Greek majority and the Turkish minority. About 80 per cent of the population are Orthodox. Cyprus established diplomatic relations with Vatican City in 1973. Maronite Rite Catholics are under the jurisdiction of the diocese of Cyprus (of the Maronites), whose bishop resides in Lebanon. Roman Rite Catholics are under the jurisdiction of the Roman Rite patriarch of Jerusalem.

There are approximately 6,700 Catholics; total population, 651,000.

Czechoslovakia: Federal socialist republic (since 1969) in Central Europe, consisting of the Czech Socialist Republic, capital Prague; and the Slovak Socialist Republic, capital Bratislava. The republics have local autonomy but are subordinate to the Federal Assembly at Prague made up of representatives from both regions. The Czech and Slovak regions of the country have separate religious and cultural backgrounds. Christianity was introduced in Slovakia in the 8th century by Irish and German missionaries and the area was under the jurisdiction of German bishops. In 863, at the invitation of the Slovak ruler Rastislav who wanted to preserve the cultural and liturgical heritage of the people, Sts. Cyril and Methodius began pastoral and missionary work in the region, ministering to the people in their own language. The saints introduced Old Slovak (Old Church Slavonic) into the liturgy and did so much to evangelize the territory that they are venerated as the apostles of Slovakia. A diocese established at Nitra in 880 had a continuous history except for a century ending in 1024. The Church in Slovakia was severely tested by the Reformation and political upheavals. After World War I, when it became part of the Republic of Czechoslovakia, it was 75 per cent Catholic. In the Czech lands, the martyrdom of Prince Wenceslaus in 929 triggered the spread of Christianity. Prague has had a continuous history as a diocese since 973. A parish system was organized about the 13th century in Bohemia and Moravia, the land of the Czechs. Mendicant orders strengthened relations with the Latin Rite in the 13th century. In the next century the teachings of John Hus in Bohemia brought trouble to the Church in the forms of schism and heresy, and initiated a series of religious wars which continued for decades following his death at the stake in 1415. Church property was confiscated, monastic communities were scattered and even murdered, ecclesiastical organization was shattered, and so many of the faithful joined the Bohemian Brethren that Catholics became a minority. The Reformation, with the way prepared by the Hussites and cleared by other factors, affected the Church seriously. A Counter Reformation got underway in the 1560's and led to a gradual restoration through the thickets of Josephinism, the Enlightenment, liberalism and troubled politics. In 1920, two years after the establishment of the Republic of Czechoslovakia, the schismatic Czechoslovak Church was proclaimed at Prague, resulting in numerous defections from the Catholic Church in the Czech region. In Ruthenia, 112,000 became Russian Orthodox between 1918 and 1930. Vigorous persecution of the church began in Slovakia before the end of World War II when Communists mounted a 1944 offensive against bishops, priests and religious. In 1945, church schools were nationalized, youth organizations were disbanded, the Catholic press was curtailed, the training of students for the priesthood was seriously impeded. Msgr. Josef Tiso, president of the Slovak Republic, was tried for "treason" in December, 1947, and was executed the following April. Between 1945 and 1949 approximately 10 per cent of the Slovak population spent some time in jail or a concentration camp. Persecution began later in the Czech part of the country, following the accession of the Gottwald regime to power early in 1948. Hospitals, schools and property were nationalized and Catholic organizations were liquidated. A puppet organization was formed in 1949 to infiltrate the Church and implement an unsuccessful plan for establishing a schismatic church. In the same year Archbishop Josef Beran of Prague was placed under house arrest. (He left the country in 1965, was made a cardinal, and died in 1969 in Rome.) A number of theatrical trials of bishops and priests were staged in 1950. All houses of religious were taken over between March, 1950, and the end of 1951. An Eastern Rite diocese, Presov, in Slovakia, was dissolved in 1950 and pressure was applied on the clergy and faithful to join the Orthodox Church. Diplomatic relations with Vatican City were terminated in 1950. About 3,000 priests were deprived of liberty in 1951 and attempts were made to force "peace priests" on the people. In 1958 it was reported that 450 to 500 priests were in jail; an undisclosed number of religious and Byzantine Rite priests had been deported; two bishops released from prison in 1956 were under house arrest; one bishop was imprisoned at Leopoldov and two at the Mirov reformatory. In Bohemia, Moravia and Silesia, five of six dioceses were without ruling bishops; one archbishop and two bishops were active but subject to "supervision"; most of the clergy refused to join the "peace priests." In 1962 only three bishops were permitted to attend the first session of the Second Vatican Council. From January to October, 1968, Church-state relations improved to some extent under the Dubcek regime: a number of bishops were reinstated; some 3,000 priests were engaged in the pastoral ministry, although 1,500 were still barred from priestly work; the "peace priests" organization was disbanded; the Eastern Rite Church, with 147 parishes, was reestablished. In 1969, an end was ordered to rehabilitation trials for priests and religious, but no wholesale restoration of priests and religious to their proper ways of life and work was in prospect. In 1972 the government ordered the removal of nuns from visible but limited apostolates to farms and mental hospitals where they would be out of sight. In 1973, the government allowed the ordination of four bishops — one in the Czech region and three in the Slovak region. Reports from Slovakia late in the same year stated that authorities there had placed severe restrictions on the education of seminarians and the functioning of priests.

Archd., 2; dioc., 10; abb., 2; bp., 6; parishes, 4,412; priests, 4,121 (3,586 dioc., 535 rel.); sem., 515; p.d., 65; m. rel., 652; w. rel., 4,847; inst., 10; Caths. (est.), 10,860,000 (75%); tot. pop. (UN est., 1972), 14,480,000.

Dahomey: Republic in west Africa, bordering on the Atlantic; member of the French Community; capitals, Cotonou, Porto Novo. Missionary work was very limited from the 16th to the 18th centuries. Effective evangelization dates from 1894. The hierarchy was established in 1955. The majority of Christians are Catholics. Dahomey maintains diplomatic relations with Vatican City.

Archd., 1; dioc., 5; abp., 1 (nat.); bp., 5 (2 nat.); parishes, 80; priests, 180 (84 dioc., 96 rel.); sem., 25; m. rel., 111; w. rel., 338; sch., 70; inst., 35; Caths., 412,374 (14%); tot. pop. (UN est., 1972), 2,830,783.

Danzig (Gdensk): Baltic seaport at the mouth of the Vistula River; incorporated into Poland after World War II. The diocese has a Christian history dating from the 10th century. Statistics are included in those for Poland.

Denmark, including the Faroe Islands and Greenland: Constitutional monarchy in northwestern Europe, north of West Germany; capital, Copenhagen. Christianity was introduced in the ninth century and the first diocese for the area was established in 831. Intensive evangelization and full-scale organization of the Church occurred from the second half of the 10th century and ushered in a period of great development and influence in the 12th and 13th centuries. Decline followed, resulting in almost total loss to the Church during the Reformation when Lutheranism became the national religion. Catholics were

considered foreigners until religious freedom was legally assured in 1849. Modern development of the Church dates from the second half of the 19th century. About 95 per cent of the population are Evangelical Lutherans. Denmark has an apostolic delegate (to Scandinavia).

Dioc., 1; bp., 1; parishes, 50; priests, 125 (37 dioc., 88 rel.); sem., 4; m. rel., 96; w. rel., 580; sch., 35; inst., 24; Caths., 26,357 (.5%); tot. pop., 5,009,945.

Dominica: Self-governing state in Caribbean; capital, Roseau. Evangelization began in 1642.

Dioc., 1; bp., 1; parishes, 16; priests, 31 (3 dioc., 28 rel.); m. rel., 28; w. rel., 33; sch., 14; inst., 1; Caths., 64,000; tot. pop., 70,000.

Dominican Republic: Caribbean republic on the eastern two-thirds of the island of Hispaniola, bordering on Haiti; capital, Santo Domingo. Evangelization began shortly after discovery by Columbus in 1492 and church organization, the first in America, was established by 1510. Catholicism is the state religion. The Dominican Republic maintains diplomatic relations with Vatican City.

Archd., 1; dioc., 4; abp., 1; bp., 5; parishes, 172; priests, 481 (110 dioc., 371 rel.); sem., 51; p.d., 4; m. rel., 475; w. rel., 1,254; sch., 253; inst., 64; Caths., 3,813,173 (92%); tot. pop., 4,130,455.

Ecuador: Republic on the west coast of South America; capital, Quito. Evangelization began in the 1530's. The first diocese was established in 1545. A synod, one of the first in the Americas, was held in 1570 or 1594. Multiphased missionary work, spreading from the coastal and mountain regions into the Amazon, made the Church highly influential during the colonial period. The Church was practically enslaved by the constitution enacted in 1824, two years after Ecuador, as part of Colombia, gained independence from Spain. Some change for the better took place later in the century, but from 1891 until the 1930's the Church labored under serious liabilities imposed by liberal governments. The concordat of 1866 was violated; foreign missionaries were barred from the country for some time; the property of religious orders was confiscated; education was taken over by the state; traditional state support was refused; legal standing was denied; attempts to control church offices were made through insistence on rights of patronage. A period of harmony and independence for the Church began after agreement was reached on Church-state relations in 1937. Ecuador maintains diplomatic relations with Vatican City.

Archd., 3; dioc., 10; prel., 1; v.a., 5; p.a., 3; card., 1; abp., 2; bp., 20; parishes, 542; priests, 1,469 (603 dioc., 866 rel.); sem., 92; m. rel., 1,259; w. rel., 4,619; sch., 930; inst., 343; Caths., 6,311,000 (93%); tot. pop., 6,801,537.

Egypt, Arab Republic of: Republic in

northeastern Africa, bordering on the Mediterranean; capital, Cairo. Alexandria was the influential hub of a Christian community established by the end of the second century; it became a patriarchate and the center of the Coptic Church, and had great influence on the spread of Christianity in various parts of Africa; Monasticism developed from desert communities of hermits in the third and fourth centuries. Arianism was first preached in Egypt in the 320's. In the fifth century, the Coptic church went Monophysite through failure to accept doctrine formulated by the Council of Chalcedon in 451 with respect to the two natures of Christ. The country was thoroughly Arabized after 640 with respect to the two natures of Christ. The country was thoroughly Arabized after 640 and was under the rule of Ottoman Turks from 1517 to 1798. English influence was strong during the 19th century. A monarchy established in 1922 lasted about 30 years, ending with the proclamation of a republic in 1953-54. By that time Egypt had become the leader of pan-Arabism against Israel. It waged two unsuccessful wars against Israel in 1948-49 and 1967. Between 1958 and 1961 it was allied with Syria and Yemen, in the United Arab Republic. Islam, the religion of some 90 percent of the population, is the state religion. Egypt maintains diplomatic relations with Vatican City.

Patriarchate, 2 (Alexandria for the Copts and for the Melkites); dioc., 6; v.a., 3; card., 1; bp., 9; parishes, 201; priests, 448 (143 dioc., 305 rel.); sem., 27; m. rel., 436; w. rel., 1,496; sch., 233; inst., 145; Caths. (est.), 139,000 (.4%); tot. pop. (Govt. est., 1972), 34,839,000.

El Salvador: Republic in Central America; capital, San Salvador. Evangelization affecting the whole territory followed Spanish occupation in the 1520's. The country was administered by the captaincy general of Guatemala until 1821 when independence from Spain was declared and it was annexed to Mexico. El Salvador joined the Central American Federation in 1825, decreed its own independence in 1841 and became a republic formally in 1856. El Salvador maintains diplomatic relations with Vatican City.

Archd., 1; dioc., 4; abp., 1; bp., 4; parishes, 228; priests, 406 (203 dioc., 203 rel.); sem., 34; m. rel., 272; w. rel., 705; sch., 151; inst., 48; Caths., 3,396,777 (91.8%); tot. pop., 3,700,197.

England: Center of the United Kingdom of Great Britain (England, Scotland, Wales) and Northern Ireland, off the northwestern coast of Europe; capital, London. The arrival of St. Augustine of Canterbury and a band of monks in 597 marked the beginning of evangelization. Real organization of the Church took place some years after the Synod of Whitby, held in 663. Heavy losses were sustained in the wake of the Danish invasion in the 780's, but recovery starting from the time of Alfred the Great and dating especially from the middle of the 10th century led to Christianization of the whole country and close Church-state relations. The Norman Conquest of 1066 opened the Church in England to European influence. The 13th century was climactic, but decline had already set in by 1300 when the country had an all-time high of 17,000 religious. In the 14th century, John Wycliff presaged the Protestant Reformation. Henry VIII, failing in 1529 to gain annulment of his marriage to Catherine of Aragon, refused to acknowledge papal authority over the Church in England, had himself proclaimed its head, suppressed all houses of religious, and persecuted persons — Sts. Thomas More and John Fisher, among others — for not subscribing to ttboxeth of Supremacy and Act of Succession. He held theline on other-than-papal doctrine, however, until his death in 1547. Doctrinal aberrations were introduced during the reign of Edward VI (1547-53), through the Order of Communion, two books of Common Prayer, and the Articles of the Established Church. Mary Tudor's attempted Catholic restoration (1553-58) was a disaster, resulting in the deaths of more than 300 Protestants. Elizabeth (1558-1603) firmed up the Established Church with formation of a hierarchy, legal enactments and multi-phased persecution. One hundred and 11 priests and 62 lay persons were among the casualties of persecution during the underground Catholic revival which followed the return to England of missionary priests from France and The Lowlands. Several periods of comparative toleration ensued after Elizabeth's death. The first of several apostolic vicariates was established in 1685; this form of church government was maintained until the restoration of the hierarchy and diocesan organization in 1850. The revolution of 1688 and subsequent developments to about 1781 subjected Catholics to a wide variety of penal laws and disabilities in religious, civic and social life. The situation began to improve in 1791, and from 1801 Parliament frequently considered proposals for the repeal of penal laws against Catholics. The Act of Emancipation restored citizenship rights to Catholics in 1829. Restrictions remained in force for some time afterwards, however, on public religious worship and activity. The hierarchy was restored in 1850. Since then the Catholic Church, existing side by side with the Established Churches of England and Scotland, has followed a general pattern of growth and development. England has a diplomatic minister to Vatican City; there is an apostolic delegate in England.

Archd., 4; dioc., 13; ap. ex., 1; card., 1; abp., 3; bp., 30; parishes, 2,472; priests, 6,607 (4,261 dioc., 2,346 rel.); sem., 658; p.d., 6; m. rel., 3,150; w. rel., 12,254; sch., 2,803; inst., 441; Caths. (est.), 4,074,000 (8.7%); tot. pop., 46,305,000.

Equatorial Guinea: Republic on the west

coast of Africa, consisting of Rio Muni on the mainland and the islands of Fernando Po and Annobon in the Gulf of Guinea: capital, Malabo (Santa Isabel). Evangelization began in 1841. There has been tension in Church-state relations since the country became independent of Spain in 1968.

Dioc., 2; bp., 2 (1 nat.); parishes, 14; priests, 41 (17 dioc., 24 rel.); sem., 23; m. rel., 31; w. rel., 74; sch., 24; inst., 3; Caths., 233,700 (77%); tot. pop. (1972 est.), 300,000.

Ethiopia (Abyssinia): Constitutional monarchy in northeast Africa; capital, Addis Ababa. The country was evangelized by missionaries from Egypt in the fourth century and had a bishop by about 340. Following the lead of its parent body, the Egyptian (Coptic) Church, the Church in the area succumbed to the Monophysite heresy in the sixth century. Catholic influence was negligible for centuries. An ordinariate for the Ethiopian Rite was established in Eritrea in 1930. An apostolic delegation was set up in Addis Ababa in 1937 and several jurisdictions were organized, some under the Congregation for the Oriental Churches and others under the Congregation for the Evangelization of Peoples. Most of the Catholics in the country are in the former Italian colony of Eritrea. Ethiopia maintains diplomatic relations with Vatican City.

Archd., 1; dioc., 2; v.a., 3; p.a., 2; abp., 1; bp., 4; parishes, 104; priests, 456 (152 dioc., 304 rel.); sem. 63; m. rel., 463; w. rel., 994; Caths., 179,169 (.68%); tot. pop., 25,984,300.

Falkland Islands: British colony off the southern tip of South America.

P.a., 1; parish, 1; priests, 2 (rel.); m. rel., 3; Caths., 230; tot. pop., 2,100.

Fiji: Independent member of the British Commonwealth, 100 inhabited islands in the southwest Pacific; capital, Suva. Marist missionaries began work in 1844 after Methodism had been firmly established. A prefecture apostolic was organized in 1863. The hierarchy was established in 1966.

Archd., 1; abp., 1; parishes, 35; priests, 83 (10 dioc., 73 rel.); sem., 8; m. rel., 125; w. rel., 275; sch., 44; inst., 3; Caths., 45,452 (8.4%); tot. pop. (UN est., 1972), 540,000.

Finland: Republic in northern Europe; capital, Helsinki. Swedes evangelized the country in the 12th century. The Reformation swept the country, resulting in the prohibition of Catholicism in 1595, general reorganization of ecclesiastical life and affairs, and dominance of the Evangelical Lutheran Church. Catholics were given religious liberty in 1781 but missionaries and conversions were forbidden by law. The first Finnish priest since the Reformation was ordained in 1903 in Paris. A vicariate apostolic for Finland was erected in 1920. A law on religious liberty, enacted in 1923, banned the foundation of monasteries. Finland maintains diplomatic relations with Vatican City.

Dioc., 1; bp., 1; parishes, 5; priests, 19 (3

dioc., 16 rel.); sem., 1; m. rel., 21; w. rel., 37; Caths., 2,959 (.06%); tot. pop., 4,634,000.

France: Republic in western Europe; capital, Paris. Christianity was known around Lyons by the middle of the second century. By 250 there were 30 bishoprics. The hierarchy reached a fair degree of organization by the end of the fourth century. Vandals and Franks subsequently invaded the territory and caused barbarian turmoil and doctrinal problems because of their Arianism. The Frankish nation was converted following the baptism of Clovis about 496. Christianization was complete by some time in the seventh century. From then on the Church, its leaders and people, figured in virtually every important development — religious, cultural, political and social — through the periods of the Carolingians, feudalism, the Middle Ages and monarchies to the end of the 18th century. The great University of Paris became one of the intellectual centers of the 13th century. Churchmen and secular rulers were involved with developments surrounding the Avignon residence of the popes and curia from 1309 until near the end of the 14th century and with the disastrous Western Schism that followed. Strong currents of Gallicanism and conciliarism ran through ecclesiastical and secular circles in France; the former was an ideology and movement to restrict papal control of the Church in the country, the latter sought to make the pope subservient to a general council. Calvinism invaded the country about the middle of the 16th century and won a strong body of converts. Jansenism with its rigorous spirit and other aberrations appeared in the next century, to be followed by the highly influential Enlightenment. The Revolution which started in 1789 and was succeeded by the Napoleonic period completely changed the status of the Church, taking a toll of numbers by persecution and defection and disenfranchising the Church in practically every way. Throughout the 19th century the Church was caught up in the whirl of imperial and republican developments and made the victim of official hostility, popular indifference and liberal opposition. In this century, the Church has struggled with problems involving the heritage of the Revolution and its aftermath, the alienation of intellectuals, liberalism, the estrangement of the working classes because of the Church's former identification with the ruling class, and the massive needs of contemporary society. France maintains diplomatic relations with Vatican City.

Archd., 18; dioc., 73; prel., 1; ap. ex., 2; ord., 1; card., 9; abp., 15; bp., 99; parishes, 38,399; priests, 44,157 (36,630 dioc., 7,527 rel.); sem., 1,919; p.d., 19; m. rel., 13,380; w. rel., 95,160; sch., 10,994; inst., 2,264; Caths. (est.), 45,321,795 (87.3%); tot. pop. (Govt. est., 1973), 51,915,000.

Gabon: Republic on the west coast of

Equatorial Africa, member of the French Community; capital, Libreville. Sporadic missionary effort took place before 1881 when effective evangelization began. The hierarchy was established in 1955. Gabon maintains diplomatic relations with Vatican City.

Archd., 1; dioc., 2; parishes, 43; priests, 105 (33 dioc., 72 rel.); sem., 1; m. rel., 118; w. rel., 156; sch., 263; inst., 35; Caths., 308,560 (52%); tot. pop., 591,000.

Gambia, The: Republic (1970) on the northwestern coast of Africa, smallest state in Africa, member of the British Commonwealth; capital, Banjui. The country was under the jurisdiction of a vicariate apostolic until 1931. The hierarchy was established in 1957. The Gambia has an apostolic delegate (the pro-nuncio to Liberia).

Dioc., 1; bp., 1; parishes, 3; priests, 22(rel.); m. rel., 26; w. rel., 18; sch., 40; inst., 1; Caths., 10,360 (2.7%); tot. pop. 380,000.

Germany: Country in northern Europe partitioned in 1949 into the Communist German Democratic Republic in the East (capital, East Berlin) and the German Federal Republic in the West (capital, Bonn). Christianity was introduced in the third century, if not earlier. Trier, which became a center for missionary activity, had a bishop by 400. Visigoth invaders introduced Arianism in the fifth century but were converted in the seventh century by the East Franks, Celtic and other missionaries. St. Boniface, the apostle of Germany, established real ecclesiastical organization in the eighth century. The Church had great influence during the Carolingian period. Bishops from that time onward began to act in dual roles as pastors and rulers, a state of affairs which led inevitably to confusion and conflict in Church-state relations and perplexing problems of investiture. The Church developed strength and vitality through the Middle Ages but succumbed to abuses which antedated and prepared the ground for the Reformation. Luther's actions from 1517 made Germany a confessional battleground. Religious strife continued until conclusion of the Peace of Westphalia at the end of the Thirty Years' War in 1648. Nearly a century earlier the Peace of Augsburg (1555) had been designed, without success, to assure a degree of tranquillity by recognizing the legitimacy of different religious confessions in different states, depending on the decisions of princes. The implicit principle that princes should control the churches emerged in practice into the absolutism and Josephinism of subsequent years. St. Peter Canisius and his fellow Jesuits spearheaded a Counter Reformation in the second half of the 16th century. Before the end of the century, however, 70 per cent of the population of north and central Germany were Lutheran. Calvinism also had established a strong presence. The Church gained internal strength in a defensive position. Through much of the 19th

century, however, its influence was eclipsed by Protestant intellectuals and other influences. It suffered some impoverishment also as a result of shifting boundaries and the secularization of property shortly after 1800. It came under direct attack in the Kulturkampf of the 1870's but helped to generate the opposition which resulted in a dampening of the campaign of Bismarck against it. Despite action by Catholics on the social front and other developments, discrimination against the Church spilled over into the 20th century and lasted beyond World War I. Catholics in politics struggled with others to pull the country through numerous postwar crises. The dissolution of the Center Party, agreed to by the bishops in 1933 without awareness of the ultimate consequences, contributed negatively to the rise of Hitler to supreme power. Church officials protested the Nazi anti-Church and anti-Semitic actions, but to no avail. After World War II Christian leadership had much to do with the recovery of Western Germany. East Germany, gone Communist under Russian auspices, initiated a program of control and repression of the Church in 1948 and 1949. With no prospect of success for measures designed to split bishops, priests, religious and lay persons, the regime has concentrated most of its attention on mind control, especially of the younger generation, by the elimination of religious schools, curtailment of freedom for religious instruction and formation, severe restriction of the religious press, and the substitution since the mid-50's of youth initiation and Communist ceremonies for the rites of baptism, confirmation, marriage, and funerals. Bishops are generally forbidden to travel outside the Republic. The number of priests is decreasing, partly because of reduced seminary enrollments ordered by the government since 1958. In 1973, the Vatican appointed three apostolic administrators and one auxiliary (all titular bishops) for the areas of three West German dioceses located in East Germany. West Germany maintains diplomatic relations with Vatican City.

Archd., 5; dioc., 18; ap. ex., 1; a.a., 1; card., 6; abp., 2; bp., 56; parishes, 11,613; priests, 25,443 (19,209 dioc., 6,234 rel.); sem., 2,096; p.d., 171; m. rel., 10,500; w. rel., 76,338; sch., 13,101; inst., 17,576. Catholics number 30,721,432; they constitute approximately 45 per cent of the West German population of 61,670,000 (UN est., 1972) and 10 per cent of the East German population of 17,050,000 (UN est., 1972).

Ghana: Republic on the western coast of Africa, bordering on the Gulf of Guinea, member of the British Commonwealth; capital, Accra. Priests visited the country in 1482, 11 years after discovery by the Portuguese, but missionary effort — hindered by the slave trade and other factors — was slight until 1880 when systematic evangelization began.

A prefecture apostolic was set up in 1943. The hierarchy was established in 1950. Ghana has an apostolic delegate.

Archd., 1; dioc., 8; abp., 1 (nat.); bp., 8 (7 nat.); parishes, 136; priests, 336 (101 dioc., 235 rel.); sem., 105; m. rel., 346; w. rel., 374; sch., 1,671; inst., 75; Caths., 1,074,742 (11.8%); tot. pop. (UN est., 1972), 9,090,000.

Gibraltar: British colony on the tip of the Spanish Peninsula on the Mediterranean. Evangelization took place after the Moors were driven out near the end of the 15th century. The Church was hindered by the British who acquired the colony in 1713. Most of the Catholics were, and are, Spanish and Italian immigrants and their descendants. A vicariate apostolic was organized in 1817. The diocese was erected in 1910.

Dioc., 1; bp., 1; parishes, 2; priests, 10 (dioc.); m. rel., 10; w. rel., 26; sch., 4; inst., 1; Caths., 19,133; tot. pop. (1972 est.), 30,000.

Gilbert Islands: British colony in the southwest Pacific in Oceania, consisting of 16 coral atolls including the Gilbert and Ellice Islands. French Missionaries of the Sacred Heart began work in the islands in 1888. A vicariate for the islands was organized in 1897. The hierarchy was established in 1966.

Dioc., 1; bp., 1; parishes, 21; priests, 19 (2 dioc., 17 rel.); m. rel., 23; w. rel., 45; sch., 48; Caths., 25,452; tot. pop., 60,000.

Greece, including Crete: Kingdom in southeastern Europe on the Balkan Peninsula; capital, Athens. St. Paul preached the Gospel at Athens and Corinth on his second missionary journey and visited the country again on his third tour. Other Apostles may have passed through also. Two bishops from Greece attended the First Council of Nicaea. After the division of the Roman Empire, the Church remained Eastern in rite and later broke ties with Rome as a result of the schism of 1054. A Latin-Rite jurisdiction was set up during the period of the Latin Empire of Constantinople, 1204-1261, but crumbled afterwards. Unity efforts of the Council of Florence had poor results. The country now has Greek Catholic and Latin jurisdictions. The Greek Orthodox Church is predominant.

Archd., 3; dioc., 4; v.a., 1; ap. ex., 1; ord., 1; abp., 3; bp., 3; parishes, 37; priests, 112 (69 dioc., 43 rel.); sem., 11; m. rel., 82; w. rel., 193; sch., 38; inst., 26; Caths., 45,478 (.4%); tot. pop., 9,500,000.

Greenland: Danish island province northeast of North America; capital, Godthaab. Catholicism was introduced about 1000. The first diocese was established in 1124 and a line of bishops dated from then until 1537. The first known churches in the western hemisphere, dating from about the 11th century, were on Greenland; the remains of 19 have been unearthed. The departure of Scandinavians and spread of the Reformation reduced the Church to nothing. The Moravian Brethren evangelized the Eskimos from the 1720's to 1901. By 1930 the Danish Church — Evangelical Lutheran — was in full possession. Since 1930 priests have been in Greenland, which is part of the Copenhagen diocese. There are about 60 Catholics in the area.

Grenada: Independent island state in the West Indies; capital, St. George's.

Dioc., 1; bp., 1; parishes, 19; priests, 23 (6 dioc., 17 rel.); sem., 2; m. rel., 24; w. rel., 26; sch., 33; Caths., 75,000; tot. pop., 110,000.

Guadeloupe and Martinique: French overseas departments in the Leeward and Windward Islands of the West Indies; capitals, Basse-Terre (Guadeloupe) and Fort-de-France (Martinique). Catholicism was introduced in the islands in the 16th century. The hierarchy was established in 1967.

Archd., 1; dioc., 1; abp., 1; bp., 1; parishes, 90; priests, 215 (97 dioc., 118 rel.); sem., 8; m. rel., 150; w. rel., 478; sch., 34; inst., 11; Caths., 617,800 (92.7%); tot. pop., 666,150.

Guam: US territory in the southwest Pacific; capital, Agana. The first Mass was offered in the Mariana Islands in 1521. The islands were evangelized by the Jesuits, from 1668, and other missionaries. The first native Micronesian bishop was ordained in 1970.

Dioc., 1; bp., 1 (nat.); parishes, 27; priests, 55 (25 dioc., 30 rel.); sem., 6; p.d., 1; m. rel., 36; w. rel., 153; sch., 14; inst., 1; Caths., 87,626; tot. pop., 110,624. (Population figures include military personnel.)

Guatemala: Republic in Central America; capital, Guatemala City. Evangelization dates from the beginning of Spanish occupation in 1524. The first diocese, for all Central American territories administered by the captaincy general of Guatemala, was established in 1534. The country became independent in 1839, following annexation to Mexico in 1821, secession in 1823 and membership in the Central American Federation from 1825. In 1870, a government installed by a liberal revolution repudiated the concordat of 1853 and took active measures against the Church. Separation of Church and state was decreed; religious orders were suppressed and their property seized; priests and religious were exiled; schools were secularized. Full freedom was subsequently granted. Guatemala maintains diplomatic relations with Vatican City.

Archd., 1; dioc., 8; prel., 2; a.a., 2; card., 1; bp., 14; parishes, 305; priests, 644 (180 dioc., 464 rel.); sem., 69; p.d., 1; m. rel., 719; w. rel., 1,018; sch., 238; inst., 167; Caths. 4,600,148 (82%); tot. pop. (UN est., 1972), 5,600,000.

Guiana, French: French overseas department on the northeast coast of South America; capital, Cayenne. Catholicism was introduced in the 17th century. The Cayenne diocese was established in 1956.

Dioc., 1; bp., 1; parishes, 20; priests, 25 (7 dioc., 18 rel.); sem., 3; m. rel., 19; w. rel., 86; sch., 12; inst., 16; Caths., 40,000; tot. pop. (1972 est.), 60,000.

Guinea: Republic on the west coast of Africa; capital, Conakry. Occasional missionary work followed exploration by the Portuguese about the middle of the 15th century; organized effort dates from 1877. The hierarchy was established in 1955. Following independence from France in 1958, Catholic schools were nationalized, youth organizations banned and missionaries restricted. Foreign missionaries were expelled in 1967. In 1971 Archbishop Tchidimbo of Conakry was sentenced to life imprisonment on a charge of conspiring to overthrow the government. Guinea has an apostolic delegate.

Archd., 1; dioc., 1; p.a., 1; abp., 1 (nat., imprisoned in 1971); bp. 1 (exiled); parishes, 22; priests, 11 (dioc.); sem., 12; m. rel., 4; w. rel., 10; Caths., 40,071 (.9%); tot. pop. (UN est., 1972), 4,110,000.

Guinea-Bissau (formerly Portuguese Guinea): Independent state on the west coast of Africa; capital, Bissau. Catholicism was introduced in the second half of the 15th century but limited missionary work, hampered by the slave trade, had meager results. Missionary work in this century dates from 1933. A prefecture apostolic was established in 1955.

P.a., 1; parishes, 12; priests, 31 (rel); m. rel., 46; w. rel., 36; sch., 78; inst., 20; Caths., 42,562; tot. pop., 487,448.

Guyana: Republic on the northern coast of South America; capital, Georgetown. In 1899 the Catholic Church and other churches were given equal status with the Church of England and the Church of Scotland, which had sole rights up to that time. Most of the Catholics are Portuguese. The Georgetown diocese was established in 1956, 10 years before Guyana became independent of England. The first native bishop was appointed in 1971.

Dioc., 1; bp., 1; parishes, 23; priests, 75 (10 dioc., 65 rel.); sem., 7; m. rel., 75; w. rel., 73; sch., 62; inst., 13; Caths., 105,000; tot. pop. (UN est., 1972), 750,000.

Haiti: Caribbean republic on the western third of Hispaniola adjacent to the Dominican Republic; capital, Port-au-Prince. Evangelization followed discovery by Columbus in 1492. Capuchins and Jesuits did most of the missionary work in the 18th century. From 1804, when independence was declared, until 1860, the country was in schism. Relations were regularized by a concordat concluded in 1860, when an archdiocese and four dioceses were established. Factors hindering the development of the Church have been a shortage of native clergy, inadequate religious instruction and the prevalence of voodoo. Political upheavals in the 1960's had serious effects on the Church. Haiti maintains diplomatic relations with Vatican City.

Archd., 1; dioc., 6; abp., 1; bp., 7; parishes, 188; priests, 391 (184 dioc., 207 rel.); sem., 41; m. rel., 413; w. rel., 792; sch., 653; inst., 218; Caths. (approx. 85% of the population), 4,309,500; tot. pop. (UN est., 1972), 5,070,000.

Honduras: Republic in Central America; capital, Tegucigalpa. Evangelization preceded establishment of the first diocese in the 16th century. Under Spanish rule and after independence from 1823, the Church held a favored position until 1880 when equal legal status was given to all religions. Honduras maintains diplomatic relations with Vatican City.

Archd., 1; dioc., 3; prel., 2; abp., 1; bp., 6; parishes, 114; priests, 202 (63 dioc., 139 rel.); sem., 16; p.d., 6; m. rel., 161; w. rel., 277; sch., 49; inst., 11; Caths., 2,666,853 (93.9%); tot. pop., 2,839,662.

Hong Kong: British crown colony at the mouth of the Canton River, adjacent to the southeast Chinese province of Kwangtung. A prefecture apostolic was established in 1841. Members of the Pontifical Institute for Foreign Missions began work there in 1858. The Hong Kong diocese was erected in 1946.

Dioc., 1; parishes, 31; priests, 313 (57 dioc., 276 rel.); sem., 28; m. rel., 423; w. rel., 797; sch., 283; inst., 39; Caths. 257,713 (5.3%); tot. pop. (UN est., 1972), 4,800,000.

Hungary: People's republic in east central Europe; capital, Budapest. The early origins of Christianity in the country, whose territory was subject to a great deal of change, is not known. Magyars accepted Christianity about the end of the 10th century. St. Stephen I (d. 1038) promoted its spread and helped to organize some of its historical dioceses. Bishops early became influential in politics as well as in the Church. For centuries the country served as a buffer for the Christian West against barbarians from the East, notably the Mongols in the 13th century. Religious orders, whose foundations started from the 1130's, provided the most effective missionaries, pastors and teachers. Outstanding for years were the Franciscans and Dominicans; the Jesuits were noted for their work in the Counter-Reformation from the second half of the 16th century onwards. Hussites and Waldensians prepared the way for the Reformation which struck at almost the same time as the Turks. The Reformation made considerable progress after 1526, resulting in the conversion of large numbers to Lutheranism and Calvinism by the end of the century. Most of them or their descendants returned to the Church later, but many Magyars remained staunch Calvinists. Turks repressed the churches, Protestant as well as Catholic, during a reign of 150 years but they managed to survive. Domination of the Church was one of the objectives of government policy during the reigns of Maria Theresa and Joseph II in the second half of the 18th century; their Josephinism affected Church-state relations until the first World War. More than 100,000 Eastern Rite schismatics were reunited with Rome about the turn of the 18th century. Secularization increased in the second half of the 19th century, which also witnessed the birth of many new Catholic organizations and movements to influence life in the nation and the Church. Catholics were involved in the social chaos and anti-religious atmosphere of the years following World War I, struggling with their compatriots for religious as well as political survival. After World War II Communist strength, which had manifested itself with less intensity earlier in the century, was great long before it forced the legally elected president out of office in 1947 and imposed a Soviet type of constitution on the country in 1949. The campaign against the Church started with the disbanding of Catholic organizations in 1946. In 1948, "Caritas," the Catholic charitable organization, was taken over and all Catholic schools, colleges and institutions were suppressed. Interference in church administration and attempts to split the bishops preceded the arrest of Cardinal Mindszenty on Dec. 26, 1948, and his sentence to life imprisonment in 1949. (He was free for a few days during the unsuccessful uprising of 1956. He then took up residence at the US Embassy in Budapest where he remained until September, 1971, when he was permitted to leave the country. He now resides in Vienna.) In 1950, religious orders and congregations were suppressed and 10,000 religious were interned. At least 30 priests and monks were assassinated, jailed or deported. About 4,000 priests and religious were confined in jail or concentration camps. The government sponsored a national "Progressive Catholic" church and captive organizations for priests and "Catholic Action," which attracted only a small minority. Signs were clear in 1965 and 1966 that a 1964 agreement with the Holy See regarding episcopal appointments had settled nothing. Six bishops were appointed by the Holy See and some other posts were filled, but none of the prelates were free from government surveillance and harassment. Four new bishops were appointed by the Holy See in January and ordained in Budapest in February, 1969; three elderly prelates resigned their sees. Shortly thereafter, peace priests complained that the "too Roman" new bishops would not deal with them. In 1972 the government accepted the appointment of five new bishops. In 1974, Pope Paul VI relieved Cardinal Mindszenty of his titles as archbishop of Esztergom and primate of Hungary in view of the pastoral interests of several dioceses of the country. (See separate article.)

Archd., 3; dioc., 8; abb., 1; ord., 1; card., 1; abp., 1; bp., 11; parishes, 2,021; priests, 3,655 (3,376 dioc., 279 rel.); sem., 242; m. rel., 350; w. rel., 41; sch., 7; inst., 102; Caths., 6,182,901 (59%); tot. pop., 10,400,000.

Iceland: Island republic between Norway and Greenland; capital, Reykjavik. Irish hermits were there in the eighth century. Missionaries subsequently evangelized the island and Christianity was officially accepted about 1000. The first bishop was ordained in 1056. The Black Death had dire effects and spiritual decline set in during the 15th century. Lutheranism was introduced from Denmark between 1537 and 1552 and made the official religion. Some Catholic missionary work was done in the 19th century. Religious freedom was granted to the few Catholics in 1874. A vicariate was erected in 1929. Iceland has an apostolic delegate (to Scandinavia).

Dioc., 1; bp., 1; parishes, 2; priests, 9 (2 dioc., 7 rel.); m. rel., 7; w. rel., 54; sch., 3; inst., 3; Caths., 1,309 (.6%); tot. pop., 212,300. (Catholic and total population figures are from the Icelandic daily newspaper.)

India: Republic on the subcontinent of south central Asia, member of the British Commonwealth; capital, New Delhi. Longstanding tradition credits the Apostle Thomas with the introduction of Christianity in the Kerala area. Evangelization followed the establishment of Portuguese posts and the conquest of Goa in 1510. Jesuits, Franciscans, Dominicans, Augustinians and members of other religious orders figured in the early missionary history. An archdiocese for Goa, with two suffragan sees, was set up in 1558. Five provincial councils were held between 1567 and 1606. The number of Catholics in 1572 was estimated to be 280,000. This figure rose to 800,000 in 1700 and declined to 500,000 in 1800. Missionaries had some difficulties with the British East India Co. which exercised virtual government control from 1757 to 1858. They also had trouble because of a conflict that developed between policies of the Portuguese government, which pressed its rights of patronage in episcopal and clerical appointments, and the Congregation for the Propagation of the Faith, which sought greater freedom of action in the same appointments. This struggle eventuated in the schism of Goa between 1838 and 1857. In 1886, when the number of Catholics was estimated to be one million, the hierarchy for India and Ceylon was restored. Jesuits contributed greatly to the development of Catholic education from the second half of the 19th century. A large percentage of the Catholic population, mostly from the lower castes, is located around Goa and Kerala and farther south. The country is predominantly Hindu. India maintains diplomatic relations with Vatican City.

Patriarchate, 1; archd., 18; dioc., 65; v.a., 1; p.a. 2; ap. ex., 5; card., 2; patriarch, 1; abp., 16; bp., 65; parishes, 3,386; priests, 9,781 (5,973 dioc., 3,808 rel.); sem., 2,268; sch., 8,677; inst., 2,794; Caths., 8,606,887 (1.5%); tot. pop. (UN est., 1972), 563,490,000.

Indonesia: Republic southeast of Asia, consisting of some 3,000 islands including Kalimantan (most of Borneo), Sulawesi (Celebes), Java, the Lesser Sundas, Moluccas, Sumatra,

Timor and West Irian (Irian Jaya, western part of New Guinea); capital, Jakarta. Evangelization by the Portuguese began about 1511. St. Francis Xavier, greatest of the modern missionaries, spent some 14 months in the area. Christianity was strongly rooted in some parts of the islands by 1600. Islam's rise to dominance began at this time. The Dutch East Indies Co., which gained effective control in the 17th century, banned evangelization by Catholic missionaries for some time but Dutch secular and religious priests managed to resume the work. A vicariate of Batavia for all the Dutch East Indies was set up in 1841. About 90 per cent of the population is Moslem. The hierarchy was established in 1961. Indonesia maintains diplomatic relations with Vatican City.

Archd., 7; dioc., 24; p.a., 2; card., 1 (nat.); abp., 6 (3 nat.); bp., 21 (3 nat.); parishes, 504; priests, 1,463 (126 dioc., 1,337 rel.); sem., 204; m. rel., 2,626; w. rel., 3,794; sch., 3,928; inst., 718; Caths., 2,540,157 (2%); tot. pop., 121,027,708.

Iran: Constitutional monarchy in southwestern Asia, between the Caspian Sea and the Persian Gulf; capital, Teheran. Some of the earliest Christian communities were established in this area outside the (then) Roman Empire. They suffered persecution in the fourth century and were then cut off from the outside world. Nestorianism was generally professed in the late fifth century. Islam became dominant after 640. Some later missionary work was attempted but without success. Religious liberty was granted in 1834, but Catholics were the victims of a massacre in 1918. Islam is the religion of perhaps 98 per cent of the population. In 1964 the country had 100,000 Monophysites, the largest group of Christians, and some 20,000 Nestorians. Catholics belong to the Latin, Armenian and Chaldean rites. Iran (Persia until 1935) maintains diplomatic relations with Vatican City.

Archd., 4; dioc., 2; abp., 3; parishes, 20; priests, 43 (11 dioc., 32 rel.); sem., 8; m. rel., 39; w. rel., 51; sch., 23; inst., 20; Caths., 25,275 (.08%); tot. pop., 30,550,000.

Iraq: Republic in southwestern Asia, between Iran and Saudi Arabia; capital, Baghdad. Some of the earliest Christian communities were established in the area, whose history resembles that of Iran. Catholics belong to the Armenian, Chaldean, Latin and Syrian rites; Chaldeans are most numerous. Islam is the religion of some 90 per cent of the population. Iraq maintains diplomatic relations with Vatican City.

Patriarchate, 1 (titular, Babylonia for the Chaldeans); archd., 8; dioc., 6; mission "sui juris," 1; patriarch, 1; abp., 8; bp., 5; parishes, 126; priests, 159 (130 dioc., 29 rel.); sem., 68; p.d., 1; m. rel., 63; w. rel., 222; sch., 45; inst., 14; Caths., 286,621 (2.8%); tot. pop. (UN est., 1972), 10,070,000.

Ireland: Republic in the British Isles; capital, Dublin. St. Patrick, who is venerated as the apostle of Ireland, evangelized parts of the island for some years after the middle of the fifth century. Conversion of the island was not accomplished, however, until the seventh century or later. Celtic monks were the principal missionaries. The Church was organized along monastic lines at first, but a movement developed in the 11th century for the establishment of jurisdiction along episcopal lines. By that time many Roman usages had been adopted. The Church gathered strength during the period from the Norman Conquest of England to the reign of Henry VIII despite a wide variety of rivalries, wars, andother disturbances. Henry introduced an age of repression of the faith which continued for many years under several of his successors. The Irish suffered from proscription of the Catholic faith, economic and social disabilities, subjection to absentee landlords and a plantation system designed to keep them from owning property, and actual persecution which took an uncertain toll of lives up until about 1714. Most of those living in the northern part of Ireland became Anglican and Presbyterian in the 1600's but the south remained strong in faith. Some penal laws remained in force until emancipation in 1829. Nearly 100 years later Ireland was divided by two enactments which made Northern Ireland, consisting of six counties, part of the United Kindgom (1920) and gave dominion status to the Irish Free State, made up of the other 26 counties (1922). This state (Eire, in Gaelic) was proclaimed the Republic of Ireland in 1949. The Catholic Church enjoys privileged status but religious freedom is guaranteed for all. Ireland maintains diplomatic relations with Vatican City.

Archd., 4; dioc., 22; card., 1; abp., 3; bp., 24; parishes, 1,224; priests, 5,839 (3,814 dioc., 2,025 rel.); sem., 632; m. rel., 4,621; w. rel., 12,962 (preceding figures include Northern Ireland); Caths. (est.), 2,852,000 (94%); tot. pop., 3,010,000.

Ireland, Northern: Part of the United Kingdom, it consists of six·of the nine counties of Ulster in the northeast corner of Ireland; capital, Belfast. History is given under Ireland, above. For 1974 developments, see Index.

Caths. (approx.), 504,000 (32%); tot. pop.; 1,534,000 (other statistics are included in Ireland).

Israel: Parliamentary democracy in the Middle East, at the eastern end of the Mediterranean; capitals, Jerusalem and Tel Aviv (diplomatic). Israel was the birthplace of Christianity, the site of the first Christian communities. Some persecution was suffered in the early Christian era and again during the several hundred years of Roman control. Moslems conquered the territory in the seventh century and, except for the period of the Kingdom of Jerusalem established by Crusaders, remained in control most of the time up until World War I. The Church survived in the area, sometimes just barely, but it did not prosper greatly or show any notable increase in numbers. The British took over the protectorate of the area after World War I. Partition into Israel for the Jews and Palestine for the Arabs was approved by the United Nations in 1947. War broke out a year later with the proclamation of the Republic of Israel. The Israelis won the war and 50 percent more territory than they had originally been ceded. War broke out again for six days in June, 1967, and in October, 1973, resulting in a Middle East crisis that shows few signs of early settlement. Caught in the middle of the conflict are hundreds of thousands of dispossessed Palestinian refugees. Judaism is the faith professed by about 85 percent of the inhabitants; approximately one-third of them are considered observants. Most of the Arab minority are Moslems. The Acre archdiocese for Melkites is situated in Israel. Maronites are subject to the bishop of Tyr, Lebanon. Latins are under the jurisdiction of the Roman patriarchate of Jerusalem. Israel has an apostolic delegate.

Caths., 35,671; tot. pop. (1973 est.), 3,200,000.

Italy: Republic in southern Europe; capital, Rome. A Christian community was formed early at Rome, probably by the middle of the first century. St. Peter established his see there. He and St. Paul suffered death for the faith there in the 60's. The early Christians were persecuted at various times there, as in other parts of the empire, but the Church developed in numbers and influence, gradually spreading out from towns and cities in the center and south to rural areas and the north. Organization, in the process of formation in the second century, developed greatly between the fifth and eighth centuries. By the latter date the Church had already come to grips with serious problems, including doctrinal and disciplinary disputes that threatened the unity of faith, barbarian invasions, and the need for the pope and bishops to take over civil responsibilities because of imperial default. The Church has been at the center of life on the peninsula throughout the centuries. It emerged from underground in 313, with the Edict of Milan, and rose to a position of prestige and lasting influence. It educated and converted the barbarians, preserved culture through the early Middle Ages and passed it on to later times, suffered periods of decline and gained strength through recurring reforms, engaged in military combat for political reasons and intellectual combat for the preservation and development of doctrine, saw and patronized the development of the arts, experienced all human strengths and weaknesses in its members, knew triumph and the humiliation of failure. For long centuries, from the fourth to the 19th, the Church was a temporal as well as spiritual power. This temporal aspect complicated its history in Italy. Since the 1870's, however, when the Papal States were annexed by the Kingdom of Italy, the history became simpler — but remained complicated — as the Church, shorn of temporal power, began to find new freedom for the fulfillment of its spiritual mission. Italy maintains diplomatic relations with Vatican City.

Patriarchate, 1; archd., 56; dioc., over 200; prel., 6; abb., 9; card., 36; abp., 54; bp., 215; parishes, 29,313; priests, 64,416 (43,159 dioc., 21,257 rel.); sem., 4,382; p.d., 9; m. rel., 32,031; w. rel., 151,638; sch., 3,698; inst., 4,561; Caths. (est.), 52,719,500 (97%); tot. pop. (UN est., 1972), 54,350,000.

Ivory Coast: Republic in western Africa, member of the French Community; capital, Abidjan. The Holy Ghost Fathers began systematic evangelization in 1895. The first native priests from the area were ordained in 1934. The hierarchy was set up in 1955. Ivory Coast maintains diplomatic relations with Vatican City.

Archd., 1; dioc., 7; abp., 1 (nat.); bp., 8 (5 nat.); parishes, 135; priests, 385 (101 dioc., 284 rel.); sem., 37; m. rel., 376; w. rel., 453; sch., 468; inst., 56; Caths., 542,811 (11%); tot. pop. (UN est., 1972), 4,530,000.

Jamaica: Parliamentary democracy in the West Indies, member of the British Commonwealth; capital, Kingston. Franciscans and Dominicans evangelized the island from about 1512 until 1655. Missionary work was interrupted after the English took possession but was resumed by Jesuits about the turn of the 19th century. A vicariate apostolic was organized in 1837. The hierarchy was established in 1967.

Archd., 1; dioc., 1; abp., 1; bp., 1; parishes, 42; priests, 120 (18 dioc., 102 rel.); sem., 8; m. rel., 114; w. rel., 248; sch., 77; inst., 8; Caths., 161,793 (8%); tot. pop., 1,921,669.

Japan: Constitutional monarchy in the northwest Pacific; capital, Tokyo. Jesuits began evangelization in the middle of the 16th century and about 300,000 converts, most of them in Kyushu, were reported at the end of the century. The Nagasaki Martyrs were victims of persecution in 1597. Another persecution took some 4,000 lives between 1614 and 1651. Missionaries, banned for two centuries, returned about the middle of the 19th century and found Christian communities still surviving in Nagasaki and other places in Kyushu. A vicariate was organized in 1846. The hierarchy was established in 1891. Religious freedom was guaranteed in 1889. Japan maintains diplomatic relations with Vatican.

Archd., 3; dioc., 13; p.a., 1; card., 1; abp., 2; bp., 15; parishes, 646; priests, 1,807 (422 dioc., 1,385 rel.); sem., 121; m. rel., 1,916; w. rel., 6,898; sch., 340; inst., 314; Caths. (Dec. 31, 1973, report of National Catholic Committee of Japan), 359,176 (.3%); tot. pop. (Govt. est., 1972), 107,332,000.

Jerusalem: The entire city, site of the first Christian community, has been under Israeli control since the Israeli-Arab war of June, 1967. There are two patriarchates in the city, Melkite and Latin. Jerusalem has an apostolic delegate.

Jordan: Constitutional monarchy in the Middle East; capital, Amman. Christianity there dates from apostolic times. Survival of the faith was threatened many times under the rule of Moslems from 636 and Ottoman Turks from 1517 to 1918, and in the Islamic Emirate of Trans-Jordan from 1918 to 1949. Since the creation of Israel, some 500,000 Palestinian refugees, some of them Christians, have been in Jordan. Islam is the state religion but religious freedom is guaranteed for all. Jordan has an apostolic delegate.

The statistics which follow are for the Melkite-Rite Catholics of the Archdiocese of Petra and Philadelphia in Jordan. Separate statistics are not available for the Latin (Roman)-Rite Catholics under the jurisdiction of the Latin patriarchate of Jerusalem.

Archd., 1; abp., 1; parishes, 35; priests, 23 (19 dioc., 4 rel.); sem., 5; m. rel., 4; w. rel., 27; sch., 21; inst., 4; Caths., 16,000 (statistics are for the Archdiocese of Petra and Philadelphia for the Melkites); tot. pop. (UN est., 1972), 2,470,000.

Kashmir and Jammu: Statistics included in India.

Kenya: Republic in eastern Africa bordering on the Indian Ocean, member of the British Commonwealth; capital, Nairobi. Systematic evangelization by the Holy Ghost Fathers began in 1892, nearly 40 years after the start of work by Protestant missionaries. The hierarchy was established in 1953. Kenya maintains diplomatic relations with Vatican City.

Archd., 1; dioc., 10; p.a., 2; card., 1 (nat.); bp., 11 (6 nat.); parishes, 185; priests, 719 (138 dioc., 581 rel.); sem., 178; m. rel., 801; w. rel., 1,526; sch., 2,578; inst., 260; Caths., 1,929,208 (15%); tot. pop., 12,263,382.

Khmer Republic (Cambodia): Republic (Oct. 9, 1970) in southeast Asia, bordering on the Gulf of Siam, Thailand, Laos and Vietnam; capital Phnom Penh. Evangelization dating from the second half of the 16th century had limited results, more among Vietnamese than Khmers. Several thousand Catholics of Vietnamese origin were forced to flee in 1970. Buddhism is the state religion. Khmer has an apostolic delegate.

V.a., 1; p.a., 2; bp., 1; parishes, 7; priests, 31 (16 dioc., 15 rel.); sem., 1; m. rel., 18; w. rel., 54; sch., 1; inst., 9; Caths. 20,315 (.3%); tot. pop., 6,750,000.

Korea: Peninsula in eastern Asia, east of China, divided into the (Communist) Democratic People's Republic in the North, formed May 1, 1948, with Pyongyang as its capital; and the Republic of Korea in the South, with Seoul as the capital. Some Catholics may have been in Korea before it became a "hermit kingdom" toward the end of the 16th century and closed its borders to foreigners. The real introduction to Catholicism came through lay converts in the last quarter of the 18th century. A priest arriving in the country in 1794 found 4,000 Catholics there who had never seen a priest. A vicariate was erected in 1831 but was not manned for several years thereafter. There were 15,000 Catholics by 1857. Four persecutions in the 19th century took a terrible toll; several thousands died in the last one, 1866-69. Freedom of religion was granted in 1883 when Korea opened its borders. Progress was made thereafter. The hierarchy was established in 1962. Since the war of 1950-1953, there have been no signs of Catholic life in the North, which has been blanketed by a news blackout. In July, 1972, both Koreas agreed to seek peaceful means of reunification. The South maintains diplomatic relations with Vatican City. In 1974, Bishop Tji of Won Ju, South Korea, was convicted by a military court and sentenced to 15 years' imprisonment on a charge of inciting rebellion. (See Index.)

North Korea: Dioc., 2; abb., 1; bp., 1; Caths. (1969), 100,000; tot. pop. (UN est., 1972), 14,680,000.

South Korea: Archd., 3; dioc., 10; p.a., 1; card., 1; abp., 2; bp., 9; parishes, 430; priests, 843 (501 dioc., 342 rel.); sem., 558; p.d., 8; m. rel., 584; w. rel., 2,090; Caths. 802,198 (2.4%); tot. pop. (UN est., 1972), 32,530,000.

Kuwait: Constitutional monarchy (sultanate or sheikdom) in southwest Asia bordering on the Persian Gulf. Remote Christian origins probably date to apostolic times. Islam is the predominant and official religion. Kuwait maintains diplomatic relations with Vatican City.

V.a., 1; parishes, 5; priests, 6 (1 dioc., 5 rel.); m. rel., 5; w. rel., 28; sch., 9; Caths., 17,700; tot. pop. (UN est., 1972), 910,000.

Laos: Constitutional monarchy in southeast Asia, surrounded by China, Vietnam, Khmer Republic, Thailand and Burma; capitals, Vientiane (administrative) and Luang Prabang (royal). Systematic evangelization by French missionaries started about 1881; earlier efforts ended in 1688. A vicariate apostolic was organized in 1899 when there were 8,000 Catholics and 2,000 catechumens in the country. Buddhism is the state religion. Laos has an apostolic delegate.

V.a., 4; bp., 4; priests, 119 (16 dioc., 103 rel.); sem., 3; m. rel., 118; w. rel., 160; sch., 51; inst., 59; Caths., 36,990 (1%); tot. pop. (UN est., 1972), 3,100,000.

Lebanon: Republic in the Middle East, north of Israel; capital, Beirut. Christianity, introduced in apostolic times, was firmly established by the end of the fourth century and has remained so despite heavy Moslem influence since early in the seventh century. The country is the center of the Maronite Rite.

Lebanon maintains diplomatic relations with Vatican City.

There are 17 ecclesiastical jurisdictions in Lebanon serving the following rites: Armenian (1 diocese); Chaldean (1 diocese); Roman (1 vicariate apostolic); Maronite (3 archdioceses and 3 dioceses); Melkite (3 archdioceses, 5 dioceses); the Syrians are served by a patriarchal vicar. The patriarchs of Antioch of the Syrians and Antioch of the Maronites reside in Lebanon.

Caths. 896,775 (30%); tot. pop., 2,960,000.

Lesotho: Constitutional monarchy, an enclave in the southeastern part of the Republic of South Africa; capital, Maseru. Oblates of Mary Immaculate, the first Catholic missionaries in the area, started evangelization in 1862. A prefecture apostolic was organized in 1894. The hierarchy was established in 1951. Lesotho maintains diplomatic relations with Vatican City.

Archd., 1; dioc., 2; abp., 1 (nat.); bp., 2 (1 nat.); parishes, 44; priests, 142 (17 dioc., 125 rel.); sem., 10; m. rel., 222; w. rel., 704; sch., 473; inst., 65; Caths., 442,743; tot. pop. (Govt. est., 1973), 1,200,000.

Liberia: Republic in western Africa, bordering on the Atlantic; capital, Monrovia. Missionary work and influence, dating interruptedly from the 16th century, were slight before the Society of African Missions undertook evangelization in 1906. Liberia maintains diplomatic relations with Vatican City.

V.a., 1; bp., 1; priests, 50 (7 dioc., 43 rel.); sem., 4; m. rel., 66; w. rel., 76; sch., 53; inst., 18; Caths., 22,998 (1%); tot. pop. (1973 est.), 1,650,000.

Libya: Arab republic in northern Africa, on the Mediterranean between the United Arab Republic (Egypt) and Tunisia; capitals are Tripoli and Benghasi. Christianity was probably preached in the area at an early date but was overcome by the spread of Islam from the 630's. Islamization was complete by 1067 and there has been no Christian influence since then. The Catholics in the country belong to the foreign colony. Islam is the state religion. Libya has an apostolic delegate (to North Africa).

V.a., 3; p.a., 1; bp., 2; parishes, 2; priests, 9 (rel.); m. rel., 94; w. rel., 94; Caths., 4,000 (.2%); tot. pop., 2,000,000.

Liechtenstein: Constitutional monarchy in central Europe, in the Alps and on the Rhine between Switzerland and Austria; capital, Vaduz. Christianity in the country dates from the fourth century; the area has been under the jurisdiction of Chur, Switzerland, since about that time. The Reformation had hardly any influence in the country. Catholicism is the state religion but religious freedom for all is guaranteed by law. Pop., 21,000.

Luxembourg: Constitutional monarchy in western Europe, between Belgium, Germany and France; capital, Luxembourg. Christianity, introduced in the fifth and sixth centuries, was firmly established by the end of the eighth century. A full-scale parish system was in existence in the ninth century. Monastic influence was strong until the Reformation, which had minimal influence in the country. The Church experienced some adverse influence from the currents of the French Revolution. Luxembourg maintains diplomatic relations with Vatican City.

Dioc., 1; bp., 1; parishes, 274; priests, 513 (416 dioc., 97 rel.); sem., 29; m. rel., 144; w. rel., 1,573; sch., 15; inst., 27; Caths. 298,720 (87.8%); tot. pop., 339,848.

Macao: Portuguese province in southeast Asia across the Pearl River estuary from Hong Kong. Christianity was introduced by the Jesuits in 1557. Diocese was established in 1576. Macao served as a base for missionary work in Japan and China.

Dioc., 1; bp., 1; parishes, 8; priests, 110 (79 dioc., 31 rel.); sem., 13; m. rel., 59; w. rel., 236; sch., 88; inst., 20; Caths., 27,000; tot. pop., 270,000.

Madeira Islands: Portuguese province, an archipelago 340 miles west of the northwestern coast of Africa; capital, Funchal. Catholicism has had a continuous history since the first half of the 15th century. Statistics are included in those for Portugal.

Malagasy Republic (Madagascar and adjoining islands): Member of the French Community, off the eastern coast of Africa; capital, Tananarive. Missionary efforts were generally fruitless from early in the 16th century until the Jesuits were permitted to start open evangelization about 1845. A prefecture apostolic was set up in 1850 and a vicariate apostolic in the north was placed in charge of the Holy Ghost Fathers in 1898. There were 100,000 Catholics by 1900. The first native bishop was ordained in 1936. The hierarchy was established in 1955. The Malagasy Republic maintains diplomatic relations with Vatican City.

Archd., 3; dioc., 14; card., 1 (nat.); abp., 2 (nat.); bp., 15 (7 nat.); parishes, 108; priests, 749 (131 dioc., 618 rel.); sem., 75; m. rel., 1,039; w. rel., 1,578; sch., 1,879; inst., 162; Caths., 1,600,000 (20%); tot. pop. (Govt. est., 1973), 7,655,134.

Malawi: Republic in the interior of eastern Africa, member of the British Commonwealth; capital, Zomba. Missionary work, begun by Jesuits in the late 16th and early 17th centuries, was generally ineffective until the end of the 19th century. The White Fathers arrived in 1889 and later were joined by others. A vicariate was set up in 1897. The hierarchy was established in 1959. Malawi maintains diplomatic relations with Vatican City.

Archd., 1; dioc., 6; abp., 1 (nat.); bp., 6 (3 nat.); parishes, 108; priests, 321 (72 dioc., 249 rel.); sem., 71; m. rel., 363; w. rel., 575; sch., 693; inst., 120; Caths., 912,240 (19%); tot. pop. (UN est., 1972), 4,670,000.

Malaysia: Parliamentary democracy in southeastern Asia, member of the British Commonwealth, federation of former states of Malaya, Sabah (former Br. North Borneo), and Sarawak; capital, Kuala Lumpur. Christianity, introduced by Portuguese colonists about 1511, was confined almost exclusively to Malacca until late in the 18th century. The effectiveness of evangelization increased from then on because of the recruitment and training of native clergy. Singapore (see separate entry), founded in 1819, became a center for missionary work. Seventeen thousand Catholics were in the Malacca diocese in 1888. Effective evangelization in Sabah and Sarawak began in the second half of the 19th century. The hierarchy was established in 1973. Malaysia has an apostolic delegate.

Archd., 1; dioc., 2; v.a., 3; abp., 1; bp., 4 (3 nat.); parishes, 101; priests, 233 (131 dioc., 102 rel.); sem., 29; m. rel., 234; w. rel., 585; sch., 301; inst., 37; Caths., 313,436 (2.8%); tot. pop. (UN est., 1972), 10,920,000.

Maldives: Republic, an archipelago 400 miles southwest of India and Ceylon; capital, Male. No serious attempt was ever made to evangelize the area, which is completely Moslem.

Tot. pop. (Govt. est., 1973), 122,673.

Mali: Republic, inland in western Africa; capital, Bamako. Catholicism was introduced late in the second half of the 19th century. Missionary work made little progress in the midst of the predominantly Moslem population. A vicariate was set up in 1921. The hierarchy was established in 1955. Mali has an apostolic delegate.

Archd., 1; dioc., 5; abp., 1 (nat.); bp., 5; parishes, 34; priests, 160 (22 dioc., 138 rel.); sem., 5; m. rel., 163; w. rel., 176; sch., 65; inst., 49; Caths., 43,245 (.8%); tot. pop., 5,136,500.

Malta: Parliamentary democracy, member of the British Commonwealth, 58 miles south of Sicily; capital, Valletta. Early catacombs and inscriptions are evidence of the early introduction of Christianity. St. Paul was shipwrecked on Malta in 60. Saracens controlled the island(s) from 870 to 1090, a period of difficulty for the Church. The line of bishops extends from 1090 to the present. Malta maintains diplomatic relations with Vatican City.

Archd., 1; dioc., 1; abp., 1; bp., 2; parishes, 72; priests, 1,069 (571 dioc., 498 rel.); sem., 107; m. rel., 726; w. rel., 1,632; sch., 87; inst., 31; Caths., 307,754 (95%); tot. pop. (Govt. est., 1972), 322,070.

Mauritania: Islamic republic on the northwest coast of Africa; capital, Nouakchott. With few exceptions, the Catholics in the country are members of the foreign colony.

Dioc., 1; bp., 1; parishes, 5; priests, 11 (1 dioc., 10 rel.); m. rel., 10; w. rel., 15; sch., 2; Caths., 6,500 (.5%); tot. pop., 1,200,000.

Mauritius: Self-governing island state, member of the British Commonwealth, 500 miles east of the Malagasy Republic; capital, Port Louis. Catholicism was introduced by Vincentians in 1722. Port Louis, made a vicariate in 1819, was a jumping-off point for missionaries to Australia, Madagascar and South Africa. Mauritius maintains diplomatic relations with Vatican City.

Dioc., 1; bp., 1; parishes, 24; priests, 90 (52 dioc., 38 rel.); sem., 10; m. rel., 68; w. rel., 311; sch., 67; inst., 15; Caths., 275,000 (33%); tot. pop., 832,000.

Melilla: Spanish possession in northern Africa. Statistics are included in those for Spain.

Mexico (United States of Mexico): Republic in Middle America. Christianity was introduced early in the 16th century. Mexico City, made a diocese in 1530, became the missionary and cultural center of the whole country. Missionary work, started in 1524 and forwarded principally by Franciscans, Dominicans, Augustinians and Jesuits, resulted in the baptism of all persons in the central plateau by the end of the century. Progress there and in the rest of the country continued in the following century but tapered off and went into decline in the 18th century, for a variety of reasons ranging from diminishing government support to relaxations of Church discipline. The wars of independence, 1810-21, in which some Catholics participated, created serious problems of adjustment for the Church. Social problems, political unrest and government opposition climaxed in the constitution of 1917 which practically outlawed the Church. Persecution took serious tolls of life and kept the Church underground, under Calles, 1924-1928, again in 1931, and under Cardenas in 1934. President Camacho, 1940-1946, ended persecution and instituted a more lenient policy. The Church, however, still labors under legal and practical disabilities. Mexico has an apostolic delegate.

Archd., 11; dioc., 50; prel., 6; v.a., 1; p.a., 1; card., 2; abp., 9; bp., 63; parishes, 3,057; priests, 9,196 (6,665 dioc., 2,531 rel.); sem., 2,264; p.d., 6; m. rel., 4,440; w. rel., 21,692; sch., 2,625; inst., 705; Caths., 48,670,811 (92%); tot. pop. (UN est., 1972), 52,640,000.

Monaco: Constitutional monarchy, an enclave on the Mediterranean coast of France near the Italian border; capital, Monaco-Ville. Christianity was introduced before 1000. Catholicism is the official religion but freedom is guaranteed for all. Monaco has a minister at Vatican City.

Dioc., 1; bp., 1; parishes, 4; priests, 35 (14 dioc., 21 rel.); sem., 1; m. rel., 59; w. rel., 79; sch., 8; inst., 3; Caths., 21,691 (89%); tot. pop., (1972 est.), 24,300.

Mongolian Peoples' Republic: Republic in north central Asia; capital Ulan Bator. Christianity was introduced by Nestorians. Some Franciscans were in the country in the 13th and 14th centuries, en route to China. Limited evangelization efforts from the 18th century had little success among the Mongols in Outer Mongolia, where Buddhism has predominated for hundreds of years. No Christians were known to be there in 1953. There may be a few Catholics in Inner Mongolia. No foreign missionaries have been in the country since 1953.

Pop. (UN est., 1972), 1,320,000.

Morocco: Constitutional monarchy in northwest Africa with Atlantic and Mediterranean coastlines; capital, Rabat. Christianity was known in the area by the end of the third century. Bishops from Morocco attended a council at Carthage in 484. Catholic life survived under Visigoth and, from 700, Arab rule; later it became subject to influence from the Spanish, Portuguese and French. Islam is the state religion. The hierarchy was established in 1955. Morocco has an apostolic delegate (to North Africa).

Archd., 2; abp., 2; parishes, 17; priests, 44 (rel.); m. rel., 172; w. rel., 585; sch., 66; inst., 16; Caths., 190,182 (.6%); tot. pop. (UN est., 1972), 15,830,000.

Mozambique: Portuguese overseas province in southeast Africa, bordering on the Indian Ocean; capital, Laurenco Marques. Christianity was introduced by Portuguese Jesuits about the middle of the 16th century. Evangelization continued from then until the 18th century when it went into decline largely because of the Portuguese government's expulsion of the Jesuits. Conditions worsened in the 1830's, improved after 1881, but deteriorated again during the anticlerical period from 1910 to 1925. Conditions improved in 1940, the year Portugal concluded a new concordat with the Holy See and the hierarchy was established. Church-state tensions have developed in recent years because of outspoken criticism by missionaries and Church leaders of Portugal's policies in Mozambique. (See Index.)

Archd., 1; dioc., 8; abp., 1; bp., 7; parishes, 131; priests, 578 (93 dioc., 485 rel.); sem., 116; p.d., 2; m. rel., 781; w. rel., 1,307; sch., 3,925; inst., 352; Caths., 1,474,130 (17%); tot. pop., 6,536,635.

Namibia (South West Africa): Territory in South Africa in dispute between the Republic of South Africa and the United Nations; capital, Windhoek. The area shares the history of the Republic of South Africa. Namibia (formerly South West Africa) has an apostolic delegate (to South Africa).

V.a., 2; bp., 2; parishes, 21; priests, 77 (3 dioc., 74 rel.); sem., 2; m. rel., 138; w. rel., 340; sch., 84; inst., 81; Caths., 122,270 (15%); tot. pop., 780,764.

Nepal: Constitutional monarchy, the only Hindu kingdom in the world, in central Asia south of the Himalayas between India and Tibet; capital, Katmandu. Little is known of the country before the 15th century. Some Jesuits passed through from 1628 and some sections were evangelized in the 18th century,

with minimal results, before the country was closed to foreigners. Conversions from Hinduism, the state religion, are not recognized in law. Christian missionary work is not allowed. Any Catholics in the country have been under the jurisdiction of the Patna diocese, India, since 1919.

Tot. pop., (1972 est.), 11,470,000.

Netherlands: Kingdom in northwestern Europe; capital, Amsterdam (seat of the government, The Hague). Evangelization, begun about the turn of the sixth century by Irish, Anglo-Saxon and Frankish missionaries, resulted in Christianization of the country by 800 and subsequent strong influence on The Lowlands. Invasion by French Calvinists in 1572 brought serious losses to the Catholic Church and made the Reformed Church dominant. Catholics suffered a practical persecution of official repression and social handicap in the 17th century. The schism of Utrecht occurred in 1724. Only one-third of the population was Catholic in 1726. The Church had only a skeleton organization from 1702 to 1853, when the hierarchy was reestablished. Despite this upturn, cultural isolation was the experience of Catholics until about 1914. From then on new vigor came into the life of the Church, and a whole new climate of interfaith relations began to develop. Before and since the Second Vatican Council, the vigor and variety of thought and practice in the Dutch Church have moved it to the vanguard position of "progressive" renewal. The Netherlands maintains diplomatic relations with Vatican City.

Archd., 1; dioc., 6; card., 3; bp., 6; parishes, 1,809; priests, 6,428 (3,360 dioc., 3,068 rel.); sem., 151; p.d., 3; m. rel., 6,828; w. rel., 22,678; Caths., 5,480,242 (41%); tot. pop., 13,333,502.

Netherlands Antilles: Autonomous part of the Kingdom of The Netherlands. Consists of two groups of islands in the Caribbean: Curacao, Aruba and Bonaire, off the northern coast of Venezuela; and St. Eustatius, Saba and the southern part of St. Martaan, southeast of Puerto Rico; capital, Willemstad on Curacao. Christianity was introduced in the 16th century.

Dioc., 1; bp., 1; parishes, 34; priests, 63 (5 dioc., 58 rel.); sem., 2; m. rel., 951; w. rel., 251; sch., 191; inst., 13; Caths., 175,000; tot. pop. (1971 est.), 230,000.

New Caledonia: French territory consisting of several islands in Oceania east of Queensland, Australia; capital, Noumea. Catholicism was introduced in 1843, nine years after Protestant missionaries began evangelization. A vicariate was organized in 1847. The hierarchy was established in 1966.

Archd., 1; abp., 1; parishes, 36; priests, 57 (9 dioc., 48 rel.); sem., 3; m. rel., 112; w. rel., 244; sch., 71; inst., 14; Caths., 80,000; tot. pop., 120,000.

New Guinea: See Papua — New Guinea.

New Hebrides: Islands in the southwest Pacific, about 500 miles west of Fiji, under joint British-French administration; capital, Vila. Effective, though slow, evangelization by Catholic missionaries began about 1887. A vicariate apostolic was set up in 1904. The hierarchy was established in 1966.

Dioc., 1; bp., 1; priests, 26 (3 dioc., 23 rel.); sem., 4; m. rel., 26; w. rel., 74; inst., 12; Caths., 13,909; tot. pop., (1972 est.), 90,000.

New Zealand: Dominion in the British Commonwealth, a group of islands in Oceania 1,200 miles southeast of Australia: capital, Wellington. Protestant missionaries were the first evangelizers. On North Island, Catholic missionaries started work before the establishment of two dioceses in 1848; their work among the Maoris was not organized until about 1881. On South Island, whose first resident priest arrived in 1840, a diocese was established in 1869. These three jurisdictions were joined in a province in 1896. The Marists were the outstanding Catholic missionaries in the area. New Zealand established diplomatic relations with Vatican City in 1973.

Archd., 1; dioc., 3; bp., 3; parishes, 285; priests, 860 (515 dioc., 345 rel.); sem., 91; m. rel., 815; w. rel., 2,444; sch., 348; inst., 29; Caths., 418,631 (14%); tot. pop. (1973 est.), 2,961,869.

Ngwane (Swaziland): Constitutional monarchy in southern Africa, almost totally surrounded by the Republic of South Africa; capital, Mbabane. Missionary work was entrusted to the Servites in 1913. A prefecture apostolic was organized in 1923. The hierarchy was established in 1951. Ngwane has an apostolic delegate (to South Africa).

Dioc., 1; bp., 1; parishes, 10; priests, 34 (3 dioc., 31 rel.); sem., 1; m. rel., 41; w. rel., 128; sch., 61; inst., 26; Caths., 37,812 (9%); tot. pop. (UN est., 1972), 420,000.

Nicaragua: Republic in Central America: capital, Managua. Evangelization began shortly after the Spanish conquest about 1524 and eight years later the first bishop took over jurisdiction of the Church in the country. Jesuits were leaders in missionary work during the colonial period, which lasted until the 1820's. Evangelization endeavor increased after establishment of the republic in 1838. In this century it was extended to the Atlantic coastal area where Protestant missionaries had begun work about the middle of the 1900's. Nicaragua maintains diplomatic relations with Vatican City.

Archd., 1; dioc., 4; prel., 1; v.a., 1; abp., 1; bp., 6; parishes, 164; priests, 310 (97 dioc., 213 rel.); sem., 45; m. rel., 267; w. rel., 484; sch., 222; inst., 49; Caths., 1,929,524 (92.6%); tot. pop., 2,082,529.

Niger: Republic in west central Africa; capital, Niamey. The first mission was set up in 1831. A prefecture apostolic was organized in 1942 and the first diocese was established in 1961. The country is predominantly Moslem. Niger maintains diplomatic relations with Vatican City.

Dioc., 1; bp., 1; parishes, 11; priests, 25 (7 dioc., 18 rel.); sem., 1; m. rel., 41; w. rel., 76; sch., 19; inst., 13; Caths., 12,300 (.2%); tot. pop. (UN est., 1972), 4,210,000.

Nigeria: Republic in western Africa; capital, Lagos. The Portuguese introduced Catholicism in the coastal region in the 15th century. Capuchins did some evangelization in the 17th century but systematic missionary work did not get underway along the coast until about 1840. A vicariate for this area was organized in 1870. A prefecture was set up in 1911 for missions in the northern part of the country where Islam was strongly entrenched. From 1967, when Biafra seceded, until early in 1970 the country was torn by civil war. The hierarchy was established in 1950. Nigeria has an apostolic delegate.

Archd., 3; dioc., 24; p.a., 1; abp., 4 (3 nat.); bp., 26 (17 nat.); parishes, 316; priests, 836 (288 dioc., 548 rel.); sem., 601; m. rel., 723; w. rel., 644; sch., 2,011; inst., 339; Caths., 3,500,000 (6%); tot. pop. (UN est., 1972), 58,020,000.

Norway: Constitutional monarchy in northern Europe, the western part of the Scandinavian peninsula; capital, Oslo. Evangelization begun in the ninth century by missionaries from England and Ireland put the Church on a firm footing about the turn of the 11th century. The first diocese was set up in 1153 and development of the Church progressed until the Black Death in 1349 inflicted losses from which it never recovered. Lutheranism, introduced from outside in 1537 and furthered cautiously, gained general acceptance by about 1600 and was made the state religion. Legal and other measures crippled the Church, forcing priests to flee the country and completely disrupting normal activity. Changes for the better came in the 19th century, with the granting of religious liberty in 1845 and the repeal of many legal disabilities in 1897. Norway was administered as a single apostolic vicariate from 1892 to 1932, when it was divided into three jurisdictions under the supervision of the Congregation for the Propagation of the Faith. Norway has an apostolic delegate (to Scandinavia).

Dioc., 1; v.a., 2; bp., 3; parishes, 21; priests, 65 (20 dioc., 45 rel.); sem., 2; m. rel., 41; w. rel., 459; sch., 4; inst., 15; Caths., 11,100 (.27%); tot. pop. 4,000,000.

Oman: See Arabian Peninsula.

Pakistan: Islamic republic in southwestern Asia, member of the British Commonwealth; capital, Islamabad. (Formerly included East Pakistan which became the independent nation of Bangladesh in 1971.) Islam, firmly established in the eighth century, is the state religion. Christian evangelization of the native population began about the middle of the 19th century, years after earlier scattered attempts. The hierarchy was established in 1950. Pakistan maintains diplomatic relations with Vatican City.

Archd., 1; dioc., 5; card., 1 bp., 8 (3 nat.); parishes, 76; priests, 224 (70 dioc., 154 rel.); sem., 41; m. rel., 234; w. rel., 575; sch., 206; inst., 119; Caths., 337,288 (.5%); tot. pop., 64,892,000.

Panama: Republic in Central America; capital, Panama City. Catholicism was introduced by Franciscan missionaries and evangelization started in 1514. The Panama diocese, oldest in the Americas, was set up at the same time. The Catholic Church has favored status and state aid for missions, charities and parochial schools, but religious freedom is guaranteed to all religions. Panama maintains diplomatic relations with Vatican City.

Archd., 1; dioc., 3; prel., 1; v.a., 1; abp., 1; bp., 6; parishes, 103; priests, 327 (85 dioc., 242 rel.); sem., 22; m. rel., 294; w. rel., 464; sch., 76; inst., 19; Caths., 1,354,717 (89.7%); tot. pop., 1,509,595.

Panama Canal Zone: Under control of the United States, which was given Canal rights following Panamanian independence from Colombian 1903. Catholic statistics are included in those reported for Panama, above.

Papua-New Guinea: Self-governing territory (formerly under Australian administration) in southwest Pacific. Consists of the eastern half of the southwestern Pacific island of New Guinea and the Northern Solomon Islands; capital, Lae. (For statistics on the Indonesian portion of New Guinea, see Indonesia.) Marists began evangelization about 1844 but were handicapped by many factors, including "spheres of influence" laid out for Catholic and Protestant missionaries. A prefecture apostolic was set up in 1896 and placed in charge of the Divine Word Missionaries. The territory suffered greatly during World War II. Hierarchy was established for New Guinea and adjacent islands in 1966. The area has an apostolic delegate (the pronuncio to Australia).

Archd., 3; dioc., 12; abp., 3; bp., 12; parishes, 236; priests, 509 (44 dioc., 465 rel.); sem., 48; p.d., 5; m. rel., 731; w. rel., 674; sch., 940; inst., 478; Caths., 706,676 (26%); tot. pop., 2,679,724.

Paraguay: Republic in central South America; capital, Asuncion. Catholicism was introduced in 1542, evangelization began almost immediately. A diocese erected in 1547 was occupied for the first time in 1556. On many occasions thereafter dioceses in the country were left unoccupied because of political and other reasons. Jesuits who came into the country after 1609 devised the reductions system for evangelizing the Indians, teaching them agriculture, husbandry, trades and other useful arts, and giving them experience in property use and community life. The reductions were communes of Indians only,

under the direction of the missionaries. About 50 of them were established in southern Brazil, Uruguay and northeastern Argentina as well as in Paraguay. They had an average population of three to four thousand. At their peak, some 30 reductions had a population of 100,000. Political officials regarded the reductions with disfavor because they did not control them and feared that the Indians trained in them might foment revolt and upset the established colonial system under Spanish control. The reductions lasted until about 1768 when their Jesuit founders and directors were expelled from Latin America. Church-state relations following independence from Spain in 1811 were tense as often as not because of government efforts to control the Church through continued exercise of Spanish patronage rights and by other means. The Church as well as the whole country suffered a great deal during the War of the Triple Alliance from 1865-70. After that time, the Church had the same kind of experience in Paraguay as in the rest of Latin America with forces of liberalism, anticlericalism, massive educational needs, poverty, a shortage of priests and other personnel. Most recently church leaders have been challenging the government to initiate long-needed economic and social reforms. Paraguay maintains diplomatic relations with Vatican City.

Archd., 1; dioc., 4; prel., 3; v.a., 2; abp., 1; bp., 9; parishes, 210; priests, 463 (199 dioc., 264 rel.); sem., 63; m. rel., 399; w. rel., 784; sch., 435; inst., 149; Caths., 2,233,418 (89.7%); tot. pop., 2,488,468.

Peru: Republic on the western coast of South America; capital, Lima. An effective diocese became operational in 1537, five years after the Spanish conquest. Evangelization, already underway, developed for some time after 1570 but deteriorated before the end of the colonial period in the 1820's. The first native-born saint of the new world was a Peruvian, Rose of Lima, a Dominican tertiary who died in 1617 and was canonized in 1671. In the new republic founded after the wars of independence the Church experienced problems of adjustment and many of the difficulties that cropped up in other South American countries: government efforts to control it through continuation of the patronage rights of the Spanish crown; suppression of houses of religious and expropriation of church property; religious indifference and outright hostility. The Church was given special status but was not made the established religion. Peru maintains diplomatic relations with Vatican City.

Archd., 7; dioc., 12; prel., 14; v.a., 8; card., 1; abp., 6; bp., 35; parishes, 942; priests, 2,374 (1,003 dioc., 1,371 rel.); sem., 190; p.d., 8; m. rel., 1,893; w. rel., 4,626; sch., 1,127; inst., 403; Caths., 13,704,021 (92%); tot. pop., 14,821,510.

Philippine Islands: Republic, an archipelago of 7,000 islands off the southeast coast of Asia; capital, Quezon City. Systematic evangelization was begun in 1564 and resulted in firm establishment of the Church by the 19th century. During the period of Spanish rule, which lasted from the discovery of the islands by Magellan in 1521 to 1898, the Church experienced difficulties with the patronage system under which the Spanish crown tried to control ecclesiastical affairs through episcopal and other appointments. This system ended in 1898 when the United States gained possession of the islands and instituted a policy of separation of Church and state. Anticlericalism flared late in the 19th century. The Aglipayan schism, an attempt to set up a nationalist church, occurred a few years later, in 1902. The republic maintains diplomatic relations with Vatican City.

Archd., 10; dioc., 28; prel., 12; v.a., 4; card., 1; abp., 9; bp., 50; parishes, 1,741; priests, 4,511 (2,215 dioc., 2,296 rel.); sem., 1,970; p.d., 1; m. rel., 3,597; w. rel., 6,769; sch., 1,633; inst., 410; Caths., 31,854,259 (82%); tot. pop., 38,810,863.

Poland: People's republic in eastern Europe; capital, Warsaw. The first traces of Christianity date from the second half of the ninth century. Its spread was accelerated by the union of the Slavs in the 10th century. The first bishopric was set up in 968. The Gniezno archdiocese, with suffragan sees and a mandate to evangelize the borderlands as well as Poland, was established in 1000. Steady growth continued thereafter, with religious orders and their schools playing a major role. Some tensions with the Orthodox were experienced. The Reformation, supported mainly by city dwellers and the upper classes, peaked from about the middle of the 16th century, resulting in numerous conversions to Lutheranism, the Reformed Church and the Bohemian Brethren. A successful Counter-Reformation, with the Jesuits in a position of leadership, was completed by about 1632. The movement served a nationalist as well as religious purpose; in restoring religious unity to a large degree, it united the country against potential invaders, the Swedes, Russians and Turks. The Counter-Reformation had bad side effects, leading to the repression of Protestants long after it was over and to prejudice against Orthodox who returned to allegiance with Rome in 1596 and later. The Church, in the same manner as the entire country, was adversely affected by the partitions of the 18th and 19th centuries. Russification hurt the Orthodox who had reunited with Rome and the Latins who were in the majority. Germans extended their Kulturkampf to the area they controlled. The Austrians exhibited some degree of tolerance. In the republic established after World War I the Church reorganized itself, continued to serve as a vital force in national life, and enjoyed generally harmonious relations with the state. Progres-

sive growth was strong until 1939 when disaster struck in the form of invasion by German and Russian forces and six years of war. In 1945, seven years before the adoption of a Soviet-type of constitution, the Communist-controlled government initiated a policy that included a constant program of atheistic propaganda; a strong campaign against the hierarchy and clergy; the imprisonment in 1948 of 700 priests and even more religious; rigid limitation of the activities of religious; censorship and curtailment of the Catholic press and Catholic Action; interference with church administration and appointments of the clergy; the "deposition" of Cardinal Wyszynski in 1953 and the imprisonment of other members of the hierarchy; the suppression of "Caritas," the Catholic charitable organization; promotion of "Progressive Catholic" activities and a small minority of "patriotic priests." Establishment of the Gomulka regime, the freeing of Cardinal Wyszynski in October, 1956, and the signing of an agreement two months later by bishops and state officials, led to some improvement of conditions. The underlying fact, however, was that the regime conceded to Catholics only so much as was necessary to secure support of the government as a more tolerable evil than the harsh and real threat of a Russian-imposed puppet government like that in Hungary. This has been the controlling principle in Church-state relations. Auxiliary Bishop Ladislaw Rubin of Gniezno sketched the general state of affairs in March, 1968. He said that there was no sign that the government had any intention of releasing its oppressive grip on the Church. As evidence of the "climate of asphyxiation" in the country he cited: persistent questioning of priests by officials concerning their activities; the prohibition against Catholic schools, hospitals and charitable works; the financial burden of a 60 per cent tax on church income. Cardinal Wyszynski denounced "enforced atheism" in a Lenten pastoral in the same year. In May, 1969, the bishops drafted a list of grievances against the government which, they said, were "only some examples of difficulties which demonstrated the situation of the Church in our homeland." The grievances were: refusal of permits to build new churches and establish new parishes; refusal of permission "for the organization of new religion classes"; pressure on Catholics who attend religious ceremonies; censorship and the lack of an independent Catholic daily newspaper; lack of representation in public life; restriction of "freedom to conduct normal pastoral work" in the western portion of the country. There was a move toward improvement in Church-state relations in 1971-72. In 1973, the Polish bishops issued a pastoral letter urging Catholics to resist the official atheism imposed by the government. In 1974 the Polish bishops expressed approval of renewed Vatican efforts at regularizing Church-state relations but insisted that they (the bishops) be consulted on every step of the negotiations.

Archd., 8; dioc., 23; ap. ex., 1; card., 2; abp., 1; bp., 65; parishes, 7,276; priests, 19,164 (15,153 dioc., 4,011 rel.); sem., 3,053; p.d., 1; m. rel., 6,358; w. rel., 25,999; sch., 30; inst., 299; Caths. (est.), 30,000,000 (89%); tot. pop. (UN est., 1972), 33,070,000.

Polynesia, French: French possession in the southern Pacific, including Tahiti and the Marquesas Islands; capital, Papeete. The first phase of evangelization in the Marquesas Islands, begun in 1838, resulted in 216 baptisms in 10 years. A vicariate was organized in 1848 but real progress was not made until after the baptism of native rulers in 1853. Persecution caused missionaries to leave the islands several times. By the 1960's, more than 95 per cent of the population was Catholic. Isolated attempts to evangelize Tahiti were made in the 17th and 18th centuries. Two Picpus Fathers began missionary work in 1831. A vicariate was organized in 1848. By 1908, despite the hindrances of Protestant opposition, disease and other factors, the Church had firm roots.

Archd., 1; dioc., 1; abp., 1; bp., 1; parishes, 82; priests, 48 (9 dioc., 39 rel.); sem., 1; m. rel., 76; w. rel., 51; sch., 20; inst., 3; Caths., 39,119; tot. pop., 130,000.

Portugal: Republic in the western part of the Iberian peninsula; capital, Lisbon. Christianity was introduced before the fourth century. From the fifth century to early in the eighth century the Church experienced difficulties from the physical invasion of barbarians and the intellectual invasion of doctrinal errors in the forms of Arianism, Priscillianism and Pelagianism. The Church survived under the rule of Arabs from about 711 and of the Moors until 1249. Ecclesiastical life was fairly vigorous from 1080 to 1185, and monastic influence became strong. A decline set in about 1450. Several decades later Portugal became the jumping-off place for many missionaries to newly discovered colonies. The Reformation had little effect in the country. Beginning about 1750, Pombal, minister of foreign affairs and prime minister, mounted a frontal attack on the Jesuits whom he succeeded in expelling from Portugal and the colonies. His anti-Jesuit campaign successful Pombal also attempted, and succeeded to some extent, in controlling the Church in Portugal until his fall from power about 1777. Liberal revolutionaries with anti-Church policies made the 19th century a difficult one for the Church. Similar policies prevailed in Church-state relations in this century until the accession of Salazar to power in 1928. In 1940 he concluded a concordat with the Holy See which regularized Church-state relations but still left the Church in a subservient condition. The prevailing spirit of church authorities in Portugal remains rather conservative. In 1971 several priests were tried for subversion for speaking out against colonialism and for taking part in guerrilla activities in Angola. Portugal maintains diplomatic relations with Vatican City.

Patriarchate, 1; archd., 2; dioc., 14; card., 3; abp., 4; bp., 14; parishes, 4,292; priests, 5,097 (4,198 dioc., 899 rel.); sem., 440; m. rel., 1,615; w. rel., 7,183; sch., 393; inst., 519; Caths., 8,388,549 (95%); tot. pop. (UN est., 1972), 8,830,000.

Puerto Rico: A US commonwealth, the smallest of the Greater Antilles, 885 miles southeast of the southern coast of Florida; capital, San Juan. Following its discovery by Columbus in 1493, the island was evangelized by Spanish missionaries and remained under Spanish ecclesiastical as well as political control until 1898 when it became a possession of the United States. The original diocese, San Juan, was erected in 1511. The present hierarchy was established in 1960.

Archd., 1; dioc., 3; card., 1; bp., 4; parishes, 204; priests, 705 (269 dioc., 436 rel.); sem., 49; m. rel., 575; w. rel., 1,621; sch., 180; inst., 144; Caths., 2,425,528 (88.8%); tot. pop., 2,728,841.

Reunion: French overseas department, 450 miles east of Madagascar; capital, Saint-Denis. Catholicism was introduced in 1667 and some intermittent missionary work was done through the rest of the century. A prefecture apostolic was organized in 1712. Vincentians began work there in 1817 and were joined later by Holy Ghost Fathers. Reunion has an apostolic delegate.

Dioc., 1; bp., 1; parishes, 64; priests, 123 (64 dioc., 59 rel.); sem., 12; m. rel., 112; w. rel., 496; sch., 43; inst., 34; Caths., 437,000; tot. pop., 468,000.

Rhodes: Greek island in the Aegean Sea, 112 miles from the southwestern coast of Asia Minor. A diocese was established about the end of the third century. A bishop from Rhodes attended the Council of Nicaea in 325. Most of the Christians followed the Eastern Churches into schism in the 11th century and became Orthodox. Turks controlled the island from 1522 to 1912. The small Catholic population, for whom a diocese existed from 1328 to 1546, lived in crossfire between Turks and Orthodox. After 1719 Franciscans provided pastoral care for the Catholics, for whom an archdiocese was erected in 1928.

Archd., 1; parishes, 2; priests, 1 (rel.); m. rel., 5; Caths., 432.

Rhodesia: Self-governing state in south central Africa; capital, Salisbury. Earlier unsuccessful missionary ventures preceded the introduction of Catholicism in 1879. Missionaries began to make progress after 1893. The hierarchy was established in 1955. In 1969, four years after the government of Ian Smith made a unilateral declaration of independence from England, a new constitution was enacted for the purpose of assuring continued white supremacy over the black majority. Catholic and Protestant prelates in the country have protested rigorously against the constitution and related enactments as opposed to human rights of the blacks and restrictive of the Church's freedom to carry out its pastoral, educational and social service functions. The first black bishop was ordained in 1973. Rhodesia has an apostolic delegate (to South Africa).

Archd., 1; dioc., 4; p.a. 1; abp., 1; bp., 5 (1 nat.); parishes, 81; priests, 374 (42 dioc., 332 rel.); sem., 72; m. rel., 506 w. rel., 1,011; sch., 190; inst., 169; Caths., 540,114 (10%); tot. pop., 5,395,696.

Rumania: Socialist republic in southeastern Europe; capital, Bucharest. Latin Christianity, introduced in the third century, all but disappeared during the barbarian invasions. The Byzantine Rite was introduced by the Bulgars about the beginning of the eighth century and established firm roots. It eventually became Orthodox, but a large number of its adherents returned later to union with Rome. Attempts to reintroduce the Latin Rite on any large scale have been unsuccessful. Communists took over the government following World War II, forced the abdication of Michael I in 1947, and enacted a Soviet type of constitution in 1952. By that time a campaign against religion was already in progress. In 1948 the government denounced a concordat concluded in 1929, nationalized all schools and passed a law on religions which resulted in the disorganization of Church administration. The 1.5 million-member Rumanian Byzantine Rite Church, by government decree, was incorporated into the Rumanian Orthodox Church, and the Orthodox bishops then seized the cathedrals of Roman Catholic bishops. Five of the six Latin Rite bishops were immediately disposed of by the government, and the last was sentenced to 18 years' imprisonment in 1951, when a great many arrests of priests and laymen were made. Religious orders were suppressed in 1949. Since 1948 more than 50 priests have been executed and 200 have died in prison. One hundred priests were reported in prison at the end of 1958. Some change for the better in Church-state relations was reported after the middle of the summer of 1964, although restrictions were still in effect. About 1,200 priests were engaged in parish work in August, 1965.

Archd., 2; dioc., 8; ord., 1; bp., 2. No recent statistics are available on the number of Catholics. There were an estimated 1,140,000 Catholics (5.9% of the population) in 1969. Tot. pop. (UN est., 1972), 20,770,000.

Rwanda: Republic in east central Africa; capital, Kigali. Catholicism was introduced about the turn of the 20th century. The hierarchy was established in 1959. Intertribal warfare between the ruling Hutus (90 per cent of the population) and the Tutsis (formerly the ruling aristocracy) has plagued the country for several years. Rwanda maintains diplomatic relations with Vatican City.

Archd., 1; dioc., 4; abp., 1; bp., 4 (nat.); parishes, 94; priests, 371 (221 dioc., 150 rel.); sem., 88; m. rel., 350; w. rel., 650; sch., 1,171; inst., 149; Caths., 1,614,743 (39.9%); tot. pop., 4,040,130.

Ryukyu Islands: Consists of Okinawa and 72 other islands in western Pacific. Statistics included in Japan.

St. Lucia: British Associated State in West Indies; capital, Castries.

Dioc., 1; parishes, 21; priests, 32 (4 dioc., 28 rel.); sem., 6; m. rel., 34; w. rel., 35; sch., 60; inst., 3; Caths., 92,000; tot. pop., 101,136.

St. Pierre and Miquelon: French overseas territory, islands near the southwest coast of Newfoundland. Catholicism was introduced about 1689.

V.a., 1; bp., 1; priests, 5 (1 dioc., 4 rel.); m. rel., 5; w. rel., 15; sch., 6; inst., 2; Caths., 5,567; tot. pop., 5,630.

Samoa: Includes the independent state of Western Samoa, American Samoa, and the New Zealand dependency of Tokelau in the southwestern Pacific. Catholic missionary work began in 1845. Most of the missions now in operation were established by 1870 when the Catholic population numbered about 5,000. Additional progress was made in missionary work from 1896. The first Samoan priest was ordained in 1892. The hierarchy was established in 1966.

Dioc., 1; card., 1; parishes, 21; priests, 32 (5 dioc., 27 rel.); sem., 8; m. rel., 47; w. rel., 105; sch., 29; Caths., 36,798; tot. pop., 174,866. (Figures are from 1970.)

San Marino: Republic, a 24-square-mile enclave in northeastern Italy; capital, San Marino. The date of initial evangelization is not known, but a diocese was established by the end of the third century. Ecclesiastically, it forms part of the diocese of Montefeltro in Italy. San Marino is represented by a minister at Vatican City.

Population (entirely Catholic), 20,000.

Sao Tome and Principe: Portuguese overseas territory, islands off the western coast of Africa in the Gulf of Guinea. Evangelization was begun by the Portuguese who discovered the islands in 1471-72. The Sao Tome diocese was established in 1534.

Dioc., 1; parishes, 12; priests, 13 (rel.); m. rel., 13; w. rel., 18; sch., 9; inst., 1; Caths., 67,816; tot. pop., 69,032.

Saudi Arabia: See Arabian Peninsula.

Scotland: Part of the United Kingdom, in the northern British Isles; capital, Edinburgh. Christianity was introduced by the early years of the fifth century. The arrival of St. Columba and his monks in 563 inaugurated a new era of evangelization which reached into remote areas by the end of the sixth century. He was extremely influential in determining the character of the Celtic Church, which was tribal, monastic, and in union with Rome.

Considerable disruption of church activity resulted from Scandinavian invasions in the late eighth and ninth centuries. By 1153 the Scottish Church took a turn away from its insularity and was drawn into closer contact with the European community. Anglo-Saxon religious and political relations, complicated by rivalries between princes and ecclesiastical superiors, were not always the happiest. Religious orders expanded greatly in the 12th century. From shortly after the Norman Conquest of England to 1560 the Church suffered adverse effects from the Hundred Years' War, the Black Death, the Western Schism and other developments. In 1560 parliament abrogated papal supremacy over the Church in Scotland and committed the country to Protestantism in 1567. The Catholic Church was proscribed, to remain that way for more than 200 years, and the hierarchy was disbanded. Defections made the Church a minority religion from that time on. Presbyterian church government was ratified in 1690. Priests launched the Scottish Mission in 1653, incorporating themselves as a mission body under a prefect apostolic and working underground to serve the faithful in much the same way their confreres did in England. About 100 heather priests, trained in clandestine places in the heather country, were ordained by the early 19th century. Catholics got some relief from legal disabilities in 1793 and more later. Many left the country about that time. Some of their numbers were filled subsequently by immigrants from Ireland. The hierarchy was restored in 1878. Scotland, though predominantly Protestant, has a better record for tolerance than Northern Ireland.

Archd., 2; dioc., 6; card., 1; abp., 1; bp., 8; parishes, 451; priests, 1,155 (921 dioc., 234 rel.); sem., 139; m. rel., 418; w. rel., 1,300; sch., 150; inst., 43; Caths., 820,928 (15%); tot. pop., 5,210,000.

Senegal: Republic, member of the French Community, in western Africa; capital, Dakar. The country had its first contact with Catholicism through the Portuguese some time after 1460. Some incidental missionary work was done by Jesuits and Capuchins in the 16th and 17th centuries. A vicariate for the area was placed in charge of the Holy Ghost Fathers in 1779. More effective evangelization efforts were accomplished after the Senegambia vicariate was organized in 1863. The hierarchy was established in 1955. Senegal maintains diplomatic relations with Vatican City.

Archd., 1; dioc., 4; p.a., 1; abp., 1 (nat.); bp., 3 (2 nat.); parishes, 42; priests, 199 (50 dioc., 149 rel.); sem., 22; m. rel., 265; w. rel., 498; sch., 128; inst., 106; Caths., 172,078 (4%); tot. pop. (1972 est.), 4,120,000.

Seychelles Islands: British colony (scheduled for independence in 1975) of 92 islands in the Indian Ocean 970 miles east of Kenya;

capital, Victoria on Mahe. Catholicism was introduced in the 18th century. A vicariate apostolic was organized in 1852. All education in the islands was conducted under Catholic auspices until 1954. The colony has an apostolic delegate (pro-nuncio to Kenya).

Dioc., 1; parishes, 17; priests, 29 (4 dioc., 25 rel.); sem., 2; m. rel., 40; w. rel., 75; sch., 32; inst., 3; Caths., 50,000; tot. pop., 55,000.

Siberia: Republic in the USSR, in northern Asia.

Dioc., 1; v.a. 1.

Sierra Leone: Republic, member of the British Commonwealth, on the western coast of Africa; capital, Freetown. Catholicism was introduced in 1858. Members of the African Missions Society, the first Catholic missionaries in the area, were joined by Holy Ghost Fathers in 1864. Protestant missionaries were active in the area before their Catholic counterparts. Educational work had a major part in Catholic endeavor. The hierarchy was established in 1950. Sierra Leone has an apostolic delegate (the pro-nuncio to Liberia).

Archd., 1; dioc., 2; abp., 1; bp., 2 (1 nat.); parishes, 26; priests, 107 (3 dioc., 104 rel.); sem., 20; m. rel., 122; w. rel., 77; sch., 421; inst., 127; Caths., 52,459 (1.9%); tot. pop. (UN est., 1972), 2,630,000.

Sikkim: Protectorate of India in the Himalayas south of Tibet; capital, Gangtok. Some evangelization took place after 1848. Buddhism is the state religion. The territory is under the jurisdiction of the diocese of Darjeeling, India.

Tot. pop., 191,000.

Singapore: Independent island republic off the southern tip of the Malay Peninsula; member of the British Commonwealth. Christianity was introduced in the area by Portuguese colonists about 1511. Singapore was founded in 1819; the first parish church was built in 1846. Singapore has an apostolic delegate.

Archd., 1; abp., 1; priests, 81 (57 dioc., 24 rel.); Caths., 71,000; tot. pop., 2,075,000 (Fides).

Solomon Islands: British protectorate in Oceania; capital, Honiara, on Guadalcanal. Evangelization of the Southern Solomons, begun earlier but interrupted because of violence against them, was resumed by the Marists in 1898. A vicariate apostolic was organized in 1912. A similar jurisdiction was set up for the Western Solomons in 1959. World War II caused a great deal of damage to mission installations. Catholic statistics for the Northern Solomons, where Catholic missionary work started in 1899 and a vicariate was set up in 1930, are included in those reported for New Guinea.

Dioc., 2; bp., 2; parishes, 27; priests, 42 (6 dioc., 36 rel.); sem., 3; m. rel., 58; w. rel., 149; sch., 77; inst., 33; Caths., 33,808; tot. pop., 194,772.

Somalia: Republic on the eastern coast of Africa; capital, Mogadishu. The country has been Moslem for centuries. Pastoral activity has been confined to immigrants. Schools and hospitals were nationalized in 1972, resulting in the departure of some foreign missionaries. Somalia has an apostolic delegate (to the Red Sea Region).

V.a., 1; priests, 14 (rel.); m. rel., 16; w. rel., 71; inst., 2; Caths., 3,200; tot. pop., 3,000,000.

Somaliland, French: See Afars and Issas.

South Africa: Republic in the southern part of Africa; capitals, Capetown (legislative) and Pretoria (administrative). Christianity was introduced by the Portuguese who discovered the Cape of Good Hope in 1498. Boers, who founded Cape Town in 1652, expelled Catholics from the region. There was no Catholic missionary activity from that time until the 19th century. After a period of British opposition, a bishop established residence in 1837 and evangelization got underway thereafter among the Bantus and white immigrants. In recent years church authorities have strongly protested the white supremacy policy of apartheid which seriously infringes the human rights of the native blacks and impedes the Church from carrying out its pastoral, educational and social service functions. The hierarchy was established in 1951. South Africa has an apostolic delegate.

Archd., 4; dioc., 17; abb., 1; p.a., 4; card., 1; abp., 4; bp., 17; parishes, 1,031; priests, 1,187 (283 dioc., 904 rel.); sem., 59; p.d., 27; m. rel., 1,414; w. rel., 4,583; sch., 849; inst., 312; Caths., 1,844,270 (8.6%); tot. pop., 21,402,470. (Catholic and total population figures are from the 1970 census.)

South West Africa: See Namibia.

Spain: Nominal monarchy on the Iberian peninsula in southwestern Europe; capital, Madrid. Christians were on the peninsula by 200; some of them suffered martyrdom during persecutions of the third century. A council held in Elvira about 304/6 enacted the first legislation on clerical celibacy in the West. Vandals invaded the peninsula in the fifth century, bringing with them an Arian brand of Christianity which they retained until their conversion following the baptism of their king Reccared, in 589. One of the significant developments of the seventh century was the establishment of Toledo as the primatial see. The Visigoth kingdom lasted to the time of the Arab invasion, 711-14. The Church survived under Moslem rule but experienced some doctrinal and disciplinary irregularities as well as harassment. Reconquest of most of the peninsula was accomplished by 1248; unification was achieved during the reign of Ferdinand and Isabella. The discoveries of Columbus and other explorers ushered in an era of colonial expansion in which Spain became one of the greatest mission-sending countries in history. In 1492, in repetition of anti-Semitic actions of 694, the expulsion of unbap-

tized Jews was decreed, leading to mass baptisms but a questionable number of real conversions in 1502. (The Jewish minority numbered about 165,000.) Activity by the Inquisition followed. Spain was not seriously affected by the Reformation. Ecclesiastical decline set in about 1650. Anti-Church actions authorized by a constitution enacted in 1812 resulted in the suppression of religious and other encroachments on the leaders, people and goods of the Church. Political, religious and cultural turmoil recurred during the 19th century and into the 20th. A revolutionary republic was proclaimed in 1931, triggering a series of developments which led to civil war from 1936 to 1939. During the conflict, which pitted leftist Loyalists against the forces of Francisco Franco, 6,632 priests and religious and an unknown number of lay persons perished in addition to thousands of victims of combat. One-man, one-party rule, established after the civil war, has come under pressure recently to liberalize its conservative stance and policy with respect to personal liberties and social and economic reforms. Generally conservative church leaders have come under the same pressure from some of their colleagues, priests and lay persons. The Catholic Church is the state religion, but the constitution provides for general religious freedom. Spain maintains diplomatic relations with Vatican City.

Archd., 13; dioc., 50; prel., 1; card., 5; abp., 10; bp., 64; parishes, 20,890; priests, 34,776 (23,966 dioc., 10,810 rel.); sem., 2,823; p.d., 1; m. rel., 21,947; w. rel., 81,951; sch., 6,937; inst., 3,516; Caths., 34,077,580 (97%); tot. pop., 34,991,532.

Spanish North Africa: Includes the cities of Ceuta and Melilla on the northern coast of Africa, which are considered part of metropolitan Spain.

Spanish Sahara: Spanish province on the northwestern coast of Africa. Islam is the religion of non-Europeans. A prefecture apostolic was set up in 1954 for the European Catholics there.

P.a., 1; priests, 9 (rel.); m. rel., 10; w. rel., 18; Caths., 16,450. (Figures are for the area covered by the prefecture apostolic of Spanish Sahara.)

Sri Lanka (formerly Ceylon): Independent socialist republic, island southeast of India; capital, Colombo. Effective evangelization began in 1543 and made great progress by the middle of the 17th century. The Church was seriously hampered during the Dutch period from about 1650 to 1795. Anti-Catholic laws were repealed by the British in 1806. The hierarchy was established in 1886. Leftist governments and other factors have worked against the Church since the country became independent in 1948. The high percentage of indigenous clergy and religious has been of great advantage to the Church. Sri Lanka has an apostolic delegate.

Archd., 1; dioc., 6; card., 1 (nat.); bp., 9 (8 nat.); parishes, 262; priests, 581 (312 dioc., 269 rel.); sem., 122; p.d., 4; m. rel., 614; w. rel., 2,333; sch., 79; inst., 177; Caths. (est.),950,000 (7%); tot. pop. (UN est., 1972), 13,030,000.

Sudan: Republic in northeastern Africa, the largest country on the continent; capital, Khartoum. Christianity was introduced from Egypt and gained acceptance in the sixth century. Under Arab rule, it was eliminated in the northern region. No Christians were in the country in 1600. Evangelization attempts begun in the 19th century in the south yielded hard-won results. By 1931 there were nearly 40,000 Catholics there, and considerable progress was made by missionaries after that time. In 1957, a year after the republic was established, Catholic schools were nationalized. An act restrictive of religious freedom went into effect in 1962, resulting in the harassment and expulsion of foreign missionaries. By 1964 all but a few Sudanese missionaries had been forced out of the southern region. The northern area, where Islam predominates, is impervious to Christian influence. Late in 1971 some missionaries were allowed to return to work in the South. Southern Sudan was granted regional autonomy within a unified country in March, 1972, thus ending often bitter fighting between the North and South dating back to 1955. Sudan maintains diplomatic relations with Vatican City.

V.a., 5; p.a., 2; bp., 2; priests, 121 (53 dioc., 68 rel.); sem., 35; m. rel., 100; w. rel., 212; sch., 37; inst., 7; Caths. (Sudan Episcopal Conference), 682,000 (4%); tot. pop. (UN est., 1972), 16,490,000.

Surinam (Dutch Guiana): Autonomous part of the Kingdom of The Netherlands, in northern South America; capital, Paramaribo, Catholicism was introduced in 1683. Evangelization began in 1817.

Dioc., 1; bp., 1; parishes, 9; priests, 56 (4 dioc., 52 rel.); sem., 2; m. rel., 90; w. rel., 145; sch., 31; inst., 22; Caths., 80,000; tot. pop., 403,000. (Figures are from 1970.)

Swaziland: See Ngwane.

Sweden: Kingdom in northwestern Europe; capital, Stockholm. Christianity was introduced by St. Ansgar, a Frankish monk, in 829/30. The Church became well established in the 12th century and was a major influence at the end of the Middle Ages. Political and other factors favored the introduction and spread of the Lutheran Church which became the state religion in 1560. The Augsburg Confession of 1530 was accepted by the government; all relations with Rome, in the country since the 12th century, were severed; monasteries were suppressed; the very presence of Catholics in the country was forbidden in 1617. A decree of tolerance for foreign Catholics was issued about 1781. Two years later a vicariate apostolic was organized for the country. In 1873 Swedes were given the legal right to leave the Lutheran Church and join

another Christian church. (Membership in the Lutheran Church is presumed by law unless notice is given of membership in another church.) In 1923 there were only 11 priests and five churches in the country. Since 1952 Catholics have enjoyed almost complete religious freedom. The hierarchy was reestablished in 1953. Hindrances to growth of the Church are the strongly entrenched established church, limited resources, a clergy shortage and the size of the country. Sweden has an apostolic delegate (to Scandinavia). Its Catholic bishop is an American, John E. Taylor, O.M.I.

Dioc., 1; bp., 1; parishes, 26; priests, 97 (28 dioc., 69 rel.); sem., 1; m. rel., 77; w. rel., 230; sch., 2; inst., 18; Caths., 63,063 (.7%); tot. pop., 8,182,230.

Switzerland: Republic in central Europe; capital, Bern. Christianity was introduced in the fourth century or earlier and was established on a firm footing before the barbarian invasions of the sixth century. Constance, established as a diocese in the seventh century, was a stronghold of the faith against the pagan Alamanni, in particular, who were not converted until some time in the ninth century. During this period of struggle with the barbarians, a number of monasteries of great influence were established. The Reformation in Switzerland was triggered by Zwingli in 1519 and furthered by him at Zurich until his death in battle against the Catholic cantons in 1531. Calvin set in motion the forces that made Geneva the international capital of the Reformation and transformed it into a theocracy. Catholics mobilized a Counter-Reformation in 1570, six years after Calvin's death. Struggle between Protestant and Catholic cantons was a fact of Swiss life for several hundred years. The Helvetic Constitution enacted at the turn of the 19th century embodied anti-Catholic measures and consequences, among them the dissolution of 130 monasteries. The Church was reorganized later in the century to meet the threats of liberalism, radicalism and the Kulturkampf. In the process, the Church, even though on the defensive, gained the strength and cohesion that characterizes it to the present time. The six dioceses in the country are immediately subject to the Holy See. In 1973, constitutional articles banning Jesuits from the country and prohibiting the establishment of convents and monasteries were repealed. There is a papal nuncio to Switzerland, but Switzerland does not have a diplomatic officer accredited to Vatican City.

Dioc., 6; abb., 2; card., 1; bp., 7; parishes, 1,639; priests, 4,441 (2,879 dioc., 1,562 rel.); sem., 245; p.d., 1; m. rel., 2,032; w. rel., 9,532; sch., 43; inst., 147; Caths., 3,131,154 (47%); tot. pop., 6,631,011.

Syria: Arab republic in southwest Asia; capital, Damascus. Christian communities were formed in apostolic times. It is believed that St. Peter established a see at Antioch before going to Rome. Damascus became a center of influence. The area was the place of great men and great events in the early history of the Church. Monasticism developed there in the fourth century. So did the Monophysite and Monothelite heresies to which portions of the Church succumbed. Byzantine Syrians who remained in communion with Rome were given the name Melkites. Christians of various persuasions — Jacobites, Orthodox and Melkites — were subject to various degrees of harassment from the Arabs who took over in 638 and from the Ottoman Turks who isolated the country and remained in control from 1516 to the end of World War II. Syria maintains diplomatic relations with Vatican City.

There are 19 ecclesiastical jurisdictions in Syria serving the following rites: Armenian (1 archdiocese, 1 diocese); Chaldean (1 diocese); Roman (1 vicariate apostolic); Maronite (1 patriarchate, whose patriarch resides in Lebanon, 2 archdioceses and 1 apostolic administration); Melkite (1 patriarchate, 5 archdioceses); Syrian (1 patriarchate, whose patriarch resides in Lebanon, 4 archdioceses). Catholics, 206,716 (3%); tot. pop. (UN est., 1972), 6,680,000.

Taiwan (Formosa): Location of the Nationalist Government of the Republic of China, an island 100 miles off the southern coast of mainland China; capital, Taipei. Attempts to introduce Christianity in the 17th century were unsuccessful. Evangelization in the 19th century resulted in some 1,300 converts in 1895. Missionary endeavor was hampered by the Japanese who occupied the island following the Sino-Japanese war of 1894-95. Nine thousand Catholics were reported in 1938. Great progress was made in missionary endeavor among the Chinese who emigrated to the island following the Communist take-over of the mainland in 1949. The hierarchy was established in 1952. Nationalist China maintains diplomatic relations with Vatican City.

Archd., 1; dioc., 6; abp., 1; bp., 5; parishes, 415; priests, 777 (220 dioc., 557 rel.); sem., 37; m. rel., 654; w. rel., 1,151; sch., 49; inst., 153; Caths., 298,637 (1.9%); tot. pop., 15,138,040.

Tanzania: Republic (consisting of former Tanganyika on the eastern coast of Africa and former Zanzibar, an island group off the eastern coast); capital, Dar es Salaam. The first Catholic mission in the former Tanganyikan portion of the republic was manned by Holy Ghost Fathers in 1868. The hierarchy was established there in 1953. Zanzibar was the landing place of Augustinians with the Portuguese in 1499. Some evangelization was attempted between then and 1698 when the Arabs expelled all priests from the territory. There was no Catholic missionary activity from then until the 1860's. The Holy Ghost Fathers arrived in 1863 and were entrusted

with the mission in 1872. Zanzibar was important as a point of departure for missionaries to Tanganyika, Kenya and other places in East Africa. A vicariate for Zanzibar was set up in 1906. Tanzania maintains diplomatic relations with Vatican City.

Archd., 2; dioc., 21; p.a., 1; a.a., 1; card., 1 (nat.); abp., 1 (nat.); bp., 21 (17 nat.); parishes, 479; priests, 1,280 (486 dioc., 794 rel.); sem., 419; p.d., 6; m. rel., 1,134; w. rel., 2,665; sch., 105; inst., 386; Caths., 2,760,087 (19.7%); tot. pop., 14,000,000.

Thailand (Siam): Constitutional monarchy in southeastern Asia; capital, Bangkok. The first Christians in the region were Portuguese traders who arrived early in the 16th century. A number of missionaries began arriving in 1554 but pastoral care was confined mostly to the Portuguese until the 1660's. Evangelization of the natives got underway from about that time. A seminary was organized in 1665, a vicariate was set up four years later, and a point of departure was established for missionaries to Tonkin, Cochin China and China. Persecution and death for some of the missionaries ended evangelization efforts in 1688. It was resumed, however, and made progress from 1824 onwards. In 1881 missionaries were sent from Siam to neighboring Laos. The hierarchy was established in 1965. Thailand maintains diplomatic relations with Vatican City.

Archd., 2; dioc., 8; abp., 2 (nat.); bp., 7 (2 nat.); parishes, 137; priests, 303 (119 dioc., 184 rel.); sem., 81; m. rel., 370; w. rel., 1,067; sch., 278; inst., 56; Caths., 157,016 (.4%); tot. pop. (UN est., 1972), 36,290,000.

Tibet: Autonomous region of China in eastern Asia, north of the Himalayas; capital, Lhasa. Christian contact and evangelization attempts have been almost fruitless. Some 1,200 Catholics were reported in Tibet about 1950. Syrians visited the area in the seventh century and evangelization attempts were made by Jesuits, 1624-35 and later, Capuchins, 1707-45, and others afterwards. They all met resistance and some met death. Missionaries do not have access to the country.

Tot. pop., 2,000,000.

Timor, Portuguese: Overseas province in the Malay archipelago; capital, Dili. A Dominican was the first priest in the territory about 1561. Twenty other Dominicans arrived in 1641 and began intensive evangelization. Some of the missionaries exercised civil as well as ecclesiastical authority until early in the 18th century. Anticlerical influences in the Portuguese government forced the missionaries out in 1834. Some improvement in Church-state relations preceded their return in 1874, but in 1910 they were expelled again and the activity of secular priests was restricted. The Catholic population numbered about 19,000 in 1930. Japanese occupation during World War II had an adverse effect on the missions. Dili was made a diocese in 1940.

Dioc., 1; bp., 1; parishes, 3; priests, 50 (42 dioc., 8 rel.); sem., 21; m. rel., 16; w. rel., 48; sch., 51; inst., 4; Caths., 187,540; tot. pop., 633,626.

Togo: Republic on the western coast of Africa; capital, Lome. The first Catholic missionaries in the area, where slave raiders operated for nearly 200 years, were members of the African Missions Society who arrived in 1563. They were followed by Divine Word Missionaries in 1914, when a prefecture apostolic was organized. At that time the Catholic population numbered about 19,000. The African Missionaries returned after their German predecessors were deported following World War I. The first native priest was ordained in 1922. The hierarchy was established in 1955. Togo has an apostolic delegate (to West Africa).

Archd., 1; dioc., 3; abp., 1 (nat.); bp., 3 (2 nat.); parishes, 58; priests, 145 (63 dioc., 82 rel.); sem., 41; m. rel., 104; w. rel., 255; sch., 360; inst., 49; Caths., 402,807 (20%); tot. pop., 1,997,178.

Tonga: Polynesian monarchy in the southwestern Pacific, consisting of about 150 islands, member of the British Commonwealth; capital Nuku'alofa. Marists started missionary work in 1842, some years after Protestants had begun evangelization. By 1880 the Catholic population numbered about 1,700. A vicariate was organized in 1937. The hierarchy was established in 1966.

Dioc., 1; bp., 1 (nat.); parishes, 12; priests, 20 (6 dioc., 14; rel.); sem., 7; m. rel., 21; w. rel., 72; sch., 19; inst., 2; Caths., 13,496; tot. pop. (UN est., 1972), 90,000.

Trinidad and Tobago: Independent nation, consisting of two islands in the Caribbean, member of the British Commonwealth; capital, Port-of-Spain. The first Catholic church in Trinidad was built in 1591, years after several missionary ventures had been launched and a number of missionaries killed. Capuchins were there from 1618 until about 1802. Missionary work continued after the British gained control early in the 19th century. Cordial relations have existed between the Church and state, both of which have manifested their desire for the development of native clergy.

Archd., 1; abp., 1; parishes, 60; priests, 136 (23 dioc., 113 rel.); sem., 8; m. rel., 142; w. rel., 227; sch., 159; inst., 19; Caths., 364,500; tot. pop., 1,069,323.

Tunisia: Republic on the northern coast of Africa; capital, Tunis. There were few Christians in the territory until the 19th century. A prefecture apostolic was organized in 1843 and the Carthage archdiocese was established in 1884. The Catholic population in 1892 consisted of most of the approximately 50,000 Europeans in the country. When Tunis became a republic in 1956, most of the Europeans left the country. The Holy See and the Tunisian government concluded an agree-

ment in 1964 which changed the Carthage archdiocese into a prelacy and handed over some ecclesiastical property to the republic. A considerable number of Moslem students are in Catholic schools, but the number of Moslem converts to the Church has been small. Tunisia maintains diplomatic relations with Vatican City.

Prel., 1; abp., 1; parishes, 23; priests, 72 (33 dioc., 39 rel.); p.d., 1; m. rel., 58; w. rel., 329; sch., 38; inst., 5; Caths., 25,000 (.4%); tot. pop., 5,430,000.

Turkey: Republic in Asia Minor and southeastern Europe, capital, Ankara. Christian communities were established in apostolic times, as attested in the Acts of the Apostles, some of the Epistles of St. Paul, and Revelation. The territory was the scene of heresies and ecumenical councils, the place of residence of Fathers of the Church, the area in which ecclesiastical organization reached the dimensions of more than 450 sees in the middle of the seventh century. The region remained generally Byzantine except for the period of the Latin occupation of Constantinople from 1204 to 1261, but was conquered by the Ottoman Turks in 1453 and remained under their domination until establishment of the republic in 1923. Christians, always a minority, numbered more Orthodox than Latins; they were all under some restriction during the Ottoman period. They suffered persecution in the 19th and 20th centuries, the Armenians being the most numerous victims. Turkey is overwhelmingly Moslem. Catholics are tolerated to a degree. Turkey maintains diplomatic relations with Vatican City.

Patriarchate, 1 (Cilicia for the Armenians, the patriarch resides in Lebanon); archd., 3; dioc., 1; v.a., 2; missions "sui juris," 1; ap. ex., 1; Caths., 27,328; tot. pop. (UN est., 1972), 36,160,000.

Uganda: Republic in eastern Africa, member of the British Commonwealth; capital, Kampala. The White Fathers were the first Catholic missionaries, starting in 1879. Persecution broke out from 1885 to 1887, taking a toll of 22 Catholic martyrs, who were canonized in 1964, and a number of Anglican victims. (Pope Paul honored all those who died for the faith during a visit to Kampala in 1969.) By 1888, there were more than 8,000 Catholics. Evangelization was resumed in 1894, after being interrupted by war, and proceeded thereafter. The first native African bishop was ordained in 1939. The hierarchy was established in 1953. Church-state relations have been erratic under the regime of Pres. Idi-Amin who has shown both benevolence and hostility toward the Church. Uganda maintains diplomatic relations with Vatican City.

Archd., 1; dioc., 11; abp., 1 (nat.); bp., 11 (9 nat.); parishes, 281; priests, 881 (338 dioc., 543 rel.); sem., 234; m. rel., 1,093; w. rel., 1,907;

sch., 1,461; inst., 141; Caths., 3,420,895 (32.7%); tot. pop. (UN est., 1972), 10,460.000.

Union of Soviet Socialist Republics: Union of 15 Soviet Socialist Republics in northern Eurasia, from the Baltic Sea to the Pacific; Russian capital, Moscow. The Orthodox Church has been predominant in Russian history. It developed from the Byzantine Church before 1064. Some of its members subsequently established communion with Rome as the result of reunion movements but most of them remained Orthodox. The government has always retained some kind of general or particular control of this church. Latins, always a minority, had a little more freedom. From the beginning of the Communist government in 1917, all churches of whatever kind — including Jews and Moslems — became the targets of official campaigns designed to negate their influence on society and/or to eliminate them entirely. An accurate assessment of the situation of the Catholic Church in Russia is difficult to make. Its dimensions, however, can be gauged from the findings of a team of research specialists made public by the Judiciary Committee of the US House of Representatives in 1964. It was reported: "The fate of the Catholic Church in the USSR and countries occupied by the Russians from 1917 to 1959 shows the following: (a) the number killed: 55 bishops; 12,800 priests and monks; 2.5 million Catholic believers; (b) imprisoned or deported: 199 bishops; 32,000 priests and 10 million believers; (c) 15,700 priests were forced to abandon their priesthood and accept other jobs; and (d) a large number of seminaries and religious communities were dissolved; 1,600 monasteries were nationalized, 31,779 churches were closed. 400 newspapers were prohibited, and all Catholic organizations were dissolved." Several Latin Rite churches are open; e.g., in Moscow, Leningrad, Odessa and Tiflis. An American chaplain is stationed in Moscow to serve Catholics at the US embassy there. Recent reports indicate that, despite repression and attempts at Russification, the strongholds of Catholicism in the USSR are Lithuania (incorporated in the USSR in 1940, together with Estonia and Latvia) and the Ukraine.

Ecclesiastical jurisdictions, 21 (including 7 in Lithuania, 2 in Latvia, 1 in Estonia); card., 1 (Cardinal Slipyi of the Ukraine, living in Rome since his release in 1963 from 18 years' imprisonment); bp., 10 (most of them, including 7 in Lithuania, are apostolic administrators or auxiliaries; some are impeded; 1 bishop was ordained in 1972, Valerians Zondaks, titular bishop of Tabaicara and auxiliary to the apostolic administration of Riga and Liepaja, Latvia); tot. pop. (Govt. est., 1973), 250,000,000. No Catholic statistics are available. Some recent reports estimate the Catholic population of Lithuania to be 3 million, in a total population of 3.1 million.

United States: See Catholic History in the United States, Statistics of the Church in the United States.

Upper Volta: Republic inland in western Africa; capital, Ouagadougou. White Fathers started the first missions in 1900 and 1901. White Sisters began work in 1911. A minor and a major seminary were established in 1926 and 1942, respectively. The first native bishop in modern times from West Africa was ordained in 1956 and the first cardinal created in 1965. The hierarchy was established in 1955. Upper Volta established diplomatic relations with Vatican City in 1973.

Archd., 1; dioc., 8; card., 1 (nat.); bp., 9 (5 nat.); parishes, 92; priests, 390 (106 dioc., 284 rel.); sem., 67; m. rel., 427; w. rel., 562; sch., 21; inst., 52; Caths., 336,506 (5.9%); tot. pop. (UN est., 1972), 5,610,000.

Uruguay: Republic (called the Eastern Republic of Uruguay) on the southeast coast of South America; capital, Montevideo. The Spanish established a settlement in 1624 and evangelization followed. Missionaries followed the reduction pattern to reach the Indians, form them in the faith and train them in agriculture, husbandry, other useful arts, and the experience of managing property and living in community. Montevideo was made a diocese in 1878. The constitution of 1830 made Catholicism the religion of the state and subsidized some of its activities, principally the missions to the Indians. Separation of Church and state was provided for in the constitution of 1917. Uruguay maintains diplomatic relations with Vatican City.

Archd., 1; dioc., 9; abp., 1; bp., 12; parishes, 215; priests, 655 (210 dioc., 445 rel.); sem., 25; p.d., 3; m. rel., 709; w. rel., 1,581; sch., 337; inst., 63; Caths., 2,675,889 (89%); tot. pop., 2,996,365.

Vatican City: See separate entry.

Venezuela: Republic in northern South America; capital, Caracas. Evangelization began in 1513-14 and involved members of a number of religious orders who worked in assigned territories, developing missions into pueblos or towns and villages of Indian converts. Nearly 350 towns originated as missions. Fifty-four missionaries met death by violence from the start of missionary work until 1817. Missionary work was seriously hindered during the wars of independence in the second decade of the 19th century and continued in decline through the rest of the century as dictator followed dictator in a period of political turbulence. Restoration of the missions got underway in 1922. The first diocese was established in 1531. Most of the bishops have been native Venezuelans. The first diocesan synod was held in 1574. Church-state relations are regulated by an agreement concluded with the Holy See in 1964. Venezuela maintains diplomatic relations with Vatican City.

Archd., 5; dioc., 17; prel., 1; v.a., 4; card., 1;

abp., 5; bp., 26; parishes, 797; priests, 2,121 (887 dioc., 1,234 rel.); sem., 120; m. rel., 1,707; w. rel., 3,735; sch., 1,030; inst., 119; Caths., 10,287,370 (92%); tot. pop., 11,151,512.

Vietnam: Country in southeastern Asia partitioned in 1954 into the Democratic Peoples' Republic of Vietnam in the North (capital, Hanoi) and the Republic of Vietnam in the South (capital, Saigon). Catholicism was introduced in 1533 but missionary work was intermittent until 1615 when Jesuits arrived to stay. One hundred thousand Catholics were reported in 1639. Two vicariates were organized in 1659. A seminary was set up in 1666 and two native priests were ordained two years later. A congregation of native women religious formed in 1670 is still active. Severe persecution broke out in 1698, three times in the 18th century, and again in the 19th. Between 100,000 and 300,000 persons suffered in some way from persecution during the 50 years before 1883 when the French moved in to secure religious liberty for the Catholics. Most of the 117 beatified Martyrs of Vietnam were killed during this 50-year period. After the French were forced out of Vietnam in 1954, the country was partitioned at the 17th parallel. The North went Communist and the Viet Cong, joined by North Vietnamese regular army troops in 1964, fought to gain control of the South. In 1954 there were approximately 1,114,000 Catholics in the North and 480,000 in the South. More than 650,000 fled to the South to avoid the government repression that has since silenced the Church in the North. In the South, the Church has continued to grow and develop despite the war. The hierarchy was established in 1960. Vietnam has an apostolic delegate.

North Vietnam: Archd., 1; dioc., 9; abp., 2; bp., 9; Caths., 750,000: tot. pop., 20,000,000.

South Vietnam; Archd., 2; dioc., 12; abp., 1; bp., 15; parishes, 631; priests, 1,996 (1,594 dioc., 402 rel.); sem., 921; m. rel., 1,716; w. rel.. 6,699; sch.. 1,420; inst., 347; Caths. (Fides), 1,905,000; (9.8%); tot. pop. 19,299,000.

Virgin Islands: Organized unincorporated US territory, about 34 miles east of Puerto Rico; capital, Charlotte Amalie on St. Thomas (one of the three principal islands). The islands were discovered by Columbus in 1493 and named for St. Ursula and her virgin companions. Missionaries began evangelization in the 16th century. A church on St. Croix dates from about 1660; another, on St. Thomas, from 1774. The Baltimore archdiocese had jurisdiction over the islands from 1804 to 1820 when it was passed on to the first of several places in the Caribbean area. Some trouble arose over a pastoral appointment in the 19th century, resulting in a small schism. The Redemptorists took over pastoral care in 1858; normal conditions have prevailed since.

Prel., 1; bp., 1; parishes, 5; priests, 16 (1 dioc., 15 rel.); sem., 1; m. rel., 17; w. rel., 26; sch., 5; Caths., 21,750; tot. pop., 72,000.

Wales: Part of the United Kingdom, on the western part of the island of Great Britain. Celtic missionaries completed evangelization by the end of the sixth century, the climax of what has been called the age of saints. Welsh Christianity received its distinctive Celtic character at this time. Some conflict developed when attempts were made — and proved successful later — to place the Welsh Church under the jurisdiction of Canterbury; the Welsh opted for direct contact with Rome. The Church made progress despite the depredations of Norsemen in the eighth and ninth centuries. Norman infiltration occurred near the middle of the 12th century, resulting in a century-long effort to establish territorial dioceses and parishes to replace the Celtic organizational plan of monastic centers and satellite churches. The Western Schism produced split views and allegiances. Actions of Henry VIII in breaking away from Rome had serious repercussions. Proscription and penal laws crippled the Church, resulted in heavy defections and touched off a 150-year period of repression in which more than 91 persons died for the faith. Methodism prevailed by 1750. Modern Catholicism came to Wales with Irish immigrants in the 19th century, when the number of Welsh Catholics was negligible. Catholic emancipation was granted in 1829. The hierarchy was restored in 1850.

Archd., 1; dioc., 1; abp., 1; bp., 2; parishes, 169; priests, 376 (205 dioc., 171 rel.); sem., 18; m. rel., 205; w. rel., 771; sch., 129; inst., 15; Caths., 141,631 (5%); tot. pop., 2,823,508.

Wallis and Futuna Islands: French territory in the southwestern Pacific. Marists, who began evangelizing the islands in 1836-7, were the first Catholic missionaries. The entire populations of the two islands were baptized by the end of 1842 (Wallis) and 1843 (Futuna). The first missionary to the latter island was killed in 1841; he was the first martyr of the Pacific. Most of the priests on the islands are native Polynesians. The hierarchy was established in 1966.

Dioc., 1; bp., 1; parishes, 5; priests, 13 (7 dioc., 6 rel.); sem., 1; m. rel., 10; w. rel., 53; sch., 9; Caths., 7,809 (statistics are for the Diocese of Wallis and Futuna).

Yemen: Arab republic in southwestern Arabia; capital, Sana. Christians perished in the first quarter of the sixth century. Moslems have been in control since the seventh century. The state religion is Islam. In 1973, for the first time in 1,400 years, Catholic personnel — priests, religious, lay persons — were invited to work in the country as staff of a government hospital; they were not to engage in proselytizing.

Tot. pop. (UN est., 1972), 6,060,000.

Yemen, Peoples Democratic Republic of:

Republic in the southern part of the Arabian peninsula; capitals, Aden and Medinat as-Shaab. No Christian community has existed there since the Moslem conquest of the seventh century. See Arabian Peninsula.

Yugoslavia: Socialist republic in southeastern Europe; capital, Belgrade. Christianity was introduced from the seventh to ninth centuries in the regions which were combined to form the nation after World War I. Since these regions straddled the original line of demarcation for the Western and Eastern Empires (and churches), and since the Reformation had little lasting effect, the Christians are nearly all either Roman Catholics or Byzantines (some in communion with Rome, the majority Orthodox). Yugoslavia was proclaimed a Socialist republic in 1945. Repression of religion became government policy. Between May, 1945, and December, 1950, persecution took the following toll: almost two-thirds of 22 dioceses lost their bishops; about 348 priests were killed; 200 priests were under arrest and in prison; 12 of 18 seminaries were closed; the Catholic press was confiscated; religious instruction was suppressed in all schools; 300 religious houses and institutions were confiscated, and nuns and other religious driven out; all Church property was expropriated; the ministry of priests was severely restricted and subject to government interference; many thousands of the faithful shared the fate of priests and religious in death, imprisonment and slave labor. Cardinal Stepinac, arrested in 1946 and the symbol of the Church under persecution in Yugoslavia, died Feb. 10, 1960. In an agreement signed June 25, 1966, the government recognized the Holy See's spiritual jurisdiction over the Church in the country and guaranteed to bishops the possibility of maintaining contact with Rome in ecclesiastical and religious matters. The Holy See confirmed the principle that the activity of ecclesiastics, in the exercise of priestly functions, must take place within the religious and ecclesiastical sphere, and that abuse of these functions for political ends would be illegal. Less than two months after the agreement was signed, a group of exiled Croatian priests issued a statement in which they accused the Yugoslav government of failing to abide by it. According to others, an improvement was noticeable. Yugoslavia maintains diplomatic relations with Vatican City.

Archd., 8; dioc., 13; a.a., 1; card., 1; abp., 8; bp., 23; parishes, 2,404; priests, 3,587 (2,341 dioc., 1,246 rel.); sem., 877; p.d., 1; m. rel., 2,095; w. rel., 6,658; sch., 4; inst., 7; Caths. (est.) 6,650,000 (32%); tot. pop. (UN est., 1972), 20,770,000.

Zaire (formerly the Congo): Republic in south central Africa; capital, Kinshasa. Christianity was introduced in 1484 and evangelization began about 1490. The first native bishop in black Africa was ordained in 1518. Subsequent missionary work was hindered by faulty methods of instruction and formation, inroads of the slave trade, wars among the tribes, and Portuguese policy based on the patronage system and having all the trappings of anti-clericalism in the 18th and 19th centuries. Modern evangelization started in the second half of the 19th century. The hierarchy was established in 1959. In the civil disorders which followed independence in 1960, some missions and other church installations were abandoned, thousands of people reverted to tribal religions and many priests and religious were killed. Zaire maintains diplomatic relations with Vatican City.

Archd., 6; dioc., 42; card., 1 (nat.); abp., 5 (4 nat.); bp., 44 (31 nat.); parishes, 671; priests, 2,766 (624 dioc., 2,142 rel.); sem., 452; p.d., 1; m. rel., 3,195; w. rel., 4,376; sch., 6,065; inst., 1,245; Caths., 9,641,940 (40%); tot. pop., 23,709,011.

Zambia: Republic in central Africa; capital, Lusaka. Portuguese priests did some evangelizing in the 16th and 17th centuries but no results of their work remained in the 19th century. Jesuits began work in the south in the 1880's and White Fathers in the north and east in 1895. Evangelization of the western region began for the first time in 1831. The number of Catholics doubled in the 20 years following World War II. Zambia maintains diplomatic relations with Vatican City.

Archd., 2; dioc., 6; p.a., 1; abp., 2 (nat.); bp., 6 (2 nat.); parishes, 166; priests, 451 (72 dioc., 379 rel.); sem., 30; p.d., 3; m. rel., 547; w. rel., 576; sch., 721; inst., 130; Caths., 894,320 (20%); tot. pop. (UN est., 1972), 4,421,000.

CATHOLIC WORLD STATISTICS

(Principal source: *Annuario Pontificio, 1974.*)

Patriarchates: 13. Eastern Rites: 8 (Asia, 6; Africa, 2). Roman Rite, 5 (Asia, 2; Europe, 2; West Indies, 1).

Archdioceses: 470 (Asia, 115; Oceania, 14; Africa, 47; Europe, 142; South America, 77; North and Middle America, 75).

Dioceses: 1,702 (Asia, 309; Oceania, 45; Africa, 271; Europe, 517; South America, 282; North and Middle America, 278).

Prelatures: 102 (Asia, 12; Africa, 1; Europe, 7; South America, 69; North and Middle America, 13).

Abbacies, 21 (Asia, 1; Oceania, 1; Africa, 1; Europe, 14; South America, 2; North and Middle America, 2).

Vicariates Apostolic: 84 (Asia, 19; Oceania, 1; Africa, 19; Europe, 4; South America, 36; North and Middle America, 5).

Prefectures Apostolic: 68 (Asia, 37; Africa, 19; South America, 11; North and Middle America, 1).

Apostolic Administrations: 11 (Asia, 2; Africa,

1; Europe, 6; North and Middle America, 2).

Missions "Sui Juris": 4 (Asia, 3; Oceania, 1).

Apostolic Exarchates, Ordinariates: 26 (Asia, 8; Oceania, 1; Europe, 13; South America, 3; North and Middle America, 1).

Cardinals: 130 (Asia, 10; Oceania, 4; Africa, 9; Europe, 73; South America, 16; North and Middle America, 18).

Patriarchs: 10. Eastern Rites, 6 (2 are cardinals). Roman Rite: 4 (2 are cardinals).

Archbishops: 394 (Asia, 90; Oceania, 12; Africa, 42; Europe, 110; South America, 68; North and Middle America, 72).

Bishops, 2,123 (Asia, 242; Oceania, 56; Africa, 287; Europe, 684; South America, 445; North and Middle America, 409).

Priests, Total: 420,606 (Asia, 26,202; Oceania, 5,566; Africa, 17,027; Europe, 253,880; South America, 33,664; North and Middle America, 84,267).

Priests, Diocesan: 271,975 (Asia, 13,298; Oceania, 2,980; Africa, 4,785; Europe, 183,679; South America, 14,724; North and Middle America, 52,509).

Priests, Religious: 148,631 (Asia, 12,904; Oceania, 2,586; Africa, 12,242; Europe, 70,201; South America, 18,940; North and Middle America, 31,758).

Seminarians: 55,982 (Asia, 6,816; Oceania, 701; Africa, 3,468; Europe, 19,630; South America, 2,645; North and Middle America, 22,722).

Permanent Deacons: 1,148 (Asia, 34; Oceania, 9; Africa, 53; Europe, 396; South America, 213; North and Middle America, 443).

Men Religious: 221,396 (Asia, 22,598; Oceania, 6,209; Africa, 18,698; Europe, 116,678; South America, 27,608; North and Middle America, 29,605).

Women Religious: 996,487 (Asia, 77,355; Oceania, 17,618; Africa, 34,713; Europe, 559,798; South America, 91,713; North and Middle America, 215,290).

Catholic Population: 669,000,000 (18.3 percent of the total world population): Asia, 53,000,000 (2.5); Oceania, 4,600,000 (23.4); Africa, 42,000,000 (11.6); Europe, 260,400,000 (40.2); America, 309,000,000 (60.2; approximately 45 percent of the North and Central American total and 90 percent of the South American).

Population figures are estimates as of Jan. 1, 1972, and include all persons baptized as Catholics. They are from the yearbook issued by the Central Statistics Office of the Church.

Totals from the *Annuario Pontificio, 1974,* amounted to more than 685,000,000.

Other sources give a figure that is considerably lower than that reported by the Central Statistics Office. (See Religious Population of the World.)

EPISCOPAL CONFERENCES

(Principal source: *Annuario Pontificio.*)

Episcopal conferences, organized and operating under general norms and particular statutes approved by the Holy See, are official bodies in and through which the bishops of a given country or territory act together as pastors of the Church.

Listed are countries with conferences, dates when statutes were approved where available, names and sees of presidents (archbishops unless otherwise noted).

AFRICA, North (Feb. 27, 1967): Cardinal Leon-Etienne Duval, Algiers.

AFRICA, South (Apr. 28, 1970): Cardinal Owen McCann, Cape Town.

ANGOLA and SAO TOME (Nov. 11, 1972): Manuel Nunes Gabriel, Luanda.

ANTILLES (Dec. 10, 1957): Samuel E. Carter, Kingston in Jamaica.

ARAB COUNTRIES: Latin Bishops (Mar. 31, 1967): Patriarch Giacomo Beltritti, Jerusalem.

ARGENTINA (Mar. 9, 1973): Adolfo Servando Tortolo, Parana.

AUSTRALIA (Apr. 3, 1971): Cardinal James Darcy Freeman, Sydney.

AUSTRIA (Dec. 20, 1969): Cardinal Franz Koenig, Vienna.

BANGLADESH (Oct. 18, 1973): Theutonius A. Ganguli, Dacca.

BELGIUM (Aug. 21, 1971): Cardinal Leo Suenens, Mechelen-Brussels.

BOLIVIA (Aug. 19, 1972): Cardinal Jose Clemente Maurer, Sucre.

BRAZIL (Jan. 23, 1971): Alois Lorscheider, Fortaleza.

BULGARIA: Bishop Metodio Dimitrow Stratiew, apostolic exarch, Sofia.

BURMA (Feb. 10, 1967): Gabriel Thohey, Rangoon.

CAMEROON (Apr. 5, 1973): Jean Zoa, Yaounde.

CANADA (Jan. 23, 1955): Jean-Marie Fortier, Sherbrooke.

CENTRAL AFRICAN REPUBLIC: Joachim N'Dayen, Bangui.

CEYLON: See Sri Lanka, Republic of.

CHAD: Paul Dalmais, N'Djamena.

CHILE (June 13, 1970): Cardinal Raul Silva Henriquez, Santiago.

CHINA (Feb. 10, 1967): Cardinal Paul Yu Pin, Nanking.

COLOMBIA (Apr. 2, 1966): Bishop Jose de Jesus Pimiento Rodriguez, Garzon.

CONGO: Cardinal Emile Biayenda, Brazzaville.

COSTA RICA (Oct. 6, 1967): Bishop Roman Arrieta Villalobos, Tileran.

CUBA (Dec. 2, 1972): Bishop Jose Maximino E. Dominguez y Rodriguez, Matanzas.

CZECHOSLOVAKIA: . . . .

DAHOMEY: Christopher Adimou, Cotonou.

DOMINICAN REPUBLIC (Oct. 6, 1967):

Octavio Beras Rojas, Santo Domingo.

ECUADOR (Mar. 3, 1967): Bernardino Echeverria Ruiz, Guayaquil.

EL SALVADOR (June 15, 1968): Bishop Benjamin Barrera y Reyes, Santa Ana.

ETHIOPIA (Dec. 15, 1966): Asrate M. Yemmeru, Addis Ababa.

FRANCE (Nov. 21, 1966): Cardinal Francois Marty, Paris.

GABON (Oct. 17, 1973): Andre Fernand Anguile, Libreville.

GAMBIA: See Liberia, Sierra Leone and Gambia.

GERMANY (Apr. 22, 1972): Cardinal Julius Doepfner, Munich and Freising. Additional conferences for West Germany and Bavaria, of which Cardinal Doepfner is president; and for Berlin, of which Cardinal Alfred Bengsch, Berlin, is president.

GHANA (Apr. 16, 1973): Bishop Dominic Kodwo Andoh, Accra.

GREAT BRITAIN (June 15, 1968): Cardinal John Heenan, Westminster (England and Wales); Cardinal Gordon J. Gray, St. Andrews and Edinburgh (Scotland).

GREECE (Apr. 17, 1967): Antonio Varthalitis, Corfu, Zante and Cefalonia.

GUATEMALA (Apr. 28, 1973): Bishop Juan Gerardi Conedera, Vera Paz.

GUINEA: Raymond-Marie Tchidimbo, Conakry.

HAITI (Mar. 11, 1972): Bishop Emmanuel Constant, Les Gonaives.

HONDURAS (Mar. 4, 1972): Hector Santos y Hernandez, Tegucigalpa.

HUNGARY (May 3, 1969): Jozsef Ijjas, Kalocsa.

INDIA (Apr. 29, 1967): Cardinal Joseph Parecattil, Ernakulam.

INDONESIA (Aug. 2, 1973): Cardinal Justin Darmojuwona, Semarang.

IRELAND (Aug. 9, 1969): Cardinal William Conway, Armagh.

ITALY (May 8, 1971): Cardinal Antonio Poma, Bologna.

IVORY COAST (Aug. 1, 1973): Bernard Yago, Abidjan.

JAPAN (Aug. 2, 1973): Cardinal Paul Yoshigoro Taguchi, Osaka.

KENYA (Jan. 18, 1969): Cardinal Maurice Otunga, Nairobi (Seychelles Islands included in this conference).

KOREA (Aug. 3, 1973): Cardinal Stephan Sou Hwan Kim, Seoul.

LAOS and KHMER REPUBLIC (CAMBODIA) (Apr. 23, 1971): Bishop Etienne Loosdregt, vicar apostolic, Vientiane.

LATVIA: Bishop Julian Vaivods, apostolic administrator, Riga and Liepaja.

LESOTHO: Alphonsus Morapeli, O.M.I., Maseru.

LIBERIA, SIERRA LEONE and GAMBIA (interterritorial episcopal conference): Thomas J. Brosnahan, Freetown and Bo.

LITHUANIA: Bishop Joseph Matulaitis-Labukas, apostolic administrator, Kaunas and Vilkaviskis.

MALAGASY REPUBLIC (June 18, 1969): Albert J. Tsiahoana, Diego-Suarez.

MALAWI (Oct. 1, 1969): James Chiona, Blantyre.

MALAYSIA and SINGAPORE (Dec. 14, 1967): Bishop Anthony D. Galvin, vicar apostolic, Miri.

MALI (June 15, 1973): Luc Auguste Sangare, Bamako.

MALTA (July 3, 1971): Michele Gonzi, Malta.

MEXICO (Apr. 29, 1972): Cardinal Jose Salazar Lopez, Guadalajara.

MOZAMBIQUE (Apr. 29, 1967): Francesco Nunes Teixeira, Quelimane.

NETHERLANDS (Dec. 2, 1972): Cardinal Bernard Alfrink, Utrecht.

NEW ZEALAND (Jan. 21, 1968): . . . .

NICARAGUA (Apr. 8, 1967): Miguel Obando Bravo, Managua.

NIGERIA: Bishop Dominic Ekandem, Ikot Ekpene.

PACIFIC (Mar. 25, 1971): Pierre Martin, former archbishop of Noumea.

PAKISTAN: Cardinal Joseph Cordeiro, Karachi.

PANAMA (Nov. 11, 1972): Bishop Daniel E. Nunez, David.

PAPUA-NEW GUINEA and SOLOMON ISLANDS (Dec. 6, 1966): Bishop Kevin W. Rowell, Aitape.

PARAGUAY (Nov. 7, 1966): Bishop Felipe Santiago Benitez Avalos, Villarrica.

PERU (Feb. 19, 1972): Cardinal Juan Landazuri Ricketts, O.F.M., Lima.

PHILIPPINE ISLANDS (Dec. 12, 1967): Teopista Alberto y Valderramo, Caceres.

POLAND (Mar. 15, 1969): Cardinal Stefan Wyszynski, Gniezno and Warsaw.

PORTUGAL (Jan. 29, 1972): Bishop Manuel D'Almeida Trindade, Aveiro.

PUERTO RICO (June 19, 1971): Cardinal Luis Aponte Martinez, San Juan.

RHODESIA (Oct. 1, 1969): Bishop Alois Haene, Gwelo.

RUMANIA: Bishop Aaron Marton, Alba Julia.

RWANDA-BURUNDI (May 5, 1969): Andre Makarakiza, Gitega.

SCANDINAVIA (Apr. 30, 1969): Bishop Paul Verschuren, Helsinki.

SENEGAL-MAURITANIA (Apr. 14, 1973): Hyacinthe Thiandoum, Dakar.

SIERRA LEONE: See Liberia, Sierra Leone and Gambia.

SPAIN (June 15, 1972): Cardinal Vicente Enrique y Tarancon, Madrid.

SRI LANKA, REPUBLIC OF (CEYLON) (Apr. 24, 1970): Cardinal Thomas Cooray, Colombo.

SUDAN (July 15, 1971): Msgr. Pio Yukwan Deng, ap. admin., prefecture apostolic of Malakal.

SWITZERLAND (Dec. 12, 1967): Bishop Francois Nestor Adam, Sion.

TANZANIA (Sept. 29, 1969): Bishop James Sangu, Mbeya.

THAILAND (Mar. 28, 1969): Bishop Robert Ratna, Ratchaburi.

TOGO: Robert Dosseh Anyron, Lome.

UGANDA: (Sept. 29, 1969): Emmanuel Nsubuga, Kampala.

UNITED STATES OF AMERICA (Dec. 19, 1970): Cardinal John Krol, Philadelphia.

UPPER VOLTA and NIGER: Cardinal Paul Zoungrana, Ouagadougou.

URUGUAY (Aug. 19, 1972): Bishop Luis Baccino, San Jose de Mayo.

VENEZUELA (Mar. 23, 1967): Crispulo Benitez Fonturvel, Barquisimeto.

VIETNAM (June 16, 1972): Paul Nguyen van Binh, Saigon.

YUGOSLAVIA (Aug. 26, 1972): Franjo Kuharic, Zagreb.

ZAIRE (Feb. 7, 1969): Bishop Leon Lesambo, Inongo.

ZAMBIA (Feb. 19, 1972): Bishop Medard J. Mazombwe, Chipata.

Territorial Conferences

Territorial as well as national episcopal conferences have been established in some places. Some conferences of this kind are still in the planning stage.

Africa: Association of Member Episcopal Conferences in Eastern Africa (AMECEA): Represents Uganda, Kenya, Tanzania, Zambia and Malawi; Cardinal Laurean Rugambwa, Dar es Salaam, Tanzania, president.

Symposium of Episcopal Conferences of Africa and Madagascar (Malagasy Republic) (SECAM): Cardinal Paul Zoungrana, Ouagadougou, Upper Volta, president.

Plenary Council of Bishops of West Africa: Abp. Robert Dosseh Anyron, Lome.

Association of Episcopal Conferences of Central Africa and Cameroon: Abp. Paul Dalmais, N'Djamena, Chad, president.

Asia: Federation of Asian Bishops' Conferences (FABC): Represents 14 Asian episcopal conferences (excluding the Middle East); headquarters in Hong Kong. Established in 1970; statutes approved experimentally Dec. 6, 1972. Cardinal Stephen Sou Hwan Kim, Seoul, president.

Europe: Council of European Bishops' Conferences: Abp. Roger Etchegaray, Marseilles, France, president.

Central and South America: Latin American Bishops' Conference (Consejo Episcopal LatinoAmericano, CELAM): Established in 1956; statutes approved experimentally Nov. 27, 1969. Represents 22 Latin American national bishops' conferences. Bishop Edoardo Pironio, Mar del Plata, Argentina, president. Address of the secretariat: Apartado Aereo 5278, Bogota, D.E., Colombia.

Episcopal Secretariat of Central America and Panama: Statutes approved experimentally Sept. 26, 1970. Bishop Roman Arrieta Villalobos, Tilaron, Costa Rica, president.

CATHOLIC INTERNATIONAL ORGANIZATIONS

(Source: *The Laity Today,* Bulletin (No. 13-14, 1973) published by the Vatican Council of the Laity.)

Guidelines

International organizations wanting to call themselves "Catholic" are required to meet standards set by the Vatican's Council of the Laity and to register with and get the approval of the Papal Secretariat of State, according to guidelines published in *Acta Apostolicae Sedis* under date of Dec. 23, 1971. The guidelines were made public in March, 1972.

Among conditions for the right of organizations to "bear the name Catholic" are:

• leaders "will always be Catholics," and candidates for office will be approved by the Secretariat of State;

• adherence by the organization to the Catholic Church, its teaching authority and teachings of the Gospel;

• evidence that the organization is really international with a universal outlook and that it fulfills its mission through its own management, meetings and accomplishments.

The guidelines also stated that leaders of the organizations "will take care to maintain necessary reserve as regards taking a stand or engaging in public activity in the field of politics or trade unionism. Abstention in these fields will normally be the best attitude for them to adopt during their term of office."

The guidelines were in line with a provision stated by the Second Vatican Council in the *Decree on the Apostolate of the Laity*: "No project may claim the name 'Catholic' unless it has obtained the consent of the lawful church authority."

They made it clear that all organizations are not obliged to apply for recognition, but that the Church "reserves the right to recognize as linked with her mission and her aims those organizations or movements which see fit to ask for such recognition."

The variety of Catholic international organizations is indicative of the wide range of their particular interests and their common concern to relate them to opportunities for giving witness to Catholic faith.

Conference

Conference of Catholic International Organizations: A permanent body for collaboration among various organizations which seek to promote the development of international life along the lines of Christian principles. Eleven international Catholic organizations participated in its foundation and first meeting in 1927 at Fribourg, Switzerland. In 1951, the conference established its general secretariat and adopted governing statutes which were approved by the Vatican Secretariat of State in 1953.

The general secretariat is located at 1, route du Jura, Fribourg, Switzerland. Other conference addresses are: 1 rue Varembe, 1200 Geneva, Switzerland (Information Center); 9, rue Cler, 750007 Paris, France (International Catholic Center for UNESCO); Avda. Corrientes 524-5, Buenos Aires, Argentina (Liaison Center for Latin America).

International Organizations

Catholic international organizations are listed below. Information includes name, date and place of establishment (when available), address of general secretariat. An asterisk indicates that the organization is a member of the Conference of Catholic International Organizations. Approximately 24 of the organizations have consultative status with other international or regional non-governmental agencies.

Ad Lucem (1932, Lille, France): 12, rue Guy de la Brosse, 75005, Paris, France. Work for the Third World.

Apostleship of Prayer (1849): Borgo Santo Spirito 5, 00193 Rome, Italy. National secretariat in most countries. (See Index.)

Apostolate of Independent Milieus (AIM) (1946, Brussels, Belgium): Piazza San Calisto 16, 00153 Rome, Italy. Evangelization of youth.

Apostolatus Maris* (**Apostleship of the Sea**) (1922, Glasgow, Scotland): Piazza San Calisto 16, 00153 Rome, Italy. (See Index.)

Associationes Juventutis Salesianae (Associations of Salesian Youth) (1847): Via Maria Ausiliatrice 32, 00152 Turin, Italy.

Blue Army of Our Lady of Fatima: (See Index.)

Caritas Internationalis* (1951, Rome, Italy): Piazza San Calisto 16, 00153, Rome, Italy. Coordinates relief aid on an international level.

Catholic Fraternity of the Sick and Infirm (1942, Verdun, France): Foyer des Malades, 49 rue Saint-Sauveur, 55100 Verdun, France.

Catholic International Education Office* (1952): 9, rue Guimard, 1040 Brussels, Belgium.

Catholic International Federation for Physical and Sports Education* (1911; present name, 1957): 5, rue Cernuschi, 75017 Paris, France.

Catholic International Union for Social Service* (1925, Milan, Italy): rue de la Poste 111, B-1030 Brussels, Belgium (general secretariat).

"Focolarini" (1943, Trent, Italy): (See Index: Focolare Movement)

General Union of Pastoral Work for Youth (1966): Via Palestro 26, 00185, Rome, Italy.

International Association of Charities of St. Vincent de Paul* (1617, Chatillon les Dombes, France): Chaussee d'Ixelles, 144, B-1050 Brussels, Belgium. (See Index: St. Vincent de Paul Society.)

International Association of Children of Mary (1847): 67 rue de Sevres, 75006 Paris, France.

International Catholic Auxiliaries (1937, Belgium): 91, rue de la Servette, 1202 Geneva, Switzerland.

International Catholic Child Bureau* (1947): 63, Largo Brancaccio, Rome, Italy.

International Catholic Confederation of Hospitals* (1951, Brussels, Belgium): Van Schaek Mathonsingel 4, Nijmegen, Netherlands.

International Catholic Conference of Guiding* (1965): 65, rue de la Glaciere, 75013 Paris, France. Founded by member bodies of interdenominational World Association of Guides and Girl Scouts.

International Catholic Film Organization* (1928, The Hague, The Netherlands): 8, rue de l'Orme, 1040 Brussels, Belgium, (general secretariat). Federation of national Catholic film offices.

International Catholic Girls' Society* (1897): 1, route du Jura, CH 1700 Fribourg, Switzerland. Welfare of Catholic girls living away from home.

International Catholic Migration Commission* (1951): 65, rue de Lausanne, 1202 Geneva, Switzerland. Coordinates Catholic activities to help migrants.

International Catholic Rural Association (1962, Rome): Piazza San Calisto 16, 00153 Rome, Italy. International body for agricultural and rural organizations.

International Catholic Scouters Conference* (1948): 21, rue de Dublin, 1050 Brussels, Belgium.

International Catholic Union of the Press*: 43, rue St. Augustin, 75002 Paris, France. Coordinates and represents at the international level the activities of Catholics and Catholic federations or associations in the field of press and information. Has four specialized branches: International Federation of Catholic Dailies and Periodicals (1928); International Federation of Catholic Journalists (1927); International Federation of Catholic Press Agencies (1950); International Catholic Association of Teachers and Scientific or Technical Research Workers on Information (1968).

International Centre for Studies in Religious Education* (1934-35, Louvain, Belgium, under name Catechetical Documentary Centre; present name, 1956): 186, rue Washington, 1050 Brussels, Belgium. Also referred to as Lumen Vitae Centre; concerned with all aspects of religious formation.

International Christian Union of Business Executives* (1931): 49, avenue d' Auderghem, 1040 Brussels, Belgium.

International Committee of Catholic Nurses* (1933): Square Vercote, 43, 1040 Brussels, Belgium.

International Cooperation for Socio-Economic Development (1965, Rome, Italy): 59-61 Avenue Adolphe Lacomble, 1040 Brussels, Belgium.

International Council of Catholic Men* (Unum Omnes) (1948): Piazza San Calisto 16, 00153 Rome, Italy.

International Crusade for the Blind (1957): 15, rue Mayet, 75006 Paris, France, Coordinates action of Catholic groups and associations for the blind and develops their apostolate.

International Federation of Catholic Parochial Youth Communities (1962, Rome, Italy): Kipdorp 30, Antwerp, Belgium.

International Federation of Catholic Rural Movements (1964, Lisbon, Portugal): 27, rue du Taciturne, 1040 Brussels, Belgium.

International Federation of Catholic Medical Associations (1954): 7 Englewood Road, Upper Darby, Pa. 19082.

International Federation of Catholic Pharmacists* (1954): 60 avenue des Pages, Le Vesinet, France.

International Federation of Catholic Universities* (1949): 77 bis, rue de Grenelle, 75007 Paris, France.

International Federation of Institutes for Social and Socio-Religious Research (1952): rue des Flamandes, 116, Leuven, Belgium.

International Military Apostolate (1967): Kaiserallee, 23, A. 2100 Korneuburg, Austria. Comprised of organizations of military men.

International Movement of Apostolate of Children (1929, France): 8, rue Duguay-Trouin, 75006 Paris, France.

International Movement of Apostolate in "Independent Milieus"* (1963): Piazza San Calisto 16, 00153 Rome, Italy. Evangelization of adults of the independent milieus (that part of population known as old or recent middle class, aristocracy, bourgeoisie or "white collar").

International Movement of Catholic Agricultural and Rural Youth* (1954, Annevoie, Belgium): Diestsevest 24, Louvain, Belgium (permanent secretariat).

International Young Catholic Students (1946, Fribourg, Switzerland; present name, 1954): 171 rue de Rennes, 75006 Paris, France.

International Young Christian Workers* (1925, Belgium): 26, rue Juste Lipse, 1040 Brussels, Belgium.

Laity and Christian Community (1966, Algiers, Algeria): 98, rue de l'Universite, 75007 Paris, France. Universal brotherhood.

Legion of Mary* (1921, Dublin, Ireland): De Montfort House, North Brunswick St., Dublin, Ireland. (See Index.)

Liga Catholica Internationalis Sobrietas (International Catholic League against Alcoholism) (1897, Brussels, Belgium): Karlstrasse 40, Lorenz-Werthmannhaus, 78 Freiburg/Br., Germany.

Medicus Mundi: Mozartstrasse 9, 51 Aachen, Germany. Place medicine at service of poor.

Movement for a Better World (1952): Centro Internationale Pio XII, Via dei Laghi Km. 10, 00040 Rocca di Papa, Italy. (See Index.)

Our Lady's Teams (Equipes Notre-Dame) (1937, France): 49, rue de la Glaciere, 75013 Paris, France. Movement for spiritual formation of couples.

Pax Christi (1950): Celebesstraat 60, The Hague, The Netherlands. (See Index.)

Pax Romana (1921, Fribourg, Switzerland, divided into two movements, 1947):

International Movement of Catholic Students* (1921): 1 route du Jura, B.P. 453, 1700 Fribourg, Switzerland, For undergraduates.

International Catholic Movement for Intellectual and Cultural Affairs* (1947): 1 route du Jura, Fribourg, Switzerland. For university graduates. Has professional secretariats at: Stradhouderskade 86, Amsterdam, The Netherlands (artists); Biesseltsebaan, 40, Nijmegen, The Netherlands (teachers); 18 rue de Varenne, 75007 Paris, France (engineers); via della Conciliazione 4d, 00193 Rome, Italy (lawyers).

St. Joan's International Alliance* (1911 in England; present title, 1931): 48, chemin des Coudries, 1121 Geneva, Switzerland. (See Index.)

Salesian Cooperators (1876): Via Maria Ausiliatrice 32, 10100 Turin, Italy. Third Salesian family founded by St. John Bosco; Members commit themselves to an apostolate at the service of the Church, giving particular attention to youth in the Salesian spirit and style.

Serra International (1953, in U.S.): (See Index.)

Society of St. Vincent de Paul (1933): 5, rue du Pre-aux-Clercs, 75007 Paris, France.

The Grail (1921), Nijmegen, The Netherlands): 5, Sayad Sokkar St. Matareya, Cairo, Egypt (temporary secretariat). (See Index.)

Third Order of St. Dominic (1285): Convento Santa Sabina, Piazza Pietro d'Illiria, Aventino 00153 Rome, Italy. (See Index.)

Third Order of St. Francis (1221, first Rule approved): Via Maria Mediatrice 25, 00165, Rome, Italy. (See Index.)

UNDA: International Catholic Association for Radio and Television* (1928, Cologne, Germany): rue de Romont 5, C.P. 211, 1701 Fribourg, Switzerland. (See Index.)

Unio Internationalis Laicorum in Servitio Ecclesiae (1965, Aachen, Germany): Breite Strasse 106-110, Postfach 102068, 5 Cologne, Germany. Consists of national and diocesan associations of persons who give professional services to the Church.

Union of Adorers of the Blessed Sacrament (1937): Largo dei Monti Parioli 3, 00197, Rome, Italy.

World Catholic Federation for the Biblical Apostolate (1969, Rome): Silberburgstr, 121 A, D 7000, Stuttgart 1, Germany.

World Federation of Catholic Youth* (1926; present title, 1968, with amalgamation of World Federation of Catholic Young Women and Girls and the International Catholic Youth Federation): 31 avenue de l'Hopital francais, 1080 Brussels, Belgium.

World Federation of Christian Life Communities* (1953): 8, Borgo Santo Spirito, C.P. 9048, Rome, Italy. First Sodality of Our Lady founded in 1563.

World Movement of Christian Workers* (1961): 201, rue Belliard, 1040 Brussels, Belgium.

World Organization of Former Students of Catholic Schools (1967, Rome): 17 rue Michel Charles, 75012 Paris, France.

World Union of Catholic Philosophical So- cieties* (1948, Amsterdam, The Netherlands): Aignerstrasse 25, 5026 Salzburg, Austria.

World Union of Catholic Teachers* (1951): Piazza San Calisto 16, 00153, Rome, Italy.

World Union of Catholic Women's Organizations* (1910): 20, rue Notre Dame des Champs, 75006 Paris, France.

Regional Organizations

European Association for Catholic Adult Education (1963, Lucerne, Switzerland): Dransdorfer Weg 15/IV, 53 Bonn, Germany.

European Forum of National Committees of the Laity (1968): Mutsaerstraat 32, B 2000 Antwerp, Belgium.

Movimiento Familiar Cristiano (1949-50, Montevideo and Buenos Aires): 7953, C.P. 480, Belo Horizonte, Brazil. Christian Family Movement of Latin America.

THE CHURCH IN PROBLEM AREAS IN 1974

Argentina: There were no reports of stress in Church-state relations in 1974. Violence of opposed factions in the Peronist movement, dating from before the return of Juan Domingo Peron to the presidency in 1973, continued to escalate. Political and economic conditions remained unsettled after his death July 1, 1974.

Bolivia: Church relations with the conservative military government of Hugo Banzer were tense. The bishops appealed in May, 1974, for a return to constitutional processes. Banzer, with the country under martial law for months, promised elections some time in 1975.

Brazil: Mixed views were expressed by bishops about the quality of relations with the government headed by Ernesto Geisel, who became president Jan. 15, 1974. Targets of criticism by bishops and others were: the cruel treatment of political prisoners; government policies considered prejudicial to the welfare and culture of Indians on the Amazonian frontier; the seizure of several diocesan radio stations; numerous arrests of persons advocating and working for economic and social development. In January, Cardinal Eugenio de Araujo Sales inveighed strongly against charges of Communist infiltration of educational and social action by the Church.

Burundi and Uganda: Intertribal rivalry and conflict continued to trouble both countries.

Chile: Churchmen were in the middle in the wake of the Allende fall in September, 1973; they were not considered conservative enough by the military regime which took over at that time, and not radical enough by leftover followers of the former Communist leader and their sympathizers. Relations were tense because of the bishops' criticisms of the government's repressive policies, particularly against political prisoners, and economic and educational measures threatening the general welfare. A "climate of insecurity and fear" prevailed, according to a statement by 28 bishops in April, 1974. It was reported the same month that the life of Cardinal Raul Silva Henriquez of Santiago had been threatened.

Colombia: The country was troubled by sporadic guerrilla campaigns, in which some priests were involved, against forces of the conservative government.

Cuba: The Church remained restricted, as it had been since 1961, with limited opportunities and personnel for ministry. The Vatican restored the status of its diplomatic mission in Havana in 1974 with the appointment of an apostolic nuncio.

Czechoslovakia: Government curbs on priests and religious remained in force. In December, 1973, and again in April priests and nuns were arrested in Slovakia for allegedly acting against the state. Hopes that some improvement in Church-state relations might result from diplomatic talks underway appeared to be dim.

Hungary: The Church remained subject to considerable control by the Communist government. Pope Paul's action in February, 1974, taking away the status and title of Cardinal Mindszenty as head of the Church in the country, even though he was in exile, had no perceptible effect in any improvement of Church-state relations.

Israel: See Vatican Policy on Jerusalem.

Italy: There was some tenseness in Church-state relations because of the Church's opposition to a divorce referendum in May, 1974. The Vatican contended that the law permitting divorce was in violation of its concordat with Italy.

Lithuania: The Church remained under tight rein in 1974. Symptomatic of continuing repression was a search of homes, offices and churches for persons responsible for "producing religious literature and literature 'slandering' the Soviet system." The search, which became known in the U.S. in February, was reported in an underground publication entitled *The Chronicle of the Lithuanian Catholic Church.* It was said that the purpose of the search was to break the backbone of the nationalist and Catholic movement in the country.

Mexico: The bishops voiced opposition in February, 1974, against a new law barring religious organizations from intervening "in any way" in education of "any type or degree"; and, in April, against an announced population control program. In March they went on record in favor of handling relations with the state themselves, without action by the Vatican or the presence of a Vatican diplomat in the country.

Northern Ireland: Catholics continued in conflict with Protestants over civil rights — employment opportunity, education, housing, political representation — as the civil war death toll mounted over 1,000 during the summer of 1974.

Panama: There were no reports of conflict with the government, whose efforts to secure control over the Canal Zone were seconded by the bishops.

Philippines: Priests, religious and lay persons were among many persons arrested in some two dozen incidents because of continuing opposition to the totalitarian policies of President Ferdinand E. Marcos. The Islands had been under martial law since September, 1972, when the government mounted a campaign against Moslem dissidents and Communist influence.

Poland: Recurrent symptoms of taut relations with the regime were protests by Cardinal Wyszynski and the bishops against government measures with respect to education, the building of churches, heavy taxation of church holdings, and interference with and harassment of priests in carrying out their ministry. While Vatican and Polish diplomats talked during 1974, the bishops made it clear in April that they wanted to be parties to any consultations. In September, the bishops' conference "was forced to deplore the slowness with which normalization, (of Church-state relations) was developing," according to a Warsaw dispatch in the Sept. 11 edition of the Italian newspaper *Avvenire.*

Portugal: Trouble for the Church seemed likely in the aftermath of the second change of government in 1974 with the accession in September of leftist radicals to positions of highest authority. Conservative policies of the bishops were already under attack during the summer.

Portuguese Colonies: A bishop and 11 missionaries were expelled from Mozambique during Holy Week, 1974, for opposition to official colonial policy. The support of such policy by some churchmen before self-determination and independence became a real possibility later in the year might strain developing Church-state relations in Mozambique, Portuguese Guinea and Angola.

Rhodesia: Church-state relations remained strained because of the bishops' opposition to racist policies of the Smith white-supremacy government.

South Africa: Work by the Church remained inhibited by the apartheid policies of the government.

South Korea: Agitation for constitutional and human rights, against the repressive policies of dictator Park Chung Hee, earned a 15-year prison sentence — on a charge of inciting to rebellion — for Bishop Daniel Tji Hak Soun of Won Ju Aug. 12, 1974. He was one of many arrested and/or imprisoned for the same "offense."

Soviet Union: While the world press gave considerable coverage in 1974 of government measures restricting the emigration and religious freedom of Jews, little was reported about the continuing repression of the unknown number of Catholics in the Ukraine and other parts of the Soviet Union.

Spain: In the midst of years-long tension between progressive and conservative Catholics and the government, the bishops' conference stood firm in support of Bishop Antonio Anoveros of Bilbao who was detained under house arrest in February, 1974. The bishop was accused of action against the government because of a letter he circulated on matters of social concern. The incident resulted in strained relations. The solidarity of the bishops was interpreted in some quarters as an indication of their readiness to press for liberalization of the tightly controlled policies characteristic of the Franco regime. Negotiations continued during the year on terms for a revision of the existing concordat between the Holy See and the Spanish government.

Racial Discrimination

During a meeting with a UN Committee on Apartheid May 22, 1974, Pope Paul VI quoted a relevant passage from his address of Dec. 21, 1973, to the College of Cardinals.

"As long as the rights of all the peoples — among them the right to self-determination and independence — are not duly recognized and honored, there cannot be true and lasting peace, even though the abusive power of arms may for a time prevail over the reactions of those opposed. For as long as, within the individual national communities, those in power do not nobly respect the rights and legitimate freedoms of the citizens, tranquility and order (even though they can be maintained by force) remain nothing but a deceptive and insecure sham, no longer worthy of a society of civilized beings. . . . We earnestly call upon all men of good will to recognize this and to give heed to the just yearnings of individuals and peoples."

The Catholic Church in Canada

The first date in the remote background of the Catholic history of Canada was July 7, 1534, when a priest in the exploration company of Jacques Cartier celebrated Mass on the Gaspe Peninsula.

Successful colonization and the significant beginnings of the Catholic history of the country date from the foundation of Quebec in 1608 by Samuel Champlain and French settlers. Montreal was established in 1642.

The earliest missionaries were Franciscan Recollects and Jesuits who arrived in 1615 and 1625, respectively. They provided some pastoral care for the settlers but worked mainly among the 100,000 Indians — Algonquins and Huron-Iroquois — in the interior and in the Lake Ontario region. Eight Jesuits, the North American Martyrs, were killed in the 1640's. Sulpician Fathers, who arrived in Canada late in the 1640's, played a part in the great missionary period which ended about 1700.

Kateri Tekakwitha, Lily of the Mohawks, the first North American Indian candidate for canonization, died in 1680.

The communities of women religious with the longest histories in Canada are the Canonesses of St. Augustine, since 1637; the Ursulines, since 1639; and the Hospitallers of St. Joseph, since 1642. Communities of Canadian origin are the Congregation of Notre Dame, founded by Marguerite Bourgeoys in 1658, and the Grey Nuns, formed by Mother d'Youville in 1738.

Start of Church Organization

Ecclesiastical organization began with the appointment of Francois Montmorency de Laval as vicar apostolic of New France in 1658 — 26 years after France canceled England's claim to possession of the country. In 1674, Quebec became the first diocese in the territory.

In 1713, the French Canadian population numbered 18,000. In the same year, the Treaty of Utrecht ceded Acadia, Newfoundland and the Hudson Bay Territory to England. The Acadians were scattered among the American Colonies in 1755.

The English acquired possession of Canada and its 70,000 French-speaking inhabitants in virtue of the Treaty of Paris in 1763. Anglo-French and Anglican-Catholic differences and tensions developed. The pro-British government at first refused to recognize the titles of church officials, hindered the clergy in their work and tried to install a non-Catholic educational system. Laws were passed which guaranteed religious liberties to Catholics (Quebec Act of 1774, Constitutional Act of 1791, legislation approved by Queen Victoria in 1851), but it took some time before actual respect for these liberties matched the legal enactments. The initial moderation of government antipathy toward the Church was caused partly by the loyalty of Catholics to the Crown during the American Revolution and the War of 1812.

Growth

The 15 years following the passage in 1840 of the Act of Union, which joined Upper and Lower Canada, were significant. New communities of men and women religious joined those already in the country. The Oblates of Mary Immaculate, missionaries par excellence in Canada, advanced the penetration of the West which had been started in 1818 by Abbe Provencher. New jurisdictions were established, and Quebec became a metropolitan see in 1844. The first Council of Quebec was held in 1851. The established Catholic school system enjoyed a period of growth.

Laval University was inaugurated in 1854 and canonically established in 1876.

Archbishop Taschereau of Quebec was named Canada's first cardinal in 1886.

The apostolic delegation to Canada was set up in 1899. It became a nunciature in 1970, with the establishment of diplomatic relations with the Vatican.

Early in this century, Canada had eight ecclesiastical provinces, 23 dioceses, three vicariates apostolic, 3,500 priests, 2.4 million Catholics, about 30 communities of men religious, and 70 or more communities of women religious. The Church in Canada was phased out of mission status and removed from the jurisdiction of the Congregation for the Propagation of the Faith in 1908.

The greatest concentration of Catholics is in the eastern portion of the country. In the northern and western portions, outside metropolitan centers, there are some of the most difficult parish and mission areas in the world. Bilingual (English-French) differences in the general population are reflected in the Church; for example, in the parallel structures of the Canadian Catholic Conference, which was established in 1943. Quebec is the center of French cultural influence. Many language groups are represented among Catholics, who include about 216,000 members of Eastern Rite in a metropolitan see and four eparchies.

Education, a past source of friction between the Church and the government, is administered by the civil provinces in a variety of arrangements authorized by the Canadian Constitution. Denominational schools have tax support in one way in Quebec and Newfoundland, and in another way in Alberta, Ontario and Saskatchewan. Several provinces provide tax support only for public schools, making private financing necessary for separate church-related schools.

ECCLESIASTICAL JURISDICTIONS OF CANADA

Provinces

Names of ecclesiastical provinces and metropolitan sees in bold face: suffragan sees in parentheses. The Winnipeg archdiocese (Latin) is not a metropolitan see.

Edmonton (Calgary, St. Paul).

Grouard-McLennan (Mackenzie-Ft. Smith, Prince George, Whitehorse).

Halifax (Antigonish, Charlottetown, Yarmouth).

Keewatin-LePas (Churchill-Hudson Bay, Labrador-Schefferville, Moosonee).

Kingston (Alexandria, Peterborough, Sault Ste. Marie).

Moncton (Bathurst, Edmundston, St. John).

Montreal (Joliette, St. Jean-de-Quebec, St. Jerome, Valleyfield).

Ottawa (Hearst, Hull, Mont-Laurier, Pembroke, Rouyn-Noranda, Timmins).

Quebec (Amos, Chicoutimi, Ste.-Anne-de-la-Pocatiere, Trois Rivieres).

Regina (Gravelbourg, Prince Albert, Saskatoon, Abbey of St. Peter).

Rimouski (Gaspe, Hauterive).

St. Boniface (no suffragans).

St. John's (Grand Falls, St. George).

Sherbrooke (Nicolet, St. Hyacinthe).

Toronto (Hamilton, London, St. Catharines, Thunder Bay).

Winnipeg — Ukrainian (Edmonton, New Westminster, Saskatoon, Toronto).

Archdioceses, Archbishops

Edmonton, Alta. (St. Albert, 1871; archdiocese, transferred Edmonton, 1912): Joseph N. MacNeil, archbishop, 1973.

Grouard-McLennan, Alta. (v. a. Athabaska-Mackenzie, 1862; Grouard, 1927; archdiocese Grouard-McLennan, 1967): Henri Legare, O.M.I., archbishop, 1972.

Halifax, N. S. (1842; archdiocese, 1852): James M. Hayes, archbishop, 1967.

Keewatin-Le Pas, Man. (v. a., 1910; archdiocese, 1967): Paul Dumouchel, O. M. I., archbishop, 1967.

Kingston, Ont. (1826; archdiocese, 1889): Joseph L. Wilhelm, archbishop, 1966.

Moncton, N.B. (1936): Donat Chiasson, archbishop, 1972.

Montreal, Que. (1836; archdiocese, 1886): Paul Gregoire, archbishop, 1968. Lawrence P. Whelan, Leo Blais, Valerien Belanger, Andre Cimichella, O. S. M., Leonard Crowley, auxiliaries.

Ottawa, Ont. (1847; archdiocese, 1886): Joseph Aurele Plourde, archbishop, 1967.

Quebec, Que. (v. a., 1658; diocese, 1674; archdiocese, 1819; metropolitan, 1844; primatial see, 1956): Cardinal Maurice Roy, archbishop, 1947. Lionel Audet, Laurent Noel, auxiliaries.

Regina, Sask. (1910; archdiocese, 1915): Charles A. Halpin, archbishop, 1973.

Rimouski, Que. (1867; archdiocese, 1946): J. Gilles Ouellet, archbishop, 1973.

St. Boniface, Man. (1847; archdiocese, 1871): Maurice Baudoux, archbishop, 1955. Antoine Hacault, auxiliary.

St. John's, Nfld. (p. a., 1784; v. a., 1796; diocese, 1847; archdiocese, 1904): Patrick J. Skinner, C. J. M., archbishop, 1951.

Sherbrooke, Que. (1874; archdiocese, 1951): J.-M. Fortier, archbishop, 1968.

Toronto, Ont. (1841; archdiocese, 1870): Philip F. Pocock, archbishop, 1971. Francis V. Allen, Thomas Fulton, auxiliaries.

Vancouver, B. C. (v. a. British Columbia, 1863; diocese New Westminster, 1890; archdiocese Vancouver, 1908): James F. Carney, archbishop, 1969.

Winnipeg, Man. (1915): Cardinal George B. Flahiff, C. S. B., archbishop, 1961.

Winnipeg, Man. (Ukrainian Byzantine Rite) (Ordinariate of Canada, 1912; ap. ex. Central Canada, 1948; ap. ex. Manitoba, 1951; archdiocese Winnipeg, 1956): Maxim Hermaniuk, C.SS.R., archbishop, 1956.

Dioceses, Bishops

Alexandria, Ont. (1890): Eugene Philippe LaRocque, bishop, 1974.

Amos, Que. (1938): Gaston Hains, bishop, 1968.

Antigonish, N. S. (Arichat, 1844; transferred, 1886): William E. Power, bishop, 1960.

Bathurst, N. B. (Chatham, 1860; transferred, 1938): Edgar Godin, bishop, 1969.

Calgary, Alta. (1912): Paul J. O'Byrne, bishop, 1968.

Charlottetown, P. E. I. (1829): Francis J. Spence, bishop, 1970.

Chicoutimi, Que. (1878): Marius Pare, bishop, 1961. Roch Pedneault, auxiliary.

Churchill-Hudson Bay, Man. (p.,a., 1925; v. a. Hudson Bay, 1931; diocese Churchill, 1967; Churchill-Hudson Bay, 1968): Omer Robidoux, O. M. I., bishop, 1970.

**Edmonton, Alta. (Ukrainian Byzantine Rite) (ap, ex., 1948; diocese, 1956): Nile Nicholas Savaryn, O.S.B.M., bishop, 1948. Martin Greschuk, auxiliary.

Edmundston, N. B. (1944): Fernand Lacroix, C. J. M., bishop, 1970.

Gaspe, Que. (1922): Bertrand Blanchet, bishop, 1973.

Grand Falls, Nfld. (Harbour Grace, 1856; present title, 1964): Alphonsus Liguori Penney, bishop, 1973.

Gravelbourg, Sask. (1930): Noel Delaquis, bishop, 1974.

Hamilton, Ont. (1856): Paul F. Reding, bishop, 1973.

Hauterive, Que. (p. a., 1882; v. a., 1905; diocese Gulf of St. Lawrence, 1945; name changed, 1960): Gerard Couturier, bishop, 1957.

Hearst, Ont. (p. a., 1918; v. a., 1920; diocese, 1938): Roger A. Despatie, bishop, 1973.

Hull, Que. (1963): Adolph Proulx, bishop, 1974.

Joliette, Que. (1904): Rene Audet, bishop, 1968.

Kamloops, B. C. (1945): Adam Exner, O.M.I., bishop, 1974.

Labrador-Schefferville (v. a. Labrador, 1945; diocese, 1967): Peter A. Sutton, O.M.I., bishop, 1974.

London, Ont. (1885; transferred Sandwich, 1859; London, 1869): G. Emmett Carter, bishop, 1964. John Sherlock, auxiliary.

Mackenzie-Fort Smith, N. W. T. (v. a. Mackenzie, 1901; diocese Mackenzie-Fort Smith, 1967): Paul Piché, O. M. I., bishop, 1967.

Mont-Laurier, Que. (1913): Andre Ouellette, bishop, 1965.

Moosonee, Ont. (v. a. James Bay, 1938; diocese Moosonee, 1967): Jules Leguerrier, O. M. I., bishop, 1967.

Nelson, B. C. (1936): Wilfred Emmett Doyle, bishop, 1958.

New Westminster, N.B. (Ukrainian Byzantine Rite) (1974): Jerome Chimij, O.S.B.M., bishop, 1974.

Nicolet, Que. (1885): Joseph A. Martin, bishop, 1950.

Pembroke, Ont. (v. a., 1882; diocese, 1898): Joseph R. Windle, bishop, 1971.

Peterborough, Ont. (1882): Francis A. Marrocco, bishop, 1968.

Prince Albert, Sask. (v. a., 1890; diocese, 1907): Laurent Morin, bishop, 1959.

Prince George, B. C. (p. a., 1908; v. a. Yukon and Prince Rupert, 1944; diocese Prince George, 1967): J. Fergus O'Grady, O. M. I., bishop, 1967.

Rouyn-Noranda, Que. (1973): Jean-Guy Hamelin, bishop, 1974.

Sainte-Anne-de-la-Pocatiere, Que. (1951): C.-H. Levesque, bishop, 1968.

St. Catharines, Ont. (1958): Thomas J. McCarthy, bishop, 1958.

St. George's, Nfld. (p. a., 1870; v. a., 1890; diocese, 1904): Richard T. McGrath. bishop, 1970.

St. Hyacinthe, Que. (1852): Albert Sanschagrin, O. M. I., bishop, 1967.

Saint-Jean-de-Quebec, (1933): Gerard Marie Coderre, bishop, 1955: Robert Lebel, auxiliary.

St. Jerome, Que. (1951): Bernard Hubert, bishop, 1971.

Saint John, N.B. (1842): Arthur J. Gilbert, bishop, 1974.

St. Paul in Alberta (1948): Raymond Roy, bishop, 1972.

Saskatoon, Sask. (1933): James P. Mahoney, bishop, 1967.

Saskatoon, Sask. (Ukrainian Byzantine Rite) (ap. ex., 1951; diocese, 1956): Andrew J. Roborecki, bishop, 1951.

Sault Ste. Marie, Ont. (1904): Alexander Carter, bishop, 1958.

Thunder Bay, Ont. (Ft. William, 1952; transferred, 1970): Norman J. Gallagher, bishop, 1970.

Timmins, Ont. (v. a. Temiskaming, 1908; diocese Haileybury, 1915; present title, 1938): Jacques Landriault, bishop, 1971.

Toronto, Ont. (Ukrainian Byzantine Rite) (ap. ex., 1948; diocese, 1956): Isidore Borecky, bishop, 1948, Michael Rusnak, C.SS.R., auxiliary.

Trois-Rivieres, Que. (1852): Georges-Leon Pelletier, bishop, 1947.

Valleyfield, Que. (1892): Guy Belanger, bishop, 1969.

Victoria, B. C. (diocese Vancouver Is., 1846; archdiocese, 1903; diocese Victoria, 1908): Remi J. De Roo, bishop, 1962.

Whitehorse, Y. T. (v.a., 1944; diocese 1967): Hubert P. O'Connor, O. M. I., bishop, 1971.

Yarmouth, N. S. (1953): Austin Emile Burke, bishop, 1968.

Military Vicariate of Canada (1951): Cardinal Maurice Roy, military vicar.

Abbacy of St. Peter, Muenster, Sask. (1921): Jerome Weber, O. S. B. (blessed, 1960).

BIOGRAPHIES OF CANADIAN BISHOPS

Allen, Francis V.: b. June 25, 1909, Toronto, Ont.; ord. priest June 10, 1933; ord. titular bishop of Avensa and auxiliary bishop of Toronto, Oct. 7, 1954.

Audet, Lionel: b. May 22, 1908, Ste. Marie de Beauce, Que.; ord. priest July 8, 1934; ord. titular bishop of Tibari and auxiliary bishop of Quebec, May 1, 1952.

Audet, Rene: b. Jan. 18, 1920, Montreal, Que.; ord. priest May 30, 1948; ord. titular bishop of Chonochora and auxiliary bishop of Ottawa, July 31, 1963; bishop of Joliette, Jan. 3, 1968.

Baudoux, Maurice: b. July 10, 1902, Louviere, Belgium; ord. priest July 17, 1929; ord.

bishop of St. Paul in Alberta, Oct. 28, 1948; titular archbishop of Preslavus and coadjutor archbishop of St. Boniface, Mar. 4, 1952; archbishop of St. Boniface, Sept. 14, 1955.

Belanger, Guy: b. Jan. 24, 1928, Valleyfield, Que.; ord. priest May 19, 1951; ord. bishop of Valleyfield, Nov. 23, 1969.

Belanger, Valerien: b. Apr. 6, 1902, Valleyfield, Que.; ord. priest May 29, 1926; ord titular bishop of Cyrene and auxiliary bishop of Montreal, May 11, 1956.

Blais, Leo: b. Apr. 28, 1904, Dollar Bay, Mich.; ord. priest June 14, 1930; ord. bishop of Prince Albert, Aug. 28, 1952; titular bishop of Geron and auxiliary bishop of Montreal, Feb. 28, 1959.

Blanchet, Bertrand: b. Sept. 19, 1932, Montagny, Que.; ord. priest May 20, 1956; ord. bishop of Gaspe, Dec. 5, 1973.

Borecky, Isidore: b. Oct. 1, 1911, Ostrovec, Ukraine; ord. priest July 17, 1938; ord. titular bishop of Amathus in Cypro and exarch of Toronto, May 27, 1948; bishop of Toronto (Ukrainians), Nov. 3, 1956.

Brodeur, Rosario L.: b. Oct. 30, 1889, Acton Vale, Que.; ord. priest June 17, 1916; ord. titular bishop of Mideo and coadjutor bishop of Alexandria, June 30, 1941; bishop of Alexandria, July 10, 1941; retired Oct. 15, 1966.

Burke, Austin Emile: b. Jan. 22, 1922, Sluice Point, N.S.; ord. priest Mar. 25, 1950; ord. bishop of Yarmouth, May 14, 1968.

Cabana, Georges: b. Oct. 22, 1894, Notre Dame de Granby, Que; ord. priest July 28, 1918; ord. titular archbishop of Anchialo and coadjutor archbishop of St. Boniface, June 30, 1941; coadjutor archbishop of Sherbrooke, Jan. 20, 1952; archbishop of Sherbrooke, May 28, 1952; retired 1968.

Carew, William A.: b. Oct. 23, 1922, St. John's, Nfld., ord. priest June 15, 1947; ord. titular archbishop of Telde, Jan. 4, 1970; nuncio to Rwanda and Burundi, 1970-74; apostolic delegate to Jerusalem and Palestine and pro-nuncio to Cyprus, 1974.

Carney, James F.: b. June 28, 1915, Vancouver, B.C.; ord. priest Mar. 21, 1942; ord. titular bishop of Obori and auxiliary bishop of Vancouver, Feb. 11, 1966; archbishop of Vancouver, Jan. 8, 1969.

Carter, Alexander: b. Apr. 16, 1909, Montreal, Que.; ord. priest June 6, 1936; ord. titular bishop of Sita and coadjutor bishop of Sault Ste. Marie, Feb. 2, 1957; bishop of Sault Ste. Marie, Nov. 22, 1958.

Carter, G. Emmett: b. Mar. 1, 1912, Montreal, Que.; ord. priest May 22, 1937; ord. titular bishop of Altiburo and auxiliary bishop of London, Ont., Feb. 2, 1962; bishop of London, Feb. 17, 1964, installed Mar. 12, 1964.

Caza, Percival: b. Aug. 13, 1896, Saint-Anicet, Que.; ord. priest June 29, 1922; ord. titular bishop of Albule and auxiliary of Valleyfield, Oct. 19, 1948; coadjutor bishop of Valleyfield, 1955; bishop of Valleyfield, Sept. 22, 1966; retired Mar. 18, 1969.

Charbonneau, Paul E.: b. May 4, 1922, Ste. Therese de Blainville, Que.; ord. priest May 31, 1947; ord. titular bishop of Thapsus and auxiliary bishop of Ottawa, Jan. 18, 1961; first bishop of Hull, May 21, 1963; retired Apr. 12, 1973 because of ill health.

Chiasson, Donat: b. Jan. 2, 1930, Paquetville, N.B.; ord. priest May 6, 1956; ord. archbishop of Moncton, June 1, 1972.

Chimij, Jerome I., O.S.B.M.: b. 1919, Radway, Alta.; ord. priest, 1944; app. first bishop of New Westminster, B.C., for the Ukrainians, July 2, 1974.

Cimichella, Andre, O.S.M.: b. Feb. 21, 1921, Grotte Santo Stefano, Italy; ord. priest May 26, 1945; ord. titular bishop of Quiza and auxiliary of Montreal, July 16, 1964.

Coderre, Gerard Marie: b. Dec. 19, 1904, St. Jacques de Montcalm, Que.; ord. priest May 30, 1931; ord. titular bishop of Aegae and coadjutor bishop of St.-Jean-de-Quebec, Sept. 12, 1951; bishop of St.-Jean-de-Quebec, Feb. 3, 1955.

Couturier, Gerard: b. Jan. 12, 1913, St. Louis du Ha Ha, Que; ord. priest Mar. 25, 1938; ord. bishop of Hauterive, Feb. 28, 1957.

Crowley, Leonard: b. Dec. 28, 1921, Montreal, Que.; ord. priest May 31, 1947; ord. titular bishop of Mons and auxiliary bishop of Montreal, Mar. 24, 1971.

Decosse, Aime: b. June 21, 1903, Somerset, Man.; ord. priest July 4, 1926; ord. bishop of Gravelbourg, Jan. 20, 1954; retired May 14, 1973.

Delaquis, Noel: b. Dec. 25, 1934, Notre-Dame-de-Lourdes, Man.; ord. priest 1958; ord. bishop of Gravelbourg, Feb. 19, 1974.

De Roo, Remi J.: b. Feb. 24, 1924, Swan Lake, Man.; ord. priest June 8, 1950; ord. bishop of Victoria, Dec. 14, 1962.

Desmarais, Joseph A.: b. Oct. 31, 1891, Upton, Que.; ord. priest July 25, 1914; ord. titular bishop of Ruspe and auxiliary bishop of St. Hyacinthe, Apr. 22, 1931; bishop of Amos, June 20, 1939; retired Oct. 31, 1968.

Despatie, Roger A.: b. Apr. 12, 1927, Sudbury, Ont.; ord. priest Apr. 12, 1952; ord. titular bishop of Usinaza and auxiliary bishop of Sault Ste. Marie, June 28, 1968; app. bishop of Hearst, Feb. 8, 1973.

Desrochers, Bruno: b. Apr. 17, 1910, St. Louis de Lotbiniere, Que.; ord. priest June 30, 1934; ord. first bishop of Sainte-Anne-de-la-Pocatiere, Sept. 21, 1951; resigned May 24, 1968; vicar general of Sainte-Anne-de-la-Pocatiere.

Douville, Arthur: b. July 22, 1894, St. Casimir de Portneuf, Que.; ord. priest May 25, 1919; ord. titular bishop of Vita and auxiliary bishop of St. Hyacinthe, Jan. 29, 1940; coadjutor bishop of St. Hyacinthe, Mar. 21, 1942; bishop of St. Hyacinthe, Nov. 27, 1942; retired June 13, 1967.

Doyle, Wilfrid E.: b. Feb. 18, 1913, Calgary, Alta.; ord. priest June 5, 1938; ord. bishop of Nelson, Dec. 3, 1958.

Dumouchel, Paul, O.M.I.: b. Sept. 19, 1911, St. Boniface, Man.; ord. priest June 24, 1936; ord. titular bishop of Sufes and vicar apostolic of Keewatin, May 24, 1955; archbishop of Keewatin-Le Pas, July 13, 1967.

Exner, Adam, O.M.I.: b. 1928, Killaly, Sask,; ord. priest 1957; ord. bishop of Kamloops, B.C., Mar. 12, 1973.

Flahiff, George F.: (See Cardinals Biographies.)

Fortier, Jean-Marie: b. July 1, 1920, Quebec, Que.; ord. priest June 16, 1944; ord. titular bishop of Pomaria and auxiliary bishop of

Ste. Anne-de-la-Pocatiere, Jan. 23, 1961; bishop of Gaspe, Jan. 19, 1965; archbishop of Sherbrooke, Apr. 20, 1968; president of the Canadian Catholic Conference, 1973.

Frenette, Emilien: b. May 6, 1905, Montreal, Que.; ord. priest May 30, 1930; ord. bishop of St. Jerome, Sept. 12, 1951; retired June 11, 1971.

Fulton, Thomas B.: b. Jan. 13, 1918, St. Catharines, Ont.; ord. priest June 7, 1941; ord. titular bishop of Cursola and auxiliary bishop of Toronto, Jan. 6, 1969.

Gagnon, Edouard, P.S.S.: b. Jan. 15, 1918, Port Daniel, Que.; ord. priest Aug. 15, 1940; ord. bishop Mar. 25, 1969; bishop of St. Paul in Alberta 1969-72; rector of Canadian College in Rome, 1972- ; president of Vatican Committee for the Family, 1973.

Gallagher, Norman J.: b. May 24, 1917, Coatbridge, Scotland; ord. priest Mar. 29, 1941; ord. titular bishop of Adrasus and auxiliary bishop of Montreal, Sept. 12, 1963; bishop of Thunder Bay, April 22, 1970.

Gilbert, Arthur J.: b. Oct. 26, 1915, Oromocto, N.B.; ord. priest June 3, 1943; ord. bishop of St. John, N.B., June 19, 1974.

Godin, Edgar: b. May 31, 1911, Neguac, N.B.; ord. priest June 15, 1941; ord. bishop of Bathurst, July 25, 1969.

Gregoire, Paul: b. Oct. 24, 1911, Verdun, Que.; ord. priest May 22, 1937; ord. titular bishop of Curubis and auxiliary bishop of Montreal, Dec. 27, 1961; archbishop of Montreal, Apr. 20, 1968.

Greschuk, Michael: b. 1924, Innistree, Alta.; ord. priest June 11, 1950; app. titular bishop of Nazianus and auxiliary bishop of Edmonton of the Ukrainians, July 2, 1974.

Hacault, Antoine: b. Jan. 17, 1926, Bruxelles, Man.; ord. priest May 20, 1951; ord. titular bishop of Media and auxiliary bishop of St. Boniface, Sept. 8, 1964.

Hains, Gaston: b. Sept. 10, 1921, Drummondville, Que.; ord. priest June 15, 1946; ord. titular bishop of Belesansa and auxiliary bishop of St. Hyacinthe, Oct. 18, 1964; coadjutor bishop of Amos, 1967; bishop of Amos, Oct. 31, 1968.

Halpin, Charles A.: b. Aug. 30, 1930, St. Eustache, Man.; ord. priest May 27, 1956; ord. archbishop of Regina, Nov. 26, 1973.

Hamelin, Jean-Guy: b. Oct. 8, 1925, St. Severin-de-Proulxville, Que.; ord. priest 1949; ord, first bishop of Rouyn-Noranda, Que., Feb. 9, 1974.

Hayes, James M.: b. May 27, 1924, Halifax, N.S.; ord. priest June 15, 1947; ord. titular bishop of Reperi and apostolic administrator of Halifax, Apr. 20, 1965; archbishop of Halifax, June 22, 1967.

Hermaniuk, Maxim, C.SS.R.: b. Oct. 30, 1911, Nove Selo, Ukraine; ord. priest Sept. 4, 1938; ord. titular bishop of Sinna and exarch of Manitoba (Ukrainians), June 29, 1951; archbishop of Winnipeg (Ukrainians), Nov. 3, 1956.

Hubert, Bernard: b. June 1, 1929, Beloeil, Que.; ord. priest May 30, 1953; ord. bishop of St. Jerome, Sept. 12, 1971.

Jennings, Edward Q.: b. Oct. 4, 1896, Saint John, N.B.; ord. priest Dec. 27, 1925; ord. titular bishop of Sala and auxiliary bishop of Vancouver, June 11, 1941; bishop of Kamloops, Feb. 22, 1946; bishop of Fort William (now Thunder Bay), May 14, 1962; resigned Sept. 18, 1969.

Johnson, Martin M.: b. Mar. 18, 1899, Toronto; ord. priest June 14, 1924; ord. first bishop of Nelson, Sept. 29, 1936; titular archbishop of Cio and coadjutor archbishop of Vancouver, Nov. 27, 1954; archbishop of Vancouver, Mar. 11, 1964; retired 1969.

Jordan, Anthony, O.M.I.: b. Nov. 10, 1901, Broxburn, Scotland; ord. priest June 23, 1929; ord. titular bishop of Vada and vicar apostolic of Prince Rupert, B.C., Sept. 8, 1945; titular archbishop of Silyum and coadjutor of Edmonton, Apr. 17, 1955; archbishop of Edmonton, Aug. 11, 1964; retired July 6, 1973.

Lacroix, Fernand, C.J.M.: b. Oct. 16, 1919, Quebec; ord. priest Feb. 10, 1946; ord. bishop of Edmundston, Oct. 20, 1970.

Lacroix, Marc, O.M.I.: b. Apr. 25, 1906, Saint Simon-de-Bagot, Que.; ord. priest May 21, 1933; ord. titular bishop of Roso and vicar apostolic of Hudson Bay, Feb. 22, 1943; bishop of Churchill-Hudson Bay, July 13, 1967; retired Oct. 25, 1968.

Landriault, Jacques: b. Sept. 23, 1921, Alfred, Ont.; ord. priest Feb. 9, 1947; ord. titular bishop of Cadi and auxiliary bishop of Alexandria, July 25, 1962; bishop of Hearst, May 27, 1964; app. bishop of Timmins, Mar. 30, 1971.

Landry, Georges: b. Dec. 3, 1895, Pomquet, N.S.; ord. priest June 24, 1921; ord. bishop of Hearst, May 1, 1946; retired Jan. 14, 1952.

LaRocque, Eugene Philippe: b. Mar. 27, 1927, Windsor, Ont.; ord. priest June 7, 1952; ord. bishop of Alexandria, Ont., Sept. 3, 1974.

Lebel, Robert: b. Nov. 8, 1924, archdiocese of Rimouski, Que.; ord. priest June 18, 1950; ord. titular bishop of Alinda and auxiliary of St. Jean de Quebec, May 12, 1974.

Le Blanc, Camille A.: b. Aug. 25, 1898, Neguac, N.B.; ord. priest Apr. 5, 1924; ord. bishop of Bathurst, Sept. 8, 1942; retired Jan. 8, 1969.

Legare, Henri, O.M.I.: b. Feb. 20, 1918, Willow Bunch, Sask.; ord. priest June 29, 1943; ord. first bishop of Labrador-Schefferville, Sept. 9, 1967; archbishop of Grouard-McLennan, Nov. 21, 1972.

Leguerrier, Jules, O.M.I.: b. Feb. 18, 1915, Clarence Creek, Ont.; ord. priest June 19, 1943; ord. titular bishop of Bavagaliana and vicar apostolic of James Bay, June 29, 1964; first bishop of Moosonee, July 13, 1967.

Levesque, Charles Henri: b. Dec. 29, 1921, St. Andre de Kamouraska, Que.; ord. priest

June 13, 1948; ord. titular bishop of Guzabeta and auxiliary bishop of Ste.-Anne-de-la-Pocatiere, Dec. 27, 1965; bishop of Ste.-Anne-de-la-Pocatiere, Aug. 17, 1968.

Levesque, Louis: b. May 27, 1908, Amqui, Que.; ord. priest June 26, 1932; ord. bishop of Hearst, Aug. 15, 1952; titular archbishop of Egnatia and coadjutor of Rimouski, Apr. 13, 1964; archbishop of Rimouski, Feb. 25, 1967; retired May 14, 1973.

Lussier, Philippe, C.SS.R.: b. Oct. 3, 1911, Weedon, Que.; ord. priest Sept. 18, 1937; ord. bishop of St. Paul in Alberta, Aug. 17, 1952; retired Aug. 17, 1968.

McCarthy, Thomas J.: b. Oct. 4, 1905, Goderich, Ont.; ord. priest May 25, 1929; ord. bishop of Nelson, Aug. 1, 1955; bishop of St. Catharines, Nov. 9, 1958.

MacEachern, Malcolm A.: b. Oct. 5, 1901, Broad Cove Chapel, N.S.; ord. priest June 11, 1927; ord. bishop of Charlottetown, Jan. 18, 1955; retired Feb. 24, 1970.

McGrath, Richard T.: b. June 17, 1912, Oderin, Placentia Bay, Nfld.; ord. priest June 24, 1936; ord. bishop of St. George's, Nfld., July 22, 1970.

MacNeil, Joseph N.: b. Apr. 15, 1924, Sydney, N.S.; ord. priest May 23, 1948; ord. bishop of St. John, N.B., June 24, 1969; archbishop of Edmonton, July 6, 1973.

Mahoney, James P.: b. Dec. 7, 1927, Saskatoon, Sask.; ord. priest June 7, 1952; ord. bishop of Saskatoon Dec. 13, 1967.

Marrocco, Francis A.: b. June 20, 1913, Peterborough, Ont.; ord. priest June 12, 1938; ord. titular bishop of Limne and auxiliary bishop of Toronto, Feb. 22, 1956; bishop of Peterborough, June 10, 1968.

Martin, Joseph A.: b. Oct. 4, 1913, Southbridge, Mass.; ord. priest May 18, 1939; ord. titular bishop of Bassiana and coadjutor bishop of Nicolet, Oct. 7, 1950; bishop of Nicolet, Nov. 8, 1950.

Melancon, Georges: b. Apr. 7, 1886, Saint-Guillaume d'Upton, Que.; ord. priest Sept. 12, 1909; ord. bishop of Chicoutimi, July 23, 1940; retired Feb. 18, 1961.

Morin, Laurent: b. Feb. 14, 1908, Montreal, Que.; ord. priest May 24, 1934; ord. titular bishop of Arsamosata and auxiliary bishop of Montreal, Oct. 30, 1955; bishop of Prince Albert, Feb. 28, 1959.

Mulvihill, James P., O.M.I.: b. Oct. 15, 1905, Old Chelsea, Ont.; ord. priest, June 24, 1937; ord. titular bishop of Caput Cilla and vicar apostolic of Whitehorse, Jan. 25, 1966; bishop of Whitehorse, July 13, 1967; retired Oct. 15, 1971.

Noel, Laurent: b. Mar. 19, 1920, Saint-Just-de-Bretenieres, Que.; ord. priest June 16, 1944; ord. titular bishop of Agathopolis and auxiliary bishop of Quebec, Aug. 29, 1963.

O'Byrne, Paul J.: b. Dec. 21, 1922, Calgary, Alta.; ord. priest Feb. 21, 1948; ord. bishop of Calgary, Aug. 22, 1968.

O'Connor, Hubert P., O.M.I.: b. Feb. 17,

1928, Huntington, Que.; ord. priest June 5, 1954; ord. bishop of Whitehorse, Dec. 8, 1971.

O'Grady, John Fergus, O.M.I.: b. July 27, 1908, Macton, Ont.; ord. priest June 29, 1934; ord. titular bishop of Aspendus and vicar apostolic of Prince Rupert, Mar. 7, 1956; first bishop of Prince George, July 13, 1967.

O'Neill, John M.: b. Oct. 26, 1903, Harbor Grace, Nfld.; ord. priest Apr. 24, 1927; ord. bishop of Grand Falls, July 7, 1940; retired Nov. 23, 1972.

O'Neill, Michael C.: b. Feb. 15, 1898, Kemptville, Ont.; ord. priest Dec. 21, 1927; ord. archbishop of Regina, Apr. 14, 1948; retired Sept. 26, 1973.

Ouellet, J. Gilles, P.M.E.: b. Aug. 14, 1922, Bromptonville, Que.; ord. priest June 30, 1946; ord. bishop of Gaspe, Nov. 23, 1968; app. archbishop of Rimouski, May 14, 1973.

Ouellette, Andre: b. Feb. 4, 1913, Salem, Mass.; ord. priest June 11, 1938; ord. titular bishop of Carre and auxiliary bishop of Mont-Laurier, Feb. 25, 1957; bishop of Mont-Laurier, Mar. 27, 1965.

Pare, Marius: b. May 22, 1903, Montmagny, Que.; ord. priest July 3, 1927; ord. titular bishop of Aegae and auxiliary bishop of Chicoutimi, May 1, 1956; bishop of Chicoutimi, Feb. 18, 1961.

Parent, Charles Eugene: b. Apr. 22, 1902, Notre Dame-de-Neiges-de-Trois-Pistoles, Que.; ord. priest Mar. 7, 1925; ord. titular bishop of Diana and auxiliary bishop of Rimouski, May 24, 1944; app. archbishop of Rimouski, Mar. 2, 1951; retired Feb. 25, 1967.

Pednault, Roch: b. Apr. 10, 1927, diocese of Chicoutimi, Que.; ord. priest Feb. 8, 1953; ord. titular bishop of Aggersel and auxiliary of Chicoutimi, Que., June 29, 1974.

Pelletier, Georges Leon: b. Aug. 19, 1904, Saint-Epiphane, Que.; ord. priest July 24, 1931; ord. titular bishop of Hephaestus and auxiliary bishop of Quebec, Feb. 24, 1943; bishop of Trois Rivieres, July 26, 1947.

Penney, Alphonsus L.: b. Sept. 27, 1924, St. John's, Nfld.; ord. priest June 29, 1949; ord. bishop of Grand Falls, Jan. 18, 1973.

Piche, Paul, O.M.I.: b. Sept. 14, 1909, Gravelbourg, Sask.; ord. priest Dec. 23, 1934; ord. titular bishop of Orcistus and vicar apostolic of Mackenzie, June 11, 1959; first bishop of Mackenzie-Fort Smith, July 13, 1967.

Plourde, Joseph Aurele: b. Jan. 12, 1915, St. Francois de Madawaska, N.B.; ord. priest May 7, 1944; ord. titular bishop of Lapda and auxiliary bishop of Alexandria, Aug. 24, 1964; archbishop of Ottawa, Jan. 12, 1967.

Pocock, Philip: b. July 2, 1906, St. Thomas, Ont.; ord. priest June 14, 1930; ord. bishop of Saskatoon, June 29, 1944; titular archbishop of Aprus and coadjutor archbishop of Winnipeg, Aug. 6, 1951; archbishop of Winnipeg, Jan. 14, 1952; titular archbishop of Isauropolis and coadjutor archbishop of Toronto,

Feb. 18, 1961; archbishop of Toronto, Mar. 30, 1971.

Power, William E.: b. Sept. 27, 1915; Montreal, Que.; ord. priest June 7, 1941; ord. bishop of Antigonish, July 20, 1960; president Canadian Catholic Conference, 1971-73.

Proulx, Adolph E.: b. Dec. 12, 1927, Hanmer, Ont., Canada; ord. priest Apr. 17, 1954; ord. titular bishop of Missua and auxiliary bishop of Sault Ste. Marie, Feb. 24, 1965; bishop of Alexandria, Apr. 28, 1967; bishop of Hull, Feb. 13, 1974.

Reding, Paul F.: b. Feb. 14, 1925, Hamilton, Ont.; ord. priest June 3, 1950; ord. titular bishop of Liberalia and auxiliary bishop of Hamilton, Sept. 14, 1966; bishop of Hamilton, Sept. 14, 1973.

Robichaud, Norbert: b. Apr. 1, 1905, St. Charles, N.B.; ord. priest May 1, 1931; ord. archbishop of Moncton, Sept. 8, 1942; retired Mar. 23, 1972.

Robidoux, Omer, O.M.L.: b. Dec. 19, 1913; ord. priest June 29, 1939; ord bishop of Churchill-Hudson Bay, May 21, 1970.

Roborecki, Andrew: b. Dec. 12, 1910, in western Ukraine; arrived Winnipeg, Man., 1912; ord. priest July 18, 1934; ord. titular bishop of Tanais and auxiliary bishop of Ukrainian Catholic Diocese of Central Canada, May 27, 1948; exarch of Saskatchewan, 1951; bishop of Saskatoon (Ukrainians), Nov. 3, 1956.

Routhier, Henri, O.M.I.: b. Feb. 28, 1900, Pincher Creek, Alta.; ord. priest Sept. 7, 1924; ord. titular bishop of Naissus and coadjutor vicar apostolic of Grouard, Sept. 8, 1945; vicar apostolic of Grouard, 1953; archbishop of Grouard-McLennan, July 13, 1967; retired Nov. 21, 1972.

Roy, Maurice: (Cardinals, Biographies.)

Roy, Raymond: b. May 3, 1919, Fisher Branch, Man.; ord. priest May 31, 1947; ord. bishop of St. Paul in Alberta, July 18, 1972.

Rusnak, Michael, C.SS.R.: b. Aug. 21, 1921, Beaverdale, Pa.; ord. priest July 3, 1949; ord. titular bishop of Tzernicus and auxiliary bishop of Toronto eparchy and apostolic visitor to Slovak Catholics of Byzantine rite in Canada, Jan. 2, 1965.

Ryan, Joseph F.: b. Mar. 1, 1897, Dundas, Ont.; ord. priest May 21, 1921; ord. bishop of Hamilton, Oct. 19, 1937; retired Mar. 27, 1973.

Sanschagrin, Albert, O.M.I.: b. Aug. 5, 1911, Saint-Tite, Que.; ord. priest May 24, 1936; ord. titular bishop of Bagi and coadjutor bishop of Amos Sept. 14, 1957; bishop of Saint-Hyacinthe, June 23, 1967.

Savaryn, Nile Nicholas, O.S.B.M.: b. May 19, 1905, Stary Sambir, Ukraine; ord. priest Aug. 23, 1931; ord. titular bishop of Jos and auxiliary bishop of the Catholic Ukrainian diocese in Canada, July 1, 1943; bishop of apostolic exarchate for western Canada, 1948; bishop of Edmonton (Ukrainians), Nov. 3, 1956.

Sherlock, John M.: b. Jan. 21, 1926, Brantford, Ont.; ord. priest 1950; ord. titular bishop of Macriana and auxiliary of London, Ont., Aug. 28, 1974.

Skinner, Patrick J., C.J.M.: b. Mar. 9, 1904, St. John's, Nfld.; ord. priest May 30, 1929; ord. titular bishop of Zenobia and auxiliary bishop of St. John's, Mar. 17, 1950; archbishop of St. John's, Mar. 23, 1951.

Smith, William J.: b. Jan. 2, 1897, Greenfield, Ont.; ord. priest June 16, 1927; ord. bishop of Pembroke, July 25, 1945; retired Feb. 17, 1971.

Spence, Francis J.: b. June 3, 1926, Perth, Ont.; ord. priest, Apr. 16, 1950; ord. titular bishop of Nova and auxiliary bishop of the military vicariate, June 15, 1967; bishop of Charlottetown, Aug. 15, 1970.

Sutton, Peter A., O.M.I.: b. Oct. 18, 1934, Chandler, Que.; ord. priest Oct. 22, 1960; ord. bishop of Labrador-Schefferville, July 18, 1974.

Tessier, Maxime: b. Oct. 9, 1906, St. Sebastien, Que.; ord. priest June 14, 1930; ord. titular bishop of Christopolis and auxiliary bishop of Ottawa, Aug. 2, 1951; coadjutor bishop of Timmins, 1953; bishop of Timmins, May 8, 1955; retired Mar. 24, 1971.

Webster, Benjamin I.: b. Mar. 7, 1898, Spofforth, Eng.; ord. priest May 26, 1923; ord. titular bishop of Paphos and auxiliary bishop of Toronto, Nov. 21, 1946; bishop of Peterborough, Apr. 21, 1954; retired 1968.

Whelan, Lawrence P.: b. Oct. 16, 1899, Montreal, Que.; ord. priest Dec. 19, 1925; ord. titular bishop of Opus and auxiliary bishop of Montreal, Aug. 15, 1941.

Wilhelm, Joseph L.: b. Nov. 16, 1909, Walkerton, Ont.; ord. priest June 9, 1934; ord. titular bishop of Saccaea and auxiliary bishop of Calgary, Aug. 22, 1963; archbishop of Kingston, Dec. 14, 1966.

Windle, Joseph R.: b. Aug. 28, 1917, Ashdad, Ont.; ord. priest May 16, 1943; ord. titular bishop of Uzita and auxiliary bishop of Ottawa, Jan. 18, 1961; coadjutor bishop of Pembroke, 1969; bishop of Pembroke, Feb. 15, 1971.

Sahelian Aid

The Canadian Catholic Organization for Development and Peace reported in March, 1974, that it had allocated $205,000 for emergency relief as well as medium and long term development to the drought-stricken Sahelian Region of West Africa.

The allocation brought to $400,000 the total amount of CCODP funds for the water-starved countries of Chad, Mali, Mauritania, Niger, Senegal, Upper Volta and Ethiopia.

The organization also reported that it had received $150,000 from Canadian Catholics for drought relief to be channelled to the African nations as soon as requests are made and approved. The Sahel was critically in need of immediate aid.

CATHOLIC POPULATION STATISTICS OF CANADA

(Source: *Annuario Pontificio*. Archdioceses are indicated by an asterisk. For dioceses marked +, see Canadian Dioceses with Interprovincial Lines.)

Canada's 10 civil provinces and two territories are divided into 17 ecclesiastical provinces consisting of 17 metropolitan sees (archdioceses) and 51 suffragan sees (50 dioceses and one abbacy); there is also one archdiocese immediately subject to the Holy See. (See listing of Ecclesiastical Provinces elsewhere in this section.)

This table presents a regional breakdown of Catholic statistics. In some cases, the totals are approximate because diocesan boundaries fall within several civil provinces.

Civil Province Dioceses	Priests Dioc.	Rel.	Tot.	Sems.	Men Rel.	Wom. Rel.	Par- ishes.	Cath. Pop.	Total Pop.
Newfoundland	117	42	159	22	137	608	86	174,515	445,053
*St. John's	54	16	70	8	77	396	39	86,051	165,513
Grand Falls	36	—	36	7	16	80	27	32,000	145,000
St. George's	26	1	27	7	12	93	20	39,464	92,328
Labrador- Schefferville+	1	25	26	—	32	39	—	17,000	42,212
Prince Edward Island									
Charlottetown	80	4	84	4	4	270	46	46,499	111,641
Nova Scotia	314	68	382	9	90	1,403	169	275,802	840,233
*Halifax	94	38	132	4	40	432	51	120,000	470,000
Antigonish	189	12	201	4	28	882	93	123,449	241,725
Yarmouth	31	18	49	1	22	89	25	32,353	128,508
New Brunswick	341	140	481	8	215	1,376	184	293,044	602,060
*Moncton	83	67	150	2	89	449	48	72,110	141,221
Bathurst	114	25	139	3	54	421	55	101,274	120,774
Edmundston	55	27	82	3	44	256	31	49,867	60,065
St. John	89	21	110	—	28	250	50	69,793	280,000
Quebec	4,767	2,999	7,766	358	7,167	30,260	1,775	5,086,075	5,858,340
*Montreal	853	1,366	2,219	61	2,537	9,368	256	1,665,000	2,203,483
*Quebec	964	599	1,563	89	1,515	7,401	266	802,487	812,125
*Rimouski	263	46	309	6	96	1,222	119	161,095	164,050
*Sherbrooke	327	160	487	15	425	1,700	133	206,047	224,246
Amos	81	38	119	—	70	393	76	93,804	97,978
Chicoutimi	306	1	307	83	167	1,175	95	255,362	256,962
Gaspe	108	22	130	6	41	452	64	100,875	110,875
Hauterive	58	35	93	1	64	296	50	100,579	102,824
Hull	104	72	176	6	108	376	56	146,868	178,546
Joliette	170	66	236	10	198	792	54	121,731	123,450
Mont Laurier	83	39	122	3	85	301	55	67,174	69,347
Nicolet	265	38	303	25	214	1,139	85	153,690	155,338
St. Anne-de-la- Pocatiere	192	10	202	8	36	576	53	90,296	90,481
St. Hyacinthe	274	103	377	12	454	1,770	106	258,993	275,653
St. Jean de Quebec	181	105	286	17	294	865	88	324,000	383,000
St. Jerome	130	126	256	5	319	434	60	178,204	211,204
Trois Rivieres	279	112	391	10	369	1,508	97	233,398	237,283
Valleyfield	129	61	190	1	175	492	62	126,472	161,475
Rouyn-Noranaa				— No separate statistics available —					
Ontario	1,541	1,346	2,887	151	2,212	5,963	976	2,022,794	8,125826
*Kingston	77	9	86	9	10	297	51	54,825	260,000
*Ottawa	275	313	588	4	602	1,539	99	224,288	514,861
*Toronto	279	460	739	36	850	590	170	650,000	3,335,000
Alexandria	46	10	56	4	23	160	32	51,430	78,731
Hamilton	148	139	287	22	176	643	106	232,640	1,212,419
Hearst	32	8	40	1	11	90	23	32,952	48,147
London	249	130	379	28	170	986	144	282,233	1,201,174
Moosonee+	1	15	16	—	36	20	14	3,700	16,500
Pembroke+	91	5	96	14	9	325	52	52,603	110,617
Peterborough	53	8	61	7	9	200	33	36,729	283,376

Civil Province / Dioceses	Priests Dioc.	Priests Rel.	Priests Tot.	Sems.	Men Rel.	Wom. Rel.	Parishes	Cath. Pop.	Total Pop.
St. Catherines	52	47	99	4	52	133	47	93,893	380,001
Sault Ste Marie	137	113	250	15	125	505	98	160,000	342,000
Thunder Bay	23	43	66	2	48	101	37	52,779	200,000
Timmins+	78	46	124	5	91	374	70	94,722	143,000
Manitoba	**141**	**249**	**390**	**14**	**323**	**1,139**	**196**	**201,647**	**997,914**
*Keewatin-LePas+	—	51	51	—	72	125	35	24,200	65,000
*St. Boniface	78	74	152	10	114	617	70	75,962	303,708
*Winnipeg	63	101	164	4	108	385	75	97,500	612,956
Churchill-Hudson Bay+	—	23	23	—	29	12	16	3,985	16,250
Saskatchewan	**197**	**211**	**408**	**20**	**253**	**1,242**	**246**	**204,974**	**937,523**
*Regina	91	73	164	10	77	350	101	95,000	490,000
Gravelbourg	25	15	40	1	25	129	27	15,054	57,523
Prince Albert	45	44	89	2	50	469	50	41,072	185,000
Saskatoon	36	43	79	7	54	209	42	41,748	185,000
St. Peter Muenster (Abbacy)	—	36	36	—	47	85	26	12,100	20,000
Alberta	**235**	**111**	**346**	**24**	**187**	**998**	**200**	**315,973**	**1,606,900**
*Edmonton	115	2	117	10	31	614	87	137,500	742,000
*Grouard-McLennan	6	31	37	—	61	115	—	30,000	88,000
Calgary	83	72	155	9	89	194	68	126,073	700,000
St. Paul	31	6	37	5	6	75	45	22,400	76,900
British Columbia	**165**	**179**	**344**	**11**	**243**	**726**	**162**	**277,536**	**1,875,072**
*Vancouver	83	95	178	7	125	415	70	150,000	1,023,960
Kamloops	16	15	31	—	23	37	18	22,400	149,000
Nelson	35	13	48	2	13	56	33	34,136	190,316
Prince George	3	33	36	2	49	50	17	33,000	130,000
Victoria	28	23	51		33	168	24	38,000	381,796
Yukon Territory									
Whitehorse+	—	22	22	—	27	22	2	6,015	22,988
Northwest Territories+									
Mackenzie-Ft. Smith	—	45	45	—	73	102	29	18,982	41,802
Eastern Rite (Ukrainian)	**184**	**82**	**266**	**9**	**114**	**148**	**156**	**199,175**	— —
*Winnipeg	44	13	57	2	13	24	41	60,060	— —
Edmonton	44	19	63	1	28	22	34	51,987	— —
Saskatoon	27	20	47	1	26	44	13	32,128	— —
Toronto	69	30	99	5	47	58	68	55,000	— —
New Westminster— No separate statistics available —									
TOTALS	**8,082**	**5,498**	**13,580**	**630**	**11,045**	**44,317**	**4,227**	**9,123,031**	**21,465,332**

Dioceses with Interprovincial Lines

The following dioceses, indicated by + in the table, have interprovincial lines.

Labrador-Schefferville includes the Labrador region of Newfoundland and the northern part of Quebec province.

Moosonee, Ont., includes part of Quebec province.

Pembroke, Ont., includes one county of Quebec province.

Timmins, Ont., includes part of Quebec province. (Some or all of the Quebec portion of Timmins may now be included in the diocese of **Rouyn-Noranda, Que.,** which was erected late in 1973 with territory taken from Timmins.)

Keewatin-Le Pas includes part of Manitoba and Saskatchewan provinces.

Churchill-Hudson Bay includes part of Northwest Territories.

Whitehorse, Y.T., includes part of British Columbia.

Northwest Territories totals do not include an area within the boundaries of the Churchill-Hudson Bay diocese.

Canadian Catechism

In a nearly unanimous vote taken during the semiannual meeting of the Canadian Catholic Conference in the fall of 1974, the bishops resolved that the "Come to the Father" catechetical series would be revised but that its basic pedagogical approach and content would be retained.

The five-member team which evaluated the English version of the program indicated that revisions would be made in the treatment of traditional devotions and practices in the Church, the place of doctrine and tradition, leadership and authority in the Church.

CANADIAN CATHOLIC CONFERENCE

The Canadian Catholic Conference was established Oct. 12, 1943, as a permanent voluntary association of the bishops of Canada, was given official approval by the Holy See in 1948, and acquired the status of an episcopal conference after the Second Vatican Council.

The CCC acts in two ways: (1) as a strictly ecclesiastical body through which the bishops act together with pastoral authority and responsibility for the Church throughout the country; (2) as an operational secretariat through which the bishops act on a wider scale for the good of the Church and society.

At the top of the CCC organizational table are the president, an executive committee, an administrative board and a plenary assembly. The membership consists of all the bishops of Canada.

Departments and Offices

The CCC has four departments with 25 offices: (I) Doctrine and Faith Department with six offices — theology (French and English), liturgy (French and English), religious education (French and English), (II) Social Life Department with five offices — social action (French), social action/family life (English), social communications (French and English), health and welfare (French); (III) Internal Relations Department with six offices — clergy (French), clergy, seminaries, education, vocations (English), religious (French and English); (IV) Missions and Ecumenism Department with eight offices — apostolic and missionary assistance (French and English), missions, Latin America (French and English), ecumenism (French and English), non-believers (French).

The general secretariat consists of general secretaries and assistants, and directors of public relations.

Administrative services, under a general director, are for purchasing, archives and library, accounting, editions, printing and expedition, personnel and publications.

Advisory councils, with a mixed membership of lay persons, religious, priests and bishops, are the National Council on Liturgy, the National Council on Fiscal Affairs, the Canadian Catholic Education Council, and the National Missionary Council.

Operations

Meetings for the transaction of business are held twice a year by the plenary assembly, every second month except July and August by the executive committee, and twice a year by the central commission.

The CCC has agencies and services operating in Ottawa, Toronto and Montreal.

All constituent organs of the CCC have French and English counterparts.

Archbishop Jean-Marie Fortier of Sherbrooke is president of the CCC; Bishop G. Emmett Carter of London, Ont., is vice-president.

Headquarters are located at 90 Parent Ave., Ottawa, KIN 7 BI, Canada.

The CCC was reorganized in 1973 to make possible the involvement of more people in the work of the Church on local levels. The CCC in Ottawa focuses attention primarily on national and international affairs. Four regional divisions — Western, Ontario, Quebec, Atlantic — concentrate on local problems and challenges. One of the major benefits of the revised structure, it was felt, would be a more efficient system of communication within and between regions.

ORGANIZATIONS

The Catholic Church Extension Society of Canada supports home missions. Address: 67 Bond St., Toronto 205, Ontario.

The Oblate Indian-Eskimo Council of Canada, 238 Argyle St., Ottawa.

The Canadian Catholic Women's League, with a membership of more than 100,000. Address: 890 St. James St., Winnipeg, Man. R3GJ7.

CANADIAN SHRINES

Our Lady of the Cape (Cap de la Madeleine), Queen of the Most Holy Rosary: The Three Rivers, Quebec, parish church, built of fieldstone in 1714 and considered the oldest stone church on the North American continent preserved in its original state, was rededicated June 22, 1888, as a shrine of the Queen of the Most Holy Rosary. Thereafter, the site increased in importance as a pilgrimage and devotional center, and in 1904 St. Pius X decreed the crowning of a statue of the Blessed Virgin which had been donated 50 years earlier to commemorate the dogma of the Immaculate Conception. In 1909, the First Plenary Council of Quebec declared the church a shrine of national pilgrimage. In 1964, the church at the shrine was given the status and title of minor basilica.

St. Anne de Beaupre: The devotional history of this shrine in Quebec, which has been called the "Lourdes of the New World," began with the reported cure of a cripple, Louis Grimont, on Mar. 16, 1658, the starting date of construction work on a small chapel of St. Anne. The original building was successively enlarged and replaced by a stone church which was given the rank of minor basilica in 1888. The present structure, a Romanesque-Gothic basilica, houses the shrine proper in its north transept. The centers of attraction are an eight-foot-high oaken statue and the great relic of St. Anne, a portion of her forearm.

St. Joseph's Oratory: The massive oratory basilica standing on the western side of Mount Royal and overlooking the city of

Montreal had its origin in a primitive chapel erected there by Brother Andre, C.S.C., in 1904. Eleven years later, a large crypt was built to accommodate an increasing number of pilgrims, and in 1924 construction work was begun on the large church. A belfry, housing a 60-bell carillon and standing on the site of the original chapel, was dedicated May 15, 1955, as the first major event of the jubilee year observed after the oratory was given the rank of minor basilica.

Martyrs' Shrine: A shrine commemorating several of the Jesuit Martyrs of North America who were killed between 1642 and 1649 in the Ontario and northern New York area is located on the former site of old Forte Sainte Marie. Before its location was fixed near Midland, Ont., in 1925, a small chapel had been erected in 1907 at old Mission St. Ignace to mark the martyrdom of Fathers Jean de Brebeuf and Gabriel Lalemant. This sanctuary has a US counterpart in the Shrine of the North American Martyrs near Auriesville, N.Y., under the care of the Jesuits.

Others

Other shrines and historic churches in Canada include the following.

In Quebec City: the Basilica of Notre Dame, dating from 1650, once the cathedral of a diocese stretching from Canada to Mexico; Notre Dame des Victoires, on the waterfront, dedicated in 1690; the Ursuline Convent, built in 1720, on du Parloir St.

In Montreal: Notre Dame Church, patterned after the famous basilica of the same name in Paris, constructed in 1829; the Shrine of Mary, Queen of All Hearts.

Near Montreal: the Chapel of Mother d'Youville, foundress of the Grey Nuns; Notre Dame de Lourdes, at Rigaud.

CONFERENCE OF RELIGIOUS

The Canadian Religious Conference is a union of major superiors of men and women in Canada. Father Albert Dumont, O.P., is the executive director. Offices are located at 324 Laurier Ave. E., Ottawa, Canada.

CANADIAN CATHOLIC PUBLICATIONS

(Sources: *Catholic Press Directory*, Canadian Catholic Conference.)

Newspapers

British Columbia Catholic, The, w; 150 Robson St., Vancouver 3, B.C.; 6,763.

Catholic Register, The, w; 67 Bond St., Toronto, Ont.; M5B 1X6; 56,000.

Monitor, The, m; P.O. Box 986, St. John's, Nfld.; 9,000.

New Freeman, The, w; Box 609, St. John, N.B.; 5,400.

Our Sunday Visitor (national), w; Noll Plaza, Huntington, Ind. 46750; 15,921.

Prairie Messenger, w; St. Peter's Press, Muenster, Sask.; SOK 2 YO; 10,971.

Teviskes, Ziburiai, (Lithuanian), w; 941 Dundas St. W., Toronto 3, Ont.; 5,560.

Western Catholic Reporter, w; 9537-76th Ave., Edmonton, Alta., T6C 4H7; 22,496.

Magazines

Annals of Good St. Anne de Beaupre, m; Basilica of St. Anne, Que.; 78,069.

Apostolat, bm; Richelieu, Que., Oblates of Mary Immaculate; 39,300.

Canadian Catholic Institutions, bm; 27 Carlton St., Toronto 2, Ont.; 5,209

Canadian League, The, 5 times a year; 890 St. James St., Winnipeg, Man. R3G 3J7; 100,000.

Centre News, q; 830 Bathurst St., Toronto, Ont.; 2,200.

Christian Communications, 6 times a year; 223 Main St., Ottawa 1, Ont.; 2,500.

Companion of St. Francis and St. Anthony, m; 15 Chestnut Park Rd., Toronto, Ont.; Conventual Franciscan Fathers; 10,000.

Field At Home, q; 10 Montcrest Blvd., Toronto 279, Ont.; 3,117.

Indian Record, 6 times a year; 1301 Wellington Crescent, Winnipeg, Man. R3N-0A9; 2,215.

Logos (Ukrainian, English and French), q; 165 Catherine St., Yorkton, Sask.; 380.

Magazine Actualite, m; 2120 Sherbrooke St. E., Montreal 133, Que.; 117,806.

Maintenant, m; 2715 Ch. Cote St., Catherine, Montreal, Que.; 10,000.

Martyrs' Shrine Message, q; R. R. No. 1, Midland, Ont.; 4,000.

Messager de Saint Antoine, m; Lac-Bouchette, Roberval, Que.

Messenger of the Sacred Heart, m; 68 Broadview Ave., Toronto, Ont.; M4K 2P9; 17,400.

Missions Etrangeres, 6 times a year; 59 Rue Desnoyers, Laval, Que.; 65,000.

Oblate Missions, bm; 17 Graham Ave., Ottawa KIS 0B6 Ont.; 6,100.

Oratory, 6 times a year; 3800 Ch. Reine-Maries, Montreal 247, Que.; 8,600.

Our Family, m; P. O. Box 249, Battleford, Sask.; SOM 0E0; Oblates of Mary Immaculate; 9,250.

Our Lady of the Atonement Annals, q; P.O. Box 370, Smoky Lake, Alta.; 900.

Redeemer's Voice, m; 165 Catherine St., Yorkton, Sask.; 1,750.

Regard de Foi, 6 times a year; 5875 Est. rue Sherbrooke, Montreal, Que.; 13,000.

Relations, m; 8100 Blvd., Saint-Laurent, Montreal 351, Que.; Jesuit Fathers; 7,955.

Restoration, m; Combermere, P.O. Ont., KOJ ILO; Madonna House; 7,177

Scarboro Mission Magazine, m; 2685 Kingston Rd., Scarboro, Ont.; 30,000.

The Catholic Church in the United States

The starting point of the mainstream of Catholic history in the United States was Baltimore at the end of the Revolutionary War, although before that time Catholic explorers had traversed much of the country and missionaries had done considerable work among the Indians in the Southeast, Northeast and Southwest.

Beginning of Organization

Father John Carroll's appointment as superior of the American missions on June 9, 1784, was the first step toward organization of the Church in this country.

At that time, according to a report he made to Rome in 1785, there were approximately 25,000 Catholics in the general population of four million. Many of them had been in the Colonies for several generations. Among them were such outstanding figures as Charles Carroll, a member of the Continental Congress and signer of the Declaration of Independence; Thomas FitzSimons of Philadelphia and Oliver Pollock, the Virginia agent, who raised funds for the militia; Commander John Barry, father of the American Navy, and numerous high-ranking army officers. For the most part, however, Catholics were an unknown minority laboring under legal and social handicaps.

Father Carroll, the brother of Charles Carroll, was named the first American bishop in 1789 and placed in charge of the Diocese of Baltimore, whose boundaries were coextensive with those of the United States. He was consecrated in England Aug. 15, 1790, and installed in his see the following Dec. 12.

Ten years later, Father Leonard Neale became his coadjutor and the first bishop ordained in the United States. Bishop Carroll became an archbishop in 1808 when Baltimore was designated a metropolitan see and the new dioceses of Boston, New York, Philadelphia and Bardstown were established. These jurisdictions were later subdivided, and by 1840 there were, in addition to Baltimore, 15 dioceses, 500 priests and 663,000 Catholics in the general population of 17 million.

Priests and First Seminaries

The number of the 24 original priests was gradually augmented with the arrival of others from France, after the Civil Constitution on the Clergy went into effect there, and other countries. Among the earliest arrivals were several Sulpicians who established the first seminary in the US, St. Mary's, Baltimore, in 1791. By 1815, 30 alumni of the school had been ordained to the priesthood. By that time, two additional seminaries were in operation: Mt. St. Mary's, established in 1809 at Emmitsburg, Md., and St. Thomas, founded two years later, at Bardstown, Ky. These and similar institutions founded later played key roles in the development and growth of the American clergy.

Early Schools

Early educational enterprises included the establishment in 1791 of a school at Georgetown which later became the first Catholic university in the US; the opening of a secondary school for girls, conducted by Visitation Nuns, in 1792 at Georgetown; and the start of a similar school in the first decade of the 19th century at Emmitsburg, Md., by Blessed Elizabeth Ann Seton and the Sisters of Charity of St. Joseph, the first religious community of American foundation.

By the 1840's, which saw the beginnings of the present public school system, more than 200 Catholic elementary schools, half of them west of the Alleghenies, were in operation. From this start, the Church subsequently built the greatest private system of education in the world.

Trusteeism

The initial lack of organization in ecclesiastical affairs, nationalistic feeling among Catholics and the independent action of some priests were factors involved in several early crises.

In Philadelphia, some German Catholics withdrew from one parish in 1789 and founded one of their own, Holy Trinity, which they maintained until 1802. Controversy over the affair reached the point of schism in 1796. Philadelphia was also the scene of the Hogan Schism, which developed in the 1820's when Father William Hogan, with the aid of lay trustees, seized control of St. Mary's Cathedral. His movement, for churches and parishes controlled by other than canonical procedures and run in extra-legal ways, was nullified by a decision of the Pennsylvania Supreme Court in 1822.

Similar troubles seriously disturbed the peace of the Church in other places, principally New York, Baltimore, Buffalo, Charleston and New Orleans.

Dangers arising from the exploitation of lay control were gradually diminished with the extension and enforcement of canonical procedures and with changes in civil law about the middle of the century.

Bigotry

Bigotry against Catholics waxed and waned during the 19th century and into the 20th. The first major campaign of this kind, which developed in the wake of the panic of 1819 and lasted for about 25 years, was mounted in 1830 when the number of Catholic immigrants began to increase to a noticeable degree. Nativist anti-Catholicism generated a great deal of violence, represented by climaxes in loss of life and property in

Charlestown, Mass., in 1834, and in Philadelphia 10 years later. Later bigotry was fomented by the Know-Nothings, in the 1850's; the Ku Klux Klan, from 1866; the American Protective Association, from 1887; and the Guardians of Liberty. Perhaps the last eruption of overt anti-Catholicism occurred during the campaign of Alfred E. Smith for the presidency in 1928. Observers feel the issue was laid to rest in the political area with the election of John F. Kennedy to the presidency in 1960.

Growth and Immigration

Between 1830 and 1900, the combined factors of natural increase, immigration and conversion raised the Catholic population to 12 million. A large percentage of the growth figure represented immigrants: some 2.7 million, largely from Ireland, Germany and France, between 1830 and 1880; and another 1.25 million during the 80's when eastern and southern Europeans came in increasing numbers. By the 1860's the Catholic Church, with most of its members concentrated in urban areas, was one of the largest religious bodies in the country.

The efforts of progressive bishops to hasten the acculturation of Catholic immigrants occasioned a number of controversies, which generally centered around questions concerning national or foreign-language parishes. One of them, called Cahenslyism, arose from complaints that German Catholic immigrants were not being given adequate pastoral care.

Immigration continued after the turn of the century, but its impact was more easily cushioned through the application of lessons learned earlier in dealing with problems of nationality and language.

Councils of Baltimore

The bishops of the growing US dioceses met at Baltimore for seven provincial councils between 1829 and 1849.

In 1846, they proclaimed the Blessed Virgin Mary patroness of the United States under the title of the Immaculate Conception, eight years before the dogma was proclaimed.

After the establishment of the Archdiocese of Oregon City in 1846 and the elevation to metropolitan status of St. Louis, New Orleans, Cincinnati and New York, the first of the three plenary councils of Baltimore was held.

The first plenary assembly was convoked on May 9, 1852, with Archbishop Francis P. Kenrick of Baltimore as papal legate. The bishops drew up regulations concerning parochial life, matters of church ritual and ceremonies, the administration of church funds and the teaching of Christian doctrine.

The second plenary council, meeting from Oct. 7 to 21, 1866, under the presidency of Archbishop Martin J. Spalding, formulated a condemnation of several current doctrinal errors and established norms affecting the organization of dioceses, the education and conduct of the clergy, the management of ecclesiastical property, parochial duties and general education.

Archbishop (later Cardinal) James Gibbons called into session the third plenary council which lasted from Nov. 9 to Dec. 7, 1884. Among highly significant results of actions taken by this assembly were the preparation of the line of Baltimore catechisms which became a basic means of religious instruction in this country; legislation which fixed the pattern of Catholic education by requiring the building of elementary schools in all parishes; the establishment of the Catholic University of America in Washington, D.C., in 1889; and the determination of six holy days of obligation for observance in this country.

The enactments of the three plenary councils have had the force of particular law for the Church in the United States.

The Holy See established the Apostolic Delegation at Washington, D.C., on Jan. 24, 1893.

Slavery and Negroes

In the Civil War period, as before, Catholics reflected attitudes of the general population with respect to the issue of slavery. Some supported it, some opposed it, but none were prominent in the Abolition Movement. Gregory XVI had condemned the slave trade in 1839, but no contemporary pope or American bishop published an official document on slavery itself. The issue did not split Catholics in schism as it did Baptists, Methodists and Presbyterians.

Catholics fought on both sides in the Civil War. Five hundred members of 20 or more sisterhoods served the wounded of both sides.

One hundred thousand of the four million slaves emancipated in 1863 were Catholics; the highest concentrations were in Louisiana, about 60,000, and Maryland, 16,000. Three years later, their pastoral care was one of the subjects covered in nine decrees issued by the Second Plenary Council of Baltimore. The measures had little practical effect with respect to integration of the total Catholic community, predicated as they were on the proposition that individual bishops should handle questions regarding segregation in churches and related matters as best they could in the pattern of local customs.

Long entrenched segregation practices continued in force through the rest of the 19th century and well into the 20th. The first effective efforts to alter them were initiated by Cardinal Joseph Ritter of St. Louis in 1947, Cardinal Patrick (then Archbishop) O'Boyle of Washington in 1948, and Bishop Vincent Waters of Raleigh in 1953.

Friend of Labor

The Church became known during the 19th century as a friend and ally of labor in seeking justice for the working man. Cardinal Gibbons journeyed to Rome in 1887, for example, to defend and prevent a condemnation of the Knights of Labor by Leo XIII. The encyclical *Rerum Novarum* was hailed by many American bishops as a confirmation, if not vindication, of their own theories. Catholics have always formed a large percentage of union membership, and some have served unions in positions of leadership.

The American Heresy

Near the end of the century some controversy developed over what was characterized as Americanism or the phantom heresy. It was alleged that Americans were discounting the importance of contemplative virtues, exalting the practical virtues, and watering down the purity of Catholic doctrine for the sake of facilitating convert work.

The French translation of Father Walter Elliott's *Life of Isaac Hecker*, which fired the controversy, was one of many factors that led to the issuance of Leo XIII's *Testem Benevolentiae* in January, 1899, in an attempt to end the matter. It was the first time the orthodoxy of the Church in the US was called into question.

Schism

In the 1890's, serious friction developed between Poles and Irish in Scranton, Buffalo and Chicago, resulting in schism and the establishment of the Polish National Church. A central figure in the affair was Father Francis Hodur, who was excommunicated by Bishop William O'Hara of Scranton in 1898. Nine years later, his ordination by the Old Catholic Archbishop of Utrecht gave the new church its first bishop.

Another schism of the period led to formation of the American Carpatho-Russian Orthodox Greek Catholic Church.

Coming of Age

In 1900, there were 12 million Catholics in the total US population of 76 million, 82 dioceses in 14 provinces, and 12,000 priests and members of about 40 communities of men religious. Many sisterhoods, most of them of European origin and some of American foundation, were engaged in Catholic educational and hospital work, of which they have always been the main support.

The Church in the United States was removed from mission status with promulgation of the apostolic constitution *Sapienti Consilio* by Pope St. Pius X on June 29, 1908.

Before that time, and even into the early 20's, the Church in this country received financial assistance from mission-aid societies in France, Bavaria and Austria. Already, however, it was making increasing contributions of its own. At the present time, it is the heaviest national contributor to the worldwide Society for the Propagation of the Faith.

American foreign missionary personnel increased from 14 or less in 1906 to 7,418 by 1974 (220 diocesan priests, 3,723 religious priests and brothers, 2,916 sisters, 101 seminarians, 458 lay persons). The first missionary seminary in the US was in operation at Techny, Ill., in 1909, under the auspices of the Society of the Divine Word. Maryknoll, the first American missionary society, was established in 1911 and sent its first priests to China in 1918. Despite these contributions, the Church in the US has not matched the missionary commitment of some other nations.

Bishops' Conference

A highly important apparatus for mobilizing the Church's resources was established in 1917 under the title of the National Catholic War Council. Its name was changed to National Catholic Welfare Conference several years later, but its objectives remained the same: to serve as an advisory and coordinating agency of the American bishops for advancing works of the Church in fields of social significance and impact — education, communications, immigration, social action, legislation, youth and lay organizations.

The forward thrust of the bishops' social thinking was evidenced in a program of social reconstruction they recommended in 1919. By 1945, all but one of their twelve points had been enacted into legislation.

The NCWC was renamed the United States Catholic Conference (USCC) in November, 1966, when the hierarchy also organized itself as a territorial conference with pastoral-juridical authority under the title, National Conference of Catholic Bishops. The USCC is carrying on the functions of the former NCWC.

Pastoral Concerns

The potential for growth of the Church in this country by immigration was sharply reduced but not entirely curtailed after 1921 with the passage of restrictive federal legislation. As a result, the Catholic population became more stabilized and, to a certain extent and for many reasons, began to acquire an identity of its own.

Some increase-from-outside has taken place in the past 50 years, however; from Canada, from central and eastern European countries, and from Puerto Rico and Latin American countries since World War II. This influx, while not as great as that of the 19th century and early 20th, has enriched the Church here with a sizable body of Eastern-Rite Catholics for whom eight ecclesiastical jurisdictions were established between 1924 and 1969. It has also created a challenge for pastoral care of the Spanish-speaking.

The Church continues to grapple with serious pastoral problems in rural areas, where about 650 counties are no-priest land. The National Catholic Rural Life Conference was established in 1922 in an attempt to make the Catholic presence felt on the land, and the Glenmary Society since its foundation in 1939 has devoted itself to this single apostolate.

Other challenges lie in the cities and suburbs where 75 percent of the Catholic population lives. Conditions peculiar to each segment of the metropolitan area have developed in recent years as the flight to the suburbs has not only altered some traditional aspects of parish life but has also, in combination with many other factors, left behind a complex of special problems in the inner city.

The Church in the US is presently in a stage of transition from a relatively stable and long established order of life and action to a new order of things. Some of the phenomena of this period are:

• differences in trends and emphasis in theology, and in interpretation and implementation of directives of the Second Vatican Council, resulting in situations of conflict;

• the changing spiritual formation, professional education, style of life and ministry of priests, which are altering influential patterns of pastoral and specialized service;

• vocations to the priesthood and religious life, which are generally in decline;

• departures from the priesthood and religious life which, while small percentage-wise, are numerous enough to be a matter of serious concern;

• decline of traditional devotional practices;

• exercise of authority along the lines of collegiality and subsidiarity;

• structure and administration, marked by a trend toward greater participation in the life and work of the Church by its members on all levels, from the parish on up;

• alienation from the Church, leading some persons into the catacombs of an underground church, "anonymous Christianity" and religious indifferentism;

• education, undergoing crisis and change in Catholic schools and seeking new ways of reaching out to the young not in Catholic schools and to adults;

• social witness in ministry to the world, which is being shaped by the form of contemporary needs — e.g., race relations, poverty, the peace movement, the Third World;

• ecumenism, involving the Church in interfaith relations.

(See Trends in the Catholic Church in the United States.)

BACKGROUND DATES IN U.S. CATHOLIC CHRONOLOGY

Dates in this section refer mostly to earlier "firsts" and developments in the background of Catholic history in the United States. For other dates, see various sections of the Almanac.

Alabama

1540: Priests crossed the territory with De Soto's expedition.

1560: Five Dominicans in charge of mission at Santa Cruz des Nanipacna.

1682: La Salle claimed territory for France.

1704: Jesuits established first parish church at Fort Louis de la Mobile.

1722: Mobile, formerly under the Quebec diocese, became part of a vicariate apostolic with Florida. Capuchins, Carmelites and Jesuits working there.

1829: Mobile-Birmingham diocese established; made two separate dioceses, 1969.

1830: Spring Hill College, Mobile, established.

1834: Visitation Nuns established an academy at Summerville.

Alaska

1779: Mass celebrated for first time on shore of Port Santa Cruz on lower Bucareli Bay on May 13 by Franciscan John Riobo.

1868: Alaska placed under jurisdiction of Vancouver Island.

1878: Father John Althoff became first resident missionary.

1886: Archbishop Charles J. Seghers, "Apostle of Alaska," murdered by a guide; had surveyed southern and northwest Alaska in 1873 and 1877, respectively.

Sisters of St. Anne first nuns in Alaska.

1894: Alaska made prefecture apostolic.

1901: Jesuits reorganized their missions, established a church at Nome.

1905: Sisters of Providence opened hospital at Nome.

1916: Alaska made vicariate apostolic.

1917: In first ordination in territory, Rev. G. Edgar Gallant raised to priesthood.

1951: Juneau diocese established.

1962: Fairbanks diocese established.

1966: Anchorage archdiocese established.

Arizona

1539: Franciscan Marcos de Niza explored the state.

1540: Franciscans Juan de Padilla, Juan de la Cruz and Marcos de Niza accompanied Coronado expedition through the territory.

1629: Spanish Franciscans began work among Moqui Indians.

1632: Franciscan Martin de Arvide killed by Indians.

1680: Franciscans Jose de Espeleta, Augustin de Santa Maria, Jose de Figueroa and Jose de Trujillo killed in Pueblo Revolt.

1700: Jesuit Eusebio Kino established mission at San Xavier del Bac, near Tucson.

1767: Jesuits expelled; Franciscans took over 10 missions.

1828: Spanish missionaries expelled by Mexican government.

1863: Jesuits returned to San Xavier.

1869: Sisters of Loretto arrived to conduct schools at Bisbee and Douglas.

1897: Tucson diocese established.

1969: Phoenix diocese established.

Arkansas

1541: Priests accompanied De Soto expedition through the territory.

1673: Marquette visited Indians in east.

1686: Henri de Tonti established trading post, first white settlement in territory.

1702: Fr. Nicholas Foucault working among Indians.

1805: Bishop Carroll of Baltimore appointed Administrator Apostolic of Arkansas.

1838: Sisters of Loretto opened first Catholic school.

1843: Little Rock diocese established. There were about 700 Catholics in state, two churches, one priest.

1853: Sisters of Mercy founded St. Mary's Convent at Fort Smith.

California

1542: Cabrillo discovered Upper (Alta) California; name of priest accompanying expedition unknown.

1602: On Nov. 12 Carmelite Andres de la Ascencion offered first recorded Mass in California on shore of San Diego Bay.

1697: Missionary work in Lower and Upper Californias entrusted to Jesuits.

1767: Jesuits expelled from territory. Spanish Crown confiscated their property, including the Pious Fund for Missions. Upper California missions entrusted to Franciscans.

1769: Franciscan Junipero Serra began establishment of Franciscan missions in California, near present San Diego. (See Franciscan Missions of Upper California.)

1775: Franciscan Luis Jayme killed by Indians at San Diego Mission.

1779: Diocese of Sonora, Mexico, which included Upper California, established.

1781: On Sept. 4 an expedition from San Gabriel Mission founded present city of Los Angeles — Pueblo "de Nuestra Senora la Reina de Los Angeles."

Franciscans Francisco Hermenegildo Garces, Juan Antonio Barreneche, Juan Marcello Diaz and Jose Matias Moreno killed by Indians.

1812: Franciscan Andres Quintana killed at Santa Cruz Mission.

1822: Interference and aggression toward missions initiated by Mexican government.

Dedication on Dec. 8 of Old Plaza Church, "Assistant Mission of Our Lady of the Angels," oldest church in Los Angeles.

1833: Missions secularized, finally confiscated.

1840: Pope Gregory XVI established Diocese of Both Californias.

1846: Peter H. Burnett, first governor of California, received into Catholic Church.

1848: Upper California ceded to the United States.

1850: Monterey diocese erected; title changed to Monterey-Los Angeles, 1859; and to Los Angeles, 1922.

1851: University of Santa Clara chartered.

1852: Lower California detached from Monterey diocese.

1853: San Francisco archdiocese established.

1855: US returned confiscated California missions to Church.

1863: Sisters of Notre Dame de Namur opened women's College of Notre Dame at Belmont.

1868: Grass Valley diocese established; transferred to Sacramento in 1886.

1922: Monterey-Fresno diocese established; became separate dioceses, 1967.

1934: Sesquicentennial of Serra's death observed; Serra Year officially declared by Legislature and Aug. 24 observed as Serra Day.

1936: Los Angeles made archdiocese. San Diego diocese established.

1952: Law exempting non-profit, religious-sponsored elementary and secondary schools from taxation upheld in referendum, Nov. 4.

1953: Archbishop James Francis McIntyre of Los Angeles made cardinal by Pius XII.

1962: Oakland, Santa Rosa and Stockton dioceses established.

1973: Archbishop Timothy Manning of Los Angeles made cardinal by Pope Paul VI.

Colorado

1858: First parish in Colorado established.

1864: Sisters of Loretto at the Foot of the Cross, first nuns in the state, established academy at Denver.

1868: Vicariate Apostolic of Colorado and Utah established.

1887: Denver diocese established.

1888: Regis College founded.

1951: Denver made archdiocese. Pueblo diocese established.

Connecticut

1651: Probably first priest to enter state was Jesuit Gabriel Druillettes; ambassador of Governor of Canada, he participated in a New England Colonial Council at New Haven.

1755: Catholic Acadians, expelled from Nova Scotia, settled in the state.

1791: Rev. John Thayer, first missionary to visit state's Catholics on regular basis, offered Mass at home of Noah Webster.

1808: Connecticut became part of Boston diocese.

1818: Religious freedom established by new constitution, although the Congregational Church remained, in practice, the state church.

1828: Father Bernard O'Cavanaugh became first resident priest in state.

1829: First Catholic church in state established at Hartford.

Catholic Press of Hartford established.

1843: Hartford diocese established.

1882: Knights of Columbus founded by Father Michael J. McGivney.

1942: Fairfield University founded.

1953: Norwich and Bridgeport dioceses established. Hartford made archdiocese.

1956: Byzantine Rite Exarchate of Stamford established; made eparchy, 1958.

Delaware

1730: Mount Cuba, New Castle County, the scene of Catholic services.

1750: Jesuit mission at Apoquiniminck administered from Maryland.

1772: First permanent parish established at Coffee Run.

1792: French Catholics from Santo Domingo settled near Wilmington.

1816: St. Peter's Church, later the cathedral of the diocese, erected at Wilmington.

1830: Daughters of Charity opened school and orphanage at Wilmington.

1868: Wilmington diocese established.

1869: Visitation Nuns established residence in Wilmington.

District of Columbia

1641: Jesuit Andrew White evangelized Anacosta Indians.

1774: Father John Carroll ministered to Catholics.

1789: Georgetown, first Catholic college in US, established.

1791: Pierre Charles L'Enfant designed the Federal City of Washington. His plans were not fully implemented until the early 1900's.

1792: James Hoban designed the White House.

1794: Father Anthony Caffrey began St. Patrick's Church, first parish church in the new Federal City.

1801: Poor Clares opened school for girls in Georgetown; first school established by nuns in US.

1802: First mayor of Washington, appointed by President Jefferson, was Judge Robert Brent.

1889: Catholic University of America founded.

1893: Apostolic Delegation established with Archbishop Francesco Satolli as the first delegate.

1919: National Catholic Welfare Conference (now the United States Catholic Conference) organized by American hierarchy to succeed National Catholic War Council.

1920: Cornerstone of National Shrine of Immaculate Conception laid.

1939: Washington made archdiocese of equal rank with Baltimore, under direction of same archbishop.

1947: Washington archdiocese received its own archbishop, was separated from Baltimore.

1967: Archbishop Patrick A. O'Boyle of Washington made cardinal by Pope Paul VI.

Florida

1513: Ponce de Leon discovered Florida.

1521: Missionaries accompanying Ponce de Leon and other explorers probably said first Masses within present limits of US.

1528: Franciscans landed on western shore.

1539: Twelve missionaries landed with De Soto at Tampa Bay.

1549: Dominican Luis Cancer de Barbastro and two companions slain by Indians near Tampa Bay.

1565: City of St. Augustine, oldest in US, founded by Pedro Menendez de Aviles, who was accompanied by four secular priests. America's oldest mission, Nombre de Dios, was established. Father Martin Francisco Lopez de Mendoza Grajales became the first parish priest of St. Augustine, where the first parish in the US was established.

1572: St. Francis Borgia, general of the Society, withdrew Jesuits from Florida.

1606: Bishop Juan de las Cabeyas de Altamirano, O.P., conducted the first episcopal visitation in the US.

1620: The chapel of Nombre de Dios was dedicated to Nuestra Senora de la Leche y Buen Parto (Our Nursing Mother of the Happy Delivery); oldest shrine to the Blessed Mother in the US.

1704: Destruction of Florida's northern missions by English and Indian troops led by Governor James Moore of South Carolina. Franciscans Juan de Parga, Dominic Criodo, Tiburcio de Osorio, Augustine Ponze de Leon, Marcos Delgado and two Indians, Anthony Enixa and Amador Cuipa Feliciano, were slain by the invaders.

1735: Bishop Francis Martinez de Tejadu Diaz de Velasco, auxiliary of Santiago, was the first bishop to take up residence in US, at St. Augustine.

1793: Florida and Louisiana were included in Diocese of New Orleans.

1857: Eastern Florida made a vicariate apostolic.

1870: St. Augustine diocese established.

1917: Convent Inspection Bill passed; repealed 1935.

1958: Miami diocese established.

1968: Miami made metropolitan see; Orlando and St. Petersburg dioceses established.

Georgia

1540: First priests to enter were chaplains with De Soto. They celebrated first Mass within territory of 13 original colonies.

1566: Pedro Martinez, first Jesuit martyr of the New World, was slain by Indians on Cumberland Island.

1569: Jesuit mission was opened at Guale Island by Father Antonio Sedeno.

1572: Jesuits withdrawn from area.

1595: Five Franciscans assigned to Province of Guale.

1597: Five Franciscan missionaries killed in coastal missions.

1606: Bishop Altamirano, O.P., conducted visitation of the Georgia area.

1612: First Franciscan province in US erected under title of Santa Elena; it included Georgia, South Carolina and Florida.

1655: Franciscans had nine flourishing missions among Indians.

1702: Spanish missions ended as result of English conquest.

1796: Augustinian Father Le Mercier was first post-colonial missionary to Georgia.

1798: Catholics granted right of refuge.

1800: First church erected in Savannah on lot given by city council.

1810: First church erected in Augusta on lot given by State Legislature.

1850: Savannah diocese established; became Savannah-Atlanta, 1937; divided into two separate sees, 1956.

1962: Atlanta made metropolitan see.

Hawaii

1825: Pope Leo XII entrusted missionary efforts in Islands to Sacred Hearts Fathers.

1827: The first Catholic missionaries arrived — Fathers Alexis Bachelot, Abraham Armand and Patrick Short, along with three lay brothers. After three years of persecution, the priests were forcibly exiled.

1836: Father Arsenius Walsh, SS. CC., a British subject, was allowed to remain in Islands but was not permitted to proselytize or conduct missions.

1839: Hawaiian government signed treaty with France granting Catholics freedom of worship and same privileges as Protestants.

1844: Vicariate Apostolic of Sandwich Islands (Hawaii) erected.

1873: Father Damien de Veuster of the Sacred Hearts Fathers arrived in Molokai and spent the remainder of his life working among lepers.

1941: Honolulu diocese established, made a suffragan of San Francisco.

Idaho

1840: Jesuit Pierre de Smet preached to the Flathead and Pend d'Oreille Indians; probably offered first Mass in state.

1842: Jesuit Nicholas Point opened a mission among Coeur d'Alene Indians near Maries.

1863: Secular priests sent from Oregon City to administer to incoming miners.

1867: Sisters of Holy Names of Jesus and Mary opened first Catholic school at Idaho City.

1868: Idaho made a vicariate apostolic.

1870: First church in Boise established.

Church lost most of missions among Indians of Northwest Territory when Commission on Indian Affairs appointed Protestant missionaries to take over.

1893: Boise diocese established.

Illinois

1673: Jesuit Jacques Marquette, accompanying Joliet, preached to Indians.

1674: Pere Marquette set up a cabin for saying Mass in what later became City of Chicago.

1675: Pere Marquette established Mission of the Immaculate Conception among Kaskaskia Indians.

1679: La Salle brought with him Franciscans Louis Hennepin, Gabriel de la Ribourde, and Zenobius Membre.

1680: Father Ribourde was killed by Kickapoo Indians.

1689: Jesuit Claude Allouez died after 32 years of missionary activity among Indians of Midwest; he had evangelized 100,000 Indians of 20 different tribes and baptized 10,000. Jesuit Jacques Gravier succeeded Allouez as vicar general of Illinois.

1730: Father Gaston, a diocesan priest, was killed at the Cahokia Mission.

1763: British conquest of the territory resulted in banishment of Jesuits.

1778: Father Pierre Gibault championed Colonial cause in the Revolution and aided greatly in securing states of Ohio, Indiana, Illinois, Michigan and Wisconsin for Americans.

1827: The present St. Patrick's Parish at Ruma, oldest English-speaking Catholic congregation in state, was founded.

1833: Visitation Nuns established residence in Kaskaskia.

1843: Chicago diocese established.

1853: Quincy diocese established; transferred to Alton, 1857; Springfield, 1923.

1860: Quincy College founded.

1877: Peoria diocese established.

1880: Chicago made archdiocese.

1887: Belleville diocese established.

1908: Rockford diocese established.

First American Missionary Congress held in Chicago.

1924: Archbishop Mundelein of Chicago made cardinal by Pope Pius XI.

1926: The 28th International Eucharistic Congress, first held in US, convened in Chicago.

1946: Blessed Frances Xavier Cabrini, former resident of Chicago, was canonized; first US citizen raised to dignity of altar. Archbishop Samuel A. Stritch of Chicago made cardinal by Pope Pius XII.

1948: Joliet diocese established.

1958: Cardinal Stritch appointed Pro-Prefect of the Sacred Congregation for the Propagation of the Faith — the first US-born prelate to be named to the Roman Curia.

1959: Archbishop Albert G. Meyer of Chicago made cardinal by Pope John XXIII.

1961: Eparchy of St. Nicholas of the Ukrainians established at Chicago.

1967: Archbishop John P. Cody of Chicago made cardinal by Pope Paul VI.

Indiana

1679: Recollects Louis Hennepin and Gabriel de la Ribourde entered state.

1686: Land near present Notre Dame University at South Bend given by French government to Jesuits for mission.

1732: Church of St. Francis Xavier founded at Vincennes.

1778: Father Gibault aided George Rogers Clark in campaign against British in conquest of Northwest Territory.

1793: First school in Indiana built at Vincennes by Father John Francis Rivet.

1834: Vincennes diocese, later Indianapolis, established.

1840: Sisters of Providence founded St. Mary-of-the-Woods College for women.

1842: University of Notre Dame founded by Holy Cross Fathers.

1843: Immigration of German farmers to Indiana swelled Catholic population.

1853: First Benedictine community established in state at St. Meinrad.

1857: Fort Wayne diocese established; changed to Fort Wayne-South Bend, 1960.

1944: Indianapolis made archdiocese. Lafayette and Evansville dioceses established.

1957: Gary diocese established.

Iowa

1673: A Peoria village on Mississippi was visited by Pere Marquette.

1679: Fathers Louis Hennepin and Gabriel de la Ribourde visited Indian villages.

1836: First permanent church, St. Raphael's, founded at Dubuque by Dominican Samuel Mazzuchelli.

1837: Dubuque diocese established.

1838: St. Joseph's Mission founded at Council Bluffs by Jesuit Father De Smet.

1843: Sisters of Charity of the Blessed Virgin Mary were first sisterhood in state.

Sisters of Charity opened Clarke College, Dubuque.

1844: Brothers of St. Joseph opened academy for boys at Dubuque.

1850: First Trappist Monastery in state, Our Lady of New Melleray, was begun.

1881: Davenport diocese established.

1882: St. Ambrose College, Davenport, established.

1893: Dubuque made archdiocese.

1902: Sioux City diocese established.

1911: Des Moines diocese established.

Kansas

1542: Franciscan Juan de Padilla, first martyr of the United States, was killed in central Kansas.

1858: St. Benedict's College founded.

1863: Sisters of Charity opened orphanage at Leavenworth, and St. John's Hospital in following year.

1877: Leavenworth diocese established; transferred to Kansas City in 1947.

1887: Dioceses of Concordia (transferred to Salina in 1944) and Wichita established.

1888: Oblate Sisters of Providence opened an orphanage for Negro boys at Leavenworth, first west of Mississippi.

1951: Dodge City diocese established.

1952: Kansas City made archdiocese.

1971: Merger of St. Benedict College (men) and St. Scholastica College (women), forming coed Benedictine College, Atchison.

Kentucky

1775: First settlers in Kentucky were Catholics.

1787: Father Charles Francis Whelan, first resident priest, ministered to settlers of Bardstown.

1806: Dominican Fathers built Priory of St. Rose, later founded St. Thomas Aquinas College.

1808: Bardstown diocese established; transferred to Louisville, 1840.

1811: Rev. Guy L. Chabrat became first priest ordained west of the Allegheny Mountains.

1812: Sisters of Loretto founded, first religious community in US without foreign affiliation.

Sisters of Charity of Nazareth founded, the second native community of women founded in the West.

1814: Nazareth College for women established.

1816: Cornerstone of St. Joseph's Cathedral, Bardstown, laid; called "The Cathedral in the Wilderness."

1817: St. Thomas Seminary founded.

1830: Hon. Benjamin J. Webb founded *Catholic Advocate*, first Catholic weekly in Kentucky.

1847: Trappist monks took up residence in Gethsemani.

1849: Cornerstone of Cathedral of the Assumption laid at Louisville.

1852: Know-Nothing troubles in state.

1853: Covington diocese established.

1937: Louisville made archdiocese. Owensboro diocese established.

1956: State Court of Appeals upheld right of Catholic Sisters to teach in state's public schools even though they wore religious habits.

Louisiana

1682: La Salle's expedition, accompanied by two priests, completed discoveries of De Soto at mouth of Mississippi. La Salle named territory Louisiana.

1699: French Catholics founded colony of Louisiana.

First recorded Mass offered Mar. 3, by Franciscan Father Anastase Douay.

1706: Father John Francis Buisson de St. Cosme was killed near Donaldsonville.

1717: Franciscan Anthony Margil established first Indian mission school of San Miguel de Linares.

1718: City of New Orleans founded by Jean Baptiste Le Moyne de Bienville.

1720: First resident priest in New Orleans was the French Recollect Prothais Boyer.

1725: Capuchin Fathers opened school for boys.

1727: Ursuline Nuns founded convent in New Orleans, oldest convent in what is now US; they conducted a school, hospital and orphan asylum.

1793: New Orleans diocese established.

1850: New Orleans made archdiocese.

1853: Natchitoches diocese established; transferred to Alexandria in 1910.

1892: Sisters of Holy Family, a Negro congregation, established at New Orleans.

1912: Loyola University of South established.

1918: Lafayette diocese established.

1925: Xavier University established in New Orleans.

1961: Baton Rouge diocese established.

1962: Catholic schools on all levels desegregated in New Orleans archdiocese.

Maine

1604: First Mass in territory celebrated by Father Nicholas Aubry, accompanying De Monts' expedition which was authorized by King of France to begin colonizing region.

1605: Colony founded on St. Croix Island; two secular priests served as chaplains.

1613: Four Jesuits attempted to establish permanent French settlement near mouth of Kennebec River.

1619: French Franciscans began work among settlers and Indians; driven out by English in 1628.

1630: New England made a prefecture apostolic in charge of French Capuchins.

1633: Capuchin Fathers founded missions on Penobscot River.

1646: Jesuits established Assumption Mission on Kennebec River.

1688: Church of St. Anne, oldest in New England, built at Oldtown.

1704: English soldiers destroyed French missions.

1724: English forces again attacked French settlements, killed Jesuit Sebastian Rale.

1853: Portland diocese established.

1854: Know-Nothing uprising resulted in burning of church in Bath.

1856: Anti-Catholic feeling continued; church at Ellsworth burned.

1864: Sisters of Congregation of Notre Dame from Montreal opened academy at Portland.

1875: James A. Healy, first bishop of Negro blood consecrated in US, became second Bishop of Portland.

Maryland

1634: Maryland established by Lord Calvert. Two Jesuits among first colonists.

First Mass offered on Island of St. Clement in Lower Potomac by Jesuit Father Andrew White.

St. Mary's founded by English and Irish Catholics.

1641: St. Ignatius Parish founded by English Jesuits at Chapel Point, near Port Tobacco.

1649: Religious Toleration Act passed by Maryland Assembly. It was repealed in 1654 by Puritan-controlled government.

1651: Cecil Calvert, second Lord Baltimore, gave Jesuits 10,000 acres for use as Indian mission.

1658: Lord Baltimore restored Toleration Act.

1672: Franciscans came to Maryland under leadership of Father Massius Massey.

1688: Maryland became royal colony as a result of the Revolution in England; Anglican Church became the official religion (1692); Toleration Act repealed; Catholics disenfranchised and persecuted until 1776.

1784: Father John Carroll appointed prefect apostolic for the territory embraced by new Republic.

1789: Baltimore became first diocese established in US, with John Carroll as first bishop.

1790: Carmelite Nuns founded convent at Port Tobacco, the first in the English-speaking Colonies.

1791: First Synod of Baltimore held.

St. Mary's Seminary, first seminary in US, established.

1793: Rev. Stephen T. Badin first priest ordained by Bishop Carroll.

1800: Jesuit Leonard Neale became first bishop consecrated in present limits of US.

1806: Cornerstone of Assumption Cathedral, Baltimore, was laid.

1808: Baltimore made archdiocese.

1809: St. Joseph's College, first women's college in US, established.

1811: Sisters of Charity of Emmitsburg approved by Bishop Carroll; first native American sisterhood.

1821: Assumption Cathedral, Baltimore, formally opened.

1829: Oblate Sisters of Charity, a Negro congregation, established at Baltimore.

First Provincial Council of Baltimore held; six others followed, in 1833, 1837, 1840, 1843, 1846 and 1849.

1836: Roger B. Taney appointed Chief Justice of Supreme Court by President Jackson.

1852: First of the three Plenary Councils of Baltimore convened. Subsequent councils were held in 1866 and 1884.

1855: German Catholic Central Verein founded.

1886: Archbishop Gibbons of Baltimore made cardinal by Pope Leo XIII.

1965: Archbishop Shehan of Baltimore made cardinal by Pope Paul VI.

Massachusetts

1630: New England made a prefecture apostolic in charge of French Capuchins.

1647: Massachusetts Bay Company enacted an anti-priest law.

1732: Although Catholics were not legally admitted to colony, a few Irish families were in Boston; a priest was reported working among them.

1755-56: Acadians landing in Boston were denied services of a Catholic priest.

1775: General Washington discouraged Guy Fawkes Day procession in which pope was carried in effigy, and expressed surprise that there were men in his army "so void of common sense as to insult the religious feelings of the Canadians with whom friendship and an alliance are being sought."

1780: The Massachusetts State Constitution granted religious liberty, but required a religious test to hold public office and provided for tax to support Protestant teachers of piety, religion and morality.

1788: First public Mass said in Boston on Nov. 2 by Abbe de la Poterie, first resident priest.

1803: Church of Holy Cross erected in Boston with financial aid given by Protestants headed by John Adams.

1808: Boston diocese established.

1831: Irish Catholic immigration increased.

1832: St. Vincent's Orphan Asylum, oldest charitable institution in Boston, opened by Sisters of Mercy.

1834: Ursuline Convent in Charlestown burned by a Nationalist mob.

1843: Holy Cross College founded.

1855: Catholic militia companies disbanded; nunneries' inspection bill passed.

1859: St. Mary's, first parochial school in Boston, opened.

1860: Portuguese Catholics from Azores settled in New Bedford.

1870: Springfield diocese established.

1875: Boston made archdiocese.

1904: Fall River diocese established.

1911: Archbishop O'Connell of Boston made cardinal by Pope Pius X.

1950: Worcester diocese established.

1958: Archbishop Richard J. Cushing of Boston made cardinal by Pope John XXIII.

1966: Apostolic Exarchate for Melkites in the US established, with headquarters in Boston.

1973: Archbishop Humberto S. Medeiros of Boston made cardinal by Pope Paul VI.

Michigan

1641: Jesuits Isaac Jogues and Charles Raymbaut preached to Chippewas; named Sault-Sainte Marie Rapids.

1660: Jesuit Rene Menard opened first regular mission in Lake Superior region.

1668: Pere Marquette founded Sainte Marie Mission at Sault-Sainte Marie.

1671: Pere Marquette founded St. Ignace Mission at Michilimackinac.

1701: Fort Pontchartrain founded on present site of Detroit and placed in command of Antoine de la Mothe Cadillac. The Chapel of Sainte-Anne-de-Detroit founded.

1706: Franciscan Father Delhalle killed by Indians at Detroit.

1823: Father Gabriel Richard elected delegate to Congress from Michigan territory; he was the first priest chosen for the House of Representatives.

1833: Father Frederic Baraga celebrated first Mass in present Grand Rapids.

Detroit diocese established, embracing whole Northwest Territory.

1843: *Western Catholic Register* founded at Detroit.

1845: St. Vincent's Hospital, Detroit, opened by Sisters of Charity.

1848: Cathedral of Sts. Peter and Paul, Detroit, consecrated.

1853: Vicariate Apostolic of Upper Michigan established.

1857: Sault-Ste. Marie diocese established; later transferred to Marquette.

1877: University of Detroit founded.

1882: Grand Rapids diocese established.

1897: Nazareth College for women founded.

1937: Detroit made archdiocese. Lansing diocese established.

1938: Saginaw diocese established.

1946: Archbishop Edward Mooney of Detroit created cardinal by Pope Pius XII.

1949: Opening of St. John's Theological (major) Seminary at Plymouth; this was first seminary in US serving an entire ecclesiastical province (Detroit).

1966: Apostolic Exarchate for Maronites in US established, with headquarters in Detroit; made an eparchy in 1972.

1969: Archbishop John Dearden of Detroit made cardinal by Pope Paul VI.

1971: Gaylord and Kalamazoo dioceses established.

Minnesota

1680: Falls of St. Anthony discovered by Franciscan Louis Hennepin.

1727: First chapel, St. Michael the Archangel, erected near town of Frontenac and placed in charge of French Jesuits.

1732: Fort Charles built; Jesuits ministered to settlers.

1736: Jesuit Jean Pierre Aulneau killed by Indians.

1739: Swiss Catholics from Canada settled near Fort Snelling; Bishop Loras of Dubuque, accompanied by Father Pellamourgues, visited the Fort and administered sacraments.

1841: Father Lucian Galtier built Church of St. Paul, thus forming nucleus of modern city of same name.

1850: St. Paul diocese established.

1851: Sisters of St. Joseph arrived in state.

1857: University of St. John founded.

1888: St. Paul made archdiocese; name changed to St. Paul-Minneapolis in 1966.

1889: Duluth, St. Cloud and Winona dioceses established.

1909: Crookston diocese established.

1958: New Ulm diocese established.

Mississippi

1540: Chaplains with De Soto expedition entered territory.

1682: Franciscans Zenobius Membre and Anastase Douay preached to Taensa and Natchez Indians. Father Membre offered first recorded Mass in the state on Mar. 29, Easter Sunday.

1698: Priests of Quebec Seminary founded missions near Natchez and Fort Adams.

1702: Father Nicholas Foucault murdered by Indians near Fort Adams.

1721: Missions practically abandoned, with only Father Juif working among Yazoos.

1725: Jesuit Mathurin de Petit carried on mission work in northern Mississippi.

1729: Indians tomahawked Jesuit Paul du Poisson near Fort Rosalie; Father Jean Souel shot by Yazoos.

1736: Jesuit Antoine Senat burned at stake by Chickasaws.

1822: Vicariate Apostolic of Mississippi and Alabama established.

1825: Mississippi made a separate vicariate apostolic.

1837: Natchez diocese established (later changed to Natchez-Jackson).

1848: Sisters of Charity opened orphan asylum and school in Natchez.

Missouri

1700: Jesuit Gabriel Marest established a mission among Kaskaskia Indians near St. Louis.

1734: French Catholic miners and traders settled Old Mines and Sainte Genevieve.

1750: Jesuits visited French settlers.

1762: Mission established at St. Charles.

1767: Carondelet mission established.

1770: First church founded at St. Louis.

1811: Jesuits established Indian mission school at Florissant.

1818: Bishop Dubourg arrived at St. Louis, with Vincentians Joseph Rosati and Felix de Andreis. St. Louis University, the diocesan (Kenrick) seminary and the Vincentian Seminary in Perryville trace their origins to them.

1826: St. Louis diocese established.

1828: Sisters of Charity opened first hospital west of the Mississippi, at St. Louis.

1832: *The Shepherd of the Valley,* first Catholic paper west of the Mississippi.

1845: First conference of Society of St. Vincent de Paul in US founded at St. Louis.

1847: St. Louis made archdiocese.

1865: A Test Oath Law passed by State Legislature (called Drake Convention) to crush Catholicism in Missouri. Law declared unconstitutional by Supreme Court in 1866.

1867: College of St. Teresa for women founded at Kansas City.

1868: St. Joseph diocese established.

1880: Kansas City diocese established.

1946: Archbishop John J. Glennon of St. Louis made cardinal by Pope Pius XII.

1956: Kansas City and St. Joseph dioceses combined into one see. Jefferson City and Springfield-Cape Girardeau dioceses established.

1961: Archbishop Joseph E. Ritter of St. Louis made cardinal by Pope John XXIII.

1969: Archbishop John J. Carberry of St. Louis made cardinal by Pope Paul VI.

Montana

1743: Pierre and Francois Verendrye, accompanied by Jesuit Father Coquart, may have explored territory.

1833: Indian missions handed over to care of Jesuits by Second Provincial Council of Baltimore.

1840: Jesuit Pierre De Smet began missionary work among Flathead and Pend d'Oreille Indians.

1841: St. Mary's Mission established by Father De Smet and two companions on the Bitter Root River in present Stevensville.

1845: Jesuit Antonio Ravalli placed in charge of St. Mary's Mission; Ravalli County named in his honor.

1859: Fathers Point and Hoecken established St. Peter's Mission near the Great Falls.

1869: Sisters of Charity founded a hospital, school and orphanage in Helena.

1877: Vicariate Apostolic of Montana established.

1884: Helena diocese established.

1904: Great Falls diocese established.

1910: Carroll College founded.

1935: Rev. Joseph M. Gilmore became first Montana priest elevated to hierarchy.

Nebraska

1541: Coronado expedition, accompanied by Franciscan Juan de Padilla, reached the Platte River.

1673: Pere Marquette visited Nebraska Indians.

1720: Franciscan Juan Miguel killed by Indians near Columbus.

1855: Father J. F. Tracy administered to Catholic settlement of St. Patrick and to Catholics in Omaha.

1856: Land was donated by Governor Alfred Cumming for a church in Omaha.

1857: Nebraska vicariate apostolic established.

1878: Creighton University established.

1881: Poor Clares, first contemplative group in state, arrived in Omaha. Duchesne College established.

1885: Omaha diocese established.

1887: Lincoln diocese established.

1912: Kearney diocese established; name changed to Grand Island, 1917.

1917: Father Flanagan founded Boy's Town for homeless boys, an institution which gained national and international recognition in subsequent years.

1945: Omaha made archdiocese.

Nevada

1774: Franciscan missionaries passed through Nevada on way to California missions.

1860: First parish, serving Genoa, Carson City and Virginia City, established.

1862: Rev. Patrick Manogue appointed pastor of Virginia City. He established a school for boys and girls, an orphanage and hospital.

1871: Church erected at Reno.

1931: Reno diocese established.

New Hampshire

1630: Territory made part of a prefecture apostolic embracing all of New England.

1784: State Constitution included a religious test which barred Catholics from public office; local support was provided for public Protestant teachers of religion.

1818: The Barber family of Claremont was visited by their son Virgil (converted to Catholicism in 1816) accompanied by Father Charles Ffrench, O.P. The visit led to the conversion of the entire Barber family.

1823: Father Virgil Barber, minister who became a Jesuit priest, built first Catholic church and school at Claremont.

1830: Church of St. Aloysius erected at Dover.

1853: New Hampshire made part of the Portland diocese.

1858: Sisters of Mercy began to teach school at St. Anne's, Manchester.

1877: Catholics obtained full civil liberty and rights.

1884: Manchester diocese established.

1893: St. Anselm's College founded; St. Anselm's Abbey canonically erected.

1937: Francis P. Murphy became first Catholic governor of New Hampshire.

New Jersey

1668: William Douglass of Bergen was refused a seat in General Assembly because he was a Catholic.

1672: Fathers Harvey and Gage visited Catholics in Woodbridge and Elizabethtown.

1701: Tolerance granted to all but "papists."

1744: Jesuit Theodore Schneider of Pennsylvania visited German Catholics of New Jersey.

1762: Fathers Ferdinand Farmer and Robert Harding working among Catholics in state.

1776: State Constitution tacitly excluded Catholics from office.

1799: Foundation of first Catholic school in state, St. John's at Trenton.

1803: First parish in northern New Jersey founded at Echo Lake.

1814: First church in Trenton erected.

1844: Catholics obtained full civil liberty and rights.

1853: Newark diocese established.

1856: Seton Hall University established.

1881: Trenton diocese established.

1937: Newark made archdiocese. Paterson and Camden dioceses established.

1947: US Supreme Court ruled on N. J. bus case, permitting children attending non-public schools to ride on buses and be given other health services provided for those in public schools.

1957: Seton Hall College of Medicine and Dentistry established: the first medical school in state; it was run by Seton Hall until 1965.

1963: Byzantine Eparchy of Passaic established.

New Mexico

1539: Territory explored by Franciscan Marcos de Niza.

1544: Franciscans Juan de la Cruz and Louis de Ubeda, lay brother, killed by Indians.

1581: Franciscans Augustin Rodriguez, Juan de Santa Maria and Francisco Lopez named the region "New Mexico"; they later died at hands of Indians.

1598: Juan de Onate founded a colony at Chamita, where first chapel in state was built.

1609: Santa Fe founded, future headquarters for missions of New Mexico.

1631: Franciscan Pedro de Miranda was killed by Indians.

1632: Franciscan Francisco Letrado was killed by Indians.

1672: Franciscan Pedro de Avila y Ayala was killed by Indians.

1675: Franciscan Alonso Gil de Avila was killed by Indians.

1680: Indians massacred 21 missionaries; missions destroyed.

1684: Franciscan Manuel Beltran was killed by Indians.

1692: Missions restored.

1696: Indians rebelled, massacred five more missionaries.

1850: Jean Baptiste Lamy appointed head of newly established Vicariate Apostolic of New Mexico.

1852: Sisters of Loretto arrived in Santa Fe.

1853: Santa Fe diocese established.

1859: Christian Brothers arrived, established first school for boys in New Mexico (later St. Michael's College).

1865: Sisters of Charity started first orphanage and hospital in Santa Fe. It was closed in 1966.

1875: Santa Fe made archdiocese.

1939: Gallup diocese established.

New York

1524: Giovanni de Verrazano was first white man to enter New York Bay.

1627: Franciscan Joseph d'Aillon discovered oil at Seneca Springs, near Cuba, N. Y.

1642: Jesuits Isaac Jogues and Rene Goupil were mutilated by Mohawks; Rene Goupil was killed by them shortly afterwards. Dutch Calvinists rescued Father Jogues.

1646: Jesuits Isaac Jogues and John Lalande were martyred by Iroquois at Ossernenon, now Auriesville.

1654: The Onondagas were visited by Jesuits from Canada.

1655: First permanent mission established near Syracuse.

1656: Church of St. Mary erected near Lake Onondaga.

Catherine Tekakwitha, "Lily of the Mohawks," was born at Ossernenon, now Auriesville (d. in Canada, 1680).

1658: Indian uprisings destroyed missions among Cayugas, Senecas and Oneidas.

1664: English took New Amsterdam and replaced French priests with their own missionaries.

Duke of York ordered religious freedom in Province of New York.

1667: Missions were restored under protection of Garaconthie, Onondaga chief.

1678: Franciscan Louis Hennepin, first white man to view Niagara Falls, celebrated Mass there.

1682: Thomas Dongan appointed governor by Duke of York.

1683: English Jesuits came to New York, later opened a school.

1700: Although Assembly enacted a bill calling for religious toleration of all Christians in 1683, other penal laws were now enforced against Catholics; all priests were ordered out of the province.

1709: Jesuit missions were abandoned.

1741: Because of an alleged popish plot to burn city of New York, four whites were hanged and 11 Negroes burned at stake.

1777: A rejected amendment of the State Constitution stated that Catholics ought not to hold lands or participate in civil rights unless they swore that no pope or priests may absolve them from allegiance to the state.

1785: Cornerstone was laid for St. Peter's Church, New York City, first permanent structure of Catholic worship in state.

Trusteeism began to cause trouble at New York.

1806: State Test Oath repealed.

1808: New York diocese established.

1828: New York State Legislature enacted a law upholding sanctity of seal of confession.

1834: First native New Yorker to become a secular priest, Rev. John McCloskey, was ordained.

1841: Fordham University and Manhattanville College established.

1847: Albany and Buffalo dioceses established.

1850: New York made archdiocese.

1853: Brooklyn diocese established.

1856: Present St. Bonaventure University and Christ the King Seminary founded at Allegany.

1858: Cornerstone of St. Patrick's Cathedral, New York City, was laid.

1868: Rochester diocese established.

1872: Ogdensburg diocese established.

1875: Archbishop John McCloskey of New York made first American cardinal by Pope Pius IX.

1878: Franciscan Sisters of Allegany were

first native American community to send members to foreign missions.

1880: William R. Grace was first Catholic mayor of New York City.

1886: Syracuse diocese established.

1911: Archbishop John M. Farley of New York made cardinal by Pope Pius X.

Catholic Foreign Mission Society of America (Maryknoll) opened a seminary for foreign missions, the first of its kind in US. The Maryknollers were also unique as the first US-established foreign mission society.

1917: Military Ordinariate established with headquarters at New York.

1919: Alfred E. Smith became first elected Catholic governor.

1924: Archbishop Patrick Hayes of New York made cardinal by Pope Pius XI.

1930: Jesuit Martyrs of New York and Canada were canonized on June 29.

1946: Archbishop Francis J. Spellman of New York made cardinal by Pope Pius XII.

1957: Rockville Centre diocese established.

1969: Archbishop Terence Cooke of New York made cardinal by Pope Paul VI.

North Carolina

1526: The Ayllon expedition attempted to establish a settlement on Carolina coast.

1540: De Soto expedition, accompanied by chaplains, entered state.

1776: State Constitution denied office to "those who denied the truths of the Protestant religion."

1805: The few Catholics in state were served by visiting missionaries.

1821: Bishop John England celebrated Mass in the ballroom of the home of William Gaston at New Bern, marking the start of organization of the first parish, St. Paul's, in the state.

1835: William Gaston, State Supreme Court Justice, succeeded in having repealed the article denying religious freedom.

1852: First Catholic church erected in Charlotte.

1868: North Carolina vicariate apostolic established.

Catholics obtained full civil liberty and rights.

1874: Sisters of Mercy arrived, opened an academy, several schools, hospitals and an orphanage.

1878: Belmont Abbey College founded.

1910: Mary Help of Christians Abbey Nullius established at Belmont.

1924: Raleigh diocese established.

North Dakota

1742: Pierre and Francois Verendrye, accompanied by Jesuit Father Coquart, explored territory.

1818: Canadian priests ministered to Catholics in area.

1839: Jesuit Father De Smet made first of

five trips among Mandan and Gros Ventre Indians.

1848: Father George Belcourt, first American resident priest in territory, reestablished Pembena Mission.

1874: Grey Nuns invited to conduct a school at Fort Totten.

1889: Fargo diocese established.

1893: Benedictines founded St. Gall Monastery at Devil's Lake. (It became an abbey in 1903.)

1909: Bismarck diocese established.

1959: Archbishop Aloysius J. Muench, bishop of Fargo, made cardinal by Pope John XXIII.

Ohio

1749: Jesuits in expedition of Celeron de Bienville preached to Indians.

First religious services were held within present limits of Ohio. Jesuits Joseph de Bonnecamp and Peter Potier celebrated Mass at mouth of Little Miami River and in vicinity of Sandusky Bay, respectively.

1751: First Catholic settlement founded among Huron Indians near Sandusky by Father de la Richardie.

1790: Benedictine Pierre Didier ministered to French immigrants.

1812: Bishop Flaget of Bardstown visited and baptized Catholics of Lancaster and Somerset Counties.

1818: Dominican Father Fenwick built St. Joseph's Church and established first Dominican convent in Ohio.

1821: Cincinnati diocese established.

1831: Xavier University founded.

1843: Seven members of Congregation of Most Precious Blood arrived in Cincinnati from France.

1845: Cornerstone laid for St. Peter's Cathedral, Cincinnati; this was first cathedral west of Alleghenies.

1847: Cleveland diocese established.

1850: Cincinnati made archdiocese.

Marianists opened St. Mary's Institute, now University of Dayton.

1865: Sisters of Charity opened hospital in Cleveland, first institution of its kind in city.

1868: Columbus diocese established.

1871: Ursuline College for women opened at Cleveland.

1910: Toledo diocese established.

1935: Archbishop John T. McNicholas, O.P., founded the Institutum Divi Thomae in Cincinnati for fundamental research in natural sciences.

1943: Youngstown diocese established.

1944: Steubenville diocese established.

1969: Byzantine Rite Eparchy of Parma established.

Oklahoma

1540: De Soto expedition, accompanied by chaplains, explored territory.

1541: Coronado expedition, accompanied by Franciscan Juan de Padilla, explored state.

1630: Spanish Franciscan Juan de Salas labored among Indians.

1700: Scattered Catholic families were visited by priests from Kansas and Arkansas.

1874: First Catholic church built by Father Smyth at Atoka.

1876: Prefecture Apostolic of Indian Territory established with Benedictine Isidore Robot as its head.

1886: First Catholic day school for Choctaw and white children opened by Sisters of Mercy at Kribs.

1891: Vicariate Apostolic of Oklahoma and Indian Territory established.

1905: Oklahoma diocese established; title changed to Oklahoma City and Tulsa, 1930.

1917: Benedictine Heights College for women founded.

Carmelite Sisters of St. Theresa of the Infant Jesus were founded at Oklahoma City.

1972: Oklahoma City made archdiocese. Tulsa diocese established.

Oregon

1603: Vizcaino explored northern Oregon coast.

1774: Franciscan missionaries accompanied Juan Perez on his expedition to coast, and Heceta a year later.

1811: Catholic Canadian trappers and traders with John J. Astor expedition founded first American settlement — Astoria.

1834: Indian missions in Northwest entrusted to Jesuits by Holy See.

1838: Abbe Blanchet appointed vicar general to Bishop of Quebec with jurisdiction over area which included Oregon Territory.

1839: First church in Pacific Northwest, under patronage of St. Paul the Apostle, was blessed at Champoig.

1843: Oregon vicariate apostolic established.

St. Joseph's College for boys opened.

1844: Jesuit Pierre de Smet established Mission of St. Francis Xavier near St. Paul.

Sisters of Notre Dame de Namur, first to enter Oregon, opened an academy for girls.

1846: Vicariate made an ecclesiastical province with Bishop Blanchet as first Archbishop of Oregon City (now Portland).

Walla Walla diocese established; suppressed in 1853.

First priest was ordained in Oregon.

1848: First Provincial Council of Oregon.

1857: Death of Dr. John McLoughlin, "Father of Oregon."

1865: Rev. H. H. Spalding, a Protestant missionary, published the Whitman Myth to hinder work of Catholic missionaries.

1874: Catholic Indian Mission Bureau established.

1875: St. Vincent's Hospital, first in state, opened at Portland.

1903: Baker diocese established.

1922: Anti-private school bill sponsored by Scottish Rite Masons was passed by popular vote, 115,506 to 103,685.

1925: US Supreme Court declared Oregon anti-private school bill unconstitutional.

1953: First Trappist monastery on West Coast established in Willamette Valley north of Lafayette.

Pennsylvania

1673: Priests from Maryland ministered to Catholics in the Colony.

1682: Religious toleration was extended to members of all faiths.

1720: Jesuit Joseph Greaton became first resident missionary of Philadelphia.

1734: St. Joseph's Church, first Catholic church in Philadelphia, was opened.

1741: Jesuit Fathers Schneider and Wappeler ministered to German immigrants.

1782: St. Mary's Parochial School opened at Philadelphia.

1788: Holy Trinity Church, Philadelphia, was incorporated; first exclusively national church organized in US.

1797: Augustinian Matthew Carr founded St. Augustine parish, Philadelphia.

1799: Prince Demetrius Gallitzin (Father Augustine Smith) built church in western Pennsylvania, at Loretto.

1808: Philadelphia diocese established.

1814: St. Joseph's Orphanage was opened at Philadelphia; first Catholic institution for children in US.

1842: University of Villanova founded by Augustinians.

1843: Pittsburgh diocese established.

1844: Thirteen persons killed, two churches and a school burned in Know-Nothing jiots at Philadelphia.

1846: First Benedictine Abbey in New World founded near Latrobe by Father Boniface Wimmer.

1853: Erie diocese established.

1868: Scranton and Harrisburg dioceses established.

1871: Chestnut Hill College, first for women in state, founded.

1875: Philadelphia made archdiocese.

1901: Altoona-Johnstown diocese established.

1913: Byzantine Rite Apostolic Exarchate of Philadelphia established; became metropolitan see, 1958.

1921: Archbishop Dennis Dougherty made cardinal by Pope Benedict XV.

1924: Byzantine Rite Apostolic Exarchate of Pittsburgh established; made an eparchy in 1963; raised to metropolitan status and transferred to Munhall, 1969.

1951: Greensburg diocese established.

1958: Archbishop John O'Hara, C.S.C., of Philadelphia made cardinal by Pope John.

1961: Allentown diocese established.

1967: Archbishop John J. Krol of Philadelphia made cardinal by Pope Paul VI.

1969: Bishop John J. Wright of Pittsburgh made cardinal by Pope Paul VI and transferred to Curia post.

Rhode Island

1663: Colonial Charter granted freedom of conscience.

1719: Laws denied Catholics the right to hold public office.

1829: St. Mary's Church, Pawtucket, was first Catholic church in state.

1837: Parochial schools inaugurated in state.

First Catholic church in Providence was built.

1851: Sisters of Mercy began work in Rhode Island.

1872: Providence diocese established.

1900: Trappists took up residence in state.

1917: Providence College founded.

South Carolina

1569: Jesuit Juan Rogel was the first resident priest in the territory.

1573: First Franciscans arrived in southeastern section.

1606: Bishop Altamirano conducted visitation of area.

1655: Franciscans had two missions among Indians; later destroyed by English.

1697: Religious liberty granted to all except "papists."

1790: Catholics given right to vote.

1820: Charleston diocese established.

1822: Bishop England founded *U.S. Catholic Miscellany,* first Catholic paper of a strictly religious nature in US.

1830: Sisters of Our Lady of Mercy, first in state, took up residence at Charleston.

1847: Cornerstone of Cathedral of St. John the Baptist, Charleston, was laid.

1861: Cathedral and many institutions destroyed in Charleston fire.

South Dakota

1842: Father Augustine Ravoux began ministrations to French and Indians at Fort Pierre, Vermilion and Prairie du Chien; printed devotional book in Sioux language the following year.

1867: Parish organized among the French at Jefferson.

1878: Benedictines opened school for Sioux children at Fort Yates.

1889: Sioux Falls diocese established.

1902: Lead diocese established; transferred to Rapid City, 1930.

1950: Mount Marty College for women founded.

1952: Blue Cloud Abbey, first Benedictine foundation in state, was dedicated.

Tennessee

1541: Cross planted on shore of Mississippi by De Soto; accompanying the expedition were Fathers John de Gallegos and Louis De Soto.

1682: Franciscan Fathers Membre and Douay accompanied La Salle to present site of Memphis; may have offered the first Masses in the territory.

1800: Catholics were served by priests from Bardstown, Ky.

1822: Non-Catholics assisted in building church in Nashville.

1837: Nashville diocese established.

1843: Sisters of Charity opened a school for girls in Nashville.

1921: Sisters of St. Dominic opened Siena College for women at Memphis.

1940: Christian Brothers College founded at Memphis.

1970: Memphis diocese established.

Texas

1541: Missionaries with De Soto and Coronado entered territory.

1553: Dominicans Diego de la Cruz, Hernando Mendez, Juan Ferrer, Brother Juan de Mina killed by Indians.

1675: Bosque-Larios missionary expedition entered region; Father Juan Larios offered first recorded Mass.

1689: Four Franciscans founded first mission, San Francisco de los Tejas.

1703: Mission San Francisco de Solano founded on Rio Grande.

1717: Franciscan Antonio Margil founded six missions in northeast.

1721: Franciscan Brother Jose Pita killed by Indians at Carnezeria.

1728: Site of San Antonio settled.

1738: Construction of San Fernando Cathedral at San Antonio.

1744: Mission of San Francisco de Solano rebuilt as the Alamo.

1750: Franciscan Francisco Xavier was killed by Indians; so were Jose Ganzabal in 1752, and Alonzo Ferrares and Jose San Esteban in 1758.

1793: Mexico secularized missions.

1825: Government of Texas secularized all Indian missions.

1830: Irish priests ministered to settlements of Refugio and San Patricio.

1841: Vicariate of Texas established.

1847: Ursuline Sisters established their first academy in territory at Galveston.

Galveston diocese established.

1852: Oblate Fathers and Franciscans arrived in Galveston to care for new influx of German Catholics.

St. Mary's College founded at San Antonio.

1854: Know-Nothing Party began to stir up hatred against Catholics.

1858: Texas Legislature passed law entitling all schools granting free scholarships and meeting state requirements to share in school fund.

1874: San Antonio diocese established.

1881: St. Edward's College founded: became first chartered college in state in 1889.

Sisters of Charity founded Incarnate Word College at San Antonio.

1890: Dallas diocese established; changed to Dallas-Ft. Worth, 1953; made two separate dioceses, 1969.

1912: Corpus Christi diocese established.

1914: El Paso diocese established.

1926: San Antonio made archdiocese. Amarillo diocese established.

1947: Austin diocese established.

1961: San Angelo diocese established.

1965: Brownsville diocese established.

1966: Beaumont diocese established.

Utah

1776: Franciscans Silvestre de Escalante and Atanasio Dominguez reached Utah (Salt) Lake; first white men known to enter the territory.

1858: Jesuit Father De Smet accompanied General Harney as chaplain on expedition sent to settle troubles between Mormons and US Government.

1866: On June 29 Father Edward Kelly offered first Mass in Salt Lake City in Mormon Assembly Hall.

1886: Utah vicariate apostolic established.

1891: Salt Lake City diocese established.

1926: College of St. Mary-of-the-Wasatch for women was founded.

Vermont

1609: Champlain expedition passed through territory.

1666: Captain La Motte built fort and shrine of St. Anne on Isle La Motte; Sulpician Father Dollier de Casson celebrated first Mass.

1668: Bishop Laval of Quebec administered confirmation in region; this was the first area in northeastern US to receive an episcopal visit.

1710: Jesuits ministered to Indians near Lake Champlain.

1793: Discriminatory measures against Catholics were repealed.

1830: Father Jeremiah O'Callaghan became first resident priest in state.

1853: Burlington diocese established.

1854: Sisters of Charity arrived to conduct St. Joseph's Orphanage at Burlington.

1904: St. Michael's College founded.

1951: First Carthusian foundation in America established at Whitingham.

Virginia

1526: Dominican Antonio de Montesinos offered first Mass on Virginia soil.

1561: Dominicans visited the coast.

1571: Father John Baptist de Segura and seven Jesuit companions killed by Indians.

1642: Priests outlawed and Catholics denied right to vote.

1689: Capuchin Christopher Plunket was captured and exiled to a coastal island where he died in 1697.

1776: Religious freedom granted.

1791: Father Jean Dubois arrived at Richmond with letters from Lafayette. The House of Delegates was placed at his disposal for celebration of Mass.

1796: A church was built at Alexandria.

1820: Richmond diocese established.

1822: Trusteeism created serious problems in diocese; Bishop Kelly resigned the see.

1848: Sisters of Charity opened an orphan asylum at Norfolk.

1866: School Sisters of Notre Dame and Sisters of Charity opened academies for girls at Richmond.

1974: Arlington diocese established.

Washington

1775: Spaniards explored the region.

1838: Fathers Blanchet and Demers, "Apostles of the Northwest," were sent to territory by archbishop of Quebec.

1840: Log church for Indians was built on Whidby Island, Puget Sound.

1843: Vicariate Apostolic of Oregon, including Washington, was established.

1844: Mission of St. Paul founded at Colville.

Six Sisters of Notre Dame de Namur began work in area.

1850: Nesqually diocese established; transferred to Seattle, 1907.

1856: Sisters of Charity established first permanent school and hospital in Northwest at Fort Vancouver.

1887: Gonzaga University founded.

1913: Spokane diocese established.

1951: Seattle made archdiocese Yakima diocese established.

West Virginia

1749: Father Joseph de Bonnecamps, accompanying the Bienville expedition, may have offered first Mass in the territory.

1821: First Catholic church in Wheeling.

1838: Sisters of Charity founded school at Martinsburg.

1848: Visitation Nuns established academy for girls at Mt. de Chantal.

1850: Wheeling diocese established.

Wheeling Hospital incorporated, the oldest Catholic charitable institution in territory.

1955: Wheeling College established.

Wisconsin

1661: Jesuit Rene Menard, first known missionary in the territory, was killed or lost in the Black River district.

1665: Jesuit Claude Allouez founded Mission of the Holy Ghost at La Pointe Chegoimegon, now Bayfield; was the first permanent mission in region.

1673: Father Marquette and Louis Joliet traveled from Green Bay down the Wisconsin and Mississippi rivers.

1762: Suppression of Jesuits in French Colonies closed many missions for 30 years.

1843: Milwaukee diocese established.

1853: St. John's Cathedral, Milwaukee, was built.

1864: Marquette University established.

1868: Green Bay and La Crosse dioceses established.

1875: Milwaukee made archdiocese.

1905: Superior diocese established.

1946: Madison diocese established.

Wyoming

1840: Jesuit Pierre de Smet offered first Mass near Green River.

1851: Father De Smet held peace conference with Indians near Fort Laramie.

1867: Father William Kelly, first resident priest, arrived in Cheyenne and built first church a year later.

1873: Father Eugene Cusson became first resident pastor in Laramie.

1875: Sisters of Charity of Leavenworth opened school and orphanage at Laramie.

1884: Jesuits took over pastoral care of Shoshone and Arapaho Indians.

1887: Cheyenne diocese established.

1949: Weston Memorial Hospital opened near Newcastle.

Catholics in Presidents' Cabinets

(For biographical data on some of these entries, see Index.)

Roger B. Taney, Attorney General 1831-33, Secretary of Treasury 1833-34; app. by Andrew Jackson.

James Campbell, Postmaster General 1853-57; app. by Franklin Pierce.

John B. Floyd, Secretary of War 1857-61; app. by James Buchanan.

Joseph McKenna, Attorney General 1897-98; app. by William McKinley.

Robert J. Wynne, Postmaster General 1904-05; app. by Theodore Roosevelt.

Charles Bonaparte, Secretary of Navy 1905-06, Attorney General 1906-09; app. by Theodore Roosevelt.

James A. Farley, Postmaster General 1933-40; app. by Franklin D. Roosevelt.

Frank Murphy, Attorney General 1939-40; app. by Franklin D. Roosevelt.

Frank C. Walker, Postmaster General 1940-45; app. by Franklin D. Roosevelt.

Robert E. Hannegan, Postmaster General 1945-47; app. by Harry S. Truman.

J. Howard McGrath, Attorney General 1949-52; app. by Harry S. Truman.

Maurice J. Tobin, Secretary of Labor; 1949-53; app. by Harry S. Truman.

James P. McGranery, Attorney General 1952-53; app. by Harry S. Truman.

Martin P. Durkin, Secretary of Labor 1953; app. by Dwight D. Eisenhower.

James P. Mitchell, Secretary of Labor 1953-61; app. by Dwight D. Eisenhower.

Robert F. Kennedy, Attorney General 1961-65; app. by John F. Kennedy, reapp. by Lyndon B. Johnson.

Anthony Celebrezze, Secretary of Health, Education and Welfare 1962-65; app. by John F. Kennedy, reapp. by Lyndon B. Johnson.

John S. Gronouski, Postmaster General

1963-65; app. by John F. Kennedy, reapp. by Lyndon B. Johnson.

John T. Connor, Secretary of Commerce 1965-67; app. by Lyndon B. Johnson.

Lawrence O'Brien, Postmaster General 1965-68; app. by Lyndon B. Johnson.

Walter J. Hickel, Secretary of Interior 1969-71; app. by Richard M. Nixon.

John A. Volpe, Secretary of Transportation 1969-72; app. by Richard M. Nixon.

Maurice H. Stans, Secretary of Commerce, 1969-72; app. by Richard M. Nixon.

Peter J. Brennan, Secretary of Labor, 1973- ; app. by Richard M. Nixon, reapp. by Gerald R. Ford.

Men who became Catholics after leaving Cabinet posts: Thomas Ewing, Secretary of Treasury under William A. Harrison, and Secretary of Interior under Zachary Taylor; Luke E. Wright, Secretary of War under Theodore Roosevelt; Albert B. Fall, Secretary of Interior under Warren G. Harding.

Catholic Justices of the Supreme Court

(For biographical data on some of these entries, see Index.)

Roger B. Taney, Chief Justice 1836-64; app. by Andrew Jackson.

Edward D. White, Associate Justice 1894-1910, app. by Grover Cleveland; Chief Justice 1910-21, app. by William H. Taft.

Joseph McKenna, Associate Justice 1898-1925; app. by William McKinley.

Pierce Butler, Associate Justice 1923-39; app. by Warren G. Harding.

Frank Murphy, Associate Justice 1940-49; app. by Franklin D. Roosevelt.

William Brennan, Associate Justice 1956-; app. by Dwight D. Eisenhower.

Sherman Minton, Associate Justice from

1949 to 1956, became a Catholic several years before his death in 1965.

Catholics Represented in National Statuary Hall

(For biographies, see Index.)

Statues of 12 Catholics deemed worthy of national commemoration by the donating states are among 91 enshrined in National Statuary Hall and other places in the US Capitol. The Hall, formerly the chamber of the House of Representatives, was erected by Act of Congress July 2, 1864.

Donating states, names and years of placement are listed. An asterisk indicates placement of a statue in the Hall itself.

Arizona: Rev. Eusebio Kino, S. J., missionary, 1965.

California: Rev. Junipero Serra, O. F. M.* missionary, 1931.

Hawaii: Father Damien, missionary, 1969.

Illinois: Gen. James Shields, statesman, 1893.

Louisiana: Edward D. White, Justice of the US Supreme Court (1894-1921), 1955.

Maryland: Charles Carroll,* statesman, 1901.

Nevada: Patrick A. McCarran,* statesman, 1960.

New Mexico: Dennis Chavez, statesman, 1966. (Archbishop Jean B. Lamy, pioneer prelate of Santa Fe, was nominated for Hall honor in 1951.)

North Dakota: John Burke,* US treasurer, 1963.

Oregon: Dr. John McLoughlin, pioneer, 1953.

West Virginia: John E. Kenna, statesman, 1901.

Wisconsin: Rev. Jacques Marquette, S. J., missionary, explorer, 1895.

CHURCH-STATE DECISIONS OF THE SUPREME COURT

(Among sources of this listing of US Supreme Court decisions was *The Supreme Court on Church and State,* Joseph Tussman, editor; Oxford University Press, New York, 1962.)

Terrett v. Taylor, 9 Cranch 43 (1815): The Court declared unconstitutional an act of the Virginia Legislature which denied property rights to Protestant Episcopal churches in the state. Religious corporations, like other corporations, have rights to their property.

Vidal v. Girard's Executors, 2 Howard 205 (1844): The Court upheld the will of Stephen Girard, which barred ministers of any religion from serving as faculty members or visitors in a school he established for orphans.

Watson v. Jones, 13 Wallace 679 (1872): The Court declared that a member of a religious organization may not appeal to secular courts against a decision made by a church tribunal within the area of its competence.

Reynolds v. United States, 98 US 145

(1879): The Court declared, in reference to the Mormon practice of polygamy, that one may not knowingly violate by external practices the law of the land on religious grounds, since such conduct would make the professed doctrines of belief superior to federal or state law. One must keep the external practice of religion within the framework of laws enacted for the common welfare. This was the first decision rendered on the Free Exercise Clause of the First Amendment.

Davis v. Beason, 133 US 333 (1890): The Court upheld the denial of the right of Mormons to vote in Idaho if they refused to sign a registration oath stating that they were not bigamists or polygamists and would not encourage or preach bigamy or polygamy.

Church of Latter-Day Saints v. United States, 136 US 1 (1890): The Court upheld an Act of Congress which annulled the charter of the Corporation of the Church of Jesus Christ of Latter-Day Saints, and declared "forfeited to the government all its real estate except a small portion used exclusively for public worship" (Tussman, *op. cit.,* p. 33). The Court held that the Corporation continually used its power to violate US laws prohibiting polygamy.

Church of the Holy Trinity v. United States, 143 US 226 (1892): The Court declared it is not "a misdemeanor for a church of this country to contract for the services of a Christian minister residing in another nation" (from the text of the decision).

Bradfield v. Roberts, 175 US 291 (1899): The Court denied that an appropriation of government funds for an institution (Providence Hospital, Washington, D.C.) run by Roman Catholic sisters violated the No Establishment Clause of the First Amendment.

Pierce v. Society of Sisters, 268 US 510 (1925): The Court denied that a state can require children to attend public schools only. The Court held that the liberty of the Constitution forbids standardization by such compulsion, and that the parochial schools involved had claims to protection under the Fourteenth Amendment.

Cochran v. Board of Education, 281 US 370 (1930): The Court upheld a Louisiana statute providing textbooks at public expense for children attending public or parochial schools. The Court held that the children and state were beneficiaries of the appropriations, with incidental secondary benefit going to the schools.

United States v. MacIntosh, 283 US 605 (1931): The Court denied that anyone can place allegiance to the will of God above his allegiance to the government, since such a person could make his own interpretation of God's will the decisive test as to whether he would or would not obey the nation's law. The Court stated that the nation, which has a duty to survive, can require citizens to bear arms in its defense.

Hamilton v. Regents of University of California, 293 US 245 (1934): The Court rejected a "claim to exemption from R.O.T.C. based on conscientious objection to war" (Tussman *op. cit.,* p. 64). If such an exemption were allowed, the liberties of the objector might be extended to the point of refusal to pay taxes in furtherance of a war or any other end condemned by his conscience. This would be an undue exaltation of the right of private judgment.

Cantwell v. Connecticut, 310 US 296 (1940): The Court declared that the right to religious freedom is violated by a statute requiring a person to secure a permit from a government official before soliciting money for alleged religious purposes from someone not of his or her sect. Such a practice would constitute censorship of religion.

Minersville School District v. Gobitis, 310 US 586 (1940): The Court upheld the right of a state to require the salute to the national flag from school children, even from those who refused to do so for sincere religious reasons.

Jones v. City of Opelika, 316 US 584 (1942): The court upheld licensing ordinances in three municipalities against "the claim by Jehovah's Witnesses that they interfere with the free exercise of religion" (Tussman, *op. cit.,* p. 91).

Murdock v. Commonwealth of Pennsylvania, 319 US 105 (1943): In a reversal of the decision handed down in Jones v. City of Opelika, the Court declared the licensing unconstitutional since it violated a freedom guaranteed under the First Amendment. The selling of religious literature by traveling preachers does not make evangelism the equivalent of a commercial enterprise taxable by the State.

Jones v. City of Opelika, 316 US 584 105 (1943): The Court declared that the Constitution denies a city the right to control the expression of men's minds and denies also the right of men to win others to their views through a program of taxes levied against such activity.

Douglas v. City of Jeannette, 319 US 157 (1943): The Court again upheld the proselytizing rights of Jehovah's Witnesses, ruling unconstitutional the action of any public authority in regulating or taxing such activity.

West Virginia State Board of Education v. Barnette, 319 US 624 (1943): In a reversal of the decision handed down in Minersville School District v. Gobitis, the Court declared unconstitutional a state statute requiring of all children a salute to the national flag and a pledge of allegiance which a child may consider contrary to sincere religious beliefs.

Prince v. Commonwealth of Massachusetts, 321 US 158 (1944): The Court upheld a "child-labor regulation against the claim that it prevents a child from performing her religious duty" (Tussman, *op. cit.,* p. 170). The Court asserted a general principle that the state has a wide range of power for limiting parental freedom and authority in things affecting the child's welfare.

United States v. Ballard, 322 US 78 (1944): The Court upheld the general principle that "the truth of religious claims is not for secular authority to determine" (Tussman, *op. cit.,* p. 181).

In Re Summers, 325 US 561 (1945): The Court upheld "the denial, to an otherwise qualified applicant, of admission to the bar on the basis of the applicant's religiously motivated 'conscientious scruples against participation in war' " (Tussman, *op. cit.,* p. 192). The petitioner was barred because he could not in good faith take the prescribed oath to support the Constitution of Illinois which required service in the state militia in times of necessity.

Girouard v. United States, 328 US 61 (1946): In a ruling related to that handed down in United States v. MacIntosh, the Court affirmed the opinion that the refusal of an alien to bear arms does not deny him citizenship.

Everson v. Board of Education, 330 US 1 (1947): The Court upheld the constitutionality of a New Jersey statute authorizing free school bus transportation for parochial as well as public school students. The Court expressed the opinion that the benefits of public welfare legislation, included under such bus transportation, do not run contrary to the concept of separation of Church and State.

McCollum v. Board of Education, 333 US 203 (1948): The Court declared unconstitutional a program for releasing children, with parental consent, from public school classes so they could receive religious instruction on public school premises from representatives of their own faiths.

Zorach v. Clauson, 343 US 306 (1952): The Court upheld the constitutionality of a New York statute permitting, on a voluntary basis, the release during school time of students from public school classes for religious instruction given off public school premises.

Kedroff v. St. Nicholas Cathedral, 344 US 94 (1952): The Court ruled against an action of New York in taking "control of St. Nicholas Cathedral away from the Moscow hierarchy" (Tussman, *op. cit.,* p. 292), on the ground that the controversy involved a matter of church government.

Fowler v. Rhode Island, 345 US 67 (1953): The Court upheld the right of a Jehovah's Witness to preach in a public park against a city ordinance which forbade such preaching. The Court held that the ordinance, as construed and applied, discriminated against the Witness and therefore amounted to preferment by the state of other religious groups.

Torcaso v. Watkins, 367 US 488 (1961): the Court declared unconstitutional a Maryland requirement that one must make a declaration of belief in the existence of God as part of the oath of office for notaries public.

McGowan v. Maryland, 81 Sp Ct 1101; Two Guys from Harrison v. McGinley, 81 Sp Ct 1135; Gallagher v. Crown Kosher Super Market, 81 Sp Ct 1128; Braunfield v. Brown, 81 Sp Ct 1144 (1961): The Court ruled that Sunday closing laws do not violate the No Establishment of Religion Clause of the First Amendment, even though the laws were religious in their inception and still have some religious overtones. The Court held that, "as presently written and administered, most of them, at least, are of a secular rather than of a religious character, and that presently they bear no relationship to establishment of religion as those words are used in the Constitution of the United States."

Engel v. Vitale, 370 US 42 (1962): The Court declared that the voluntary recitation in public schools of a prayer composed by the New York State Board of Regents is unconstitutional on the ground that it violates the No Establishment of Religion Clause of the First Amendment.

Abington Township School District v. Schempp and **Murray v. Curlett, 83 Sp Ct 1560** (1963): The Court ruled that Bible reading and recitation of the Lord's Prayer in public schools, with voluntary participation by students, are unconstitutional on the ground that they violate the No Establishment of Religion Clause of the First Amendment.

Sherbert v. Verner, 83 A Sp Ct 1790 (1963): The Court ruled that individuals of any religious faith may not, because of their faith or lack of it, be deprived of the benefits of public welfare legislation.

Chamberlin v. Dade County,1 83 Sp Ct 1864 (1964): The Court reversed a decision of the Florida Supreme Court concerning the constitutionality of prayer and devotional Bible reading in public schools during the school day, as sanctioned by a state statute which specifically related the practices to a sound public purpose.

Board of Education v. Allen, No. 660 (1968): The Court declared constitutional the New York school book loan law which requires local school boards to purchase books with state funds and lend them to parochial and private school students.

Flast v. Cohen, No. 416 (1968): The Court held that individual taxpayers can bring suits to challenge federal expenditures on grounds that they violate the principle of separation of Church and State even though generally taxpayers cannot challenge federal expenditures in court.

Walz v. Tax Commission of New York (1970): The Court upheld the constitutionality of a New York statute exempting church-owned property from taxation.

Earle v. DiCenso, Robinson v. DiCenso, Lemon v. Kurtzman, Tilton v. Richardson (1971): In Earle v. DiCenso and Robinson v. DiCenso, the Court ruled unconstitutional a 1969 Rhode Island statute which provided salary supplements to teachers of secular subjects in parochial schools; in Lemon v. Kurtzman, the Court ruled unconstitutional a 1968 Pennsylvania statute which authorized the state to purchase services for the teaching of secular subjects in nonpublic schools. The principal argument against constitutionality in these cases was that the statutes and programs at issue entailed excessive entanglement of government with religion. In Tilton v. Richardson, the Court held that this argument did not apply to a prohibitive degree with respect to federal grants, under the Higher Education Facilities Act of 1963, for the construction of facilities for nonreligious purposes by four church-related institutions of higher learning, three of which were Catholic, in Connecticut.

Amish Decision (1972): In a case appealed on behalf of Yoder, Miller and Yutzy, the Court ruled that Amish parents were exempt from a Wisconsin statute requiring them to send their children to school until the age of 16. The Court said in its decision that secondary schooling exposed Amish children to attitudes, goals and values contrary to their beliefs, and substantially hindered "the religious development of the Amish child and his integration into the way of life of the Amish faith-community at the crucial adolescent state of development."

Committee for Public Education and Religious Liberty, et al., v. Nyquist, et al., No. 72-694 (1973): The Court ruled that provisions of a 1972 New York statute were unconstitutional on the grounds that they were violative of the No Establishment Clause of the First Amendment and had the "impermissible effect" of advancing the sectarian activities of church-affiliated schools. The programs ruled unconstitutional concerned: (1) maintenance and repair grants, for facilities and equipment, to ensure the health, welfare and safety of students in nonpublic, non-profit elementary and secondary schools serving a high concentration of students from low income families; (2) tuition reimbursement ($50 per grade school child, $100 per high school student) for parents (with income less than $5,000) of children attending nonpublic elementary or secondary schools; tax deduction from adjusted gross income for parents failing to qualify under the above reimbursement plan, for each child attending a nonpublic school.

Sloan, Treasurer of Pennsylvania, et al., v. Lemon, et al., No. 72-459 (1973): The Court ruled unconstituional a Pennsylvania Parent Reimbursement Act for Nonpublic Education which provided funds to reimburse parents (to a maximum of $150) for a portion of tuition expenses incurred in sending their children to nonpublic schools. The Court held that there was no significant difference between this and the New York tuition reimbursement program (above), and declared that the Equal Protection Clause of the Fourteenth Amendment cannot be relied upon to sustain a program held to be violative of the No Establishment Clause.

Levitt, et al., v. Committee for Public Education and Religious Liberty, et al., No. 72-269 (1973): The Court ruled unconstitutional the Mandated Services Act of 1970 under which New York provided $28 million ($27 per pupil from first to seventh grade, $45 per pupil from seventh to 12th grade) to reimburse nonpublic schools for testing, recording and reporting services required by the state. The Court declared that the act provided "impermissible aid" to religion in contravention of the No Establishment Clause.

In related decisions handed down June 25, 1973, the Court: (1) affirmed a lower court decision against the constitutionality of an Ohio tax credit law benefiting parents with children in nonpublic schools; (2) reinstated an injunction against a parent reimbursement program in New Jersey; (3) affirmed South Carolina's right to grant construction loans to church-affiliated colleges, and dismissed an appeal contesting its right to provide loans to students attending church-affiliated colleges (**Hunt v. McNair, Durham v. McLeod**).

Wheeler v. Barrera (1974): The Court ruled that nonpublic school students in Missouri must share in federal funds for educationally deprived students on a comparable basis with public school students under Title I of the Elementary and Secondary Education Act of 1965.

THE WALL OF SEPARATION

Thomas Jefferson, in a letter written to the Danbury (Conn.) Baptist Association Jan. 1, 1802, coined the metaphor, "a wall of separation between Church and State," to express a theory concerning interpretation of the religion clauses of the First Amendment: "Congress shall make no law respecting an establishment of religion or prohibiting the free exercise thereof."

The metaphor was cited for the first time in judicial proceedings in 1879, in the opinion by Chief Justice Waite in Reynolds v. United States. It did not, however, figure substantially in the decision.

Accepted as Rule

In 1947 the wall of separation gained acceptance as a constitutional rule, in the decision handed down in Everson v. Board of Education. Associate Justice Black, in describing the principles involved in the No Establishment Clause, wrote:

"Neither a state nor the Federal Government can set up a church. Neither can pass laws which aid one religion, aid all religions, or prefer one religion over another. Neither can force nor influence a person to go to or to remain away from church against his will or force him to profess a belief or disbelief in any religion. No person can be punished for entertaining or professing religious beliefs or disbeliefs, for church attendance or non-attendance. No tax in any amount, large or small, can be levied to support any religious activities or institutions, whatever they may be called, or whatever form they may adopt to teach or practice religion. Neither a state nor the Federal Government can, openly or secretly, participate in the affairs of any religious organizations or groups and vice versa. In the words of Jefferson, the clause against establishment of religion by law was intended to erect 'a wall of separation between Church and State.' "

Mr. Black's associates agreed with his statement of principles, which were framed without reference to the Freedom of Exercise

Clause. They disagreed, however, with respect to application of the principles, as the split decision in the case indicated. Five members of the Court held that the benefits of public welfare legislation — in this case, free bus transportation to school for parochial as well as public school students — did not run contrary to the concept of separation of Church and State embodied in the First Amendment.

Different Opinions

Inside and outside the legal profession, opinion is divided concerning the wall of separation and the balance of the religion clauses of the First Amendment.

The view of absolute separationists, carried to the extreme, would make government the adversary of religion. The bishops of the United States, following the McCollum decision in 1948, said that the wall metaphor had become for some persons the "shibboleth of doctrinaire secularism."

Proponents of governmental neutrality toward religion are of the opinion that such neutrality should not be so interpreted as to prohibit incidental aid to religious institutions providing secular services.

In the realm of practice, federal and state legislatures have enacted measures involving incidental benefits to religious bodies. Examples of such measures are the tax exemption of church property; provision of bus rides, book loans and lunch programs to students in church-related as well as public schools; military chaplaincies; loans to church-related hospitals; the financing of studies by military veterans at church-related colleges under GI bills of rights.

CHURCH TAX EXEMPTION

The exemption of church-owned property was ruled constitutional by the US Supreme Court May 4, 1970, in the case of Walz v. The Tax Commission of New York.

Suit in the case was brought by Frederick Walz, who purchased in June, 1967, a 22-by-29-foot plot of ground in Staten Island valued at $100 and taxable at $5.24 a year. Shortly after making the purchase, Walz instituted a suit in New York State, contending that the exemption of church property from taxation authorized by state law increased his own tax rate and forced him indirectly to support churches in violation of his constitutional right to freedom of religion under the First Amendment. Three New York courts dismissed the suit, which had been instituted by mail. The Supreme Court, judging that it had probable jurisdiction, then took the case.

In a 7-1 decision affecting Church-state relations in every state in the nation, the Court upheld the New York law under challenge.

Chief Justice Warren E. Burger, who wrote the majority opinion, said that Congress from its earliest days had viewed the religion clauses of the Constitution as authorizing statutory real estate tax exemption to religious bodies. He declared: "Nothing in this national attitude toward religious tolerance and two centuries of uninterrupted freedom from taxation has given the remotest sign of leading to an established church or religion, and on the contrary it has operated affirmatively to help guarantee the free exercise of all forms of religious beliefs."

Justice William O. Douglas wrote in dissent that the involvement of government in religion as typified in tax exemption may seem inconsequential but: "It is, I fear, a long step down the establishment path. . . . Perhaps I have been misinformed. But, as I read the Constitution and the philosophy, I gathered that independence was the price of liberty."

Burger rejected Douglas' "establishment" fears. If tax exemption is the first step toward establishment, he said, "the second step has been long in coming."

The basic issue centered on the following question: Is there a contradiction between federal constitutional provisions against the establishment of religion, or the use of public funds for religious purposes, and state statutes exempting church property from taxation?

In the Walz' decision, the Supreme Court ruled that there is no contradiction.

Legal Background

The US Constitution makes no reference to tax exemption.

There was no discussion of the issue in the Constitutional Convention nor in debates on the Bill of Rights.

In the Colonial and post-Revolutionary years, some churches had established status and were state-supported. This state of affairs changed with enactment of the First Amendment, which laid down no-establishment as the federal norm. This norm was adopted by the states which, however, exempted churches from tax liabilities.

No establishment, no hindrance, was the early American view of Church-state relationships.

This view, reflected in custom law, was not generally formulated in statute law until the second half of the 19th century, although specific tax exemption was provided for churches in Maryland in 1798, in Virginia in 1800, and in North Carolina in 1806.

The first major challenge to church property exemption was initiated by the Liberal League in the 1870's. It reached the point that President Grant included the recommendation in a State of the Union address in 1875, stating that church property should bear its own proportion of taxes. The plea fell on deaf ears in Congress, but there was some support for the idea at state levels. The exemption, however, continued to survive various challenges.

At the present time, 36 state constitutions contain either mandatory or permissive provisions for exemption. Statues provide for exemption in all other states.

There has been considerable litigation challenging this special exemption, but most of it focused on whether a particular property satisfied statutory requirements. Few cases before Walz focused on the strictly constitutional question, whether directly under the First Amendment or indirectly under the Fourteenth Amendment.

Objections

Objectors to the tax exempt status of churches feel that churches should share, through taxation, in the cost of the ordinary benefits of public services they enjoy, and/or that the amount of "aid" enjoyed through exemption should be proportionate to the amount of social good they do.

According to one opinion, exemption is said to weaken the independence of churches from the political system which benefits them by exemption.

In another view, exemption is said to involve the government in decisions regarding what is and what is not religion.

Unrelated Income

Taxation of the unrelated business income of churches is a different matter. In a joint statement on this subject issued in May, 1969, the US Catholic Conference and the National Council of Churches said they favored "elimination of the specific exemption of churches from taxation on income from regularly conducted commercial business activities which are unrelated to their exempt functions."

The two groups prefaced the statement with the observation:

"Under existing law many types of organizations are granted exemption from the income tax. Certain exempt organizations, including charitable, educational and some religious organizations, labor unions, business leagues, etc., are nevertheless subjected to tax upon their incomes from any unrelated business; and rents derived from debt-financed property (under leases for periods in excess of five years) are included in unrelated business taxable income.

"The tax upon unrelated business taxable income does not apply to churches, or conventions or associations of churches.

"Such exemption makes available to churches a potential advantage over taxpaying organizations engaged in commercial business activities."

Periodic agitation over the question whether churches should be taxed or should pay for services they enjoy at public expense has been fruitless.

U.S. STATISTICAL SUMMARY

(Principal source: *The Official Catholic Directory, 1974.* Comparisons are with figures reported in the previous edition.)

Catholic Population: 48,465,438; 22.95 per cent of total population; increase, 5,011.

Jurisdictions: 32 archdioceses; 132 dioceses (including Guam); 1 exarchate; 1 prelacy; 1 abbacy; the military ordinariate.

Cardinals: 11 (7 head archiepiscopal sees, 1 is an official in the Roman Curia, 3 are retired).

Archbishops: 56 (32 residential archbishops, including 7 cardinals; 3 coadjutors or auxiliaries; 16 retired, including 3 cardinals; 5 serving outside the U.S.).

Bishops: 318 (214 residential and titular bishops; 50 retired; 54 serving outside the United States).

Abbots: 61.

Priests: 56,712; decrease, 257. Includes diocesan or secular priests, 36,058 (decrease, 165); religious order priests, 20,654 (decrease, 92).

Brothers: 9,233; increase, 32.

Sisters: 139,963; decrease, 3,091.

Seminarians: 19,348; decrease, 2,432. Includes: diocesan seminarians, 11,765 (decrease, 1,160); religious order seminarians, 7,583 (decrease, 1,272).

Infant Baptisms: 916,564; decrease, 58,507.

Converts: 74,741; increase, 816.

Marriages: 406,908; decrease, 8,579.

Deaths: 415,412; decrease, 10,928.

Parishes: 18,433; increase, 49.

Seminaries, Diocesan: 109; increase, 2.

Religious Seminaries, Novitiates, Scholasticates: 293; decrease, 11.

Colleges and Universities: 258; decrease, 4. Students, 407,081; decrease, 11,002.

High Schools: 1,702; decrease, 51. Students, 911,130; decrease, 17,944.

Elementary Schools: 8,647; decrease, 185. Students, 2,717,898; decrease, 156,353.

Teachers: 174,711; decrease, 8,547. Includes: priests, 7,076 (decrease, 965); scholastics, 551 (increase, 176); brothers 3,735 (decrease, 326); sisters, 59,759 (decrease, 7,239); lay teachers, 103,590 (decrease, 193).

Public School Students in Religious Instruction Programs: 5,253,738; decrease, 271,074. Includes: high school students, 1,171,322 (decrease, 119,846); elementary school students, 4,082,416 (decrease, 151,228).

Catholic Hospitals: 798; decrease, 15. Patients treated, 27,288,276; increase, 2,042,173.

Nurses' Schools: 153; decrease, 18. Student nurses, 20,128; decrease, 550.

Homes for Invalids and Aged: 472; increase, 29. Guest facilities, 49,213; increase, 2,091.

Orphanages: 195; children, 15,494.

Children in Foster Homes: 19,301.

U.S. Catholic Jurisdictions, Hierarchy, Statistics

The organizational structure of the Catholic Church in the United States consists of 32 provinces with as many archdioceses (metropolitan sees), 131 suffragan sees (130 dioceses, 1 prelacy), two jurisdictions immediately subject to the Holy See — the Eparchy of St. Maron in Detroit for the Maronites and the Abbacy of Mary Help of Christians (Belmont, N.C.) — 1 apostolic exarchate for the Melkites, and the Military Ordinariate. With the exception of the abbacy, each of these jurisdictions is under the direction of an archbishop or bishop, called an ordinary, who has apostolic responsibility and authority for the pastoral service of the people in his care.

The structure includes the territorial episcopal conference known as the National Conference of Catholic Bishops. In and through this body, which is strictly ecclesiastical and has defined juridical authority, the bishops exercise their collegiate pastorate over the Church in the entire country (see Index).

Related to the NCCB is the United States Catholic Conference, a civil corporation and operational secretariat through which the bishops, in cooperation with other members of the Church, act on a wider-than-ecclesiastical scale for the good of the Church and society in the United States (see Index).

The representative of the Holy See to the Church in this country is the Apostolic Delegate, Archbishop Jean Jadot (see Index).

ECCLESIASTICAL PROVINCES

(Sources: *The Official Catholic Directory, 1974,* NC News Service.)

The 32 ecclesiastical provinces bear the names of archdioceses, i.e., of metropolitan sees.

Anchorage: Archdiocese of Anchorage and suffragan sees of Fairbanks, Juneau. Geographical area: Alaska.

Atlanta: Archdiocese of Atlanta (Ga.) and suffragan sees of Savannah (Ga.), Charlotte and Raleigh (N.C.), Charleston (S.C.). Geographical area: Georgia, North Carolina (except Belmont Abbacy), South Carolina.

Baltimore: Archdiocese of Baltimore (Md.) and suffragan sees of Wilmington (Del.), Arlington and Richmond (Va.), Wheeling (W. Va.). Geographical area: Maryland (except five counties), Delaware, Virginia, West Virginia.

Boston: Archdiocese of Boston (Mass.) and suffragan sees of Fall River, Springfield and Worcester (Mass.), Portland (Me.), Manchester (N.H.), Burlington (Vt.). Geographical area: Massachusetts, Maine, New Hampshire, Vermont.

Chicago: Archdiocese of Chicago and suffragan sees of Belleville, Joliet, Peoria, Rockford, Springfield. Geographical area: Illinois.

Cincinnati: Archdiocese of Cincinnati and suffragan sees of Cleveland, Columbus, Steubenville, Toledo, Youngstown. Geographical area: Ohio.

Denver: Archdiocese of Denver (Colo.) and suffragan sees of Pueblo (Colo.), Cheyenne (Wyo.). Geographical area: Colorado, Wyoming.

Detroit: Archdiocese of Detroit and suffragan sees of Gaylord, Grand Rapids, Kalamazoo, Lansing, Marquette, Saginaw. Geographical area: Michigan.

Dubuque: Archdiocese of Dubuque and suffragan sees of Davenport, Des Moines, Sioux City. Geographical area: Iowa.

Hartford: Archdiocese of Hartford (Conn.) and suffragan sees of Bridgeport and Norwich (Conn.), Providence (R.I.). Geographical area: Connecticut, Rhode Island.

Indianapolis: Archdiocese of Indianapolis and suffragan sees of Evansville, Fort Wayne-South Bend, Gary, Lafayette. Geographical area: Indiana.

Kansas City (Kans.): Archdiocese of Kansas City and suffragan sees of Dodge City, Salina, Wichita. Geographical area: Kansas.

Los Angeles: Archdiocese of Los Angeles and suffragan sees of Fresno, Monterey, San Diego. Geographical area: Southern California.

Louisville: Archdiocese of Louisville (Ky.) and suffragan sees of Covington and Owensboro (Ky.), Memphis and Nashville (Tenn.). Geographical area: Kentucky, Tennessee.

Miami: Archdiocese of Miami and suffragan sees of Orlando, St. Augustine, St. Petersburg. Geographical area: Florida.

Milwaukee: Archdiocese of Milwaukee and suffragan sees of Green Bay, La Crosse, Madison, Superior. Geographical area: Wisconsin.

Munhall (Byzantine Rite): Metropolitan See of Munhall, Pa. and Eparchies of Passaic (N.J.), Parma (Ohio).

Newark: Archdiocese of Newark and suffragan sees of Camden, Paterson, Trenton. Geographical area: New Jersey.

New Orleans: Archdiocese of New Orleans (La.) and suffragan sees of Alexandria, Baton Rouge and Lafayette (La.), Birmingham and Mobile (Ala.), Natchez-Jackson (Miss.). Geographical area; Louisiana, Alabama, Mississippi.

New York: Archdiocese of New York and suffragan sees of Albany, Brooklyn, Buffalo, Ogdensburg, Rochester, Rockville Centre, Syracuse. Geographical area: New York.

Oklahoma City: Archdiocese of Oklahoma City (Okla.) and suffragan sees of Tulsa (Okla.) and Little Rock (Ark.). Geographical area: Oklahoma, Arkansas.

Omaha: Archdiocese of Omaha and suffragan sees of Grand Island, Lincoln. Geographical area: Nebraska.

Philadelphia: Archdiocese of Philadelphia and suffragan sees of Allentown, Altoona-Johnstown, Erie, Greensburg, Harrisburg, Pittsburgh, Scranton. Geographical area: Pennsylvania.

Philadelphia (Byzantine Rite): Metropolitan See of Philadelphia (Byzantine Rite) and Eparchies of St. Nicholas of the Ukrainians in Chicago and Stamford, Conn. The jurisdiction extends to all Ukrainian Catholics in the US from the ecclesiastical province of Galicia in the Ukraine.

Portland: Archdiocese of Portland (Ore.) and suffragan sees of Baker (Ore.), Boise (Ida.), Great Falls and Helena (Mont.). Geographical area: Oregon, Idaho, Montana.

St. Louis: Archdiocese of St. Louis and suffragan sees of Jefferson City, Kansas City-St. Joseph, Springfield-Cape Girardeau. Geographical area: Missouri.

St. Paul and Minneapolis: Archdiocese of St. Paul and Minneapolis (Minn.) and suffragan sees of Crookston, Duluth, New Ulm, St. Cloud and Winona (Minn.), Bismarck and Fargo (N.D.), Rapid City and Sioux Falls

(S.D.). Geographical area: Minnesota, North Dakota, South Dakota.

San Antonio: Archdiocese of San Antonio (Tex.) and suffragan sees of Amarillo, Austin, Beaumont, Brownsville, Corpus Christi, Dallas, Fort Worth, Galveston-Houston and San Angelo (Tex.). Geographical area: Texas (except the Diocese of El Paso).

San Francisco: Archdiocese of San Francisco (Calif.) and suffragan sees of Oakland, Sacramento, Santa Rosa and Stockton (Calif.), Agaña (Guam), Honolulu (H.I.), Reno (Nev.), Salt Lake City (Utah). Geographical area: Northern California, Nevada, Utah, Hawaii, Guam.

Santa Fe: Archdiocese of Santa Fe (N.M.) and suffragan sees of Gallup (N.M.), Phoenix and Tucson (Ariz.), El Paso (Tex.). Geographical area: New Mexico, Arizona, Diocese of El Paso (Tex.).

Seattle: Archdiocese of Seattle and suffragan sees of Spokane, Yakima. Geographical area: Washington.

Washington: Archdiocese of Washington, D.C., and suffragan see of Prelacy of Virgin Islands. Geographical area: District of Columbia, five counties of Maryland, Virgin Islands.

ARCHDIOCESES, DIOCESES, ARCHBISHOPS, BISHOPS

(Sources: *The Official Catholic Directory, 1974:* NC News Service.)

Archdioceses are indicated by an asterisk.

Albany, N.Y. (1847): Edwin B. Broderick, bishop, 1969.

Former bishops: John McCloskey, 1847-64; John J. Conroy, 1865-77; Francis McNeirny, 1877-94; Thomas M. Burke, 1894-1915; Thomas F. Cusack, 1915-18; Edmund F. Gibbons, 1919-54; William A. Scully, 1954-69.

Alexandria, La. (1853): Lawrence P. Graves, bishop, 1973.

Established at Natchitoches, transferred, 1910.

Former bishops: Augustus M. Martin, 1853-75; Francis X. Leray, 1877-79, administrator, 1879-83; Anthony Durier, 1885-1904; Cornelius Van de Ven, 1904-32; D. F. Desmond, 1933-45; Charles P. Greco, 1946-73.

Allentown, Pa. (1961): Joseph McShea, bishop, 1961.

Altoona-Johnstown, Pa. (1901): James J. Hogan, bishop, 1966.

Established as Altoona, name changed, 1957.

Former bishops: Eugene A. Garvey, 1901-20; John J. McCort, 1920-36; Richard T. Guilfoyle, 1936-57; Howard J. Carroll, 1958-60; J. Carroll McCormick, 1960-66.

Amarillo, Tex. (1926): Lawrence M. DeFalco, bishop, 1963.

Former bishops; Rudolph A. Gerken, 1927-33; Robert E. Lucey, 1934-41; Laurence J. Fitzsimons, 1941-58; John L. Morkovsky, 1958-63.

Anchorage,* Alaska (1966): Joseph T. Ryan, archbishop, 1966.

Arlington, Va. (1974): Thomas J. Welsh, bishop, 1974.

Atlanta,* Ga. (1956; archdiocese, 1962): Thomas A. Donnellan, archbishop, 1968.

Former ordinaries: Francis E. Hyland, 1956-61; Paul J. Hallinan, first archbishop, 1962-68.

Austin, Tex. (1947): Vincent M. Harris, bishop, 1971.

Former bishop: Louis J. Reicher, 1947-71.

Baker, Ore. (1903): Thomas J. Connolly, bishop, 1971.

Established as Baker City, name changed, 1952.

Former bishops: Charles J. O'Reilly, 1903-18; Joseph F. McGrath, 1919-50; Francis P. Leipzig, 1950-71.

Baltimore,* Md. (1789; archdiocese, 1808): William D. Borders, archbishop, 1974. T. Austin Murphy, F. Joseph Gossman, auxiliaries.

Former ordinaries: John Carroll, 1789-1815, first archbishop; Leonard Neale, 1815-17; Ambrose Marechal, S.S., 1817-28; James Whitfield, 1828-34; Samuel Eccleston, S.S., 1834-51; Francis P. Kenrick, 1851-63; Martin J. Spalding, 1864-72; James R. Bayley, 1872-77; Cardinal James Gibbons, 1877-1921; Michael J. Curley, 1921-47; Francis P. Keough, 1947-61, Cardinal Lawrence J. Shehan, 1961-74.

Baton Rouge, La. (1961): Joseph V. Sullivan, bishop, 1974.

Former bishop: Robert E. Tracy, 1961-74.

Beaumont, Tex. (1966): Warren L. Boudreaux, bishop, 1971.

Former bishop: Vincent M. Harris, 1966-71.

Belleville, Ill. (1887): Albert R. Zuroweste, bishop, 1948.

Former bishops: John Janssen, 1888-1913; Henry Althoff, 1914-47.

Birmingham, Ala. (1969): Joseph G. Vath, bishop, 1969.

Bismarck, N. Dak. (1909): Hilary B. Hacker, bishop, 1957.

Former bishops: Vincent Wehrle, O.S.B., 1910-39; Vincent J. Ryan, 1940-51; Lambert A. Hoch, 1952-56.

Boise, Ida. (1893): Sylvester Treinen, bishop, 1962.

Former bishops: Alphonse J. Glorieux, 1893-1917; Daniel M. Gorman, 1918-27; Edward J. Kelly, 1928-56; James J. Byrne, 1956-62.

Boston,* Mass. (1808; archdiocese, 1875): Cardinal Humberto S. Medeiros, archbishop, 1970. Thomas J. Riley, Joseph F. Maguire, Lawrence J. Riley, auxiliaries.

Former ordinaries: John L. de Cheverus, 1810-23; Benedict J. Fenwick, S.J., 1825-46; John B. Fitzpatrick, 1846-66; John J. Williams, 1866-1907, first archbishop; Cardinal William O'Connell, 1907-44; Cardinal Richard Cushing, 1944-70.

Bridgeport, Conn. (1953): Walter W. Curtis, bishop, 1961.

Former bishop: Lawrence J. Shehan, 1953-61.

Brooklyn, N.Y. (1853): Francis J. Mugavero, bishop, 1968. John J. Boardman, Charles R. Mulrooney, Joseph P. Denning, John J. Snyder, auxiliaries.

Former bishops: John Loughlin, 1853-91; Charles E. McDonnell, 1892-1921; Thomas E. Molloy, 1921-56; Bryan J. McEntegart, 1957-68.

Brownsville, Tex. (1965): John J. Fitzpatrick, bishop, 1971.

Former bishops: Adolph Marx, 1965; Humberto S. Medeiros, 1966-70.

Buffalo, N.Y. (1847): Edward D. Head, bishop, 1973. Pius A. Benincasa, Bernard J. McLaughlin, auxiliaries.

Former bishops: John Timon, C.M., 1847-67; Stephen V. Ryan, C.M., 1868-96; James E. Quigley, 1897-1903; Charles H. Colton, 1903-15; Dennis J. Dougherty, 1915-18; William Turner, 1919-36; John A. Duffy, 1937-44; John F. O'Hara, C.S.C., 1945-51; Joseph A. Burke, 1952-62; James McNulty, 1963-72.

Burlington, Vt. (1853): John A. Marshall, bishop, 1972.

Former bishops: Louis De Goesbriand, 1853-99; John S. Michaud, 1899-1908; Joseph J. Rice, 1910-38; Matthew F. Brady, 1938-44; Edward F. Ryan, 1945-56; Robert F. Joyce, 1957-71.

Camden, N.J. (1937): George H. Guilfoyle, bishop, 1968. James L. Schad, auxiliary.

Former bishops: Bartholomew J. Eustace, 1938-56; Justin J. McCarthy, 1957-59; Celestine J. Damiano, 1960-67.

Charleston, S.C. (1820): Ernest L. Unterkoefler, bishop, 1964.

Former bishops: John England, 1820-42; Ignatius W. Reynolds, 1844-55; Patrick N. Lynch, 1858-82; Henry P. Northrop, 1883-1916; William T. Russell, 1917-27; Emmet M. Walsh, 1927-49; John J. Russell, 1950-58; Paul J. Hallinan, 1958-62; Francis F. Reh, 1962-64.

Charlotte, N.C. (1971): Michael J. Begley, bishop, 1972.

Cheyenne, Wyo. (1887): Hubert M. Newell, bishop, 1951.

Former bishops: Maurice F. Burke, 1887-93; Thomas M. Lenihan, 1897-1901; James J. Keane, 1902-11; Patrick A. McGovern, 1912-51.

Chicago,* Ill. (1843; archdiocese, 1880): Cardinal John Cody, archbishop, 1965; Thomas J. Grady, William E. McManus, Alfred L. Abramowicz, Nevin Hayes, O. Carm., auxiliaries.

Former ordinaries: William Quarter, 1844-48; James O. Van de Velde, S.J., 1849-53; Anthony O'Regan, 1854-58; James Duggan, 1859-70; Thomas P. Foley, administrator, 1870-79; Patrick A. Feehan, 1880-1902, first archbishop; James E. Quigley, 1903-15; Cardinal George Mundelein, 1915-39; Cardinal Samuel Stritch, 1939-58; Cardinal Albert Meyer, 1958-65.

Cincinnati,* Ohio (1821; archdiocese, 1850): Joseph L. Bernardin, archbishop, 1972. Nicholas Elko, auxiliary.

Former ordinaries: Edward D. Fenwick, O.P., 1822-32; John B. Purcell, 1833-83, first archbishop; William H. Elder, 1883-1904; Henry Moeller, 1904-1925; John T. McNicholas, O.P., 1925-50; Karl J. Alter, 1950-69; Paul F. Leibold, 1969-72.

Cleveland, Ohio (1847): James A. Hickey, bishop, 1974. William M. Cosgrove, auxiliary.

Former bishops: L. Amadeus Rappe, 1847-70; Richard Gilmour, 1872-91; Ignatius F. Horstmann, 1892-1908; John P. Farrelly, 1909-21; Joseph Schrembs, 1921-45; Edward F. Hoban, 1945-66; Clarence G. Issenmann, 1966-74.

Columbus, Ohio (1868): Edward J. Herrmann, bishop, 1973. Edward G. Hettinger, auxiliary.

Former bishops: Sylvester H. Rosecrans, 1868-78; John A. Watterson, 1880-99; Henry Moeller, 1900-03; James J. Hartley, 1904-44; Michael J. Ready, 1944-57; Clarence Issenmann, 1957-64; John J. Carberry, 1965-68; Clarence E. Elwell, 1968-73.

Corpus Christi, Tex. (1912): Thomas J. Drury, bishop, 1965.

Former bishops; Paul J. Nussbaum, C.P., 1913-20; Emmanuel B. Ledvina, 1921-49; Mariano S. Garriga, 1949-65.

Covington, Ky. (1853): Richard Ackerman, C.S.Sp., bishop, 1960.

Former bishops: George A. Carrell, S.J., 1853-68; Augustus M. Toebbe, 1870-84; Camillus P. Maes, 1885-1914; Ferdinand Brossart, 1916-23; Francis W. Howard, 1923-44; William T. Mulloy, 1945-59.

Crookston, Minn. (1909): Kenneth J. Povish, bishop, 1970.

Former bishops: Timothy Corbett, 1910-38; John H. Peschges, 1938-44; Francis J. Schenk, 1945-60; Laurence A. Glenn, 1960-70.

Dallas, Tex. (1890): Thomas Tschoepe, bishop, 1969.

Former bishops: Thomas F. Brennan, 1891-92; Edward J. Dunne, 1893-1910; Joseph P. Lynch, 1911-54; Thomas K. Gorman, 1954-69.

Davenport, Ia. (1881): Gerald F. O'Keefe, bishop, 1966.

Former bishops: John McMullen, 1881-83; Henry Cosgrove, 1884-1906; James Davis, 1906-26; Henry P. Rohlman, 1927-44; Ralph L. Hayes, 1944-66.

Denver,* Colo. (1887; archdiocese, 1941): James V. Casey, archbishop, 1967. George R. Evans, Richard C. Hanifen, auxiliaries.

Former ordinaries: Joseph P. Machebeuf, 1887-89; Nicholas C. Matz, 1889-1917; J. Henry Tihen, 1917-31; Urban J. Vehr, 1931-67, first archbishop.

Des Moines, Ia. (1911): Maurice J. Dingman, bishop, 1968.

Former bishops: Austin Dowling, 1912-19; Thomas W. Drumm, 1919-33; Gerald T. Bergan, 1934-48; Edward C. Daly, O.P., 1948-64; George J. Biskup, 1965-67.

Detroit,* Mich. (1833; archdiocese, 1937): Cardinal John F. Dearden, archbishop, 1958. Thomas J. Gumbleton, Walter J. Schoenherr, Arthur H. Krawczak, Joseph L. Imesch, auxiliaries.

Former ordinaries: Frederic Rese, 1833-71; Peter P. Lefevere, administrator, 1841-69; Caspar H. Borgess, 1871-88; John S. Foley, 1888-1918; Michael J. Gallagher, 1918-37; Cardinal Edward Mooney, 1937-58, first archbishop.

Dodge City, Kans. (1951): Marion F. Forst, bishop, 1960.

Former bishop: John B. Franz, 1951-59.

Dubuque,* Iowa (1837; archdiocese, 1893): James J. Byrne, archbishop, 1962. Francis J. Dunn, auxiliary.

Former ordinaries: Mathias Loras, 1837-58; Clement Smyth, O.C.S.O., 1858-65; John Hennessy, 1866-1900, first archbishop; John J. Keane, 1900-11; James J. Keane, 1911-29; Francis J. Beckman, 1930-46; Henry P. Rohlman, 1946-54; Leo Binz, 1954-61.

Duluth, Minn. (1889): Paul F. Anderson, bishop, 1969.

Former bishops: James McGolrick, 1889-1918; John T. McNicholas, O.P., 1918-25;

Thomas A. Welch, 1926-59; Francis J. Schenk, 1960-69.

El Paso, Tex. (1914): Sidney M. Metzger, bishop, 1942.

Former bishop: Anthony J. Schuler, S.J., 1915-42.

Erie, Pa. (1853): Alfred M. Watson, bishop, 1969.

Former bishops: Michael O'Connor, 1853-54; Josue M. Young, 1854-66; Tobias Mullen, 1868-99; John E. Fitzmaurice, 1899-1920; John M. Gannon, 1920-66; John F. Whealon, 1966-69.

Evansville, Ind. (1944): Francis Raymond Shea, bishop, 1970.

Former bishops: Henry J. Grimmelsman, 1944-65; Paul F. Leibold, 1966-69.

Fairbanks, Alaska (1962): Robert L. Whelan, S.J., bishop, 1968.

Former bishop: Francis D. Gleeson, S.J., 1948-68.

Fall River, Mass. (1904): Daniel A. Cronin, bishop, 1970. James J. Gerrard, auxiliary.

Former bishops: William Stang, 1904-07; Daniel F. Feehan, 1907-34; James E. Cassidy, 1934-51; James L. Connolly, 1951-70.

Fargo, N. Dak. (1889): Justin A. Driscoll, bishop, 1970.

Established at Jamestown, transferred, 1897.

Former bishops: John Shanley, 1889-1909; James O'Reilly, 1910-34; Aloysius J. Muench, 1935-59; Leo F. Dworschak, 1960-70.

Fort Wayne-South Bend, Ind. (1857): Leo A. Pursley, bishop, 1957. Joseph R. Crowley, auxiliary.

Established as Fort Wayne, name changed, 1960.

Former bishops: John H. Luers, 1858-71; Joseph Dwenger, C.Pp. S., 1872-93; Joseph Rademacher, 1893-1900; Herman J. Alerding, 1900-24; John F. Noll, 1925-56.

Fort Worth, Tex. (1969): John J. Cassata, bishop, 1969.

Fresno, Calif. (1967): Hugh A. Donohoe, bishop, 1969.

Former bishop: Timothy Manning, 1967-69.

Gallup, N. Mex. (1939): Jerome J. Hastrich, bishop, 1969.

Former bishop: Bernard T. Espelage, O.F.M., 1940-69.

Galveston-Houston, Tex. (1847): Wendelin J. Nold, bishop, 1950. John L. Morkovsky, coadjutor, apostolic administrator.

Established as Galveston, name changed, 1959.

Former bishops: John M. Odin, C.M., 1847-61; Claude M. Dubuis, 1862-92; Nicholas A. Gallagher, 1892-1918; Christopher E. Byrne, 1918-50.

Gary, Ind. (1957): Andrew G. Grutka, bishop, 1957.

Gaylord, Mich. (1971): Edmund C. Szoka, bishop, 1971.

Grand Island, Neb. (1912): John J. Sullivan, bishop, 1972.

Established at Kearney, transferred, 1917.

Former bishops: James A. Duffy, 1913-31; Stanislaus V. Bona, 1932-44; Edward J. Hunkeler, 1945-51; John L. Paschang, 1951-72.

Grand Rapids, Mich. (1882): Joseph Breitenbeck, bishop, 1969. Joseph C. McKinney, auxiliary.

Former bishops: Henry J. Richter, 1883-1916; Michael J. Gallagher, 1916-18; Edward D. Kelly, 1919-26; Joseph G. Pinten, 1926-40; Joseph C. Plagens, 1941-43; Francis J. Haas, 1943-53; Allen J. Babcock, 1954-69.

Great Falls, Mont. (1904): Eldon B. Schuster, bishop, 1968.

Former bishops: Mathias C. Lenihan, 1904-30; Edwin V. O'Hara, 1930-39; William J. Condon, 1939-67.

Green Bay, Wis. (1868): Aloysius J. Wycislo, bishop, 1968. John B. Grellinger, Mark Schmitt, auxiliaries.

Former bishops: Joseph Melcher, 1868-73; Francis X. Krautbauer, 1875-85; Frederick X. Katzer, 1886-91; Sebastian G. Messmer, 1892-1903; Joseph J. Fox, 1904-14; Paul P. Rhode, 1915-45; Stanislaus V. Bona, 1945-67.

Greensburg, Pa. (1951): William G. Connare, bishop, 1960.

Former bishop: Hugh L. Lamb, 1951-59.

Harrisburg, Pa. (1868): Joseph T. Daley, bishop, 1971.

Former bishops: Jeremiah F. Shanahan, 1868-86; Thomas McGovern, 1888-98; John W. Shanahan,1899-1916; Philip R. McDevitt, 1916-35; George L. Leech, 1935-71.

Hartford,* Conn. (1843; archdiocese, 1953): John F. Whealon, archbishop, 1969. John F. Hackett, Joseph F. Donnelly, auxiliaries.

Former ordinaries: William Tyler, 1844-49; Bernard O'Reilly, 1850-56; F. P. MacFarland, 1858-74; Thomas Galberry, O.S.A., 1876-78; Lawrence S. McMahon, 1879-93; Michael Tierney, 1894-1908; John J. Nilan, 1910-34; Maurice F. McAuliffe, 1934-44; Henry J. O'Brien, 1945-68, first archbishop.

Helena, Mont. (1884): Raymond Hunthausen, bishop, 1962.

Former bishops: John B. Brondel, 1884-1903; John P. Carroll, 1904-25; George J. Finnigan, C.S.C., 1927-32; Ralph L. Hayes, 1933-35; Joseph M. Gilmore, 1936-62.

Honolulu, H.I. (1941); John J. Scanlan, bishop, 1968.

Former bishop: James J. Sweeney, 1941-68.

Indianapolis,* Ind. (1834; archdiocese, 1944); George J. Biskup, archbishop, 1970.

Established at Vincennes, transferred, 1898.

Former ordinaries: Simon G. Bruté, 1834-39; Celestine de la Hailandiere, 1839-47; John S. Bazin, 1847-48; Maurice de St. Palais, 1849-77; Francis S. Chatard, 1878-1918; Joseph Chartrand, 1918-33; Joseph E. Ritter, 1934-46, first archbishop; Paul C. Schulte, 1946-70.

Jefferson City, Mo. (1956): Michael F. McAuliffe, bishop, 1969.

Former bishop: Joseph Marling, C.Pp.S., 1956-69.

Joliet, Ill. (1948): Romeo Blanchette, bishop, 1966. Raymond J. Vonesh, auxiliary.

Former bishop: Martin D. McNamara, 1949-66.

Juneau, Alaska (1951): Francis T. Hurley, bishop, 1971.

Former bishops: Dermot O'Flanagan, 1951-68; Joseph T. Ryan, administrator, 1968-71.

Kalamazoo, Mich. (1971): Paul V. Donovan, bishop, 1971.

Kansas City,* Kans. (1877; archdiocese, 1952): Ignatius J. Strecker, archbishop, 1969.

Established as vicariate apostolic, 1850, became Diocese of Leavenworth, 1877, transferred to Kansas City 1947.

Former ordinaries: J. B. Miege, vicar apostolic, 1851-74; Louis M. Fink, O.S.B., vicar apostolic, 1874-77, first bishop, 1877-1904; Thomas F. Lillis, 1904-10; John Ward, 1910-29; Francis Johannes, 1929-37; Paul C. Schulte, 1937-46; George J. Donnelly, 1946-50; Edward Hunkeler, 1951-69, first archbishop.

Kansas City-St. Joseph, Mo. (Kansas City, 1880; St. Joseph, 1868; united 1956): Charles H. Helmsing, bishop, 1962.

Former bishops (Kansas City): John J. Hogan, 1880-1913; Thomas F. Lillis, 1913-38; Edwin V. O'Hara, 1939-56; John P. Cody, 1956-61.

Former bishops (St. Joseph): John J. Hogan, 1868-80, administrator, 1880-93; Maurice F. Burke, 1893-1923; Francis Gilfillan, 1923-33; Charles H. Le Blond, 1933-56.

La Crosse, Wis. (1868): Frederick W. Freking, bishop, 1965.

Former bishops: Michael Heiss, 1868-80; Kilian C. Flasch, 1881-91; James Schwebach, 1892-1921; Alexander J. McGavick, 1921-48; John P. Treacy, 1948-64.

Lafayette, Ind. (1944): Raymond J. Gallagher, bishop, 1965.

Former bishops: John G. Bennett, 1944-57; John J. Carberry, 1957-65.

Lafayette, La. (1918): Gerard L. Frey, bishop, 1973.

Former bishops: Jules B. Jeanmard, 1918-56; Maurice Schexnayder, 1956-72.

Lansing, Mich. (1937): Alexander Zaleski, bishop, 1965. James Sullivan, auxiliary.

Former bishop: Joseph H. Albers, 1937-65.

Lincoln, Neb. (1887): Glennon P. Flavin, bishop, 1967.

Former bishops: Thomas Bonacum, 1887-1911; J. Henry Tihen, 1911-17; Charles J. O'Reilly, 1918-23; Francis J. Beckman, 1924-30; Louis B. Kucera, 1930-57; James V. Casey, 1957-67.

Little Rock, Ark. (1843): Andrew J. McDonald, bishop, 1972.

Former bishops: Andrew Byrne, 1844-62;

Edward Fitzgerald, 1867-1907; John Morris, 1907-46; Albert L. Fletcher, 1946-72.

Los Angeles,* Calif. (1840; archdiocese, 1936): Cardinal Timothy Manning, archbishop, 1970. John J. Ward, William R. Johnson, Juan A. Arzube, auxiliaries.

Former ordinaries: Francisco Garcia Diego y Moreno, O.F.M., 1840-46; Joseph S. Alemany, O.P., 1850-53; Thaddeus Amat, C.M., 1854-78; Francis Mora, 1878-96; George T. Montgomery, 1896-1903; Thomas J. Conaty, 1903-15; John J. Cantwell, 1917-47, first archbishop; Cardinal James McIntyre, 1948-70.

Louisville,* Ky. (1808; arc]diocese, 1937): Thomas J. McDonough, archbishop, 1967. Charles G. Maloney, auxiliary.

Established at Bardstown, transferred, 1841.

Former ordinaries: Benedict J. Flaget, S.S. 1810-32; John B. David, S.S., 1832-33; Benedict J. Flaget, S.S., 1833-50; Martin J. Spalding, 1850-64; Peter J. Lavialle, 1865-67; William G. McCloskey, 1868-1909; Denis O'Donaghue, 1910-24; John A. Floersh, 1924-67, first archbishop.

Madison, Wis. (1946): Cletus F. O'Donnell, bishop, 1967.

Former bishop: William P. O'Connor, 1946-67.

Manchester, N.H. (1884): Vacant as of Aug. 20, 1974.

Former bishops: Denis M. Bradley, 1884-1903; John B. Delany, 1904-06; George A. Guertin, 1907-32; John B. Peterson, 1932-44; Matthew F. Brady, 1944-59; Ernest J. Primeau, 1960-74.

Marquette, Mich. (1857): Charles A. Salatka, bishop, 1968.

Former bishops: Frederic Baraga, 1857-68; Ignatius Mrak, 1869-78; John Vertin, 1879-99; Frederick Eis, 1899-1922; Paul J. Nussbaum, C. P., 1922-35; Joseph C. Plagens, 1935-40; Francis Magner, 1941-47; Thomas L. Noa, 1947-68.

Memphis, Tenn. (1970): Carroll T. Dozier, bishop, 1971.

Miami,* Fla. (1958; archdiocese, 1968): Coleman F. Carroll, bishop, 1958, first archbishop, 1968. Rene H. Gracida, auxiliary.

Milwaukee,* Wis. (1843; archdiocese, 1875): William E. Cousins, archbishop, 1959. Leo J. Brust, auxiliary.

Former ordinaries: John M. Henni, 1844-81, first archbishop; Michael Heiss, 1881-90; Frederick X. Katzer, 1891-1903; Sebastian G. Messmer, 1903-30; Samuel A. Stritch, 1930-39; Moses E. Kiley, 1940-53; Albert G. Meyer, 1953-58.

Mobile, Ala. (1829): John L. May, bishop, 1969.

Former bishops: Michael Portier, 1829-59; John Quinlan, 1859-83; Dominic Manucy, 1884; Jeremiah O'Sullivan, 1885-96; Edward P. Allen, 1897-1926; Thomas J. Toolen, 1927-69.

Monterey in California (1967): Harry A. Clinch, bishop, 1967.

Formerly Monterey-Fresno, 1922.

Former bishops (Monterey-Fresno): John J. Cantwell, administrator, 1922-24; John B. MacGinley, first bishop, 1924-32; Philip G. Sher, 1933-53; Aloysius J. Willinger, 1953-67.

Munhall,* Pa. (Byzantine Rite) (1924; metropolitan, 1969): Stephen J. Kocisko, eparch, 1968, first metropolitan, 1969. John Bilock, auxiliary.

Former ordinaries: Basil Takach 1924-48; Daniel Ivancho, 1948-54; Nicholas T. Elko, 1955-67.

Nashville, Tenn. (1837): Joseph A. Durick, bishop, 1969.

Former bishops: Richard P. Miles, O.P., 1838-60; James Whelan, O.P., 1860-64; Patrick A. Feehan, 1865-80; Joseph Rademacher, 1883-93; Thomas S. Byrne, 1894-1923; Alphonse J. Smith, 1924-35; William L. Adrian, 1936-69.

Natchez-Jackson, Miss. (1837): Joseph B. Brunini, bishop, 1968. Joseph Howze, auxiliary.

Former bishops: John J. Chanche, S.S., 1841-52; James Van de Velde, S.J., 1853-55; William H. Elder, 1857-80; Francis A. Janssens, 1881-88; Thomas Heslin, 1889-1911; John E. Gunn, S.M., 1911-24; Richard O. Gerow, 1924-67.

Newark,* N.J. (1853; archdiocese, 1937): Peter L. Gerety, archbishop, 1974. John J. Dougherty, Joseph A. Costello, auxiliaries.

Former ordinaries: James R. Bayley, 1853-72; Michael A. Corrigan, 1873-80; Winand M. Wigger, 1881-1901; John J. O'Connor, 1901-27; Thomas J. Walsh, 1928-52, first archbishop; Thomas A. Boland, 1953-74.

New Orleans,* La. (1793; archdiocese, 1850): Philip M. Hannan, archbishop, 1965. L. Abel Caillouet, Harold R. Perry, S. V. D., auxiliaries.

Former ordinaries: Luis Penalver y Cardenas, 1793-1801; John Carroll, administrator, 1809-15; W. Louis Dubourg, S.S., 1815-25; Joseph Rosati, C.M., administrator, 1826-29; Leo De Neckere, C.M., 1829-33; Anthony Blanc, 1835-60, first archbishop; Jean Marie Odin, C.M., 1861-70; Napoleon J. Perche, 1870-83; Francis X. Leray, 1883-87; Francis A. Janssens, 1888-97; Placide L. Chapelle, 1897-1905; James H. Blenk, S.M., 1906-17; John W. Shaw, 1918-34; Joseph F. Rummel, 1935-64; John P. Cody, 1964-65.

New Ulm, Minn. (1957): Alphonse J. Schladweiler, bishop, 1958.

New York,* N.Y. (1808; archdiocese, 1850): Cardinal Terence J. Cooke, archbishop, 1968. John J. Maguire, coadjutor archbishop, 1965. Joseph M. Pernicone, Edward E. Swanstrom, Patrick V. Ahern, James P. Mahoney, Anthony F. Mestice, auxiliaries.

Former ordinaries: Richard L. Concanen, O.P., 1808-10; John Connolly, O.P., 1814-25; John Dubois, S.S., 1826-42; John J. Hughes,

1842-64, first archbishop; Cardinal John Mc-Closkey, 1864-85; Michael A. Corrigan, 1885-1902; Cardinal John Farley, 1902-18; Cardinal Patrick Hayes, 1919-38; Cardinal Francis Spellman, 1939-67.

Norwich, Conn. (1953): Vincent J. Hines, bishop, 1960.

Former bishop: Bernard J. Flanagan, 1953-59.

Oakland, Calif. (1962): Floyd L. Begin, bishop, 1962.

Ogdensburg, N. Y. (1872): Stanislaus Brzana, bishop, 1968.

Former bishops: Edgar P. Wadhams, 1872-91; Henry Gabriels, 1892-1921; Joseph H. Conroy, 1921-39; Francis J. Monaghan, 1939-42; Bryan J. McEntegart, 1943-53; Walter P. Kellenberg, 1954-57; James J. Navagh, 1957-63; Leo R. Smith, 1963; Thomas A. Donnellan, 1964-68.

Oklahoma City,* Okla. (1905; archdiocese, 1972); John R. Quinn, 1971, first archbishop 1972.

Former bishops: Theophile Meerschaert, 1905-24; Francis C. Kelley, 1924-48; Eugene J. McGuinness, 1948-57; Victor J. Reed, 1958-71.

Omaha,* Nebr. (1885; archdiocese, 1945): Daniel E. Sheehan, archbishop, 1969.

Former ordinaries: James O'Gorman, O.C.S.O., 1859-74, vicar apostolic; James O'Connor, vicar apostolic, 1876-85, first bishop, 1885-90; Richard Scannell, 1891-1916; Jeremiah J. Harty, 1916-27; Francis Beckman, administrator, 1926-28; Joseph F. Rummel, 1928-35; James H. Ryan, 1935-47, first archbishop; Gerald T. Bergan, 1948-69.

Orlando, Fla. (1968): Vacant as of Aug. 20, 1974.

Former bishop: William Borders, 1968-74.

Owensboro, Ky. (1937): Henry J. Soenneker, bishop, 1961.

Former bishop: Francis R. Cotton, 1938-60.

Parma, Ohio (Byzantine Rite) (1969): Emil Mihalik, eparch, 1969.

Passaic, N.J. (Byzantine Rite) (1963): Michael J. Dudick, eparch, 1968.

Former bishop: Stephen Kocisko, 1963-68.

Paterson, N. J. (1937): Lawrence B. Casey, bishop, 1966.

Former bishops: Thomas H. McLaughlin, 1937-47; Thomas A. Boland, 1947-52; James A. McNulty, 1953-63; James J. Navagh, 1963-65.

Peoria, Ill. (1877): Edward W. O'Rourke, bishop, 1971.

Former bishops: John L. Spalding, 1877-1908; Edmund M. Dunne, 1909-29; Joseph H. Schlarman, 1930-51; William E. Cousins, 1952-58; John B. Franz, 1959-71.

Philadelphia,* Pa. (1808; archdiocese, 1875): Cardinal John Krol, archbishop, 1961. Gerald V. McDevitt, John J. Graham, Martin Lohmuller, auxiliaries.

Former ordinaries: Michael Egan,

O. F. M., 1810-14; Henry Conwell, 1820-42; Francis P. Kenrick, 1842-51; John N. Neumann, C.SS.R., 1852-60; James F. Wood, 1860-83, first archbishop; Patrick J. Ryan, 1884-1911; Edmond F. Prendergast, 1911-18; Cardinal Dennis Dougherty, 1918-51; Cardinal John O'Hara, C.S.C., 1951-60.

Philadelphia,* Pa. (Byzantine Rite) (1924; metropolitan, 1958): Ambrose Senyshyn, O.S.B.M., metropolitan, 1961. Basil Losten, auxiliary.

Former ordinaries: Stephen Ortynsky, O.S.B.M., 1907-16; Constantine Bohachevsky, 1924-61.

Phoenix, Ariz. (1969): Edward A. McCarthy, bishop, 1969.

Pittsburgh, Pa. (1843): Vincent M. Leonard, bishop, 1969. John B. McDowell, Anthony G. Bosco, auxiliaries.

Former bishops: Michael O'Connor, 1843-53, 1854-60; Michael Domenec, C.M., 1860-76; J. Tuigg, 1876-89; Richard Phelan, 1889-1904; J. F. Regis Canevin, 1904-20; Hugh C. Boyle, 1921-55; John F. Dearden, 1950-58; John J. Wright, 1959-69.

Portland, Me. (1853): Vacant as of Aug. 20, 1974. Edward C. O'Leary, auxiliary.

Former bishops: David W. Bacon, 1855-74; James A. Healy, 1875-1900; William H. O'Connell, 1901-06; Louis S. Walsh, 1906-24; John G. Murray, 1925-31; Joseph E. McCarthy, 1932-55; Daniel J. Feeney, 1955-69; Peter L. Gerety, 1969-74.

Portland,* Ore. (1846): Cornelius M. Power, archbishop, 1974.

Established as Oregon City, name changed, 1928.

Former ordinaries: Francis N. Blanchet, 1846-80 vicar apostolic, first archbishop; Charles J. Seghers, 1880-84; William H. Gross, C.SS.R., 1885-98; Alexander Christie, 1899-1925; Edward D. Howard, 1926-66; Robert J. Dwyer, 1966-74.

Providence, R. I. (1872): Louis E. Gelineau, bishop, 1972. Kenneth A. Angell, auxiliary.

Former bishops: Thomas F. Hendricken, 1872-86; Matthew Harkins, 1887-1921; William A. Hickey, 1921-33; Francis P. Keough, 1934-47; Russell J. McVinney, 1948-71.

Pueblo, Colo. (1941): Charles A. Buswell, bishop, 1959.

Former bishop: Joseph C. Willging, 1942-59.

Raleigh, N. C. (1924): Vincent S. Waters, bishop, 1945. George E. Lynch, auxiliary.

Former bishops: William J. Hafey, 1925-37; Eugene J. McGuinness, 1937-44.

Rapid City, S. Dak. (1902): Harold J. Dimmerling, bishop, 1969.

Established at Lead, transferred, 1920.

Former bishops: John Stariha, 1902-09; Joseph F. Busch, 1910-15; John J. Lawler, 1916-48; William T. McCarty, C.SS.R., 1948-69.

Reno, Nev. (1931): Joseph Green, bishop, 1967.

Former bishops: Thomas K. Gorman,

1931-52; Robert J. Dwyer, 1952-66.
Richmond, Va. (1820): Walter F. Sullivan, bishop, 1974. J. Louis Flaherty, auxiliary.
Former bishops: Patrick Kelly, 1820-22; Richard V. Whelan, 1841-50; John McGill, 1850-72; James Gibbons, 1872-77; John J. Keane, 1878-88; Augustine Van de Vyver, 1889-1911; Denis J. O'Connell, 1912-26; Andrew J. Brennan, 1926-45; Peter L. Ireton, 1945-58; John J. Russell, 1958-72.
Rochester, N. Y. (1868): Joseph L. Hogan, bishop, 1969. Dennis W. Hickey, John E. McCafferty, auxiliaries.
Former bishops: Bernard J. McQuaid, 1868-1909; Thomas F. Hickey, 1909-28; John F. O'Hern, 1929-33; Edward F. Mooney, 1933-37; James E. Kearney, 1937-66; Fulton J. Sheen, 1966-69.
Rockford, Ill. (1908): Arthur J. O'Neill, bishop, 1968.
Former bishops: Peter J. Muldoon, 1908-27; Edward F. Hoban, 1928-42; John J. Boylan, 1943-53; Raymond P. Hillinger, 1953-56; Loras T. Lane, 1956-68.
Rockville Centre, N. Y. (1957): Walter P. Kellenberg, bishop, 1957. Vincent J. Baldwin, John R. McGann, auxiliaries.
Sacramento, Calif. (1886): Alden J. Bell, bishop, 1962. John S. Cummins, auxiliary.
Former bishops: Patrick Manogue, 1886-95; Thomas Grace, 1896-1921; Patrick J. Keane, 1922-28; Robert J. Armstrong, 1929-57; Joseph T. McGucken, 1957-62.
Saginaw, Mich. (1938): Francis F. Reh, bishop, 1969.
Former bishops: William F. Murphy, 1938-50; Stephen S. Woznicki, 1950-68.
St. Augustine, Fla. (1870): Paul F. Tanner, bishop, 1968.
Former bishops: Augustin Verot, S.S., 1870-76; John Moore, 1877-1901; William J. Kenny, 1902-13; Michael J. Curley, 1914-21; Patrick J. Barry, 1922-40; Joseph P. Hurley, 1940-67.
St. Cloud, Minn. (1889): George H. Speltz, bishop, 1968. James S. Rausch, auxiliary.
Former bishops: Otto Zardetti, 1889-94; Martin Marty, O.S.B., 1895-96; James Trobec, 1897-1914; Joseph F. Busch, 1915-53; Peter Bartholome, 1953-68.
St. Louis,* Mo. (1826; archdiocese, 1847): Cardinal John J. Carberry, archbishop, 1968. George J. Gottwald, Joseph A. McNicholas, Charles R. Koester, Edward T. O'Meara, auxiliaries.
Former ordinaries: Joseph Rosati, C.M., 1827-43; Peter R. Kenrick, 1843-95, first archbishop; John J. Kain, 1895-1903; Cardinal John Glennon, 1903-46; Cardinal Joseph Ritter, 1946-67.
St. Maron of Detroit (Maronite Rite) (1966; eparchy, 1972): Francis Zayek, exarch, 1966, first eparch, 1972.
St. Nicholas in Chicago (Byzantine Rite Eparchy of St. Nicholas of the Ukrainians) (1961): Jaroslav Gabro, eparch, 1961.

St. Paul and Minneapolis,* Minn. (1850; archdiocese, 1888): Leo Binz, archbishop, 1962. Leo C. Byrne, coadjutor archbishop, 1967. Raymond A. Lucker, ohn R. Roach, auxiliaries.
Former ordinaries: Joseph Cretin, 1851-57; Thomas L. Grace, O.P., 1859-84; John Ireland, 1884-1918, first archbishop; Austin Dowling, 1919-30; John G. Murray, 1931-56; William O. Brady, 1956-61.
St. Petersburg, Fla. (1968): Charles McLaughlin, bishop, 1968.
Salina, Kans. (1887): Cyril J. Vogel, bishop, 1965.
Established at Concordia, transferred, 1944.
Former bishops: Richard Scannell, 1887-91; John J. Hennessy, administrator, 1891-98; John F. Cunningham, 1898-1919; Francis J. Tief, 1921-38; Frank A. Thill, 1938-57; Frederick W. Freking, 1957-64.
Salt Lake City, Utah (1891): J. Lennox Federal, bishop, 1960.
Former bishops: Lawrence Scanlan, 1891-1915; Joseph S. Glass, C.M., 1915-26; John J. Mitty, 1926-32; James E. Kearney, 1932-37; Duane G. Hunt, 1937-60.
San Angelo, Tex. (1961): Stephen A. Leven, bishop, 1969.
Former bishops: Thomas J. Drury, 1962-65; Thomas Tschoepe, 1966-69.
San Antonio,* Tex. (1874; archdiocese, 1926): Francis Furey, archbishop, 1969. Patrick Flores, auxiliary.
Former ordinaries: Anthony D. Pellicer, 1874-80; John C. Neraz, 1881-94; John A. Forest, 1895-1911; John W. Shaw, 1911-18; Arthur Jerome Drossaerts, 1918-40, first archbishop; Robert E. Lucey, 1941-69.
San Diego, Calif. (1936): Leo T. Maher, bishop, 1969. Gilbert Espinoza Chavez, auxiliary.
Former bishops: Charles F. Buddy, 1936-66; Francis J. Furey, 1966-69.
San Francisco,* Calif. (1853): Joseph T. McGucken, archbishop, 1962. William J. McDonald, Norman F. McFarland, auxiliaries.
Former ordinaries: Joseph S. Alemany, O.P., 1853-84; Patrick W. Riordan, 1884-1914; Edward J. Hanna, 1915-35; John Mitty, 1935-61.
Santa Fe,* N. Mex. (1850; archdiocese, 1875): Robert Sanchez, archbishop, 1974.
Former ordinaries: John B. Lamy, 1850-85, first archbishop; John B. Salpointe, 1885-94; Placide L. Chapelle, 1894-97; Peter Bourgade, 1899-1908; John B. Pitaval, 1909-18; Albert T. Daeger, O.F.M., 1919-32; Rudolph A. Gerken, 1933-43; Edwin V. Byrne, 1943-63; James P. Davis, 1964-74.
Santa Rosa, Calif. (1962): Mark J. Hurley, bishop, 1969.
Former bishop: Leo T. Maher, 1962-69.
Savannah, Ga. (1850): Raymond Lessard, bishop, 1973.
Former bishops: Francis X. Gartland,

1850-54; John Barry, 1857-59; Augustin Verot, S.S., 1861-70; Ignatius Persico, O.F.M. Cap., 1870-72; William H. Gross, C.SS.R., 1873-85; Thomas A. Becker, 1886-99; Benjamin J. Keiley, 1900-22; Michael Keyes, S.M., 1922-35; Gerald P. O'Hara, 1935-59; Thomas J. McDonough, 1960-67; Gerard L. Frey, 1967-72.

Scranton, Pa. (1868): J. Carroll McCormick, bishop, 1966.

Former bishops: William O'Hara, 1868-99; Michael J. Hoban, 1899-1926; Thomas C. O'Reilly, 1928-38; William J. Hafey, 1938-54; Jerome D. Hannan, 1954-65.

Seattle,* Wash. (1850; archdiocese, 1951): Thomas A. Connolly, bishop, 1950, first archbishop, 1951.

Established as Nesqually, name changed, 1907.

Former ordinaries; Augustin M. Blanchet, 1850-79; Aegidius Junger, 1879-95; Edward J. O'Dea, 1896-1932; Gerald Shaughnessy, S.M., 1933-50.

Sioux City, Ia. (1902): Frank Greteman, bishop, 1970.

Former bishops: Philip J. Garrigan, 1902-19; Edmond Heelan, 1919-48; Joseph M. Mueller, 1948-70.

Sioux Falls, S. Dak. (1889): Lambert A. Hoch, bishop, 1956.

Former bishops: Martin Marty, O.S.B., 1889-94; Thomas O'Gorman, 1896-1921; Bernard J. Mahoney, 1922-39; William O. Brady, 1939-56.

Spokane, Wash. (1913): Bernard J. Topel, bishop, 1955.

Former bishops: Augustine F. Schinner, 1914-25; Charles D. White, 1927-55.

Springfield-Cape Girardeau, Mo. (1956): Bernard F. Law, bishop, 1973.

Former bishops:: Charles Helmsing, 1956-62; Ignatius J. Strecker, 1962-69; William Baum, 1970-73.

Springfield, Ill. (1853): William A. O'Connor, bishop, 1949.

Former bishops: Henry D. Juncker, 1857-68; Peter J. Baltes, 1870-86; James Ryan, 1888-1923; James A. Griffin, 1924-48.

Springfield, Mass. (1870): Christopher J. Weldon, bishop, 1950.

Former bishops: Patrick T. O'Reilly, 1870-92; Thomas D. Beaven, 1892-1920; Thomas M. O'Leary, 1921-49.

Stamford, Conn. (Byzantine Rite) (1956); Joseph M. Schmondiuk, eparch, 1961.

Former eparch: Ambrose Senyshyn, O.S.B.M., 1956-61.

Steubenville, Ohio (1944): John K. Mussio, bishop, 1945.

Stockton, Calif. (1962): Merlin J. Guilfoyle, bishop, 1969.

Former bishop: Hugh A. Donohoe, 1962-69.

Superior, Wis. (1905): George A. Hammes, bishop, 1960.

Former bishops: Augustine F. Schinner,

1905-13; Joseph M. Koudelka, 1913-21; Joseph G. Pinten, 1922-26; Theodore M. Reverman, 1926-41; William P. O'Connor, 1942-46; Albert G. Meyer, 1946-53; Joseph Annabring, 1954-59.

Syracuse, N. Y. (1886): David F. Cunningham, bishop, 1970. Francis J. Harrison, auxiliary.

Former bishops: Patrick A. Ludden, 1887-1912; John Grimes, 1912-22; Daniel J. Curley, 1923-32; John A. Duffy, 1933-37; Walter A. Foery, 1937-70.

Toledo, Ohio (1910): John A. Donovan, bishop, 1967. Albert H. Ottenweller, auxiliary.

Former bishops: Joseph Schrembs, 1911-21; Samuel A. Stritch, 1921-30; Karl J. Alter, 1931-50; George J. Rehring, 1950-67.

Trenton, N. J. (1881): George W. Ahr, bishop, 1950; John C. Reiss, auxiliary.

Former bishops: Michael J. O'Farrell, 1881-94; James A. McFaul, 1894-1917; Thomas J. Walsh, 1918-28; John J. McMahon, 1928-32; Moses E. Kiley, 1934-40; William A. Griffin, 1940-50.

Tucson, Ariz. (1897): Francis J. Green, bishop, 1960.

Former bishops: Peter Bourgade, 1897-99; Henry Granjon, 1900-22; Daniel J. Gercke, 1923-60.

Tulsa, Okla. (1972): Bernard J. Ganter, bishop, 1973.

Washington,* D.C. (1939): William Baum, archbishop, 1973. Thomas W. Lyons, Eugene A. Marino, S.S.J., auxiliaries.

Former ordinaries: Michael J. Curley, 1939-47; Cardinal Patrick O'Boyle, 1948-73.

Wheeling, W. Va. (1850): Joseph H. Hodges, bishop, 1962. James E. Michaels, S.S.C., auxiliary.

Former bishops: Richard V. Whelan, 1850-74; John J. Kain, 1875-93; Patrick J. Donahue, 1894-1922; John J. Swint, 1922-62.

Wichita, Kans. (1887): David M. Maloney, bishop, 1967.

Former bishops: John J. Hennessy, 1888-1920; Augustus J. Schwertner, 1921-39; Christian H. Winkelmann, 1940-46; Mark K. Carroll, 1947-67.

Wilmington, Del. (1868): Thomas Mardaga, bishop, 1968.

Former bishops: Thomas A. Becker, 1868-86; Alfred A. Curtis, 1886-96; John J. Monaghan, 1897-1925; Edmond Fitzmaurice, 1925-60; Michael Hyle, 1960-67.

Winona, Minn. (1889): Loras J. Watters, bishop, 1969.

Former bishops: Joseph B. Cotter, 1889-1909; Patrick R. Heffron, 1910-27; Francis M. Kelly, 1928-49; Edward A. Fitzgerald, 1949-69.

Worcester, Mass. (1950): Bernard J. Flanagan, bishop, 1959. Timothy J. Harrington, auxiliary.

Former bishop: John J. Wright, 1950-59.

Yakima, Wash. (1951): Vacant as of Aug. 20, 1974.

Former bishops: Joseph P. Dougherty, 1951-69; Cornelius M. Power, 1969-74.

Youngstown, Ohio (1943): James W. Malone, bishop, 1968. William A. Hughes, auxiliary.

Former bishops: James A. McFadden, 1943-52; Emmet M. Walsh, 1952-68.

Apostolic Exarchate for Melkites (1966): Archbishop Joseph Tawil, exarch, 1969.

Former exarch: Justin Najmy, 1966-68.

Military Ordinariate (1917): Cardinal Terence J. Cooke, military vicar, 1968. William Moran, military delegate.

Former military vicars: Cardinal Patrick Hayes, 1917-38; Cardinal Francis Spellman, 1939-67.

Abbacy of Belmont, N. C. (1910): Edmund F. McCaffrey, O.S.B., abbot, 1970.

Former abbots: Leo M. Haid, O.S.B., 1910-24; Vincent G. Taylor. O.S.B., 1925-59; Walter A. Coggin, O.S.B., 1960-70.

Military Ordinariate

The Military Ordinariate or Vicariate, is the diocese which serves members of the armed forces of the United States wherever they are. It has jurisdiction over: military and Veterans Administration hospital chaplains; personnel of the armed forces and members of their families and dependents habitually living with them; members of the Coast Guard, National Guard, Air National Guard and Civil Air Patrol when on active duty; persons living on military installations and/or attached to military offices or VA facilities.

The ordinariate was canonically established on a permanent basis by a decree of the Sacred Consistorial Congregation dated Sept. 8, 1957. Cardinal Terence J. Cooke, Archbishop of New York, is Military Vicar. Offices of the ordinariate are located at 30 East 51st St., New York, N.Y. 10022.

MISSIONARY BISHOPS

Africa

Nigeria: Sokoto (diocese), Michael J. Dempsey, O.P.

South Africa: De Aar (diocese), Joseph A. De Palma, S.C.J.

Keimos (diocese), John Minder, O.S.F.S.

Southwest Africa (Namibia): Keetmanshoop (vicariate apostolic), Edward F. Schlotterback, O.S.F.S.

Tanzania: Arusha (diocese), Dennis V. Durning, C. S.Sp.

Musoma (diocese), John Rudin, M.M.

Nachingwea (diocese), Bernard R. Cotey, S.D.S.

Shinyanga (diocese), Edward A. McGurkin, M.M.

Asia

Burma: Prome (diocese), Thomas A. Newman, M.S.

China: Chowtsun (diocese), Henry A. Pinger, O.F.M. Expelled.

Wuchow (diocese), Frederick A. Donaghy, M.M. Expelled.

India: Bhagalpur (diocese), Urban McGarry, T.O.R.

Patna (diocese), Augustine F. Wildermuth, S.J.

Indonesia: Agats (diocese), Alphonse A. Sowada, O.S.C.

Israel: Acre (archdiocese, Melkite Rite), Joseph Raya.

Korea: Inchon (diocese), William J. McNaughton, M.M.

Cheju-Do (prefecture), Harold W. Henry, S.S.C., ap. admin.

Pakistan: Multan (diocese), Ernest B. Boland, O. P.

Philippine Islands: Marbel (prelacy), Reginald Arliss, C. P.

Tagum (prelacy), Joseph W. Regan, M. M.

Taiwan: Taichung (diocese), William F. Kupfer, M. M.

Thailand: Udon Thani (diocese), Clarence J. Duhart, C. SS. R.

Turkey: Izmir (archdiocese), John H. Boccella, T. O. R.

Central America, West Indies

Bahamas: Nassau (diocese), Paul L. Hagarty, O. S. B.

Dominican Republic: San Juan de la Maguana (diocese), Thomas F. Reilly, C. SS. R.

Guatemala: Guatemala (archdiocese), Richard J. Ham, M. M., auxiliary.

Huehuetenango (diocese), Hugo Gerbermann, M. M.

Honduras: Comayagua (diocese), Bernardino Mazzarella, O. F. M.

Olancho (prelacy), Nicholas D'Antonio Salza, O.F.M.

Honduras, British: Belize (diocese), Robert L. Hodapp, S. J.

Nicaragua: Bluefields (vicariate apostolic), Salvator Schlaefer, O. F. M. Cap.

Virgin Islands: (prelacy), Edward Harper, C. SS. R.

Europe

Sweden: Stockholm (diocese), John E. Taylor, O. M. I.

Oceania

Caroline and Marshall Islands (vicariate apostolic), Martin J. Neylon, S. J.

Fiji Islands: Suva (archdiocese), George H. Pearce, S. M.

New Guinea: Goroko (diocese), John E. Cohill, S. V. D.

Kavieng (diocese), Alfred M. Stemper, M. S. C.

Madang (archdiocese), Adolph A. Noser, S. V. D.

Mendi (diocese), Firmin Schmidt, O. F. M. Cap.

Mount Hagen (diocese), George Bernarding, S. V. D.

Wewak (diocese), Leo Arkfeld, S. V. D.

South America

Bolivia: Coroico (prelacy), Thomas R. Manning, O. F. M.

La Paz (archdiocese), Andrew B. Schierhoff, auxiliary.

Santa Cruz (diocese), Charles A. Brown, M. M., auxiliary.

Brazil: Abaete do Tocantina (prelacy), Angelo Frosi, S. X.

Belem do Para (archdiocese), Jude Prost, O. F. M., auxiliary.

Borba (prelacy), Adrian J. M. Veigle, T. O. R.

Cristalandia (prelacy), James A. Schuck, O. F. M.

Jatai (diocese), Benedict D. Coscia, O. F. M. Mathias Schmidt, O. S. B., auxiliary.

Paranagua (diocese), Bernard Nolker, C. SS. R.

Santarem (prelacy), James C. Ryan, O. F. M.

Sao Salvador da Bahia (archdiocese), Thomas W. Murphy, C.SS.R., auxiliary.

Paraguay: Coronel Oviedo (prelacy), Jerome Pechillo, T. O. R.

Peru: Chimbote (prelacy), James C. Burke, O.P.

Chulucanas (prelacy), John McNabb, O.S.A.

CATHOLIC POPULATION OF THE UNITED STATES

(Source: *The Official Catholic Directory, 1974;* figures as of Jan 1, 1974. Archdioceses are indicated by an asterisk; for dioceses marked +, see Dioceses with Interstate Lines.)

Section, State Diocese	Catholics	Dioc.	Priests Rel.	Total	Bros.	Sisters	Parishes	Missions
NEW ENGLAND	5,557,477	4,393	2,286	6,679	777	14,964	1,683	231
Maine, Portland	262,694	249	96	345	51	1,048	142	64
New Hampshire, Manchester	264,747	302	82	384	76	1,324	126	39
Vermont, Burlington	148,496	192	55	247	15	416	100	41
Massachusetts	2,923,682	2,286	1,488	3,774	379	8,220	788	52
*Boston	1,893,050	1,430	978	2,408	200	5,401	408	19
Fall River	320,000	232	170	402	37	840	113	16
Springfield	371,092	290	148	438	35	1,053	137	15
Worcester	339,540	334	192	526	107	926	130	2
Rhode Island, Providence	606,840	373	218	591	115	1,380	155	4
Connecticut	1,351,018	991	347	1,338	141	2,576	372	31
*Hartford	827,701	610	142	752	88	1,418	218	10
Bridgeport	327,867	234	136	370	22	807	84	4
Norwich+	195,450	147	69	216	31	351	70	17
MIDDLE ATLANTIC	13,185,859	9,979	4,445	14,424	2,736	39,426	3,894	456
New York	6,504,375	4,734	2,252	6,986	1,832	19,035	1,724	228
*New York	1,800,000	1,144	922	2,066	1,007	7,768	407	57
Albany	517,716	435	230	665	125	1,620	211	55
Brooklyn	1,346,220	1,029	273	1,302	362	2,961	228	—
Buffalo	925,482	639	489	1,128	91	2,819	297	17
Ogdensburg	176,151	195	44	239	28	465	122	40
Rochester	358,850	391	94	485	43	1,139	160	28
Rockville Centre	990,151	498	94	592	127	1,457	129	10
Syracuse	389,805	403	106	509	49	806	170	21
New Jersey	3,003,106	2,022	883	2,905	420	6,056	683	42
*Newark	1,520,163	937	424	1,361	242	2,783	253	7
Camden	331,807	399	53	452	21	696	122	9
Paterson	310,273	297	247	544	79	1,091	102	6
Trenton	840,863	389	159	548	78	1,486	206	20
Pennsylvania	3,678,378	3,223	1,310	4,533	484	14,335	1,487	186
*Philadelphia	1,375,096	1,058	520	1,578	276	6,303	311	18
Allentown	260,340	306	110	416	33	1,043	151	21
Altoona-Johnstown	150,626	153	82	235	26	394	120	16
Erie	210,748	284	57	341	15	886	126	—
Greensburg	225,079	189	101	290	13	452	117	30
Harrisburg	193,022	178	65	243	9	947	103	17
Pittsburgh	911,928	577	275	852	94	3,011	320	23
Scranton	351,539	478	100	578	18	1,299	239	61

Section, State Diocese	Catholics	Priests Dioc.	Rel.	Total	Bros.	Sisters	Par- ishes	Mis- sions
SOUTH ATLANTIC	2,527,692	2,083	2,140	4,223	598	7,326	1,141	297
Delaware, Wilmington+	114,963	116	84	200	22	410	54	19
Maryland, *Baltimore+	455,902	364	397	761	156	2,373	145	18
District of Columbia								
*Washington+	389,482	376	789	1,165	226	803	126	3
Virginia, Richmond+	250,000	200	178	378	33	734	125	27
West Virginia, Wheeling+	95,617	129	73	202	11	515	101	71
North Carolina	74,419	112	74	186	13	376	116	41
Belmont Abbey	417	2	27	29	6	—	1	—
Charlotte	37,581	46	32	78	2	260	56	19
Raleigh	36,421	64	15	79	5	116	59	22
South Carolina, Charleston	48,091	84	58	142	23	262	66	31
Georgia	98,639	136	102	238	31	390	83	51
*Atlanta	61,166	69	62	131	27	200	41	21
Savannah	37,473	67	40	107	4	190	42	30
Florida	1,000,579	566	385	951	83	1,463	325	36
*Miami	631,600	273	197	470	50	753	120	6
Orlando	112,260	122	27	149	1	175	58	5
St. Augustine	81,375	86	40	126	—	189	72	16
St. Petersburg	175,344	85	121	206	32	346	75	9
EAST NORTH CENTRAL	10,423,397	8,074	4,535	12,609	2,008	35,878	4,171	468
Ohio	2,305,915	1,993	943	2,936	528	8,223	946	54
*Cincinnati	517,888	448	386	834	263	2,376	262	—
Cleveland	904,674	627	260	887	144	2,866	237	3
Columbus	193,640	229	75	304	34	840	108	12
Steubenville	57,000	158	15	173	15	172	73	21
Toledo	331,752	281	114	395	18	1,382	149	16
Youngstown	300,961	250	93	343	54	587	117	2
Indiana	722,703	763	590	1,353	285	4,325	465	39
*Indianapolis	203,530	241	176	417	89	2,144	164	21
Evansville	87,942	126	19	145	10	666	75	6
Ft. Wayne-South Bend	159,076	132	244	376	123	922	82	7
Gary	188,568	145	95	240	50	413	85	2
Lafayette	83,587	119	56	175	13	180	59	3
Illinois	3,546,900	2,265	1,612	3,877	621	10,884	1,108	122
*Chicago	2,476,300	1,252	1,093	2,345	354	7,030	456	6
Belleville	115,100	176	43	219	28	529	129	18
Joliet	350,086	197	176	373	169	1,115	110	9
Peoria	216,752	259	112	371	21	772	171	46
Rockford	208,294	183	96	279	15	457	99	7
Springfield	180,368	198	92	290	34	981	143	36
Michigan	2,345,558	1,410	605	2,015	217	4,991	791	127
*Detroit	1,569,104	693	406	1,099	181	3,000	328	8
Gaylord	72,762	59	18	77	3	167	58	23
Grand Rapids	150,429	164	43	207	10	623	84	16
Kalamazoo	83,416	59	28	87	20	346	45	18
Lansing	205,707	143	62	205	—	383	80	6
Marquette	95,589	141	15	156	1	166	92	44
Saginaw	168,551	151	33	184	2	306	104	12
Wisconsin	1,502,321	1,643	785	2,428	357	7,455	861	126
*Milwaukee	696,560	666	507	1,173	216	3,994	265	19
Green Bay	320,015	337	168	505	97	1,076	193	31
La Crosse	199,497	319	48	367	31	1,042	178	21
Madison	200,948	211	33	244	12	831	138	—
Superior	85,301	110	29	139	1	512	87	55
EAST SOUTH CENTRAL	613,087	950	440	1,390	334	4,508	603	159
Kentucky	342,515	532	161	693	173	3,270	281	56
*Louisville	189,650	274	124	398	150	1,605	125	22
Covington	103,500	188	22	210	13	1,104	82	34
Owensboro	49,365	70	15	85	10	561	74	—

Section, State Diocese	Catholics	Dioc.	Priests Rel.	Total	Bros.	Sisters	Parishes	Missions
Tennessee	95,146	129	44	173	76	383	85	24
Memphis	40,183	51	24	75	55	160	29	4
Nashville	54,963	78	20	98	21	223	56	20
Alabama	90,515	149	165	314	33	529	129	34
Birmingham	42,436	65	80	145	14	238	58	19
Mobile	48,079	84	85	169	19	291	71	15
Mississippi, Natchez-Jackson	84,911	140	70	210	52	326	108	45
WEST NORTH CENTRAL	3,205,727	4,249	1,874	6,123	752	16,699	2,730	613
Minnesota	1,003,319	1,014	372	1,386	181	4,592	709	123
*St. Paul and Minneapolis	532,504	376	140	516	67	1,544	218	9
Crookston	43,681	50	19	69	—	341	51	29
Duluth	94,426	97	40	137	3	356	83	39
New Ulm	70,324	124	1	125	—	164	83	12
St. Cloud	145,434	178	155	333	82	1,401	146	34
Winona	116,950	189	17	206	29	786	128	—
Iowa	524,713	957	106	1,063	88	2,809	541	87
*Dubuque	230,763	413	76	489	80	1,697	194	41
Davenport	103,276	205	17	222	8	557	119	20
Des Moines	79,056	131	6	137	—	215	89	6
Sioux City	111,618	208	7	215	—	340	139	20
Missouri	736,831	987	785	1,772	327	4,347	489	83
*St. Louis	499,405	604	532	1,136	244	3,257	248	9
Jefferson City	68,603	141	11	152	15	212	88	27
Kansas City-St. Joseph	130,020	163	206	369	56	651	94	15
Springfield-Cape Girardeau	38,803	79	36	115	12	227	59	32
North Dakota	168,895	236	79	315	28	829	196	98
Bismarck	73,159	92	48	140	23	379	79	45
Fargo	95,736	144	31	175	5	450	117	53
South Dakota	136,922	176	108	284	28	652	172	79
Rapid City	36,000	132	59	191	26	549	50	48
Sioux Falls	100,922	44	49	93	2	103	122	31
Nebraska	317,011	441	186	627	66	1,435	280	98
*Omaha	203,949	236	166	402	56	1,067	136	19
Grand Island	52,117	80	3	83	—	160	53	37
Lincoln	60,945	125	17	142	10	208	91	42
Kansas	318,036	438	238	676	34	2,035	343	45
*Kansas City	138,000	130	157	287	21	873	97	21
Dodge City	32,817	65	6	71	—	221	52	8
Salina	58,348	88	44	132	7	430	98	—
Wichita	88,871	155	31	186	6	511	96	16
WEST SOUTH CENTRAL	3,464,559	1,913	1,632	3,545	663	7,135	1,483	672
Arkansas, Little Rock	55,100	109	64	173	49	573	80	36
Louisiana	1,206,258	641	545	1,186	302	2,099	466	178
*New Orleans	585,546	246	328	574	222	1,250	164	22
Alexandria	73,500	123	46	169	18	240	86	60
Baton Rouge	151,844	85	69	154	22	225	66	26
Lafayette	395,368	187	102	289	40	384	150	70
Oklahoma	108,668	178	64	242	22	508	124	71
*Oklahoma City	65,715	114	38	152	14	293	71	47
Tulsa	42,953	64	26	90	8	215	53	24
Texas	2,094,533	985	959	1,944	290	3,955	813	387
*San Antonio	538,619	192	217	409	162	1,511	158	71
Amarillo	71,307	74	20	94	1	140	60	27
Austin	138,402	100	62	162	37	170	80	32
Beaumont	75,000	54	31	85	1	110	37	18
Brownsville	277,124	28	82	110	15	167	61	50
Corpus Christi	184,122	72	82	154	9	373	72	46
Dallas	110,924	98	115	213	16	383	55	14
El Paso+	226,453	85	74	159	19	332	72	54
Fort Worth	72,629	58	38	96	17	194	49	25
Galveston-Houston	338,774	180	209	389	13	526	120	18
San Angelo	61,179	44	29	73	—	49	49	32

Section, State Diocese	Catholics	Dioc.	Priests Rel.	Total	Bros.	Sisters	Par- ishes	Mis- sions
MOUNTAIN	1,524,861	1,104	790	1,894	266	3,253	761	701
Montana	115,403	232	56	288	13	262	134	113
Great Falls	67,681	98	40	138	3	146	76	66
Helena	47,722	134	16	150	10	116	58	47
Idaho, Boise	61,272	86	24	110	2	194	66	36
Wyoming, Cheyenne+	45,000	66	7	73	4	94	39	30
Colorado	410,119	256	273	529	40	1,196	183	106
*Denver	303,969	162	206	368	31	934	123	44
Pueblo	106,150	94	67	161	9	262	60	62
New Mexico	344,266	178	141	319	142	542	144	296
*Santa Fe	298,604	157	82	239	114	372	90	251
Gallup+	45,662	21	59	80	28	170	54	45
Arizona	407,588	174	216	390	28	694	119	94
Phoenix	225,219	83	127	210	21	317	64	25
Tucson	182,369	91	89	180	7	377	55	69
Utah, Salt Lake City	51,093	54	39	93	21	139	38	11
Nevada, Reno	90,120	58	34	92	16	132	38	15
PACIFIC	5,455,666	2,792	2,433	5,225	1,078	10,221	1,493	414
Washington	467,009	370	331	701	49	1,330	221	64
*Seattle	343,680	206	229	435	35	699	126	37
Spokane	72,383	94	96	190	14	566	57	20
Yakima	50,946	70	6	76	—	65	38	7
Oregon	277,920	251	140	391	90	1,092	156	57
*Portland	254,273	203	130	333	90	1,000	125	27
Baker	23,647	48	10	58	—	92	31	30
California	4,463,625	2,107	1,797	3,904	822	7,325	1,001	226
*Los Angeles	1,984,429	680	760	1,440	311	3,007	319	40
*San Francisco	827,950	317	517	834	160	1,790	150	11
Fresno	282,316	121	52	173	19	243	84	47
Monterey	95,000	82	42	124	28	236	43	12
Oakland	346,341	145	185	330	165	678	84	3
Sacramento	218,227	188	65	253	49	386	89	45
San Diego	547,000	425	114	539	30	714	165	29
Santa Rosa	71,360	95	26	121	57	159	36	25
Stockton	91,002	54	36	90	3	112	31	14
Alaska	42,112	28	48	76	10	73	49	29
*Anchorage	24,000	12	13	25	2	24	16	5
Fairbanks	13,312	6	33	39	8	31	24	20
Juneau	4,800	10	2	12	—	18	9	4
Hawaii, Honolulu	205,000	36	117	153	107	401	66	38
EASTERN RITES	532,113	521	79	600	21	553	474	21
*Philadelphia	49,813	125	14	139	4	225	101	8
Stamford	87,650	52	17	69	4	70	57	1
St. Nicholas of Chicago	29,857	36	11	47	—	19	36	4
*Munhall	150,625	83	9	92	5	156	83	—
Passaic	97,740	83	15	98	4	41	83	2
Parma	29,211	49	7	56	—	38	46	—
St. Maron of Detroit	65,541	57	1	58	—	4	43	4
Melkite Exarchate	21,676	36	5	41	4	—	25	2
MILITARY ORDINARIATE	1,975,000	—	—	—	—	—	—	—
TOTALS 1974	48,465,438	36,058	20,654	56,712	9,233	139,963	18,433	4,032
Totals 1973	48,460,427	36,223	20,746	56,969	9,201	143,054	18,384	4,040
Totals 1964	44,874,371	35,077	22,251	57,328	12,132	180,015	17,445	4,594

Dioceses with Interstate Lines

Diocesan lines usually fall within a single state and in some cases include a whole state.

The following dioceses, with their statistics as reported in tables throughout the Almanac, are exceptions.

Norwich, Conn., includes Fisher's Island, N.Y.

Wilmington, Del., includes nine counties of Maryland and two of Virginia. (See Boundary Changes below.)

Baltimore, includes all of Maryland except

nine counties under the jurisdiction of Wilmington and five under Washington.

Washington, D.C., includes five counties of Maryland.

Richmond includes all of Virginia except two counties under the jurisdiction of Wilmington ar.d 18 under Wheeling; Richmond also includes eight counties of West Virginia. (See Boundary Changes below.)

Wheeling includes all of West Virginia except eight counties under the jurisdiction of Richmond; it also includes 18 counties of Virginia. (See Boundary Changes below.)

El Paso, Tex., includes seven counties of New Mexico.

Gallup, N.M., has jurisdiction over several counties of Arizona.

Cheyenne, Wyo., includes all of Yellowstone National Park.

Boundary Changes

Since establishment of the Diocese of Arlington June 4, 1974: Richmond and Arlington include the entire state of Virginia; Wheeling includes the entire state of West Virginia; Wilmington includes the entire state of Delaware and nine counties of Maryland.

These boundary changes are not reflected in 1974 statistical tables throughout the Almanac.

PERCENTAGE OF CATHOLICS IN U.S. POPULATION

(Source: *The Official Catholic Directory, 1974*; figures are as of Jan. 1, 1974. Total general population figures at the end of the table are U.S. Census Bureau estimates for Jan. 1 of the respective years. Archdioceses are indicated by an asterisk; for dioceses marked +, see Dioceses with Interstate Lines.)

Section, State Diocese	Catholic Pop.	Total Pop.	Cath. Pct.
NEW ENGLAND	**5,557,477**	**13,046,825**	**42.59**
Maine, Portland	262,694	993,663	26.43
New Hampshire.			
Manchester	264,747	784,000	33.76
Vermont, Burlington	148,496	465,000	31.93
Massachusetts	2,923,682	6,777,612	43.13
*Boston	1,893,050	4,818,000	39.29
Fall River	320,000	530,000	60.37
Springfield	371,092	791,643	46.87
Worcester	339,540	637,969	53.22
Rhode Island			
Providence	606,840	949,723	63.89
Connecticut	1,351,018	3,076,827	43.90
*Hartford	827,701	1,724,900	47.98
Bridgeport	327,867	818,300	40.06
Norwich +	195,450	533,627	36.62
MIDDLE ATLANTIC	**13,185,859**	**38,441,345**	**34.30**
New York	6,504,375	18,909,338	34.39
*New York	1,800,000	5,300,000	33.96
Albany	517,716	1,550,667	33.38
Brooklyn	1,346,220	4,588,485	29.33
Buffalo	925,482	1,778,355	51.75
Ogdensburg	176,151	382,353	46.07
Rochester	358,850	1,439,600	24.92
Rockville Centre	990,151	2,661,321	37.20
Syracuse	389,805	1,208,557	32.25
New Jersey	3,003,106	7,688,654	39.05
*Newark	1,520,163	3,019,160	50.35
Camden	331,807	1,104,400	30.04
Paterson	310,273	1,010,016	30.07
Trenton	840,863	2,555,078	32.90
Pennsylvania	3,678,378	11,843,353	31.05
*Philadelphia	1,375,096	3,901,000	35.24
Allentown	260,340	980,000	26.56
Altoona-Johnstown	150,626	627,403	24.00
Erie	210,748	858,582	24.54
Greensburg	225,079	695,101	32.38
Harrisburg	193,022	1,575,000	12.25

Section, State Diocese	Catholic Pop.	Total Pop.	Cath. Pct.
Pittsburgh	911,928	2,293,825	39.75
Scranton	351,539	912,442	38.52
SOUTH ATLANTIC	**2,527,692**	**31,226,475**	**8.09**
Delaware			
Wilmington +	114,963	850,979	13.50
Maryland			
*Baltimore +	455,902	2,366,726	19.26
District of Columbia			
*Washington +	389,482	2,055,634	18.94
Virginia			
Richmond +	250,000	4,648,494	5.37
West Virginia			
Wheeling +	95,617	2,093,583	4.56
North Carolina	74,419	5,208,375	1.42
Belmont Abbey	417	482	86.51
Charlotte	37,581	2,727,500	1.37
Raleigh	36,421	2,480,393	1.46
South Carolina			
Charleston	48,091	2,665,000	1.80
Georgia	98,639	3,580,000	2.75
*Atlanta	61,166	2,000,000	3.05
Savannah	37,473	1,580,000	2.37
Florida	1,000,579	7,757,684	12.89
*Miami	631,600	2,806,365	22.50
Orlando	112,260	1,436,800	7.81
St. Augustine	81,375	1,690,000	4.81
St. Petersburg	175,344	1,824,519	9.61
EAST NORTH CENTRAL	**10,423,397**	**40,823,792**	**25.53**
Ohio	2,305,915	10,720,051	21.51
*Cincinnati	517,888	2,670,727	19.39
Cleveland	904,674	3,004,834	30.10
Columbus	193,640	1,813,723	10.67
Steubenville	57,000	546,000	10.43
Toledo	331,752	1,443,318	22.98
Youngstown	300,961	1,241,449	24.24

Section, State Diocese	Catholic Pop.	Total Pop.	Cath. Pct.
Indiana	722,703	5,187,201	13.93
*Indianapolis	203,530	2,022,366	10.06
Evansville	87,942	435,177	20.20
Ft. Wayne-S. Bend	159,076	973,937	16.33
Gary	188,568	768,841	24.52
Lafayette	83,587	986,880	8.46
Illinois	3,546,900	11,210,359	31.63
*Chicago	2,476,300	5,936,200	41.71
Belleville	115,100	807,682	14.25
Joliet	350,086	1,005,920	34.80
Peoria	216,752	1,434,428	15.11
Rockford	208,294	934,938	22.27
Springfield	180,368	1,091,191	16.52
Michigan	2,345,558	9,193,156	25.51
*Detroit	1,569,104	4,707,312	33.33
Gaylord	72,762	294,968	24.66
Grand Rapids	150,429	916,671	16.41
Kalamazoo	83,416	796,912	10.46
Lansing	205,707	1,466,075	14.03
Marquette	95,589	304,347	31.40
Saginaw	168,551	706,871	23.84
Wisconsin	1,502,321	4,513,025	33.28
*Milwaukee	696,560	2,006,317	34.71
Green Bay	320,015	728,512	43.92
La Crosse	199,497	667,849	29.87
Madison	200,948	803,792	25.00
Superior	85,301	306,555	27.82
EAST SOUTH CENTRAL	**613,087**	**12,772,829**	**4.79**
Kentucky	342,515	3,379,743	10.13
*Louisville	189,650	1,201,974	15.77
Covington	103,500	1,500,000	6.90
Owensboro	49,365	677,769	7.28
Tennessee	95,146	3,803,168	2.50
Memphis	40,183	1,178,168	3.41
Nashville	54,963	2,625,000	2.09
Alabama	90,515	3,373,006	2.68
Birmingham	42,436	2,143,875	1.97
Mobile	48,079	1,229,131	3.91
Mississippi.			
Natchez-Jackson	84,911	2,216,912	3.83
WEST NORTH CENTRAL	**3,205,727**	**16,295,069**	**19.67**
Minnesota	1,003,319	3,767,968	26.62
*St. Paul & Minneapolis	532,504	2,017,225	26.39
Crookston	43,681	215,227	20.29
Duluth	94,426	390,227	24.19
New Ulm	70,324	279,054	25.20
St. Cloud	145,434	349,853	41.57
Winona	116,950	516,382	22.64
Iowa	524,713	2,781,456	18.86
*Dubuque	230,763	956,078	24.13
Davenport	103,276	687,310	15.02
Des Moines	79,056	625,185	12.64
Sioux City	111,618	512,883	21.76
Missouri	736,831	4,709,509	15.64
*St. Louis	499,405	1,933,811	25.82
Jefferson City	68,603	671,029	10.22

Section, State Diocese	Catholic Pop.	Total Pop.	Cath. Pct.
Kansas City- St. Joseph	130,020	1,271,000	10.22
Springfield- Cape Girardeau	38,803	833,669	4.65
North Dakota	168,895	617,760	27.33
Bismarck	73,159	244,777	29.88
Fargo	95,736	372,983	25.66
South Dakota	136,922	660,000	20.74
Rapid City	36,000	178,000	20.22
Sioux Falls	100,922	482,000	20.93
Nebraska	317,011	1,510,121	20.99
*Omaha	203,949	711,156	28.67
Grand Island	52,117	296,232	17.59
Lincoln	60,945	502,733	12.12
Kansas	318,036	2,248,255	14.14
*Kansas City	138,000	882,028	15.64
Dodge City	32,817	205,923	15.93
Salina	58,348	333,729	17.48
Wichita	88,871	826,575	10.74
WEST SOUTH CENTRAL	**3,464,559**	**20,166,110**	**17.18**
Arkansas			
Little Rock	55,100	1,923,295	2.86
Louisiana	1,206,258	3,729,428	32.34
*New Orleans	585,546	1,370,980	42.71
Alexandria	73,500	1,083,132	6.78
Baton Rouge	151,844	572,608	26.51
Lafayette	395,368	702,708	56.26
Oklahoma	108,668	2,583,414	4.20
*Oklahoma City	65,715	1,451,914	4.52
Tulsa	42,953	1,131,500	3.79
Texas	2,094,533	11,929,973	17.55
*San Antonio	538,619	1,288,621	41.79
Amarillo	71,307	750,000	9.50
Austin	138,402	939,600	14.72
Beaumont	75,000	586,598	12.78
Brownsville	277,124	355,180	78.02
Corpus Christi	184,122	527,000	34.93
Dallas	110,924	2,384,300	4.65
El Paso +	226,453	654,213	34.61
Fort Worth	72,629	1,323,000	5.48
Galveston-Houston	338,774	2,564,500	13.21
San Angelo	61,179	556,961	10.98
MOUNTAIN	**1,524,861**	**8,470,156**	**18.00**
Montana	115,403	681,021	16.94
Great Falls	67,681	351,858	19.23
Helena	47,722	329,163	14.49
Idaho, Boise	61,272	756,000	8.10
Wyoming, Cheyenne +	45,000	355,000	12.67
Colorado	410,119	2,201,985	18.62
*Denver	303,969	1,805,277	16.83
Pueblo	106,150	396,708	26.75
New Mexico	344,266	945,000	36.43
*Santa Fe	298,604	708,000	42.17
Gallup +	45,662	237,000	19.26
Arizona	407,588	1,885,400	21.61
Phoenix	225,219	1,191,600	18.90
Tucson	182,369	693,800	26.28
Utah			
Salt Lake City	51,093	1,157,000	4.41
Nevada, Reno	90,120	488,750	18.43

Section, State Diocese	Cath. Pop.	Total Pop.	Cath. Pct.	Section, State Diocese	Cath. Pop.	Total Pop.	Cath. Pct.
PACIFIC	**5,455,666**	**27,428,560**	**19.89**	San Diego	547,000	2,801,333	19.52
				Santa Rosa	71,360	513,231	13.93
Washington	467,009	3,398,100	13.74	Stockton	91,002	525,833	17.30
*Seattle	343,680	2,573,000	13.35	Alaska	42,112	296,120	14.22
Spokane	72,383	483,398	14.97	*Anchorage	24,000	160,000	15.00
Yakima	50,946	341,702	14.90	Fairbanks	13,312	93,120	14,29
Oregon	277,920	2,251,567	12.34	Juneau	4,800	43,000	11.16
*Portland	254,273	1,979,267	12.84	Hawaii, Honolulu	205,000	832,000	24.63
Baker	23,647	272,300	8.68				
California	4,463,625	20,650,773	21.61	**EASTERN RITES**	**532,113**	—	—
*Los Angeles	1,984,429	9,421,470	21.06	**MILITARY**			
*San Francisco	827,950	2,542,655	32.56	**ORDINARIATE**	**1,975,000**		
Fresno	282,316	1,166,336	24.20				
Monterey	95,000	379,010	25.06	**TOTALS 1974**	**48,465,438**	**211,216,000**	**22.95**
Oakland	346,341	1,731,705	20.00	Totals 1973	48,460,427	209,712,000	23.10
Sacramento	218,227	1,569,200	13.90	Totals 1964	44,874,371	190,818,000	23.51

INFANT BAPTISMS AND CONVERTS IN THE UNITED STATES

(Source: *The Official Catholic Directory, 1974:* figures as of Jan. 1, 1974. Archdioceses are in-dicated by an asterisk; for dioceses marked +, see Dioceses with Interstate Lines.)

Section, State Diocese	Infant Baptisms	Converts	Section, State Diocese	Infant Baptisms	Converts
NEW ENGLAND	**88,461**	**2,198**	Pittsburgh	14,654	1,062
			Scranton	5,551	291
Maine, Portland	5,018	380	**SOUTH ATLANTIC**	**50,394**	**6,356**
New Hampshire			Delaware, Wilmington +	2,730	165
Manchester	5,468	110	Maryland, *Baltimore +	7,938	792
Vermont, Burlington	2,998	173	District of Columbia		
Massachusetts	45,504	748	*Washington +	8,921	977
*Boston	28,485	362	Virginia, Richmond +	5,904	737
Fall River	5,333	91	West Virginia, Wheeling +	1,766	431
Springfield	6,052	190	North Carolina	1,773	440
Worcester	5,634	105	Belmont Abbey	22	4
Rhode Island			Charlotte	777	203
Providence	8,031	160	Raleigh	974	233
Connecticut	21,442	627	South Carolina, Charleston	1,269	348
*Hartford	12,723	382	Georgia	2,458	653
Bridgeport	5,268	134	*Atlanta	1,586	339
Norwich +	3,451	111	Savannah	872	314
MIDDLE ATLANTIC	**236,963**	**10,326**	Florida	17,635	1,813
			*Miami	9,792	614
New York	123,490	4,503	Orlando	2,715	300
*New York	36,151	1,242	St. Augustine	1,880	452
Albany	9,131	670	St. Petersburg	3,248	447
Brooklyn	28,532	539			
Buffalo	11,025	473	**EAST NORTH CENTRAL**	**176,296**	**21,464**
Ogdensburg	3,424	253	Ohio	39,503	4,833
Rochester	7,889	531	*Cincinnati	9,575	1,184
Rockville Centre	19,474	316	Cleveland	13,598	1,212
Syracuse	7,864	479	Columbus	3,673	812
New Jersey	50,409	1,512	Steubenville	1,155	207
*Newark	22,996	586	Toledo	6,737	873
Camden	7,007	343	Youngstown	4,765	545
Paterson	7,021	166	Indiana	13,876	2,581
Trenton	13,385	417	*Indianapolis	4,147	1,031
Pennsylvania	63,064	4,311	Evansville	1,591	235
*Philadelphia	24,325	1,082	Ft. Wayne-South Bend	3,100	524
Allentown	4,928	246	Gary	3,225	347
Altoona-Johnstown	2,581	372	Lafayette	1,813	444
Erie	4,242	470	Illinois	57,474	7,636
Greensburg	3,100	324	*Chicago	38,006	5,096
Harrisburg	3,683	464	Belleville	2,022	388

Section, State Diocese	Infant Baptisms	Converts	Section, State Diocese	Infant Baptisms	Converts
Illinois			**Kansas**		
Joliet	6,070	326	Dodge City	710	137
Peoria	4,541	813	Salina	1,139	225
Rockford	3,747	377	Wichita	1,798	391
Springfield	3,088	636			
Michigan	36,923	4,102	**WEST SOUTH CENTRAL**	**96,781**	**6,434**
*Detroit	20,955	1,753			
Gaylord	1,486	169	**Arkansas, Little Rock**	1,141	382
Grand Rapids	2,963	436	**Louisiana**	24,740	1,665
Kalamazoo	1,797	323	*New Orleans	11,569	601
Lansing	4,309	793	Alexandria	1,768	405
Marquette	1,845	164	Baton Rouge	3,146	264
Saginaw	3,568	464	Lafayette	8,257	395
Wisconsin	28,520	2,312	**Oklahoma**	2,140	759
*Milwaukee	12,604	907	*Oklahoma City	1,572	502
Green Bay	6,187	372	Tulsa	568	257
La Crosse	4,081	446	**Texas**	68,760	3,628
Madison	3,945	405	*San Antonio	16,162	466
Superior	1,703	182	Amarillo	2,705	174
			Austin	3,151	310
EAST SOUTH CENTRAL	**12,344**	**2,850**	Beaumont	1,602	261
			Brownsville	8,737	66
Kentucky	6,645	992	Corpus Christi	7,677	158
*Louisville	3,705	499	Dallas	4,295	535
Covington	1,942	320	El Paso +	10,279	189
Owensboro	998	173	Fort Worth	2,017	328
Tennessee	1,978	1,004	Galveston-Houston	9,938	1,021
Memphis	856	394	San Angelo	2,197	120
Nashville	1,122	610			
Alabama	1,764	599	**MOUNTAIN**	**39,599**	**3,762**
Birmingham	787	273			
Mobile	977	326	**Montana**	2,951	365
Mississippi, Natchez-Jackson	1,957	255	Great Falls	1,480	215
			Helena	1,471	150
WEST NORTH CENTRAL	**64,554**	**9,527**	**Idaho, Boise**	1,717	358
			Wyoming, Cheyenne +	1,163	160
Minnesota	20,887	2,218	**Colorado**	11,316	846
*St. Paul and Minneapolis	11,349	873	*Denver	8,559	703
Crookston	909	81	Pueblo	2,757	143
Duluth	1,885	171	**New Mexico**	8,205	892
New Ulm	1,412	172	*Santa Fe	7,224	270
St. Cloud	2,901	305	Gallup +	981	622
Winona	2,431	616	**Arizona**	10,709	683
Iowa	10,703	1,764	Phoenix	5,718	448
*Dubuque	4,496	620	Tucson	4,991	235
Davenport	2,341	411	**Utah, Salt Lake City**	1,457	210
Des Moines	1,712	370	**Nevada, Reno**	2,081	248
Sioux City	2,154	363			
Missouri	13,416	2,357	**PACIFIC**	**124,830**	**8,899**
*St. Louis	8,632	1,174			
Jefferson City	1,391	254	**Washington**	7,588	1,302
Kansas City-St. Joseph	2,619	603	*Seattle	4,965	902
Springfield-Cape Girardeau	774	326	Spokane	1,377	265
North Dakota	3,714	467	Yakima	1,246	135
Bismarck	1,548	173	**Oregon**	4,167	815
Fargo	2,166	294	*Portland	3,616	680
South Dakota	2,820	356	Baker	551	135
Rapid City	827	115	**California**	107,381	6,419
Sioux Falls	1,993	241	*Los Angeles	57,831	2,654
Nebraska	6,511	1,107	*San Francisco	11,499	627
*Omaha	4,067	567	Fresno	7,249	347
Grand Island	1,092	189	Monterey	2,511	177
Lincoln	1,352	351	Oakland	6,076	609
Kansas	6,503	1,258	Sacramento	4,881	512
*Kansas City	2,856	505			

Section, State Diocese	Infant Baptisms	Converts	Section, State Diocese	Infant Baptisms	Converts
California			Eastern Rites		
San Diego	13,165	1.164	St. Nicholas of Chicago	288	10
Santa Rosa	1,630	147	*Munhall	783	41
Stockton	2,539	182	Passaic	704	56
Alaska	744	104	Parma	480	65
*Anchorage	374	62	St. Maron of Detroit	508	27
Fairbanks	299	27	Melkite Exarchate	288	—
Juneau	71	15			
Hawaii, Honolulu	4,950	259	**MILITARY ORDINARIATE**	**22,204**	**2,662**
EASTERN RITES	**4,138**	**263**			
			TOTALS 1974	**916,564**	**74,741**
*Philadelphia	739	51	Totals 1973	975,071	73,925
Stamford	348	13	Totals 1964	1,322,315	123,986

CATHEDRALS IN THE UNITED STATES

A cathedral is the principal church in a diocese, the one in which the bishop has his seat *(cathedra)*. He is the actual rector, although many functions of the church, which usually serves a parish, are the responsibility of a priest serving as the administrator. Because of the dignity of a cathedral, the dates of its dedication and its patronal feast are observed throughout a diocese.

The pope's cathedral, the Basilica of St. John Lateran, is the highest-ranking church in the world.

(Archdioceses are indicated by asterisk.)

Albany, N.Y.: Immaculate Conception.
Alexandria, La.: St. Francis Xavier.
Allentown, Pa.: St. Catherine of Siena.
Altoona-Johnstown, Pa.: Blessed Sacrament (Altoona); St. John Gualbert (Johnstown Co-Cathedral).
Amarillo, Tex.: Sacred Heart.
Anchorage,* Alaska: Holy Family.
Atlanta,* Ga.: Christ the King.
Arlington, Va.: St. Thomas More.
Austin, Tex.: St. Mary.
Baker, Ore.: St. Francis de Sales.
Baltimore,* Md.: Mary Our Queen; Basilica of the Assumption of the Blessed Virgin Mary (Co-Cathedral).
Baton Rouge, La.: St. Joseph.
Beaumont, Tex.: St. Anthony.
Belleville, Ill.: St. Peter.
Belmont Abbey, N.C.: Mary Help of Christians.
Birmingham, Ala.: St. Paul.
Bismarck, N.D.: Holy Spirit.
Boise, Ida.: St. John the Evangelist.
Boston,* Mass.: Holy Cross.
Bridgeport, Conn.: St. Augustine.
Brooklyn, N.Y.: St. James.
Brownsville, Tex.: Immaculate Conception.
Buffalo, N.Y.: St. Joseph.
Burlington, Vt.: Immaculate Conception (destroyed by fire in 1972).
Camden, N.J.: Immaculate Conception.
Charleston, S.C.: St. John the Baptist.
Charlotte, N.C.: St. Patrick.
Cheyenne, Wyo.: St. Mary.

Chicago, Ill.: Holy Name.
Cincinnati,* Ohio: St. Peter in Chains.
Cleveland, Ohio: St. John the Evangelist.
Columbus, Ohio: St. Joseph.
Corpus Christi, Tex.: Corpus Christi.
Covington, Ky.: Basilica of the Assumption.
Crookston, Minn.: Immaculate Conception.
Dallas, Tex.: Sacred Heart.
Davenport, Ia.: Sacred Heart.
Denver,* Colo.: Immaculate Conception.
Des Moines, Ia.: St. Ambrose.
Detroit,* Mich.: Blessed Sacrament.
Dodge City, Kans.: Sacred Heart.
Dubuque,* Ia.: St. Raphael.
Duluth, Minn.: Holy Rosary.
El Paso, Tex.: St. Patrick.
Erie, Pa.: St. Peter.
Evansville, Ind.: Most Holy Trinity (Pro-Cathedral).
Fairbanks, Alaska: Sacred Heart.
Fall River, Mass.: St. Mary of the Assumption.
Fargo, N.D.: St. Mary.
Fort Wayne-S. Bend, Ind.: Immaculate Conception (Fort Wayne); St. Matthew (South Bend Co-Cathedral).
Fort Worth, Tex.: St. Patrick.
Fresno, Calif.: St. John.
Gallup, N.M.: Sacred Heart.
Galveston-Houston, Tex.: St. Mary (Galveston); Sacred Heart (Houston Co-Cathedral).
Gary, Ind.: Holy Angels.
Gaylord, Mich.: St. Mary.
Grand Island, Nebr.: Nativity of Blessed Virgin Mary.
Grand Rapids, Mich.: St. Andrew.
Great Falls, Mont.: St. Ann.
Green Bay, Wis.: St. Francis Xavier.
Greensburg, Pa.: Blessed Sacrament.
Harrisburg, Pa.: St. Patrick.
Hartford,* Conn.: St. Joseph.
Helena, Mont.: St. Helena.
Honolulu, H.I.: Our Lady of Peace.
Indianapolis,* Ind.: Sts. Peter and Paul.
Jefferson City, Mo.: St. Joseph.
Joliet, Ill.: St. Raymond.

Juneau, Alaska: Nativity of the Blessed Virgin Mary.
Kalamazoo, Mich.: St. Augustine.
Kansas City,* Kans.: St. Peter the Apostle.
Kansas City-St. Joseph, Mo.: Immaculate Conception (Kansas City); St. Joseph (St. Joseph Co-Cathedral).
La Crosse, Wis.: St. Joseph.
Lafayette, Ind.: St. Mary.
Lafayette, La.: St. John the Evangelist.
Lansing, Mich.: St. Mary.
Lincoln, Nebr.: Cathedral of the Risen Christ.
Little Rock, Ark.: St. Andrew.
Los Angeles,* Calif.: St. Vibiana.
Louisville,* Ky.: Assumption.
Madison, Wis.: St. Raphael.
Manchester, N.H.: St. Joseph.
Marquette, Mich.: St. Peter.
Memphis, Tenn.: Immaculate Conception.
Miami,* Fla.: St. Mary.
Milwaukee,* Wis.: St. John.
Mobile, Ala.: Immaculate Conception (Minor Basilica).
Monterey, Calif.: San Carlos Borromeo.
Munhall,* Pa. (Byzantine Rite): St. John the Baptist.
Nashville, Tenn.: Incarnation.
Natchez-Jackson, Miss.: Our Lady of Sorrows (Natchez); St. Peter (Jackson Co-Cathedral).
Newark,* N.J.: Sacred Heart.
New Orleans,* La.: Cathedral (Basilica) of St. Louis.
New Ulm, Minn.: Holy Trinity.
New York,* N.Y.: St. Patrick.
Norwich, Conn.: St. Patrick.
Oakland, Calif.: St. Francis de Sales.
Ogdensburg, N.Y.: St. Mary.
Oklahoma City,* Okla.: Our Lady of Perpetual Help.
Omaha,* Nebr.: St. Cecilia.
Orlando, Fla.: St. Charles Borromeo.
Owensboro, Ky.: St. Stephen.
Parma, Ohio (Byzantine Rite): St. John the Baptist.
Passaic, N.J. (Byzantine Rite): St. Michael.
Paterson, N.J.: St. John the Baptist.
Peoria, Ill.: St. Mary.
Philadelphia,* Pa.: Sts. Peter and Paul.
Philadelphia,* Pa. (Byzantine Rite): Immaculate Conception.
Phoenix, Ariz.: Sts. Simon and Jude.
Pittsburgh, Pa.: St. Paul.
Portland, Me.: Immaculate Conception.
Portland,* Ore.: Immaculate Conception.
Providence, R.I.: Sts. Peter and Paul.
Pueblo, Colo.: Sacred Heart.
Raleigh, N.C.: Sacred Heart.
Rapid City, S.D.: Our Lady of Perpetual Help.
Reno, Nev.: St. Thomas Aquinas.
Richmond, Va.: Sacred Heart.
Rochester, N.Y.: Sacred Heart.
Rockford, Ill.: St. Peter.
Rockville Centre, N.Y.: St. Agnes.

Sacramento, Calif.: Blessed Sacrament.
Saginaw, Mich.: St. Mary.
St. Augustine, Fla.: St. Augustine.
St. Cloud, Minn.: St. Mary.
St. Louis,* Mo.: St. Louis.
St. Maron of Detroit (Maronite Rite): St. Maron.
St. Nicholas in Chicago (Byzantine Rite): St. Nicholas.
St. Paul and Minneapolis,* Minn.: St. Paul (St. Paul); Basilica of St. Mary (Minneapolis Co-Cathedral).
St. Petersburg, Fla.: St. Jude the Apostle.
Salina, Kans.: Sacred Heart.
Salt Lake City, Utah: The Madeleine.
San Angelo, Tex.: Sacred Heart.
San Antonio,* Tex.: San Fernando.
San Diego, Calif.: St. Joseph.
San Francisco,* Calif.: St. Mary (Assumption).
Santa Fe,* N.M.: San Francisco de Asis.
Santa Rosa, Calif.: St. Eugene.
Savannah, Ga.: St. John the Baptist.
Scranton, Pa.: St. Peter.
Seattle,* Wash.: St. James.
Sioux City, Ia.: Epiphany.
Sioux Falls, S.D.: St. Joseph.
Spokane, Wash.: Our Lady of Lourdes.
Springfield, Ill.: Immaculate Conception.
Springfield, Mass.: St. Michael.
Springfield-Cape Girardeau, Mo.: St. Agnes (Springfield); St. Mary (Cape Girardeau Co-Cathedral).
Stamford, Conn. (Byzantine Rite): St. Vladimir (Pro-Cathedral).
Steubenville, Ohio: Holy Name.
Stockton, Calif: Annunciation.
Superior, Wis.: Christ the King.
Syracuse, N.Y.: Immaculate Conception.
Toledo, Ohio: Blessed Virgin Mary of the Holy Rosary.
Trenton, N.J.: St. Mary.
Tucson, Ariz.: St. Augustine.
Tulsa, Okla.: Holy Family.
Washington,* D.C.: St. Matthew.
Wheeling, W. Va.: St. Joseph.
Wichita, Kans.: Immaculate Conception.
Wilmington, Del.: St. Peter.
Winona, Minn.: Sacred Heart.
Worcester, Mass.: St. Paul.
Yakima, Wash.: St. Paul.
Youngstown, Ohio: St. Columba.
Apostolic Exarchate of the Melkites: Our Lady of the Annunciation (Boston, Mass.).

BASILICAS IN U.S., CANADA

Basilica is a title assigned to certain churches because of their antiquity, dignity, historical importance or significance as centers of worship. Major basilicas have the papal altar and holy door, which is opened at the beginning of a Jubilee Year; minor basilicas enjoy certain ceremonial privileges.

Among the major basilicas are the patriarchal basilicas of St. John Lateran, St. Peter, St. Paul Outside the Walls and St. Mary

Major in Rome; St. Francis and St. Mary of the Angels in Assisi, Italy. The first four have the Holy Doors which are opened and closed at the start and end of Holy Years.

The patriarchal basilica of St. Lawrence, Rome, is a minor basilica.

The dates in the listings below indicate when the churches were designated as basilicas.

Alabama: Mobile, Cathedral of the Immaculate Conception (Mar. 10, 1962).

California: San Francisco, Mission Dolores (Feb. 8, 1952); Carmel, Old Mission of San Carlos (Feb. 5, 1960).

Illinois: Chicago, Our Lady of Sorrows (May 4, 1956), Queen of All Saints (Mar. 26, 1962).

Indiana: Vincennes, Old Cathedral (Mar. 14, 1970).

Iowa: Dyersville, St. Francis Xavier (May 11, 1956).

Kentucky: Trappist, Our Lady of Gethsemani (May 3, 1949); Covington, Cathedral of Assumption (Dec. 8, 1953).

Louisiana: New Orleans, St. Louis King of France (Dec. 9, 1964).

Maryland: Baltimore, Assumption of the Blessed Virgin Mary (Sept. 1, 1937).

Massachusetts: Roxbury, Perpetual Help ("Mission Church") (Sept. 8, 1954).

Minnesota: Minneapolis, St. Mary (Feb. 1, 1926).

Missouri: Conception, Basilica of Immaculate Conception (Sept. 14, 1940); St. Louis, St. Louis King of France (Jan. 27, 1961).

New York: Brooklyn, Our Lady of Perpetual Help (Sept. 5, 1969); Buffalo, St. Adalbert's (Aug. 11, 1907); Lackawanna, Our Lady of Victory (1926).

Ohio: Carey, Shrine of Our Lady of Consolation (Oct. 21, 1971).

Pennsylvania: Latrobe, St. Vincent Basilica, Benedictine Archabbey (Aug. 22, 1955); Conewago, Basilica of the Sacred Heart (June 30, 1962).

Wisconsin: Milwaukee, St. Josaphat (Mar. 10, 1929).

Manitoba: St. Boniface, Cathedral Basilica of St. Boniface (June 10, 1949).

Newfoundland: St. John's, Cathedral Basilica of St. John the Baptist.

Nova Scotia: Halifax, St. Mary's Basilica (June 14, 1950).

Ontario: Ottawa, Basilica of Notre Dame; London, St. Peter's Cathedral (Dec. 13, 1961).

Prince Edward Island: Charlottetown, Basilica of St. Dunstan.

Quebec: Sherbrooke, Cathedral Basilica of St. Michael (July 31, 1959). Montreal, Cathedral Basilica of St. James the Greater; St. Joseph of Mount Royal. Cap-de-la-Madeleine, Basilica of Our Lady of the Cape (Aug. 15, 1964). Quebec, Basilica of Notre Dame; St. Anne de Beaupre, Basilica of St. Anne.

CHANCERY OFFICES OF U.S. ARCHDIOCESES AND DIOCESES

A chancery office, under this or another title, is the central administrative office of an archdiocese or diocese.

(Archdioceses are indicated by asterisk.)

Albany, N.Y.: 465 State St., Box 6297, Quail Station. 12206.

Alexandria, La.: 2315 Texas Ave., P. O. Box 5665. 71301.

Allentown, Pa.: 1729 Turner St. 18104.

Altoona-Johnstown, Pa.: Logan Blvd., Hollidaysburg, Pa. 16648.

Amarillo, Tex.: 1800 N. Spring St., P. O. Box 5644. 79107.

Anchorage,* Alaska: 811 Sixth Ave., P. O. Box 2239. 99501.

Arlington, Va.: 200 N. Glebe Rd. 22203.

Atlanta,* Ga.: 756 W. Peachtree St. N.W. 30308.

Austin, Tex.: N. Congress and 16th, P. O. Box 13327. Capitol Sta. 78711.

Baker, Ore.: Baker and First Sts., P. O. Box 826, 97814.

Baltimore,* Md.: 320 Cathedral St. 21201.

Baton Rouge, La.: P. O. Box 2028. 70821.

Beaumont, Tex.: 703 Archie St., P. O. Box 3948. 77704.

Belleville, Ill.: 5312 W. Main St., Box 896. 62203.

Belmont Abbey, N.C.: Belmont, N.C., 28012.

Birmingham, Ala.: P. O. Box 2086. 35201.

Bismarck, N.D.: 420 Raymond St., Box 1575. 58501.

Boise, Ida.: Box 769, 420 Idaho St. 83701.

Boston,* Mass.: 2121 Commonwealth Ave., Brighton, Mass. 02135.

Bridgeport, Conn.: 250 Waldemere Ave. 06604.

Brooklyn, N.Y.: 75 Greene Ave. 11238.

Brownsville, Tex.: P. O. Box 2279. 78520.

Buffalo, N.Y.: 35 Lincoln Parkway. 14222.

Burlington, Vt.: 52 Williams St. 05401.

Camden, N.J.: 1845 Haddon Ave., P. O. Box 709, 01801.

Charleston, S.C.: 119 Broad St. P. O. Box 818. 29402.

Charlotte, N.C.: P. O. Box 3776. 28203.

Cheyenne, Wyo.: Box 426. 82001.

Chicago,* Ill.: 211 E. Chicago Ave. 60611.

Cincinnati,* O.: 29 E. 8th St. 45202.

Cleveland, O.: 350 Chancery Bldg., Cathedral Sq., 1027 Superior Ave. 44114.

Columbus, O.: 198 E. Broad St. 43215.

Corpus Christi, Tex.: 620 Lipan St. 78401.

Covington, Ky.: 1140 Madison Ave., P. O. Box 192. 41012.

Crookston, Minn.: 1200 Memorial Dr., P. O. Box 610. 56716.

Dallas, Tex.: 3915 Lemmon Ave., P. O. Box 19507. 75219.

Davenport, Ia.: P.O. Box 2253. 52804.
Denver,* Colo.: 938 Bannock St. 80204.
Des Moines, Ia.: 2910 Grand Ave., P. O. Box 1816. 50306.
Detroit,* Mich.: 1234 Washington Blvd. 48226.
Dodge City, Kans.: 910 Central Ave., P. O. Box 849. 67801.
Dubuque,* Ia.: 1229 Mt. Loretta Ave. 52001.
Duluth, Minn.: 215 W. 4th St. 55806.
El Paso, Tex.: 1012 N. Mesa St. 79902.
Erie, Pa.: 205 W. 9th St. 16501.
Evansville, Ind.: 219 N. W. Third St. 47708.
Fairbanks, Alaska: 1316 Peger Rd. 99701.
Fall River, Mass.: 362 Highland Ave., Box 2577. 02722.
Fargo, N. D.: 504 Black Bldg., Box 1750. 58102.
Fort Wayne-South Bend, Ind.: P. O. Box 390, Fort Wayne. 46801.
Fort Worth, Tex.: 1206 Throckmorton St. 76102.
Fresno, Calif.: P. O. Box 1668, 1550 N. Fresno St. 93717.
Gallup, N. Mex.: 406 W. Aztec St., P. O. Box 1338. 87301.
Galveston-Houston, Tex.: 1700 San Jacinto St., Houston. 77002.
Gary, Ind.: 668 Pierce St., P. O. Box 474. 46401.
Gaylord, Mich.: M-32 West, P. O. Box 700. 49735.
Grand Island, Nebr.: 311 W. 17th St., P. O. Box 996. 68801.
Grand Rapids, Mich.: 265 Sheldon Ave. S. E. 49502.
Great Falls, Mont.: 725 Third Ave. N., P. O. Box 1399. 59403.
Green Bay, Wis.: Box 66. 54305.
Greensburg, Pa.: 723 E. Pittsburgh St. 15601.
Harrisburg, Pa.: 111 State St. P. O. Box 2153. 17105.
Hartford,* Conn.: 134 Farmington Ave. 06105.
Helena, Mont.: 612 Harrison Ave., P. O. Box 1729. 59601.
Honolulu, H. I.: 1184 Bishop St. 96813.
Indianapolis,* Ind.: 1350 N. Pennsylvania St. 46206.
Jefferson City, Mo.: 605 Clark Ave. P. O. Box 417. 65101.
Joliet, Ill.: 425 Summit St. 60435.
Juneau, Alaska: 416 5th St. 99801.
Kalamazoo, Mich.: 215 N. Westnedge. Ave. 49005.
Kansas City,* Kans.: 2220 Central Ave., P. O. Box 2328. 66110.
Kansas City-St. Joseph, Mo.: P. O. Box 1037, Kansas City. 64141.
La Crosse, Wis.: P.O. Box 982. 54601.
Lafayette in Indiana: 610 Lingle Ave. 47902.
Lafayette, La.: P. O. Drawer 3387. 70501.
Lansing, Mich.: 300 W. Ottawa. 48933.

Lincoln, Nebr.: 3400 Sheridan Blvd., P. O. Box 80328. 68501.
Little Rock, Ark.: 2415 N. Tyler St. 72207.
Los Angeles,* Calif.: 1531 W. 9th St. 90015.
Louisville,* Ky.: 212 E. College St., P. O. Box 1073. 40201.
Madison, Wis.: 15 E. Wilson St. 53701.
Manchester, N. H.: 153 Ash St. 03105.
Marquette, Mich.: 444 S. Fourth St., P. O. Box 550. 49855.
Memphis, Tenn.: 1325 Jefferson Ave., 38104.
Mami,* Fla.: 6301 Biscayne Blvd. 33138.
Milwaukee,* Wis.: 345 N. 95th St. 53226.
Mobile, Ala.: 400 Government St., P. O. Box 1966. 36606.
Monterey, Calif.: 580 Fremont Blvd. 93940.
Munhall,* Pa. (Byzantine Rite) 54 RiverviewAve., Pittsburgh. 15214.
Nashville, Tenn.: 421 Charlotte Ave. 37219.
Natchez-Jackson, Miss.: 237 E. Amite St., P. O. Box 2248, Jackson. 39205.
Newark,* N. J.: 31 Mulberry St. 07102.
New Orleans,* La.: 7887 Walmsley Ave. 70125.
New Ulm, Minn.: Chancery Drive. 56073.
New York,* N. Y.: 1011 First Ave. 10022.
Norwich, Conn.: 201 Broadway, P. O. Box 587. 06360.
Oakland, Calif.: 2900 Lakeshore Ave. 94610.
Ogdensburg, N. Y.: 622 Washington St. 13669.
Oklahoma City,* Okla.: 1521 N. Hudson, Oklahoma City. 73103.
Omaha,* Nebr.: 100 N. 62nd St. 68132.
Orlando, Fla.: P. O. Box 7700. 32804.
Owensboro, Ky.: c/o Chancellor's Residence, 4003 Frederica St. 42301.
Parma, Ohio (Byzantine Rite): 1900 Carlton Rd. 44134.
Passaic, N.J. (Byzantine Rite): 101 Market St. 07055.
Paterson, N. J.: 24 De Grasse St. 07505.
Peoria, Ill.: 607 N. E. Madison Ave. 61603.
Philadelphia,* Pa.: 222 N. 17th St. 19103.
Philadelphia,* Pa. (Byzantine Rite): 815 N. Franklin St. 19123.
Phoenix, Ariz.: 400 E. Monroe St. 85004.
Pittsburgh, Pa.: 111 Blvd. of the Allies. 15222.
Portland, Me.: 510 Ocean Ave., Woodfords P. O. Box H. 04103.
Portland in Oregon*: 2838 E. Burnside St. 97207.
Providence, R. I.: Cathedral Sq. 02903.
Pueblo, Colo.: 1426 Grand Ave. 81003.
Raleigh, N. C.: P. O. Box 1949. 27602.
Rapid City, S. D.: 520 Cathedral Dr., P. O. Box 752. 57701.
Reno, Nev.: 515 Court St. 89501. P. O. Box 1211, 89504.
Richmond, Va.: 807 Cathedral Pl. 23220.
Rochester, N.Y.: 1150 Buffalo Rd. 14624.

Rockford, Ill.: 1245 N. Court St. 61101.

Rockville Centre, N.Y.: 50 N. Park Ave. 11570.

Sacramento, Calif.: 1119 K St., P. O. Box 1706. 95808.

Saginaw, Mich.: 2555 Wieneke Rd. 48603.

St. Augustine, Fla.: Suite 1648, Gulf Life Tower, Jacksonville, Fla. 32207.

St. Cloud, Minn.: P. O. Box 1248. 56301.

St. Louis,* Mo.: 4445 Lindell Blvd. 63108.

St. Maron of Detroit, Mich.: 11470 Kercheval, P. O. Box 3307, Jefferson Sta., Detroit, Mich. 48214.

St. Nicholas in Chicago (Byzantine Rite): 2245 W. Rice St. 60622.

St. Paul and Minneapolis,* Minn.: 226 Summit Ave., St. Paul. 55102.

St. Petersburg, Fla.: 6363 9th Ave. N. 33710. P. O. Box 13109. 33733.

Salina, Kans.: 421 Country Club Rd., P. O. Box 999. 67401.

Salt Lake City, Utah: 333 E. S. Temple. 84111.

San Angelo, Tex.: 116 S. Oakes. Box 1829. 76901.

San Antonio,* Tex.: 9123 Lorene Lane, P. O. Box 32648. 78284.

San Diego, Calif.: Alcala Park. 92110.

San Francisco,* Calif.: 445 Church St. 94114.

Santa Fe,* N. Mex.: 202 Morningside Dr. S. E., Albuquerque. 87108.

Santa Rosa, Calif.: 398 10th St., P. O. Box 1499. 95403.

Savannah, Ga.: 225 Abercorn St., P. O. Box 8789. 31402.

Scranton, Pa.: 300 Wyoming Ave. 18503.

Seattle,* Wash.: 907 Terry Ave. 98104.

Sioux City, Ia.: P. O. Box 1530. 51102.

Sioux Falls, S.D.: 423 N. Duluth Ave. 57104.

Spokane, Wash.: 1023 W. Riverside Ave. 99201.

Springfield, Illinois: 524 E. Lawrence Ave. 62705.

Springfield, Mass.: 76 Elliot St. 01105. P.O. Box 1730, 01101.

Springfield-Cape Girardeau, Mo.: 410 Landers Bldg., Springfield. 65806.

Stamford, Conn. (Byzantine Rite): 161 Glenbrook Rd. 06902.

Steubenville, Ohio: 422 Washington St., P. O. Box 969. 43952.

Stockton, Calif.: 1105 N. Lincoln St. 95203. P. O. Box 4237. 95204.

Superior, Wis.: 1201 Hughitt Ave. 54880.

Syracuse, N.Y.: 240 E. Onondaga St., 13202.

Toledo, Ohio: 2544 Parkwood Ave. 43610.

Trenton, N.J.: 701 Lawrenceville Rd. 08638.

Tucson, Ariz.: 192 S. Stone Ave., Box 31, 85702.

Tulsa, Okla.: P. O. Box 2009. 74101.

Washington,* D.C.: 1721 Rhode Island Ave. N. W. 20036.

Wheeling, W. Va.: 1300 Byron St. 26003.

Wichita, Kans.: 424 N. Broadway. 67202.

Wilmington, Del.: P. O. Box 2030. 19899.

Winona, Minn.: 275 Harriet St. 55987.

Worcester, Mass.: 49 Elm St. 01609.

Yakima, Wash.: 228 Liberty Bldg., P.O. Box 901. 98901.

Youngstown, Ohio: 144 W. Wood St. 44503.

Apostolic Exarchate of the Melkites: 19 Dartmouth St., W. Newton, Mass. 02165.

NATIONAL CATHOLIC CONFERENCES

The two conferences described below are related in membership and directive control but distinct in nature, purpose and function.

The National Conference of Catholic Bishops (NCCB) is a strictly ecclesiastical body in and through which the bishops of the United States act together, officially and with authority as pastors of the Church. It is the sponsoring organization of the United States Catholic Conference.

The United States Catholic Conference (USCC) is a civil corporation and operational secretariat in and through which the bishops, together with other members of the Church, act on a wider scale for the good of the Church and society. It is sponsored by the National Conference of Catholic Bishops.

The principal officers of both conferences are: Cardinal John J. Krol, president; Archbishop Leo C. Byrne, vice president; Archbishop Thomas A. Donnellan, treasurer; Bishop James S. Rausch, general secretary.

Headquarters of both conferences are located at 1312 Massachusetts Ave. N. W., Washington, D. C. 20005.

NCCB

The National Conference of Catholic Bishops, established by action of the US hierarchy Nov. 14, 1966, is a strictly ecclesiastical body with defined juridical authority over the Church in this country. It was set up with the approval of the Holy See and in line with directives from the Second Vatican Council. Its constitution was formally ratified during the November, 1967, meeting of the US hierarchy.

The NCCB is the successor to the Annual Meeting of the Bishops of the United States, whose pastoral character was originally approved by Pope Benedict XV Apr. 10, 1919.

The address of the Conference is 1312 Massachusetts Ave. N. W., Washington, D. C. 20005.

Pastoral Council

The conference, one of many similar territorial conferences envisioned in the conciliar *Decree on the Pastoral Office of Bishops in the Church* (No. 38), is "a council in which the bishops of a given nation or territory (in this case, the United States) jointly exercise their pastoral office to promote the greater good which the Church offers mankind, especially through the forms and methods of the apostolate fittingly adapted to the circumstances of the age."

Its decisions, "provided they have been approved legitimately and by the votes of at least two-thirds of the prelates who have a deliberative vote in the conference, and have been recognized by the Apostolic See, are to have juridically binding force only in those cases prescribed by the common law or determined by a special mandate of the Apostolic See, given either spontaneously or in response to a petition of the conference itself."

All bishops who serve or have served the Church in the US, its territories and possessions, have full membership and voting rights in the NCCB.

Officers, Committees

The conference operates through a number of bishops' committees with functions in specific areas of work and concern. Their basic assignments are to prepare materials on the basis of which the bishops, assembled as a conference, make decisions, and to put suitable action plans into effect.

The principal officers are: Cardinal John J. Krol, president; Archbishop Leo C. Byrne, vice president; Archbishop Thomas A. Donnellan, treasurer; Bishop James S. Rausch, general secretary.

These officers, with several other bishops, hold positions on executive-level committees — Executive Committee, the Committee on Budget and Finance, the committee on Personnel and Administrative Services, and the Committee on Research, Plans and Programs. They also, with other bishops, serve on the NCCB Administrative Committee.

The standing committees and their chairmen (Archbishops and Bishops) are as follows.

American Board of Catholic Missions, William G. Connare.

Arbitration, Edward W. O'Rourke.

Boundaries of Dioceses and Provinces, Cardinal John J. Krol.

Canon Law, Bernard J. Flanagan.

Church in Latin America, John J. Fitzpatrick.

Doctrine, George W. Ahr.

Ecumenical and Interreligious Affairs, William W. Baum.

Lay Apostolate, Francis J. Furey.

Liaison with Priests, Religious and Laity, Warren L. Boudreaux.

Liturgy, Walter W. Curtis.

Men Religious, Aloysius J. Wycislo.

Missions, Glennon P. Flavin.

Nomination of Bishops, Cardinal John J. Krol.

North American College, Louvain, Stephen A. Leven.

North American College, Rome, Daniel A. Cronin.

Pastoral Research and Practices, John R. Quinn.

Permanent Diaconate, Daniel E. Sheehan.

Priestly Formation, Loras J. Watters.

Priestly Life and Ministry, Thomas J. Grady.

Vocations, Raymond J. Vonesh.

Welfare Emergency Relief, Cardinal John J. Krol.

Women Religious, James J. Byrne.

Ad hoc committees and their chairmen are as follows.

Bicentennial, Cardinal John F. Dearden.

Campaign for Human Development, Raymond J. Gallagher.

Farm Labor, Joseph F. Donnelly.

Holy Year, Cardinal Timothy Manning.

Liaison with National Office for Black Catholics, Joseph A. McNicholas.

Migration and Tourism, Robert E. Tracy.

National Catechetical Directory, John F. Whealon.

Nominations to Conference Offices (chair vacant).

Pro-Life Activities, Cardinal John P. Cody.

Spanish-Speaking, James S. Rausch.

Women in Society and Church, Leo C. Byrne.

USCC

The United States Catholic Conference, Inc. (USCC), is the operational secretariat and service agency of the National Conference of Catholic Bishops for carrying out the civic-religious work of the Church in this country. It is a civil corporation related to the NCCB in membership and directive control but distinct from it in purpose and function.

The address of the Conference is 1312 Massachusetts Ave. N.W., Washington, D.C. 20005.

Service Secretariat

The USCC, as of Jan. 1, 1967, took over the general organization and operations of the former National Catholic Welfare Conference, Inc., whose origins dated back to the National Catholic War Council of 1917. The council underwent some change after World War I and was established on a permanent basis Sept. 24, 1919, as the National Catholic Welfare Council to serve as a central agency for organizing and coordinating the efforts of US Catholics in carrying out the social mission of the Church in this country. In 1923, its name was changed to National Catholic Welfare Conference, Inc., and clarification was made of its nature as a service agency of the bishops and the Church rather than as a conference of bishops with real juridical authority in ecclesiastical affairs.

The Official Catholic Directory states that the USCC assists "the bishops in their service to the Church in this country by uniting the people of God where voluntary collective action on a broad interdiocesan level is needed. The USCC provides an organizational structure and the resources needed to insure coordination, cooperation, and assistance in the public, educational and social concerns of the Church at the national or interdiocesan level."

Officers, Departments

The principal officers of the USCC are Cardinal John J. Krol, president; Archbishop Leo C. Byrne, vice president; Archbishop Thomas A. Donnellan, treasurer; Bishop James S. Rausch, general secretary. These officers, with several other bishops, hold positions on executive-level committees — the Executive Committee; the Committee on Research, Plans and Programs; the Committee on Budget and Finance; the Committee on Personnel and Administrative Services. They also serve on the Administrative Board.

The Executive Committee, organized in 1969, is authorized to handle matters of urgency between meetings of the Administrative Board and the general conference, to coordinate items for the agenda of general meetings, and to speak in the name of the USCC.

The major departments and their chairmen (Archbishops and Bishops) are: Communications, Joseph L. Bernardin; Education, William D. Borders; Social Development and World Peace, John J. Dougherty. Each department is supervised by a committee composed of an equal number of episcopal and non-episcopal members, including lay persons.

A National Advisory Council of bishops, priests, men and women religious, lay men and women advises the Administrative Board on overall plans and operations of the USCC.

The administrative general secretariat, in addition to other duties, supervises staff-service offices of Finance and Administration, General Counsel, Government Liaison, and Research, Plans and Programs.

USCC committees, bureaus and offices are divisions under the departments, as follows:
  • **Communications:** Office of Communi-

cations. Communications Development, National Catholic Office for Information, Film and Broadcasting, NC News Service. Creative Services.
  • **Education:** Elementary and Secondary Education, Higher Education, Religious Education Family Life, Youth Activities.
  • **Social Development and World Peace:** Health Affairs, Chaplains' Services, Justice and Peace, Rural Life, Spanish-Speaking, Urban Affairs, Latin America, Migration and Refugee Services.
  • **Campaign for Human Development,** for anti-poverty programs.
  • **Related Organizations:** National Conference of Catholic Laity, National Catholic Community Service.

Most of the 35 organizations and associations affiliated with the USCC are covered in separate Almanac entries.

NCCB-USCC REGIONS

For meeting and other operational purposes, the members of the National Conference of Catholic Bishops and the U.S. Catholic Conference are grouped in the following geographical regions.

I. Maine, Vermont, New Hampshire, Massachusetts, Rhode Island, Connecticut.

II. New York.

III. New Jersey, Pennsylvania.

IV. Delaware, District of Columbia, Florida, Georgia, Maryland, North Carolina, South Carolina, Virgin Islands, Virginia, West Virginia.

V. Alabama, Kentucky, Louisiana, Mississippi, Tennessee.

VI. Michigan, Ohio.

VII. Illinois, Indiana, Wisconsin.

VIII. Minnesota, North Dakota, South Dakota, Wyoming, Colorado.

IX. Iowa, Kansas, Missouri, Nebraska.

X. Arizona, Arkansas, New Mexico, Oklahoma, Texas.

XI. California, Hawaii, Nevada, Utah, Caroline-Marshall Islands, Guam.

XII. Idaho, Montana, Alaska, Washington, Oregon.

MEETINGS OF THE CONFERENCE OF BISHOPS
November 12 to 16, 1973

The meeting, held in Washington, D. C., was attended by more than 250 members of the hierarchy. The presiding officer was Cardinal John J. Krol, president of the National Conference of Catholic Bishops and the U.S. Catholic Conference.

The bishops acted on the following items.

Bicentennial Observance: Adopted "Justice in the World" as the theme of Catholic observance of the nation's bicentennial in 1976. The Committee for the Observance of the Bicentennial, declared Cardinal John F. Dearden, "hopes to highlight the Christian princi-

ples concerning the dignity of man, his God-given freedoms, and the continued need for justice in our day."

Catholic Relief Services: Received from Bishop Edward E. Swanstrom, executive director, a report on 30 years of CRS operations. He said: "In the past 30 years 11.6 million tons of supplies valued at $2.42 billion have been channeled into CRS programs. These relief goods have reached into 137 countries; during this time, as many as 40 million needy men, women and children have been helped in one year."

Deacons: Received a committee report stating that at least 59 U.S. dioceses had permanent diaconate programs in operation and that 411 permanent deacons (374 married, 37 unmarried) were engaged in a wide variety of ministries.

Eucharistic Congress: Agreed by a voice vote to support the 41st International Eucharistic Congress in 1976 in Philadelphia, given the approval of Pope Paul and the Permanent Committee for International Eucharistic Congresses.

Farm Workers: Passed resolutions in support of the Cesar Chavez-led United Farm Workers of America in their struggle with growers and the Teamsters for union recognition and contracts. Regarding union elections, the bishops went "on record in support of the field workers in the agriculture industry to free, secret-ballot elections which will determine whether or not they want union representation and which union they want to represent them." The bishops called "upon the growers and Teamsters to accede to this demand of the UFW of America without further delay." On the subject of the UFWA boycott, they said they endorsed and supported "the UFW's consumer boycott of table grapes and head lettuce until such time as free, secret-ballot elections are held."

First Confession and Communion: Heard a report by Bishop William D. Borders, chairman of the Education Committee, that a 1973 Vatican document on this subject requires that children be given the opportunity of receiving the sacrament of penance as well as the Eucharist on reaching the age of reason.

Human Rights: Passed unanimously a resolution of support for the United Nations Universal Declaration of Human Rights, which they called "a testament of vital importance to the global family."

In-Hand Reception of Holy Communion: For the second time since 1969, defeated by a vote of 121 to 113 a motion to seek Vatican permission to introduce in-hand reception of Holy Communion in the U.S. The vote was far short of the two-thirds majority required for passage. (The practice was being followed in 26 countries, including Canada.)

Liturgical Changes: Adopted motions to seek Vatican authorization for a number of changes in the sacramentary and for several prayers and commemorations for special U.S. feasts and holidays.

Marriage Court Norms: Decided to send a personal delegation to Pope Paul to seek indefinite extension beyond July 1, 1974, of more than 20 special norms for handling cases concerning the validity of marriage in U.S. marriage tribunals. The procedural norms, expediting decision in such cases, were authorized on an experimental basis in 1970.

Mary: Issued a 20,000-word pastoral letter on Mary entitled "Behold Your Mother, Woman of Faith," concerning Marian doctrine and devotion. (Its contents were closely related to "The Mother of Jesus in Catholic Understanding" and Pope Paul's apostolic exhortation entitled *Marialis Cultus;* see separate Almanac entries.)

Media Morals: Voted to establish an ad hoc committee to direct the "development of a detailed programmatic proposal" on morality in the mass communications media and their impact on the morals of society.

Middle East: Passed a resolution calling for "a comprehensive political solution" to Arab-Israeli conflicts. They urged "recognition of the right of Israel to exist as a sovereign state with secure boundaries; recognition of the rights of the Palestinian Arabs, especially the refugees . . .; acceptance as the basis for negotiations . . . of the stipulations set forth in the United Nations Security Council Resolution 242 of 22 November 1967" (withdrawal of Israeli troops from occupied Arab territories). The resolution said of Jerusalem: "We believe it necessary to insure access to the city through a form of international guarantee. Moreover, the character of the city as a religiously pluralist community, with equal protection of the religious and civil rights of all citizens, must be guaranteed in the name of justice."

Ministries: Agreed by a large majority to seek Vatican permission to establish two new lay ministries open to women as well as men — ministries of religious education and of music.

Penal Reform: Published "The Reform of Correctional Institutions in the 1970's," upholding the rights of inmates and urging greater involvement by the Church and community in efforts for the rehabilitation of inmates. (See separate entry.)

Priests: Without registering approval or disapproval of their contents, voted to permit distribution of two reports on priestly ministry and research and scholarship derived from a four-year, $500,000 study of the priesthood sponsored by the NCCB.

The bishops also replaced their Ad Hoc Committee for Priestly Life and Ministry with a permanent committee under the chairmanship of Auxiliary Bishop Thomas J. Grady of Chicago. (Msgr. Colin A. MacDonald was later named executive director of the committee.)

Privacy Invasion, Proxy Decisions: Heard Bishop Mark J. Hurley, moderator of the Secretariat on Human Values, warn that progress in science and computerized technology pose mounting threats to individual human rights and freedoms. The gathering and use of computerized data by government and private agenices endanger rights to privacy, while proxy decisions by "some superauthority" have the potential to affect the weaker members of society with such practices as experimentation on prisoners, psychosurgery, fetal experimentation, amniocentesis and euthanasia.

Regional Meetings: Assigned "Communication and the Church as a Form of Evangelization in the Contemporary World," as the theme of regional NCCB meetings to be held in the spring of 1974.

Religious: Approved proposals to ask the chairmen of regional conferences of the NCCB to invite major superiors of men religious to regional convocations, and to ask the NCCB president to consider setting up joint committees with the Conference of Major Superiors of Men.

Right to Life: Approved a resolution of "opposition to the Supreme Court's rulings on abortion" of Jan. 22, 1973. The resolution said, in part: "We are convinced that the decision of the Supreme Court is wrong, and must be reversed. The only certain way to repair effectively the damage perpetrated by the Court's opinions is to amend the Constitution to provide clearly and definitively a constitutional base for legal protection of unborn human beings. . . . We wish to state once again, as emphatically as possible, our endorsement of and support for a constitutional amendment that will protect the life of the unborn. . . . We wish to make it clear beyond doubt . . . that we consider the passage of a pro-life constitutional amendment a priority of the highest order, one to which we are committed by our determination to uphold the dignity of the human being and by our conviction that this nation must provide protection for the life, liberty and pursuit of happiness for all human beings, before as well as after birth."

Seminaries: Were told by Bishop Loras J. Watters, chairman of the Committee on Priestly Formation, that reports from around the country noted "frequent deviations" from the bishops' own 1972 "Program of Priestly Formation." Spiritual formation problems, he said, included "a lack of integration between the spiritual formation and the academic and pastoral," "a lack of communal prayer," and difficulty in attaining daily participation in the liturgy. On the academic side, he reported that "some seminaries do not have four full academic years of theology as required by Rome," and that many students beginning the study of theology had "very little or no philosophy" in their academic background.

Synod Delegates: Elected the following representatives to the 1974 assembly of the Synod of Bishops: Cardinals John J. Krol, John F. Dearden and John J. Carberry, and Archbishop Joseph L. Bernardin; Cardinal Timothy Manning and Coadjutor Archbishop Leo C. Byrne, first and second alternates.

Vocations to Diocesan Priesthood: Were told by Msgr. Andrew McGowan, president of the National Conference of Diocesan Vocation Directors, that the number of vocations to the diocesan priesthood is "totally inadequate to meet the institutional needs" of the Church in the United States. "Clearly, un-mistakably, despite rumors to the contrary and occasional evidences of good news," he said, the number of vocations is so low that it is impossible to meet current needs, much less the greater needs of the future.

Regional Meetings

"The Use of Modern Means of Communication as Instruments of Evangelization" was the topic of two- to four-day meetings of bishops in the 12 regions of the United States toward the end of April, 1974. The purposes of the meetings were to stimulate communication efforts on local and national levels, to develop topics for presentation at the 1974 assembly of the Synod of Bishops in Rome, and to formulate items for the agenda of the annual November meeting of the National Conference of Catholic Bishops and the United States Catholic Conference.

Discussions of ways and means of doing that resulted in "a convergence of views and consensus on major points," according to a summary report on the meetings issued by Archbishop Joseph L. Bernardin, chairman of the Communications Committee.

Major points covered in the meetings included the following.

Catholic Press: Strong support was urged, especially for newspapers, along with efforts to increase circulation and readership. The possibility of consolidating some diocesan newspapers was suggested.

Parish-Level Communications: These can be achieved and improved by means of bulletins, adult education, the use of audio-visual materials, in and through parish councils, effective homily plans. Homilies were described in one meeting as "the best medium of adult education available to the Church."

Diocesan-Level Communications: Emphasis fell on the need for "a well staffed, well funded office of communication in every diocese." Interdiocesan collaboration and the establishment of regional communication centers were considered ways of increasing professionalism and ranges of service. "Ideally," according to the summary report, "there should be one high-quality communication center in each region, jointly funded and utilized by all dioceses of the region. Functions of such a center would include production, placement, training and research."

National-Level Communications: There was general agreement in favor of the continuing development and strengthening of the operations of the USCC Communications Department and NC News Service, the principal source of national Catholic news and feature services.

Radio and Television: The potential of the electronic media in religious broadcasting has hardly been tapped, was the tenor of many discussions. "Dioceses need to be more active in radio and television," and need also "an effective 'mix' of media and media-related activities" for effective communication. High priority was given to the need for professionalism in developing local and network production and programming.

Personnel: The professionalism characteristic of the communications industry has been matched in religious broadcasting and those who do it. The related training of suitable personnel is indispensable.

Participants in the regional meetings asked that the 1974 assembly of the Synod of Bishops "provide the Church with a description of evangelization which includes perennial Gospel truths but also reflects contemporary attitudes and is adaptable to varied cultures."

All the meetings except one — of the bishops of Pennsylvania and New Jersey — held sessions open to members of the press and other interested parties. Communications experts addressed most of the assemblies, and observers participated in more than a few exchanges of ideas.

STATE CATHOLIC CONFERENCES

These conferences are agencies of bishops and dioceses in the various states. Their general purposes are to develop and sponsor cooperative programs designed to cope with pastoral and common-welfare needs, and to represent the dioceses before governmental bodies, the public, and in private sectors. Their membership consists of representatives from the dioceses in the states — bishops, clergy and lay persons in various capacities.

The **National Association of State Catholic Conference Directors** maintains liaison with the general secretariat of the US Catholic Conference.

Theodore N. Staudt of Ohio is president.

Alaska Catholic Conference, 416 5th St., Juneau, Alaska 99801; exec. dir., Frank W. Matulich.

Arizona Catholic Conference, 400 E. Monroe St., Phoenix, Ariz. 85004; exec. dir., G. A. (Jack) Bradley.

California Catholic Conference, 926 J St., Suite 1100, Sacramento, Calif. 95814; exec. dir., Rev. Msgr. John S. Cummins.

Colorado Catholic Conference, 938 Bannock St., Denver, Colo. 80204; Sr. Loretta A. Madden.

Connecticut Catholic Conference, 134 Farmington Ave., Hartford, Conn. 06105; exec. dir., William Wholean.

Florida Catholic Conference, P.O. Box 1571, Tallahassee, Fla. 32302; exec. dir., Thomas A. Horkan.

Georgia Catholic Conference, 335 Ivy St., N.E., Atlanta, Ga. 30303; exec. secy., Rev. Michael A. Morris.

Illinois Catholic Conference, 201 E. Ohio St., Chicago, Ill. 60611; exec. dir., Rev. William J. Lion.

Indiana Catholic Conference, Room 442, Illinois Building, Indianapolis, Ind. 46204; exec. dir., Raymond R. Rufo.

Iowa Catholic Conference, 918 Insurance Exchange Building, Des Moines, Iowa 50309; exec. dir., Timothy McCarthy.

Kansas Catholic Conference, 601 Minnesota Ave., Kansas City, Kan. 66101; exec. dir., Vincent W. DeCoursey.

Kentucky Catholic Conference, 605 Bank of Commerce Building, Lexington, Ky. 40507; exec. dir. and general counsel, Donald P. Moloney.

Louisiana Catholic Conference, 1100 Chartres St., New Orleans, La. 70116; exec. dir., Emile Comar.

Maryland Catholic Conference, 320 Cathedral St., Baltimore, Md. 21201; exec. dir., James Shaneman.

Massachusetts Catholic Conference, 60 School St., Boston, Mass. 02107; exec. dir., Joseph J. Reilly.

Michigan Catholic Conference, P.O. Box 157, Lansing, Mich. 48901; exec. dir., Thomas M. Bergeson.

Minnesota Catholic Conference, 145 University Ave., W., St. Paul, Minn. 55103; exec. dir., John F. Markert.

Missouri Catholic Conference, P.O. Box 1022, Jefferson City, Mo. 65101; acting exec. dir., Louis DeFeo.

Montana Catholic Conference, P.O. Box 404, Helena, Mont. 59601; exec. dir., John Frankino.

Nebraska Catholic Conference, 521 S. 14th St., Lincoln, Nebr. 68508; exec. dir., Paul V. O'Hara.

New Jersey Catholic Conference, 495 W. State St., Trenton, N.J. 08618; exec. dir., Edward J. Leadem.

New York State Catholic Committee, 11 N. Pearl St., Albany, N.Y. 12207; exec. secy., Charles J. Tobin, Jr.

North Dakota Catholic Conference, 304 Ave. A. West, Bismarck, N. Dak. 58501; exec. dir., Edwin C. Becker.

Ohio, Catholic Conference of, 22 South Young St., Columbus, Ohio 43215; exec. dir., Theodore N. Staudt.

Pennsylvania Catholic Conference, 509 N. Second St., Harrisburg, Pa. 17105; exec. dir., Howard J. Fetterhoff.

Tennessee Catholic Conference, 2015 West End Ave., Nashville, Tenn. 37203; acting coordinator, Rev. Philip Breen.

Texas Catholic Conference, 702 Commodore Perry Hotel, Austin, Tex. 78701; exec. dir., Rev. John McCarthy.

Virginia, Office of Lay Activities, 813 Cathedral St., Richmond, Va. 23220; exec. secy., Charles Brower.

Washington Catholic Conference, 301 Security Building, Olympia, Wash. 98501; general counsel, Francis J. Walker.

Wisconsin Catholic Conference, 16 N. Carroll St., Madison, Wis. 53703; exec. dir., Charles M. Phillips.

Biographies of American Bishops

(Sources: Almanac survey, *The Official Catholic Directory*, NC News Service.)

A

Abramowicz, Alfred L.: b. Jan. 27, 1919, Chicago, Ill.; educ. St. Mary of the Lake Seminary (Mundelein, Ill.), Gregorian Univ. (Rome); ord. priest May 1, 1943; ord. titular bishop of Paestum and auxiliary bishop of Chicago, June 13, 1968.

Ackerman, Richard Henry, C.S.Sp.: b. Aug. 30, 1903, Pittsburgh, Pa.; educ. Duquesne Univ. (Pittsburgh, Pa.), St. Mary's Scholasticate (Norwalk, Conn.), Univ. of Fribourg (Switzerland); ord. priest Aug. 28, 1926; ord. titular bishop of Lares and auxiliary bishop of San Diego, May 22, 1956; app. bishop of Covington, Apr. 4, 1960.

Ahern, Patrick V.: b. Mar. 8, 1919, New York, N.Y.; educ. Manhattan College and Cathedral College (New York City), St. Joseph's Seminary (Yonkers, N. Y.), St. Louis Univ. (St. Louis, Mo.), Notre Dame Univ. (Notre Dame, Ind.); ord. priest Jan. 27, 1945; ord. titular bishop of Naiera and auxiliary bishop of New York, Mar. 19, 1970.

Ahr, George William: b. June 23, 1904, Newark, N.J.; educ. St. Vincent College (Latrobe, Pa.), Seton Hall College (S. Orange, N.J.), North American College (Rome); ord. priest July 29, 1928; ord. bishop of Trenton, Mar. 20, 1950.

Alter, Karl Joseph: b. Aug. 18, 1885, Toledo, O.; educ. St. John's Univ. (Toledo, O.), St. Mary's Seminary (Cleveland, O.); ord. priest June 4, 1910; ord. bishop of Toledo, June 17, 1931; app. archbishop of Cincinnati, June 14, 1950; resigned 1969.

Anderson, Paul F.: b. Apr. 20, 1917, Roslindale, Mass.; educ. Boston College (Chestnut Hill, Mass.), St. John's Seminary (Brighton, Mass.); ord. priest Jan. 6, 1943; ord. titular bishop of Polignando and coadjutor bishop of Duluth, Oct. 17, 1968; bishop of Duluth, Apr. 30, 1969.

Angell, Kenneth A.: b. 1930, Providence, R.I.; educ. St. Mary's Seminary (Baltimore, Md.); ord. priest 1956; app. titular bishop of Septimunicia and auxiliary bishop of Providence, R.I., Aug. 13, 1974.

Arkfeld, Leo, S.V.D.: b. Feb. 4, 1912, Butte, Nebr.; educ. Divine Word Seminary (Techny, Ill.), Sacred Heart College (Girard, Pa.); ord. priest Aug. 15, 1943; ord. titular bishop of Bucellus and vicar apostolic of Central New Guinea, Nov. 30, 1948; name of vicariate changed to Wewak, May 15, 1952; first bishop of Wewak, Nov. 15, 1966.

Arliss, Reginald, C.P.: b. Sept. 8, 1906, East Orange, N.J.; educ. Immaculate Conception Seminary (Jamaica, N.Y.) and other Passionist houses of study; ord. priest Apr. 28, 1934; missionary in China for 16 years, expelled 1951; missionary in Philippines; rector of the Pontifical Philippine College Seminary in Rome, 1961-69; ord. titular bishop of Cerbali and prelate of Marbel, Philippines, Jan. 30, 1970.

Arzube, Juan: b. June 1, 1918, Guayaquil, Ecuador; educ. Rensselaer Polytechnic Institute (Troy, N.Y.), St. John's Seminary (Camarillo, Calif.); ord. priest 1954; ord. titular bishop of Civitate and auxiliary bishop of Los Angeles, Mar. 25, 1971.

B

Baldwin, Vincent J.: b. July 13, 1907, Brooklyn, N.Y.; educ. Cathedral College (Brooklyn, N.Y.), Institute of Philosophy (Huntington, N.Y.), Capranica College (Rome); ord. priest July 26, 1931, Rome; ord. titular bishop of Bencenna and auxiliary bishop of Rockville Centre, July 26, 1962; app. episcopal vicar, Nov. 3, 1971.

Bartholome, Peter William: b. Apr. 2, 1893, Bellechester, Minn.; educ. Campion College (Prairie du Chien, Wis.), St. Paul Seminary (St. Paul, Minn.), Apollinare (Rome); ord. priest June 12, 1917; ord. titular bishop of Lete and coadjutor bishop of St. Cloud, Mar. 3, 1942; bishop of St. Cloud, May 31, 1953; resigned 1968; assigned the titular see of Tanaramusa.

Baum, William W.: b. Nov. 21, 1926, Dallas, Tex.; educ. Kenrick Seminary (St. Louis, Mo.), Angelicum (Rome); ord. priest May 12, 1951; executive director of NCCB commission on ecumenical affairs, 1964-67; appointed member of joint working group of the World Council of Churches and Vatican Secretariat for Promoting Christian Unity, 1965; ord. bishop of Springfield-Cape Girardeau, Apr. 6, 1970; app. archbishop of Washington, Mar. 5, 1973; installed May 9, 1973.

Begin, Floyd L.: b. Feb. 5, 1902, Cleveland, O.; educ. St. John's Cathedral College (Cleveland, O.), North American College and Apollinare (Rome); ord. priest July 31, 1927; ord. titular bishop of Sala and auxiliary bishop of Cleveland, May 1, 1947; app. first bishop of Oakland, Feb. 21, 1962.

Begley, Michael J.: b. Mar. 12, 1909, Mattineague, Mass.; educ. Mt. St. Mary Seminary (Emmitsburg, Md.); ord. priest May 26, 1934; ord. first bishop of Charlotte, N.C., Jan. 12, 1972.

Bell, Alden J.: b. July 11, 1904, Peterborough, Ont., Canada; educ. St. Joseph's College (Mountain View, Calif.), St. Patrick's Seminary (Menlo Park, Calif.), Catholic Univ. (Washington, D.C.); ord. priest May 14, 1932; ord. titular bishop of Rhodopolis and auxiliary bishop of Los Angeles, June 4, 1956; app. bishop of Sacramento, Mar. 30, 1962.

Benincasa, Pius A.: b. July 8, 1913, Niagara Falls, N.Y.; educ. Propaganda Univ. and

Lateran Univ. (Rome); ord. priest Mar. 27, 1937; served in Vatican Secretariat of State, 1954-64; ord. titular bishop of Buruni and auxiliary bishop of Buffalo, June 29, 1964.

Bernardin, Joseph L.: b. Apr. 2, 1928, Columbia, S.C.; educ. St. Mary's Seminary (Baltimore, Md.), Catholic Univ. (Washington, D.C.); ord. priest Apr. 26, 1952; ord. titular bishop of Lugura and auxiliary bishop of Atlanta, Apr. 26, 1966; general secretary of the USCC and NCCB, 1968-72; app. archbishop of Cincinnati, Nov. 21, 1972; installed Dec. 19, 1972.

Bernarding, George, S.V.D.: b. Feb. 15, 1912, Carrick, Pa.; educ. Divine Word Seminary (Girard, Pa.); ord. priest Aug. 13, 1939; ord. titular bishop of Belabitene and first vicar apostolic of Mount Hagen, New Guinea, Apr. 21, 1960; first bishop of Mount Hagen, Nov. 15, 1966.

Bilock, John M.: b. June 20, 1916, McAdoo, Pa.; educ. St. Procopius College and Seminary (Lisle, Ill.); ord. priest Feb. 3, 1946; vicar general of Byzantine archeparchy of Munhall, 1969; ord. titular bishop of Pergamum and auxiliary bishop of Munhall, May 15, 1973.

Binz, Leo: b. Oct. 31, 1900, Stockton, Ill.; educ. Loras College (Dubuque, Ia.), St. Mary's Seminary (Baltimore, Md.), Sulpician Seminary (Washington, D.C.), North American College, Propaganda Univ., Gregorian Univ. (Rome); ord. priest Mar. 15, 1924; ord. titular bishop of Pinara and coadjutor bishop and apostolic administrator of Winona, Dec. 21, 1942; app. titular archbishop of Silyum and coadjutor archbishop of Dubuque, Oct. 15, 1949; app. assistant at the papal throne, June 11, 1954; archbishop of Dubuque, Dec. 2, 1954; app. archbishop of St. Paul, Dec. 16, 1961, installed Feb. 28, 1962; title changed to St. Paul and Minneapolis, 1966.

Biskup, George J.: b. Aug. 23, 1911, Cedar Rapids, Ia.; educ. Loras College (Dubuque, Ia). North American College (Rome), State Univ. of Iowa (Iowa City, Ia); ord. priest Mar. 19, 1937; ord. titular bishop of Hemeria and auxiliary bishop of Dubuque, Apr. 24, 1957; app. bishop of Des Moines, Jan. 30, 1965; app. titular archbishop of Tamalluma and coadjutor of Indianapolis, July 26, 1967; archbishop of Indianapolis, Jan. 14, 1970.

Blanchette, Romeo: b. Jan. 6, 1913, St. George, Ill.; educ. St. Mary of the Lake Seminary (Mundelein, Ill.), Gregorian Univ. (Rome); ord. priest Apr. 3, 1937; vicar general of Joliet, 1950-66; ord. titular bishop of Maxita and auxiliary of Joliet, Apr. 3, 1965; app. bishop of Joliet, July 19, 1966, installed Aug. 31, 1966.

Boardman, John J.: b. Nov. 7, 1894, Brooklyn N. Y.; educ. St. John's College (Brooklyn, N. Y.), St. John's Seminary (Brooklyn, N.Y.); ord. priest May 21, 1921; ord. titular bishop of Gunela and auxiliary bishop of Brooklyn, June 11, 1952; named assistant at

the papal throne; treasurer of the Society for the Propagation of the Faith.

Boccella, John H., T. O. R.: b. June 25, 1912, Castelfranci, Italy; came to US at the age of two; educ. St. Francis College and Seminary (Loretto, Pa.), Angelicum Univ. (Rome), Catholic Univ. (Washington, D. C.); ord. priest Mar. 29, 1941; provincial of Third Order Regular in US, 1945-47; minister general of Third Order Regular, 1947-68; ord. archbishop of Izmir, Turkey, Apr. 17, 1968.

Bokenfohr, John, O.M.I.: b. Jan. 28, 1903, West Point, Nebr.; ord. priest July 11, 1927; ord. bishop of Kimberley, S. Africa, May 3, 1963; resigned July 17, 1974.

Boland, Ernest B., O.P.: b. July 10, 1925, Providence, R. I.; educ. Providence College (Rhode Island), Dominican Houses of Study (Somerset, Ohio; Washington, D. C.); ord. priest June 9, 1955; ord. bishop of Multan, Pakistan, July 25, 1966.

Boland, Thomas A.: b. Feb. 17, 1896, Orange, N.J.; educ. Seton Hall College (South Orange, N.J.), North American College (Rome), Fordham Univ. (New York City); ord. priest Dec. 23, 1922; ord. titular bishop of Irina and auxiliary bishop of Newark, July 25, 1940; app. bishop of Paterson, June 21, 1947; app. archbishop of Newark, Nov. 15, 1952, installed Jan. 14, 1953; resigned Apr. 2, 1974.

Borders, William D.: b. Oct. 9, 1913, Washington, Ind.; educ. St. Meinrad Seminary (St. Meinrad, Ind.), Notre Dame Seminary (New Orleans, La.), Notre Dame Univ. (Notre Dame, Ind.); ord. priest May 18, 1940; ord. first bishop of Orlando, June 14, 1968; app. archbishop of Baltimore, Apr. 2, 1974, installed June 26, 1974.

Bosco, Anthony G.: b. Aug. 1, 1927, New Castle, Pa.; educ. St. Vincent Seminary (Latrobe, Pa.), Lateran Univ. (Rome); ord. priest June 7, 1952; ord. titular bishop of Labicum and auxiliary of Pittsburgh, June 30, 1970.

Boudreaux, Warren L.: b. Jan. 25, 1918, Berwick, La.; educ. St. Joseph's Seminary (St. Benedict, La.), St. Sulpice Seminary (Paris, France), Notre Dame Seminary (New Orleans, La.), Catholic Univ. (Washington, D. C.); ord. priest May 30, 1942; ord. titular bishop of Calynda and auxiliary bishop of Lafayette, La., July 25, 1962; app. bishop of Beaumont, June 5, 1971.

Breitenbeck, Joseph M.: b. Aug. 3, 1914, Detroit, Mich.; educ. University of Detroit, Sacred Heart Seminary (Detroit, Mich.), North American College and Lateran Univ. (Rome), Catholic Univ. (Washington, D.C.); ord. priest May 30, 1942; ord. titular bishop of Tepelta and auxiliary bishop of Detroit, Dec. 20, 1965; app. bishop of Grand Rapids, Oct. 15, 1969, installed Dec. 2, 1969.

Brizgys, Vincas: b. Nov. 10, 1903, Plynial, Lithuania; ord. priest June 5, 1927; ord. titular bishop of Bosano and auxiliary bishop of Kaunas, Lithuania, May 10, 1940; taken into custody and deported to Germany, 1944; liberated by Americans, 1945; US citizen, 1958.

Broderick, Edwin B.: b. Jan. 16, 1917, New York, N. Y.; educ. Cathedral College (New York City), St. Joseph's Seminary (Yonkers, N. Y.), Fordham Univ. (New York City); ord. priest May 30, 1942; ord. titular bishop of Tizica and auxiliary of New York, Apr. 21, 1967; bishop of Albany May 10, 1969.

Brown, Charles, A., M.M.: b. Aug. 20, 1919, New York, N. Y.; educ. Cathedral College (New York City), Maryknoll Seminary (Maryknoll, N. Y.); ord. priest June 9, 1946; ord. titular bishop of Vallis and auxiliary bishop of Santa Cruz, Bolivia, Mar. 27, 1957.

Brunini, Joseph B.: b. July 24, 1909, Vicksburg, Miss.; educ. Georgetown Univ. (Washington, D. C.), North American College (Rome), Catholic Univ. (Washington, D.C.); ord. priest Dec. 5, 1933; ord. titular bishop of Axomis and auxiliary bishop of Natchez-Jackson, Jan. 29, 1957; apostolic administrator of Natchez-Jackson, 1966; app. bishop of Natchez-Jackson, Dec. 2, 1967, installed Jan. 29, 1968.

Brust, Leo J.: b. Jan. 7, 1916, St. Francis, Wis.; educ. St. Francis Seminary (Milwaukee, Wis.), Canisianum (Innsbruck, Austria), Catholic Univ. (Washington, D. C.); ord. priest May 30, 1942; ord. titular bishop of Suelli and auxiliary bishop of Milwaukee, Oct. 16, 1969.

Brzana, Stanislaus J.: b. July 1, 1917, Buffalo, N.Y.; educ. Christ the King Seminary (St. Bonaventure, N.Y.), Gregorian Univ. (Rome); ord. priest June 7, 1941; ord. titular bishop of Cufruta and auxiliary bishop of Buffalo, June 29, 1964; bishop of Ogdensburg, Oct. 22, 1968.

Burke, James C., O.P.: b. Nov. 30, 1926, Wilkes-Barre, Pa.; educ. King's College (Wilkes-Barre, Pa.), Providence College (R.I.); ord. priest June 8, 1956; ord. titular bishop of Lamiggiga and prelate of Chimbote, Peru, May 25, 1967.

Buswell, Charles A.: b. Oct. 15, 1913, Homestead, Okla.; educ. St. Louis Preparatory Seminary (St. Louis, Mo.), Kenrick Seminary (Webster Groves, Mo.), American College, Univ., of Louvain (Belgium); ord. priest July 9, 1939; ord. bishop of Pueblo, Sept. 30, 1959.

Byrne, James J.: b. July 28, 1908, St. Paul, Minn.; educ. Nazareth Hall Preparatory Seminary and St. Paul Seminary (St. Paul, Minn.), Univ. of Minnesota (Minneapolis, Minn.), Louvain Univ. (Belgium); ord. priest June 3, 1933; ord. titular bishop of Etenna and auxiliary bishop of St. Paul, July 2, 1947; app. bishop of Boise, June 16, 1956; app. archbishop of Dubuque, Mar. 19, 1962, installed May 8, 1962.

Byrne, Leo Christopher: b. Mar. 19, 1908, St. Louis, Mo.; educ. Kenrick Seminary (St. Louis, Mo.); ord. priest June 10, 1933; ord.

titular bishop of Sabadia and auxiliary bishop of St. Louis, June 29, 1954; installed as coadjutor bishop of Wichita, April 25, 1961; apostolic administrator of Wichita, 1963; app. titular archbishop of Plestra and coadjutor of St. Paul and Minneapolis, Aug. 2, 1967; elected vice-president of NCCB/USCC, Nov. 18, 1971.

C

Caillouet, L. Abel.: b. Aug. 2, 1900, Thibodaux, La.; educ. St. Joseph's Preparatory Seminary (St. Benedict, La.), St. Mary's Seminary (Baltimore, Md.), North American College (Rome); ord. priest Mar. 7, 1925; ord. titular bishop of Setea and auxiliary bishop of New Orleans, Oct. 28, 1947.

Carberry, John J.: (See Cardinals, Biographies.)

Carroll, Coleman Francis: b. Feb. 9, 1905, Pittsburgh, Pa.; educ. Duquesne Univ. (Pittsburgh, Pa.), St. Vincent Seminary (Latrobe, Pa.), Catholic Univ. (Washington, D.C.); ord. priest June 15, 1930; ord. titular bishop of Pitanae and auxiliary bishop of Pittsburgh, Nov. 10, 1953; app. first bishop of Miami, installed Oct. 7, 1958; became first archbishop, 1968.

Carroll, Mark K.: b. Nov. 19, 1896, St. Louis, Mo.; educ. St. Louis Preparatory Seminary and St. Louis Theological Seminary (St. Louis, Mo.); ord. priest June 10, 1922; ord. bishop of Wichita, Apr. 23, 1947; retired, 1963, but retained title; resigned, 1967.

Casey, James V.: b. Sept. 22, 1914, Osage, Ia.; educ. Loras College (Dubuque, Ia.), North American College (Rome), Catholic Univ. (Washington, D.C.); ord. priest Dec. 8, 1939; ord. titular bishop of Citium and auxiliary bishop of Lincoln, Apr. 24, 1957; bishop of Lincoln, June 14, 1957; app. archbishop of Denver, Feb. 22, 1967, installed May 17, 1967.

Casey, Lawrence B.: b. Sept. 6, 1905, Rochester, N.Y.; educ. St. Bernard's Seminary (Rochester, N.Y.); ord. priest June 7, 1930; ord. titular bishop of Cea and auxiliary bishop of Rochester, May 5, 1953; app. bishop of Paterson, installed May 12, 1966.

Cassata, John J.: b. Nov. 8, 1908, Galveston, Tex.; educ. St. Mary's Seminary (La Porte, Tex.), North American College, Urbana Univ. and Gregorian Univ. (Rome); ord. priest Dec. 8, 1932; ord. titular bishop of Bida and auxiliary bishop of Dallas-Fort Worth, June 5, 1968; app. bishop of Fort Worth, Aug. 27, 1969, installed Oct. 21, 1969.

Chavez, Gilbert Espinoza: b. May 9, 1932, Ontario, Calif.; educ. St. Francis Seminary (El Cajon, Calif.); Immaculate Heart Seminary (San Diego), Univ. of California; ord. priest 1960; ord. titular bishop of Magarmel and auxiliary of San Diego, June 21, 1974.

Clinch, Harry A.: b. Oct. 27, 1908, San Anselmo, Calif.; educ. St. Joseph's College (Mountain View, Calif.), St. Patrick's Seminary (Menlo Park, Calif.); ord. priest June 6, 1936; ord. titular bishop of Badiae and auxiliary bishop of Monterey-Fresno, Feb. 27, 1957; app. first bishop of Monterey in California, installed Dec. 14, 1967.

Cody, John P.: (See Cardinals, Biographies.)

Cohill, John Edward, S.V.D.: b. Dec. 13, 1907, Elizabeth, N.J.; educ. Divine Word Seminary (Techny, Ill.); ord. priest Mar. 20, 1936; ord. first bishop of Goroko, New Guinea, Mar. 11, 1967.

Comber, John W., M.M.: b. Mar. 12, 1906, Lawrence, Mass.; educ. St. John's Preparatory College (Danvers, Mass.), Boston College (Boston, Mass.), Maryknoll Seminary (Maryknoll, N.Y.); ord. priest Feb. 1, 1931; superior general of Maryknoll, 1956-66; ord. titular bishop of Foratiana, Apr. 9, 1959.

Connare, William G.: b. Dec. 11, 1911, Pittsburgh, Pa.; educ. Duquesne Univ. (Pittsburgh, Pa.), St. Vincent Seminary (Latrobe, Pa.); ord. priest June 14, 1936; ord. bishop of Greensburg, May 4, 1960.

Connolly, James L.: b. Nov. 15, 1894, Fall River, Mass.; educ. St. Charles College (Catonsville, Md.), St. Mary's Seminary (Baltimore, Md.), Catholic Univ. (Washington, D.C.), Louvain Univ. (Belgium); ord. priest Dec. 21, 1923; rector of St. Paul (Minn.) minor seminary 1940-43, major seminary 1943-45; ord. titular bishop of Mylasa and coadjutor of Fall River, May 24, 1945; bishop of Fall River, May 17, 1951; resigned Oct. 30, 1970.

Connolly, Thomas Arthur: b. Oct. 5, 1899, San Francisco, Calif.; educ. St. Patrick's Seminary (Menlo Park, Calif.), Catholic Univ. (Washington, D.C.); ord. priest June 11, 1926; ord. titular bishop of Sila and auxiliary bishop of San Francisco, Aug. 24, 1939; app. coadjutor bishop of Seattle, Feb. 28, 1948; succeeded as bishop of Seattle, May 18, 1950; first archbishop of Seattle, June 23, 1951.

Connolly, Thomas J.: b. July 18, 1922, Tonopah, Nev.; educ. St. Patrick's Seminary (Menlo Park, Calif.), Catholic Univ. (Washington, D.C.), Lateran Univ. (Rome); ord. priest Apr. 8, 1947; ord. bishop of Baker, June 30, 1971.

Cooke, Terence J.: (See Cardinals, Biographies.)

Coscia, Benedict Dominic, O.F.M.: b. Aug. 10, 1922, Brooklyn, N.Y.; educ. St. Francis College (Brooklyn, N.Y.), Holy Name College (Washington, D.C.); ord. priest June 11, 1949; ord. bishop of Jatai, Brazil, Sept. 21, 1961.

Cosgrove, William M.: b. Nov. 26, 1916, Canton, Ohio; educ. John Carroll Univ. (Cleveland, O.); ord. priest Dec. 18, 1943; ord. titular bishop of Trisipa and auxiliary bishop of Cleveland, Sept. 3, 1968.

Costello, Joseph A.: b. May 9, 1915, Newark, N.J.; educ. Seton Hall Univ. (S. Orange,

N.J.), Immaculate Conception Seminary (Darlington, N.J.); ord. priest June 7, 1941; ord. titular bishop of Choma and auxiliary bishop of Newark, Jan. 24, 1963.

Cotey, Bernard R., S.D.S.: b. June 15, 1921, Milwaukee, Wis.; educ. Divine Savior Seminary (Lanham, Md.), Marquette Univ. (Milwaukee, Wis.); ord. priest June 7, 1949; ord. first bishop of Nachingwea, Tanzania, Oct. 20, 1963.

Cousins, William E.: b. Aug. 20, 1902, Chicago, Ill.; educ. Quigley Seminary (Chicago, Ill.), St. Mary of the Lake Seminary (Mundelein, Ill.); ord. priest Apr. 23, 1927; ord. titular bishop of Forma and auxiliary bishop of Chicago, Mar. 7, 1949; app. bishop of Peoria, May 21, 1952; archbishop of Milwaukee, Jan. 27, 1959.

Cronin, Daniel A.: b. Nov. 14, 1927, Newton, Mass.; educ. St. John's Seminary (Boston, Mass.), North American College and Gregorian Univ. (Rome); ord. priest Dec. 20, 1952; attaché apostolic nunciature (Addis Ababa), 1957-61; served in papal Secretariat of State, 1961-68; ord. titular bishop of Egnatia and auxiliary bishop of Boston, Sept. 12, 1968; bishop of Fall River, Dec. 16, 1970.

Crowley, Joseph R.: b. Jan. 12, 1915, Fort Wayne, Ind.; educ. St. Mary's College (St. Mary, Ky.), St. Meinrad Seminary (St. Meinrad, Ind.); served in US Air Force, 1942-46; ord. priest May 1, 1953; editor of *Our Sunday Visitor* 1958-67; ord. titular bishop of Maraguis and auxiliary bishop of Fort Wayne-South Bend, Aug. 24, 1971; named vicar general and diocesan director of religious education, Feb. 1, 1972.

Cummins, John S.: b. Mar. 3, 1928, Oakland, Calif.; educ. St. Patrick's Seminary (Menlo Park, Calif.), Catholic Univ. (Washington, D.C.), Univ. of California; ord priest 1953; executive director of the California Catholic Conference; app. titular bishop of Lambaesis and auxiliary bishop of Sacramento, Feb. 26, 1974.

Cunningham, David F.: b. Dec. 3, 1900, Walkerville, Mont.; educ. St. Michael's College (Toronto, Canada), St. Bernard's Seminary (Rochester, N.Y.), Catholic Univ. (Washington, D.C.); ord. priest June 12, 1926; ord. titular bishop of Lampsacus and auxiliary bishop of Syracuse, June 8, 1950; app. coadjutor bishop of Syracuse with right of succession, 1967; bishop of Syracuse, Aug. 4, 1970.

Curtis, Walter W.: b. May 3, 1913, Jersey City, N.J.; educ. Fordham Univ. (New York City), Seton Hall Univ. (South Orange, N.J.), Immaculate Conception Seminary (Darlington, N.J.), North American College and Gregorian Univ. (Rome), Catholic Univ. (Washington, D.C.); ord. priest Dec. 8, 1937; ord. titular bishop of Bisica and auxiliary bishop of Newark, Sept. 24, 1957; app. bishop of Bridgeport, 1961, installed Nov. 21, 1961.

D

Daley, Joseph T.: b. Dec. 21, 1915, Connerton, Pa.; educ. St. Charles Borromeo Seminary (Philadelphia, Pa.); ord. priest June 7, 1941; ord. titular bishop of Barca and auxiliary bishop of Harrisburg, Pa., Jan. 7, 1964; coadjutor bishop of Harrisburg, Aug. 2, 1967; bishop of Harrisburg, Oct. 19, 1971.

Danglmayr, Augustine: b. Dec. 11, 1898, Muenster, Tex.; educ. Subiaco College (Arkansas), St. Mary's Seminary (La Porte, Tex.), Kenrick Seminary (St. Louis, Mo.); ord. priest June 10, 1922; ord. titular bishop of Olba, Oct. 7, 1942; auxiliary bishop of Dallas-Ft. Worth, 1942-69.

D'Antonio Salza, Nicholas, O.F.M.: b. July 10, 1916, Rochester, N.Y.; educ. St. Anthony's Friary (Catskill, N.Y.); ord. priest June 7, 1942; ord. titular bishop of Giufi Salaria and prelate of Olancho, Honduras, July 25, 1966.

Dargin, Edward Vincent: b. Apr. 25, 1898, New York, N.Y.; educ. Fordham Univ. (New York City), St. Joseph Seminary (Dunwoodie, N.Y.), Catholic Univ. (Washington, D.C.); ord. priest Sept. 23, 1922; ord. titular bishop of Amphipolis and auxiliary bishop of New York, Oct. 5, 1953; app. episcopal vicar, 1966. Retired.

Davis, James Peter: b. June 9, 1904, Houghton, Mich.; educ. St. Joseph's College (Mountain View, Calif.), St. Patrick's Seminary (Menlo Park, Calif.); ord. priest May 19, 1929; ord. bishop of San Juan, Puerto Rico, Oct. 6, 1943; app. first archbishop of San Juan, July 30, 1960; app. archbishop of Santa Fe, installed Feb. 25, 1964; resigned June 4, 1974.

Dearden, John Francis: (See Cardinals, Biographies.)

De Falco, Lawrence M.: b. Aug. 25, 1915, McKeesport, Pa.; educ. St. Vincent's College (Latrobe, Pa.), St. John's Seminary (Little Rock, Ark.), Gregorian Univ. (Rome); ord. priest June 11, 1942; ord. bishop of Amarillo, May 30, 1963.

Deksnys, Anthony L.: b. May 9, 1906, Buteniskis, Lithuania; educ. Metropolitan Seminary and Theological and Philosophical Faculty at Vytautas the Great Univ. (all at Kaunas, Lithuania), Univ. of Fribourg (Switzerland); ord. priest May 30, 1931; served in US parishes at Mt. Carmel, Pa., and East St. Louis, Ill.; ord. titular bishop of Lavellum, June 15, 1969; assigned to pastoral work among Lithuanians in Western Europe.

Dempsey, Michael J., O.P.: b. Feb. 22, 1912, Providence, R.I.; entered Order of Preachers (Dominicans), Chicago province, 1935; ord. priest June 11, 1942; ord. bishop of Sokoto, Nigeria, Aug. 15, 1967.

Denning, Joseph P.: b. Jan. 4, 1907, Flushing, L. I.; educ. Cathedral College (Brooklyn, N. Y.), Immaculate Conception Seminary (Huntington, L. I.), St. Mary's Seminary

(Baltimore, Md.); ord. priest May 21, 1932; ord. titular bishop of Mallus and auxiliary bishop of Brooklyn, Apr. 22, 1959.

De Palma, Joseph A., S.C.J.: b. Sept. 4, 1913, Walton, N. Y.; ord. priest May 20, 1944; superior general of Congregation of Priests of the Sacred Heart, 1959-67; ord. first bishop of De Aar, South Africa, July 19, 1967.

Dimmerling, Harold J.: b. Sept. 23, 1914, Braddock, Pa.; educ. St. Fidelis Preparatory Seminary (Herman, Pa.), St. Charles Seminary (Columbus, O.), St. Francis Seminary (Loretto, Pa.); ord. priest May 2, 1940; ord. bishop of Rapid City, Oct. 30, 1969.

Dingman, Maurice J.: b. Jan. 20, 1914, St. Paul, Ia.; educ. St. Ambrose College (Davenport, Ia.), North American College and Gregorian Univ. (Rome), Catholic Univ. (Washington, D. C.); ord. priest Dec. 8, 1939; ord. bishop of Des Moines, June 19, 1968.

Donaghy, Frederick Anthony, M.M.: b. Jan. 13, 1903, New Bedford, Mass.; educ. Holy Cross College (Worcester, Mass.), St. Mary's Seminary (Baltimore, Md.), Maryknoll Seminary (Maryknoll, N. Y.); ord. priest Jan. 29, 1929; ord. titular bishop of Setea and vicar apostolic of Wuchow, China, Sept. 21, 1939; title changed to bishop of Wuchow, Apr. 11, 1946; expelled by Communists.

Donahue, Stephen Joseph: b. Dec. 10, 1893, New York, N. Y.; educ. Cathedral College (New York, N. Y.), St. Joseph's Seminary (Dunwoodie, N. Y.), North American College (Rome); ord. priest May 22, 1918; ord. titular bishop of Medea and auxiliary bishop of New York, May 1, 1934. Retired.

Donnellan, Thomas A.: b. Jan. 24, 1914, New York, N. Y.; educ. Cathedral College and St. Joseph's Seminary (New York, N.Y.), Catholic Univ. (Washington, D. C.); ord. priest June 3, 1939; ord. bishop of Ogdensburg, Apr. 9, 1964; app. archbishop of Atlanta, installed July 16, 1968.

Donnelly, Joseph F.: b. May 1, 1909, Norwich, Conn.; educ. St. Mary's Seminary and Univ. (Baltimore, Md.), Catholic Univ. (Washington, D.C.), Fairfield Univ. (Fairfield, Conn.); ord. priest June 29, 1934; director of Hartford Archdiocesan Labor Institute, 1942-65; chairman of Connecticut State Board of Mediation and Arbitration 1949-65; ord. titular bishop of Nabala and auxiliary bishop of Hartford, Jan. 28, 1965.

Donohoe, Hugh A.: b. June 28, 1905, San Francisco, Calif.; educ. St. Patrick's Preparatory and Major Seminaries (Menlo Park, Calif.), Catholic Univ. (Washington, D. C.); ord. priest June 14, 1930; ord. titular bishop of Taium and auxiliary bishop of San Francisco, Oct. 7, 1947; app. first bishop of Stockton, Jan. 27, 1962; app. bishop of Fresno, Aug. 27, 1969, installed Oct. 7, 1969.

Donovan, John A.: b. Aug. 5, 1911, Chatham, Ont., Canada; educ. Sacred Heart Seminary (Detroit, Mich.), North American College and Gregorian Univ. (Rome); ord. priest Dec. 8, 1935; ord. titular bishop of Rhasus and auxiliary bishop of Detroit, Oct. 26, 1954; app. bishop of Toledo, installed Apr. 18, 1967.

Donovan, Paul V.: b. Sept. 1, 1924, Bernard, Iowa; educ. St. Gregory's Seminary (Cincinnati, Ohio), Mt. St. Mary's Seminary (Norwood, Ohio), Lateran Univ. (Rome); ord. priest May 20, 1950; ord. first bishop of Kalamazoo, Mich., July 21, 1971.

Dougherty, John J.: b. Sept. 16, 1907, Jersey City, N. J.; educ. Seton Hall Univ. (S. Orange, N. J.), Immaculate Conception Seminary (Darlington, N. J.), North American College, Gregorian Univ., Pontifical Biblical Institute (Rome); ord. priest July 23, 1933; ord. titular bishop of Cotenna and auxiliary bishop of Newark, Jan. 24, 1963.

Dozier, Carroll T.: b. Aug. 18, 1911, Richmond, Va.; educ. Holy Cross College (Worcester, Mass.), Gregorian Univ. (Rome); ord. priest, Mar. 19, 1937, Rome; ord. first bishop of Memphis, Jan. 6, 1971.

Driscoll, Justin A.: b. Sept. 30, 1920, Bernard, Ia.; educ. Loras College (Dubuque, Ia.), Catholic Univ. (Washington, D. C.); ord. priest July 28, 1945; president of Loras College, 1967-70; ord. bishop of Fargo, Oct. 28, 1970.

Drury, Thomas J.: b. Jan. 4, 1908, Co. Sligo, Ireland; educ. St. Benedict's College (Atchison, Kans.), Kenrick Seminary (St. Louis, Mo.); ord. priest June 2, 1935; ord. first bishop of San Angelo, Tex., Jan. 24, 1962; app. bishop of Corpus Christi, installed Sept. 1, 1965.

Dudick, Michael J.: b. Feb. 24, 1916, St. Clair, Pa.; educ. St. Procopius College and Seminary (Lisle, Ill.); ord. priest Nov. 13, 1945; ord. bishop of Byzantine Rite Eparchy of Passaic, Oct. 24, 1968.

Duhart, Clarence James, C.SS.R.: b. Mar. 23, 1912, New Orleans, La.; ord. priest June 29, 1937; ord. bishop of Udon Thani, Thailand, Apr. 21, 1966.

Dunn, Francis J.: b. Mar. 22, 1922, Elkader, Ia.; educ. Loras College (Dubuque, Ia) Kenrick Seminary (St. Louis, Mo.), Angelicum (Rome, Italy); ord. priest Jan. 11, 1948; chancellor of Dubuque, Aug. 27, 1960; ord. titular bishop of Turris Tamallani and auxiliary bishop of Dubuque, Aug. 27, 1969, app. vicar general, Aug. 28, 1969.

Durick, Joseph Aloysius: b. Oct. 13, 1914, Dayton, Tenn.; educ. St. Bernard Minor Seminary (St. Bernard, Ala.), St. Mary's Seminary (Baltimore, Md.), Urban Univ. (Rome); ord. priest May 23, 1940; ord. titular bishop of Cerbal and auxiliary bishop of Mobile-Birmingham, Mar. 24, 1955; app. coadjutor bishop of Nashville, Tenn., installed Mar. 3, 1964; apostolic administrator, 1966; bishop of Nashville, Sept. 10, 1969.

Durning, Dennis V., C.S.Sp.: b. May 18,

1923, Germantown, Pa.; educ. St. Mary's Seminary (Ferndale, Conn.); ord. priest June 3, 1949; ord. first bishop of Arusha, Tanzania, May 28, 1963.

Dworschak, Leo F.: b. Apr. 6, 1900, Independence, Wis.; educ. St. John's Univ. (Collegeville, Minn.), Catholic Univ. (Washington, D.C.); ord. priest May 29, 1926; ord. titular bishop of Tium and coadjutor bishop of Rapid City, Aug. 22, 1946; app. auxiliary bishop of Fargo, Apr. 10, 1947; bishop of Fargo, May 10, 1960; retired, 1970.

Dwyer, Robert Joseph: b. Aug. 1, 1908, Salt Lake City, Utah; educ. St. Patrick's Seminary (Menlo Park, Calif.), Catholic Univ. (Washington, D.C.); ord. priest June 11, 1932; ord. bishop of Reno, Aug. 5, 1952; app. archbishop of Portland, Ore., Dec. 14, 1966, installed Feb. 6, 1967; resigned Jan. 22, 1974.

E

Elko, Nicholas T.: b. Dec. 14, 1909, Donora, Pa.; educ. Duquesne Univ. (Pittsburgh, Pa.), Seminary of Uzhorod (Czechoslovakia); ord. priest Sept. 30, 1934; ord. titular bishop of Apollonias and apostolic administrator of Byzantine-Rite exarchy of Pittsburgh, Mar. 6, 1955; succeeded as exarch of Pittsburgh, Sept. 5, 1955; became eparch when Pittsburgh was raised to eparchy, July, 1963; app. titular archbishop of Dara, 1967, and ordaining prelate for Byzantine Rite in Rome; head of Oriental liturgical commission; app. auxiliary bishop of Cincinnati, Aug. 10, 1971.

Etteldorf, Raymond P.: b. Aug. 12, 1911, Ossian, Ia.; educ. Loras College (Dubuque, Ia.), Gregorian Univ. (Rome); ord. priest Dec. 8, 1937; secretary general of Supreme Council for direction of Pontifical Missionary Works, 1964-68; secretary of Pontifical Commission for Economic Affairs, 1968-69; ord. titular archbishop of Tindari, Jan. 6, 1969; papal representative to New Zealand and the Pacific Islands, 1968-74; pro-nuncio to Ethiopia, 1974.

Evans, George R.: b. Sept. 25, 1922, Denver, Colo.; educ. Notre Dame Univ. (Notre Dame, Ind.), St. Thomas Seminary (Denver, Colo.), Apollinare Univ. (Rome, Italy); ord, priest May 31, 1947; ord. titular bishop of Tubyza and auxiliary bishop of Denver, Apr. 23, 1969.

F

Fearns, John M.: b. June 25, 1897, New York, N.Y.; educ. St. Joseph's Seminary (Yonkers, N.Y.), North American College and Gregorian Univ. (Rome); ord. priest Feb. 19, 1922; ord. titular bishop of Geras and auxiliary bishop of New York, Dec. 10, 1957; app. episcopal vicar, 1966. Retired.

Federal, Joseph Lennox: b. Jan. 13, 1910, Greensboro, N.C.; educ. Belmont Abbey College (Belmont Abbey, N.C.), Niagara Univ. (Niagara Falls, N.Y.), Univ. of Fribourg (Switzerland), North American College and Gregorian Univ. (Rome); ord. priest Dec. 8, 1934; ord. titular bishop of Appiaria and auxiliary bishop of Salt Lake City, Apr. 11, 1951; app. coadjutor with right of succession, May, 1958 bishop of Salt Lake City, Mar. 31, 1960.

Fitzpatrick, John J.: b. Oct. 12, 1918, Trenton, Ont., Canada; educ. Urban Univ. (Rome), Our Lady of the Angels Seminary (Niagara Falls, N.Y.); ord. priest Dec. 13, 1942; ord. titular bishop of Cenae and auxiliary bishop of Miami, Aug. 28, 1968; bishop of Brownsville, Tex., May 28, 1971.

Flaherty, J. Louis: b. May 13, 1910, Norfolk, Va.; educ. Holy Cross College (Worcester, Mass.), North American College and Gregorian Univ. (Rome), Catholic Univ. (Washington, D.C.); ord. priest Dec. 8, 1936; ord. titular bishop of Tabuda and auxiliary bishop of Richmond, Oct. 5, 1966.

Flanagan, Bernard Joseph: b. Mar. 31, 1908, Proctor, Vt.; educ. Holy Cross College (Worcester, Mass.), North American College (Rome), Catholic Univ. (Washington, D.C.); ord. priest Dec. 8, 1931; ord. first bishop of Norwich, Nov. 30, 1953; app. bishop of Worcester, installed, Sept. 24, 1959.

Flavin, Glennon P.: b. Mar. 2, 1916, St. Louis, Mo.; educ. Kenrick Seminary (St. Louis, Mo.); ord. priest Dec. 20, 1941; ord. titular bishop of Joannina and auxiliary bishop of St. Louis, May 30, 1957; app. bishop of Lincoln, installed Aug. 17, 1967.

Fletcher, Albert Lewis: b. Oct. 28, 1896, Little Rock, Ark.; educ. Little Rock College and St. John's Seminary (Little Rock, Ark.); ord. priest June 4, 1920; ord. titular bishop of Samos and auxiliary bishop of Little Rock, Apr. 25, 1940; bishop of Little Rock, Dec. 7, 1946; resigned July 4, 1972.

Flores, Felixberto C.: b. Jan. 13, 1921, Agana, Guam; educ. St. John's Seminary (Brighton, Mass.), Fordham Univ. (New York); ord. priest Apr. 30, 1949; ord. titular bishop of Stonj, May 17, 1970, and apostolic administrator of the diocese of Agana, Guam; installed second residential bishop of Agana, July 12, 1972.

Flores, Patrick F.: b. July 26, 1929, Ganado, Tex.; educ. St. Mary's Seminary (Houston, Tex.); ord. priest May 26, 1956; ord. titular bishop of Itolica and auxiliary bishop of San Antonio, May 5, 1970; first Mexican-American bishop.

Foery, Walter Andrew: b. July 6, 1890, Rochester, N.Y.; educ. St. Andrew's Preparatory Seminary and St. Bernard's Seminary (Rochester, N.Y.); ord. priest June 10, 1916; ord. bishop of Syracuse, Aug. 18, 1937; resigned 1970.

Forst, Marion F.: b. Sept. 3, 1910, St. Louis, Mo.; educ. St. Louis Preparatory Seminary (St. Louis, Mo.), Kenrick Seminary (Webster Groves, Mo.); ord. priest June 10, 1934; ord. bishop of Dodge City, Mar. 24, 1960.

Franz, John B.: b. Oct. 29, 1896, Springfield, Ill.; educ. Quincy College (Quincy, Ill.), Kenrick Seminary (Webster Groves, Mo.), Catholic Univ. (Washington, D.C.); ord. priest June 13, 1920; ord. first bishop of Dodge City, Aug. 29, 1951; app. bishop of Peoria, installed Nov. 4, 1959; resigned May 24, 1971.

Freking, Frederick W.: b. Aug. 11, 1913, Heron Lake, Minn.; educ. St. Mary's College (Winona, Minn.), North American College and Gregorian Univ. (Rome), Catholic Univ. (Washington, D.C.); ord. priest July 31, 1938; ord. bishop of Salina, Nov. 30, 1957; app. bishop of La Crosse, Dec. 30, 1964, installed Feb. 24, 1965.

Frey, Gerard L.: b. May 10, 1914, New Orleans, La.; educ. Notre Dame Seminary (New Orleans, La.); ord. priest Apr. 2, 1938; ord. bishop of Savannah, Aug. 8, 1967; app. bishop of Lafayette, La., Nov. 7, 1972, installed Jan, 7, 1973.

Frosi, Angelo, S. X.: b. Jan. 31, 1924, Baffano Cremona, Italy; ord. priest May 6, 1948; ord. titular bishop of Magneto, May 1, 1970, and prelate of Abaete do Tocantins, Brazil.

Furey, Francis J.: b. Feb. 22, 1905, Summit Hill, Pa.; educ. St. Charles Borromeo Seminary (Overbrook, Pa.), Pontifical Major Roman Seminary (Rome); ord. priest Mar. 15, 1930; ord. titular bishop of Temnus and auxiliary bishop of Philadelphia, Dec. 22, 1960; app. coadjutor bishop of San Diego with right of succession, July, 1963; bishop of San Diego, 1966-69; archbishop of San Antonio, Aug. 6, 1969.

Furlong, Philip J.: b. Dec. 8, 1892, New York, N.Y.; educ. Cathedral College (New York, N.Y.), St. Joseph's Seminary (Yonkers, N.Y.); ord. priest May 18, 1918; ord. titular bishop of Araxa and auxiliary to military vicar, Jan. 25, 1956. Retired.

G

Gabro, Jaroslav: b. July 31, 1919, Chicago, Ill.; educ. St. Procopius College (Lisle, Ill.), St. Charles College (Catonsville, Md.), St. Basil's College (Stamford, Conn.), St. Josaphat's Seminary and Catholic Univ. (Washington, D.C.); ord. priest Sept. 27, 1945; ord. first eparch of the eparchy of St. Nicholas of the Ukrainians, in Chicago, Oct. 26, 1961, installed Dec. 12, 1961.

Gallagher, Raymond J.: b. Nov. 19, 1912, Cleveland, Ohio; educ. John Carroll Univ. and Our Lady of the Lake Seminary (Cleveland, O.); ord. priest Mar. 25, 1939; secretary of the National Conference of Catholic Charities 1961-65; ord. bishop of Lafayette in Indiana, Aug. 11, 1965.

Ganter, Bernard J.: b. 1929, Galveston, Tex.; educ. Texas A & M Univ. (College Sta., Tex.), St. Mary's Seminary (La Porte, Tex.), Catholic Univ. (Washington, D.C.); ord.

priest May 22, 1952; chancellor of Galveston-Houston diocese, 1969-73; ord. first bishop of Tulsa, Feb. 7, 1973.

Gelineau, Louis E.: b. May 3, 1928, Burlington, Vt.; educ. St. Michael's College (Winooski, Vt.), St. Paul's Univ. Seminary (Ottawa, Ont.), Catholic Univ. (Washington, D.C.); ord. priest June 5, 1954; ord. bishop of Providence, R.I., Jan. 26, 1972.

Gerbermann, Hugo, M.M.: b. Sept. 11, 1913, Nada, Tex.; educ. St. John's Minor and Major Seminary (San Antonio, Tex.), Maryknoll Seminary (Maryknoll, N.Y.); ord. priest Feb. 7, 1943; missionary work in Ecuador and Guatemala; ord. titular bishop of Amathus and prelate of Huehuetenango, Guatemala, July 22, 1962; first bishop of Huehuetenango, Dec. 23, 1967.

Gerety, Peter L.: b. July 19, 1912, Shelton, Conn.; educ. Sulpician Seminary (Paris, France); ord. priest June 29, 1939; ord. titular bishop of Crepedula and coadjutor bishop of Portland, Me., with right of succession, June 1, 1966; app. apostolic administrator of Portland, 1967; bishop of Portland, Me., Sept. 15, 1969; app. archbishop of Newark, Apr. 2, 1974; installed June 28, 1974.

Gerow, Richard Oliver: b. May 3, 1885, Mobile, Ala.; educ. McGill Institute (Mobile, Ala.), Mt. St. Mary's College (Emmitsburg, Md.), North American College (Rome); ord. priest June 5, 1909; ord. bishop of Natchez-Jackson, Oct. 15, 1924; retired from active administration of diocese, 1966; resigned, 1967.

Gerrard, James J.: b. June 9, 1897, New Bedford, Mass.; educ. St. Laurent College (Montreal, Que.), St. Bernard's Seminary (Rochester, N.Y.); ord. priest May 26, 1923; ord. titular bishop of Forma and auxiliary bishop of Fall River, Mar. 19, 1959.

Gleeson, Francis D., S.J.: b. Jan. 17, 1895, Carrollton, Mo.; educ. Mount St. Michael's Scholasticate (Spokane, Wash.), St. Francis Xavier College (Ona, Spain); entered the Society of Jesus, 1912; ord. priest July 29, 1926; ord. titular bishop of Cotenna and vicar apostolic of Alaska, Apr. 5, 1948; first bishop of Fairbanks, Aug. 8, 1962; retired Nov. 15, 1968.

Glenn, Laurence A,: b. Aug. 25, 1900, Bellingham, Wash.; educ. St. John's Univ. (Collegeville, Minn.), Catholic Univ. (Washington, D.C.); ord. priest June 11, 1927; ord. titular bishop of Tuscamia and auxiliary bishop of Duluth, Sept. 12, 1956; app. bishop of Crookston, Jan. 27, 1960, installed Apr. 20, 1960; resigned 1970.

Glennie, Ignatius T., S.J.: b. Feb. 5, 1907, Mexico City; educ. Mt. St. Michael's Scholasticate (Spokane, Wash.), Pontifical Seminary (Kandy, Ceylon), St. Mary's College (Kurdeong, India); entered Society of Jesus, 1924; ord. priest Nov. 21, 1938; ord. bishop of Trincomalee, Ceylon, Sept. 21, 1947; title of see changed to Trincomalee-Batticaloa (Sri Lanka), 1967; resigned Mar. 25, 1974.

Gorman, Thomas Kiely: b. Aug. 30, 1892, Pasadena, Calif.; educ. St. Mary's Seminary (Baltimore, Md.), Catholic Univ. (Washington, D.C.), Louvain Univ. (Belgium); ord. priest June 23, 1917; ord. bishop of Reno, July 22, 1931; installed as titular bishop of Rhasus and coadjutor bishop of Dallas-Fort Worth, with right of succession, May 8, 1952; bishop of Dallas-Fort Worth, Aug. 20, 1954; resigned 1969.

Gossman, F. Joseph: b. Apr. 1, 1930, Baltimore, Md.; educ. St. Charles College (Catonsville, Md.), St. Mary's Seminary (Baltimore, Md.), North American College (Rome), Catholic Univ. (Washington, D.C.); ord. priest Dec. 17, 1955; ord. titular bishop of Agunto and auxiliary bishop of Baltimore, Sept. 11, 1968; named urban vicar, June 13, 1970.

Gottwald, George J.: b. May 12, 1914, St. Louis, Mo.; educ. Kenrick Seminary (Webster Groves, Mo.); ord. priest June 9, 1940; ord. titular bishop of Cedamusa and auxiliary bishop of St. Louis, Aug. 8, 1961.

Gracida, Rene H.: b. June 9, 1923, New Orleans, La.; educ. Rice Univ. and Univ. of Houston (Houston, Tex.), Univ. of Fribourg (Switzerland); ord. priest May 23, 1959; ord. titular bishop of Masuccaba and auxiliary bishop of Miami, Jan. 25, 1972.

Grady, Thomas J.: b. Oct. 9, 1914, Chicago, Ill.; educ. St. Mary of the Lake Seminary (Mundelein, Ill.), Gregorian Univ. (Rome), Loyola Univ. (Chicago, Ill.); ord. priest Apr. 23, 1938; ord. titular bishop of Vamalla and auxiliary bishop of Chicago, Aug. 24, 1967.

Graham, John J.: b. Sept. 11, 1913, Philadelphia, Pa.; educ. St. Charles Borromeo Seminary (Philadelphia, Pa.), Pontifical Roman Seminary (Rome, Italy); ord. priest Feb. 26, 1938; ord. titular bishop of Sabrata and auxiliary bishop of Philadelphia, Jan. 7, 1964.

Graner, Lawrence L., C.S.C.: b. Apr. 3, 1901, Franklin, Pa.; educ. Holy Cross Seminary (Notre Dame, Ind.), Holy Cross Mission Seminary (Washington, D.C.); entered Congregation of the Holy Cross, 1924; ord. priest June 24, 1928; ord. bishop of Dacca, India, Apr. 23, 1947; title changed to archbishop of Dacca, July 15, 1950; retired 1967.

Graves, Lawrence P.: b. May 4, 1916, Texarkana, Ark.; educ. St. John's Seminary (Little Rock, Ark.), North American College (Rome), Catholic Univ. (Washington, D.C.); ord. priest June 11, 1942; ord. titular bishop of Vina and auxiliary bishop of Little Rock, Apr. 25, 1969; app. bishop of Alexandria, May 22, 1973, installed July 22, 1973.

Graziano, Lawrence, O.F.M.: b. Apr. 5, 1921, Mt. Vernon, N.Y.; educ. Mt. Alvernia Seminary (Wappingers Falls, N.Y.); ord. priest Jan. 26, 1947; ord. titular bishop of Limata and auxiliary bishop of Santa Ana, El Salvador, Sept. 21, 1961; app. coadjutor bishop of San Miguel, El Salvador, with right of succession, 1965; bishop of San Miguel, Jan. 10, 1968; resigned, 1969; assigned titular see of Valabria.

Greco, Charles Paschal: b. Oct. 29, 1894, Rodney, Miss.; educ. St. Joseph's Seminary (St. Benedict, La.), Louvain Univ. (Belgium), Dominican Univ. (Fribourg, Switzerland); ord. priest July 25, 1918; ord. bishop of Alexandria Feb. 25, 1946; retired May 22, 1973.

Green, Francis J.: b. July 7, 1906, Corning, N.Y.; educ. St. Patrick's Seminary (Menlo Park, Calif.); ord. priest May 15, 1932; ord. titular bishop of Serra and auxiliary bishop of Tucson, Sept. 17, 1953; named coadjutor of Tucson with right of succession, May 11, 1960; bishop of Tucson, Oct. 26, 1960.

Green, Joseph: b. Oct. 13, 1917, St. Joseph, Mich.; educ. St. Joseph Seminary (Grand Rapids, Mich.). St. Gregory Seminary (Cincinnati, O.), St. Mary's Seminary (Norwood, O.), Lateran Univ. (Rome); ord. priest July 14, 1946; ord. titular bishop of Trisipa and auxiliary bishop of Lansing, Aug. 28, 1962; app. bishop of Reno, installed May 25, 1967.

Grellinger, John B.: b. Nov. 5, 1899, Milwaukee, Wis.; educ. Marquette Univ. and St. Francis Seminary (Milwaukee, Wis.), Urban Univ. and Gregorian Univ. (Rome); ord. priest July 14, 1929; ord. titular bishop of Syene and auxiliary bishop of Green Bay, July 14, 1949.

Greteman, Frank H.: b. Dec. 25, 1907, Willey, Ia.; educ. Loras Academy and Loras College (Dubuque, Ia.), North American College (Rome), Catholic Univ. (Washington, D.C.); ord. priest Dec. 8, 1932; ord. titular bishop of Vissalsa and auxiliary bishop of Sioux City, May 26, 1965; bishop of Sioux City, Dec. 9, 1970.

Grutka, Andrew G.: b. Nov. 17, 1908, Joliet, Ill.; educ. St. Procopius College and Seminary (Lisle, Ill.), Urban Univ. and Gregorian Univ. (Rome); ord. priest Dec. 5, 1933; app. moderator of lay activities in Gary diocese, 1955; ord. first bishop of Gary, Feb. 25, 1957; app. member of Pontifical Marian Academy, Jan. 5, 1970; elected president of Catholic Communications Foundation, Jan. 6, 1971.

Guilfoyle, George H.: b. Nov. 13, 1913, New York, N.Y.; educ. Georgetown Univ. (Washington, D.C.), Fordham Univ. (New York City), St. Joseph's Seminary (Dunwoodie, N.Y.), Columbia Univ. (New York City); ord. priest Mar. 25, 1944; ord. titular bishop of Marazane and auxiliary bishop of New York, Nov. 30, 1964; app. bishop of Camden, installed Mar. 4, 1968.

Guilfoyle, Merlin J.: b. July 15, 1908, San Francisco, Calif.; educ. St. Joseph's College (Mountain View, Calif.), St. Patrick's Seminary (Menlo Park, Calif.), Catholic Univ. (Washington, D.C.); ord. priest June 10, 1933; ord. titular bishop of Bulla and auxiliary bishop of San Francisco, Sept. 21, 1950; app. bishop of Stockton, Nov. 19, 1969, installed Jan. 13, 1970.

Gumbleton, Thomas J.: b. Jan. 26, 1930, Detroit, Mich.; educ. St. John Provincial Seminary (Detroit, Mich.), Pontifical Lateran Univ. (Rome); ord. priest June 2, 1956; ord. titular bishop of Ululi and auxiliary bishop of Detroit, May 1, 1968.

H

Hacker, Hilary B.: b. Jan. 10, 1913, New Ulm, Minn.; educ. St. Paul Seminary (St. Paul, Minn.), Gregorian Univ. (Rome); ord. priest June 4, 1938; ord. bishop of Bismarck, N. Dak., Feb. 27, 1957.

Hackett, John F.: b. Dec. 7, 1911, New Haven, Conn.; educ. St. Thomas Seminary (Bloomfield, Conn.), Seminaire Ste. Sulpice (Paris); ord. priest June 29, 1936; ord. bishop of Helenopolis in Palaestina and auxiliary bishop of Hartford, Mar. 19, 1953.

Hagarty, Paul Leonard, O.S.B.: b. Mar. 20, 1909, Greene, Ia.; educ. Loras College (Dubuque, Ia.), St. John's Seminary and St. John's Univ. (Collegeville, Minn.); entered Order of St. Benedict, 1931; ord. priest June 6, 1936; ord. titular bishop of Arba and vicar apostolic of the Bahamas, Oct. 19, 1950; first bishop of Nassau, July 5, 1960.

Ham, J. Richard, M.M.: b. July 11, 1921, Chicago, Ill.; educ. Maryknoll Seminary (New York); ord. priest June 12, 1948; missionary to Guatemala, 1958; ord. titular bishop of Puzia di Numidia and auxiliary bishop of Guatemala, Jan. 6, 1968.

Hammes, George A.: b. Sept. 11, 1911, St. Joseph Ridge, Wis.; educ. St. Lawrence Seminary (Mt. Calvary. Wis.), St. Louis Preparatory Seminary (St. Louis, Mo.), Kenrick Seminary (Webster Groves, Mo.), Sulpician Seminary, Catholic Univ. (Washington, D.C.); ord. priest May 22, 1937; ord. bishop of Superior, May 24, 1960.

Hanifen, Richard C.: b. 1931, Denver, Colo,; educ. Regis College and St. Thomas Seminary (Denver, Colo.), Catholic Univ. (Washington, D.C.), Lateran Univ. (Rome); ord. priest June 6, 1959; app. titular bishop of Abercorn and auxiliary bishop of Denver, July 23, 1974.

Hannan, Philip M.: b. May 20, 1913, Washington, D.C.; educ. St. Charles College (Catonsville, Md.), Catholic Univ. (Washington, D.C.), North American College (Rome); ord. priest Dec. 8, 1939; ord. titular bishop of Hieropolis and auxiliary bishop of Washington, D.C., Aug. 28, 1956; app. archbishop of New Orleans, installed Oct. 13, 1965.

Harper, Edward, C.SS.R.: b. July 23, 1910, Brooklyn, N.Y.; educ. Redemptorist Houses of Study; ord. priest June 18, 1939; ord. titular bishop of Heraclea Pontica and first prelate of Virgin Islands, Oct. 6, 1960.

Harrington, Timothy J.: b. Dec. 19, 1918, Holyoke, Mass.; educ. Holy Cross College (Worcester, Mass.), Grand Seminary (Montreal, Que.), Boston College School of Social Work; ord. priest Jan. 19, 1946; ord. titular bishop of Rusuca and auxiliary bishop of Worcester, Mass., July 2, 1968.

Harris, Vincent M.: b. Oct. 14, 1913, Conroe, Tex.; educ. St. Mary's Seminary (La Porte, Tex.), North American College and Gregorian Univ. (Rome), Catholic Univ. (Washington, D.C.); ord. priest Mar. 19, 1938; ord. first bishop of Beaumont, Tex., Sept. 28, 1966; app. titular bishop of Rotaria and coadjutor bishop of Austin, Apr. 27, 1971; bishop of Austin, Nov. 15, 1971.

Harrison, Francis J.: b. Aug. 12, 1912; Syracuse, N.Y.; educ. Notre Dame Univ. (Notre Dame, Ind.), St. Bernard's Seminary (Rochester, N.Y.), ord. priest June 4, 1937; ord. titular bishop of Aquae in Numidia and auxiliary bishop of Syracuse, Apr. 22, 1971.

Hastrich, Jerome J.: b. Nov. 13, 1914, Milwaukee, Wis.; educ. Marquette Univ., St. Francis Seminary (Milwaukee, Wis.); ord. priest Feb. 9, 1941; ord. titular bishop of Gurza and auxiliary bishop of Madison, Sept. 3, 1963; app. bishop of Gallup, N.Mex., Sept. 3, 1969.

Hayes, James Thomas Gibbons, S.J.: b. Feb. 11, 1889, New York City; educ. St. Francis Xavier's College (New York City), Jesuit Novitiate (St. Andrew-on-the-Hudson, N.Y.), Jesuit House of Studies (Tronchiennes, Belgium); entered the Society of Jesus, Aug. 14, 1907; ord. priest June 29, 1921; ord. bishop of Cagayan, P.I., June 18, 1933; first archbishop of Cagayan, June 29, 1951; resigned Oct. 13, 1970.

Hayes, Nevin W., O.Carm: b. Feb. 17, 1922, Chicago, Ill.; ord. priest June 8, 1946; prelate nullius of Sicuani, Peru, 1959; ord. titular bishop of Nova Sinna and prelate of Sicuani, Aug. 5, 1965; app. auxiliary bishop of Chicago, Feb. 2, 1971.

Head, Edward D.: b. Aug. 5, 1919, White Plains, N. Y.; educ. Cathedral College, St. Joseph's Seminary, Columbia Univ. (New York City); ord. priest Jan. 27, 1945; director of New York Catholic Charities; ord. titular bishop of Ardsratha and auxiliary bishop of New York, Mar. 19, 1970; app. bishop of Buffalo, Jan. 23, 1973, installed Mar. 19, 1973.

Helmsing, Charles H.: b. Mar. 23, 1908, Shrewsbury, Mo.; educ. St. Louis Preparatory Seminary (St. Louis, Mo.), Kenrick Seminary (Webster Groves, Mo.); ord. priest June 10, 1933; ord. titular bishop of Axomis and auxiliary bishop of St. Louis, Apr. 19, 1949; first bishop of Springfield-Cape Girardeau, Aug. 24, 1956; bishop of Kansas City-St. Joseph, 1962, installed Apr. 3, 1962.

Henry, Harold W., S.S.C.: b. July 11, 1909, Northfield, Minn.; convert, 1922; educ. St. Columban's Seminary (Omaha, Nebr.); ord. priest Dec. 21, 1932; ord. titular bishop of Coridala and vicar apostolic of Kwang Ju, Korea, May 11, 1957; title changed to archbishop of Kwang Ju, 1962, when see was raised to metropolitan rank; transferred to titular see of Thubunae in Numidia, June 28, 1971, and named apostolic administrator of prefecture apostolic of Cheju-Do, Korea.

Herrmann, Edward J.: b. Nov. 6, 1913, Baltimore, Md.; educ. Mt. St. Mary's Seminary (Emmitsburg, Md.), Catholic Univ. (Washington, D.C.); ord. priest June 12, 1947; ord. titular bishop of Lamzella and auxiliary bishop of Washington, D.C., Apr. 26, 1966; app. bishop of Columbus, June 26, 1973.

Hettinger, Edward Gerhard: b. Oct. 14, 1902, Lancaster, O.; educ. St. Vincent's College (Beatty, Pa.); ord. priest June 2, 1928; ord. titular bishop of Teos and auxiliary bishop of Columbus, Feb. 24, 1942.

Hickey, Dennis W.: b. Oct. 28, 1914, Dansville, N. Y.; educ. Colgate Univ. and St. Bernard's Seminary (Rochester, N. Y.); ord. priest June 7, 1941; ord. titular bishop of Rusuccuru and auxiliary bishop of Rochester, N. Y., Mar. 14, 1968.

Hickey, James A.: b. Oct. 11, 1920, Midland, Mich.; educ. Sacred Heart Seminary (Detroit, Mich.), Catholic Univ. (Washington, D. C.), Lateran Univ. and Angelicum (Rome), Michigan State Univ.; ord. priest June 15, 1946; ord. titular bishop of Taraqua and auxiliary bishop of Saginaw, Apr. 14, 1967; rector of North American College, Rome, 1969-74; app. bishop of Cleveland, June 5, 1974; installed July 16, 1974.

Hines, Vincent J.: b. Sept. 14, 1912, New Haven, Conn.; educ. St. Thomas Seminary (Bloomfield, Conn.), St. Sulpice Seminary (Paris), Lateran Univ. (Rome); ord. priest May 2, 1937; ord. bishop of Norwich, Conn., Mar. 17, 1960.

Hoch, Lambert A.: b. Feb. 6, 1903, Elkton, S. D.; educ. Creighton Univ. (Omaha, Nebr.), St. Paul Seminary (St. Paul, Minn.); ord. priest May 30, 1928; ord. bishop of Bismarck, Mar. 25, 1952; app. bishop of Sioux Falls Dec. 5, 1956.

Hodapp, Robert L., S.J.: b. Oct. 1, 1910. Mankato, Minn.; educ. St. Stanislaus Seminary (Florissant, Mo.), St. Louis Univ. (St. Louis, Mo.); ord. priest June 18, 1941; ord. bishop of Belize, Br. Honduras, June 26, 1958.

Hodges, Joseph H.: b. Oct. 8, 1911, Harper's Ferry, W. Va.; educ. St. Charles College (Catonsville, Md.), North American College (Rome); ord. priest Dec. 8, 1935; ord. titular bishop of Rusadus and auxiliary bishop of Richmond, Oct. 15, 1952; named coadjutor bishop of Wheeling with right of succession, May 24, 1961; bishop of Wheeling, Nov. 23, 1962.

Hogan, James J.: b. Oct. 17, 1911, Philadelphia, Pa.; educ. St. Charles College (Catonsville, Md.), St. Mary's Seminary (Baltimore), Gregorian Univ. (Rome), Catholic Univ. (Washington, D.C.); ord. priest Dec. 8, 1937; ord. titular bishop of Philomelium and auxiliary bishop of Trenton, Feb. 25, 1960; app.

bishop of Altoona-Johnstown, installed July 6, 1966.

Hogan, Joseph L.: b. Mar. 11, 1916, Lima, N. Y.; educ. St. Bernard's Seminary (Rochester, N. Y.), Canisius College (Buffalo, N. Y.), Angelicum (Rome); ord. priest June 6, 1942; ord. bishop of Rochester, Nov. 28, 1969.

Howard, Edward Daniel: b. Nov. 5, 1877, Cresco, Ia.; educ. St. Joseph's College (Dubuque, Ia.), St. Mary's College (St. Mary's, Kans.), St. Paul Seminary (St. Paul, Minn.); ord. priest June 12, 1906; ord. titular bishop of Isauropolis and auxiliary bishop of Davenport, Apr. 8, 1924; app. archbishop of Oregon City, Apr. 30, 1926; title changed to archbishop of Portland, Sept. 26, 1928; resigned, 1966; assigned titular see of Albule.

Hughes, William A.: b. 1922, Youngstown, O.; educ. St. Charles College (Catonsville, Md.), St. Mary's Seminary (Cleveland, O.) Notre Dame Univ. (Notre Dame, Ind.); ord priest Apr. 6, 1946; app. titular bishop of Inis Cathaig and auxiliary bishop of Youngstown, July 23, 1974.

Howze, Joseph L.: b. Aug. 30, 1924, Daphne, Ala.; convert to Catholicism, 1948; educ. St. Bonaventure Univ. (St. Bonaventure, N.Y.); ord. priest May 7, 1959; ord. titular bishop of Massita and auxiliary bishop of Natchez-Jackson, Jan. 28, 1973.

Hunthausen, Raymond G.: b. Aug. 21, 1921, Anaconda, Mont.; educ. Carroll College (Helena, Mont.), St. Edward's Seminary (Kenmore, Wash.), St. Louis Univ. (St. Louis, Mo.), Catholic Univ. (Washington, D.C.), Fordham Univ. (New York City), Notre Dame Univ. (Notre Dame, Ind.); ord. priest June 1, 1946; ord. bishop of Helena, Aug. 30, 1962.

Hurley, Francis T.: b. Jan. 12, 1927, San Francisco, Calif.; educ. St. Patrick's Seminary (Menlo Park, Calif.), Catholic Univ. Washington, D.C.); ord. priest June 16, 1951; assigned to NCWC in Washington, D.C., 1957; assistant (1958) and later (1968) associate secretary of NCCB and USCC; ord. titular bishop of Daimlaig and auxiliary bishop of Juneau, Alaska, Mar. 19, 1970; app. bishop of Juneau, July 20, 1971.

Hurley, Mark J.: b. Dec. 13, 1919, San Francisco, Calif.; educ. St. Patrick's Seminary (Menlo Park, Calif.), Univ. of California (Berkeley), Catholic Univ. (Washington, D.C.), Lateran Univ. (Rome), Univ. of Portland (Portland, Ore.); ord. priest Sept. 23, 1944; ord. titular bishop of Thunusuda and auxiliary bishop of San Francisco, Jan. 4, 1968; app. bishop of Santa Rosa, Nov. 19, 1969.

I-J

Imesch, Joseph L.: b. June 21, 1931, Detroit, Mich.; educ. Sacred Heart Seminary (Detroit, Mich.), North American College, Gregorian Univ. (Rome); ord. priest Dec. 16, 1956; ord. titular bishop of Pomaria and auxiliary bishop of Detroit, Apr. 3, 1973.

Issenmann, Clarence G.: b. May 30, 1907, Hamilton, O.; educ. St. Joseph's College (Rensselaer, Ind.), St. Gregory's Seminary (Cincinnati, O.), St. Mary of the West Seminary (Norwood, O.); ord. priest June 29, 1932; ord. titular bishop of Phytea and auxiliary bishop of Cincinnati, May 25, 1954; bishop of Columbus, 1957-64; app. titular bishop of Filaca, coadjutor bishop of Cleveland and apostolic administrator *"sede plena,"* 1964; bishop of Cleveland, 1966; resigned June 5, 1974, because of ill health.

Johnson, William R.: b. Nov. 19, 1918, Tonopah, Nev.; educ. Los Angeles College and St. John's Seminary (Camarillo, Calif.), Catholic Univ. (Washington, D.C.); ord. priest May 28, 1944; ord. titular bishop of Blera and auxiliary bishop of Los Angeles, Mar. 25, 1971

Joyce, Robert F.: b. Oct. 7, 1896, Proctor, Vt.; educ. Univ. of Vermont (Burlington, Vt.), Grand Seminary (Montreal, Canada); ord. priest May 26, 1923; ord. titular bishop of Citium and auxiliary bishop of Burlington, Oct. 28, 1954; installed as bishop of Burlington, Feb. 26, 1957; resigned Dec. 14, 1971.

K

Kearney, James Edward: b. Oct. 28, 1884, Red Oak, Ia.; educ. St. Joseph's Seminary (Dunwoodie, N.Y.), Catholic Univ. (Washington, D.C.); ord. priest Sept. 19, 1908; ord. bishop of Salt Lake, Oct. 28, 1932; app. bishop of Rochester, July 31, 1937; retired Oct. 21, 1966.

Kellenberg, Walter P.: b. June 3, 1901, New York, N.Y.; educ. Cathedral College (New York, City), St. Joseph Seminary (Dunwoodie, N.Y.); ord. priest June 2, 1928; ord. titular bishop of Joannina and auxiliary bishop of New York, Oct. 5, 1953; app. bishop of Ogdensburg, Jan. 19, 1954; app. first bishop of Rockville Centre Apr. 16, 1957, installed May 27, 1957.

Kennally, Vincent, S.J.: b. June 11, 1895, Boston, Mass.; educ. Woodstock College (Woodstock, Md.), Weston College (Weston, Mass.); ord. priest June 20, 1928; ord. titular bishop of Sassura and vicar apostolic of the Caroline and Marshall Islands, Mar. 25, 1957; retired Sept. 20, 1971.

Klonowski, Henry T.: b. Mar. 8, 1898, Scranton, Pa.; educ. Univ. of Scranton (Scranton, Pa.), St. Francis Seminary (St. Francis, Wis.) St. Cyril and Methodius Seminary (Orchard Lake, Mich.), Capranica College, Angelicum and Gregorian Univ. (Rome); ord. priest Aug. 8, 1920; ord. titular bishop of Daldis and auxiliary bishop of Scranton, July 2, 1947; retired May, 1973.

Kocisko, Stephen: b. June 11, 1915, Minneapolis, Minn.; educ. Nazareth Hall Minor Seminary (St. Paul, Minn.), Pontifical Ruthenian College, Urban Univ. (Rome); ord.

priest Mar. 30, 1941; ord. titular bishop of Teveste and auxiliary bishop of apostolic exarchate of Pittsburgh, Oct. 23, 1956; installed as first eparch of the eparchy of Passaic, Sept. 10, 1963; app. eparch of Byzantine-Rite diocese of Pittsburgh, installed Mar. 5, 1968; app. first metropolitan of Munhall, installed June 11, 1969.

Koester, Charles R.: b. Sept. 16, 1915, Jefferson City, Mo.; educ. Conception Academy (Conception, Mo.), St. Louis Preparatory Seminary and Kenrick Seminary (St. Louis, Mo.), North American College (Rome); ord. priest Dec. 20, 1941; ord. titular bishop of Suacia and auxiliary bishop of St. Louis, Feb. 11, 1971.

Krawczak, Arthur H.: b. Feb. 2, 1913, Detroit, Mich.; educ. Sacred Heart Seminary, Sts. Cyril and Methodius Seminary (Orchard Lake, Mich.), Catholic Univ. (Washington, D.C.); ord. priest May 18, 1940; ord. titular bishop of Subbar and auxiliary bishop of Detroit, May 3, 1973.

Krol, John J.: (See Cardinals, Biographies.)

Kupfer, William F., M.M.: b. Jan. 28, 1909, Brooklyn, N.Y.; educ. Cathedral College (Brooklyn, N.Y.) Maryknoll Seminary (Maryknoll, N.Y.); ord. priest June 11, 1933; missionary in China; app. prefect apostolic of Taichung, Formosa, 1951; ord. first bishop of Taichung, July 25, 1962.

L

Lardone, Francesco: b. Jan. 12, 1887, Moretta, Italy; educ. Pontifical Schools of Theology and Canon Law and Royal Univ. (Turin); ord. priest June 29, 1910; became an American citizen, 1937; ord. titular archbishop of Rhizaeum and apostolic nuncio to Haiti and the Dominican Republic, June 30, 1949; app. apostolic nuncio to Peru, Nov. 21, 1953; papal representative to Turkey (first apostolic delegate, then internuncio), 1959-66.

Law, Bernard F.: b. Nov. 4, 1931, Torreon, Mexico; educ. Harvard Univ. (Cambridge, Mass.), St. Joseph Seminary (St. Benedict, La.), Pontifical College Josephinum (Worthington, O.); ord. priest May 21, 1961; editor of *Mississippi Register* (now *Mississippi Today),* 1963-68; director of NCCB Committee on Ecumenical and Interreligious Affairs, 1968-71; vicar general of Natchez-Jackson diocese, 1971-73; ord. bishop of Springfield-Cape Girardeau, Mo., Dec. 5, 1973.

Leech, George Leo: b. May 21, 1890, Ashley, Pa.; educ. St. Charles Borromeo Seminary (Overbrook, Pa.), Catholic Univ. (Washington, D.C.); ord. priest May 29, 1920; ord. titular bishop of Mela and auxiliary bishop of Harrisburg, Oct. 17, 1935; bishop of Harrisburg Dec. 19, 1935; resigned Oct. 19, 1971; app. titular bishop of Allegheny.

Leipzig, Francis P.: b. June 29, 1895, Chilton, Wis.; educ. St. Francis Seminary (Milwaukee, Wis.), Mt. Angel Seminary (St. Benedict, Ore.), St. Patrick's Seminary (Menlo

Park, Calif.); ord. priest Apr. 14, 1920; ord. bishop of Baker, Sept. 12, 1950; retired June 30, 1971.

Lemay, Leo, S.M.: b. Sept. 23, 1909, Lawrence, Mass.; educ. Marist College (Washington, D.C.), Gregorian Univ. (Rome); ord. priest Apr. 15, 1933; ord. titular bishop of Agbia and vicar apostolic of North Solomon Islands, Sept. 21, 1960; first bishop of Bougainville, Nov. 15, 1966; resigned Aug. 6, 1974.

Leonard, Vincent M.: b. Dec. 11, 1908, Pittsburgh, Pa.; educ. Duquesne Univ. (Pittsburgh, Pa.), St. Vincent Seminary (Latrobe, Pa.); ord. priest June 16, 1935; ord. titular bishop of Arsacal and auxiliary bishop of Pittsburgh, Apr. 21, 1964; app. bishop of Pittsburgh, installed July 2, 1969.

Lessard, Raymond W.: b. 1931, Grafton, N.D.; educ. St. Paul Seminary (St. Paul, Minn.), North American College (Rome); ord. priest Dec. 16, 1956; served on staff of the Congregation for Bishops in the Roman Curia, 1964-75; ord. bishop of Savannah, Apr. 27, 1973.

Leven, Stephen A.: b. Apr. 30, 1905, Blackwell, Okla.; educ. St. Gregory's College (Shawnee, Okla.), St. Benedict's College (Atchison, Kans.), St. Mary's Seminary (La Porte, Tex.), American College (Louvain, Belgium); ord. priest June 10, 1928; ord. titular bishop of Bure and auxiliary bishop of San Antonio, Feb. 8, 1956; app. bishop of San Angelo, Tex., installed Nov. 25, 1969.

Lohmuller, Martin J.: b. Aug. 21, 1919, Philadelphia, Pa.; educ. St. Charles Borromeo Seminary (Philadelphia, Pa.), Catholic Univ. (Washington, D.C.); ord. priest June 3, 1944; ord. titular bishop of Ramsbury and auxiliary bishop of Philadelphia, Apr. 2, 1970.

Losten, Basil: b. May 11, 1930, Chesapeake City, Md.; educ. St. Basil's College (Stamford, Conn.), Catholic University (Washington, D.C.); ord. priest June 10, 1957; ord. titular bishop of Arcadiopolis in Asia and auxiliary bishop of Ukrainian archeparchy of Philadelphia, May 25, 1971.

Lucey, Robert Emmet: b. Mar. 16, 1891, Los Angeles, Calif.; educ. St. Vincent's College (Los Angeles, Calif.), St. Patrick's Seminary (Menlo Park, Calif.), North American College (Rome); ord. priest May 14, 1916; ord. bishop of Amarillo, May 1, 1934; app. archbishop of San Antonio, Jan. 23, 1941; retired June 4, 1969.

Lucker, Raymond A.: b. Feb. 24, 1927, St. Paul, Minn.; educ. St. Paul Seminary (St. Paul, Minn.); University of Minnesota (Minneapolis), Angelicum (Rome); ord. priest June 7, 1952; director of USCC department of education, 1968-71; ord. titular bishop of Meta and auxiliary bishop of St. Paul and Minneapolis, Sept. 8, 1971.

Lynch, George E.: b. Mar. 4, 1917, New York, N.Y.; educ. Fordham Univ. (New

York), Mt. St. Mary's Seminary (Emmitsburg, Md.), Catholic Univ. (Washington, D.C.); ord. priest May 29, 1943; ord. titular bishop of Satafi and auxiliary bishop of Raleigh Jan. 6, 1970.

Lyons, Thomas W.: b. 1924, Washington, D.C.; educ. St. Charles College (Catonsville, Md.), St. Mary's Seminary (Baltimore, Md.); ord. priest 1948; app. titular bishop of Mortlach and auxiliary bishop of Washington, D.C., July 16, 1974.

M

McAuliffe, Michael F.: b. Nov. 22, 1920, Kansas City, Mo.; educ. St. Louis Preparatory Seminary (St. Louis, Mo.), Catholic Univ. (Washington, D.C.); ord. priest May 31, 1945; ord. bishop of Jefferson City, Aug. 18, 1969.

McCafferty, John E.: b. Jan. 6, 1920, New York, N.Y.; educ. St. Andrew's and St. Bernard's Seminaries (Rochester, N.Y.), Catholic Univ. (Washington, D.C.); ord. priest Mar. 17, 1945; ord. titular bishop of Tanudaia and auxiliary bishop of Rochester, Mar. 14, 1968.

McCarthy, Edward A.: b. Apr. 10, 1918, Cincinnati, O.; educ. Mt. St. Mary Seminary (Norwood, O.), Catholic Univ. (Washington, D.C.), Lateran and Angelicum (Rome); ord. priest May 29, 1943;; ord. titular bishop of Tamascani and auxiliary bishop of Cincinnati, June 15, 1965; first bishop of Phoenix, Ariz., Dec. 2, 1969.

McCauley, Vincent, C.S.C.: b. Mar. 8, 1906, Council Bluffs, Ia.; educ. Notre Dame Univ. (Notre Dame, Ind.), Holy Cross Seminary (Washington, D.C.); ord. priest June 24, 1943; ord. first bishop of Fort Portal, Uganda, May 18, 1961; resigned because of ill health, Dec. 1, 1972; general secretary of Episcopal Conferences of East Africa (AMECEA).

McCormick, J. Carroll: b. Dec. 15, 1907, Philadelphia, Pa.; educ. College Ste. Marie (Montreal), St. Charles Seminary (Overbrook, Pa.), Minor and Major Roman Seminary (Rome); ord. priest July 10, 1932; ord. titular bishop of Ruspae and auxiliary bishop of Philadelphia, Apr. 23, 1947; app. bishop of Altoona-Johnstown, installed Sept. 21, 1960; app. bishop of Scranton, installed May 25, 1966.

McDevitt, Gerald V.: b. Feb. 23, 1917, Philadelphia, Pa.; educ. St. Charles Seminary (Philadelphia, Pa.), Pontifical Roman Seminary (Rome); ord. priest May 30, 1942; ord. titular bishop of Tigias and auxiliary bishop of Philadelphia, Aug. 1, 1962.

McDonald, Andrew J.: b. Oct. 24, 1923, Savannah, Ga.; educ. St. Mary's Seminary (Baltimore, Md.), Catholic Univ. (Washington, D.C.), Lateran Univ. (Rome); ord. priest May 8, 1948; ord. bishop of Little Rock, Sept. 5, 1972.

McDonald, William J.: b. June 17, 1904,

Mooncoin, Ireland; educ. St. Kieran's College and Seminary (Kilkenny, Ireland), Catholic Univ. (Washington, D. C.); ord. priest June 10, 1928; rector of Catholic Univ. of America, 1957-67; ord. titular bishop of Aquae Regiae and auxiliary bishop of Washington, May 19, 1964; app. auxiliary bishop of San Francisco, July 26, 1967.

McDonough, Thomas J.: b. Dec. 5, 1911, Phil/adelphia, Pa.; educ. St. Charles Seminary (Overbrook, Pa.), Catholic Univ. (Washington, D. C.); ord. priest May 26, 1938; ord. titular bishop of Thenae and auxiliary bishop of St. Augustine, Apr. 30, 1947; app. auxiliary bishop of Savannah, Jan. 2, 1957; named bishop of Savannah, installed Apr. 27, 1960; app. archbishop of Louisville, installed May 2, 1967.

McDowell, John B.: b. July 17, 1921, New Castle, Pa.; educ. St. Vincent College, St. Vincent Theological Seminary (Latrobe, Pa.), Catholic Univ. (Washington, D.C.); ord. priest Nov. 4, 1945; ord. titular bishop of Tamazuca, and auxiliary bishop of Pittsburgh, Sept. 8, 1966.

McEleney, John J., S.J.: b. Nov. 13, 1895, Woburn, Mass.; educ. Boston College (Boston, Mass.), Jesuit Scholasticate (New England Province); entered Society of Jesus, 1918; ord. priest June 18, 1930; app. provincial of New England Province, 1944; ord. titular bishop of Zeugma and vicar apostolic of Jamaica, Apr. 15, 1950; title changed to bishop of Kingston, Feb. 29, 1956; archbishop of Kingston, Sept. 14, 1967; retired 1970.

McFarland, Norman F.: b. Feb. 21, 1922, Martinez, Calif.; educ. St. Patrick's Seminary (Menlo Park, Calif.), Catholic Univ. (Washington, D. C.); ord. priest June 15, 1946; ord. titular bishop of Bida and auxiliary bishop of San Francisco, Sept. 8, 1970.

McGann, John R.: b. Dec. 2, 1924, Brooklyn, N.Y.; educ. Cathedral College (Brooklyn, N.Y.), Immaculate Conception Seminary (Huntington, L.I.); ord. priest June 3, 1950; ord. titular bishop of Morosbisdus and auxiliary bishop of Rockville Centre, Jan. 7, 1971; vicar general and episcopal vicar.

McGarry, Urban, T.O.R.: b. Nov. 11, 1911, Warren, Pa.; ord. priest Oct. 3, 1942, in India; prefect apostolic of Bhagalpur, Aug. 7, 1956; ord. first bishop of Bhagalpur, India, May 10, 1965.

McGucken, Joseph T.: b. Mar. 13, 1902, Los Angeles, Calif.; educ. St. Patrick's Seminary (Menlo Park, Calif.), North American College (Rome); ord. priest Jan. 15, 1928; ord. titular bishop of Sanavus and auxiliary bishop of Los Angeles, Mar. 19, 1941; app. coadjutor bishop of Sacramento with right of succession, Oct. 26, 1955; bishop of Sacramento, Jan. 14, 1957; archbishop of San Francisco, installed Apr. 3, 1962.

McGurkin, Edward A., M.M.: b. June 22, 1905, Hartford, Conn.; educ. Maryknoll Seminary (Maryknoll, N. Y.); ord. priest

Sept. 14, 1930; ord. first bishop of Maswa, Tanganyika, Oct. 3, 1956; title of see changed to Shinyanga (Tanzania), 1957.

McIntyre, J. Francis L.: (See Cardinals, Biographies.)

McKinney, Joseph C.: b. Sept. 10, 1928, Grand Rapids, Mich.; educ. St. Joseph's Seminary (Grand Rapids, Mich.), Seminaire de Philosophie (Montreal, Canada), Urban Univ. (Rome, Italy); ord. priest Dec. 20, 1953; ord. titular bishop of Lentini and auxiliary bishop of Grand Rapids, Sept. 26, 1968.

McLaughlin, Bernard J.: b. Nov. 19, 1912, Buffalo, N. Y.; educ. Urban Univ. (Rome, Italy); ord. priest Dec. 21, 1935, at Rome; ord. titular bishop of Mottola and auxiliary bishop of Buffalo, Jan. 6, 1969.

McLaughlin, Charles B.: b. Sept. 26, 1913, New York, N. Y.; educ. Cathedral College (New York City), St. Joseph's Seminary (Yonkers, N.Y.), St. John's Seminary (Little Rock, Ark.); ord. priest June 6, 1941; ord. titular bishop of Risinium and auxiliary bishop of Raleigh, Apr. 15, 1964; app. first bishop of St. Petersburg, installed June 17, 1968.

McManus, James E., C.SS.R.: b. Oct. 10, 1900, Brooklyn, N.Y.; educ. Redemptorist Preparatory College (North East, Pa.), Mt. St. Alphonsus Seminary (Esopus, N. Y.), Catholic Univ. (Washington, D. C.); entered Congregation of the Most Holy Redeemer, 1921; ord. priest June 19, 1927; ord. bishop of Ponce, Puerto Rico, July 1, 1947; founder of Catholic Univ. of Ponce; transferred to titular see of Benda and app. auxiliary bishop of New York, Nov. 18, 1963; retired 1970.

McManus, William E.: b. Jan. 27, 1914, Chicago, Ill.; educ. St. Mary of the Lake Seminary (Mundelein, Ill.), Catholic Univ. (Washington, D.C.); ord priest Apr. 15, 1939; ord. titular bishop of Mesarfelta and auxiliary bishop of Chicago, Aug. 24, 1967.

McNabb, John C., O.S.A.: b. Dec. 11, 1925, Beloit, Wis.; educ. Villanova Univ. (Villanova, Pa.), Augustinian College and Catholic Univ. (Washington, D.C.), De Paul Univ. (Chicago, Ill.); ord. priest May 24, 1952; ord. titular bishop of Saia Maggiore and prelate of Chulucanas, Peru, June 17, 1967.

McNaughton, William J., M.M.: b. Dec. 7, 1926, Lawrence, Mass.; educ. Maryknoll Seminary (Maryknoll, N.Y.); ord. priest June 13, 1953; ord. titular bishop of Thuburbo Minus and vicar apostolic of Inchon, Korea, Aug. 24, 1961; title changed to bishop of Inchon, Mar. 10, 1962.

McNicholas, Joseph A.: b. Jan. 13, 1923, St. Louis, Mo.; educ. Cardinal Glennon College, Kenrick Seminary and St. Louis Univ. (all in St. Louis, Mo.); ord. priest June 7, 1949; ord. titular bishop of Scala and auxiliary bishop of St. Louis, Mar. 25, 1969.

McShea, Joseph M.: b. Feb. 22, 1907, Latimer, Pa.; educ. St. Charles Seminary (Philadelphia, Pa.), Major Pontifical Roman Seminary (Rome); ord. priest Dec. 6, 1931; ord. titular bishop of Mina and auxiliary bishop of Philadelphia, Mar. 19, 1952; app. first bishop of Allentown, installed Apr. 11, 1961.

Maginn, Edward J.: b. Jan. 4, 1897, Glasgow, Scotland; educ. Holy Cross College (Worcester, Mass.), St. Joseph's Seminary (Yonkers, N.Y.); ord. priest June 10, 1922; ord. titular bishop of Curium and auxiliary bishop of Albany, Sept. 12, 1957; apostolic administrator of Albany, 1966-69; retired July 8, 1972.

Maguire, John J.: b. Dec. 11, 1904, New York, N.Y.; educ. Cathedral College (New York City), St. Joseph's Seminary (Dunwoodie, N.Y.), North American College (Rome); ord. priest Dec. 22, 1928; ord. titular bishop of Antiphrae and auxiliary bishop of New York, June 29, 1959; app. titular archbishop of Tabalta and coadjutor archbishop of New York, Sept. 15, 1965.

Maguire, Joseph F.: b. Sept. 4, 1919, Boston, Mass.; educ. Boston College, St. John's Seminary (Boston, Mass.); ord. priest June 29, 1945; ord. titular bishop of Macteris and auxiliary bishop of Boston, Feb. 2, 1972.

Maher, Leo T.: b. July 1, 1915, Mount Union, Ia.; educ. St. Joseph's College (Mountain View, Calif.), St. Patrick's Seminary (Menlo Park, Calif.); ord. priest Dec. 18, 1943; ord. first bishop of Santa Rosa, April 5, 1962; bishop of San Diego, Oct. 4, 1969.

Mahoney, James P.: b. Aug. 16, 1925, Kingston, N.Y.; educ. St. Joseph's Seminary (Dunwoodie, N.Y.); ord. priest May 19, 1951; ord. titular bishop of Ipagro and auxiliary bishop of New York, Sept. 15, 1972.

Malone, James W.: b. Mar. 8, 1920, Youngstown, O.; educ. St. Charles Preparatory Seminary (Catonsville, Md.), St. Mary's Seminary (Cleveland, O.), Catholic Univ. (Washington, D.C.); ord. priest May 26, 1945; ord. titular bishop of Alabanda and auxiliary bishop of Youngstown, Mar. 24, 1960; apostolic administrator, 1966; bishop of Youngstown, installed June 20, 1968.

Maloney, Charles G.: b. Sept. 9, 1912, Louisville, Ky.; educ. St. Joseph's College (Rensselaer, Ind.), North American College (Rome); ord. priest Dec. 8, 1937; ord. titular bishop of Capsa and auxiliary bishop of Louisville, Feb. 2, 1955.

Maloney, David M.: b. Mar. 15, 1912, Littleton, Colo.; educ. St. Thomas Seminary (Denver, Colo.), Gregorian Univ. and Apollinare Univ. (Rome); ord. priest Dec. 8, 1936; ord. titular biahop of Ruspe and auxiliary bishop of Denver, Jan. 4, 1961; app. bishop of Wichita, Kans., Dec. 6, 1967.

Manning, Thomas R., O.F.M.: b. Aug. 29, 1922, Baltimore, Md.; educ. Duns Scotus College (Cincinnati, O.), Holy Name College (Washington, D.C.); ord. priest June 5, 1948; ord. titular bishop of Arsamosata and prelate of Coroico, Bolivia, July 14, 1959.

Manning, Timothy: (See Cardinals, Biographies.)

Marcinkus, Paul C.: b. Jan. 15, 1922, Cicero, Ill.; ord. priest May 3, 1947; served in Vatican secretariat from 1952; ord. titular bishop of Orta, Jan. 6, 1969; secretary (1968-71) and president (1971-) of Institute for Works of Religion (Vatican Bank).

Mardaga, Thomas J.: b. May 14, 1913, Baltimore, Md.; educ. St. Charles College (Catonsville, Md.), St. Mary's Seminary (Baltimore, Md.); ord. priest May 14, 1940; ord. titular bishop of Mutugenna and auxiliary bishop of Baltimore, Jan. 25, 1967; app. bishop of Wilmington, installed Apr. 6, 1968.

Marino, Eugene A., S.S.J.: b. 1934, Biloxi, Miss.; educ. Epiphany Apostolic College and Mary Immaculate Novitiate (Newburgh, N.Y.), St. Joseph's Seminary (Washington, D.C.), Catholic Univ. (Washington, D.C.), Loyola Univ. (New Orleans, La.), Fordham Univ. (New York City); ord. priest 1962; app. titular bishop of Walla Walla and auxiliary bishop of Washington, D.C., July 16, 1974.

Marling, Joseph M., C.Pp.S.: b. Aug. 31, 1904, Centralia, W. Va.; educ. St. Joseph's College (Collegeville, Ind.), St. Charles Seminary (Carthagena, O.), Catholic Univ. (Washington, D.C.); ord. priest Feb. 21, 1929; ord. titular bishop of Thasus and auxiliary bishop of Kansas City, Mo., Aug. 6, 1947; app. first bishop of Jefferson City, Aug. 24, 1956; resigned 1969; assigned titular see of Lesina.

Marshall, John A.: b. Apr. 26, 1928, Worcester, Mass.; educ. Holy Cross College (Worcester, Mass.), Sulpician Seminary (Montreal), North American College and Gregorian Univ. (Rome), Assumption College, (Worcester); ord. priest Dec. 19, 1953; ord. bishop of Burlington, Jan. 25, 1972.

May, John L.: b. Mar. 31, 1922, Evanston, Ill.; educ. St. Mary of the Lake Seminary (Mundelein, Ill.); ord. priest May 3, 1947; general secretary and vice-president of the Catholic Church Extension Society, 1959; ord. titular bishop of Tagarbala and auxiliary bishop of Chicago, Aug. 14, 1967; bishop of Mobile, Ala., Sept. 29, 1969.

Mazzarella, Bernardino N., O.F.M.: b. Apr. 20, 1904, Mirabella Eclano, Italy; educ. St. Anthony Seminary (Catskill, N.Y.), Franciscan Houses of Study (Province of Immaculate Conception); ord. priest June 5, 1931; ord. titular bishop of Hadrianopolis in Pisidia and prelate nullius of Olancho, Honduras, Oct. 18, 1957; installed as first bishop of Comayagua, Honduras, May 17, 1963.

Medeiros, Humberto S.: (See Cardinals, Biographies.)

Mendez, Alfred, C.S.C.: b. June 3, 1907, Chicago, Ill.; educ. Notre Dame Univ. (Notre Dame, Ind.), Institute of Holy Cross (Washington, D.C.); ord. priest June 24, 1935; ord. first bishop of Arecibo, Puerto Rico, Oct. 28, 1960; resigned Jan. 24, 1974.

Mestice, Anthony F.: b. Dec. 6, 1923, New York, N.Y.; educ. St. Joseph Seminary (Yonkers, N.Y.); ord. priest June 4, 1949; ord. titular bishop of Villa Nova and auxiliary bishop of New York Apr. 27, 1973.

Metzger, Sidney Matthew: b. July 11, 1902, Fredericksburg, Tex.; educ. St. John's Seminary (San Antonio, Tex.), North American College (Rome); ord. priest Apr. 3, 1926; ord. titular bishop of Birtha and auxiliary bishop of Santa Fe, Apr. 10, 1940; app. coadjutor bishop of El Paso, Dec. 26, 1941; bishop of El Paso, Dec. 1, 1942.

Michaels, James E., S.S.C.: b. May 30, 1926, Chicago, Ill.; educ. Columban Seminary (St. Columban, Neb.), Gregorian Univ. (Rome); ord. priest Dec. 21, 1951; ord. titular bishop of Verbe and auxiliary bishop of Kwang Ju, Korea, Apr. 14, 1966; app. auxiliary bishop of Wheeling, Apr. 3, 1973.

Mihalik, Emil J.: b. Feb. 6, 1920, Pittsburgh, Pa.; educ. St. Procopius Seminary (Lisle, Ill.), Duquesne Univ. (Pittsburgh, Pa.); ord. priest Sept. 21, 1945; ord. first bishop of Byzantine Rite diocese of Parma, O., June 12, 1969.

Minder, John, O.S.F.S.: b. Nov. 1, 1923, Philadelphia, Pa.; ord. priest June 3, 1950; ord. bishop of Keimos, South Africa, Jan. 10, 1968.

Moran, William J.: b. Jan. 15, 1906, San Francisco, Calif.; educ. St. Patrick's Seminary (Menlo Park, Calif.); ord. priest June 20, 1931; Army chaplain, 1933; ord. titular bishop of Centuria and auxiliary to the military vicar, Dec. 13, 1965.

Morkovsky, John Louis: b. Aug. 16, 1909, Praha, Tex.; educ. St. John's Seminary (San Antonio, Tex.), North American College, Urban Univ. and Gregorian Univ. (Washington, D. C.); ord. priest Dec. 5, 1933; ord titular bishop of Hieron and auxiliary bishop of Amarillo, Feb. 22, 1956; app. bishop of Amarillo, Aug. 27, 1958; titular bishop of Tigava and coadjutor bishop of Galveston-Houston with right of succession, June 11, 1963; apostolic administrator; president Texas Conference of Churches, 1970-72.

Morrow, Louis La Ravoire, S. D. B.: b. Dec. 24, 1892, Weatherford, Tex.; educ. Salesian School and Palafox (Puebla, Mexico); professed in Salesians of St. John Bosco, Sept. 29, 1912; ord. priest May 21, 1921; ord. bishop of Krishnagar, India, Oct. 29, 1939; resigned Oct. 31, 1969.

Mueller, Joseph M.: b. Dec. 1, 1894, St. Louis, Mo.; educ. Pontifical College Josephinum (Worthington, O.); ord. priest June 14, 1919; ord. titular bishop of Sinda and coadjutor bishop of Sioux City, Oct. 16, 1947; bishop of Sioux City, Sept. 20, 1948; resigned Oct. 15, 1970.

Mugavero, Francis John: b. June 8, 1914, Brooklyn, N. Y.; educ. Cathedral College (Brooklyn, N. Y.), Immaculate Conception Seminary (Huntington, N. Y.), Fordham Univ. (New York City); ord. priest May 18, 1940; ord. bishop of Brooklyn, Sept. 12, 1968.

Mulrooney, Charles R.: b. Jan. 13, 1906, Brooklyn, N. Y.; educ. Cathedral College (Brooklyn, N. Y.), St. Mary's Seminary (Baltimore, Md.), Sulpician Seminary (Washington, D. C.); ord. priest June 10, 1930; ord. titular bishop of Valentiniana and auxiliary bishop of Brooklyn, April 22, 1959.

Murphy, T. Austin: b. May 11, 1911, Baltimore, Md.; educ. St. Charles College (Catonsville, Md.), St. Mary's Seminary (Baltimore, Md.); ord priest June 10, 1937; ord. titular bishop of Appiaria and auxiliary bishop of Baltimore, July 3, 1962.

Murphy, Thomas W., C.SS.R. b. Dec. 17, 1917, Omaha, Nebr.; educ. St. Joseph's College (Kirkwood, Mo.); ord. priest June 29, 1943; ord. first bishop of Juazeiro, Brazil, Jan. 2, 1963; resigned Jan. 30, 1974; app. titular bishop of Sululos and auxiliary bishop of Sao Salvador da Bahia, Brazil, Jan. 31, 1974.

Mussio, John K.: b. June 13, 1902, Cincinnati, O.; educ. Xavier Univ. (Cincinnati, O.), Notre Dame Univ. (Notre Dame, Ind.), St. Gregory Preparatory Seminary (Cincinnati, O.), Mt. St. Mary Seminary (Norwood, O.), Angelicum (Rome); ord. priest Aug. 15, 1935; ord. bishop of Steubenville, May 1, 1945.

N

Nelson, Knute Ansgar, O.S.B.: b. Oct. 1, 1906, Copenhagen, Denmark; educ. Abbey of Maria Laach (Germany), Brown Univ. (Providence, R. I.); professed in the Order of St. Benedict, May 30, 1932; ord. priest May 22, 1937; became an American citizen, Mar. 4, 1941; ord. titular bishop of Bilta and coadjutor bishop of Stockholm, Sweden, Sept. 8, 1947; succeeded as bishop of Stockholm, Oct. 1, 1957; retired; titular bishop of Dura. 1962.

Newell, Hubert M.: b. Feb. 16, 1904, Denver, Colo.; educ. Regis College and St. Thomas Seminary (Denver, Colo.), Catholic Univ. (Washington, D.C.); ord. priest June 15, 1930; ord. titular bishop of Zapara and coadjutor bishop of Cheyenne, Sept. 24, 1947; bishop of Cheyenne, Nov. 10, 1951.

Newman, Thomas A., M.S.: b. Nov. 3, 1903, Waterbury, Conn.; educ. LaSalette Seminary (Ipswich, Mass.), Gregorian Univ. (Rome); ord. priest June 29, 1929; ord. first bishop of Prome, Burma, May 21, 1961.

Neylon, Martin J., S.J.: b. Feb. 13, 1920, Buffalo, N. Y.; ord. priest June 18, 1950; ord. titular bishop of Libertina and coadjutor vicar apostolic of the Caroline and Marshall Islands, Feb. 2, 1970; vicar apostolic of Caroline and Marshall Is., Sept. 20, 1971.

Noa, Thomas L.: b. Dec. 18, 1892, Iron Mountain, Mich.; educ. St. Francis Seminary (St. Francis, Wis.), North American College (Rome); ord. priest Dec. 23, 1916; ord. titular bishop of Salona and coadjutor bishop of Sioux City, Mar. 19, 1946; app. bishop of Marquette, Aug. 25, 1947; resigned 1968.

Nold, Wendelin J.: b. Jan. 18, 1900, Bonham, Tex.; educ. St. Mary's Seminary (La Porte, Tex.), North American College (Rome); ord. priest Apr. 11, 1925; ord. titular bishop of Sasima and coadjutor bishop of Galveston, Feb. 25, 1948, succeeded as bishop of Galveston, Apr. 1, 1950; title of see changed to Galveston-Houston, 1959.

Nolker, Bernard, C.SS.R.: b. Sept. 25, 1912, Baltimore, Md.; educ. St. Mary's College (North East, Pa.), St. Mary's College (Ilchester, Md.), Mt. St. Alphonsus Seminary (Esopus, N. Y.); ord. priest June 18, 1939; ord. first bishop of Paranagua, Brazil, Apr. 25, 1963.

Noser, Adolph A., S. V. D.: b. July 4, 1900, Belleville, Ill.; educ. Quincy College (Quincy, Ill.), St. Mary's Mission House (Techny, Ill.), Angelicum (Rome); received into the Society of the Divine Word, 1921; ord. priest Sept. 27, 1925; ord. titular bishop of Capitolias and vicar apostolic of Accra, Gold Coast, British West Africa, Aug. 22, 1947; title changed to bishop of Accra, Apr. 18, 1950; transferred to titular see of Hierpiniana and vicariate apostolic of Alexishaven, New Guinea, Jan. 8, 1953; first archbishop of Madang, Nov. 15, 1966.

O

O'Boyle, Patrick A.: (See Cardinals, Biographies.)

O'Brien, Henry Joseph: b. July 21, 1896, New Haven, Conn.; educ. St. Thomas Seminary (Hartford, Conn.), St. Bernard's Seminary (Rochester, N. Y.), Louvain Univ. (Belgium); ord. priest July 8, 1923; ord. titular bishop of Sita and auxiliary bishop of Hartford, May 14, 1940; bishop of Hartford, Apr., 1945; first archbishop of Hartford, Aug. 6, 1953; retired Nov. 20, 1968.

O'Connor, Martin J.: b. May 18, 1900, Scranton, Pa.; educ. St. Thomas College (Scranton, Pa.), St. Mary's Seminary (Baltimore, Md.), North American College, Urban Univ. and Apollinaris (Rome); ord. priest Mar. 15, 1924; ord. titular bishop of Thespia and auxiliary bishop of Scranton, Jan. 27, 1943; rector of North American College 1946-1964; app. titular archbishop of Laodicea in Syria, Sept. 5, 1959; apostolic nuncio to Malta, 1965-69; president emeritus Pontifical Commission for Social Communication.

O'Connor, William A.: b. Dec. 27, 1903, Chicago, Ill.; educ. Quigley Seminary (Chicago, Ill.), St. Mary of the Lake Seminary (Mundelein, Ill.), Urban Univ. (Rome); ord. priest Sept. 24, 1927; ord. bishop of Springfield, Ill., Mar. 7, 1949.

O'Donnell, Cletus F.: b. Aug. 22, 1917, Waukon, Ia.; educ. St. Mary Seminary (Mundelein, Ill.), Catholic Univ. (Washington, D.C.); ord. priest May 3, 1941; ord. titular bishop of Abritto and auxiliary bishop of Chicago, Dec. 21, 1960; app. bishop of Madison, Feb. 22, 1967, installed Apr. 25, 1967.

O'Keefe, Gerald: b. Mar. 30, 1918, St. Paul,

Minn,; educ. College of St. Thomas, St. Paul Seminary (St. Paul, Minn.); ord. priest Jan. 29, 1944; ord. titular bishop of Candyba and auxiliary bishop of St. Paul July 2, 1916; bishop of Davenport, Oct. 20, 1966, installed Jan. 4, 1967.

O'Leary, Edward C.: b. Aug. 21, 1920, Bangor, Me.; educ. Holy Cross College (Worcester, Mass.), St. Paul's Seminary (Ottawa, Canada); ord. priest June 15, 1946; ord. titular bishop of Moglena and auxiliary bishop of Portland, Me., Jan. 25, 1971.

O'Meara, Edward T.: b. Aug. 3, 1921, St. Louis, Mo.; educ. Cardinal Glennon College and Kenrick Seminary (St. Louis, Mo.), Angelicum (Rome); ord. priest Dec. 21, 1946; app. national director of Society for the Propagation of the Faith, 1967; ord. titular bishop of Thisiduo and auxiliary bishop of St. Louis, Feb. 13, 1972.

O'Neill, Arthur J.: b. Dec. 14, 1917, East Dubuque, Ill.; educ. Loras College (Dubuque, Ia.), St. Mary's Seminary (Baltimore, Md.); ord. priest Mar. 27, 1943; ord. bishop of Rockford, Oct. 11, 1968.

O'Rourke, Edward W.: b. Oct. 31, 1917, Downs, Ill.; educ. St. Mary's Seminary (Mundelein, Ill.), Aquinas Institute of Philosophy and Theology (River Forest, Ill.); ord. priest May 28, 1944; exec. dir. National Catholic Rural Life Conference, 1960-71; ord. and installed bishop of Peoria, July 25, 1971.

Ottenweller, Albert F.: b. Apr. 5, 1916, Stanford, Mont.; educ. St. Joseph's Seminary (Rensselaer, Ind.), Catholic Univ. (Washington, D.C.); ord. priest 1943; ord. titular bishop of Perdices and auxiliary bishop of Toledo, May 31, 1974.

P

Pardy, James V., M.M.: b. Mar. 9, 1898, Brooklyn, N. Y.; educ. St. Francis College (Brooklyn), Fordham Univ. (New York City), Catholic Univ. (Washington, D. C.); ord. priest. Jan. 26, 1930; ord. titular bishop of Irenopolis and first vicar apostolic of Cheong Ju, Korea, Sept. 16, 1958; title changed to bishop of Cheong Ju, Mar. 10, 1962; retired 1969; assigned titular see of Umbriatico.

Paschang, John L.: b. Oct. 5, 1895, Hemingford, Nebr.; educ. Conception College (Conception, Mo.), St. John Seminary (Collegeville, Minn.), Catholic Univ. (Washington, D. C.); ord. priest June 12, 1921; ord. bishop of Grand Island, Oct. 9, 1951; resigned July 25, 1972.

Pearce, George H., S.M.: b. Jan. 9, 1921, Brighton, Mass.; educ. Marist College and Seminary (Framington, Mass.); ord. priest Feb. 2, 1947; ord. titular bishop of Attalea in Pamphylia and vicar apostolic of the Samoa and Tokelau Islands, June 29, 1956; title changed to bishop of Apia, 1966; app. archbishop of Suva, Fiji Islands, June 22, 1967.

Pechillo, Jerome, T.O.R.: b. May 16, 1919,

Brooklyn, N. Y.; educ. Catholic Univ. (Washington, D. C.); ord. priest June 10, 1947; ord. titular bishop of Novasparsa and prelate of Coronel Oviedo, Paraguay, Jan. 25, 1966.

Pernicone, Joseph M.: b. Nov. 4, 1903, Regalbuto, Sicily; educ. Cathedral College (New York City), St. Joseph's Seminary (Dunwoodie, N. Y.), Catholic Univ. (Washington, D. C.); ord. priest Dec. 18, 1926; ord. titular bishop of Hadrianapolis and auxiliary bishop of New York, May 5, 1954; app. episcopal vicar, 1966.

Perry, Harold R., S. V. D.: b. Oct. 9, 1916, Lake Charles, La.; educ. St. Augustine Seminary (Bay St. Louis, Miss.), St. Mary's Seminary (Techny, Ill.); ord. priest Jan. 6, 1944; app. provincial of southern province of Society of the Divine Word, 1964; ord. titular bishop of Mons in Mauretania and auxiliary bishop of New Orleans, Jan. 6, 1966.

Pinger, Henry A., O.F.M.: b. Aug. 16, 1897, Lindsay, Nebr.; educ. Our Lady of Angels Seminary (Cleveland, O.), St. Anthony's Seminary (St. Louis, Mo.); professed in the Order of Friars Minor, June 18, 1918; ord. priest June 27, 1924; ord. titular bishop of Capitolias and vicar apostolic of Chowtsun, China, Sept. 21, 1937; title changed to bishop of Chowtsun, Apr. 11, 1946; imprisoned by Reds in 1951, released in 1956; expelled.

Povish, Kenneth J.: b. Apr. 19, 1924, Alpena, Mich.; educ. St. Joseph's Seminary (Grand Rapids, Mich.), Sacred Heart Seminary (Detroit, Mich.), Catholic Univ. (Washington, D. C.); ord. priest June 3, 1950; ord. bishop of Crookston, Sept. 29, 1970.

Power, Cornelius M.: b. Dec. 18, 1913, Seattle, Wash.; educ. St. Patrick's College (Menlo Park, Calif.), St. Edward's Seminary (Kenmore, Wash.), Catholic Univ. (Washington, D. C.); ord. priest June 3, 1939; ord. bishop of Yakima, May 1, 1969, installed May 29, 1969; app. archbishop of Portland, Ore., Jan. 22, 1974, installed Apr. 17, 1974.

Primeau, Ernest J.: b. Sept. 17, 1909, Chicago, Ill.; educ. Loyola Univ. (Chicago, Ill.), St. Mary of the Lake Seminary (Mundelein, Ill.), Lateran Univ. (Rome); ord. priest Apr. 7, 1934; ord. bishop of Manchester, Feb. 25, 1960; resigned Jan. 30, 1974; app. director of Villa Stritch, Rome, 1974.

Prost, Jude, O.F.M.: b. Dec. 6, 1915, Chicago, Ill.; educ. Our Lady of the Angels Seminary (Cleveland, O.), St. Joseph's Seminary (Teutopolis, Ill.); ord. priest June 24, 1942; ord. titular bishop of Fronta and auxiliary bishop of Belem do Para, Brazil, Nov. 1, 1962.

Pursley, Leo A.: b. Mar. 12, 1902, Hartford City, Ind.; educ. Mt. St. Mary's Seminary (Cincinnati, O.); ord. priest June 11, 1927; ord. titular bishop of Hadrianapolis in Pisidia and auxiliary bishop of Fort Wayne, Sept. 19, 1950; app. apostolic administrator of Fort

Wayne, Mar. 9, 1955; installed as bishop of Fort Wayne, Feb. 26, 1957; title of see changed to Fort Wayne-South Bend, 1960.

Q

Quinn, John R.: b. Mar. 28, 1929, Riverside, Calif.; educ. St. Francis Seminary (El Cajon, Calif.), North American College (Rome); ord. priest July 19, 1953; ord. titular bishop of Thisiduo and auxiliary bishop of San Diego, Dec. 12, 1967; bishop of Oklahoma City and Tulsa, Nov. 30, 1971; first archbishop of Oklahoma City, Dec. 19, 1972.

R

Rausch, James S.: b. Sept. 4, 1928, Albany, Minn.; educ. St. Thomas College (St. Paul, Minn.), Univ. of Minnesota (Minneapolis), Gregorian Univ. (Rome); ord. priest June 2, 1956; associate general secretary of USCC, 1970-72; general secretary of NCCB-USCC, 1972-; ord. titular bishop of Summa and auxiliary bishop of St. Cloud, Apr. 26, 1973.

Raya, Joseph M.: b. July 20, 1917, Zahle, Lebanon; educ. St. Louis College (Paris, France), St. Anne's Seminary (Jerusalem); ord. priest July 20, 1941; came to US, 1949, became US citizen; ord. archbishop of Acre, Israel, of the Melkites, Oct. 20, 1968.

Regan, Joseph W., M.M.: b. Apr. 5, 1905, Boston, Mass.; educ. Boston College (Boston, Mass.), St. Bernard's Seminary (Rochester, N. Y.), Maryknoll Seminary (Maryknoll, N.Y.); ord. priest Jan. 27, 1929; missionary in China 15 years; in Philippines since 1952; ord. titular bishop of Isinda and prelate of Tagum, Philippine Islands, Apr. 25, 1962.

Reh, Francis F.: b. Jan. 9, 1911, New York, N.Y.; educ. St. Joseph's Seminary (Dunwoodie, N.Y.), North American College and Gregorian Univ. (Rome); ord. priest Dec. 8, 1935; ord. bishop of Charleston, S.C., June 29, 1962; named titular bishop of Macriana in Mauretania, 1964; rector of North American College, 1964-68; bishop of Saginaw, installed Feb. 26, 1969.

Rehring, George John: b. June 10, 1890, Cincinnati, O.; educ. Mt. St. Mary of the West Seminary (Cincinnati, O.), Collegium Angelicum (Rome); ord. priest Mar. 28, 1914; ord. titular bishop of Lunda and auxiliary bishop of Cincinnati, Oct. 7, 1937; app. bishop of Toledo, July 26, 1950; retired 1967.

Reicher, Louis J.: b. June 14, 1890, Piqua, O.; educ. St. Mary's Seminary (Cincinnati, O.), St. Mary's Seminary (La Porte, Tex.); ord. priest Dec. 6, 1918; ord. first bishop of Austin, Apr. 14, 1948; resigned Nov. 15, 1971.

Reilly, Thomas F., C.SS.R.: b. Dec. 20, 1908, Boston, Mass.; educ. Mt. St. Alphonsus Seminary (Esopus, N.Y.), Catholic Univ. (Washington, D.C.); ord. priest June 10, 1933; ord. titular bishop of Themisonium and prelate of San Juan de la Maguana, Dominican Republic, Nov. 30, 1956; first bishop of San Juan de la Maguana, Nov. 21, 1969.

Reiss, John C.: b. May 13, 1922, Red Bank, N.J.; educ. Catholic Univ. (Washington, D.C.), Immaculate Conception Seminary (Darlington, N.J.); ord. priest May 31, 1947; ord. titular bishop of Simidicca and auxiliary bishop, of Trenton, Dec. 12, 1967.

Riley, Lawrence J.: b. Sept. 6, 1914; Boston, Mass.; educ. Boston College and St. John's Seminary (Boston, Mass.); ord. priest Sept. 21, 1940; ord. titular bishop of Daimlaig and auxiliary bishop of Boston, Feb. 2, 1972.

Riley, Thomas J.: b. Nov. 30, 1900, Waltham, Mass.; educ. Boston College (Boston, Mass.), St. John's Seminary (Brighton, Mass.), Louvain Univ. (Belgium); ord. priest May 20, 1927; ord. titular bishop of Regiae and auxiliary bishop of Boston, Dec. 21, 1959.

Roach, John R.: b. July 31, 1921, Prior Lake, Minn.; educ. St. Paul Seminary (St. Paul, Minn.); Univ. of Minnesota (Minneapolis); ord. priest June 18, 1946; ord. titular bishop of Cenae and auxiliary bishop of St. Paul and Minneapolis, Sept. 8, 1971.

Rudin, John J., M.M.: b. Nov. 27, 1916, Pittsfield, Mass.; educ. Maryknoll Seminary (Maryknoll, N.Y.), Gregorian Univ. (Rome); ord. priest June 11, 1944; ord. first bishop of Musoma, Tanzania, Oct. 3, 1957.

Russell, John J.: b. Dec. 1, 1897, Baltimore, Md.; educ. St. Charles College (Catonsville, Md.), St. Mary's Seminary (Baltimore, Md.), North American College (Rome); ord. priest July 8, 1923; ord. bishop of Charleston, Mar. 14, 1950; bishop of Richmond, July 3, 1958; retired Apr. 30, 1973.

Ryan, James C., O.F.M.: b. Nov. 17, 1912, Chicago, Ill.; educ. St. Joseph's Seraphic Seminary (Westmont, Ill.), Our Lady of the Angels Seminary (Cleveland, O.); ord. priest June 24, 1938; ord. titular bishop of Margo and prelate of Santarem, Brazil, April 9, 1958.

Ryan, Joseph T.: b. Nov. 1, 1913, Albané N.Y.; educ. Manhattan College (New York City); ord. priest June 3, 1939; national secretary of Catholic Near East Welfare Assn. 1960-65; ord. first archbishop of Anchorage, Alaska, Mar. 25, 1966.

S

Salatka, Charles A.: b. Feb. 26, 1918, Grand Rapids, Mich.; educ. St. Joseph's Seminary (Grand Rapids, Mich.), Catholic Univ. (Washington, D.C.), Lateran Univ. (Rome); ord. priest Feb. 24, 1945; ord. titular bishop of Cariana and auxiliary bishop of Grand Rapids, Mich., Mar. 6, 1962; app. bishop of Marquette, installed Mar. 25, 1968.

Sanchez, Robert: b. Mar. 20, 1934, Socorro, N.M.; educ. Immaculate Heart Seminary (Santa Fe, N.M.), Gregorian Univ. (Rome), Catholic Univ. (Washington, D.C.); ord. priest 1956; ord. archbishop of Santa Fe, N.M., July 25, 1974.

Scanlan, John J.: b. May 24, 1906, County Cork, Ireland; educ. National Univ. of Ireland (Dublin), All Hallows College (Dublin); ord. priest June 22, 1930; US citizen 1938; ord. titular bishop of Cenae and auxiliary bishop of Honolulu, Sept. 21, 1954; bishop of Honolulu, installed May 1, 1968.

Schad, James L.: b. July 20, 1917, Philadelphia, Pa.; educ. St. Mary's Seminary (Baltimore, Md.); ord. priest Apr. 10, 1943; ord. titular bishop of Panatoria and auxiliary bishop of Camden, Dec. 8, 1966.

Schexnayder, Maurice: b. Aug. 13, 1895, Wallace, La.; educ. Chenet Institute (New Orleans, La.), St. Joseph's Seminary (St. Benedict, La.), St. Mary's Seminary (Baltimore, Md.), North American College (Rome); ord. priest Apr. 11, 1925; ord. titular bishop of Tuscamia and auxiliary bishop of Lafayette, La., Feb. 22, 1951; bishop of Lafayette, La., May 24, 1956; retired Nov. 7, 1972.

Schierhoff, Andrew B.: b. Feb. 10, 1922, St. Louis, Mo.; ord. priest Apr. 14, 1948; missionary in Bolivia from 1956; ord. titular bishop of Cerenza and auxiliary of La Paz, Bolivia, Jan. 6, 1969.

Schladweiler, Alphonse: b. July 18, 1902, Milwaukee, Wis.; educ. St. Joseph College (Teutopolis, Ill.), St. Paul's Seminary (St. Paul, Minn.), Univ. of Minnesota (Minneapolis, Minn.); ord. priest June 9, 1929; ord. first bishop of New Ulm, Jan. 29, 1958.

Schlaefer, Salvator, O.F.M. Cap.: b. June 27, 1920, Campbellsport, Wis.; ord. priest June 5, 1946; missionary in Bluefields, Nicaragua from 1947; ord. titular bishop of Fiumepiscense and vicar apostolic of Bluefields, Nicaragua, Aug. 12, 1970.

Schlotterback, Edward F., O.S.F.S.: b. Mar. 2, 1912, Philadelphia, Pa.; educ. Catholic Univ. (Washington, D.C.); ord. priest Dec. 17, 1938; ord. titular bishop of Balanea and vicar apostolic of Keetmanshoop, Namibia, July 11, 1956.

Schmidt, Firmin M., O.F.M.Cap.: b. Oct. 12, 1918, Catherine, Kans.; educ. Catholic Univ. (Washington, D.C.); ord. priest June 2, 1946; app. prefect apostolic of Mendi, Papua-New Guinea, Apr. 3, 1959; ord. titular bishop of Conana and first vicar apostolic of Mendi, Dec. 15, 1965; first bishop of Mendi, Nov. 15, 1966.

Schmidt, Mathias, O.S.B.: b. 1931, Wortonville, Kans.; ord. priest May 30, 1957; missionary in Brazil; ord. titular bishop of Mutugenna and auxiliary bishop of Jatai, Brazil, Sept. 10, 1972.

Schmitt, Adolph G., C.M.M.: b. Apr. 20, 1905, Bimpar, Bavaria; educ. Aloysianum Preparatory Seminary (Lehr, Bavaria), Mariannhill Seminary, and University of Wuerzburg (Bavaria); entered Mariannhill Mission Society, 1926; ord. priest Mar. 19, 1931; became US citizen, 1945; ord. titular bishop of Nasai and vicar apostolic of Bulawayo, Rhodesia, Apr. 2, 1951; bishop of Bulawayo, Jan. 1, 1955; resigned May 18, 1974.

Schmitt, Mark: b. Feb. 14, 1923, Algoma, Wis., educ. Salvatorian Seminary (St. Nazianz, Wis.), St. John's Seminary (Collegeville, Minn.); ord. priest May 22, 1948; ord. titular bishop of Ceanannus Mor and auxiliary bishop of Green Bay, June 24, 1970.

Schmondiuk, Joseph: b. Aug. 6, 1912, Wall, Pa.; educ. St. Joseph's Preparatory College High School (Philadelphia, Pa.), Pontifical Ruthenian College, Angelicum and Urban Univ. (Rome); ord. priest Mar. 29, 1936; ord. titular bishop of Zeugma in Syria and auxiliary bishop of apostolic exarchate of Philadelphia, Nov. 8, 1956; title of see changed to metropolitan, 1958; app. eparch of Stamford, 1961.

Schoenherr, Walter J.: b. Feb. 28, 1920, Detroit, Mich.' educ. Sacred Heart Seminary (Detroit, Mich.), Mt. St. Mary Seminary (Norwood, O); ord. priest Oct. 27, 1945; ord. titular bishop of Timidana and auxiliary bishop of Detroit, May 1, 1968.

Schuck, James A., O.F.M.: b. Jan. 17, 1913, Treverton, Pa.; educ. St. Joseph's Seminary (Callicoon, N.Y.), St. Bonaventure's University (St. Bonaventure, N.Y.), Holy Name College (Washington, D.C.); ord. priest June 11, 1940; ord. titular bishop of Avissa and prelate of Cristalandia, Brazil, Feb. 24, 1959.

Schulte, Paul Clarence: b. Mar. 18, 1890, Fredericktown, Mo.; educ. St. Francis Solanus College (Quincy, Ill.), Kenrick Seminary (Webster Groves, Mo.); ord. priest June 11, 1915; ord. bishop of Leavenworth, Sept. 21, 1937; archbishop of Indianapolis, July 27, 1946; resigned Jan. 14, 1970; assigned titular see of Elicrora.

Schuster, Eldon B.: b. Mar. 10, 1911, Calio, N. Dak.; educ. Loras College (Dubuque, Ia.), Catholic Univ. (Washington, D.C.), Oxford Univ. (England), St. Louis Univ. (St. Louis, Mo.); ord. priest May 27, 1937; ord. titular bishop of Amblada and auxiliary bishop of Great Falls, Mont., Dec. 21, 1961; app. bishop of Great Falls, Dec. 2, 1967, installed Jan. 23, 1968.

Senyshyn, Ambrose, O.S.B.M.: b. Feb. 23, 1903, Stary Sambor, Galicia; educ. Monastery Colleges at Krechiev and Iawriev, Dobromil and Crystynopol (Galicia); ord. priest Aug. 23, 1931; ord. titular bishop of Maina and auxiliary bishop of the Ukrainian-Greek Catholic Diocese of the United States, Oct. 22, 1942; app. first bishop of Byzantine Ukrainian Rite exarchate of Stamford, Aug. 8, 1956; eparch of Stamford, 1958; app. metropolitan of Ukrainian archeparchy of Philadelphia, 1961.

Shea, Francis R.: b. Dec. 4, 1913, Knoxville, Tenn.; educ. St. Mary's Seminary (Baltimore, Md.), North American College (Rome), Peabody College (Nashville, Tenn.); ord. priest Mar. 19, 1939; ord. bishop of Evansville, Ind., Feb. 3, 1970.

Sheehan, Daniel E.: b. May 14, 1917, Emerson, Nebr.; educ. Creighton Univ. (Omaha, Nebr.), Kenrick Seminary (Webster Groves, Mo.), Catholic Univ. (Washington, D.C.): ord. priest May 23, 1942; ord. titular bishop of Capsus and auxiliary bishop of Omaha, Mar. 19, 1964; app. archbishop of Omaha, installed Aug. 11, 1969.

Sheen, Fulton J.: b. May 8, 1895, El Paso, Ill.; educ. St. Viator College (Kankakee, Ill.), St. Paul seminary (St. Paul, Minn.), Catholic Univ. (Washington, D.C.), Louvain Univ. (Belgium), Collegium Angelicum (Rome); ord. priest Sept. 20, 1919; app. national director of the Pontifical Society for the Propagation of the Faith, 1950; ord. titular bishop of Caesariana and auxiliary bishop of New York, June 11, 1951; app. bishop of Rochester, installed Dec. 15, 1966; resigned Oct. 15, 1969; titular archbishop of Newport.

Shehan, Lawrence Joseph: (See Cardinals, Biographies.)

Smith, Eustace J., O.F.M.: b. Aug. 22, 1908, Medford, Mass.; educ. St. Joseph's Seraphic Seminary (Callicoon, N.Y.), Holy Name College (Washington, D.C.). Antonianum, Pontifical Biblical Institute (Rome), Franciscan Biblical Institute (Jerusalem); ord. priest June 12, 1934; ord. titular bishop of Apamea Cibotus and vicar apostolic of Beirut, Feb. 2, 1956.

Snyder, John J.: b. Oct. 25, 1925, New York, N.Y.; educ. Cathedral College (Brooklyn, N.Y.), Immaculate Conception Seminary (Huntington, N.Y.); ord. priest June 9, 1951; ord. titular bishop of Forlimpopli and auxiliary bishop of Brooklyn, Feb. 2, 1973.

Soenneker, Henry J.: b. May 27, 1907, Melrose, Minn.; educ. Pontifical Josephinum College (Worthington, O.), Catholic Univ. (Washington, D.C.); ord. priest May 26, 1934; ord. bishop of Owensboro, Apr. 26, 1961.

Sowada, Alphonse A., O.S.C.: b. June 23, 1933, Avon, Minn.; educ. Holy Cross Scholasticate (Fort Wayne, Ind.), Catholic Univ. (Washington, D.C.); ord. priest May 31, 1958; missionary in Indonesia from 1958; ord. bishop of Agats, Indonesia, Nov. 23, 1969.

Speltz, George H.: b. May 12, 1912, Altura, Minn.; educ. St. Mary's College, St. Paul's Seminary (St. Paul, Minn.), Catholic Univ. (Washington, D.C.); ord. priest June 2, 1940; ord. titular bishop of Claneus and auxiliary bishop of Winona, Mar. 25, 1963; app. coadjutor bishop of St. Cloud, Apr. 4, 1966; bishop of St. Cloud, Jan. 31, 1968.

Stanton, Martin W.: b. Apr. 17, 1897, Jersey City, N.J.; educ. St. Peter's College (Jersey City, N.J.), Immaculate Conception Seminary (Darlington, N.J.), Fordham Univ. (New York City); ord. priest June 14, 1924; ord. titular bishop of Citium and auxiliary bishop of Newark, Sept. 24, 1957. Retired.

Stemper, Alfred M., M.S.C.: b. Jan. 2, 1913, Black Hammer, Minn.; ord. priest June

26, 1940; ord. titular bishop of Eleutheropolis and vicar apostolic of Kavieng, New Guinea, Oct. 28, 1957; first bishop of Kavieng, Nov. 15, 1966.

Strecker, Ignatius J.: b. Nov. 23, 1917, Spearville, Kans.; educ. St. Benedict's College (Atchison, Kans.), Kenrick Seminary (Webster Groves, Mo.), Catholic Univ. (Washington, D.C.); ord. priest Dec. 19, 1942; ord. bishop of Springfield-Cape Girardeau, Mo., June 20, 1962; archbishop of Kansas City, Kans., Oct. 28, 1969.

Sullivan, James S.: b. July 23, 1929, Kalamazoo, Mich.; ord. priest June 4, 1955; ord. titular bishop of Siccessi and auxiliary bishop of Lansing, Sept. 21, 1972.

Sullivan, John J.: b. July 5, 1920, Horton, Kans.; educ. Kenrick Seminary (St. Louis, Mo.); ord. priest Sept. 23, 1944; vicepresident of Catholic Church Extension Society and national director of Extension Lay Volunteers, 1961-68; ord. bishop of Grand Island, Sept. 19, 1972.

Sullivan, Joseph V.: b. Aug. 15, 1919, Kansas City, Mo.; educ. Sulpician Seminary (Washington, D.C.), Catholic Univ. (Washington, D.C.); ord. priest June 1, 1946; ord. titular bishop of Tagamuta and auxiliary bishop of Kansas City-St. Joseph, Apr. 3, 1967; app. Bishop of Baton Rouge, Aug. 13, 1974.

Sullivan, Walter F.: b. June 10, 1928, Washington, D.C.; ord. priest May 9, 1953; ord. titular bishop of Selsea and auxiliary bishop of Richmond, Va., Dec. 1, 1970; app. bishop of Richmond, June 4, 1974.

Swanstrom, Edward E.: b. Mar. 20, 1903, New York, N.Y.; educ. Fordham Univ. (New York City), St. John's Seminary (Brooklyn, N.Y.), New York School of Social Work; ord. priest June 2, 1928; director of Catholic Relief Services; ord. titular bishop of Arba and auxiliary bishop of New York, Oct. 28, 1960.

Szoka, Edmund C.: b. Sept. 14, 1927, Grand Rapids, Mich.; educ. Sacred Heart Seminary (Detroit, Mich.), St. John's Provincial Seminary (Plymouth, Mich.), Lateran Univ. (Rome). ord. priest June 5, 1954; ord. first bishop of Gaylord, Mich., July 20, 1971.

T

Tanner, Paul F.: b. Jan. 15, 1905, Peoria, Ill.; educ. Marquette Univ. (Milwaukee, Wis.), Kenrick Seminary (Webster Groves, Mo.), St. Francis Seminary (Milwaukee, Wis.), Catholic Univ. (Washington, D.C.): ord. priest May 30, 1931; assistant director NCWC Youth Department 1940-45; assistant general secretary of NCWC 1945-58; general secretary of NCWC (now USCC) 1958-68; ord. titular bishop of Lamasba, Dec. 21, 1965; bishop of St. Augustine, Mar. 27, 1968.

Tawil, Joseph: b. Dec. 25, 1913, Damascus, Syria; ord. priest July 20, 1936; ord. titular archbishop of Mira and patriarchal vicar for eparchy of Damascus of the Patriarchate of

Antioch for the Melkites, Jan. 1, 1960; apostolic exarch for faithful of the Melkite rite in the US, Oct. 31, 1969.

Taylor, John E., O.M.I.: b. Nov. 15, 1914, East St. Louis, Ill.; educ. Angelicum Univ., Gregorian Univ. (Rome), Univ. of Ottawa (Ottawa, Canada); ord. priest May 25, 1940; ord. bishop of Stockholm, Sweden, Sept. 21, 1962.

Toolen, Thomas Joseph: b. Feb. 28, 1886, Baltimore, Md.; educ. St. Mary's Seminary (Baltimore, Md.), Catholic Univ. (Washington, D.C.); ord. priest Sept. 27, 1910; ord. bishop of Mobile, May 4, 1927; personal title of archbishop conferred, July 14, 1954; retired 1969; assigned titular see of Glastonbury.

Topel, Bernard J.: b. May 31, 1903, Bozeman, Mont.; educ. Carroll College (Helena, Mont.), Grand Seminary (Montreal), Catholic Univ. (Washington, D.C.), Harvard Univ. (Cambridge, Mass.), Notre Dame Univ. (Notre Dame, Ind.); ord. priest June 7, 1927; ord. titular bishop of Binda and coadjutor bishop of Spokane, Sept. 21, 1955; bishop of Spokane, Sept. 25, 1955.

Tracy, Robert E.: b. Sept. 14, 1909, New Orleans, La.; educ. St. Joseph's Preparatory Seminary (St. Benedict, La.), Notre Dame Seminary (New Orleans); ord. priest June 12, 1932; national chaplain of Newman Federation; 1954-56; ord. titular bishop of Sergentiza and auxiliary bishop of Lafayette, La., May 19, 1959; app. first bishop of Baton Rouge, Aug. 10, 1961; resigned Mar. 21, 1974.

Treinen, Sylvester: b. Nov. 19, 1917, Donnelly, Minn.; educ. Crosier Seminary (Onamia, Minn.), St. Paul Seminary (St. Paul, Minn.); ord. priest June 11, 1946; ord. bishop of Boise, July 25, 1962.

Tschoepe, Thomas: b. Dec. 17, 1915, Pilot Point, Tex.; educ. Pontifical College Josephinum (Worthington, O.); ord. priest May 30, 1943; ord. bishop of San Angelo, Tex., Mar. 9, 1966; app. bishop of Dallas, Tex., Aug. 27, 1969.

U-V

Unterkoefler, Ernest L.: b. Aug. 17, 1917, Philadelphia, Pa.; educ. Catholic Univ. (Washington, D.C.); ord. priest May 18, 1944; ord. titular bishop of Latopolis and auxiliary bishop of Richmond, Va., Feb. 22, 1962; app. bishop of Charleston, 1964, installed Feb. 22, 1965.

Vath, Joseph G.: b. Mar. 12, 1918, New Orleans, La.; educ. Notre Dame Seminary (New Orleans, La.), Catholic Univ. (Washington, D.C.); ord. priest June 7, 1941; ord. titular bishop of Novaliciana and auxiliary bishop of Mobile-Birmingham, May 26, 1966; app. first bishop of Birmingham, Oct. 8, 1969.

Veigle, Adrian J.M., T.O.R.: b. Sept. 15, 1912, Lilly, Pa.; educ. St. Francis College

(Loretto, Pa.), Pennsylvania State College; ord. priest May 22, 1937; ord. titular bishop of Gigthi and prelate of Borba, Brazil, June 9, 1966.

Vogel, Cyril J.: b. Jan. 15, 1905, Pittsburgh, Pa.; educ. Duquesne Univ. (Pittsburgh, Pa.), St. Vincent's Seminary (Latrobe, Pa.); ord. priest June 7, 1931; ord. bishop of Salina, June 17, 1965.

Vonesh, Raymond J.: b. Jan. 25, 1916, Chicago, Ill.; educ. St. Mary of the Lake Seminary (Mundelein, Ill.). Gregorian Univ. (Rome); ord. priest May 3, 1941; ord. titular bishop of Vanariona and auxiliary bishop of Joliet, Ill., Apr. 3, 1968.

W-Z

Walsh, James Edward, M.M.: b. Apr. 30, 1891, Cumberland, Md.; educ. Mt. St. Mary's College (Emmitsburg, Md.), Maryknoll Foreign Mission Seminary (Maryknoll, N.Y.); entered Catholic Foreign Mission Society (Maryknoll, N.Y.), 1912; ord. priest Dec. 7, 1915; ord. titular bishop of Sata and vicar apostolic of Kongmoon, China, May 22, 1927; superior general of Maryknoll, July 21, 1936, until Aug. 7, 1946; app. general secretary, Catholic Central Bureau, Shanghai, China, Aug. 24, 1948; placed under house arrest in October, 1958, detained in Shanghai hospital; sentenced to 20 years' imprisonment for "espionage," Mar., 1960; released 1970.

Ward, John J.: b. Sept. 28, 1920, Los Angeles, Calif.; educ. St. John's Seminary (Camarillo, Calif.), Catholic Univ. (Washington, D.C.); ord. priest May 4, 1946; ord. titular bishop of Bria and auxiliary of Los Angeles, Dec. 12, 1963.

Waters, Vincent S.: b. Aug. 15, 1904, Roanoke, Va.; educ. Belmont Abbey College (Belmont, N.C.), St. Charles College (Catonsville, Md.), St. Mary's Seminary (Baltimore, Md.), North American College (Rome); ord. priest Dec. 8, 1931; ord. bishop of Raleigh, May 15, 1945.

Watson, Alfred M.: b. July 11, 1907, Erie, Pa.; educ. St. Mary's Seminary (Baltimore, Md.), Catholic Univ. (Washington, D.C.); ord. priest May 10, 1934; ord. titular bishop of Nationa and auxiliary bishop of Erie, June 29, 1965; app. bishop of Erie, 1969, installed May 13, 1969.

Watters, Loras J.: b. Oct. 14, 1915, Dubuque, Ia.; educ. Loras College (Dubuque, Ia.), Gregorian Univ. (Rome), Catholic Univ. (Washington, D.C.); ord. priest June 7, 1941; ord. titular bishop of Fidoloma and auxiliary bishop of Dubuque, Aug. 26, 1965; bishop of Winona, installed Mar. 13, 1969.

Weldon, Christopher J.: b. Sept. 6, 1905, New York, N.Y.; educ. Montreal College (Canada), St. Joseph's Seminary (Dunwoodie, N.Y.), Catholic Univ. (Washington, D.C.); ord. priest Sept. 21, 1939; ord. bishop of Springfield, Mass., Mar. 24, 1950.

Welsh, Thomas J.: b. Dec. 20, 1921, Weatherly, Pa.; educ. St. Charles Borromeo Seminary (Philadelphia, Pa.), Catholic Univ. (Washington, D.C.); ord. priest May 30, 1946; ord. titular bishop of Scattery Island and auxiliary bishop of Philadelphia, Apr. 2, 1970; app. first bishop of Arlington, Va., June 4, 1974, installed Aug. 13, 1974.

Whealon, John F.: b. Jan. 15, 1921, Barberton, O.; educ. St. Charles College (Catonsville, Md.), St. Mary's Seminary (Cleveland, O.); ord. priest May 26, 1945; ord. titular bishop of Andrapa and auxiliary bishop of Cleveland, July 6, 1961; app. bishop of Erie, Dec. 9, 1966, installed Mar. 7, 1967; archbishop of Hartford, installed Mar. 19, 1969.

Whelan, Robert L., S.J.: b. Apr. 16, 1912, Wallace, Ida.; educ. St. Michael's College (Spokane, Wash.), Alma College (Alma, Calif.); ord. priest June 17, 1944; ord. titular bishop of Sicilibba and coadjutor bishop of Fairbanks, Alaska, with right of succession, Feb. 22, 1968; bishop of Fairbanks, Nov. 30, 1968.

Wildermuth, Augustine F., S.J.: b. Feb. 20, 1904, St. Louis, Mo.; educ. St. Stanislaus Seminary (Florissant, Mo.), St. Michael's Scholasticate (Spokane, Wash.), Sacred Heart College (Shembaganur, S. India), St. Mary's College (Kurseong, India), Gregorian Univ. (Rome); entered Society of Jesus, 1922; ord. priest July 25, 1935; ord. bishop of Patna, India, Oct. 28, 1947.

Wright, John J.: (See Cardinals, Biographies.) Prefect of the Sacred Congregation for the Clergy.

Wycislo, Aloysius John: b. June 17, 1908, Chicago, Ill.; educ. St. Mary's Seminary (Mundelein, Ill.), Catholic Univ. (Washington, D.C.); ord. priest Apr. 4, 1934; ord. titular bishop of Stadia and auxiliary bishop of Chicago, Dec. 21, 1960; app. bishop of Green Bay, installed Apr. 16, 1968.

Zaleski, Alexander M.: b. June 24, 1906, Laurel, N.Y.; educ. St. Mary's College and Sts. Cyril and Methodius Seminary (Orchard Lake, Mich.), American College (Louvain, Belgium), Biblical Institute (Rome); ord. priest July 12, 1931; ord. titular bishop of Lyrbe and auxiliary bishop of Detroit, May 23, 1950; app. coadjutor bishop of Lansing and apostolic administrator "sede plena," 1964; bishop of Lansing, Dec. 1, 1965.

Zayek, Francis: b. Oct. 18, 1920, Manzanillo, Cuba; ord. priest Mar. 17, 1946; ord. titular bishop of Callinicum and auxiliary bishop for Maronites in Brazil, Aug. 5, 1962; named apostolic exarch for Maronites in US, with headquarters in Detroit; installed June 11, 1966; first eparch of St. Maron of Detroit, Mar. 25, 1972.

Zuroweste, Albert R.: b. Apr. 26, 1901, East St. Louis, Ill.; educ. St. Francis College (Quincy, Ill.), Kenrick Seminary (Webster Groves, Mo.), Catholic Univ. (Washington, D.C.); ord. priest June 8, 1924; ord. bishop of Belleville, Jan. 29, 1948.

RETIRED U.S. PRELATES

Information includes name of the prelate and see held at the time of retirement; archbishops are indicated by an asterisk.

The preferred form of address of retired prelates is *Former Archbishop* or *Bishop of* (last see held).

Karl J. Alter* (Cincinnati), Peter W. Bartholome (St. Cloud), John Bokenfohr, O.M.I. (Kimberley, S. Africa), Mark K. Carroll (Wichita), James L. Connolly (Fall River), Augustine Danglmayr (Ft. Worth, auxiliary),

Edward V. Dargin (New York, auxiliary), James P. Davis* (Santa Fê), Stephen J. Donahue (New York, auxiliary), Leo P. Dworschak (Fargo), Robert Dwyer* (Portland, Ore.), John M. Fearns (New York, auxiliary), Albert L. Fletcher (Little Rock), Walter A. Foery (Syracuse), John B. Franz (Peoria), Philip J. Furlong (Military Vicariate, delegate),

Richard O. Gerow (Natchez-Jackson), Francis D. Gleeson, S.J. (Fairbanks), Laurence A. Glenn (Crookston), Ignatius T. Glennie, S.J. (Trincomalee-Batticaloa, Sri Lanka), Thomas K. Gorman (Dallas-Ft. Worth), Lawrence L. Graner* (Dacca, Bangladesh), Lawrence Graziano, O.F.M. (San Miguel, El Salvador), Charles P. Greco (Alexandria),

James T. Hayes, S.J.* (Cagayan, Philippines), Edward D. Howard* (Portland, Ore.), Clarence G. Issenmann (Cleveland), Robert F. Joyce (Burlington), James E. Kearney (Rochester),

Vincent Kennally, S.J. (Caroline and Marshall Islands, vicar apostolic). Henry T. Klonowski (Scranton, auxiliary), George L. Leech (Harrisburg), Francis P. Leipzig (Baker), Leo Lemay, S.M. (Bougainville, Solomon Is.), Robert E. Lucey* (San Antonio),

Cardinal J. Francis McIntyre* (Los Angeles), John J. McEleney, S.J.* (Kingston, Jamaica), James E. McManus, C.SS.R. (New York, auxiliary), Edward J. Maginn (Albany, auxiliary), Joseph M. Marling, C.PP.S. (Jefferson City), Alfred Mendez, C.S.C. (Arecibo, P.R.).

Louis La Ravoire Morrow, S.D.B. (Krishnagar, India), Joseph M. Mueller (Sioux City), Knute Ansgar Nelson, O.S.B. (Stockholm, Sweden), Thomas L. Noa (Marquette), Cardinal Patrick O'Boyle* (Washington, D.C.), Henry J. O'Brien* (Hartford),

Martin J. O'Connor* (Prefect Emeritus, Pontifical Commission for Social Communications), James V. Pardy, M.M. (Cheong Ju, Korea), John L. Paschang (Grand Island), Ernest J. Primeau (Manchester).

George J. Rehring (Toledo), Louis J. Reicher (Austin), John J. Russell (Richmond), Maurice Schexnayder (Lafayette, La.), Adolph G. Schmitt, C.M.M. (Bulawayo, Rhodesia), Paul C. Schulte* (Indianapolis), Fulton J. Sheen* (Rochester; titular archbishop, Newport). Cardinal Lawrence J. Shehan* (Baltimore), Eustace J. Smith, O.F.M. (Beirut, vicar apostolic), Martin W. Stanton, (Newark, auxiliary), Thomas J. Toolen* (Mobile-Birmingham; personal title of archbishop), Robert E. Tracy (Baton Rouge), James E. Walsh, M.M. (Kongmoon, China, vicar apostolic).

U.S. BISHOPS OVERSEAS

Cardinal John J. Wright, prefect of the Congregation for the Clergy; Archbishop Raymond P. Etteldorf, pro-nuncio to Ethiopia; Bishop Anthony L. Deksnys, pastoral work among Lithuanians in Western Europe; Bishop Paul C. Marcinkus, president of Institute for Works of Religion (Vatican Bank). (See also Missionary Bishops.)

BISHOP-BROTHERS

See separate entries for biographical data. The asterisk indicates brothers who were bishops at the same time.

There have been nine pairs of brother-bishops in the history of the US hierarchy.

Most recently: Francis T. Hurley* of Juneau and Mark J. Hurley* of Santa Rosa, both living; Coleman F. Carroll* present archbishop of Miami, and the late Howard Carroll* of Altoona-Johnstown.

The others, all deceased, were: Francis Blanchet* of Oregon City (Portland) and Augustin Blanchet* of Walla Walla; John S. Foley of Detroit and Thomas P. Foley of Chicago; Francis P. Kenrick,* apostolic administrator of Philadelphia, bishop of Philadelphia and Baltimore, and Peter R. Kenrick* of St. Louis; Matthias C. Lenihan of Great Falls and Thomas M. Lenihan of Cheyenne; James O'Connor, vicar apostolic of Nebraska and bishop of Omaha, and Michael O'Connor of Pittsburgh and Erie; Jeremiah F. and John W. Shanahan, both of Harrisburg; Sylvester J. Espelage, O.F.M.,* of Wuchang, China, who died 10 days after the ordination of his brother, Bernard T. Espelage,* O.F.M., of Gallup.

AMERICAN BISHOPS OF THE PAST

Information includes dates, place of birth if outside the US, date of ordination to the priesthood, sees held, and, in the case of non-residential bishops, name of the titular see.

A

Adrian, William H. (1883-1972): ord. Apr. 15, 1911; bp. Nashville, 1936-69 (ret.).

Albers, Joseph (1891-1965): ord. June 17, 1916; aux. bp. Cincinnati (Lunda), 1929-37; first bp. Lansing, 1937-65.

Alemany, Joseph Sadoc, O.P. (1814-1888): b. Spain; ord. Mar. 11, 1837; bp. Monterey, (now Los Angeles), 1850-53; first abp. San Francisco, 1853-84 (res.).

Alencastre, Stephen P., S.S.CC. (1876-1940): b. Madeira; ord. Ar. 5, 1902; coad. v.a. Sandwich Is. (Arabissus), 1924-36; v.a. Sandwich (now Hawaiian Is.,) 1936-40.

Alerding, Herman J. (1845-1924): b. Germany; ord. Sept. 22, 1869; bp. Fort Wayne, 1900-24.

Allen, Edward P. (1853-1926): ord. Dec. 17, 1881; bp. Mobile, 1897-1926.

Althoff, Henry (1873-1947): ord. July 26, 1902; bp. Belleville, 1914-47.

Amat, Thaddeus, C.M. (1811-1878): b. Spain; ord. Dec. 23, 1837; bp. Monterey (now Los Angeles), 1854-78.

Anderson, Joseph (1865-1927): ord. May 20, 1892; aux. bp. Boston (Oyrina), 1909-27.

Anglim, Robert, C.SS.R. (1922-1973): ord. Jan. 6, 1948; prelate Coari, Brazil (Gaguari), 1966-73.

Annabring, Joseph (1900-1959): b. Hungary; ord. May 3, 1927; bp. Superior, 1954-59.

Appelhans, Stephen A., S.V.D. (1905-1951): ord. May 5, 1932; v.a. East New Guinea (Catula), 1948-51.

Armstrong, Robert J. (1884-1957): ord. Dec. 10, 1910; bp. Sacramento, 1929-57.

Arnold, William R. (1881-1965): ord. June 13, 1908; delegate of US military vicar (Phocaea), 1945-65.

Atkielski, Roman R. (1898-1969): ord. May 30, 1931; aux. bp. Milwaukee (Stobi), 1947-69.

B

Babcock, Allen J. (1898-1969): ord. Mar. 7, 1925; aux. bp. Detroit (Irenopolis), 1947-54; bp. Grand Rapids, 1954-69.

Bacon, David W. (1815-1874): ord. Dec. 13, 1838; first bp. Portland, Me., 1855-74.

Baltes, Peter J. (1827-1886): b. Germany; ord. May 31, 1852; bp. Alton (now Springfield), Ill., 1870-86.

Baraga, Frederic: See Index.

Barron, Edward (1801-1854): b. Ireland; ord. 1829; v.a. The Two Guineas (Constantina), 1842-44 (res.), missionary in US.

Barry, John (1799-1859): b. Ireland; ord. Sept. 24, 1825; bp. Savannah, 1857-59.

Barry, Patrick J. (1868-1940): b. Ireland; ord. June 9, 1895; bp. St. Augustine, 1922-40.

Baumgartner, Apollinaris, O.F.M. Cap. (1899-1970): ord. May 30, 1926; v.a. Guam (Joppa), 1945-65; first bp. Agana, Guam, 1965-70.

Bayley, James Roosevelt: See Index.

Bazin, John S. (1796-1848): b. France; ord. July 22, 1822; bp. Vincennes (now Indianapolis), 1847-48.

Beaven, Thomas D. (1851-1920): ord. Dec. 18, 1875; bp. Springfield, Mass., 1892-1920.

Becker, Thomas A. (1832-1899): ord. June 18, 1859; first bp. Wilmington, 1868-86; bp. Savannah, 1886-99.

Beckman, Francis J. (1875-1948): ord. June 20, 1902; bp. Lincoln, 1924-30; abp. Dubuque, 1930-46 (res.).

Benjamin, Cletus J. (1909-1961): ord. Dec. 8, 1935; aux. bp. Philadelphia (Binda), 1960-61.

Bennett, John G. (1891-1957): ord. June 27, 1914; first bp. Lafayette, Ind., 1944-57.

Bergan, Gerald T. (1892-1972): ord. Oct. 28, 1915; bp. Des Moines, 1934-38; abp. Omaha, 1948-69 (ret.).

Bidawid, Thomas M. (1910-1971): b. Iraq; ord. May 15, 1935; US citizen; first abp. Ahwaz, Iran (Chaldean Rite), 1968-70: Chaldean patriarchal vicar for United Arab Republic, 1970-71.

Blanc, Anthony (1792-1860): b. France; ord. July 22, 1816; bp. New Orleans, 1835-50; first abp. New Orleans, 1850-60.

Blanchet (brothers): **Augustin M.** (1797-1887): b. Canada; ord. June 3, 1821; bp. Walla Walla, 1846-50; first bp. Nesqually (now Seattle), 1850-79 (res.). **Francis N.** (1795-1883): b. Canada; ord. July 19, 1819; v.a. Oregon Territory (Philadelphia, Adrasus), 1843-46; first abp. Oregon City (now Portland), 1846-80 (res.)

Blenk, James H., S.M. (1856-1917): b. Germany; ord. Aug. 16, 1885; bp. San Juan, 1899-1906; abp. New Orleans, 1906-17.

Boeynaems, Libert H., SS.CC. (1857-1926): b. Belgium; ord. Sept. 11, 1881; v.a. Sandwich (now Hawaiian) Is. (Zeugma), 1903-26.

Bohachevsky, Constantine (1884-1961): b. Austrian Galicia; ord. Jan. 31, 1909; ap. ex. Ukrainian Byzantine Catholics in US (Amisus), 1924-58; first metropolitan of Byzantine Rite archeparchy of Philadelphia, 1958-61.

Boileau, George, S.J. (1912-1965): ord. June 13, 1948; coad. bp. Fairbanks (Ausuccura), 1964-65.

Bona, Stanislaus (1888-1967): ord. Nov. 1, 1912; bp. Grand Island, 1932-44; coad. bp. Green Bay (Mela), 1944-45; bp. Green Bay, 1945-67.

Bonacum, Thomas (1847-1911): b. Ireland; ord. June 18, 1870; first bp. Lincoln, 1887-1911.

Borgess, Caspar H. (1826-1890): b. Germany; ord. Dec. 8, 1848; coad. bp. and ap. admin. Detroit (Calydon), 1870-71; bp. Detroit, 1871-87 (res.).

Bourgade, Peter (1845-1908): b. France; ord. Nov. 30, 1869; v.a. Arizona (Thaumacus), 1885-97; first bp. Tucson, 1897-99; abp. Santa Fe, 1899-1908.

Boylan, John J. (1889-1953): ord. July 28, 1915; bp. Rockford, 1943-53.

Boyle, Hugh C. (1873-1950): ord. July 2, 1898; bp. Pittsburgh, 1921-50.

Bradley, Denis (1846-1903): b. Ireland; ord. June 3, 1871; first bp. Manchester, 1884-1903.

Brady, John (1842-1910): b. Ireland; ord. Dec. 4, 1864; aux. bp. Boston (Alabanda), 1891-1910.

Brady, Matthew F. (1893-1959): ord. June 10, 1916; bp. Burlington, 1938-44; bp. Manchester, 1944-59.

Brady, William O. (1899-1961): ord. Dec. 21, 1923; bp. Sioux Falls, 1939-56; coad. abp. St. Paul (Selymbria), June-Oct. 1956; abp. St. Paul, 1956-61.

Brennan, Andrew J. (1877-1956): ord. Dec. 17, 1904; aux. bp. Scranton (Thapsus), 1923-26; bp. Richmond, 1926-45 (res.).

Brennan, Thomas F. (1853-1916): b. Ireland; ord. July 14, 1880; first bp. Dallas, 1891-92; aux. bp. St. John's, Newfoundland (Usula), 1893-1905 (res.).

Broderick, Bonaventure (1868-1943): ord. July 26, 1896; aux. bp. Havana, Cuba (Juliopolis), 1903-05 (res.).

Brondel, John B. (1842-1903): b. Belgium; ord. Dec. 17, 1864; bp. Vancouver Is., 1879-84: first bp. Helena, 1884-1903.

Brossart, Ferdinand (1849-1930): b. Germany; ord. Sept. 1, 1892; bp. Covington, 1916-23 (res.).

Brute, Simon G. (1779-1839): b. France; ord. June 11, 1808; first bp. Vincennes (now Indianapolis), 1834-39.

Buddy, Charles F. (1887-1966): ord. Sept. 19, 1914; first bp. San Diego, 1936-66.

Burke, Joseph A. (1886-1962): ord. Aug. 3, 1912; aux. bp. Buffalo (Vita), 1943-52; bp. Buffalo, 1952-62.

Burke, Maurice F. (1845-1923): b. Ireland; ord. May 22, 1875; first bp. Cheyenne, 1887-93; bp. St. Joseph, 1893-1923.

Burke, Thomas M. (1840-1915): b. Ireland; ord. June 30, 1864; bp. Albany, 1894-1915.

Busch, Joseph F. (1866-1953): ord. July 28, 1889; bp. Lead (now Rapid City), 1910-15; bp. St. Cloud, 1915-53.

Byrne, Andrew (1802-1862): b. Ireland; ord. Nov. 11, 1827; first bp. Little Rock, 1844-62.

Byrne, Christopher E. (1867-1950): ord. Sept. 23, 1891; bp. Galveston, 1918-50.

Byrne, Edwin V. (1891-1963): ord. May 22, 1915; first bp. Ponce, 1925-29; abp. San Juan, 1929-43; abp. Santa Fe, 1943-63.

Byrne, Patrick J., M.M. (1888-1950): ord. June 23, 1915; apostolic delegate to Korea (Gazera), 1949-50.

Byrne, Thomas S. (1841-1923): ord. May 22, 1869; bp. Nashville, 1894-1923.

C

Canevin, J. F. Regis (1853-1927): ord. June 4, 1879; coad. bp. Pittsburgh (Sabrata), 1903-04; bp. Pittsburgh, 1904-21 (res.).

Cantwell, John J. (1874-1947): b. Ireland; ord. June 18, 1899; bp. Monterey-Los Angeles, 1917-22; bp. Los Angeles, 1917-36; first abp. Los Angeles, 1936-47.

Carrell, George A., S. J. (1803-1868): ord. Dec. 20, 1827; first bp. Covington, 1853-68.

Carroll, Howard J. (1902-1960): ord. Apr. 2, 1927; bp. Altoona-Johnstown, 1958-60.

Carroll, James J. (1862-1913): ord. June 15, 1889; bp. Nueva Segovia, P. I., 1908-12 (res.).

Carroll, John: See Index.

Carroll, John P. (1864-1925): ord. July 7, 1886; bp. Helena, 1904-25.

Cartwright, Hubert J. (1900-1958): ord. June 11, 1927; coad. bp. Wilmington (Neve), 1956-58.

Cassidy, James E. (1869-1951): ord. Sept. 8, 1898; aux. bp. Fall River (Ibora), 1930-34; bp. Fall River, 1934-51.

Chabrat, Guy Ignatius, S.S. (1787-1868): b. France; ord. Dec. 21, 1811; coad. bp. Bardstown (Bolina), 1834-47 (res.).

Chanche, John J., S.S. (1795-1852): ord. June 5, 1819; bp. Natchez (now Natchez-Jackson), 1841-52.

Chapelle, Placide L. (1842-1905): b. France; ord. June 28, 1865; coad. abp. Santa Fe (Arabissus), 1891-94; abp. Santa Fe, 1894-97; abp. New Orleans, 1897-1905.

Chartrand, Joseph (1870-1933): ord. Sept. 24, 1892; coad. bp. Indianapolis (Flavias), 1910-18; bp. Indianapolis, 1918-33.

Chatard, Francis S. (1834-1918): ord. June 14, 1862; bp. Vincennes (now Indianapolis—title changed in 1898), 1878-1918.

Cheverus, John Lefebvre de (1768-1836): b. France; ord. Dec. 18, 1790; bp. Boston, 1810-23 (returned to France, made cardinal 1836).

Christie, Alexander (1848-1925): ord. Dec. 22, 1877; bp. Vancouver Is., 1898-99; abp. Oregon City (now Portland), 1899-1925.

Clancy, William (1802-1847): b. Ireland; ord. May 24, 1823; coad. bp. Charleston (Oreus). 1834-37; v.a. British Guiana, 1837-43.

Collins, John J., S.J. (1856-1934): ord. Aug. 29, 1891; v.a. Jamaica (Antiphellus), 1907-18.

Collins, Thomas P., M.M. (1915-1973): ord. June 21, 1942; v.a. Pando, Bolivia (Sufetula), 1961-68 (res.).

Colton, Charles H. (1848-1915): ord. June 10, 1876; bp. Buffalo, 1903-15.

Conaty, Thomas J. (1847-1915): b. Ireland; ord. Dec. 21, 1872; rector of Catholic University, 1896-1903; tit. bp. Samos, 1901-03; bp. Monterey-Los Angeles (now Los Angeles), 1903-15.

Concanen, Richard L., O.P. (1747-1810): b. Ireland; ord. Dec. 22, 1770; first bp. New York. 1808-10 (detained in Italy, never reached his see).

Condon, William J. (1895-1967): ord. Oct. 14, 1917; bp. Great Falls, 1939-67.

Connolly, John, O.P. (1750-1825): b. Ireland; ord. Sept. 24, 1774; bp. New York, 1814-25.

Conroy, John J. (1819-1895): b. Ireland; ord. May 21, 1842; bp. Albany, 1865-77 (res.).

Conroy, Joseph H. (1858-1939): ord. June 11, 1881; aux. bp. Ogdensburg (Arindela), 1912-21; bp. Ogdensburg, 1921-39.

Conwell, Henry (1748-1842): b. Ireland; ord. 1776; bp. Philadelphia, 1820-42.

Corbett, Timothy (1858-1939): ord. June 12, 1886; first bp. Crookston, 1910-38 (res.).

Corrigan, Joseph M. (1879-1942): ord. June 6, 1903; rector of Catholic University, 1936-42; tit. bp. Bilta, 1940-42.

Corrigan, Michael A. (1839-1902): ord. Sept. 19, 1863; bp. Newark, 1873-80; coad. abp. New York (Petra), 1880-85; abp. New York, 1885-1902.

Corrigan, Owen (1849-1929): ord. June 7, 1873; aux. bp. Baltimore (Macri), 1908-29.

Cosgrove, Henry (1834-1906): ord. Aug. 27, 1857; bp. Davenport, 1884-1906.

Cote, Philip, S.J. (1896-1970): ord. Aug. 14, 1927; v. a. Suchow, China (Polystylus), 1935-46; first bp. Suchow, 1946-70 (imprisoned by Chinese Communists, 1951; expelled from China, 1953; ap. admin. Islands of Quemoy and Matsu, 1969-70).

Cotter, Joseph B. (1844-1909): b. England; ord. May 3, 1871; first bp. Winona, 1889-1909.

Cotton, Francis R. (1895-1960): ord. June 17, 1920; first bp. Owensboro, 1938-60.

Cowley, Leonard P. (1913-1973): ord. June 4, 1938; aux. bp. St. Paul and Minneapolis, (Pertusa), 1958-73.

Crane, Michael J. (1863-1928): ord. June 15, 1889; aux. bp. Philadelphia (Curium), 1921-28.

Cretin, Joseph (1799-1857): b. France; ord. Dec. 20, 1823; bp. St. Paul, 1851-57.

Crimont, Joseph R., S.J. (1858-1945): b. France; ord. Aug. 26, 1888; v. a. Alaska (Ammaedara), 1917-45.

Crowley, Timothy J., C.S.C. (1880-1945): b. Ireland; ord. Aug. 2, 1906; coad. bp. Dacca (Epiphania), 1927-29; bp. Dacca, 1929-45.

Cunningham, John F. (1842-1919): b. Ireland; ord. Aug. 8, 1865; bp. Concordia, 1898-1919.

Curley, Daniel J. (1869-1932): ord. May 19, 1894; bp. Syracuse, 1923-32.

Curley, Michael J. (1879-1947): b. Ireland; ord. Mar. 19, 1904; bp. St. Augustine, 1914-21; abp. Baltimore, 1921-39; title changed to abp. Baltimore and Washington, 1939-47.

Curtis, Alfred A. (1831-1908): convert, 1872; ord. Dec. 19, 1874; bp. Wilmington, 1886-96 (res.).

Cusack, Thomas F. (1862-1918): ord. May 30, 1885; aux. bp. New York (Temiscyra), 1904-15; bp. Albany, 1915-18.

Cushing, Richard J.: See Index.

D

Daeger, Albert T., O.F.M. (1872-1932): ord. July 25, 1896; abp. Santa Fe, 1919-32.

Daly, Edward C., O.P. (1894-1964): ord. June 12, 1921; bp. Des Moines, 1948-64.

Damiano, Celestine (1911-1967): ord. Dec. 21, 1935; apostolic delegate to South Africa (Nicopolis in Epiro), 1952-60; bp. Camden, 1960-67.

Danehy, Thomas J., M.M. (1914-1959): ord. Sept. 17, 1939; ap. admin. v. a. Pando, Bolivia (Bita), 1953-59.

David, John B., S.S. (1761-1841): b. France; ord. Sept. 24, 1785; coad. bp. Bardstown

(Mauricastrum), 1819-32; bp. Bardstown (now Louisville), 1832-33 (res.).

Davis, James (1852-1926): b. Ireland; ord. June 21, 1878; coad. bp. Davenport (Milopotamus), 1904-06; bp. Davenport, 1906-26.

De Cheverus, John L.: See Cheverus, John.

De Goesbriand, Louis (1816-1899): b. France; ord. July 13, 1840; first bp. Burlington, 1853-99.

De la Hailandiere, Celestine (1798-1882): b. France; ord. May 28, 1825; bp. Vincennes (now Indianapolis), 1839-47 (res.).

Delany, John B. (1864-1906): ord. May 23, 1891; bp. Manchester, 1904-06.

Demers, Modeste, (1809-1871): b. Canada; ord. Feb. 7, 1836; bp. Vancouver Is., 1846-71.

Dempsey, Michael R. (1918-1974): ord. May 1, 1943; aux. bp. Chicago (Truentum), 1968-74,

De Neckere, Leo, C.M. (1799-1833): b. Belgium; ord. Oct. 13, 1822; bp. New Orleans, 1829-33.

De Saint Palais, Maurice (1811-1877): b. France; ord. May 28, 1836; bp. Vincennes (now Indianapolis), 1849-77.

Desmond, Daniel F. (1884-1945): ord. June 9, 1911; bp. Alexandria, 1933-45.

Dinand, Joseph N., S.J. (1869-1943): ord. June 25, 1903; v. a. Jamaica (Selinus), 1927-29 (res.).

Dobson, Robert (1867-1942): ord. May 23, 1891; aux. bp. Liverpool, Eng. (Cynopolis), 1922-42.

Domenec, Michael, C.M. (1816-1878): b. Spain; ord. June 30, 1839; bp. Pittsburgh, 1860-76; bp. Allegheny, 1876-77 (res.).

Donahue, Joseph P. (1870-1959): ord. June 8, 1895; aux. bp. New York (Emmaus), 1945-59.

Donahue, Patrick J. (1849-1922): b. England; ord. Dec. 19, 1885; bp. Wheeling, 1894-1922.

Donnelly, George J. (1889-1950): ord. June 12, 1921; aux. bp. St. Louis (Coela), 1940-46; bp. Leavenworth (now Kansas City — title changed in 1947), 1946-50.

Donnelly, Henry E. (1904-1967): ord. Aug. 17, 1930; aux. bp. Detroit (Tymbrias), 1954-67.

Doran, Thomas F. (1856-1916): ord. July 4, 1880; aux. bp. Providence (Halicarnassus), 1915-16.

Dougherty, Dennis (1865-1951): ord. May 31, 1890; bp. Nueva Segovia, P.I., 1903-08; bp. Jaro, P.I., 1908-15; bp. Buffalo, 1915-18; abp. Philadelphia, 1918-1951; cardinal, 1921.

Dougherty, Joseph P. (1905-1970): ord. June 14, 1930; first bp. Yakima, 1951-69; aux. bp. Los Angeles (Altino), 1969-70.

Dowling, Austin (1868-1930): ord. June 24, 1891; first bp. Des Moines, 1912-19; abp. St. Paul, 1919-30.

Drossaerts, Arthur J. (1862-1940): b. Holland; ord. June 15, 1889; bp. San Antonio 1918-26; first abp. San Antonio, 1926-40.

Drumm, Thomas W. (1871-1933): b. Ire-

land; ord. Dec. 21, 1901; bp. Des Moines, 1919-33.

Dubois, John, S.S. (1764-1842): b. France; ord. Sept. 28, 1787; bp. New York, 1826-42.

Dubourg, William L., S.S. (1766-1833): b. Santo Domingo; ord. 1788; bp. Louisiana and the Two Floridas (now New Orleans), 1815-25; returned to France; bp. Montauban, 1826-33; abp. Besancon 1833.

Dubuis, Claude M. (1817-1895): b. France; ord. June 1, 1844; bp. Galveston, 1862-92 (res.).

Dufal, Peter, C.S.C. (1822-1898): b. France; ord. Sept. 29, 1852; v.a. Eastern Bengal (Delcon), 1860-78; coad. bp. Galveston, 1878-80 (res.).

Duffy, James A. (1873-1968): ord. May 27, 1899; bp. Kearney (see transferred to Grand Island, 1917), 1913-31 (res.).

Duffy, John A. (1884-1944): ord. June 13, 1908; bp. Syracuse, 1933-37; bp. Buffalo, 1937-44.

Duggan, James (1825-1899): b. Ireland; ord. May 29, 1847; coad. bp. St. Louis (Gabala), 1857-59; bp. Chicago, 1859-80 (res.). Inactive from 1869 because of illness.

Dunn, John J. (1869-1933): ord. May 30, 1896; aux. bp. New York (Camuliana), 1921-33.

Dunne, Edmund M. (1864-1929): ord. June 24, 1887; bp. Peoria, 1909-29.

Dunne, Edward (1848-1910): b. Ireland; ord. June 29, 1871; bp. Dallas, 1893-1910.

Durier, Anthony (1832-1904): b. France; ord. Oct. 28, 1856; bp. Natchitoches (now Alexandria), La., 1885-1904.

Dwenger, Joseph, C.Pp.S. (1837-1893): ord. Sept. 4, 1859; bp. Fort Wayne, 1872-93.

E

Eccleston, Samuel, S.S. (1801-1851): ord. Apr. 24, 1825; coad. bp. Baltimore (Thermae), Sept.-Oct., 1834; abp. Baltimore, 1834-51.

Egan, Michael, O.F.M. (1761-1814): b. Ireland; first bp. Philadelphia, 1810-14.

Eis, Frederick (1843-1926): b. Germany; ord. Oct. 30, 1870; bp. Sault Ste. Marie and Marquette (now Marquette), 1899-1922 (res.).

Elder, William (1819-1904): ord. Mar. 29, 1846; bp. Natchez (now Natchez-Jackson), 1857-80; coad. bp. Cincinnati (Avara), 1880-83; abp. Cincinnati, 1883-1904.

Elwell, Clarence F. (1904-1973): ord. Mar. 17, 1929; aux. bp. Cleveland (Cone) 1962-68; bp. Columbus, 1968-73.

Emmet, Thomas A., S.J. (1873-1950): ord. July 30, 1909; v.a. Jamaica (Tuscamia), 1930-49 (res.).

England, John: See Index.

Escalante, Alonso Manuel, M.M. (1906-1967): b. Mexico; ord. Feb. 1, 1931; v.a. Pando, Bolivia (Sora), 1943-60 (res.).

Espelage (brothers): **Bernard T., O.F.M.** (1892-1971): ord. May 16, 1918; bp. Gallup,

1940-69 (res.). **Sylvester J., O.F.M.** (1877-1940): ord. Jan. 18, 1900; v.a. Wuchang, China (Oreus), 1930-40.

Eustace, Bartholomew J. (1887-1956): ord. Nov. 1, 1914; bp. Camden, 1938-56.

F

Fahey, Leo F. (1898-1950): ord. May 29, 1926; coad. bp. Baker City (Ipsus), 1948-50.

Farley, John: See Index.

Farrelly, John P. (1856-1921): ord. Mar. 22, 1880; bp. Cleveland, 1909-21.

Fedders, Edward L., M.M. (1913-1973): ord. June 11, 1944; prelate Juli, Peru (Antiochia ad Meadrum, 1963-73.

Feehan, Daniel F. (1855-1934): ord. Dec. 29, 1879; bp. Fall River, 1907-34.

Feehan, Patrick A. (1829-1902): b. Ireland; ord. Nov. 1, 1852; bp. Nashville, 1865-80; first abp. Chicago, 1880-1902.

Feeney, Daniel J. (1894-1969): ord. May 21, 1921; aux. bp. Portland, Me. (Sita), 1946-52; coad. bp. Portland, 1952-55; bp. Portland, 1955-69.

Feeney, Thomas J., S.J. (1894-1955): ord. June 23, 1927; v.a. Caroline and Marshall Is. (Agnus), 1951-55.

Fenwick, Benedict J., S.J. (1782-1846): ord. June 11, 1808; bp. Boston, 1825-46.

Fenwick, Edward D., O.P. (1768-1832): ord. Feb. 23, 1793; first bp. Cincinnati, 1822-32.

Fink, Michael, O.S.B. (1834-1904): b. Germany; ord. May 28, 1857; coad. v.a., 1871-74, and v.a., 1874-77, Kansas and Indian Territory (Eucarpia); first bp. Leavenworth (now Kansas City), 1877-1904.

Finnigan, George, C.S.C. (1885-1932): ord. June 13, 1915; bp. Helena, 1927-32.

Fitzgerald, Edward (1833-1907): b. Ireland; ord. Aug. 22, 1857; bp. Little Rock, 1866-1907.

Fitzgerald, Edward A. (1893-1972): ord. July 25, 1916; aux, bp. Dubuque (Cantanus), 1946-49; bp. Winona, 1949-69 (res.).

Fitzgerald, Walter J., S.J. (1883-1947): ord. May 16, 1918; coad. v.a. Alaska (Tymbrias), 1939-45; v.a. Alaska, 1945-47.

Fitzmaurice, Edmond (1881-1962): b. Ireland; ord. May 28, 1904; bp. Wilmington, 1925-60 (res.).

Fitzmaurice, John E. (1837-1920): b. Ireland; ord. Dec. 21, 1862; coad. bp. Erie (Amisus), 1898-99; bp. Erie, 1899-1920.

Fitzpatrick, John B. (1812-1866): ord. June 13, 1840; aux. bp. Boston (Callipolis), 1843-46; bp. Boston, 1846-66.

Fitzsimon, Laurence J. (1895-1958): ord. May 17, 1921; bp. Amarillo, 1941-58.

Flaget, Benedict, S.S.: See Index.

Flannelly, Joseph F. (1894-1973): ord. Sept. 1, 1918; aux. bp. New York (Metelis), 1948-70 (res.).

Flasch, Kilian C. (1831-1891): b. Germany; ord. Dec. 16, 1859; bp. La Crosse, 1881-91.

Floersh, John (1886-1968): ord. June 10, 1911; coad. bp. Louisville (Lycopolis), 1923-24; bp. Louisville, 1924-37; first abp. Louisville, 1937-67 (res.).

Foley (brothers): **John S.** (1833-1918): ord. Dec. 20, 1856; bp. Detroit, 1888-1918. **Thomas** (1822-1879): ord. Aug. 16, 1846; coad. bp. and ap. admin. Chicago (Pergamum), 1870-79.

Foley, Maurice P. (1867-1919): ord. July 25, 1891; bp. Tuguegarao, P.I., 1910-16; bp. Jaro, P.I., 1916-19.

Ford, Francis X., M.M.: See Index.

Forest, John A. (1838-1911): b. France; ord. Apr. 12, 1863; bp. San Antonio, 1895-1911.

Fox, Joseph J. (1855-1915): ord. June 7, 1879; bp. Green Bay, 1904-14 (res.).

G

Gabriels, Henry (1838-1921): b. Belgium; ord. Sept. 21, 1861; bp. Ogdensburg, 1892-1921.

Galberry, Thomas, O.S.A. (1833-1878): b. Ireland; ord. Dec. 20, 1856; bp. Hartford, 1876-78.

Gallagher, Michael J. (1866-1937): ord. Mar. 19, 1893; coad. bp. Grand Rapids (Tiposa in Mauretania), 1915-16; bp. Grand Rapids, 1916-18; bp. Detroit, 1918-37.

Gallagher, Nicholas (1846-1918): ord. Dec. 25, 1868; coad. bp. Galveston (Canopus), 1882-92; bp. Galveston, 1892-1918.

Gannon, John M. (1877-1968): ord. Dec. 21, 1901; aux. bp. Erie (Nilopolis), 1918-20; bp. Erie, 1920-66 (res.).

Garcia Diego y Moreno, Francisco, O.F.M. (1785-1846): b. Mexico; ord. Nov. 14, 1808; bp. Two Californias (now Los Angeles), 1840-46.

Garriga, Mariano S. (1886-1965): ord. July 2, 1911; coad. bp. Corpus Christi (Syene), 1936-49; bp. Corpus Christi, 1949-65.

Garrigan, Philip (1840-1919): b. Ireland; ord. June 11, 1870; first bp. Sioux City, 1902-19.

Gartland, Francis X. (1808-1854): b. Ireland; ord. Aug. 5, 1832; first bp. Savannah, 1850-54.

Garvey, Eugene A. (1845-1920): ord. Sept. 22, 1869; first bp. Altoona (now Altoona-Johnstown), 1901-20.

Gercke, Daniel J. (1874-1964): ord. June 1, 1901; bp. Tucson, 1923-60 (res.).

Gerken, Rudolph A. (1887-1943): ord. June 10, 1917; first bp. Amarillo, 1927-33; abp. Santa Fe, 1933-43.

Gibbons, Edmund F. (1868-1964): ord. May 27, 1893; bp. Albany, 1919-54 (res.).

Gibbons, James: See Index.

Gilfillan, Francis (1872-1933): b. Ireland; ord. June 24, 1895; coad. bp. St. Joseph (Spiga), 1922-23; bp. St. Joseph 1923-33.

Gill, Thomas E. (1908-1973): ord. June 10, 1933; aux. bp. Seattle (Lambesis) 1956-73.

Gilmore, Joseph M. (1893-1962): ord. July 25, 1915; bp. Helena, 1936-62.

Gilmour, Richard (1824-1891): b. Scotland;

ord. Aug. 30, 1852; bp. Cleveland, 1872-91.

Girouard, Paul J., M.S. (1898-1964): ord. July 26, 1927; first bp. Morondava, Madagascar, 1956-64.

Glass, Joseph S., C.M. (1874-1926): ord. Aug. 15, 1897; bp. Salt Lake City, 1915-26.

Glennon, John: See Index.

Glorieux, Alphonse J. (1844-1917): b. Belgium; ord. Aug. 17, 1867; v.a. Idaho (Apollonia), 1885-93; bp. Boise, 1893-1917.

Goesbriand, Louis J. de (1816-1899): b. France; ord. July 13, 1840; first bp. Burlington, 1853-99.

Gorman, Daniel (1861-1927): ord. June 24, 1893; bp. Boise, 1918-27.

Grace Thomas (1841-1921): b. Ireland; ord. June 24, 1876; bp. Sacramento, 1896-1921.

Grace, Thomas L., O.P. (1814-1897): ord. Dec. 21, 1839; bp. St. Paul, 1859-84 (res.).

Granjon, Henry (1863-1922): b. France; ord. Dec. 17, 1887; bp. Tucson, 1900-22.

Griffin, James A. (1883-1948): ord. July 4, 1909; bp. Springfield, Ill., 1924-48.

Griffin, William A. (1885-1950): ord. Aug. 15, aux. bp. Newark (Sanavus), 1938-40; bp. Trenton, 1940-50.

Griffin, William R. (1883-1944): ord. May 25, 1907; aux. bp. La Crosse (Lydda), 1935-44.

Griffiths, James H. (1903-1964): ord. Mar. 12, 1927; aux. bp. New York and delegate of US military vicar (Gaza), 1950-64.

Grimes, John (1852-1922): b. Ireland; ord. Feb. 19, 1882; coad. bp. Syracuse (Hemeria), 1909-12; bp. Syracuse, 1912-22.

Grimmelsman, Henry J. (1890-1972): ord. Aug. 15, 1915; first bp. Evansville, 1945-65 (res.).

Gross, William H., C.SS.R. (1837-1898): ord. Mar. 21, 1863; bp. Savannah, 1873-85; abp. Oregon City (now Portland), 1885-98.

Guertin, George A. (1869-1932): ord. Dec. 17, 1892; bp. Manchester, 1907-32.

Guilfoyle, Richard T. (1892-1957): ord. June 2, 1917; bp. Altoona (now Altoona-Johnstown), 1936-57.

Gunn, John E., S.M. (1863-1924); b. Ireland; ord. Feb. 2, 1890; bp. Natchez (now Natchez-Jackson), 1911-24.

H

Haas, Francis J. (1889-1953): ord. June 11, 1913; bp. Grand Rapids, 1943-53.

Hafey, William (1888-1954): ord. June 16, 1914; first bp. Raleigh, 1925-37; coad. bp. Scranton (Appia), 1937-38; bp. Scranton, 1938-54.

Hagan, John R. (1890-1946): ord. Mar. 7, 1914; aux. bp. Cleveland (Limata), 1946.

Haid, Leo M., O.S.B. (1849-1924): ord. Dec. 21, 1872; v.a. N. Carolina (Messene), 1888-1910; abbot Mary Help of Christians abbacy, 1910-24.

Hallinan, Paul J. (1911-1968): ord. Feb. 20, 1937; bp. Charleston, 1958-62; first abp. Atlanta, 1962-68.

Hanna, Edward J. (1860-1944): ord. May 30, 1885; aux. bp. San Francisco (Titiopolis), 1912-15; abp. San Francisco, 1915-35 (res.).

Hannan, Jerome D. (1896-1965): ord. May 22, 1921; bp. Scranton, 1954-65.

Harkins, Matthew (1845-1921): ord. May 22, 1869; bp. Providence, 1887-1921.

Hartley, James J. (1858-1944): ord. July 10, 1882; bp. Columbus, 1904-44.

Harty, Jeremiah J. (1853-1927): ord. Apr. 28, 1878; abp. Manila, 1903-16; abp. Omaha, 1916-27.

Hayes, Patrick J.: See Index.

Hayes, Ralph L. (1884-1970): ord. Sept. 19, 1909; bp. Helena 1933-35; rector North American College, 1935-44; bp. Davenport, 1944-66 (res.).

Healy, James A. (1830-1900): ord. June 10, 1854; bp. Portland 1875-1900.

Heelan, Edmond (1868-1948): b. Ireland: ord. June 24, 1890; aux. bp. Sioux City (Gerasa), 1919-20; bp. Sioux City, 1920-48.

Heffron, Patrick (1860-1927): ord. Dec. 22, 1884; bp. Winona, 1910-27.

Heiss, Michael (1818-1890): b. Germany; ord. Oct. 18, 1840; bp. a Crosse, 1868-80; coad. abp. Milwaukee, 1880-81; abp. Milwaukee, 1881-90.

Hendrick, Thomas A. (1849-1909): ord. June 7, 1873; bp. Cebu, P.I., 1904-09.

Hendricken, Thomas F. (1827-1886): b. Ireland; ord. Apr. 25, 1853; bp. Providence, 1872-86.

Hennessy, John (1825-1900): b. Ireland; ord. Nov. 1, 1850; bp. Dubuque, 1866-93; first abp. Dubuque, 1893-1900.

Hennessy, John J. (1847-1920): b. Ireland; ord. Nov. 28, 1869; first bp. Wichita, 1888-1920; ap. admin. Concordia (now Salina), 1891-98.

Henni, John M. (1805-1881): b. Switzerland; ord. Feb. 2, 1829; first bp. Milwaukee, 1844-75; first abp. Milwaukee, 1875-81.

Heslin, Thomas (1845-1911): b. Ireland; ord. Sept. 8, 1869; bp. Natchez (now Natchez-Jackson), 1889-1911.

Heston, Edward L. (1907-73): ord. Dec. 22, 1934; sec. Sacred Congregation for Religious and Secular Institutes, 1969-71; pres. Pontifical Commission for Social Communications, 1971-73; tit. abp. Numidea, 1972.

Hickey, David F., S.J. (1882-1973): ord. June 27, 1917; v.a. Belize, Br. Honduras (Bonitza), 1948-56; first bp. Belize, 1956-57 (res.).

Hickey, Thomas F. (1861-1940): ord. Mar. 25, 1884; coad. bp. Rochester (Berenice), 1905-09; bp. Rochester, 1909-28 (res.).

Hickey, William A. (1869-1933): ord. Dec. 22, 1893; coad. bp. Providence (Claudiopolis), 1919-21; bp. Providence, 1921-33.

Hillinger, Raymond P. (1904-1971): ord. Apr. 2, 1932; bp. Rockford, 1953-56; aux. bp. Chicago (Derbe), 1956-71.

Hoban, Edward F. (1878-1966): ord. July 11, 1903; aux. bp. Chicago (Colonia), 1921-

28; bp. Rockford, 1928-42; coad. bp. Cleveland (Lystra), 1942-45; bp. Cleveland, 1945-66.

Hoban, Michael J. (1853-1926): ord. May 22, 1880; coad. bp. Scranton (Halius), 1896-99; bp. Scranton, 1899-1926.

Hogan, John J. (1829-1913): b. Ireland; ord. Apr. 10, 1852; first bp. St. Joseph, 1868-80; first bp. Kansas City, 1880-1913.

Horstmann, Ignatius (1840-1908): ord. June 10, 1865; bp. Cleveland, 1892-1908.

Howard, Francis W. (1867-1944): ord. June 16, 1891; bp. Covington, 1923-44.

Hughes, John J.: See Index.

Hunkeler, Edward J. (1894-1970): ord. June 14, 1919; bp. Grand Island, 1945-51; bp. Kansas City, Kans. 1951-52; first abp. Kansas City, 1952-69 (res.).

Hunt, Duane G. (1884-1960): ord. June 27, 1920; bp. Salt Lake City, 1937-60.

Hurley, Joseph P. (1894-1967): ord. May 29, 1919; bp. St. Augustine, 1940-67.

Hyland, Francis E. (1901-1968): ord. June 11, 1927; aux. bp. Savannah-Atlanta (Gomphi), 1949-56; bp. Atlanta, 1956-61 (res.).

Hyle, Michael W. (1901-1967): ord. Mar. 12, 1927; coad bp. Wilmington, 1958-60; bp. Wilmington, 1960-67.

I

Ireland, John: See Index.

Ireton, Peter L. (1882-1958): ord. June 20, 1906; coad. bp. Richmond (Cyme), 1935-45; bp. Richmond, 1945-58.

J

Janssen, John (1835-1913): b. Germany; ord. Nov. 19, 1858; first bp. Belleville, 1888-1913.

Janssens, Francis A. (1843-1897): b. Holland; ord. Dec. 21, 1867; bp. Natchez, 1881-88; abp. New Orleans, 1888-97.

Jeanmard, Jules B. (1879-1957): ord. June 10, 1903; first bp. Lafayette, La., 1918-56 (res.).

Johannes, Francis (1874-1937): b. Germany; ord. Jan. 3, 1897; coad. bp. Leavenworth (Thasus), 1928-29; bp. Leavenworth (now Kansas City), 1929-37.

Jones, William A., O.S.A. (1865-1921): ord. Mar. 15, 1890; bp. San Juan, 1907-21.

Junger, Aegidius (1833-1895): b. Germany; ord. June 27, 1862; bp. Nesqually (now Seattle), 1879-95.

K

Kain, John J. (1841-1903): ord. July 2, 1866; bp. Wheeling, 1875-93; coad. abp. St. Louis (Oxyrynchus), 1893-95; abp. St. Louis, 1895-1903.

Katzer, Frederick X. (1844-1903): b. Austria; ord. Dec. 21, 1866; bp. Green Bay, 1886-91; abp. Milwaukee, 1891-1903.

Keane, James J. (1856-1929): ord. Dec. 23, 1882; bp. Cheyenne, 1902-11; abp. Dubuque, 1911-29.

Keane, John J. (1839-1918): b. Ireland; ord. July 2, 1866; bp. Richmond, 1878-88; rector of Catholic University, 1888-97; consultor of Congregation for Propagation of the Faith, 1897-1900; abp. Dubuque, 1900-11 (res.).

Keane, Patrick J. (1872-1928): b. Ireland; ord. June 20, 1895; aux. bp. Sacramento (Samaria), 1920-22; bp. Sacramento, 1922-28.

Kearney, Raymond A. (1902-1956): ord. Mar. 12, 1927; aux. bp. Brooklyn (Lysinia), 1935-56.

Keiley, Benjamin J. (1847-1925): ord. Dec. 31, 1873; bp. Savannah, 1900-22 (res.).

Kelleher, Louis J. (1889-1946): ord. Apr. 3, 1915; aux. bp. Boston (Thenae), 1945-46.

Kelley, Francis C. (1870-1948): b. Canada; ord. Aug. 23, 1893; bp. Oklahoma, 1924-48.

Kelly, Edward D. (1860-1926): ord. June 16, 1886; aux. bp. Detroit (Cestrus), 1911-19; bp. Grand Rapids, 1919-26.

Kelly, Edward J. (1890-1956): ord. June 2, 1917; bp. Boise, 1928-56.

Kelly, Francis M. (1886-1950): ord. Nov. 1, 1912; aux. bp. Winona (Mylasa), 1926-28; bp. Winona, 1928-49 (res.).

Kelly, Patrick (1779-1829): b. Ireland; ord. July 18, 1802; first bp. Richmond, 1820-22 (returned to Ireland; bp. Waterford and Lismore, 1822-29).

Kennedy, Thomas F. (1858-1917): ord. July 24, 1887; rector North American College, 1901-17; tit. bp. Hadrianapolis, 1907-15; tit. abp. Seleucia, 1915-17.

Kenny, William J. (1853-1913): ord. Jan 15, 1879; bp. St. Augustine, 1902-13.

Kenrick (brothers): Francis P. (1796-1863): b. Ireland; ord. Apr. 7, 1821; coad. bp. Philadelphia (Aratha), 1830-42; bp. Philadelphia, 1842-51; abp. Baltimore, 1851-63. **Peter** (1806-1896): b. Ireland; ord. Mar. 6, 1932; coad. bp. St. Louis (Adrasus), 1841-43; bp., 1843-47, and first abp. 1847-95, St. Louis (res.).

Keough, Francis P. (1890-1961): ord. June 10, 1916; bp. Providence, 1943-47; abp. Baltimore, 1947-61.

Keyes, Michael, S.M. (1876-1959): b. Ireland; ord. June 21, 1907; bp. Savannah, 1922-35 (res.).

Kiley, Moses E. (1876-1953): b. Nova Scotia; ord. June 10, 1911; bp. Trenton, 1934-40; abp. Milwaukee, 1940-53.

Kogy, Lorenz S., O.M. (1895-1963): b. Georgia, Russia; ord. Nov. 15, 1917; U.S. citizen, 1944; patriarchal vicar for Armenian diocese of Beirut (Comana), 1951-63.

Koudelka, Joseph (1852-1921): b. Austria; ord. Oct. 8, 1875; aux. bp. Cleveland (Germanicoplis), 1908-11; aux. bp. Milwaukee, 1911-13; bp. Superior, 1913-21.

Kowalski, Rembert, O.F.M. (1884-1970): ord. June 22, 1911; v.a. Wuchang, China (Ipsus), 1942-46; first bp. Wuchang, 1946-70 (in exile from 1953).

Kozlowski, Edward (1860-1915): b. Poland;

ord. June 29, 1887; aux. bp. Milwaukee (Germia), 1914-15.

Krautbauer, Francis X. (1824-1885): b. Germany; ord. July 16, 1850; bp. Green Bay, 1875-85.

Kucera, Louis B. (1888-1957): ord. June 8, 1915; bp. Lincoln, 1930-57.

L

Lamb, Hugh (1890-1959): ord. May 29, 1915; aux. bp. Philadelphia (Helos), 1936-51; bp. Greensburg, 1951-59.

Lamy, Jean B.: See Index.

Lane, Loras (1910-1968): ord. Mar. 19, 1937; aux. bp. Dubuque (Bencenna), 1951-56; bp. Rockford, 1956-68.

Lane, Raymond A., M.M. (1894-1974): ord. Feb. 8, 1920; v.a. Fushun, Manchukuo (Hypaepa), 1940-46; sup. gen. Maryknoll, 1946-56.

Laval, John M. (1854-1937): b. France; ord. Nov. 10, 1877; aux. bp. New Orleans (Hierocaesarea), 1911-37.

Lavialle, Peter J. (1819-1867): b. France; ord. Feb. 12, 1844; bp. Louisville, 1865-67.

Lawler, John J. (1862-1948): ord. Dec. 19, 1885; aux. bp. St. Paul (Hermopolis), 1910-16; bp. Lead (now Rapid City), 1916-48.

Le Blond, Charles H. (1883-1958): ord. June 29, 1909; bp. St. Joseph, 1933-56 (res.).

Ledvina, Emmanuel (1868-1952): ord. Mar. 18, 1893; bp. Corpus Christi, 1921-49 (res.).

Lefevere, Peter P. (1804-1869): b. Belgium; ord. Nov. 30, 1831; coad. bp. and admin. Detroit (Zela), 1841-69.

Leibold, Paul F. (1914-1972): ord. May 18, 1940; aux. bp. Cincinnati (Trebenna), 1958-66; bp. Evansville, 1966-69; abp. Cincinnati, 1969-72.

Lenihan (brothers): **Mathias C.** (1854-1943): ord. Dec. 20, 1879; bp. Great Falls, 1904-30 (res.). **Thomas M.** (1844-1901): b. Ireland; ord. Nov. 19, 1868; bp. Cheyenne, 1897-1901.

Leray, Francis X. (1825-1887): b. France; ord. Mar. 19, 1852; bp. Natchitoches (now Alexandria, La.), 1877-79; coad. bp. New Orleans and admin. of Natchitoches (Jonopolis), 1879-83; abp. New Orleans, 1883-87.

Ley, Felix, O.F.M. Cap. (1909-1972): ord. June 14, 1936; ap. admin. Ryukyu Is., (Caporilla), 1968-72.

Lillis, Thomas F. (1861-1938): ord. Aug. 15, 1885; bp. Leavenworth (now Kansas City, Kans.), 1904-10; coad. bp. Kansas City, Mo. (Cibyra), 1910-13; bp. Kansas City, Mo., 1913-38.

Lootens, Louis (1827-1898): b. Belgium; ord. June 14, 1851; v. a. Idaho and Montana (Castabala), 1868-76 (res.).

Loras, Mathias (1792-1858): b. France; ord. Nov. 12, 1815; first bp. Dubuque, 1837-58.

Loughlin, John (1817-1891): b. Ireland; ord. Oct. 18, 1840; first bp. Brooklyn, 1853-91.

Lowney, Denis M. (1863-1918): b. Ireland;

ord. Dec. 17, 1887; aux. bp. Providence (Hadrianopolis), 1917-18.

Ludden, Patrick A. (1838-1912): b. Ireland; ord. May 21, 1865; first bp. Syracuse, 1887-1912.

Luers, John (1819-1871): b. Germany; ord. Nov. 11, 1846; first bp. Fort Wayne, 1858-71.

Lynch, Joseph P. (1872-1954): ord. June 9, 1900; bp. Dallas (Dallas-Fort Worth, 1953), 1911-54.

Lynch, Patrick N. (1817-1882): b. Ireland; ord. Apr. 5, 1840; bp. Charleston, 1858-82.

M

McAuliffe, Maurice F. (1875-1944): ord. July 29, 1900; aux. bp. Hartford (Dercos), 1925-34; bp. Hartford, 1934-44.

McCarthy, Joseph E. (1876-1955): ord. July 4, 1903; bp. Portland, Me., 1932-55.

McCarthy, Justin J. (1900-1959): ord. Apr. 16, 1927; aux. bp. Newark (Doberus), 1954-57; bp. Camden, 1957-59.

McCarty, William T., C.SS.R. (1889-1972): ord. June 10, 1915; military delegate (Anea), 1943-47; coad. bp. Rapid City, 1947-48; bp. Rapid City, 1948-69 (res.).

McCloskey, James P. (1870-1945): ord. Dec. 17, 1898, bp. Zamboanga, P.I., 1917-20; bp. Jaro, P.I., 1920-45.

McCloskey, John: See Index.

McCloskey, William G. (1823-1909): ord. Oct. 6, 1852; bp. Louisville, 1868-1909.

McCormick, Patrick J. (1880-1953): ord. July 6, 1904; aux. bp. Washington (Atenia), 1950-53.

McCort, John J. (1860-1936): ord. Oct. 14, 1883; aux. bp. Philadelphia (Azotus), 1912-20; bp. Altoona, 1920-36.

McDevitt, Philip R. (1858-1935): ord. July 14, 1885; bp. Harrisburg, 1916-35.

McDonnell, Charles E. (1854-1921): ord. May 19, 1878; bp. Brooklyn, 1892-1921.

McDonnell, Thomas J. (1894-1961): ord. Sept. 20, 1919; aux. bp. New York (Sela), 1947-51; coad. bp. Wheeling, 1951-61.

McEntegart, Bryan (1893-1968): ord. Sept. 8, 1917; bp. Ogdensburg, 1943-53; rector Catholic University (Aradi), 1953-57; bp. Brooklyn, 1957-68.

McFadden, James A. (1880-1952): ord. June 17, 1905; aux. bp. Cleveland (Bida), 1932-43; first bp. Youngstown, 1943-52.

MacFarland, Francis P. (1819-1874): ord. May 1, 1845; bp. Hartford, 1858-74.

McFaul, James A. (1850-1917): b. Ireland; ord. May 26, 1877; bp. Trenton, 1894-1917.

McGavick, Alexander J. (1863-1948): ord. June 11, 1887; aux. bp. Chicago (Marcopolis), 1899-1921; bp. La Crosse, 1921-48.

McGeough, Joseph F. (1903-1970): ord. Dec. 20, 1930; internuncio Ethiopia, 1957-60; apostolic delegate (Hemesa) S. Africa, 1960-67; nuncio Ireland, 1967-69.

McGill, John (1809-1872): ord. June 13, 1835; bp. Richmond, 1850-72.

MacGinley, John B. (1871-1969): b. Ireland; ord. June 8, 1895; bp. Nueva Caceres, 1910-24; first bp. Monterey-Fresno, 1924-32 (res.).

McGolrick, James (1841-1918): b. Ireland; ord. June 11, 1867; first bp. Duluth, 1889-1918.

McGovern, Patrick A. (1872-1951): ord. Aug. 18, 1895; bp. Cheyenne, 1912-51.

McGovern, Thomas (1832-1898): b. Ireland; ord. Dec. 27, 1861; bp. Harrisburg, 1888-98.

McGrath, Joseph F. (1871-1950): b. Ireland; ord. Dec. 21, 1895; bp. Baker City (now Baker), 1919-50.

McGuinness, Eugene (1889-1957): ord. May 22, 1915; bp. Raleigh, 1937-44; coad. bp. Oklahoma City and Tulsa (Ilium), 1944-48; bp. Oklahoma City and Tulsa, 1948-57.

McLaughlin, Thomas H. (1881-1947): ord. July 26, 1904; aux. bp. Newark (Nisa), 1935-37; first bp. Paterson, 1937-47.

McMahon, John J. (1875-1932): ord. May 20, 1900; bp. Trenton, 1928-32.

McMahon, Lawrence S. (1835-1893): ord. Mar. 24, 1860; bp. Hartford, 1879-93.

McManaman, Edward P. (1900-1964): ord. Mar. 12, 1927; aux. bp. Erie (Floriana), 1948-64.

McMullen, John (1832-1883): b. Ireland; ord. June 20, 1858; first bp. Davenport, 1881-83.

McNamara, John M. (1878-1960): ord. June 21, 1902; aux. bp. Baltimore (Eumenia), 1928-47; aux. bp. Washington, 1947-60.

McNamara, Martin D. (1898-1966): ord. Dec. 23, 1922; first bp. Joliet, 1949-66.

McNeirny, Francis (1828-1894): ord. Aug. 17, 1854; coad. bp. Albany (Rhesaina), 1872-77; bp. Albany, 1877-94.

McNicholas, John T., O.P. (1877-1950): b. Ireland; ord. Oct. 10, 1901; bp. Duluth, 1918-25; abp. Cincinnati, 1925-50.

McNulty, James A. (1900-1972): ord. July 12, 1925; aux. bp. Newark (Methone), 1947-53; bp. Paterson, 1953-63; bp. Buffalo, 1963-72.

McQuaid, Bernard J.: See Index.

McSorley, Francis J., O.M.I. (1913-1971): ord. May 30, 1939; v.a. Jolo, P.I. (Sozusa), 1958-71.

McVinney, Russell J. (1898-1971): ord. July 13, 1924; bp. Providence, 1948-71.

Machebeuf, Joseph P. (1812-1889): b. France; ord. Dec. 17, 1836; v. a. Colorado and Utah (Epiphania), 1868-1887; first bp. Denver, 1887-89.

Maes, Camillus P. (1846-1915): b. Belgium; ord. Dec. 19, 1868; bp. Covington, 1885-1915.

Magner, Francis (1887-1947): ord. May 17, 1913; bp. Marquette, 1941-47.

Mahoney, Bernard (1875-1939): ord. Feb. 27, 1904; bp. Sioux Falls, 1922-39.

Maloney, Thomas F. (1903-1962): ord. July 13, 1930; aux. bp. Providence (Andropolis), 1960-62.

Manogue, Patrick: See Index.

Manucy, Dominic (1823-1885): ord. Aug.

15, 1850; v. a. Brownsville (Dulma), 1874-84; bp. Mobile, Mar.-Sept., 1884 (res.); reappointed v. a. Brownsville (Maronea) (now diocese of Corpus Christi), 1884-85.

Marechal, Ambrose, S.S. (1766-1828): b. France; ord. June 2, 1792; abp. Baltimore, 1817-28.

Markham, Thomas F. (1891-1952): ord. June 2, 1917; aux. bp. Boston (Acalissus), 1950-52.

Martin, Augustus M. (1803-1875): b. France; ord. May 31, 1828; first bp. Natchitoches (now Alexandria), 1853-75.

Marty, Martin, O.S.B. (1834-1896): b. Switzerland; ord. Sept. 14, 1856; v. a. Dakota (Tiberias), 1880-89; first bp. Sioux Falls, 1889-95; bp. St. Cloud, 1895-96.

Marx, Adolph, (1915-1965): b. Germany; ord. May 2, 1940; aux. bp. Corpus Christi (Citrus), 1956-65; first bp. Brownsville, 1965.

Matz, Nicholas C. (1850-1917): b. France; ord. May 31, 1874; coad. bp. Denver (Telmissus), 1887-89; bp. Denver, 1889-1917.

Meerschaert, Theophile (1847-1924): b. Belgium; ord. Dec. 23, 1871; v. a. Oklahoma and Indian Territory (Sidyma), 1891-1905; first bp. Oklahoma, 1905-24.

Melcher, Joseph (1806-1873): b. Austria; ord. Mar. 27, 1830; first bp. Green Bay, 1868-73.

Messmer, Sebastian (1847-1930): b. Switzerland; ord. July 23, 1871; bp. Green Bay, 1892-1903; abp. Milwaukee, 1903-30.

Meyer, Albert (1903-1965): ord. July 11, 1926; bp. Superior, 1946-53; abp. Milwaukee, 1953-58; abp. Chicago, 1958-65; cardinal, 1959

Michaud, John S. (1843-1908): ord. June 7, 1873; coad. bp. Burlington (Modra), 1892-99; bp. Burlington, 1899-1908.

Miege, John B., S.J. (1815-1884): b. France; ord. Sept. 12, 1844; v. a. Kansas and Indian Territory (now Kansas City) (Messene), 1851-74 (res.).

Miles, Richard P., O.P. (1791-1860): ord. Sept. 21, 1816; first bp. Nashville, 1838-60.

Minihan, Jeremiah F. (1903-1973); ord. Dec. 21, 1929; aux. bp. Boston (Paphus), 1954-73.

Misner, Paul B., C.M. (1891-1938): ord. Feb. 23, 1919; v.a. Yukiang, China (Myrica), 1935-38.

Mitty, John J. (1884-1961): ord. Dec. 22, 1906; bp. Salt Lake, 1926-32; coad. abp. San Francisco (Aegina), 1932-35; abp. San Francisco, 1935-61.

Moeller, Henry (1849-1925): ord. June 10, 1876; bp. Columbus, 1900-03; coad. abp. Cincinnati (Areopolis), 1903-04; abp. Cincinnati, 1904-25.

Molloy, Thomas E. (1884-1956): ord. Sept. 19, 1908; aux. bp. Brooklyn (Lorea), 1920-21; bp. Brooklyn, 1921-56.

Monaghan, Francis J. (1890-1942): ord. May 29, 1915; coad. bp. Ogdensburg (Mela), 1936-39; bp. Ogdensburg, 1939-42.

Monaghan, John J. (1856-1935): ord. Dec. 18, 1880; bp. Wilmington, 1897-1925 (res.).

Montgomery, George T. (1847-1907): ord. Dec. 20, 1879; coad. bp. Monterey-Los-Angeles (Thmuis), 1894-96; bp. Monterey-Los Angeles (now Los Angeles), 1896-1903; coad. abp. San Francisco (Auxum), 1903-07.

Mooney, Edward (1882-1958): ord. Apr. 10, 1909; ap. del. India (Irenopolis), 1926-31; ap. del. Japan, 1931-33; bp. Rochester, 1933-37; first abp. Detroit, 1937-58; cardinal, 1946.

Moore, John (1835-1901): b. Ireland; ord. Apr. 9, 1860; bp. St. Augustine, 1877-1901.

Mora, Francis (1827-1905): b. Spain; ord. Mar. 19, 1856; coad. bp. Monterey-Los Angeles (Mosynopolis), 1873-78; bp. Monterey-Los Angeles, 1878-96 (res.).

Morris, John (1866-1946): ord. June 11, 1892; coad. bp. Little Rock (Acmonia), 1906-07; bp. Little Rock, 1907-46.

Mrak, Ignatius (1810-1901): b. Austria; ord. July 31; 1837; bp. Sault Ste. Marie and Marquette (now Marquette), 1869-78 (res.).

Muench, Aloysius: See Index.

Muldoon, Peter J. (1862-1927): ord. Dec. 18, 1886; aux. bp. Chicago (Tamasus), 1901-08; first bp. Rockford, 1908-27.

Mullen, Tobias (1818-1900): b. Ireland; ord. Sept. 1, 1844; bp. Erie, 1868-99 (res.).

Mulloy, William T. (1892-1959): ord. June 7, 1916; bp. Covington, 1945-59.

Mundelein, George (1872-1939): ord. June 8, 1895; aux. bp. Brooklyn (Loryma), 1909-15; abp. Chicago, 1915-39; cardinal, 1924.

Murphy, Joseph A., S.J. (1857-1939): b. Ireland; ord. Aug. 26, 1888; v. a. Belize, Br. Honduras (Birtha), 1923-39.

Murphy, William F. (1885-1950): ord. June 13, 1908; first bp. Saginaw, 1938-50.

Murray, John G. (1877-1956): ord. Apr. 14, 1900; aux. bp. Hartford (Flavias), 1920-25; bp. Portland, 1925-31; abp. St. Paul, 1931-56.

N

Navagh, James J. (1901-1965): ord. Dec. 21, 1929; aux. bp. Raleigh (Ombi), 1952-57; bp. Ogdensburg, 1957-63; bp. Paterson, 1963-65.

Neale, Leonard (1746-1817): ord. June 5, 1773; coad. bp. Baltimore (Gortyna), 1800-15; abp. Baltimore, 1815-17.

Neraz, John C. (1828-1894): b. France; ord. Mar. 19, 1853; bp. San Antonio, 1881-1894.

Neumann, John, Bl.: See Index.

Niedhammer, Matthew A., O.F.M. Cap. (1901-1970): ord. June 8, 1927; v. a. Bluefields, Nicaragua (Caloe), 1943-70.

Nilan, John J. (1855-1934): ord. Dec. 2, 1878; bp. Hartford, 1910-34.

Noll, John F.: See Index.

Northrop, Henry P. (1842-1916): ord. June 25, 1865; v.a. North Carolina (Rosalia), 1881-83; bp. Charleston, 1883-1916.

Nussbaum, Paul J., C.P. (1870-1935): ord. May 20, 1894; first bp. Corpus Christi, 1913-

20 (res.); bp. Sault Ste. Marie and Marquette (now Marquette), 1922-35.

O

O'Brien, William D. (1878-1962): ord. July 11, 1903; aux. bp. Chicago (Calynda), 1934-62.

O'Connell, Denis J. (1849-1927): b. Ireland; ord. May 26, 1877; aux. bp. San Francisco (Sebaste), 1908-12; bp. Richmond, 1912-26 (res.).

O'Connell, Eugene (1815-1891): b. Ireland; ord. May 21, 1842; v. a. Marysville (Flaviopolis), 1861-68; first bp. Grass Valley, 1868-84 (res.).

O'Connell, William H. (1859-1944): ord. June 7, 1884; bp. Portland, 1901-06; coad. bp. Boston (Constantia), 1906-07; abp. Boston, 1907-44; cardinal, 1911.

O'Connor (brothers), **James** (1823-1890): b. Ireland; ord. Mar. 25, 1848; v a. Nebraska (Dibon), 1876-85; first bp. Omaha, 1885-90. **Michael, S.J.** (1810-1872): b. Ireland; ord. June 1, 1833; first bp. Pittsburgh, 1843-53; first bp. of Erie, 1853-54; bp. Pittsburgh, 1854-60 (resigned, joined Jesuits).

O'Connor, John J. (1855-1927): ord. Dec. 22, 1877; bp. Newark, 1901-27.

O'Connor, William P. (1886-1973): ord. Mar. 10, 1912; bp. Superior, 1942-46; first bp. Madison, 1946-67 (res.).

O'Dea, Edward J. (1856-1932): ord. Dec. 23, 1882; bp. Nesqually (now Seattle — title changed in 1907), 1896-1932.

Odin, John M., C.M. (1800-1870): b. France; ord. May 4, 1823; v. a. Texas (Claudiopolis), 1842-47; first bp. Galveston, 1847-61; abp. New Orleans, 1861-70.

O'Donaghue, Denis (1848-1925): ord. Sept. 6, 1874; aux. bp. Indianapolis (Pomaria), 1900-10; bp. Louisville, 1910-24 (res.).

O'Dowd, James T. (1907-1950): ord. June 4, 1932; aux. bp. San Francisco (Cea), 1948-50.

O'Farrell, Michael J. (1832-1894): b. Ireland; ord. Aug. 18, 1855; first bp. Trenton, 1881-94.

O'Flanagan, Dermot (1901-1973): b. Ireland; ord. Aug. 27, 1929; first bp. Juneau, 1951-68 (res.).

O'Gara, Cuthbert, C.P. (1886-1968): b. Canada; ord. May 26, 1915; v.a. Yuanling, China (Elis), 1934-46; first bp. Yuanling, 1946-68 (imprisoned, 1951, and then expelled, 1953, by Chinese Communists).

O'Gorman, James, O.C.S.O. (1804-1874): b. Ireland; ord. Dec. 23, 1843; v.a. Nebraska (now Omaha) (Raphanea), 1859-74.

O'Gorman, Thomas (1843-1921): ord. Nov. 5, 1865; bp. Sioux Falls, 1896-1921.

O'Hara, Edwin V.: See Index.

O'Hara, Gerald P. (1888-1963): ord. Apr. 3, 1920; aux. bp. Philadelphia (Heliopolis), 1929-35; bp. Savannah (title changed to Savannah-Atlanta in 1937), 1935-59 (res.); regent of Rumania nunciature, 1946-50 (expelled); nuncio to Ireland, 1951-54; ap. del. to Great Britain, 1954-63.

O'Hara, John F., C.S.C. (1886-1960): ord. Sept. 9, 1916; delegate of US military vicar (Mylasa), 1940-45; bp. Buffalo, 1945-51; abp. Philadelphia, 1951-60; cardinal, 1958.

O'Hara, William (1816-1899): b. Ireland; ord. Dec. 21, 1842; first bp. Scranton, 1868-99.

O'Hare, William F., S.J. (1870-1926): ord. June 25, 1903; v.a. Jamaica (Maximianopolis), 1920-26.

O'Hern, John F. (1874-1933): ord. Feb. 17, 1901; bp. Rochester, 1929-33.

O'Leary, Thomas (1875-1949): ord. Dec. 18, 1897; bp. Springfield, Mass., 1921-49.

Olwell, Quentin, C.P. (1898-1972); ord. Feb. 4, 1923; prelate Marbel, P.I. (Thabraca), 1961-69 (ret.).

O'Regan, Anthony (1809-1866): b. Ireland; ord. Nov. 29, 1834; bp. Chicago, 1854-58 (res.).

O'Reilly, Bernard (1803-1856): b. Ireland; ord. Oct. 16, 1831; bp. Hartford, 1850-56.

O'Reilly, Charles J. (1860-1923): b. Canada; ord. June 29, 1890; first bp. Baker City (now Baker), 1903-18; bp. Lincoln, 1918-23.

O'Reilly, James (1855-1934): b. Ireland; ord. June 24, 1880; bp. Fargo, 1910-34.

O'Reilly, Patrick T. (1833-1892): b. Ireland; ord. Aug. 15, 1857; first bp. Springfield, Mass., 1870-92.

O'Reilly, Peter J. (1850-1924): b. Ireland; ord. June 24, 1877; aux. bp. Peoria (Lebedus), 1900-24.

O'Reilly, Thomas C. (1873-1938): ord. June 4, 1898; bp. Scranton, 1928-38.

Ortynsky, Stephen, O.S.B.M. (1866-1916): b. Poland; ord. July 18, 1891; first Ukrainian Byzantine Rite bishop in US (Daulia), 1907-16.

O'Shea, John A., C.M. (1887-1969): ord. May 30, 1914; v.a. Kanchow, China (Midila), 1928-46; first bp. Kanchow, 1946-69 (expelled by Chinese Communists, 1953).

O'Shea, William F., M.M. (1884-1945): ord. Dec. 5, 1917; v.a. Heijon, Japan (Naissusz), 1939-45; prisoner of Japanese 1941-42.

O'Sullivan, Jeremiah (1842-1896): b. Ireland; ord. June 30, 1868; bp. Mobile, 1885-96.

P

Paschang, Adolph J., M.M. (1895-1968): ord. May 21, 1921; v.a. Kong Moon, China (Sasima), 1937-46; first bp. Kong Moon, 1946-68 (expelled by Communists, 1951).

Pellicer, Anthony (1824-1880): ord. Aug. 15, 1850; first bp. San Antonio, 1874-80.

Penalver y Cardenas, Luis (1749-1810): b. Cuba; ord. Apr. 4, 1772; first bp. Louisiana and the Two Floridas (now New Orleans), 1793-1801; abp. Guatemala, 1801-06 (res.).

Perche, Napoleon J. (1805-1883): b. France; ord. Sept. 19, 1829; abp. New Orleans, 1870-83.

Persico, Ignatius, O.F.M. Cap. (1823-1895):

b. Italy; ord. Jan. 24, 1846; bishop from 1854; bp. Savannah-Atlanta, 1870-72; cardinal, 1893.

Peschges, John H. (1881-1944): ord. Apr. 15, 1905; bp. Crookston, 1938-44.

Peterson, John B. (1871-1944): ord. Sept. 15, 1899; aux. bp. Boston (Hippos), 1927-32; bp. Manchester, 1932-44.

Phelan, Richard (1828-1904): b. Ireland; ord. May 4, 1854; coad. bp. Pittsburgh (Cibyra), 1885-89; bp. Pittsburgh, 1889-1904.

Pitaval, John B. (1858-1928): b. France; ord. Dec. 24, 1881; aux. bp. Santa Fe (Sora), 1902-09; abp. Santa Fe, 1909-18 (res.).

Plagens, Joseph C. (1880-1943): b. Poland; ord. July 5, 1903; aux. bp. Detroit (Rhodiapolis), 1924-35; bp. Sault Ste. Marie and Marquette (title changed to Marquette, 1937), 1935-40; bp. Grand Rapids, 1941-43.

Portier, Michael (1795-1859): b. France; ord. May 16, 1818; v.a. Two Floridas and Alabama (Olena), 1826-29; first bp. Mobile, 1829-59.

Prendergast, Edmond (1843-1918): b. Ireland; ord. Nov. 17, 1865; aux. bp. Philadelphia (Scilium), 1897-1911; abp. Philadelphia, 1911-18.

Purcell, John B. (1800-1883): b. Ireland; ord. May 20, 1826; bp., 1833-50, and first abp., 1850-83, Cincinnati.

Q

Quarter, William (1806-1848): b. Ireland; ord. Sept. 19, 1829; first bp. Chicago, 1844-48.

Quigley, James E. (1855-1915): b. Canada; ord. Apr. 13, 1879; bp. Buffalo, 1897-1903; abp. Chicago, 1903-15.

Quinlan, John (1826-1883): b. Ireland; ord. Aug. 30, 1852; bp. Mobile, 1859-83.

Quinn, William Charles, C.M. (1905-1960): ord. Oct. 11, 1931; v.a. Yukiang, China (Halicarnassus), 1940-46; first bp. Yukiang, 1946-60 (expelled by Chinese Communists, 1951).

R

Rademacher, Joseph (1840-1900): ord. Aug. 2, 1863; bp. Nashville, 1883-93; bp. Fort Wayne, 1893-1900.

Rappe, Louis Amadeus (1801-1877): b. France; ord. Mar. 14, 1829; first bp. Cleveland, 1847-70 (res.).

Ready, Michael J. (1893-1957): ord. Sept. 14, 1918; bp. Columbus, 1944-57.

Reed, Victor J. (1905-1971): ord. Dec. 21, 1929; aux. bp. Oklahoma City and Tulsa (Limasa), 1957-58; bp. Oklahoma City and Tulsa, 1958-71.

Reilly, Edmond J. (1897-1958): ord. Apr. 1, 1922; aux. bp. Brooklyn (Nepte), 1955-58.

Rese, Frederic (1791-1871): b. Germany; ord. Mar. 15, 1823; first bp. Detroit, 1833-71. Inactive from 1841 because of ill health.

Reverman, Theodore (1877-1941): ord. July 26, 1901; bp. Superior, 1926-41.

Reynolds, Ignatius A. (1798-1855): ord.

Oct. 24, 1823; bp. Charleston, 1844-55.

Rhode, Paul P. (1871-1945): b. Poland; ord. June 17, 1894; aux. bp. Chicago (Barca), 1908-15; bp. Green Bay, 1915-45.

Rice, Joseph J. (1871-1938): ord. Sept. 29, 1894; bp. Burlington, 1910-38.

Rice, William A., S. J.(1891-1946): ord. Aug. 27, 1925; v.a. Belize, Br. Honduras (Rusicade), 1939-46.

Richter, Henry J. (1838-1916): b. Germany; ord. June 10, 1865; first bp. Grand Rapids, 1883-1916.

Riordan, Patrick W. (1841-1914): b. Canada; ord. June 10, 1865; coad. abp. San Francisco (Cabasa), 1883-84; abp. San Francisco, 1884-1914.

Ritter, Joseph E.: See Index.

Robinson, Pascal C., O. F. M. (1870-1948): b. Ireland; ord. Dec. 21, 1901; ap. visitor to Palestine, Egypt, Syria and Cyprus (Tyana), 1927-29; ap. nuncio to Ireland, 1929-48.

Rohlman, Henry P. (1876-1957): b. Germany; ord. Dec. 21, 1901; bp. Davenport, 1927-44; coad. abp. Dubuque (Macra), 1944-46; abp. Dubuque, 1946-54 (res.).

Rooker, Fraderick Z. (1861-1907): ord. July 25, 1888; bp. Jaro, P.I., 1903-07.

Ropert, Gulstan F., SS. CC. (1839-1903): b. France; ord. May 26, 1866; v.a. Sandwich (now Hawaiian) Is. (Panopolis), 1892-1903.

Rosati, Joseph, C. M.: See Index.

Rosecrans, Sylvester (1827-1878): ord. June 5, 1853; aux. bp. Cincinnati (Pompeiopolis), 1862-68; first bp. Columbus, 1868-78.

Rouxel, Gustave A. (1840-1908): b. France; ord. Nov. 4, 1863; aux. bp. New Orleans (Curium), 1899-1908.

Rummel, Joseph (1876-1964): b. Germany; ord. May 24, 1902; bp. Omaha, 1928-35; abp. New Orleans, 1935-64.

Russell, William T. (1863-1927): ord. June 21, 1889; bp. Charleston, 1917-27.

Ryan, Edward F. (1879-1956): ord. Aug. 10, 1905; bp. Burlington, 1945-56.

Ryan, James (1848-1923): b. Ireland; ord. Dec. 24, 1871; bp. Alton (now Springfield), Ill., 1888-1923.

Ryan, James H. (1886-1947): ord. June 5, 1909; rector Catholic University, 1928-35; tit. bp. Modra, 1933-35; bp., 1935-45, and first abp. Omaha, 1945-47.

Ryan, Patrick J. (1831-1911): b. Ireland; ord. Sept. 8, 1853; coad. bp. St. Louis (Tricomia), 1872-84; abp. Philadelphia, 1884-1911.

Ryan, Stephen, C. M. (1826-1896): b. Canada; ord. June 24, 1849; bp. Buffalo, 1868-96.

Ryan, Vincent J. (1884-1951): ord. June 7, 1912; bp. Bismarck, 1940-51.

S

Salpointe, John B. (1825-1898): b. France; ord. Dec. 20, 1851; v.a. Arizona (Dorylaeum), 1869-84; coad. abp. Santa Fe (Anazarbus), 1884-85; abp. Santa Fe, 1885-94 (res.).

Scanlan, Lawrence (1843-1915): b. Ireland; ord. June 28, 1868; v.a. Utah (Laranda), 1887-91; bp. Salt Lake (now Salt Lake City), 1891-1915.

Scannell, Richard (1845-1916): b. Ireland; ord. Feb. 26, 1871; first bp. Concordia (now Salina), 1887-91; bp. Omaha, 1891-1916.

Schenk, Francis J. (1901-1969): ord. June 13, 1926; bp. Crookston, 1945-60; bp. Duluth, 1960-69.

Scher, Philip G. (1880-1953): ord. June 6, 1904; bp. Monterey-Fresno, 1933-53.

Schinner, Augustine (1863-1937): ord. Mar. 7, 1886; first bp. Superior, 1905-13; first bp. Spokane, 1914-25 (res.).

Schlarman, Joseph H. (1879-1951): ord. June 29, 1904; bp. Peoria, 1930-51.

Schott, Lawrence F. (1907-1963): ord. July 15, 1935; aux. bp. Harrisburg (Eluza), 1956-63.

Schrembs, Joseph (1866-1945): b. Germany; ord. June 29, 1889; aux. bp. Grand Rapids (Sophene), 1911; bp. Toledo, 1911-21; bp. Cleveland, 1921-45.

Schuler, Anthony J., S. J. (1869-1944): ord. June 27, 1901; first bp. El Paso, 1915-42 (res.).

Schwebach, James (1847-1921): b. Luxembourg; ord. June 16, 1870; bp. La Crosse, 1892-1921.

Schwertner, August J. (1870-1939): ord. June 12, 1897; bp. Wichita, 1921-39.

Scully, William (1894-1969): ord. Sept. 20, 1919; coad. bp. Albany (Pharsalus), 1945-54; bp. Albany, 1954-69.

Sebastian, Jerome D. (1895-1960): ord. May 25, 1922; aux. bp. Baltimore (Baris in Hellesponto), 1954-60.

Seghers, Charles J.: See Index.

Seidenbusch, Rupert, O. S. B. (1830-1895): b. Germany; ord. June 22, 1853; v.a. Northern Minnesota (Halia), 1875-88 (res.).

Seton, Robert J. (1839-1927): b. Italy; ord. Apr. 15, 1865; tit. abp. Heliopolis, 1903-27. Grandson of Bl. Elizabeth Seton.

Shahan, Thomas J. (1857-1932): ord. June 3, 1882; rector, Catholic University of America, 1909-27; tit. bp. Germanicopolis, 1914-32.

Shanahan (brothers): **Jeremiah F.** (1834-1886): ord. July 3, 1859; first bp. Harrisburg, 1868-86. **John W.** (1846-1916): ord. Jan. 2, 1869; bp. Harrisburg, 1899-1916.

Shanley, John (1852-1909): ord. May 30, 1874; first bp. Jamestown (see transferred to Fargo in 1897), 1889-1909.

Shanley, Patrick H., O.C.D. (1896-1970): b. Ireland; ord. Dec. 21, 1930; US citizen; prelate Infanta, P.I. (Sophene), 1953-60 (res.).

Shaughnessy, Gerald, S.M. (1887-1950): ord. June 20, 1920; bp. Seattle, 1933-50.

Shaw, John W. (1863-1934): ord. May 26, 1888; coad. bp. San Antonio (Castabala), 1910-11; bp. San Antonio, 1911-18; abp. New Orleans, 1918-34.

Sheehan, Edward T., C.M. (1888-1933): ord. June 7, 1916; v. a. Yukiang, China (Calydon), 1929-33.

Sheil, Bernard J. (1886-1969): ord. May 21,

1910; aux. bp. Chicago (Pegae), 1928-69; tit. abp. Selge, 1959-69. Founder of Catholic Youth Organization.

Smith, Alphonse (1883-1935): ord. Apr. 18, 1908; bp. Nashville, 1924-35.

Smith, Leo R. (1905-1963): ord. Dec. 21, 1929; aux. bp. Buffalo (Marida), 1952-63; bp. Ogdensburg, 1963.

Smyth, Clement, O.C.S.O. (1810-1865):b. Ireland; ord. May 29, 1841; coad. bp. Dubuque (Thennesus), 1857-58; bp. Dubuque, 1858-65.

Spalding, John L.: See Index.

Spalding, Martin J.: See Index.

Spellman, Francis J.: See Index.

Spence, John S. (1909-1973): ord. Dec. 5, 1933; aux. bp. Washington (Aggersel), 1964-73.

Stang, William (1854-1907): b. Germany; ord. June 15, 1878; first bp. Fall River, 1904-07.

Stariha, John (1845-1915): b. Austria; ord. Sept. 19, 1869; first bp. Lead (now Rapid City), 1902-09 (res.).

Steck, Leo J. (1898-1950): ord. June 8, 1924; aux. bp. Salt Lake City (Ilium), 1948-50.

Stock, John (1918-1972): ord. Dec. 4, 1943; aux. bp. Philadelphia (Ukrainian Rite) (Pergamum), 1971-72.

Stritch, Samuel: See Index.

Sullivan, Bernard, S.J. (1889-1970): ord. June 26, 1921; bp. Patna, India, 1929-46 (res.).

Sweeney, James J. (1898-1968): ord. June 20, 1925; first bp. Honolulu, 1941-68.

Swint, John J. (1879-1962): ord. June 23, 1904; aux. bp. Wheeling (Sura), 1922; bp. Wheeling, 1922-62.

T

Takach, Basil (1879-1948): b. Austria-Hungary; ord. Dec. 12, 1902; first ap. ex. Pittsburgh Byzantine Rite exarchy (Zela), 1924-48.

Thill, Francis A. (1893-1957): ord. Feb. 28, 1920; bp. Concordia (title changed to Salina in 1944), 1938-57.

Tief, Francis J. (1881-1965): ord. June 11, 1908; bp. Concordia (now Salina), 1921-38 (res.).

Tierney, Michael (1839-1908): b. Ireland; ord. May 26, 1866; bp. Hartford, 1894-1908.

Tihen, J. Henry (1861-1940): ord. Apr. 26, 1886; bp. Lincoln, 1911-17; bp. Denver, 1917-31 (res.).

Timon, John, C. M. (1797-1867): ord. Sept. 23, 1826; first bp. Buffalo, 1847-67.

Toebbe, Augustus M. (1829-1884): b. Germany; ord. Sept. 14, 1854; bp. Covington, 1870-84.

Treacy, John P. (1890-1964): ord. Dec. 8, 1918; coad. bp. La Crosse (Metelis), 1945-48; bp. La Crosse, 1948-64.

Trobec, James (1838-1921): b. Austria; ord. Sept. 8, 1865; bp. St. Cloud, 1897-1914 (res.).

Tuigg, John (1820-1889): b. Ireland; ord. May 14, 1850; bp. Pittsburgh, 1876-89.

Turner, William (1871-1936): b. Ireland; ord. Aug. 13, 1893; bp. Buffalo, 1919-36.

Tyler, William (1806-1849): ord. June 3, 1829; first bp. Hartford, 1844-49.

V

Van de Velde, James O., S.J. (1795-1855): b. Belgium; ord. Sept. 16, 1827; bp. Chicago, 1849-53; bp. Natchez, 1853-55.

Van de Ven, Cornelius (1865-1932): b. Holland; ord. May 31, 1890; bp. Natchitoches (title changed to Alexandria in 1910), 1904-32.

Van de Vyver, Augustine (1844-1911): b. Belgium; ord. July 24, 1870; bp. Richmond, 1889-1911.

Verdaguer, Peter (1835-1911): b. Spain; ord. Dec. 12, 1862; v. a. Brownsville (Aulon), 1890-1911.

Vehr, Urban J. (1891-1973): ord. May 29, 1915; bp. 1931-41, and first abp. Denver, 1941-67 (res.).

Verot, Augustin, S.S. (1805-1876): b. France; ord. Sept. 20, 1828; v. a. Florida (Danaba), 1858-61; bp. Savannah, 1861-70; bp. St. Augustine, 1870-76.

Vertin, John (1844-1899): b. Austria; ord. Aug. 31, 1866; bp. Sault Ste. Marie and Marquette (now Marquette), 1879-99.

W

Wade, Thomas, S. M. (1893-1969): ord. June 15, 1922; v. a. Northern Solomons (Barbalissus), 1930-69.

Wadhams, Edgar (1817-1891): convert, 1846; ord. Jan. 15, 1850; first bp. Ogdensburg, 1872-91.

Walsh, Emmet (1892-1968): ord. Jan. 15, 1916; bp. Charleston, 1927-49; coad. bp. Youngstown (Rhaedestus), 1949-52; bp. Youngstown, 1952-68.

Walsh, James A., M.M. (1867-1936): ord. May 20, 1892; co-founder with Thomas F. Price of Maryknoll, first US-established foreign mission society and first sponsor of a US foreign mission seminary; superior of Maryknoll, 1911-36; tit. bp. Syene, 1933-36.

Walsh, Louis S. (1858-1924): ord. Dec. 23, 1882; bp. Portland, Me., 1906-24.

Walsh, Thomas J. (1873-1952): ord. Jan. 27, 1900; bp. Trenton, 1918-28; bp., 1928-37, and first abp., 1937-52, Newark.

Ward, John (1857-1929): ord. July 17, 1884; bp. Leavenworth (now Kansas), 1910-29.

Watterson, John A. (1844-1899): ord. Aug. 9, 1868; bp. Columbus, 1880-99.

Wehrle, Vincent, O.S.B. (1855-1941): b. Switzerland; ord. Apr. 23, 1882; first bp. Bismarck, 1910-39 (res.).

Welch, Thomas A. (1884-1959): ord. June 11, 1909; bp. Duluth, 1925-59.

Whelan, James, O. P. (1822-1878): b. Ireland; ord. Aug. 2, 1846; coad. bp. Nashville

(Marcopolis), 1859-60; bp. Nashville, 1860-64 (res.).

Whelan, Richard V. (1809-1874): ord. May 1, 1831; bp. Richmond, 1841-50; bp. Wheeling, 1850-74.

White, Charles (1879-1955): ord. Sept. 24, 1910; bp. Spokane, 1927-55.

Whitfield, James (1770-1834): b. England; ord. July 24, 1809; coad. bp. Baltimore (Apollonia), 1828; abp. Baltimore, 1828-34.

Wigger, Winand (1841-1901): ord. June 10, 1865; bp. Newark, 1881-1901.

Willging, Joseph C. (1884-1959): ord. June 20, 1908; first bp. Pueblo, 1942-59.

Williams, John J. (1822-1907): ord. May 17, 1845; bp., 1866-75, and first abp., 1875-1907, Boston.

Willinger, Aloysius J., C.SS.R. (1886-1973): ord. July 2, 1911; bp. Ponce, P.R., 1929-46; coad. bp. Monterey-Fresno, 1946-53; bp. Monterey-Fresno, 1953-67 (res.).

Winkelmann, Christian H. (1883-1946): ord. June 11, 1907; aux. bp. St. Louis (Sita), 1933-39; bp. Wichita, 1939-46.

Wood, James F. (1813-1883): convert, 1836; ord. Mar. 25, 1844; coad. bp. Philadelphia (Antigonea), 1857-60; bp., 1860-75, and first abp., 1875-83, Philadelphia.

Woznicki, Stephen (1894-1968): ord. Dec. 22, 1917; aux. bp. Detroit (Peltae), 1938-50; bp. Saginaw, 1950-68.

Y-Z

Young, Josue (1808-1866): ord. Apr. 1, 1838; bp. Pittsburgh, 1853-54; bp. Erie, 1854-66.

Zardetti, Otto (1847-1902): b. Switzerland; ord. Aug. 21, 1870; first bp. St. Cloud, 1889-94; abp. Bucharest, Rumania, 1894-95 (res.).

NORTH AMERICAN COLLEGE

The North American College was founded by the bishops of the United States in 1859 as a residence and house of formation for US seminarians and graduate students in Rome. The first ordination of an alumnus took place June 14, 1862. Pontifical status was granted the college by Leo XIII Oct. 25, 1884.

Students living at the college study theology and related subjects in the various seminaries in Rome, principally at the Pontifical Gregorian University.

The college is directed by an American rector and staff, and operates under the auspices of a US bishops' committee which was set up in 1924.

The present rector, the 14th, is Msgr. Harold P. Darcy.

NATIONAL SHRINE

The National Shrine of the Immaculate Conception is dedicated to the honor of the Blessed Virgin Mary, who was declared patroness of the United States in 1846.

The shrine project was launched in 1914; the site and foundation stone were blessed in 1920; the crypt, an underground church, was completed in 1926; the main church and superstructure were dedicated Nov. 20, 1959; more than 56 chapels and additional interior furnishings have been installed since the dedication. The shrine has a distinctive bell tower and carillon.

The shrine is the seventh largest religious building in the world, with normal seating and standing accommodations for 6,000 persons. Eight thousand persons attended one function in 1971.

Approximately one million persons visit the shrine each year. Open daily, it is located adjacent to the Catholic University of America, Fourth St. and Michigan Ave. N. E., Washington, D. C., 20017.

The shrine director is Msgr. John J. Murphy.

JOHN XXIII CENTER

The John XXIII Center for Eastern Christian Studies was established in 1951 by Father Feodor Wilcock and a group of other Eastern-Rite Jesuits. It operates a wide variety of ecumenical activities related to Eastern Christian studies. One of its projects is the John XXIII Institute, believed to be the only academic institution outside of Rome offering a degree in the theology of the Eastern tradition of Christianity.

Father James H. McCarthy, S.J., is head of the Center, which is located 2502 Belmont Ave., Fordham Univ., Bronx, N.Y. 10458.

INTER COM

The Inter-Community Association of Missioners is a post-Vatican II professional organization of Catholic priests engaged in the full-time ministry of renewal through the preaching of missions and retreats.

The association's membership exceeds 400 priests, representing 24 religious orders.

According to the mind of the Second Vatican Council and its frequent insistence on preaching the Word of God, INTER COM is a service and research organization. The apostolate of parish missions is maintained and enhanced by improving the image of the missioner, by in-service training of veteran missioners and improving their sermon content and presentation, by recruiting younger members of the clergy to this apostolate, by demonstrating cooperation among preaching orders, and by annual seminars for ongoing education, shared experiences, and experimentation on new formats and presentations.

The association also plans and fosters general area missions, makes available potential resources of preachers, and has originated a bold and innovative program for the certification of preachers who qualify.

The general chairman is Father Jude Mead, C.P. Address: 3800 Franklin Ave., Baltimore, Md. 21229.

Religious

Religious orders and congregations, collectively called **religious institutes,** are special societies in the Church. Their members, called **religious,** live a community kind of life according to rules and constitutions approved by Church authority and strive for Christian perfection not only by fulfilling the obligations common to all the faithful but also through the profession and observance of public vows of obedience, chastity and poverty. In church law, their way of life is called the state of perfection or the religious life.

Religious Institutes

The particular goal of each institute and the means of realizing it in practice are stated in the rule and constitutions proper to the institute. Local bishops, with permission of the Holy See, can give approval for rules and constitutions of **institutes of diocesan rank. Pontifical rank** belongs to institutes approved by the Holy See. General jurisdiction over all religious is exercised by the Congregation for Religious and Secular Institutes. General legislation concerning religious is contained in Canons 487 to 681 of the Code of Canon Law and in subsequent enactments, especially since the Second Vatican Council.

All religious institutes are commonly called religious orders, despite the fact that there are differences between orders and congregations. The best known **orders** include the Benedictines, Trappists, Franciscans, Dominicans, Carmelites and Augustinians, for men; and the Carmelites, Poor Clares, Dominicans of the Second Order and Visitation Nuns, for women. Members of the orders have solemn vows; their communities have papal enclosure and exemption, and are bound to perform the Liturgy of the Hours (Divine Office) in choir as a common practice. Members of the **congregations** have simple vows. The orders are older than the congregations, which did not appear until the 16th century.

Contemplative institutes devote themselves exclusively to divine worship by prayer, penance and other spiritual exercises in a life of retirement. They do not engage in the active ministry. Examples are the Trappists and Carthusians, the Carmelite and Poor Clare nuns. **Active institutes** are geared primarily for the ministry and many kinds of apostolic work. **Mixed institutes** combine elements of the contemplative and active ways of life. While most institutes of men and women can be classified as active, all of them have some contemplative aspects.

Historical Development

The basis of the life of religious institutes was the invitation Christ extended to men (Mt. 19:16ff.) to follow him with special dedication in a life like his own, which was that of a poor and chaste man under obedience to the Father.

In the earliest years of Christianity, some men and women dedicated themselves to the service of God in a special manner. Among them were holy women, deaconesses and virgins mentioned in the Acts of the Apostles, and confessors and ascetics like St. Clement of Rome, St. Ignatius of Antioch and St. Polycarp.

In the third and fourth centuries, there were traces of a kind of religious profession, and the root idea of the life began to produce significant results in the solitary and community hermitages of Egypt and Syria under the inspiration of men like St. Paul of Thebes, St. Anthony the Abbot and St. Pachomius.

St. Basil, "Father of Monasticism in the East," exerted a deep and still continuing influence on the development of religious life among men and women. His opposite number in the West was St. Benedict, whose rule or counsels, dating from about 530, set the pattern of monastic life for men and women which prevailed for nearly six centuries and which still endures. Before his time, St. Augustine framed guidelines for community life which are still being followed by some men and women religious.

Mendicant orders, whose members were freer than the monks for works of the active ministry, made their appearance early in the 13th century and began to change some of the established aspects of religious life. Religious women, however, continued to live in the monastic manner.

A significant change in religious life developed in the 16th century when several communities of men with simple rather than solemn vows were approved; among them were **clerics regular** like the Jesuits and Barnabites. Some of these communities are considered to be orders, although they differ in some respects from the older orders.

The Sisters of Charity, in 1633, were the first community of women with simple vows to gain Church approval. Since that time, the number and variety of female communities have greatly increased. Women religious, no longer restricted to the hidden life of prayer, became engaged in many kinds of work including education, health and social service, and missionary endeavor.

Clerical communities of men—i. e., those whose membership is predominantly composed of priests — are similarly active in many types of work. Their distinctive fields are education, home and foreign missions, retreats, special assignments and the communications media, as well as the internal life and conduct of their own communities. They also engage in the ordinary pastoral ministry which is the principal work of diocesan or secular priests.

They are generally called **regular clergy** because of the rule of life (*regula* in Latin) they follow.

Non-clerical or lay institutes of men are the various brotherhoods whose non-ordained members (called **lay brothers,** or simply **brothers**) are engaged in educational and hospital work, missionary endeavors, and other special fields.

Some of the institutes of men listed below have a special kind of status because their members, while living a common life like that which is characteristic of religious, do not profess the vows of religious. Examples are the Maryknoll Fathers, the Oratorians of St. Philip Neri, the Paulists and Sulpicians. They are called **societies of the common life without vows.**

RENEWAL OF RELIGIOUS LIFE

Following are key excerpts from the *Decree on the Appropriate Renewal of Religious Life* promulgated by the Second Vatican Council.

Norms

"A life consecrated by a profession of the counsels (of poverty, chastity and obedience) is of surpassing value. Such a life has a necessary role to play in the circumstances of the present age. That this kind of life and its contemporary role may achieve greater good for the Church, this sacred Synod issues the following decrees. They concern only the general principles which must underlie an appropriate renewal of the life and rules of religious communities. These principles apply also to societies living a community life without the exercise of vows, and to secular institutes, though the special character of both groups is to be maintained. After the Council, the competent authority will be obliged to enact particular laws opportunely spelling out and applying what is legislated here" (No. 1).

"The appropriate renewal of religious life involves two simultaneous processes: (1) a continuous return to the sources of all Christian life and to the original inspiration behind a given community and (2) an adjustment of the community to the changed conditions of the times. . . .

"(a) Since the fundamental norm of the religious life is a following of Christ as proposed by the gospel, such is to be regarded by all communities as their supreme law.

"(b) It serves the best interests of the Church for communities to have their own special character and purpose. Therefore loyal recognition and safekeeping should be accorded to the spirit of founders, as also to all the particular goals and wholesome traditions which constitute the heritage of each community.

"(c) All communities should participate in the life of the Church. According to its individual character, each should make its own and foster in every possible way the enterprises and objectives of the Church in such fields as these: the scriptural, liturgical, doctrinal, pastoral, ecumenical, missionary, and social.

"(d) Communities should promote among their members a suitable awareness of contemporary human conditions and of the needs of the Church. . . .

"(e) Since the religious life is intended above all else to lead those who embrace it to an imitation of Christ and to union with God through the profession of the evangelical counsels, the fact must be honestly faced that even the most desirable changes made on behalf of contemporary needs will fail of their purpose unless a renewal of spirit gives life to them. Indeed such an interior renewal must always be accorded the leading role even in the promotion of external works" (No. 2).

"The manner of living, praying, and working should be suitably adapted to the physical and psychological conditions of today's religious and also, to the extent required by the nature of each community, to the needs of the apostolate, the requirements of a given culture, the social and economic circumstances anywhere, but especially in missionary territories."

Allowance should be made for prudent experimentation in the direction of renewal and adaptation (No. 3).

". . . The hope of renewal must be lodged in a more diligent observance of rule and of constitution rather than in a multiplication of individual laws" (No. 4).

Various Communities

"The members of each community should recall above everything else that by their profession of the evangelical counsels they have given answer to a divine call to live for God alone not only by dying to sin (cf. Rom. 6:11) but also by renouncing the world. They have handed over their entire lives to God's service in an act of special consecration which is deeply rooted in their baptismal consecration and which provides an ampler manifestation of it.

"Inasmuch as their self-dedication has been accepted by the Church, they should realize that they are committed to her service as well.

". . . The members of each community should combine contemplation with apostolic love. By the former they adhere to God in mind and heart; by the latter they strive to associate themselves with the work of redemption and to spread the Kingdom of God" (No. 5).

"Members of those communities which are totally dedicated to contemplation give themselves to God alone in solitude and silence and through constant prayer and ready penance. No matter how urgent may be the needs of the active apostolate, such communities will always have a distinguished part to play in Christ's Mystical Body. . . . Their manner of living should be revised according to the aforementioned principles and standards of appropriate renewal, though their withdrawal from the world and the practices of their contemplative life should be maintained at their holiest" (No. 7).

Communities geared for apostolic action "should skillfully harmonize their observances and practices with the needs of the apostolate to which they are dedicated," with due regard for diversity (No. 8). This norm applies to monastic institutes, which should preserve their special character; to communities which "closely join the apostolic life with choral prayer and monastic observances"; and to "the lay religious life, for both men and women" (Nos. 9 and 10).

[See Secular Institutes for a quotation from the decree on the subject.]

The Vows, Authority

"That chastity which is practiced 'on behalf of the heavenly Kingdom' (Mt. 19:12), and which religious profess, deserves to be esteemed as a surpassing gift of grace. For it liberates the human heart in a unique way (cf. 1 Cor. 7:32-35) and causes it to burn with greater love for God and all mankind. It is therefore an outstanding token of heavenly riches, and also a most suitable way for religious to spend themselves readily in God's service and in works of the apostolate. . . .

"Since the observance of total continence intimately involves the deeper inclinations of human nature, candidates should not undertake the profession of chastity nor be admitted to its profession except after a truly adequate testing period and only if they have the needed degree of psychological and emotional maturity" (No. 12).

"Poverty voluntarily embraced in imitation of Christ provides a witness which is highly esteemed, especially today. Let religious painstakingly cultivate such poverty, and give it new expressions if need be. . . .

". . . Members of a community ought to be poor in both fact and spirit, and have their treasures in heaven (cf. Mt. 6:20).

". . . Communities as such should aim at giving a kind of corporate witness to their own poverty. . . .

"To the degree that their rules and constitutions permit, religious communities can rightly possess whatever is necessary for their temporal life and their mission. Still, let them avoid every appearance of luxury, of excessive wealth, and accumulation of possessions" (No. 13).

"Through the profession of obedience, religious offer to God a total dedication of their own wills as a sacrifice of themselves; they thereby unite themselves with greater steadiness and security to the saving will of God. . . . Under the influence of the Holy Spirit, religious submit themselves to their superiors, whom faith presents as God's repre-

sentatives, and through whom they are guided into the service of all their brothers in Christ. . . . In this way . . . religious assume a firmer commitment to the ministry of the Church and labor to achieve the mature measure of the fullness of Christ (cf. Eph. 4:13).

"Therefore, in a spirit of faith and of love for God's will, let religious show humble obedience to their superiors in accord with the norms of the rule and constitution. . . . Let them bring to the execution of commands and to the discharge of assignments entrusted to them the resources of their minds and wills, and their gifts of nature and grace. Lived in this manner, religious obedience will not diminish the dignity of the human person but will rather lead it to maturity in consequence of that enlarged freedom which belongs to the sons of God.

". . . Each superior should himself be docile to God's will in the exercise of his office. Let him use his authority in a spirit of service for the brethren. . . . Governing his subjects as God's own sons, and with regard for their human personality, a superior will make it easier for them to obey gladly. Therefore he must make a special point of leaving them appropriately free with respect to the sacrament of penance and direction of conscience. Let him give the kind of leadership which will encourage religious to bring an active and responsible obedience to the offices they shoulder and the activities they undertake. Therefore a superior should listen willingly to his subjects and encourage them to make a personal contribution to the welfare of the community and of the Chruch. Not to be weakened, however, is the superior's authority to decide what must be done and to require the doing of it.

"Let chapters and councils faithfully acquit themselves of the governing role given to them; each should express in its own way the fact that all members of the community have a share in the welfare of the whole community and a responsibility for it" (No. 14).

Vicars' Conference

Sixty vicars and associate vicars for religious elected Father William Hughes of Rockville Centre, N.Y., president of the newly formed Conference of Vicars for Religious at an early May, 1972, meeting in Cleveland.

They also approved a constitution committing the conference: to assist vicars with cooperation, communications services and continuing education; to increase the service of dioceses to religious, and to respond to the needs of religious on regional, national and international levels; to carry on liaison with the Congregation for Religious and Secular Institutes, the National Conference of Catholic Bishops and other organizations concerned with religious.

RELIGIOUS INSTITUTES OF MEN IN THE UNITED STATES

(Sources: Catholic Almanac survey; _Official Catholic Directory._)

The number of priests and brothers, as of Jan. 1, 1973, is given at the end of entries.

African Missions, Society of S.M.A.: Founded 1856, at Lyons, France, by Bishop Melchior de Marion Bressilac. General motherhouse, Rome, Italy; American provincialate, 23 Bliss Ave., Tenafly, N.J. 07670. Missionary work in West Africa, Bahama Islands and inner city parishes. 81 priests.

Assumptionists (Augustinians of the Assumption), AA.: Founded 1845, at Nimes, France, by Rev. Emmanuel d'Alzon; in US, 1946. General motherhouse, Rome, Italy; US province, 329 W. 108th St., New York, N.Y. 10025. Educational, parochial, ecumenical, retreat, foreign mission work, 100 priests, 41 brothers.

Atonement, Franciscan Friars of the, S.A.: Founded 1898, at Garrison, N.Y., by Fr. Paul James Francis. General motherhouse, Graymoor, Garrison, N.Y. 10524. Ecumenical, charitable, mission work. 132 priests, 96 brothers.

Augustinians (Order of St. Augustine), O.S.A.: Established canonically in 1256 by Pope Alexander IV; in US, 1796. General motherhouse, Rome, Italy.

St. Thomas of Villanova Province (1796), Villanova, Pa. 19085. 341 priests, 10 brothers.

Our Mother of Good Counsel Province (1941), Tolentine College, 20300 Governors Hwy., Olympia Fields, Ill. 60461. 159 priests, 32 brothers.

St. Augustine Province, 2060 N. Vermont Ave., Los Angeles, Calif. 90027. 42 priests.

Our Mother of Good Counsel Vice-Province, St. Augustine Priory, Richland, N.J. 08350. 21 priests, 3 brothers.

Augustinian Recollects, O.A.R.: Founded 1588; in US, 1944. General motherhouse, Rome, Italy; US provincial residence, 57 Ridgeway Ave., West Orange, N.J. 07052. Missionary, parochial, education work. 80 priests, 12 brothers.

Barnabites (Clerics Regular of St. Paul), C.R.S.P.: Founded 1530, in Milan, Italy, by St. Anthony M. Zaccaria. Generalate, Rome, Italy; American headquarters, 40 Agassiz Circle, Buffalo, N.Y. 14214. Parochial, educational, mission work. 16 priests.

Basil the Great, Order of St. (Ukrainian), O.S.B.M.: General motherhouse, Rome, Italy; US province, 31-12 30th St., Long Island City, N.Y. 11106. Parochial work among Byzantine Ukrainian Rite Catholics. 45 priests, 2 brothers.

Basilian Fathers (Congregation of the Priests of St. Basil), C.S.B.: Founded 1822, at Annonay, France. General motherhouse, 95 St. Joseph St., Toronto, Ont., M5S 2R9, Canada. Educational, parochial work. 155 priests (in US).

Basilian Salvatorian Fathers: Founded 1684, at Saida, Lebanon, by Eftimios Saifi; in US, 1953. General motherhouse, Saida, Lebanon; American headquarters, East and Pleasant Sts., Methuen, Mass. 01844. Educational, parochial work among Eastern Rite peoples. 25 priests.

Benedictines (Order of St. Benedict), O.S.B.: Founded 529, in Italy, by St. Benedict of Nursia: in US, 1846.

American Cassinese Federation (1855), Rt. Rev. Martin Burne, O.S.B., pres., St. Mary's Abbey, Morristown, N.J. 07960. 16 abbeys, 2 priories and 2 monasteries in the US. 1,166 priests, 290 brothers.

Benedictine Federation of the Americas (formerly Swiss-American Congregation) (1870), Rt. Rev. David Melancon, O.S.B., pres., St. Joseph Abbey, St. Benedict, La. 70457. 12 abbeys, 1 priory in US. 530 priests, 250 brothers.

English Benedictine Congregation: St. Anselm's Abbey, 'S. Dakota Ave. and 14th St. N.E., Washington, D.C. 20017. 29 priest monks, 7 monks; Abbey of St. Gregory, Cory's Lane, Portsmouth, R.I. 02871. 31 choir religious; Priory of St. Mary and St. Louis, 500 S. Mason Rd., St. Louis, Mo. 63141. 12 priests.

Congregation of St. Ottilien for Foreign Missions, St. Paul's Abbey, Newton, N.J. 07860. 27 priests, 9 brothers; Benedictine Mission House, Schuyler, Neb. 68661. 2 priests, 9 brothers.

Hungarian Congregation, Woodside Priory, 302 Portola Rd., Portola Valley, Calif. 94025. 11 priests, 5 brothers.

Congregation of the Annunciation, St. Andrew Priory, Valyermo, Calif. 93563. 23 choir monks.

Houses not in Congregations: Mount Saviour Monastery, Pine City, N.Y. 14871. 24 monks; Conventual Priory of St. Gabriel the Archangel, Weston, Vt. 05161. 4 priests, 10 choir monks.

Benedictines, Sylvestrine, O.S.B.: Founded 1231, in Italy by Sylvester Gozzolini. General motherhouse, Rome, Italy; US headquarters, 17320 Rosemont Rd., Detroit, Mich. 48219. 27 priests, 5 brothers.

Bethlehem Missionaries, Society of, S.M.B.: Founded 1921, at Immensee, Switzerland, by Rt. Rev. Canon Peter Bondolfi. General motherhouse, Immensee, Switzerland; US headquarters, 5630 E. 17th Pkwy., Denver, Colo. 80220. Foreign mission work. 12 priests, 1 brother.

Blessed Sacrament, Congregation of the, S.S.S.: Founded 1856, at Paris, France, by St. Pierre Julien Eymard; in US, 1900. General motherhouse, Rome, Italy; US headquarters, 184 E. 76th St., New York, N.Y. 10021. Perpetual adoration and Eucharistic apostolate. 124 priests, 72 brothers.

Camaldolese Congregation, Cam. O.S.B.:
Founded 1012, at Camaldoli, near Arezzo,
Italy, by St. Romuald; in US. 1958. General
motherhouse, Arezzo, Italy; US foundation,
Immaculate Heart Hermitage, Big Sur, Calif.
93920. 10 priests, 9 brothers.

**Camaldolese Hermits of the Congregation
of Monte Corona, Er. Cam.:** Founded 1520,
from Camaldoli, Italy, by Bl. Paul Gius-
tiniani. General motherhouse, Frascati
(Rome), Italy; US foundation, Bloomingdale,
O. 43910. 5 hermits (3 priests).

**Camillians (Clerics Regular, Ministers of
the Sick), O.S.Cam.:** Founded 1582, at
Rome, by St. Camillus de Lellis; in US, 1923.
General motherhouse, Rome, Italy; North
American province, 10100 W. Blue Mound
Rd., Wauwatosa, Wis. 53226. 14 priests, 17
brothers.

**Carmelites (Order of Our Lady of Mt. Car-
mel), O. Carm.:** General motherhouse,
Rome, Italy. Educational, charitable work.

Most Pure Heart of Mary Province (1864),
45 E. Dundee Rd., Barrington, Ill. 60010. 311
priests, 40 brothers.

St. Elias Province (1931), 69-34 52nd Ave.,
Maspeth, N.Y. 11378. 87 priests, 6 brothers.

Carmelites, Order of Discalced, O.C.D.: Established 1562, a Reform Order of Our Lady
of Mt. Carmel; in US, 1935. General motherhouse, Rome, Italy. Parochial, foreign mission work.

St. Therese of Oklahoma Province (1935),
1125 S. Walker St., P.O. Box 26127, Oklahoma City, Okla. 73126. 31 priests, 4 brothers.

Washington Province of Discalced Carmelites (1947), 1810 Volney Rd., Youngstown,
Ohio 44511. 79 priests, 22 brothers.

Anglo-Irish Province, P.O. Box 446, Redlands, Calif. 92373. 36 priests, 7 brothers.

Polish Province, 1628 Ridge Rd., Munster,
Ind. 46321. 8 priests, 2 brothers.

Carthusians, Order of, O. Cart.: Founded
1084, in France, by St. Bruno; in US, 1951.
General motherhouse, St. Pierre de Char-
treuse, France; US charterhouse, Arlington,
Vt. 05250. Cloistered, contemplatives. 6
priests, 4 brothers.

Christ, Society of, S.Ch.: Founded 1932,
General Motherhouse, Poznan, Poland; US
address, 15 Asselin St., Warren, R.I. 02885.

Cistercians, Order of, S.O. Cist.: Founded
1098, by St. Robert. Headquarters, Rome,
Italy.

Our Lady of Spring Bank Abbey, 34639 W.
Fairview Rd., Oconomowoc, Wis. 53066. 12
priests, 4 brothers.

Our Lady of Gerowval Monastery, Rose
Hill, Miss. 39356.

Our Lady of Dallas Monastery, Rt. 2, Box
1, Irving, Tex. 75062. 34 priests.

Cistercian Monastery of Our Lady of Fatima, Hainesport, Mt. Laurel Rd. (Mt. Laurel
Twp), Moorestown, P.O. 295, N.J. 08057.

St. Mary's Monastery, Route 1, New Ring-
gold, Pa. 17960.

**Cistercians of the Strict Observance, Order
of (Trappists), O.C.S.O.:** Founded 1098, in
France, by St. Robert; in US, 1848. Generalate, Rome, Italy. Number in each community is given at end of each entry.

Our Lady of Gethsemani Abbey (1848),
Trappist P.O., Ky. 40073. 110.

Our Lady of New Melleray Abbey (1849),
Dubuque, Iowa 52001. 66.

St. Joseph's Abbey (1825), Spencer, Mass.
01562. 70.

Holy Spirit Monastery (1944), Conyers,
Ga. 30207. 58.

Our Lady of Guadalupe Abbey (1947), Lafayette, Ore. 97127. 40.

Our Lady of the Holy Trinity Abbey
(1947), Huntsville, Utah 84317. 47.

Abbey of the Genesee, (1951), Piffard,
N.Y. 14533. 35.

Our Lady of Mepkin Abbey (1949),
Moncks Corner, S. Car. 29461. 30.

Our Lady of the Holy Cross Abbey (1950),
Berryville, Va. 22611. 33.

Our Lady of the Assumption Abbey, Rt. 5,
Ava, Mo. 65608. 16.

Our Lady of New Clairvaux Abbey (1955),
Vina, Calif. 96092. 28.

St. Benedict's Monastery (1956), Snow-
mass, Colo. 81654. 21.

**Claretians (Missionary Sons of the Immacu-
late Heart of Mary), C.M.F.:** Founded 1849,
at Vich, Spain, by St. Anthony Mary Claret.
General motherhouse, Rome, Italy. Mission,
parochial, educational work.

Western Province, 1119 Westchester Pl.,
Los Angeles, Calif. 90019. 96 priests, 18
brothers.

Eastern Province, 400 N. Euclid Ave. Oak
Park, Ill. 60302. 41 priests, 5 brothers.

**Clerics Regular Minor (Adorno Fathers)
C.R.M.:** Founded 1589, at Naples, Italy, by
Ven. Augustine Adorno and St. Francis
Caracciolo. General motherhouse, Rome,
Italy; US address, 575 Darlington Ave., Ram-
sey, N.J. 07446. 7 priests.

**Columban Fathers (St. Columban Foreign
Mission Society):** Founded 1918. US head-
quarters, St. Columbans, Nebr. 68056.
Foreign mission work. 157 priests.

**Consolata Society for Foreign Missions,
I.M.C.:** Founded 1901, at Turin, Italy, by Fa-
ther Joseph Allamano. General motherhouse,
Rome, Italy; US headquarters, P.O. Box C,
Lincoln Hwy., Somerset, N.J. 08873. 38
priests, 1 brother.

**Crosier Fathers (Canons Regular of the
Order of the Holy Cross), O.S.C.:** Founded
1210, in Belgium by Bl. Theodore De Celles.
Generalate, Amersfoort, Netherlands; US
province, 2620 E. Wallen Rd., Fort Wayne,
Ind. 46825. Mission, retreat, educational
work. 106 priests, 49 brothers.

Cross, Congregation of Holy, C.S.C.:
Founded 1837, in France; in US, 1841. Generalate, Rome, Italy. Educational and pastoral work; home missions and retreats; foreign

missions; social services and apostolate of the press.

Indiana Province (1841), 1304 E. Jefferson Blvd., South Bend, Ind. 46617. 414 priests, 46 brothers.

Eastern Province (1952), 835 Clinton Ave., Bridgeport, Conn. 06604. 165 priests, 28 brothers.

Southern Province (1968), 812 Audubon St., New Orleans, La. 70118. 64 priests, 3 brothers.

Divine Word, Society of the, S.V.D.: Founded 1875, in Holland, by Fr. Arnold Janssen; in US, 1897. General motherhouse, Rome, Italy.

Northern Province of the Blessed Virgin (1964), Techny, Ill. 60082. 101 priests, 56 brothers.

Sacred Heart Province (Eastern Province) (1940), 1025 Michigan Ave. N.E., Washington, D.C. 20017. 72 priests, 38 brothers.

St. Augustine's Province (Southern Province) (1940), 201 Ruella Ave., Bay St. Louis, Miss. 39520. 68 priests, 10 brothers.

St. Therese Province (Western Province) (1964), 2181 W. 25th St., Los Angeles, Calif. 90018. 50 priests, 10 brothers.

Dominicans (Order of Friars Preachers), O.P.: Founded early 13th century, in France by St. Dominic. General headquarters, Rome, Italy. Preaching, literary, scientific pursuits.

St. Joseph Province (1806), 869 Lexington Ave., New York, N.Y. 10021. 480 priests, 40 brothers.

Holy Name of Jesus Province (1912), 5877 Birch Ct., Oakland, Calif. 94609. 150 priests, 32 brothers.

St. Dominic Province (1873), 5375 Notre Dame de Grace Ave., Montreal Que. HAA 1L2, Canada. 35 priests, 10 brothers (in US).

St. Albert the Great Province (1939), 1909 S. Ashland Ave., Chicago, Ill. 60608. 333 priests, 45 brothers.

Spanish Province, US foundation (1926), P.O. Box 277, San Diego, Tex. 78384. 7 priests.

Edmund, Society of St., S.S.E.: Founded 1843, in France, by Fr. Jean Baptiste Muard. General motherhouse, Edmundite Generalate, Winooski, Vt. 05404. Educational, missionary work. 100 priests, 15 brothers.

Eudists (Congregation of Jesus and Mary), C.J.M.: Founded 1643, in France, by St. John Eudes. General motherhouse, Rome, Italy; Canadian province, 6125 1 ère Ave., Charlesbourg, Quebec G1H 2V9, P.Q., Canada. Educational, missionary work. 12 priests in Buffalo diocese.

Francis, Third Order Regular of St., T.O.R.: Founded 1221, in Italy; in US, 1910. General motherhouse, Rome, Italy. Educational, parochial, missionary work.

Most Sacred Heart of Jesus Province (1910), 601 Pitcairn Pl., Pittsburgh, Pa. 15232. 163 priests, 42 brothers.

Immaculate Conception Province, 2006 Edgewater Parkway, Silver Springs, Md. 20903. 67 priests, 14 brothers.

Commissariat of the Spanish Province of the Immaculate Conception (1924), 205 East Jersey St., Elizabeth, N.J. 07206. 37 priests, 2 brothers.

St. Jerome's, House of Studies, 1359 Monroe St., N.E., Washington, D.C. 20017. 1 priest, 1 brother.

Francis de Sales, Oblates of St., O.S.F.S.: Founded 1871, by Fr. Louis Brisson. General motherhouse, Rome, Italy. Educational work.

Wilmington-Philadelphia Province (1906), 2200 Kentmere Parkway, Box 1452, Wilmington, Del. 19899. 273 priests, 41 brothers.

Toledo-Detroit Province (1966), 2109 Richmond Rd., Box 3322, Toledo, Ohio 43607. 95 priests, 19 brothers.

Franciscans (Order of Friars Minor), O.F.M.: Founded 1209 in Italy, by St. Francis of Assisi; in US, 1844. General motherhouse, Rome, Italy. Preaching, missionary, educational, parochial, charitable work.

St. John the Baptist Province (1844), 1615 Vine St., Cincinnati, Ohio 45210. 352 priests, 123 brothers.

Sacred Heart Province (1858), 3140 Meramec St., St. Louis, Mo. 63118. 469 priests, 128 brothers.

Assumption of the Blessed Virgin Mary Province (1887), Pulaski, Wis. 54162. 216 priests, 118 brothers.

Most Holy Name of Jesus Province (1901), 135 W. 31st St., New York, N.Y. 10001. 671 priests, 130 brothers.

St. Barbara Province (1915), 1500 34th Ave., Oakland, Calif. 94601. 228 priests, 82 brothers.

Immaculate Conception Province, 147 Thompson St., New York, N.Y. 10012. 188 priests, 40 brothers.

Holy Cross Custody (1912), 1400 Main St., P.O. Box 608, Lemont, Ill. 60439. 28 priests, 3 brothers.

Most Holy Savior Custody, 232 S. Home Ave., Pittsburgh, Pa. 15202. 35 priests, 6 brothers.

St. John Capistran Commissariat (1928), 1290 Hornberger Ave., Roebling, N.J. 08554. 21 priests, 13 brothers.

St. Stephen Transylvanian Commissariat (1948), 517 S. Belle Vista Ave., Youngstown, Ohio 44509. 12 priests, 4 brothers.

Holy Family Croatian Custody, (1927), 4848 S. Ellis Ave., Chicago, Ill. 60615. 47 priests, 1 brother.

St. Casimir Lithuanian Vicariate, Kennebunkport, Me. 04046. 34 priests, 8 brothers.

Holy Gospel Province (Mexico), US foundation, 2400 Marr St., El Paso, Tex. 79903. 4 priests, 4 brothers.

Saints Francis and James Province (Jalisco, Mexico), US foundation, 504 E. Santa Clara

St., Hebbronville, Tex. 78361. 3 priests, 2 brothers.

Eastern District, Commissariat of the Holy Land, Mt. St. Sepulchre, 14th and Quincy Sts. N.E., Washington, D.C. 20017. 12 priests, 22 brothers.

St. Mary of the Angels Custody, Byzantine Slavonic Rite, P.O. Box 70, Sybertsville, Pa. 18251.

Academy of American Franciscan History, P.O. Box 34440, Washington, D.C. 20034. 18 priests, 2 brothers.

Franciscans (Order of Friars Minor Capuchin), O.F.M. Cap.: Established in 1528 as a separate jurisdiction of the order founded in 1209 by St. Francis of Assisi; first US province established after 1873. General motherhouse, Rome, Italy. Missionary, parochial work, chaplaincies.

St. Joseph Province (1857), 1740 Mt. Elliott Ave., Detroit, Mich. 48207. 245 priests, 66 brothers.

St. Augustine Province (1873), 220 37th St., Pittsburgh, Pa. 15201. 253 priests, 37 brothers.

St. Mary Province (1952), 30 Gedney Park Dr., White Plains, N.Y. 10605. 215 priests, 45 brothers.

New Jersey Provincial Commissariat (1918), St. Francis Friary, Newton, N.J. 07860. 58 priests, 18 brothers.

California Vice-Province (St. Patrick's Province of Ireland), 1721 Hillside Dr., Burlingame, Calif. 94010. 50 priests, 6 brothers.

Sts. Adalbert and Stanislaus Province (Warsaw, Poland), Manor Dr., Oak Ridge, N.J. 07438. 13 priests, 1 brother.

Franciscans (Order of Friars Minor Conventual), O.F.M. Conv.: Established in 1517 as a separate jurisdiction of the order founded in 1209 by St. Francis of Assisi; first US foundation, 1852. General curia, Rome, Italy. Missionary, educational, parochial work.

Immaculate Conception Province (1852), 812 N. Salina St., Syracuse, N.Y. 13208. 247 priests, 32 brothers.

St. Anthony of Padua Province (1903), 1300 Dundalk Ave., Baltimore, Md. 21222. 217 priests, 22 brothers.

St. Bonaventure Province (1939), 955 E. Ringwood Rd., Lake Forest, Ill. 60045. 84 priests, 35 brothers.

Our Lady of Consolation Province (1926), Mt. St. Francis, Ind. 47146. 148 priests, 41 brothers.

Glenmary Missioners (The Home Missioners of America): Founded 1939, in US. General headquarters, State Rt. 4 and Crescentville Rd., Fairfield, Ohio 45014. Home mission work. 74 priests, 31 brothers.

Holy Family, Congregation of the Missionaries of the, M.S.F.: Founded 1895, in Holland, by Rev. John P. Berthier. General motherhouse, Rome, Italy; US headquarters, 10415 Midland Blvd., St. Louis, Mo. 63114.

Belated vocations for the missions. 58 priests, 11 brothers.

Holy Family, Sons of the, S.F.: Founded 1864, at Barcelona, Spain, by Joseph Manyanet; in US, 1920. General motherhouse, Barcelona, Spain; US address, P.O. Box 1228, Santa Cruz, N. Mex. 87567. 14 priests.

Holy Ghost Fathers, C.S.Sp.: Founded 1703, in Paris, by Claude Francois Poullart des Places; in US, 1872. General motherhouse, Rome, Italy. Missions, education.

Eastern Province (1872), 915 Dorseyville Rd., Pittsburgh, Pa. 15238. 213 priests, 26 brothers.

Western Province (1964), 4626 Pennsylvania St., Denver, Colo. 80216. 79 priests, 3 brothers.

Holy Ghost, Missionaries of the, M.Sp.S.: Founded 1914, at Mexico City, Mexico, by Felix Rougier. General motherhouse, Mexico City; US headquarters, 4433 Santa Fe Ave., Vernon, Calif. 90058. Missionary work. 5 priests, 2 brothers.

Immaculate Heart Missioners (Missionhurst), C.I.C.M.: Founded 1862, by Very Rev. Theophile Verbist. General motherhouse, Rome, Italy; US province, 4651 N. 25th St., P.O. Box BB, Arlington, Va. 22207. Home and foreign mission work. 77 priests, 17 brothers.

Jesuits (Society of Jesus), S.J.: Founded 1534, in France, by St. Ignatius Loyola; in US, 1833. Generalate, Rome, Italy. Missionary, educational, literary work.

Maryland Province (1833), 5704 Roland Ave., Baltimore, Md. 21210. 499 priests, 56 brothers.

New York Province (1943), 501 E. Fordham Rd., Bronx, N.Y. 10458. 869 priests, 82 brothers.

Missouri Province (1863), 4511 W. Pine Blvd., St. Louis, Mo. 63108. 424 priests, 64 brothers.

New Orleans Province (1907), 6301 Strafford Pl., P.O. Box 6378, New Orleans, La. 70174. 308 priests, 48 brothers.

California Province (1909), College at Prospect Aves., P.O. Box 519, Los Gatos, Calif. 95030. 487 priests, 65 brothers.

New England Province (1926), 393 Commonwealth Ave., Boston, Mass. 02115. 756 priests, 52 brothers.

Chicago Province, 509 N. Oak Park Ave., Oak Park, Ill. 60302. 370 priests, 39 brothers.

Oregon Province (1932), 2222 N.W. Hoyt, Portland, Ore. 97210. 387 priests, 50 brothers.

Detroit Province (1955), 602 Boulevard Center Blvd., Cass at W. Grand Blvd., Detroit, Mich. 48202. 284 priests, 57 brothers.

Wisconsin Province (1955), 2120 W. Clybourn St., Suite 200, Milwaukee, Wis. 53233. 460 priests, 49 brothers.

Joseph, Congregation of St., C.S.J.: General motherhouse, Rome, Italy; US vice province, 551 W. O'Farrell St., San Pedro, Calif.

90731. Parochial, missionary, educational work. 15 priests, 5 brothers.

Joseph, Oblates of St., O.S.J.: Founded 1878, in Italy, by Bishop Joseph Marello. General motherhouse, Rome, Italy. Parochial, educational work.

Eastern Province, 28 Memorial Ave., Exeter, Pa. 18643. 14 priests, 3 brothers.

Western Province, 1333 58th St., Sacramento, Calif. 95819. 26 priests, 8 brothers.

Josephite Fathers, C.J.: General motherhouse, Ghent, Belgium; US foundation, 989 Brookside Ave., Santa Maria, Calif. 93454. 12 priests.

Josephite Fathers (St. Joseph's Society of the Sacred Heart), S.S.J.: Founded 1866, in England, by Cardinal Vaughan; in US, 1871. General motherhouse, 1130 N. Calvert St., Baltimore, Md. 21202. Work in Negro missions. 205 priests, 27 brothers.

LaSalette, Missionaries of Our Lady of, M.S.: Founded 1852, by Msgr. de Bruillard; in US, 1892. Motherhouse, Rome, Italy.

Our Lady of Seven Dolors Province (1933), P.O. Box 6127, Hartford, Conn. 06106. 135 priests, 35 brothers.

Immaculate Heart of Mary Province (1945), P.O. Box 538, Attleboro, Mass. 02703. 87 priests, 36 brothers.

Mary Queen Province (1961), 4650 S. Broadway, St. Louis, Mo. 63111. 86 priests, 8 brothers.

Mary Queen of Peace Vice Province (1967), 5270 N. Lake Dr., Milwaukee, Wis. 53217. 30 priests, 9 brothers.

Legionaries of Christ (Missionaries of the Sacred Heart of Jesus and the Sorrowful Virgin), L.C.: Founded 1941, in Mexico, by Rev. Maciel. General motherhouse, Rome, Italy; US novitiate, 393 Derby Ave., Orange, Conn. 06477. 7 priests.

Marian Fathers, M.I.C.: Founded 1673; US foundation, 1913. General motherhouse, Rome, Italy. Educational, parochial, mission, publication work.

St. Casimir Province (1930), 6336 S. Kilbourn Ave., Chicago, Ill. 60629. 50 priests, 8 brothers.

St. Stanislaus Kostka Province (1948), Eden Hill, Stockbridge, Mass. 01262. 25 priests, 14 brothers.

Marianists (Society of Mary; Brothers of Mary), S.M.: Founded 1817, at Bordeaux, France, by Rev William-Joseph Chaminade; in US, 1849. General motherhouse, Rome, Italy. Educational work.

Cincinnati Province (1849), 2765 Ridgeway Rd., Dayton, Ohio. 45419. 89 priests, 321 brothers.

St. Louis Province (1908), Marycliff, Glencoe, Mo. 63038. 81 priests, 323 brothers.

Pacific Province (1948), Cupertino, Calif. 95014. 36 priests, 153 brothers.

New York Province (1961), 4301 Roland Ave., Baltimore, Md. 21210. 36 priests, 120 brothers.

Mariannhill, Congregation of the Missionaries of, C.M.M.: Trappist monastery, begun in 1882 by Abbot Francis Pfanner in Natal, South Africa, became an independent modern congregation in 1909; in US, 1920. Generalate, Rome, Italy; US-Canadian headquarters, 23715 Ann Arbor Trail, Dearborn Heights, Mich. 48127. Foreign mission work. 20 priests, 5 brothers.

Marist Fathers (Society of Mary), S.M.: Founded 1816, at Lyons, France, by Jean Claude Colin; in US, 1863. General motherhouse, Rome, Italy. Educational, foreign mission, pastoral work.

Washington Province (1924), 220 Taylor St. N.E., Washington D.C. 20017. 118 priests, 4 brothers.

Northeastern Province (1924), 72 Beacon St., Chestnut Hill, Mass. 02167. 125 priests, 16 brothers.

San Francisco Western Province (1961), 625 Pine St., San Francisco, Calif. 94108. 35 priests, 7 brothers.

Mary Immaculate, Oblates of, O.M.I.: Founded 1816, in France, by Charles Joseph Eugene de Mazenod; in US, 1849. General motherhouse, Rome, Italy. Educational, mission work.

Southern US Province (1904), Room 211, 1015 Jackson-Keller Rd., San Antonio, Tex. 98213. 256 priests, 20 brothers.

Our Lady of Hope, Eastern Province (1883), 350 Jamaicaway, Boston, Mass. 02130. 226 priests, 12 brothers.

St. John the Baptist Province (1921), 216 Nesmith St., Lowell, Mass. 01852. 160 priests, 27 brothers.

Central Province (1924), 104 N. Mississippi River Blvd., St. Paul, Minn. 55104. 175 priests, 25 brothers.

Western Province (1953), 290 Lenox Ave., Oakland, Calif. 94610. 64 priests, 7 brothers.

Italian Province, US foundation, St. Nicholas Church, Palisades Park, N.J. 07650. 5 priests.

Maryknoll Fathers (Catholic Foreign Mission Society of America), M.M.: Founded 1911, in US, by Frs. Thomas F. Price and James A. Walsh. General Center, Maryknoll, N.Y. 10545. 868 priests, 123 brothers.

Mekhitarist Order of Vienna, C.M.Vd.: Established 1773. General headquarters, Vienna, Austria; US addresses, Our Lady Queen of Martyrs Church, 1327 Pleasant Ave., Los Angeles, Calif. 90033 and Holy Cross Church, 100 Mt. Auburn St., Cambridge, Mass. 02138. Work among Armenians in US.

Mercedarians (Order of Our Lady of Mercy), O.de M.: Founded 1218, in Spain, by St. Peter Nolasco. General motherhouse, Rome, Italy; US headquarters, LeRoy, N.Y. 14482. 13 priests, 2 brothers.

Mercy, Congregation of Priests of (Fathers of Mercy), C.P.M.: Founded 1808, in France, by Rev. Jean Baptiste Rauzan; in US, 1839.

General motherhouse, Cold Spring, N.Y. 10516. Mission work.

Mill Hill Missionaries (St. Joseph's Society for Foreign Missions), M.H.M.: Founded 1866, in England, by Cardinal Vaughan; in US, 1951. General motherhouse, London, England; American headquarters, Albany, N.Y. 12203. 38 priests, 5 brothers.

Missionaries of the Holy Apostles, M.Ss.A.: Founded 1962, Washington, D.C., by Eusebe M. Menard. General headquarters, 1335 Quincy St. N.E., Washington, D.C. 20017. 31 priests, 3 brothers (in North and South America).

Missionary Fathers of St. Charles, Congregation of the, C.S.: Founded 1887, at Piacenza, Italy, by Bishop John Baptist Scalabrini. General motherhouse, Rome, Italy.

St. Charles Borromeo Province (1888), 27 Carmine St., New York, N.Y. 10014. 86 priests, 5 brothers.

St. John Baptist Province (1903), 546 N. East Ave., Oak Park, Ill. 60302. 74 priests, 4 brothers.

Monks of the Brotherhood of St. Francis (Monks of New Skete, Byzantine Rite): Founded 1966, in US. New Skete Monastery, Cambridge, N.Y. 12816. 8 monks.

Montfort Fathers (Missionaries of the Company of Mary), S.M.M.: Founded 1715, by St. Louis Marie Grignon de Montfort; in US, 1948. General motherhouse, Rome, Italy; US headquarters, 101-18 104th St., Ozone Park, N.Y. 11416. Mission work. 63 priests, 7 brothers.

Oratorian Fathers (Congregation of the Oratory of St. Philip Neri), C.O.: Founded 1575, at Rome, by St. Philip Neri. Central administration, Rome, Italy; a confederation of autonomous houses. US addresses: P.O. Box 11586, Rock Hill, S.C. 29730; P.O. Box 1688, Monterey, Calif. 93940; 4040 Bigelow Blvd., Pittsburgh, Pa. 15213; P.O. Box 211, Yarnell, Ariz. 85362, 24 priests, 5 brothers.

Pallottines (Society of the Catholic Apostolate), S.A.C.: Founded 1835, at Rome, by St. Vincent Pallotti. General motherhouse, Rome, Italy. Charitable, educational, parochial, mission work.

Immaculate Conception Province (1952), 309 N. Paca St., Baltimore, Md. 21201. 34 priests, 12 brothers.

Mother of God Province (1946), 5424 W. Blue Mound Rd., Milwaukee, Wis. 53208. 41 priests, 7 brothers.

Irish Province, US address: 3352 4th St., Wyandotte, Mich. 48192. 30 priests.

Christ the King Province (Poland), 303 Goundry St., North Tonawanda, N.Y. 14120. 9 priests, 1 brother.

Queen of Apostles Province (1909), 448 E. 116th St., New York, N.Y. 10029. 16 priests.

Paraclete, Servants of the, s.P.: Founded 1947, Santa Fe, N.M., archdiocese. General motherhouse, Rome, Italy; US motherhouse, Jemez Springs, N.M. 87025. Devoted to care of priests. 48 priests, 9 brothers.

Paris Foreign Missions Society, M.E.P.: Founded 1662, at Paris, France. Headquarters, Paris, France; US establishment, 930 Ashbury St., San Francisco, Calif. 94117. Mission work and training of native clergy. 3.

Passionists (Congregation of the Passion), C.P.: Founded 1720, in Italy, by St. Paul of the Cross. General motherhouse, Rome, Italy.

St. Paul of the Cross Province (1852), 1901 West St., Union City, N.J. 07087. 403 priests, 60 brothers.

Holy Cross Province (Western Province), 5700 N. Harlem Ave., Chicago, Ill. 60631. 198 priests, 27 brothers.

Patrick's Missionary Society, St., S.P.S.: Founded 1932, at Wicklow, Ireland, by Msgr. Patrick Whitney; in US, 1953. International headquarters, Kiltegan Co., Wicklow, Ireland. US foundations: 35 S. 29th St., Camden, N.J. 08105; 70 Edgewater Rd., Cliffside Park, N.J. 07010; 19536 Eric Dr., Saratoga, Calif. 95070; 1347 W. Granville Ave., Chicago, Ill. 60626. 26 priests.

Pauline Fathers (Order of St. Paul the First Hermit), O.S.P.: Founded 1215; established in US, 1955. General motherhouse, Czestochowa, Jasna Gora, Poland; US headquarters, P.O. Box 151, Doylestown, Pa. 18901. 15 priests, 11 brothers.

Pauline Fathers (Society of St. Paul for the Apostolate of Communications), S.S.P.: Founded 1914, by Very Rev. James Alberione; in US, 1932. Motherhouse, Rome, Italy; American province, Old Lakeshore Rd., Derby, N.Y. 14047. 16 priests, 38 brothers.

Paulists (Missionary Society of St. Paul the Apostle), C.S.P.: Founded 1858, in New York, by Fr. Isaac Thomas Hecker. General offices, 86 Dromore Rd., Scarsdale, N.Y. 10583. Missionary, ecumenical, pastoral work. 229 priests.

Piarists (Order of the Pious Schools), Sch.P.: Founded 1617, at Rome, Italy, by St. Joseph Calasanctius. General motherhouse, Rome, Italy. American headquarters, 1339 Monroe St. N.E., Washington, D.C. 20017. Educational work. 58 priests, 2 brothers.

Pontifical Institute for Foreign Missions, P.I.M.E.: Founded 1850, in Italy, at request of Pope Pius XI. General motherhouse, Rome, Italy; US headquarters, 9800 Oakland Ave., Detroit, Mich. 48211. Foreign mission work. 42 priests, 4 brothers.

Precious Blood, Society of, C.Pp.S.: Founded 1815, in Italy, by St. Gaspar del Bufalo. General motherhouse, Rome, Italy.

Cincinnati Province, 3500 Montgomery Rd., Cincinnati, Ohio. 45207. 272 priests, 71 brothers.

Kansas City Province, Ruth Ewing Rd., Liberty, Mo. 64068. 104 priests, 9 brothers.

Pacific Province, 24 Ursuline Rd., Santa

Rosa, Calif. 95401. 32 priests, 2 brothers.

Atlantic Vicariate, 65 Highland Ave., Rochester, N.Y. 14620. 17 priests, 2 brothers.

Premonstratensians (Order of the Canons Regular of Premontre; Norbertines), O. Praem.: Founded 1120, at Premontre, France, by St. Norbert. Generalate, Rome, Italy. Educational, parish work.

St. Norbert Abbey, 1016 N. Broadway, DePere, Wis. 54115. 127 priests, 7 brothers.

Daylesford Abbey, 220 S. Valley Rd., Paoli, Pa. 19301. 56 priests, 5 brothers.

St. Michael's Seminary and Novitiate, 1042 Star Route, Orange, Calif. 92667. 8 priests.

Providence, Sons of Divine, F.D.P.: Founded 1893, at Tortona, Italy, by Don Aloysius Orione; in US, 1933. General motherhouse, Tortona, Italy; US address, 111 Orient Ave., E. Boston, Mass. 02128.

Redemptorists (Congregation of the Most Holy Redeemer), C.SS.R.: Founded 1732, in Italy, by St. Alphonsus Mary Liguori. General motherhouse, Rome, Italy. Mission work.

Baltimore Province (1850), 7509 Shore Rd., Brooklyn, N.Y. 21209. 618 priests, 74 brothers.

St. Louis Province (1875), Box 6, Glenview, Ill. 60025. 364 priests, 58 brothers.

Oakland Province (1952), 3696 Clay St., San Francisco, Calif. 94118. 91 priests, 13 brothers.

New Orleans Vice-Province, 1527 3rd St., New Orleans, La., 70130.

Resurrectionists (Priests of the Congregation of the Resurrection), C.R.: Founded 1836, in France, under direction of Bogdan Janski. Motherhouse, Rome, Italy; US address, 5235 W. Belden Ave., Chicago, Ill. 60618. Parochial, educational, mission work. 124 priests, 7 brothers.

Rosminians (Institute of Charity), I.C.: Founded 1828, in Italy, by Antonio Rosmini-Serbati. General motherhouse, Rome, Italy; US address, 2327 W. Heading Ave., Peoria, Ill. 61604. Charitable work. 30 priests.

Sacred Heart, Missionaries of the, M.S.C.: Founded 1854, by Rev. Jules Chevelier. General motherhouse, Rome, Italy; US province, 305 S. Lake St., P.O. Box 270, Aurora, Ill. 60507. 111 priests, 36 brothers.

Sacred Heart of Jesus, Priests of the, S.C.J.: Founded 1877, in France. General motherhouse, Rome, Italy; US headquarters, Sacred Heart Monastery, Hales Corners, Wis. 53130. Educational, preaching, mission work. 127 priests, 69 brothers.

Sacred Hearts, Fathers of the (Picpus Fathers), SS.CC.: Founded 1805, in France, by Fr. Coudrin. General motherhouse, Rome, Italy. Mission, educational work.

Eastern Province (1946), 3 Adams St. (Box 111), Fairhaven, Mass. 02719. 99 priests, 9 brothers.

Western Province (1970), 3 St. James Pk., Los Angeles, Calif. 90018. 41 priests, 2 brothers.

Hawaiian Province, Box 797, Kaneohe, Oahu, Hawaii 96744. 66 priests, 12 brothers.

Sacred Hearts of Jesus and Mary, Missionaries of the, M.SS.CC.: Founded at Naples, Italy, by Ven. Gaetano Errico. General motherhouse, Rome, Italy; US headquarters, 2249 Shore Rd., Linwood, N.J. 08221. 8 priests.

Salesians of St. John Bosco (Society of St. Francis de Sales), S.D.B.: Founded 1841, by St. John (Don) Bosco. General motherhouse, Rome, Italy.

St. Philip the Apostle Province (1902), 148 Main St., New Rochelle, N.Y. 10802. 175 priests, 72 brothers.

San Francisco Province (1926), 1100 Franklin St., San Francisco, Calif. 94109. 96 priests, 51 brothers.

Salvatorians (Society of the Divine Savior), S.D.S.: Founded 1881, in Rome, by Fr. Francis Jordan; in US, 1896. General motherhouse, Rome, Italy; US province, 1735 Hi-Mount Blvd., Milwaukee, Wis. 53208. Educational, parochial, mission work; campus ministries, chaplaincies. 149 priests, 83 brothers.

Scalabrinians: See Missionary Fathers of St. Charles, Congregation of the.

Servites (Order of Friar Servants of Mary), O.S.M.: Founded 1237, at Florence, Italy, by Seven Holy Founders. Generalate, Rome, Italy. General apostolic ministry.

Eastern Province (1967) 3401 S. Home Ave., Berwyn, Ill. 60402. 124 priests, 32 brothers.

Western Province (1967), 5210 Somerset St., Buena Park, Calif. 90621. 58 priests, 12 brothers.

Somascan Fathers, C.R.S.: Founded 1534, at Somasca, Italy, by St. Jerome Emilian. General motherhouse, Rome, Italy; US addresses: 628 Hanover St., Manchester, N.H. 03104; Pine Haven Boys Center, River Rd., Suncook, N.H. 03275. 6 priests, 2 brothers.

Sons of Mary Missionary Society: Founded 1952, in the Boston archdiocese, by Rev. Edward F. Garesche, S.J. Headquarters, 567 Salem End Rd., Framingham, Mass. 01701. Dedicated to health of the sick; medical, pastoral and social work in home and foreign missions. 24 professed members.

Stigmatine Fathers and Brothers (Congregation of the Sacred Stigmata), C.S.S.: Founded 1816, by Ven. Gaspare Bertoni. General motherhouse, Rome, Italy; US headquarters, 554 Lexington St., Waltham, Mass. 01254. Parish work, Christian living center, information center. 94 priests, 9 brothers.

Sulpicians (Society of Priests of St. Sulpice), S.S.: Founded 1641, at Paris, by Rev. Jean Jacques Olier. General motherhouse, Paris, France; US province, 5408 Roland Ave., Baltimore, Md. 21210. Education of seminarians and priests. 172 priests.

Theatines (Congregation of Clerics Regular): C.R.: Founded 1524, at Rome, by St. Cajetan. General motherhouse, Rome, Italy;

US headquarters, 1050 S. Birch St., Denver, Colo. 80222. 25 priests.

Trappists: See Cistercians of the Strict Observance.

Trinitarians (Order of the Most Holy Trinity), O.SS.T.: Founded 1198, by St. John of Matha. General motherhouse, Rome, Italy; US headquarters, Park Heights Ave., Box 5742, Baltimore, Md. 21208. 41 priests, 36 brothers.

Trinity, Missionary Servants of the Most Holy, S.T.: Founded 1929, by Fr. Thomas Augustine Judge. Generalate, 503 Rock Creek Church Rd. N.W., Washington, D.C. 20010. Home mission work. 157 priests, 50 brothers.

Verona Fathers (Sons of the Sacred Heart of Jesus), F.S.C.J.: Founded 1885, in Italy. General motherhouse, Rome, Italy; US headquarters, 8108 Beechmont Ave., Cincinnati, Ohio 45230. Mission work. 45 priests, 4 brothers.

Viatorian Fathers (Clerics of St. Viator), C.S.V.: Founded 1831, in France, by Fr. Louis Joseph Querbes. General motherhouse, Rome, Italy: US headquarters, 1212 E. Euclid, Arlington Hts., Ill. 60004. Educational work. 149 priests, 20 brothers.

Vincentians (Congregation of the Mission; Lazarists), C.M.: Founded 1625, in Paris, by St. Vincent de Paul; in US, 1867. General motherhouse, Rome, Italy. Educational work.

Eastern Province (1867), 500 E. Chelten Ave., Philadelphia, Pa. 19144. 332 priests, 16 brothers.

Western Province (1888), 1849 Cass Ave., St. Louis, Mo. 63106. 229 priests, 24 brothers.

Utica Vice-Province (1903), 10475 Cosby Manor Rd., Utica, N.Y. 13502. 54 priests, 7 brothers.

American Italian Branch, Our Lady of Pompei Church, 3600 Claremont St., Baltimore, Md. 21224. 6 priests.

American Spanish Branch (Barcelona, Spain), St. Peter's Rectory, 117 Warren St., Brooklyn, N.Y. 11201. 12 priests.

American Spanish Branch (Zaragoza, Spain), Holy Agony Church, 1834 3rd Ave., New York, N.Y. 10029. 16 priests.

Los Angeles Vice-Province (1958), 649 W. Adams Blvd., Los Angeles, Calif. 90007. 70 priests, 3 brothers.

New Orleans Vice-Province (1958), P.O. Box 337, Beaumont, Tex. 77709. 62 priests, 1 brother.

Vocationist Fathers (Society of Divine Vocations), S.D.V.: Founded 1920, in Italy; in US, 1962. General motherhouse, Naples, Italy; US address, 170 Broad St., Newark, N.J. 07104.

White Fathers, W.F.: Founded 1868, at Algiers, by Cardinal C.M.A. Lavigerie. General motherhouse, Rome, Italy; US headquarters, 777 Belvidere Ave., Plainfield, N.J. 07062. Foreign missions. 57 priests, 9 brothers.

Xaverian Missionary Fathers, S.X.: Founded 1895, by Archbishop Conforti, at Parma, Italy. General motherhouse, Rome, Italy; U.S. province, 12 Helene Ct., Wayne, N.J. 07470. Foreign mission work. 26 priests, 1 brother.

INSTITUTES OF BROTHERS

Alexian Brothers, C.F.A.: Founded 14th century in western Germany and Belgium during the Black Plague. Motherhouse, Aachen, Germany; generalate, Signal Mountain, Tenn. 37377. Hospital and general health work. 229.

Charity, Brothers of, F.C.: Founded 1807, in Belgium, by Canon Peter J. Triest. General motherhouse, Rome, Italy: American District House, 7720 Doe Lane, Philadelphia, Pa. 19118. Charitable, educational work.

Christian Brothers, Congregation of, C.F.C. (formerly Christian Brothers of Ireland): Founded 1802 at Waterford, Ireland, by Edmund Ignatius Rice. General motherhouse, Rome, Italy. Educational work.

American Province, Eastern US (1916), 21 Pryor Terr., New Rochelle, N.Y. 10801. 354.

American Province, Western US (1966), Brother Rice Provincialate, 1500 Benicia Rd., Vallejo, Calif. 94590. 186.

Christian Instruction, Brothers of (La Mennais Brothers), F.I.C.: Founded 1817, at Ploermel, France, by Abbe Jean Marie de la Mennais and Abbe Gabriel Deshayes. General motherhouse, Rome, Italy; American province, Notre Dame Institute, Alfred, Me. 04002. 114.

Christian Schools, Brothers of the (Christian Brothers), F.S.C.: Founded 1680, at Reims, France, by St. Jean Baptiste de la Salle. General motherhouse, Rome, Italy; US Conference, 100 De La Salle Dr., P.O. Box 356, Lockport, Ill. 60441. Educational, charitable work. 1,919.

Cross, Congregation of Holy, C.S.C.: Founded 1837, in France, by Rev. Basil Moreau; US province, 1841. Generalate, Rome, Italy. Educational work.

Midwest Province (1841), Box 460, Notre Dame, Ind. 46556. 372.

Southwest Province (1956), St. Edward's University, Austin, Tex. 78704. 188.

Eastern Province (1956), 24 Ricardo St., West Haven, Conn. 06516. 216.

Francis, Brothers of Poor of St. C.F.P.: Founded 1857. Motherhouse, Aachen, Germany; US province, Box 120, Mt. Alverno, Fayetteville, Ohio. 45118. Educational work, especially with poor and emotionally disturbed youth. 90.

Francis Xavier, Brothers of St. (Xaverian Brothers), C.F.X.: Founded 1839, in Belgium, by Theodore J. Ryken. Generalate, Rome, Italy. Educational work.

Sacred Heart Province, 10516 Summit Ave., Kensington, Md. 20795. 265.

St. Joseph Province, 704 Brush Hill Rd., Milton, Mass. 02186. 235.

Franciscan Brothers of Brooklyn, O.S.F.: Founded in Ireland; established at Brooklyn, 1858. Generalate, 135 Remsen St., Brooklyn, N.Y. 11201. Educational work. 190.

Franciscan Brothers of the Holy Cross, F.F.S.C.: Founded 1862, in Germany. Generalate, Hausen, Linz Rhein, Germany; US region, St. James Trade School, R.R. 1, Springfield, Ill. 62707. Educational work. 24.

Franciscan Missionary Brothers of the Sacred Heart of Jesus, O.S.F.: Founded 1927, in the St. Louis, Mo., archdiocese. Motherhouse, R.R. 3, Eureka, Mo. 63025. Care of aged, infirm, homeless men and boys. 28.

Good Shepherd, Society of Brothers of the, B.G.S.: Founded 1951, by Bro. Mathias Barrett. Motherhouse, P.O. Box 389, Albuquerque, N.M. 87103. Operate shelters and refuges for aged and homeless men; homes for handicapped men and boys, alcoholic rehabilitation center. 56.

Holy Eucharist, Brothers of the, F.S.E.: Founded in US, 1957. Generalate, P.O. Box 178, Cottonport, La. 71327. Teaching, social, clerical, nursing work.

Immaculate Heart of Mary, Brothers of the, F.I.C.M.: Founded 1948, at Steubenville, Ohio, by Bishop John K. Mussio. Motherhouse, 609 N. 7th St., Steubenville, Ohio 43952. Educational, charitable work. 18.

Immaculate Heart of Mary, Brothers of Charity: Founded 1958, in US. Motherhouse, 201 Highway 60, Riverside, Calif. 92507.

John of God, Hospitaller Order of St., O.H.: Founded 1537, in Spain. General motherhouse, Rome, Italy; US headquarters, 2035 W. Adams Blvd., Los Angeles, Calif. 90018. Nursing work and related fields. 42.

Joseph, Brothers of St., F.S.J.: Founded 1962, in US. Motherhouse, Rt. 13, Box 767, Oklahoma City, Okla. 73132.

Marist Brothers, F.M.S.: Founded 1817, in France, by Bl. Marcellin Champagnat. General motherhouse, Rome, Italy; US address, 1044 Northern Blvd., Roslyn, N.Y. 11576. Educational, social, catechetical work. 228.

Mercy, Brothers of, F.M.M.: Founded 1856, in Germany. General motherhouse, Montabaur, Germany. American headquarters, 4520 Ransom Rd., Clarence, N.Y. 14031. Hospital work. 39.

Mercy, Brothers of Our Lady of, C.F.M.M.: Founded 1844, in The Netherlands by Abp. J. Zwijsen. Generalate, Tilburg, The Netherlands; US region, 2336 South "C" St., Oxnard, Calif. 93030. 15.

Patrician Brothers (Brothers of St. Patrick), F.S.P.: Founded 1808, in Ireland, by Bishop Daniel Delaney; US novitiate, 7820 Bolsa Ave., Midway City, Calif. 92655. Educational work. 15.

Pius X, Brothers of St.: Founded 1952, at La Crosse, Wis., by Bishop John P. Treacy. Motherhouse, Box 438, DeSoto, Wis. 54624.

Education, health fields, agriculture, religious education, social work. 14.

Rosary, Brothers of the Holy, F.S.R.: Founded 1956, in US. Address, 101 Boynton Lane, Reno, Nev. 89502. 9.

Sacred Heart, Brothers of the, S.C.: Founded 1821, in France, by Rev. Andre Coindre. General motherhouse, Rome, Italy, Educational work.

New Orleans Province (1847), P.O. Box 89, Bay St. Louis, Miss. 39520. 153.

New England Province (1945), "Cor Jesu Terrace," Pascoag, R.I. 02859. 302.

New York Province (1960), R.D. 1, Box 215, Belvidere, N.J. 07823. 71.

MEN SUPERIORS

The Conference of Major Superiors of Men of the USA is a consultative board for discussion of the affairs of men religious in this country, and a liaison body for establishing and maintaining contact among religious institutes and with the Holy See, bishops, diocesan clergy, and Catholic and civic associations. The conference, which was formed in 1956, was officially established Mar. 23, 1960, by decree of the Congregation for Religious and Secular Institutes.

The general objective of the conference is to promote the spiritual and apostolic welfare of religious priests and brothers in the US.

Conference membership consists of 255 major superiors of institutes with a combined total of approximately 40,000 members.

The Rev. Joseph Francis, S.V.D., is president of the conference. The executive secretary is Brother Thomas Page More, C.F.X.

The national secretariat is located at 1330 New Hampshire Ave. N.W., Suite 114, Washington, D.C. 20036.

Approximately 140 members attended the 17th annual assembly of the conference in June, 1974, in Chicago. "The American Religious as Evangelizer" was the subject of the meeting, at which attention was directed to the theme of the 1974 assembly of the Synod of Bishops as it applied to American religious.

The conference passed a resolution asking for humane treatment of political prisoners and the protection of human rights in Chile. A second resolution called on the Congregation for Religious and Secular Institutes to reconsider an earlier decision excluding brother members of clerical institutes from the office of superior.

BROTHERS' ASSEMBLY

The National Assembly of Religious Brothers was founded in 1972 as a grassroots organization open to members of all-brother institutes as well as mixed institutes of priests and brothers. It is a service organization for its members and those affected by their apostolates.

The primary objectives of the assembly are

"to encourage actively the development of the religious life of its members and of all brothers, to be concerned and involved with the needs of the Church and society, to establish realistic and effective means of communication and cooperation" with other church groups, and to seek "effective representation for its members in matters concerning their religious and professional lives."

Membership in the assembly is open to the 9,700 brothers in the U.S. involved in education, social work, parish ministry, health serv-

ices, clerical and administrative work, and a wide variety of other service-oriented tasks.

The national office is located at 11601 Georgia Ave., Wheaton, Md. 20902.

Marist Brother Dominic Lozeau of Poughkeepsie, N.Y., was elected president of the assembly at its third annual convention June 20 to 23, 1974, in St. Louis.

"Prayer in the Life of the Religious Brother" was the theme of the 1974 convention, which was attended by representatives of 39 institutes in the U.S. and Canada.

MEMBERSHIP OF RELIGIOUS INSTITUTES OF MEN

Below are world membership statistics from *Annuario Pontificio, 1974*, of institutes of men of pontifical right with 500 or more members; the number of priests is in parentheses. Also listed are institutes with less than 500 members with houses in the U.S.

Most of the institutes reported decreases in membership between 1972 and 1973. Institutes which did not report any change in membership are indicated by an asterisk.

Jesuits (20,908)	30,860
Franciscans (Friars Minor) (15,762)	23,301
Salesians* (11,471)	20,423
Brothers of Christian Schools*	14,517
Franciscans (Capuchins)* (9,536)	13,606
Benedictines* (7,058)	10,819
Marist Brothers	8,181
Dominicans (6,169)	8,086
Redemptorists* (5,432)	7,540
Oblates of Mary Immaculate* (5,287)	6,029
Society of the Divine Word (3,176)	5,319
Vincentians (4,085)	5,197
Holy Spirit, Congregation (3,449)	4,441
Franciscans (Conventuals)* (2,868)	4,259
Augustinians (2,831)	3,847
White Fathers* (3,001)	3,604
Discalced Carmelites (2,497)	3,577
Passionists* (2,704)	3,568
Trappists* (1,671)	3,357
Christian Brothers	3,317
Claretians (2,044)	3,011
Priests of the Sacred Heart (2,002)	2,870
Missionaries of the Sacred Heart of Jesus (2,057)	2,846
Marianists* (588)	2,827
Holy Cross Fathers* (1,077)	2,638
Brothers of the Sacred Heart* (10)	2,373
Carmelites (Ancient Observance)* (1,754)	2,371
Marists* (1,701)	2,266
Hospitallers of St. John of God (116)	2,020
Pallottines* (1,430)	2,020
Piarists (1,507)	1,917
Picpus Fathers (1,441)	1,825
Brothers of Christian Instruction of Ploermel	1,773
Verona Fathers (1,094)	1,745
Congregation of the Immaculate Heart of Mary (1,430)	1,717
Brothers of Christian Instruction of St. Gabriel* (2)	1,703

Montfort Fathers* (1,258)	1,683
Society of African Missions* (1,408)	1,643
Servants of Mary* (1,029)	1,642
Assumptionists (1,219)	1,506
Cistercians (Common Observance) (974)	1,480
Viatorians (506)	1,477
Premonstratensians (1,189)	1,452
Augustinians (Recollects) (1,062)	1,370
Blessed Sacrament Fathers (896)	1,338
Salvatorians* (863)	1,280
Pious Society of St. Paul (510)	1,213
Canons Regular of St. Augustine*	1,190
Brothers of Charity	1,162
Mill Hill Missionaries* (989)	1,150
Oblates of St. Francis de Sales* (774)	1,136
Consolata Fathers* (830)	1,132
Carmelites of BVM* (644)	1,128
Missionaries of Holy Family (833)	1,123
Ministers of Sick (Camillians) (686)	1,084
Maryknollers* (869)	1,047
Columbans	1,034
Sons of Divine Providence* (736)	1,032
La Salette Missionaries* (718)	1,004
Mercedarians* (616)	963
Franciscans (Third Order Regular) (605)	894
Xaverian Missionary Fathers (596)	854
Pontifical Institute for Foreign Missions* (614)	830
Brothers of Immaculate Conception	818
Congregation of St. Joseph (551)	782
Brothers of Our Lady of Mercy	779
Scalabrinians (599)	766
Paris Foreign Mission Society* (737)	756
Legionaries of Christ (83)	709
Crosier Fathers (474)	678
Sulpicians* (650)	650
Miss. of Most Precious Blood* (492)	647
Brothers of Our Lady of Lourdes	616
Xaverian Brothers	607
Eudists (515)	599
Mariannhill Missionaries (335)	576
Third Order Capuchin Religious of Our Lady of Sorrows* (259)	551
Servants of Charity (374)	532
Trinitarians (390)	529
Barnabites (401)	506
Congr. of St. Basil (Canada)* (441)	502
St. Patrick's Mission Society* (335)	495
Resurrectionists* (353)	489

Oratorians (395)	477
Carthusians (270)	457
Stigmatine Fathers* (360)	452
Rosminians (314)	438
Somascan Fathers (268)	423
Priests of the Sacred Heart of Jesus (338)	411
Bethlehem Missionaries* (299)	395
Society of Christ* (224)	391
Missionaries of Holy Spirit (197)	382
Oblates of St. Joseph* (274)	375
Marian Fathers* (265)	361
Paulists* (249)	315
Alexian Brothers	260
Josephite Fathers* (S.S.J.) (209)	260
Missionary Servants of Most	

Holy Trinity (209)	260
Atonement Friars (138)	251
Vocationist Fathers* (156)	226
Order of St. Paul the First Hermit* (118)	218
Sylvestrine Benedictines (138)	211
Bros. of Poor of St. Francis	182
Sons of Holy Family* (112)	173
Brothers of Mercy	171
Theatines (120)	164
Josephites (C.J.) (138)	159
Basilian Salvatorian Fathers* (98)	135
Franciscan Bros. of Holy Cross	126
Priests of St. Edmund* (101)	124
Glenmary Missioners (76)	111
Camaldolese (28)	88
Servants of Holy Paraclete* (45)	53

RELIGIOUS INSTITUTES OF WOMEN IN THE UNITED STATES

(Sources: Catholic Almanac survey, *Official Catholic Directory.*)

The number in parentheses indicates the number of professed members, as of Jan. 1, 1973, of institutes with more than 50 members in the U.S.

Adorers, Handmaids of the Blessed Sacrament and of Charity, Sisters, A.A.S.C.: Founded 1850, in Spain; in US, 1961. General motherhouse, Madrid, Spain; US foundation, 2637 Homedale St., San Diego, Calif. 92139.

Africa, Missionary Sisters of Our Lady of (White Sisters), S.A.: Founded 1869, at Algiers, Algeria, by Cardinal Lavigerie; in US, 1929. General motherhouse, Frascati, Italy; US headquarters, 5335 16th St., N.W., Washington, D.C. 20011. Medical, educational, catechetical and social work in Africa.(50)

African Sisters of Our Lady of Good Counsel, O.L.G.S.: Founded 1939, in Africa; in US, 1962. General motherhouse, Uganda; US foundation, 783 Grove St., Worcester, Mass. 01605.

Agnes, Sisters of St., C.S.A.: Founded 1858, in US, by Caspar Rehrl. General motherhouse, 390 E. Division St., Fond du Lac, Wis. 54935. Educational, hospital, social work. (783)

Ann, Sisters of St., S.S.A.: Founded 1834, in Italy; in US, 1952. General motherhouse, Turin, Italy; US headquarters, Mount St. Ann, Ebensburg, Pa. 15931.

Anne, Sisters of St., S.S.A.: Founded 1850, at Vaudreuil, Que., Canada; in US, 1866. General motherhouse, Lachine, Que., Canada; US address, 720 Boston Post Rd., Marlboro, Mass. 01752. Educational, social work. (301)

Anthony, Missionary Servants of St., M.S.S.A.: Founded 1929, in US, by Rev. Peter Baque. General motherhouse, 100 Peter Baque Rd., San Antonio, Tex. 78209. Social work.

Apostolate, Sisters Auxiliaries of the, A.A.: Founded 1903, in Canada; in US, 1911. General motherhouse, 689 Maple Terr., Monongah, W. Va. 26554. Educational, social work.

Assumption, Little Sisters of the, L.S.A.: Founded 1865, in France; in US, 1891. General motherhouse, Paris, France; US motherhouse, 1195 Lexington Ave., New York, N.Y. 10028. Social work. (71)

Assumption, Oblate Sisters of the, O.A.: Founded in France; in US, 1956. US address, 1015 Pleasant St., Worcester, Mass. 01602.

Assumption, Religious of the, R.A.: Founded 1839, in France; in US, 1919. General motherhouse, Paris, France; US novitiate, 3480 W. Schoolhouse Lane, Germantown, Philadelphia, Pa. 19144. Educational work.

Assumption of the Blessed Virgin, Sisters of the, S.A.S.V.: Founded 1853, in Canada; in US, 1891. General motherhouse, Nicolet, Que., Canada; American province, North Main St., Petersham, Mass. 01366. Educational, mission, social work. (253)

Basil the Great, Sisters of the Order of St. (Munhall Byzantine Rite), O.S.B.M.: Founded fourth century, by St. Basil the Great. Motherhouse, Mount St. Macrina. West National Pike, Uniontown, Pa. 15401. Educational, social work. (140)

Basil the Great, Sisters of the Order of St. (Ukrainian Byzantine Rite), O.S.B.M.: Founded fourth century, in Cappadocia, by St. Basil the Great; in US, 1911. Generalate, Rome, Italy; US motherhouse, 710 Fox Chase Rd., Philadelphia, Pa. 19111. Educational, social work. (119)

Benedictine Nuns of the Primitive Observance, O.S.B.; Founded c. 529, in Italy; in US, 1948. US motherhouse, Regina Laudis Monastery, Bethlehem, Conn. 06751. Cloistered.

Benedictine Sisters, O.S.B.: Founded c. 529, in Italy; in US, 1852. General motherhouse, Eichstatt, Bavaria, Germany. US addresses: St. Vincent's Archabbey, Latrobe, Pa. 15650; St. Walburga Convent, Boulder, Colo. 80302. (59)

Benedictine Sisters (Bedford, N.H.), O.S.B.: Founded in US, 1957. Regina Pacis, 75 Wallace Rd., Bedford, N.H. 03102.

Benedictine Sisters, Missionary, O.S.B.: Founded 1885. General motherhouse, Tutzing, Bavaria; US motherhouse, 300 N. 18th St., Norfolk, Nebr. 68701. (88)

Benedictine Sisters, Olivetan, O.S.B.: Founded 1887, in US. General motherhouse, 223 E. Jackson Ave., Jonesboro, Ark. 72401. Educational, hospital work. (108)

Benedictine Sisters of Perpetual Adoration of Pontifical Jurisdiction, Congregation of the, O.S.B.: Founded 529, in Italy; in US, 1874. General motherhouse, 8300 Morganford Rd., St. Louis, Mo. 63123. (248)

Benedictine Sisters of Pontifical Jurisdiction, O.S.B.: Founded c. 529, in Italy. No general motherhouse in US. Three congregations:

Congregation of St. Scholastica (1922). Pres., Sister Joan Chittister, O.S.B., St. Benedict Convent, 706 W. First St., Oil City, Pa. 16301. Seventeen motherhouses in US. (1,996)

Congregation of St. Gertrude the Great (1937). St. Scholastica Convent, Fort Smith, Ark. 72901. Thirteen motherhouses in US. (1,873)

Congregation of St. Benedict (1947). St. Benedict's Priory, St. Joseph, Mo. 56374. Seven motherhouses in US. (1,901)

Bethany, Congregation of Oblates of, C.O.B.: Founded 1902 in France; in US, 1959. Motherhouse, Canada; US address: 4538 Lindell Blvd., St. Louis, Mo. 63108.

Bethany, Sisters of, C.V.D.: Founded 1928, in El Salvador; in US 1949. US address: 850 N. Hobart Blvd., Los Angeles, Calif. 90029.

Bethlemita Sisters, Daughters of the Sacred Heart of Jesus, S.C.I.F.: Founded 1861, in Guatemala. Motherhouse, Bogota, Colombia; US address, 330 W. Pembroke St., Dallas, Tex. 75208.

Blessed Virgin Mary, Institute of the (Loreto Sisters), I.B.V.M.: Founded 17th century in Bavaria; in US, 1954. General motherhouse, Dublin, Ireland; US address, 6351 N. 27th Ave., Phoenix, Ariz. 85017.

Blessed Virgin Mary, Institute of the (Sisters of Loretto), I.B.V.M.: Founded 1609, in Belgium; in US, 1880. US address, Box 508, Wheaton, Ill. 60187. Educational work. (464, total membership)

Bon Secours, Sisters of, C.B.S.: Founded 1824, in France; in US, 1881. General motherhouse, Rome, Italy; US motherhouse, Marriottsville Rd., Marriottsville, Md. 21104. Hospital work. (90)

Bridgettine Sisters (Order of the Most Holy Savior), O.SS.S.: Founded 1344, at Vadstena, Sweden, by St. Bridget; in US, 1957. General motherhouse, Rome, Italy; US address, Vikingsborg, Darien, Conn. 06820.

Brigid, Congregation of St., C.S.B.: Founded 1807, in Ireland; in US, 1953. US regional house, 5118 Loma Linda Dr., San Antonio, Tex. 78201.

Carmel, Congregation of Our Lady of Mount, O. Carm.: Founded 1825, in France; in US, 1833. General motherhouse, P.O. Box 476, Lacombe, La. 70445. Educational work. (161)

Carmel, Institute of Our Lady of Mount, O. Carm.: Founded 1854, in Italy; in US, 1947. General motherhouse, Florence, Italy; US headquarters, 5 Wheatland St., Peabody, Mass. 01960. Domestic work.

Carmelite Missionaries, C.M.: Founded Barcelona, Spain; in US, 1962. General motherhouse, Rome, Italy; US foundation, 106 Abbey St., Winters, Calif. 95694.

Carmelite Missionaries of St. Theresa, C.M.S.T.: Founded 1903, in Mexico. General motherhouse, Mexico City, Mexico; US novitiate, 10910 Old Katy Rd., Houston, Tex. 77043. (76)

Carmelite Sisters for the Aged and Infirm, O. Carm.: Founded 1929, at New York, by Cardinal Patrick Hayes, Motherhouse, Avila-on-Hudson, Germantown, N.Y. 12526. Social work. (427)

Carmelite Sisters of Charity, C.a.Ch.: Founded by St. Joaquina de Vedruna. General motherhouse, Rome, Italy; US address, 19950 Anita Ave., Castro Valley, Calif.

Carmelite Sisters of Corpus Christi, O.Carm.: Founded 1908, in England; in US, 1920. US address, 21 Battery St., Newport, R.I. 02840. Home and foreign mission work. (145)

Carmelite Sisters of St. Therese of the Infant Jesus, C.S.T.: Founded 1917, in US. General motherhouse, 1300 Classen Dr., Oklahoma City, Okla. 73103. Educational, social work.

Carmelite Sisters of the Divine Heart of Jesus, C.D.C.J.: Founded 1891, in Germany; in US, 1912. General motherhouse, Sittard, Holland. US provincial houses: 1230 Kavanaugh Pl., Milwaukee, Wis. 52313; 10341 Manchester Rd., St. Louis, Mo. 63122; 4130 Alameda St., Corpus Christi, Tex. 78416. Educational, social, mission work. (184 in US and Canada)

Carmelite Sisters of the Sacred Heart, O.C.D.: Founded 1904, in Mexico. General motherhouse, Guadalajara, Mexico; US motherhouse, 920 E. Alhambra Rd., Alhambra, Calif. 91801. Educational, hospital work, day nurseries. (110)

Carmelites, Calced, O.Carm.: Founded 1536, at Naples, Italy; in US, 1930. Five monasteries in US. Cloistered.

Carmelites, Discalced, O.C.D.: Founded 1562, Spain; in US, 1790. Sixty-five independent monasteries throughout the US. Cloistered. (829)

Casimir, Sisters of St., S.S.C.: Founded 1907, in US. General motherhouse, 2601 W. Marquette Rd., Chicago, Ill. 60629. Educational, hospital, social work. (430)

Cenacle, Congregation of Our Lady of the Retreat in the, R.C.: Founded 1826; in US, 1892. General motherhouse, Rome, Italy. US provinces: The Cenacle, Mt. Kisco, N.Y. 10549; 200 Lake St., Brighton, Mass. 02135; 513 Fullerton Pkwy., Chicago, Ill. 60614. (385)

Charity, Daughters of Divine, F.D.C.: Founded 1868, at Chanty, Austria; in US, 1913. General motherhouse, Rome, Italy. US provinces: 56 Meadowbrook Rd., White Plains, N.Y. 10605; 39 N. Portage Path, Akron, O. 44303; 1315 N. Woodward Ave., Bloomfield Hills, Mich. 48013. Educational, hospital work. (241)

Charity, Irish Sisters of, R.S.C.: Founded 1815, in Ireland; in US, 1953. Motherhouse, Dublin, Ireland; US headquarters, 10664 St. James Dr., Culver City, Calif. 90243. (52)

Charity, Little Missionary Sisters of, P.M.C.: Founded 1915, in Italy; in US, 1949. General motherhouse, Rome, Italy; US headquarters, 120 Orient Ave., E. Boston, Mass. 02128.

Charity, Sisters of (of Seton Hill), S.C.: Founded 1870, at Altoona, Pa., from Cincinnati foundation. Generalate, Mt. Thor Rd., Greensburg, Pa. 15601. Educational, hospital, social work. (667)

Charity, Sisters of (Grey Nuns of Montreal), S.G.M.: Founded 1738, in Canada; in US, 1855. General motherhouse, Pierrefonds, Roxboro 910, Que., Canada; US motherhouse, 10 Pelham Rd., Lexington, Mass. 02173. (140)

Charity, Sisters of (of Leavenworth), S.C.L.: Founded 1858, in US. General motherhouse, Leavenworth, Kans. 66048. (763)

Charity, Sisters of (of Nazareth), S.C.N.: Founded 1812, in US. General motherhouse, Nazareth P. O., Nelson Co., Ky. 40048. (1,321)

Charity, Sisters of (of St. Augustine), C.S.A.: Founded 1851, at Cleveland, O. General motherhouse, 5232 Broadview Rd., Richfield, O. 44286. (270)

Charity, Sisters of Christian, S.C.C.: Founded 1849, in Germany; in US, 1873. General motherhouse, Rome, Italy. US provinces: Mallinckrodt Convent, Mendham, N.J. 07945; Maria Immaculata Convent, Ridge Rd. at Walnut, Wilmette, Ill. 60011, Educational, other work. (960)

Charity, Vincentian Sisters of, V.S.C.: Founded 1835, in Austria; in US, 1902. General motherhouse, 8200 McKnight Rd., Pittsburgh, Pa. 15237. (332)

Charity, Vincentian Sisters of, V.S.C.: Founded 1928, at Bedford, O. General motherhouse, 1160 Broadway, Bedford, O. 44146. (113)

Charity of Cincinnati, Ohio, Sisters of, S.C.: Founded 1809. General motherhouse, Mt. St. Joseph, Ohio 45051. Educational, hospital, social work. (1,240)

Charity of Ottawa, Sisters of (Grey Nuns of the Cross), S.C.O.: Founded 1845, at Ottawa, Canada; in US, 1857. General motherhouse, Ottawa, Canada; US provincial house, 975 Varnum Ave., Lowell, Mass. 01854. Educational, hospital work, extended health care. (157)

Charity of Our Lady, Mother of Mercy, Sis-ters of, S.C.M.M.: Founded 1832, in Holland; in US, 1874. General motherhouse, Rome, Italy; US provincialate, 80 Taylor Ave., East Haven Conn. 06512. (38)

Charity of Our Lady of Mercy, Sisters of, O.L.M.: Founded 1829, in US. General motherhouse, Charleston, S. C. 29412. Educational, hospital work. (81)

Charity of Quebec, Sisters of (Grey Nuns), S.C.Q.: Founded 1849, at Quebec; in US, 1890. General motherhouse, Ave. de'Estimauville, Quebec 5, P. Q., Canada. Social work. (82)

Charity of St. Elizabeth, Sisters of (Convent, N.J.), S.C.: Founded 1859, at Newark, N. J. Generalate, Convent, N. J. 07961. Educational, hospital work. (1,385)

Charity of St. Hyacinthe, Sisters of (Grey Nuns), S.C.S.H.: Founded 1840, at St. Hyacinthe, Canada; in US, 1878. General motherhouse, 665 Ste-Anne St., La Providence (St. Hyacinthe), P. Q., Canada. (146)

Charity of St. Joan Antida, Sisters of, S.C.S.J.A.: Founded 1799, in France; in US, 1932. General motherhouse, Rome, Italy; US motherhouse, 8560 N. 76th Pl., Milwaukee, Wis. 53223. (64)

Charity of St. Louis, Sisters of, S.C.S.L.: Founded 1803, in France; in US, 1910. General motherhouse, Rome, Italy; US provincial house, 422 Robin Ct., Cheshire, Conn. 06410. (59)

Charity of St. Vincent de Paul, Daughters of, D. C.: Founded 1633, in France; in US 1809, at Emmitsburg, Md., by Bl. Elizabeth Ann Seton. General motherhouse, Paris, France. US provinces: Emmitsburg, Md. 21727; 7800 Natural Bridge Rd., Normandy, St. Louis, Mo. 63121; 9400 New Harmony Rd., Evansville, Ind. 47712; 96 Menands Rd., Albany, N.Y. 12204; 2600 Altamont Rd., Los Altos, Calif. 94022. (2,128)

Charity of St. Vincent de Paul, Sisters of, Halifax, S.C.H.: Founded 1856, at Halifax, N. S., from Emmitsburg, Md., foundation. Generalate, Mt. St. Vincent, Halifax, N. S., Canada. Educational, hospital, social work. (1,458, total membership)

Charity of St. Vincent de Paul, Sisters of, New York, S.C.: Founded 1817, from Emmitsburg, Md. General motherhouse, Mt. St. Vincent on Hudson, New York, N. Y. 10471. Educational, hospital work. (1,100)

Charity of St. Vincent de Paul, Sisters of (Tyrol), C.S.V.P.: Founded 1825, at Tyrol, Austria. General motherhouse, Zams, Oberintal, Tyrol, Austria; US motherhouse, 705 Clyman St., Watertown, Wis. 53094.

Charity of the Blessed Virgin Mary, Sisters of, B.V.M.: Founded 1833, in US. General motherhouse, Mt. Carmel, Dubuque, Ia. 52001. Educational work. (1,814)

Charity of the Incarnate Word, Congregation of the Sisters of, C.C.V.I.: Founded 1869, at San Antonio, Tex., by Bishop C. M. Dubuis. General motherhouse, 4515 Broadway, San Antonio, Tex. 78209. (644)

Charity of the Incarnate Word, Congregation of the Sisters of (Houston, Tex.), C.C.V.I.: Founded 1866, in US, by Bishop C. M. Dubuis. General motherhouse, 6510 Lawndale Ave., Houston, Tex. 77023. Educational, hospital, social work. (426)

Charity of the Sacred Heart, Daughters of, F.C.S.C.J.: Founded 1823, at LaSalle de Vihiers, France; in US, 1905. General motherhouse, La Salle de Vihiers, France; US motherhouse, Littleton, N. H. 03561. (132)

Charles Borromeo, Missionary Sisters of St. (Scalabrini Srs.): Founded 1895, in Italy; in US, 1941. American novitiate, 1414 N. 37th Ave., Melrose Park, Ill. (52)

Child Jesus, Sisters of the Poor, P.C.J.: Founded 1844, at Aix-la-Chapelle, Germany; in US, 1924. General motherhouse, Simpelveld, Holland; American provincialate, 4567 Olentangy River Rd., Columbus, O. 43214.

Chretienne, Sisters of Ste., S.S.CH.: Founded 1807, in France; in US, 1903. General motherhouse, Metz, France; American provincial house, 297 Arnold St., Wrentham, Mass. 02093. Educational, hospital, mission work. (146)

Christ, Adorers of the Blood of, A.S.C.: Founded 1834, in Italy; in US, 1870. General motherhouse, Rome, Italy. US provinces: Ruma (P.O. Red Bud R.R.1.), Ill. 62278; 1165 Southwest Blvd., Wichita, Kans. 67213; Columbia, Pa. 17512. Educational, hospital work. (875)

Christ the King, Sister Servants of, S.S.C.K.: Founded 1936, in US. General motherhouse, Mt. Calvary, Wis. 53057

Christ the Teacher, Sisters of (Byzantine Rite): Founded 1960, at Pittsburgh, Pa. General motherhouse, 66 Riverview Ave., Pittsburgh, Pa.

Christian Doctrine, Sisters of Our Lady of, R.C.D.: Founded 1910, at New York. Motherhouse, Marydell, Suffern, N.Y. 10901. (57)

Christian Education, Religious of, R.C.E.: Founded 1817, in France; in US, 1905. General motherhouse, Paris, France; US provincial residence, 8 Old Mystic St., Arlington, Mass. 02174. (84)

Cistercian Nuns: Established in US, 1958. Motherhouse, Frauenthal, Switzerland; in US, Valley of Our Lady Monastery, Rt. 1, Prairie du Sac, Wis. 53378.

Cistercian Nuns of the Strict Observance, Order of, O.C.S.O.: Founded 1125, in France, by St. Stephen Harding; in US, 1949. General motherhouse France. US abbeys: Arnold St. (R.F.D. Box 500), Wrentham, Mass. 02093; Box 97, Sonalta, Ariz. 85637; Whitethorn, Calif. 95489; R.R. 3, Dubuque, Ia. 52001. (63)

Clergy, Congregation of Our Lady, Help of the, C.L.H.C.: Founded 1961, in US. Motherhouse, Maryvale Convent, Maple Ave., Higganum, Conn. 06441.

Clergy, Servants of Our Lady Queen of the,

S.R.C.: Founded 1929, in Canada; in US, 1936. General motherhouse, Lac-au-Saumon, P.Q. GOJ 1 MO, Canada.

Colettines: See Franciscan Poor Clare Nuns.

Columban, Missionary Sisters of St., S.S.C.: Founded 1922, in Ireland; in US, 1930. General motherhouse, Wicklow, Ireland; US region, 950 Metropolitan Ave., Hyde Park, Mass. 01236. (65)

Consolata Missionary Sisters, M.C.: Founded 1910, in Italy; in US, 1954. General motherhouse, Turin, Italy; US headquarters, 6801 Belmont Rd., Belmont, Mich. 49306.

Cordi-Marian Missionary Sisters, M.C.M.: Founded 1921, in Mexico; in US, 1926. General motherhouse, 2910 Morales St., Morales, Mexico.

Cross, Daughters of the, D.C.: Founded 1640, in France; in US, 1855. General motherhouse, 1000 Fairview St., Shreveport, La. 71104. Educational work.

Cross, Daughters of, of Liege, F.C.: Founded 1883, in Liege, Belgium; in US, 1958. US address, 165 W. Eaton Ave., Tracy, Calif. 95376.

Cross, Sisters of the Holy, C.S.C.: Founded 1841, at Le Mans, France; in US, 1843. General motherhouse, Notre Dame, Ind. 46556. Educational, hospital work.(1,217)

Cross and of the Seven Dolors, Sisters of the Holy, C.S.C.: Founded 1847, in Canada; in US, 1881. General motherhouse, Montreal, Que., Canada; US provincial house, Pittsfield, N.H. 03263. Educational work. (438)

Cross and Passion, Sisters of the (Passionist Sisters), C.P.: Founded 1852; in US, 1924. General motherhouse, Bolton, England; US address: Mt. St. Joseph, Wakefield, R.I. 02878 (94)

Cross and Passion of Our Lord Jesus Christ, Nuns of the (Passionist Nuns), C.P.: Founded 1771, in Italy, by St. Paul of the Cross; in US, 1910. Five convents in the US. Contemplatives. (82)

Crucified, Augustinian Daughters of the: Founded 1840, in Italy. General motherhouse, Rome, Italy; US novitiate, 420 Lincoln Hwy., Malvern, Pa. 19355.

Cyril and Methodius, Sisters of Sts., SS.C.M.: Founded 1909, in US, by Rev. Matthew Jankola. General motherhouse, Danville, Pa. 17821. Educational, hospital work. (403)

Disciples of the Divine Master, P.D.D.M.: Founded 1924; in US, 1948. General motherhouse, Rome, Italy; US headquarters, 12830 Warren Ave., Dearborn, Mich. 48126. (50)

Divine Compassion, Sisters of, R.D.C.: Founded 1886, in US. General motherhouse, 52 N. Broadway, White Plains, N.Y. 10603. Educational work. (214)

Divine Love, Oblates to, Sisters, R.O.D.A.: Founded 1923, in Italy; in US, 1947. General motherhouse, Rome, Italy; US novitiate,

Beekman Rd., Hopewell Junction, N.Y. 12533.

Divine Spirit, Congregation of the, C.D.S.: Founded 1956, in US, by Archbishop John M. Gannon. Motherhouse, 409 W. 6th St., Erie, Pa. 16507. Educational, social work; care of aged. (57)

Dominicans

Dominican Nuns of the Second Order of Perpetual Adoration, O.P.: Founded 1206, in France; in US, 1880. Twelve independent monasteries. Cloistered. (382)

Dominican Oblates of Jesus, D.O.J.: Founded 1946 in Spain, General motherhouse, Madrid, Spain; US foundation, La Salette Convent, 85 New Park Ave., Hartford, Conn. 06106.

Dominican Rural Missionaries, O.P.: Founded 1932, in France; in US, 1951, at Abbeville, La. General motherhouse, Luzarches, France; US motherhouse, 1318 S. Henry St., Abbeville, La. 70510.

Dominican Sisters of Bethany, O.P.: Founded 1914, in The Netherlands; in US, 1961. General motherhouse, Bracciano, Italy; US headquarters, 1501 W. Touhy Ave., Chicago, Ill. 60626. Social service work.

Dominican Sisters of Bethany, Congregation, O.P.: Founded 1866, in France. Motherhouse, France; US novitiate, 204 Ridge St., Millis, Mass. 02054.

Dominican Sisters of the Perpetual Rosary, O.P.: Founded 1880, at Calais, France. Eight independent monasteries. Contemplative. (125)

Dominican Sisters of the Presentation, O.P.: Founded 1684, in France; in US, 1906. General motherhouse, Tours, France; US headquarters, 3012 El St., Dighton, Mass. 02715. Hospital work. (72)

Dominican Sisters of the Roman Congregation of St. Dominic, O.P.: Founded 1621, in France; in US, 1904. General motherhouse, Rome, Italy; US province, 200 Ivy St., Brookline, Mass. 02146. Educational work. (90)

Eucharistic Missionaries of St. Dominic, O.P.: Founded 1927, in Louisiana. General motherhouse, 1101 Aline St., New Orleans, La. 70115. Parish mission work. (59)

Maryknoll Sisters of St. Dominic, M.M.: Founded 1912, in New York. Center, Maryknoll, N.Y. 10545. (1,128)

Religious Missionaries of St. Dominic, O.P.: General motherhouse, Rome, Italy. US foundations: 808 S. Wright St., Alice, Texas 78332; 1123 N. Staples St., Corpus Christi, Tex. 78401; 432 N. Oak St., Santa Paula, Calif. 93060.

Sisters of the Third Order of St. Dominic, O.P.: Thirty congregations in the US. Educational, hospital work. Names of congregations are given below, followed by the date of foundation, location of motherhouse and number of professed sisters.

St. Catharine of Siena, 1822. St. Catharine, Ky. 40061. (661)

St. Mary of the Springs, 1830. Columbus Ohio 43219. (645)

Most Holy Rosary, 1849. Sinsinawa, Wis. 53824. (1,622)

Most Holy Name of Jesus, 1850. San Rafael, Calif. 94901. (280)

Holy Cross, 1853. Albany Ave., Amityville, N. Y. 11701. (1,326)

Most Holy Rosary, 1859. Mt. St. Mary on Hudson, Newburgh, N. Y. 12550. (469)

St. Cecilia, 1860. Eighth Ave. N. and Clay St., Nashville, Tenn. 37208. (126)

St. Mary, 1860. 4601 Cleveland Ave., New Orleans, La. 70119, (148)

St. Catherine of Siena, 1862. 5635 Erie St., Racine, Wis. 53402. (472).

Our Lady of the Sacred Heart, 1873. 1237 W. Monroe St., Springfield, Ill. 62704. (511).

Our Lady of the Rosary, 1876. Sparkill, N. Y. 10976. (728)

Queen of the Holy Rosary, 1876. Mission San Jose, Calif. 94538. (473).

Most Holy Rosary, 1877. Adrian, Mich. 49221. (2,076).

Our Lady of the Sacred Heart, 1877. 2025 E. Fulton St., Grand Rapids, Mich. 49503. (658).

St. Dominic, 1878. Blauvelt, N. Y. 10913. (433).

Immaculate Conception (Dominican Sisters of the Sick Poor), 1879. P. O. Box 231, Ossining, N. Y. 10562. Social work. (106).

St. Catherine de Ricci, 1880. 2850 N. Providence Rd., Media, Pa. 19063. (146).

Sacred Heart of Jesus, 1881. Mt. St. Dominic, Caldwell, N. J. 07006. (476).

Sacred Heart, 1882. 6501 Almeda Rd., Houston, Tex. 77021. (263).

St. Thomas Aquinas, 1888. 423 E. 152nd St., Tacoma, Wash. 98445. (179).

Most Holy Cross, 1890. P. O. Box 280, Edmonds, Wash. 98020. (151).

St. Catherine of Siena, 1891. 37 Park St., Fall River, Mass. 02721. (128).

St. Rose of Lima (Servants of Relief for Incurable Cancer), 1896. Hawthorne, N. Y. 10532. (121).

Immaculate Conception, 1902. 3600 Broadway, Great Bend, Kans. 67530. Pontifical Institute. (226).

St. Catherine of Siena, 1911. 4600 93rd St., Kenosha, Wis. 53140. (100)

St. Rose of Lima, 1923. 775 Drahner Rd., Oxford, Mich. 48051. (100).

Immaculate Conception, 1929. Biala Nizna, Poland: US provincial house, 9000 W. 81st St., Justice, Ill. 60458.

Immaculate Heart of Mary, 1929. Akron, Ohio 44313. (195).

Immaculate Heart of Mary, W. 3102 Fort George Wright Dr., Spokane, Wash. 99204. (70).

St. Catherine of Siena of Oakford, Republic of South Africa, 1955. General motherhouse, Natal, Republic of South Africa; US motherhouse, 1855 Miramonte Ave., Mountain View, Calif. 94040.

(End, Listing of Dominicans)

Dorothy, Institute of the Sisters of St., S.S.D.: Founded 1834, in Italy; in US, 1911. General motherhouse, Rome, Italy; US motherhouse, Villa Fatima, Taunton, Mass. 02780. (82).

Eucharist, Religious of the, R.E.: Founded 1857, in Belgium; in US, 1900. General motherhouse, Belgium; US foundation, 2907 Ellicott Terr., N.W., Washington, D.C. 20008.

Family, Congregation of the Sisters of the Holy, S.S.F.: Founded 1842, in US. General motherhouse, 6901 Chef Menteur Hway., New Orleans, La. 70126. Educational, hospital work. (286).

Family, Little Sisters of the Holy, P.S.S.F.: Founded 1880, in Canada; in US, 1900. General motherhouse, Sherbrooke, Que., Canada. Domestic work. (110).

Family, Sisters of the Holy, S.H.F.: Founded 1872, in US. General motherhouse, P. O. Box 3248, Mission San Jose, Calif. 94538. Educational, social work. (271).

Family of Nazareth, Sisters of the Holy, C.S.F.N.: Founded 1875, in Italy; in US, 1885. General motherhouse, Rome, Italy. US provinces: 353 N. River Rd., Des Plaines, Ill. 60616; Grant and Frankford Aves., Torresdale, Philadelphia, Pa. 19114; 285 Bellevue Rd., Pittsburgh, Pa. 15229; Marian Heights, 1428-1, Monroe Turnpike, Monroe, Conn. 06868; 1814 Egyptian Way, Box 757, Grand Prairie, Tex. 75050. (1,489).

Filippini, Religious Teachers, M.P.F.: Founded 1692, in Italy; in US, 1910. General motherhouse, Rome, Italy; US interprovincial motherhouse, Villa Walsh, Morristown, N. J. 07960. Educational work. (460).

Francis de Sales, Oblate Sisters of St., O.S.F.S.: Founded 1866, in France; in US, 1951. General motherhouse, Troyes, France; US headquarters, Childs, Md. 21916. Educational, social work.

Franciscans

Bernardine Sisters of the Third Order of St. Francis, O.S.F.: Founded 1457, at Cracow, Poland; in US, 1894. General motherhouse, 647 Spring Mill Rd., Villanova, Pa. 19085. Educational, hospital, social work. (1,000).

Congregation of the Servants of the Holy Infancy of Jesus, O.S.F.: Founded 1855, in Germany; in US, 1929. General motherhouse, Wuerzburg, Germany; American motherhouse, P. O. Box 708, Plainfield, N. J. 07061. (82).

Congregation of the Third Order of St. Francis of Mary Immaculate, O.S.F.: Founded 1865, in US, by Fr. Pamphilus da Magliano, O.F.M. General motherhouse, 520 Plainfield Ave., Joliet, Ill. 60435. Educational work. (636).

Conventuals of the Third Order of St. Francis of the Mission of the Immaculate Virgin, O.S.F.: Founded 1893, in New York. General motherhouse, Hastings-on-Hudson, N. Y. 10706. Educational, hospital work. (186).

Daughters of St. Francis of Assisi, D.S.F.: Founded 1890, in Austria-Hungary; in US, 1946. Provincial motherhouse, 507 N. Prairie St., Lacon, Ill. 61540. Nursing, CCD work.

Felician Sisters (Congregation of the Sisters of St. Felix), C.S.S.F.: Founded 1855, in Poland; in US, 1874. General motherhouse, Rome, Italy. US provinces: 36800 Schoolcraft Rd., Livonia, Mich. 48150; 600 Doat St., Buffalo, N.Y. 14211; 3800 Peterson Ave., Chicago, Ill. 60645; South Main St., Lodi, N.Y. 07644; 1500 Woodcrest Ave., Coraopolis, Pa. 15108; 1315 Enfield St., Enfield, Conn. 06082; Monument Rd., Ponca City, Okla. 74601. (3,216)

Franciscan Handmaids of the Most Pure Heart of Mary, F.H.M.: Founded 1917, in US. General motherhouse, 15 W. 124th St., New York, N.Y. 10027. Educational, social work. (47)

Franciscan Hospitaller Sisters of the Immaculate Conception, F.H.I.C.: Founded 1876, in Portugal; in US, 1960. General motherhouse, Oporto, Portugal; US foundation, 1395 E. Santa Clara St., San Jose, Calif. 95116.

Franciscan Missionaries of Mary, F.M.M.: Founded 1877, in India; in US, 1904. General motherhouse, Rome, Italy; US provincialate, 225 E. 45th St., New York, N.Y. 10017. Foreign mission work. (283)

Franciscan Missionaries of Our Lady, O.S.F.: Founded 1854, at Calais, France; in US, 1913. General motherhouse, Desvres, France; US motherhouse, 4200 Essen Lane, Baton Rouge, La. 70809. Hospital work. (51)

Franciscan Missionaries of St. Joseph (Mill Hill Sisters), F.M.S.J.: Founded 1883, at Rochdale, Lancashire, England; in US, 1952. General motherhouse, Eccleshall, Stafford, England; US headquarters, St. Clare Convent, 4 Reber St., Albany, N.Y. 12205.

Franciscan Missionaries of the Divine Motherhood, F.M.D.M.: Founded 1935, in England; US foundation, East Greenbush, N.Y. 12061.

Franciscan Missionary Sisters for Africa, O.S.F.: American foundation, 1953. Generalate, Ireland; US headquarters, 172 Foster St., Brighton, Mass. 02135.

Franciscan Missionary Sisters of Giglio, S.F.M.G.: First foundation in US, 1961. General motherhouse, Assisi, Italy; US address, St. Hyacinth College and Seminary, Granby, Mass. 01033.

Franciscan Missionary Sisters of Our Lady of Sorrows, O.S.F.: Founded 1937, in China, by Bishop R. Palazzi, O.F.M.; in US, 1849. US address, 2385 Laurel Glen Rd., Santa Cruz, Calif. 95060. Educational, social, domestic, retreat and foreign mission work.

Franciscan Missionary Sisters of the Divine Child, F.M.D.C.: Founded 1927, at Buffalo, N.Y., by Bishop William Turner. General motherhouse, 6380 Main St., Williamsville, N.Y. 14221. Educational, social work. (70)

Franciscan Missionary Sisters of the Immaculate Conception, O.S.F.: Founded 1874, in Mexico; in US, 1927. US provincial house, 1519 Woodworth St., San Fernando, Calif. 91340. (97)

Franciscan Missionary Sisters of the Sacred Heart, F.M.S.C.: Founded 1860, in Italy; in US, 1865. Generalate, Rome, Italy; US provincialate, 120 Franklin St., Peekskill, N.Y. 10566. Educational and social welfare apostolates and specialized services.

Franciscan Nuns of the Most Blessed Sacrament, F.SS.S.: Motherhouse, 5817 Old Leeds Rd., Birmingham, Ala. 35210.

Franciscan Poor Clare Nuns (Poor Clares, Order of St. Clare, Poor Clares of St. Colette), P.C., O.S.C., P.C.C.: Founded 1212, at Assisi, Italy, by St. Francis of Assisi; in US, 1875. Proto-monastery, Assisi, Italy; twenty-four autonomous monasteries in the US. (461)

Franciscan Sisters, Daughters of the Sacred Hearts of Jesus and Mary, O.S.F.: Founded 1860, in Germany; in US, 1872. Generalate, Rome, Italy; US motherhouse, P.O. Box 667, Wheaton, Ill. 60187. Educational, hospital, social work. (303)

Franciscan Sisters of Allegany, N.Y., O.S.F.: Founded 1859, at Allegany, N.Y., by Fr. Pamphilus da Magliano, O.F.M. General motherhouse Allegany, N.Y. 14706. Educational, hospital, foreign mission work. (831)

Franciscan Sisters of Baltimore, O.S.F.: Founded 1868, in England; in US, 1881. General motherhouse, 3725 Ellerslie Ave., Baltimore, Md. 21218. Educational work. (80)

Franciscan Sisters of Chicago, O.S.F.: Founded 1894, in US. General motherhouse, 1220 Main St., Lemont, Ill. 60439. Educational, hospital, social work. (319)

Franciscan Sisters of Christian Charity, O.S.F.: Founded 1869, in US. Motherhouse, Rt. 5, Manitowoc, Wis. 54220. Educational, hospital work. (977)

Franciscan Sisters of Little Falls, Minn., O.S.F.: Founded 1891, in US. General motherhouse, Little Falls, Minn. 56345. Health, education, social services. (386)

Franciscan Sisters of Mary Immaculate of the Third Order of St. Francis of Assisi, F.M.I.: Founded 16th century, in Switzerland; in US, 1932. General motherhouse, Rome, Italy; US provincial house, Box 5664, Amarillo, Tex. 79107. (84)

Franciscan Sisters of Our Lady of Perpetual Help, O.S.F.: Founded 1901, in US, from Joliet, Ill., foundation. General motherhouse, 201 Brotherton Lane, St. Louis, Mo. 63135. Educational, hospital work. (320)

Franciscan Sisters of Our Lady of the Holy Angels, B.M.V.A.: Founded 1863, at Neu-

wied, Germany; in US, 1923. General motherhouse, Rhine, Germany; US motherhouse, 1925 Norfolk Ave., St. Paul, Minn. 55116. Educational, hospital, social work.

Franciscan Sisters of Ringwood, F.S.R.: Founded 1927, at Passaic, N.J. General motherhouse, St. Francis, Ringwood, N.J. 07456. Educational work. (68)

Franciscan Sisters of St. Elizabeth, F.S.S.E.: Founded 1866, at Naples, Italy; in US, 1919. General motherhouse, Rome; US address, 449 Park Rd., Parsippany, N.J. 07054.

Franciscan Sisters of St. Joseph, F.S.S.J.: Founded 1897, in US. General motherhouse, 5286 S. Park Ave., Hamburg, N.Y. 14075. Educational, hospital work. (442)

Franciscan Sisters of the Atonement, Third Order Regular of St. Francis (Graymoor Sisters), S.A.: Founded 1898, in US, as Anglican community; entered Church, 1909. General motherhouse, Graymoor, Garrison P.O., N.Y. 10524. Mission work. (334)

Franciscan Sisters of the Immaculate Conception, O.S.F.: Founded in Germany; in US, 1928. General motherhouse, Kloster, Bonlanden, Germany; US province, N. Davis Rd., E. Aurora, N.Y. 14052.

Franciscan Sisters of the Immaculate Conception, O.S.F.: Founded 1901, in US. General motherhouse, 1000 30th St., Rock Island, Ill. 61201. Hospital work.

Franciscan Sisters of the Immaculate Conception, Missionary, O.S.F.: Founded 1873, in US. General motherhouse, Rome, Italy; US address, 790 Centre St., Newton, Mass. 02158. Educational work. (456)

Franciscan Sisters of the Immaculate Conception and St. Joseph for the Dying, O.S.F.: Founded 1919, in US. General motherhouse, 485 Church St., Monterey, Calif. 93940.

Franciscan Sisters of the Poor, S.F.P.: Founded 1845, at Aix-la-Chapelle, Germany, by Mother Frances Schervier; in US, 1858. Community service center, 23 Middagh St., Brooklyn, N.Y. 11201. Hospital, social work. (403)

Franciscan Sisters of the Sacred Heart, O.S.F.: Founded 1876, in US. General motherhouse, Mokena, Ill. 60448. Educational, hospital, mission work. (384)

Franciscan Sisters of the Third Order of the Immaculate Conception, F.S.I.C.: Founded 1879, in Spain; in US, 1958. General motherhouse, Murcia, Spain; US foundation, 1525 N. 18th St., Philadelphia, Pa. 19121.

Hospital Sisters of the Third Order of St. Francis, O.S.F.: Founded 1844, in Germany; in US, 1875. General motherhouse, Muenster, Germany; US motherhouse, Box 42, Springfield, Ill. 62705. Hospital work. (652)

Little Franciscan Sisters of Mary, P.F.M.: Founded 1889, in US. General motherhouse, Baie St. Paul, Que., Canada. US province, 55 Moore Ave., Worcester, Mass. Educational, hospital, social work.

Missionaries of the Third Order of St. Francis of Our Lady of the Prairies, O.L.P.: Founded 1960, in US. General motherhouse, Powers Lake, N.D. 58773.

Missionary Sisters of the Immaculate Conception of the Mother of God, S.M.I.C.: Founded 1910, in Brazil; in US, 1922, Generalate, P.O. Box 204, 662 East Dr., Oradell, N.J. 07649. Mission, educational, hospital work. (134)

Mothers of the Helpless, M.D.: Founded 1873, in Spain; in US, 1916. General motherhouse, Valencia, Spain; US address, 432 W. 20th St., New York, N.Y. 10011.

Philip Neri Missionary Teachers, Sisters of St., R.F.: Founded 1858, in Spain; in US, 1956. Motherhouse, Barcelona, Spain; US novitiate, Route 4, Box 131, Stuart, Fla. 33494.

Poor Clares of Perpetual Adoration, P.C.P.A.: Founded 1854, at Paris, France; in US, 1921, at Cleveland, Ohio. Four monasteries. Contemplative, cloistered, perpetual adoration. (80)

School Sisters of St. Francis, O.S.F.: Founded 1874, in US. General motherhouse, 1501 S. Layton Blvd., Milwaukee, Wis. 53215. (2,171)

School Sisters of St. Francis (Bethlehem, Pa.), O.S.F.: Founded 1843, in Austria; in US, 1913. General motherhouse, Rome, Italy; US province, Bethlehem, Pa. 18017. Educational work. (96)

School Sisters of St. Francis (Pittsburgh, Pa.), O.S.F.: Founded 1913, in US. Provincial motherhouse, 934 Forest Ave., Pittsburgh, Pa. 15202. Educational, nursing work. (151)

School Sisters of the Third Order of St. Francis (Savannah, Mo.), O.S.F.: Founded 1842, in Austria; in US, 1924. Provincial house, La Verna Hts., Savannah, Mo. 64485. Educational, hospital work. (50)

School Sisters of the Third Order of St. Francis (Panhandle, Tex.), O.S.F.: Founded 1845, in Austria; in US, 1942. General motherhouse, Vienna, Austria; center and novitiate, Sancta Maria Convent, Panhandle, Tex. 79068. Educational, social work.

Sisters of Charity of Our Lady, Mother of the Church, S.C.M.C.: Established 1970, in US. Motherhouse, Baltic, Conn. 06330. Teaching, nursing, care of aged, and dependent children. (87)

Sisters of Our Lady of Mercy (Mercedarians), S.O.L.M.: General motherhouse, Rome, Italy; US addresses: 70 Bay 47th St. Brooklyn, N.Y. 11214; St. Edward School, Pine Hill, N.J. 08021.

Sisters of Mercy of the Holy Cross, S.C.S.C.: Founded 1856, in Switzerland; in US. 1912. General motherhouse, Ingenbohl, Switzerland; US provincial house, Merrill, Wis. 54452. (94)

Sisters of St. Elizabeth, S.S.E.: Founded 1931, at Milwaukee, Wis. General motherhouse, 745 N. Brookfield Rd., Brookfield, Wis. 53005.

Sisters of St. Francis (Clinton, Iowa), O.S.F.: Founded 1868, in US. General motherhouse, Bluff Blvd. and Springdale Dr., Clinton, Ia. 57232. Educational, hospital, social work. (250)

Sisters of St. Francis (Millvale, Pa.), O.S.F.: Founded 1865, Pittsburgh, Pa. General motherhouse, 146 Hawthorne Rd., Millvale P. O., Pittsburgh, Pa. 15209. Educational, hospital work. (417)

Sisters of St. Francis of Christ the King, O.S.F.: Founded 1869, in Austria. General motherhouse, Rome, Italy; US provincial house, Lemont, Ill. 60439. Educational work, home for aged. (150)

Sisters of St. Francis of Penance and Christian Charity, O.S.F.: Founded 1835, in Holland; in US, 1874. General motherhouse, Rome, Italy. US provinces: 4421 Lower River Rd., Stella Niagara, N.Y. 14144; 2851 W. 52nd Ave., Denver, Colo. 80221; 3910 Bret Harte Dr., P.O. Box 1028, Redwood City, Calif. 94064. (718)

Sisters of St. Francis of Philadelphia, O.S.F.: Founded 1855, at Philadelphia, by Bl. John N. Neumann. General motherhouse, Glen Riddle, Pa. 19037. Educational, hospital work. (1,642)

Sisters of St. Francis of the Congregation of Our Lady of Lourdes, O.S.F.: Founded 1916, in US. General motherhouse, 6832 Convent Blvd., Sylvania, O. 43560. Educational, hospital work. (498)

Sisters of St. Francis of the Holy Cross, O.S.F.: Founded 1881, in US, by Rev. Edward Daems, O.S.C. General motherhouse, Rt. 1, Green Bay (Bay Settlement), Wis. 54301. Educational, nursing work; home for aged. (176)

Sisters of St. Francis of the Holy Eucharist, O.S.F.: Founded 1424, in Switzerland; in US, 1893. General motherhouse, Ashland and Prewitt Sts., Nevada, Mo. 64772. Educational, social work.

Sisters of St. Francis of the Immaculate Conception, O.S.F.: Founded 1890, in US. General motherhouse, 2408 W. Heading Ave., Peoria, Ill. 61604. Educational, social work. (117)

Sisters of St. Francis of the Immaculate Heart of Mary, O.S.F.: Founded 1241, in Bavaria; in US, 1913. General motherhouse, Rome, Italy; US motherhouse, Hankinson, N.D. 58041. Educational, hospital work. (144)

Sisters of St. Francis of the Martyr St. George, O.S.F.: Founded in 1859, in Germany; in US, 1923. General motherhouse, Thuine, Hanover, Germany; US motherhouse, Alton, Ill. 62002. Social, hospital, foreign mission work. (60)

Sisters of St. Francis of the Perpetual Adoration, O.S.F.: Founded 1863, in Germany; in US, 1875. General motherhouse, Olpe, Germany. US provinces: Box 766, Mishawaka, Ind. 46544; P.O. Box 1060, Colorado Springs, Colo. 80901. Educational, hospital work. (741)

Sisters of St. Francis of the Providence of God, O.S.F.: Founded 1922, in US, by Msgr. M. L. Krusas. General motherhouse, Grove and McRoberts Rds., Pittsburgh, Pa. 15234. Educational, hospital work. (234)

Sisters of St. Joseph of the Third Order of St. Francis, S.S.J.: Founded 1901, in US. General motherhouse, 107 S. Greenlawn Ave., South Bend, Ind. 46617. Educational, hospital work. (1,020)

Sisters of St. Mary of the Third Order of St. Francis, S.S.M.: Founded 1872, in US. General motherhouse, 1100 Bellevue Ave., St. Louis, Mo. 63117. Hospital, social work. (418)

Sisters of the Holy Infant Jesus, H.I.J.: Founded 1662, at Rouen, France; in US, 1950. General motherhouse, Paris, France. US addresses: 20 Reiner St., Colma, Calif. 94014; St. John the Baptist School, Healdsburg, Calif. 95448; St. Veronica's School, South San Francisco, Calif. 94015.

Sisters of the Sorrowful Mother (Third Order of St. Francis), S.M.M.: Founded 1883, in Italy; in US, 1889. General motherhouse, Rome, Italy. US provinces: 6618 N. Teutonia Ave., Milwaukee, Wis. 53209; 9 Pocono Rd., Denville, N.J. 07834; Rt. 3, Box 168, Broken Arrow, Okla. 74012. Educational, hospital work. (525)

Sisters of the Third Franciscan Order Minor Conventuals, O.S.F.: Founded 1860, at Syracuse, N.Y. General motherhouse, 1024 Court St., Syracuse, N.Y. 13208. Educational, hospital work. (537)

Sisters of the Third Order of St. Francis, O.S.F.: Founded 1877, in US, by Bishop John L. Spalding. Motherhouse, Edgewood Hills, E. Peoria, Ill. 61611. Hospital work. (208)

Sisters of the Third Order of St. Francis, O.S.F.: Founded 1894, in US. Motherhouse, Maryville, Mo. 64468. Hospital work. (71)

Sisters of the Third Order of St. Francis, O.S.F.: Founded 1861, at Buffalo, N.Y., from Philadelphia foundation. General motherhouse, 400 Mill St., Williamsville, N.Y. 14221. Educational, hospital work. (331)

Sisters of the Third Order of St. Francis (Oldenburg, Ind.), O.S.F.: Founded 1851, in US. General motherhouse, Oldenburg, Ind. 47036. Educational work. (734)

Sisters of the Third Order of St. Francis of Assisi, O.S.F.: Founded 1849, in US. General motherhouse, 3221 S. Lake Dr., Milwaukee, Wis. 53207. Educational work. (767)

Sisters of the Third Order of St. Francis of Penance and Charity, O.S.F.: Founded 1869, in US, by Rev. Joseph Bihn. Motherhouse, St. Francis Ave., Tiffin, O. 44883. Educational, hospital work. (230)

Sisters of the Third Order of St. Francis of the Holy Family, O.S.F.: Founded 1875, in US. General motherhouse, Dubuque, Ia. 52001. Education, hospital work. (788)

Sisters of the Third Order of St. Francis of the Perpetual Adoration, F.S.P.A.: Founded 1849, in US. General motherhouse, 912 Market St., La Crosse, Wis. 54601. Educational, health care. (1,031)

Sisters of the Third Order Regular of St. Francis of the Congregation of Our Lady of Lourdes, O.S.F.: Founded 1877, in US. General motherhouse, Assisi Heights, Rochester, Minn. 55901. Education, hospitals. (780)

(End, Listing of Franciscans)

Good Shepherd Sisters (Servants of the Immaculate Heart of Mary), S.C.I.M.: Founded 1850, in Canada; in US, 1882. General motherhouse, Quebec, Canada; Provincial House, Bay View, Saco, Maine 04072. Educational, social work. (213)

Good Shepherd, Sisters of Our Lady of Charity of the, R.G.S.: Founded 1641, in France; in US, 1843. Generalate, Rome, Italy. US provinces: 575 N. Bend Rd., Cincinnati, O. 45224; Mt. St. Florence, Peekskill, N.Y. 10566; 3601 Reservoir Rd. N. W., Washington, D.C. 10007; 7654 Natural Bridge Rd., St. Louis, Mo. 63121; 5100 Hodgson Rd., St. Paul, Minn. 55112. (1,605, including 582 Contemplatives of the Cross).

Graymoor Sisters: See Franciscan Sisters of the Atonement.

Grey Nuns of the Sacred Heart, G.N.S.H.: Founded 1921, in US. General motherhouse, Quarry Rd., Yardley, Pa. 19067. (373)

Guadalupe, Sisters of, O.L.G.: Founded 1946, in Mexico City. General motherhouse, Mexico City, Mexico; US address, St. Mary's College, Winona, Minn. 55987. (60)

Guardian Angels, Sisters of the Holy, S.A.C.: Founded 1839, in France. General motherhouse, Madrid, Spain; US foundation, 1245 S. Van Ness, Los Angeles, Calif. 90019.

Handmaids of Mary Immaculate, A.M.I.: Founded 1952, in Helena, Montana. Motherhouse, (temporary), Marian Center, Detroit, Mich.

Handmaids of the Precious Blood, Congregation of, H.P.B.: Founded 1947, at Jemez Springs, N. M. General motherhouse, Villa Cor Jesu, Jemez Springs, N. M. 87025.

Helpers, Society of, H.H.S.: Founded 1856, in France; in US, 1892. General motherhouse, Paris, France; US motherhouse, 303 Barry Ave., Chicago, Ill. 60657. (94)

Hermanas Catequistas Guadalupanas, H.C.G.: Founded 1923, in Mexico; in US, 1950. General motherhouse, Mexico; US foundation, 7815 Somerset Rd., San Antonio, Tex. 78211.

Holy Child Jesus, Society of the, S.H.C.J.: Founded 1846, in England; in US, 1862. General motherhouse, Rome, Italy. US provinces: 1341 Montgomery Ave., Rosemont, Pa. 19010; Westchester Ave., Rye, N. Y.

10580; 5905 N. Commercial St., Portland, Ore. 97217. (503)

Holy Faith, Sisters of the, S.H.F.: Founded 1856, in Ireland; in US, 1953. General motherhouse, Dublin, Ireland; US address, 1050 N. Texas St., Fairfield Calif. 94533.

Holy Ghost, Sisters of the, C.H.G.: Founded 1913, in US, by Most Rev. J. F. Regis Canevin. General motherhouse, 5246 Clarwin Ave., West View, Pittsburgh, Pa. 15229. Educational, nursing work; care of aged. (121)

Holy Ghost and Mary Immaculate, Sister Servants of, S.H.G.: Founded 1893, in US. General motherhouse, 301 Yucca St., San Antonio, Tex. 78203. Education, hospital work. (237)

Holy Heart of Mary, Servants of the, S.S.C.M.: Founded 1860, in France; in US, 1889. General motherhouse, Montreal, Que., Canada; US motherhouse, 145 S. 4th St., Kankakee, Ill. 60901. Educational, hospital, social work. (136)

Holy Names of Jesus and Mary, Sisters of the, S.N.J.M.: Founded 1843, in Canada; in US, 1859. General motherhouse, 1420 Mt. Royal Blvd., Outremont, Montreal, Canada; four provinces in US. (1,453).

Holy Spirit, Daughters of the, D.H.S.: Founded 1706, in France; in US, 1902. General motherhouse, Bretagne, France; US motherhouse, 72 Church St., Putnam, Conn. 06260. Educational work, district nursing. (395).

Holy Spirit, Mission Sisters of the, M.S.Sp.: Founded 1932, at Cleveland, O. Motherhouse, 1030 N. River Rd., Saginaw, Mich. 48603.

Holy Spirit, Missionary Sisters, Servants of the: Founded 1889, in Holland; in US, 1901. Generalate, Rome, Italy; US motherhouse, Techny, Ill. 60082. (300)

Holy Spirit, Sisters of the, C.S.Sp.: Founded 1890, in Rome, Italy; in US, 1929. General motherhouse, 10102 Granger Rd., Garfield Hts., Ohio 44125. Educational, social, nursing work.

Holy Spirit of Perpetual Adoration, Sister Servants of the: Founded 1896, in Holland; in US, 1915. General motherhouse, Steyl, Holland; US motherhouse, 2212 Green St., Philadelphia, Pa. 19130. (80)

Home Mission Sisters of America (Glenmary Sisters): Founded 1952, in US. Motherhouse, 4580 Colerain Ave., Cincinnati, O. 45223.

Home Visitors of Mary, Sisters, H.V.M.: Founded 1949, in Detroit, Mich. Motherhouse, 356 Arden Park, Detroit, Mich. 48002.

Humility of Mary, Congregation of, C.H.M.: Founded 1854, in France; in US, 1864. US address, Ottumwa, Ia. 52501. (335)

Humility of Mary, Sisters of the, H.M.: Founded 1854, in France; in US, 1864. US address, Villa Maria, Pa. 16155. (491)

Immaculate Conception, Little Servant Sisters of the: Founded 1850, in Poland; in US,

1926. General motherhouse, Poland; US motherhouse, 184 Amboy Ave., Woodbridge, N.J. 07095.

Immaculate Conception, Sisters of the, C.I.C.: Founded 1874, in US. General motherhouse, 5205 Avron Blvd., Metairie, La. 70002.

Immaculate Conception of the Blessed Virgin Mary, Sisters of the (Lithuanian), M.I.C.: Founded 1918, at Mariampole, Lithuania; in US, 1936. General motherhouse, Mariampole, Lithuania; US headquarters, Putnam, Conn. 06260.

Immaculate Heart of Mary, Daughters of the, I.H.M.: Founded 1952, in US. General motherhouse, Wintersville, Steubenville P.O., Ohio 43952.

Immaculate Heart of Mary, Missionary Sisters, I.C.M.: Founded 1897, in India; in US, 1919. Generalate, Rome, Italy; US address, 1710 N. Glebe Rd., Arlington, Va. 22207. Educational social, foreign mission work. (74)

Immaculate Heart of Mary, Sisters of the, C.M.F.: Founded 1848, in Spain; in US, 1878. General motherhouse, Barcelona, Spain. US province, 35 E. 15th St., Tucson, Ariz. 85701. Educational work. (72)

Immaculate Heart of Mary, Sisters of the (California Institute of the Most Holy and Immaculate Heart of the B.V.M.), I.H.M.: Founded 1848, in Spain; in US, 1871. Generalate, 3431 Waverly Dr., Los Angeles, Calif. 90027. (59)

Immaculate Heart of Mary, Sisters, Servants of the, I.H.M.: Founded 1845, in US, by Rev. Louis Florent Gillet. US jurisdictions: 610 W. Elm St., Monroe, Mich. 48161; Villa Maria, Immaculata, Pa. 19345; Marywood, Scranton, Pa. 18509; 2857 Palmerston St., Troy, Mich. 48084; 8961 Laurence St., Allen Park, Mich. 48101. Educational work. (5,402)

Incarnate Word and Blessed Sacrament, Congregation of, I.W.B.S., S.I.W.: Founded 1625, in France; in US, 1853. US motherhouses: 6618 Pearl Rd., Parma Heights, Cleveland, O. 44130; 4600 Bissonnet St., Bellaire, Tex. 77401; 1101 Northeast Water St., Victoria, Tex. 77901; 2930 S. Alameda St., Corpus Christi, Tex. 78404. Educational, hospital work. (573)

Infant Jesus, Sisters of the (Nursing Sisters of the Sick Poor), C.I.J.: Founded 1835, in France; in US, 1905. General motherhouse, 310 Prospect Park W., Brooklyn, N.Y. 11215. (162)

Jeanne d'Arc, Sisters of Ste.: Founded 1914, in America, by Rev. Marie Clement Staub, A.A. General motherhouse, 1681 Chemin St. Louis, Quebec, Canada; US novitiate, 29 Whitman Rd., Worcester, Mass. 01609. Spiritual and temporal service of priests. (271 in US and Canada)

Jesus, Congregation of Daughters of, F.J.: Founded 1834, in France; in US, 1904. General motherhouse, Kermaria, Locmine,

France; American motherhouse, 9040 84th Ave., Edmonton, Alberta, Canada. Educational, hospital work.

Jesus, Daughters of, F.I.: Founded 1871, in Spain; in US, 1950. General motherhouse, Rome, Italy; US convent, 6020 St. Charles Ave., New Orleans, La. 70118. (51)

Jesus, Little Sisters of: Founded 1939, in Sahara; in US, 1952. General motherhouse, Rome, Italy; US headquarters, 700 Irving St. N.W., Washington, D.C. 20017.

Jesus, Society of the Sisters, Faithful Companions of, F.C.J.: Founded 1820, in France; in US, 1896. General motherhouse, Kent, England. US convents: Columbus St., Fitchburg, Mass. 01420; 20 Atkins St., Providence, R.I. 02908; 5 Lincoln St., Centredale, R.I. 02911; Corys Lane, Portsmouth, R.I. 02871. (64)

Jesus Crucified, Congregation of: Founded 1930, in France; in US, 1955. General motherhouse, Brou, France; US foundations: Regina Mundi Priory, Devon, Pa. 19333; St. Paul's Priory, 61 Narragansett, Newport, R.I.

Jesus Crucified and the Sorrowful Mother, Poor Sisters of, C.J.C.: Founded 1924, in US, by Rev. Alphonsus, C.P. General motherhouse, Thatcher St., Brockton, Mass. 02402. Educational, home nursing work. (97)

Jesus-Mary, Religious of, R.J.M.: Founded 1818, at Lyons, France; in US, 1877. General motherhouse, Rome, Italy; US province, 8908 Riggs Rd., Hyattsville, Md. 20782. Educational work. (299)

Jesus, Mary and Joseph, Missionaries of, M.J.M.J.: Founded 1942, in Spain; in US, 1956. General motherhouse, Madrid, Spain; US regional house, 12940 Up River Rd., Corpus Christi, Tex. 78410. (50)

Jesus the Priest, Oblate Sisters of, O.J.S.: Founded 1937, in Mexico City; in US, 1950. Motherhouse, Mexico City, Mexico; US address, La Salle Institute, Glencoe, Mo. 63038.

John the Baptist, Sisters of St., C.S.J.B.: Founded 1878, in Italy; in US, 1906. General motherhouse, Rome, Italy; US provincialate, Anderson Hill Rd., Purchase, N.Y. 10577. Educational work. (183)

Joseph, Little Daughters of St., L.D.S.J.: Founded 1857, in Canada; in US, 1931. General motherhouse, 2333 W. Sherbrooke St., Montreal, Que., Canada. Spiritual and temporal welfare of priests.

Joseph, Missionary Servants of St., M.S.S.J.: Founded 1874, in Spain; in US, 1957. General motherhouse, Salamanca, Spain; US address, 203 N. Spring St., Falls Church, Va. 22046.

Joseph, Religious Daughters of St., F.S.J.: Founded 1875, in Spain. General motherhouse, Spain; US foundation, 319 Humphreys Ave., Los Angeles, Calif. 90022.

Joseph, Religious Hospitallers of St., R.H.S.J.: Founded 1636, in France; in US, 1894. General motherhouse, 251 Pine Ave.

W., Montreal, Que., Canada. Hospital work. (86)

Joseph, Sisters of St., C.S.J.: Founded 1650, in France; in US, 1836, at St. Louis. US motherhouses (number of professed members is given in parentheses):

637 Cambridge St., Brighton, Mass. 02135 (1,534); 1515 W. Ogden Ave., La Grange Park, Ill., 60525 (223); 480 S. Batavia St., Orange, Calif. 92666 (400); Mt. St. Joseph Convent, Chestnut Hill, Philadelphia, Pa. 19118 (2,521).

St. Joseph Convent, Brentwood, N.Y. 11717 (1,643); 23 Agassiz Circle, Buffalo, N.Y. 14214 (326); Mt. St. Joseph's Convent, Rutland, Vt. 05701 (113); 3430 Rocky River Dr. N.W., Cleveland, O. 44111 (313); Main St. and Division Rd., Tipton, Ind. 46072 (122); Nazareth, Mich. 49074 (595); 362 W. Main St., Watertown, N.Y. 13601 (153); Mt. Gallitzin Motherhouse, Baden, Pa. 15005 (519); 819 W. 8th St., Erie, Pa. 16502.

4095 East Ave., Rochester, N.Y. 14610 (762); 13th and Washington Sts., Concordia, Kans. 66901 (518); Holyoke, Mass. 01040 (715); 1412 E. 2nd St., Superior, Wis. 54880 (36); Pogue Run Rd., Wheeling, W. Va. 26003 (230); 3700 E. Lincoln St., Wichita, Kans. 67218 (350)

Joseph, Sisters of St., S.S.J.: Founded 1650, at Le Puy, France; in US, 1902. General motherhouse, Le Puy, France; US motherhouse, 127 Howland St., Fall River, Mass. 02724. Educational, hospital work. (100)

Joseph, Sisters of St., C.S.J.: Founded 1823, in France; in US, 1855. General motherhouse, Bourg, France. US provinces: Marywood Rd., Crookston, Minn. 56716; 1200 Mirabeau Ave., New Orleans, La. 70122; 6532 Beechmont Ave., Cincinnati, O. 45230. (333)

Joseph, Sisters of St. (Lyons, France), C.S.J.: Founded 1650, in France; in US, 1906. General motherhouse, Lyons, France; US motherhouse, 93 Halifax St., Winslow, Me. 04901. Educational, hospital work. (110)

Joseph, Sisters of St., of Peace, C.S.J.: Founded 1884, in England. General executive office, 1330 Massachusetts Ave., Suite 101, Washington, D.C. 20005. Educational, hospital, social service work. (497)

Joseph of Carondelet, Sisters of St., C.S.J.: Founded 1650, in France; in US, 1836, at St. Louis. US headquarters, 2307 S. Lindbergh Blvd., St. Louis, Mo. 63131. (4,030)

Joseph of Chambery, Sisters of St.: Founded 1650, in France; in US, 1885. Generalate, Rome, Italy; US motherhouse, 27 Park Rd., West Hartford, Conn. 06119. Educational, hospital, social work. (386)

Joseph of Cluny, Sisters of St., S.J.C.: Founded 1807, in France. General motherhouse, Paris, France; US provincial house, Cluny Convent, Brenton Rd., Newport, R.I. 02840. (52)

Joseph of St. Augustine, Fla., Sisters of St.,

S.S.J.: General motherhouse, 241 St. George St., St. Augustine, Fla. 32084. Educational, hospital, social work. (187)

Joseph of St. Mark, Sisters of St., S.S.J.S.M.: Founded 1845, in France; in US, 1937. General motherhouse, Alsace-Lorraine, France; US motherhouse, 21800 Chardon Rd., Euclid, Cleveland, O. 44117. Social, domestic work. (52)

Lamb of God, Sisters of the, A.D.: Founded 1945, in France; in US, 1958. General motherhouse, France; US foundation, 1516 Parish Ave., Owensboro, Ky. 42301.

Loretto at the Foot of the Cross, Sisters of, S.L.: Founded 1812 in US, by Rev. Charles Nerinckx. General motherhouse, Nerinx, Ky. 40049. Educational work. (852)

Louis, Congregation of Sisters of St., S.S.L.: Founded 1842, in France; in US, 1849. General motherhouse, Monaghan, Ireland; US novitiate, 22300 Mulholland Dr., Woodland Hills, Calif. 91364. Educational work. (108)

Love of God, Sisters of the, R.A.D.: Founded 1864, in Spain; in US, 1958. Motherhouse, Spain; US address, Fairhaven, Mass. 02719.

Marian Sisters of the Diocese of Lincoln: Founded 1954. Motherhouse, 68462 Marycrest, Waverly, Nebr. 68462.

Marian Society of Dominican Catechists, O.P.: Founded 1954. General motherhouse, Boyce, La. 71409. Diocesan community.

Marianites of Holy Cross, Congregation of the Sisters, M.S.C.: Founded 1841, in France; in US, 1843. General motherhouse, Sarthe, France; US provinces: 4123 Woodland Dr., New Orleans, La. 70114; Great Rd., Princeton, N.J. 08540. (293)

Marist Sisters, Congregation of Mary, S.M.: Founded 1824, in France. General motherhouse, Rome, Italy; US convents: Dearborn Hts., Mich. 48125; E. Detroit, Mich.; Wheeling, W. Va. 26002.

Maronite Antonine Sisters: Established in US, 1966. US address, Box 519 N. Lipkey Rd., R.D. 1, North Jackson, Ohio 44451.

Martha of Prince Edward Island, Sisters of St., C.S.M.: Founded 1916, in Canada; in US, 1961. General motherhouse, 141 Mt. Edward Rd., Charlottetown, P.E.I., Canada.

Marthe, Sisters of Sainte (of St. Hyacinthe), S.M.S.H.: Founded 1883, in Canada; in US, 1929. General motherhouse, St. Joseph de Hyacinthe, Que., Canada.

Mary, Company of, O.D.N.: Founded 1607, in France; in US, 1926. General motherhouse, Rome, Italy; US motherhouse, 16791 E. Main St., Tustin, Calif. 92680. (86)

Mary, Daughters of the Heart of, D.H.M.: Founded 1790, in France; in US, 1851. Generalate, Paris, France; US provincialate, 103 E. 20th St., New York, N.Y. 10003. Educational work. (288)

Mary, Little Company of, Nursing Sisters, L.C.M.: Founded 1877, in England; in US, 1893. General motherhouse, Rome, Italy; US provincial house, 9350 S. California Ave., Evergreen Park, Ill. 60642. (80)

Mary, Missionary Sisters of the Society of (Marist Sisters), S.M.S.M.: Founded 1845, et St. Brieuc, France; in US, 1922. General motherhouse, Rome, Italy; US provincialate, 591 Springs Rd., Bedford, Mass. 01730. Foreign missions. (115)

Mary, Servants of, O.S.M.: Founded 13th century, in Italy; in US, 1893. General motherhouse, Louvain, Belgium; US provincial motherhouse, 7400 Military Ave., Omaha, Nebr. (224)

Mary, Servants of (Servite Sisters), O.S.M.: Founded 1894, in Austria; in US, 1952. General motherhouse, Vienna, Austria; US novitiate, Sublimity, Ore. 97385. Nursing work.

Mary, Servants of (Servite Sisters), O.S.M.: Founded 13th century, in Italy; in US, 1912. General motherhouse, Ladysmith, Wis. 54848. (137)

Mary, Sisters of St., of Oregon, S.S.M.O.: Founded 1886, in Oregon, by Bishop William H. Gross, C.Ss.R. General motherhouse, 4440 S.W. 148th Ave., Beaverton, Ore. 97005. Educational, nursing work. (245)

Mary, Sisters Servants of, O.S.M.: Founded 1861, in Italy; in US, 1916. Generalate, Rome, Italy; US motherhouse, 13811 S. Western Ave., Blue Island, Ilt. 60406. Educational, hospital work.

Mary, Sisters Servants of (Trained Nurses), S. de M.: Founded 1851, at Madrid, Spain; in US, 1914. General motherhouse, Rome, Italy; US motherhouse, 800 N. 18th St., Kansas City, Kans. 66102. Home nursing. (339)

Mary and Joseph, Daughters of, D.M.J.: Founded 1817, in Belgium; in US, 1926. Generalate, Rome, Italy; American provincial house, 12935 San Vicente Blvd., Los Angeles, Calif. 90049. (100)

Mary Help of Christians, Daughters of (Salesian Sisters of St. John Bosco), F.M.A.: Founded 1872, in Italy, by St. John Bosco; in US, 1908. General motherhouse, Rome, Italy; US motherhouse, North Haledon, N.J. 07508. Education, youth work. (269)

Mary of Namur, Sisters of St., S.S.M.N.: Founded 1819, at Namur, Belgium; in US, 1863. General motherhouse, Namur, Belgium. US provinces: 20 Rich St., Buffalo, N.Y. 17211; 3300 Hemphill St., Ft. Worth, Tex. (398)

Mary of Providence, Daughters of St., D.S.M.P.: Founded 1872, at Como, Italy; in US, 1913. General motherhouse, Rome, Italy; US provincial house, 4200 N. Austin Ave., Chicago, Ill. 60634. Educational work. (105)

Mary of the Catholic Apostolate, Sisters of the, S.A.C.: Founded 1926 at Schoenstatt, Germany; in US, 1949. General motherhouse, Schoenstatt, Germany. US addresses: Star Route 1, Box 100, Rockport, Tex. 78382;

W. 284-N.698 Cherry Lane, Waukesha, Wis. 53186. (74)

Mary of the Immaculate Conception, Daughters of, D.M.: Founded 1904, in US, by Msgr. Lucian Bojnowski. General motherhouse, New Britain, Conn. 06053. Educational, hospital work. (152)

Mary Immaculate, Daughters of (Marianist Sisters), F.M.I.: Founded 1816, in France, by Very Rev. William-Joseph Chaminade. General motherhouse, Rome, Italy; US foundation, 251 W. Ligustrum Dr., San Antonio, Tex. 78228. Educational work.

Mary Immaculate, Religious of, R.M.I.: Founded 1876, in Spain; in US, 1954. General motherhouse, Rome, Italy: US foundation 719 Augusta St., San Antonio, Tex. 78215.

Mary Immaculate, Sisters Servants of, S.S.M.I: Founded 1892, in Austria; in US, 1935. General motherhouse, Rome, Italy; US province, 209 W. Chestnut Hill Ave., Philadelphia, Pa. 19118. Educational, hospital work. (90)

Mary Immaculate of Mariowka, Sister Servants of, S.S.M.I.: Founded 1878 in Poland. General motherhouse, Poland; American provincialate, 1220 Tugwell Dr., Catonsville, Md. 21228.

Mary Reparatrix, Society of, S.M.R.: Founded 1857, in France; in US, 1908. Generalate, Rome, Italy; US province, 14 E. 29th St., New York, N.Y. 10016. (68)

Medical Mission Sisters (Society of Catholic Medical Missionaries, Inc.), S.C.M.M.: Founded 1925, in US. Generalate, Rome, Italy; US headquarters, 8400 Pine Rd., Philadelphia, Pa. 19111. Medical work, especially in mission areas. (150)

Medical Missionaries of Mary, M.M.M.: Founded 1937, in Ireland, by Mother Mary Martin, M.M.M.: in US, 1950. General motherhouse, Drogheda, Ireland; US motherhouse, 1 Arlington St., Winchester, Mass. 01890. Medical aid in missions.

Mercedarian Missionaries of Berriz, M.M.B.: Founded 1930, in Spain; in US, 1946. General motherhouse, Berriz, Spain; US vice provincial house, 918 E. 9th St., Kansas City, Mo. 64106. (113)

Mercy, Daughters of Our Lady of, D.M.: Founded 1837, in Italy, by St. Mary Joseph Rossello; in US, 1919. General motherhouse, Savona, Italy; US motherhouse, Catawba Ave., Newfield, N.J. 08344. Educational, hospital work. (106)

Mercy, Missionary Sisters of Our Lady of, M.O.M.: Founded 1938, in Brazil; in US, 1955. General motherhouse, Brazil; US address, 388 Franklin St., Buffalo, N.Y. 14202.

Mercy, Sisters of, R.S.M.: Founded 1831, in Ireland, by Mother Mary Catherine McAuley. US motherhouses (number of professed members is given in parentheses):

634 New Scotland Ave., Albany, N.Y. 12208 (352); 273 Willoughby Ave., Brooklyn, N.Y. 11205 (398); S. 5245 Murphy Rd., Orchard Park, N.Y. 14127 (396); Mansfield Ave., Burlington, Vt. 05401 (157): 1125 Prairie Dr., N.E., Cedar Rapids, Ia. 52402 (213); 444 E. Grandview Blvd., Erie, Pa. 16504 (190); 249 Steele Rd., W. Hartford, Conn. 06117 (573).

Windham, N.H. 03087 (387); Merion, Pa. 10968 (653); 3333 Fifth Ave., Pittsburgh, Pa. 15213 (418); 605 Stevens Ave., Portland, Me. 04103 (306); Belmont, N. Car. 28012 (163); 1437 Blossom Rd., Rochester, N.Y. 14610 (344); Rt. 3, Box 3216, Auburn, Calif. 95603 (150).

2300 Adeline Dr., Burlingame, Calif. 94010 (397); US Route 22 at Tirrell Rd., North Plainfield, N.J. 07061 (552); 46 High St., Worcester, Mass. 01608 (111).

Mercy, Sisters of, of the Union in the United States of America, R.S.M.: Founded 1831 in Ireland, by Mother M. Catherine McAuley; union formed in 1929. General motherhouse, 10000 Kentsdale Dr., Box 3446, Bethesda, P.O., Washington, D.C. 20034. (5,637)

Mercy, Sisters of, Daughters of Christian Charity of St. Vincent de Paul, S.M.D.C.: Founded 1842, in Hungary; US foundation, Rt. 1, Box 353, Hewitt, N.J. 07421.

Mercy of the Blessed Sacrament, Sisters of, R.M.S.S.: Founded 1910 in Mexico City. General motherhouse, Mexico; US foundation, 555 E. Mountain View, Barstow, Calif. 92311.

Mill Hill Sisters: See Franciscan Missionaries of St. Joseph.

Minim Daughters of Mary Immaculate, C.F.M.M.: Founded 1886, in Mexico; in U.S. 1926. General motherhouse, Leon, Guanajuato, Mexico; US address, Box 1865, Nogales, Ariz. 85621. (50)

Misericorde Sisters, S.M.: Founded 1848, in Canada; in US, 1887. General motherhouse. 12435 Ave. Misericorde, Montreal 9, Canada. Hospital work. (67)

Mission Helpers of the Sacred Heart, M.H.S.H.: Founded 1890, in US. General motherhouse, 1001 W. Joppa Rd., Towson, Md. 21204. Religious education, social work. (191)

Missionary Catechists of the Sacred Hearts of Jesus and Mary (Violetas), M.C.: Founded 1927, in Mexico; in US, 1943. Motherhouse, Tlalpan, Mexico; US address, 209 W. Murray St., Victoria, Tex. 77901. (136)

Missionary Sisters of the Catholic Apostolate (Pallottine Sisters), S.A.C.: Founded in Rome, 1843; in US, 1912. Generalate, Rome, Italy; US provincialate, Rt. 2, 15270 Old Halls Ferry Rd., Florissant, Mo. 63034.(113)

Most Pure Virgin Mary, Missionary Daughters of the: Founded 1903, at Mexico City; in US, 1916. General motherhouse, Aguascalientes, Mexico. Educational work.

Mother of God, Missionary Sisters of the, M.S.M.G.: Byzantine, Ukrainian Rite, Stamford. Motherhouse, 711-719 N. Franklin St., Philadelphia, Pa. 19123.

Mother of God, Sisters Poor Servants of the, S.M.G.: Founded 1869, at London, England; in US, 1947. General motherhouse, Maryfield, Roehampton, London. US addresses: High Point, N.C. 27260; Norton, Va. 24273; 1800 Geary St., Philadelphia, Pa. 19145. Hospital work.

Nazareth, Poor Sisters of: Founded 1924, in US. General motherhouse, Hammersmith, London, England; US novitiate, 3333 Manning Ave., Los Angeles, Calif. 90064. (56)

Notre Dame, School Sisters de: Founded 1853, in Czechoslovakia; in US, 1910. General motherhouse, Horazdovice, Czechoslovakia; US motherhouse, 3501 State St., Omaha, Nebr. 68112. Educational work. (123)

Notre Dame, School Sisters of, S.S.N.D.: Founded 1833, in Germany; in US, 1847. General motherhouse, Rome, Italy. US provinces: 700 W. Highland Rd., Mequon, Wis. 53092; 6401 N. Charles St., Baltimore, Md. 21212; 320 E. Ripa Ave., St. Louis, Mo. 63125; Good Counsel Hill, Mankato, Minn. 56011; Wilton, Conn. 06897; Rt. 2, Box 4, Irving, Tex. 75060; R.R. 1, DeKalb, Ill. 60115. (5,752)

Notre Dame, Sisters of, S.N.D.: Founded 1850, at Coesfeld, Germany; in US, 1874. General motherhouse, Rome, Italy. US provinces: 13000 Auburn Rd., Chardon, O. 44024; 1601 Dixie Highway, Covington, Ky. 41011; 3837 Secor Rd., Toledo, O. 43623; 624 W. Potrero Rd., Thousand Oaks, Calif. 91360. (1,559)

Notre Dame, Sisters of the Congregation of, C.N.D.: Founded 1653, in Canada; in US, 1860. General motherhouse, Montreal, Que., Canada; US motherhouse, 223 West Mountain Rd., Ridgefield, Conn. 06877. Education. (342)

Notre Dame de Namur, Sisters of, S.N.D.: Founded 1803, in France; in US, 1840. General motherhouse, Rome, Italy. US provinces:— Dartmouth St., Boston, Mass. 02116; 1561 N. Benson Rd., Fairfield, Conn. 06430; Ilchester, Md. 21083; 701 E. Columbia Ave., Reading, Cincinnati, O. 45215; Bohlman Rd., Saratoga, Calif. 95070. Educational work. (2,585)

Notre Dame de Sion, Congregation of, N.D.S.: Founded 1843, in France; in US, 1892. Generalate, Rome, Italy; US provincial house, 3823 Locust St., Kansas City, Mo. 64109. Creation of better understanding and relations between Christians and Jews.

Notre Dame des Anges, Missionary Sisters of, M.N.D.A.: Founded 19)2, in Canada; in US, 1949. General motherhouse, Lennoxville, Canada; US headquarters, 320 N. Main St., Union City, Conn. 06770.

Our Lady of LaSalette, Sisters of, S.M.S.: Founded 1930, in France. General mother-

house, France; US novitiate, Attleboro, Mass.]2703.

Our Lady of Sorrows, Sisters of, O.L.S.: Founded 1839, in Italy; in US, 1947. General motherhouse, Rimini, Italy; US headquarters, 10450 Ellerbe Rd., Shreveport, La. 71106.

Pallottine Sisters of the Catholic Apostolate, C.S.A.C.: Founded 1843, at Rome, Italy; in US, 1889. General motherhouse, Rome; US motherhouse, Harriman Heights, Harriman, N.Y. 10926. Educational work. (150)

Parish Visitors of Mary Immaculate, P.V.M.I.: Founded 1920, in New York. General motherhouse, Box 658, Monroe, Orange Co., N.Y. 10950. Mission work. (126)

Passionist Sisters: See Cross and Passion, Sisters of the.

Paul, Daughters of St., Missionary Sisters of the Catholic Editions, D.S.P.: Founded 1915, at Alba, Piedmont, Italy; in US, 1932. General motherhouse, Rome, Italy; US provincial house, 50 St. Paul's Ave., Jamaica Plain, Mass. 02130. Apostolate of the communications arts. (114)

Peter Claver, Missionary Sisters of St., S.S.P.C.: Founded 1894; in US, 1914. General motherhouse, Rome, Italy; US address, 667 Woods Mill Rd. S., Chesterfield, Mo. 63017.

Pious Schools, Sisters of, Sch., P.: Founded 1829 in Spain; in US, 1954. General motherhouse, Rome, Italy; US headquarters, 12500 N. Maclay St., Sylmar, Calif. 91342.

Poor, Little Sisters of the, L.S.P.: Founded 1839, in France; in US, 1868. General motherhouse, St. Pern, France. US provinces: 110-30 221st St., Queens Village, N.Y. 11429; 601 Maiden Choice Lane, Baltimore, Md. 21228; 80 W. Baldwin Rd., Palatine, Ill. 60067. Social work. (697)

Poor Clare Missionary Sisters (Misionaras Clarisas), M.C.: Founded Mexico. General motherhouse, Rome, Italy; US novitiate, 11712 Stuart Dr., Garden Grove, Calif. 92640.

Poor Clare Nuns: See Franciscan Poor Clare Nuns.

Poor Clares of Ireland, P.C.: General motherhouse, Newry, Ireland; US foundation, 37 E. Emerson, Chula Vista, Calif. 92011.

Poor Handmaids of Jesus Christ (Ancilla Domini Sisters), P.H.J.C.: Founded 1851, in Germany; in US, 1868. General motherhouse, Dernbach, Westerwald, Germany; US motherhouse, Donaldson, Ind. 46513. Educational, hospital work. (472)

Precious Blood, Daughters of Charity of the Most: Founded 1872, at Pagani, Italy; in US, 1908. General motherhouse, Rome, Italy; US novitiate, 46 Preakness Ave., Paterson, N.J. 07502. Social work.

Precious Blood, Missionary Sisters of the, C.P.S.: Founded 1885, at Mariannhill, South

Africa; in US, 1925. Generalate, Rome, Italy: US motherhouse, New Holland Ave., P.O. Box 43, Shillington, Pa. 19607. Home and foreign mission work. (51)

Precious Blood, Sisters Adorers of the, A.P.B.: Founded 1861, in Canada; in US, 1890. General motherhouses: 2520, rue Girouard, St. Hyacinthe, Que., Canada (French); 667 Talbot St., London 12, Ont., Canada (English). Contemplatives. (115)

Precious Blood, Sisters of the, C.Pp.S.: Founded 1834, in Switzerland; in US, 1844. Generalate, 4000 Denlinger Rd., Dayton, Ohio 45426. Educational, hospital work. (637)

Precious Blood, Sisters of the Most, C.Pp.S.: Founded 1845, in Steinerberg, Switzerland; in US, 1870. General motherhouse, 204 N. Main St., O'Fallon, Mo. 63366. Educational work. (507)

Presentation, Sisters of St. Mary of the S.M.P.: Founded 1829, in France; in US, 1903. General motherhouse, Broons, Cotes-du-Nord, France. US motherhouse, Valley City, N. Dak. 58072. Educational, hospital work. (112)

Presentation of Mary, Sisters of the, P.M.: Founded 1796, in France; in US, 1873. General motherhouse, Rome, Italy. US provinces: Manchester, N.H. 03104; Methuen, Mass. 01844. (768)

Presentation of the B.V.M., Sisters of the, P.B.V.M.: Founded 1777, in Ireland; in US, 1854. US motherhouses: 2360 Carter Rd., Dubuque, Ia. 52001; R.D. 2, Box 101, Newburgh, N.Y. 12550; 8931 Callaghan Rd., San Antonio, Tex. 78230; 2340 Turk St., San Francisco, Calif. 94118; Watervliet, N.Y. 12189.

Route 1, Fargo, N. Dak. 58102; 250 S. Davis Dr., P.O. Box 1113, Warner Robbins, Ga. 31093; Aberdeen, S. Dak. 57401; 1300 E. Cedar, Globe, Ariz. 85501; 1555 E. Dana, Mesa, Ariz. 85201; 366 South St., Fitchburg, Mass. 01420. (1,383)

Providence, Daughters of Divine, F.D.P.: Founded 1832, Italy; in US, 1964. General motherhouse, Rome, Italy; US foundation, 1029 N. Atlanta St., Metairie, La. 70003.

Providence, Missionary Catechists of Divine, M.C.D.P.: Founded 1930, as a filial society; adjunct branch of Sisters of Divine Providence (San Antonio). Formation house, 2318 Castroville Rd., San Antonio, Tex. 78237. (64)

Providence, Oblate Sisters of, O.S.P.: Founded 1829, in US. General motherhouse, 701 Gun Rd., Baltimore, Md. 21227. Educational work. (262)

Providence, Sisters of, S.P.: Founded 1861, in Canada; in US, 1873. General motherhouse, Brightside, Holyoke, Mass. 01040. (350)

Providence, Sisters of, S.P.: Founded 1843, in Canada; in US, 1854. General motherhouse, Montreal, Canada. US provinces:

Providence Hts., Pine Lake, Issaquah, Wash. 98027; 9 E. 9th Ave., Spokane, Wash. 99202. (558)

Providence, Sisters of (of St. Mary-of-the-Woods), S.P.: Founded 1806, in France; in US, 1840. General motherhouse, St. Mary-of-the-Woods, Ind. 47876. (1,282)

Providence, Sisters of Divine, C.D.P.: Founded 1762, in France; in US, 1866. General motherhouse, Box 197, Helotes, Tex. 78023. Educational, hospital work. (628)

Providence, Sisters of Divine, C.D.P.: Founded 1851, in Germany; in US, 1876. General motherhouse, Rome, Italy. US provinces: 9000 Babcock Blvd., Allison Park, Pa. 15101; 8351 Florissant Rd., Normandy, Mo. 63121; Box 2, Rte. 80, Kingston, Mass. 02360. Educational, hospital work. (673)

Providence, Sisters of Divine (of Kentucky), C.D.P.: Founded 1762, in France; in US, 1889. General motherhouse, Moselle, France; US province, Melbourne, Ky. 41059. Educational, hospital work, domestic work. (396)

Providence and of the Immaculate Conception, Sisters of, S.P.I.C.: Founded 1837, in Belgium. General motherhouse, Belgium; US address, 2041 Mt. Diablo Blvd., Walnut Creek, Calif. 94596.

Redeemer, Oblates of the Most Holy, O.SS.R.: Founded 1864, in Spain. General motherhouse, Spain; US foundation, 60-80 Pond St., Jamaica Plain, Mass. 02130.

Redeemer, Order of the Most Holy, O.SS.R.: Founded 1731, by St. Alphonsus Liguori; in US, 1957. US addresses: Esopus, N.Y. 12429; Liguori, Mo. 63057.

Redeemer, Sisters of the Divine, S.D.R.: Founded 1849, in Niederbronn, France; in US, 1912. General motherhouse, Rome, Italy; US motherhouse, 999 Rock Run Road, Elizabeth, Pa. 15037. Educational, hospital work; care of the aged. (132)

Redeemer, Sisters of the Holy, S.H.R.: Founded 1849, in Alsace; in US, 1924. General motherhouse, Wuerzburg, Germany; US regional house, Huntingdon Valley, Pa. 19006. Personalized medical care in hospitals, homes for aged and private homes. (127)

Refuge, Sisters of Our Lady of Charity of, O.L.C.R.: Founded 1641, at Caen, France; in US, 1855. US federation, P.O. Box 327, Wisconsin Dells, Wis. 53965. Social work. (247)

Religious Conceptionist Missionaries, R.C.M.: Founded 1892, in Spain; in US, 1962. General motherhouse, Madrid, Spain; US foundation, 867 Oxford, Clovis, Calif. 93612.

Reparation of the Congregation of Mary, Sisters of, S.R.C.M.: Founded 1903, in US. Motherhouse, Monsey, N.Y. 10952.

Resurrection, Sisters of the, C.R.: Founded 1891, in Italy; in US, 1900. General motherhouse, Rome, Italy. US provinces: 7432 Talcott Ave., Chicago, Ill. 60631; Castleton-on-Hudson, N.Y. 12033. Educational work. (345)

Rita of the Immaculate Heart, Daughters of St., D.S.R.: Motherhouse, Berry Ave., Versailles, Ky. 40383.

Rosary, Congregation of Our Lady of the Holy, R.S.R.: Founded 1874, in Canada; in US, 1899. General motherhouse, C.P. 2020, Rimouski, Que., Canada. Educational work.

Rosary, Missionary Sisters of Our Lady of the Holy, H.R.S.: Founded 1924, in Ireland; in US, 1954. Motherhouse, Killeshandra, Co. Cavan, Ireland. US novitiate, 214 Ashwood Rd., Villanova, Pa. 19085. African missions.

Sacrament, Missionary Sisters of the Most Blessed, M.SS.S.: General motherhouse, Madrid, Spain; US foundations: 1111 Wordin Ave., Bridgeport, Conn. 06605.

Sacrament, Nuns of the Perpetual Adoration of the Blessed, A.P.: Founded 1807, in Rome, Italy; in US, 1925. US monasteries: 145 N. Cotton Ave., El Paso, Tex. 79901; 771 Ashbury St., San Francisco, Calif. 94117.

Sacrament, Oblate Sisters of the Blessed, O.S.B.S.: Founded 1935, in US; motherhouse, Marty, S.D. 57361. Care of American Indians.

Sacrament, Religious Mercedarians of the Blessed, R.M.SS.: Founded 1910, in Mexico; in US, 1926. General motherhouse, Mexico City, Mexico; US convent, 222 W. Cevallos St., San Antonio, Tex. 78204.

Sacrament, Servants of the Blessed, S.S.S.: Founded 1858, in France, by St. Pierre Julien Eymard; in US, 1947. General motherhouse, Rome, Italy; US motherhouse, 101 Silver St., Waterville, Me. 04901. Contemplative.

Sacrament, Sisters of Perpetual Adoration of the Blessed (of Guadalupe), A.P.: Founded 1879, in Mexico; in US, 1925. General motherhouse, Mexico City, Mexico.

Sacrament, Sisters of the Blessed, for Indians and Colored People, S.B.S.: Founded 1891, in US. General motherhouse, Cornwells Heights, Pa. 19020. (489)

Sacrament, Sisters of the Most Holy, M.H.S.: Founded 1851, in France; in US, 1872. General motherhouse, 409 W. St. Mary Blvd. (P.O. Box 2429), Lafayette, La. 70501. (131)

Sacrament, Sisters Servants of the Blessed, S.S.B.S.: Founded 1904, in Mexico. General motherhouse, Guadalajara, Mexico. US address, 536 Rockwood Ave., Calexico, Calif. 92231.

Sacramentine Nuns (Religious of the Order of the Blessed Sacrament and Our Lady), O.S.S.: Founded 1639, in France; in US, 1912. US monasteries: 23 Park Ave., Yonkers, N.Y. 10703; US 31, Conway, Mich. 49722. Perpetual adoration of the Holy Eucharist.

Sacred Heart, Daughters of Our Lady of the: Founded 1882, in France; in US, 1955. General motherhouse, Rome, Italy; US address, 424 E. Browning Rd., Bellmawr, N.J. 08031. Educational work.

Sacred Heart, Missionary Sisters of the (Cabrini Sisters), M.S.C.: Founded 1880, in Italy, by St. Frances Xavier Cabrini; in US, 1889. General motherhouse, Rome, Italy; US provincialate, 223 E. 19th St., New York, N.Y. 10003. Educational, health, social and catechetical work. (391)

Sacred Heart, Religious of the Apostolate of the, R.A.: General motherhouse, Madrid, Spain; US address, 1120 6th St., Miami Beach, Fla., 33139.

Sacred Heart, Society Devoted to the, S.D.S.H.: Founded 1940, in Hungary; in US, 1956. US motherhouse, 728 S. Hudson Ave., Los Angeles, Calif. 90005. Educational work.

Sacred Heart, Society of the, R.S.C.J.: Founded 1800, in France; in US, 1818. General motherhouse, Rome, Italy. US provinces: 1177 King St., Greenwich, Conn. 06830; 2047 W. Fargo, Chicago, Ill. 60645; 4535 Maryland Ave., St. Louis, Mo. 63108; 453 Miller Ave., S. San Francisco, Calif. 94080; 842 Commonwealth Ave., Newton, Mass. 02159. Educational work. (906)

Sacred Heart of Jesus, Apostles of, A.S.C.J.: Founded 1894, in Italy; in US, 1902. General motherhouse, Rome, Italy; US motherhouse, 265 Benham St., Hamden, Conn. 06514. Educational, social work. (243)

Sacred Heart of Jesus, Congregation of Oblates of, O.S.C.: Founded 1843, in France; in US, 1955. US address, 314 S. 4th St., Camden, N.J. 08103.

Sacred Heart of Jesus, Handmaids of the, A.C.J.: Founded 1877, in Spain. General motherhouse, Rome, Italy; US province, 2025 Church Rd., Wyncote, Pa. 19095. Educational, retreat work. (60)

Sacred Heart of Jesus, Missionary Sisters of the Most, M.S.C.: Founded 1899, in Germany; in SS, 1908. General motherhouse, Rome, Italy; US province, Hyde Park, Reading, Pa. 19605. Educational, hospital, social work. (315)

Sacred Heart of Jesus, Oblate Sisters of the, O.S.H.J.: Founded 1894; in US, 1949. General motherhouse, Rome, Italy; US motherhouse, 50 Warner Rd., Hubbard, Ohio 44425. Educational, social work.

Sacred Heart of Jesus, Servants of the Most: Founded 1894, in Poland; in US, 1959. General motherhouse, Cracow, Poland; in US, 231 Arch St., Cresson, Pa. 16630.

Sacred Heart of Jesus, Sisters of the, S.S.C.J.: Founded 1816, in France; in US, 1903. General motherhouse, St. Jacut, Brittany, France; US provincial house, 5922 Blanco Rd., San Antonio, Tex. 78216. Educational, hospital, domestic work. (91)

Sacred Heart of Jesus and of the Poor, Servants of the (Mexican), S.S.H.J.P.: Founded 1885, in Mexico; in US, 1907. General motherhouse, Apartado 92, Puebla, Pue, Mexico; US regional house, 237 Tobin Pl., El Paso, Tex. 79905. (70)

Sacred Heart of Jesus for Reparation, Congregation of the Handmaids of the: Founded

1918, in Italy; in US, 1958. US address, Sunshine Park, R.D. 3, Steubenville, Ohio 43952.

Sacred Heart of Mary, Religious of the, R.S.H.M.: Founded 1848, in France; in US, 1877. Generalate, Rome, Italy. US provinces; 15 E. 81st St., New York, N.Y. 10028; 945 Tremonto Rd., Santa Barbara, Calif. 93103. (580)

Sacred Hearts, Religious of the Holy Union of the, S.U.S.C.: Founded 1826, in France; in US, 1886. Generalate, Rome, Italy. US provinces: 492 Rock St., Fall River, Mass. 02720; Main St., Groton, Mass. 01450. Educational work. (368)

Sacred Hearts and of Perpetual Adoration, Sisters of the, SS.CC.: Founded 1797, in France; in US, 1908. General motherhouse, Rome, Italy; US motherhouse, 330 Main St., N. Fairhaven, Mass. 02719. Educational work.

Sacred Hearts of Jesus and Mary, Sisters of the, S.H.J.M.: Established 1953, in US. General motherhouse, Essex, England; US address, 310 San Carlos Ave., El Cerrito, Calif. 94530.

Savior, Company of the, C.S.: Founded 1952, in Spain; in US, 1962. General motherhouse, Madrid, Spain; US foundation, 820 Clinton Ave., Bridgeport, Conn. 06608.

Savior, Sisters of the Divine, S.D.S.: Founded 1888, in Italy; in US, 1895. General motherhouse, Rome, Italy; US motherhouse, 4311 N. 100th St., Milwaukee, Wis. 53222. Educational, hospital work. (238)

Saviour, Daughters of Most Holy: Founded 1849, in Germany; in US, 1951. American province, 547 B St., Santa Rosa, Calif. 95401.

Social Service, Sisters of, S.S.S.: Founded 1908, in Hungary; in US, 1926. General motherhouse, 1120 Westchester Pl., Los Angeles, Calif. 90019. (134)

Social Service, Sisters of, S.S.S.: Founded in Hungary, 1923. US motherhouse, 440 Linwood Ave., Buffalo, N.Y. 14209. Social work.

Teresa of Jesus, Society of St., S.T.J.: Founded 1876, in Spain; in US, 1910. General motherhouse, Rome, Italy; US provincial house, 4018 S. Presa St., San Antonio, Tex. 78223. (110)

Thomas of Villanova, Congregation of Sisters of St., S.S.T.V.: Founded 1661, in France; in US, 1948. General motherhouse, Neuilly-sur-Seine, France; US foundation W. Rocks Rd., Norwalk, Conn. 06851.

Trinity, Missionary Servants of the Most Blessed, M.S.B.T.: Founded 1912, in US, by Very Rev. Thomas A. Judge. General motherhouse, 3501 Solly St., Philadelphia, Pa. 19136. Educational, social work. (446)

Trinity, Sisters of the Most Holy, O.Ss.T.: Founded 1198, in Rome; in US, 1920. General motherhouse, Rome, Italy; US motherhouse, 21320 Euclid Ave., Euclid, Ohio 44117. Educational work.

Ursula of the Blessed Virgin, Society of the

Sisters of St., S.U.: Founded 1606, in France; in US, 1902. General motherhouse, Tours, France; US novitiate, Rhinebeck, N.Y. 12572. Educational work. (74)

Ursuline Nuns (Roman Union), O.S.U.: Founded 1535, in Italy; in US, 1727. Generalate, Rome, Italy. US provinces: 1 Berrian Rd., New Rochelle, N.Y. 10804; Crystal Heights Rd., Crystal City, Mo. 63019; 639 Angela Dr., Santa Rosa, Calif. 95401; 71 Lowder St., Dedham, Mass. 02026; 401 Findley St., Toronto, O. 43694. (1,155)

Ursuline Nuns of the Congregation of Paris, O.S.U.: Founded 1535, in Italy; in US, 1727. US motherhouses: St. Martin, O. 45170; East Miami St., Paola, Kans. 66071; 3115 Lexington Rd., Louisville, Ky. 40206; 2600 Lander Rd., Cleveland, O. 44124; Maple Mount, Ky. 42356; 2413 Collingwood Blvd., Toledo, O. 43620; 4250 Shields Rd., Canfield, O. 44406; 1339 E. McMillan St., Cincinnati, O. 45206. (1,943)

Ursuline Nuns of the Congregation of Tildonk, Belgium, R.U.: Founded 1535, in Italy; in US, 1924. Generalate, Haecht, Belgium; US address, Blue Point, L.I., N.Y. 11715. Educational, foreign mission work. (119)

Ursuline Sisters, O.S.U.: General motherhouse, Blackrock, Cork, Ireland; US address, Torch Hill Rd., Columbus, Ga. 31903.

Ursuline Sisters of Mount Calvary, O.S.U.: Founded 1535, in Italy; in US, 1910. General motherhouse, Mount Calvary, Germany; US motherhouse, 1026 N. Douglas Ave., Belleville, Ill. 62221. Educational work.

Venerini Sisters, Religious, M.P.V.: Founded 1685, in Italy; in US, 1909. General motherhouse, Rome, Italy; US provincialate; 23 Edward St., Worcester, Mass. 01605. (70)

Verona, Missionary Sisters of, M.S.V.: Founded 1875, in Italy; in US, 1950. US address, 1307 Lakeside Ave., Richmond, Va. 23228. Hospital, social, educational work.

Victory Missionary Sisters, Our Lady of, O.L.V.M.: Founded 1922, in US. Motherhouse, Victory Noll, Box 109, Huntington, Ind. 46750. Educational, social work. (358)

Vincent de Paul, Sisters: See Charity of St. Vincent de Paul, Sisters of.

Visitation Nuns, V.H.M.: Founded 1610, in France; in US, 1799. North American federations: 2002 Bancroft Pkwy., Wilmington, Del. 19806 (Pres., Mother Mary Gabrielle Muth); Visitation Monastery, Springfield, Mo. 65804 (Pres., Mother Anne Madeleine Ernstmann). Contemplative. Educational work. (549)

Visitation of the Congregation of the Immaculate Heart of Mary, Sisters of the, S.V.M.: Founded 1952, in US. Motherhouse, 900 Alta Vista St., Dubuque, Ia. 52201. Educational work.

Vocationist Sisters (Sisters of the Divine Vocations): Founded 1921, in Italy. General motherhouse, Naples, Italy; US foundation, 172 Broad St., Newark, N.J. 07104.

White Sisters: See Africa, Missionary Sisters of Our Lady of.

White Sisters of Charity of St. Vincent de Paul of Zagreb: Founded 1845, in Croatia; in US, 1955. General motherhouse, Zagreb, Yugoslavia; US foundation, 171 Knox Ave., West Seneca, N.Y. 14224.

Wisdom, Daughters of, D.W.: Founded 1703, in France, by St. Louis Marie Grignon de Montfort; in US, 1904. General motherhouse, Vendee, France; US motherhouse, 385 S. Ocean Ave., Islip, N.Y. Educational, hospital work. (253)

Xaverian Missionary Society of Mary, Inc., M.M.: Founded 1945, in Italy; in US, 1954. General motherhouse, Parma, Italy; US address, 242 Salisbury St., Worcester, Mass. 01609.

Xavier Mission Sisters (Catholic Mission Sisters of St. Francis Xavier), X.M.S.: Founded 1946, at Warren, Mich., by Cardinal Edward Mooney. General motherhouse, 35750 Moravian Dr., Fraser, Mich. 48026. Educational, hospital, social work in missions.

ORGANIZATIONS OF WOMEN RELIGIOUS

Leadership of Women

The Leadership Conference of Women Religious in the United States of America is an association of the major superiors of religious communities of women, with the purpose of promoting the spiritual and apostolic welfare of the sisterhoods of the US.

Organized in the late 50's and approved by the Congregation for Religious and Secular Institutes June 13, 1962, it has a membership of approximately 600. Its original name, changed in 1971, was the Conference of Major Superiors of Women. With its formerly affiliated Sister Formation Conference, it inaugurated measures for the religious and professional development of sisters and has contributed greatly to the renewal of religious life in this country.

The officers are: Sisters: Francis Borgia Rothluebber, O.S.F., president; Francine Zeller, O.S.F., vice president; Rosemary Ferguson, O.P., secretary; Mary Daniel Turner, S.N.D. de N., executive director.

The national secretariat is located at 1325 Massachusetts Ave., N.W., Washington, D.C. 20005.

The 1974 assembly of the conference met Aug. 25 to 29, in Houston. Its theme was "The Gospel: Vision and Mandate."

Formation Conference

The Sister Formation Conference was organized in 1952 for the purpose of promoting the spiritual and professional formation of sisters belonging to American institutes. In 1970 it became independent of the Leadership Conference of Women Religious with which it had been affiliated.

The presiding officer of the conference is Sister Mary Lou Wirtz, O.S.F. The executive director is Sister Ruth McGoldrick, S.P.

The national secretariat is located at 1325 Massachusetts Ave. N.W., Washington, D.C. 20005.

National Assembly

More than 2,000 delegates attending a convention in Cleveland Apr. 17 to 19, 1970, voted overwhelmingly in favor of a proposal to establish the National Assembly of Women Religious and to make it "a voice" of sisters in the United States.

The assembly's primary goal is "to challenge women religious to communicate a valid concept of the role of the consecrated celibate women in the Church today, and to study, evaluate, establish priorities and make recommendations concerning areas in which women religious are critically needed."

The assembly is intended to be a forum for communication among women religious and "a voice through which they can speak to the Church and to the world."

NAWR's current agenda derives from a comprehensive "Ministry of Justice" resolution adopted at its 1972 convention in Minneapolis and reaffirmed in 1973 in New York. In the statement the sisters committed themselves to "a ministry of justice by the continuous use of our organized power to affect local and international policy for the liberation of all peoples from oppression." The resolution has been put into effect through the sponsorship of regional workshops designed to help sisters bring about significant changes in their respective areas of service.

Membership in the NAWR is open to individual sisters, councils of sisters (official organization of sisters in a diocese), organizations of women religious (de facto groups of sisters which are not official diocesan bodies), clergy and lay associates.

NAWR reported a 1974 membership of 90 diocesan councils and 2,500 individuals. Service publications of the assembly include *NAWR Trends*.

Principal officers in 1974 were Sisters: Catherine Pinkerton, C.S.J., chairperson; Marjorie Fisher, R.S.C.J., treasurer; Mary Rehman, C.H.M., administrative assistant.

Offices are located at 201 E. Ohio St., Chicago, Ill., 60611.

The 1974 NAWR convention was held Aug. 14 to 18 in St. Louis.

Black Sisters

(Source: Sister Mary Shawn Copeland, O.P., executive director.)

The National Black Sisters' Conference

was organized in August, 1968, for the express purpose of enabling the sisters to determine their priorities in relation to their black people. Five years after its founding, 80 per cent of its 325 members had apostolates in black communities. The conference includes black sisters from 123 religious congregations in the United States and Islands.

A major concern of the conference is the development of continuance of black vocations to religious life in the unique contemporary black life style, for fulfillment in bringing about the liberation of black people.

The conference foresees the establishment of a central formation experience or opportunity for the formation of black sisters in the religious life style. It has initiated efforts to make it possible for black sisters to transfer from the congregations to which they belong to other institutes in which they might find greater opportunities for personal and apostolic fulfillment. Evaluations are being made of the priorities of various congregations in terms of their apostolates, life styles and formation. Only the names of those congregations which meet the conference's criteria will be circulated among black women interested in religious life.

Project RACE (Religious Active for Rural Evolvement) was initiated by the conference in southeastern Louisiana to provide tutorial and recreational programs for the children of sugar cane workers, and year-long engagement by staff members in community development and organization.

Other priorities include work with the National Office for Black Catholics and efforts to bring about a redistribution of black sisters to meet the demands of the black community in a better way and to unify the total work of the Church in focusing on the most productive channels of freedom for black people.

The conference is concerned with national and local social issues and is committed to public stands and concrete action where these may be indicated. Immediate concerns are black community schools, alternative black educational systems, prison reform, and community organization.

The conference publishes a newsletter, *Signs of Soul,* four times a year, and has published the following: "Black Religious Women as Part of the Answer," "Celibate Black Commitment," and "Black Survival: Past, Present and Future."

Sister Helen Marie Christian, R.S.M., is president of the conference. The associate director is Sister Mary Shawn Copeland, O.P.

Headquarters are located at 3508 Fifth Ave. Pittsburgh, Pa. 15213.

Participants in the August, 1974, convention of the conference in Atlanta were urged by Ida Lewis, editor and publisher of *Encore,* to regard the education and enlightenment of black youth as their first priority.

National Coalition

Recognition and development of the role of women in the Church and society, along with advocacy for social activism, are the principal characteristics of the Coalition of American Nuns, organized in July, 1969, under the leadership of Sister Margaret Traxler, S.S.N.D.

Sister Ann Gillen of Chicago is the executive director.

Sisters Uniting

Sisters Uniting, formed in March, 1971, in Chicago, describes itself as a group that works "to facilitate cooperation and coordination" of six national associations: the Association of Contemplative Sisters, the National Sister Formation Conference, the National Sister Vocation Conference, the National Coalition of American Nuns, the Leadership Conference of Women Religious, and the National Association of Women Religious.

Consortium

The Consortium Perfectae Caritatis ("Association of Perfect Love"), named after the Latin title of the Second Vatican Council's *Decree on the Appropriate Renewal of Religious Life,* was organized in March, 1971, at a Washington, D.C., meeting of nearly 150 sisters from 48 communities in the United States and Canada.

The stated purposes of the association are: (1) to bring together those who accept the conciliar documents of Vatican Council II regarding religious life, subsequent papal statements, and interpretations and directives emanating from the Congregation for Religious and Secular Institutes; (2) to communicate and share with each other experiences in implementing the conciliar plan of renewal.

Five hundred sisters representing 70 American and 50 European communities attended the first international assembly of Consortium Feb. 23 to Mar. 4, 1974, in Rome. In radical departure from renewal conferences based on current sociological surveys and psychological studies, the assembly reexamined the role of women religious in the Church from the perspectives of historic continuity and spiritual theology. The theme, "Religious Woman — a Minister of Faith," developed a panoramic view of women religious and their historic contribution to the faith and life of the Church through the ministry of consecrated virginity.

Mother Mary Elise, S.N.D., of Chardon, O., is head of the group's national council. The secretary is Sister Mary Florice, S.N.D.

The association publishes *Consortium* bi-monthly.

The mailing address of the magazine is P.O. Box 1092, Washington, D.C. 20013.

Las Hermanas

Las Hermanas is a national organization of

women religious of Hispanic origin formed in 1971 in Houston for the purpose of being "actively present to the ever-changing needs" of the Spanish-speaking.

Accordingly, the organization has three projects in operation: cultural awareness workshops designed to make groups of women religious and civic/governmental agencies more aware of the needs of Spanish-speaking Catholics; Proyecto Mexico, an educational program for Mexican sisters seeking involvement in parish ministry; a nine-month pastoral, educational and renewal institute for priests, religious and lay persons in the Spanish-speaking apostolate.

Las Hermanas, which has sister associates and lay affiliates, is directed by a national co-ordinating team headed by Sisters Carmelita Espinoza, R.G.S., Maria de Jesus Ybarra, O.D.N. and Mario Barron, C.S.J.

The mailing address is P. O. Box 28185, San Antonio, Tex. 78228.

The fifth national convention of Las Hermanas was held Aug. 9 to 12, 1974, in Kansas City, Kans.

Contemplatives

The Association of Contemplative Sisters was founded by nearly 140 representatives of 57 communities in the US and Canada who took part in a two-week seminar for contemplatives held in August, 1969, at Woodstock College, Md. It has a membership of approximately 1,000.

The purposes of the association are to encourage and foster healthy development of the contemplative life so that contemplative women may serve the Church more effectively, and to provide a vehicle of communication between the nuns, their communities and the Church at large.

The association publishes the *Contemplative Review*, edited by Sister Mary Roman, Carmelite Monastery, Beckley Hill, Barre, Vt. 05641.

Sister Jean Alice McGoff, O.C.D., is president of the association.

The central office is located at 2500 Cold Spring Rd., Indianapolis, Ind. 46222.

Vocation Conference

The National Sisters Vocation Conference, formed in September, 1970, is a national organization dedicated to deepening the under-standing of the role of women, especially women religious, in the Church through work in the vocation apostolate.

The conference seeks to coordinate and provide informational and other services to persons and organizations in the vocation apostolate, and to assist prospective candidates for religious life.

Its 1974 membership was approximately 1,400.

The national director is Sister M. Cathleen Toomey, R.S.M.

The national office is located at 1307 S. Wabash Ave., Chicago, Ill. 60605.

Other Conferences

International Organizations: The Union of Superiors General (Men), which was established in 1957, had its statutes approved by the Congregation for Religious and Secular Institutes in 1967, and has Pedro Arrupe, S.J., as president; the International Union of Superiors General (Women), which was established in 1965, had its statutes approved in 1967, and has M. Mary Linscott, of the Sisters of Our Lady of Namur, as president.

Regional Organization: The Latin American Confederation of Religious, which was established in 1959, had its statutes approved in 1967, and has Manuel Edwards, SS.CC., as president.

Other Conferences: National conferences of superiors of religious, generally separate for men and women, have been established in 17 countries in Europe, 14 in North and Central America, 10 in South America, 18 in Africa, and 18 in Asia and Australia.

STUDY ON ENTRANCES AND DEPARTURES OF NUNS

A *Study on Entrances and Departures in Religious Communities of Women in the United States 1965-1972* documented the decline in the number of women entering religious communities and variations in the number of those departing from 1965 to 1971. The study, published in March, 1973, was conducted by Sister Margaret Mary Modde, O.S.F., director of the National Sisters Vocation Conference.

(A second but more limited study of the same subject, for the period from Jan. 1, 1972, to May 1, 1974, was published in 1974. See Follow-Up Study, below.)

Study findings were based on data supplied by 274 participating communities with a membership of 103,014. (The total number of religious communities of women in the U.S.

in 1972 was approximately 455, with an overall membership of 145,000.)

Findings

• The study reported that "the average yearly number entering and remaining (in the participating communities from 1965 to 1972) was 768, and the total average decrease was 3,841."

"This represented a .75 per cent increase in membership and a 3.72 decrease in membership, or a net 2.97+ per cent decrease each year." Continuation of this trend over the next five years "would represent a total decrease of 13.8 per cent" (14,216 sisters). There were signs, however, that these trends might not continue, since other statistics indicated that "the peak year for departures was 1970" and that there was "a slight increase in the entrance rate from 1971 to 1972."

• "Of the total number of women entering (13,476) the participating religious communities between 1965-1971, 44 per cent remained (5,907) and 56 per cent (7,569) did not remain."

• "Of the total number of departures of sisters, 34 per cent were due to deaths, 66 per cent were due to dispensation of perpetual vows or termination of temporary vows."

• "The average yearly net increase in religious communities from 1965-1972 was 768+ members, while the average yearly net decrease was 3,841 members. Approximately, the average yearly decrease due to deaths was 1,346, dispensation, 1,551, and termination of vows, 944+."

Entering and Remaining

The following table "shows the number of young women who entered these (participating) religious communities of women between 1965-1971 and the number of these young women remaining today."

Year	Entering	Remaining
1965	4,110	1,466
1966	3,481	1,272
1967	2,394	1,044
1968	1,486	744
1969	790	474
1970	662	472
1971	506	410
Total	13,476	5,907

"The sharp drop in entrances into religious communities began between 1966-1967 and . . . consistently continued until 1972 when there was a slight increase of 47 over the previous year." Five hundred and 53 entered communities in 1972.

Departures

This table shows "the departures from these (participating) religious communities of women between 1965-1972 by death, dispensation of vows or termination of vows."

Year	Deaths	Dispensed	Termination	Total
1965	1,285	491	571	2,347
1966	1,389	727	694	2,810
1967	1,329	1,328	1,089	3,746
1968	1,330	1,494	1,274	4,098
1969	1,445	2,163	1,395	5,003
1970	1,410	2,456	1,216	5,082
1971	1,441	2,269	816	4,526
1972	1,138	1,478	501	3,117
Total	10,767	12,406	7,556	30,729

"The greatest number of dispensations, 2,456, was granted in 1970, whereas the greatest number of sisters leaving at the termination of temporary vows, 1,395, occurred in 1969, and the highest number of deaths, 1,445, also occurred in 1969.

"The combined greatest loss of sisters, that is, due to death, dispensation and/or termination of vows, occurred in 1970, with 5,082."

FOLLOW-UP STUDY

A second *Study on Entrances and Departures in Religious Communities of Women in the United States, Jan. 1, 1972, to May 1, 1974,* by Sister Margaret Mary Modde, O.S.F., was published in 1974 by the National Sisters Vocation Conference.

Findings were based on data supplied by 178 communities with a membership of 62,210 — 42.9 per cent of the approximately 414 communities in the country, with a total membership of 139,963.

Entering and Remaining

Seven hundred and eight women entered participating communities during the survey period and 537 remained at its end, for a retention rate of 75.8 per cent. This rate was higher than the 44 per cent registered in the 1965-72 survey, possibly because of entrances at a later age than previously and the effectiveness of more individualized formation programs.

Departures

The following table shows the departures from communities participating in the study from Jan. 1, 1972, to Jan. 1, 1973 (indicated by 1972-3) and from Jan. 1, 1973, to May 1, 1974 (indicated by 1973-4).

Year	Deaths	Dispensed	Termination	Total
1972-3	838	1,186	258	2,282
1973-4	987	1,304	183	2,474
Total	1,825	2,490	441	4,756

Observations

The study noted: "Of the total decrease in membership (4,756) of religious communities during the period of this study, 62 per cent of the total was due to dispensation or termination of vows and 38 per cent was due to deaths."

There was "a total net decrease of 6.8 per cent in membership of the participating communities" during the period of the study.

"If this trend continues, the decrease in membership over the next five years would be 8,440."

One statistical table in the study, of figures compiled by *The Official Catholic Directory,* showed that membership in religious communities of women in the U.S. peaked at 181,421 in 1966 and recorded a low of 139,963 in 1974. The year of greatest loss, 9,174, was 1969.

A superior of the Daughters of Mary, Help of Christians, reported in the fall of 1974 that her community, unlike many others with few candidates, was not suffering from any dearth of vocations.

SECULAR INSTITUTES

(Sources: Almanac survey; *Directory of Secular Institutes with Foundations in the U.S.A.,* published by the National Center for Church Vocations; *Annuario Pontificio.*)

Secular institutes are societies of men and women living in the world who dedicate themselves by vow or promise to observe the evangelical counsels and to carry on apostolic works suitable to their talents and opportunities in the areas of their everyday life.

"Secular institutes are not religious communities but they carry with them in the world a profession of evangelical counsels which is genuine and complete, and recognized as such by the Church. This profession confers a consecration on men and women, laity and clergy, who reside in the world. For this reason they should chiefly strive for total self-dedication to God, one inspired by perfect charity. These institutes should preserve their proper and particular character, a secular one, so that they may everywhere measure up successfully to that apostolate which they were designed to exercise, and which is both in the world and, in a sense, of the world" (*Decree on the Appropriate Renewal of Religious Life,* No. 11; Second Vatican Council).

A secular institute reaches maturity in several stages. It begins as an association of the faithful, technically called a pious union, with the approval of a local bishop. Once it has proved its viability, he can give it the status of an institute of diocesan right, in accordance with norms and permission emanating from the Congregation for Religious and Secular Institutes. On issuance of a separate decree from this congregation, an institute of diocesan right becomes an institute of pontifical right.

Secular institutes, which originated in the latter part of the 18th century, were given full recognition and approval by Pius XII Feb. 2, 1947, in the apostolic constitution *Provida Mater Ecclesia.* On Mar. 25 of the same year a special commission for secular institutes was set up within the Congregation for Religious. Institutes were commended and confirmed by Pius XII in a motu proprio of Mar. 12, 1948, and were the subject of a special instruction issued a week later, Mar. 19, 1948.

The **United States Conference of Secular Institutes (CSI)** was established in October, 1972, following the organization of the World Conference of Secular Institutes in Rome. Its membership is open to all canonically erected secular institutes with members living in the United States. The conference was organized to offer secular institutes an opportunity to exchange experiences, to do research in order to help the Church carry out its mission, and to search for ways and means to make known the existence of secular institutes in the U.S. Address: 7007 Bradley Blvd., Bethesda, Md. 20034.

Institutes in the U.S.

Caritas Christi (Cultural Crossroads, Inc.): Originated in Marseilles, 1937; for women. Established as a secular institute of pontifical right Mar. 19, 1955. Address: Rev. Austin Green, O.P., national priest-assistant, 1909 S. Ashland Ave., Chicago, Ill. 60608.

Company of St. Paul: Originated in Milan, Italy, 1920; for lay people and priests. Approved as a secular institute of pontifical right June 30, 1960. Address: P. O. Box 6267, Washington, D.C. 20015.

Company of St. Ursula, Daughters of St. Angela Merici ("The Angelines"): Founded in Brescia, Italy, 1935; for women. Approved as a secular institute of pontifical right 1958. Addresses: Secretary, Via Martinengo da Barco 8, 25100 Brescia, Italy; P. O. Box 4254, Grand Central Station P. O., New York, N.Y. 10017.

Cordimarian Filiation (Daughters of the Immaculate Heart of Mary): Originated in Spain, 1850, by St. Anthony M. Claret; for women. Final approval by the Holy See, Dec. 8, 1959. Address, Rev. Joseph Gallego, C.M.F., 4541 S. Ashland Ave., Chicago, Ill. 60609. International membership of approximately 2,000.

DeSales Secular Institute: Founded in Vienna, Austria, 1940; for women. Pontifical right. Address: Rev. Joseph Griffin, O.S.F.S., DeChantal National Center, 2019 Delaware Ave., Wilmington, Del. 19806.

Diocesan Laborer Priests: Approved as a secular institute of pontifical right. The specific aim of the institute is the promotion, sustenance and cultivation of apostolic, religious and priestly vocations. Delegate for US, Rev. John Queralt, 3706 15th St. N.E., Washington, D.C. 20017.

Institute of Apostolic Oblates: Founded in Rome, Italy, 1947; for women. U.S. addresses: 8113 Fillmore Dr., Stanton, Calif. 90680; 311 Central Ave., Brooklyn, N.Y. 11221.

Institute of the Cenacle: Originated in Italy, 1952; for priests and laymen. Received formal decree of approval from the Congregation for Religious and Secular Institutes Oct. 29, 1953. Address: Via Aurelia 183, 00165, Rome, Italy. Msgr. Georges Roche, general superior; Rev. Royce Hughes, American superior, Via Concordia 1, 00183 Rome, Italy.

Institute of Secular Missionaries: Founded in Vitoria, Spain, 1939; for women. Approved as a secular institute, 1955. Address: 109 W. Fifth Ave., Covington, Ky. 41011.

Institute of the Heart of Jesus: Originated in France Feb. 2, 1791; restored Oct. 29, 1918; for diocesan priests. Received final approval from the Holy See as a secular institute of pontifical right Feb. 2, 1952. Canon Jean Canivez, superior general. Addresses: Central House, 202 Avenue du Maine, Paris 14me, France; US address, Rev. David Scheider, Notre Dame High School, Batavia, N.Y.

14020. International membership of approximately 1,900.

Mission of Our Lady of Bethany: Founded in Plessis-Chevet, France, 1948; for women. Approved as an institute of diocesan right 1965. Address: Sister Mary Joan, O.P., Dominican Sisters of Bethany, 204 Ridge St., Millis, Mass. 02054.

Missionaries of the Kingship of Christ: Originated in Assisi, Italy, 1919; for women. Established as an institute of pontifical right with decree of praise July 12, 1948; received final approbation Aug. 3, 1953. American establishment originated, 1950; first members received, Oct. 4, 1951; separate territory in the USA established May 9, 1970. Address: Rev. Stephen Hartdegen, O.F.M., Holy Name College, 14th and Shepherd Sts. N.E., Washington, D.C. 20017. International membership of women, approximately 4,000. Separate divisions for women, men, diocesan priests.

Oblate Missionaries of Mary Immaculate: Founded, 1952, and approved as a secular institute Feb. 2, 1962; for women. Addresses: Oblate Missionaries of Mary Immaculate, 1054 Lisbon St., Lewiston, Me. 04240; 7535 Boulevard Parent, Trois Rivieres, P. Q., Canada. International membership of approximately 1,000.

Rural Parish Workers of Christ the King: Originated in Cottleville, Mo., 1942; for women. An approved secular institute of the Archdiocese of St. Louis. Dedicated to the service of neighbor, especially in rural areas. Address: Box 300, Rt. 1, Cadet, Mo. 63630.

Schoenstatt Sisters of Mary: Originated in Schoenstatt, Germany, 1926; for women. Established as a secular institute of diocesan right May 20, 1948; of pontifical right Oct. 18, 1948. Addresses: Schoenstatt Sisters of Mary, W. 284 N. 698 Cherry Lane, Waukesha, Wis. 53186; House Schoenstatt, Star Rt. 1, Box 100, Rockport, Tex. 78382. International membership of more than 2,500.

Secular Institute of Pius X: Originated in Manchester, N.H., 1940; for priests and laymen. Approved as a secular institute, 1959 (first secular institute of diocesan right founded in the US to be approved by the Holy See). Addresses: P. O. Box 357, Manchester, N.H. 03101. C.P. 1815, Quebec City, P.Q., Canada.

Society of Our Lady of the Way: Originated, 1936; for women. Approved as a secular institute of pontifical right Jan. 3, 1953. Address: Society of Our Lady of the Way, 2339 N. Catalina Ave., Los Angeles, Calif. 90027. International membership of more than 400.

Teresian Institute: Founded in Spain 1911; for women. Address: 235 Cypress St., Newton Centre, Mass. 02159.

Voluntas Dei: Originated in Canada, 1958; for secular priests and laymen. Approved as a secular institute May 6, 1965. Address: Institute Voluntas Dei, 7385, Blvd. Parent, Trois-Rivieres, Que., Canada. International membership of approximately 150.

The *Annuario Pontificio* (1974) lists the following **secular institutes of pontifical right which are not established in the US:**

For men: Institute of Prado (originated Dec. 25, 1856; decree of praise, Oct. 28, 1959). Christ the King (originated, 1936; decree of praise, Oct. 27, 1963).

For women: Alliance in Jesus through Mary, Apostles of the Sacred Heart, Catechists of the Sacred Heart of Jesus (Ukrainian), Daughters of the Sacred Heart, Daughters of the Queen of the Apostles, Institute of the Blessed Virgin Mary (della Strada), Missionaries of the Sick, Institute of Notre Dame du Travail, Institute of Our Lady of Life, Oblates of Christ the King, Workers of Divine Love, Faithful Servants of Jesus.

Associations

Caritas: Originated in New Orleans, 1950; for women. Address: 3316 Feliciana St., New Orleans, La. 70126.

Daughters of Our Lady of Fatima: Originated in Lansdowne, Pa., 1949; for women. Received diocesan approval, Jan., 1952. Address: Miss Mary C. Long, Fatima House, Rolling Hills Rd., Ottsville, Pa. 18942.

Focolare Movement: Inaugurated in Trent, Italy, in 1943, by Chiara Lubich and a small group of companions; for men and women. Approved as an association of the faithful, 1962. It is not a secular institute by statute, but vows are observed by many single persons among its totally dedicated core membership of 1,500. Centers are located in 30 countries throughout the world. US centers are located in Boston, Chicago (where it was introduced in 1955), and New York. National headquarters : 250 E. 73rd St., Apt. 21D, New York, N.Y. 10021 (women); 206 Skillman Ave., Brooklyn, N.Y. 11211 (men).

Jesus Caritas Fraternity of Fr. Charles de Foucauld: Originated in Ars, France, 1952; for women. Established as an association of perfection May 31, 1962. Address: Miss A. M. de Commaille, 185 Claremont Ave., New York, N. Y. 10027. International membership of approximately 550.

Madonna House Apostolate: Originated in Toronto, Canada, 1930; for priests and lay persons. The constitutions of Madonna House were approved on a diocesan basis in July, 1956. Address: Madonna House, Combermere, Ontario, Canada—Catherine Doherty (women), Jack Scanlan (men), Rev. T. Callahan (priests). International membership.

Pax Christi: Lay institute of men and women dedicated to witnessing to Christ, with special emphasis on service to the poor in Mississippi. Addresses: St. Francis Center, 708 Ave. I, Greenwood, Miss. 38930; LaVerna House, 2108 Altawoods Blvd., Jackson, Miss. 39204.

THIRD ORDERS SECULAR

Third orders secular are societies of the faithful living in the world who seek to deepen their Christian life and apostolic commitment in association with and according to the spirit of various religious institutes. Members are called Tertiaries, Lay Franciscans, etc. The orders are called "third" because their foundation followed the establishment of the first (for men) and second (for women) religious orders with which they are associated.

Augustine, Third Order Secular of St.: Founded, 13th century; approved Nov. 7, 1400.

Carmel, (The Lay Carmelite Order) (Calced): Founded, 13th century; approved by Pope Nicholas V, Oct. 7, 1452. Address: Aylesford, National Scapular Center, I-55 and Cass Ave. N. Westmont, Ill. 60559. Approximately 15,000 members in US.

Carmel, Third Order Secular of Our Blessed Lady of Mt., and St. Teresa of Jesus (Discalced): Rule based on the Carmelite reform established by St. Teresa and St. John of the Cross, 16th century; approved Mar. 23, 1594; rule revised and given for five-year experimental period Oct. 26, 1970. Addresses of provincial directors: 514 Warren St., Brookline, Mass. 02146; .Mt. Carmel Center, 4600 W. Davis, Dallas, Tex. 75211; P.O. Box 3079 San Jose, Calif. 95116. Approximately 3,150 members in US.

Dominic, Third Order Secular of St. (The Dominican Laity): Founded in the 13th century. Addresses of provincial directors: 141 E. 65th St., New York, N.Y. 10021; 1909 S. Ashland Ave., Chicago, Ill. 60608; St. Albert's College, 5890 Birch Ct., Oakland, Calif. 94618.

Francis, Third Order Secular of St. (Secular Franciscans): Founded, 1209 by St. Francis of Assisi; approved Aug. 30, 1221. Address: National Secretary, Third Order of St. Francis, 1615 Vine St., Cincinnati, Ohio 45210. Approximately 2.2 million in the world, 59,000 English speaking in North America.

Mary, Third Order of: Founded, Dec. 8, 1850; rule approved by the Holy See, 1857. Addresses of provincial directors: 87 Lacy St., Marietta, Ga. 30060; 7 Harvard St., P. O. Box 66, Charlestown, Mass. 02129; 625 Pine St., San Francisco, Calif. 94108. Approximately 14,000 in the world, 6,600 in US.

Mary, Third Order Secular of Servants of (Servite): Founded, 1233; approved, 1424. Address: Director of Third Order, 323 W. Illinois St., Chicago, Ill. 60610. Approximately 2,500 in US.

Mercy, Secular Third Order of Our Lady of (Mercedarian): Founded, 1219 by St. Peter Nolasco; approved the same year.

Norbert, Third Order of St.: Founded, 1122 by St. Norbert; approved by Pope Honorius II, 1126. Address: St. Norbert Abbey, De Pere, Wis. Approximately 5,300 in US and Canada.

Trinity, Third Order Secular of the Most Holy: Founded, about 1198; approved, 1219. Address: Bro. Gary MacPherson, Holy Trinity Monastery, Pikesville, Md. 21208.

Oblates of St. Benedict are lay persons affiliated with a Benedictine abbey or monastery who strive to direct their lives, as circumstances permit, according to the spirit and Rule of St. Benedict.

MISSIONS UNDER ATTACK

Cardinal Agnelo Rossi, writing in the Mar. 28, 1974, edition of *L'Osservatore Romano*, criticized "self-styled theologians" and other Catholics seeking "to snuff out the Church's missionary zeal."

The prefect of the Congregation for the Evangelization of Peoples wrote:

"In the midst of a ferment of ideas about secularization and secularism, fostered and spread in various forms, even by persons linked with bishops' conferences, some voices openly assert that nowadays one need be concerned only for the local church.

"Others will say: 'Enough with evangelization. Today we must speak of dialogue, since it is more consistent with every man's religious freedom as underlined by the (Second Vatican) Council.'

"Or, finally, others declare: 'It isn't enough to worry about souls. Now the really urgent problem is to free man from oppression, from wretched poverty and from social injustices, using dynamic and efficacious methods such as Marxism .and, if necessary, violent revolution.'"

The cardinal commented: "In this way, for one reason or another, such persons put the missions to one side, considering them only as historic events of times vanished forever, or as an aspect of colonialism or westernization.

"Naturally, this outlook serves only to discourage and weaken the missionary spirit, vital to the Church. It discourages the Church's missionaries, as if they were the final remnants of a class doomed to disappear."

In a reference to "self-styled theologians," Cardinal Rossi called it "incredible" that such assertions be advanced "in an epoch which has seen the Second Vatican Council solemnly and unequivocally confirm the primary mission of the entire Church to evangelize."

He also called it. ironic that the missions should be downgraded "when two-thirds of mankind still does not know Our Lord Jesus Christ."

Cardinal Rossi declared: "When in our very house people try with sophistries to snuff out the Church's missionary zeal, (the Congregation for the Evangelization of Peoples) cannot be silent. It must make its voice heard and recall again, not to protesters themselves who will always be in the world and do not sincerely want to be converted, but to the faithful people."

Missionary Activity of the Church

The following excerpts concerning the Church's missionary activity are from the decree of the same name promulgated by the Second Vatican Council.

Doctrine

"The pilgrim Church is missionary by her very nature" (No. 2).

Christ "founded His Church as the sacrament of salvation, and sent His apostles into all the world just as He Himself had been sent by His Father (cf. Jn. 20:21). He gave them this command: 'Go, therefore, and make disciples of all nations, baptizing them in the name of the Father, and of the Son, and of the Holy Spirit, teaching them to observe all that I have commanded you' (Mt. 28:19ff). 'Go into the whole world; preach the gospel to every creature. He who believes and is baptized shall be saved, but he who does not believe shall be condemned' (Mk. 16:15ff).

". . . The mission of the Church . . . is fulfilled by that activity which makes her fully present to all men and nations" (No. 5).

" 'Missions' is the term usually given to those particular undertakings by which the heralds of the gospel are sent out by the Church and go forth into the whole world to carry out the task of preaching the gospel and planting the Church among peoples or groups who do not yet believe in Christ. These undertakings are brought to completion by missionary activity and are commonly exercised in certain territories recognized by the Holy See" (and placed under the general direction of the Congregation for the Evangelization of Peoples) (No. 6).

Distinctive Purpose

"The specific purpose of this missionary activity is evangelization and the planting of the Church among those peoples and groups where she has not yet taken root. Thus from the seed which is the Word of God, particular native Churches can be adequately established and flourish the world over, endowed with their own vitality and maturity. Thus too, sufficiently provided with a hierarchy of their own which is joined to a faithful people, and adequately fitted out with requisites for living a full Christian life, they can make their contribution to the good of the Church universal.

". . . Missionary activity among the nations differs from pastoral activity exercised among the faithful, as well as from undertakings aimed at restoring unity among Christians. And yet these two other activities are most closely connected with the missionary zeal of the Church, because the division among Christians damages the most holy cause of preaching the gospel to every creature and blocks the way to the faith for many. Hence, by the same mandate which makes missions necessary, all the baptized are called to be gathered into one flock, and thus to be able to bear unanimous witness before the nations to Christ their Lord. And if they are not yet capable of bearing full witness to the same faith, they should at least be animated by mutual esteem and love" (No. 6).

"Missionary activity is nothing else and nothing less than a manifestation or epiphany of God's will, and the fulfillment of that will in the world and in world history. In the course of this history God plainly works out the history of salvation by means of mission. By the preaching of the word and by the celebration of the sacraments, whose center and summit is the most holy Eucharist, missionary activity brings about the presence of Christ, the Author of salvation" (No. 9).

The three phases of missionary activity are:

• **Christian Witness,** to establish the presence of the Church: "The Church must be present in these groups of men through those of her children who dwell among them or are sent to them. For, wherever they live, all Christians are bound to show forth, by the example of their lives and by the witness of their speech, that new man which they put on at baptism, and that power of the Holy Spirit by whom they were strengthened at confirmation. Thus other men, observing their good works, can glorify the Father (cf. Mt. 5:16) and can better perceive the real meaning of human life and the bond which ties the whole community of mankind together" (No. 11).

• **Preaching the Gospel and Gathering Together the People of God,** through proclamation of the Gospel to conversion and on to transition to full Christian life. In this process: "The Church strictly forbids forcing anyone to embrace the faith, or alluring or enticing people by unworthy techniques. By the same token, she also strongly insists on a person's right not to be deterred from the faith by unjust vexations on the part of others" (No. 13).

• **Forming the Christian Community,** with the objective of developing, sustaining and self-supporting churches in mission lands through the various ministries of lay persons, bishops, priests, deacons and religious (Nos. 15 to 18).

Concerning the role of lay persons, the decree said: "Laymen cooperate in the Church's work of evangelization. As witnesses and at the same time as living instruments, they share in her saving mission. This is especially so if they have been called by God and have been accepted by the bishop for this work" (No. 41).

UNITED STATES FOREIGN MISSIONARIES

(Data on US foreign missionary personnel in the following tables were gathered by, and are reproduced with permission of, the United States Catholic Mission Council, 1325 Massachusetts Ave. N.W., Washington, D.C., 20005.

(For additional information about the Church in mission areas, see News Events and other Almanac entries.)

FIELD DISTRIBUTION, 1974

(Under this and following headings, Alaska, Hawaii, etc., are considered abroad because they are outside the 48 contiguous states.)

Africa: Men, 620; women 501; total, 1,121. Largest numbers in Tanzania, 198; Kenya, 146; Ghana, 115; Zambia, 104; Uganda, 83.

Near East: Men, 36; women, 24; total, 60. Largest numbers in Israel, 20; Lebanon, 18; Egypt, 14.

Far East: Men, 1,275; women, 570; total, 1,845. Largest numbers in Philippines, 557; Japan, 365; Taiwan, 209; India, 177; Korea, 173; Hong Kong, 94.

Oceania: Men, 407; women, 476; total, 883. Largest groups in Hawaii, 262; New Guinea, 243; Guam, 116.

Europe: Men, 21; women, 22; total, 43. Largest groups in Finland, 11; Sweden, 8, Denmark, 7.

North America: Men, 101; women, 140; total, 241. Largest group in Alaska.

Caribbean Islands: Men, 382; women, 375; total, 757. Largest groups in Puerto Rico, 355; Jamaica, 166; Haiti, 76.

Central America: Men, 470; women, 282; total, 752. Largest groups in Mexico, 223; Guatemala, 194.

South America: Men, 960; women, 756; total, 1,716. Largest groups in Peru, 511; Brazil, 488; Bolivia, 285; Chile, 206.

MEN RELIGIOUS, 1974

Sixty-nine mission-sending groups had 3,824 priests and brothers in overseas assignments.

Jesuits: 712 in 37 countries; largest group, 125 in Philippines.

Maryknoll Fathers: 673 in 19 countries; largest group, 79 in Tanzania.

Franciscans (O.F.M.): 230 in 16 countries; largest group, 83 in Brazil.

Divine Word Missionaries: 194 in 14 countries; largest group, 68 in New Guinea.

Redemptorists: 168 in 6 countries; largest group, 80 in Brazil.

Oblates of Mary Immaculate: 167 in 15 countries; largest group, 33 in Mexico.

Capuchins (O.F.M. Cap.): 166 in 10 countries; largest group, 39 in Nicaragua.

Marianists: 159 in 13 countries; largest group, 61 in Hawaii.

Benedictines: 107 in 13 countries; largest group, 20 in Brazil.

Columbans: 90 in 8 countries; largest group, 38 in Philippines.

Dominicans: 74 in 7 countries; largest group, 22 in Nigeria.

Holy Cross Fathers: 69 in 8 countries; largest group, 26 in Bangladesh.

Holy Cross Brothers: 68 in 7 countries; largest group, 21 in Brazil.

Holy Ghost Fathers: 61 in 6 countries; largest group, 26 in Puerto Rico.

Brothers of Christian Schools: 59 in 9 countries; largest group, 23 in Philippines.

Passionists: 57 in 4 countries; largest group, 29 in Philippines.

Conventual Franciscans (O.F.M. Conv.): 51 in 5 countries; largest group, 20 in Zambia.

La Salette Fathers: 50 in 4 countries; largest group, 18 in Philippines.

Vincentians: 43 in 8 countries; largest group, 26 in Panama.

Marist Fathers: 36 in 7 countries; largest group, 15 in New Guinea.

Marist Brothers: 31 in 7 countries; largest group, 13 in Philippines.

Missionaries of the Sacred Heart: 29 in 2 countries; larger group, 23 in New Guinea.

Sacred Heart Brothers: 29 in 5 countries; largest group, 14 in Zambia.

White Fathers: 29 in 9 countries; largest group, 8 in Tanzania.

African Missionary Fathers: 25 in 3 countries; largest group in Liberia.

Augustinians: 24 in 2 countries; larger group, 15 in Peru.

Xaverian Brothers: 21 in 2 countries; larger group, 11 in Kenya.

Xaverian Missionary Fathers: 21 in 6 countries; largest group, 9 in Sierra Leone.

Missionhurst: 20 in 5 countries; largest group, 14 in Dominican Republic.

Precious Blood Fathers: 20 in 2 countries; larger group, 14 in Chile.

Thirty-nine other mission-sending institutes had 19 or less members in overseas assignments.

DIOCESAN PRIESTS, 1974

Two hundred and 20 diocesan priests from 82 dioceses were in overseas assignments in 1974.

The largest groups were from Boston (24 in 6 countries) and St. Louis (12 in 3 countries).

Many diocesan priests in overseas assignments were members of the **Missionary Society of St. James the Apostle,** founded by Cardinal Richard J. Cushing of Boston in 1958. Its director is Father Dennis A. Dever, 24 Clark St., Boston, 02109.

SISTERS, 1974

One hundred and 60 mission-sending groups had 2,916 sisters in overseas assignments.

Maryknoll Sisters: 538 in 23 countries; largest

group, 89 in Hawaii.

Marists: 169 in 14 countries; largest group, 35 in Fiji.

Sisters of the Third Order of St. Dominic: 100 in 13 countries; largest group, 23 in Peru.

School Sisters of Notre Dame: 97 in 16 countries; largest group, 21 in Puerto Rico.

Religious Sisters of Mercy: 92 in 10 countries; largest group, 55 in Guam.

Servants of the Immaculate Heart of Mary: 72 in 7 countries; largest group, 30 in Peru.

Sisters of Notre Dame De Namur: 72 in 7 countries; largest group, 23 in Kenya.

Franciscan Missionaries of Mary: 68 in 18 countries; largest group, 9 in Australia.

Daughters of Charity: 62 in 9 countries; largest group, 32 in Bolivia.

Benedictines: 62 in 11 countries; largest group, 15 in Colombia.

Medical Mission Sisters: 59 in 11 countries; largest group, 16 in Ghana.

Sisters of St. Joseph (Brentwood, N.Y.): 51 in 2 countries; larger group, 50 in Puerto Rico.

Ursulines of the Roman Union: 43 in 14 countries; largest group, 9 in Mexico.

Sisters of the Holy Cross: 42 in 4 countries; largest group, 19 in Brazil.

Franciscan Sisters of Allegany, N.Y.: 38 in 3 countries; largest group, 24 in Jamaica.

Servants of the Holy Spirit: 37 in 7 countries; largest group, 12 in Ghana.

Sisters of St. Joseph (Carondolet): 36 in 2 countries; larger group, 25 in Peru.

Sisters of the Third Franciscan Order, Minor Conventuals (Syracuse, N.Y.): 36 in 3 countries; largest group, 23 in Hawaii.

Sisters of the Holy Child Jesus: 32 in 4 countries; largest group, 14 in Nigeria.

Religious Sisters of Mercy of the Union in the U.S.A.: 30 in 5 countries; largest group, 9 in Honduras.

Graymoor Sisters: 27 in 3 countries; largest group, 19 in Canada.

Sisters of Notre Dame: 27 in 2 countries; larger group, 14 in India.

Bernardines: 26 in 3 countries; 9 each in Liberia and Puerto Rico.

Adorers of the Blood of Christ: 23 in 5 countries; largest group, 7 in Liberia.

Sisters of the Most Precious Blood (O'Fallon, Mo.): 22 in 3 countries; largest group, 11 in Finland.

Felician Sisters: 21 in Brazil.

Franciscans of the Sorrowful Mother: 21 in 5 countries; largest group, 9 in Barbados.

Sisters of St. Francis of Millvale: 20 in 2 countries; larger group, 17 in Puerto Rico.

Sisters of St. John the Baptist: 20 in 3 countries; largest group, 10 in Zambia.

Missionary Sisters of the Immaculate Heart of Mary: 20 in 10 countries; largest group, 5 in Virgin Islands.

Missionary Sisters of St. Columban: 20 in 5 countries; largest group, 9 in Philippines.

One hundred and 29 other mission-sending institutes had 19 or less members in overseas assignments.

LAY VOLUNTEERS, 1974

Four hundred and 58 lay volunteers of 35 sponsoring organizations were in overseas assignments in 1974.

Catholic Medical Mission Board: 146 in 18 countries; largest group, 31 in Haiti.

Catholic Relief Services: 87 in 42 countries; largest group, 8 in India.

Lay Mission Helpers: 60 in 13 countries; largest group, 13 in New Guinea.

Jesuit Volunteer Corps: 54 in 2 countries; larger group, 50 in Alaska.

Frontier Apostolate: 18 in Canada.

Milwaukee Latin American Office: 10 in 5 countries; largest group, 5 in Colombia.

Regis College Lay Apostolate: 9 in 3 countries; largest group, 7 in Hawaii.

The 28 other sponsoring organizations had 8 or less members in overseas assignments.

U.S. Mission Council

The United States Catholic Mission Council, which took over and expanded functions of the former Mission Secretariat, started operations Sept. 1, 1970, "to provide a forum and organ for the evaluation, coordination and fostering, in the United States, of the worldwide missionary effort of the Church."

Structurally, the council is made up of five seven-member committees representing the National Conference of Catholic Bishops, the Conference of Major Superiors of Men, the Leadership Conference of Women Religious, the National Conference of Catholic Laity and mission agencies. Heads of the committees form the executive board which meets at least quarterly to oversee the implementation of policies and programs determined at annual meetings of the whole committee.

Typical activities of the council are educational efforts related to the Church's teaching about its missionary nature, the sponsorship of conferences on theological and pastoral foundations of missionary endeavor, liaison and cooperation with missionary bodies of other Christian churches, the encouragement of mission studies, training programs and refresher courses for departing and returning missionaries, gathering data on missionary activity, and general mission animation.

Brother Thomas Page More, C.F.X., is executive secretary of the council, with offices at 1325 Massachusetts Ave. N.W., Room 500, Washington, D.C. 20005.

Mission Committees: Diocesan mission committees may be greatly assisted by local mission committees in parishes, religious communities, universities, colleges, high schools, and other centers of Catholic life and action. Through such local committees the vision of the whole missionary Church can be more effectively brought to the individual person.

U.S. Foreign Missionaries, 1956-1974

Year	Diocesan Priests	Religious Priests	Religious Brothers	Religious Sisters	Seminarians	Lay Persons	Total
1956		2914*		2212			5126
1958	19	3477*		2532		96	6124
1960	14	3018	575	2827	170	178	6782
1962	31	3172	720	2764	152	307	7146
1964	80	3438	782	3137	157	532	8126
1966	215	3731	901	3706	201	549	9303
1968	282	3727	869	4150	208	419	9655
1970	373	3117	666	3824	90	303	8373
1972+	246	3182	634	3121	97	376	7656
1973	237	3913*		3012		529	7691
1974	220	3084	639	2916	101	458	7418

*Includes religious brothers and seminarians.
+A corrected total for 1972 should read 7937, indicating losses of 436 from 1970 to 1972 and 246 from 1972 to 1973.

Field Distribution by Areas, 1956-1974

	1956	1958	1960	1962	1964	1966	1968	1970	1972	1973	1974
Africa	445	617	781	901	1025	1184	1157	1141	1107	1229	1121
Far East	1555	1809	1959	2110	2332	2453	2470	2137	1955	1962	1845
Near East	103	110	111	75	122	142	128	39	59	54	60
Oceania	809	951	986	992	846	953	1027	900	826	811	883
Europe	102	153	203	93	69	38	33	38	39	40	43
North America	168	357	337	224	220	211	251	233	234	253	241
Caribbean Islands	887	928	991	967	1056	1079	1198	1067	819	796	757
Central America	329	392	433	537	660	857	936	738	728	763	752
South America	728	807	981	1247	1796	2386	2455	2080	1889	1783	1716
TOTALS	5126	6124	6782	7146	8126	9303	9655	8373	7656	7691	7418

HOME MISSIONS

The expression "home missions" is applied to places in the U.S. where the local Church is not fully established, i.e., where it does not have resources, human and otherwise, which are needed to begin or, if begun, to survive and grow. These areas share the name "missions" with their counterparts in foreign lands because they too need outside help to provide the personnel and means for making the Church present and active there in carrying out its mission for the salvation of men.

Dioceses in the Southeast, the Southwest, and the Far West are most urgently in need of outside help to carry on the work of the Church. Millions of persons live in counties in which there are no resident priests. Many others live in rural areas beyond the reach and influence of a Catholic center. According to the most recent statistics compiled by the Glenmary Research Center there are 639 priestless counties in the United States. Many states generally thought to be well off from a pastoral standpoint include areas in which the Catholic Church and the ministry of priests are virtually unknown.

About 20 per cent of the total U.S. population and less than three per cent of the Catholic population live within the boundaries of the 17 "most missionary" dioceses of the country. A "Survey of the Catholic Weakness" conducted by the National Catholic Rural Life Conference disclosed that the Catholic Church ranked 33rd among 38 religious bodies in percentage of rural membership.

Mission Workers

A number of forces are at work to meet the pastoral needs of these missionary areas and to establish permanent churches and operating institutions where they are required. In many dioceses, one or more missions and stations are attended from established parishes and are gradually growing to independent status. Priests, brothers and sisters belonging to scores of religious institutes are engaged full-time in the home missions. Lay persons, some of them in affiliation with special groups and movements, are also involved.

Group 7 was organized by the Glenmary Home Missioners for this purpose in 1971. Membership is open to Catholic adults, 21-years-old and older, willing to make a minimum commitment of two years. Twenty-six members of Group 7 are working in Georgia, Mississippi, North Carolina, Tennessee and Virginia.

The Society for the Propagation of the Faith, which conducts an annual collection for mission support in all parishes of the U.S., allocates 40 per cent of this sum for disbursement to home missions through the American Board of Catholic Missions.

The Catholic Church Extension Society provides one million dollars or more a year for the building of mission installations and related needs.

Special mission support is the purpose of the Commission for the Catholic Missions among the Colored People and the Indians.

Diocesan, parochial and high school mission societies frequently undertake projects in behalf of the home missions.

Glenmary Missioners

The Glenmary Home Missioners, founded by Father W. Howard Bishop in 1939, is the only home mission society established for the sole purpose of carrying out the pastoral ministry in small towns and the rural districts of the United States. With 77 priests and 27 professed brothers as of June 1, 1974, the Glenmary Missioners had 41 mission bases and 47 satellite missions in the archdioceses of Atlanta and Cincinnati, and in the dioceses of Altoona-Johnstown, Birmingham, Charlotte, Covington, Dallas, Harrisburg, Little Rock, Nashville, Natchez-Jackson, Tulsa, Owensboro, Savannah and Wheeling.

The Rev. Charles M. Hughes is president.

National headquarters are located in Fairfield, O. The mailing address is P. O. Box 46404, Cincinnati, O. 45246.

Regional offices for information are at 429 Unquowa Rd., Fairfield, Conn. 06430, and P. O. Box 8, Techny, Ill. 60082.

Sisters

The Glenmary Home Mission Sisters of America, founded July 16, 1952, had 21 professed members engaged in work in six social and catechetical centers, one home nursing center, one house of study and one promotional center, in the archdioceses of Cincinnati and St. Louis, and the dioceses of Charlotte, Columbus, Covington, Dallas, Owensboro and Savannah. Much of this work was concentrated in rural areas where poverty was prevalent. In September, 1971, members of the community began work in religious education research in Nashville and in campus ministry in the Savannah diocese. The community also conducts an associate program for laywomen interested in work in home mission areas for two or more years.

Sister Mary Joseph Wade, elected in 1967, is superior general. The community has headquarters at 4580 Colerain Ave., Cincinnati, Ohio 45223.

Negro Missions

The Commission for Catholic Missions among the Colored People and the Indians reported the following (1973) statistics for 71 dioceses in which it supplied financial assistance: 838,848 Catholics, 656 churches, 1,002 priests, 23,692 infant baptisms, 6,452 adults received into the Church, 402 schools, 108,659 students. The total number of black Catholics was estimated to be more than 900,000.

The commission, using figures different in some respects from those given above, reported: "The past year . . . 38 additional priests were to be counted among the 1,014 pastors or assistant pastors of missions and parishes composed entirely or predominantly of Negro members. These parishes now number 666, 20 more than previously reported. Thirty-eight more schools were reported to have achieved a large or entirely Negro enrollment, bringing the number of schools of this type up to 412. Correspondingly higher were the reported number of their teachers, approximately 5,000."

"Nearly two out of three Catholic Negroes now live in the 50 largest eastern, mid-western and far western cities. In the centers of these rapidly changing cities 341 large and small parishes with entirely or predominantly Negro congregations are under the care of 711 priests. Their elementary and high schools, now numbering 278, have almost 85,000 pupils enrolled."

The commission report, which was limited in scope, did not cover all aspects of the Church's ministry to the black population, which was estimated to number more than 22 million.

Indian Missions

The Commission for Catholic Missions among the Colored People and the Indians reported the following (1973) statistics for 43 dioceses in which it supplied financial assistance: 152,670 Catholics, 397 churches, 259 priests, 4,459 infant baptisms, 609 adults received into the Church, 40 schools, 7,049 students.

Missions were located in 25 states: 157 in the Southwest, 63 in the Northwest, 60 in the Dakotas, 45 in Alaska, 36 in the Great Lakes area, and 40 in other states.

The commission reported: "The work of the Church that is directed especially to Indians is carried on almost entirely on the Indian reservations. . . . The bases of this ministry are 125 missions where one or more priests reside; to most of them one or several outmissions are attached, or stations without chapels. The other outstanding feature of this apostolate are the 40 Catholic schools on reservations, now attended by 7,049 Indian pupils. Three hundred and 59 priests and about 600 nuns, scholastics and religious brothers are engaged "in church and school activities."

Special work for Indians "who have left their reservations is conducted on a small scale" through the operation of Indian centers. Nine of them are located in large towns and cities near reservations.

According to the most recent census reports, it was estimated that 300,000 Indians were living on federal reservations and 307,000 in urban areas. An estimated 25,000 Catholic Indians were not on reservations.

Support Bodies

The Catholic Church Extension Society: This society was established for the purpose of preserving and extending the Church in the US and its dependencies principally through the collection and disbursement of funds for missions. Since the time of its founding in 1905, more than $50 million have been received and expended for this purpose. Disbursements in 1973 amounted to $3.3 million.

Works of the society are supervised by a board of governors consisting of twelve members: Cardinal John Cody, archbishop of Chicago, chancellor; Rev. Joseph A. Cusack, president; five bishops or priests, and five lay-men. Society headquarters are located at 1307 S. Wabash Ave., Chicago, Ill. 60605.

Commission for Catholic Missions among the Colored People and the Indians: Organized in 1886, this commission provided financial support ($2,547,000 in 1973) for religious works among Negroes and Indians in the United States. Funds are raised by an annual collection in all parishes of the country.

Cardinal John J. Krol is head of the board of directors. Rev. J. B. Tennelly, S.S., D.D., is secretary. Commission headquarters are located at 2021 H St. N.W., Washington, D.C. 20006.

MINISTRY TO THE SPANISH-SPEAKING

The U.S. Census Bureau, in a report based on a nationwide survey and dated March, 1973, indicated that there were approximately 10.8 million persons of Spanish origin in this country. They included about: 6.5 million of Mexican origin; 1.5 million of Puerto Rican origin; 700,000 of Cuban origin; two million of Central or South American or other Hispanic origin. They comprised nearly 5.2 per cent of the nation's population.

According to other estimates, the total figure was considerably higher.

Every state has some Spanish-speaking residents, ranging from 2,000 in North Dakota to more than 2.5 million in California.

Nearly three-fourths of the Spanish-speaking live in California, New Mexico, Texas, Florida and New York.

Most of the Spanish-speaking in the southwestern states are Mexican American. Large numbers of Mexican Americans are also in the Chicago area, Ohio, northern Indiana and southern Michigan.

Puerto Ricans, although concentrated especially in and near New York City, also have large settlements in Chicago and Philadelphia. New York City alone has about three out of every five persons of Puerto Rican birth or parentage in the U.S.

Most persons of Cuban origin live in Florida, particularly in the Miami and Tampa areas. There are smaller concentrations in New York City, northeastern New Jersey, Los Angeles, Long Beach, Calif., Chicago and urban areas of northwestern Indiana.

The vast majority of the Spanish-speaking in the U.S. have been baptized in the Catholic Church.

Variable Conditions

Pastoral ministry to the Spanish-speaking in the United States varies, depending on differences among the people and the availability of personnel to carry it out.

The pattern in cities with large numbers of Spanish-speaking is built around special churches, centers or other agencies where pastoral and additional forms of service are provided in a manner suited to the needs, language and culture of the people. Services in some places are extensive and include legal advice, job placement, language instruction, recreational and social assistance, specialized counseling, replacement services. In many places, however, even where there are special ministries, the needs are generally greater than the means required to meet them.

Some of the urban dwellers have been absorbed into established parishes and routines of church life and activity. Many Spanish-speaking communities, especially those with transients, remain in need of special ministries.

An itinerant form of ministry best meets the needs of the scores of thousands of migrant workers who follow the crops in various areas of the country. Some of these ministries are carried out from centers and include other services — health, instruction for children, etc. — in addition to opportunities for attending Mass and receiving the sacraments.

Pastoral care for the Spanish-speaking was the central concern of the 1972 Primer Encuentro Nacional Hispano de Pastoral, a national meeting of diocesan bishops and their delegates sponsored by the U.S. Catholic Conference. Needs pinpointed in deliberations were for: greater participation by the Spanish-speaking in leadership and decision-making at all levels in the Church in the U.S.; the development of programs for Christian leadership formation; the establishment of nationally coordinated regional centers of pastoral research and reflection.

Special ministries for the Spanish-speaking have been in operation for a long time in dioceses of the Southwest. The total number of dioceses with such ministries is more than 50. More than 20 others have migrant ministries in operation.

Organizations

USCC Division for the Spanish-Speaking: The purpose of this division of the Department of Social Development and World Peace, U.S. Catholic Conference, is to promote pastoral ministry to and the integral development of the Spanish-speaking. Accordingly, its programs center around leadership development, the establishment of local offices for on-the-scene operations, communication and informational services for, by and about the Spanish-speaking.

Paul Sedillo, Jr., is director of the national office, at 1312 Massachusetts Ave. N.W., Washington, D.C. 20005.

In the Southwest, 55 Mexican-American priests organized **PADRES** in October, 1969, to help the Church identify more closely with the social, economic and educational needs of the Spanish-speaking. PADRES is the abbreviation of the Spanish title, "Padres Asociados para Derechos Religiosos, Educativos y Sociales."

Leadership development among the Spanish-speaking poor is the first of five goals of PADRES, which has a nationwide membership of 1,113 — including 256 Hispanic — priests. Bishop Patrick F. Flores is the national chairman. Father Juan Romero is the executive director. Offices are located at 2518 W. Commerce St., San Antonio, Tex. 78207.

An analogous organization of Chicano sisters, **Las Hermanas,** was organized in 1971 (see separate entry).

Mexican American Cultural Center: Founded by the Texas Catholic Conference at a meeting held in Austin Sept. 29, 1971, MACC is a center of research, education, leadership formation and publication. Cooperating with PADRES and Las Hermanas, and with the additional endorsement of the U.S. Catholic Conference, it is dedicated to the liberation and integral development of Mexican-American and other Spanish-speaking peoples. It coordinates programs in social and spiritual development of the Spanish-speaking; bi-cultural/bi-lingual learning environments; community services for cultural and leadership development; intensive courses in pastoral ministry for the Spanish-speaking.

Ruben R. Alfano is program director of the center, which is located at 3019 French Pl., P. O. Box 28240, San Antonio, Tex. 78284.

Miami Apostolate

The Spanish-Speaking Apostolate in metropolitan Miami is one of the most extensive in the country. It serves a population of well over 400,000 people: more than 300,000 Cubans who have established residence there since Fidel Castro rose to power Jan. 1, 1959; a permanent Latin population of more than 50,000; and some 100,000 migrant workers. Directly involved in the apostolate are 90 Spanish-speaking priests and 88 religious brothers and sisters. Spanish-speaking priests are assigned to 39 parishes.

Centro Hispano Catolico (Spanish Catholic Center), founded by Archbishop Coleman F. Carroll in October, 1959, provides many forms of assistance to new arrivals from Latin countries, including: pastoral counseling, orientation to life in the U.S., employment services, medicine-food-clothing distribution, day nursery and kindergarten care, programs for senior residents, and home visits. Located in the center are Archdiocesan Offices for Immigration Services and the Latin American Affairs Office which fosters cultural relations with Latin American countries.

The staff of the center consists of a chaplain, one Sister of St. Philip Neri, four Sisters of Social Service, and more than a score of lay persons. Sister Suzanne, S.S.S., is supervisor. of the center. The executive director and episcopal vicar for Spanish-speaking peoples in the archdiocese is Msgr. Orlando Fernandez. The center is located at 130 N. E. 2nd St., Miami, Fla. 33132.

Officers of the Migration and Refugee Service, U.S. Catholic Conference, in Miami figured largely in the work of receiving and resettling many of the refugees who have come to this country via the Cuban airlift and Spain.

All told, 298,833 persons were resettled between 1961 and the end of 1973. The states with the highest numbers of resettled Cubans were New York (80,909), New Jersey (59,238), California (39,618), and Illinois (22,356).

APPALACHIA COMMITTEE

The Catholic Committee of Appalachia, chaired by Bishop Michael Begley of Charlotte, consists of bishops, priests, religious and lay persons engaged in ministry in the 13-state region of Appalachia.

The committee belongs to the Commission on Religion in Appalachia, an ecumenical group with members from 17 denominations.

MISSION FUNDS

The Pontifical Society for the Propagation of the Faith reported in May, 1974, that it had distributed the sum of $36,580,509.55 for the support of missionary works in 1973. The sums to the respective continents were: $15,771,758.22   (Africa), $3,148,238.80 (America), $15,038,082.75   (Asia), $1,341,148.39   (Oceania), $1,281,281.39 (Europe).

The allocations were made from a total of $40,133,581 raised by national organizations of the society in 1972. The largest contribution, $18,482,541, was from the United States.

National Association of Boards of Education: Founded in 1972, it provides assistance in the formation of parochial and diocesan boards of education, and offers members a variety of services, including consultation and publications. The membership is approximately 1,700. Mary-Angela Harper, Ph.D., is executive director. Address: Suite 350, One Dupont Circle, Washington, D.C. 20036.

Education

Following are a résumé and excerpts of the principal themes stated in the Declaration on Christian Education issued by the Second Vatican Council.

All men have an inalienable right to education for personal and social development, and for attainment of their ultimate end (salvation). Christians have a right to a Christian education.

Parents are the primary and principal educators, and the first school is the family in which children learn to live in the society of men and of the Church.

Parents, who entrust others with a share in the work of educating their children, need the help of the community. Civil society, therefore, has the responsibility of aiding parents and secondary educators, as the common good demands, by building schools and providing other educational institutions.

Roles in Education

"The office of educating belongs by a unique title to the Church, not merely because she deserves recognition as a human society capable of educating, but most of all because she has the responsibility of announcing the way of salvation to all men, of communicating the life of Christ to those who believe, and of assisting them with ceaseless concern so that they may grow into the fullness of that same life" (No. 3).

"In discharging her educative function, the Church is preoccupied with all appropriate means to that end. But she is particularly concerned with the means which are proper to herself, of which catechetical training is foremost. . . . The Church seeks to penetrate and ennoble with her own spirit those other means which belong to the common heritage of mankind, and which contribute mightily to the refinement of spirit and the molding of men. Among these are the media of social communication, many groups devoted to spiritual and physical development, youth associations, and especially schools" (No. 4).

"Parents, who have the first and the inalienable duty and right to educate their children, should enjoy true freedom in their choice of schools. Consequently, public authority, which has the obligation to oversee and defend the liberties of citizens, ought to see to it, out of a concern for distributive justice, that public subsidies are allocated in such a way that, when selecting schools for their children, parents are genuinely free to follow their consciences.

"For the rest, it is incumbent upon the state to provide all citizens with the opportunity to acquire an appropriate degree of cultural enrichment, and with the proper preparation for exercising their civic duties and rights. Therefore, the state itself ought to protect the right of children to receive an adequate schooling. . . . must keep in mind the principle of subsidiarity, so that no kind of school monopoly arises. For such a monopoly would militate against the native rights of the human person, the development and spread of culture itself, the peaceful association of citizens, and the pluralism which exists today in very many societies" (No. 6).

"The Church is keenly aware of her very grave obligation to give zealous attention to the moral and religious education of all her children. To those large numbers of them who are being trained in schools which are not Catholic, she needs to be present with her special affection and helpfulness. This she does through the living witness of those who teach and direct such students, through the apostolic activity of their schoolmates, but most of all through the services of the priests and laymen who transmit to them the doctrine of salvation in a way suited to their age and circumstances, and who afford them spiritual assistance through programs which are appropriate under the prevailing conditions of time and setting.

"The Church reminds parents of the serious duty which is theirs of taking every opportunity — or of making the opportunity — for their children to be able to enjoy these helps and to pace their development as Christians with their growth as citizens of the world. For this reason, the Church gives high praise to those civil authorities and civil societies that show regard for the pluralistic character of modern society, and take into account the right of religious liberty, by helping families in such a way that in all schools the education of their children can be carried out according to the moral and religious convictions of each family" (No. 7).

Catholic School Purposes

"The Church's involvement in the field of education is demonstrated especially by the Catholic school. No less than other schools does the Catholic school pursue cultural goals and the natural development of youth. But it has several distinctive purposes.

• "It aims to create for the school community an atmosphere enlivened by the gospel spirit of freedom and charity.

• "It aims to help the adolescent in such a way that the development of his own personality will be matched by the growth of that new creation he became by baptism.

• "It strives to relate all human culture eventually to the news of salvation, so that the light of faith will illumine the knowledge which students gradually gain of the world, of life, and of mankind."

"The Catholic school retains its immense importance in . . . our times." (No. 8).

BASIC TEACHINGS FOR CATHOLIC RELIGIOUS EDUCATION

Following is the text of Basic Teachings for Catholic Religious Education, a document by the U.S. bishops listing the essential elements of faith which must be stressed in the religious formation of Catholics of all ages. The text, in preparation for two years, was approved by the Congregation for the Clergy and the U.S. bishops, and was released for publication Jan. 11, 1973. It reflects the contents of the General Catechetical Directory approved by Pope Paul VI Mar. 18, 1971, and is one of several contributions toward the development of a National Catechetical Directory still in preparation.

(This text, copyrighted by the National Conference of Catholic Bishops, was circulated by the NC Documentary Service, *Origins,* Vol. 2, No. 31.)

INTRODUCTION

All religious education is formation in Christ, given to make "faith become living, conscious and active, through the light of instruction." Religious education is proclaiming to others the gospel of the risen Lord, while showing that this "Good News" alone gives meaning to life. So the faith, prayer and lived example of the teacher are of great importance.

No list of documents can bring about real religious education, but certain basic teachings are necessary for doctrinal substance and stability.

This text sets down the principal elements of the Christian message. These basic teachings are here specified by the American bishops, who as bishops hold in the Church special responsibility for determining the content of faith instruction. It is necessary that these basic teachings be central in all Catholic religious instruction, be never overlooked or minimized, and be given adequate and frequent emphasis.

This text makes clear what must be stressed in the religious formation of Catholics of all ages. The bishops have in mind every type of religious education: in the home, in Catholic schools, in programs of the Confraternity of Christian Doctrine, in courses of adult education in religion.

The most effective methodology is expected in teaching basic beliefs. Due consideration should be shown for the listener's level of maturity and understanding. "In this instruction a proper sequence should be observed, as well as a method appropriate to the matter that is being treated, and to the natural disposition, ability, age and circumstances of life of the listener."

It is necessary that the authentic teachings of the Church, and those only, be presented in religious instruction as official Catholic doctrine. Religion texts or classroom teachers should never present merely subjective theorizing as the Church's teaching.

"For this reason, a distinction must be borne in mind between, on the one hand, the area that is devoted to scientific investigation and, on the other, the area that concerns the teaching of the faithful. In the first, experts enjoy the freedom required by their work and are free to communicate to others, in books and commentaries, the fruits of their research. In the second, only those doctrines may be attributed to the Church which are declared to be such by her authentic Magisterium."

This document is not to be confused with either the *General Catechetical Directory* or the planned *National Catechetical Directory* (to which this document will be helpful input). This document should, however, be read in the light of the *General Catechetical Directory,* by which its admittedly limited scope can readily be understood.

This text does not give guidance concerning a hierarchical order of importance of doctrines, or concerning methods of religious instruction. This only specifies the doctrinal basics which the bishops expect in teaching Catholic doctrine. This is intended for parents and catechists, for priests, deacons and religious, for writers and publishers of catechetical texts — to use as adult study and in reviewing the content of religious education programs.

John Henry Cardinal Newman described the knowledge of religion expected in his day: "We want a laity . . . who know their religion, who enter into it, who know just where they stand, who know what they hold and what they do not, who know their creed so well that they can give an account of it, who know so much history that they can defend it."

A century later, the bishops want all this. But they ask and pray for much more — for a laity transformed by the gospel message, who put the gospel to work in every action of their daily lives, whose joy and simplicity and concern for others are so radiant that all men recognize them as Christ's disciples by the love they have for one another.

THREE THEMES

There are three themes, chosen from others, which carry through all religious education. These are:

First Theme: The Importance of Prayer — The People of God have always been a praying people. Religious educators then, who are mature in the faith and faithful to this tradition, will teach prayer. This teaching will take place through experiences of prayer, through the example of prayer, and through the learning of common prayers. Religious education, at home or in the classroom, given by a teacher who values prayer, will provide both the instruction and the experience.

People can pray together as a community when they share some common prayers. So it is important that some of the Church's great prayers be understood, memorized and said frequently. Among these are the Sign of the Cross, the Our Father, the Hail Mary, the Apostles' Creed, an Act of Contrition, and the Rosary.

But there is more to prayer than memorized formulas. Talking with God spontaneously and familiarly, and listening to him, is prayer. Informal prayer, suited to the person's age and capacity, should be explained and encouraged. Praise and thankfulness in prayer bring balance and strength in the difficulties, as well as the joys, of life.

By instruction in prayer, through all levels of religious education, the learner is gradually led on to a more mature prayer — to meditation, contemplation, and union with God.

Second Theme: Participating in the Liturgy — As members of the Christian community, all are called to participate actively in the liturgical prayer of the Church. Religious education therefore must involve the student in his faith community and in that community's liturgy.

Liturgy itself educates. It teaches, it forms community, it forms the individual. It makes possible worship of God and a social apostolate to men.

The Mass, the Church's "great prayer," is the highest, most noble form of the Church's liturgy. Effective instruction will therefore help every Christian participate actively in the eucharistic celebration of his own witnessing faith community.

It is especially important, therefore, that the eucharistic celebration engage younger members of the parish in genuine worship. The parish community takes on new dimension and vitality from their participation in every Mass, especially when the community comes together on Sundays and holy days. The young of the parish are influenced by the example of their elders, and grow by their own full sharing in the Sacrifice of the Mass.

Third Theme: Familiarity with the Holy Bible — A life of prayer is nourished by reading the Bible, which is in itself a form of prayer.

The Word of God is life-giving. It nourishes and inspires, strengthens and sustains. It is the primary source, with Tradition, of Church teaching.

Religious education should encourage love and respect for the Scriptures. This will happen as one is gradually introduced to the Scriptures and given a background knowledge which will prepare him for reading and understanding them. At an appropriate level, each one should have his own copy of the Bible.

In studying and teaching the Bible, the instructor should follow the approach of the Second Vatican Council. The Bible has God as its author and helps us to know and love Jesus Christ.

The Bible is likewise to be taught as a collection of divinely inspired books, each with its human author, its history of composition, and type of literature (or literary form). These help us understand "what meaning the sacred writers really intended, and what God wanted to manifest by means of their words."

The words of St. Paul should describe the Catholic student of religion: "From your infancy you have known the Sacred Scriptures, the source of the wisdom which, through faith in Jesus Christ, leads to salvation. All Scripture is inspired of God and is useful for teaching — for reproof, correction, and training in holiness, so that the man of God may be fully competent and equipped for every good work" (2 Tm. 3:15-16).

Scripture and Tradition stand together as the "one sacred deposit of the word of God, which is committed to the Church." The importance of Tradition is described by the Second Vatican Council: "This Tradition, which comes from the apostles, develops in the Church with the help of the Holy Spirit. For there is a growth in the understanding of the realities and the words which have been handed down . . . ." Catholics therefore should be well instructed in Tradition as well as Scripture.

BASIC TEACHINGS

1. The Mystery of the One God — Father, Son, Holy Spirit: The "history of salvation" is the story of God's dealing with men. Through it, the one true God in three Persons — the Father, the Son, the Holy Spirit — reveals himself to man and saves man from sin.

In the Old Testament God revealed himself as the one true personal God, transcendent above this world. By these Old Testament words and actions, God prepared for the later revelation of the Trinity.

This mystery was expressed in the person, words, and works of Jesus Christ. Jesus revealed himself as the eternal and divine Son of God; more fully revealed the Father; and made known a third divine Person, the Holy Spirit, whom the Father and he, as risen Lord, sent to his Church.

Thus, the divine Teacher gives his disciples authoritative knowledge of the true God, and calls them to become sons of God through the gift of the Spirit which he bestows on them.

Catechetical instruction should foster an ever-increasing awareness of the Triune God. It should enable students to grasp, through faith, the great truth that, beginning at baptism, they are called to a lifelong developing intimacy with the three divine Persons.

2. True Worship of God in a World Which Ignores Him: Religious education must stimulate an unshakable belief that God is all-good. "The living God" (Mt. 16:16) is holy, just, and merciful. Infinitely wise and perfect, he has made firm commitments to men and bound them to himself by solemn covenants. He has each of us always in view. He frees us, saves us, and loves us with the love of a father, the love of a spouse. Instruction about God's goodness should awaken joy in the God who is the cause of our eternal hope and should prompt us to worship him.

We worship God especially in the sacred liturgy, offering ourselves to him through our Lord Jesus Christ. We commit ourselves to carrying out his will in our every activity, and to use and increase the talents he has given us. And from his goodness we receive the graces needed to profess the truth in love and to bring forth the fruits of love, justice and peace, all to his glory.

The sad fact is that many people today pay little or no attention to God, while others are persuaded that God is distant, indifferent, or altogether absent. That is because modern life is man-centered, not God-centered. Its climate is unfavorable to faith. Yet, no matter how hidden, some desire for God is lodged in every man.

3. Knowledge of God and the Witness of Christian Love: Sacred Scripture testifies that man can come to know God through the things God has made. The Church holds and teaches that from reflection on created things human reason can come to a knowledge of God as the beginning and end of all that is.

Yet unbelievers need help to find God. They ask, "Show us a sign." We who are committed to Christ can do so, as the first generation Christians did. How? By the compelling witness of a life which shows a steadfast and mature faith in God, which is lived in personal love of Christ, and which carries out works of justice and charity.

True, our final goal is in eternity. But faith in God and union with Christ also entail an obligation to work at solving the problems which beset men here and now. And so Christians must show by their actions that faith in God, far from freeing them of concern for the world's troubles, impels them to be involved and to press for their solution.

4. Jesus Christ, Son of God, the Firstborn of All Creation, and Savior: The greatest of God's works is the taking on of human flesh (incarnation) by his Son, Jesus Christ. The Son came on earth and entered human history so as to renew the world from within and be for it an abiding source of supernatural life and salvation from sin.

He is the firstborn of all creation. He is before all. All things hold together in him, just as all have been created in him, through him, and for him.

Obedient unto death, he was exalted as Lord of all, and through the reality of his resurrection was made known to us as God's Son in power. Being the firstborn of the dead, he gives eternal life to all. In him we are created new men. Through him all creatures will be saved from the slavery of corruption. "There is no salvation in anyone else" (Acts 4:12). Nor has there ever been, from the very beginning.

5. Creation, the Beginning of the History of Man's Salvation: The entire universe was created out of nothing. This includes our world in which salvation and redemption are in fact accomplished through Jesus Christ.

In the Old Testament, God's creative action showed his power and proved that he is always with his people. The creation of angels and of the world is the beginning of the mystery of salvation. And the creation of man is the first gift leading to Christ. In Christ's resurrection from the dead the same all-powerful action of God stands out splendidly.

For this reason, creation is to be presented not in isolation, but as directly relating to the salvation accomplished by Jesus Christ. So, too, when a Christian considers the doctrine of creation, he must not only recall the first action by which God "created the heavens and the earth," but should also remember God's continuing activity as he works out the salvation of men.

God is actively and lovingly present in human history from start to finish, using his limitless power in our behalf. Just as his presence shines forth in the history of Israel, just as he was powerfully at work in the life, death, and resurrection of his Incarnate Son, so is he present among us today and will be for all generations. He will bring his saving work to final completion only at the end of the world, when there will be "new heavens and a new earth."

6. Jesus Christ, the Center of All God's Saving Works: The Christian knows that in Jesus Christ he is joined to all history and all men. The story of man's salvation, set in the midst of the ongoing history of the world, is the carrying out of God's plan for us. Its aim is to form his people into "the whole Christ . . . that perfect man who is Christ come to full stature" (Eph. 4:13).

Realizing this, the Christian addresses himself to his appointed task of making creation give glory to God. He does so to the full extent of his abilities and opportunities, through the power of Jesus the Savior.

7. Jesus Christ, True Man and True God in the Unity of the Divine Person: Head and Lord of the universe, the Son of God was "manifested in the flesh" (1 Tm. 3:16). This is "a wonderful mystery of our faith" *(ibid.)*.

The man, Jesus Christ, lived among men. As man, he thought with a human mind, acted with a human will, loved with a human heart. By becoming man, he joined himself in a real way with every human being except in sin. He accorded the human person a degree of respect and concern such as no one before had done.

He lived among men, was close to them, reached out to all — the virtuous and sinners, the poor and the rich, fellow-citizens and foreigners, and was especially solicitous for the suffering and the rejected. In him, God's love for man is seen.

And well it might be. For Jesus is also truly divine. He is not only the perfect man, but God's only-begotten Son: "God from God, light from light, true God from true God, begotten not made, of one substance with the father" (Nicene Creed).

In explaining the incarnation and the divinity of Christ, the teacher must take care to follow Christian Tradition as expressed in Sacred Scripture and by the Fathers and councils of the Church. The instruction should convey the age-old witness of Christian life about this truth: in Christ there is all fullness of divinity.

8. Jesus Christ, Savior and Redeemer of the World: Christ appeared in the history of man and the world, a history subject to sin. Christ steps into the world as God made man, to be its Savior and Redeemer. God so loved sinners that he gave his Son, reconciling the world to himself. It was by the obedience of the Son to the will and command of his Father that all men were saved (cf. Rom. 5:19).

As the Messiah fulfilling Old Testament prophecy and history, Jesus carried out his earthly mission. He preached the gospel of the kingdom of God and summoned men to interior conversion and faith. He persisted in his ministry despite the resistance of religious leaders of his day and their threats on his life.

Out of filial love for his Father and redemptive love of us, he gave himself up to death, and passed through it to the glory of the Father.

By his death and resurrection he redeemed mankind from slavery to sin and to the devil. Risen truly and literally, the Lord became the unfailing source of life and of the outpouring of the Holy Spirit upon the human race, and is the firstborn among many brethren, and created in himself a new humanity.

9. The Holy Spirit in the Church and in the Life of the Christian: The Holy Spirit carries out Christ's work in the world. As Christ is present where a human being is in need (Mt. 25:31, ff.), so the Spirit is at work when persons answer God's invitation to love him and one another. The coming of the consoling Paraclete was promised by Christ. He pledged that the Spirit of Truth would be within us and remain with us. And the Holy Spirit did come at Pentecost, never to depart. The Spirit is present in a special way in the community of those who acknowledge Christ as Lord, the Church. The Church, then, is enlivened by the Spirit. Our lives also are to be guided by that same Holy Spirit, the Third Person of the Trinity.

Catechetical instruction must underscore the importance and the work of the abiding Spirit of Truth in the Church and in our lives. For this the teachings of the Second Vatican Council will be useful.

10. The Sacraments, Actions of Christ in the Church (the Universal Sacrament): The saving work of Christ is continued in the Church. Through the gift of the Holy Spirit, the Church enjoys the presence of Christ and carries on his ministry and saving mission.

The Church has been entrusted with special means for carrying on Christ's works: namely, the sacraments which he instituted. They are outward signs both of God's grace and man's faith. They effectively show God's intention to sanctify man and man's willingness to receive this sanctification. In this way they bring us God's grace.

The Church itself is in a true sense the universal sacrament. The Church is not only the People of God, but, "by her relationship with Christ, the Church is, as it were, a sacrament (or sign and instruction) of intimate union with God and of the unity of all mankind."

Sacraments are the principal actions through which Christ gives his Spirit to Christians and makes them a holy people. He has entrusted the sacraments to the Church, but they are always to be thought of as actions of Christ himself, from whom they get their power. Thus, it is Christ who baptizes, Christ who offers himself in the Sacrifice of the Mass through the ministry of the priests, and Christ who forgives sins in the sacrament of penance.

"The purpose of the sacraments is to sanctify men, to build up the body of Christ, and finally to give worship to God. Because they are signs, they also instruct . . . the very act of celebrating them disposes the faithful more effectively to receive the grace in a fruitful manner, to worship God duly, and to practice charity. It is therefore of capital importance that the faithful easily understand the sacramental signs, and with great eagerness have frequent recourse to the sacraments, instituted to nourish Christian life."

Catechetical instruction, then, must teach the seven sacraments according to this full meaning. Since they are sacraments of faith, the right attitude of faith must be encouraged, as well as the sincerity and generosity required for celebrating and receiving them worthily.

The sacraments must be seen as sources of grace for individuals and communities, in addition to being remedies for sin and the effects of sin. Therefore, the Christian's union with God in grace is to be presented as in an important measure connected with the sacraments.

11. Religious Instruction on the Sacraments: In religious education each sacrament is to be taught, with careful attention to its individual nature. The instructor should carefully explain the external ritual, or the "sign" for each, and should explain that sacraments, when worthily received, bring God's grace. The teacher should help the student appreciate the lifelong human and ecclesial goal of sacramental living. Such instruction will encourage the students to think about the meaning of the visible signs, as well as the invisible reality of God's saving love which these signs express.

Here, in broad outline, we note:

Baptism is the sacrament of rebirth as a child of God sanctified by the Spirit, of unity with Jesus in his death and resurrection, of cleansing from original sin and personal sins, and of welcome into the community of the Church. It permanently relates him to God with a relationship that can never be erased. It joins him to the priestly, prophetic, and kingly works of Christ.

Confirmation is the sacrament by which those born anew in baptism now receive the seal of the Holy Spirit, the gift of the Father and the Son. Confirmation, as the sealing of the candidate with the Spirit, is linked with the other sacraments of Christian initiation, baptism and the Eucharist. Religious instruction should emphasize the idea of initiation and explain the sealing of the Spirit as preparation for the witness of a mature Christian life, and for the apostolate of living in the world and extending and defending the faith.

Penance brings to the Christian God's merciful forgiveness for sins committed after baptism. Sacramental absolution, which follows upon sincere confession of sin, true sorrow, and resolution not to sin again, is a means of obtaining pardon from God. Usually given to the individual, it also brings about a reconciliation with the faith community, the Church, which is wounded by our sins. Religious instruction should teach this sacrament as bringing individualized direction toward spiritual growth, toward eliminating habits of sin and working for perfection. Confession is for the Catholic the sacramental way of obtaining pardon for sins, of submitting his offenses to the mercy and forgiving grace of God. If one has fallen into serious sin, sacramental confession is the ordinary way established in the Church to reconcile the sinner with Christ and with his Church. It is also true that a sinner can be restored to grace by perfect sorrow or perfect contrition in the sense of the Church's Tradition. Therefore every Catholic, from his early years, should be instructed how to receive and best profit from the regular reception of this sacrament.

Holy Orders in a special way conforms certain members of the People of God to Christ the Mediator. It puts them in positions of special service for building up the Body of Christ and gives a sacred power to fulfill that ministry of service. Through this sacrament Christ bestows a permanent charism of the Holy Spirit enabling the recipients to guide and shepherd the faith community, proclaim and explain the gospel, and guide and sanctify God's people. Representing Christ, they primarily offer the Sacrifice of the Mass. Also as his representatives, they administer the sacrament of penance for the forgiveness of sins, and the sacrament of the anointing of the sick.

The Anointing of the Sick is the sacrament for the seriously ill, infirm and aged. It is best received as soon as the danger of death begins, from either sickness or old age. By this anointing and the accompanying prayers for the restoration of health, the entire Church through the priests asks the Lord to lighten their sufferings, forgive their sins, and bring them to eternal salvation. The Church encourages the sick to contribute to the spiritual good of the entire People of God by associating themselves freely to the sufferings and death of Christ.

12. The Eucharist, Center of All Sacramental Life: The Eucharist has primacy among the sacraments. It is of the greatest importance for uniting and strengthening the Church. The eucharistic celebration is carried out in obedience to the words of Jesus at the Last Supper: "Do this in memory of me."

When a priest pronounces the words of eucharistic consecration, the underlying reality of bread and wine is changed into the body and blood of Christ, given for us in sacrifice. That change has been given the name "transubstantiation." This means that Christ himself, true God and true man, is really and substantially present, in a mysterious way, under the appearances of bread and wine.

This Sacrifice (of the Mass) is not merely a ritual which commemorates a past sacrifice. In it, through the ministry of priests, Christ perpetuates the Sacrifice of the Cross in an unbloody manner. At the same time, the Eucharist is a meal which recalls the Last Supper, celebrates our unity together in Christ, and anticipates the messianic banquet of the kingdom. In the Eucharist Jesus nourishes Christians with his own self, the Bread of Life, so that they may become a people more acceptable to God and filled with greater love of God and neighbor.

To receive the Eucharist worthily the Christian must be in the state of grace (cf. 1 Cor. 11: 27-28).

Having been nourished by the Lord himself, the Christian should with active love eliminate all prejudices and all barriers to brotherly cooperation with others. The Eucharist is a sacrament of unity. It is meant to unite the faithful more closely each day with God and with one another.

The Eucharist, reserved in our churches, is a powerful help to prayer and service of others. Religious instruction should stress the gratitude, adoration and devotion due to the Real Presence of Christ in the Blessed Sacrament reserved.

13. The Sacrament of Matrimony: Particular attention must be given to religious education concerning matrimony. In modern society it is necessary to emphasize that marriage was instituted by the Creator himself and given by him certain purposes, laws and blessings. Students are to be acquainted with the vision and teaching of the Second Vatican Council concerning marriage and the family, concerning the indissolubility of marriage and the evil of divorce.

Christ raised marriage of the baptized to the dignity of a sacrament. The spouses, expressing their personal and irrevocable consent, are the ministers of the sacrament. Therefore they live together in Christ's grace. They imitate — and in a way represent — Christ's own love for his Church. By this sacrament Christian spouses are, as it were, consecrated to uphold the dignity of matrimony and to carry out its duties. It should be made clear that the Church discourages the contracting of mixed marriages in order to encourage a full union of mind and life in matrimony.

Following the Second Vatican Council, the religion teacher should show that marriage is the basis of family life. Special attention should be given to the unity and unbreakable quality of matrimony, as decreed by God. The purposes of marriage should be explained in accord with the teachings of the Second Vatican Council:

"Marriage and conjugal love are by their nature ordained toward the begetting and education of children.... Hence, while not making the other purposes of matrimony of less account, the true practice of conjugal love, and the whole meaning of the family life which results from it, have this aim: that the couple be ready with stout hearts to cooperate with the love of the Creator and the Savior, who through them will enlarge and enrich his own family day by day ... Marriage to be sure is not instituted solely for procreation [but also that] the mutual love of the spouses, too, be embodied in a rightly ordered manner, that it grow and ripen."

Similarly, there must be a clear presentation of the Church's teaching concerning chastity in marriage, moral methods of regulating births, and the protection due to human life once a child has been conceived.

The teacher should explain the vocation of every family to function perfectly as a community — that is, a group of persons sharing life together at a deep, personal level. Each member of the family has this obligation. Such a community will reach out to affect constructively the Church, the civic and the world community.

14. The New Man in the Spirit: When man accepts the Spirit of Christ, God introduces

him to a way of life completely new. It empowers a man to share in God's own life. He is joined to the Father and to Christ in a vital union which not even death can break.

The indwelling Holy Spirit gives a man hope and courage, heals his weakness of soul, enables him to master passion and selfishness. The Spirit prompts man to pursue what is good and to advance in such virtues as charity, joy, peace, patience, kindness, longanimity, humility, fidelity, modesty, continence, and chastity. The presence of the Holy Spirit makes prayer possible and effective.

God's dwelling in the soul is a matchless grace and manifold gift. Its effects have been expressed in many ways. Thus, a sinner is said to be "justified by God" or "given new life by the Holy Spirit," or "given a share in Christ's life in himself," or to receive grace. The root meaning is that a person dies to sin, shares in the divinity of the Son through the Spirit of adoption, and enters into close communion with the most Holy Trinity.

In the history of salvation, it is divinely appointed that man is to receive this sanctifying grace of adoption as God's child and to inherit eternal life. Because of the grace of Christ the Savior, man is given supernatural life, meaning and dignity far beyond what his own nature confers.

15. Human and Christian Freedom: God's plan is that man, united with Jesus Christ, should give a free answer to God's call. At the outset, God endowed human nature with freedom. But this has been badly impaired by the sin of humanity, original sin. The resultant weakness is overcome by grace, so that man can live with holiness in the faith of Jesus Christ.

The Church knows that, because of psychological difficulties or external conditions, freedom can be reduced slightly or considerably or altogether. Hence conditions most favorable to the exercise of genuine human freedom must be promoted, not only for man's temporal welfare but also for the higher good of grace and eternal salvation. Accordingly, the Church will seek to communicate a true sense and appreciation of freedom, will defend freedom against unjust force of every kind, and will summon Christians to work together with all men of good will to safeguard freedom.

16. The Sins of Man: In working out his salvation, man finds that the greatest problem is sin.

Original sin is the first obstacle. How does it affect him?

"Although he was made by God in a state of holiness, from the very dawn of history man abused his liberty, at the urging of the evil one. Man set himself against God and sought to find fulfillment apart from God."

"Through one man sin entered the world, and with sin death, death thus coming to all men inasmuch as all sinned" (Rom. 5: 12).

"It is human nature so fallen, stripped of the grace that clothed it, injured in its own natural powers and subjected to the dominion of death, that is transmitted to all men — and it is in this sense that every man is born in sin." This sin of mankind is multitudinous, has caused incalculable sorrow and ruin, and weighs down on every man.

In addition to the effects of original sin, there is personal sin, that committed by the individual. By it a person, acting knowingly and deliberately, violates the moral law. The sinner fails in love of God. He turns away from, or even back from his lifetime goal of doing God's will. He may even, by serious offense (mortal sin), rupture his relationship with the Father.

It is important that the awareness of sin not be lost or lessened. The Christian must have clear knowledge of right and wrong, so as to be able to choose with an informed conscience to love God and avoid offending him.

Religious instruction must not be silent about the reality of sin, the kinds of sin and the degree of gravity and personal wilfulness which indicate mortal sin. Instruction must remind the student of the sufferings and the death on the cross which Christ endured to destroy the effects of sin.

But it must go on to speak eloquently of God's forgiveness. Even though a man sin, he can be pardoned. The power of grace is greater than that of sin. The superabundant love of God restores the penitent and draws him toward salvation.

17. The Moral Life of Christians: Christ directed his apostles to teach the observance of everything that he had commanded. Catechetical instruction must include both the things which are to be believed and those which are to be done or avoided if we are to respond generously to God's love.

Christian morality defines a way of living worthy of a human being and of an adopted son of God. It is a positive response to God, by growing in the new life given through Jesus Christ. It is supported and guided by the grace and gifts of the Holy Spirit.

Christian freedom needs to be guided in questions of day-to-day living. Each person must have a right conscience and follow it. Conscience is not feeling nor self-will, although these may affect the degree of culpability. Conscience is a personal judgment that something is right or wrong because of the will and law of God.

So the conscience of the Catholic Christian must pay respectful and obedient attention to the teaching authority of God's Church. It is the duty of this teaching authority, or magisterium, to give guidance for applying the enduring norms and values of Christian morality to specific situations of everyday life.

The Christian must know that there are moral values which are absolute and never to

be disregarded or violated by anyone in any situation. Fidelity to them may require heroism of the sort which we see in the lives of the saints and the deaths of the martyrs.

Obedience to the Holy Spirit includes a faithful observance of the commandments of God, the laws of the Church, and just civil laws. All civil laws are not necessarily just, because at times evil laws permit what God forbids. "Better for us to obey God than men!" (Acts 5:29) Christian witness is especially powerful when it defends the values of God rather than those of the world.

18. The Perfection of Christian Love: The special characteristic of Christian moral teaching is its total relationship to the love of God, or charity. All commandments and norms for this moral teaching are summed up in faith working through charity. Love of God is the soul of morality. God is love, and in God's plan that love reaches out in Jesus Christ, to unite men in mutual love.

It follows, then, that responding freely and perfectly to God and God's will means keeping his commandments and living in his love. It means accepting and practicing the "new commandment" of charity.

Sustained by faith, man is to live a life of love of God and of his fellow men. This is his greatest responsibility, and the source of his greatest dignity. A man's holiness, whatever his vocation or state of life may be, is the perfection of love of God.

Following the Second Vatican Council, religious instruction should speak of the importance for humanity and for the Church of those women and men who, accepting a religious vocation, show in this special and needed way their love of God and true service to mankind. Such instruction should acknowledge the excellence which the Christian message gives to virginity consecrated in Christ.

19. Specifics in the Teaching of Morality: The duties and obligations flowing from love of God and man are to be taught in specific, practical fashion. The follower of Christ is to know the Christian response to the challenges and temptations of contemporary living. The Church has a duty to apply moral principles to current problems, personal and social.

The specifics of morality are to be taught within the overall framework of the Ten Commandments of God and the Sermon on the Mount, especially the Beatitudes (see Appendix A). Also included should be the spiritual and corporal works of mercy, the theological and moral virtues, the seven capital sins, etc. Whatever approach is used, the student should know the Ten Commandments as part of his religious heritage (see Appendix A). Teaching morality also should include instruction on the laws of the Church (see Appendix B). The Bible and the lives of the saints supply concrete examples of moral living.

Toward God the Christian has a lifelong

obligation of love and service. The will of God must be put first in the scale of personal values, and must be kept there throughout life. One must have toward God the attitude of a son to an all-good, all-loving father, and must never think or live as if independent of God. He must gladly give to God genuine worship and true prayer, both liturgical and private.

Man must not put anyone or anything in place of God. This is idolatry, which has its variations in superstition, witchcraft, occultism. Honoring God, man is never to blaspheme nor perjure himself. Honoring God, one is to show respect for persons, places and things related specially to God.

Atheism, heresy, and schism are to be rejected in the light of man's duties to God.

Toward his fellow man the Christian has specific obligations in love. Like Christ, he will show that love by concern for the rights of his fellow man — his freedom, his housing, his food, his health, his right to work, etc. The Christian is to show to all others the justice and charity of Christ — to reach out in the spirit of the Beatitudes to help all others, to build up a better society in the local community and justice and peace throughout the world. His judgment and speech concerning others are to be ruled by the charity due all sons of God. He will respect and obey all lawful authority in the home, in civil society, and in the Church.

Many are the sins against neighbor. It is sinful to be selfishly apathetic toward others in their needs. It is sinful to violate the rights of others — to steal, deliberately damage another's good name or property, cheat, not to pay one's debts. Respecting God's gift of life, the Christian cannot be anti-life and must avoid sins of murder, abortion, euthanasia, genocide, indiscriminate acts of war. He must not use immoral methods of family limitation. Sins of lying, detraction and calumny are forbidden, as are anger, hatred, racism and discrimination. In the area of sexuality, the Christian is to be modest in behavior and dress. In a sex-saturated society, the follower of Christ must be different. For the Christian there can be no premarital sex, fornication, adultery, or other acts of impurity or scandal to others. He must remain chaste, repelling lustful desires and temptations, self-abuse, pornography and indecent entertainment of every description.

Toward self the follower of Christ has certain duties. He must be another Christ in the world of his own day, a living example of Christian goodness. He must be humble and patient in the face of his own imperfections, as well as those of others. He must show a Christlike simplicity toward material things and the affluence of our society. The follower of Christ must be pure in words and actions even in the midst of corruption.

To be guarded against is the capital sin of pride, with its many manifestations. So too with sloth — spiritual, intellectual and physical. The Christian must resist envy of others' success and of their financial and material possessions. He is not to surrender self-control and abuse his bodily health by intemperance in drugs, alcohol, food.

Obviously this listing does not cover all morality or all immorality. But it indicates the practical approach which will help the Christian to form a right conscience, choose always what is right, avoid sin and the occasions of sin, and live in this world according to the Spirit of Christ in love of God.

20. The Church, People of God and Institution for Salvation: The Church, founded by Christ, had its origin in his death and resurrection. It is the new People of God, prepared for in the Old Testament and given life, growth, and direction by Christ in the Holy Spirit. It is the work of God's saving love in Christ.

In the Catholic Church are found the deposit of faith, the sacraments, and the ministries inherited from the apostles. Through these gifts of God, the Church is able to act and grow as a community in Christ, serving mankind and giving men his saving word and activity.

The Church shares in the prophetic office of Christ. Assembled by God's Word, it accepts that Word and witnesses to it in every quarter of the globe. So the Church is missionary by its very nature, and every member of the Church shares the command from Christ to carry the good news to all mankind.

The Church is also a priestly people.

By God's design, it is a society with leaders — i.e., with a hierarchy. As such, it is a people guided by its bishops who are in union with the pope, the bishop of Rome, the vicar of Christ. He has succeeded to the office of Peter in his care and guidance of the whole flock of Christ and is the head of the college of bishops. To them the community of faith owes respect and obedience, for "in exercising his office of father and pastor, a bishop should stand as one who serves."

Religious instruction should treat the role of the pope and of the bishops in their office of teaching, sanctifying and governing the Church. It should explain the gift of infallibility in the Church, and the way and manner in which the teaching authority of the Church guides the faithful in truth.

The Holy Spirit preserves the Church as the body of Christ and his bride, so that — despite the sins of its members — it will never fail in faithfulness to him and will meet him in holiness at the end of the world. The Spirit also helps the Church constantly to purify and renew itself and its members. To help its members, the Spirit-guided Church can modernize in those areas that permit change.

21. The Church as a Community: The

Church is a community sharing together the life of Christ, a people assembled by God. Within this assembly there is a basic equality of all persons. There are different responsibilities in the Church. For example, the ministerial priesthood is essentially different from the "priesthood of the people." But all are united and equal as the one People of God.

In the Church every individual has a call from God, a vocation to holiness. Each deserves respect, since all join in the one cause of Christ. The pope and the bishops coordinate this work, in every rite, diocese, parish and mission. In each, no matter how small or poor or isolated, "Christ is present, and by his power the one, holy, catholic and apostolic Church is gathered together."

22. The Quest for Unity: Christ willed that all who believe in him be one, so that the world might know that he was sent by the Father. Christian unity, then, in faith and love, is God's will. Prayer and work for Christian unity are essential to Catholic life, and religious education must bring this out. Catholics should be deeply, personally concerned over the present, sad divisions of Christians. Catholics should take the first steps in ecumenical dialogue and should try to make the Church more faithful to Christ and to its heritage from the apostles.

We recognize the unique fullness of the Catholic Church which we believe to be the ordinary means of salvation, and which we desire to share with all men. But we also recognize that Catholics can be enriched by the authentic insights into the gospel as witnessed by other religious traditions.

A still wider unity must be a concern of Catholic life and education: the unity of all men under God. Following the Second Vatican Council, religious education must show Christlike respect for all men of good will, beginning with our elder brothers in faith, the Jewish people, and reaching out to those others who with us believe in God.

Religious instruction is, then, to show a sensitive appreciation of the dignity and unique value of every human being. The Church rejects as unchristian any unjust discrimination or injustice because of race, national origin, ethnic origin, color, sex, class, or religion. God has given to every man intrinsic dignity, freedom and eternal importance. "If anyone says, 'My love is fixed on God,' yet hates his brother, he is a liar. One who has no love for the brother he has seen cannot love the God he has not seen" (1 Jn. 4:20).

23. The Church as the Institution for Salvation: The Church is a community of the People of God with Christ as leader and head. It is a structured institution to which Christ has given the mission of bringing the message of salvation to all men. "Established by Christ as a fellowship of life, charity and truth, this messianic people is also used by him as an instrument for the redemption of all, and is sent forth into the whole world as the light of the world and the salt of the earth."

The Church is not of this world, and can never conform itself to this world. But it both speaks and listens to the world, and strives to be seen by the world as faithful to the gospel. So "Christians cannot yearn for anything more ardently than to serve the men of the modern world ever more generously and effectively. Therefore, holding faithfully to the gospel and benefiting from its resources, and united with every man who loves and practices justice, Christians have shouldered a gigantic task demanding fulfillment in this world. Concerning this task they must give a reckoning to him who will judge every man on the last day."

In, but not of this world, the Church is "inspired by no earthly ambition." Only in heaven will it be perfect. Engaged in the world, it always has heaven in view, toward which the People of God are journeying.

24. Mary, Mother of God, Mother and Model of the Church: The Gospel of Luke gives us Mary's words: "My spirit finds joy in God my Savior, for he has looked upon his servant in her lowliness; all ages to come shall call me blessed" (Lk 1: 47-48).

Religious instruction should lead students to see Mary as singularly blessed and relevant to their own lives and needs. Following venerable Christian Tradition as continued in the Second Vatican Council, the teacher should explain the special place of the Virgin Mary in the history of salvation and in the Church.

The "ever-virgin mother of Jesus Christ our Lord and God," she is in the Church in a place highest after Christ, and also is very close to us as our spiritual Mother. In religious instruction there should be explanations of her special gifts from God (being Mother of God, being preserved from all stain of original sin, being assumed body and soul to heaven). The special veneration due to Mary — Mother of Christ, Mother of the Church, our spiritual Mother — should be taught by word and example.

The Church likewise honors the other saints who are already with the Lord in heaven. They inspire us by the heroic example of their lives. To them we pray, asking their intercession with God for us.

The teacher should remind students of reverence toward the bodies of those who have gone before us in death, and our duty of praying for deceased relatives, friends and all the faithful departed.

25. Final Reunion with God: During this earthly life, Christians look forward to their final reunion with God. They long for the coming of "our Lord Jesus Christ, who will give a new form to this lowly body of ours and remake it according to the pattern of his glorified body" (Phil. 3:21).

But the final realities will come about only

when Christ returns with power to bring history to its appointed end. Then as judge of the living and the dead he will hand over his people to the Father. Then only will the Church reach perfection and enter into the fullness of God. Until the Lord's arrival in majesty, "some of his disciples are pilgrims on earth, some have finished this life and are being purified, and others are in glory, beholding clearly God himself Three and One, as he is."

Religious instruction on death, judgment, and eternity should be given in a spirit of consoling hope, as well as salutary fear (cf. Thes. 4:18). The Lord's resurrection means that death has been conquered. So we have reason to live, and to face death, with courage and joy. The renewed funeral liturgy sets the tone for religious instruction on death. In the risen Christ we live, we die, and we shall live again. We look ahead to a homecoming with God our loving Father.

Religious instruction should treat seriously the awesome responsibility which each person has about his eternal destiny. The importance of the individual judgment after death, of the refining and purifying punishments of purgatory, of the dreadful possibility of the eternal death of hell, and of the last judgment should be taught in the light of Christian hope.

On the day of the last judgment each person will fully reach his eternal destiny. Then all of us will be revealed "before the judgment place of Christ, so that each one may receive what he deserves, according to what he has done, good or bad, in his bodily life" (2 Cor. 5:10). Then "the evildoers shall rise to be damned," and "those who have done right shall rise to live" (cf. Jn. 5:29) — to a life eternally with God beyond what the heart of man can imagine, to receive the good things that God has prepared for those who love him.

APPENDIX A

The Ten Commandments of God are of special importance in teaching specifics of morality. The Old Testament, the New Testament and the long use of the Church testify to this. A summary presentation of the Ten Commandments of God taken from the *New American Bible* translation is:

1. I, the Lord, am your God. You shall not have other gods besides me.

2. You shall not take the name of the Lord, your God, in vain.

3. Remember to keep holy the Sabbath day.

4. Honor your father and your mother.

5. You shall not kill.

6. You shall not commit adultery.

7. You shall not steal.

8. You shall not bear false witness against your neighbor.

9. You shall not covet your neighbor's wife.

10. You shall not covet anything that belongs to your neighbor.

The Beatitudes are likewise of particular importance in teaching specifics of morality. The traditional listing of the Beatitudes, as taken from the *New American Bible* translation, is:

1. Blest are the poor in spirit: the reign of God is theirs.

2. Blest are the sorrowing: they shall be consoled.

3. Blest are the lowly: they shall inherit the land.

4. Blest are they who hunger and thirst for holiness: they shall have their fill.

5. Blest are they who show mercy: mercy shall be theirs.

6. Blest are the single-hearted: for they shall see God.

7. Blest are the peacemakers: they shall be called sons of God.

8. Blest are those persecuted for holiness' sake: the reign of God is theirs. (Mt. 5:3-10)

APPENDIX B

From time to time the Church has listed certain specific duties of Catholics. Some duties expected of Catholic Christians today include the following. (Those traditionally mentioned as precepts of the Church are marked with an asterisk.)

1. To keep holy the day of the Lord's resurrection: to worship God by participating in Mass every Sunday and holy day of obligation:* to avoid those activities that would hinder renewal of soul and body, e.g., needless work and business activities, unnecessary shopping, etc.

2. To lead a sacramental life: to receive Holy Communion frequently and the sacrament of penance regularly — minimally, to receive the sacrament of penance at least once a year (annual confession is obligatory only if serious sin is involved)* — minimally, to receive Holy Communion at least once a year between the first Sunday of Lent and Trinity Sunday.*

3. To study Catholic teaching in preparation for the sacrament of confirmation, to be confirmed, and then to continue to study and advance the cause of Christ.

4. To observe the marriage laws of the Church:* to give religious training (by example and word) to one's children; to use parish schools and religious education programs.

5. To strengthen and support the Church:* one's own parish community and parish priests; the worldwide Church and the Holy Father.

6. To do penance, including abstaining from meat and fasting from food on the appointed days.*

7. To join in the missionary spirit and apostolate of the Church.

Msgr. Wilfrid H. Paradis is project director for the National Catechetical Directory.

CATECHETICAL CONSULTATION

Initial preparatory work for the development of a National Catechetical Directory was completed early in 1974 with the conclusion of a first round of nationwide consultations of priests, religious and lay persons.

The purpose of the project, under the direction of Msgr. Wilfrid H. Paradis since June 13, 1973, is to compile a comprehensive U.S.-oriented guidebook for religious education that will incorporate the basic features of the *General Catechetical Directory* approved by Pope Paul Mar. 18, 1971, *Basic Teachings for Catholic Religious Education* (see foregoing article), and related recommendations on content and programs by persons concerned with religious education.

Following the first set of local consultations, 63 of 114 diocesan coordinators reported in May, 1974, that the content of religious education was the matter of greatest interest and concern in their areas.

The priority-of-interest listing of other subjects was reported as follows: the sacraments (by 62 directors), parents as educators (by 35), adult education (by 34), methods of education (by 30). Social concerns and action rated ninth and ecumenism, 16th. The lowest ratings were given to the subjects of religious freedom, the potential of lay persons, suffering, and questions concerning the end of the world, the last judgment, heaven and hell.

In addition to the priority-of-interest listing from diocesan coordinators, the national project office received more than 17,000 recommendations from priests, religious and lay persons.

A second round of consultations, to be based on a tentative draft of the directory, was scheduled for January through April, 1975.

Concern about Content

Concern about the content of religious education is "a question of language," commented Sister Mariella Frye, associate national project director. She said concern was expressed that the Christian message is not being transmitted unless "it is couched in language close to that which they (the respondents to a questionnaire) learned as children. . . . The concern is that the entire content of the Christian message be taught and not watered down."

Msgr. Paradis said: "Perhaps the reaction of those suffering frustration and disappointment with regard to (current religious education) content was best expressed by the coordinator from New Ulm (Minn.), who reported that 'doctrine seems blurred for many who are annoyed and upset by the uncertainty.' There is, he added, 'overwhelming evidence among our rural people that they really want a clear, concise, simple presentation of the Message.' With regard to morality, he continued: 'Many think leaders have done a copout and teach their own thing.' "

CATHOLIC SCHOOLS AND STUDENTS IN THE UNITED STATES

(Source: *The Official Catholic Directory, 1974;* figures are as of Jan. 1, 1974. Archdioceses are indicated by an asterisk.)

Section, State Diocese	Univs. Colleges	Students	High Schools	Students	Elem. Schools	Students
NEW ENGLAND	33	45,160	157	71,747	632	184,128
Maine, Portland	2	993	5	1,193	24	7,108
New Hampshire, Manchester	5	3,299	6	2,954	39	11,636
Vermont, Burlington	4	2,633	3	1,519	15	3,326
Massachusetts	11	27,094	94	39,904	312	91,997
*Boston	6	20,283	67	25,834	202	58,935
Fall River	1	1,600	8	3,962	29	9,080
Springfield	1	420	8	5,288	47	14,818
Worcester	3	4,791	11	4,820	34	9,164
Rhode Island, Providence	4	3,765	15	6,573	70	20,469
Connecticut	7	7,376	34	19,604	172	49,592
*Hartford	4	1,380	17	10,655	95	27,704
Bridgeport	2	5,690	11	5,822	56	16,590
Norwich	1	306	6	3,127	21	5,298
MIDDLE ATLANTIC	73	118,233	440	293,354	2,334	874,036
New York	34	45,994	203	136,583	1,018	418,951
*New York	18	17,788	78	47,945	300	123,340
Albany	3	2,832	17	7,887	84	19,451
Brooklyn	2	9,483	31	30,720	190	127,600
Buffalo	7	12,399	29	15,532	168	45,708
Ogdensburg	1	181	5	1,644	32	6,905

Section, State Diocese	Univs. Colleges	Students	High Schools	Students	Elem. Schools	Students
New York						
Rochester	—	—	9	8,471	85	26,111
Rockville Centre	1	1,079	17	16,180	89	48,157
Syracuse	2	2,232	17	8,204	70	21,679
New Jersey	**13**	**17,818**	**97**	**57,222**	**491**	**172,127**
*Newark	6	16,043	50	25,556	223	80,312
Camden	—		12	8,269	72	24,126
Paterson	6	1,040	14	6,747	76	19,414
Trenton	1	735	21	16,650	120	48,275
Pennsylvania	**26**	**54,421**	**140**	**99,549**	**825**	**282,958**
*Philadelphia	10	24,976	52	60,026	309	152,080
Allentown	2	733	10	6,150	80	17,986
Altoona-Johnstown	2	2,022	3	2,269	41	9,219
Erie	3	5,334	12	4,528	55	15,748
Greensburg	2	1,639	3	1,202	50	10,036
Harrisburg	—	—	11	5,826	58	13,630
Pittsburgh	3	9,851	36	13,481	152	48,764
Scranton	4	9,866	13	6,067	80	15,495
SOUTH ATLANTIC	**15**	**28,874**	**137**	**62,623**	**552**	**185,102**
Delaware, Wilmington	—	—	9	4,576	29	11,008
Maryland, *Baltimore	4	6,123	25	12,589	93	36,002
District of Columbia, *Washington	4	17,239	31	12,540	84	31,103
Virginia, Richmond	1	621	15	5,514	51	17,395
West Virginia, Wheeling	1	526	10	2,789	36	6,576
North Carolina	2	847	3	881	40	9,769
Belmont Abbey	1	622	—	—	—	—
Charlotte	1	225	2	698	19	5,019
Raleigh	—	—	1	183	21	4,750
South Carolina, Charleston	—	—	4	1,332	31	6,381
Georgia	—	—	8	3,804	33	10,324
*Atlanta	—	—	3	1,812	15	4,569
Savannah	—	—	5	1,992	18	5,755
Florida	3	3,518	32	18,598	155	56,544
*Miami	2	2,448	17	9,387	62	25,688
Orlando	—	—	5	2,761	27	9,017
St. Augustine	—	—	3	2,112	27	8,905
St. Petersburg	1	1,070	7	4,338	39	12,934
EAST NORTH CENTRAL	**52**	**99,483**	**362**	**226,956**	**2,262**	**703,473**
Ohio	**14**	**24,636**	**100**	**65,120**	**546**	**182,932**
*Cincinnati	5	15,764	27	20,482	131	48,417
Cleveland	4	5,266	29	21,011	181	67,501
Columbus	1	1,000	15	6,160	53	14,504
Steubenville	1	998	6	1,589	18	3,916
Toledo	2	718	17	9,599	97	27,819
Youngstown	1	890	6	6,279	66	20,775
Indiana	**9**	**16,411**	**34**	**16,860**	**229**	**58,212**
*Indianapolis	2	1,323	14	6,393	86	21,496
Evansville	—		5	2,297	31	6,824
Ft. Wayne-S. Bend	5	12,105	8	4,179	46	12,839
Gary	1	1,921	5	3,410	47	13,409
Lafayette	1	1,062	2	581	19	3,644
Illinois	**12**	**36,724**	**116**	**84,717**	**703**	**240,429**
*Chicago	6	29,115	74	61,782	406	163,234
Belleville	1	760	5	3,367	58	11,559
Joliet	3	4,714	9	6,276	67	19,918
Peoria	—	—	10	4,348	57	15,033
Rockford	—	—	8	4,611	52	14,545
Springfield	2	2,135	10	4,333	63	16,140

Section, State Diocese	Univs. Colleges	Students	High Schools	Students	Elem. Schools	Students
Michigan	8	**14,900**	74	**39,421**	346	**109,795**
*Detroit	5	12,045	50	28,176	169	69,010
Gaylord	—	—	5	1,085	21	4,564
Grand Rapids	1	1,536	6	3,609	46	10,174
Kalamazoo	1	482	3	1,432	23	4,522
Lansing	1	837	4	2,882	36	9,584
Marquette	-	--	1	121	13	3,234
Saginaw	-	--	5	2,116	38	8,707
Wisconsin	9	**6,812**	38	**20,838**	438	**112,105**
*Milwaukee	4	3,572	16	11,309	178	52,717
Green Bay	2	1,963	10	4,093	104	25,818
La Crosse	1	601	9	4,145	78	17,642
Madison	1	580	3	1,291	55	11,517
Superior	1	96	-	--	23	4,411
EAST SOUTH CENTRAL	10	**7,741**	60	**25,686**	295	**72,217**
Kentucky	5	**5,012**	32	**13,568**	160	**37,025**
*Louisville	3	2,462	12	7,083	78	19,778
Covington	1	1,590	15	4,747	54	11,804
Owensboro	1	960	5	1,738	28	5,443
Tennessee	2	**1,197**	10	**5,499**	41	**12,170**
Memphis	1	825	5	3,182	16	5,975
Nashville	1	372	5	2,317	25	6,195
Alabama	3	**1,532**	5	**3,080**	53	**13,731**
Birmingham	2	666	2	1,092	24	5,356
Mobile	1	866	3	1,988	29	8,375
Mississippi, Natchez-Jackson	-	—	13	**3,539**	41	**9,291**
WEST NORTH CENTRAL	37	**45,344**	189	**79,661**	991	**238,291**
Minnesota	9	**11,211**	32	**14,849**	242	**62,196**
*St. Paul and Minneapolis	3	5,048	15	9,194	116	37,650
Crookston	-	--	2	406	12	2,140
Duluth	1	1,015	1	530	16	2,499
New Ulm	-	--	3	888	33	5,615
St. Cloud	3	2,956	4	1,221	39	8,692
Winona	2	2,192	7	2,610	26	5,600
Iowa	8	**6,380**	35	**15,458**	180	**39,659**
*Dubuque	3	2,865	13	6,318	89	19,452
Davenport	4	2,733	8	2,666	25	5,503
Des Moines	-	--	3	2,090	22	5,137
Sioux City	1	782	11	4,384	44	9,567
Missouri	8	**17,228**	52	**26,741**	296	**75,916**
*St. Louis	6	13,594	36	20,120	187	53,942
Jefferson City	-	--	2	881	36	7,138
Kansas City-St. Joseph	2	3,634	11	5,030	48	11,679
Springfield-Cape Girardeau	-	--	3	710	25	3,157
North Dakota	2	**1,011**	9	**2,753**	37	**7,841**
Bismarck	1	749	7	1,988	21	4,552
Fargo	1	262	2	765	16	3,289
South Dakota	2	**1,002**	7	**1,763**	29	**6,069**
Rapid City	-	--	2	382	4	957
Sioux Falls	2	1,002	5	1,381	25	5,112
Nebraska	2	**4,923**	35	**11,029**	105	**25,722**
*Omaha	2	4,923	22	7,959	68	20,439
Grand Island	-	--	7	1,366	10	1,377
Lincoln	-	--	6	1,704	27	3,906
Kansas	6	**3,589**	19	**7,068**	102	**20,888**
*Kansas City	3	1,967	8	3,926	49	11,602
Dodge City	1	413	-	--	13	1,693

Section, State Diocese	Univs. Colleges	Students	High Schools	Students	Elem. Schools	Students
Kansas						
Salina	1	609	7	1,222	12	2,158
Wichita	1	600	4	1,920	28	5,435
WEST SOUTH CENTRAL	**12**	**17,074**	**132**	**51,964**	**526**	**159,117**
Arkansas, Little Rock	-	--	6	**1,955**	**39**	**6,762**
Louisiana	**4**	**7,625**	**64**	**28,958**	**200**	**80,641**
*New Orleans	4	7,625	30	18,346	105	50,138
Alexandria	-	--	7	2,259	26	6,735
Baton Rouge	-	--	9	3,308	26	10,450
Lafayette	-	--	18	5,045	43	13,318
Oklahoma	**1**	**354**	**5**	**2,144**	**32**	**5,597**
*Oklahoma City	1	354	2	1,017	20	3,292
Tulsa	-	--	3	1,127	12	2,305
Texas	**7**	**9,095**	**57**	**18,907**	**255**	**66,117**
*San Antonio	3	4,432	19	5,235	58	14,872
Amarillo	-	--	2	306	12	1,727
Austin	1	1,190	1	272	17	4,051
Beaumont	-	--	2	661	10	2,231
Brownsville	-	--	2	731	8	1,998
Corpus Christi	-	--	4	1,056	25	6,368
Dallas	1	1,561	7	3,303	34	10,677
El Paso	-	--	4	1,401	24	5,204
Fort Worth	-	--	3	1,099	15	4,028
Galveston-Houston	2	1,912	11	4,704	46	14,037
San Angelo	-	--	2	139	6	924
MOUNTAIN	**6**	**7,442**	**42**	**13,336**	**207**	**52,804**
Montana	**2**	**2,094**	**9**	**1,794**	**24**	**5,255**
Great Falls	1	998	5	850	19	4,261
Helena	1	1,096	4	944	5	994
Idaho, Boise	**1**	**50**	**1**	**415**	**13**	**2,219**
Wyoming, Cheyenne	-	--	1	**184**	**8**	**2,005**
Colorado	**1**	**1,210**	**12**	**2,808**	**60**	**16,074**
*Denver	1	1,210	9	2,331	48	14,287
Pueblo	-	--	3	477	12	1,787
New Mexico	**2**	**4,088**	**5**	**1,916**	**33**	**7,628**
*Santa Fe	2	4,088	4	1,761	23	5,636
Gallup	-	--	1	155	10	1,992
Arizona	-	--	9	**4,218**	**49**	**14,833**
Phoenix	-	--	7	3,243	27	9,373
Tucson	-	--	2	975	22	5,460
Utah, Salt Lake City	-	--	3	**863**	**9**	**1,910**
Nevada, Reno	-	--	2	**1,138**	**11**	**2,880**
PACIFIC	**19**	**37,313**	**176**	**84,931**	**794**	**238,975**
Washington	**4**	**7,020**	**18**	**6,680**	**92**	**21,966**
*Seattle	2	3,702	12	4,776	64	15,764
Spokane	2	3,318	5	1,466	21	4,688
Yakima	-	--	1	438	7	1,514
Oregon	**2**	**2,782**	**11**	**3,914**	**57**	**11,808**
*Portland	2	2,782	10	3,764	53	11,140
Baker	-	--	1	150	4	668
California	**12**	**26,746**	**137**	**69,953**	**611**	**193,807**
*Los Angeles	4	7,660	68	36,564	272	99,842
*San Francisco	5	14,896	26	14,177	107	33,827
Fresno	-	--	2	1,034	24	5,280
Monterey	-	--	4	1,304	15	3,562
Oakland	2	1,672	11	6,303	56	15,590
Sacramento	-	--	10	3,485	41	10,349
San Diego	1	2,518	9	4,654	71	19,454
Santa Rosa	-	--	5	1,300	13	2,952
Stockton	-	--	2	1,132	12	2,951

Section, State Diocese	Univs. Colleges	Students	High Schools	Students	Elem. Schools	Students
Alaska	-	--	2	359	4	546
*Anchorage	-	--	-	--	1	110
Fairbanks	-	--	2	359	2	289
Juneau	-	--	-	--	1	147
Hawaii, Honolulu	1	765	8	4,025	30	10,848
EASTERN RITES	1	417	7	1,472	54	9,755
*Philadelphia	1	417	1	380	19	3,201
Stamford	-	--	4	338	9	1,247
St. Nicholas of Chicago	-	--	1	158	4	889
*Munhall	-	--	-	--	7	2,129
Passaic	-	--	-	--	8	1,183
Parma	-	--	1	596	6	1,058
St. Maron of Detroit	-	--	-	--	1	48
Melkite Exarchate	-	--	-	--	-	--
TOTALS 1974	258	407,081	1,702	911,730	8,647	2,717,898
Tmtals 1973	262	418,083	1,753	929,674	8,832	2,874,251
Totals 1964	295	366,172	2,458	1,068,424	10,902	4,556,616

REPORT ON CATHOLIC EDUCATION

The status of Catholic educational institutions in the U.S. at the beginning of 1974, 1973 and 1964 were reflected in figures (as of Jan. 1) reported by *The Official Catholic Directory, 1974.*

Colleges and Universities: 258 (37 less than in 1964). The decreases were due not only to closings but also to some changes of status, from claimed religious affiliation to institutional independence. Students: 407,081 (11,002 less than in 1973 and 40,909 more than in 1964). The all-time high enrollment of 435,716 was registered in 1969.

High Schools: 1,702 in 1974 (51 less than in 1973 and 756 less than in 1964). Students: 911,730 in 1974 (17,944 less than in 1973 and 156,694 less than in 1964).

Elementary Schools: 8,647 in 1974 (185 less than in 1973 and 2,255 less than in 1964). Students: 2,717,898 in 1974 (156,353 less than in 1973 and 1,838,718 less than in 1964).

Public School Students receiving religious instruction on released time: 5,253,738 in 1974 (271,074 less than in 1973 and 936,807 more than in 1964). High School Students: 1,171,322 in 1974 (119,846 less than in 1973 and 77,815 less than in 1964). Elementary School Students: 4,082,416 in 1974 (151,228 less than in 1973 and 1,014,622 more than in 1964).

Teachers, Full-Time: 174,711 in 1974 (8,547 less than in 1973 and 16,088 less than in 1964).

Priests: 7,076 in 1974 (965 less than in 1973 and 4,621 less than in 1964).

Scholastics: 551 in 1974 (176 more than in 1973 and 575 less than in 1964).

Brothers: 3,735 (326 less than in 1973 and 1,665 less than in 1964).

Sisters: 59,759 (7,239 less than in 1973 and

44,682 less than in 1964).

Lay persons: 103,590 (193 less than in 1973 and 35,455 more than in 1964). Lay teachers comprised 59.29 per cent of the total faculty in 1974, 56.63 per cent in 1973 and 35.64 per cent in 1964. They outnumbered priests and religious teachers for the first time in 1971 (106,844 to 93,594).

Costs: The costs of elementary and secondary education — borne by parents, parochial and diocesan subsidy — have soared in recent years. Some parents have found it economically prohibitive to send their children to available schools. Diocesan administrators, forced to close some schools, have amalgamated and clustered others for regional rather than strictly parochial service. Hardest hit are schools in inner-city areas.

Aside from construction and maintenance expenses, the costliest budget items are salaries for lay teachers whose pay scales are higher than those of priests and religious. Salaries for the latter are rising, however, for a variety of reasons; one of them is the need of religious communities for greater income to provide for the care of their retired teachers.

Sisters Remain Committed

Trends behind the decrease (7,239 in 1974) in the number of sisters teaching in Catholic schools are smaller numbers of young women joining religious communities, the departure of sisters from religious life, and the withdrawal of some sisters from teaching to take up other forms of apostolic work. By and large, however, the decrease does not indicate any wholesale lack of interest on the part of women religious in Catholic education and schools.

Problems and Causes

Causes of enrollment drops include rising costs, population shifts from cities to suburban areas, lower birth rates, and attitudinal changes of parents wondering whether the schools will survive, whether they are worth what they cost, and whether they are really so important for religious as well as general education.

School spokesmen, however, have reaffirmed again and again that Catholic schools will not be phased out of existence.

Questioning continues about the high percentage (60 to 75) of church funds allocated to schools in which less than 50 per cent, overall, of Catholic children are enrolled while much less is available for religious education programs for public school students and adults.

School administrators anticipated little immediate effect from the June 25, 1973, rulings of the Supreme Court against the constitutionality of several forms of public aid to non-public school education (see Church-State Decisions of the Supreme Court). Msgr. Roland P. DuMaine, assistant superintendent of schools in the San Francisco archdiocese, said that "our schools are not deprived of any existing benefit" as a result of the decisions.

New Programs Needed

Educators have called attention to past emphasis on the role of Catholic schools in education and the neglect of other aspects of the Church's total teaching function. Programs along the lines envisaged in *To Teach as Jesus Did,* a statement issued by the U.S. bishops in 1972, would extend the Church's educational effort to involve the total community — adults, parents as cooperators in the religious development of their children, college and university students through the campus ministry, lower-level students not in Catholic schools.

Doctrinal Concern

Opinions of parents and educators, as well as bishops who have the prime magisterial responsibility in the Church, remain divided over the merits of some aspects of current religious education programs. At the extremes are those who resist any change at all in traditional catechetical programs and those who appear to be more concerned about ecumenical, psychological and sociological relevance than wholeness of the doctrine which is essential to Catholic belief, practice, experience and witness.

This state of affairs has produced chain reactions of confusion in religious education and, for some parents, lack of confidence in Catholic schools.

U.S. bishops and educators are taking steps to resolve problems of religious education and to provide directives for the teaching of doctrine in line with the *General Catechetical Directory* issued by the Congregation for the Clergy in 1971. In 1972 the bishops published a statement, *To Teach as Jesus Did,* emphasizing the central significance of total Christian education and formation in the pastoral mission of the Church. They followed this up early in 1973 with publication of a document entitled *Basic Teachings for Catholic Religious Education* (see separate entry for text). The best of all of these documents, along with other contents, will form the substance of a future *National Catechetical Directory.*

1974-75 SCHOOL SCENE

Distinctive features in the Catholic school scene at the opening of the 1974-75 year were summarized as follows by John Maher in an NC News story dated Sept. 3, 1974.

Catholic education officials around the United States found enrollment declines continuing to diminish, or even reverse, and morale high among faculty, students and parents as the school year opened in September, 1974.

Many of the officials also said that, although they were determined to seek additional federal and state aid, they realized that there was little likelihood that great amounts of government aid would be given. That realization, however, was leading to greater financial accountability and responsibility, they said.

The officials also noted increased efforts to recruit students for Catholic schools and the trend toward establishing kindergartens as a means of introducing parents to Catholic education at an early stage in their children's lives.

Reflecting the tightness of the educational job market, applications for teaching positions in Catholic schools were up sharply everywhere.

NCEA

The National Catholic Educational Association, founded in 1904, is a voluntary organization of educational institutions and individuals concerned with Catholic education in the US. Its objectives are to promote and encourage the principles and ideals of Christian education and formation by suitable service and other activities.

The NCEA has 14,000 institutional and individual members. Its official publication is *Momentum.* Numerous service publications are issued to members.

Bishop Raymond J. Gallagher of Lafayette, Ind., is chairman of the association. The Rev. John F. Meyers is president.

Headquarters are located at: Suite 350, One Dupont Circle, Washington, D.C. 20036.

Father Meyers, following his election to the presidency of NCEA in 1974, said that the Church's qualitative goal is "a good Catholic education for all."

LEGAL STATUS OF CATHOLIC EDUCATION

The right of private schools to exist and operate in the United States is recognized in law. It was confirmed by the US Supreme Court in 1925 when the tribunal ruled (Pierce v. Society of Sisters, see Church-State Decisions of the Supreme Court) that an Oregon state law requiring all children to attend public schools was unconstitutional.

Private schools are obliged to comply with the education laws in force in the various states regarding such matters as required basic curricula, periods of attendance, and standards for proper accreditation.

The special curricula and standards of private schools are determined by the schools themselves. Thus, in Catholic schools, the curricula include not only the subject matter required by state educational laws but also other fields of study, principally, education in the Catholic faith.

The Supreme Court has ruled that the First Amendment to the US Constitution, in accordance with the No Establishment of Religion Clause of the First Amendment, prohibits direct federal and state aid from public funds to church-affiliated schools. (See several cases in Church-State Decisions of the Supreme Court.)

Permissible Aid

This prohibition does not extend to child-benefit and public-purpose programs of aid under federal or state laws, even though some incidental and secondary benefit accrues to church-related schools.

Statutes authorizing such programs have been ruled constitutional on the grounds that they:

- have a "secular legislative purpose";
- neither inhibit nor advance religion as a "principal or primary effect";
- do not foster "excessive government entanglement with religion."

Programs of aid to nonpublic school education called "certainly constitutional" by Father Charles M. Whelan, S.J., constitutional lawyer and professor of law at Fordham University, are: bus transportation, textbook loans, school lunches and health services, and "secular, neutral or non-ideological services, facilities and materials provided in common to all school children," public and nonpublic.

Programs of these types were in operation in approximately 28 states, as of December, 1973.

Aid is provided most commonly in the form of auxiliary services such as transportation of students to and from school (23 states), textbook loans (14 states), instructional materials (five states), health services (14 states), guidance and counseling (three states), testing (five states), special education (eight states), vocational education (two

states). A number of states offer free lunch programs and even cooperative central purchasing arrangements.

Twenty-two states had no provision for auxiliary services of any kind: Alabama, Alaska, Arizona, Arkansas, Colorado, Florida, Georgia, Hawaii, Idaho, Maryland, Montana, Nevada, North Carolina, Oklahoma, Oregon, South Carolina, Tennessee, Texas, Utah, Virginia, Washington, and Wyoming.

With respect to college and university education in church-affiliated institutions, the Supreme Court has upheld the constitutionality of statutes providing student loans and, under the Federal Higher Education Facilities Act of 1963, construction loans and grants for secular-purpose facilities.

Catholic schools are exempt from real estate taxation in all of the states. Since Jan. 1, 1959, nonprofit parochial and private schools have also been exempt from several federal excise taxes.

Shared Time

In a shared time program of education, students enrolled in Catholic or other church-related schools take some courses (e.g., religion, social studies, fine arts) in their own schools and others (e.g., science, mathematics, industrial arts) in public schools. Such a program, outlined in 1956 by Dr. Erwin L. Shaver of the Massachusetts Council of Churches, has been given serious consideration in recent years by Catholic and other educators. Its constitutionality has not been seriously challenged, but practical problems — relating to teacher and student schedules, transportation, adjustment to new programs, and other factors — are knotty.

Limited shared time programs involving Catholic school students have been in operation since 1927 in Caledonia, Minn., since 1945 in Rutland, Vt., and for a number of years in several communities in Connecticut, Illinois, Michigan, Minnesota, Pennsylvania and Ohio. Since 1964, programs have also been reported operative in Iowa, New Jersey, Oregon, Washington and Wisconsin.

Released Time

Several million children of elementary and high school age of all denominations have the opportunity of receiving religious instruction on released time. Under released time programs they are permitted to leave their public schools during school hours to attend religious instruction classes held off the public school premises. They are released at the request of their parents. Public school authorities merely provide for their dismissal, and take no part in the program.

The first released time program was set up at Gary, Ind., in 1914. In 1905 a proposal had been made by Dr. George U. Wenner, to the

Interfaith Conference on Federation, that public school pupils be given a day off a week for religious instruction in their churches. In 1876 a court decision in Vermont left to the discretion of local school boards whether they would release public school students for religious instruction.

In New York, where released time began in 1917, a law was passed in 1940 which authorized school boards to permit the release of public school pupils from class, at the request of their parents, to attend religious instruction off public school premises. The US Supreme Court upheld the constitutionality of the measure in the case of Zorach v. Clauson in 1952.

Released time programs are operative in most states at this time.

ESEA

The first major federal aid to education program in US history containing provisions benefitting parochial school students was enacted by the first session of the 89th Congress and signed into law by President Lyndon B. Johnson on Apr. 11, 1965. The 1965 Elementary and Secondary School Aid Law was passed by the House of Representatives (263 to 153) on Mar. 26 and by the Senate (73 to 18) on Apr. 9.

Provisions

The principal provisions of the $1.3 billion program were stated in three of the eight titles of the law.

• 1. One billion dollars was allocated to public school districts under a formula based chiefly on the number of children in schools who came from families earning less than $2,000 a year. The grant was intended to cover half of the cost of education for each eligible pupil.

Parochial and other private school pupils in the same low-income bracket were to benefit by extensions to them by local public school districts of shared services or facilities. Public school districts were required to take these children into account when making plans to aid needy students.

• 2. About $100 million was provided to buy textbooks for pupils, materials and volumes for school libraries, and some instructional equipment. All were to be owned by a public agency, such as a local school district or library, but they could be loaned to children attending nonpublic schools.

• 3. Another $100 million was to be used to establish educational centers to benefit both public and private school pupils with cultural enrichment programs and other special services. Public agencies would operate these centers, but the legislation required that private school educators and others from outside the public schools take part in planning for them.

Avoids Impasse

President Johnson presented his program to the Congress on Jan. 12, 1965, in a special message which indicated his intention of avoiding the separation of Church and State impasse which had blocked all earlier aid proposals pertaining to nonpublic, and especially church-affiliated, schools. The aim of the program, under public control, is to serve the public purpose by aiding disadvantaged pupils in public and nonpublic schools.

Program Regulations

Regulations for the administration of programs under the new law were issued Sept. 15, 1965, by the US Office of Education. The leading norms are as follows.

• Participation of Nonpublic School Children: Must be "substantially comparable" to that of public school children.

• Special Projects: Can include "broadened health services, school breakfasts for poor children, and guidance and counseling services" in addition to strictly educational offerings. Public school teachers can go to private schools to offer special services, and mobile or portable equipment can be placed on private school premises temporarily.

• Aid for Textbooks and Library Resources: Materials are to be loaned by public agencies to private school teachers and pupils, not to the schools themselves.

To be distributed to private school pupils on an equal basis with public school student numbers, the materials must be approved for use in public schools and can include books, periodicals, documents, pamphlets, photographic works, musical scores, maps, charts, globes, sound recordings, films and video tapes.

If constitutional restrictions prevent a state from allowing its agencies to act as channels for aid to teachers and pupils in private schools, the regulations provide that the US Commissioner of Education can provide for the distribution of the books and materials himself.

Amendment, Benefits

ESEA, since its passage, has been refunded in several stages and amended in some respects but has remained substantially the same as enacted.

The most recent refunding ($25 billion) was enacted with passage of the Education Amendments of 1974 (H.R. 69) and their signing into law by President Gerald R. Ford Aug. 21, 1974. The amendments provided, among other things, for the broadening of bilingual education and increased funding for education of the handicapped. They also embodied a forward-funding mechanism to ensure program continuity, and a prohibition against busing past the school nearest a child's home unless a court should find it necessary to protect the constitutional rights of minority children.

The law has benefitted many disadvantaged pupils in public and nonpublic schools. Spokesmen for Catholic education, however, have called attention of the Congress to the fact that provisions of the law have not been applied to a disproportionately large number of eligible students in Catholic schools. (See Wheeler v. Barrera, under 1973,1974 Supreme Court Decisions.)

1973, 1974 SUPREME COURT DECISIONS

The U.S. Supreme Court handed down landmark decisions June 25, 1973, against the constitutionality of programs of aid to nonpublic school education on the elementary and secondary levels. Grounds for the decisions were that the programs violated the No Establishment Clause of the First Amendment, that they had the "impermissible effect" of advancing sectarian activities, and that they were generative of religious divisiveness.

The decisions (see Church-State Decisions of the Supreme Court) struck down provisions in New York statutes for maintenance and repair grants for certain nonpublic school facilities (9 to 0), tuition reimbursement (6 to 3) or tax credits (6 to 3) for parents with children in nonpublic schools, and payment to nonpublic schools for specified services mandated by the state (8 to 1). A Pennsylvania reimbursement program shared the same fate as its New York counterpart (6 to 3).

Voting with the majority in all cases were Justices William O. Douglas, William J. Brennan, Jr., Potter Stewart, Thurgood Marshall, Harry A. Blackmun and Lewis F. Powell, Jr. Chief Justice Warren E. Burger and Justice William H. Rehnquist dissented in the 6 to 3 decisions but joined the majority in the 8 to 1 decision. Justice Byron R. White dissented in all but the 9 to 0 decision.

In different decisions with the same thrust, the Court had ruled on June 28, 1971, against the constitutionality of a Rhode Island statute providing salary supplements for teachers of secular subjects in parochial schools in the state, and of a purchase-of-services program for instruction in secular subjects in nonpublic schools in Pennsylvania.

Analysis of Decisions

The two sets of decisions indicated that the Court would strike down any program containing the potential for massive subsidies, either direct or indirect, for education in church-affiliated elementary and secondary schools. So commented Father Charles M. Whelan, S.J., constitutional lawyer and professor of law at Fordham University.

In an analysis of the rulings, Father Whelan said that it seemed "reasonably clear" that all five programs at issue suffered from "three fatal defects":

• "Roman Catholic schools got the lion's share of the benefits."

• The total amount of money involved in the programs, although small, "could easily be expanded to provide massive subsidies for education in parochial schools."

• "There was no way for public schools, parents and students to benefit as well as nonpublic schools, parents and students."

The primary argument against the programs was the "effect" argument. Father Whelan called this a development parallel with the "excessive entanglement" argument in the Lemon decision. He said that the "narrow channel between the Scylla and Charybdis of effect and entanglement" spoken of by Justice Powell (who delivered the majority opinion) will probably "prove too narrow in the immediate future for any new programs specially designed to insure the survival, much less the well-being, of nonpublic elementary and secondary schools."

College Aid Upheld

In two other decisions also handed down June 25, 1973, the Supreme Court sustained the constitutionality of construction loans to church-affiliated colleges (**Hunt v. McNair**, 6 to 3) and loans to students attending such colleges and majoring in studies of religion or preparing for the ministry (**Durham v. McLeod**, 6 to 3). The dissenting Justices were Douglas, Brennan and Marshall.

Father Whelan, along with other observers, speculated about the inconsistency of these decisions, in favor of aid to higher education which is not compulsory, with the others, against aid on the elementary and secondary levels of compulsory education.

Wheeler v. Barrera

The Supreme Court, in Wheeler v. Barrera, ruled 8 to 1 June 10, 1974, that nonpublic school students must share in federal funds for educationally deprived students on a comparable basis with public school students under Title I of the Elementary and Secondary Education Act.

The ruling was made in response to a suit brought by parents of parochial school students in Kansas City, Mo. They contended that the state was in violation of ESEA since no state-paid teachers were being assigned to work with disadvantaged children on the premises of parochial schools during regular school hours. The state argued that such services were in violation of the Missouri constitution.

In a 24-page opinion for the Court, Justice Harry Blackmun found that services provided eligible nonpublic-school students in Missouri were "plainly inferior, both qualitatively and quantitatively," to those given public school pupils. The Court asserted that comparable but not necessarily identical programs would have to be offered nonpublic school students. It was left to Missouri officials to determine which of "numerous" forms of comparable aid should be provided.

The lone dissenter from the Court's opinion was Justice William Douglas.

Commenting on the decision, Dr. Edward R. D'Alessio, director of the Division of Elementary and Secondary Education, U.S. Catholic Conference, noted its "strong emphasis" on the principle of comparability of services for nonpublic school students.

"Apart from ESEA," he said, "the concept of 'comparable' services is well worth exploring for its possible application to other programs of aid to education."

D'Alessio said that emphasis on the needs of children, if applied "across the board," would "go a long way toward enabling government to respond to the educational needs of the child, particularly the disadvantaged, regardless of the school he or she attends. In short, the Barrera case marks a positive turn away from the negative thinking that has characterized some recent aid-to-education decisions."

UNIVERSITIES AND COLLEGES IN THE UNITED STATES

Listed below are institutions of higher learning established under Catholic auspices. Some of them are now independent.

Information includes: name of each institution; indication of male (m), female (w), co-educational (c) student body; name of founding group or group with which the institution is affiliated; year of foundation; number of students, in parentheses.

Albertus Magnus College (w): 700 Prospect St., New Haven, Conn. 06511. Dominican Sisters; 1925 (480).

Albuquerque, University of (c): St. Joseph Pl. N.W., Albuquerque, N.M. 87105. Sisters of St. Francis; 1940 (2,880).

Allentown College of St. Francis de Sales (c); Center Valley, Pa. 18034. Oblates of St. Francis de Sales; 1965 (508).

Alvernia College (w): Reading, Pa. 19607. Franciscan Sisters; 1958 (225).

Alverno College (w): 3401 S. 39th St. Milwaukee, Wis. 53215. School Sisters of St. Francis; 1936; independent (1,181).

Anna Maria College (c): Sunset Lane, Paxton, Mass. 01612. Sisters of St. Anne; 1946 (603).

Annhurst College (w): R.R. 2 Woodstock, South Woodstock, Conn. 06281. Daughters of the Holy Spirit; 1941 (205).

Aquinas College (c): 1607 Robinson Rd. S. E., Grand Rapids, Mich. 49506. Sisters of St. Dominic; 1922 (1,536).

Assumption College (c): 500 Salisbury St., Worcester, Mass. 01609. Assumptionist Fathers; 1904 (1,714).

Avila College (c): 11901 Wornall Rd., Kansas City, Mo. 64145. Sisters of St. Joseph of Carondelet; 1867 (1,065).

Barat College (w): 700 Westleigh Rd., Lake Forest, Ill. 60045. Religious of the Sacred Heart; 1919 (484).

Barry College (w): 11300 N. E. 2nd Ave., Miami, Fla. 33161. Dominican Sisters; 1940 (1,387).

Bellarmine College (c): 2000 Norris Pl., Louisville, Ky. 40205; Louisville archdiocese; 1950 (1,306).

Belmont Abbey College (m): Belmont, N. C. 20812. Benedictine Fathers; 1878 (565).

Benedictine College (formerly St. Benedict and Mt. St. Scholastica Colleges) (c): Atchison, Kans. 66002. Benedictines (1,060).

Biscayne College (m): 16400 N. W. 32nd Ave., Miami, Fla. 33054. Augustinian Fathers; 1962 (1,115).

Boston College (University Status) (c): Newton, Mass. 02167. Jesuit Fathers; 1863 (12,218).

Brescia College (c): 120 W. 7th St., Owensboro, Ky. 42301. Ursuline Sisters; 1925 (960).

Briar Cliff College (c): W. 33rd and Rebecca Sts., Sioux City, Ia. 51104. Sisters of St. Francis of the Holy Family; 1930 (782).

Cabrini College (c): Radnor, Pa. 19087. Missionary Srs. of Sacred Heart; 1957 (434).

Caldwell College (w): Caldwell, N. J. 07006. Dominican Sisters; 1939 (868).

Canisius College (c): 2001 Main St., Buffalo, N. Y. 14208. Jesuit Fathers; 1870; independent (3,912).

Cardinal Stritch College (c): 6801 N. Yates Rd., Milwaukee, Wis. 52317. Sisters of St. Francis of Assisi; 1932 (1,024).

Carlow College (w): 3333 5th Ave., Pittsburgh, Pa. 15213. Sisters of Mercy; 1929 (800).

Carroll College (c): Helena, Mont. 59601. Diocesan Clergy; 1909 (1,096).

Catholic University of America (c): Fourth St. and Michigan Ave. N.E., Washington, D.C. 20017. Hierarchy of the United States; 1889. Pontifical University (6,795).

Catholic University of Puerto Rico (c): Ponce, P. R. Hierarchy of Puerto Rico; Pontifical University (6,651).

Chaminade College (c): 3140 Waialae Ave., Honolulu, H. I. 96816. Marianists; 1955 (909).

Chestnut Hill College (w): Philadelphia, Pa. 19118. Sisters of St. Joseph; 1871 (528).

Christian Brothers College (c): 650 E. Parkway S., Memphis, Tenn. 38104. Brothers of the Christian Schools; 1871 (825).

Clarke College (w): 1550 Clarke Dr., Dubuque, Iowa 52001. Sisters of Charity; 1843 (658).

Creighton Universtiy (c): 2500 California St., Omaha, Neb. 68131. Jesuit Fathers; 1878 (4,341).

Dallas, University of (c): Irving, Tex. 75060. Diocesan; 1956 (1,561).

Dayton, University of (c): 300 College Park, Dayton, Ohio 45409. Marianists; 1850 (6,733).

De Paul University (c): 2323 N. Seminary Ave., Chicago, Ill. 60614. Vincentians; 1898 (9,567).

Detroit, University of (c): McNicholas Rd. at Livernois, Detroit, Mich. 48221. Jesuit Fathers; 1877 (8,672).

Dominican College (w): 2401 E. Holcombe Blvd., Houston, Tex. 77021. Dominican Sisters; 1964; (292).

Dominican College (c): 5915 Erie St., Racine, Wis. 53402. Dominican Sisters; 1935; independent (774).

Dominican College of Blauvelt (c): Blauvelt, N. Y. 10913. Dominican Sisters; 1952 (815).

Dominican College of San Rafael (c): San Rafael, Calif. 94901. Dominican Sisters; 1890; independent (677).

Don Bosco College (m): P.O. Box 6, Newton, N.J. 07860. Salesian Fathers; 1928 (180).

Duquesne University (c): 801 Bluff St., N.W., Pittsburgh, Pa. 15219. Holy Ghost Fathers; 1878 (8,348).

D'Youville College (w): 320 Porter Ave., Buffalo, N. Y. 14201. Grey Nuns of the Sacred Heart; 1908; independent (1,236).

Edgecliff College (c): Edgecliff Victory Pkwy., Cincinnati, Ohio 45206. Sisters of Mercy; 1935 (787).

Edgewood College (c): 855 Woodrow St., Madison, Wis. 53711. Dominican Sisters; 1927 (580).

Emmanuel College (w): 400 The Fenway, Boston, Mass. 02115. Sisters of Notre Dame de Namur; 1919 (968).

Fairfield University (c): Fairfield, Conn. 06433. Jesuit Fathers; 1942 (4,500).

Felician College (w): S. Main St., Lodi, N.J. 07644. Felician Sisters; 1923 (518).

Fontbonne College (w): Wydown and Big Bend Blvds., St. Louis, Mo. 63105. Sisters of St. Joseph of Carondelet; 1923 (650).

Fordham University (c): Fordham Rd. and Third Ave., New York, N. Y. 10458. Jesuit Fathers; 1841; independent (13,800).

Fort Wright College (c): W. 4000 Randolph Rd., Spokane, Wash. 99204. Sisters of the Holy Names of Jesus and Mary; 1939 (360).

Gannon College (c): 109 W. 6th St., Erie, Pa. 16501. Diocesan Clergy; 1944 (3,214).

Georgetown University (c): 37th and O Sts. N.W., Washington, D.C. 20007. Jesuit Fathers; 1789 (9,747).

Georgian Court College (w): Lakewood, N.J. 08701. Sisters of Mercy; 1908 (735).

Gonzaga University (c): Spokane, Wash. 99202. Jesuit Fathers; 1887 (2,958).

Great Falls, College of (c): 1301 29th St. S., Great Falls, Mont. 59401. Sisters of Charity of Providence; 1932 (998).

Gwynedd-Mercy College (w): Gwynedd

Valley, Pa. 19437. Sisters of Mercy; 1948 (599).

Holy Cross College (c): Worcester, Mass. 01610. Jesuit Fathers; 1843 (2,475).

Holy Family College (w): Grant and Frankford Aves., Philadelphia, Pa. 19114. Sisters of Holy Family of Nazareth; 1954 (383).

Holy Names, College of the (c): 3500 Mountain Blvd., Oakland, Calif. 94619. Sisters of the Holy Names of Jesus and Mary; 1800 (716).

Illinois Benedictine College (c): Lisle, Ill. 60532. Benedictine Fathers; 1890 (1,183).

Immaculata College (w): Immaculata, Pa. 19345. Sisters, Servants of the Immaculate Heart of Mary; 1920 (633).

Incarnate Word College (c): 4301 Broadway, San Antonio, Tex. 78209. Sisters of Charity of the Incarnate Word; 1881 (1,554).

Iona College (c): 715 North Ave., New Rochelle, N.Y. 10801. Congregation of Christian Brothers; 1940; independent (4,314).

John Carroll University (c): North Park and Miramar Blvds., Cleveland, Ohio. 44118. Jesuit Fathers; 1886 (3,671).

Kansas Newman College (formerly Sacred Heart College) (c): 3100 McCormick Ave., Wichita, Kans. 67213. Sisters Adorers of the Most Precious Blood; 1933 (604).

King's College (c): Wilkes-Barre, Pa. 18702. Holy Cross Fathers; 1946 (2,378).

Ladycliff College (c): Highland Falls, N.Y. 10928. Franciscan Sisters; 1933; independent (482).

La Roche College (c): 9000 Babcock Blvd., Allison Park, Pittsburgh, Pa. 15237. Sisters of Divine Providence; 1963 (565)

La Salle College (c): 20th St. and Olney Ave., Philadelphia, Pa. 19141. Brothers of the Christian Schools; 1863 (6,222)

Le Moyne College (c): Syracuse, N.Y. 13214. Jesuit Fathers; 1946; independent (1,654).

Lewis University (c): Lockport, Ill. 60441. Christian Brothers; 1930 (2,653).

Lone Mountain College (c): 2800 Turk St., San Francisco, Calif. 94118. Religious of the Sacred Heart; 1930 (793).

Loras College (c): 1450 Alta Vista St., Dubuque, Ia. 52001. Archdiocese of Dubuque; 1839 (1,403).

Loretto Heights College (c): 3001 S. Federal Blvd., Denver, Colo. 80236. Sisters of Loretto; 1918; independent (746).

Loyola College (c): 4501 N. Charles St., Baltimore, Md. 21210, Jesuits; 1852 (3,875).

Loyola University (c): 820 N. Michigan Ave., Chicago, Ill. 60611. Jesuit Fathers; 1870 (15,202).

Loyola University (c): 6363 St. Charles Ave., New Orleans, La. 70118. Jesuit Fathers; 1904 (4,499).

Loyola Marymount University (c): 7101 W. 80th St., Los Angeles, Calif. 90045. Jesuit Fathers; Religious of Sacred Heart of Mary, Sisters of St. Joseph of Orange; 1911 (4,887).

Madonna College (c): 3600 Schoolcraft Rd., Livonia, Mich. 48150. Felician Sisters; 1937 (831).

Manhattan College (m): 4513 Manhattan College Pkwy., New York, N.Y. 10471. Brothers of the Christian Schools; 1853; independent (4,127). Coed arrangements with Mt. St. Vincent College.

Marian College (w): Fond du Lac, Wis. 54935. Sisters of St. Agnes; 1936 (450).

Marian College (c): 3200 Cold Springs Rd., Indianapolis, Ind. 46222. Sisters of St. Francis (Oldenburg, Ind.); 1937 (959).

Marist College (c): Poughkeepsie, N.Y. 12601. Marist Brothers of the Schools; 1946; independent (1,878).

Marquette University (c): 615 N. 11th St., Milwaukee, Wis. 53233. Jesuit Fathers; 1881; independent (10,671).

Mary College (c): Route 2, Box 119, Bismarck, N.D. 58501. Benedictine Sisters; 1959 (749).

Mary Manse College (c): 2436 Parkwood Ave., Toledo, Ohio 43620. Ursuline Nuns; 1922 (722).

Marycrest College (c): 1607 W. 12th St., Davenport, Iowa 52804. Sisters of the Humility of Mary; 1939 (1,010).

Marygrove College (c): 8425 W. McNicholas Rd., Detroit, Mich. 48221. Sisters, Servants of the Immaculate Heart of Mary; 1910 (1,458).

Marymount College (c): Salina, Kans. 67401. Sisters of St. Joseph of Concordia; 1922 (609).

Marymount College (w): Tarrytown, N.Y. 10591. Religious of the Sacred Heart of Mary; 1907; independent (1,006).

Marymount Manhattan College (w): 221 E. 71st St., New York, N.Y. 10021. Religious of the Sacred Heart of Mary; 1948; independent (1,316).

Maryville College (c): 13550 Conway Rd., St. Louis, Mo. 63141. Religious of the Sacred Heart; 1872 (1,021).

Marywood College (c): Scranton, Pa. 18509. Sisters, Servants of the Immaculate Heart of Mary; 1915 (2,625).

Mater Dei College (w): Riverside Dr., Ogdensburg, N.Y. 13669. Sisters of St. Joseph; 1960 (181).

Medaille College (c): 18 Agassiz Circle, Buffalo, N.Y. 14214. Sisters of St. Joseph; 1937 (414).

Mercy College (c): 555 Broadway, Dobbs Ferry, N.Y. 10522. Sisters of Mercy; 1950; independent (1,716).

Mercy College (c): 8200 W. Outer Dr., Detroit, Mich. 48219. Sisters of Mercy; 1941 (1,895).

Mercyhurst College (c): 501 E. 38th St., Erie, Pa. 16501. Sisters of Mercy; 1926 (1,477).

Merrimack College (c): North Andover, Mass. 01845. Augustinians. 1947 (2,049).

Misericordia (w): Dallas, Pa. 18612. Sisters of Mercy; 1932 (1,101).

Molloy College (w): 1000 Hempstead Ave., Rockville Centre, N.Y. 11570. Dominican Sisters; 1955 (1,079).

Mount Angel College (c): Mt. Angel, Ore. 97362. Benedictine Sisters; 1954, independent (287).

Mount Marty College (c): Yankton, S.D. 57078. Benedictine Sisters; 1950 (571).

Mt. Mary College (w): 2900 W. Menomonee River Pkwy., Milwaukee, Wis. 53222. School Sisters of Notre Dame; 1913 (907).

Mt. Mercy College (c): Elmhurst Dr., Cedar Rapids, Ia. 52402. Sisters of Mercy; 1928 (809).

Mt. St. Agnes College: Merged with Loyola College (Maryland).

Mt. St. Joseph College (w): 670 Tower Hill Rd., Wakefield, R.I. 02879. Passionist Sisters; 1953 (140).

Mt. St. Joseph on the Ohio, College of (w): Mt. St. Joseph, Ohio 45051. Sisters of Charity; 1920 (749).

Mt. St. Mary College (w): Hooksett, N.H. 03106. Sisters of Mercy; 1934; independent (229).

Mt. St. Mary College (c): Newburgh, N.Y. 12550. Dominican Sisters; 1954 (743).

Mt. St. Mary College (m): Emmitsburg, Md. 21727. Diocesan Clergy; 1808 (1,160).

Mt. St. Mary's College (c): 12001 Chalon Rd., Los Angeles, Calif. 90049. Sisters of St. Joseph of Carondelet; 1925 (1,280).

Mt. St. Vincent, College of (w): Mt. St. Vincent-on-Hudson, New York, N.Y. 10471. Sisters of Charity; 1847; independent (1,130). Coed arrangements with Manhattan College.

Mount Senario College (c): Ladysmith, Wis. 54848. Servants of Mary; independent (243).

Mundelein College (w): 6363 N. Sheridan Rd., Chicago, Ill. 60626. Sisters of Charity of the Blessed Virgin Mary; 1929 (805).

Nazareth College (c): Nazareth, Mich. 49074. Sisters of St. Joseph; 1924 (482).

Nazareth College (w): East Ave., Rochester, N.Y. 14610. Sisters of St. Joseph; 1924; independent (1,917).

New Rochelle, College of (w): 29 Castle Pl., New Rochelle, N.Y. 10805. Ursuline Nuns; 1904; independent (2,351).

Newton College (w): 885 Centre St., Newton, Mass. 02159. Religious of the Sacred Heart; 1946; independent (832), scheduled to merge with Boston College in June, 1975.

Niagara University (c): Niagara Falls, N.Y. 14109. Vincentian Fathers; 1856 (3,585).

Notre Dame, College of (c): Belmont, Calif. 94002. Sisters of Notre Dame de Namur; 1868; independent (1,392).

Notre Dame College (w): 4545 College Rd., Cleveland, Ohio 44121. Sisters of Notre Dame; 1922 (515).

Notre Dame College (w): Manchester, N.H. 03104. Sisters of the Holy Cross; 1950 (328).

Notre Dame College (w): 320 E. Ripa Ave., St. Louis, Mo. 63125. School Sisters of Notre Dame; 1896 (340).

Notre Dame of Maryland, College of (c): 4701 N. Charles St., Baltimore, Md. 21210. School Sisters of Notre Dame; 1873 (680).

Notre Dame University (c): Notre Dame, Ind. 46556. Holy Cross Fathers; 1842 (8,344).

Ohio Dominican College (c): Columbus, Ohio 43219. Dominican Srs.; 1911 (1,000).

Our Lady of Angels College (w): Aston, Pa. 19014. Sisters of St. Francis; 1965 (395).

Our Lady of Holy Cross College (c): 4123 Woodland Dr., New Orleans, La. 70114. Congregation of Sisters Marianites of Holy Cross (446).

Our Lady of the Elms College (w): Chicopee, Mass. 01013. Sisters of St. Joseph; 1928 (420).

Our Lady of the Lake College (c): 411 S.W. 24th St., San Antonio, Tex. 78285. Sisters of Divine Providence; 1912 (2,283).

Portland, University of (c): Willamette Blvd. at Fiske St., Portland, Ore. 97203. Holy Cross Fathers; 1901; independent (2,024).

Providence College (c): River Ave. and Eaton St., Providence, R.I. 02918. Dominican Fathers; 1917 (2,835).

Quincy College (c): 1831 College Ave., Quincy, Ill. 62301. Franciscan Fathers; 1860 (1,569).

Regis College (c): W. 50th Ave. and Lowell Blvd. Denver, Colo. 80221. Jesuit Fathers; 1888 (1,210).

Regis College (w): Wellesley St., Weston, Mass. 02193. Sisters of St. Joseph; 1927 (807).

Rivier College (w): Nashua, N.H. 03060. Sisters of the Presentation of Mary; 1933; independent (1,095).

Rockhurst College (c): 5225 Troost Ave., Kansas City, Mo. 64110. Jesuit Fathers; 1910 (2,341).

Rosary College (c): 7900 Division St., River Forest, Ill. 60305. Dominican Sisters; 1901 (1,292).

Rosary Hill College (c): 4380 Main St., Buffalo, N.Y. 14226. Sisters of St. Francis of Penance and Christian Charity; 1947; independent (1,331).

Rosemont College (w): Rosemont, Pa. 19010. Society of the Holy Child Jesus; 1921 (607).

Sacred Heart College (w): Belmont, N.C. 28012. Sisters of Mercy; 1935 (225).

Sacred Heart University (c): Fairfield (P.O. Bridgeport), Conn. 06604. Diocese of Bridgeport; 1963; independent (1,190).

St. Ambrose College (c): Davenport, Ia. 52803. Diocese of Davenport; 1882 (1,236).

St. Anselm's College (c): Manchester N.H. 03102. Benedictine Fathers; 1889 (1,557).

St. Basil's College (m): 195 Glenbrook Rd., Stamford, Conn. 06902. Byzantine Rite Diocese of Stamford; 1939 (23).

St. Benedict College (w): St. Joseph, Minn. 56374. Benedictine Sisters; 1913 (1,362).

St. Bernard College (c): St. Bernard, Ala. 35138. Benedictine Fathers; 1892 (464).

St. Bonaventure University (c): St. Bonaventure, N.Y. 14778. Franciscan Fathers; 1856 (2,431).

St. Catherine College (w): 2004 Randolph St., St. Paul, Minn. 55116. Sisters of St. Joseph of Carondelet; 1905 (1,537).

St. Edward's University (c): Austin, Tex. 78704. Holy Cross Brothers; 1885 (1,190).

St. Elizabeth, College of (w): Convent Station, N.J. 07961. Sisters of Charity; 1899; independent (584).

St. Francis College (c): 605 Pool Rd., Biddeford, Me. 04005. Franciscan Fathers; 1943; independent (509).

St. Francis College (c): 180 Remsen St., Brooklyn, N.Y. 11201. Franciscan Brothers; 1884; independent (2,824).

St. Francis College (c): 2701 Spring St., Fort Wayne, Ind. 46808. Sisters of St. Francis; 1937 (1,592).

St. Francis College (c): 500 Wilcox, Joliet, Ill. 60435. Franciscan Sisters; 1925 (878).

St. Francis College (c): Loretto, Pa. 15940. Franciscan Fathers; 1847 (1,542).

St. John College (c): Cleveland, Ohio 44114. Diocesan College; 1928 (678).

St. John Fisher College (m): 3690 East Ave., Rochester, N.Y. 14618. Basilian Fathers; 1951; independent (1,374).

St. John's University (c): Grand Central and Utopia Pkwys., Jamaica, N.Y. 11432 (Queens Campus); 300 Howard Ave., Grymes Hill, Staten Island, N.Y. 10301 (Staten Island Campus). Vincentian Fathers; 1870 (13,626).

St. John's University (m): Collegeville, Minn. 56321. Benedictine Fathers; 1857 (1,735). Coed in graduate school.

St. Joseph College (w): 1678 Asylum Ave., West Hartford, Conn. 06117. Sisters of Mercy; 1932 (941). Coed in graduate school.

St. Joseph's College (c): Standish (P.O. N. Windham), Me. 04062. Sisters of Mercy, 1915 (507).

St. Joseph's College (c): Rensselaer, Ind. 47978; Calumet Campus, 4721 Indianapolis Blvd., East Chicago, Ind. 46312. Society of the Precious Blood; 1889 (1,062 at Rensselaer; 1,661 at Calumet Campus, East Chicago).

St. Joseph's College (c): City Ave. at 54th St., Philadelphia, Pa. 19131. Jesuit Fathers; 1851 (2,294).

St. Joseph's College (c): 245 Clinton Ave., Brooklyn, N.Y. 11205. Sisters of St. Joseph; 1916; independent (527).

St. Joseph the Provider, College of (c): Clement Rd., Rutland, Vt. 05701. Sisters of St. Joseph; 1954 (195).

St. Leo College (c): St. Leo, Fla. 33574. Benedictine Fathers; 1889; independent (1,070).

St. Louis University (c): 221 N. Grand Blvd., St. Louis, Mo. 63103. Jesuit Fathers; 1818 (11,089).

St. Martin's College (c): Olympia, Wash. 98503. Benedictine Fathers; 1895 (543).

St. Mary, College of (w): 1901 S. 72nd St., Omaha, Neb. 68124. Sisters of Mercy; 1923; independent (568).

St. Mary College (w): Leavenworth, Kans. 66048. Sisters of Charity of Leavenworth; 1923 (481).

St. Mary of the Plains College (c): Dodge City, Kans. 67801. Sisters of St. Joseph of Wichita; 1952 (413).

St. Mary-of-the-Woods College (w): St. Mary-of-the-Woods, Ind. 47876. Sisters of Providence; 1840 (364).

St. Mary's College (w): Notre Dame, Ind. 46556. Sisters of the Holy Cross; 1844 (1,505).

St. Mary's College (m): Orchard Lake, Mich. 48034. Secular Clergy (140).

St. Mary's College (c): Moraga, Calif. 94575. Brothers of the Christian Schools; 1863 (1,012).

St. Mary's College (c): Winona, Minn. 55987. Brothers of the Christian Schools; 1913 (1,152).

St. Mary's Dominican College (w): 7214 St. Charles Ave., New Orleans, La. 70118. Dominican Sisters; 1910 (872).

St. Mary's University (c): 2700 Cincinnati Ave., San Antonio, Tex. 78228. Society of Mary (Marianists); 1852 (3,692).

St. Michael's College (c): Winooski Park, Vt. 05404. Society of St. Edmund; 1904 (1,733).

St. Norbert College (c): De Pere, Wis. 54178. Norbertine Fathers; 1898 (1,500).

St. Peter's College (c): 2641 Kennedy Blvd., Jersey City, N.J. 07306. Jesuit Fathers; 1872 (4,402).

St. Rose, College of (c): 432 Western Ave., Albany, N.Y. 12203. Sisters of St. Joseph of Carondelet; 1920; independent (1,563).

St. Scholastica, College of (c): College St. and Kenwood Ave., Duluth, Minn. 55811. Benedictine Sisters; 1912 (1,015).

St. Teresa, College of (c): Winona, Minn. 55987. Sisters of St. Francis; 1907 (1,040).

St. Thomas, College of (m): St. Paul, Minn. 55101. Archdiocese of St. Paul; 1885 (2,456).

St. Thomas, University of (College Status) (c): 3812 Montrose Blvd., Houston, Tex. 77006. Basilian Fathers; 1947 (1,605).

St. Thomas Aquinas College (c): Sparkill, N.Y. 10976. Dominican Sisters (750).

St. Vincent's College (m): Latrobe, Pa. 15650. Benedictine Fathers; 1846 (975).

St. Xavier College (c): 3700 W. 103rd St., Chicago, Ill. 60655. Sisters of Mercy; chartered 1846 (1,219).

Salve Regina College (c): Ochre Point Ave., Newport, R.I. 02840. Sisters of Mercy; 1934 (725).

San Diego, University of (c): Alcala Park, San Diego, Calif. 92110. Diocesan Clergy; 1954 (1,352).

San Francisco, University of (c): 2131 Fulton St., San Francisco, Calif. 95053. Jesuit Fathers; 1851 (5,962).

Santa Clara, University of (c): Santa Clara, Calif. 95053. Jesuit Fathers; 1851 (6,170).

Santa Fe, College of (c): Santa Fe, N. Mex. 87501. Brothers of the Christian Schools; 1947 (1,208).

Scranton, University of (c): Scranton, Pa. 18510. Jesuit Fathers; 1888 (3,762).

Seattle University (c): Broadway and East Madison, Seattle, Wash. 98122. Jesuit Fathers; 1891 (3,149).

Seton Hall University (c): South Orange, N.J. 07079. Diocesan Clergy; 1856 (9,719).

Seton Hill College (w): Greensburg, Pa. 15601. Sisters of Charity of Seton Hill; 1883 (660).

Siena College (c): Loudonville, N.Y. 12211. Franciscan Fathers; 1937 (2,046).

Siena Heights College (c): Adrian, Mich. 49221. Dominican Sisters; 1919 (847).

Silver Lake College of Holy Family (c): R.F.D. 5, Manitowoc, Wis. 54220. Franciscan Sisters of Christian Charity; 1935 (463).

Spalding College (c): 851 S. 4th St., Louisville, Ky. 40203. Sisters of Charity of Nazareth; 1920 (1,071).

Spring Hill College (c): Mobile, Ala. 36608. Jesuit Fathers; 1830 (944).

Steubenville, College of (c): Steubenville, Ohio 43952. Franciscan Fathers; 1946 (998).

Stonehill College (c): North Easton, Mass. 02356. Holy Cross Fathers; 1948 (1,611).

Thomas More College (c): Turkey Foot Rd., Box 85, Fort Mitchell, Covington, Ky. 41017. Diocese of Covington; 1921 (1,589).

Trinity College (w): Colchester Ave., Burlington, Vt. 05401. Sisters of Mercy; 1925 (497).

Trinity College (w): Michigan Ave. and Franklin St. N.E., Washington, D.C. 20017. Sisters of Notre Dame de Namur; 1897 (500).

Ursuline College (w): Lander Rd. and Fairmont Blvd., Cleveland, Ohio 44124. Ursuline Nuns; 1871 (404).

Villa Maria College (w): 2551 W. Lake Rd., Erie, Pa. 16505. Sisters of St. Joseph; 1925 (643).

Villanova University (c): Villanova, Pa. 19086. Augustinian Fathers; 1842 (10,305).

Viterbo College (c): La Crosse, Wis. 54601. Franciscan Sisters; 1931 (701).

Walsh College (c): 2020 Easton St. N.W., Canton, Ohio 44720. Brothers of Christian Instruction; 1951 (894).

Wheeling College (c): 316 Washington Ave., Wheeling, W. Va. 26003. Jesuit Fathers; 1954 (590).

White Plains, College of (c): 52-78 N. Broadway, White Plains, N.Y. 10603. Sisters of the Divine Compassion; 1923; independent (667).

Xavier University (c): Victory Pkwy. and Dana Ave., Cincinnati, Ohio 45207. Jesuit Fathers; 1831 (6,259).

Xavier University (c): Palmetto and Pine

Sts., New Orleans, La. 70125. Sisters of the Blessed Sacrament; 1925 (1,808).

Catholic Junior Colleges

Ancilla Domini College (c): Donaldson, Ind. 46513. Ancilla Domini Sisters; 1937 (167).

Aquinas Junior College (c): Harding Rd., Nashville, Tenn. 37205. Dominican Sisters; 1961 (102).

Cullman College (c): Cullman, Ala. 35055. Benedictine Sisters; 1940 (202).

Donnelly College (c): 1236 Sandusky Ave., Kansas City, Kans. 66102. Diocesan College. Benedictine Sisters; 1949 (426).

Elizabeth Seton College (c): 1061 N. Broadway, Yonkers, N.Y. 10701. Sisters of Charity; 1960 (422).

Harriman College (c): Harriman Heights Rd., Harrimman, N.Y. 10926. Sisters of the Catholic Apostolate (185).

Hilbert College (c): 5200 S. Park Ave., Hamburg, N.Y. 14075. Franciscan Sisters; 1960; independent(585).

Holy Cross Junior College (c): Notre Dame, Ind. 46556. Brothers of Holy Cross; 1966 (255).

Immaculata College of Washington (w): 4300 Nebraska Ave. N.W., Washington, D.C. Sisters of Providence; 1922 (197).

Lourdes Junior College (w): Sylvania, Ohio 43560. Franciscan Srs. (186).

Manor Junior College (w): Fox Chase Manor, Jenkintown, Pa. 19046. Sisters of St. Basil the Great; 1947 (417).

Maria College (w): 700 New Scotland Ave., Albany, N.Y. 12208. Sisters of Mercy; 1963 (482).

Maria Regina College (w): 1024 Court St., Syracuse, N.Y. 13208. Franciscan Sisters; 1963 (401).

Marymount College (w): 2807 N. Glebe Rd., Arlington, Va. 22007. Religious of the Sacred Heart of Mary; 1950 (621).

Marymount College (c): 6717 Palos Verdes Dr., South Palos Verdes Estates, Calif. 90274. Religious of the Sacred Heart of Mary (248).

Mt. Aloysius Junior College (c): Cresson, Pa. 16630. Sisters of Mercy; 1939 (480).

Mt. St. Clare College (c): Bluff Blvd., and Springdale Dr., Clinton, Ia. 52732. Sisters of Third Order of St. Francis; 1918 (205).

Ottumwa Heights College (c): Grandview Ave., Ottumwa, Ia. 52501. Sisters of the Humility of Mary; 1925 (382).

Presentation College (c): Aberdeen, S.D. 57401. Sisters of the Presentation; 1951 (431).

St. Catharine College (c); St. Catharine, Ky. 40061. Dominican Sisters; 1931 (118).

St. Gertrude, College of (c): Cottonwood, Ida. 83522. Benedictine Sisters.

St. Gregory's College (c): Shawnee, Okla. 74801. Benedictine Fathers; 1876 (354).

St. Joseph College of Florida (c): 720 S. Indian River, Jensen Beach, Fla. 33457. Sisters of St. Joseph (318).

St. Joseph's College (c): Bennington, Vt. 05201. Sisters of St. Joseph (215).

St. Mary's College (c): 200 N. Main St., O'Fallon, Mo. 63366. Sisters of the Most Precious Blood; 1921 (395).

St. Mary's College (c): 2600 S. 5th St., Minneapolis, Minn. 55406 (838).

Springfield College in Illinois (c): 1500 N. Fifth St., Springfield, Ill. 62702. Ursuline Nuns; 1929 (566).

Tombrock College (w): New St., P.O. Box 628, W. Paterson, N.J. 07424. Missionary Srs. of the Immaculate Conception; 1964. Closed 1974; may reopen in 1975.

Trocaire College (w): 110 Red Jackett Pkwy., Buffalo, N.Y. 14220. Sisters of Mercy; 1958 (733).

Villa Julie College (w): Green Spring Valley Rd., Stevenson, Md. 21153. Sisters of Notre Dame de Namur; 1952 (355).

Villa Maria College of Buffalo (c): 240 Pine Ridge Rd., Buffalo, N.Y. 14225. Felician Srs.; 1960 (424).

CAMPUS MINISTRY

"Campus ministry is a pastoral apostolate of service to the members of the entire college community through concern and care for persons, the proclamation of the Gospel, and the celebration of the liturgy," according to a set of guidelines drawn up by an eight-member commission of the National Catholic Educational Association. The general purpose of the ministry is to make the Church present and active in the academic community.

Ideally, according to the guidelines, elements of the ministry — carried on by teams of priests, men and women religious, and lay persons — include liturgical leadership; pastoral counseling; coordination of expressions and energies for religious life on campus; Christian witness on social and moral issues; objective and independent mediation between various groups on campus; participation in religious aspects of the work of the administration, faculty and students.

Status, Agencies

The dimensions and challenge of the campus ministry are evident from estimates that approximately 75 to 80 per cent of 1.8 million Catholics in colleges and universities are on secular or non-Catholic private campuses. Serving them are about 750 full-time and 1,000 part-time campus ministry personnel.

The Division of Higher Education, under the Department of Education of the US Catholic Conference, has responsibility for continuing support of ministry in this field. Rev. Laurence T. Murphy, M.M., is director of the division, with offices at 1312 Massachusetts Ave. N.W., Washington, D.C. 20005.

Information and services are furnished by the National Committee of Diocesan Directors of Campus Ministry. This is a committee of members elected from each of the 12 ecclesiastical regions of the US, and is an advisory body to the Division of Higher Education.

The autonomous Catholic Campus Ministry Association, whose former equivalent was the National Newman Chaplain's Association, is headed by Rev. Dr. Patrick H. O'Neill, O.S.A., 408 E. Lyman Ave., Winter Park, Fla.·32789.

Training Programs

Frank J. Lewis Chaplains' Schools for Campus Ministry Orientation, held in June, 1973, in Detroit and San Diego, provided orientation and direction for men and women new to the ministry. Forty campus ministers attended each of the schools, which were funded by the Frank J. Lewis Foundation.

The National Center for Campus Ministry, for specialized ministerial training and education, serves as a national focus for religious and moral concern in higher education.

Designed by an ecumenical team of chaplains and educators active on public, private and church-related campuses, it is sponsored by the Catholic bishops of the US and is funded by Catholic and non-Catholic individual donors and foundations. It is governed by a board of directors representing major American religious and academic traditions.

The center coordinates local and regional programs of training and continuing education, as well as research projects. Information concerning its operations is available from the National Center for Campus Ministry, 1312 Massachusetts Ave. N.W., Washington, D.C. 20005. Rev. Laurence T. Murphy, M.M., president of the board of trustees, is the interim director.

Newman Background

Special ministry on secular campuses in the US began in 1893 when the first student unit of the Newman movement or apostolate was formed at the University of Pennsylvania. Similar units were formed later at other colleges and universities, and in 1915 various groups throughout the country organized a national student federation. Father John Keough of Philadelphia, who became the first national chaplain of the federation in 1917, was a prime mover in publicizing and developing the movement.

The bishops of the US formally recognized the movement in 1941, and in 1962 approved a National Newman Apostolate structure consisting of: the National Newman Student Federation (dating from 1915), the John Henry Cardinal Newman Honorary Society (1938), the National Newman Chaplains' Association (1950), the National Newman Alumni Association (1957), the National Newman Association of Faculty and Staff (1959), and the National Newman Foundation (1959).

Developments in recent years led to dismantling of the whole Newman structure and its replacement by other organizations and programs considered better related to existing conditions on campuses and in the Church and society in general.

DIOCESAN AND INTERDIOCESAN SEMINARIES

Information, according to states, includes names of archdioceses and dioceses, and names and addresses of seminaries. Types of seminaries, when not clear from titles, are indicated in most cases. Interdiocesan seminaries are generally conducted by religious orders for candidates for the priesthood from several dioceses. The list does not include houses of study only for members of religious communities.

Arizona: Tucson — Regina Cleri Seminary (minor), 8800 E. 22nd St. 85710.

California: Los Angeles — St. John's Seminary (major), 5012 E. Seminary Rd., Camarillo. 93010; St. John's Seminary College, 5118 E. Seminary Rd., Camarillo. 93010; Our Lady Queen of Angels (minor), Box 1071, San Fernando. 91341.

Sacramento — St. Pius X Seminary (minor), Twin Cities Rd. and Midway Ave., Galt. 95632.

San Diego — St. Francis Seminary, 5102 San Pedro Ave. 92111.

San Francisco — St. Patrick's Seminary (major), 320 Middlefield Rd., Menlo Park. 94025; St. Patrick's College Seminary, P.O. Box 151, Menlo Park. 94040; St. Joseph High School (minor), Menlo Park. 94040.

Colorado: Denver — St. Thomas Theological Seminary (major), 1300 S. Steele St.

Connecticut: Hartford — St. Thomas Seminary (minor), 467 Bloomfield Ave., Bloomfield. 06002.

Stamford Byzantine Rite — Ukrainian Catholic Seminary (major), 161 Glenbrook Rd. 06902; St. Basil's Preparatory School, Clovelly Rd. 06902.

District of Columbia: Washington — Theological School of Catholic University of America, 401 Michigan Ave., N.E. 20017.

Florida: Miami — St. John Vianney Minor Seminary, 2900 S.W. 87th Ave. 33165; St. Vincent de Paul Seminary (major), Military Trail, P.O. Box 460, Boynton Beach. 33435.

Hawaii: Honolulu — St. Stephen's Seminary, P.O. Box 698, Kaneohe. 96744.

Illinois: Belleville — St. Henry's Preparatory Seminary, 5901 W. Main St. 62223.

Chicago — Quigley Preparatory Seminary, 103 East Chestnut St. 60611 (North), 7740 South Western Ave. 60620 (South); St. Mary of the Lake Seminary, Mundelein. 60060; Niles Campus of St. Mary of the Lake Seminary, 7135 N. Harlem Ave. 60648.

Joliet — St. Charles Borromeo Seminary, High School, Rt. 53A and Airport Rd. 60441.

Springfield — Immaculate Conception

Seminary, 1903 E. Lakeshore Dr. 62708.

Indiana: Gary — Bishop Noll Institute, 1519 Hoffman St., Hammond. 46320.

Indianapolis — St. Meinrad Major and Minor Seminary (interdiocesan), St. Meinrad. 47577.

Iowa: Davenport — St. Ambrose Seminary, 518 W. Locust St. 52803.

Dubuque — Seminary of St. Pius X, Loras College. 52001.

Kansas: Kansas City — Savior of the World Seminary, 1201 Parallel Ave. 66109.

Kentucky: Covington — Seminary of St. Pius X, Erlanger. 41018.

Louisville — St. Thomas Seminary (preparatory), 1816 Norris Pl. 40205.

Louisiana: Baton Rouge — St. Joseph Cathedral Prep School, 3300 Hundred Oaks Ave. 70821.

Lafayette — Immaculata Seminary (preparatory), Carmel Ave. 70501. Box 3847. 70501.

New Orleans — Notre Dame Seminary, 2901 S. Carrollton Ave. 70118; St. John Vianney Preparatory School, 3810 Monroe St. 70118.

Maryland: Baltimore — St. Mary's Seminary and University, 5400 Roland Ave. 21210; Mt. St. Mary's Seminary, Emmitsburg. 21727.

Massachusetts: Boston — St. John's Seminary, Brighton. 02135; Pope John XXIII National Seminary, 558 South Ave., Weston. 02193.

Melkite Exarchate — St. Basil's Seminary for Eastern Rites, 30 East St., Methuen. 01844.

Michigan: Detroit — Sacred Heart Seminary College, Inc., 2701 Chicago Blvd. 48206; Sts. Cyril and Methodius Seminary, Orchard Lake. 48034; St. John's Provincial Seminary (major for dioceses in Detroit province), P.O. Box 298, Plymouth. 48170.

Grand Rapids — St. Joseph's Minor Seminary, 600 Burton St., S.E., 49507.

St. Maron of Detroit Eparchy — Our Lady of Lebanon Maronite Seminary, 7164 Alaska Ave. N.W., Washington, D.C. 20012.

Minnesota: St. Cloud — St. John's Seminary, Collegeville. 56321.

St. Paul and Minneapolis — St. Paul Seminary, 2260 Summit Ave., St. Paul. 55105; St. John Vianney Seminary, 2215 Summit Ave., St. Paul. 55105.

Winona — Immaculate Heart of Mary Seminary, Terrace Heights. 55987.

Missouri: Jefferson City — St. Thomas Aquinas Preparatory Seminary, 245 N. Levering Ave. Hannibal. 63401.

Kansas City-St. Joseph — St. John's Diocesan Seminary (high school), 2015 E. 72nd St. Kansas City. 64132.

St. Louis — St. Louis Roman Catholic Theological Seminary (Kenrick Seminary), 7800 Kenrick Rd. 63119; Cardinal Glennon College, (major), 5200 Glennon Dr. 63119;

St. Louis Preparatory Seminary, 5200 Shrewsbury Ave. 63119 (South), 3500 St. Catherine St., Florissant 63033 (North).

Springfield-Cape Girardeau — Sacred Heart House of Studies, 625 E. Locust St., Springfield. 65803.

Montana: Helena — Diocesan Preparatory Seminary, Carroll College. 59601.

New Jersey: Newark — Immaculate Conception Seminary (major), Darlington. 07446; Seton Hall Divinity School, South Orange. 07079.

New Mexico: Gallup — Cristo Rey Minor Seminary, 406 W. Aztec. 87301; Cristo Rey College Seminary, 205 E. Wilson. 87301.

Santa Fe — Immaculate Heart of Mary Seminary, Mt. Carmel Rd. 87501.

New York: Brooklyn — Cathedral Preparatory Seminary of the Immaculate Conception, 555 Washington Ave. 11238; Cathedral College of the Immaculate Conception, 7200 Douglaston Parkway, Douglaston. 11362; Cathedral Preparatory Seminary of the Immaculate Conception, 56-25 92nd St., Elmhurst. 11373.

Buffalo — Diocesan Preparatory Seminary, 844 Delaware Ave. 14209; Christ the King Seminary (interdiocesan); East Aurora. 14052.

New York — St. Joseph's Seminary (major), Dunwoodie, Yonkers. 10704; Cathedral College (minor), 555 West End Ave. 10024.

Ogdensburg — Wadhams Hall, Riverside Dr. 13669.

Rochester — St. Bernard's Seminary, 2260 Lake Ave. 14612.

Rockville Centre — Immaculate Conception Diocesan Seminary, Lloyd Harbor, Huntington, L.I. 11743; St. Pius X Preparatory Seminary, 1220 Front St., Uniondale, L.I. 11553.

North Dakota: Fargo — Cardinal Muench Seminary, RFD 2. 58102.

Ohio: Cincinnati — Mt. St. Mary's Seminary of the West, 5440 Moeller Ave., Norwood. 45212; St. Gregory's Minor Seminary, 6616 Beechmont Ave., Cincinnati. 45230.

Cleveland — St. Mary's Seminary, 1227 Ansel Rd. 44108; Borromeo Seminary, 28700 Euclid Ave. Wickliffe. 44092.

Columbus — College of St. Charles Borromeo, 2010 E. Broad St. 43209; Pontifical College Josephinum (interdiocesan), Worthington. 43085.

Steubenville — St. John Vianney Seminary (major and minor), Bloomingdale. 43910.

Toledo — Seminary of the Holy Spirit, 5201 Airport Highway. 43615.

Pennsylvania: Erie — St. Mark's Seminary, 429 E. Grandview Blvd. 16504.

Munhall Greek Rite — Byzantine Catholic Seminary of Sts. Cyril and Methodius, 3605 Perrysville Ave., Pittsburgh.

Philadelphia — Theological Seminary of St. Charles Borromeo, Overbrook. 19151.

Philadelphia Ukrainian Rite — St. Josaphat's Seminary, 201 Taylor St. N.E., Washington, D.C. 20017.

Pittsburgh — St. Paul Seminary, 2900 Noblestown Rd. 15205; St. Fidelis Seminary (interdiocesan), Herman. 16039.

Scranton — St. Pius X Seminary, Dalton. 18414.

Rhode Island: Providence — Our Lady of Providence Seminary (major), Warwick Neck Ave., Warwick. 02889.

South Dakota: Sioux Falls — Minor Seminary, 3100 W. 41st St. 57105.

Texas: Corpus Christi — Corpus Christi Minor Seminary, Rt. 1, Box 500. 78415.

Dallas — Holy Trinity Seminary (major), P.O. Drawer 5378, Irving. 75062.

El Paso — St. Charles Seminary High School, P.O. Box 17548. 79917.

Galveston-Houston — St. Mary's Seminary, 9845 Memorial Dr. Houston. 77024.

San Antonio — The Assumption Seminary 2600 W. Woodlawn Ave. 78228.

Virginia: Richmond — St. John Vianney Minor Seminary, Rt. 2, Box 389. 23233.

Washington: Seattle — St. Thomas the Apostle (major, for provinces of Seattle, Portland in Oregon and Anchorage, Alaska), Kenmore. 98028; St. Edward's Seminary (minor), Kenmore. 98028.

Spokane — Bishop White Seminary, E. 429 Sharp Ave. 99202; Mater Cleri Seminary, Colbert. 99005.

West Virginia: Wheeling — St. Joseph Preparatory Seminary, Rt. 6, Vienna. 26101; Seminary House of Studies, 1252 National Rd., Wheeling. 26003.

Wisconsin: Green Bay — Sacred Heart Center, Oneida. 54155.

Madison — Holy Name Seminary (minor), High Point Rd., R.R. 2. 53711.

Milwaukee — St. Francis School of Pastoral Ministry, 3257 S. Lake Dr. 53207; St. Francis de Sales College, 3501 S. Lake Dr. 53207; De Sales Seminary High School, 3501 S. Lake Dr. 53207.

U.S. SEMINARIES AND STUDENTS, 1962-1974
(Source: *The Official Catholic Directory.*)

Year	Dioc. Seminaries	Total Dioc. Students	Religious Seminaries Scholasticates	Total Rel. Students	Total Seminarians
1962	98	23,662	447	22,657	46,319
1963	107	25,247	454	22,327	47,574
1964	112	26,701	459	22,049	48,750
1965	117	26,762	479	22,230	48,992
1966	126	26,252	481	21,862	48,114
1967	123	24,293	452	21,086	45,379
1968	124	22,232	437	17,604	39,836
1969	122	19,573	407	14,417	33,990
1970	118	17,317	383	11,589	28,906
1971	110	14,987	340	10,723	25,710
1972	106	13,554	326	9,409	22,963
1973	107	12,925	304	8,855	21,780
1974	109	11,765	293	7,583	19,348

Breakdown

The peak enrollment year for diocesan seminaries was 1965, when they had a total of 26,762 students. The comparative figure at the beginning of 1974 was 11,765, a decrease of 54.5 per cent.

The peak year for seminaries of religious institutes was 1962, when the total enrollment was 22,657. The comparative figure at the beginning of 1974 was 7,583, a decrease of 66.5 per cent.

The total all-time high enrollment of 48,992 in 1965 was down to 19,348 at the beginning of 1974, a decrease of 60.5 per cent.

Reasons

Many reasons have been advanced for the decline in the number of candidates for the priesthood and religious life.

Obvious ones are defections from both ways of life; the impact of changes rightly or wrongly attributed to the Second Vatican Council; the slow pace of institutional renewal in the priesthood, the religious life and the Church in general, coupled with confused expectations; opportunities for apostolic service in other vocations; the problem of adjusting personalist strivings with the needs for institutional commitment; the difficulty of submitting oneself to the other as well as this-worldly demands of these vocations in the contemporary cultural and social climate.

The basic reason, however, is a crisis of faith, stated Cardinal Gabriel Garrone, prefect of the Congregation for Catholic Education, in a Vatican Radio interview in April, 1972.

He said that the progressive decrease in vocations "is in direct relation to the crisis in the priesthood" and religious life.

This crisis in turn, he added, is "linked to the crisis of faith, and the crisis of faith is linked to the absolutely unprecedented conditions of the present-day life of men and of society."

The cardinal said: "Our fundamental concern must spring from the fact that we live in a very complex and very new environment; and that we, therefore, run the risk of remaining passive, either through discouragement or cowardice, or else we lose sight of the most fundamental impulse of all in the matter of vocations — faith."

CARA STUDY

The decline in the numbers of seminaries and seminarians in the United States was confirmed in a study conducted by the Center for Applied Research in the Apostolate and published in May, 1973, under the title, *An Overview: Seminary Enrollment 1967-72.*

The study was based on the enrollment records of (1) 275 seminaries in operation in the 1967-68 academic year and (2) 181 of these seminaries still operating in the 1972-73 academic year.

The study was prefaced with the qualification: "It is not a study of the total number of students preparing for the Catholic priesthood in the United States nor does it intend to conclude with exact statistics in this area."

Seminary High Schools

The number of seminary high schools under study declined from 138 to 80 between October, 1967, and October, 1972. Total enrollment decreased from 14,825 to 7,570, a loss of 49 per cent. Enrollment in the surviving 80 schools fell from 10,789 to 7,570, a drop of 30 per cent.

Various reasons were given for the closing of high school seminaries. One writer cited "lack of students, lack of personnel, lack of funds to keep the much-too-large-for-our-needs facility going." Also influential was the argument that "the ideal atmosphere in which a high school student can best mature is in the milieu of his own family and peers, both male and female," rather than in the closed environment of a seminary, especially a boarding high school.

Closings resulted in the shift of some students to other seminary high schools. Several dioceses instituted a "home seminary program," as in Cincinnati, Louisville, San Diego and Oakland. Similar programs were adopted by some religious institutes which had ceased to recruit students on the high school level.

"The future of the seminary high school," said the CARA report, "depends in large part upon the convictions of the individual bishop and his senate or the (religious) provincial and his council. This conviction will be based upon their evaluation of the importance of the seminary high school, the rate of enrollment and the perseverance of students vs. the financial commitment, and the viability of other alternatives to the seminary high school for providing the diocese or religious community with candidates for the priesthood."

Seminary Colleges

The report covered 64 seminary colleges with independent academic programs in October, 1967: 46 four year colleges, 8 senior colleges (philosophates, the first two years of the major seminary), 10 junior colleges (the last two years of the minor seminary). By October, 1972, 18 of these had closed — 10 four year colleges, 2 senior colleges and 6 junior colleges — leaving 46 seminary colleges. Total enrollment dropped from 7,554 to 3,940, a loss of 48 per cent.

Reasons for the decline in enrollment, the study observed, "would have to include these four important areas of consideration: (1) the decline in vocations, (2) the increase in the number of houses of study on college campuses, (3) the increase in the number of students preparing for the priesthood on the college level who are being trained outside of the customary seminary system, i.e., neither in a seminary with an independent academic program nor in a Catholic college while residing in a house of formation, and (4) the increasing number of college students who are not making a vocational decision until after college."

CARA reported that it had "on file a listing of 106 seminary college houses of studies, i.e., residences on or near college campuses in which only spiritual formation is provided with all or almost all of the academic training provided by a neighboring college."

Despite this development, it was said that "there seems to be no strong indication that such residences will soon replace the seminary college with its own complete program of academics, spiritual formation, and pastoral experience. Moreover, the experience of the more established college seminary residences seems to indicate that the religious orders and dioceses operating such establishments have suffered the same decline in the number of students studying for the priesthood as the seminaries with independent academic programs."

Exact figures are not available for the number of the college students applying for admission to theologates without prior seminary training. On the basis of a sampling of admissions to six theologates, however, the CARA study advanced "the hypothesis that about 6 per cent of the students now entering theologates to study for the priesthood have never before been in a seminary."

A problem resulting from such admissions is that "professors of the theological sciences are finding it increasingly difficult to present their subjects with any significant depth." One professor of philosophy, Father George McLean, O.M.I., of the Catholic University of America, noted: "Some (professors) thought that many central courses were being taught in superficial terms due to the deficiencies in philosophical background of the students. Others remarked on the anti-intellectual and anti-speculative bias in students whose lack of philosophical background limited them to dealing, in the words of one theology professor, 'with theology only on the level of elementary metaphors or common sense.' "

Seminary Theologates

The study reported that "in October, 1967, there were 73 Catholic seminary theologates with independent academic programs. The total enrollment in these seminaries was 6,168.

"Between June, 1968, and October, 1972, a total of 19, or 26 per cent, of the 73 seminary theologates ceased to operate their own independent programs. Of these, 8 had closed, 10 had amalgamated . . . and 1 had moved to a university campus and had become a house of residence. The total enrollment in seminary theologates with independent academic programs also decreased from 6,168 in 1967-68 to 5,063 (including the enrollment figures of the 10 schools which had amalgamated), a decline of 1,105, or 18 per cent.

"If we consider for the purpose of our study only the 54 independent seminary theologates which were in operation in 1967 and continue to operate with independent academic programs in 1972, the decline in enrollment is even less. These 54 seminary theologates had a total enrollment in 1967-68 of 5,122, and in 1972-73 an enrollment of 4,497. This represents a decline of 625 or 12 per cent. Thus, whether the loss of enrollment in the seminary theologates with independent academic programs is placed at 12 per cent or 18 per cent, the decline is considerably less than in the seminary colleges."

Possible reasons for this less rapid decline in theologate enrollment might be: "(1) while the number of young men entering seminary colleges is less, the percentage of students persevering and entering theologates is greater; (2) the enrollment of the theologates is being sustained by the ever increasing number of students entering from colleges which are entirely outside the seminary system; and (3) the impact of the decline in the seminary colleges' enrollment has not yet fully hit the seminary theologates."

A significant development in theologates has been the amalgamation of formerly independent institutions by pooling students, faculties and academic resources. Two examples are the Catholic Theological Union in Chicago, formed in 1968 by four religious orders, and the Washington Theological Coalition, organized in 1969 by six religious orders. At least nine other clusters or consortia of schools have been established, some with ecumenical dimensions.

The CARA study also noted these developments in theologates: "the increasing stress placed upon academic excellence, the emphasis given to the study of Protestant as well as Catholic theology, the hiring of lay men and lay women, sisters and Protestant ministers to teach on the faculties of Catholic seminary theologates, the greater freedom allowed the seminarians in their contacts with all peoples, the development of a whole new area of pastoral ministerial training, the stress placed upon the individual's responsibility for his own personal development, especially his spiritual formation."

Table

Following is a table of the enrollment statistics of the seminary high schools, seminary colleges and seminary theologates covered in the study, and the percentage of decline for each year from 1967-68 to 1972-73.

Yr	HS	Coll	Theol	Total	Decl
'67	10,789	6,311	5,122	22,222	—
'68	9,722	6,120	5,042	20,884	6.0%
'69	8,954	5,519	4,864	19,337	7.4%
'70	8,377	4,915	4,689	17,981	7.0%
'71	7,969	4,268	4,568	16,805	6.5%
'72	7,570	3,940	4,497	16,007	4.7%

TEACHING OF LITURGY

Liturgical education in 45 representative U.S. theologates was called deficient in a report on a study conducted jointly by the Center for Applied Research in the Apostolate and the U.S. Bishops' Committee on the Liturgy.

The study, "The Teaching and Celebration of Liturgy in the Catholic Seminary Theologates of the United States," was based on a survey conducted by CARA during the 1973-74 academic year. A summary of a CARA-copyrighted report on the study by Father Thomas Krosnicki, an associate director of the bishops' committee, was circulated by NC News in September, 1974.

Findings

Findings were drawn from data supplied by 45 theologates, 74 per cent of the total of 61 asked to participate in the study.

Twenty-seven seminaries indicated that liturgy was not considered a major subject in their curricula. The number of required courses in liturgy varied from none to seven. The average number required was two.

"Theology is insufficiently related to practical piety as expresssd in the liturgy, and pastoral preparation is insufficiently related to the priestly task of presiding over and interpreting the liturgy."

"Not all seminary faculties understand that liturgy is by nature an integrative discipline, affecting many areas of seminary study and practice. As long as this lack of understanding remains, it can be expected that seminarians will view the study of the liturgy from an impoverished perspective, and will emerge as celebrants without an informed understanding of the liturgy. Consequently, as long as these conditions continue, we can expect that the quality of liturgical celebration and catechesis will suffer as they already have in the decade since Vatican II."

Where efforts are made at integration, they are in the area of sacramental theology.

Most seminary professors teaching liturgy are working only part time in this field, and most do not have professional degrees in liturgy. "Some of the professors," however, "are outstanding liturgists although they hold no liturgical degree as such."

"The degree of responsibility that the professors of liturgy have for the prayer and worship life in the seminary covers the complete span of 'none' to 'full responsibility.' "

Liturgical celebration and the immediate preparation of seminarians as future celebrants "often function in isolation from the seminary liturgists and sometimes in contradiction to norms being taught in the classroom."

There is a need to train seminarians to be able to judge what is good liturgy and what is counterfeit. "The future presidents of the liturgical assembly need to equip themselves with the ability to preside with a sense of security in their role and in a manner that enhances the total celebration. Such style-presence is not viewed simply as a matter of communication techniques. One's personal faith-prayer is fundamental."

"Homiletics (the art of preaching) continues to be an especially problematic area ... seminarians are often being prepared to preach in a deficient manner. This situation has already appeared as a crisis on the parochial level."

PONTIFICAL UNIVERSITIES

(Principal source: *Annuario Pontificio.*)

These universities, listed according to country of location, have been canonically erected and authorized by the Sacred Congregation for Catholic Education to award degrees in stated fields of study.

Argentina: Catholic University of S. Maria of Buenos Aires (June 16, 1960). Theology, philosophy, psychology, pedagogy, letters, law and political science, economic and social science, physics and mathematics, engineering, fine arts (with music). Rector, Most rev. Octavio N. Derisi, titular bishop of Raso.

Belgium: Catholic University of Louvain (Dec. 9, 1425; 1834), with autonomous institutions for French- (Louvain) and Flemish- (Leuven) speaking. Theology, canon law, philosophy, letters, psychology and educational science, law, economics and social science, medicine, science. Rectors: Msgr. Edouard Massaux (French), Dr. Pieter De Somer (Flemish).

Brazil: Pontifical Catholic University of Rio de Janeiro (Jan. 20, 1947). Theology, philosophy, science and letters, law, social institute, industrial and civil engineering. Rector, Pedro Belisario Velloso Rebello, S.J.

Pontifical Catholic University of Rio Grande do Sul, Porto Alegre (Nov. 1, 1950). Philosophy, science and letters, law, political and economic science, engineering, odontology. Rector, Prof. Jose Otao Stefani.

Pontifical Catholic University of Sao Paulo (Jan. 25, 1947). Theology, law, philosophy, science and letters, industrial engineering, economic and social science, medicine, journalism. Rector, Prof. Jose Geraldo Ataliba Noguerira.

University of Campinas (Sept. 8, 1956). Philosophy, science, letters, law, economics, odontology, music. Rector, Prof. Benedito Jose Barreto Fonseca.

Canada: Laval University, Quebec (Mar. 15, 1876). Theology, philosophy, arts and letters, law, commerce, medicine and pharmacy, science, social science, agriculture and forestry. Rector, Dr. Kerwin Larkin.

St. Paul University, Ottawa (Feb. 5, 1889). Theology, canon law, philosophy, missiology. Rector, Rev. Marcel Patry, O. M. I.

University of Sherbrooke (Nov. 21, 1957). Theology, art, law, science, commerce, medicine. Rector, Msgr. Roger Maltais.

Chile: Catholic University of Chile, Santiago (June 21, 1888). Theology, philosophy, letters, education, juridical, political and social science, physics and mathematics, architecture, agronomy, economics, medicine, technology. Rector, Prof. Fernando Castillo Velasco.

Catholic University of Valparaiso (Nov. 1, 1961). Philosophy and pedagogy, juridical and social science, commerce, physics and mathematics, chemical engineering, polytechnics, architecture, agriculture. Rector, Dr. Raul Allard Neumann.

Colombia: Bolivarian Pontifical Catholic University, Medellin (Aug. 16, 1945). Law, social and political science, pedagogy, philosophy, economics and commerce, letters, mechanical, electrical and chemical engineering, architecture and civic planning, fine arts. Rector, Msgr. Felix Henao Botero.

Pontifical Xaverian University, Bogota (July 31, 1937). Theology, canon law, philosophy, letters, pedagogy, law, economics, social science, medicine, dentistry, engineering, architecture. Rector, Rev. Alfonso Borrero, S.J.

Cuba: Catholic University of St. Thomas of Villanueva, Havana (May 4, 1957). Philosophy and letters, pedagogy and figurative art, law, commercial science, art and economics, science and technology. Taken over by the Castro government in May, 1961.

Ecuador: Catholic University of Ecuador, Quito (July 16, 1954). Law and economics, philosophy, pedagogy and letters, engineering, agriculture. Rector, Rev. Hernan Malo Gonzalez, S.J.

El Salvador: José Simeón Cañas University, San Salvador (Sept. 15, 1965). Economic science, mechanical, electronic, chemical engineering. Rector, Rev. Luis Achaerando, S.J.

Ethiopia: University of Asmara (Sept. 8, 1960). Letters and pedagogy, juridic, political and economic sciences, mathematics, engineering and architecture. President, Dr. Tekle Aseffa.

France: Catholic Faculties of Lille (Nov. 18, 1875). Theology, law, letters, medicine and pharmacy, science, engineering. Rector, Msgr. Gerard Leman.

Catholic Faculties of Lyons (Nov. 22, 1875). Theology, canon law, philosophy, law and economics, letters, science. Rector, Canon Paul Chevallier.

Catholic Institute of Paris (Aug. 11, 1875). Theology, canon law, philosophy, pedagogy, economic and social science, letters, science. Rector, Msgr. Paul Poupard.

Catholic Institute of Toulouse (Nov. 15,1877). Theology, canon law, philosophy, letters and science, Rector, Msgr. Xavier Ducros.

Catholic University of the West, Angers (Sept. 16, 1875). Theology (philosophy), law, economics, letters, science. Rector, Canon Louis Collin.

Guatemala: Rafael Landivar University, Guatemala (Oct. 18, 1961). Letters, law, administrative science. Rector, Prof. José Falla Aris.

Ireland: St. Patrick's College, Maynooth (Mar. 29, 1896). Theology, canon law, philosophy, arts and science, sociology, education, Celtic studies. Rector, Msgr. Jeremiah Newman.

Italy: Catholic University of the Sacred Heart, Milan (Dec. 25, 1920). Jurisprudence, political and social science, economics and commerce, letters and philosophy, medicine and surgery, pedagogy, agriculture. Rector, Prof. Giuseppe Lazzati.

Japan: *Jochi Daigaku* (University of Sophia), Tokyo (Mar. 29, 1913). Theology, philosophy, letters, languages, law, economics and commerce, science and polytechnics. Rector, Rev. Giuseppe Pittau, S. J.

Lebanon: St. Joseph University of Beirut (Mar. 25, 1881). Theology, Oriental letters, law, engineering, economics, medicine and pharmacy. Rector, Rev. Eduard Mouracade, S.J.

Netherlands: Roman Catholic University, Nijmegen (June 29, 1923). Theology, law, letters, philosophy, medicine, natural science.

Nicaragua: Central American University, Managua (1961). Law, letters and pedagogy, civil and electronic engineering, administrative and economic science, veterinary science. Rector, Arturo Dibar, S.J.

Panama: University of S. Maria la Antigua, Panama (May 27, 1965). Letters, philosophy and pedagogy, science, administra-

tion and commerce. Rector, Carlos Ariz.

Paraguay: Catholic University of Our Lady of the Assumption, Asuncion (Feb. 2, 1965). Philosophy and pedagogy, law, political and social science, administrative science. Rector, Rev. Juan Oscar Usher Taponier.

Peru: Catholic University of Peru, Lima (Sept. 30, 1942). Theology, philosophy, history and letters, jurisprudence and political science, economic and commercial science, civil engineering, education, agriculture. Rector, Felipe MacGregor, S.J.

Philippine Islands: University of Santo Tomas, Manila (Nov. 20, 1645). Theology, canon law, philosophy, pedagogy, law, letters, science, engineering and architecture, fine arts, medicine and surgery, pharmacy, commerce and administration, music. Rector, Rev. Leonardo Legazpi, O.P.

Poland: Catholic University of Lublin (July 25, 1920). Theology, philosophy, canon law, social-economic science, letters. Rector, Msgr. Albert Krapiec, O.P.

Portugal: Portuguese Catholic University (Oct. 1, 1971). Theology, philosophy, humane sciences. Rector, Jose Bacelar e Oliveira, S.J.

Puerto Rico: Catholic University of Puerto Rico, Ponce (Aug. 15, 1972). Arts, science, commerce, pedagogy, law. Rector, Dr. Francisco J. Carreras.

Spain: Catholic University of Navarra, Pamplona (Aug. 6, 1960). Theology, canon law, philosophy and letters, jurisprudence, medicine, science, pharmacy, political, economic and commercial science, industrial engineering, agriculture, journalism, Superior Institute of Business Studies. Rector, Prof. Francisco Ponz-Piedrafita.

Pontifical University of Comillas (Mar. 29, 1904). Theology, canon law, philosophy. Rector, Rev. Mariano Madurga, S.J.

Pontifical University of Salamanca (Sept. 25, 1940). Theology, canon law, social sciences, philosophy. Rector, Rev. Fernando Sebastian Aguilar, C. M. F.

University of Deusto, Bilbao (Aug. 10, 1963). Theology, law, economics and social science, philosophy and letters, science. Rector, Rev. Pedro Pi Ferrer, S.J.

Taiwan: Fu Jen Catholic University (Nov. 15, 1923, at Peking; reconstituted at Taipeh, Sept. 8, 1961). Theology, art, law, economics, science. Rector, Cardinal Paul Yu Pin.

United States: Catholic University of America, Washington, D. C. (Mar. 7, 1889). Pontifical faculties of theology, canon law, philosophy. Rector, Prof. Clarence C. Walton.

Georgetown University, Washington, D.C. (Mar. 30, 1833). Arts and science, language, law, economics, diplomatic and consular science, medicine and odontology. Rector, Rev. Robert Henle, S.J.

Niagara University, Niagara Falls (June 21, 1956). Arts and science, economics, education. Rector, Kenneth T. Slattery, C.M.

Venezuela: Catholic University "Andres Bello," Caracas (Sept. 29, 1963). Letters and education, law, economics, social science, physical and natural science, pharmacy, civil and industrial engineering, architecture. Rector, Rev. Pio Bello, S. J.

Zaire: University of Kinshasa, Kinshasa (Apr. 25, 1957). Theology, law, medicine, letters and philosophy, science, political, social and economic science. Rector, Most Rev. Tharcisse Tshibangu, titular bishop of Scampa.

Ecclesiastical Faculties

(Source: *Annuario Pontificio*)

These faculties in Catholic seminaries and universities, listed according to country of location, have been canonically erected and authorized by the Sacred Congregation for Catholic Education to award degrees in stated fields of study. In addition to those listed here, there are other faculties of theology or philosophy in state universities and for members of certain religious orders only.

Australia: Faculty of Theology, Sydney (Feb. 2, 1954). Pres., Rev. Patrick Murphy.

Canada: Institute of Medieval Studies, Toronto (Oct. 18, 1939). Pres., Very Rev. Edward Synan, C.S.B.

Germany: Theological Faculty, Paderborn (June 11, 1966). Pres., Rev. Eduard Stakemeier.

Theological Faculty of the Major Episcopal Seminary, Trier (June 5, 1950). Pres., Rev. Klaus Kremer.

Philosophical Faculty, Munich (1925; Oct. 25, 1971). Pres., Very Rev. Albert Keller, S. J.

Theological Faculty, Eichstatt (July 25, 1972), Pres., Andreas Bauch.

Theological-Philosophical Faculty, Frankfurt. Pres., Otto Semmelroth, S.J.

Great Britain: Heythrop Athenaeum of Ecclesiastical Studies (Nov. 1, 1964). Theology, philosophy. Pres., Rev. Frederick Copleston, S.J.

India: Institute of Philosophy and Theology, Poona (July 27, 1926). Theology, philosophy. Rector, Rev. Eriberto Alphonso, S.J.

Institute of Theology, Alwaye, Kerala (Feb. 24, 1972). Pres., Rev. Dominic Fernandez, O.C.D.

Italy: Interregional Theological Faculty, Milan (Aug. 8, 1935). Pres. Most Rev. Carlo Colombo, titular bishop of Vittoriana.

Pontifical Theological Faculty of the Most Sacred Heart of Jesus, Cagliari, of the Pontifical Regional Seminary of Sardinia (July 5, 1927). Pres., Rev. Giuseppe Bosio.

Pontifical Ambrosian Institute of Sacred Music, Milan (Mar. 12, 1940). Pres., Msgr. Ernesto Moneta Caglio.

Theological Faculty of Southern Italy, Naples (Mar. 16, 1918, at the Pontifical Campano Seminary; Oct. 31, 1941, at Major Archiepiscopal Seminary). Pres. Gustavo Galeota, S.J. Has Pastoral Ignatian Institute,

Messina. Pres., Pietro Schiavone, S.J.

Pontifical Faculty of Educational Science, Turin (Jan. 31, 1966). Pres., Sr. Ernestine Marchesa, F.M.A.

Madagascar: Superior Institute of Theology, Ambatoroka (Apr. 21, 1960). Pres., Very Rev. Ermengildo Ranaivo.

Peru: Pontifical and Civil Faculty of Theology, Lima (July 25, 1571). Pres., Hawkins Garaycoa, M.Sp.S.

Poland: Theological Faculty, Poznan (July 23, 1969). Dean, Rev. Peter Michal.

Spain: Theological Faculty of Barcelona, of the Major Seminary of Barcelona and the College of St. Francis Borgia of San Cugat del Valles (Mar. 7, 1968). Pres., Rev. Pedro Tena.

Theological Faculty, Granada (Feb. 11, 1940). Pres. Matias Garcias, S.J.

Theological Faculty of the North, of the Metropolitan Seminary of Burgos and the Diocesan Seminary of Vitoria (Feb. 6, 1967). Pres., Very Rev. Jose Zunzunegui.

United States: St. Mary's Faculty of Theology, Baltimore (May 1, 1822). Pres., Rev. William J. Lee, S.S.

St. Mary of the Lake Faculty of Theology, Chicago (Sept. 30, 1929). Pres., Rev. William LeSaint, S.J.

Vietnam, South: Theological Faculty, Dalat (July 31, 1965). Pres., Rev. Giuseppe Raviolo, S.J.

The Pontifical College Josephinum (Theological Seminary and Preparatory Department) at Worthington, Ohio, is a regional pontifical seminary. Established Sept. 1, 1888, it is immediately subject to the Holy See. Rector, Msgr. Thomas P. Campbell.

Institutes of Higher Studies in Rome

(Source: *Annuario Pontificio*.)

Pontifical Gregorian University (1552). Theology, canon law, philosophy, psychology, science of religion, church history, missiology, social sciences. Rector, Very Rev. Herve Carrier. Associated with the university are:

The **Pontifical Biblical Institute** (May 7, 1909), with faculties of Scripture and ancient Oriental studies. Rector, Rev. C. Martini.

The **Pontifical Institute of Oriental Studies** (Oct. 15, 1917), with faculties of Oriental ecclesiastical studies and Oriental canon law. Rector, Very Rev. Georges Dejaifve.

Pontifical Lateran University (1773). Theology, canon law, civil law, philosophy, moral theology, literature. Rector, Msgr. Pietro Pavan.

Pontifical Urban University (1627). Theology, philosophy, missiology. Rector, Rev. Pietro Chiocchetta.

Pontifical University of St. Thomas Aquinas (Angelicum) (1580), of the Order of Preachers. Theology, canon law, philosophy, social sciences, spirituality. Rector, Very Rev. Paul Gundolf Gieraths, O.P.

Pontifical Athenaeum of St. Anselm (1687), of the Benedictines. Theology, philosophy, liturgy, monastic studies. Rector, Very Rev. Basil Studer, O.S.B.

Pontifical Athenaeum Antonianum (of St. Anthony) (May 17, 1933), of the Order of Friars Minor. Theology, canon law, philosophy, and the affiliated School of Biblical Studies in Jerusalem. Rector, Rev. Roberto Zavalloni, O.F.M.

Pontifical Athenaeum Salesianum (May 3, 1940), of the Salesians of Don Bosco. Canon law, theology, philosophy, pedagogy, Higher Latin Studies (Feb. 22, 1964). Rector, Rev. Antonio Javierre, S.D.B.

Pontifical Institute of Sacred Music (1911). President, Msgr. Ferdinand Haberl.

Pontifical Institute of Christian Archeology (Dec. 11, 1925). Rector, Prof. Antonio Ferrua, S.J.

Pontifical Theological Faculty "St. Bonaventure" (Dec. 18, 1587), of the Order of Friars Minor Conventual. President, Very Rev. Orlando Todisco, O. F. M. Conv.

Pontifical Theological Faculty of Sts. Teresa of Jesus and John of the Cross (Teresianum) (July 16, 1935), of the Carmelites. Theology, spirituality. President, Very Rev. Roberto Moretti, O. Carm.

Pontifical Theological Faculty "Marianum" (1398), of the Servants of Mary. President, Very Rev. Elio Peretto.

Pontifical Institute of Arabic Studies (1926), of the White Fathers. President, Very Rev. Michael Fitzgerald.

PONTIFICAL ACADEMY OF SCIENCES

(Sources: *Annuario Pontificio,* NC News Service.)

The Pontifical Academy of Sciences was constituted in its present form by Pius XI Oct. 28, 1936, in virtue of *In Multis Solaciis,* a document issued on his own initiative.

The academy is the only supranational body of its kind in the world, with a pope-selected, life-long membership of outstanding mathematicians and experimental scientists from many countries. The normal complement of members is 70; the total number, however, includes additional honorary and supernumerary members. Non-Catholics as well as Catholics belong to the academy.

Purposes of the academy are to honor pure science and its practitioners, to promote the freedom of pure science and to foster research.

The academy originated as the Accademia Linceorum (lynxes) in Rome Aug. 17, 1603. Pius IX reorganized this body and gave it a new name — Pontificia Accademia dei Nuovi Lincei — in 1847. It was taken over by the Italian state in 1870 and called the Accademia Nationale dei Lincei, Leo XIII reconstituted it with a new charter in 1887. Pius XI designated the Vatican Gardens as the site of academy headquarters in 1922 and gave it its present title and status in 1936. Four years later he gave the title of Excellency to its members.

In addition to four supernumerary members, membership as of June 20, 1974, numbered 51 in the following countries: England, 7; U.S. and France, 6; Italy, 4; Canada, 3; Germany, Japan, Netherlands, and Spain, 2 each; Argentina, Australia, Austria, Belgium, Brazil, Chile, Greece, Finland, Mexico, Monaco, Pakistan, Peru, Portugal, Sweden, Switzerland, Vatican City and Venezuela, 1 each.

On July 4, 1974, Pope Paul VI named six scientists to the Pontifical Academy of Sciences — three from the U.S., one each

from Nigeria, England and France. U.S. members were: Rita Levi Montalcini, professor of biology at Washington Univ., St. Louis, Mo. (the first woman ever named to the Academy); Severo Ochoa, professor of biochemistry at New York University's School of Medicine (Nobel prize winer, 1959); Marshall Warren Nierenberg, director of the department of genetic biochemistry, National Heart Institute, Bethesda, Md. (Nobel prize winner, 1968). The others named were: Thomas Adeoye Lambo, vice-director general of the World Health Organization (Nigeria); George Porter, professor of physical chemistry at the University of Sheffield (England); and Jerome Lejeune, professor of general genetics of the medical faculty of the University of Paris (France).

Scientists from the US who presently hold membership in the Academy are: Edward Adalbert-Doisy, professor of biochemistry at St. Louis University School of Medicine (May 29, 1948); Franco Rasetti, professor emeritus of physics at John Hopkins University, Baltimore, Md. (Oct. 28, 1936); George Speri Sperti, director of the Institutum Divi Thomae in the Athanaeum of Ohio (Oct. 28, 1936); Hugh Stott Taylor, professor of chemistry at Princeton University (Oct. 28, 1936); William Wilson Morgan, director of Yerkes Observatory, Williams Bay, Wis. (Sept. 24, 1964); Albert Szent-Gyorgyi, director of muscle research at the Marine Biological Laboratory, Woods Hole, Mass. (Apr. 10, 1970).

Deceased US members of the Academy were: George D. Birkhoff, Alexis Carrel, Herbert Sidney Langfeld, Robert A. Millikan, Thomas H. Morgan, Theodore von Karman, Victor F. Hess, Peter Debye.

Other members of the Academy and the dates of their selection are as follows:

Argentina: Luis F. Leloir (Apr. 22, 1968).
Australia: Keith E. Bullen (Apr. 22, 1968).
Austria: Hans Tuppy (Apr. 10, 1970).

Belgium: Christian de Duve (Apr. 16, 1970).

Brazil: Carlos Chagas (Aug. 18, 1961).

Canada: Herbert Charles Best (Apr. 5, 1955); Ernesto Gherzi, S.J. (Oct. 28, 1936); Gerhard Herzberg (Sept. 24, 1964).

Chile: Eduardo Cruz-Coke (May 29, 1948).

England: Hermann Alexander Bruck (Apr. 5, 1955); Sir James Chadwick (Apr. 8, 1961); Paul Adrien Dirac (Aug. 18, 1961); Alan Lloyd Hodgkin (Apr. 22, 1968); Alfred R. Ubbelohde (Apr. 22, 1968); Peter C. C. Garnham (Apr. 10, 1970); Robert Stoneley (Apr. 10, 1970).

Finland: Arthur Ilmari Virtanen (Apr. 5, 1955).

France: Louis de Broglie (Apr. 5, 1955); Gaston Maurice Julia (Apr. 5, 1955); Jean Lecomte (Sept. 24, 1964); Pierre Raphael Lepine (Sept. 24, 1964); Louis Leprince-Ringuet (Aug. 18, 1961); Georges Chaudron (April 10, 1970).

Germany: Werner Carl Heisenberg (Apr. 5, 1955); Wolfgang Gentner (Apr. 10, 1970).

Greece: George Joakimoglou (Apr. 10, 1970).

Italy: Giovanni Battista Bonino (May 23, 1942); Bettolo Giovanni Battista Marini (Apr. 22, 1968); Domenico Marotta (Apr. 8, 1961); Mauro Picone (Apr. 10, 1970).

Japan: Paul San-Ichiro Mizushima (Aug. 18, 1961); Hideki Yukawa (Apr. 8, 1961).

Mexico: Manuel Sandoval Vallarta (Aug. 18, 1961).

Monaco: Rudolf L. Mossbauer (Apr. 10, 1970).

Netherlands: F. J. J. Buytendijk (Oct. 28, 1936); Jan Hendrik Oort (Aug. 18, 1961).

Pakistan: Salimuzzanam Siddiqui (Sept. 24, 1964).

Peru: Alberto Hurtado (Aug. 18, 1961).

Portugal: Antonio De Almeida (Apr. 8, 1961).

Spain: Jose Garcia Sineriz (May 23, 1942); Manuel Lora Tomayo (Sept. 24, 1964).

Sweden: Sven Horstadius (Aug. 18, 1961).

Switzerland: Leopold Ruzicka (Dec. 5, 1942).

Vatican City: Daniel J. Kelly O'Connell, S.J. (Sept. 24, 1964).

Venezuela: Marcel Roche (Apr. 10, 1970).

Supernumerary members are: Patrick Treanor, S.J., director of the Vatican Observatory; Joseph Junkes, S.J., prefect of the Astrophysics Laboratory of the Vatican Observatory; Alfons Stickler, S.D.B., prefect of the Vatican Library; Msgr. Martino Giusti, prefect of the Secret Vatican Archives.

President of the Academy is Carlos Chagas (Nov. 5, 1972).

PONTIFICAL URBAN UNIVERSITY

The Pontifical Urban University was founded by Pope Urban VIII Aug. 1, 1627, for the express purpose of training priests from mission countries.

In the nearly 350 years of its existence, the university has had great influence on the missionary activity of the Church. At the present time, many of the more than 250 native bishops in mission countries are among its alumni, as well as a large number of their priests.

UNION PRO DEO

The International Union Pro Deo was inaugurated in Belgium by Father Felix Morlion, O.P., in a series of courses in political and social philosophy, and subsequently spread to other parts of Europe, North and South America. At the invitation of Pope Pius XII, an international study center was established in Rome in 1944. Four years later, the Pro Deo International University of Social Studies was founded, and has since been the headquarters of the movement.

The Congregation for Catholic Education has supervisory authority over the Union, which was given the status of a moral entity Jan. 25, 1965.

AGRIMISSIO

Agrimissio is a service agency aiding religious institutes, other organizations (including the Food and Agriculture Organization of the United Nations) and technicians working in rural development in mission territories. It was established in 1970 by the Union of Superiors General, the International Union of Superiors General and the National Catholic Rural Life Conference.

Msgr. Luigi Ligutti, permanent observer of the Holy See to the FAO from 1948 to 1970, is president; Father B. Coutinho is the executive secretary. Headquarters are located at Piazza S. Calisto, 16, Rome, Italy.

FIDES

International Fides Service, the news agency of the Congregation for the Evangelization of Peoples, issues a periodic service of news, comment and background information concerning the missions.

The office address is Via di Propaganda, 1 C, 00187, Rome, Italy.

ICCM

The International Council of Catholic Men announced in January, 1974, that its 1974-75 program would emphasize active participation in Holy Year 1975 and a rejection of "the spirit and practice of materialism."

Board members said in a statement: "In the harassed pursuit of alleged prosperity, the idea of God and the supernatural disappears; and justice, brotherhood and charity are trampled underfoot. No reconciliation is possible without education to deep respect for man and nature, a respect that corresponds to God's own way of acting with regard to man and all creatures."

Social Services

Catholic Charities is the ordinary title of an umbrella-type of agency which supervises social work under the auspices of archdioceses and dioceses in the United States.

The first central, over-all diocesan agency in the US was established in 1903. There are now more than 500 diocesan and branch agencies of Catholic Charities in this country.

The principal fields of service in which diocesan organizations and their member agencies are engaged are family counseling, child welfare, health services for unmarried mothers, community services, day care centers, neighborhood center programs, and care of the aged. Community organization and social action are also functions of Catholic Charities.

National Conference

The National Conference of Catholic Charities, organized in 1910, serves diocesan organizations by providing a field service, developing a literature, providing an informational service, promoting research, assisting with organization, improving standards, and representing agencies of Catholic Charities among other national organizations and offices, both voluntary and governmental. It has over 500 institutional, 1,500 individual and 650 organizational members.

Closely affiliated with the conference is the National Association of Directors of Catholic Charities and the Conference of Religious, an organization of religious engaged in social and charitable work. Also affiliated are the Society of St. Vincent de Paul of the US, the Association of Ladies of Charity of the US, and the National Christ Child Society.

The conference is the representative of the International Conference of Catholic Charities before the UN Economic and Social Council and before UNICEF. It has consultative status with both agencies.

NCCC initiated steps in 1972 to augment its traditional services to social service agencies with greater emphasis on social action and advocacy.

Msgr. Lawrence J. Corcoran is secretary of the conference.

Offices are located at 1346 Connecticut Ave. N.W., Washington, D.C. 20036.

Vincent de Paul Society

The Society of St. Vincent de Paul, originally called the Conference of Charity, is an association of Catholic laymen devoted to personal service of the poor through the spiritual and corporal works of mercy. The first conference was formed at Paris in 1833 by Frederic Ozanam and his associates.

The first conference in the US was organized in 1845 at St. Louis. There are now approximately 4,200 units of the society in this country, with a membership of about 36,000.

In the past 50 years, members of the society in this country have distributed among poor persons financial and other forms of assistance valued at approximately $180 million.

US Vincentian councils and conferences participating in "twinning" programs assist their poorer counterparts abroad by sending them correspondence, information and financial aid on a continuing basis.

Under the society's revised regulations, women are being admitted to membership. Increasing emphasis is being given to stores and rehabilitation workshops of the society through which persons with marginal income can purchase refurbished goods at minimal cost. Handicapped persons are employed in renovating goods and store operations.

Henri Jacob of Paris, France, is president of the Council General, the governing body of the society. There are approximately 700,000 members in the world.

The office of the US Superior Council is located at 4140 Lindell Blvd., St. Louis, Mo. 63108.

Service Organizations

Catholic Hospital Association: Founded in 1915, is a service organization for about 830 Catholic-sponsored health care facilities located throughout the United States.

Through research, its monthly *Hospital Progress,* annual meetings and conferences, it keeps institutional and individual members up-to-date on unique Catholic apostolic aspects of medical, moral, educational and professional developments in the health field.

The Catholic Health Services Leadership Program, a major CHA activity, is designed to develop the relationships and maximize the potential strengths and resources of religious congregations, dioceses and their multi-faceted health care facilities and services.

The Catholic Health Assembly (annual meeting) offers CHA constituents the opportunity to dialogue the best methods to strengthen and unify the corporate health commitment of religious congregations and dioceses — the sponsoring groups that operate Catholic hospitals and nursing homes.

Sister Grace Marie Hiltz, S.C., is president of the association. Sister Mary Maurita, R.S.M., is the executive vice-president.

Executive offices are located at 1438 S. Grand Boulevard, St. Louis, Mo. 63104.

The Official Catholic Directory, 1974, reported 688 Catholic general hospitals with 158,170 beds treating 26,968,607 patients annually; 110 special hospitals and sanatoria with 9,724 beds treating 319,669; and 153 nurses' schools with 20,128 students.

National Association of Catholic Chaplains: Founded in 1965, it operates under the auspices of the Department of Social Development and World Peace, U.S. Catholic Conference. Membership is approximately 1,200.

The association conducts two pastoral institutes for general hospital chaplains annually, one in Washington, D.C., and another in Menlo Park, Calif. By the summer of 1974, nearly 750 chaplains had attended these institutes.

Father Thomas Forker, chaplain of Pilgrim State Hospital, New York, is president of the association. Father David Baeten is the executive secretary.

The office of the association is located at 1312 Massachusetts Ave. N. W., Washington, D.C. 20005.

FACILITIES FOR RETIRED AND AGED PERSONS

This list covers residence, health care and other facilities for the retired and aged under Catholic auspices. Information includes name, type of facility if not evident from the title, address, and total capacity (in parentheses); unless noted otherwise, facilities are for both men and women.

(Sources: Almanac survey, *The Official Catholic Directory, 1974*)

Alabama: Allen Memorial Home (Nursing Home), 735 S. Washington Ave., Mobile 36603 (50).

Good Samaritan Hospital Nursing Home, 1107 Voeglin St., Selma 36701 (26).

Sacred Heart Home of the Little Sisters of the Poor, 1655 McGill Ave., Mobile 36604 (108).

Villa Mercy (Skilled Nursing Home), Daphne 36526 (45).

Arizona: Sacred Heart Home for the Aged, Little Sisters of the Poor, 1110 N. 16th St., Phoenix 85006 (170).

Villa Maria de Guadalupe Nursing Home, 701 E. Adams St., Tucson 85719 (25).

Arkansas: Benedictine Manor (Retirement Home), 2nd and Grand Sts., Hot Springs 71901 (50).

St. Joseph's Home (Nursing Home), Brinkley 72021 (28).

St. Joseph's Home for the Aged, Camp Robinson Rd., N. Little Rock 72118 (9).

California: Casa Manana Inn, 3700 N. Sutter St., Stockton 95204 (175).

Catholic Women's Center (Residence for Elderly Single Women), 195 E. San Fernando St., San Jose 95112 (50).

Little Flower Haven (Residential Care Facility for Retired), 8585 La Mesa Blvd., La Mesa 92041 (94).

Little Sisters of the Poor, 2700 E. First St., Los Angeles 90033 (160).

Little Sisters of the Poor, 2647 E. 14th St., Oakland 94601 (100).

Little Sisters of the Poor, 300 Lake St., San Francisco 94118 (186).

Madonna Residence (Hotel for Women over 60), 270 McAllister St., San Francisco 94102 (82).

Marian Residence (Retirement Home), 124 S. College Dr., Santa Maria 93454 (85).

Nazareth House, 2121 N. 1st St., Fresno 93703 (80).

Nazareth House, 3333 Manning Ave., Los Angeles 90064 (107).

Nazareth House, 245 Nova Albion Way, Terra Linda, San Rafael 94903 (109).

Our Lady of Fatima Villa (Nursing Home, Women), 20400 Saratoga-Los Gatos Rd., Saratoga 95070 (85).

Our Lady's Home, 3431 Foothill Blvd., Oakland 94601 (200).

St. Francis Home (Elderly and Retired Women), 1718 W. 6th St., Santa Ana 92703 (71).

Villa Siena, 1855 Miramonte, Mountain View 94040 (23).

Colorado: Little Sisters of the Poor, 3630 W. 30th Ave., Denver 80211 (100).

St. Elizabeth Retreat (Retirement Home), 2825 W. 32nd Ave., Denver 80211 (95).

Connecticut: Notre Dame Convalescent Home, West Rocks Rd., Norwalk 06851 (60).

Regina Pacis Villa (Residence), RFD No. 1, Pomfret Center 06259 (16).

St. Joseph Guest Home (Women, Employed and Retired), 311 Greene St., New Haven 06511 (93).

St. Joseph's Home for the Aged, 88 Jackson St., Willimantic 06226 (37).

St. Joseph's Manor (Residence, Rest Home, Chronic Disease Hospital), 6448 Main St., Trumbull 06611 (285).

St. Joseph's Residence, Little Sisters of the Poor, 1365 Enfield St., Enfield, Conn. 06082 (94).

St. Lucian's Home of the Aged, 532 Burritt St., New Britain 06053 (85).

St. Mary's Home (Residence and Health Care Facility), 291 Steele Rd., W. Hartford 06117 (177).

Villa Maria Rest Home for the Aged, West St., Thompson 06277 (30).

Delaware: St. Joseph's Home, Little Sisters of the Poor, 401 N. Bancroft Pkwy., Wilmington 19805 (97).

District of Columbia: St. Joseph's Home, Little Sisters of the Poor, 220 H St., N.E., Washington 20002 (167).

Florida: All Saints Nursing Home for the

Aged, 2040 Riverside Ave., Jacksonville 32204 (54).

Cor Jesu Convalescent Center (Skilled Nursing Facility), 4918 N. Habana Ave., Tampa 33614 (90).

Florida Manor (Residence), P.O. Box 5577, Orlando 32805.

Haven of Our Lady of Peace (Residence and Health Care Facility), 5203 9th Ave., Pensacola 32504 (88).

Lourdes Residence, 305 S. Flagler Dr., W. Palm Beach 33401 (142).

Marian Towers, Inc. (Retirement Home), 1705 North Bay Rd., Miami Beach 33160.

Pennsylvania Retirement Residence, 208 Evernia St., W. Palm Beach 33401 (230).

St. Elizabeth Gardens (Retirement Home), 801 N.E. 33rd St., Pompano Beach 33064.

St. Joseph's Residence, 3485 N.W. 30th St., Ft. Lauderdale 33311.

St. Joseph's Manor (Residence), 2335 Lakeview Ave. S., St. Petersburg 33712 (64).

Villa Maria (Residence), 1050 N.E. 123rd St., N. Miami 33161.

Villa Maria Nursing and Rehabilitation Center, 1050 N.E. 125th St., N. Miami 33161 (180).

Idaho: St. Benedict's Hospital Home for the Aged, Jerome 83338 (40).

Illinois: Addolorato Villa (Residence), Highway 83, McHenry Rd., Wheeling 60090 (103).

Holy Family Villa (Residence), Lemont 60439 (108).

Huber Memorial Home (Women), 1000 30th St., Rock Island 61201 (22).

Maryhaven-West (Residence, Nursing Care), 1700 E. Lake St., Glenview 60025 (148).

Mayslake Village (Retirement Facility), 1801 35th St., Oak Brook 60521 (325).

Meredith Memorial Home, Public Square, Belleville 62220 (86).

Mother Theresa Home, 1270 Main St., Lemont 60439 (56).

Our Lady of Angels Retirement Home, 1291 Wyoming, Joliet 60435 (100).

Our Lady of the Snows Apartment Community (Retirement Apartment Community with Lifetime Contract), 9500 Route 460, Belleville 62223 (175).

Rosary Hill Convalescent Home, 9000 W. 81st St., Justice 60458 (60).

St. Andrew Home, 7000 N. Newark Ave., Chicago 60648 (199).

St. Ann's Home and Infirmary, Waukegan and Techny Rds., Techny 60082 (175).

St. Ann's Home for the Aged, 770 State St., Chester 62233 (45).

St. Augustine's Home, Little Sisters of the Poor, 2358 Sheffield Ave., Chicago 60614 (110).

St. Benedict Home (Sheltered and Interme-

diate Care), 6930 W. Touhy Ave., Niles 69648 (52).

St. Joseph's Home for the Elderly, 80 W. Baldwin Rd., Palatine 60067 (208).

St. Joseph's Home for the Aged, 2650 N. Ridgeway Ave., Chicago 60647 (175).

St. Joseph's Home, 2223 W. Heading Ave., Peoria 61604 (200).

St. Joseph's Home for the Aged, 649 E. Jefferson St., Freeport 61032 (118).

St. Joseph's Home, S. 6th St. Rd., Springfield 62703 (93).

St. Patrick's Residence (Sheltered and Intermediate Care;Skilled Nursing Facility), 22 E. Clinton St., Joliet 60431 (207).

Villa Scalabrini (Residence), Northlake 60161 (146).

Villa Saint Cyril (Residence), 1111 St. John's Ave., Highland Park 60035 (80).

Indiana: Providence Home of Our Lady of the Holy Rosary, Jasper 47546 (37).

Providence Retirement Home, 703 E. Spring St., New Albany 47150 (73).

Regina Pacis Home (Residence and Extended and Intermediate Care Facility), 3900 Washington Ave., Evansville 47715 (51).

Sacred Heart Home (Residence and Comprehensive Nursing), R.R. 2, Avilla 46710 (130).

St. Anne Home (Residence and Comprehensive Nursing), 1900 Randalia Dr., Ft. Wayne 46805 (119).

St. Anthony's Rest Home, 201 Franciscan Rd., Crown Point 46307 (122).

St. Augustine Home, Little Sisters of the Poor, 2345 W. 86th St., Indianapolis 46260 (184).

St. John's Home for the Aged, Little Sisters of the Poor, 1236 Lincoln Ave., Evansville 47714 (130).

St. Paul Hermitage (Residence and Comprehensive Nursing), 501 N. 17th St., Beech Grove 46107 (104).

Iowa: The Alverno Residence for Retired Citizens, Clinton 52732 (131).

Bishop Drumm Home for the Aged, 1409 Clark St., Des Moines 50314 (145).

Holy Spirit Retirement Home (Nursing Home), 1701 W. 25th St., Sioux City 51103 (78).

Kahl Home for the Aged and Infirm (Health Facility), 1101 W. 9th St., Davenport 52802 (126).

The Marian Home, 23 N. 7th St., Fort Dodge 50501 (50).

Mary of the Angels Home (Women, Employed and Retired), 605 Bluff St., Dubuque 52001 (92).

Ritter Home for Retired Women, 1837 Sunnyside Ave., Burlington 52601 (10).

St. Anthony Nursing Home, 406 E. Anthony St., Carroll 51401 (78).

St. Francis Home (Custodial, Nursing Home), 901 Davis Ave., Dubuque 52001 (101).

Kansas: Mt. St. Joseph Home for the Aging (Health Care Facility), 2601 Ridge Ave., Kansas City 66102 (47).

St. Ann's Home, 323 E. 5th St., Concordia 66901 (76).

St. John's Rest Home, Victoria 67671 (45).

St. Joseph's Home for the Aging, 924 N. Topeka, El Dorado 67042 (58).

Villa Maria Home for the Aging, 116 S. Central, Mulvane 67110 (57).

Kentucky: Carmel Home (Residence and Nursing Home), Old Hartford Rd., Owensboro 42301 (82).

Carmel Manor (Residence), Carmel Manor St., Ft. Thomas, 41075 (99).

Cardome Residence for Women, Georgetown 40324 (30).

Home for Senior Citizens, P.O. Box R. 1, Philpot 42366 (68).

Madonna Manor Nursing Home, 2344 Amsterdam Rd., Covington 41016 (Cottages for Senior Citizens: 8, with 34 Apartments).

St. Charles Nursing Home, Kyles Lane, Covington 41011 (143).

St. Joseph's Home for the Aged Poor, 622 S. 10th St., Louisville 40203 (185).

St. Margaret of Cortona Home (Women), 1310 Leestown Pike, Lexington 40508 (24).

Taylor Manor Nursing Home, Versailles 40383 (78).

Louisiana: Bethany M.H.S. Nursing Home (Women), P.O. Box 2308, Lafayette 70501 (40).

Christopher Inn Apartments (Residence for Senior Citizens), 2110 Royal St., New Orleans 20116 (250).

Consolata Home (Nursing Home), New Iberia 70560 (74).

Lafon Home of the Holy Family, 1125 N. Tonti St., New Orleans 70119 (75).

Little Sisters of the Poor, 4201 Woodland Dr., New Orleans 70114 (135).

Ollie Steele Burden Manor (Retirement Home and Skilled Nursing Care), 4200 Essen Lane, Baton Rouge 70809 (44).

Our Lady of Prompt Succor Home (Nursing and Extended Care Facility), 751 E. Prudhomme Lane, Opelousas 70570.

St. Joseph's Home (Nursing Home), 2301 Sterlington Rd., Monroe 71201 (110).

St. Margaret's Daughters' Home, 504 Tricou St., New Orleans 70117 (82).

Wynhoven Apartments (Residence for Senior Citizens), 4600 - 10th St., Marrero 70072.

Maine: Deering Pavilion (Apartments for Senior Citizens), 289 Congress St., Portland 04112 (200 units).

Marcotte Nursing Home, 100 Campus Ave., Lewiston 04240 (377).

Mt. St. Joseph Home (Nursing Home), Highwood St., Waterville 04901 (76).

Northern Maine Security Home (Residence and Intermediate Care Facility), Eagle Lake 04789 (71).

St. John Valley Security Home (Boarding-Nursing Home), 40 Riverview St., Madawaska 04756 (82).

Villa Muir, Home for Women, Bay View, Saco 04072 (15).

Maryland: Carroll Manor (Residence and Nursing Home), 4922 La Salle Rd., Hyattsville 20782 (210).

Little Sisters of the Poor, St. Martin's Home (for the Aged), 601 Maiden Choice Lane, Baltimore 21228 (236).

Sacred Heart Home, 5805 Queens Chapel Rd., Hyattsville 20782 (102).

Stella Maris Hospice (Long-term Geriatrics), 2300 Dulaney Valley Rd., Towson 21204 (355).

Villa Rosa (Nursing Home), Lottsford Vista Rd., Mitchellville 20716 (59).

Massachusetts: Beaven-Kelly Home for Aged Men (Rest Home), 1245 Main St., Brightside, Holyoke 01040 (55).

Catholic Memorial Home, 2446 Highland Ave., Fall River 02720 (293).

Don Orione Home, 111 Orient Ave., East Boston 02128 (180).

D'Youville Manor (Nursing Home), 981 Varnum St., Lowell 01854 (207).

Little Sisters of the Poor, St. Joseph's Home, 424 Dudley St., Boston 02119 (116).

Little Sisters of the Poor, 186 Highland Ave., Somerville 02143 (148).

Madonna Manor (Nursing Home), Washington St., N. Attleboro 02760 (129).

Marian Manor (Nursing Home), 40 Old Harbor St., S. Boston, 02127 (376).

Marian Manor (Nursing Home), 33 Summer St., Taunton 02780 (129).

Maristhill Nursing Home, 66 Newton St., Waltham 02154 (120).

Our Lady's Haven (Nursing Home), 71 Center St. Fairhaven 02719 (131).

Protectory of Mary Immaculate (Nursing Home), 189 Maple St., Lawrence 01841 (123).

Sacred Heart Home, 359 Summer St., New Bedford 02740 (197).

St. Francis Home for Aged, 37 Thorne St., Worcester 01604 (86).

St. Joseph's Manor for Elderly Ladies, 321 Centre St., Dorchester 02122 (95).

St. Joseph's Manor Nursing Home, 261 Thatcher St., Brockton 02154 (56).

St. Luke's Home, 85 Springfield St., Springfield 01105 (192).

St. Patrick's Manor (Nursing Home), 863 Central St., Framingham 01701 (280).

Michigan: Bishop Noa Home for Senior Citizens, Escanaba 49829 (107).

Burtha M. Fisher Home (Residence and Nursing Home), 17550 Southfield Rd., Detroit 48235 (183).

Carmel Hall (Residence and Nursing

Home), 2560 Woodward Ave., Detroit 48201 (500).

Kundig Center (Residence), 2936 Ash St., Detroit 48208 (140).

Lourdes Nursing Home, 2380 Watkins Lake Rd., Pontiac 48054 (108).

Marian Hall (Residence), 529 Detroit St., Flint 48502 (114).

Marycrest Manor (Nursing Home), 15475 Middlebelt Rd., Livonia 48154 (92).

Marydale Center for the Aged (Board and Apartments), 3147 Tenth Ave., Port Huron 48060 (44).

St. Ann's Home for Retired People, 2161 Leonard St. N.W., Grand Rapids 49304 (113).

St. Catherine Cooperative House for Elderly Women, 1641 Webb Ave., Detroit 48206 (13).

St. Elizabeth Briarbank (Residence), 1315 N. Woodward Ave., Bloomfield Hills 48013 (56).

St. Francis Home (Nursing Home), 915 N. River Rd., Saginaw 48603 (100).

St. John Vianney Cooperative House for Men, 4806 Mt. Elliot, Detroit 48207 (30).

St. Joseph's Home for the Aged, 4800 Cadieux Rd., Detroit 48224 (100).

Stapleton Center (Residence), 9341 Agnes St., Detroit 48214 (20).

Villa Elizabeth, 2100 Leonard St. N.E., Grand Rapids 49505 (109).

Villa Franciska (Residence, Women), 565 W. Long Lake Rd., Bloomfield Hills 48013 (18).

Minnesota: Assumption Nursing Home, Cold Spring 56320 (68).

Divine Providence Community Home, Sleepy Eye 56085 (40).

Divine Providence Home (Skilled Nursing Home), Ivanhoe 56142 (51).

Holy Trinity Home for Aged, Graceville 56240 (17).

Little Sisters of the Poor (Skilled Nursing and Intermediate Care), 90 Wilkin St., St. Paul 55102 (114).

Madonna Towers (Retirement Apartments), 4001 19th Ave. N.W., Rochester 55901 (145).

Mary Randorf Home of Sacred Heart Parish (Nursing Home), 222 5th St. N., Staples 56479 (84).

Mother of Mercy Nursing Home, Albany 56307 (62).

Regina Nursing Home and Retirement Residence, Hastings 55033 (138).

Sacred Heart Hospice (Nursing Home), 1200 Twelfth St. S.W., Austin 55912 (60).

St. Alexander Nursing Home, 1500 5th St. N., New Ulm 56073 (61).

St. Ann's Home, 330 E. 3rd St., Duluth 55805 (200).

St. Anne Hospice (Residence and Nursing Care), 1347 W. Broadway, Winona 55987 (123).

St. Elizabeth's Hospital and Nursing Home, Campbell Ave., Wabasha 55981 (69).

St. Francis Home, W. 4th Ave., Shakopee 55379 (35).

St. Francis Nursing Home, Breckenbridge 56520 (132).

St. Joseph's Home, (Residence and Extended Health Care), 1824 Minnesota Blvd. S.E., St. Cloud 56301 (118).

St. Joseph's Home for the Elderly (Nursing Home), 215 Broadway N.E., Minneapolis 55413 (118).

St. Mary's Extended Care Center, 25512 S. 7th St., Minneapolis 55406 (240).

St. Mary's Home, Winsted 55395 (74).

St. Mary's Home, 1925 Norfolk Ave., St. Paul 55116 (90).

St. Mary's Villa (Nursing Home), Pierz 56364 (66).

St. Otto's Home (Nursing Home), Little Falls 56345 (159).

St. Raphael's Home (Residence and Health Care Facility), 511 9th Ave. N., St. Cloud 56301 (93).

St. Therese Home (Residence and Health Care Facility), 8000 Bass Lake Rd., New Hope 55428 (304).

St. Vincent's Rest Home (Nursing Home), 223 E. 7th St., Crookston 56716 (73).

St. William's Nursing Home, Parkers Prairie 56361 (61).

Villa of St. Francis Nursing Home, Morris 56267 (104).

Missouri: Chariton Apartments (Retirement Apartments), 4249 Michigan Ave., St. Louis 63117 (122 units; 150 residents).

Hotel Alverne (Retirement Home), 1014 Locust St., St. Louis 63101 (251).

LaVerna Heights (Retirement Home and Nursing Care, Women), 104 E. Park Ave., Savannah 64485 (60).

Little Sisters of the Poor, 5331 Highland Ave., Kansas City 64110 (240).

Little Sisters of the Poor, St. Charles Home, 3400 S. Grand Blvd., St. Louis 63118 (134).

Mercy Villa Professional Nursing Home, 1015 N. Main St., Springfield 65802 (134).

Mother of Good Counsel Home for Chronic Sick, 6825 Natural Bridge Rd., Normandy, 63121 (110).

Our Lady of Mercy Home (Residence and Nursing Home), 918-24 E. 9th St., Kansas City 64106 (126).

Our Lady of Perpetual Help Nursing Home, 3419 Gasconada St., St. Louis 63118 (113).

St. Agnes Home, 10341 Manchester Rd., Kirkwood 63122 (130).

St. Anne Home (Nursing Home), 5351 Page Blvd., St. Louis 63112 (190).

St. Joseph Hill Nursing Care Facility

(Men), Highway FF, Eureka 63025 (125).

St. Joseph's Home for the Aged, 1550 W. Main St., Jefferson City 65101 (70).

St. Joseph's Home for the Aged, 723 First Capitol Dr., St. Charles 63301 (101).

St. Louis Residence, Little Sisters of the Poor, 3225 N. Florissant Ave., St. Louis 63107 (250).

Montana: Holy Family Nursing Home, Holy Family Hospital, St. Ignatius 59865 (4).

Nebraska: Madonna Professional Care Center (Nursing Care), 2200 S. 52nd St., Lincoln 68502 (182).

Mt. Carmel Home, Keens' Memorial (Nursing Home), 18th St., and 5th Ave., Kearney 68847 (74).

St. Joseph's Home, P.O. Box 1129, Norfolk 68701 (52).

St. Joseph's Home, 320 E. Decatur St., West Point 68788 (60).

St. Joseph's Villa, David City 68632. (44).

St. Vincent's Home, 4500 Ames Ave., Omaha 68104 (259).

New Hampshire: Mount Carmel Nursing Home, 235 Myrtle St., Manchester 03104 (118).

Notre Dame Hospital, Geriatrics Department (Extended Health Care, Women), Manchester 03102 (28).

St. Ann Home, 201 Dover Point Rd., Dover 03820 (52).

St. Francis Home (Nursing Home), Court St., Laconia 03246 (49).

St. Teresa Manor (Nursing Home), 519 Bridge St., Manchester 03104 (50).

St. Vincent de Paul Nursing Home, Providence Ave., Berlin 03570 (72).

New Jersey: Holy Family Residence (Women), New St., P.O. Box 536, W. Paterson 07424 (60).

Little Sisters of the Poor, 70 Dey St., Paterson 07503. (141).

Mater Dei Nursing Home, Rt. 40, P.O. Newfield, Upper Pittsgrove Township 08344 (64).

Morris Hall, Home for the Aged (Residence and Nursing Home), 2361 Lawrenceville Rd., Lawrenceville 08648 (90).

Mount St. Andrew Villa (Residence), 55 W. Midland Ave., Paramus 07652 (58).

Our Lady's Residence (Nursing Home), Glendale and Clematis Aves., Pleasantville 08232 (104).

St. Ann's Home for the Aged (Residence and Nursing Care, Women), 198 Old Bergen Rd., Jersey City 07305 (105).

St. Joseph's Rest Home for Aged Women, 46 Preakness Ave., Paterson 07502 (30).

St. Joseph's Villa, Peapack 07977 (12).

St. Mary's Catholic Home (Skilled Nursing Home), Kresson Rd., Cherry Hill 08034 (94).

St. Rose of Lima Home, 1 S. 8th St., Newark 07107 (170).

Villa Maria (Residence), 641 Somerset St., N. Plainfield 07061 (75).

New Mexico: Good Shepherd Manor (Shelter Care Home for Aged Men), Little Brothers of the Good Shepherd, P.O. Box 10248, Albuquerque 87114 (27).

New York: Bernardine Apartments, 240 E. Onondaga St., Syracuse 13202.

Ferncliff Nursing Home, P.O. Box 386, River Rd., Rhinebeck 12572 (320).

Frances Schervier Home and Hospital, 2975 Independence Ave., New York 10453 (364).

The Heritage (Residence), 1500 Portland Ave., Rochester 14621 (249).

Holy Family Home, 410 Mill St., Williamsville 14221 (96).

Josephine Baird Home (Skilled Nursing Home), 340 W. 55th St., New York 10019 (173).

Little Sisters of the Poor, 391 Central Ave., Albany 12206 (103).

Little Sisters of the Poor, 660 E. 183rd St., Bronx 10458 (200).

Little Sisters of the Poor, 1608 8th Ave., Brooklyn 11215 (152).

Little Sisters of the Poor, 135 W. 106th St., New York 10025 (137).

Little Sisters of the Poor, 110-30 221st St., Queens Village 11429.

Little Sisters of the Poor, 192 9th St., Troy 12180 (110).

Loretto Rest (Residence), E. Brighton and Glen Aves., Syracuse 13205 (206).

Madonna Home of Mercy Hospital (Nursing Home and Extended Care Facility) (120), and Mercy Hospital Health Related Facility (Residence) (58), Watertown 13601.

Madonna Residence for the Elderly, 1 Prospect Park W., Brooklyn, 11215 (290).

Marillac House (Apartments for Active or Retired Senior Citizens), 301 Orchard, Fayettville 13066 (52 units).

Mary Manning Walsh Home (Nursing Home), 1339 York Ave., New York 10021 (347).

Mercy General Hospital Nursing Home Unit, Tupper Lake 12986 (26).

Mt. Carmel Home (Nursing Home, Women), 539 W. 54th St., New York 10019 (92).

Mt. Loretto Convalescent and Rest Home, R.D., 3, Amsterdam 12010 (87).

Nazareth Nursing Home, 291 W. North St., Buffalo 14201 (100).

Our Lady of Consolation Residence (Nursing Home), Albany and Schlegel Aves., Amityville 11701 (110).

Ozanam Hall Queens Nursing Home, 42-41 201st St., Bayside 11361 (432).

Providence Rest Home (Women), 3304 Waterbury Ave., Bronx 10465 (154).

Resurrection Rest Home (Nursing Home and Health Related Facility), Castleton 12011 (54).

Sacred Heart Home (Health Care Facility) (91), and Brothers of Mercy Apartments for Elderly (100 units), 4520 Ransom Rd., Clarence 14031.

Sacred Heart Nursing Home, 8 Mickle St., Plattsburgh 12901 (74).

St. Ann's Home (Nursing Home and Extended Care Facility), 1500 Portland Ave., Rochester 14621 (354).

St. Anthony's Home for the Aged, 5285 S. Park Ave., Hamburg 14075 (90).

St. Columban's on the Lake (Retirement Home), Silver Creek 14136 (50).

St. Elizabeth Home, 5539 Broadway, Lancaster 14086 (100).

St. Francis Home (Nursing and Intermediate Care Facility), 147 Reist St., Williamsville 14221 (96).

St. Joseph's Guest House, 350 Cuba Hill Rd., Huntington 11743.

St. Joseph's Home (Nursing Home), 420 Lafayette St., Ogdensburg 13669 (82).

St. Joseph's Nursing Home, 2535 Genesee St., Utica 13501.

St. Luke Manor for Chronically Ill, 17 Wiard St., Batavia 14020 (20).

St. Patrick's Home for the Aged and Infirm, 66 Van Cortland Park S., Bronx 10463 (214).

St. Teresa's Nursing Home, 120 Highland Ave., Middletown 10940 (92).

St. Vincent's Home for the Aged, 319 Washington Ave., Dunkirk 14048 (36).

St. Zita's Home (Women), 143 W. 14th St., New York 10011.

Uihlein Mercy Center (Nursing Home), Lake Placid 12946 (96).

North Carolina: Maryfield Nursing Home, Greensboro Rd., High Point 27260 (60).

North Dakota: Holy Family Guest Home (Nursing Home), Carrington 58421 (40).

Manor St. Joseph (Residence), Edgeley 58533 (50).

St. Anne's Guest Home, 813 Lewis Blvd., Grand Forks 58201 (100).

St. Olaf Guest (Retirement) Home, Powers Lake 58773 (20).

Ohio: Alvernia Rest Home, 6765 State Rd., Cleveland 44134 (143).

Assumption Nursing Home, 550 Chalmers Ave., Youngstown 44511 (84).

Franciscan Terrace (Residence and Nursing Care), 60 Compton Rd., Cincinnati 45215 (144).

House of Loreto (Nursing Home), 2812 Harvard Ave. N.W., Canton 44709 (98).

Jennings Hall (Skilled Nursing Home), 10204 Granger Rd., Garfield Heights, Cleveland 44125 (122).

Kirby Manor (Retirement Apartments),

11500 Detroit Ave., Cleveland 44102 (202 suites).

Little Sisters of the Poor, 476 Riddle Rd., Cincinnati 45220 (100).

Little Sisters of the Poor, 4291 Richmond Rd., Cleveland 44122 (212).

Maria-Joseph Home for the Aged and Lourdes Hall Nursing Home, 4950 Salem Ave., Dayton 45416 (150).

Mt. St. Joseph (Nursing Home), 21800 Chardon Rd., Euclid 44117 (100).

Sacred Heart Home, 4900 Navarre Ave., Oregon 43616 (246).

St. Augustine Manor (Nursing Home), 7818 Detroit Ave., Cleveland 44102 (184).

St. Edward Nursing Home, 3131 Smith Rd., Akron 44313 (95).

St. Francis Home for the Aged, 182 St. Francis Ave., Tiffin 44883 (106).

St. Joseph's Hospice for the Aged (Nursing Home), 219 N. Chapel St., Louisville 44641 (58).

St. Margaret's Hall (Residence and Nursing Facility), 1960 Madison Rd., Cincinnati 45206 (145).

St. Raphael Home (Residence and Nursing Facility), 1550 Roxbury Rd., Columbus 43212 (80).

St. Rita's Nursing Home, 880 Greenlawn Ave., Columbus 43223 (100).

St. Theresa Residence for the Aged, 6760 Belkenton Ave., Cincinnati 45236 (125).

Schroder Manor, 1302 Millville Ave., Hamilton 45013 (15).

The Siena Home (Skilled Nursing Home), 235 W. Orchard Spring Dr., Dayton 45415 (98).

Villa Maria Nursing Home, Green Springs 44836 (150).

Villa Maria Rest Home, 609 N. 7th St., Steubenville 43952 (26).

Villa Sancta Anna Home for Aged, 25000 Chagrin Blvd., Beachwood 44122 (68).

Oklahoma: St. Ann's Nursing Home, 3825 N.W. 19th St., Oklahoma City 74107 (82).

Oregon: Benedictine Nursing Center, S. Main St., Mt. Angel 97362 (105).

Mt. St. Joseph's Residence and Extended Care Center, 3060 S.E. Stark St., Portland 97214 (317).

St. Anthony's Hospital Extended Care Facility, Pendleton 97801 (65).

St. Catherine's Residence and Nursing Center, 3959 Sheridan Ave., North Bend 97459 (99).

St. Elizabeth's Nursing Home, Baker 97814 (49).

Sisters of St. Mary of Oregon Maryville Nursing Home, 14645 S.W. Farmington, Beaverton 97005 (120).

Pennsylvania: Ascension Manor (Apartment House), 911 N. Franklin St., Philadelphia 19123 (140 units).

Blessed John Neumann Nursing Home, 10400 Roosevelt Blvd., Philadelphia 19116 (196).

Christ the King Manor, 1100 W. Long Ave., Du Bois 15801 (100).

Corpus Christi Residence for Women, 7165 Churchland St., Pittsburgh 15206.

Drueding Infirmary, Master and Lawrence Sts., Philadelphia 19122 (50).

Garvey Manor (Nursing Home), Logan Blvd., Holidaysburg, 16648 (152).

Holy Family Home, Little Sisters of the Poor, 5300 Chester Ave., Philadelphia 19143 (220).

Holy Family Manor (Skilled Nursing Facility), 1200 Spring St., Bethlehem 18018 (200).

James P. Wall Memorial Home, 1028 Benton Ave., Pittsburgh 15212 (118).

Little Flower Manor, Springfield and Providence Rds. Darby 19023 (75).

Little Sisters of the Poor, 5324 Penn Ave., Pittsburgh 15224 (115).

Little Sisters of the Poor, 2500 Adams Ave., Scranton 18509 (67).

Maria Joseph Manor, Danville 17821 (87).

Marian Manor (Residence and Nursing Care), 2695 Winchester Dr., Pittsburgh 15220 (176).

Mt. Trexler Skilled Nursing Unit of Sacred Heart Hospital, Limeport 18060 (65).

Our Lady Help of Christians Home b)nursing Home, Women), 56th St. and City Line Ave., Philadelphia 19131 (17).

Sacred Heart Manor (Residence and Health Care), 6445 Germantown Ave., Philadelphia 19119 (169).

St. Ann — Villa Laboure (Residence), 449b. Locust Ave., Philadelphia 19144 (16).

St. Anne Home (Residence and Nursing Care, Women), R.D. 2, Columbia 17512 (120).

St. Anne Home for the Elderly (Skilled Nursing Facility), 685 Angela Dr., Greensburg 15601 (125).

St. Basil's Home for Women, Uniontown 15401 (18).

St. Bernadette Home for the Aged and Convalescent, 1525 N. 18th St., Philadelphia 19121 (174).

St. Ignatius Nursing Home, 4401 Haverford Ave., Philadelphia 19104 (176).

St. Joseph Home for the Aged (Women, Married Couples), Holland, Pa. 18966 (92).

St. Joseph Manor (Skilled Nursing Facility), 1616 Huntingdon Pike, Meadowbrook 19046 (100).

St. Leonard's Guest Home, 601 N. Montgomery St., Hollidaysburg 16648 (24).

St. Mary's Home for the Aged, 607 E. 26th St., Erie 16504 (122).

St. Mary's Manor for Sighted and Unsighted, 701 Lansdale Ave., Lansdale 19446 (160).

St. Mary's Villa (Nursing Home), Elmhurst 18416 (121).

Shenango Valley Home for Senior Citizens (Residence and Nursing Care), 2250 Shenango Freeway, Sharon 16146 (100).

Sisters of the Holy Ghost, Home for Aged Women, Hampton Heights, Allison Park 15101 (17).

Villa de Marillac Nursing Home (Women), 5300 Stanton Ave., Pittsburgh 15206 (50).

Villa St. Elizabeth, 1301 Museum Rd., Reading 19602 (49).

Villa Teresa (Nursing Home), 1051 Avila Rd., Harrisburg 17109 (178).

Vincentian Home for the Chronically Ill., Perrymount Rd., Pittsburgh 15237 (153).

Rhode Island: Holy Trinity Home for Aged of the Little Sisters of the Poor, 964 Main St., Pawtucket 02860 (135).

Scalabrini Villa (Rest — Nursing Home), 860 Quidnessett Rd., North Kingstown 02852 (70).

L'Hospice St. Antoine (Residence), Mendon Rd. (P.O. Woonsocket), North Smithfield 02895 (249).

The St. Clare Home for Aged People, 309 Spring St., Newport 02840 (38).

South Carolina: Carter Mary Home, 1660 Ingram Rd., Charleston 29407 (8).

South Dakota: Brady Memorial Home (Intensive Care Nursing Facility), 500 S. Ohlman St., Mitchell 57301 (60).

Maryhouse, Pierre 57501 (47).

Mother Joseph Manor (Skilled Nursing Facility), 1002 North Jay St., Aberdeen 57401 (60).

St. William's Home for the Aged, 101 Viola St., Milbank 57252 (35).

Tekakwitha Nursing Home, Sisseton 57262 (102).

Tennessee: Alexian Brothers Rest Home (Retired Men and Women), Signal Mountain 37377 (97).

Ave Maria Guild Home (Nursing Home), 2805 Charlie Bryan Rd., Memphis 38134 (73).

Texas: Home for Aged Women, 920 S. Oregon St., El Paso 79901 (24).

Mother of Perpetual Help Home (Intermediate Care Facility), 319 E. Madison Ave., Brownsville 78520 (46).

Mt. Carmel Home, 4130 S. Alameda St., Corpus Christi 78411 (92).

The Regis (Retirement Home and Nursing Care), 400 Austin Ave., Waco 76701 (260).

St. Ann's Home for the Aged (Nursing Home), P.O. Box 1338, Panhandle 79068 (52).

St. Anthony's Center (Residence and Extended Health Care), 6301 Almeda Rd., Houston 77021 (279).

St. Benedict's Nursing Home, Alamo and Johnson Sts., San Antonio 78204 (186).

St. Francis Village, Inc. (Retired and Elderly), Crowley. Mailing address — P.O. Box 16310, Ft. Worth 76133 (400).

St. Joseph Residence, 330 W. Pembroke St., Dallas 75208 (49).

Virgen de San Juan Nursing Home, San Juan 78589 (46).

Utah: St. Joseph Villa (Nursing Home), 474 Westminster Ave., Salt Lake City 84115 (89).

Vermont: Loretto Home for Aged, 59 Meadow St., Rutland 05701 (55).

Michaud Memorial Manor (Residence), Derby Line 05830 (24).

St. Joseph's Home for Aged, 243 N. Prospect St., Burlington 05401 (56).

Virginia: Fulton Catholic Home, Inc. (Aging Poor), 810 Louisiana St., Richmond 23231 (15).

St. Sophia's Home for the Aged, 16 N. Harvie St., Richmond 23220 (114).

Washington: Cathedral Plaza Apartments (Retirement Apartments), W. 1120 Sprague Ave., Spokane 99204 (150).

The De Paul Retirement Apartments, 4831 35th Ave. S.W., Seattle 98126 (105 units).

Fahy Garden Apartments, Dean and Cedar Sts., Spokane 99201 (30).

Fahy West Apartments, W. 1517 Dean Ave., Spokane 99201 (55).

Highline Nursing Home, 609 Highline Dr., E. Wenatchee 98802 (80).

The Josephinum (Retirement Home), 1902 2nd Ave., Seattle 98101 (228).

Mt. St. Vincent Nursing Center, 4831 35th Ave., N.W., Seattle 98126 (198).

St. Joseph Nursing Home, 1006 North H St., P.O. Box 229, Aberdeen 98520 (33).

St. Joseph Nursing Home, 708 E. Mission Ave., Spokane 99202 (83).

West Virginia: Knights of St. George Home, Wellsburg 26070 (30).

Welty Home for the Aged (Women), 21 Washington Ave., Wheeling 26003 (44).

Wisconsin: Divine Savior Nursing Home, 715 W. Pleasant St., Portage 53901 (106).

The Henry Boyle Catholic Home for the Aged (Nursing Home), 271 N. Park Ave., Fond du Lac 54935 (37).

Hope Nursing Home, 438 Ashford Ave., Lomira 53048 (40).

McCormick Memorial Home for the Aged, 212 Iroquois St., Green Bay 54301 (70).

Marycrest (Residence, Women), 600 Third Ave., Durand 54736 (16).

Maryhill Manor Nursing and Retirement Home, 973 Main St., Niagara 54151 (51).

Milwaukee Catholic Home (Retirement Apartments and Skilled Nursing Care), 2301 E. Bradford Ave., Milwaukee 53211 (150).

Nazareth House (Skilled Nursing Facility), Stoughton 53589 (100).

Sacred Heart Hospital Nursing Home, Tomahawk 54487 (31).

St. Ann Rest Home, 2020 S. Muskego Ave., Milwaukee 53204 (54).

St. Anne's Home for the Elderly (Aged Poor), 3800 N. 92nd St., Milwaukee 53222 (220).

St. Camillus Health Center (Skilled Nursing Home), 10100 W. Bluemound Rd., Wauwatosa 53226 (186).

St. Catherine Infirmary (Nursing Home), 5635 Erie St., Racine 53402 (41).

St. Elizabeth's Nursing Home (Women), 745 N. Brookfield Rd., Brookfield 53005 (18).

St. Francis Home, 709 S. 10th St., La Crosse 54601 (69).

St. Francis Home (Skilled Nursing Facility), 2325 E. 3rd St. Superior 54880 (49).

St. Joan Antida Nursing Home, 6640 W. Beloit Rd., W. Allis 53219 (79).

St. Joseph's Home, 705 Clyman St., Watertown 53094 (88).

St. Joseph's Home, 9244 29th Ave., Kenosha 53140 (82).

St. Joseph's Home, 5301 W. Lincoln Ave., W. Allis 53219 (130).

St. Joseph Home and Hospital (Skilled Nursing Facility), River Falls 54022 (52).

St. Joseph's Hospital Home for the Aged, Arcadia 54612 (61).

St. Joseph's Nursing Home, 2415 Cass St., La Crosse 54601 (78).

St. Joseph's Nursing Home, 400 Water Ave., Hillsboro 54634 (75).

St. Joseph on the Flambeau Nursing Home, Ladysmith 54848 (104).

St. Joseph Residence, Inc. (Nursing Home), 1925 Division St., New London 54961 (107).

St. Mary's Home for the Aged (Residence and Nursing Care), 2005 Division St., Manitowoc 54220 (150).

St. Mary's Nursing Home (Women), 3516 W. Center St., Milwaukee 53210 (130).

St. Mary's Residential Care Home, 203 W. Wisconsin St., Sparta 54656 (30).

St. Mary's Ringling Manor (Nursing Home), 1208 Oak St., Baraboo 53913 (81).

St. Monica's Senior Citizens Home (Retirement Apartments and Rooms), 3920 N. Green Bay Rd., Racine 53404 (102).

St. Paul Home (Residence and Skilled Nursing Home), 509 W. Wisconsin Ave., Kaukauna 54130 (54).

South Milwaukee Nursing Home, 3601 S. Chicago Ave., S. Milwaukee 53172 (96).

Villa Clement (Nursing and Convalescent Center), W. Allis 53214 (190).

Villa St. Vincent, 610 S. Pearl St., New London 54961 (52).

Concern for the aging and aged was one of the features of the Respect Life Program sponsored in October, 1974, by the Committee for Pro-Life Activities of the National Conference of Catholic Bishops. The program, in its third year, was planned for adoption in parishes across the country.

Other concerns of the program included the right of the unborn to life.

FACILITIES FOR HANDICAPPED CHILDREN AND ADULTS

Source: *Directory of Catholic Special Facilities and Programs in the United States for Handicapped Children and Adults,* published by the National Catholic Educational Association, One Dupont Circle — Suite 350, Washington, D. C. 20036; edited by the Rev. Msgr. Elmer H. Behrmann, Ph. D., and Sister Ann Dolores Moll, S. L., executive secretary and secretary, respectively, of the Special Education Department, NCEA.

This listing covers facilities and programs with an educational or training concept. Information about other services for the handicapped can generally be obtained from the Catholic Charities Office or its equivalent (c/o Chancery Office) in any diocese. (See Index for listing of addresses of chancery offices in the US.)

Abbreviation code: b, boys; c, coeducational; d, day; g, girls; r, residential. Other information includes chronological age for admission. The number in parentheses at the end of an entry indicates total capacity or enrollment.

Deaf and Hard of Hearing

California: St. Joseph's Center for Deaf and Hard of Hearing, 4025 Grove St., Oakland. 94609.

Illinois: Holy Redeemer Day Classes for Deaf (c; 6-13 yrs.), 9536 S. Millard Ave., Evergreen Park. 60642 (30).

Holy Trinity Day Classes for the Deaf (c; 3-14 yrs.), 1910 W. Taylor, Chicago. 60612 (50).

St. Mary of Perpetual Help High School (day classes, c; 14-20 yrs.), 1023 W. 32nd St., Chicago. 60608 (18).

St. Timothy Day Classes for the Deaf (c; 3-14 yrs.), 6330 N. Washtenaw, Chicago. 60645 (24).

Louisiana: Chinchuba Institute (r&d,c; 2-16 yrs.), P.O. Box 187, Marrero. 70072 (73).

Massachusetts: Boston School for the Deaf (r&d,c; 4 yrs. and older), 800 N. Main St., Randolph. 02368 (304).

Missouri: St. Joseph Institute for the Deaf (r&d,c; 3½-15 yrs.), 1483 82nd Blvd., University City. 63132 (170).

New Jersey: Mt. Carmel Guild Pre-School Deaf Program (d.c.), 17 Mulberry St., Newark. 07102 (80).

New York: Cleary School for Deaf Children (d.c; 2½ yrs. and older), 301 Smithtown Blvd., Lake Ronkonkoma, L.I. 11779 (72).

Nassau Day Classes (c; 3-14 yrs.), 75 Post Ave., Westbury. 11590 (54).

St. Francis de Sales School for the Deaf (d.c; 3-16 yrs.), 697 Carroll St., Brooklyn. 11215 (170).

St. Joseph's School for the Deaf (d,c; 3-10 yrs.), 1000 Hutchinson River Pkwy, Bronx. 10465 (270).

St. Mary's School for the Deaf (r&d,c; 3-21 yrs.), 2253 Main St., Buffalo. 14214 (390).

Ohio: St. Rita School for the Deaf (r,c; 4 yrs. and older), 1720 Glendale-Milford Rd., Cincinnati. 45215 (150).

Pennsylvania: Abp. Ryan Memorial Institute for Deaf (r&d,c; pre-school through 8th grade), 3509 Spring Garden St., Philadelphia. 19104 (80).

De Paul Institute (r&d,c; 2-18 yrs.), Castlegate Ave., Pittsburgh. 15226 (173).

Wisconsin: St. John's School for the Deaf (r&d,c; 3-20 yrs.), 3680 S. Kinnickinnic Ave., Milwaukee. t3207 (160).

Emotionally And/Or Socially Maladjusted

Arizona: Good Shepherd School for Girls (r; 12-21 yrs.), 1820 W. Northern Ave., Phoenix. 85021 (189). Also has after care off-campus division.

Arkansas: Monastery of Our Lady of Charity (r,g; 6 yrs. and older), 1125 Malvern Ave., Hot Springs. 71901 (50).

California: Boys Town of the Desert (r; 12-16 yrs.), 14700 Manzanita Park Rd., Beaumont. 92223 (80).

Hanna Boys Center (r; 10-15 yrs.), Box 100, Sonoma. 95476 (120).

Junipero Serra Boys Club (r; 16-18 yrs.), 316 N. Union Ave., Los Angeles. 90026 (32).

Pelletier High School (r,g; 12-18 yrs.), 1500 S. Arlington Ave., Los Angeles. 90019 (105).

Rancho San Antonio (r,b; 12-16 yrs.), 21000 Plummer St., Chatsworth. 91311 (93).

University Mound School for Girls (r; 13-17 yrs.), 501 Cambridge St., San Francisco. 94134 (96).

Colorado: Mt. St. Vincent Home (r,c; 5-14 yrs.), 4159 Lowell Blvd., Denver. 80211 (48).

Neuville Center (r,g; 8th-12th grade), 15151 E. Quincy Ave., Denver. 80232 (60).

Connecticut: Highland Heights—St. Francis Home for Children (r,c; 8-12 yrs.), 651 Prospect St. 06505 (28).

Mt. St. John (r,b; 11-16 yrs.), Kirtland St., Deep River. 06417 (95).

Georgia: Village of St. Joseph (r&d,c; 6-16 yrs.), 2969 Butner Rd. S.W., Atlanta. 30331.

Hawaii: Child Development Center (therapeutic day treatment center; preschool), 2345 Nuuanu Ave., Honolulu. 96817 (10).

Illinois: Group Home—Dominican Sisters of Bethany (r,g; 13-16 yrs.), 1434 W. Estes Ave., Chicago. 60626 (8).

Group Home, The Marcella Residence (g; 14-18 yrs.), 4633 N. Dover, Chicago. 60640 (10).

House of the Good Shepherd, Heart of Mary High School (r,g; 13-18 yrs.), 1126 W. Grace St., Chicago. 60613 (90).

St. Joseph Carondelet Child Center (r,c; 5-14 yrs.), 739 E. 35th St., Chicago. 60616 (48).

Indiana: Father Gibault School for Boys (r;

10-16 yrs.), 5901 Dixie Bee Rd., Terre Haute. 47802 (108).

Hoosier "Boys" Town (r; 10-15 yrs.), Schererville. 46375 (80).

St. Vincent Villa (r.c; 6-13 yrs.), 2000 N. Wells St., Ft. Wayne. 46808 (60).

St. Vincent Villa Pre-School (d,c), 2000 N. Wells St., Ft. Wayne. 46808 (37).

Kentucky: Boys' Haven (r; 14-19 yrs.), 3201 Bardstown Rd., Louisville. 40205 (51).

Maryhurst School (r,g; 13-17 yrs.), 2214 Bank St., Louisville. 40212.

Our Lady of the Highlands (r,g; teen-age high school age), 938 Highland Ave., Ft. Thomas. 41075 (60).

Louisiana: Our Lady of the River School (r,g), 3225 River Rd., Bridge City. 70094 (60).

Maryland: Christ Child Institute for Children (d,c), Edson Lane, Rockville. 20852 (28).

Good Shepherd Center (r,g; 14-18 yrs.), 4100 Maple Ave., Baltimore. 21227 (120).

Massachusetts: Cushing Hall (r,b; 13-16 yrs.), 279 Tilden Rd., Scituate. 02066 (40). Diagnostic treatment center.

McAuley Nazareth Home for Boys (r; 6-10 yrs.), 77 Mulberry St., Leicester. 01524 (30).

Nazareth Child Study Center (r&d,c; 18 mo.-14 yrs.), 420 Pond St., Jamaica Plain, Mass. 02130 (160).

Our Lady of Lourdes School (r,g; 12-16 yrs.), 280 Tinkham Rd., Springfield. 01129 (80).

Our Lady of Providence Children's Center (r,c; 6-12 yrs.), 2112 Riverdale St., W. Springfield. 01089 (40).

Michigan: Barat House, League of Catholic Women (r,g; 12-16 yrs.), 5250 John R. St., Detroit. 48202 (24).

Boysville of Michigan, Inc. (r; 13-18 yrs.), 8744 Clinton-Macon Rd., Clinton. 49236 (180).

Don Bosco Hall (r,b; 13-17 years.), 10001 Petoskey Ave., Detroit. 48204 (52).

Villa Maria, Sisters of the Good Shepherd (r,g; 13-18 yrs.), 1315 Walker St. N.W., Grand Rapids. 49504 (50).

Vista Maria School (r,g; 12-17 yrs.), 20651 W. Warren Ave., Detroit. 48223 (125).

Minnesota: Carmel Heights (r,g; 13-19 yrs.), 1600 Eighth Ave. East, Duluth. 55805 (20).

Oak Grove High School, Home of the Good Shepherd, (r,g; 14-17 yrs.), 5100 Hodgson Rd., St. Paul. 55112 (60).

St. Cloud Children's Home (r,c; 12-16 yrs.), 1726 7th Ave. S., St. Cloud. 56301 (60).

Missouri: Child Center of Our Lady of Grace (r&d,c; 4-12 yrs.), 7900 Natural Bridge Rd., St. Louis. 63121 (100).

Marillac School (r&d,c; 7-11 yrs.), 310 W. 106th St., Kansas City. 64114 (115 day, 30 boarders).

Marygrove School for Girls (r; 12-17 yrs.), 2705 Mullanphy Lane, Florissant. 63031 (70).

Nebraska: Father Flanagan's Boys' Home (r; 10-16 yrs.), Boys Town, Nebr. 68010 (820).

Mary House (r, g; 14-18 yrs.), 519 S. 40th St., Omaha. 68105. Group home (5).

Walden Center (g, 13-18 yrs.), 602 S. 38th Ave., Omaha. 68105. Short term crisis center.

Nevada: St. Yves High School (r,g; 13-17 yrers.), 7000 North Jones Blvd., Las Vegas, 89106 (60).

New Jersey: Collier School (r,g; 12-17 yrs.), Rest Hill, Wickatunk. 07765 (60).

New York: The Astor Home for Children (r,c; 6-11 yrs., boys; 6-9 yrs., girls), 36 Mill St., Rhinebeck. 12572 (52).

Baker Hall (r,b; 12-17 yrs.), 150 Martin Rd., Lackawanna. 14218 (90).

Holy Angels Home (r,g; 11-17 yrs.), 1326 Winton Rd. N., Rochester. 14609 (39).

LaSalle School for Boys (r&d; 11-18 yrs.), 391 Western Ave., Albany. 12203 (145).

Lincoln Hall (r,b; 12-16 yrs.), Lincolndale. 10540 (270).

Madonna Heights School for Girls (r; 12-16 yrs.), Burrs Lane, Huntington. 11743 (98).

Our Lady of Charity School (r,g; 12-18 yrs.), Hamburg. 14075 (50).

Saint Anne Institute (r,g; 12-18 yrs.), 25 W. Lawrence St., Albany. 12206 (190).

St. Helena's Residence (r,g; 12-17 yrs.), 337 E. 17th St., New York. 10003 (20).

St. John's of Rockaway Beach (r,b; 10-14 yrs.), 144 Beach 111th St., Rockaway Park. 11694 (112). Also conducts group homes in Rockaway and Richmond Hill.

Villa Loretto (r,g; 15 ½-18 yrs.), Peekskill. 10566 (140).

North Dakota: Home on the Range for Boys (r; 12-18 yrs.), Sentinel Butte. 58654 (49).

Ohio: Carmelita Hall (r,g; 14-19 yrs.), 2903 Ridgewood Dr., Parma. 44134 (16).

Children's Village of St. Vincent de Paul (Parmadale) (r,c; 3-16 yrs.), 6753 State Rd., Parma. 44134 (240).

Marycrest School for Girls (r,g; 14-18 yrs.), 7800 Brookside Rd., Independence. 44131 (70).

Mount Alverno School (r,b; 12-15 yrs.), Mount Alverno Rd., Cincinnati. 45238 (84).

Our Lady of the Woods School, Girls Town of America (r; 13-18 yrs.), 575 N. Bend Rd., Cincinnati. 45224 (80).

Rosemont School (r,g; 12-18 yrs.), 2440 Dawnlight Ave., Columbus. 43211 (92).

St. Anthony Home for Boys (r; 13-17 yrs.), 8301 Detroit Ave. N.W., Cleveland. 44102 (60).

Oklahoma: Tulsa Vianney Girls Residence (r; 12-17 yrs.), 4001 E. 101st St., Tulsa. 74135 (59).

Oregon: Christie School (r,g; 9-16 yrs.), Marylhurst. 97036 (40).

St. Mary's Home for Boys (r; 8-18 yrs.), 16535 S.W. Tualatin Valley Highway, Beaverton. 97005 (40).

Villa St. Rose School for Girls (r; 12-18 yrs.), 597 N. Dekum St., Portland. 97217 (65).

Pennsylvania: Claver School for Girls (r;

13-17 yrs.), 5301 Chew Ave., Philadelphia. 19138 (45).

Gannondale School for Girls (r; 12-17 yrs.), 4635 E. Lake Rd., Erie. 16511 (48).

Gilmary School for Girls (r; 14-18 yrs.), Flaugherty Run Rd., Coraopolis. 15108 (96).

Harborcreek School for Boys (r; 10-15 yrs.), 5712 Iroquois Ave., Harborcreek. 16421 (65).

Lourdesmont School (r,g; 14-17 yrs.), 537 Venard Rd., Clarks Summit. 18411 (60-75).

Pauline Auberle Foundation (r,b; 13-19 yrs.), 1101 Hartman St., McKeesport. 15132 (55).

St. Gabriel Hall (r,b; 10-17 yrs.), P.O. Box 390, Phoenixville. 19460 (177).

St. Michael's School for Boys (r,b; 12-15 yrs.), Hoban Heights. 18620 (100).

Tekakwitha Hills School (r,g; 13-18 yrs.), 8550 Verree Rd., Philadelphia. 19111 (70).

Toner Institute (r,b; 9-13 yrs.), Castlegate Ave., Pittsburgh. 15226 (66).

Tennessee: DeNeuville Heights School for Girls (r; 13-18 yrs.), 3060 Baskin St., Memphis. 38127 (52).

Texas: Mt. St. Michael Jr. and Sr. High School (r,g; 12-18 yrs.), 4500 W. Davis St., Dallas. 75211 (120).

St. Joseph Center (r&d,c; 10-15 yrs.), 901 S. Madison St., Dallas. 75219 (60).

Washington: Good Shepherd Home (r,g; 13-17 yrs.), 4649 Sunnyside Ave. N., Seattle. 98103 (70).

Marian Heights High School (r,g; 13-18 yrs.), 3754 W. Indian Trail Rd., Spokane. 99208 (60). Also conducts a group home.

Morning Star Boys Ranch (r,b; 11-14 yrs.), Box 781-A Route 3, Spokane. 99203 (30).

Wisconsin: Cedarcrest Girls Residence (r,g; 12-16 yrs.), 8830 W. Bluemound Rd., Milwaukee. 53226 (55).

Our Lady of Charity High School (r,g; 12-21 yrs.), 2640 West Point Rd., Green Bay. 54303 (102).

St. Aemilian Child Care Center, Inc. (r&d,b; 6-12 yrs.), 8901 W. Capitol Dr., Milwaukee. 53222 (47).

St. Charles Boys Home (r; 12-18 yrs.), 151 S. 84th St., Milwaukee. 53214 (56).

St. Joseph's Children's Home (r,c; 6-15 yrs., boys; 6-12 yrs., girls), 1200 15th Ave. E., Superior. 54880 (40).

St. Michael's Home for Children (r,c; 9-18 yrs.), 3222 South Ave., La Crosse. 54601 (83).

St. Vincent Group Home (r,g; 13-21 yrs.), 3310 N. Dousman St., Milwaukee. 53212 (22).

Wyoming: St. Joseph's Children's Home (r,c; 6-13 yrs.), South Main, Torrington. 82240 (45).

Mentally Retarded

California: Helpers of the Mentally Retarded, Inc., 2626 Fulton St., San Francisco. 94118. Conducts two facilities: Helpers Home for Girls (permanent home; 18 years and older), 2626 Fulton St., San Francisco. 94118 (6); Helpers Home for Boys (permanent home; 18 years and older), 383 14th Ave., San Francisco, 94118 (6).

Kennedy Child Study Center (d,c; 5-13 yrs.), 1339 - 20th St., Santa Monica. 90404 (80). Also conducts a developmental nursery (18 mos.-3 yrs.) and a preschool for children from culturally deprived areas (3-5 yrs.).

St. Madeleine Sophie's Preschool Training Center (c; 2-9 yrs.), 2111 E. Madison Ave., El Cajon. 92021 (60).

St. Vincent School (r&d,g; 8-14 yrs.), P.O. Drawer V, 4300 Calle Real, Santa Barbara. 93102 (175).

Tierra del Sol (d,c; 12 yrs. and older), 9919 Sunland Blvd., Sunland. 91040 (100).

Connecticut: Special Education Department, 162 Oak St., Bridgeport. 06604.

Sacred Heart Educational Center (d,c; 5 yrs. to adult), Holy Family Academy, Baltic. 06380 (45).

District of Columbia: Lt. Joseph P. Kennedy Jr. Institute (d,c; 6-18 yrs.), 801 Buchanan St. N.E., Washington. 20017 (120).

St. Gertrude's School of Arts and Crafts (r&d,g; 6-12 yrs.), 4801 Sargent Rd. N.E., Washington. 20017 (48).

Florida: Department of Special Education, 1325 W. Flagler St., Miami. 33135.

Marian Center School for Exceptional Children (r&d,c; 3-14 yrs.), 15701 Northwest 37th Ave., Opa Locka. 33054 (140).

Morning Star School (d,c; 4-15 yrs.), 725 Mickler Rd., Jacksonville. 32211 (70).

Morning Star School (d,c; 4-18 yrs.), 954 Leigh Ave., Orlando. 32804 (45).

Morning Star School (d,c; 4-16 yrs.), 4660 - 80th Ave., N., Pinellas Park. 33565 (50).

Morning Star School (d,c; 4-16 yrs.), 302 E. Linebaugh Ave., Tampa. 33612 (50).

Hawaii: Special Education Center of Oahu (d,c; 4-21 yrs.), 5275 Kalanianole Hwy., P. O. Box 7028, Honolulu. 96821 (80).

Illinois: Bartlett Developmental Learning Center (r&d,c; 6-16 yrs.), 801 W. Bartlett Rd., Bartlett. 60103 (80).

Good Shepherd Manor (permanent home for men; 18 yrs. to death), P.O. Box 260, Momence. 60954 (125).

Kennedy Job Training Center (c; 16 yrs. and older), 123rd and Wolf Rd., Palos Park. 60464 (110).

Lt. Joseph P. Kennedy, Jr., School (r&d,b; 6-12 yrs.), 123rd & Wolf Rd., Palos Park. 60464 (164).

Misericordia Home (r,c; 1 mo.-6 yrs.), 2916 W. 47th St., Chicago. 60632 (136).

Mt. St. Joseph (sheltered care home for older retarded girls and women; 20-45 yrs.), Route 3, Box 261, Lake Zurich. 60047 (158; long waiting list).

St. Agnes Special Education Classes (d,c; 5½-10 yrs.), 3835 S. Washtenaw, Chicago. 60632 (15).

St. Francis School for Exceptional Children (r,c; 6-12 yrs.), 1209 S. Walnut Ave., Freeport. 61032 (27).

St. Jude School (d,c; 6-16 yrs.), 2nd & Spring Ave., Aviston. 62216 (30).

St. Mary of Providence (r&d,g; 4-14 yrs.), 4200 N. Austin Ave., Chicago. 60634 (190).

St. Rose Center (d,g; 6-15 yrs.), 4911 S. Hoyne Ave., Chicago. 60609 (60).

Special Education Program of the East St. Louis Deanery (d,c; 6-16 yrs.), 8213 Church Lane, East St. Louis. 62203 (45).

Indiana: Cara Pre-School (d,c; 4-8 yrs.), 18th and Poplar Sts., Terre Haute. 47803 (13).

Marian Day School (d,c; 6-16 yrs.), 625 Bellemeade Ave., Evansville. 47713 (56).

St. Bavo Special Class (d,c; 6-15 yrs.), 512 W. 8th St., Mishawaka. 46544 (12).

St. Mary Child Center School (d,c; 6-16 yrs.), 311 N. New Jersey St., Indianapolis. 46204 (32).

Trainable and Educable Special Education Classes (d,c; 6-18), P.O. Box 121, Batesville. 47006 (30).

Kansas: Department of Special Education, Diocese of Wichita, 619 S. Maize Rd., Wichita. 67209.

Holy Family Center (d,c; 6-18 yrs.), 619 S. Maize Rd., Wichita. 67209 (65).

Hope, Inc. (d,c; 16 yrs. and older), 1500 Polk, Great Bend. 67530 (35).

Lakemary Center, Inc. (r&d,c; 3-16 yrs.), 100 Lakemary Dr., Paola. 66071 (60r,60d).

Kentucky: Good Counsel School (d,c; 6-16 yrs.), 116 W. 6th St., Covington. 41011 (120).

Laboratory Classes for the Mentally Retarded, Ursuline College (d,c; 4½-15 yrs.), 3105 Lexington Rd., Louisville. 40206 (35-40).

Msgr. Pitt Learning Center (d,c; 5 yrs. and older), 1202 S. Shelby, Louisville. 40203 (70).

Msgr. Pitt Pre-Job Training and Work Study Program (d,c; 16-20 yrs.), 1202 S. Shelby, Louisville. 40203 (20).

Louisiana: Department of Special Education, Archdiocese of New Orleans, 1522 Chippewa St., New Orleans. 70130. Conducts day classes, a special day school, and a vocational rehabilitation center for the mentally retarded.

Department of Special Education, Diocese of Baton Rouge, 555 N. 23rd St., Baton Rouge. 70805. Conducts 12 classes in 6 special centers and a vocational rehabilitation center.

Holy Angels Institute (r,c; teen-age, 14 yrs. and older; nursery, 2 mo. to kindergarten age), 10450 Ellerbe Rd., Shreveport. 71106 (140).

Regina Caeli Center (d,c; 6-16 yrs.), 3903 Kingston, Lake Charles. 70601 (45).

St. Mary's Training School (r,c; 4-16 yrs.), P.O. Box 295, Clarks. 71415 (172).

Maryland: The Benedictine School for Exceptional Children (r,c; 6-16 yrs.), Ridgely. 21660 (100). Also conducts Habilitation Center (r,c; 17-25 yrs.) and a half-way house.

The Education Center (d,c; 6-16 yrs.), 7027 Bellona Ave., Baltimore. 21212 (150).

St. Bernardine Special Education School (d,c; 6-12 yrs.), 3814 Edmondson Ave., Baltimore. 21229 (55).

St. Elizabeth School for Special Education (d,c; 12 yrs. and older), 801 Argonne Dr., Baltimore. 21218 (160).

St. Francis School for Special Education (d,c; 5-13 yrs.), 2226 Maryland Ave., Baltimore. 21218 (92).

St. Maurice Day School (d,c; 5-16 yrs.), 10100 Kendale Dr., Potomac. 20854 (108).

Massachusetts: Cardinal Cushing School and Training Center for Exceptional Children (r&d,c; 6 yrs. and older), Hanover. 02339 (165).

Nazareth Hall on the Cape (d,c; 6-15 yrs.), 261 South St., Hyannis. 02601 (25).

Nazareth Hall for Exceptional Children (d,c; 7-14 yrs.), 887 Highland Ave., Fall River, 02720 (70).

Nazareth Hall School (d,c; 5-16 yrs.), 204 Commonwealth Ave., Attleboro Falls. 02763.

Nazareth Vocational Center (c; 14-21 yrs.), 707 Highland Ave., Fall River. 02720 (24).

Our Lady of Mercy School (d,c; 7-16 yrs.), 25 West Chester St., Worcester. 01605 (90).

St. Coletta Day School (d,c; 7-12 yrs., admission age), 85 Washington St., Braintree. 02184 (58).

Michigan: Department of Special Education, Archdiocese of Detroit, 305 Michigan Ave., Detroit. 48222. Conducts 10 educable classes in 5 centers.

Felician Sisters Home for Mentally Retarded Infants (from birth to 5 yrs.), 1012 S. Jefferson St., Saginaw. 48601. A demonstration project.

Our Lady of Providence School (r&d,g; 6-16 yrs.), 16115 Beck Rd., Northville. 48167 (130).

Robert F. Kennedy High School (c; 14-18 yrs.), 5930 McClellan Ave., Detroit. 48213 (90).

St. Louis School (r,b; 8-14 yrs.), 16195 Old U.S. 12, Chelsea. 48118 (60).

Work Evaluation Program (c; 17 yrs. and older), Holy Trinity School, Lacrosse and 6th St., Detroit. 48226. (10). Vocational program sponsored by Detroit Special Education Dept.

Minnesota: Christ Child School for Exceptional Children (d,c; 4-21 yrs.), 2078 Summit Ave., St. Paul. 55103 (124).

St. Gertrude's School (d,c; 7-16 yrs.), 30 Eighth Ave., S., St. Cloud. 56301 (23).

Missouri: Department of Special Education, Archdiocese of St. Louis, 4472 Lindell Blvd., St. Louis. 63108. Conducts 22 special day classes (c; 6-16 yrs.) and 2 day classes for pre-school children.

Good Shepherd Manor (custodial care facility for boys and men; 16-40 yrs.), 3220 E. 23rd St., Kansas City. 64127 (40).

St. Joseph's Vocational Center (c; 16-21

yrs.), 5341 Emerson Ave., St. Louis. 63120 (124).

St. Mary's Special School (r,c; 6-16 yrs.), 5341 Emerson Ave., St. Louis. 63120 (137).

St. Peter's Special Classes (d,c; 6-15 yrs.), 314 W. High St., Jefferson City. 65101 (30).

Universal Sheltered Workshop, 4208 W. Florissant Ave., St. Louis. 63115. Provides sheltered terminal employment to adult mentally retarded.

Nebraska: Villa Marie School (r&d,c; 7-16 yrs.), Rt. 1, Box 109, Waverly. 68462 (25).

New Jersey: Alhambra Pavilion Day Care and Child Study Center (c; 4-8 yrs.), 21 Centre St., Newark. 07102 (40).

Archbishop Damiano School (d,c; 3½-15 yrs.), 532 Delsea Dr., Westville Grove. 08093 (90).

Child Study Center (d,c; 4-8 yrs.), 272 Main St., Ridgefield Park. 07660 (17).

Department of Special Education, Diocese of Camden, 721 Cooper St., Camden, N.J. 08101. Conducts day classes.

Department of Special Education, Diocese of Paterson (d,c; 3-9 yrs.), 16 Jackson St., Paterson. 07505 (18).

Immaculate Conception Special Class (d,c; 6 yrs. and older), 171 Division St., Trenton. 08611 (11).

McAuley School for Exceptional Children (d,c; 5-9 yrs.), Rt. 22 at Terrill Rd., N. Plainfield. 07061 (30).

Marian Center (d,c; 7-14 yrs.), Delsea Dr. and Chestnut Sts., Vineland. 08360 (30).

Mount Carmel Guild — Department of Special Education, Archdiocese of Newark, 17 Mulberry St., Newark. 07102. Conducts day classes for the mentally retarded. Also conducts work training programs.

St. Cecilia Special Class (c; 7-13 yrs.), 21 Vernon St., Iselin. 08830 (30).

New Mexico: Notre Dame on the Rio Grande (custodial facility for males, 13 yrs. and older; no maximum age), 305 Lagunita Rd. S.W., Albuquerque. 87105 (15).

St. Joseph's Manor (custodial facility for males, 16 years and older; no maximum age), P.O. Box 487, Bernalillo. 87004. (24).

New York: Cantalician Center for Learning (d,c; 6-18 yrs.), 3233 Main St., Buffalo. 14214 (200).

Catholic Charities Learning Center for Exceptional Children (d,c; 3-6 yrs.), 305 Garfield Pl., Brooklyn. 11215 (18).

Cobb Memorial School (r,c; 6-10 yrs.), Altamont. 12009 (50).

Immaculate Heart of Mary Children's Home (r,c; 6-12 yrs.), William and Kennedy Sts., Buffalo. 14206. Conducts special class for retarded children in the home.

Marianne Hall — Special Education (d,c; 3-15 yrs.), 114 Michaels Ave., Syracuse, 13208 (12).

Maryhaven School for Exceptional Children (r&d,c; 7-16 yrs.), 450 Myrtle Ave., Port Jefferson. 11777 (90). Also conducts a voca-

tional rehabilitation center (d,c; 16 yrs. and older).

St. Catherine Child Care Center (r,c; birth to 5 yrs.), 30 N. Main St., Albany. 12203 (20).

St. Joseph School for Exceptional Children (r&d,c; 7-14 yrs.), Bennett Rd., Dunkirk. 14048 (30).

St. Rita's Home for Children (r,c; birth to 3 yrs.), 2110 Millersport Hwy., Buffalo. 14221 (64).

School for the Disabled (d,c; 5 yrs. and older), Maxwell Rd. — Rt. 9, Newtonville. 12128 (40). For mentally retarded and cerebral palsied.

School of the Holy Childhood (d,c; 7-18 yrs.), 215 Andrews St., Rochester. 14604 (85).

Special Education Department, Diocese of Brooklyn, 345 Adams St., Brooklyn, 11201. Conducts 14 special day classes in 7 parish schools.

Special Education Department, Archdiocese of New York, 451 Madison Ave., New York. 10022. Conducts 13 special day classes in 9 parish schools.

North Carolina: Holy Angels Nursery (r,c; birth to 6 yrs.), Belmont. 28012 (72).

Ohio: Department of Mental Retardation, Diocese of Cleveland, 2346 W. 14th St., Cleveland. 44113.

Good Shepherd Manor (permanent care of men 18 years and older), P.O. Box 387, Wakefield. 45687 (104).

Mary Immaculate School for Exceptional Children (d,c; 6-16 yrs.), 3837 Secor Rd., Toledo. 43623 (100).

Marymount Rehabilitation Services (vocational rehabilitation; 16 yrs. and older), 12215 Granger Rd., Cleveland. 44125.

Mt. Aloysius (r,b; 10-21 yrs.), Tile Plant Rd., New Lexington. 43764 (100).

Our Lady of Angels Special School (d,c; 7-21 yrs.), 3570 Rocky River Dr., Cleveland. 44111. Also conducts Seton High School Work Study Program (c; 16-21 yrs.).

Our Lady of the Elms Special Education (d,c; 6-14 yrs.), 1230 W. Market St., Akron. 44313 (64).

Rose Mary, The Johanna Graselli Rehabilitation and Education Center (r,c; 2-15 yrs.), 19350 Euclid Ave., Cleveland. 44117 (40).

St. John's Villa (d,c; 6-14 yrs.), W. Main St., Carrollton. 44615 (150).

St. Joseph Center (d,c; 7-16 yrs.), 2346 W. 14th St., Cleveland. 44113 (75).

Sheltered Workshop and Training Center (c; 16 yrs. and older), 1904 W. 22nd St., Cleveland. 44143 (25).

Oregon: Emily School for Retarded Children (d,c; 4-18 yrs.), 830 N. E. 47th Ave., Portland. 97213 (30).

Our Lady of Providence Children's Nursing Center (r; nursing care), 830 N. E. 47th Ave., Portland. 97213.

Pennsylvania: Clelian Heights School for Exceptional Children (r&d,c; 6-16 yrs.), R.D. 3, Box 304A, Greensburg. 15601 (100). Also conducts re-socialization program (r&d,g; 16-20 yrs.).

Department of Special Education, Diocese of Pittsburgh, 162 Steuben St., Pittsburgh. 15220. Conducts a program consisting of eight special day classes.

Don Guanella School (r,b; 7-14 yrs.), Sproul Road, Route 27, Springfield. 19064 (200).

McGuire Memorial (r&d,c; infancy to 7 yrs.), 2119 Mercer Rd., New Brighton. 15066 (150).

Mercy Day School: Center for Special Learning (d,c; 6-18 yrs.), 830 S. Woodward St., Allentown. 18103 (80).

Our Lady of Confidence Day School (c; 3-21 yrs.), 1099 W. Luzerne St., Philadelphia. 19140 (240).

St. Anthony School for Exceptional Children (r&d,c; 6-16 yrs.), 13th St. and Hulton Rd., Oakmont. 15139 (150). Also conducts a work adjustment center (c; 16 yrs. and older).

St. Joseph Day School (c; 6-18 yrs.), 619 Mahantongo St., Pottsville. 17901 (40).

St. Joseph's Children and Maternity Hospital Day School (c), 2010 Adams Ave., Scranton. 18509 (24).

St. Katherine School (d,c; 7-17 yrs.), Lancaster and Bowman Ave., Philadelphia. 19151 (270).

St. Mary of Providence Institute (r&d,g; 6-14 yrs.), Elverson. 19520 (120).

Rhode Island: St. Joseph's Pine Harbor (r,c; 3-16 yrs.), Singleton Rd., Pascoag. 02859 (70).

Tennessee: Madonna Day School for Retarded Children (d,c; 7-16), 4189 Leroy, Memphis. 38108 (50).

Texas: Katherine A. Ryan Center for Mentally Retarded Children (d,c), 4301 Broadway, San Antonio. 78209 (40).

Notre Dame of Dallas Special School (d,c; 6-12 yrs.), yrs.), Rt. 2, Box 4, Irving. 75062. (108).

Virginia: St. Coletta School (d,c; 5-18 yrs.), 1305 N. Jackson, Arlington. 22201 (45).

St. Mary's Infant Home (r,c; 3 days-9 yrs.), 317 Chapel St., Norfolk. 23504 (50).

Washington: Antonian School for Special Children (r&d,c; 6-18 yrs.), Cheney Rural Rt. 3, Box 14B, Cheney. 99004 (31).

Marian School (d,c; 6-18 yrs.), Fort Wright College, Spokane. 99204. (45).

Wisconsin: St. Coletta School, Jefferson. 53549. Offers the following programs:

a complete program of special education from kindergarten through elementary and advanced levels (r&d,c);

a work training center in preparation for job placement (r,c; 17-20 yrs.)'

a custodial care center (r,c; 45-85 yrs.);

a half-way house to give guidance and assist with problems (r,c; 18-24 yrs.);

a sheltered workshop to provide employment for the mentally retarded in a sheltered environment (r,c; 25-45 yrs.).

St. Coletta Day School (c; 8-16 yrs.), 1725 N. 54th St., Milwaukee. 53208 (16).

Orthopedically Handicapped

Alabama: Father Purcell Memorial (r,c; birth to 14 yrs.), 1918 Fairview Ave., Montgomery. 36108 (54).

Kentucky: Redwood School and Rehabilitation Center, United Cerebral Palsy of Northern Kentucky, Inc., (d,c; 18 mo. and older), 71 Orphanage Rd., Fort Mitchell, 41017 (77).

Pennsylvania: St. Edmond's Home for Crippled Children (r,c; 2-10 yrs.)., 320 S. Roberts Rd., Rosemont. 19010 (50).

Visually Handicapped

Illinois: Department of Vision and Hearing (itinerant program for the visually handicapped; 6-20 yrs.), 126 N. Desplaines St., Chicago. 60606.

St. Raphael Day School for the Blind (c), 6011 S. Justine St., Chicago. 60636 (6).

Maine: Blind Children's Resource Center, Sacred Heart School (d,c; 6-14 yrs.), 273 Minot Ave., Auburn (15).

Blind Children's Resource Center, Cathedral School (d,c; grades 1-8), 14 Locust St., Portland. 04111 (17).

New Jersey: Mt. Carmel Guild Special Education, Department for the Visually Handicapped (itinerant teaching program for grade and high school children), 17 Mulberry St., Newark. 07102 (56).

St. Joseph's School for the Multiple Handicapped Blind (r&d,c; 4-21 yrs.), 253 Baldwin Ave., Jersey City. 07306 (37).

New York: Catholic Charities Special Services Division (itinerant program, c; 6-20 yrs.), 75 Post Ave., Westbury. 11590 (42).

Catholic Guild for the Blind (itinerant teaching program, c; 5-17 yrs.), 191 Joralemon St., Brooklyn. 11201.

Lavelle School for the Blind (r&d,c; 3-20 yrs.), 221st St. and Paulding Ave., Bronx. 10469 (220).

St. Peter's School Resource Room (c; kindergarten through 8th grade), 2331 Fifth Ave., Troy. 12180 (15).

Pennsylvania: St. Lucy Day School (d,c; 5-14 yrs.), 929 S. Farragut St., Philadelphia. 19143 (49).

Genetic Research

Msgr. James T. McHugh, director of the Family Life Division, U.S. Catholic Conference, called "interesting and salutary" the recommendation of a scientists' panel that research into the creation of hybrid human genes be curtailed.

He said July 19, 1974, that the suggestion, made by a committee of the National Academy of Sciences, showed that at least some scientists were alert to the ethical implications of their research.

OTHER SOCIAL SERVICES

Cancer Hospitals or Homes: The following homes or hospitals specialize in the care of cancer patients. They are listed according to state.

Penrose Cancer Hospital, Sisters of Charity of Cincinnati, 2215 N. Cascade Ave., Colorado Springs, Colo. 80907.

Our Lady of Perpetual Help Free Cancer Home, Servants of Relief for Incurable Cancer, 760 Washington St., S.W., Atlanta, Ga. 30315 (54).

Rose Hawthorne Lathrop Home, Servants of Relief for Incurable Cancer, 1600 Bay St., Fall River, Mass. 02724 (40).

Our Lady of Good Counsel Free Cancer Home, Servants of Relief for Incurable Cancer, 2076 St. Anthony Ave., St. Paul, Minn. 55104 (49).

Calvary Hospital, Little Company of Mary Sisters, 1600 Macombs Ave., Bronx, N.Y. 10452 (111).

St. Rose's Free Home for Incurable Cancer, Servants of Relief for Incurable Cancer, 71 Jackson St., New York, N.Y. 10002 (94).

Rosary Hill Home, Servants of Relief for Incurable Cancer, Hawthorne, N.Y. 10532 (82).

Holy Family Home, staffed by Dominican Sisters of St. Rose of Lima, 6707 State Rd., Cleveland, O. 44134.

Sacred Heart Free Home for Incurable Cancer, Dominican Sisters, 1315 W. Hunting Park Ave., Philadelphia, Pa. 19140 (60).

Drug Addiction: A national office was established in the framework of the US Catholic Conference in 1972: Catholic Office of Drug Education (CODE), 1312 Massachusetts Ave. N.W., Washington, D.C. 20005. Director, Rev. Roland Melody, S.T.

Rehabilitation centers have been established in several dioceses.

Alcoholics: Some priests and religious throughout the US are committed in a special way to the personal rehabilitation and pastoral care of alcoholics through participation in Alcoholics Anonymous and other programs. Facilities for the rehabilitation of alcoholics include:

St. Christopher's Inn, Atonement Friars, Graymoor, Garrison, N.Y. 10524 (capacity, 200).

Matt Talbot Inn, 9305 Superior Ave., Cleveland, Ohio 44106 (capacity, 25 men).

Mt. Carmel Hospital for Alcoholism (40 beds), and Mt. Carmel Rehabilitation Center for Male Alcoholics (100 beds), 396 Straight St., Paterson, N.J. 07501.

Sacred Heart Rehabilitation Center, 569 Elizabeth St., Detroit, Mich. 48201.

The National Clergy Conference on Alcoholism was established to conduct workshops in various dioceses to instruct priests on ways of dealing with problem drinkers.

Convicts: Priests serve as full- or part-time chaplains in penal and correctional institutions throughout the country. Limited efforts have been made to assist in the rehabilitation of released prisoners in Halfway House establishments.

Facilities for Homeless Men: Representative of places where meals are provided, and in some cases lodging and other services as well, are:

St. Anthony's Dining Room, 121 Golden Gate Ave., San Francisco, Calif. 94102, where more than 11 million free meals have been served since 1950. Founded by Rev. Alfred Boeddeker, O.F.M.

Oznam Inn, Little Brothers of the Good Shepherd, 843 Camp St., New Orleans, La. 70130: Under sponsorship of the St. Vincent de Paul Society.

St. Vincent's Dining Room, 205 E. 2nd St., Reno, Nev. 87301.

St. Vincent's Dining Room, 650 S. Main St., Las Vegas, Nev. 89101.

Good Shepherd Refuge, Little Brothers of the Good Shepherd, 601 2nd St., Albuquerque, N.M.

Holy Name Centre for Homeless Men, Inc., 18 Bleeker St., New York, N.Y. 10012. Provides social services and counselling for alcoholic men, and aid to transients and those in need.

St. Christopher Inn, Graymoor, Garrison, N.Y. 10524.

Good Samaritan Inn, Little Brothers of the Good Shepherd, 1450 E. Broad St., Columbus, Ohio 43205.

St. John's Hospice for Men, Little Brothers of the Good Shepherd, 1221 Race St., Philadelphia, Pa. 19107.

St. Joseph's House of Hospitality, 61 Tannehill St., Pittsburgh, Pa. 15219.

Unwed Mothers: Residential and care services for unwed mothers are the specific work of Sisters of the Good Shepherd in their numerous convents in the US.

Organizations for Handicapped

(See separate article for a listing of facilities for the handicapped.)

Blind

The Carroll Rehabilitation Center for the Visually Impaired (formerly the Catholic Guild for All the Blind): Located at 770 Centre St., Newton, Mass. 02158, it conducts St. Paul's Rehabilitation Center for the Blind, St. Raphael's Geriatric Adjustment Center, a college preparatory program and programs in research, community mobility, volunteer and special services, casework and counseling, and professional training. It maintains a large program of services for trainees not in residence on campus. It also publishes a quarterly newspaper, *Listen,* with a circulation of approximately 30,000. The executive director is Paul Cifrino.

American Federation of Catholic Workers for the Blind and Visually Handicapped, Inc.: The Federation, founded in 1954 in Pittsburgh, Pa., is an association of independent agencies and individuals who work for and with the blind in their own local areas. The president is Edward T. Ruch, American Foundation for the Blind, 15 West 16th St., New York, N.Y. 10010.

Xavier Society for the Blind: The Society is located at 154 E. 23rd St., New York, 10010. Founded in 1900 by Rev. Joseph Stadelman, S.J., it is a center for publications for the blind and maintains a circulating library of approximately 7,000 volumes in Braille, along with a growing list of titles in large type and on tape. Its many publications include *The Catholic Review,* a monthly selection of articles of current interest from the Catholic press presented for the visually handicapped in Braille, on tape, and in large print. Xavier maintains the National Catholic Educational Index, listing all transcribed and recorded textbooks used currently in the overall Catholic educational system. The director of Xavier is Rev. Anthony F. La Bau, S.J.

The Deaf

Approximately 250 priests, 120 sisters and 30 brothers are engaged in special work among some 60,000 deaf persons in the U.S.

International Catholic Deaf Association: Established in 1949, the association has more than 5,000 members in 105 chapters, mostly in the U.S. It is affiliated with the Council of Organizations Serving the Deaf, the recognized official organization of all national associations working with the deaf in this country. In 1971, the ICDA cooperated with the National Association for the Deaf in conducting a census of the deaf funded by the US Department of Health, Education and Welfare. New data was sought regarding the number — greatly increased since rubella outbreaks from 1963 to 1965 — location and needs of the deaf, for service planning and programming. The ICDA publishes *The Deaf Catholic,* a bimonthly. The ICDA chaplain is Rev. Lawrence Murphy, St. John's School for the Deaf, Milwaukee, Wis. 53207.

Mentally Retarded

National Apostolate for the Mentally Retarded: Established in 1968, the apostolate has headquarters at Trinity College, P.O. Box 4588, Washington, D.C. 20017. It publishes the quarterly *NAMR Journal* and a monthly newsletter, and has available a bibliography on the religious education of the retarded. Rev. Patrick Cullen is president of the apostolate; the executive director is Rev. Robert Malloy, O.F.M. Cap.

Service Agency

Special Education Department, National Catholic Educational Association: Established in 1954 to coordinate under one agency information and service functions for all areas of special education under Catholic auspices. Prior to 1954, its functions were carried out by a special office of the NCEA. Rev. Msgr. E. H. Behrmann is executive secretary of the department, with offices at 4472 Lindell Blvd., St. Louis, Mo. 63108.

INSTITUTIONAL PROTECTION

Congress passed a bill in the summer of 1974 providing for the establishment of a commission to study the ethics of government-sponsored biomedical research on human subjects, including research on fetuses and programs involving prisoners, minors and the mentally incompetent.

The U.S. Catholic Conference opposed the bill because of the wording of a conscience clause in the legislation. While the clause allows individuals to refuse to participate in procedures contrary to their religious beliefs or moral convictions, without fear of any penalty, its language does not provide the same protection for institutions, including Catholic hospitals.

The USCC felt so strongly about the omission of institutional protection from the conscience clause that James Robinson, director of the USCC Office of Government Liaison, sent telegrams to all Congressmen opposing the bill. The deletion of conscience protection for institutions, he said, "presents a threat to religious freedom."

Democratic Senator Joseph Biden of Delaware, who voted against the bill, called the omission of institutional protection "a grave infringement upon civil liberties."

Robinson said he feared that courts might interpret the omission as a sign from Congress that "institutions do not have rights worth protecting."

According to Robinson, the effect of the omission was uncertain. He noted, however, that the omission of institutional protection language in the bill in no way negated a conscience clause enacted into law in 1973. That clause prohibits courts or the government from forcing institutions to perform abortion or sterilization procedures against their religious convictions. The clause provides further that federal funds may not be withheld from an institution refusing to perform such procedures on religious or moral grounds.

It was felt in some quarters that no conscience clause would have been better than the "individuals only" version produced by a House-Senate conference committee.

A bill passed by the Senate in 1973 included a comprehensive conscience clause which would have protected institutions from participation in any health care program or research activity funded by the federal government which was against their religious or moral convictions.

There is great variety in retreat and renewal programs, with orientations ranging from the traditional to teen encounters. Central to all of them are celebration of the liturgy and deepening of a person's commitment to faith and witness in life.

Features of many of the forms are as follows.

Traditional Retreats: Centered around conferences and the direction of a retreat master; oriented to the personal needs of the retreatants; including such standard practices as participation in Mass, reception of the sacraments, private and group prayer, silence and meditation, discussions.

Team Retreat: Conducted by a team of several leaders or directors (priests, religious, lay persons) with division of subject matter and activities according to their special skills and the nature and needs of the group.

Closed Retreat: Involving withdrawal for a period of time — overnight, several days, a weekend — from everyday occupations and activities.

Open Retreat: Made without total disengagement from everyday involvements, on a part-time basis.

Private Retreat: By one person, on a kind of do-it-yourself basis with the one-to-one assistance of a director.

Special Groups: With formats and activities geared to particular groups; e.g., members of Alcoholics Anonymous, vocational groups and apostolic groups.

Marriage Encounters: Usually weekend periods of husband-wife reflection and dialogue; introduced into the US from Spain in 1967.

Charismatic Renewal: Featuring elements of the movement of the same name; "Spirit-oriented"; communitarian and flexible, with spontaneous and shared prayer, personal testimonies of faith and witness.

Christian Community: Characterized by strong community thrust.

Teen Encounters, SEARCH: Formats adapted to the mentality and needs of youth, involving experience of Christian faith and commitment in a community setting.

Christian Maturity Seminars: Similar to teen encounters in basic concept but different to suit persons of greater maturity.

Cursillo: see separate entry.

Movement for a Better World: see separate entry.

Conferences

Retreats International: The first organization for promoting retreats in the US was started in 1904 in California. Its initial efforts and the gradual growth of the movement led to the formation in 1928 of the National Catholic Laymen's Retreat Conference, the forerunner of Retreats International. Henry J. Balling, Jr., president; Lyle M. Becker, executive secretary. Address: 2999 W. Spencer St., Appleton, Wis. 54911.

Retreats International-Women's Division: Successor to the National Laywomen's Retreat Movement, which was founded in 1936 in Chicago as an association of retreat houses, retreat leagues, diocesan organizations, schools and convents conducting or sponsoring retreats for women. Marjorie Samberg is the president. Coadjutor Archbishop Leo C. Byrne of St. Paul and Minneapolis is the episcopal advisor. Mailing address: 229 W. Fulton, Celina, Ohio 45822.

HOUSES OF RETREAT AND RENEWAL

(Sources: Almanac survey: *The Official Catholic Directory, 1974.*)

Abbreviation code: m, men; w, women; mc, married couples. Houses and centers without code generally offer facilities to all groups. An asterisk after an abbreviation indicates that the facility is primarily for the group designated but that special groups are also accommodated. Houses furnish information concerning the types of programs they offer.

Alabama: Blessed Trinity Shrine Retreat, P.O. Holy Trinity, Holy Trinity 36859.

Visitation Sacred Heart Retreat House, 2300 Spring Hill Ave., Mobile 36607.

Alaska: Holy Spirit Retreat House, Star Route A, Box 388, Anchorage 99502.

Arizona: Franciscan Renewal Center, Casa de Paz y Bien, 5802 E. Lincoln Dr., Box 220, Scottsdale 85252.

Picture Rocks Retreat — A Christian Renewal Center, 7101 W. Picture Rocks Rd., Cortaro 85230.

California: Cenacle Retreat House (w*), 5340 Fair Oaks Blvd., Carmichael 95608.

Christ the King Retreat Center, Box 156, Citrus Heights 95610.

Christian Brothers Retreat House (students), 2233 Sulphur Springs Ave., St. Helena 94574.

El Carmelo Retreat House (Christian Renewal Center), 926 E. Highland Ave., P.O. Box 446, Redlands 92373.

El Retiro San Inigo (m), Box 128, Los Altos 94022.

Holy Spirit Retreat House, 4316 Lanai Rd., Encino 91316.

La Casa de Maria, 800 El Bosque Rd., Santa Barbara 93108.

Manresa Retreat House (m*), P.O. Box K, Azusa 91702.

Mary and Joseph Retreat House, 5300 Crest Rd., Rancho Palos Verdes 90274.

Mater Dolorosa Retreat House (m*), 700 N. Sunnyside Ave., Sierra Madre 91024.

New Camaldoli Immaculate Heart Hermitage (m, private), Big Sur 93920.

Poverello of Assisi Retreat House, 1519 Woodworth St., San Fernando 91340.

Retreat House of the Sacred Heart (w), 920 E. Alhambra Rd., Alhambra 91801.

St. Andrew's Priory Retreat House, Valyermo 93563.

St. Andrew's Priory Youth Center (y), Valyermo 93563.

St. Anthony's Retreat House, P.O. Box 248, Three Rivers 93271.

St. Charles Priory, Benet Hill, Oceanside 92054.

St. Clare's Retreat (w*), 2381 Laurel Glen Rd. Santa Cruz 95060.

St. Francis Retreat (m*), P.O. Box 1070, San Juan Bautista 95045.

St. Raymond's Dominican Retreat (y), 1666 Hidden Valley Rd., Thousand Oaks 91360.

San Damiano Retreat, P.O. Box 767, Danville 94526.

Serra Retreat (m*), P.O. Box 127, Malibu 90265.

Sisters of Social Service (one-day retreats), 1120 Westchester Pl., Los Angeles 90019.

Vallombrosa Center (w*), 250 Oak Grove Ave., Menlo Park 94025.

Villa Maria del Mar, 2-1918 East Cliff Dr., Santa Cruz 95062.

Colorado: El Pomar Renewal Center, 1661 Mesa Ave., Colorado Springs 80906.

Sacred Heart Retreat House (m), Box 185, Sedalia 80135.

Connecticut: Cenacle Center for Meditation and Spiritual Renewal (w*), Wadsworth St., Box 550,Middletown 06457.

Holy Family Retreat (m*), 303 Tunxis Rd., West Hartford 06107.

Holy Ghost Retreat House (m), Box 607, New Canaan 06840.

Immaculata Retreat House, Route 32, Windham Rd., Willimantic 06226.

Our Lady of Calvary Retreat House (w), Cotton Rd., Farmington 06032.

Villa Maria Retreat House (w*), 159 Sky Meadow Dr., Stamford 06903.

Delaware: St. Francis Renewal Center, 1901 Prior Rd., Wilmington 19809.

District of Columbia: Washington Retreat House (w*), 4000 Harewood Rd. N.E., Washington 20017.

Florida: Cenacle Retreat House, 1400 S. Dixie Highway, Lantana 33462.

Franciscan Center (ecumenical), 3010 Perry Ave., Tampa 33603.

Holy Name Priory (private), San Antonio 33576.

Mary Queen of Apostles Dominican Retreat House, 7275 S.W. 124th St., Kendall 33156.

Our Lady of Florida Retreat House (m*), 1300 US Hwy. No. 1, North Palm Beach 33408.

St. Leo's Abbey (m), St. Leo 33574.

Georgia: Ignatius House, 6700 Riverside Dr. N.W., Atlanta 30328.

Monastery of the Holy Spirit (m), R.R. 1, Conyers 30207.

Illinois: Aylesford Renewal Center, US 66 at Cass Ave., N, Westmont 60559.

Bellarmine Hall (m*), Box 268, Barrington 60010.

Bishop Lane Retreat House, R.R. 2, Box 214 A, Rockford 61102.

Cabrini Contact Center, 9430 Golf Rd., Des Plaines 60016.

Cenacle Retreat House (w), 513 Fullerton Parkway, Chicago 60614.

Cenacle Retreat House (w), 11600 Longwood Dr., Chicago, 60643.

Cenacle Retreat and Conference Center, P.O. Box 340, Warrenville 60555.

Childerley Retreat House (university students), 506 McHenry Rd., Wheeling 60090.

King's House, N. 66th St., Belleville 62223.

King's House of Retreats, Box 313, Henry 61537.

La Salle Manor, Christian Brothers Retreat House (y), Plano 60545.

Laymen's Retreat House, Techny 60082.

St. Francis Retreat (m*), Mayslake, 1717 31st St., Oak Brook 60521.

St. Mary's Retreat House, P.O. Box 608, 1400 W. Main St., Lemont 60439.

St. Peter's Friary (m), 110 W. Madison St., Chicago 60602.

Viatorian Villa, 3015 N. Bayview Lane, McHenry 60050.

Villa Redeemer, Box 6, Glenview 60025.

Indiana: Alverna Retreat House, 8140 Spring Mill Rd., Indianapolis 46260.

Lourdes Retreat House (m), Box 156, Cedar Lake 46303.

Our Lady of Fatima Retreat House, 5353 E. 56th St., Indianapolis 46226.

Our Lady of Fatima Retreat House, Notre Dame 46556.

Our Lady of Lourdes Retreat House (m), 12915 Parrish St., P.O. Box 156, Cedar Lake 46303.

St. Jude Guest House, St. Meinrad 47577.

Sarto Retreat Center, 4200 N. Kentucky Ave., Evansville 47711.

Seven Dolors Shrine Retreat House, R.R. 12, Box 31, Valparaiso 46383.

Iowa: American Martyrs Retreat House,

P.O. Box 605, Cedar Falls 50613.
Colfax Interfaith Spiritual Center, Box 37,
Colfax, 50054.

Kansas: Villa Christi Retreat House, 3033
W. Second St., Wichita 67203.

Kentucky: Marydale Center, Donaldson
Rd., Erlanger 41018.
Our Lady of Gethsemañi (m, private), The
Guestmaster, Abbey of Gethsemani, Trappist
40073.

Louisiana: Abbey Christian Life Center, St.
Joseph's Abbey, St. Benedict 70457.
Ave Maria Retreat House, Route 1, Box
0368 AB, Marrero 70072.
Cenacle Retreat House (w), 5500 St. Mary
St., Metairie 70004.
Manresa House of Retreats (m), P.O. Box
89, Convent 70723.
Maryhill Retreat House (Christian Life
Center), 600 Maryhill Rd., Pineville 71360.
Our Lady of the Oaks Retreat House, P.O.
Box D, Grand Coteau 70541.

Maine: St. Paul's Center, Oblate Fathers
Retreat House (French-English), 136 State
St., Augusta 04330.

Maryland: CYO Retreat House (y*), 15523
York St.,Sparks 21152.
Christian Brothers Retreat House (y), Rt.
15 South, Adamstown 21712.

Loyola Retreat House-on-Potomac (m*),
Faulkner 20632. City Office, 1028 Connecti-
cut Ave. N.W., Washington, D.C. 20036.
Manresa-on-Severn, P.O. Box 9, Annapolis
21404.
Marriottsville Spiritual Center (w), Mar-
riottsville 21104.
Pine Lane Spiritual Center (y*), Winches-
ter Rd., Annapolis 21404.
St. Joseph Spiritual Center, 3800 Frederick
Ave., Baltimore 21229.

Massachusetts: Calvary Apostolic Center,
Passionist Community, 59 South St., Shrews-
bury 01545.
Campion Hall Jesuit Retreat House, Great
Pond Rd., North Andover 01845.
Cenacle Retreat House, 200 Lake St.,
Brighton, Boston 02135.
Christian Formation Center, River Rd.,
Andover 01810
Eastern Point Retreat House, Gonzaga
Hall, Gloucester 01930.
Espousal Center, 554 Lexington St., Wal-
tham 02154.
Holy Cross Fathers Retreat House, Wash-
ington St., N. Easton 02356.
Jesuit Center, Sullivan Square, Charles-
town, Boston 02129.
La Salette Center for Christian Living, 947
Park St., Attleboro 02703.
Loretto Retreat House, Jeffrey's Neck Rd.,
Ipswich 01938.

Marian Center, 1365 Northampton St.,
Holyoke 01040.
Miramar Retreat House, Duxbury, 02332.
Mother of God Retreat House (boys), Old
Groveland Rd., Bradford 01830.
Mt. Carmel Christian Life Center, Oblong
Rd., Williamstown 01267.
Sacred Heart Juniorate (boys), Fellows
Rd., P.O. Box 271, Ipswich 01938.
St. Gabriel's Retreat House, 159 Washing-
ton St., Brighton, Boston 02135.

Michigan: Blessed Sacrament Retreat
House, Sacramentine Sisters, Conway 49722.
Capuchin Retreat, Box 188, Washington
48094.
Christian Friendship House (y), 1975 N.
River Rd., St. Clare 48079.
Manresa Jesuit Retreat House, 1390 Quar-
ton Rd., Bloomfield Hills 48013.
Mary Reparatrix Retreat Center (w*),
17330 Quincy Ave., Detroit 48221.
Marygrove Renewal Center, Garden
49835.
Portiuncula in the Pines,P.O. Box 250, De
Witt 48820.
Queen of Angels Retreat, 3400 S. Washing-
ton Blvd., Saginaw.
St. Basil's Center, 3990 Giddings Rd., Pon-
tiac 48057.
St. Lazare Retreat House, W. Spring Lake
Rd., Spring Lake 49456.
St. Mary's Retreat House (w*); 775 W.
Drahner Rd., Oxford 48051.
St. Paul of the Cross Retreat House, 23333
Schoolcraft, Detroit 48223.

Minnesota: Cenacle Retreat House, 1221
Wayzata Blvd., Wayzata 55391.
Christian Brothers Retreat Center (y), Rt.
1, Box 18, Marine-on-St. Croix 55047.
Christian Community Center, Assisi
Heights, Rochester 55901.
Fiat Retreat House (y), 2120 Park Ave. S.,
621 First Ave. S., Minneapolis 55404.
Fitzgerald Center, Immaculate Heart of
Mary Seminary, Terrace Heights, Winona
55987.
Franciscan Retreats, Conventual Francis-
can Friars, Prior Lake 55372.
Jesuit Retreat House (m), 8243 N. Demon-
treville Trail, North St. Paul 55109.
King's House of Retreats, 621 S. First
Ave., Buffalo 55313.
Maryhill Retreat House, 260 Summit Ave.,
St. Paul 55102.
St. John Abbey (summer months), College-
ville 56321.

Mississippi: St. Augustine's (m*), Divine
Word Missionaries, Box 311, Bay St. Louis
39520.

Missouri: Cenacle Retreat House (w*), 900
S. Spoede Rd., St. Louis 63131.
Family Life Center, St. Pius X Abbey,
Abbey Rd., 111Pevely 63070.

Holy Family Retreat House, Conception 64432.

Immacolata Retreat House, RFD 4, Box 434, Liberty 64068.

Marianist Apostolic Center, Glencoe 63038.

Our Lady of Assumption Abbey (m), Trappists, Rt. 5, Ava 65608.

Pallottine Renewal Center, RR 2, 15270, Old Halls Ferry Rd., Florissant 63034.

Passionist Retreat of Our Lady, Retreat House, Passionist Fathers and Brothers, Warrenton 63383.

The White House Retreat (m), 7400 Christopher Dr., St. Louis 63129.

Montana: Ursuline Retreat Center (w), 2300 Central Ave., Great Falls 59401.

Nebraska: Catholic Women's Retreat League, 1034 S. 38th Ave., Omaha 68105.

Good Counsel, R.R. 1, Box 110, Waverly 68462.

St. Columbans Foreign Mission Society, St. Columbans 68056.

New Hampshire: The Common - St. Joseph Monastery, Peterborough 03458.

New Hampshire Monastery, Hundred Acres, New Boston 03070.

Oblate Fathers Retreat House, Hudson 03051.

St. Francis Friary and Retreat House, 860 Central Rd., Rye Beach 03871.

New Jersey: Blackwood Center, St. Pius X House, Box 216, Blackwood 08012.

Blessed Trinity Missionary Retreat Cenacle (w*), 1190 Long Hill Rd., Stirling 07980.

Carmel Retreat House, 1071 Ramapo Valley Rd., Mahwah; mailing address, P.O. Box 285, Oakland 07436.

Cenacle Retreat House, River Rd., Highland Park 08904.

Christ House, Rt. 15, Lafayette 07848

Good Shepherd Center, 74 Kahdena Rd., Morristown 07960.

Loyola House of Retreats, 161 James St., Morristown 07960.

Queen of Peace Retreat House, Route 206, Newton 07860.

St. Bonaventure Retreat House (m), 174 Ramsey St., Paterson 07501.

St. Joseph's Villa (w), Srs. of St. John the Baptist, Peapack 07977.

San Alfonso Retreat House, 755 Ocean Ave., Long Branch 07740.

Stella Maris Convent, 981 Ocean Ave., Elberon 07741.

Villa Pauline Retreat and Guest House (w*), Hilltop Rd., Mendham 07945.

New Mexico: Dominican Retreat House, Our Lady Queen of Peace, 5825 Coors Rd. S.W., Albuquerque 87105.

Holy Cross Retreat House, P.O. Box 158, Mesilla Park 88047.

Our Lady of Guadalupe Monastery (families - pentecostal), Pecos 87552.

New York: Bishop Molloy Retreat House (m), 178th and Wexford Terr., Jamaica, L.I. 11432.

Cardinal Spellman Retreat House, Passionist Fathers, 5801 Palisade Ave., Bronx (Riverdale) 10471.

Cenacle Center for Spiritual Renewal, Cenacle Rd., Lake Ronkonkoma, L.I., 11779.

Cenacle Retreat House, 693 East Ave., Rochester 14607.

Christ the King Retreat House, 500 Brookford Rd., Syracuse 13224.

Cormaria Retreat House (w*), Sag Harbor, L.I. 11963.

Dominican Retreat House, 1945 Union St., Schenectady 12309.

Gonzaga Retreat House (priests and religious), Monroe 10950.

Holy Cross Passionist Apostolic Center, Rt. 5, Dunkirk 14048 (5,000).

Jesuit Retreat House, North American Martyrs Shrine, Auriesville 12016.

John XXIII Center for Renewal and Ecumenism, Assumptionists, Cassadaga 14718.

Marian Shrine, Don Bosco Retreat House, Filor's Lane, West Haverstraw 10993.

Monastery of the Precious Blood (w), Ft. Hamilton Parkway and 54th St., Brooklyn 11219.

Mount Alvernia Retreat House, Wappingers Falls 12590.

Mount Augustine Retreat House and Apostolic Center, 144 Campus Rd., Staten Island 10301.

Mount Manresa Retreat House, 239 Fingerboard Rd., Staten Island 10305.

Notre Dame Retreat House, Box 74, Foster Rd., Canandaigua 14424.

Queen of Apostles Retreat House, North Haven, Sag Harbor 11963.

Regina Maria Retreat House (w*), 77 Brinkerhoff St., Plattsburgh 12901.

Retreat House of Mary Reparatrix, 14 E. 29th St., New York 10016.

St. Andrew's House, 89 A St. Andrew's Rd., Walden 12586.

St. Columban's Retreat House, Derby 14047.

St. Francis Retreat House, Capuchin Fathers, Garrison 10524.

St. Gabriel (y*), Burns Rd., Shelter Island Heights 11965.

St. Ignatius Retreat House, 6969 Strickler Rd., Clarence Center 14032.

St. Ignatius Retreat House, Searington Rd., Manhasset, L.I. 11030.

St. Josaphat's Retreat House, East Beach Rd., Glen Cove 11542.

St. Joseph Center (Spanish Center), 523 W. 142nd St., New York 10031.

Stella Maris Retreat House (w), Skaneateles 13152.

North Carolina: Maryhurst Retreat House (w*), P.O. Box 1390, Pinehurst 28374.

North Dakota: Queen of Peace Retreat, 1310 N. Broadway, Fargo 58102.

Ohio: Catholic Women's Retreat League of Columbus, c/o Miss Josephine Roundtree, president, 92 S. 4th St., Newark 43055.

Franciscan Renewal Center, 320 West St., Carey 43316.

Friarhurst Retreat House, 8136 Wooster Pike, Cincinnati 45227.

Holy Cross Center, Passionist Community, 1055 St. Paul Pl., Cincinnati 45202.

Jesuit Retreat House, 5629 State Rd., Cleveland 44134.

Loyola of the Lakes, 700 Killinger Rd., Clinton 44216.

Loyola Retreat House, P.O. Box 289, Milford 45150.

Maria Stein Retreat-Renewal Center, Box 128, Maria Stein 45860.

Marianist Center, 4435 East Patterson Rd., Dayton 45430.

Men of Milford Retreat House (private), Box 348, Milford 45150.

Our Lady of the Pines (w*), 1250 Tiffin St., Fremont 43420.

Sacred Heart, 3128 Logan Ave., Box 3902, Youngstown 44505.

St. Joseph Christian Life Center, 18485 Lake Shore Blvd., Cleveland 44119.

Shrine Center for Renewal, Diocese of Columbus, 5277 E. Broad St., Columbus 43213.

Oregon: Loyola Jesuit Retreat House, 3220 S.E. 43rd St., Portland 97206.

Mt. Angel Abbey, St. Benedict 97373.

Our Lady of Peace Retreat (w*), 3600 S. W. 170th Ave., Beaverton 97005.

Trappist Abbey Retreat (m, y, private), P.O. Box 97, Lafayette 97127.

Pennsylvania: Bl. Raphaela Mary Retreat House, 616 Coopertown Rd., Haverford 19041.

Byzantine Catholic Seminary (m), 3605 Perrysville Ave., Pittsburgh 15214.

Cenacle Retreat House (w*), 4721 Fifth Ave., Pittsburgh 15213.

Convent of the Precious Blood (days of recollection), New Holland Ave., Shillington 19607.

Dominican Retreat House (w*), Ashbourne Rd. and Juniper Ave., Elkins Park 19117.

Mt. St. Ann Retreat, (w*), P.O. Box 328, Ebensburg 15931.

St. Alphonsus Retreat House (m*), Box 218, Tobyhanna 18466 (1,200).

St. Emma Retreat House, 1001 Harvey St., Greensburg 15601.

St. Fidelis Seminary, Herman 16039.

St. Francis Retreat House, 3918 Chipman Rd., Easton 18042.

St. Francis Retreat House (w), Monocacy Manor, Bethlehem 18017.

St. Francis Retreat House, 1201 Beechwood Blvd., Pittsburgh 15206.

St. Gabriel's Retreat House (w), 631 Griffin Pond Rd., Clarks Summit 18411.

St. Joseph's-in-the-Hills (m*), Malvern 19355.

St. Paul of the Cross Retreat House, 148 Monastery Ave., Pittsburgh 15203.

St. Vincent Retreat Houe (m*, summer), Latrobe 15650.

Villa Maria Retreat House, Box 218, Wernersville 19585.

Villa of Our Lady of the Poconos (w*), Mt. Pocono 18344.

Rhode Island: Corpus Christi Carmel Retreat House, 21 Battery St., Newport 02840.

Ephpheta House — A Center for Renewal, 10 Manville Hill Rd; mailing address, P.O. Box 1, Manville 02838.

Our Lady of Peace Retreat House, Ocean Rd., Narragansett 02882.

South Carolina: Springbank Christian Center, Dominican Retreat House, Kingstree 29556.

Tennessee: Nazareth, House of the Lord, 1306 Dellwood Ave., Memphis 88127.

Texas: Cenacle Retreat House, 420 N. Kirkwood, Houston 77024.

Christian Holiday House, Oblate Fathers, P.O. Box 635, Dickinson 77539.

Holy Name Retreat House (m*), 430 Bunker Hill Rd., P.O. Box 19306, Houston 77024.

Montserrat Jesuit Retreat House, P.O. Box 398, Lake Dallas 75065.

Our Lady of the Pillar Christian Renewal Center, 2507 N.W. 36th St., San Antonio 78228.

Saint Joseph Retreat House, 127 Oblate Dr., San Antonio.

San Juan Retreat House, ("El Rancho Alegre"), Diocese of Brownsville, P.O. Box 998, San Juan 78589.

Utah: Our Lady of the Holy Trinity Retreat House (m), Huntsville 84317.

Virginia: Dominican Retreat, 7103 Old Dominion Dr., McLean 22101.

Franciscan Center for Spiritual Renewal, Rt. 642, Box 825, Winchester 22601..

Holy Family Retreat House, Box 3151, Hampton 23363.

St. Ann Retreat House, Bristow 22013.

Washington: Camp Field Retreat Center, P.O. Box 128, Leavenworth 98826.

Immaculate Heart Retreat House, Route 3, Box 653, Spokane 99203.

Palisades Retreat, P.O. Box 2214, Tacoma.

St. Peter the Apostle Diocesan Retreat

Center, P.O. Box 86, Cowiche 98923.

Wisconsin: Cenacle Retreat House (w*), 3288 N. Lake Dr., Milwaukee 53211.

Holy Hill Retreat Center, Hubertus 53033.

Holy Name Retreat House (m), Chambers Island; mailing address, 131 S. Madison St., P.O. Box 337, Green Bay 54305.

Jesuit Retreat House (m), 4800 Fahrnwald Rd., Oshkosh 54901.

Monte Alverno Retreat House, 1000 N. Ballard Rd., Appleton 54911.

Mother of Perpetual Help, 1800 N. Timber Trail Lane, Oconomowoc 53066.

Our Lady of Spring Bank Manor, Cistercian Fathers, Oconomowoc 53066.

St. Benedict Center (ecumenical retreat and conference center), Fox Bluff, P.O. Box 5070, Madison 53705.

St. Vincent Pallotti Center, Rt. 3, Box 47, Elkhorn 53121.

Siena Center, 5635 Erie St., Racine 53402.

Wyoming: St. Stephen's Indian Mission (private), St. Stephen's 82524.

CANA, PRE-CANA CONFERENCES

These special-purpose conferences are not a part of retreat programs, and the movement they represent is not related to the retreat movement. With the latter, however, they share the purpose of deepening religious experience.

Cana Conferences: Cana Conferences for married couples focus on four general areas: the relationships between husband and wife, parents and children, God and the family, society and the family. Treatment of these subjects, techniques of presentation, methods of discussion, and integrated religious activities are determined by the ordinary or special interests of different conference groups. Priests, medical doctors, marriage experts from other disciplines, and married couples may serve as lecturers or discussion leaders. Most conference groups are open to mixed-religion couples.

The movement, called Cana after the marriage feast at Cana (Jn. 2:1-11), traces its origin to Family Renewal Days given in 1943 in New York City by Father John P. Delaney, S.J. The name was changed to Cana Conference by Father Edward Dowling, S.J. The bishops of the United States, in their annual statement in 1949, commended the conferences and urged their promotion throughout the country.

The movement is autonomous and has no central headquarters. It is serviced nationally by the Family Life Division of the US Catholic Conference.

Pre-Cana Conferences: These pre-marriage conferences for engaged couples are analogous to Cana Conferences for married couples. Their purpose is a spiritual, intellectual, emotional, and practical preparation for Christian marriage.

TEEN-AGE MARRIAGES

A special screening program for teen-age couples wanting to marry was introduced in the St. Louis archdiocese in the spring of 1974. Its announced purpose is to gauge their "maturity and readiness for marriage."

Elements of the program are interviews with parish priests on a variety of topics related to personal and marital matters, recommendations by priests concerned, and, where necessary, special counseling.

In some cases, the procedures might lead to advice for the postponement of marriage.

Pastoral Concern

Cardinal John J. Carberry, in writing to priests of the archdiocese about the program, said: "We priests are indeed deeply concerned with the number of teen-age marriages which often bring unhappiness or end in divorce. It is to be noted that the use of the program in no way violates the natural right of marriage, which is God-given. It places its emphasis upon the intelligent use of that right."

Father Robert G. Ditch, who helped to formulate the program and develop a questionnaire to be used in it, said: "What it means for teen-agers is that a Catholic marriage is . . . more than getting a date reserved in the parish schedule. This program is not meant to stop them from marrying, but to get them to know more about it; to have them better informed about it."

He noted that the U.S. divorce rate for couples under the age of 19 is 50 per cent.

Questionnaire

The questionnaire to be used in the program, Father Ditch said, is not simply a check-off list but a uniform way of getting teen-agers to look at each other as potential marriage partners. "The questions are inroads to eight areas of discussion: personality, immaturity, maturity, dependence, communication, courtship, marital adjustment, and planning for the future. Often they are subjects that the couple have never discussed between themselves. When the topics are brought to light, they suddenly discover what problems might lie ahead."

Father Ditch acknowledged the possibility of alienation from the Church in cases where a recommendation might be made for no marriage or for postponement. "Hopefully," he said, "the couple will not see an arbitrary infringing on their rights, but will recognize the hazards and conflicts they bring to each other."

The St. Louis program is to run for two years, after which it will be evaluated for results and developments.

Other dioceses with similar programs include Hartford, New Ulm, Rochester and Spokane.

Lay Persons and Their Apostolate

The identity and role of lay persons in the life and mission of the Church were defined in two documents issued by the Second Vatican Council.

According to the *Dogmatic Constitution on the Church* (No. 31):

"The term laity is here understood to mean all the faithful except those in holy orders and those in a religious state sanctioned by the Church. These faithful are by baptism made one body with Christ and are established among the People of God. They are in their own way made sharers in the priestly, prophetic, and kingly functions of Christ. They carry out their own part in the mission of the whole Christian people with respect to the Church and the world.

"A secular quality is proper and special to laymen. . . .

"The laity, by their very vocation, seek the kingdom of God by engaging in temporal affairs and by ordering them according to the plan of God. They live in the world, that is, in each and in all of the secular professions and occupations. They live in the ordinary circumstances of family and social life, from which the very web of their existence is woven.

"They are called there by God so that by exercising their proper function and being led by the spirit of the gospel they can work for the sanctification of the world from within, in the manner of leaven. In this way they can make Christ known to others, especially by the testimony of a life replendent in faith, hope, and charity. The layman is closely involved in temporal affairs of every sort. It is therefore his special task to illumine and organize these affairs in such a way that they may always start out, develop, and persist according to Christ's mind, to the praise of the Creator and the Redeemer."

Call to the Apostolate

In its *Decree on the Lay Apostolate,* the council developed these concepts and outlined the principal features of this apostolate.

"Incorporated into Christ's Mystical Body through baptism and strengthened by the power of the Holy Spirit through confirmation, they are assigned to the apostolate by the Lord Himself. They are consecrated into a royal priesthood and a holy people (cf. 1 Pt. 2:4-10) in order that they may offer spiritual sacrifices through everything they do, and may witness to Christ throughout the world. . . .

"The apostolate is carried on through the faith, hope, and charity which the Holy Spirit diffuses in the hearts of all members of the Church. Indeed, the law of love, which is the Lord's greatest commandment, impels all the faithful to promote God's glory through the spread of His kingdom and to obtain for all men that eternal life which consists in knowing the only true God and Him whom He sent, Jesus Christ (cf. Jn. 17:3). On all Christians therefore is laid the splendid burden of working to make the divine message of salvation known and accepted by all men throughout the world.

"For the exercise of this apostolate, the Holy Spirit who sanctifies the People of God through the ministry and the sacraments gives to the faithful special gifts as well (cf. 1 Cor. 12:7), 'alloting to everyone according as he will' (1 Cor. 12:11). Thus may the individual, 'according to the gift that each has received, administer it to one another' and become 'good stewards of the manifold grace of God' (1 Pt. 4:10), and build up thereby the whole body in charity (cf. Eph. 4:16). From the reception of these charisms or gifts . . . there arise for each believer the right and duty to use them in the Church and in the world for the good of mankind and for the upbuilding of the Church. In so doing, believers need to enjoy the freedom of the Holy Spirit who 'breathes where he wills' (Jn. 3:8). At the same time, they must act in communion with their brothers in Christ, especially with their pastors" (No. 3).

"The layman's religious program of life should take its special quality from his status as a married man and a family man, or as one who is unmarried or widowed, from his state of health, and from his professional and social activity. He should not cease to develop earnestly the qualities and talents bestowed on him in accord with these conditions of life, and he should make use of the gifts which he has received from the Holy Spirit" (No. 4).

Goals and Methods

"The mission of the Church is not only to bring to men the message and grace of Christ, but also to penetrate and perfect the temporal sphere with the spirit of the gospel" (No. 5).

"The mission of the Church concerns the salvation of men, which is to be achieved by belief in Christ and by His grace. Hence the apostolate of the Church and of all her members is primarily designed to manifest Christ's message by words and deeds and to communicate His grace to the world. . . .

(The lay apostolate) "does not consist only in the witness of one's way of life; a true apostle looks for opportunities to announce Christ by words addressed either to nonbelievers with a view to leading them to faith, or to believers with a view to instructing and strengthening them, and motivating them toward a more fervent life" (No. 6).

"The temporal order must be renewed in such a way that, without the slightest detriment to its own proper laws (and values), it can be brought into conformity with the higher principles of the Christian life and adapted to the shifting circumstances of time, place, and person. Outstanding among the works of this type of apostolate is that of Christian social action. This sacred Synod desires to see it extended now to the whole temporal sphere, including culture" (No. 7).

"The apostolate of the social milieu, that is, the effort to infuse a Christian spirit into the mentality, customs, laws, and structures of the community in which a person lives, is so much the duty and responsibility of the laity that it can never be properly performed by others" (No. 13).

"The individual apostolate . . . is the origin and condition of the whole lay apostolate, even in its organized expression, and admits

of no substitute" (No. 16).

"The group apostolate is highly important also because the apostolate must often be implemented through joint action, in both the church communities and various other spheres. For the associations established to carry on the apostolate in common sustain their members, form them for the apostolate, and rightly organize and regulate their apostolic work so that much better results can be expected than if each member were to act on his own" (No. 18).

"Deserving of special honor and commendation in the Church are those lay people, single or married, who devote themselves and their professional skill, either permanently or temporarily, to the service of associations and their activities" (No. 22).

USCC-RELATED AGENCIES

The following agencies are engaged in carrying out programs of the United States Catholic Conference. Additional agencies are reported in other Almanac entries.

Division of Religious Education/CCD (Confraternity of Christian Doctrine): Its objective is the religious education of Catholic children who are not in Catholic schools, out-of-school youths and adults. Recent figures indicate that some five and one-half million Catholic children and youths participate in CCD programs from pre-kindergarten through high school. An adult religious education program is carried out through group discussions of texts or films, forums, and particularly in extensive catechist training courses for all academic levels.

The modern revival and expansion of the confraternity dates from publication of the encyclical *Acerbo Nimis* by St. Pius X in 1905. His directive that the CCD be established in every parish was incorporated in the Code of Canon Law and reaffirmed by the Second Vatican Council in the *Decree on the Bishops' Pastoral Office in the Church.*

The CCD is a parish-based organization operating under a priest-director and a board or commission of lay persons.

Responsibility for many details of a local CCD unit ideally rests with a lay coordinator or administrator who is a trained professional in theology and/or religious education. This is a recent development in religious education outside the parish school system. Another noteworthy new development in CCD programs is growing emphasis on training parents to prepare their children for reception of First Communion, penance and confirmation.

On the diocesan level, CCD work is coordinated by a director appointed by the bishop, with a staff of assistants — priests, religious, lay persons. In some dioceses, the program operates under an office of religious education or other agency with a similar title. The diocesan office oversees the work of local and regional units, conducts teacher-training courses, issues guidelines for a unified program, conducts diocesan or regional meetings for CCD teachers and other workers.

On the national level, the Division of Religious Education/CCD (formerly called the National Center of the Confraternity of Christian Doctrine and since 1969 under the Department of Education, US Catholic Conference) contributes in many ways to the operation of religious education programs throughout the country. On the international level, it participates in programs of the Congregation of the Clergy in the religious education field.

Publications under the direction of the division include *The Living Light* and other catechical publications.

Father Charles C. McDonald is director of the division.

Offices are located at 1312 Massachusetts Ave. N.W., Washington, D.C. 20005.

National Council of Catholic Laity: A coalition of the National Council of Catholic Men and the National Council of Catholic Women and other national lay groups representing 15,000 organizations in the United States. It provides services and leadership training institutes to diocesan and other groups, and also to individuals. Several national commissions develop programs and make them available to their counterparts on diocesan and other levels and to all NCCL affiliates. The NCCL publication is *People*, which also serves the National Council of Catholic Men and the National Council of Catholic Women.

The principal officers are Jean Eckstein, president, and Margaret Mealey, executive director.

Offices are located at 1312 Massachusetts Ave. N.W. Washington, D.C. 20005.

National Council of Catholic Men: A federation of more than 9,000 Catholic organizations of men. Through a parish service bureau and a network of diocesan councils, it provides programs of information and action, national conferences and leadership training, and a medium through which Catholic men may be heard nationally on matters of common interest. NCCM is a constituent of the National Council of Catholic Laity.

The president is William H. Sandweg.

Offices are located at 1312 Massachusetts Ave. N.W., Washington, D.C. 20005.

National Council of Catholic Women: A service agency for 10,000 affiliated organizations of Catholic women. Education in Christian principles and related action are its objectives. It provides affiliated groups with informational services, leadership training, and programs developed by five national commissions. It is a constituent of the National Council of Catholic Laity.

The principal officers are Mrs. G. Sam Zilly, president, and Margaret Mealey, executive director.

Offices are located at 1312 Massachusetts Ave., N.W., Washington, D.C. 20005.

Associates of the National Council of Catholic Women encourages membership in and promotion of the work of the NCCW. Offices are located at 5410 Connecticut Ave. N.W., Washington, D.C. 20015.

National Catholic Rural Life Conference: Founded in 1923 through the efforts of Bishop Edwin V. O'Hara for the purpose of promoting the general welfare of rural people by a program of extensive services, publications and rural-related activities. Publications include the official monthly *Catholic Rural Life.*

The conference has approximately 5,000 members among rural pastors, farmers, teachers, sociologists, economists, agricultural agents and officials. There are 95 officially appointed diocesan rural life directors.

St. Isidore the Farmer is patron of the conference.

Archbishop Ignatius J. Strecker of Kansas City, Kans., is president. Co-directors are Msgr. John G. Weber and Father John J. McRaith.

National headquarters are located at 3801 Grand Ave., Des Moines, Ia. 50312.

National Catholic Community Service: Established by the US hierarchy in November, 1940, to serve members of the armed forces, defense production workers and their families. It has continued since then to serve the spiritual, social, welfare and recreational needs of the nation's defense forces, and patients in Veterans' Administration hospitals.

NCCS has responsibility for USO services through staff in locations in the United States and overseas — in Rome and Naples, Italy; Athens, Greece; Frankfurt, Germany; Thailand. A VA program is in operation in 150 hospitals throughout the country.

During World War II, in cooperation with the United Service Organizations, NCCS conducted over 500 operations in this country

and abroad. It is a member agency of the USO and of the VA Voluntary Service National Advisory Committee.

Alice C. Collins, is the executive director.

Headquarters are located at 1312 Massachusetts Ave. N.W., Washington, D.C. 20005.

Catholic Relief Services—USCC: The official overseas aid and development agency of American Catholics; it is a separately incorporated organization of the U.S. Catholic Conference.

CRS was founded in 1943 by the bishops of the United States to help civilians in Europe and North Africa caught in the disruption and devastation of World War II.

Initially, CRS collected, purchased and shipped to war-torn countries huge quantities of food, clothing, medicines and other relief supplies which were distributed to hundreds of thousands of displaced persons, prisoners of war, bombed-out families, widows, orphans and other war victims.

As conditions in Europe improved in the late 1940s and early 1950s, the works conducted by CRS spread to other continents and areas — Asia, Africa and Latin America, wherever people were in want or distress — helping all in need, regardless of race, religion or color.

In addition to aiding the poverty-stricken and victims of natural and other disasters, the programs of CRS also encompass long-range development projects designed to help individuals, families and entire communities raise their standards of living and attain economic viability. Such projects run the gamut from simple road-clearing projects that link isolated villages with better marketplaces and building crude dams to digging intricate irrigation systems, providing potable water sources, establishing small industries, and constructing schools and community centers.

CRS operations are funded, for the most part, from the proceeds of two annual collections in parishes throughout the U.S. — of money (usually on the third — Laetare — Sunday of Lent) and of clothing (in November, near Thanksgiving, yielding more than 18 million pounds of clothing a year). Support is also received from private philanthropic foundations in the U.S., Europe and Australasia. Assistance from the federal government takes three forms: (a) food availabilities under Title II of Public Law 480; (b) defrayment of ocean freight costs on U.S. government-donated foods and all accredited relief supplies generated by CRS itself; and (c) grants for refugee relief and resettlement.

In the year ending June 30, 1973, the CRS global program in 70 countries had a total value in excess of $138 million.

Bishop Edward E. Swanstrom, auxiliary of New York, is the executive director.

CRS headquarters are located at 1011 First Ave., New York, N.Y. 10022.

Family Life Division — USCC: Established in 1931 as a central service agency for assisting, developing and coordinating family life programs throughout the United States. Since 1969 it has expanded its scope of interest and concern to the whole social mission of the Church.

Until this change was made, the division's activities were largely educational, with respect to: growth of the Christian person, preparation for marriage, husband-wife relationships, parent-children relationships, family-Church-community relationships, and services to family life programs. Accordingly, it promoted Cana and Pre-Cana conferences, couple-centered groups, and the development of marriage courses in secondary and higher education. It also carried out representative functions for the bishops of the US in matters pertaining to family life. The division is continuing many of these and other services.

The recent thrust of the division's wide concern and activity has been in the direction of exerting pressure on the social structure to improve circumstances for a decent family life.

Approximately 130 US dioceses have family life directors who are associated with the division.

Msgr. James T. McHugh is the director.

Division headquarters are located at 1312 Massachusetts Ave. N.W., Washington, D.C. 20005.

SPECIAL APOSTOLATES AND GROUPS

Apostleship of the Sea: An international Catholic organization for the moral, social and spiritual welfare of seafarers, founded in 1922 in Glasgow, Scotland. Approved by the Holy See in 1922, it is under the top-level direction of the Pontifical Commission for Migrants and Other Travellers, Piazza San Calisto 16, Rome, Italy—00153. The US unit is the National Catholic Apostleship of the Sea Conference, founded in 1947. It serves 80 chaplains in 73 US ports on seacoasts and the Great Lakes. Conference operations include a hospitality and welcoming program carried on through 15 maritime centers in: Chicago, Ill.; Houston, Tex.; Jacksonville, Fla.; Lake Charles and New Orleans, La.; Green Bay and Milwaukee, Wis.; Mobile, Ala.; New York, N.Y.; Oakland, San Francisco, San Pedro and Wilmington, Calif.; Seattle, Wash.; Tampa, Fla. Recent developments include emphasis on interfaith cooperation on the port level in seamen's work, and investigations on how the Apostleship of the Sea can assist in all phases of the various apostolates for people on the move. Bishop Robert E. Tracy of Baton Rouge is the episcopal promoter of the conference. The Rev. James P. Keating, of Chicago, is secretary and national director. The national office is located at 9501 S. Ewing Ave., Chicago, Ill. 60617.

Catholic Central Union of America (1855): One of the oldest Catholic lay organizations in the US, the Union is devoted to the development and vigor of Christian principles in personal, social, cultural, economic and civic life. It was the first society ever given an official mandate for Catholic Action by a committee of the American bishops, in 1936. A bureau in St. Louis is the center for the separate but coordinated direction of the Union. The headquarters is also a publishing house (the monthly *Social Justice Review, The Catholic Woman's Journal,* other publications), a library of German-Americana and Catholic Americana, a clearing-house for information, and a center for works of charity. Aid is given to home and foreign missions, and maintenance and direction are provided for St. Elizabeth's Settlement and Day Nursery in St. Louis. Union membership is approximately 20,000. Joseph Gervais of Rochester, N. Y. is president; Harvey J. Johnson is director of the Central Bureau located at 3835 Westminster Place, St. Louis, Mo. 63108. (See also: National Catholic Women's Union.)

Catholic Medical Mission Board (1928): Founded by Dr. Paluel Flagg and the Rev. Edward Garesche, S.J. Its purposes are to gather and ship medical supplies, and to recruit and assign medical and paramedical personnel to overseas mission hospitals and dispensaries. Since its foundation, it has shipped approximately 33 million pounds of supplies. In 1973 more than $6 million in medicines were shipped to 2,722 mission distribution centers in 53 countries. Also in 1973, 87 medical volunteers were placed in 15 countries; 42 additional volunteers were similarly assigned during the first three months of 1974. The Rev. Joseph J. Walter, S.J., is the director. Office: 10 W. 17th Street, New York, N. Y. 10011.

Center for Applied Research in the Apostolate (CARA): A research and development agency in the field of the Church's worldwide religious and social mission. Its purpose is to gather information for the use of decision-makers in evaluating the present status of the Church's mission of service and in planning programs of development toward greater effectiveness of its multiphased ministry in the future. CARA has research and planning programs focused on: church personnel (recruitment, selection, training, utilization, effectiveness, retirement, health, due process); town and country, formed in 1967 when the Glenmary Home Missioners merged their research center with CARA; overseas areas, with respect to Africa, Oceania, Asia and Latin America; the campus ministry; urban affairs; social theology, diocesan planning, religious life, and other subjects. CARA was incorporated as a non-profit corporation in the District of Columbia Aug. 5, 1964. Offices are located at 1234 Massachusetts Ave., N.W., Washington, D.C. 20005.

Christian Family Movement (CFM) (1947): Originating in Chicago and having a membership of married couples, its purpose is to Christianize family life and create communities conducive to Christian family life. Since 1968, CFM in the US has included couples from all Christian churches. The International Confederation of Christian Family Movements has a membership of 135,000 couples. Ray and Dorothy Maldoon are the US national president couple. National and international headquarters: 1655 Jackson Blvd., Chicago, Ill. 60612. Spanish-speaking CFM, organized in 1969 under the title **Movimiento Familiar Cristiano (MFC)**, serves some 2,000 couples in 42 major cities. Headquarters: 1655 Jackson Blvd., Chicago, Ill. 60612.

Christian Life Communities: Formerly known as Sodalities of Our Lady, they are groups of men and women, adults and youth, joined with other people who are involved or wish to be involved in living their full Christian vocation and commitment in the world. The governing principles and operating norms of Sodalities were revised in the spirit of documents of the Second Vatican Council by the General Council of the World Federation of Sodalities in October, 1967. The new principles were confirmed, on an experimental basis, by Paul VI Mar. 25, 1968. In August, 1970, they were amended by the General Council and submitted to the Holy See for approval. The communities (5,000 in the world, 184 in the US) have greater freedom than previous rules permitted with respect to overall structure, spiritual program (although the Spiritual Exercises of St. Ignatius remain a specific source and characteristic of the spirituality), and apostolic endeavor. The US National Federation functions under lay officers and a board of directors composed of lay persons, priests and religious, with Bishop Maurice J. Dingman of Des Moines as episcopal moderator. The World Federation office is located in Rome. National office: 3109 S. Grand Blvd., St. Louis, Mo. 63118.

Cursillo Movement: An instrument of Christian renewal designed to form and stimulate persons to engage in apostolic action individually and in the organized apostolate, in accordance with the mission which individuals have to transform the environments in which they live into Christian environments. The movement originated in Spain, where the first cursillo was held near Palma, Mallorca, in 1949. It was introduced in the US in 1957 and is functioning in more than 120 dioceses. The method of the movement involves a three-day weekend called a cursillo and a follow-up program known as the post-cursillo. The weekend is an intensive experience in Christian community living centered on Christ and built around 15 talks (10 by lay-

men, five by priests), active participation in discussions and related activities, the celebration of the liturgy. The follow-up program focuses on small weekly reunions of three to five persons and larger group reunions, called ultreyas, in which participants share experiences and insights derived from their prayer life, study and apostolic action. The movement operates within the framework of diocesan and parish pastoral plans, and functions autonomously in each diocese under the direction of the bishop. Responsibility for growth and effectiveness rests with a diocesan leaders' school, a diocesan secretariat, or both. Bishop Joseph Green of Reno is episcopal advisor to the movement. Gerry Hughes is coordinator of the National Cursillo Center, P.O. Box 21226, Dallas, Tex. 75211.

Frontier Apostles (1956): Volunteers for a minimum of two years' service in their professional line (priests, sisters and seminarians, lay persons) in the Diocese of Prince George, British Columbia, Canada. More than 1,300 have served since the start of the corps by Bishop Fergus O'Grady; about 80 per cent of 160 now serving are connected with schools of the diocese. Address: Bishop O'Grady, College Rd., Prince George, B.C.

Grail, The (1921): An international movement of women concerned about the full development of all peoples, working in education, social and cultural areas. Founded by Rev. Jacques van Ginneken, S.J., in The Netherlands, it was introduced in the US in 1940. Working in 22 countries, Grail participants include women from Australia, Brazil, Canada, East Africa, Egypt, France, Germany, India, Indonesia, Italy, Japan, Mexico, The Netherlands, Portugal, Scotland, South Africa, Surinam, United States, West Africa. Chairman of the Co-ordinating Committee, US Grail: Mary A. Kane. US headquarters: Grailville, Loveland, Ohio 45140. International Secretariat: 5, rue Sayed Sokkar, Matareya, Cairo, Egypt.

Group 7 (1971): Started by the Glenmary Home Missioners to recruit Catholic men and women 21 years of age and older for periods of two years or more in the US home mission apostolate, particularly in the 17-state area of Appalachia, the South and Southeast. The purpose of participants is to give individual and group witness to Christian faith in personal and family life, work of their own choice, and community activities. The sponsoring Missioners prepare members for the apostolate, assist them with ongoing educational and instructional programs, and keep them in touch with each other through regular communications. Father John McNearney is director of Group 7. Headquarters: Box 46404, Cincinnati, O. 45246.

International Liaison (1965): A placement office for volunteer lay personnel sponsored by the Archdiocese of Newark. It provides liaison services between volunteers and missions and voluntary agencies, with respect to programs in operation in the US and abroad, and has working relations with sister offices in various US dioceses, Canada and campus ministries. In 1973, Maryknoll (Catholic Foreign Mission Society of America) affiliated with International Liaison. Father George Mader is the director. Office: 39 Lackawanna Pl., Bloomfield, N.J. 07003.

Jesuit Volunteer Corps (1956): Established by the Oregon Province of the Jesuits, for service to the underprivileged. There are 250 volunteers working among Eskimos and Indians in Alaska; Indians in the Western states; in inner-city areas, primarily in the Northwest; in Zambia, Africa; in Micronesia and in some Northwest Jesuit high schools. The Rev. L. Gooley, S.J., is the director. Headquarters: P.O. Box 3928, Portland Ore. 97208.

Lay Mission-Helpers Association (1955): It trains and assigns men and women for work in overseas apostolates for periods of three years. In 1973, 50 members were in overseas assignments and eight in home missions. Overseas assignments included a wide variety of work in Cameroons, Ghana, Kenya, Malawi, New Guinea, Republic of South Africa, Lesotho, Rhodesia, Sierra Leone, Tanzania, West Irian. and Thailand. Affiliated is the Mission Doctors Association, which recruits, prepares and sends Catholic physicians and dentists, and their families, to mission hospitals and clinics throughout the world for tours of three years. The Rev. Msgr. Lawrence O'Leary is director of both associations. Headquarters: 1531 West Ninth St., Los Angeles, Calif. 90015.

Legion of Mary (1921): Founded at Dublin, its purposes are exclusively spiritual, viz., the sanctification of its members and service to others. It is one of the largest lay organizations in the Church. US address for information: The Legion of Mary, St. Louis Regional Senatus, Box 1313, St. Louis, Mo. 63188. The supreme governing body has offices at De Montfort House, North Brunswick St., Dublin 7, Ireland.

Movement for a Better World (1952): An international movement whose US contingent of some 30 persons conducts retreats with a distinctive communitarian thrust for the purpose of motivating Christian witness and action for making a better world. The founder and general director of worldwide MBW is Father Riccardo Lombardi, S.J. US office: Summit Bldg., 8555-16th St., Suite 402, Silver Spring, Md. 20910. The movement publishes *Atmosphere.*

Opus Dei: An association of Catholic faithful who strive to practice the Christian virtues, in their own states in life and through the exercise of their own professions or occupations in order to carry on an apostolate of witness to Christ. Since the purpose is strictly spiritual, members are free to hold the most diverse views on temporal matters, thus assuring a real pluralism of opinions in all cultural, economic, political and similar areas. Founded by Msgr. Josemaria Escriva de Balaguer in 1928 in Spain, it received full approval from the Holy See June 16, 1950. Members of more than 80 nationalities from all continents form separate branches for men and women. In the US, Opus Dei conducts corporate works in the East, Midwest and on the West coast. The directors' offices are located at 9 East 96th Street (15A), New York, N.Y. 10028. Elsewhere, the association conducts universities, training schools for farmers and workers, and numerous educational and charitable centers.

Pax Christi (1948): International Catholic peace movement. Originated in Lourdes, France, as a union of French and German Catholics to symbolize a mutual effort to heal wounds inflicted by World War II, spread to Poland and Italy, and acquired its international title when it merged with the English organization Pax. A general secretariat is located at The Hague, The Netherlands. **Pax Christi-USA**, established in 1973, has a membership of 400. Eileen Egan and Gordon C. Zahn are co-chairpersons. *Thirdly Publication* is issued three times a year. Address: 1335 N St. N.W., Washington, D.C. 20005.

Regis College Lay Apostolate (1950): Founded by Sister Mary John Sullivan, C.S.J., it enlists college graduates for a year of teaching service in home and overseas missions. More than 450 lay apostles from Regis College and more than 400 from other colleges have served since the beginning of the program. Headquarters: Regis College, Weston, Mass. 02193

St. Joan's International Alliance (1911): An organization and movement for equal opportunities for women as well as men in all fields — social, economic, political, cultural — and for full participation of women in the service of the Church. It originated in London, England, as The Catholic Women's Suffrage Society, became an international organization with the present title in 1931 and a member of the Conference of International Catholic Organizations in 1973. Membership is open to men and women. The alliance has consultative status with the United Nations. The international secretariat is located in Geneva, Switzerland; Magdalene Leroy-Boy is the president. The U.S. branch was founded in 1965; its president is Bernice McNeela. Address: 435 W. 119 St., New York, N.Y. 10027.

Southwest Volunteer Apostolate: Recruits and places volunteers for work among the Indians and Spanish-speaking of the Diocese of Gallup. The executive secretary is Fred Reed. Mailing address: P. O. Box 626, Gallup, N.M.

Young Christian Movement (YCM) (1812):

An international apostolic movement, formerly known as the Young Christian Workers, which seeks to train and involve young adults, single and between the ages of 18 and 30, in a variety of people-oriented situations. Groups meet weekly to discuss social and moral issues and to become involved in the solution of problems affecting their individual lives and the community. Membership is international, in 91 countries. The assistant national chaplain is Father Patrick J. O'Connor. The national office is located at 1655 W. Jackson Blvd., Chicago, Ill. 60612. International headquarters: Brussels, Belgium.

Center of Concern (1972): An ecumenical public interest group working to sensitize North Americans to the problems of people in the Third World. It has a large communications network throughout the world and publishes a newsletter, "Focus," and a social justice action sheet, "Action," Irving Friedman is the chairperson. Address: 3700 13th St. N.E., Washington, D.C. 20017.

LAOS: An ecumenical agency for training and recruiting volunteers with professional skills for work in developing nations and in areas of need in the US. LAOS aims to increase public awareness of forces which dehumanize people and to promote action for a world of justice, brotherhood and peace. Address: 4920 Piney Branch Rd. N.W., Washington, D.C. 20011.

CATHOLIC YOUTH ORGANIZATIONS

Angelic Warfare Confraternity (Cord of St. Thomas Confraternity) (1649), 141 E. 65th St., New York, N.Y. 10021. Apostolate for preservation of personal chastity; St. Thomas Aquinas is its patron. Director, Brendan Larnen, O.P.

Black Christian Students (1968): 3517 W. 13th Pl., Chicago, Ill. 60623. For black youth in high schools and parishes in the Chicago area, with emphasis on the Christian dimension of black identity, awareness, culture and future directives. BCS, with plans to spread elsewhere, originated from a group in Young Christian Students, with which it maintains liaison. National Coordinator, Maurice Blackwell; liaison (with YCS), Rev. Vincent J. Giese.

Boy Savior Youth Movement (1874): 30 W. 16th St., New York, N.Y. 10011; 18,000 in 55 schools.

Boy Scouts in the Catholic Church: The National Catholic Committee on Scouting, an affiliate of the Division of Youth Activities of the USCC, works in cooperation with the Boy Scouts of America, North Brunswick, N.J., in promoting the basic principles of Catholicism among more than one million Catholics among the BSA membership of six million. *Boy's Life.* Committee Chairman, Thomas F. Hawkins, Oak Brook, Ill. National chaplain, Rev. Kenneth F. O'Connell, 328 W. 14th St., New York, N.Y. 10014.

Camp Fire Girls, Inc. (1910): 1740 Broadway, New York, N.Y. 10019. The Division of Youth Activities of the USCC acts as advisor in matters pertaining to Catholic participation in the Camp Fire Girls program. To help young people learn and grow in their individual ways through participation in enjoyable activities. Open to girls from six through high school. Membership: over 600,000 (no exact statistics available on number of Catholic girls participating).

Catholic Central Youth Union of America: 3835 Westminster Pl., St. Louis, Mo. 63108. To develop lay leadership in Catholic social action. Membership: 12-25 age group—approximately 100.

Catholic Youth Organization (CYO): Name of official, parish-centered diocesan Catholic youth programs throughout the country. The National CYO Federation is a constituent member of the Division of Youth Activities of the USCC; 1312 Massachusetts Ave. N.W., Washington, D.C. 20005. CYO promotes a program of spiritual, social and physical activities. The original CYO was organized by Bishop Bernard Sheil of Chicago in 1930.

Columbian Squires (1925): P. O. Drawer 1670, New Haven, Conn. 06507. Junior organization of the Knights of Columbus. To train and develop leadership through active participation in well-organized four-point program of activities. Membership: 13- to 18-year-old Catholic boys. More than 700 circles (local units) active in the U.S., Canada, Puerto Rico, Mexico, Philippines and Guatemala. *Columbian Squires,* monthly. Director, William L. Piedmont.

Forest Rangers, Catholic Order of Foresters: 305 W. Madison St., Chicago, Ill. 60606. To develop physical, mental and moral lives of members. *Catholic Forester.* Membership: youth up to 16 years of age—approximately 39,000 in 1,170 subordinate courts in US and Canada. High Chief Ranger, Louis E. Caron.

Girl Scouts of the U.S.A.: 830 Third Ave., New York, N.Y. 10022. Girls from all archdioceses and dioceses in the US and its possessions participate in Girl Scouting. The Division of Youth Activities of the USCC is affiliated with Girl Scouts of the U.S.A. *Girl Scout Leader; The American Girl.* Membership: nearly four million (no exact statistics available on number of Catholic girls participating).

Junior Catholic Daughters of America: 10 W. 71st St., New York, N.Y. 10023. A major department of the Catholic Daughters of America. Promote spiritual, cultural and recreational activities under proper leadership; develop articulate Catholic leadership. Membership: Juniors (11 to 18 years old); Juniorettes (6 to 11 years old). National Director, Miss Carole Kelly.

Junior Daughters of Isabella: 375 Whitney Ave., New Haven, Conn. 06511. To promote religious, educational, civic and athletic training of Catholic girls. Membership: Catholic girls 10-22 in junior circles in 11 states and one foreign country.

League of Tarcisians of the Sacred Heart (1917): 3 Adams St., Fairhaven, Mass. 02719. Organize children in their schools as junior apostles of the Sacred Heart. Director, Rev. Francis Larkin, SS. CC.

National Catholic Forensic League (1952): To develop articulate Catholic leaders through an inter-diocesan program of speech and debate activities. *Newsletter*, quarterly. Membership: 900 schools; membership open to Catholic, private and public schools through the local diocesan league. President (1972-74), Rev.Frederick J. Easterly, C.M., St. John Vianney Seminary, 2900 S.W. 87th Ave., Miami, Fla. 33165.

National Christ Child Society Inc. (1886): 5151 Wisconsin Ave. N.W., Washington, D.C. 20016. Founder, Mary V. Merrick. A welfare organization for the care of underprivileged children. Membership: approximately 10,000 adult and junior members in 33 cities in US. President, Mrs. Robert Rasmussen.

Pontifical Association of the Holy Childhood (1843): 800 Allegheny Ave., Box 6758, Pittsburgh, Pa. 15233. *It's Our World*, 4 times a year. National Director, Rev. Francis W. Wright, C.S.Sp.

St. Dominic Savio Classroom Club: 148 Main St., New Rochelle, N. Y. To promote a program of spiritual, intellectual and recreational activities. *Notes to Savios*, monthly. Membership: students in fifth grade in elementary school through second year of high school — 500,000 members, 2,500 moderators and one million crusaders throughout the world.

Young Christian Students: 1655 W. Jackson Blvd., Chicago, Ill. 60612. A student movement for Christian social change. Membership: 500 in high schools and parishes.

Fraternities and Sororities

Alpha Delta Gamma (1924): P. O. Box 54321, Los Angeles, Calif. 90054. Fraternity. *Alphadelity*. Membership: 6,250 in 18 college chapters and 11 alumni associations.

Delta Epsilon Sigma (1939): Loras College, Dubuque, Ia. 52001. National scholastic honor society for students, faculty and alumni of Catholic colleges and universities. Membership: 20,105 in 100 chapters. Secretary, Rev. Dr. Neil W. Tobin.

Kappa Gamma Pi (1926): A national Catholic college women's honor society for graduates who, in addition to academic excellence, have shown outstanding leadership in extracurricular activities. *Kappa Gamma Pi News*,

quarterly. Membership: approximately 16,000 in 123 colleges; 40 alumnae chapters in metropolitan areas. National Moderator, Rev. Cyril F. Meyer, C.M., St. John's Univ., Jamaica, N.Y. 11432. President, Dr. Sally Ann Vonderbrink, 5747 Colerain Ave., Cincinnati, O. 45239.

Phi Kappa Theta (1959): 332 Main St., Worcester, Mass. 01608. National collegiate fraternity with a Catholic heritage. Continuation of Phi Kappa Fraternity, founded at Brown Univ. in 1889, and Theta Kappa Phi Fraternity, founded at Lehigh Univ. in 1919. *The Temple Magazine* quarterly, and newsletter, *The Sun*. Membership: 4,000 undergraduate and 24,000 alumni in 75 collegiate and 25 alumni chapters. President, Rev. J. Raymond Favret. Executive Director, Robert L. Wilcox.

Youth Division, USCC

The Division of Youth Activities of the United States Catholic Conference, established in 1940, is a coordinating and service agency for Catholic youth work throughout the country. The Rev. Msgr. Thomas J. Leonard of Philadelphia is director of the division.

The organization within the division is the National CYO Federation, which serves diocesan organizations.

The Division of Youth Activities maintains liaison with the US Youth Council, the World Assembly of Youth, the World Federation of Catholic Youth, and other groups.

The division has offices at 1312 Massachusetts Ave. N.W., Washington, D.C. 20005.

YOUTH TALKS

In January, 1974, Holy Name societies began marking the 700th anniversary of the organization's founding with a membership drive geared especially to attract the participation of youth.

"Youth Talks to Adults," a seminar program run by parish groups, was the vehicle adopted to enlist the interest of young men in the society and its activities.

The program was designed around a panel of seven or eight teen-agers from different cultures and backgrounds giving short presentations and discussing questions on such topics as communicating with parents, the legalization of marijuana, the Church and race relations, vocations and Catholic schools.

In addition to the youth membership drive during the anniversary year, the organization planned work to reanimate parish societies and promote more spiritual and social programs.

Cardinal John J. Krol said in a letter to Holy Name men that the Church and the nation "have a great need for men who conduct their lives in fidelity to the spirit of this ancient lay confraternity."

ASSOCIATIONS, MOVEMENTS, SOCIETIES IN THE U.S.

(Principal source: Almanac survey.)
See Index for other associations, movements and societies covered elsewhere.

A

Academy of American Franciscan History (1944), Box 34440, Washington, D.C. 20034. Dir., Rev. Antonine Tibesar, O.F.M.

Academy of California Church History (1946), P.O. Box 1668, Fresno, Calif. 93717. Pres., Msgr. James Culleton.

Albertus Magnus Guild (1953). Society of Catholic scientists. Pres., Rev. William D. Sullivan, S.J., Boston College, Chestnut Hill, Mass. 02167.

American Benedictine Academy (1947), 2nd and Division Sts., Atchison, Kans. 66002. Scholarly Benedictine society; *The American Benedictine Review,* edited by Timothy Fry, O.S.B.

American Catholic Correctional Chaplains Association (1952), 275 in 475 institutions. Pres., Rev. John Foley, Massachusetts Correctional Institution, Box 100, S. Walpole, Mass. 02032.

American Catholic Historical Association (1919), The Catholic University of America, Washington, D.C. 20017. *The Catholic Historical Review,* quarterly. Pres., Rev. Eric W. Cochrane (1974), Sec., Rev. Robert Trisco.

American Catholic Philosophical Association (1926), Catholic University of America, Washington, D.C. 20017; 1,600. *New Scholasticism,* quarterly, *Proceedings,* annually. Pres., Jude P. Dougherty, Nat. Sec., George F. McLean, O.M.I.

American Committee on Italian Migration (1952), 9 E. 35th St., New York, N.Y. 10016; 32,000. *ACIM Dispatch,* 4 times a year. Sec., Rev. Joseph A. Cogo, C.S.

American Slovenian Catholic Union (KSKJ) (1894), 351-353 N. Chicago St., Joliet, Ill. 60431; 45,000. *Glasilo,* weekly. Sup. Sec., Robert L. Kosmerl.

Apostleship of Prayer (1849-France; 1861-US): 114 E. 13th St., New York, N.Y. 10003. *Monthly Leaflet,* 1,400,000. Promotes Daily Offering and Sacred Heart devotion.

Apostolate of Christian Action, P.O. Box 24, Fresno, Calif. 93707. *Divine Love,* quarterly. Pres., Stephen Oraze.

Archconfraternity of Christian Mothers (Christian Mothers) (1881), 220 37th St., Pittsburgh, Pa. 15201; over 3,400 branches. Monthly newsletter and quarterly bulletin. Dir. Gen., Very Rev. Bertin Roll, O.F.M. Cap.

Archconfraternity of Our Lady of Perpetual Help and St. Alphonsus (1871), 526 59th St., Brooklyn, N.Y. 11220. 1,250 branches.

Archconfraternity of Perpetual Adoration (1893), St. John's Abbey, Collegeville, Minn. 56321. Dir. Gen., Rt. Rev. John Eidenschink, O.S.B.

Archconfraternity of the Holy Ghost (1912), Holy Ghost Preparatory School, Cornwells Heights, Pa. 19020 (US headquarters). Nat. Dir., Very Rev. Henry J. Brown, C.S.Sp.

Association for Social Economics (formerly the Catholic Economic Association) (1941), De Paul University, 2323 N. Seminary Ave., Chicago, Ill. 60614; 1,000. *Review of Social Economy,* semiannually. Pres. Joseph McGuire.

Association for the Sociology of Religion (formerly the American Catholic Sociological Society) (1938), Loyola Marymount University, Los Angeles, Calif. 90045. *Sociological Analysis,* quarterly. Exec. Sec., Dr. Loretta Morris.

Association of Catholic Trade Unionists (1937), 58 Washington Square South, New York, N.Y. 10012. Exec. Sec., John C. Donohue.

Association of Marian Helpers (1946), Stockbridge, Mass. 01262; 525,000, mostly in U.S. *The Marian Helpers Bulletin,* quarterly.

Association of Romanian Catholics of America (1948), 4309 Olcott Ave., E. Chicago, Ind. 46312.

B

Blue Army of Our Lady of Fatima (1946), Ave Maria Institute, Washington, N.J. 07882; world-wide membership. *Soul,* bimonthly. Pres., Bishop Joao Pereira Venancio of Leiria, Portugal.

C

Canon Law Society of America (1939), 134 Farmington Ave., Hartford, Conn. 06105. To further research and study in canon law; 1,400. Pres., Rev. Donald B. Heintschel.

Catholic Accountants Guild of the Diocese of Brooklyn (1947), 611 Eighth Ave., Brooklyn, N.Y. 11211; 125. Mod., Rev. Msgr. Thomas G. Hagerty. Other similar guilds have been established in a number of cities.

Catholic Aid Association (1878), 49 W. Ninth St., St. Paul, Minn. 55102; 73,000. *Catholic Aid News,* monthly. Fraternal life insurance society. Pres., F. L. Spanner.

Catholic Alliance for Communications (formerly Catholic Institute of the Press, 1944), 1011 First Ave., New York, N.Y. 10022. To foster Christian principles and action among working members of the communications fields. Pres., Thomas A. Brennan.

Catholic Alumni Clubs International (1957), To advance social, cultural and spiritual well-being of members. Membership limited to single Catholics with professional education; 7,000 in 50 clubs in U.S. and Canada. International Pres., R.S. Miller, Jr., 7052 Vernon Ave., St. Louis, Mo. 63130.

Catholic Apostolate of Radio, Television and Advertising (1954), 1011 First Ave., New

York, N.Y. 10022; 1,700 in New York City. Pres., Anthony Cervini.

Catholic Art Association (1937), Box 113, Rensselaerville, N.Y. 12147; 800. Pres., Rev. Thomas W. Phelan.

Catholic Audio-Visual Educators Association (CAVE) (1953), Pres., Rev. Joseph Breslin, Cardinal O'Hara High School, Eagle and Spoul Rds., Springfield, Pa. 19064.

Catholic Aviation League of Our Lady of Loreto (1949), O'Hare International Airport, P.O. Box 66123, Chicago, Ill. 60666. Pres., Arthur Fennell.

Catholic Bible Society of America, Inc. (1957), P.O. Box 2296, Dallas, Tex. 75221. Place Bibles in hospitals of Diocese of Dallas and elsewhere. Pres. Mrs. James S. Adams.

Catholic Biblical Association of America (1936), Catholic University of America, Washington, D.C. 20017; 764. *The Catholic Biblical Quarterly.* Pres., Rev. John E. Huesman, S.J.

Catholic Big Brothers, Inc. (of Archdiocese of New York) (1918), 1011 First Ave., New York, N.Y. 10022; Newsletter, quarterly. To provide opportunities for male identification to fatherless boys, 8-15 years of age, through services of qualified adult male volunteers.

Catholic Big Sisters, Inc., (of the Archdiocese of New York), 135 E. 22nd St., New York, N.Y. 10010. Voluntary organization providing adjunctive services to Family Court, for girls up to 16 and boys up to 10 years of age. Dir., Hortense Baffa.

Catholic Business Education Association (1945); 2,001. Pres., Sister Mary Matthew McCloskey, R.S.M., Box 1169, Vicksburg, Miss. 39180.

Catholic Commission on Intellectual and Cultural Affairs (CCICA) (1946), 620 Michigan Ave. N.E., Washington, D.C. 20017; 325. Exec. Dir., Rev. William J. Rooney.

Catholic Council on Working Life, 1307 S. Wabash Ave., Chicago, Ill. 60605. Pres., Martin Burns.

Catholic Daughters of America (1903), 10 W. 71st St., New York, N.Y. 10023; over 200,000. *Share Magazine.* Nat. Regent, Mrs. Winifred L. Trabeaux.

Catholic Evidence Guild (1918, in England; 1931, in US), c/o 127 W. 31st St., New York, N.Y. 10001. Lay movement for spread of Catholic truth by means of outdoor speaking.

Catholic Family Life Insurance (1868), 1572 E. Capitol Dr., Milwaukee, Wis. 53211; 43,000. *The Family Friend,* quarterly. Pres., David L. Springob.

Catholic Guardian Society (1913), 1011 First Ave., New York, N.Y. 10022. Exec. Dir., James P. O'Neill.

Catholic Home Bureau for Dependent Children (1898), 1011 First Ave., New York, N.Y. 10022. Exec. Dir., Sr. M. Una McCormack.

Catholic Interracial Council of New York, Inc. (1934), 55 Liberty St., New York, N.Y. 10005. *Interracial Review,* quarterly. Pres.,

Robert F. Wagner, Exec. Dir., John J. Garra.

Catholic Interracial Councils: See National Catholic Conference for Interracial Justice.

Catholic Knights of America (1877), 217 E. 8th St., Cincinnati, O. 45202; 19,560. *Catholic Knights of America Journal,* monthly. Fraternal insurance society.

Catholic Knights of St. George (1881), 709 Brighton Rd., Pittsburgh, Pa. 15233; 67,000. *Knight of St. George,* monthly. Fraternal insurance society. Pres., Joseph J. Miller.

Catholic Kolping Society (1923), 125 N. Stratton La., Mt. Prospect, Ill. 60056; 2,180. *Kolping Banner,* monthly. Fraternal society.

Catholic Lawyers' Guild. Organization usually on a diocesan basis, under different titles.

Catholic League (1943), 1200 N. Ashland Ave., Chicago, Ill. 60622. Exec. Dir., Most Rev. Alfred Abramowicz.

Catholic Library Association (1921), 461 W. Lancaster Avenue, Haverford, Pa., 19041; 4,000. *Catholic Library World,* monthly (Sept.-April), bimonthly (May-June, July-Aug.); *Catholic Periodical and Literature Index.* Pres., Dr. Mary-Jo Di Muccio, Exec. Dir., Matthew R. Wilt.

Catholic Near East Welfare Association (Near East Missions) (1926), 1011 First Ave., New York, N.Y. 10022. *Near East Missions,* weekly column in 70 diocesan newspapers. Aids missionary activity in 18 countries (under jurisdiction of the Sacred Congregation for the Oriental Church) in Europe, Africa and Asia, including the Holy Land. Nat. Sec., Rev. Msgr. John G. Nolan.

Catholic Negro-American Mission Board (1907), 335 Broadway, Room 1102, New York, N.Y. 10013; 15,000. *Educating in Faith,* monthly. Dir., Rev. Benjamin M. Horton, S.S.J.

Catholic One Parent Organization (COPO) (1961), 39 Lackawanna Pl., Bloomfield, N.J. 07003. To give widows and widowers an opportunity to meet others in the same situation, blending social and spiritual programs. Moderator, Rev. Joseph M. Doyle.

Catholic Order of Foresters (1883), 305 W. Madison St., Chicago, Ill. 60606; 178,634 in 28 states and Canada. *The Catholic Forester,* bimonthly. Fraternal and insurance society. High Chief Ranger, Louis E. Caron.

Catholic Pamphlet Society (1938), 2171 Fillmore Ave., Buffalo, N.Y. 14214. Sec., Rev. Msgr. Eugene H. Selbert.

Catholic Peace Fellowship (1964), North Broadway, Upper Nyack, N.Y. 10960; 6,500, *CPF Bulletin.* Peace education and action, development of the pacifist tradition within the Catholic Church. Nat. Sec., Thomas C. Cornell.

Catholic Press Association of the US, Inc. (1911), 432 Park Ave. S., New York, N.Y. 10016; 378. *The Catholic Journalist* bimonthly; *Catholic Press Directory,* annually. Pres., John F. Fink, Exec. Dir., James A. Doyle.

Catholic Renascence Society (1940), c/o Exec. Sec., Sister Celestine Cepress, Viterbo College, La Crosse, Wis. 54601. *Renascence,* quarterly.

Catholic School Press Association (1931), 1135 W. Kilbourn Ave., Milwaukee, Wis. 53233. *Catholic School Editor,* quarterly. Dir., Warren G. Bovee.

Catholic Theological Society of America (1946), Office of Secretary, St. Mary of the Lake Seminary, Mundelein, Ill. 60060; 1,104; *Proceedings* annually. Pres., Bro. Luke Salm, F.S.C. (1974-1975).

Catholic Traditionalist Movement (1964), 210 Maple Ave., Waterbury, N.Y. 11590.

Catholic Truth Society (1922), 2816 E. Burnside St., Portland, Ore. 97214; Exec. Dir., Gorman Hogan.

Catholic Union of the Sick in America, Inc. (CUSA) (1947), 184 E. 76th St., New York, N.Y. 10021; 1,200. Admin. Leader, Rev. Joseph La Montagne, S.S.S.

Catholic War Veterans (1935), 2 Massachusetts Ave. N.W., Washington, D.C. 20001; 2,000 posts, *Catholic War Veteran,* bimonthly.

Catholic Worker Movement (1933), 36 E. First St., New York, N.Y. 10003. *The Catholic Worker,* 9 times a year. Lay apostolate founded by Peter Maurin and Dorothy Day; has Houses of Hospitality in 17 U.S. cities and several communal farms in various parts of the country. Promotes pacifism and anarchism in that it is decentralist, and believes in what the popes have termed the principle of subsidiarity, urging decentralization in the school system, community control, and in the economic field credit unions, cooperatives and unions of workers and mutual aid.

Catholic Workman (**Katolicky Delnik**) (1891), New Prague, Minn. 56071; 18,487; *Catholic Workman,* monthly. Fraternal and insurance society. Pres. Rudy G. Faimon.

Catholic Writers' Guild of America (1919), 65 East 89th St., New York, N. Y. 10028; 200. Exec. Secs., Rev. Bernard J. McMahon.

Catholics United for the Faith (1968), 222 North Ave., New Rochelle, N.Y. 10801; 12,000 in 120 chapters in U.S., 5 in Canada and 1 in Rome. Pres., H. Lyman Stebbins.

Central Association of the Miraculous Medal (1915), 475 E. Chelten Ave., Philadelphia, Pa. 19144. *Miraculous Medal,* quarterly. Dir., Rev. Donald L. Doyle, C.M.

Chaplains' Aid Association, Inc. (1917), 1011 First Ave., New York, N.Y. 10022. Pres., Most Rev. Philip J. Furlong.

Christopher Movement (1945), 12 E. 48th St., New York, N. Y. 10017. Without formal organization or meetings, the movement stimulates personal initiative and responsible action in line with Christian principles, particularly in the fields of education, government, industrial relations and communications. Christopher radio and TV programs are broadcast by 4,000 stations; a million and one-quarter copies of *Christopher News Notes* are distributed seven times a year without subscription fee; 401 weekly newspapers carry the syndicated column *What One Person Can Do;* 28 daily newspapers carry the syndicated column *It's Your Life;* over two million copies of 27 Christopher books are in circulation. Dir., Rev. Richard Armstrong, M.M.

Composers' Forum for Catholic Worship, Inc. (1970), P.O. Box 8554, Sugar Creek, Mo. 64054; 1,000. Research center for the creation of new music for the liturgy. Exec. Dir., Robert I. Blanchard.

Confraternity of the Immaculate Conception of Our Lady of Lourdes (1874), Box 561, Notre Dame, Ind. 46556.

Confraternity of the Most Holy Rosary: See Rosary Altar Society.

Convert Movement Our Apostolate (CMOA) (1945), formerly Convert Makers of America, St. Charles Seminary, 209 Flagg Place, Staten Island, N.Y. 10304. *Bulletin* quarterly. To train and assist lay persons to discuss and present the Faith to interested persons on a one-to-one basis.

Crusade for a More Fruitful Preaching and Hearing of the Word of God, Inc. (1937), Allendale, N.J.; *Voices from the Pew,* 2 times a year for seminarians. Pres., Mrs. Barbara Durbin.

Czech Catholic Union of Texas (K.J.T.) (1889), 214 Colorado St., La Grange, Tex. 78945; 14,855. *Nasinec,* weekly, and *K. J. T. News,* monthly. Fraternal and insurance society. Pres., Cyrill Svrek.

D

Damien-Dutton Society (1944), 214 Commercial Ave., New Brunswick, N.J. 08901; 24,000. *Damien Dutton Call,* quarterly. Provides medicine, rehabilitation and research for conquest of leprosy. Pres., Howard E. Crouch, Dir., Sr. Mary Augustine, S.M.S.M.

Daughters of Isabella (1897), 375 Whitney Ave., New Haven, Conn. 06511; 120,000. Supreme Reg., Mrs. Marie Heyer.

E

Edith Stein Guild, Inc. (1955), Promotes Judaeo-Christian understanding and assists Jewish converts; 860. ESG *Newsletter.* Address, 144-80 Sanford Ave., Flushing, N. Y. 11355.

Enthronement of the Sacred Heart in the Home (1907), 3 Adams St., Fairhaven, Mass. 02719; over 2,000,000. Nat. Dir., Rev. Francis Larkin, SS.CC.

Eucharistic Guard for Nocturnal Adoration (1938), National Center, 800 North Country Club Rd., Tucson, Ariz. 85716. Dir., Rev. James T. Weber.

Eymard League (1948), 194 E. 76 St., New York, N.Y. 10021; approximately 26,000. *Eymard League Bulletin,* quarterly. Nat. Dir., Rev. Ralph A. Lavigne, S.S.S.

F

Family Communion Crusade, Inc. (1950), Barre, Mass. 01005. Exec. Dir., Rev. Hector C. Lemieux, S.S.S.

Family Rosary Crusade (1942), and **Crusade for Family Prayer,** 773 Madison Ave., Albany, N.Y. 12208. Dir., Rev. Patrick Peyton, C.S.C.

Federation of Diocesan Liturgical Commissions (1969), Pevely, Mo. 63070. *Federation Notes.* Exec. Dir., Rev. Maur Burbach, O.S.B.

First Catholic Slovak Ladies' Association, USA (1892), 24950 Chagrin Blvd., Beachwood, Ohio 44122; 100,000. *Fraternally Yours,* monthly. Fraternal insurance society. Exec. Sec., Frances L. Mizenko.

First Catholic Slovak Union (Jednota) (1890), 3289 E. 55th St., Cleveland, Ohio 44127; 115,097. *Jednota,* weekly. Exec. Sec., Stephen F. Ungvarsky.

First Friday Clubs (1936). Organized on local basis; about 90 clubs in US, others elsewhere. Objectives are to spread devotion to the Sacred Heart, encourage members to receive Holy Communion on First Fridays and to meet at breakfast, luncheon or dinner for discussions of Catholic interest.

Franciscan Apostolate of the Way of the Cross (1949), 174 Ramsey St., Paterson, N.J. 07501. Stations Crucifix available on request. Dir., Rev. Cassian J. Kirk, O.F.M.

Friendship House (1938), 21 E. Van Buren St., Chicago, Ill. 60605. *Community,* quarterly. Religious-oriented group, lay and clergy, working in human relations and social problems. Nat. Dir., Bill Bianchi.

G

Gabriel Richard Institute, (1949), 2315 Orleans Ave., Detroit, Mich. 48207. Conducts leadership technique courses in 18 dioceses.

Gregorian Institute of America (1942), 7404 S. Mason Ave., Chicago, Ill. 60638. Pres., Edward J. Harris.

Guard of Honor of the Immaculate Heart of Mary (1932), 135 West 31st St., New York, N.Y. 10001. An archconfraternity approved by the Holy See whose members cultivate devotion to the Blessed Virgin Mary, particularly through a daily Guard Hour of Prayer.

Guild of Catholic Lawyers (1928), Empire State Bldg., 350 Fifth Ave., Room 316, New York, N.Y. 10001; 600. Pres., Marion I. Guilfoyle.

Guild of Our Lady of Ransom (1948), 409 W. Broadway (Room No. 5), S. Boston, Mass. 02127. For aid to inmates and former inmates of Massachusetts prisons. Exec. Dir., and Treas., Rev. John J. Foley, Catholic Chaplain, Massachusetts State Prison.

Guild of St. Paul (1937), 601 Hill'n Dale, Lexington, Ky. 40503; 13,542; Nat. Spir. Dir., Rt. Rev. Msgr. Leonard Nienaber; Pres., Robert Parks.

H

Holy Name Society (in US) (1909), 141 E. 65th St., New York, N.Y. 10021; 5,000,000. Promote reverence for and devotion to the Holy Name of Jesus and develop lay apostolate programs in line with renewal aims of the Second Vatican Council, Nat. Dir., Rev. Brendan Larnen, O.P.

Holy Name Society, National Association (1970), 141 E. 65th St., New York, N.Y. 10021. Association of diocesan and parochial Holy Name Societies. Pres., James T. Flanagan.

Hungarian Catholic League of America, Inc. (1945), 30 E. 30th St., New York, N.Y. 10016; local branches in 15 states. *Catholic Hungarian Sunday,* weekly.

I

Illinois Club for Catholic Women (1920), 820 North Michigan, Chicago, Ill. 60611. *Triune-News,* monthly. Pres., Mrs. Lydon Wild.

International Catholic Truth Society (1898); 407 Bergen St., Brooklyn, N.Y. 11217. Propagate and preserve the Faith by free distribution of Catholic literature.

Italian Catholic Federation of California, Central Council (1924), 678 Green St., San Francisco, Calif. 94133; 25,000. *Bollettino,* monthly. Sec., Armand De Martini.

J

John Carroll Society, The. (1951), 1660 K St. N.W.,Washington, D.C. 20006. Sec., Martin J. McNamara, Esq.

Judean Society, Inc. (1966), 1075 Space Park Way No. 336, Mt. View, Calif. 94040; over 700; *The Challenge* To offer divorced Catholic women friendship and self-help activities; to educate concerning rights under canon law; to inform the public regarding the life style of divorced Catholic women. Nat. Dir., Frances A. Miller.

K

Knights of Peter Claver (1909), Claver Bldg., 1821 Orleans Ave., New Orleans, La. 70116; 17,000. *The Claverite,* bimonthly. Fraternal and aid society. Sup. Knight, Ernest Granger, Sr.

Knights of St. John, Supreme Commandery (1886), 1603 S. Bedford Ave., Evansville, Ind. 47713. Sup. Sec., Brig. Gen. Clarence J. Schu.

Knights of St. John, Supreme Ladies' Auxiliary (1900), 831 Emmett St., Schenectady, N.Y. 12307; 20,000. Sup. Sec., Miss Adelaide Mahoney.

Knights of the Immaculate (1917), National Center, 8000 39th Ave., Kenosha, Wis. 53141; canonically established with international headquarters in Rome. A pious association for spiritual renewal, personal and social, under the patronage of the Blessed Virgin Mary.

L

Ladies of Charity in the United States, Association of (1960), 1849 Cass Ave., St. Louis, Mo. 63106; 34,000. International Association founded by St. Vincent de Paul in 1617. Pres., Mrs. Dow King, Jr.

League of St. Dymphna, National Shrine of St. Dymphna, Massillon, Ohio 44646. For persons with mental and nervous disorders. Director, Rev. M. M. Herttna.

Lithuanian Catholic Religious Aid, Inc. (1961), 64-09 56th Rd. Maspeth, N.Y. 11378; 194. To assist the persecuted Church in Lithuania. Pres., Most Rev. Vincent Brizgys.

Lithuanian Roman Catholic Alliance of America (1889), 73 S. Washington St., Wilkes-Barre, Pa. 18701; 158 branches. *Garsas,* monthly. Fraternal insurance organization. Pres., Thomas E. Mack.

Little Flower Mission League (1957), P.O. Box 178, Cottonport, La. 71327. Sponsored by the Brothers of the Holy Eucharist.

Little Flower Society (1923), 11343 S. Michigan Ave., Chicago, Ill. 60628; 40,000, *Little Flower News,* monthly. Nat. Dir., Rev. Quentin Duncan, O. Carm.

Liturgical Conference, The, 1330 Massachusetts Avenue N.W., Washington, D.C. 20005. *Liturgy, Living Worship, Homily Service,* monthlies. Education, research and publication programs for vitalizing and enriching Christian liturgical life, and field service training program. Pres., Elizabeth G. Sullivan.

Loyal Christian Benefit Association (1890), 305 W. 6th St., Erie, Pa. 16512; 56,623. *The Fraternal Leader,* bimonthly. Pres., Miss Bertha M. Leavy.

M

Mariological Society of America (1949), 350. *Marian Studies,* annually. St. Joseph Hospital, 601 N.E. Harbor Blvd., Port Charlotte, Fla. 33950.

Markham Prayer Card Apostolate (Apostolate To Aid the Dying) (1931), Franciscan Sisters of the Poor, 60 Compton Rd., Cincinnati, Ohio 45215. Dir., Rev. Herman H. Kenning.

Melkite Association of North America (1958), 5804 Tanglewood Dr., Bethesda, Md. 20034; 20,000. Promote and stimulate the spiritual and social welfare of Greek Catholic Melkites in America. Pres., Baddia J. Rashid.

Missionary Association of Catholic Women (1916), 1425 N. Prospect Ave., Milwaukee, Wis. 53202. Pres., Mrs. Joseph Gockel.

Missionary Cenacle Apostolate (M.C.A.) (1909), 149 E. 39th St., New York, N.Y. 10016; about 1,000.

Missionary Union of the Clergy in the USA (1936), 366 Fifth Ave., New York, N.Y. 10001; *Worldmission,* quarterly. Nat. Dir., Most Rev. Edward T. O'Meara.

Morality in Media, Inc. (1962), 487 Park Ave., New York, N.Y. 10022; 42,000. Newsletter, 8 times a year. To stop traffic in pornography constitutionally and effectively, and promote principles of love, truth and taste in the media. Pres., Rev. Morton A. Hill, S.J.

N

National Alliance of Czech Catholics (1917), 2636 S. Central Park, Chicago, Ill. 60623; 450 parishes.

National Association of Church Personnel Administrators (1973), Pres., Rev. Daniel Johnson, 149 Church St., Hamden, Conn. 06415.

National Association of Laity (1967), 683 W. 3rd St., Bloomsburg, Pa. 17815; 4,000 in 18 chapters, Pres., Dr. Joseph Skehan.

National Association of Priest Pilots (1964), Pres., Rev. Richard Skriba, 5157 S. California Ave., Chicago, Ill. 60632.

National Catholic Bandmasters' Association (1953), Box 523, Notre Dame University, Notre Dame, Ind. 46556. *The School Musician Magazine.*

National Catholic Cemetery Conference (1949), 710 N. River Rd., Des Plaines, Ill. 60016. *The Catholic Cemetery,* monthly. Pres., Rev. Msgr. Charles Grahmann.

National Catholic Conference for Interracial Justice (1960), 1307 S. Wabash Ave., Chicago, Ill. 69605. *Commitment,* quarterly. Serves 150 Catholic human relations and urban affairs groups; sponsors educational programs on societal problems. Exec. Dir., Rev. James J. Sheehan.

National Catholic Development Conference (1968), 130 E. 40th St., New York, N.Y. 10016. Professional association of organizations and individuals engaged in raising funds for Catholic charitable activities. Pres., Rev. Robert W. Dahlke, S.J., Exec. Dir., George T. Holloway.

National Catholic Guidance Conference (1962), division of American Personnel and Guidance Association, 1607 New Hampshire Ave. N.W., Washington, D.C. 20009. 35 diocesan councils, 73 institutions, 535 individuals. *Counseling and Values,* and *Newsletter,* quarterlies. Pres., James J. Lee, Univ. of Wisconsin, Madison, Wis. 53706.

National Catholic Music Educators Association (1942), 4637 Eastern Ave. N.E., Washington, D.C. 20018; affiliate of NCEA; 4,583. *Musart,* quarterly during school year. Pres., Rev. William A. Volk, C.PP.S., Exec. Dir., Carolyn J. Fraley.

National Catholic Pharmacists Guild of the United States (1962 in US), 300 in US. *The Catholic Pharmacist.* Exec. Dir., John P. Winkelmann, 1012 Surrey Hills Dr., St. Louis, Mo. 63117.

National Catholic Society of Foresters (1891), 59 E. Van Buren St., Chicago, Ill. 60605; 78,411. *National Catholic Forester,* bimonthly. A fraternal insurance society. Pres., Mrs. Lucy Domino.

National Catholic Stewardship Council (1962), 1234 Massachusetts Ave. N.W., Washington, D.C. 20005. To exchange ideas on ways and means of assisting those engaged in promotion of stewardship and support of the Church. Exec. Dir., Rev. Francis A. Novak, C.SS.R.

National Catholic Women's Union (1916), 3835 Westminster Pl., St. Louis, Mo. 63108; 28,000. *The Catholic Woman's Journal*,10 times a year. Auxiliary of the Catholic Central Union of America.

National Center for Church Vocations (1969), 305 Michigan Ave., Detroit, Mich. 48226. Established by National Conference of Catholic Bishops and the Conferences of Major Superiors of men and women to coordinate Church vocations work in the US. Exec. Dir., Rev. Edward J. Baldwin.

National Church Goods Association, 6469 N. Nokomis Ave., Chicago, Ill. 60646. Pres., David R. Malhame.

National Clergy Conference on Alcoholism, 2749 N. Marshfield Ave., Chicago, Ill. 60614. Exec. Dir., Rev. John P. Cunningham.

National Federation of Catholic Physicians' Guilds (1927), 2825 N. Mayfair Rd., Milwaukee, Wis. 53222; 6,700 in 88 autonomous guilds in US and Canada, *Linacre Quarterly.* Pres., John J. Brennan, M.D.

National Federation of Laymen, Inc. (1968), P.O. Box 56058, Chicago, Ill. 60656; representatives in 31 regions of the U.S. Chairman, Edward J. Kraus.

National Organization for Continuing Education of Roman Catholic Clergy, Inc. (1973). Membership, 73 dioceses, 33 religious communities. Pres., Rev. Joseph H. Voor, 2000 Norris Pl., Louisville, Ky. 40205.

Nocturnal Adoration Society of the United States (1882), 194 E. 76th St., New York, N. Y. 10021; 38,000 in 555 units. Nat. Dir., Rev. Hector C. Lemieux, S.S.S.

O

Order of the Alhambra, International (1904), 4200 Leeds Ave., Baltimore, Md. 21229. 11,000 in US and Canada. Fraternal society dedicated to assisting retarded children. Supreme Commander, Anthony Comorat.

P

Paulist League (1924), 415 W. 59th St., New York, N.Y. 10019; 24,300. Dir., Rev. Edward J. Gorry, C.S.P.

Philangeli (Friends of the Angels) (1949 in England; 1956 in U.S.), 1212 E. Euclid St., Arlington Heights, Ill. 60004; approximately 500,000 in 60 countries. To encourage devotion to the angels. Nat. Dir., Rev. Emmett M. Walsh, C.S.V.

Pious Union of Prayer (1898), St. Joseph's Home, P.O. Box 288, Jersey City, N.J. 07303; 90,000.*Orphans' Messenger and Advocate of the Blind,* quarterly.

Pious Union of the Holy Spirit (1900), 30 Gedney Park Dr., White Plains, N.Y. 10605. Pres., Rev. Jerome McHugh, O.F.M. Cap.

Pontifical Mission for Palestine (1949), c/o Catholic Near East Welfare Association, 1011 First Ave., New York, N.Y. 10022. Field offices in Beirut, Lebanon, Jerusalem and Amman, Jordan. The papal relief agency for 1.5 million Palestinian refugees in Lebanon, Syria, Jordan, and the Gaza Strip. Distributes food, clothing, other essentials; maintains medical clinics, orphanages, libraries, refugee camp schools and chapels, the Pontifical Mission Center for the Blind (Gaza), the Pontifical Mission Libraries (Jerusalem, Bethlehem, Nazareth), the Epheta Institute for Deaf-Mutes (Bethlehem). Pres., Rev. Msgr. John G. Nolan.

Priests' Eucharistic League (1887), 194 E. 76th St., New York, N.Y. 10021; 17,500. *Emmanuel,* monthly. Nat. Dir., Rev. Raymond A. Tartre, S.S.S.

Pro Maria Committee (1952), 22 Second Ave., Lowell, Mass. 01854. Promote devotion to Our Lady of Beauraing (See Index). Dir., Rev. J. Debergh, O.M.I.

The Providence Association of the Ukrainian Catholics in America (Ukrainian Catholic Fraternal Benefit Society) (1912), 817 N. Franklin St., Philadelphia, Pa. 19123. *America* (Ukrainian-English).

R

Raskob Foundation for Catholic Activities, Inc. (1945), 1205 Hotel Du Pont, Wilmington, Del. 19898. Exec. Vice Pres., Gerard S. Garey.

Reparation Society of the Immaculate Heart of Mary, Inc. (1946), 100 E. 20th St., Baltimore, Md. 21218. *Fatima Findings,* monthly. Dir. Rev. John Ryan, S.J.

Rosary Altar Society (Confraternity of the Most Holy Rosary) (1891, in US), 141 E. 65th St., New York, N. Y. 10021; 3,000,000. *The Rosary Bulletin,* monthly. Prov. Dir., Rev. Brendan Larnen, O.P.

Rosary League (1901), Franciscan Sisters of the Atonement, Graymoor, Garrison, N.Y. 10524. 1,600. *Sparks,* quarterly.

S

Sacred Heart Auto League, Walls, Miss. 38680; 400,000. To promote careful, prayerful driving. Dir., Rev. Gregory Bezy, S.C.J.

St. Ansgar's Scandinavian Catholic League (1910), 40 W. 13th St., New York, N.Y. 10011; 2,000. *St. Ansgar's Bulletin,* annually.

St. Anthony's Guild (1924), Paterson, N.J. 07509. *Anthonian,* quarterly. Dir., Rev. Salvator Fink, O.F.M.

St. Apollonia Guild (1958), 2186 Draper Ave., St. Paul, Minn. 55113. For Catholic dentists. Pres., Dr. Terrance L. Tri.

St. Jude League (1928), 221 W. Madison St., Chicago, Ill. 60606. *St. Jude Journal,* bimonthly. Dir., Rev. Mark J. Brummel, C.M.F.

St. Margaret of Scotland Guild, Inc. (1938), Graymoor, Garrison, N.Y. 10524; 2,200. Moderator, Bro. Gerard Hand, S.A.

St. Martin de Porres Guild (1936), 141 E. 65th St., New York, N.Y. 10021. Gen. Dir., Rev. Timothy Shea, O.P.

St. Thomas Aquinas Foundation of the Dominican Fathers of the United States (STAF), 141 E. 65th St., New York, N.Y. 10021. Nat. Mod., Very Rev. Thomas H. McBrien, O.P.

Seraphic Society for Vocations (1944), St. Joseph Franciscan Seminary, P.O. Box 245, Westmont, Ill. 60559. Dir., Bro. Quentin Holmes, O.F.M.

Serra International (1938), 22 W. Monroe St., Chicago, Ill. 60603; 12,500 members in 360 clubs in more than 27 countries. *Serran,* bimonthly. Fosters vocations to the priesthood, and religious life, trains Catholic lay leadership. Formally aggregated to the Pontifical Society for Priestly Vocations, 1951. Pres., Edward B. Dillon, Jr.

Slovak Catholic Federation of America (1911), 2430 California Ave., Pittsburgh, Pa. 15212; 300,000. *Good Shepherd (Dobry Pastier)* monthly. The following fraternal organizations hold continuous membership: First Catholic Slovak Union, First Catholic Slovak Ladies Assn.; Slovak Catholic Sokol; Penna. Slovak Catholic Union; Ladies Penna. Slovak Catholic Union; First Slovak Wreath of the Free Eagle.

Slovak Catholic Sokol (1905), 205 Madison St., Passaic, N.J. 07055; 51,965. *Katolicky Sokol,* weekly; *Priatel Dietok,* monthly.

Society for the Propagation of the Faith (1822), 366 Fifth Ave., New York, N.Y. 10001; 3,000,000 in 156 dioceses in US. *Mission,* bimonthly; *Worldmission,* quarterly. Is subject to direction of Sacred Congregation for the Propagation of the Faith. Nat. Dir., Most Rev. Edward T. O'Meara.

Society of Retired Catholic Persons (1962), 1100 W. Wells St., Milwaukee Wis. 53233; 5,000. Organization for economic advantage, social activities and apostolic work for retired persons. Pres., Merlin Victora.

Society of St. Peter the Apostle for Native Clergy (1898), 366 Fifth Ave., New York, N.Y. 10001; 156 branches. Organized as the Pope's own mission aid society for the maintenance of diocesan seminaries and diocesan seminarians in mission countries.

Spiritual Life Institute of America (1961), Star Route One, Sedona, Arizona 86336. *Desert Call,* seasonal. An ecumenical movement to foster the contemplative spirit in America. Founder, Rev. William McNamara, O.C.D. Second foundation: Primitive Wilderness Hermitage, Kemptville, Yarmouth Co., Nova Scotia, Canada.

T

Te Deum International (1940), 611 S. 6th

St., Springfield, Ill. 62701; 27 chapters. For Catholic adult education on current and international affairs.

Theresians of America (1961), 5326 E. Pershing Ave., Scottsdale, Ariz. 85254; 6,000. Spiritual, intellectual and apostolic organization concerned with the vocation to Christian womanhood in both religious and lay states. Nat. Dir. and founder, Very Rev. Msgr. Elwood C. Voss.

U

Una Voce in the United States (1967), P.O. Box 446, Grand Central Station, New York, N.Y. 10017; 5,000. Pres., John A. McManemin.

United Societies of U.S.A. (1903), 613 Sinclair St., McKeesport, Pa. 15132; 50,000 in 169 lodges in 7 states. *Unity,* quarterly newsletter. Pres., Nicholas M. Kish.

United States Catholic Historical Society (1885), Office of Executive Secretary, St. Joseph's Seminary, Yonkers, N.Y. 10704; 360. *Historical Records and Studies* and a monograph series, annually. Pres., J. G. E. Hopkins.

V

Vernacular Society (1946), P.O. Box 207, Passaic, N.J. 07055; 500. *Vernacular,* newsletter. Pres., Reinhold Kissner.

W-Y

Western Catholic Union (1877), W.C.U. Bldg., 506-510 Maine St., Quincy, Ill. 62301; 27,282 in 126 branches in 9 states. *Western Catholic Union Record,* monthly.

William J: Kerby Foundation (1941), The Catholic University of America, Washington, D.C. 20017. Pres., Charles Cronin.

Wisconsin Council of Catholic Women (1915), 810 Farwell Dr., Madison, Wis. 53704. Pres., Mrs. Patrick McCormick.

Word of God Institute (1972), 487 Michigan Ave. N.E., Washington, D.C. 20017. For renewed biblical preaching. Dir., Rev. John Burke, O.P.

Young Ladies' Institute (1887), 50 Oak St., San Francisco, Calif. 94102. Grand Sec,, Mrs. Valda Britschgi.

Young Men's Institute (1883), 50 Oak St., San Francisco, Calif. 94102; 4,500. *Institute Journal,* bimonthly. Grand Sec., B. G. Merdinger.

Knights of Columbus

The Knights of Columbus, which originated as a fraternal benefit society of Catholic men, was founded by Father Michael J. McGivney and chartered by the General Assembly of Connecticut Mar. 29, 1882.

In line with their general purpose to be of service to the Church, the Knights are active in many apostolic works and community programs.

Since January, 1947, the Knights have

sponsored a program of Catholic advertising in secular publications with national circulation. This has brought some 6 million inquiries and led to more than 600,000 enrollments in courses in the Catholic faith. In recent years the Knights have broadened this program to include other media for spreading Christian and religious ideals. As a result substantial contributions have been made to support the work of the John LaFarge Institute in New York, the Catholic Communications Foundation in New York, and the Center for Applied Research in the Apostolate (CARA) in Washington.

K. of C. scholarship funds — two at the Catholic University of America, another for disbursement at other Catholic colleges in the US, one at Canadian colleges and another for the Philippines — have provided college educations for more than 1,200 students since 1914.

The order promotes youth activity through sponsorship of the Columbian Squires and through cooperation with other organized youth groups.

K. of C. membership, as of Mar. 31, 1974, was 1,174,887 in 5,858 councils in the U.S., Canada, the Philippines, Cuba, Mexico, Puerto Rico, Panama, Guatemala, Guam and the Virgin Islands. Insurance assets, as of Dec. 31, 1973, amounted to $514,535,122 and total insurance in force, $2,430,755,438.

The Knights' publication, *Columbia,* has the greatest circulation (almost 1.2 million) of any Catholic monthly in the US.

John W. McDevitt is Supreme Knight. Virgil C. Dechant is Supreme Secretary.

International headquarters are located at One Columbus Plaza, New Haven, Conn. 06507.

BLACK CATHOLICS

The National Office for Black Catholics, organized in August, 1970, is a central agency with the general purposes of promoting participation by black Catholics in the Church and of making more effective the apostolate of the Church in the black community. Its executive director is Brother Joseph Davis, S.M. Its liaison officer with the National Conference of Catholic Bishops and the U.S. Catholic Conference is Auxiliary Bishop Joseph A. McNicholas of St. Louis. Offices are located at 734 15th St. N.W., Washington, D.C. 20005.

The NOBC has affiliates in various cities throughout the country and a participating membership of approximately 3,000.

Three of its member bodies are:
• The National Black Catholic Clergy Caucus, formed at a charter meeting in April, 1968, in Detroit. Its president, elected in January, 1973, is Auxiliary Bishop Joseph Howze of Natchez-Jackson. Brother Joseph C. Hager, S.M., is the executive director.
• The National Black Catholic Sisters'

Conference (see separate entry).
• The National Black Catholic Lay Caucus.

At a six-state regional conference of the National Black Catholic Lay Caucus held in San Diego in May, 1974, executive director James McNeil called on black Catholics to "present a revolutionary Christian witness to the poor and the oppressed," and to "be an agent of education for change."

Caucus president John Guillory said that black Catholics are "committed to the black community and to change for a better life." He also spoke of their concern for the survival of the Church in their communities.

CATHOLIC RIGHTS LEAGUE

A group of Catholics concerned about anti-Catholic bias and bigotry in the United States announced in May, 1973, the formation of the Catholic League for Religious and Civil Rights.

Patterned after the Jewish Anti-Defamation League and the National Association for the Advancement of Colored People, its stated purpose is to promote and champion the rights of Catholics and of other religious minorities expressed in the Declaration of Independence and the Bill of Rights; and to adopt programs and procedures to correct discriminatory practices against Catholics and others because of their religion."

Father Kenneth Baker, S.J., a member of the board of directors, said its activities would be:
• "public exposure of anti-Catholicism," to be carried on "by way of information and education of the public about the facts;
• "negotiating with offenders (privately, as much as possible) and trying to get them to cease and desist from anti-Catholic prejudices;
• "litigation, as a last resort, against inveterate and notorious offenders."

League founders made it clear that the organization has no official standing with the Church. They said its existence, operations and success would depend entirely on the funding and supporting activity of its membership — which was open to persons of all faiths but was expected to be mostly Catholic.

The American Civil Liberties Union, Americans United for Separation of Church and State, other organizations, "judicial anti-Catholicism," and offensive segments of the communications and entertainment media were expected to be targets of league action.

The league publishes *The Catholic League Newsletter.*

Father Virgil G. Blum, S.J., professor of political science at Marquette University, is president of the league. The executive director is Stuart D. Hubbell, an attorney, of Traverse City, Mich.

The league's mailing address is 714 N. 27th St., Milwaukee, Wisc. 53233.

Communications

Following are excerpts from a 23,000-word Pastoral Instruction on the Mass Media written by the Pontifical Commission for Social Communications and made public June 3, 1971. The most extensive document on the subject ever issued by the Vatican, it supplements and applies the contents of the much shorter Decree on the Instruments of Social Communication promulgated by the Second Vatican Council Dec. 4, 1963. The Latin title of the Instruction is Communio et Progressio ("Unity and Advancement"), from its first two words.

[These excerpts are from the text circulated by NC News Service.]

Purpose of the Media; "The unity and advancement of men living in society: these are the chief aims of social communication and of all the means it uses. These means include the press, the cinema, radio and television."

"In the Christian faith, the unity and brotherhood of man are the chief aims of all communication."

The Common Good: "The total output of the media in any given area should be judged by the contribution it makes to the common good."

Requirements of Communication: "Every communication must comply with certain essential requirements, and these are sincerity, honesty and truthfulness. Good intentions and a clear conscience do not thereby make a communication sound and reliable. A communication must state the truth. It must accurately reflect the situation with all its implications. The moral worth and validity of any communication does not lie solely in its theme or intellectual content. The way in which it is presented, the way in which it is spoken and treated, and even the audience for which it is designed — all these factors must be taken into account."

Every Man a Partner: "The torrent of information and opinion pouring through (the) channels (of communication) makes every man a partner in the business of the human race. This interchange creates the proper conditions for that mutual and sympathetic understanding which leads to universal progress."

Questions: "How can we ensure that (the) swift and haphazard and endless stream of news is properly evaluated and understood? The media are bound to seek a mass audience, and so they often adopt a neutral stance in order to avoid giving offense to any section of their audience. How, in a society that is committed to the rights of dissent, is the distinction between right and wrong, true and false, to be made?"

"How, in the face of competition to capture a large popular audience, are the media to be prevented from appealing to and inflaming the less admirable tendencies in human nature? How can one avoid the concentration of the power to communicate in too few hands, so that any real dialogue is killed? How can one avoid allowing communications made indirectly and through machinery to weaken direct human contact — especially when these communications take the form of pictures and images? When the media invite men to escape into fantasy, what can be done to bring them back to present reality? How can one stop the media from encouraging mental idleness and passivity? And how can one be certain that the incessant appeal to emotion does not sap reason?"

Public Opinion: "The means of social communication are a public forum where every man may exchange ideas. The public expression and the confrontation of different opinions that occur within this dialogue influence and enrich the development of society and further its progress."

"Public opinion is an essential expression of human nature organized in society."

"If public opinion is to emerge in the proper manner, it is absolutely essential that there be freedom to express ideas and attitudes. In accordance with the express teaching of the Second Vatican Council, it is necessary to declare unequivocally that freedom of speech for individuals and groups must be permitted so long as the common good and public morality are not endangered."

Propaganda: "The process of promoting — in what is sometimes referred to as a 'propaganda campaign' — with a view to influencing public opinion is justified only when it serves the truth, promotes causes that are in the public interest, and its objectives and methods accord with the dignity of man."

Weight of Opinions: "Not every opinion that is given publicity should be taken as a true expression of that public opinion which is held by a significant number of people. A number of differing opinions can flourish at the same time in the same area, although one usually has a greater following than the others. The opinion of the majority, however, is not necessarily the best or the closest to the truth."

"Views openly and commonly expressed which reflect the aspirations of the people should always be carefully considered. This is especially binding on those in authority, whether civil or religious."

Right To Be Informed and To Inform: "If public opinion is to be formed in a proper manner, it is necessary that, right from the start, the public be given free access both to the sources and channels of information, and be allowed freedom to express its own views. Freedom of opinion and the right to be informed go hand in hand."

"With the right to be informed goes the

duty to seek information. Information does not simply occur; it has to be sought."

"The right to information is not merely the prerogative of the individual; it is essential to the public interest."

Safety of Correspondents: "The safety of (news) correspondents should be ensured in every possible way because of the service they render to man's right to know about what is happening. This is particularly true in the case of wars, which involve and concern the whole human race. The Church utterly condemns the use of violence against newsmen or against anyone in any way involved in the passing on of news."

Privacy and secrecy: "The right to information is not limitless. It has to be reconciled with other existing rights. There is the right of privacy which protects the private life of families and individuals. There is the right of secrecy which obtains if necessity or professional duty or the common good itself requires it. Indeed, whenever public good is at stake, discretion and discrimination and careful judgment should be used in the preparation of news."

Advertising: Advertising must respect the truth, taking into account accepted advertising conventions."

"If harmful or utterly useless goods are touted to the public, if false assertions are made about goods for sale, if less admirable human tendencies are exploited, those responsible for such advertising harm society and forfeit their good name and credibility. More than this, unremitting pressure to buy articles of luxury can arouse false wants that hurt both individuals and families by making them ignore what they really need. And those forms of advertising which, without shame, exploit the sexual instincts simply to make money, or which seek to penetrate into the subconscious recesses of the mind in a way that threatens the freedom of the individual, these forms of advertising must be shunned. It is desirable that advertisers make definite rules for themselves lest their sales methods affront human dignity or harm the community."

"Serious harm can be done (to developing countries) if advertising and commercial pressure become so irresponsible that communities seeking to rise from poverty to a reasonable standard of living are persuaded to seek this progress by satisfying wants that have been created artificially."

News Reporting: "Not only must news reporting keep to the facts and bear down on the most important ones, but the meaning of what is reported should be brought out by explanation."

Censorship: "Censorship should be used only in the very last extremity."

Communication in the Church: "The Church looks for ways of multiplying and strengthening the bonds of union between her members. For this reason, communication and dialogue among Catholics are indispensable. The Church lives her life in the midst of the whole community of man. She must therefore maintain contacts and lines of communication in order to keep a relationship with the whole human race. This is done both by giving information and by listening carefully to public opinion inside and outside the Church. By holding a continuous discussion with the contemporary world, she tries to help in solving the problems that men face at the present time."

Dialogue and Public Opinion: "Since the Church is a living body, she needs public opinion in order to sustain a giving and taking between her members."

"Catholics should be fully aware of the real freedom to speak their minds which stems from a 'feeling for the faith' and from love."

"Those who exercise authority in the Church will take care to ensure that there is responsible exchange of freely held and expressed opinion among the People of God. More, they will set up norms and conditions for this to take place."

Freedom of Expression: "While the individual Catholic follows the magisterium (teaching authority of the Church), he can and should engage in free research so that he may better understand revealed truths or explain them to a society subject to incessant change."

Constructive Dialogue: "Free dialogue within the Church does no injury to her unity and solidarity. It nurtures concord and the meeting of minds by permitting the free play of the variations of public opinion. But, in order that this dialogue may go on in the right direction, it is essential that charity be in command even when there are differing views. Everyone in this dialogue should be animated by the desire to serve and to consolidate unity and cooperation. There should be a desire to build, not to destroy. There should be a deep love for the Church and a compelling desire for its unity."

Scientific Investigation and Doctrine: "Distinction must be borne in mind between, on the one hand, the area that is devoted to scientific investigation and, on the other, the area that concerns the teaching of the faithful. In the former area, experts enjoy the freedom required by their work and are free to communicate to others in books and commentaries the fruits of their research. In the second area, only those doctrines may be attributed to the Church which are declared to be such by her authentic teaching authority. These doctrines, obviously, can be aired in public without fear."

"It sometimes happens, however, because of the very nature of social communication, that new opinions circulating among theologians at times circulate too soon and in the wrong places. Such opinions, which might be confused with the authentic doctrine of the Church, should be examined critically. It must also be remembered that the real significance of such theories is often badly distorted by popularization and by the style of presentation used in the media."

Flow of Information in the Church: "Since the development of public opinion within the Church is essential, individual Catholics have the right to all the information they need to play their active role in the life of the Church."

The normal flow of life and the smooth functioning of government within the Church requires a steady two-way flow of information between the ecclesiastical authorities at all levels and the faithful as individuals and as organized groups. This applies to the whole world. To make this possible, various institutions are required. These might include news agencies, official spokesmen, meeting facilities, pastoral councils, all properly financed."

Attitude on Secrecy: "On those occasions when the affairs of the Church require secrecy, rules normal in civil affairs apply.

"On the other hand, the spiritual riches which are an essential attribute of the Church demand that the news she gives out . . . be distinguished by integrity, truth and openness. When ecclesiastical authorities are unwilling to give information or are unable to do so, then rumor is unloosed; and rumor is not a bearer of the truth but of dangerous half-truths. Secrecy should therefore be restricted to matters that involve the good name of individuals or that touch upon the rights of people, whether singly or collectively."

Church-World Dialogue: "The Church needs to know contemporary reactions to ideas and events, whether they be Catholic or not. The greater the extent to which these means of social communication reflect these reactions, the more they contribute toward this knowledge required by the Church."

"It is the mission of those with responsible positions in the Church to announce without fail or pause the full truth by the means of social communication, so as to give a true picture of the Church and her life. Since the media are often the only channels of information that exist between the Church and the world, a failure to use them amounts to 'burying the talent given by God.' "

Media and the Gospel: "During his life on earth, Christ showed himself to be the perfect Communicator, while the Apostles used what means of communication were available in their time. It is now necessary that the same message be carried by the means of social communication that are available today. Indeed, it would be difficult to suggest that Christ's command was being obeyed unless all the opportunities offered by the . . . media to extend to vast numbers of people the announcement of his Good News were being used."

The Catholic Press: "The Catholic press . . . can be marvelously effective in bringing a knowledge of the Church to the world and a knowledge of the world to the Church. It does this by imparting information and by stimulating those processes by which public opinion is formed. There is, however, no advantage in founding new publications if quantity is achieved at the cost of quality and if the new injure the old."

"That part of the Catholic press which is of general interest published news and opinions and background articles about all the facets and the problems and worries of modern life. This it does in the light of Christian principles. It is the task of the Catholic press to balance, to complete and, if necessary, to correct the news and comments about religion and the Christian life."

Papal statements issued since publication of this document have reiterated the importance of the media for the total development of individuals and whole communities.

PRESS STATISTICS

The *1974 Catholic Press Directory,* published by the Catholic Press Association, reported 434 newspapers and magazines in the United States, Canada and the West Indies, with a total circulation of 22,767,256. The figures reflected an increase in the number of newspapers ($+4$) but a decrease in circulation ($-296,574$); the number of magazines increased ($+5$) as did the circulation ($+258,812$).

Newspapers

United States: 143; circulation, 5,057,957.
  National newspapers: 6; circulation, 641,093.
    (*National Catholic Register,* 89,860; *National Catholic Reporter,* 40,075; *Our Sunday Visitor,* 384,147; *Twin Circle,* 72,288; *The Wanderer,* 46,223; *Priests USA,* 8,500.)
  Diocesan newspapers published locally: 120; circulation, 4,153,185.
  Diocesan newspapers with a *Register* title, 9; circulation, 59,553.
  Diocesan editions of *Our Sunday Visitor:* 6; circulation, 130,717.
  Other-language newspapers, 2; circulation 73,409. (*Jednota,* weekly newspaper of the First Catholic Slovak Union, and *L'Union,* the official quarterly magazine of the Union Saint Jean Baptiste.)
Canada and West Indies: 9; circulation, 148,989.
  National newspaper, Canada, 1 (*Our Sunday Visitor*); circulation, 15,921.
  Diocesan newspapers, Canada, 6; circulation, 110,630.
  Diocesan newspapers, West Indies, 2; circulation, 22,438.

Magazines

United States and Canada: 282; circulation, 17,560,310.

English-language magazines: 253; circulation, 16,996,376.

Other-language magazines: 29; circulation, 563,934.

The magazine with the largest circulation (1,132,659) is *Columbia,* the official organ of the Knights of Columbus.

Among magazines with status in the secu-lar communications field are *America* and *Commonweal.*

The oldest Catholic weekly newspaper in the U.S. is *The Pilot* of Boston, established in 1829 (under a different title).

Our Sunday Visitor, Inc., started publication in April, 1974, of a Spanish-language weekly, *El Visitante Dominical.*

CATHOLIC NEWSPAPERS AND MAGAZINES IN THE U.S.

(Sources: *Catholic Press Directory, 1974;* Almanac survey; NC News Service.)

Abbreviation code: a, annual; bm, bimonthly; m, monthly; q. quarterly; w, weekly.

Newspapers

A-B

Advocate, The, w; 37 Evergreen Pl., E. Orange, N.J. 07018; Newark archdiocese; 49,227.

Alive, m; 400 East Monroe, Phoenix, Ariz. 85004; Phoenix diocese; 10,000.

Anchor, The, w; 410 Highland Ave., Fall River, Mass. 02722; Fall River diocese; 25,586.

Arizona Register, biweekly; 64 W. Ochoa St., Tucson, Ariz. 85701; 17,000.

Beacon, The, w; Box A, Pequannock, N.J. 07440; Paterson diocese; 50,112.

Bishop's Bulletin, bm; 423 W. Duluth Ave., Sioux Falls, S. Dak. 57104; 22,000.

Byzantine Catholic World, w; 3643 Perrysville Ave., Pittsburgh, Pa. 15214; Munhall Byzantine archdiocese; 13,000.

C

Catholic Accent, w; P.O. Box 850, Greensburg, Pa. 15601; Greensburg diocese; 49,587.

Catholic Advance, The, w; 424 N. Broadway, Wichita, Kans. 67202; Wichita diocese; 12,548.

Catholic Banner, w; 119 Broad St., Charleston, S.C. 29401; Charleston diocese; 6,147.

Catholic Bulletin, w; 244 Dayton Ave., St. Paul, Minn. 55102; St. Paul and Minneapolis archdiocese, New Ulm diocese; 57,303.

Catholic Chronicle, w; 1933 Spielbusch Ave., Toledo, O. 43624; Toledo diocese; 44,324.

Catholic Commentator, The, w; P.O. Box 14746, Baton Rouge, La. 70808; Baton Rouge diocese; 37,804.

Catholic Crosswinds, semi-monthly; P.O. Box 194, Pueblo, Colo. 81002; Pueblo diocese; 24,018.

Catholic Exponent, w; 440 Ohio Edison Bldg., Youngstown O. 44503; Youngstown diocese; 42,913.

Catholic Free Press, w; 247 Mill St., Worcester, Mass. 01602; Worcester diocese; 21,920.

Catholic Herald, The, w; 5890 Newman Ct., Sacramento, Calif. 95819; Sacramento diocese; 12,785.

Catholic Herald Citizen, w; P.O. Box 736, Milwaukee, Wis. 53201; Milwaukee archdiocese, Madison diocese; 155,671.

Catholic Herald Citizen — Superior Edition, w; 1512 N. 12th St., Superior, Wis. 54880.

Catholic Hungarian's Sunday, w; 517 S. Belle Vista Ave., Youngstown, O. 44509; 3,450.

Catholic Keys to the News, The, w; P.O. Box 1037, Kansas City, Mo. 64141; Kansas City-St. Joseph diocese; 14,500.

Catholic Light, w; 300 Wyoming Ave., Scranton, Pa. 18503; Scranton diocese; 54,037.

Catholic Messenger, w; 407 Brady St., Davenport, Ia. 52805; Davenport diocese; 27,883.

Catholic Mirror, w; 306 Securities Bldg., Des Moines, Ia. 50309; 18,900.

Catholic Missourian, w; P.O. Box 1107; Jefferson City, Mo. 65101; Jefferson City diocese; 16,950.

Catholic News, The, w; 68 W. Broad St., Mt. Vernon, N.Y. 10552; New York archdiocese; 40,238.

Catholic News of Western New York, w; 501 Virginia St., Buffalo, N.Y. 14202; Buffalo diocese; 118,113.

Catholic News-Register, w; 425 Summit St., Joliet, Ill. 60435; Joliet diocese; 11,100.

Catholic Northwest Progress, w; 907 Terry Ave., Seattle, Wash. 98104; Seattle archdiocese, Yakima diocese; 39,966.

Catholic Observer, biweekly; 57 Observer St., Springfield, Mass. 01104; Springfield diocese; 13,308.

Catholic Post, The, w; 409 N. Monroe Ave., Peoria, Ill. 61603; Peoria diocese; 38,513.

Catholic Register, w; Box 126-C, Logan Blvd., Hollidaysburg, Pa. 16648; Altoona-Johnstown diocese.

Catholic Review, w; 320 Cathedral St., Baltimore, Md. 21203; Baltimore archdiocese; 62,237.

Catholic Sentinel, w; 2816 E. Burnside St., Portland, Ore. 97214; Portland archdiocese, 20,833; Baker diocese, 2,026.

Catholic Spirit, The, biweekly; 161 Edgington Lane, Wheeling, W. Va. 26003; Wheeling diocese; 22,217

Catholic Standard, w; 1711 N. St., N.W., Washington, D.C. 20036; Washington archdiocese; 43,117.

Catholic Standard and Times, w; 222 N. 17th St., Philadelphia, Pa. 19103; Philadelphia archdiocese, Allentown diocese; 62,243.

Catholic Star Herald, w; 1845 Haddon

Ave., Camden, N.J. 08103; Camden diocese; 37,643.

Catholic Sun, The, w; 204 E. Jefferson St., Syracuse, N.Y. 13202; Syracuse diocese; 37,852.

Catholic Telegraph, w; 326 W. 7th St., Cincinnati, O. 45202; Cincinnati archdiocese; 53,051.

Catholic Times, w; 197 E. Gay St., Columbus, O. 43216; Columbus diocese; 34,304.

Catholic Transcript, w; 785 Asylum Ave., Hartford, Conn. 06105; Hartford archdiocese, Bridgeport and Norwich dioceses; 57,824.

Catholic Universe Bulletin, w; 1027 Superior Ave. N.E., Cleveland, O. 44114; Cleveland diocese; 78,956.

Catholic Virginian, w; 14 N. Laurel St., Richmond, Va. 23220; Richmond diocese; 36,906.

Catholic Voice, The, w; 2918 Lakeshore Ave., Oakland, Calif. 94610; Oakland diocese; 88,964.

Catholic Voice, The, w; 6060 N.W. Radial, Omaha, Nebr. 68104; Omaha archdiocese; 20,737.

Catholic Week, w; P.O. Box 349, Mobile, Ala. 36601; Mobile diocese; 9,562.

Catholic Weekly, The, w; 1520 Court St., Saginaw, Mich. 48605; Saginaw diocese; 24,049.

Catholic Weekly, The, w; 1628 Lambden Rd., Flint, Mich. 48501; Lansing diocese; 16,075.

Catholic Witness, The, w; 2300 Market St., Harrisburg, Pa. 17103; Harrisburg diocese; 50,548.

Church Today, every 3 weeks; 2315 Texas Ave., Alexandria, La. 71301; Alexandria diocese; 16,100.

Church World, w; 19 Commercial St., Portland, Me. 04104; Portland diocese; 13,812.

Clarion Herald, w; 523 Natchez St., New Orleans, La. 70130; New Orleans archdiocese; 103,272.

Concern, m (exc. Aug.); 153 Ash St., Manchester, N.H. 03105; Manchester diocese; 14,024.

Courier, The, w; 270 Hamilton St., Winona, Minn. 55987; Winona diocese; 11,152.

Courier Journal, w; 67 Chestnut St., Rochester N.Y. 14604; Rochester diocese; 70,970.

Criterion, The, w; P.O. Box 174, Indianapolis, Ind. 46206; Indianapolis archdiocese; 40,304.

Crociato, Il (Ital.-Eng.), w; 1 Hanson Pl., Brooklyn, N.Y. 11217; 4,210.

D-F

Dakota Catholic Action, 9 times a year; P.O. Box A, Douglas, N. Dak. 58735; Bismarck diocese; 15,000.

Delmarva Dialog, w; 1925 Delaware Ave., Wilmington, Del. 19899; Wilmington diocese; 31,000.

Denver Catholic Register, w; 938 Bannock St., Denver, Colo. 80201; Denver archdiocese; 23,725.

Draugas (Lithuanian), daily; 4545 W. 63rd St., Chicago, Ill. 60629; Lithuanian Catholic Press Society.

Eastern Catholic Life, w; 101 Market St., Passaic, N.J. 07055; Passaic Byzantine eparchy; 14,045.

Eastern Kansas Register, The, w; 2220 Central, Kansas City, Kans. 66110; Kansas City archdiocese; 29,872.

Eastern Montana Catholic Register, w; 725 Third Ave. N., Great Falls, Mont. 59401; Great Falls diocese; 5,665.

Evangelist, The, w; 39 Philip St., Albany, N.Y. 12207; Albany diocese; 93,300.

Florida Catholic, The, w; 620 N. Magnolia Ave., Orlando, Fla. 32802; Orlando and St. Petersburg dioceses; 44,200.

G-L

Gary Edition of Our Sunday Visitor, w; 3855 Broadway, Gary, Ind. 46409; 38,670.

Georgia Bulletin, w; 756 W. Peachtree St. N.W., Atlanta, Ga. 30308; Atlanta archdiocese; 13,500

Globe, The, w; P.O. Box 1678, Sioux City, Ia. 51102; Sioux City diocese; 25,050.

Guardian, The, w; 2500 N. Tyler St., Little Rock, Ark. 72207; Little Rock diocese; 10,938.

Harmonizer, The, w; Noll Plaza, Huntington, Ind. 46750; Fort Wayne-S. Bend diocese; 23,024.

Hawaii Catholic Herald, w; 1184 Bishop St., Honolulu, H.I. 96813; Honolulu diocese; 8,279.

Idaho Register, w; 420 Idaho St., Boise, Idaho 83702; Boise diocese; 11,811.

Inland Register, w; 1023 W. Riverside, Spokane, Wash. 99201; Spokane diocese; 9,900.

Inside Passage, w; 329 Fifth St., Juneau, Alaska 99801; Juneau and Fairbanks dioceses; 3,050.

Intermountain Catholic Register, The, w; P.O. Box 2489, Salt Lake City, Utah 84110; Salt Lake City diocese; 6,282.

Jednota (Slovak-Eng.), w; 1655 W. Harrisburg Pike, Middletown, Pa. 17057; 37,909.

Lafayette Edition of Our Sunday Visitor, w; 610 Lingle Ave., Lafayette, Ind. 47901; 8,774.

Lake Shore Visitor, w; 2-M Commerce Bldg., Erie, Pa. 16512; Erie diocese; 18,684.

Liberte, La (French-English), biweekly; 275 Rollstone St., Fitchburg, Mass. 01421.

Long Island Catholic, The, w; 53 N. Park Ave., Rockville Centre, N.Y. 11570; Rockville Centre diocese; 171,771.

M

Message, The, w; 208 N.W. Third St., Evansville, Ind. 47708; Evansville diocese; 10,876.

Messenger, The, w; 224 W. Washington St., Belleville, Ill. 62220; Belleville diocese; 22,889.

Messenger, The, w; 1044 Scott St., Covington, Ky. 41012; Covington diocese; 9,913.

Michigan Catholic, The, w; 644 Selden St., Detroit, Mich. 48201; Detroit archdiocese; 108,148.

Mirror, The, w; M.P.O. Box 847, Springfield, Mo. 65801; Springfield-Cape Girardeau diocese; 11,173.

Mississippi Today, w; P.O. Box 2130, Jackson, Miss. 39205; Natchez-Jackson diocese; 11,997.

Monitor, The, w; 441 Church St., San Francisco, Calif. 94114; San Francisco archdiocese, Stockton and Santa Rosa diocese; 32,215.

Monitor, The, w; 139 N. Warren St., Trenton, N.J. 08607; Trenton diocese; 77,773.

Morning Star, The, w; 515 Cathedral S., Lafayette, La. 70501; Lafayette diocese; 29,864.

N

Narod Polski (Polish-Eng.), semi-monthly; 1331 Augusta Blvd., Chicago, Ill. 60622; 50,000.

Nasa Nada (Eng.-Croatian), w; 1414 W. 119th St., Crown Point, Ind. 46307; 6,250.

National Catholic Register, w; Box 680, Huntington, Ind. 46750, 89,860.

National Catholic Reporter, The, w; P.O. Box 281, Kansas City, Mo. 64141; published by laymen; 40,075.

Nevada Register, m; P.O. Box 1989, Reno, Nev. 89505; Reno diocese; 3,999.

New Day, The, w; 202 Morningside Dr. S.E., Albuquerque, N.M. 87108; Albuquerque diocese; 3,900.

New Star, The, w; 2208 W. Chicago Ave., Chicago, Ill. 60622; St. Nicholas of Chicago Ukrainian diocese; 11,235.

New World, The, w; 109 N. Dearborn St., Chicago, Ill. 60602; Chicago archdiocese; 163,841.

North Carolina Catholic, w; P.O. Box 10686, Raleigh, N.C. 27605; Raleigh diocese; 5,100.

North Country Catholic, w; P.O. Box 326, Ogdensburg, N.Y. 13669; Ogdensburg diocese; 14,800.

Northwestern Kansas Register, w; P.O. Box 958, Salina, Kans. 67401; 8,500.

O-R

Observer, The, w; P.O. Box 2079, Monterey, Calif. 93940; Monterey diocese; 9,500.

Observer, The, w; 1260 N. Church St., Rockford, Ill. 61101; Rockford diocese; 11,433.

One Voice, w; P.O. Box 10822, Birmingham, Ala. 35202; Birmingham diocese; 10,837.

Our Northland Diocese, m; 1200 Memorial Dr., Crookston, Minn. 56716; Crookston diocese; 12,770.

Our Sunday Visitor, w; Noll Plaza, Huntington, Ind. 46750; national edition and official publication for 7 dioceses; Our Sunday Visitor, Inc.; 384,147.

Outlook, m (Sept.-June); 215 W. 4th St., Duluth, Minn. 55806; Duluth diocese; 25,000.

Pilot, The, w; 49 Franklin St., Boston, Mass. 02110; Boston archdiocese; 120,500.

Pittsburgh Catholic, The, w; 110 Third Ave., Pittsburgh, Pa. 15222; Pittsburgh diocese; 106,548.

Polish American Journal, m; 413 Cedar Ave., Scranton, Pa. 18505; 27,889.

Priests — USA, m; 1307 S. Wabash Ave., Chicago, Ill. 60605; National Federation of Priests' Councils; 8,500.

Providence Visitor, w; 184 Broad St., Providence, R.I.; Providence diocese; 37,500.

Record, The, w; 433 S. 5th St., Louisville, Ky. 40202; Louisville archdiocese; 15,589.

S

St. Cloud Visitor, w; 810 Germain St., St. Cloud, Minn. 56301; St. Cloud diocese; 28,711.

St. Joseph's-Blatt (German-Eng.), bm; St. Benedict, Ore. 97373; Manfred F. Ellenberger; 1,652.

St. Louis Review, w; 462 N. Taylor Ave., St. Louis, Mo. 63108; St. Louis archdiocese; 79,982.

Shlakh — The Way, w; 805 N. Franklin St., Philadelphia, Pa. 19123; Philadelphia archeparchy. Stamford and Chicago eparchies; 11,443.

Southern Cross, The, w; P.O. Box 81869, San Diego, Calif. 92138; San Diego diocese; 43,120.

Southern Cross, The w; P.O. Box 10027; Savannah, Ga. 31402; Savannah diocese; 10,035.

Southern Nebraska Register, w; P.O. Box 80329, Lincoln, Nebr. 68501; Lincoln diocese; 14,720.

Southwest Kansas Register, w; P.O. Box 1317, Dodge City, Kans. 67801; Dodge City diocese; 8,250.

Spirit, The, w; 203 S. Monroe Ave., Green Bay, Wis. 54305; Green Bay diocese; 33,200.

Steubenville Register, w; 419 S. 4th St., Steubenville, O. 43952; Steubenville diocese; 9,250.

T

Tablet, w; 1 Hanson Pl., Brooklyn, N.Y. 11243; Brooklyn diocese; 108,825.

Tennessee Register, The, w; 421 Charlotte Ave., Nashville, Tenn. 37219; Nashville diocese; 12,117.

Texas Catholic, w; 3915 Lemmon Ave., Dallas, Tex. 75219; Dallas and Fort Worth dioceses; 23,371.

Texas Catholic Herald, The, w; 1700 San

Jacinto St., Houston, Tex. 77002; Galveston-Houston diocese; 66,687.

Texas Catholic Herald — Austin Edition, w; P.O. Box 13327, Capital Sta., Austin, Tex. 78711; Austin diocese; 8,200.

Texas Catholic Herald — Beaumont, w; P.O. Box 3944, Beaumont, Tex. 77704; Beaumont diocese; 14,600.

Texas Concho Register, biweekly; 116 S. Oakes, San Angelo, Tex. 76901; San Angelo diocese; 3,679.

Texas Gulf Coast Catholic, w; P.O. Box 2584, Corpus Christi, Tex. 78403; Corpus Christi diocese; 7,000.

Tidings, The, w; 1530 W. 9th St., Los Angeles, Calif. 90015; Los Angeles archdiocese; 69,137.

Times-Review, The, w; P.O. Box 991, La Crosse, Wis. 54601; La Crosse diocese; 17,026.

Today's Catholic (formerly Alamo Register), w; P.O. Box 12429, San Antonio, Tex.; San Antonio archdiocese; 20,247.

Twin Circle, w; P.O. Box 25986, Los Angeles, Calif. 90025; 72,288.

U-W

U.P. Catholic, w; P.O. Box 548, Marquette, Mich. 49855; Marquette diocese; 11,303.

Vermont Catholic Tribune, w; 209 College St., Burlington, Vt. 05401; Burlington diocese; 29,500.

Voice, The, w; 6201 Biscayne Blvd., Miami, Fla. 33138; Miami archdiocese; 57,634.

Voice of the Southwest, w; P.O. Box 68, Lumberton, N. Mex. 87547; Gallup diocese; 1,571.

Wanderer, The, w; 128 E. 10th St., St. Paul, Minn. 55101; 46,223.

WestMont Word, w; 520 N. Ewing, Helena, Mont. 59601; Helena diocese; 9,660.

West River Catholic, m; 520 Cathedral Dr., Rapid City, S. Dak. 57701; Rapid City diocese; 9,500.

West Texas Register, biweekly; 1800 N. Spring, Amarillo, Tex. 79107; Amarillo diocese; 2,837.

Western Catholic Edition of Our Sunday Visitor, w; 514 E. Lawrence Ave., Springfield, Ill. 62703; Springfield diocese; 38,933.

Western Michigan Catholic, w; 154 Louis St., N.W., Grand Rapids, Mich. 49502; Grand Rapids diocese; 10,681.

Western Nebraska Register, w; 607 W. Division St., Grand Island, Nebr. 68801; Grand Island diocese; 4,341.

Witness, The, w; 845 Bluff St., Dubuque, Ia. 52001; Dubuque archdiocese; 24,831.

Wyoming Catholic Register, w; 206 E. 24th St., Cheyenne, Wyo. 82001; 5,441.

Magazines, Other Periodicals

A

Act, 10 times a year; 1655 Jackson Blvd., Chicago, Ill. 60612; 4,000.

A.D. Correspondence, 26 times a year; Notre Dame, Ind. 46556; 3,889.

AIM (Aids in Ministry), q; Box 306, Cranbury, N.J.; 3,911.

America, w; 106 W. 56th St., New York, N.Y. 10019; 50,096.

American Benedictine Review, q; 2nd and Division Sts., Atchison, Kans. 66002; 1,350.

American Ecclesiastical Review, m; 620 Michigan Ave. N.E., Washington, D.C. 20017; 2,300.

American Midland Naturalist, q; Notre Dame, Ind. 46556; 1,650.

Americas, The, q; Box 34440, Washington, D.C. 20034; Academy of American Franciscan History; 1,035.

Amerikanski Slovenec (Slovenian), w; 6117 St. Clair Ave., Cleveland, O. 44103; Slovenian Catholic Union; 16,000.

Annals of Our Lady of the Angels, m; 253 Knickerbocker Rd., Tenafly, N.J. 07670; 21,000.

Anthonian, q; Paterson, N.J. 07509; St. Anthony's Guild; 160,000.

Anthropological Quarterly, q; 620 Michigan Ave. N.E., Washington, D.C. 20017; Catholic Anthropological Conference; 750.

Apostolate of Our Lady, m; Carey, O. 43316; Our Lady of Consolation National Shrine; 26,500.

Apostolate of the Little Flower, bm; P.O. Box 5280, 906 Kentucky Ave., San Antonio, Tex. 78201; Discalced Carmelite Fathers; 34,840.

Ave Maria (Polish), 6 times a year; 600 Doat St., Buffalo, N.Y. 14211; Felician Srs.; 5,100.

B

Bells of St. Ann, 3 times a year; Belcourt, N.D. 58316; St. Ann's Indian Mission; 26,466.

Benedictine Orient, bm; 2400 Maple Ave., Lisle, Ill. 60532; 7,252.

Benedictine Magazine, q; Mt. St. Scholastica, Atchison, Kans. 66002; 710.

Bernardine Bulletin, The, semiannually; 647 Spring Mill Rd., Villanova, Pa. 19085; Bernardine Srs.; 14,000.

Best Sellers, semimonthly; Univ. of Scranton, Scranton, Pa. 18510; 2,590.

Better World, q; Belford, N.J. 07718; Mary Productions Guild; 3,000.

Bible Today, The, 6 times a year; Liturgical Press, Collegeville, Minn. 56321; 14,260.

Brothers' Newsletter, q; Passionist Monastery, P.O. Box 150, West Springfield, Mass. 01089; National Assembly of Religious Brothers; 4,500.

C

Call Board, The, 5 times a year; 227 W. 45th St., New York, N.Y. 10036; Catholic Actors' Guild; 1,200.

Catechist, The, m (exc. Dec., June-Aug.); 2285 Arbor Blvd., Dayton, O. 45439; 31,000.

Catholic Action News, m; P.O. Box 1750, Fargo, N. Dak. 58102; Fargo diocese; 17,200.

Catholic Aid News, m; 49 W. 9th St., St. Paul, Minn. 55102; 24,000.

Catholic Apostolate Newsletter, bm; 5424 Blue Mound Rd., Milwaukee, Wis. 53208; Pallottine Fathers; 13,000.

Catholic Biblical Quarterly, q; 620 Michigan Ave. N.E., Washington, D.C. 20017; Catholic Biblical Assn.; 3,450.

Catholic Cemetery, The, m; 710 N. River Rd., Des Plaines, Ill. 60016; 2,291.

Catholic Charities Review, m (exc. July-Aug.), 1346 Connecticut Ave. N.W., Washington, D.C. 20036; 7,000.

CCH Echoes, q; 1400 State St., Alton, Ill. 62002; Catholic Children's Home; 250.

Catholic Digest, The, m; P.O. Box 3090, St. Paul, Minn. 55165; 526,036.

Catholic Family Leader, bm; 1312 Massachusetts Ave. N.W., Washington, D.C. 20005; Family Life Division, USCC; 6,785.

Catholic Forester Magazine, bm; 305 W. Madison St., Chicago, Ill. 60606; Catholic Order of Foresters; 137,261.

Catholic Historical Review, q; 620 Michigan Ave. N.E., Washington, D.C. 20017; American Catholic Historical Assn.; 2,050.

Catholic Institutional Management, bm; 6305 Brookside Plaza, Kansas City, Mo. 64113; 38,616.

Catholic Journalist, The, bm; 432 Park Ave. S., New York, N.Y. 10016; Catholic Press Association; 1,578.

C.K. of A. Journal, m; 217 E. 8th St., Cincinnati, O. 45202; Catholic Knights of America; 18,600.

C.L. of C. Index, m; 195 E. Broad St., Columbus, O. 43215; 7,730.

Catholic Lawyer, q; St. John's University, Jamaica, N.Y. 11432; St. Thomas More Institute for Legal Research; 3,500.

Catholic Library World, m; 461 W. Lancaster Ave., Haverford, Pa. 19041; Catholic Library Association; 3,504.

Catholic Life Magazine, m (exc. July-Aug.); 9800 Oakland Ave., Detroit, Mich. 48211; PIME Missionaries; 15,260.

Catholic Mind, The, m (exc. July-Aug.); 106 W. 56th St., New York, N.Y. 10019; 5,700.

Catholic Periodical and Literature Index, bm; 461 W. Lancaster Ave., Haverford, Pa. 19041; Catholic Library Association; 1,769.

Catholic Press Directory, a; 432 Park Ave. S., New York, N.Y. 10016; Catholic Press Assn.; 1,466.

Catholic Quote, m; Valparaiso, Nebr. 68065; 6,450.

Catholic Review (Braille), m; 154 E. 23rd St., New York, N.Y. 10010; Xavier Society for the Blind; 2,800.

Catholic School Editor, The, q; 1135 W. Kilbourn Ave., Milwaukee, Wis. 53233; Catholic School Press Assn.; 300.

Catholic University of America Law Review,
q; 620 Michigan Ave. N.E., Washington, D.C. 20017; 1,500.

Catholic War Veteran, bm; 2 Massachusetts Ave. N.W., Washington, D.C. 20001; 100,000.

Catholic Woman's Journal, m; 3835 Westminster Pl., St. Louis, Mo. 63108; 1,344.

Catholic Worker, 9 times a year; 36 E. First St., New York, N.Y. 10003; Dorothy Day; 82,000.

Catholic Workman, m; 107 N. Central Ave., New Prague, Minn. 56071; 7,500.

Catholic Youth Work Annual, a; 1312 Massachusetts Ave. N.W., Washington, D.C. 20005; 7,000.

Chicago Studies, 3 times a year; P.O. Box 665, Mundelein, Ill. 60060; 4,000.

Christopher News Notes, 7 times a year; 12 E. 48th St., New York, N.Y. 10017; The Christophers; 1,150,000.

Classical Bulletin, 6 times a year; 221 N. Grand Blvd., St. Louis, Mo. 63103; 1,700.

Classical Folia, biennial; College of Holy Cross, Worcester, Mass. 01610; Institute of Early Christian Iberian Studies; 600.

Claverite, The, bm; 1821 Orleans Ave., New Orleans, La. 70116; Knights of Peter Claver; 8,000.

Columban Mission, m (exc. June, Aug.); St. Columbans, Nebr. 68056; Columban Fathers; 244,333.

Columbia, m; One Columbus Plaza, New Haven, Conn. 06507; Knights of Columbus; 1,132,659.

Columbian, The, w; 188 W. Randolph St., Chicago, Ill. 60601; 24,950.

Comment/Media Today, 9 times a year; 39 Lackawanna Pl., Bloomfield, N.J. 07003; Christian Communications Apostolate; 2,500.

Commitment, q; 1307 S. Wabash Ave., Chicago, Ill. 60605; National Catholic Conference for Interracial Justice; 24,000.

Commonweal, w; 232 Madison Ave., New York, N.Y. 10016; 24,769..

Community, q; 21 E. Van Buren St., Chicago, Ill. 60605; Friendship House; 1,700.

Consolata Missions, q; P.O. Box C, Somerset, N.J. 08873; 32,000.

Continuum, q; St. Xavier College, Chicago, Ill. 60655.

Cord, The, m; St. Bonaventure University, St. Bonaventure, N.Y. 14778; 1,186.

Counseling and Values, q; 802 Finch Bldg., St. Paul, Minn. 55101; National Catholic Guidance Conference, Inc.; 3,886.

Critic, The, bm; 180 N. Wabash Ave., Chicago, Ill. 60601; Thomas More Association; 28,476.

Cross and Crown, q; P.O. Box 627, Oak Park, Ill. 60303; 6,500.

Crossroads Radio, m; 1089 Elm St., W. Springfield, Mass. 01089; 4,400.

Crusader's Almanac, The, q; 1400 Quincy

St. N.E., Washington, D.C. 20017; Commissariat of the Holy Land; 105,000.

D

Damien-Dutton Call, q; 214 Commercial Ave., New Brunswick, N.J. 08901; 15,000.

Daystar, a; 172 Foster St., Brighton, Mass. 02135; Franciscan Missionary Sisters of Africa; 1,750.

Diakonia, q; Fordham Univ., Bronx, N.Y. 10458; John XXIII Center for Eastern Christian Studies; 1,015.

Divine Love, q; P.O. Box 24, Fresno, Calif. 93707; 200,000.

Divine Word Messenger, q; Bay St. Louis, Miss. 39520; 12,500.

Divine Word Missionaries, q; Techny, Ill. 60082.

E

Educating in Faith, m; 335 Broadway, New York, N.Y. 10013; Catholic Negro-American Mission Board; 16,500.

Emmanuel, m (bm July-Aug.); 194 E. 76th St., New York, N.Y. 10021; Blessed Sacrament Fathers; 19,205.

Encounter, 3 times a year; 200 Lake St., Boston, Mass. 02135; Religious of the Cenacle; 7,000.

Eucharist, bm; 194 E. 76th St., New York, N.Y. 10021; 15,884.

Extension, m; 1307 S. Wabash Ave., Chicago, Ill. 60605; Catholic Church Extension Society.

F

Family, m; 50 St. Paul's Ave., Boston, Mass. 02130; Daughters of St. Paul; 40,000.

Family Digest, m; Noll Plaza, Huntington, Ind. 46750; 157,185.

Family Friend, q; P.O. Box 5663, Milwaukee, Wis. 53211; 22,000.

Fatima Findings, m; 100 E. 20th St., Baltimore, Md. 21218; Reparation Society of the Immaculate Heart of Mary; 4,231.

Franciscan Herald, m; 1434 W. 51st St., Chicago, Ill. 60609; Third Order of St. Francis; 4,865.

Franciscan Message, m (exc. July-Aug.); Franciscan Publishers, Pulaski, Wis. 54162; 3,335.

F.M.A. Focus, q; P.O. Box 598, Mt. Vernon, N.Y. 10550; Franciscan Mission Associates; over 150,000.

Franciscan Reporter, q; 3140 Meramec St., St. Louis, Mo. 63138; 34,050.

Franciscan Studies, a; St. Bonaventure, N.Y. 14778; Franciscan Institute; 706.

Fraternal Leader, bm; 305 W. 6th St., Erie, Pa. 16512; Loyal Christian Benefit Association; 45,400.

Freeing the Spirit, q; 1325 Massachusetts Ave. N.W., Washington, D.C. 20005; National Office for Black Catholics.

Friar, m; Butler, N.J. 07405; Franciscan Fathers; 21,150.

G-I

Glenmary's Challenge, q; 4119 Glenmary Terrace, Fairfield, Ohio 45014; Glenmary Home Missioners; 102,000.

Good Shepherd (Slovak and English), m; 205 Madison St., Passaic, N.J. 07055; Slovak Catholic Federation of America; 3,700

Grain and Fire, q; P.O. Box 178, Cottonport, La. 71327; Brothers of the Holy Eucharist; 600.

Homiletic and Pastoral Review, m; 86 Riverside Dr., New York, N.Y. 10024; 19,948.

Hospital Progress, m; 1438 S. Grand Blvd., St. Louis, Mo. 63104; Catholic Hospital Association; 11,500.

Immaculata, m; 8000 39th Ave., Kenosha, Wis. 53141; Franciscan Fathers; 24,500.

Impact, 6 times a year; 734 15th St., N.W., Washington, D.C. 20005; National Office for Black Catholics; 2,000.

Institute Journal, bm; 50 Oak St., San Francisco, Calif. 94102; Young Men's Institute; 10,000.

It's Our World, 4 times a year; P.O. Box 6758, Pittsburgh, Pa. 15212; Pontifical Assn. of the Holy Childhood; 297,000.

J-K

Jesuit, The, q; 39 E. 83rd St., New York, N.Y. 10028; 300,000.

Jesuit, (New Orleans Edition), q; 1607 Pere Marquette Bldg., New Orleans, La. 70112; 42,000.

Jesuit Blackrobe, q; 3601 W. Fond du Lac Ave., Milwaukee, Wis. 53216; 58,000.

Jesuit Bulletin, 4 times a year; 4511 W. Pine Blvd., St. Louis, Mo. 63108; Jesuit Seminary Aid Association; 64,000.

Josephite Harvest, The, bm; 1130 N. Calvert St., Baltimore, Md. 21202; Josephite Missionaries; 50,000.

Jurist, The, q; Catholic University of America, Washington, D.C. 20017; School of Canon Law; 2,185.

Katolicky Sokol (Catholic Falcon) (Slovak-English), w; 205 Madison St., Passaic, N.J. 07055; Slovak Catholic Sokol; 19,400.

Katolik (Czech), w; 1637 S. Allport St., Chicago, Ill. 60608; 5,000.

Kinship, q; 4580 Colerain Ave., Cincinnati, O. 45223; Glenmary Home Mission Sisters; 13,500.

Knights of St. John, q; 1603 S. Bedford Ave., Evansville, Ind. 47713; 7,400.

Kolping Banner, m; 125 N. Stratton Lane, Mt. Prospect, Ill. 60056; Catholic Kolping Society; 2,253.

L

Laivas (Lithuanian), m; 4545 W. 63rd St., Chicago, Ill. 60629.

Land of Cotton, q; 2048 W. Fairview Ave., Montgomery, Ala. 36108; 73,754.

La Paloma, m; 124 Festival, El Paso, Tex. 79912; El Paso diocese newsletter.

Latin America Calls, 9 times a year; P.O. Box 6066, Washington, D.C. 20005; Division for Latin America, USCC; 100,000.

Leaves, bm; 23715 Ann Arbor Trail, Dearborn Heights, Mich. 48127; Mariannhill Fathers; 196,300.

Liguorian, m; 1 Liguori Rd., Liguori, Mo. 63057; Redemptorist Fathers; 448,572.

Linacre Quarterly, q; 2825 N. Mayfair Rd., Milwaukee, Wis. 53222; Federation of Catholic Physicians Guilds; 9,720.

Listen, q; 770 Centre St., Newton, Mass. 02158; Carroll Rehabilitation Center for the Visually Impaired; 30,000.

Little Bronzed Angel, m; St. Paul's Indian Mission, Marty, S.D. 53761; Benedictine Fathers; 20,000.

Little Flower Magazine, bm; 1125 S. Walker, Oklahoma City, Okla. 73126; Discalced Carmelite Fathers; 20,000.

Liturgy, 10 times a year, 1330 Massachusetts Ave., N.W. Washington, D.C. 20005; 4,491.

Living Light, The, q; Our Sunday Visitor, Inc., Huntington, Ind. 46750, publisher; edited by National Center of Religious Education — CCD, USCC; 4,804.

M

Marian, The, 5 times a year; 4545 W. 63rd St., Chicago, Ill. 60629, Marian Fathers.

Marian Helpers Bulletin, q; Stockbridge, Mass. 01262; Association of Marian Helpers and of the Congregation of Marian Fathers; 757,000.

Marquette Today, q; 1834 W. Wisconsin Ave., Milwaukee, Wis. 53233; 56,000.

Marriage, m; Abbey Press, St. Meinrad, Ind. 47577; 55,000.

Mary Magazine and Aylesford News, bm; Cass Ave. N. at I-55, Westmont, Ill. 60559; Carmelite Fathers; 24,835.

Maryknoll Magazine, m; Maryknoll, N.Y. 10545; Catholic Foreign Mission Society; more than 200,000.

Master's Work, q; Waukegan and Willow Rds., Techny, Ill. 60082; Holy Spirit Missionary Sisters; 6,000.

Mediatrix, q; 6301 12th Ave., Brooklyn, N.Y. 11219; 7,000.

Medical Mission News, bm; 10 W. 17th St., New York, N.Y. 10011; Catholic Medical Mission Board, Inc. 41,500.

Men of Malvern, bm; Malvern, Pa. 19355; 44,000.

Mercy Profile, q; 2303 Grandview Ave., Cincinnati, O. 45206; Sisters of Mercy; 17,000.

Messenger, The, m; 16010 Detroit Ave., Lakewood, O. 44107; 11,000.

Messenger of the Holy Family, bm; 2500 Ashby Rd., St. Louis, Mo. 63114; 4,600.

MHS Review, bm; 232 S. Home Ave., Pittsburgh, Pa. 15202; 3,150.

Miesiecznik Franciszkanski (Polish), m;

Franciscan Printery, Pulaski, Wis. 54162; Franciscan Fathers; 11,400.

Miraculous Medal, The, q; 475 E. Chelten Ave., Philadelphia, Pa. 19144; Central Association of the Miraculous Medal; 108,216.

Mission, bm; 366 Fifth Ave., New York, N.Y. 10001; Society for Propagation of the Faith; 3,140,000.

Mission, bm; Red Lion and Knight Rds., Philadelphia, Pa. 19114; Sisters of the Blessed Sacrament; 4,800.

Mission Helper, The, q; 1001 W. Joppa Rd., Baltimore, Md. 21204; Mission Helpers of the Sacred Heart; 7,400.

Missionhurst, 9 times a year; 4651 N. 25th St., Arlington, Va. 22207; Immaculate Heart of Mary Mission Society, Inc.; 382,500.

Mission Intercom, 10 times a year; 1325 Massachusetts Ave. N.W., Washington, D.C. 20005; US Catholic Mission Council; 2,500.

Missionaries of Africa Report, bm; 1622 21st St. N.W., Washington, D.C. 20009; Society of Missionaries of Africa (White Fathers); 18,829.

Modern Schoolman, The, q; 3700 W. Pine Blvd., St. Louis, Mo. 63108; St. Louis University; 900.

Momentum, 4 times a year; Suite 350, One Dupont Circle, Washington, D.C. 20036; National Catholic Educational Association; 16,000.

Mother Cabrini Messenger, bm; 2520 Lakeview Ave., Chicago, Ill. 60614; Mother Cabrini League; 85,000.

Mount Loretto Review, a; 6581 Hylan Blvd., Staten Island, N.Y. 10309; 100,000.

Musart, q (during school year); 4637 Eastern Ave. N.W., Washington, D.C. 20018; National Catholic Music Educators Association; 4,029.

Mwangaza, q; 172 Foster St., Brighton, Mass. 02135; Franciscan Missionary Sisters for Africa; 1,750.

My Daily Visitor, m; Noll Plaza, Huntington, Ind. 46750; Our Sunday Visitor, Inc.; 15,405.

N

Narod (Czech-Eng.), w; 1637 S. Allport St., Chicago, Ill. 60608; Benedictine Abbey Press; 5,000.

National Catholic Forester, bm; 59 E. Van Buren St., Chicago, Ill. 60605; 57,900.

National Jesuit News, m; 5430 S. University, Chicago, Ill. 60615; 6,900.

New Catholic World, bm; 1865 Broadway, New York, N.Y. 10023; 14,800.

New Covenant, m; P.O. Box 102, Main St. Station, Ann Arbor, Mich. 48107; Charismatic Renewal Services; 20,895.

New Scholasticism, q; Notre Dame, Ind. 46556; American Catholic Philosophical Association; 2,550.

News and Views, q; 3900 Westminster Pl., St. Louis, Mo. 63108; Sacred Heart Program; 210,000.

North American Voice of Fatima, m; 1023 Swann Rd., Youngstown, N.Y. 14174; 13,000.

Notre Dame Magazine, bm; Notre Dame Univ., Notre Dame, Ind. 46556; 72,000.

Now, q; 35750 Moravian, Fraser, Mich. 48026; Xavier Mission Srs.; 16,040.

O

Oblate World and Voice of Hope, bm; 350 Jamaica Way, Boston, Mass. 02130; Oblates of Mary Immaculate; 35,000.

Official Guide to Catholic Educational Institutions, a; 200 Sunrise Highway, Rockville Centre, L.I., N.Y. 11570; 52,479.

OMI Missions, q; P.O. Box 96, San Antonio, Tex, 78295; 21,000.

OMI Philippine Mission, q; P.O. Box 1467, San Antonio, Tex. 78295; 21,000.

Orphan's Messenger and Advocate of the Blind, q; P.O. Box 288, Jersey City, N.J. 07303; St. Joseph's Home, 94,701.

Our Lady of the Snows, bm; 15 S. 59th St., Belleville, Ill. 62223; Shrine of Our Lady of the Snows; 212,000.

Our Lady's Digest, bm; Olivet, Ill. 61860; La Salette Fathers.

Our Lady's Missionary, m; Topsfield, Rd., Ipswich, Mass. 01938; La Salette Fathers; 45,000.

P

Pacemaker, m; 500 17th Ave., Seattle, Wash. 98122; Providence Hospital; 3,500.

Padres' Trail, 10 times a year; St. Michael's Mission, St. Michael, Ariz. 86511; Franciscan Fathers; 7,052.

Paraclete, 5 times a year; P.O. Box 2000, Wheaton, Md. 20902; Holy Ghost Fathers; 155,000.

Parish Visitor, q; 328 W. 71st St., New York, N.Y. 10023; Parish Visitors of Mary Immaculate; 3,000.

Passionist Orbit, q; 5700 N. Harlem Ave., Chicago, Ill. 60631; Passionist Fathers; 50,000.

Pastoral Life, m; Route 224, Canfield, Ohio 44406; Society of St. Paul; 7,430.

Paulist Fathers News, bm; 415 W. 59th St., New York, N.Y. 10019; 31,400.

People, bm; 1312 Massachusetts Ave. N.W., Washington, D.C. 20005; National Council of Catholic Laity; 30,000.

Perpetual Help World, q; 294 E. 150th St., Bronx, NY. 10451; Redemptorists.

Perspective 21, 3 times a year; 400 Sette Dr., Paramus, N.J. 07652.

Philosophy Today, q; Carthagena Station, Celina, Ohio 45822; 1,300.

Pilgrim, q; Jesuit Fathers, Auriesville, N.Y. 12016; Shrine of Our Lady of Martyrs; 25,000.

Pope Speaks, The, q; 3622 12th St. N.E., Washington, D.C. 20017; John O'Neill; 4,820.

Priatel Dietok (Children's Friend) (Slo-

vak), m; 205 Madison St., Passaic, N.J. 07055; Junior Catholic Sokol; 7,600.

Priest, The, m; Noll Plaza, Huntington, Ind. 46750; Our Sunday Visitor, Inc.; 10,146.

Probe, m; (Oct.-June), 720 N. Rush St., Chicago, Ill. 60611; NAWR; 2,500.

Professional Placement Newsnotes, bm; 10 W. 17th St., New York, N.Y. 10011; 5,800.

Q-R

Queen, bm; 40 S. Saxon Ave., Bay Shore, N.Y. 11706; Montfort Fathers; 10,247.

Reign of the Sacred Heart, m; Hales Corners, Wis. 53130; 110,000.

Religion Teacher's Journal, 9 times a year; P.O. Box 180, W. Mystic, Conn. 06388; 35,750.

Religious Book Review, 5 times a year; Box 296, Williston Park, N.Y. 11596; 9,514.

Renascence, q; Marquette University, Milwaukee, Wis. 53233; Catholic Renascence Society; 782.

Response, The, bm (Sept.-June); 39 Lackawanna Pl., Bloomfield, N.J. 07003; International Liaison of Newark archdiocese; 530.

Review for Religious, bm; 539 N. Grand Blvd., St. Louis, Mo. 63103; 18,904.

Review of Politics, q; Univ. of Notre Dame, Notre Dame, Ind. 46556; 2,100.

Review of Social Economy, semiannual; 2323 N. Seminary Ave., Chicago, Ill. 60614; Association for Social Economics; 916.

Roses and Gold from Our Lady of the Ozarks, m; 1749 Grand Ave., Carthage, Mo. 64836; 33,000.

Roze Maryi (Polish). m; Eden Hill, Stockbridge, Mass. 01262; 7,000.

S

Sacred Music, q; Route 2, Box 1, Irving, Tex. 75062; 1,500.

St. Anthony Messenger, m; 1615 Republic St., Cincinnati, O. 45210; Franciscan Fathers; 251,061.

St. Joseph's Advocate, q; Mill Hill Missionaries, Albany, N.Y. 12203; 7,500.

St. Maron's Diocese of Detroit-USA/Diocesan Newsletter, bm; 11470 Kercheval, Detroit, Mich. 48214; 4,500.

Salesian Bulletin, bm; 148 Main St., New Rochelle, N.Y. 10802; Salesian Fathers; 90,000.

Salesian Missions, q; 148 Main St., New Rochelle, N.Y. 10802; Salesians of St. John Bosco; 930,000.

Salvatorian, The, q; Society of the Divine Savior, Salvatorian Center, Wis. 53061; 173;503.

Sandal Prints, bm; 1820 Mt. Elliott Ave., Detroit, Mich. 48207; Capuchin Fathers; 9,238.

School Guide, a; 68 W. Broad St., Mt. Vernon, N.Y. 10552; 125,000.

School Sister, The, q; Notre Dame of the Lake, Mequon, Wis. 53092; 24,731.

Science Studies, a; St. Bonaventure University, St. Bonaventure, N.Y. 14778; 690.

Scouting Bulletin of the Catholic Committee on Scouting, q; North Brunswick, N.J. 08902; 7,500.

Serenity, q; 601 Maiden Choice Lane, Baltimore, Md. 21228; Little Sisters of the Poor; 35,000.

Share, m (Sept.-June); Maryknoll, N.Y. 10545; Maryknoll Junior Edition; 28,000.

Shepherd's Call, The, q; 601 Second St. S.W., Albuquerque, N.M. 87103; 7,750.

Sign, The, m; Monastery Place, Union City, N.J. 07087; Passionist Fathers; 127,531.

Silent Advocate, bm; St. Rita School for the Deaf, 1720 Glendale-Milford Rd., Cincinnati, O. 45215; 50,000.

Sisters Today, m; St. John's Abbey, Collegeville, Minn. 56321; 22,541.

Social Justice Review, m (exc. July-Aug.); 3835 Westminster Pl., St. Louis, Mo. 63108; Catholic Central Union of America; 1,722.

Sociological Analysis, q; Box 813, Fisk University, Nashville, Tenn. 37203.

Sodalis Polonia, 9 times a year; St. Mary's College, Orchard Lake, Mich. 48033; Sts. Cyril and Methodius Seminary; 1,580.

Sons of Mary Missionary Society, q; 567 Salem End Rd., Framingham, Mass. 01701; 2,500.

Sophia, q; 19 Dartmouth St., West Newton, Mass. 02165; Melkite Exarchate in US; 3,000.

Soul, bm; Ave Maria Institute, Washington, N.J. 07882; Blue Army; 100,000.

Spirit, q; Seton Hall University, South Orange, N.J. 08824; poetry magazine; 862.

Spirit and Life, 6 times a year; Clyde, Mo. 64432; Benedictine Srs. of Perpetual Adoration; 7,000.

Spiritual Book News, 7 times a year; Notre Dame, Ind. 46556; 5,596.

Spiritual Life, q; 2131 Lincoln Rd. N.E., Washington, D.C. 20002; Discalced Carmelites; 13,000.

Spotlite, bm; 305 S. Lake St.; Aurora, Ill. 60507; Missionaries of the Sacred Heart; 33,000.

Squires Newsletter, m; Columbus Plaza, New Haven, Conn. 06507; Columbian Squires; 18,395.

Sword, 3 times a year; 31 N. Broadway, Joliet, Ill. 60435; 400.

T

Theological Studies, q; 475 Riverside Dr., New York, N.Y. 10027; Jesuit Fathers; 7,000.

Theology Digest, q; 3701 Lindell Blvd., St. Louis, Mo. 63108; 8,095.

Theresian, News, The, 3 times a year; 5326 E. Pershing Ave., Scottsdale, Ariz. 85254; 5,000.

Thomist, The, q; 487 Michigan Ave. N.E., Washington, D.C. 20017; Dominican Fathers; 1,100.

Thought, q; 441 E. Fordham Rd., Bronx,

N.Y. 10458; Fordham University; 1,930.

Today's Catholic Teacher, m (Sept.-May); 2451 E. Riva Rd., Suite 200, Dayton, O. 45439; 68,831.

Today's Parish, bm; Twenty-Third Publications, P.O. Box 180, West Mystic, Conn. 06388; 8,500.

Trinity Missions, 4 times a year; P.O. Box 30, Silver Springs, Md. 20910; 300,000.

Triumph, m; 278 Broadview Ave., Warrenton, Va. 22186.

U-V

Ultreya Magazine, m; 931 S. Hampton Rd., Dallas, Tex. 75207; Cursillo Movement; 6,000.

L'Union (French), q; 1 Social St., Woonsocket, R.I. 02895; 35,500.

UNIREA, The Union (Romanian and English), m; 4309 Olcott Ave., East Chicago, Ind. 46312; 2,000.

U.S. Catholic, m; 221 W. Madison St., Chicago, Ill. 60606; Claretian Fathers; 50,715.

Verona Fathers Missions, 4 times a year; 2104 St. Michael's St., Cincinnati, O. 45204; 20,000.

Victorian, q; 780 Ridge Rd., Lackawanna, N.Y. 14218; Our Lady of Victory Homes of Charity; 27,186.

Vox Regis, 3 times a year; St. Bonaventure, N.Y. 14778; Christ the King Seminary; 1,300.

W-Z

Waif's Messenger, m; 1140 W. Jackson Blvd., Chicago, Ill. 60607; Mission of Our Lady of Mercy; 49,579.

Way — Catholic Viewpoints, 10 times a year; 109 Golden Gate Ave., San Francisco, Calif. 94102; Franciscan Fathers of California, Inc.; 2,500.

Western Catholic Union Record, m; 906 W.C.U. Bldg., Quincy, Ill. 62301; Western Catholic Union; 19,259.

Word of God, w; 2187 Victory Blvd., Staten Island, N.Y. 10314; Society of St. Paul; 30,000.

Working for Boys, q; 601 Winchester St., Newton Highlands, Mass. 02161; Xaverian Brothers; 26,568.

Worldmission, q; 366 5th Ave., New York, N.Y. 10001; Society for the Propagation of the Faith; 3,200.

Worship, 10 times a year; St. John's Abbey, Collegeville, Minn. 56321; 9,133.

Xaverian Missions Newsletter, 9 times a year; 101 Summer St., Holliston, Mass. 01746; Xaverian Missionary Fathers; 22,500.

Your Edmundite Missions Newsletter, bm; 1428 Broad St., Selma, Ala. 36701; Southern Missions of Society of St. Edmund; 73,150.

Youth Program Service, bm; 1312 Massachusetts Ave. N.W., Washington, D.C. 20005; 7,000.

Zeal, q; St. Elizabeth Mission Society of the Sisters of St. Francis, Allegany, N.Y. 14706; 1,800.

Books

The **Official Catholic Directory**, annual, P. J. Kenedy and Sons, 866 Third Ave., New York, N.Y. 10022; circulation 13,197. First edition, 1817.

The **Catholic Almanac**, annual; Our Sunday Visitor, Inc., Huntington, Ind. 46750, publisher; editorial offices, 620 Route 3, Clifton, N.J. 07013. First edition, 1904. (See publication history.)

The **American Catholic Who's Who**, biennial; NC Publications, 1312 Massachusetts Ave., N.W., Washington, D.C. 20005. First volume, 1934-35; 2,000.

International English Language Periodicals

Australasian Catholic Record, q; St. Patrick's Seminary, Manly, New South Wales, Australia.

Biblical Theology, tri-annual; 44 Old Manse Rd., Newtownabbey, Co. Antrim, N. Ireland BT37 ORX.

Christ to the World, bm; Via G, Nicoterra 31, 00195, Rome, Italy.

Clergy Review, m; 48 Great Peter St., London, S.W. 1, England.

Communio, q; Gonzaga Univ., Spokane, Wash. 99202.

Doctrine and Life, m and **Supplement to Doctrine and Life**, bm; Dominican Publications, St. Saviour's, Dublin 1, Ireland.

Downside Review, q; Newman Bookshop, 87 St. Aldates, Oxford, England.

Dublin Review, q; 14 Howick Place, London, S.W. 1, England.

Eastern Churches Review, semi-annual; 9 Alfred St., Oxford, England.

Furrow, m; St. Patrick's College, Maynooth, Ireland.

Heythrop Journal q; Heythrop College, Cavendish Sq., London W1M, OAN, England.

IDOC International, m; 235 E. 49th St., New York, N.Y. 10017.

International Philosophical Quarterly, q; Fordham University, Bronx, N.Y. 10458.

Irish Theological Quarterly, q; St. Patrick's College, Maynooth, Ireland.

Life and Worship, q; Fowler Wright Books, Ltd., Tenbury Wells, Worcs., England

L'Osservatore Romano, w; Vatican City.

Louvain Studies, semi-annual; Naamsestraat 100, Louvain, Belgium.

Lumen Vitae, q; International Center for Studies in Religious Education, 184, rue Washington, 1050 Brussels, Belgium.

The **Middle East Quarterly**, 235 E. 49th St., New York, N.Y. 10017.

Month, m; 114 Mount St., London, W. 1, England.

New Blackfriars, m; edited by English Dominicans, Blackfriars, Oxford, England.

One in Christ, q; Benedictine Priory, Priory Close — Southgate, London N. 14 4AT, Eng. (U.S. agency, Grailville, Loveland, O. 45140).

Philosophical Studies, annual; St. Patrick's College, Maynooth, Ireland.

Recusant History, tri-annual; Catholic Record Society, 114 Mount St., London, W. 1, England.

Religion and Society, q; Christian Institute for the Study of Religion and Society, 17 Miller Rd., P.O. Box 604, Bangalore 560 006, S. India.

Scripture in Church, q; Dominican Publications, St. Saviour's, Dublin 1, Ireland.

Studies in Religion/Sciences Religieuses (bilingual), q; Univ. of Toronto Press, Front Campus, Toronto, Ont. M5S 1A6.

Sursum Corda, bm; Box 79, Box Hall, Vic., Australia 3128.

Tablet, The w; 48 Great Peter St., SW1P 2HB, London, England.

Teaching All Nations, q; East Asian Pastoral Institute, Box 1815, Manila, Philippines.

Theology, m; S.P.C.K. Holy Trinity Church, Marylebone Rd., London, N.W. 1, England.

Catholic News Agencies

(Source: The Catholic Press Association.)

Argentina: Agencia Informativa Catolica Argentina (AIC), Rodriguez Pena 846, Casilla de Correo Central 2886, Buenos Aires.

Austria: Katholische Presse-Agentur (Kathpress), Wollzeile 2a, Vienna 1.

Belgium: Centre d'Information de Presse (CIP), 38 avenue des Arts, Brussels.

Germany: Katholische Nachrichten Agentur (KNA), Kaiser Friedrichstrasse, 9, Bonn.

Hong Kong: Catholic Centre Press Bureau, P.O. Box 2984, Hong Kong.

Indonesia: Agence "PAX," Dj. Kramat Raya 134, Djakarta IV/5.

Japan: TO-SEI, 10-1 Rokubancho, Chiyodaku, Tokyo.

Mexico: Documentacion e Informacion Catolica, Aristoteles 239, Mexico 1. Central National de Communicacion Social (CENCOS), Medellin 33, Mexico 7.

Pakistan: Catholic News Service (CNSP), 111 Depot Lines, Karachi 3.

Peru: Noticias Aliadas, Apartado 5594, Lima.

Spain: Prensa Asociada (PA), Alfonso XI, 4—Apartado 14530, Madrid 14.

Switzerland: Katholische Internationale Presse-Agentur (KIPA), Case Postale 1054 CH 1701, Fribourg.

Taiwan: Catholic I-Shi News Agency, 120 Yun-Ho St., Taipeh.

Tanzania: News Letter, P.O. Box 3133, Dar-es-Salaam.

Uganda: Catholic News Bulletin, P.O. Box 2886, Kampala.

United States of America: NC News Service (NC), 1312 Massachusetts Ave. N.W., Washington, D.C. 20005.

Yugoslavia: Aktuslnosti Krscanska Sadasnjost (AKSA), Yugoslav Catholic Center for Documentation and Information, Belgrade.

Zaire: Documentation et Information Africaine (DIA), B.P. 2598, Kinshasa.

Missions: Agenzia Internationale Fides (AIF), Palazzo di Propagande Fide, Via di Propaganda I-c, Rome, Italy.

Agencies distributing news related to Catholicism as well as other news are:

France: Agence France Presse (AFP), 13 Place de la Bourse, Paris 2e.

Italy: Agenzia Nazionale Stampa Associata (ANSA), Via Propaganda 27, Rome.

Spain: LOGOS, Mateo Inurria 15, Apartado 466, Madrid—16.

U.S. Press Services

NC News Service (NC), established in 1920, provides a worldwide daily news report by wire throughout the continental U.S. and by mail to Canadian and overseas subscribers, serving more than 200 Catholic periodicals, foreign news agencies and Vatican Radio. It also provides feature and photo services; "Origins," a documentary and text service; "Catholic Trends," a fortnightly newsletter to church administrators; "Know Your Faith," a weekly religious education package. NC is represented in all U.S. dioceses and more than 20 foreign countries. It has a three-member bureau in Rome. It is a division of the Communications Department, United States Catholic Conference, with offices at 1312 Massachusetts Ave. N.W., Washington, D.C. 20005. The director and editor-in-chief is A. E. P. Wall.

Religious News Service (RNS) provides Catholic and other religious news in daily foreign and domestic reports, photos and features; "The Religious News Reporter," a weekly 15-minute radio and/or TV package; "The Week in Religion," a feature. RNS was inaugurated in 1933 by the National Conference of Christians and Jews as an independent news agency. Its offices are located at 43 W. 57th St., New York, N.Y. 10019. Lillian R. Block is managing editor.

Eastern Rite Information Service (ER), for Eastern Church news; 2208 W. Chicago Ave., Chicago, Ill. 60622.

Catholic Press Features (CPF), for articles and columns; 6 Boston Rd., Bellerose, N.Y. 11426.

Spanish-Language Service: A weekly news summary, *Resumen Semanal de Noticias*, issued by NC News Service, is used by a number of diocesan newspapers. Some papers carry features of their own in Spanish.

CATHOLIC WRITERS' MARKET
(Source: Almanac survey.)

Editors call the following suggestions to the attention of writers:

Manuscripts should be typewritten, double-spaced, on one side of the page.

Writers should know the editorial policy, purpose and style of the publication to which they submit manuscripts. Sample copies may easily be obtained, often for the mere cost of postage. Some editors suggest that writers send outlines of proposed material, in order to facilitate editorial decision and direction. "Timely" copy should be submitted considerably in advance of the date of proposed publication; some editors advise a period of three months. Authors are urged to avoid sermonizing. Writers should not expect extensive criticism of their work, although they should profit from advice and direction when these are given. Editors are not required to state their reasons for rejecting manuscripts. Replies regarding the acceptance or rejection of copy are usually made within a few weeks.

All writers should send to editors stamped, self-addressed envelopes for the return of material. Those who write to Canadian editors may use international reply coupons, not US stamps.

Payment is made on acceptance or publication. Rates are sometimes variable because of the reputation of the writer, the quality and length of the manuscript, the amount of editorial work required for its final preparation.

America: 106 W. 56th St., New York, N.Y. 10019. Ed., Rev. Donald R. Campion, S.J. Weekly, circulation 50,000; $12 per year.

ARTICLES on important public issues evaluated scientifically and morally; serious and authenticated articles on family life, education, religion; occasionally, "thought" pieces; 1,000-2,000 words—3¢ a word. VERSE, short and modern, befitting a Catholic publication but not necessarily religious —$7.50 and up. No fiction.

American Ecclesiastical Review: 620 Michigan Ave. N.E., Washington, D.C. 20017. Editor-in-chief, Bro. James P. Clifton, C.F.X. Monthly, exc. July-Aug., circulation 2,200; $10 per year.

ARTICLES, mostly theological: 3,000 words.

Annals of Good St. Anne de Beaupre, The: Basilica of St. Anne, Quebec, Canada. Ed., Rev. J. C. Nadeau, C.SS.R. Monthly, circulation 78,000; $3 per year.

FICTION: Stories of general Catholic interest, preferably with slant on devotion to St. Anne; 1,500-1,600 words — 1½-2¢ a word. ARTICLES of solid general interest to Catholics: on aspects of devotion to St. Anne, relative to history of the devotion in North America or elsewhere: on educational or social problems, or situations that should be of concern to all — especially Christians: 1,200-1,800 words — 2¢ a word, Payment on acceptance; report within a month.

Catechist: 2285 Arbor Blvd., Dayton, O. 45439. Ed., Robert Hawking. Monthly Sept.

through May (exc. Dec.), circulation 31,000; $6 per year.

ARTICLES of interest to teachers of religion in parochial schools and CCD programs: 1,500-1,800 words — rate varies. PHOTOGRAPHS, black and white — rate varies.

Catholic Digest: St. Paul, Minn. 55105. Mss. to Rev. Kenneth Ryan, editor. Monthly, circulation 535,000; $4.97 per year.

ARTICLES, factual, of interest to Catholics: 1,500-2,500 words — $200 and up (reprint magazine, uses only two or three original mss per month). PICTURE STORIES, $75 and up. SPECIAL DEPARTMENTS — Open Door, In Our Parish, Hearts Are Trumps, Flights of Fancy, In Our House: short incidents — nominal prices paid to contributors. No fiction or verse.

Catholic Free Press: 247 Mill St. Worcester, Mass. 01602. Ed., Owen J. Murphy, Jr. Weekly, circulation 22,196; $5 per year. Official newspaper of the Diocese of Worcester.

ARTICLES on liturgical subjects, domestic and world affairs, etc.; illustrated features and human interest articles: 500-3,000 words $7-$25. No fiction.

Columban Mission: St. Columbans, Nebr. 68056. Ed., Rev. Michael Harrison. Monthly (exc. June, Aug.); circulation 240,000; $2 per year.

ARTICLES mostly staff written: occasionally accept feature or factual articles on social and religious aspects of Oriental and Latin American life: 2,000 words — $70-$100. PHOTOGRAPHS of Oriental and Latin American subjects and photo stories — $5.

Columbia: Columbus Plaza, New Haven, Conn. 06507. Ed., Elmer Von Feldt. Monthly, circulation 1,175,000; $3 per year. Official organ of the Knights of Columbus.

ARTICLES dealing with current events, social problems, Catholic apostolic activities: 1,000-3,000 words (must be accompanied by glossy photos) — $100 to $300. FICTION, Christian viewpoint: up to 3,000 words — up to $300. SATIRE: 1,000 words — $100. CARTOONS, pungent, wordless humor — $25. COVERS — $600.

Commonweal: 232 Madison Ave., New York, N.Y. 10016. Ed., James O'Gara. Weekly, circulation 27,000; $15 per year.

ARTICLES, political, religious and literary subjects: 1,000-3,000 words — 2¢ a word. VERSE, serious poetry of high literary merit — about 40¢ a line.

Cross and Crown: 6851 S. Bennett Ave., Chiago, Ill. 60649. Ed., Very Rev. John J. McDonald, O.P. Quarterly, circulation 6,500; $4 four year.

ARTICLES concerning any phase of the spiritual life: minimum 3,000-4,000 words—$4 a page. No fiction or poetry.

Crusader's Almanac: Franciscan Monastery, 1400 Quincy St. N.E., Washington, D.C. 20017. Ed., **Rev.** Terence W. Kuehn, O.F.M.

Quarterly, circulation 105,000; 50¢ per year.

ARTICLES about the Holy Land, Bible and Crusades given preference — 1¢ a word.

Divine Word Messenger: 201 Ruella Ave., Bay Saint Louis, Miss. 39520. Ed., Rev. George G. Wilson, S.V.D. Quarterly, circulation 12,537; $2 per year.

ARTICLES: Catholic Church and American Negro; also general, social, religious, pious, moral themes: 500-1,500 words — 2¢ a word.

Emmanuel; 194 E. 76th Street, New York, N.Y. 10021. Editor-in-Chief, Rev. Raymond A. Tartre, S.S.S. Monthly, bimonthly July-Aug., circulation 17,500; $4 per year.

ARTICLES, clerical spirituality, Eucharistic, pastoral, theological, Scriptural: 2,000-3,000 words — $40.

Eucharist: 194 E. 76th St., New York, N.Y. 10021. Ed., Rev. William J. O'Halloran, S.S.S. Bimonthly, circulation 14,671; $3 per year.

ARTICLES, presenting meaning of Eucharist in Catholic spirituality: average length 1,500 words — 2-3¢ a word.

Family Digest: Noll Plaza, Huntington, Ind. 46750. Ed., Robert A. Willems. Monthly, circulation 166,830; $5 per year.

ARTICLES of timely interest to the young and growing Catholic family — personality profiles, interviews, social concerns, education, humor, inspiration and family interrelationships; 1,000 words or less — 5¢ a word. REPRINTS — $25. PHOTOS, professional quality b/w — $10 each; limited color, $25. PHOTO STORIES — same rates. CARTOONS — $10 each for exclusives. FILLERS — $5 each for exclusives based on personal experience.

Franciscan Message: Franciscan Publishers, Pulaski, Wis. 54162, Ed., Rev. Lawrence Janowski, O.F.M. Monthly (except July-Aug.), circulation 3,000; $3 per year.

ARTICLES, factual, current Catholic interest. Solid theology and/or scriptural background desirable, also personal experience: 1,500-2,000 words — 2¢ a word.

Friar: Butler, N.J. 07405. Ed., Rev. Rudolf Harvey, O.F.M. Monthly (bimonthly July-Aug.), circulation 19,600; $5 per year.

ARTICLES, Franciscan themes, current events, biography, popular instruction: 2,000 words. Rates vary. CARTOONS.

Hospital Progress: 1438 S. Grand Blvd., St. Louis, Mo. 63104. Ed., R. J. Stephens. Monthly, circulation 17,000; $7 per year.

Official organ of the Catholic Hospital Association.

ARTICLES, hospital-oriented; administrative procedures and theories; hospital departmental services: 1,500-5,000 words — $1 per column inch. BOOK REVIEWS, hospital oriented — payment by agreement.

Institute Journal: 50 Oak St., San Francisco, Calif. 94102. Ed., James R. Mullen. Bimonthly, $1 per year.

FICTION — no fixed rate. PHOTOGRAPHS — $15.

It's Our World: 800 Allegheny Ave., Pittsburgh, Pa. 15233. Ed., Thomas F. Haas. Four times a year (two issues: Grades 1-4, 5-8); circulation 3,000,000.

ARTICLES, with mission themes suitable for children: 600-800 words — usual rates.

Josephite Harvest, The: 1130 N. Calvert St., Baltimore, Md. 21202. Ed., Rev. John G. Barnett, S.S.J. Bimonthly; circulation 50,000; $2 per year.

ARTICLES concerning the missions: 1¢ a word, and up — by previous arrangement only.

Living Light, The, An Interdisciplinary Review of Christian Education: Published by Our Sunday Visitor, Huntington, Indiana 46750. Editorial offices, National Center of Religious Education-CCD, 1312 Massachusetts Ave. N.W., Washington D.C. 20005. Quarterly, circulation 4,630; $8 per year.

ARTICLES on religious education, catechetics, Scripture: under 3,000 words — 2¢ per word.

Marian Helpers Bulletin: Eden Hill, Stockbridge, Mass. 01262. Ed., Bro. Robert M. Doyle, M.I.C. Quarterly, circulation over 525,000; $1 per year.

ARTICLES of general interest on devotional, spiritual, moral and social topics: 300-900 words — $25-$35 per article.

Marriage: Abbey Press, St. Meinrad, Ind. 47577. Ed., John J. McHale, Monthly, circulation 62,000; $5 per year.

ARTICLES should deal with the relationship between husband and wife; interviews with marriage authorities and interesting couples, profiles, personal essays on marriage: maximum 2,500 words — 5¢ a word minimum.

Maryknoll: Maryknoll, N.Y. 10545. Ed., Rev. Miguel d'Escoto, M.M. Monthly, circulation more than 300,000; $1.00 per year.

ARTICLES must apply in some way to the hopes and aspirations, the culture, the problems and challenges of peoples in Asia, Africa and Latin America: 1,000-1,500 words — average payment, $100. Outline wanted before submission of material. PHOTOS: More interested in photo stories than in individual black and whites and color transparencies. Photo stories — up to $150, black and white; up to $200, color. Individual photos — $15, black and white; $25, color. Transparencies returned after use. Query to be made before sending photos.

Messenger of the Sacred Heart, The: 833 Broadway Ave., Toronto, Ont., Canada, M4K 2P9. Ed., Rev. F.J. Power, S.J. Monthly, circulation 23,000; $2.50 per year.

FICTION: stories which appeal to men, written with humor—good family reading: maximum, 2,000 words — 2¢ a word. ARTICLES of Catholic interest: 2,500 words — 2¢ a word Payment upon acceptance.

Miraculous Medal, The: 475 E. Chelten Ave., Philadelphia, Pa. 19144. Ed., Rev. Donald L. Doyle, C.M. Quarterly, circulation 112,000.

FICTION, of general interest. Catholic in principle: 1,500-2,000 words — 2¢ a word and up. VERSE, religious in theme or turn; preferably about Our Lady: maximum 20 lines — 50¢ a line and up. Payment on acceptance. No articles.

My Daily Visitor: Noll Plaza, Huntington, Ind. 46750. Mng. Ed., Paul A. Manoski. Monthly, circulation 16,611; $4 per year.

A pocket-sized booklet of reflections for each day of the month, combined with Mass prayers for the Sundays and holy days of the month.

MATERIAL: Daily reflections based on the feast of the day or the liturgical season: maximum 165 words per page (each day's reflection is printed on a separate page) — $100 for series of reflections.

New Catholic World: 1865 Broadway, New York, N.Y. 10023. Mng. Ed., Robert Heyer. Bimonthly, circulation 16,000; $4.50 per year. Thematic issues.

FICTION, anything but pietistic: 1,800-2,000 words. ARTICLES, related to themes of issue (query editor): about 1,800-2,000 words. VERSE, not over 22 lines. Rates of payment supplied.

O.M.I. Missions Magazine (Southern Province): P.O. Box 96, San Antonio, Tex. 78291. Ed., John A. Lewis; Dir., Rev. John A. Hakey, O.M.I. Quarterly, circulation 20,000; $3 per year.

ARTICLES: Photo and mission stories of Oblate Fathers in their missionary work; profiles of Oblate priests and brothers; articles of general Catholic interest — 1½-2¢ a word. Finished manuscripts only.

OMI Missions Magazine (Philippine Province): P.O. Box 1467, San Antonio, Tex. 78295. Ed., John A. Lewis; Dir., Rev. Cullen F. Deckert, O.M.I. Quarterly, circulation 20,000; $3 per year.

ARTICLES: Photo and mission stories of Oblate Fathers in their missionary work; profiles of Oblate priests and brothers; articles of general Catholic interest — 1½-2¢ a word. Finished manuscripts only.

Orphan's Messenger and Advocate of the Blind: St. Joseph's Home, P.O. Box 288, Jersey City, N.J. 07303. Ed., Sr. Eleanor Quin. Quarterly, circulation 94,701; $1 per year.

FICTION, all types, family problems and themes with good morals: 1,000-1,500 words — 1¢ to 2¢ a word. ARTICLES, timely topics or religious: 500-1,000 words — 1¢ to 3¢ a word. PHOTOGRAPHS and DRAWINGS accepted occasionally — rate varies.

Our Family: Box 249, Battleford, Sask., Canada SOM OEO. Ed., Rev. A. James Materi, O.M.I. Monthly, circulation 9,369; $4 per year.

FICTION, adult only; stories that reflect

lives, problems and concerns of audience; love, romance, adventure, intrigue; 1,800-3,000 words — 1¢-2¢ a word. ARTICLES related to family living; religion, education, social, biographical, marriage, courtship, domestic, institutional: 1,800-3,000 words — 1¢-2¢ a word. POETRY, in the market for many more poems; should deal with man in search for himself, for God, for others, for love, for meaning in life, for commitment: 8-30 lines — $3-$10. PHOTOS — $5-$10, more if used on cover. Usually buys first North American serial rights; will consider purchasing second or reprint rights.

Our Sunday Visitor: Noll Plaza, Huntington, Ind. 46750. Ed., Richard B. Scheiber. Weekly newspaper-magazine, circulation 347,872; $6.50 per year.

ARTICLES, no limitation on subjects other than those imposed by good taste and orthodoxy. Picture and text stories, profiles of individuals and organizations; articles that reflect moral, cultural, historical, social, economic and certain political concerns about the US and the world; articles on current problems. Practical, factual and anecdotal material is sought: 1,200-2,000 words—$75-$100, usual payment. Queries are preferred to unsolicited completed manuscripts. PHOTOGRAPHS, picture stories preferred rather than individual photos. Picture stories (color) — $100 and up.No fiction or poetry.

Priest, The: Noll Plaza, Huntington, Ind. 46750. Ed., Rev. Jordan Aumann, O.P. (Mss. to the Editor, 1111 N. Richmond St., Chicago, Ill. 60622.) Monthly, circulation 10,672; $8 per year.

ARTICLES of benefit to priests and seminarians in any of the following areas: priestly spirituality, contemporary theology, liturgy, apostolate and ministry, pastoral notes, Scripture. Controversial subject matter acceptable provided it does not go beyond the realm of orthodoxy or respect for authority or demands of fraternal charity: 6-15 double-spaced pages—$25 to $100 (about $5 per manuscript page).

Queen of All Hearts: 40 S. Saxon Ave., Bay Shore, N.Y. 11706. Ed., Rev. James McMillan, S.M.M.; Mng. Ed., Rev. Roger M. Charest S.M.M. Bimonthly; circulation 10,145; $3 per year.

FICTION: short stories, preferably with a Marian theme: 1,000-2,000 words. ARTICLES that bring out the importance of devotion to Mary. PHOTOGRAPHS with human interest, especially relating to the Madonna. VERSE with Marian theme. Payment varies. No artwork or fillers.

Review for Religious: 612 Humboldt Bldg., 539 N. Grand Blvd., St. Louis, Mo. 63103. Ed., R. F. Smith, S.J. Bimonthly, circulation 19,244; $6 per year.

ARTICLES, of interest to religious: 3,000-10,000 words — $6 per printed page.

St. Anthony Messenger: 1615 Republic St.,

Cincinnati, O. 45210. Ed., Rev. Jeremy Harrington, O.F.M. Monthly, circulation 260,000; $6 per year.

FICTION: Written out of a totally Christian background, illuminating the truth of human nature for adults. No preachiness, sentimentality. FACT ARTICLES: 3,000-3,500 words. Outstanding personalities. Information and comment on major movements in the Church: application of Christian faith to daily life; real-life solutions in the areas of a) family life, education; b) personal living (labor, leisure, art, psychology, spirituality). Human interest narrative. Humor. Photos and picture stories. Query letters welcome.

Salesian Missions: 148 Main St., New Rochelle, New York. Ed., Rev. Edward J. Cappelletti, S.D.B. Bimonthly, circulation 825,000; $2 per year.

ARTICLES: mission interest; pertaining to Salesian Society, life, spirit and educational system of St. John Bosco; adolescent interest and education—2¢ a word and up. PHOTOGRAPHS—$5-$6. Suggest queries before submitting material. Payment on acceptance. Early report.

Sign, The: Monastery Pl., Union City, N.J. 07087. Ed., Rev. Augustine P. Hennessy, C.P. Monthly, circulation 155,000; $6 per year.

FICTION of general Catholic interest: 1,000-3,500 words—$200-$300. ARTICLES of Catholic and general interest: 1,000-3,000 words — $200-$300. PHOTOGRAPHS, DRAWINGS

Social Justice Review: 3835 Westminster Pl., St. Louis, Mo. 63108. Ed., Harvey J. Johnson, Monthly, exc. July-Aug., circulation 1,741; $6 per year.

ARTICLES: research, editorial and review: 2,000-4,000 words—$3 per column. No fiction.

Spiritual Life: 2131 Lincoln Rd., N.E., Washington, D.C. 20002. Ed., Rev. Christopher Latimer, O.C.D. Quarterly, circulation 13,300; $4 per year.

ARTICLES, must follow scope of magazine: 3,000-5,000 words — rate varies. Sample copy and instructions for writers sent upon request.

Today's Catholic Teacher: 2451 E. River Rd., Suite 200, Dayton, O. 45439. Ed., Ruth A. Matheny. Monthly Sept. through May (exc. Dec.), circulation 70,000; $6 per year.

ARTICLES of professional and personal interest to teachers, administrators, pastors, parish councils and school board members concerning Catholic schools and CCD programs: 600-800 words, 1,500-3,000 words—$20-$75. Premium payment for superior content and writing presentation. Black and white photos helpful. Payment on publication.

Triumph: 278 Broadview Ave., Warrenton, Va. 22186. Ed., Michael Lawrence. Monthly, circulation, 8,000; $10 per year.

ARTICLES: Should follow general scope of the magazine: 1,000-3,500 words—2½¢ per word on publication. BOOK REVIEWS, inquire of editor first: 1,000-2,500 words—2½¢ per word on publication.

WAY—Catholic Viewpoints: 109 Golden Gate Ave. San Francisco, Calif. 94102. Ed., Simon Scanlon, O.F.M. Ten times a year, circulation 8,404; $4 per year.

ARTICLES, in keeping with the purpose of the magazine, to bear effective witness to the ideals and aims of the Order of St. Francis: to view the world through Christian eyes; to point up the relationship between abstract belief and concrete action in the modern world: 1,500-2,200 words—$30 to $50. PHOTOGRAPHS: bought with articles.

Working for Boys: 601 Winchester St., Newton Highlands, Mass. 02161. Ed., Brother Jerome, C.F.X. (Mss. to Bro. Jason, C.F.X., Assoc. Ed., Xaverian Brothers High School, Westwood, Mass, 02090.) Quarterly, circulation 27,253; 25¢ per year.

FICTION, preferably seasonal: 800-1,000 words—3¢ a word. ARTICLES, preferably seasonal: All Souls, Christmas, Easter, Summer: 800-1,000 words—3¢ a word. VERSE, seasonal, 4-16 lines—25¢-50¢ a line.

Worship: St. John's Abbey, Collegeville, Minn. 56321. Ed., Rev. Aelred Tegels, O.S.B. Monthly (exc. July-Aug.), circulation 9,000; $8 per year.

ARTICLES related to the engagement of the magazine in ongoing study of both the theoretical and pastoral dimensions of liturgy; examines historical traditions of worship in their doctrinal context, the experience of worship in Christian churches, the findings of contemporary theology, psychology, communications, cultural anthropology, and sociology insofar as they have a bearing on public worship: 3,000-5,000 words—2¢ a word for commissioned articles. No fiction or poetry.

DIRECTORY OF PUBLISHERS

This list includes Catholic publishers, some major Protestant publishers, other publishing houses which issue Catholic titles.

Abbey Press, St. Meinrad, Ind. 47577.

Abingdon Press, 201 Eighth Ave., S., Nashville, Tenn. 37202.

Abrams, Harry A., 110 E. 59th St., New York, N.Y. 10022.

Academy Guild Press, 2435 E. McKinley St., Fresno, Calif. 93621.

Alba House, 2187 Victory Blvd., Staten Island, N. Y. 10314.

Alba House Communications, Canfield, O. 44406.

Alleluia Press, Alendale, N.J. 07401.

Allyn and Bacon, Inc., Rockleigh, N.J. 07647.

America Press, 106 W. 56th St., New York, N. Y. 10019.

Arlington House, 81 Centre Ave., New Rochelle, N.Y. 10801.

Association Press, 291 Broadway, New York, N.Y. 10007.

Augsburg Publishing House, 426 S. 5th St., Minneapolis, Minn. 55415.

Ave Maria Institute, Washington, N. J. 07882.

Ave Maria Press, Notre Dame, Ind. 46556.

Bantam Books, Inc., 666 Fifth Ave., New York, N.Y. 10019.

Barnes and Noble, Inc., 105 Fifth Ave., New York, N. Y. 10003.

Beacon Press, 25 Beacon St., Boston, Mass. 02108.

Benziger, Inc., 866 Third Ave., New York, N.Y. 10022.

Bobbs-Merrill, Inc., 4 W. 58th St., New York, N.Y. 10019.

Brown, William C., Co., 135 S. Locust St., Dubuque, Ia. 52001.

Bruce Books, 866 3rd Ave., New York, N.Y. 10022.

Cardinal Mindszenty Foundation, P.O. Box 1321, St. Louis, Mo. 63105.

Carmelite Press, 6413 Dante Ave., Chicago, Ill. 60637.

Carmelite Third Order Press, Aylesford, I-55 and Cass Ave. N., Westmont, Ill. 60559.

Catechetical Guild, Noll Plaza, Huntington, Ind. 46750. A division of Our Sunday Visitor, Inc., for the production of audiovisual materials for religious education programs.

Catholic Bible House, Box 2651, Charlotte, N. C. 28201.

Catholic Book Publishing Co., 257 W. 17th St., New York, N. Y. 10011.

Catholic Library Association, 461 W. Lancaster Ave., Haverford, Pa. 19041.

Catholic Press, Inc. 1725 S. Indiana Ave., Chicago, Ill. 60616.

Catholic University of America Press, 620 Michigan Ave. N.E., Washington, D. C. 20017.

Cistercian Publications, Institute of Cistercian Studies, Western Michigan Univ., Kalamazoo, Mich. 49001.

Claretian Publications, 221 W. Madison St., Chicago, Ill. 60606.

Conception Abbey Press, Conception, Mo. 64433.

Concordia Publishing House, 3558 S. Jefferson Ave., St. Louis, Mo. 63118.

Confraternity of the Precious Blood, 5300 Fort Hamilton Parkway, Brooklyn, N.Y. 11219.

Consortium Press, 821 Fifteenth St. N.W., Washington, D.C. 20005.

Continuum Books, Seabury Press, 815 Second Ave., New York, N.Y. 10017.

Crawley, John J. and Co., Inc., 336 Mountain Rd., Union City, N.J. 07087.

Crowell-Collier and Macmillan, Inc., 866 Third Ave., New York, N. Y. 10022.

Daughters of St. Paul, 78 Fort Pl., Staten Is., N.Y. 10301.

Delaney Publications, 720 N. Rush St., Chicago, Ill. 60611.

Dell Publishing Co., Inc., 750 Third Ave., New York, N. Y. 10017.

Devin-Adair Co., 1 Park Ave., Greenwich, Conn. 06870.

Dimension Books, Inc., Box 811, Denville, N. J. 07834.

Divine Word Publications, Techny, Ill. 60082.

Dodd, Mead and Co., 79 Madison Ave., New York, N. Y. 10016.

Donohue, M. A., and Co., 711 S. Dearborn St., Chicago, Ill. 60605.

Doubleday and Co., Inc., 277 Park Ave., New York, N. Y. 10017.

Duquesne University Press, Pittsburgh, Pa. 15219.

Eerdmans Publishing Co., 255 Jefferson Ave. S.E., Grand Rapids, Mich. 49502.

Farrar, Straus and Giroux, Inc., 19 Union Sq. W., New York, N. Y. 10003.

Fawcett Publications, Fawcett Pl., Greenwich, Conn. 06830.

Fides Publishers, Inc., Notre Dame, Ind. 46556.

Fordham University Press, 441 E. Fordham Rd., Bronx, N. Y. 10458.

Fortress Press, 2900 Queen Lane, Philadelphia, Pa. 19129.

Franciscan Herald Press, 1434 W. 51st St. Chicago, Ill. 60609.

Franciscan Marytown Press, 8000 39th Ave., Kenosha, Wis. 53141.

Franciscan Publishers, Pulaski, Wis. 54162.

Golden Press, Inc., 850 Third Ave., New York, N. Y. 10022.

Harcourt, Brace, Jovanovich, Inc., 757 Third Ave., New York, N.Y. 10017.

Harper and Row, 49 E. 53rd St., New York, N. Y. 10016.

Harvard University Press, Cambridge, Mass. 02138.

Hawthorn Books, Inc., 260 Madison Ave., New York, N.Y. 10016.

Herder, B., Book Co., 314 N. Jefferson, St. Louis, Mo. 63103.

Hi-Time Publishers, Inc., Box 7337, Milwaukee, Wis. 53213.

Holt, Rinehart and Winston, Inc., 383 Madison Ave., New York, N.Y. 10017.

Houghton Mifflin Co., 2 Park St., Boston, Mass. 02107.

IDOC, 235 E. 49th St., New York, N.Y. 10017.

Image Books (see Doubleday and Co.).

Immaculata Press, Putnam, Conn. 06260.

John Day Co., 257 Park Ave. S., New York, N.Y. 10010.

John Knox Press, 341 Ponce de Leon Ave. N.E., Atlanta, Ga. 30308.

K. of C. Information Bureau, P.O. Box 1971, New Haven, Conn. 06509.

Kenedy, P.J., and Sons, 866 3rd Ave., New York, N. Y. 10022.

Knopf, Alfred A., Inc., 201 E. 50th St., New York, N. Y. 10022.

Liguorian Books, Liguori, Mo. 63057.

Lippincott, J. B., Co., E. Washington Sq., Philadelphia, Pa. 19105.

Little, Brown and Co., 34 Beacon St., Boston, Mass. 02106.

Liturgical Conference, 1330 Massachusetts Ave. N. W., Washington, D. C. 20005.

Liturgical Press, Collegeville, Minn. 56321.

Loyola University Press, 3441 N. Ashland Ave., Chicago, Ill. 60657.

Lumen Christi Press, P. O. Box 13176, Houston, Tex. 77019.

McGraw-Hill Book Co., 1221 Ave. of the Americas, New York, N. Y. 10036.

Macmillan Company, 866 Third Ave., New York, N. Y. 10022.

McKay Co., David, 750 Third Ave., New York, N. Y. 10017.

Marian Library, University of Dayton, Dayton, O. 45409.

Marquette Univ. Press, 1131 W. Wisconsin Ave., Milwaukee, Wis. 53233.

Maryknoll Publications, Maryknoll, N. Y. 10545.

Mine Publications, 25 Groveland Terrace, Minneapolis, Minn. 55403.

Mission Helpers of the Sacred Heart, 1001 W. Joppa Rd., Baltimore, Md. 21204.

Montfort Publications, 40 S. Saxon Ave., Bay Shore, L.I., N.Y. 11706.

NC Publications, 1312 Massachusetts Ave. N.W. Washington, D.C. 20005.

National Center of Religious Education—CCD, 1312 Massachusetts Ave. N.W., Washington, D.C.

Nelson, Thomas Inc. 407 Seventh Ave. S., Nashville, Tenn. 37203.

New American Library, 1301 Ave. of the Americas, New York, N. Y. 10019.

Newman Press (see Paulist/Newman).

Notre Dame University Press, Notre Dame, Ind. 46556.

Orbis Books, Maryknoll, N.Y. 10545.

Our Sunday Visitor, Inc., Noll Plaza, Huntington, Ind. 46750.

Oxford University Press, Inc., 200 Madison Ave., New York, N. Y. 10016.

Paulist/Newman Press, 400 Sette Dr., Paramus, N. J. 07652.

Penguin Books, Inc., 7110 Ambassador Rd., Baltimore, Md. 21207.

Pflaum/Standard, 38 W. 5th St., Dayton, O. 45402.

Philosophical Library, 15 E. 40th St., New York, N. Y. 10016.

Pio Decimo Press, Box 53, Baden Sta., St. Louis, Mo. 63147.

Pocket Books, Inc., 630 Fifth Ave., New York, N. Y. 10020.

Popular Library, Inc., 355 Lexington Ave., New York, N. Y. 10017.

Prentice-Hall, Inc., Englewood Cliffs, N. J. 07632.

Putnam's, G. P. Sons, 200 Madison Ave., New York, N. Y. 10016.

Random House, Inc., 201 E. 50th St., New York, N. Y. 10022.

Regina Press, Midland Ave., Hicksville, N.Y. 11801.

Regnery, Henry, 114 W. Illinois St., Chicago, Ill. 60610.

Romig, Walter, 979 Lakepointe Rd., Grosse Pointe, Mich. 48230.

Sadlier, William H., 11 Park Pl., New York, N. Y. 10007.

St. Anthony Messenger Press, 1615 Republic St., Cincinnati, O. 45210.

St. John's University Press, Grand Central and Utopia Pkwys., Jamaica, N. Y. 11432.

St. Martin's Press, 175 Fifth Ave., New York, N.Y. 10010.

St. Norbert Abbey Press, Box 192, De Pere, Wis. 54115.

St. Paul Editions, 50 St. Paul's Ave., Boston, Mass. 02130.

Scott, Foresman and Co., 99 Bauer Dr,, Oakland, N. J. 07436.

Scribner's, Chas., Sons, 597 Fifth Ave., New York, N. Y. 10017.

Sheed and Ward, 64 University Pl., New York, N.Y. 10003. (Continuing as independent editorial subsidiary of Universal Press Syndicate, 475 Fifth Ave., New York, N.Y. 10017.)

Silver Burdett Co., Park Ave. and Columbia Rd., Morristown, N. J. 07960.

Simon and Schuster, Inc., 630 Fifth Ave., New York, N. Y. 10020.

Taplinger Publishing Co., 200 Park Ave. S.,

New York, N. Y. 10003.

Templegate, 719 E. Adams St., Springfield, Ill. 62705.

Thomas More Association, 180 N. Wabash Ave., Chicago, Ill. 60661.

Twenty-Third Publications, P.O. Box 180, W. Mystic, Conn. 06388.

Twin Circle Guild, 86 Riverside Dr., New York, N. Y. 10024.

United States Catholic Conference, 1312 Massachusetts Ave. N.W., Washington, D.C. 20005.

US Center for the Catholic Biblical Apostolate, 1312 Massachusetts Ave. N.W., Washington, D.C. 20005.

Universal Publications, P.O. Box 722, Patagonia, Ariz. 85624.

Viking Press, 625 Madison Ave., New York, N. Y. 10022.

Westminster Press, Juniper and Walnut Sts., Philadelphia, Pa. 19107.

BOOK CLUBS

Catholic Book Club (1928), 106 W. 56th St., New York, N. Y. 10019. Sponsors Campion Award.

Catholic Digest Book Club (1954), Catholic Digest Magazine, P.O. Box 3090, St. Paul, Minn. 55165.

Herald Book Club (1958), Franciscan Herald Press, 1434 W. 51st St., Chicago, Ill. 60609.

Thomas More Book Club (1939), Thomas More Association, 180 N. Wabash Ave., Chicago, Ill. 60601. The Association sponsors the Thomas More Association Medal.

RADIO, TELEVISION, THEATRE

Radio

Christian in Action: Originated in 1941, produced in cooperation with the Division for Film and Broadcasting, NCCB/USCC. A 15-minute weekly program currently employing a youth-oriented music and commentary format; heard on more than 50 stations (ABC).

Christopher Radio Program: Produced by Rev. Richard Armstrong, M.M. Features 15-minute interview-discussion series, weekly, on 937 stations; a one-minute Christopher "Thought for Today," daily, on more than 2,600 stations. Address: 12 E. 48th St., New York, N.Y. 10017.

Crossroads: Originated in 1954 as the Hour of the Crucified, produced by the Passionist Fathers and Brothers. Weekly, on nearly 325 stations and Armed Forces Radio. Director: Rev. Cyril Schweinberg, C.P.; Associate Director: Bro. Damian Carroll, C.P. Address: 1089 Elm St., West Springfield, Mass. 01089.

Encuentro (Spanish-language version of Crossroads): Originated in October, 1972. Weekly, on over 30 Spanish-language stations in U.S. and Latin America. Producer: Bro. John Regis McHale, C.P. Address: 1089 Elm

St., W. Springfield, Mass. 01089.

Guideline: Produced in cooperation with the Division for Film and Broadcasting, NCCB/USCC. Weekly program designed to set forth the teachings of the Catholic Church and to discuss issues the Church faces in the contemporary world; heard on approximately 90 stations (NBC).

Sacred Heart Program: Originated in 1939, produced by the Jesuit Fathers. Features five 15-minute programs and one half-hour program weekly on radio, and one 15-minute TV program weekly. Director, Rev. Denis E. Daly, S.J. Address: 3900 Westminster Place, St. Louis, Mo. 63108.

Television

Directions: Originated in 1960, this weekly half-hour program sustains a news-oriented approach to reporting social, moral and religious issues within a Catholic context. The Division for Film and Broadcasting, NCCB/USCC, cooperates in the production of some 11 segments a year, which are carried at variable dates on more than 100 stations (ABC).

Look Up and Live: Originated in 1954, this

half-hour series sustains a variety of formats from dramatizations to studio discussions. The Division for Film and Broadcasting, NCCB/USCC, cooperates in producing 14 half-hours a year, in addition to interfaith and seasonal specials; carried on approximately 120 stations (CBS).

Religious Specials: The Division for Film and Broadcasting, NCCB/USCC, cooperates in the production of four one-hour Catholic specials a year and occasional seasonal or tri-faith presentations. These programs offered a varied format: film, dramatizations, panel discussions, music and commentary, etc. Catholic portions are telecast on approximately 175 stations (NBC).

Theatre

The Blackfriars Theatre: The oldest experimental theatre under Catholic auspices in the United States, suspended operations in March, 1972, 32 years after it became the first off-Broadway theatre in New York City. Founded in 1931 in Washington, D.C., under the sponsorship of the Blackfriars Guild, it produced 75 original plays in 41 years; the last one, which opened Feb. 23, 1972, was *The Red Hat*. The Guild founders and long-time promoters of the theatre were Dominican Fathers Urban Nagle (1905-65) and Thomas F. Carey (1904-72). President, Rev. Terence Quinn, C.P. Address: 141 E. 65th St., New York, N.Y. 10021.

Catholic University Speech and Drama Department: Established in 1937. Offers degree courses in theatre arts, produces six plays a year in The Hartke Theatre, has touring company of graduates (see National Players). Chairman of the department, Rev. Gilbert V. Hartke, O.P. Address: Catholic University of America, Washington, D.C. 20017.

National Players: Originated in 1949, is the professional touring company of graduates of the Catholic University Speech and Drama Department; oldest classical touring company in the US. Operates a theatre at Olney, Md.

Catholic Actors' Guild of America, Inc.: Established in 1914 to provide varied services to people in the theatre. Has more than 1,000 members, publishes *The Call Board* bimonthly. President, Cyril Richard. Address: Piccadilly Hotel, 227 W. 45th St., New York, N.Y. 10036. The Actors' Chapel is located in St. Malachy's Church, 239 W. 49th St., New York, N.Y.

National Theatre Arts Conference: Originated in 1937. It is primarily a program service organization; membership, 750. President and Director, Sister Honor Murphy, Dominican College, Racine, Wis. 53402.

Communications Services

Christopher TV Series, "Christopher Closeup": Originated in 1951. Half-hour and quarter-hour interviews in color, weekly, on more than 150 stations. Address: 12 E. 48th St., New York, N.Y. 10017.

Family Theater: Films for TV. Address: 7201 Sunset Blvd., Hollywood, Calif. 90046.

Franciscan Communications Center: An audio-visual media center of the Franciscan movement, dedicated to the production of public service broadcasting material and audio-visual media for religious education. Creators and producers of TeleSPOTS and AudioSPOTS, 10- to 60-second public service messages for radio and TV; TeleKETICS films and media kits (Images of Faith, Lifelines, etc.), for religious, moral and value education. Address: 1229 South Santee St., Los Angeles, Calif. 90015.

Mary Productions "Airtime": Originated in 1950. Offers royalty-free scripts for stage, film, radio and tape production. Address: Mary Productions Guild, 58 Lenison Ave., Belford, N.J. 07718.

Paulist Communications: Contracts with dioceses and parishes to provide public service programs free to radio stations and scripts to priest-broadcasters; contacts stations for dioceses. Address: P.O. Box 1057, Pacific Palisades, Calif. 90272.

Paulist Productions: Producers and distributors of the INSIGHT Film Series (available for TV at no charge), and the educational series VIGNETTES. Purchase and rental information available. Address: P.O. Box 1057, Pacific Palisades, Calif. 90272.

Sacred Heart Program — TV: Originated in 1954, produced by the Jesuit Fathers. Director, Rev. Denis E. Daly, S.J. Address: 3900 Westminster Pl., St. Louis, Mo. 63108.

St. Bernardine Communicators Guild: Offers vocation tapes to individuals and organizations for broadcast on local stations. Address: 6801 N. Yates Rd., Milwaukee, Wis. 53217.

Tele-Vue I Productions: Films for TV, mostly educational, for sale and rental. Address: Rev. Paul W. Stauder, 24 S. Illinois St., Belleville, Ill. 62220.

UNDA-USA: A national professional and autonomous Catholic association for broadcasters and allied communicators organized in 1972. It succeeded the Catholic Broadcasters Association of America which in 1948 had replaced the Catholic Forum of the Air organized in 1938. It is a member of the international Catholic association for radio and television known as UNDA (the Latin word for "wave," symbolic of air waves of communication). UNDA-USA publishes a newsletter five times a year for members and presents the Gabriel Awards (see Index) annually for excellence in broadcasting. President, Rev. Kenny C. Sweeney. Address: 136 West Georgia St., Indianapolis, Ind. 46225.

Division for Film and Broadcasting (DFB): A unit of the Department of Communications of the National Conference of Catholic Bishops and the United States Catholic

Conference, was formed in January, 1972, through a reorganization of the former National Catholic Office for Motion Pictures and the National Catholic Office for Radio and Television.

DFB provides a national service of information, training and cooperation for diocesan communications offices throughout the country. It sponsors workshops, seminars and institutes in film and broadcasting, and publishes SHARE, a packet of film and broadcasting information, twice monthly.

For the motion picture medium, DFB publishes the twice-monthly *Catholic Film Newsletter* which reviews all current nationally released 35 mm films and provides information about resources for film utilization and education (16 mm films, books, magazines, festivals). The critical reviews are addressed to the moral as well as artistic dimensions of motion pictures and are the result of a consensus based on the reactions of DFB's professional staff and board of consultors. All films reviewed are also classified according to the DFB rating system. Film classification supplements appear every two months as part of the *Newsletter*. In addition, the publication carries information and evaluative studies on trends and issues pertinent to television, with an emphasis on educational material.

The division maintains a 16mm film library of Catholic program material and a consultation service for educational and religious film program directors.

For the broadcast media, DFB is responsible for cooperating with the three major networks (NBC, ABC, and CBS) in the production of all regularly scheduled network radio and television programs involving Catholic participation (see Radio and Television).

For the Catholic press, DFB publishes a weekly film/broadcast service consisting of reviews, information, articles and photos.

Special projects are undertaken with individual publications, religious and general.

DFB also plays a liaison role for the NCCB/USCC with the film and broadcasting industries, national media, and religious agencies and organizations. It is a member of OCIC and UNDA, the international Catholic organizations for film and broadcasting, respectively. Consultations and information services are also provided for the Pontifical Commission for Social Communications and the communications offices of national episcopal conferences throughout the world.

Rev. Patrick J. Sullivan, S.J., is the director.

Address: 1011 First Ave., New York, N.Y. 10022.

Foundation

The Catholic Communications Foundation (CCF) was established by the Catholic Fraternal Benefit Societies in 1968 in New York to lend support and assistance to development of the broadcasting apostolate of the Church.

The CCF, in addition to making financial grants (more than $300,000 from 1969 to 1974) for religious programs and programming services, has promoted the development of diocesan communications capabilities and has funded scholarship programs at the Institute for Religious Communications at Loyola University, New Orleans.

CCF officers are Bishop John A. Donovan, chairman of the board; Bishop Andrew A. Grutka, president and treasurer; John B. Heinz and Charles E. Reilly, Jr., executive vice president and secretary, respectively. Serving on the board are several US bishops, communications executives, and representatives of the fraternal societies.

Address: Suite 1224, 500 Fifth Ave., New York, N.Y. 10036.

DIOCESAN COMMUNICATIONS OFFICES, DIRECTORS

(Principal source: *1974 Directory of Catholic Communications Personnel,* published by the National Catholic Office for Information. Archdioceses are designated by an asterisk.

Alabama: Birmingham — Rev. Martin Muller (Communications), Box 6147, Birmingham 35209.

Mobile — Rev. Michael J. Dyer (Ed., *The Catholic Week*), Rev. James G. Walsh, C.S.P. (Radio-TV), 557 Dauphin St., Mobile 36602.

Alaska: Anchorage* — Rev. Richard Saudis, 811 6th Ave., Box 2239, Anchorage 99510.

Fairbanks — Rev. James E. Poole, S.J., Box 101, Nome 99762.

Juneau — Rev. Robert J. Mihelyi (Communications), 329 5th St., Juneau 99801.

Arizona: Phoenix — Jerry Burns (Media Director), 400 E. Monroe, Phoenix 85004.

Tucson — Msgr. John F. Burns (Information), Box 31, Tucson 85702.

Arkansas: Little Rock — Msgr. B. Francis McDevitt (Communications, Radio-TV), 617 Louisiana St., Little Rock 72201.

California: Fresno — Mr. Joseph Jasmin (Information), Box 4273, Fresno 93744.

Los Angeles* — Rev. John C. Urban (Communications), 1531 W. 9th St., Los Angeles 90015.

Monterey — Rev. Felix Migliazzo (Ed., *The Observer*), Box 88, Monterey 93940.

Oakland — Mr. William Bettencourt (Public Relations), Rev. Richard Mangini, 2918 Lakeshore Ave., Oakland 94610.

Sacramento — Rev. James T. Murphy (Information), Box 1407, Sacramento 95807; Rev. James F. Church (Radio-TV), 1121 K St., Sacramento 95814.

San Diego — Mr. Michael Newman (Communications), Box 81869, San Diego 92138; Rev. Eugene Fischer (Radio-TV), P.O. Box 11277, San Diego 92111.

San Francisco* — Rev. Miles Riley (Communications Center), Rev. Harry G. Schlitt (Radio-TV), Sister Janet Marie (Film and Audio Distributor), 50 Oak St., San Francisco; Gerard E. Sherry (Information), 441 Church St., San Francisco 94114.

Santa Rosa — Msgr. Walter J. Tappe, 398 10th St., Box 1297, Santa Rosa 95403.

Stockton — Rev. Lawrence J. McGovern (Information), Box 4237, 1105 N. Lincoln St., Stockton 95204.

Colorado: Denver* — Rev. C. B. Woodrich (Information), 938 Bannock St., Denver 80204; Rev. Maurice J. McInerney (Radio-TV), 29 W. Kiowa St., Colorado Springs 80902.

Pueblo — Rev. Edward W. Wichmann (Communications), Box 194, Pueblo 81002.

Connecticut: Bridgeport — Rev. Alfred J. Sienkiewicz (Radio-TV), 385 Scofieldtown Rd., Stamford 06903.

Hartford* — Rev. Edmund S. Nadolny (Communications), 477 Connecticut Blvd., E. Hartford 06108.

Norwich — Mr. Thomas R. Bride (Information), Box 587, Norwich 06360.

Stamford (Ukrainian Diocese) — Msgr. Emil Manastersky, 161 Glenbrook Rd., Stamford 06902.

Delaware: Wilmington — Mr. F. Eugene Donnelly (Public Relations), Box 2030, Wilmington 19899

District of Columbia: Washington* — Msgr. John F. Donoghue (Communications), Mr. Chester F. Craigie (Public Affairs), 1721 Rhode Island Ave. N.W., Washington 20036; Msgr. Leonard F. Hurley (Radio-TV), Box 18, Germantown, Md. 20767.

Florida: Miami* — Mr. John E. Shields (Public Relations), 6301 Biscayne Blvd., Miami 33138; Msgr. Joseph H. O'Shea (Radio-TV), Rev. Jose Hernando (Spanish Speaking Radio-TV), Rev. Frank E. Cahill (Programming and Production), 6200 Northeast 4th Ct., Miami 33138.

Orlando — Rev. Richard Steinkamp (Communications), 550 N. Bumby, Orlando 32803.

St. Augustine — Rev. R. Joseph James (Diocesan News Service), Box 8625, Jacksonville 32211; Msgr. Harold Jordan (Radio-TV), 2403 Atlantic Blvd., Jacksonville 32207.

St. Petersburg — Rev. J. Keith Symons, Box 13109, St. Petersburg 33733.

Georgia: Atlanta* — Rev. Jerry E. Hardy, 756 W. Peachtree St. N.W., Atlanta 30308.

Savannah — Rev. Francis J. Donohue (Communications), Box 9207, Savannah 31402.

Hawaii: Honolulu — Msgr. Francis A. Marzen, 1184 Bishop St., Honolulu 96813.

Idaho: Boise — Rev. David J. Kundtz (Dir., Idaho Catholic Office, Radio-TV), Box 2835, Boise 83701.

Illinois: Belleville — Rev. James Blazine

(Communications), 5312 W. Main St. P.O. Box 896, Belleville 62223.

Chicago* — Rev. James P. Roache (Communications), Rev. John S. Banahan (Radio-TV), Box 1979, Chicago 60690; Rev. James F. Moriarty (Multimedia Communications), Suite 1100, 1 N. Wacker Dr., Chicago 60606.

Joliet — Rev. Edwin J. Joyce, 425 Summit St., Joliet 60435; Rev. William F. Irwin, St. Patrick Church, Wilton Center, R.R. No. 1, Manhattan 60442.

Peoria — Rev. Tom Royer, 612 E. Park Ave., Champaign 61820.

Rockford — Rev. Thomas Monahan (Communications), 1260 N. Church St., Rockford 61101.

St. Nicholas in Chicago for Ukrainians — Msgr. Jaroslav Swyschuk (Eastern Rite Information Bureau), 2208 W. Chicago Ave., Chicago 60622.

Springfield — Rev. Richard L. Paynic (Information), Box 15, Springfield 62705.

Indiana: Evansville — Rev. Joseph L. Ziliak, (Information), 208 N.W. 3rd St., Evansville 47708; Rev. Jean F. Vogler (Radio-TV), 3109 Bayard Park Dr., Evansville 47714.

Fort Wayne-South Bend — Msgr. James P. Conroy (Communications), Noll Plaza, Huntington 46750.

Gary — Rev. John J. Savio, 6060 Miller Ave., Gary 46403.

Indianapolis* — Mr. Charles J. Schisla (Communications), 136 W. Georgia St., Indianapolis 46225.

Lafayette — Rev. Paul Dehner (Information), 3810 W. Jefferson Rd., Kokomo 46901.

Iowa: Davenport — Rev. Francis C. Henricksen (Communications), 407 Brady St., Box 939, Davenport 52805.

Des Moines — Sister Janet M. Hudspeth, O.P. (Communications), 2910 Grand Ave., Box 1816, Des Moines 50306.

Dubuque* — Mr. John W. Dalton, 1229 Mt. Loretta Ave. Dubuque 52001.

Sioux City — Rev. Albert O. Grindler, 710 19th St., Box 1678, Sioux City 51102; Msgr. Frank Brady (Radio-TV), 1212 Morningside Ave., Sioux City 51106.

Kansas: Dodge City — Msgr. A. J. Felling (Communications), Box 849, Dodge City 67801.

Kansas City* — Rev. H. J. Wickey (Information), Box 2329, Kansas City 66110.

Salina — Rev. L. E. Pierce (Information), Box 958, Salina 67401.

Wichita — Rev. Eugene J. Gerber, 424 N. Broadway, Wichita 67202.

Kentucky: Covington — Rev. Patrick A. Doyle, 1044 Scott St., Covington 41012; Rev. James Quill (Radio-TV), Thomas More College, P.O. Box 85, Covington 41017.

Louisville* — Rev. John H. Morgan, 1305 W. Market St., Louisville 40203.

Owensboro — Msgr. George Hancock (Information), 4003 Frederica St., Owensboro

42301; Rev. Leonard Reisz (Radio-TV), St. Peter Church, Waverly 42462.

Louisiana: Alexandria — Mr. Al Nassif (Information), Box 5047, Alexandria 71301.

Baton Rouge — Mr. William Hammack (Information), Box 14746, Baton Rouge 70808.

Lafayette — Msgr. Richard Mouton (Information), P.O. Box D, Abbeville 70510; Msgr. Marcel Murie (Radio-TV), Box 156, Lawtell 70550.

New Orleans* — Mr. Thomas M. Finney (Communications, Public Relations), 7887 Walmsley Ave., New Orleans 70125; Rev. Jean C. Meyer (Radio-TV), 3615 Claire Ave., Gretna 70053; Mr. Allan Jacobs (Provincial Communications Director), 3030 I-10 Service Rd., Suite B-4, Metairie 70001.

Maine: Portland — Mr. Clarence F. McKay (Communications), 510 Ocean Ave., Portland 04103.

Maryland: Baltimore* — Mr. James E. Shaneman (Information), Ms. Ruth Dee (Telecommunications), 320 Cathedral St., Baltimore 21201.

Massachusetts: Boston* — Mr. George E. Ryan (News Bureau), 49 Franklin St., Boston 02110; Msgr. Walter L. Flaherty (Radio-TV), 55 Chapel St., Newton 02160.

Fall River — Msgr. Daniel F. Shallow (Information), P.O. Box 7, Fall River 52722; Rev. John F. Hogan, (TV), 494 Slocum Rd., N. Dartmouth 02747.

Springfield — Msgr. David P. Welch, 57 Observer St., Box 1570, Springfield 01101; Rev. Cyril Schweinberg, C.P. (Radio-TV), 1089 Elm St., W. Springfield 01089.

Worcester — Rev. John W. Barrett (Communications), 247 Mill St., Worcester 01602.

Melkite Apostolic Exarchate — Rev. James E. King, 19 Dartmouth St., W. Newton 02165.

Michigan: Detroit* — Mr. John F. Lynch (Communications), Sr. Maureen Rogers, O.P. (Radio-TV), 305 Michigan Ave., Detroit 48226.

Gaylord — Rev. Ronald V. Gronowski (Communications), 2425 Frederick St., Alpena 49707.

Grand Rapids — Msgr. Hugh M. Beahan, 423 First St. N.W., Grand Rapids 49504.

Kalamazoo — Rev. Robert E. Consani (Communications), 200 E. Front St., Mattawan 49071.

Lansing — Rev. Donald L. Eder (Communications), Chancery Office, 505 N. Capitol Ave., Lansing 48933.

Marquette — Rev. Raymond Moncher (Communications), 310 W. Washington St., Marquette 49855.

Saginaw — Rev. Alcuin Mikulanis, O.F.M. (Communications), Mr. Robert Young (Press Officer), 2555 Wieneke Rd., Saginaw 48603.

St. Maron's Diocese of Detroit (Maronite Rite) — Msgr. Joseph Abi-Nader, Box 3307

— Jefferson Sta., Detroit 48214.

Minnesota: Crookston — Rev. John O'Toole, Box 605, Crookston 56716.

Duluth — Rev. George M. Schroeder (Information), 215 W. 4th St., Duluth 55806.

New Ulm — Rev. Donald J. Eichinger (Communications), Church of the Japanese Martyrs, Sleepy Eye 56085.

St. Cloud — Ms. Rosemary Borgert (Information), 810 St. Germain St., Box 1068, St. Cloud 56301.

St. Paul and Minneapolis* — Rev. Robert C. Nygaard (Communications), 226 Summit Ave., St. Paul 55102.

Winona — Msgr. W. T. Magee (Communications), Box 949, Winona 55987.

Mississippi: Natchez-Jackson — James Bonney, Box 2130, Jackson 39205; Rev. Patrick Farrell (Radio-TV), P.O. Box 2248, Jackson 39205.

Missouri: Jefferson City — Rev. Hugh Behan (Information), Box 1107, Jefferson City 65101; Rev. John Long (Radio-TV), St. Stanislaus Church, Wardsville — Rt. 4, Jefferson City 65101.

Kansas City-St. Joseph — Rev. John Weiss, Box 1037, Kansas City 64141.

St. Louis* — Rev. Edward O'Donnell (Information), 462 N. Taylor Ave., St. Louis 63108; Rev. Joseph M. O'Brien (Radio-TV), 4140 Lindell Blvd., St. Louis 63108.

Springfield-Cape Girardeau — Mr. Robert G. Lee (Communications), M.P.O. Box 847, Springfield 65801.

Montana: Great Falls — Rev. Richard Hopkins, 725 3rd Ave. N., Box 2107, Great Falls 59403.

Helena — Rev. Maurice Medina (Communications), Box 1175, Helena 59601; Rev. James H. Provost (Information), Box 1729, Helena 59601.

Nebraska: Grand Island — Rev. Bernard M. Berger (Communications), P.O. Box 477, Grand Island 68801.

Lincoln — Rev. James D. Dawson (Information), Box 80328, Lincoln 68501.

Omaha* — Sister Patricia Kowalski (Communications), 100 N. 62nd St., Omaha 68132.

Nevada: Reno — Rev. Lawrence M. Quilici (Communications — Southern Nevada), 1111 Michael Way, Las Vegas 89108; Rev. Thomas Meger (Communications — Northern Nevada), Box 1211, Reno 89504.

New Hampshire: Manchester — Rev. Philip P. Bruni (Communications), 153 Ash St., Manchester 03105.

New Jersey: Camden — Mr. Charles Germain (Information), 1845 Haddon Ave., Box 709, Camden 08101.

Newark* — Msgr. Paul J. Hayes (Communications), 39 Lackawanna Pl., Bloomfield 07003; Rev. James Pindar (Radio-TV), Seton Hall Univ., S. Orange 07079.

Passaic (Byzantine Rite Eparchy) — Msgr. Thomas Dolinay 101 Market St., Passaic 07055.

Paterson — Rev. Bruce Welch (Communications), 74 Kahdena Rd., Morristown 07960; Mr. Gerald M. Costello (Information), 163-165 Newark-Pompton Turnpike (Box A), Pequannock 07440.

Trenton — Msgr. William E. Maguire, 139 N. Warren St., Trenton 08608.

New Mexico: Gallup — Rev. Cormac Antram, O.F.M., Box 48, Houck 86506.

Santa Fe* — Mrs. Eileen Stanton (Communications), 202 Morningside Dr. S.E., Albuquerque 87108.

New York: Albany — Rev. William H. Kennedy (Communications), 40 N. Main Ave., Albany 12203.

Brooklyn — Rev. Thomas J. Flanagan (Public Information), Mr. Frank DeRosa (Press Relations), 75 Greene Ave., Brooklyn 11238.

Buffalo — Msgr. Anthony J. Caligiuri (Communications), 35 Lincoln Pky., Buffalo 14222; Msgr. John J. McMahon (Radio-TV), 100 S. Elmwood Ave., Buffalo 14202.

New York* — Msgr. Eugene V. Clark (Communications), Rev. James B. Lloyd (Radio-TV), Rev. Jose Alvarez (Spanish Media), 1011 First Ave., New York, N.Y. 10022.

Ogdensburg — Rev. David W. Stinebrickner (Information), 622 Washington St., Ogdensburg 13669; Rev. John L. Downs (Radio-TV), St. Cecilia's Rectory, 23 Grove St., Adams 13605.

Rochester — Mr. James M. Noonan (Communications), 1150 Buffalo Rd., Rochester 14624; Rev. Louis J. Hohman (Episcopal Advisor), 67 Chestnut St., Rochester 14604.

Rockville Centre — Rev. Daniel S. Hamilton (Information), 53 N. Park Ave., Box 395, Rockville Centre 11571; Rev. William J. Ayres (Radio-TV), 40 Grove Pl., Babylon 11702.

Syracuse — Rev. Robert F. Lavin, 721 Main St., Phoenix 13135.

North Carolina: Charlotte — Rev. William G. Wellein, 335 Springdale Ave., Winston-Salem 27104.

Raleigh — Rev. James F. Keenan, Box 1149, Washington 27889.

Belmont Abbey — Rev. Peter Stragand, O.S.B., Belmont 28012.

North Dakota: Bismarck — Rev. John J. Owens, Holy Cross Church, Douglas 58735.

Fargo — Sister Mary Ethel (Ed., *Catholic Action News*), Box 1750, Fargo 58102

Ohio: Cincinnati* — Mr. Daniel J. Kane (Communications), Rev. Theodore Kosse (Radio-TV), 426 E. 5th St., Cincinnati 45202.

Cleveland — Rev. Joseph Kraker (Communications), Mr. J. Jerome Lackamp (Radio-TV), 1027 Superior Ave., Cleveland 44114.

Columbus — Rev. John Geiger (Mng. Ed., *Catholic Times*), 197 E. Gay St., Columbus 43215.

Parma (Byzantine Rite Eparchy) — Rev. Joseph Pohorlak, 5390 W. 220th St., Fairview Park 44126.

Steubenville — Rev. James C. Marshall, 422 Washington St., Box 969, Steubenville 43952.

Toledo — Mr. Jim Richards (Information), 2544 Parkwood Ave., Toledo 43610.

Youngstown — Mr. Patrick DiSalvatore (Communications), Sister Nancy Dawson, O.S.U. (Radio-TV), 144 W. Wood St., Youngstown 44114.

Oklahoma: Oklahoma City* — Rev. Gerald K. Mayfield (Communications), P.O. Box 332, Oklahoma City 73101.

Tulsa — Most Rev. Bernard J. Ganter, Bishop of Tulsa, Box 2009, Tulsa 74101.

Oregon: Baker — Rev. Joseph B. Hayes, St. Patrick Church, Box 730, Vale 97918.

Portland — Mr. Gorman Hogan, 2816 E. Burnside, Portland 92714; Rev. Leo Remington (Radio-TV), 2838 E. Burnside, Portland 97214.

Pennsylvania: Allentown — Msgr. Vincent E. Lewellis (Information), 1729 Turner St., Allentown 18104.

Altoona-Johnstown — Msgr. Edward W. O'Malley (Information), 126C Logan Blvd., Hollidaysburg 16648.

Erie — Msgr. E. James Caldwell (Publicity and Information), Box 4047, Erie 16512.

Greensburg — Mr. John Quigley (Communications), Ms. Colleen Wood (Radio-TV), Box 850, Greensburg 15601.

Harrisburg — Rev. David T. McAndrew (Communications), 610 Church St., Box 787, Harrisburg 17108.

Munhall* (Byzantine Rite) — Msgr. Edward V. Rosack (Information), 624 Park Rd., Cambridge 15003; Most Rev. John M. Bilock (Radio-TV), 54 Riverview Ave., Pittsburgh 15214.

Philadelphia* — Mr. Edward F. Devenney (Communications), Rev. Leo J. McKenzie (Radio-TV), 222 North 17th St., Philadelphia 19103.

Philadelphia* (Ukrainian) — Rev. Ronald Popivchak, 519 Union Ave., Bridgeport 19405.

Pittsburgh — Msgr. Daniel H. Brennan (Communications), Mr. Joseph Williams (Public Information), 111 Boulevard of the Allies, Pittsburgh 15222.

Scranton — Rev. Joseph P. Gilgallon, 300 Wyoming Ave., Box 708, Scranton 18503.

Rhode Island: Providence — Mr. Brian L. Wallin (Communications), Cathedral Square, Providence 02903.

South Carolina: Charleston — Rev. Robert J. Millard (Communications), P.O. Box 4937, Charleston Hts. 29405.

South Dakota: Rapid City — Rev. William J. O'Connell, Box 752, Rapid City 57701.

Sioux Falls — Msgr. Louis J. Delahoyde, 423 N. Duluth Ave., Sioux Falls 57104.

Tennessee: Memphis — Rev. Thomas Donahue, 203 S. White Station Rd., Memphis 38117.

Nashville — Mr. Joseph A. Sweat (Public Affairs), 421 Charlotte Ave., Nashville 37219.

Texas: Amarillo — Msgr. Leroy T. Matthiesen (Information), Msgr. Richard F. Vaughan (Radio-TV), Box 5644, 1800 N. Spring, Amarillo 79107.

Austin — Rev. Victor Goertz (Ed., *Texas Catholic Herald*), 1401 Washington Ave., Waco 76702.

Beaumont — Rev. Edmund Paulauskas, P.O. Box 3948, Beaumont 77704.

Brownsville — Mr. Allan Porter (Communications), Box 2279, Brownsville 78520.

Corpus Christi — Mr. John J. Foley (Public Relations), 818 Antelope, Corpus Christi 78401.

Dallas — Mr. Norman D. Phillips (Information), Box 19507, Dallas 75219; Mr. Ed Hallack, KDFW, 400 N. Griffin St., Dallas 75202.

El Paso — Mr. Andrew Sparke (Information), 1013 E. San Antonio, El Paso 79901.

Fort Worth — Rev. Eugene Witkowski, 1206 Throckmorton St., Ft. Worth 76102; Mr. Frank Mills (Radio-TV), 2243 Mistletoe Blvd., Ft. Worth 76110.

Galveston-Houston — Rev. John L. Fos, 1700 San Jacinto St., Houston 77002; Mr. Paul Kelly (Radio-TV), 1700 San Jacinto St., Houston 77002.

San Angelo — Mr. Frank Trudo (Communications), 1705 Kenwood Dr., San Angelo 76901.

San Antonio* — Rev. Emil J. Wesselsky (Communications), 6815 S. Zarzamora, San Antonio 78224.

Utah: Salt Lake City — Msgr. W. H. McDougall (Information), 331 E. S. Temple St., Salt Lake City 84111; Rev. Thomas J. Meersman (Radio-TV), Box 447, Kearns 84118.

Vermont: Burlington — Rev. Charles P. Davignon (Communications), 52 Williams St., Burlington 05401.

Virginia: Richmond — Mr. Bob Edwards (Communications), Suite 3, 811 Cathedral Pl., Richmond 23220.

Washington: Seattle* — Rev. James Eblen (Communications), 907 Terry Ave., Seattle 98104.

Spokane — Mr. Dan Morris, W. 1023 Riverside Ave., P.O. Box 48, Spokane 99210.

Yakima — Rev. Robert J. Shields, Box 366, White Salmon 98672.

West Virginia: Wheeling — Mr. Frank L. Sweeney, Box 230, Wheeling 26003.

Wisconsin: Green Bay — Mr. Reinhart J. Wessing (Communications), Box 909, Green Bay 54305.

La Crosse — Rev. Dennis J. Lynch (Communications), 1732 State St., La Crosse 54601.

Madison — Rev. Joseph P. Higgins, Box 111, Madison 53701; Rev. Stephen Umhoefer

(Radio-TV), High Point Rd. Rt. 2, Madison 53711.

Milwaukee* — Msgr. Ralph R. Schmit (Radio-TV), 4063 N. 64th St., Milwaukee 53216.

Superior — Rev. Robert Urban (Information), 1512 N. 12th St., Superior 54880.

Wyoming: Cheyenne — Rev. Philip Colibraro (Information), Box 97, Pine Bluffs 82082.

National Office

The National Catholic Office for Information, successor to the NCWC Bureau of Information, serves as the official spokesman for both the United States Catholic Conference and the National Conference of Catholic Bishops in relating to the news media.

The office prepares and distributes news releases; handles inquiries from the press; arranges news media coverage of bishops' meetings; offers public information and public relations counsel on a day-to-day basis to the office of the general secretary of the USCC and the NCCB, and to other agencies and staff members; performs a number of special research and writing functions on behalf of the conferences and their staffs.

The office also provides services and coordination for diocesan information offices.

William Ryan is director of the office, which is located at 1312 Massachusetts Ave. N.W., Washington, D.C. 20005.

APPALACHIAN INDUSTRIES

Appalachian Industries, specializing in woodworking, was started in 1967 by Father Patrick O'Donnell, a Glenmary Missioner assigned to Lewis and Carter Counties in northeastern Kentucky.

Its purposes are to attract new businesses and to develop local enterprises, thereby giving people of the area reasons to remain in local employment rather than moving to cities for the sake of higher income. The training of craftsmen and their establishment as independent contractors is a primary objective.

Industries — specializing in custom-designed walnut and cherry tables, benches, chairs in Shaker simplicity and Danish contemporary styles — has a market outlet in Appalachian Studios and runs a retail gift shop in Vanceburg.

Appalachian Studios is located on Route 59 south of Vanceburg. The mailing address is Route 1, Box 6-A, Vanceburg, Ky. 41179.

Credit Unions

The Credit Union National Association, Inc., reported in April, 1974, that there were 838 Catholic credit unions in the United States and 248 in Canada.

Many of the Catholic credit unions were parish organized and operated according to standard union requirements.

Honors and Awards

Pontifical Orders

The Pontifical Orders of Knighthood are secular orders of merit whose membership depends directly on the pope. Details regarding the various orders are handled by a special agency in the Secretariat of Briefs, an office in the Papal Secretariat of State.

Supreme Order of Christ (Militia of Our Lord Jesus Christ): The highest of the five pontifical orders of knighthood, the Supreme Order of Christ was approved Mar. 14, 1319, by John XXII as a continuation in Portugal of the suppressed Order of Templars. Members were religious with vows and a rule of life until the order lost its religious character toward the end of the 15th century. Since that time it has existed as an order of merit. Paul VI, in 1966, restricted awards of the order to Christian heads of state.

Order of the Golden Spur (Golden Militia): Although the original founder is not certainly known, this order is one of the oldest knighthoods. Indiscriminate bestowal and inheritance diminished its prestige, however, and in 1841 Gregory XVI replaced it with the Order of St. Sylvester and gave it the title of Golden Militia. In 1905 St. Pius X restored the Order of the Golden Spur in its own right, separating it from the Order of St. Sylvester. Paul VI, in 1966, restricted awards of the order to Christian heads of state.

Order of Pius IX: Founded by Pius IX June 17, 1847, the order is awarded for outstanding services for the Church and society, and may be given to non-Catholics as well as Catholics. The title to nobility formerly attached to membership was abolished by Pius XII in 1939. In 1957 Pius XII instituted the Class of the Grand Collar as the highest category of the order; in 1966, Paul VI restricted this award to heads of state "in solemn circumstances." The other three classes are of Knights of the Grand Cross, Knight Commanders with and without emblem, and Knights. The new class was created to avoid difficulties in presenting papal honors to Christian or non-Christian leaders of high merit.

Order of St. Gregory the Great: First established by Gregory XVI in 1831 to honor citizens of the Papal States, the order is conferred on persons who are distinguished for personal character and reputation, and for notable accomplishment. The order has civil and military divisions, and three classes of knights.

Order of St. Sylvester: Instituted Oct. 31, 1841, by Gregory XVI to absorb the Order of the Golden Spur, this order was divided into two by St. Pius X in 1905, one retaining the name of St. Sylvester and the other assuming the title of Golden Militia. Membership consists of three degrees: Knights of the Grand Cross, Knight Commanders with and without emblem, and Knights.

Ecclesiastical Order

Order of the Holy Sepulchre: Critical opinion is divided regarding various details of the history of the order. It is certain, however, that these knights first appeared in the Holy Land and were in existence at the end of the 11th century. Some assign earlier dates or origin, claiming as founders St. James the Apostle, first bishop of Jerusalem, and St. Helena, builder of the Basilica of the Holy Sepulchre. Others hold that Godfrey of Bouillon instituted the order in 1099 and that it took its name from the Holy Sepulchre where its members were knighted.

The order lost a great deal of prestige after the fall of the Latin Kingdom of Jerusalem and the consequent departure of the knights from the Holy Land. It was united with the Knights of St. John in 1489, came under the grand mastership of Alexander VI in 1496 and shortly thereafter was split into three national divisions, German, French and Spanish. Pius IX re-established the Latin patriarchate of Jerusalem in 1847 and gave the patriarch the faculty of conferring the order of knighthood. This right had been held by the Franciscan custos following the appointment of the Friars as guardians of the Holy Land in 1342. Three classes of membership were designated in 1868. Leo XIII later instituted the Cross of Honor (which does not confer knighthood) in three classes — gold, silver and bronze — and also the Dames of the Holy Sepulchre. From 1907 to 1928 the pope was grand master, an office now held by a cardinal. Revised statutes for the order went into effect in 1949, 1962 and 1967. The 1949 constitution enjoined the knights "to revive in modern form the spirit and ideal of the Crusades with the weapons of faith, the apostolate, and Christian charity."

The Order of the Holy Sepulchre now has five classes: 12 Knights of the Collar and four degrees, with separate divisions of each for men and women — Grand Cross, Commanders with Plaque, Commanders and Knights. Three honorary decorations are awarded, vis., Palm of the Order, Cross of Merit (which may be bestowed on non-Catholics), and the Pilgrim's Shell.

Investiture ceremonies combine a profession of faith with the ancient ritual of knighthood dubbing. Candidates do not take monastic vows but pledge an upright Christian life and loyalty to the pope.

The grand master of the order is Cardinal Maximilien de Furstenberg.

There are four lieutenancies of the order in the United States.

Knights of Malta

The Sovereign Military Hospitaller Order of St. John of Jerusalem of Rhodes and of Malta traces its origin to a group of men who maintained a Christian hospital in the Holy Land in the 11th century. The group was approved as a religious order — the Hospitallers of St. John — by Paschal II in 1113.

The order, while continuing its service to the poor, principally in hospital work, assumed military duties in the following century and included knights, chaplains and sergeants-at-arms among its members. All the knights were professed monks with the vows of poverty, chastity and obedience. Headquarters were located in the Holy Land until the last decade of the 13th century and on Rhodes after 1308 (whence the title, Knights of Rhodes).

After establishing itself on Rhodes, the order became a sovereign power like the sea republics of Italy and the Hanseatic cities of Germany, flying its own flag, coining its own money, floating its own navy, and maintaining diplomatic relations with many nations.

The order was forced to abandon Rhodes in 1522 after the third siege of the island by the Turks under Sultan Suliman I. Eight years later, the Knights were given the island of Malta, where they remained as a bastion of Christianity until near the end of the 18th century. Headquarters have been located in Rome since 1834.

The title of Grand Master of the Order, in abeyance for some time, was restored by Leo XIII in 1879. A more precise definition of both the religious and the sovereign status of the order was embodied in a new constitution of 1961 and a code issued in 1966.

Religious aspects of the order are subject to regulation by the Holy See. At the same time the sovereignty by the order, which is based on international law, is recognized by the Holy See and by 38 countries with which full diplomatic relations are maintained.

The four main classifications of members are: Knights of Justice, who are religious with the vows of poverty, chastity and obedience; Knights of Obedience, who make a solemn promise of obedience to the Grand Master; Knights of Honor and Devotion and of Grace and Devotion, of noble lineage; and Knights of Magistral Grace. There are also chaplains, Dames and Donats of the order.

The order, with five grand priories, three sub-priories and 32 national associations, is devoted to hospital and charitable work of all kinds in some 60 countries.

The Grand Master, who is the sovereign head of the order, has the title of Most Eminent Highness with the rank of Cardinal. He must be of noble lineage and under solemn vows for a minimum period of 10 years.

The present Grand Master is Fra' Angelo de Mojana di Cologna, a lawyer of Milan, who was elected for life May 8, 1962, by the Council of State.

The address of headquarters of the order is Via Condotti, Palazzo Malta, 00187 Roma, Italia.

Papal Medals

Pro Ecclesia et Pontifice: This decoration ("For the Church and the Pontiff") had its origin in 1888 as a token of the golden sacerdotal jubilee of Leo XIII; he bestowed it on those who had assisted in the observance of his jubilee and on persons responsible for the success of the Vatican Exposition. The medal bears the likeness of Leo XIII on one side; on the other, the tiara, the papal keys, and the words *Pro Ecclesia et Pontifice*. Originally, the medal was issued in gold, silver or bronze. St. Pius X ordered that it be of gold only. It is awarded in recognition of service to the Church and the papacy.

Benemerenti: Several medals ("To a well-deserving person") have been conferred by popes for exceptional accomplishment and service. The medals, which are made of gold, silver or bronze, bear the likeness and name of the reigning pope on one side; on the other, a laurel crown and the letter "B."

These two medals may be given by the pope to both men and women. Their bestowal does not convey any title or honor of knighthood.

AMERICAN CATHOLIC AWARDS

Aquinas Medal, by the American Catholic Philosophical Association for outstanding contributions to the field of Catholic philosophy.

Jacques Maritain (1951), Etienne Gilson (1952), Gerald Smith, S.J. (1955), Gerald B. Phelan (1959), Rudolf Allers (1960), James A. McWilliams, S.J. (1961) Charles De Koninck (1964), James Collins (1965).

Martin C. D'Arcy (1967), Dr. Josef Pieper (1968), Leo R. Ward (1969), Bernard Lonergan, S.J. (1970), Henry B. Veatch (1971), Joseph Owens, C.SS.R. (1972), A. Hilary Armstrong (1973), Cornelio Fabro (1974).

Bellarmine Medal (1955), by Bellarmine College (Louisville, Ky.), to persons in national or international affairs who, in controversial matters, exemplify the characteristics of St. Robert Bellarmine in charity, justice and temperateness.

Jefferson Caffrey (1955), Gen. Carlos Romulo (1956), US Rep. John W. McCormack (1957), Frank M. Folsom (1958), Robert D. Murphy (1959), James P. Mitchell (1960), Frederick H. Boland (1961);

Gen. Alfred M. Gruenther (1962), Henry Cabot Lodge (1963), R. Sargent Shriver (1964), Irene Dunne (1965), Sen. Everett M. Dirksen (1966), Nicholas Katzenbach (1967), Danny Thomas (1968), J..Irwin Miller(1969),

Theodore M. Hesburgh, C.S.C. (1970), Sen. John Sherman Cooper (1971), (no award, 1972), Dr. William B. Walsh (1973).

Borromeo Award (1960), by Carroll College (Helena, Mont.), for zeal, courage and devotion in the spirit of St. Charles Borromeo.

William D. Murray (1960), Robert E. Sullivan (1961), Vincent H. Walsh (1962), Leo V. Kelly (1963), Joseph A. Kimmet (1964), Dr. W. E. Long (1965), Frank E. Blair (1968), Gough, Booth, Shanahan and Johnson (1971), Egon E. Mallman, S.J. (1973), Christian Brothers of Ireland (1974).

Campion Award (1955), by the Catholic Book Club for distinguished service in Catholic letters.

Jacques Maritain (1955), Helen C. White (1956), Paul Horgan (1957), James Brodrick, S.J. (1958), Sister M. Madeleva (1959), Frank J. Sheed and Maisie Ward (1960), John La Farge, S.J. (1961), Harold C. Gardiner, S.J. (1962);

T. S. Eliot (1963), Barbara Ward (1964), Msgr. John T. Ellis (1965), John Courtney Murray, S.J. (1966), Phyllis McGinley (1967), Dr. George N. Shuster (1968), G. B. Harrison (1970), Walter and Jean Kerr (1971).

Cardinal Gibbons Medal (1949) by the Alumni Association of the Catholic University of America for distinguished and meritorious service to the Church, the United States or the Catholic University.

Carlton J. H. Hayes (1949), Gen. Carlos P. Romulo (1950), Fulton Oursler (1951), Most Rev. Fulton J. Sheen (1953), J. Edgar Hoover (1954), Gen. J. Lawton Collins (1955), US Sen. John F. Kennedy and Ignatius Smith, O.P. (1956), Most Rev. Bryan J. McEntegart (1957), Thomas E. Murray (1958);

Gen. Alfred M. Gruenther (1959), Karl F. Herzfeld (1960), Charles G. Fenwick (1961), Luke W. Hart (1962), John W. McCormack (1963), John A. McCone (1964), R. Sargent Shriver (1965), James J. Norris (1967), Danny Thomas (1968), Theodore Hesburgh, C.S.C. (1969), Dr. Carroll Hochwalt (1970), Danny Thomas (1971), Cardinal Patrick O'Boyle (1972), Helen Hayes (1973).

Cardinal Spellman Award (1947), by the Catholic Theological Society for outstanding achievement in the field of theology.

Revs. Francis J. Connell, C.SS.R., Emmanuel Doronzo, O.M.I., Gerald Yelle, S.S., William R. O'Connor, John C. Murray, S.J. (1947); Eugene Burke, C.S.P. (1948), Bernard J. J. Lonergan, S.J. (1949), John C. Murray, S.J. (1950), Msgr. William R. O'Connor (1951), Emmanuel Doronzo, O.M.I. (1952), Gerald Kelly, S.J. (1953), Francis J. Connell, C.SS.R. (1954), Edmond D. Benard (1955), John C. Ford, S.J. (1956);

Gerard Yelle, S.S. (1957), Msgr. Joseph C. Fenton (1958), Juniper Carol, O.F.M. (1959), Rev. John Quasten (1960), Cyril C. Vollert, S.J. (1961), Walter J. Burghardt, S.J. (1962), Rev. Francis Dvornik (1963), Barnabas

Ahern, C.P. (1964), Godfrey Diekmann, O.S.B. (1965), Paul K. Meagher, O.P. (1966), John L. McKenzie, S.J. (1967), Dr. Martin R. P. McGuire (1968), Richard J. McCormick, S.J. (1969), Avery Dulles, S.J. (1970), Raymond E. Brown, S.S. (1971).

For recipients after 1971, see John Courtney Murray Award.

Catholic Action Medal (1934), by St. Bonaventure University (Allegany, N. Y.).

Alfred E. Smith (1934), Michael Williams (1935), Joseph Scott (1936), Patrick Scanlan (1937), George J. Gillespie (1938), William F. Montavon (1939), John J. Craig (1940), John S. Burke (1941), Dr. George Speri Sperti (1942), Francis P. Matthews (1943);

Jefferson Caffrey (1944), John A. Coleman (1945), David Goldstein (1946), Clement Lane (1947), Paul W. Weber (1948), Bruce M. Mohler (1949), Edward M. O'Connor (1950), Richard F. Pattee (1951), James M. O'Neill (1952), John E. Swift (1953);

Frank M. Folsom (1954), Walter L. McGuiness (1955), Carlton J. H. Hayes (1956), Thomas E. Murray (1957), Paul V. Murray (1958), Dr. John L. Madden (1959), Christopher H. Dawson (1960), Stephen Kuttner (1961), Charles De Koninck (1962), Lt. Gen. G. Trudeau (1963), Frank J. Sheed (1964), Danny Thomas (1965), Walter and Jean Kerr (1966), Sir Hugh Stott Taylor (1967), Maurice Lavanoux (1968).

CIP Award (1948), by the Catholic Institute of the Press (now the Catholic Alliance for Communications) for service in the communications media.

Bob Considine (1948), Neil MacNeil (1949), Fulton Oursler (1950), Leo McCarey (1951), Dr. James M. O'Neill (1952), H. I. Phillips (1953), Martin Quigley (1954), Gene Lockhart (1955), Jim Bishop (1956), Arthur Daley and Red Smith (1957);

Clare Boothe Luce (1958), John La Farge, S.J. (1959), Phyllis McGinley (1960), Edwin O'Connor (1961), Barrett McGurn (1962), Paul Horgan (1963), Daniel Callahan (1964), NBC-TV and CBS-TV (1965), Gary MacEoin (1966).

Catholic Press Association Award (1959), by the Catholic Press Association for distinguished contribution to Catholic journalism.

Dale Francis (1959), Frank A. Hall (1960), John C. Murray, S.J. (1961), Albert J. Nevins, M.M. (1962), Floyd Anderson (1963), Rev. Patrick O'Connor (1964), John Cogley (1965), Joseph Breig (1966), John Reedy, C.S.C. (1967), Bishop James P. Shannon (1968), no award (1969), Msgr. Robert G. Peters (1970), Francis A. Fink (1971), Jeremy Harrington (1972), Robert E. Burns (1973), Gerard E. Sherry (1974).

Cecilia Medal (1952), by the Music Department of Boys Town (Nebr.) for outstanding work in liturgical music.

Winifred T. Flanagan (1952), Dom Francis Missia (1953), Omer Westendorf (1954), Dom

Ermin Vitry (1955), William A. Reilly (1956), Flor Peeters (1957), Roger Wagner (1958), Most Rev. Gerald T. Bergan (1959), Francis T. Brunner, C.SS.R. (1960), Jean Langlois (1961);

James B. Welch (1962), W. Ripley Dorr (1963), C. Alexander Peloquin (1964), Dr. Louise Cuyler (1965), Dr. Eugene Selhorst (1966), Dr. Paul Manz (1967), Myron J. Roberts (1968), Norman T. Letter (1969), Rev. Elmer Pfeil (1969), Rev. Richard Schuler (1970).

Christian Culture Award (1941), by Assumption University (Canada) to outstanding exponents of Christian ideals.

Sigrid Undset (1941), Jacques Maritain (1942), Philip Murray (1943), Frank J. Sheed (1944), Arnold M. Walter (1945), Henry Ford II (1946), George S. Sperti (1947), Richard Pattee (1948), Étienne Gilson (1949), Paul Doyon (1950), Christopher Dawson (1951), John C.H. Wu (1952);

Charles Malik (1953), Ivan Mestrovic (1954), F. W. Foerster (1955), Paul Martin (1956), Robert Speaight (1957), Allen Tate (1958), Barbara Ward (1959), John Cogley (1960), Peter Drucker (1961), Benjamin E. Mays (1962), John Quincy Adams (1963);

William Foxwell Albright (1964), Dr. Karl Stern (1965), John Howard Griffin (1966), Edith K. Peterkin (1967), Dr. Mircea Eliade (1968), Dr. James D. Collins (1969), Dorothy Day (1970), Dr. Marshall McLuhan (1971), James M. Cameron (1972), Jean Vanier (1973), Robert J. Kreyche (1974).

Christian Wisdom Award (1958), by Loyola University (Chicago) to outstanding American or European theologians.

John C. Murray, S.J. (1958), Martin C. D'Arcy, S.J. (1959), Gustave A. Weigel, S.J. (1960), Etienne Gilson (1962).

Collegian Award (1949), by "The Collegian," weekly student newspaper of La Salle College (Phila.), for public service in the field of communications.

Ed Sullivan (1949), Morley Cassidy (1950), Bob Considine (1951), Red Smith (1952), George Sokolsky (1953), Edward R. Murrow (1954), David Lawrence (1955), Jim Bishop (1956), Richard W. Slocum (1957), Chet Huntley (1958);

John C. O'Brien (1959), Walter Cronkite (1960), David Brinkley (1961), James Reston (1962), Charles Collingwood (1963), Art Buchwald (1964), Nancy Dickerson (1965), Charles Schulz (1966), Sandy Grady (1967), Harrison E. Salisbury (1968), Ralph W. Howard (1969).

Damien-Dutton Award (1953), by the Damien-Dutton Society for service toward conquest of leprosy or for the promotion of better understanding of social problems connected with the disease.

Stanley Stein (1953), Joseph Sweeney, M.M. (1954), Sister Marie Suzanne (1955), Dr. Perry Burgess (1956), John Farrow

(1957), Dr. H. Windsor Wade (1958), Sister Hilary Ross (1959), Msgr. Louis J. Mendelis (1960), Dr. Kensuke Mitsuda (1961), Pierre d'Orgeval, SS.CC. (1962);

Eunice Weaver (1963), Dr. Robert Cochrane (1964), John F. Kennedy, posthumously (1965), The Peace Corps (1966), Dr. Howard A. Rusk (1967), Dr. Frans Hemerijckx (1968), Dr. Victor G. Heiser (1969), Dr. Dharmendra (1970), Dr. Chapman H. Binford (1971), Dr. Patricia Smith (1972), Dr. Jacinto Convit (1973), Dr. Jose N. Rodriguez (1974).

Dinneen Award (1957), by the National Theatre Arts Conference.

Emmett Lavery (1957), Euphemia Van Rensselaer Wyatt (1958), Therese M. Cuny (1959), Urban Nagle, O.P. (1961), George Schaefer (1964), Walter Kerr (1965), Alfred Lunt and Lynn Fontanne (1966), Roger Stevens (1967), Pearl Bailey (1969), Gabriel V. Hartke, O.P. (1970), John Michael Tebelak (1971).

Edith Stein Award (1955), by the Edith Stein Guild for service toward better understanding between Christians and Jews.

Sister Noemi de Sion (1956), Authur B. Klyber, C.SS.R. (1957), Rev. John M. Oesterreicher (1958), John J. O'Connor (1959), Victor J. Donovan, C.P. (1960), Jacques and Raissa Maritain (1961), Gerard E. Sherry (1962), Mother Kathryn Sullivan, R.S.C.J. (1963), Paulist Press (1964), Rev. Edward N. Flannery (1965), Mother Katherine Hargrove, R.S.C.J. (1966), Gregory Baum, O.S.A. (1967), Sr. Rose Albert Thering (1968), Msgr. Vincent O. Genova (1969), Dr. Joseph Lichten (1970), Philip Scharper (1971), Rabbi Marc Tanenbaum (1972), Leon Paul (1973).

Emmanuel D'Alzon Medal (1954), by Assumptionists to persons exemplifying the ideals of their founder.

Jacques Maritain (1954), Michael F. Doyle (1955), Cardinal Richard J. Cushing (1956), Mother Mary St. Elizabeth (1956), Most Rev. John J. Wright (1959), Paolino Gerli (1960), Most Rev. Honoré van Waeyenbergh (1961), J. Peter Grace (1963), Danny Thomas (1967), Miss Mary Dowd, posthumously (1970).

Father McKenna Award (1950), by the national headquarters of the Holy Name Society, for outstanding service to the society's ideals.

Msgr. John J. Murphy, Msgr. Henry J. Watterson, Msgr. Frederic J. Allchin (1950), Eustace Struckhoff, O.F.M., Msgr. Joseph A. McCaffrey, Msgr. Francis P. Connelly, Rev. Raymond E. Jones, Msgr. Joseph E. Maguire, Msgr. Edward J. Kelly, Msgr. J. Frederick Kriebs, Rev. Thomas E. O'Connell, Very Rev. Charles L. Elslander, Rev. Joseph J. Heim, Msgr. F. Borgias Lehr (1951);

Rev. Francis J. Hannegan (1954), Rev. Charles A. Hoot, Rev. Louis A. Hinnebusch, O.P., Rev. John O. Purcell, Rev. Paul M.

Lackner (1955), Msgr. F. J. Timoney (1958), Rev. Thomas F. McNicholas (1960), James A. Quinn, O.P., and Rev. John C. Griffith (1961), Msgr. Joseph A. Aughney (1962), Msgr. Cornelius P. Higgins (1963), Msgr. Charles P. Mynaugh (1964), Msgr. Charles P. Muth, Rev. Patrick J. Foley (1971), Rev. Msgr. Robert T. Kickham (1973).

Franciscan International Award (1958), by the Conventual Franciscans (Prior Lake, Minn.) for outstanding contributions to the American way of life.

Mr. and Mrs. Ignatius A. O'Shaughnessy (1959), Archbishop William O. Brady (1960), Lawrence Welk (1961), Charles Kellstad (1962), Dr. Finn J. Larsen (1963), Dr. Charles W. Mayo (1964), Ara Parseghian (1965), F. K. Weyerhaueser (1966);

Alcoholics Anonymous (1967), James T. Griffin (1968), George S. Harris (1969), Baroness Catherine DeHueck Doherty (1970), Harry Reasoner (1971), Dr. Billy Graham (1972), Dr. and Mrs. John C. Willke (1973), Gov. Patrick J. Lucey (1974).

Good Samaritan Award (1968), by the National Catholic Development Conference to recognize the concern for one's fellowman exemplified by the Good Samaritan.

Bishop Edward E. Swanstrom (1968), Berard Scarborough, O.F.M. (1969), Bishop Joseph B. Whelan, C.S.Sp. (1970), Mother Teresa (1971), Bishop Michael R. Dempsey (1972), Msgr. Ralph W. Beiting (1973).

Hoey Awards (1942), by the Catholic Interracial Council of New York (55 Liberty St., New York, N.Y. 10004) for the promotion of interracial justice.

Frank A. Hall and Edward La Salle (1942), Philip Murray and Ralph H. Metcalfe (1943), Mrs. Edward V. Morrell and John L. Yancey (1944), Paul D. Williams and Richard Barthe (1945), Richard Reid and Charles L. Rawlings (1946), Julian J. Reiss and Clarence T. Hunter (1947), Mrs. Anna McGarry and Ferdinand L. Rousseve (1948), John J. O'Connor and M. C. Clarke (1949), J. Howard McGrath and Lou Montgomery (1950), Mrs. Roger L. Putnam and Francis M. Hammond (1951);

Charles F. Vatterot, Jr., and Joseph J. Yancey (1952), Joseph J. Morrow and John B. King (1953), Mrs. Gladys D. Woods and Collins J. Seitz (1954), Millard F. Everett and Dr. James W. Hose (1955), Frank M. Folsom and Paul G. King (1956), George Meany and James W. Dorsey (1957), James T. Harris and Robert S. Shriver, Jr. (1958), Percy H. Steele, Jr., and John P. Nelson (1959);

William Duffy, Jr., and George A. Moore (1960), Ralph Fenton and Mrs. Osma Spurlock (1961), Benjamin Muse and Dr. Eugene T. Reed (1962), James T. Carey and Percy H. Williams (1963), Arthur J. Holland and Frederick O'Neal (1964), Gerard E. Sherry and James R. Dumpson (1965), Jane M. Hoey and Mrs. Roy Wilkins (1966), Dr. Frank

Horne and Lt. Gov. Malcolm Wilson (1967), E. H. Molisani and John Strachan (1968);

Harold E. McGannon and Hulan E. Jack (1969), George P. McManus, Alfred B. Del Bello, Maceo A. Thomas and Cleo Joseph L. Froix, M.D. (1970), Most Rev. Francis J. Mugavero and Most Rev. Harold R. Perry (1971), Joseph F. Crangle and Alen E. Pinado (1972), Meade H. Esposito and Robert B. Boyd (1973).

Honor et Veritas Award (1959), by the Catholic War Veterans to outstanding Americans.

Cardinal Francis J. Spellman (1960), Gen. Douglas MacArthur (1961), U. S. Sen. Thomas J. Dodd (1962), Gen. William Westmoreland (1966), Dean Rusk (1967), Col. Martin T. Riley (1968), Theodore M. Hesburgh (1969), Kenneth D. Wells (1970), Danny Thomas (1971), Thomas V. Cuite (1972), Lawrence Welk (1973).

Insignis Medal (1951), by Fordham University for extraordinary distinction in the service of God through excellence in professional performance.

Dr. Carlos Espinosa Davila, Arthur H. Hayes (1955), Pierre Harmel, Victor Andres Belaunde (1956), M. E. Michelet (1957), Daniel Linehan, S.J., Dr. Victor F. Hess (1958), Dr. George N. Shuster, John H. Tully, Albert Conway (1959), Charles F. Vatterot, Cardinal Agagianian, Charles Norman and Lucy W. Shaffer, David C. Cronin, S.J. (1960);

Cardinal Spellman (1961), Edward P. Gilleran (1962), Joseph A. Martino, William J. Tracy (1963), Brother James M. Kenny, S.J., and Austin Ripley (1966), Vincent T. Lombardi (1967), Melkite Patriarch Maximos V Hakim of Antioch (1968), Joseph and Marian Kaiser (1970), Joseph P. Routh (1973).

John Courtney Murray Award (1972), by the Catholic Theological Society for distinguished achievement in theology. Originated in 1947 as the Cardinal Spellman Award.

Rev. Charles E. Curran (1972).

John Gilmary Shea Prize (1944), by the American Catholic Historical Association for scholarly works on the history of the Catholic Church broadly considered.

Carlton J. H. Hayes (1946), John H. Kennedy (1950), George W. Pare (1951), Rev. Philip Hughes (1954), Annabelle M. Melville (1955), Rev. John Tracy Ellis (1956), Rev. Thomas J. McAvoy, C.S.C. (1957), Rev. John M. Daley, S.J. (1958), Rev. Robert A. Graham, S.J. (1959);

Rev. Maynard Geiger, O.F.M. (1960), Rev. John C. Murray, S.J. (1961), Francis Dvornik (1962), Oscar Halecki (1963), Helen C. White (1964), John T. Noonan (1965), Rev. Robert I. Burns, S.J. (1966 and 1967), Rev. Edward S. Surtz, S.J. (1968), Robert Brentano (1969), David M. Kennedy (1970), Jaroslav Pelikan (1971), John T. Noonan (1972), Robert E. Quirk (1973).

John La Farge Memorial Award for Inter-

racial Justice (1965), by the Catholic Interracial Council of New York.

Cardinal Francis J. Spellman (1965), U.S. Sen. Jacob K. Javits (1966), Gov. Nelson Rockefeller (1967), George F. Meany (1968), Whitney M. Young, Jr. (1969), Harry Van Arsdale, Jr. (1970), John V. Lindsay (1971), Earl W. Brydges (1972), Louis K. Lefkowitz (1973), Arthur Levitt (1974).

Laetare Medal (1883), by the University of Notre Dame for distinguished accomplishment for Church or nation by an American Catholic.

John Gilmary Shea (1883), Patrick J. Keeley (1884), Eliza Allen Starr (1885), Gen. John Newton (1886), Edward Preuss (1887), Patrick V. Hickey (1888), Mrs. A. H. Dorsey (1889), William J. Onahan (1890), Daniel Dougherty (1891), Henry F. Brownson (1892);

Patrick Donahoe (1893), Augustin Daly (1894), Mrs. James Sadlier (1895), Gen. William S. Rosecrans (1896), Dr. Thomas A. Emmet (1897), Timothy E. Howard (1898), Mary G. Caldwell (1899), John Creighton (1900), Wm. B. Cochran (1901), Dr. J. B. Murphy (1902);

Charles J. Bonaparte (1903), Richard C. Kerens (1904), Thomas B. Fitzpatrick (1905), Dr. Francis Quinlan (1906), Katherine E. Conway (1907), James C. Monaghan (1908), Frances Tiernan (Christian Reid) (1909), Maurice F. Egan (1910), Agnes Repplier (1911), Thomas M. Mulry (1912);

Charles G. Hebermann (1913), Edward Douglass White (1914), Mary V. Merrick (1915), Dr. James J. Walsh (1916), Admiral William S. Benson (1917), Joseph Scott (1918), George Duval (1919), Dr. Lawrence F. Flick (1920), Elizabeth Nourse (1921), Charles P. Neil (1922);

Walter G. Smith (1923), Charles D. Maginnis (1924), Dr. Edward F. Zahm (1925), Edward N. Hurley (1926), Margaret Anglin (1927), Jack J. Spalding (1928), Alfred E. Smith (1929), Frederick P. Kenkel (1930), James J. Phelan (1931), Dr. Stephen J. Maher (1932);

John McCormack (1933), Mrs. Nicholas F. Brady (1934), Frank Spearman (1935), Richard Reid (1936), Jeremiah Ford (1937), Dr. Irvin Abell (1938), Josephine Brownson (1939), Gen. Hugh A. Drum (1940), William T. Walsh (1941), Helen C. White (1942);

Thomas F. Woodlock (1943), Anne O'Hare McCormick (1944), G. Howland Shaw (1945), Carlton J. H. Hayes (1946), William G. Bruce (1947), Frank C. Walker (1948), Irene Dunne (Mrs. Francis Griffin) (1949), Gen. Joseph L. Collins (1950), John H. Phelan, (1951), Thomas E. Murray (1952);

I. A. O'Shaughnessy (1953), Jefferson Caffrey (1954), George Meany (1955), Gen. Alfred M. Gruenther (1956), Clare Boothe Luce (1957), Frank M. Folsom (1958), Robert D. Murphy (1959), George N. Shuster

(1960), Pres. John F. Kennedy (1961), Dr. Francis J. Braceland (1962);

Adm. George W. Anderson, Jr. (1963), Phyllis McGinley (1964), Frederick D. Rossini (1965), Mr. and Mrs. Patrick F. Crowley (1966), J. Peter Grace (1967), R. Sargent Shriver (1968), Justice William J. Brennan, Jr. (1969), Dr. William D. Walsh (1970), Walter and Jean Kerr (1971), Dorothy Day (1972), Rev. John A. O'Brien (1973), James A. Farley (1974).

Magnificat Medal (1947), by Mundelein College (Chicago) to Catholic college alumnae for leadership in social action.

Mrs. Henry Mannix (1948), Mrs. Felix H. Lapeyre (1949), Mrs. Mary B. Finan (1950), Mrs. John J. Daly (Mary Tinley) (1951), Mrs. K. Cary Clem (1952), Mrs. Robert E. Garritty (1953), Dr. Jeannette E. Vidal (1954), Mrs. Ben Regan (1955), Marion McCandless (1956), Mrs. Donald Gunn (1957);

Ellen Collins (1958), Ruth M. Fox (1959), Margaret J. Mealey (1960), Mrs. George Vergara (1961), Josephine Sobrino (1962), Mrs. Patrick F. Crowley (1963), Ann M. Lally (1964).

Marianist Award (1949), by the University of Dayton for outstanding contributions to Mariology (until 1966); for outstanding contributions to mankind (from 1967).

Juniper Carol, O.F.M. (1950), Daniel A. Lord, S.J. (1951), Patrick J. Peyton, C.S.C. (1952), Roger Brien, S.G.G. (1953), Emil Neubert, S.M. (1954), Joseph A. Skelly, C.M. (1955), Frank Duff (1956), Eugene F. Kennedy and John McShain (1957), Winifred A. Feely (1958), Abp. John F. Noll (1959), Eamon R. Carroll, O. Carm. (1960), Coley Taylor (1961), Abbe Rene Laurentin (1963), Philip C. Hoelle, S.M. (1964), Cyril O. Vollert, S.J. (1965), Eduardo Frei Montalvo (1967).

Marian Library Medal (1953), by the Marian Library of the University of Dayton for books in English on the Blessed Virgin Mary. Starting in 1971, the medal will be awarded every four years, at the time of an International Mariological Congress, to a scholar for Mariological studies.

Most Rev. Fulton J. Sheen (1953), Msgr. John S. Kennedy (1954), Rev. William G. Most (1955), Ruth Cranston (1956), Juniper Carol, O.F.M. (1957), Donald C. Sharkey and Joseph Debergh, O.M.I. (1958);

Edward O'Connor, C.S.C. (1959), John J. Delaney (1960), Sister Mary Pierre, S.M. (1961), Marion A. Habig, O.F.M. (1962), Titus F. Cranny, S.A. (1963), Hilda C. Graef (1964), Edward Schillebeeckx, O.P. (1965), Cyril Vollert, S.J. (1966), Thomas O'Meara, O.P. (1967), Charles Balic, O. F. M. (1971).

Mater et Magistra Award (1963), by the College of Mt. St. Joseph on the Ohio to women for social action in the pattern and spirit of the encyclical *Mater et Magistra*.

Jane Hoey (1963), Mary Dolan (1964),

Mrs. Anne Fremantle (1966), Margaret Mealey (1967), Mrs. Arthur L. Zepf, Sr. (1968), Alice R. May (1969).

Mendel Medal (1928), by Villanova University for scientists.

Dr. John A. Kolmer (1929), Dr. Albert F. Zahm (1930), Dr. Karl F. Herzfeld (1931), Dr. Francis P. Garvan (1932), Dr. Hugh Stott Taylor (1933), Abbe Georges Lemaitre (1934), Dr. Francis Owen Rice (1935), Rev. Julius A. Nieuwland, C.S.C. (1936), Pierre Teilhard de Chardin, S.J. (1937), Dr. Thomas Parran (1938);

Rev. John M. Cooper (1939), Dr. Peter J. W. Debye (1940), Dr. Eugene M. K. Geiling (1941), Dr. Joseph A. Becker (1942), Dr. George Speri Sperti (1943), Dr. John C. Hubbard (1946), Frank N. Piasecki (1954), James B. Macelwane, S.J. (1955), Dr. William J. Thaler (1960), Dr. James A. Shannon (1961), Maj. Robert M. White (1963), Dr. Charles A. Hufnagel (1965), Dr. Alfred M. Bongiovanni (1968).

Msgr. John P. Monaghan Social Action Award by the Assn. of Catholic Trade Unionists; originally (1948), the Quadragesimo Anno Medal.

John Quincy Adams (1948), Brother Justin, F.S.C. (1949), Joseph Bierne (1950), Rev. Raymond A. McGowan (1951), Philip Murray (1952), Charles M. Halloran (1953), US Sen. Robert F. Wagner, Sr. (1954), Rev. John P. Monaghan (1955), John C. Cort (1956), Msgr. Joseph F. Connolly (1957);

George Meany (1958), Robert F. Kennedy (1959), Thomas Carey (1960), James B. Carey (1961), Rev. Joseph Hammond (1966), Paul Jennings (1967), Matthew Guinan (1968), David Sullivan (1969), Vincent McDonnell (1970).

Peace Award (1950), by the Third Order Secular of St. Francis.

Myron C. Taylor (1950), John Foster Dulles (1951), John W. McCormack (1952), John C. Wu (1953), Ralph Bunche (1954), John R. Gariepy (1956), Most Rev. Richard J. Cushing (1957), Patrick McGeehan, Sr. (1958), Victor Andres Belaunde (1959), J. Edgar Hoover (1960), George K. Hunton (1961);

Mrs. Lester Auberlin (1962), Rev. Martin Luther King (1963), Most Rev. John J. Wright (1964), Pope Paul VI (1965), Cardinal Wyszynski (1966), Bishop Fred Pierce Corson (1967), Robert F. Kennedy, posthumously (1968), Msgr. Robert Fox (1969), Bishop James Walsh, M.M. (1970), Jean Vanier (1972), Mother Teresa of Calcutta (1974).

Peter Guilday Prize (1972), by the American Catholic Historical Association for articles accepted by the editors of the *Catholic Historical Review* which are the first scholarly publications of their authors.

James P. Gaffey (1972).

Pius XII Marian Award (1955), by the Montfort Fathers for promotion of the devotion of consecration to the Immaculate Heart of Mary.

Denis M. McAuliffe, O. P. (1955), James M. Keane, O. S. M. (1956), Rev. John Cantwell (1957), Marie Delicia Unson (1958), Rev. Herman J. Vincent of St. Henry's Parish, Bridge City, Tex., and parishioners of St. Helen's Mission, Orangefield, Tex. (1959), Leo Dillon (1960), De Montfort Groups of Detroit, Mich., and Rev. Thomas Kerwin, their spiritual director (1961), Frank Duff (1965), Mr. and Mrs. Thomas F. Larkin, Jr. (1973).

Poverello Medal (1949), by The College of Steubenville (Ohio), "in recognition of great benefactions to humanity, exemplifying in our age the Christ-like spirit of charity which filled the life of St. Francis of Assisi."

Alcoholics Anonymous Fellowship (1949), Edward F. Hutton (1950), the Court of Last Resort, New York, N. Y. (1951), The Lions International (1952), Variety Clubs International (1953), Llewellyn J. Scott (1954), Dr. Jonas E. Salk and Associates (1955), Mother Anna Dengel (1956), Catherine de Hueck Doherty (1957), D. M. Hamill (1958);

Daniel W. Egan, T. O. R. (1959, posthumously), Mrs. Emma C. Zeis (1960), Donald H. McGannon (1961), Jane Wyatt (1962), Birgit Nilsson (1963), Arthur Joseph Rooney (1964), Joe E. Brown (1965), Project Hope (1966), Lena F. Edwards (1967), VISTA (1968), Jack Twyman (1969), The Salvation Army (1970), Most Rev. John K. Mussio (1971). Bro. George J. Hungerman, F.M.S.I., M.D. (1972), The Dismas Committee of the St. Vincent de Paul Society (1973).

Regina Medal (1959), by the Catholic Library Association for outstanding contributions to children's literature.

Eleanor Farjeon (1959), Anne Carroll Moore (1960), Padraic Colum (1961), Frederick G. Melcher (1962), Ann Nolan Clark (1963), May Hill Arbuthnot (1964), Ruth Sawyer Durand (1965), Leo Politi (1966), Bertha Mahoney Miller (1967), Marguerite de Angeli (1968), Lois Lenski (1969), Ingri and Edgar Parin d'Aulaire (1970), Tasha Tudor (1971) Miendert DeJong (1972); Frances Clarke Sayers (1973), Robert McCloskey (1974).

Rerum Novarum Award (1949), by St. Peter's College (Jersey City, N. J.) for outstanding work in the interests of industrial peace.

Raymond Reiss (1949), Justin McAghon (1950), Frederick W. Mansfield (1951), Most Rev. Karl J. Alter (1952), Martin P. Durkin (1953), Christopher W. Hoey (1954), James P. Mitchell (1955), George Meany (1956), Henry Ford II (1957), Hugh E. Sheridan (1958);

Joseph F. Finnegan (1959), Cardinal Richard Cushing (1960), Joseph D. Keenan (1961), (no award 1962), Louis C. Seaton (1963).

Richard Reid Memorial Award (1963), by

the Catholic Institute of the Press (now the Catholic Alliance for Communications) in memory of its cofounder.

Thomas A. Brennan (1963), James A. Connolly (1964), John J. Sheehan (1965), Arthur Hull Hays (1966), Victor L. Ridder (1968), Bob Considine, (1969).

The Saint De La Salle Medal, by Manhattan College, for significant contribution to the moral, cultural or educational life of the nation.

John F. Brosnan (1951), Cardinal Francis Spellman (1952), Most Rev. Joseph P. Donahue (1953), Most Rev. Edwin V. O'Hara, posthumously (1950), Sr. Mary Emil, I.H.M. (1957), Msgr. Joseph E. Schieder (1958), Very Rev. Bro. Bertrand, O. S. F. (1959), Dr. Roy J. Deferrari (1960).

John Courtney Murray, S.J. (1961), Bro. Clair Stanislaus, F.S.C. (1962), Most Rev. Bryan J. McEntegart (1963), Sr. M. Rose Eileen, C.S.C. (1964), Mother Kathryn Sullivan, R.S.C.J. (1965), Bro. Bernard Peter, F.S.C. (1966), Dr. William Hughes Mulligan (1967), C. Alfred Koob, O. Praem. (1968), Theodore M. Hesburgh, C.S.C. (1970), Most Rev. Edwin B. Broderick (1971), Very Rev. Bro. Charles Henry, F.S.C. (1972), Mary Shea Giordano (1973).

St. Francis Xavier Medal (1954), by Xavier University (Cincinnati) to persons exemplifying the spirit of St. Francis Xavier.

Most Rev. Fulton J. Sheen, Rev. Leo Kampsen, Msgr. Frederick G. Hochwalt (1954), James Keller, M.M. (1955), Gen. Carlos P. Romulo (1956), Stan Musial, Aloysius A. Breen, S.J., Edwin G. Becker (1957), Msgr. (Maj. Gen.) Patrick J. Ryan, Msgr. (Maj. Gen.) Terrence P. Finnegan, Msgr. (Rear Adm.) George A. Rosso (1958);

Neal Ahern and T. L. Bouscaren, S.J. (1959), Celestine J. Steiner, S.J. (1960), Philip J. Scharper (1961), Charles Dismas Clark, S.J. (1962), Pres. John F. Kennedy (posthumously) and J. Paul Spaeth (1963), James B. Donovan (1964), Charles H. Keating, Jr. (1965), Frank Blair (1967), Martin H. Work (1968), Lt. Col. William A. Anders (1969), Bishop James E. Walsh, M.M. (1970), Lawrence Welk, Rev. Msgr. Ralph N. Beiting (1971), Paul L. O'Connor, S.J. (1972), James F. Maguire, S.J., Edward P. VonderHaar (posthumously) (1973), Daniel J. O'Conor, Jr. (1974).

St. Vincent de Paul Medal (1948), by St. John's University (Jamaica, N.Y.), for outstanding service to Catholic charities.

Francis D. McGarey (1948), John A. Coleman (1949), Aloysius L. Fitzpatrick (1950), Frank J. Lewis (1951), Howard W. Fitzpatrick (1952), Richard F. Mulroy (1953), Harry J. Kirk (1954), Bernard J. Keating (1955), John M. Nolan (1956), John R. Gariepy (1957);

Charles E. McCarthy (1958), Frederick V. Goess (1959), Maurice J. Costello (1960),

Thomas F. Hanley (1961), John J. Lynch (1962), William A. Walters (1963), George E. Heneghen (1964), James A. Quigney (1965), Henry J. Shields (1966);

Eugene McGovern (1967), George J. Krygier (1968), James A. Cousins (1969), Edward T. Reilly (1970), T. Raber Taylor (1971), Luke J. Smith (1972).

Serra Award of the Americas (1947), by the Academy of American Franciscan History for service to Inter-American good will.

Sumner Welles (1947), Pablo Martinez del Rio (1948), Dr. Herbert E. Bolton (1949), Gabriela Mistral (1950), Carlos E. Castaneda (1951), Victor A. Belaunde (1952), Clarence Haring (1953), Alceu Amoroso Lima (1954), France V. Scholes (1956);

Silvio Zavala (1957), John Tate Lanning (1958), John Basadre (1959), Arthur Preston Whitaker (1960), Marcel Bataillon (1961), Javier Malagon y Barcelo (1962), Dr. George P. Hammond (1964), Augustin Millares Carlo (1970).

Signum Fidei Medal (1942), by the Alumni Association of La Salle College (Phila.) for contribution to the advancement of Christian principles.

Brother E. Anselm, F.S.C. (1942), Karl H. Rogers (1943), Very Rev. Edward V. Stanford, O.S.A. (1944), Mrs. Edward V. Morrell (1945), Cardinal Dennis Dougherty (1946), Max Jordan (1947), John J. Sullivan (1948), Dr. Louis H. Clerf (1949), Most Rev. Gerald P. O'Hara (1950), Most Rev. Fulton J. Sheen (1951);

John H. Harris (1952), James Keller, M.M, (1953), John M. Haffert (1954), Dr. Francis J. Braceland (1955), Matthew H. McCloskey (1956), Henry Viscardi, Jr. (1957), no award (1958), Dr. Joseph J. Toland, Jr. (1959), Luke E. Hart (1960), Joseph E. McCafferty (1961);

Martin H. Work (1962), R. Sargent Shriver (1963), Mother M. Benedict, M.D. (1964), Sen. Eugene McCarthy (1965), William B. Ball (1966), Frank Folsom (1967), Rev. Leon H. Sullivan (1968), Rev. William J. Finley (1969);

Dr. James W. Turpin (1970), Lisa A. Richette, Esq. (1971), Rev. Melvin Floyd (1972), Elwood E. Kieser, C.S.P. (1973), Msgr. Philip J. Dowling (1974).

Soteriological Award (1967), by the Confraternity of the Passion (Third Order of the Passionists, St. Michael's Monastery, Union City, N. J.) for outstanding exemplification of sharing in the Passion of Christ in contemporary society.

Most Rev. Cuthbert M. O'Gara, C.P. (1967), Mrs. Martin Luther King, Jr. (1968), Veronica's Veil Players (1969), Mother Mary Teresa Benedetti, C.P. (1970), Dr. Billy Graham (1971), Mrs. Flo Kuhn (1972), Rev. Martin J. Tooker, C.P. (1973).

Stella Maris Medal (1960), by Mary Manse College (Toledo, O.) for service.

Alice R. May (1960), **Emma Endres**

Kountz (1961), Elizabeth M. Zepf (1962), Judge Geraldine F. Macelwane (1963), Ven. Mother Mary Adelaide, O.S.F. (1964), Marian Rejent, M.D. (1966), Mrs. Irene Hubbard McCarthy (1967), Sr. Ruth Hickey, S.G.M. (1969), Mrs. Ella Phillips Stewart (1970), Sr. M. Lawrence Wilson (1971), Mrs. Carol Pietrykowski (1972), Miss Rita O'Grady (1973).

Thomas More Association Medal (1954), by the Thomas More Association for distinguished contribution to Catholic literature during the year.

Doubleday and Co., Inc. (1954), Alfred A. Knopf, Inc. (1955), P. J. Kenedy and Sons, Inc. (1956), Farrar, Straus and Cudahy, Inc. (1957), Hawthorn Books (1958), Sheed and Ward, Inc. (1959), J. B. Lippincott Co. (1960), Doubleday and Co., Inc. (1961), Random House, Inc. (1962);

William Morrow and Co., Inc. (1963), Harper and Row (1964), Farrar, Straus and Giroux (1965), Doubleday and Co., Inc. (1966), Herder and Herder (1967), Hans Kueng (1968), John L. McKenzie, S.J. (1969), Daniel Callahan (1970). Daniel Berrigan, S.J. (1971), Andrew Greeley and Eugene Kennedy, M.M. (1972), Graham Greene (1973).

Vercelli Medal (1947), by the Holy Name Society for distinguished service to ideals of the society.

William Bruce, Paul M. Brennan, Joseph Scott, Stephen Barry, Patrick Kennedy (1947), R. W. Hoogstraet (1948), William H. Collins (1949), Ward D. Hopkins (1950), Charles A. Burkholder, James C. Connell, James T. Vocelle, Edwin J. Allen, Fred A. Muth, Austin J. Roche, Michael Lawlor (1951), Michael L. Roche (1953), Maurice J. O'Sullivan, Lucien T. Vivien, Jr. (1954);

John A. Lee, Sr., Daniel M. Hamill, Clarence F. Boggan, Louis J. Euler, Henry J. McGreevy, Ralph F. Nunlist (1955), James J. McDonnell (1957), Joseph J. Wilson (1958), William J. Meehan (1959), Paul Meade (1960), William T. Tavares (1961), David M. Martin (1962), Bert M. Walz (1963), Herbert Michelbrook (1964), Alfred A. McGarraghy (1965), Frank J. Beuerlein (1968), Humbert J. Campana (1970), Richard Asmus (1971), Charles J. Little (1973), William J. Burke, Jr. (1974).

CPA AWARDS

Catholic Press Association Awards for material published in 1973 were presented during the 64th CPA convention held Apr. 23 to 26, 1974, in Denver, Colo.

Newspapers

Awards were presented to newspapers in three categories of circulation: small — 1,000 to 13,000; medium — 13,000-38,000; large — 38,000 and over.

General excellence: *The Church World*, Portland, Me. (small); *The Monitor*, San Francisco (medium); *The National Catholic Reporter*, Kansas City, Mo. (large).

Best front page: *Mississippi Today*, Jackson (small); *The Record*, Louisville, Ky. (medium), *The St. Louis Review* (large).

Best campaign in the public interest: *The Church World* (small), for a nine-month right-to-life campaign; *The Catholic Free Press*, Worcester, Mass. (medium), for a campaign to prevent the closing of a maternity ward; *The Long Island Catholic*, Rockville Centre, N.Y. (large), for a presentation on revenue-sharing.

Awards without reference to circulation categories:

Best news story originating with a newspaper: *The Catholic Post*, Peoria, Ill., for "Peoria School Scene of Long Gun Battle," by Pat Sweeney.

Best background, in-depth, interpretative reporting: *The Evangelist*, Albany, N.Y., for "De-tailing Death" by James Breig.

Best editorial: *The Catholic Voice*, Oakland, Calif., for "America Is Losing Her Soul" by Father Richard A. Mangini.

Best editorial page or section: *The Eastern Kansas Register*, Kansas City, Kan.

Best human interest feature story: *The Witness*, Dubuque, Ia., for "The Happiest Man on Earth" by David Cushing, with photo by Steve Lansing.

Culture and arts column originating with a newspaper: *The Catholic Voice*, Oakland for "Arts of Leisure" by Ray Orrock.

Spiritual life column originating with a newspaper: *The Evangelist*, for its column by Sister Frances Eustace.

General commentary column originating with a newspaper: *The Catholic Bulletin*, St. Paul, Minn., for "Tracts for the Times" by Father Marvin R. O'Connell.

Syndicated column on spiritual life: Inter/Syndicate for its column by Father Richard P. McBrien.

Syndicated column of general commentary: Inter/Syndicate and its column by Father Andrew M. Greeley entitled "The Church — 1973."

Best youth coverage: *Western Catholic Reporter*, Edmonton, Alberta, Canada.

Best photo story originating with a newspaper: *The Catholic Sun*, Syracuse, N.Y., for "Young People Who Care" by J. R. Costello.

Best photograph originating with a newspaper: *The National Catholic Reporter*, for picture of Dorothy Day and pickets by Bob Fitch.

Best example of circulation promotion: *The New World*, Chicago, and *The Catholic Exponent*, Youngstown, O.

Best news story, background piece, editorial or treatment dealing with justice and peace. *The Idaho Register*, Boise, for its five-part series by Father William Taylor on injustice in Colombia.

Best special issue, section or supplement:

The Catholic Standard, Washington, D.C.

Best example of advertising promotion: *The Catholic Northwest Progress,* Seattle.

Magazines

General excellence: *U.S. Catholic* (general interest); *Maryknoll* (missions); *Catholic Lawyer* (professional and special interest); *The American Benedictine Review* (scholarly); *My Daily Visitor* (devotional); *Pastoral Life* (clergy and religious); *National Jesuit News* (religious orders).

Best color cover: *The Catechist* (four-color); *Momentum* (two or three-color); *The Catechist* (single color).

Best short story: *The Sign,* for "Memories Are Priceless" by Whitfield Cook.

Best article originating with a magazine: *Columbia,* for "Abortion Is Killing" by Dr. and Mrs. J. C. Willke.

Best editorial: *America,* for "A White House Homily — Undelivered."

Best regular column originating with a magazine: *National Jesuit News,* for "Movies by Malcolm" by Father Malcolm W. Gordon, S.J.

Best single photo originating with a magazine: *Momentum,* for "Latin American Girl" by Carl Balcerak.

Best photo story originating with a magazine: *U.S. Catholic,* for "The White Man's Forked Tongue" by Paul Conklin.

Best illustration of an article, story or poem with art work or photography: *The Catechist,* for "Religious Education — Family Style" by Robert Cyphers (illustrator), Richard Reichert (author), Joe Loverti (designer).

Best poetry: "Thought for Erogenesis" by Duane Edwards.

Best treatment of peace and justice: *St. Anthony Messenger,* for "Brazil Bishop's Fight for Human Rights" by Gary MacEoin.

Best special issue, section or supplement: *Commonweal,* for its 50th anniversary issue.

Best single piece of promotion: *Today's Catholic Teacher* for the booklet, "The Catholic School Textbooks Market Guide."

Special award by the judges: *U.S. Catholic,* for its sustained editorial/circulation promotional campaign.

Books

Christian life and inspiration: *Time and Myth,* John Dunne, Doubleday & Co.

Theology: *Theology of Liberation,* Gustavo Gutierrez; Orbis Books.

Scripture: *Virginal Conception and Bodily Resurrection of Jesus,* Raymond Brown, S.S.; Paulist Press; and *This Man Jesus,* Bruce Vawter, C.M.; Doubleday & Co.

Religious history and biography: *The Asian Journal,* Thomas Merton; New Directions.

Catechetics: *Catechetics in Context,* Berard Marthaler; Our Sunday Visitor.

Fiction: *Catholics,* Brian Moore; Holt, Rinehart & Winston.

Marriage and family: *Divorce and Remarriage in the Catholic Church,* Lawrence Wrenn; Paulist Press.

Young people: *Good News for Little Christians,* Sister Marjorie Gilbert with Edward Wakin; Our Sunday Visitor.

CHRISTOPHER AWARDS

Christopher Awards were presented Feb. 28, 1974, in New York City to book authors and to the producers, directors and writers of the feature-length motion pictures and network television specials cited below. The award is a bronze medallion inscribed with the Christopher motto, "It is better to light one candle than to curse the darkness."

Award winners were selected on the basis of their affirmation of the highest values of the human spirit, artistic and technical accomplishment, and a significant degree of public acceptance of their work.

Special Christopher Awards were presented to Frank Sheed and Maisie Ward for their outstanding contribution to religious book publishing.

Books for Adults

Erma Brenner, *A New Baby! A New Life!,* illustrated by Symeon Shimin; McGraw-Hill.

Hope Chamberlain, *A Minority of Members — Women in the U.S. Congress;* Praeger.

Sharon R. Curtin, *Nobody Ever Died of Old Age;* Atlantic-Little, Brown.

Allen F. Davis, *American Heroine: The Life and Legend of Jane Addams;* Oxford.

Barbara Howes, editor, *The Eye of the Heart — 42 Great Short Stories by Latin American Writers;* Bobbs-Merrill.

Kenneth Koch, *Rose, Where Did You Get That Red?;* Random House.

A. W. Reed, *Myths and Legends of Australia,* illustrated by Roger Hart; Taplinger.

Dougal Robertson, *Survive the Savage Sea;* Praeger.

Ronald B. Taylor, *Sweatshops in the Sun — Child Labor on the Farm;* Beacon.

Books for Young People

N. M. Bodecker, *It's Raining Said John Twaining — Danish Nursery Rhymes,* Athanaeum, a Margaret K. McElderry Book; preschool.

Martha Alexander, *I'll Protect You From the Beasts;* Dial; ages 5-8.

Carol Fenner, *Gorilla, Gorilla,* illustrated by Symeon Shimin; Random House; ages 5-8.

Dr. Michael Fox, *The Wolf,* illustrated by Charles Frace; Coward, McCann & Geoghegan; ages 8-12.

Kristin Hunter, *Guests in the Promised Land;* Scribners; ages 12 and up.

Robert A. Liston, *The Right to Know — Censorship in America;* Franklin Watts; ages 12 and up.

Motion Pictures

"Tom Sawyer," Readers' Digest Production; family.

"Bang the Drum Slowly," Paramount, and "The New Land," Warner Brothers; adults and adolescents.

Television Specials

"ABC News Closeup: Food: Green Grow the Profits."

"Appointment with Destiny: Peary's Race for the North Pole," CBS.

"B.J. and Eddie Outward Bound," ABC.

"Bill Moyers' Journal: An Essay on Watergate," WNET.

"CBS Reports: You and the Commercial."

"A Child's Christmas in Wales," CBS.

"A Conversation with Dr. Abraham Joshua Heschel," NBC.

"The Forbidden City," NBC.

"If That's a Gnome . . . This Must Be Zurich," NBC.

"I Heard the Owl Call My Name," CBS.

"A Man Whose Name Was John," ABC.

"The Man Without a Country," ABC.

"New Hopes for Health," ABC.

"Rookie of the Year," ABC.

"The Selfish Giant," CBS.

"Street of the Flower Boxes," NBC.

"The World Turned Upside Down," ABC.

GABRIEL AWARDS

Gabriel Awards are presented annually for excellence in radio and television broadcasting by UNDA-USA, the Catholic fraternal association for broadcasters and allied communicators.

Awards presented May 30, 1974, for outstanding achievement in the 1973 broadcasting year are listed below.

Television

"GE Theater: I Heard the Owl Call My Name," CBS-TV, produced by Tomorrow Entertainment, Inc.

"Christmas at the Worcester Art Museum," WSMW-TV, Worcester, Mass.

"The Sins of the Fathers," NBC.

"Close-Up: Fire," ABC News.

"Come Along . . . With Ulysses S. Grant," WABC-TV.

"The Littlest Junkie: A Children's Story," WABC-TV.

"The Questions of Abraham," CBS News.

"Montage: They Shall Take Up Serpents," WKYC-TV, Cleveland, Ohio.

"Paper Chains" (from the "Everyman" Series), WMAQ-TV, Chicago, produced by the Church Federation of Greater Chicago.

"Close-Up: Life, Liberty and the Pursuit of Coal," ABC News.

"Street of the Flower Boxes," NBC.

"Ladybug's Garden," WNYS-TV, Syracuse, N.Y., produced by Ladybug's Garden Productions, Inc., Camillus, N.Y.

"6th Grade Report," Buckeye Cablevision, Inc., Toledo, Ohio.

"Love Tells the Truth" (TeleSPOTS), Franciscan Communications Center, Los Angeles, Calif.

"Anti-Drug Spots," WJCT-TV, Jacksonville, Fla.

"The Orphanage," WABC-TV, produced by Rosenfeld, Sirowitz and Lawson, New York.

Award for Outstanding Contributions to Children's Programming: Robert Keeshan (Captain Kangeroo), CBS.

Station Award: KPIX-TV, San Francisco, Calif.

Radio

"John the Baptist," WOWO Radio, Fort Wayne, Ind.

"The Battered American Marriage," NBC News.

"Dear Jack . . . BZ Remembers JFK," WBZ Radio, Boston, Mass.

"Abortion: An Investigative Report," WCAU Radio, Philadelphia, Pa.

"Love Notes for Listeners 'Water,' " KCBS-FM, produced by the Archdiocesan Communications Center, San Francisco, Calif.

"In Touch," WJW Radio, North Royalton, Ohio, produced by the Greater Cleveland Interchurch Council and the Catholic Diocese of Cleveland.

"What's It All About," TRAV, Atlanta, Ga.

"I'll Never Tell," Archdiocesan Communications Center, San Francisco, Calif.

"Mail Bag," KBPS Radio, Portland, Ore.

"For What It's Worth," WRIF Radio, Detroit, produced by the Metropolitan Detroit Council of Churches.

"Your Last Contest," WIXY Radio, Cleveland, Ohio.

"Lovewords," KRLD Radio, Dallas, Tex., produeced by Harry O'Connor, Hollywood, Calif.

"Listening Is the Beginning of Understanding," (Church of Jesus Christ of Latter-Day Saints), produced by Bonneville Program Services, Salt Lake City, Utah.

"Country Crossroads," Radio and TV Commission of the Southern Baptist Convention, Fort Worth, Tex.

In addition, 18 other TV and 9 radio programs were awarded certificates of merit by UNDA.

Newswriters' Award

The Supple Memorial Award for 1974 was presented in June to Marjorie Hyer of the *Washington Post.* The former NC News Service correspondent was honored for analytical articles on the abortion issue after the 1973 rulings of the Supreme Court, and a number of other articles relating religious news to national significance.

OBSCENITY LAWS AND THE SUPREME COURT

Between 1967 and the beginning of the 1972-73 term, five Supreme Court Justices handed down 22 or more decisions in which they overturned obscenity convictions in 14 states and overruled 98 jurists of lower courts.

These rulings, along with the following decisions of the entire Supreme Court, served as precedents for decisions handed down June 21, 1973, in Miller v. California, Paris Adult Theater v. Slaton, and related cases.

Roth Test

Roth v. United States, Alberts v. California (1957): The Court ruled that obscene literature is not within the area of speech or press protected by the Constitution. The ruling was based on the observation: "Implicit in the history of the First Amendment is the rejection of obscenity as utterly without redeeming social importance. This rejection for that reason is mirrored in the universal judgment that obscenity should be restrained."

The Court gave this test of obscenity: "Whether to the average person, applying community standards, the dominant theme of the material taken as a whole appeals to prurient interest."

In connection with this definition, the Court indicated that material relating to sex is not necessarily obscene. Determiing standards of obscenity were said to be:

• The quality of the material must be of such a nature that it has the inherent "capacity to attract individuals eager for a forbidden look: that is, it must consist of material which goes substantially beyond customary limits of candor in the description or representation of nudity, sex or shameful acts."

• It must be offensive to the community conscience and not merely to a group in the community. This standard, however, does not outlaw the enactment of statutes designed to prevent the deliberate distribution of obscene literature to children.

• The offensive material must constitute the dominant theme. Unrelated excerpts or incidental passages are not sufficient to render a book obscene.

Smith v. California: The Court ruled unconstitutional a Los Angeles ordinance making it a criminal offense to have an obscene book in one's possession for the purpose of sale, on the ground that the ordinance did not make "knowledge" of the obscene contents an essential element of the crime.

Roth Test Modified

Manual Enterprises v. Day (1962): The Court reversed a Circuit Court of Appeals decision which had substantiated findings of the Post Office Department that homosexual material could not be mailed because it was obscene and because the magazine in question indicated where obscene material could be obtained. One opinion supporting the decision held that the allegedly objectionable material was not of such a nature as to be considered "patently offensive" by community standards of the nation. This line of thought represented a modification of the community standards test stated in Roth.

Jacobellis v. Ohio (1964): The Court reversed the conviction of a motion picture operator for exhibiting "The Lovers." The opinion noted that "a work cannot be proscribed unless it is utterly without social importance," and that the term "community standards" used in Roth does not refer to a local standard but rather to a national standard.

Tralins v. Gerstein, Grove Press, Inc., v. Gerstein: The Court ruled that Florida courts had erred in finding two publications obscene, *Pleasure Is My Business* and *Tropic of Cancer.*

Three major decisions were handed down Mar. 21, 1966, when the Court sustained the convictions of **Ralph Ginzburg**, publisher of *Eros* magazine, and **Edward Mishkin**, publisher of books on sadism and masochism, while reversing a Massachusetts ban on John Clelan's 18th century novel, *Fanny Hill.*

In the Ginzburg ruling it said that, when material is neither obviously obscene nor obviously not obscene, courts may take the advertising and promotional activities of distributors into account as an indication of their intentions.

In the Mishkin case, the Court said legal obscenity is present when the material appeals to the prurient interest of the special audience to which it is addressed.

In the *Fanny Hill* decision, the Court declared that the presence of "redeeming social value" can render a work immune to a ban on grounds of obscenity

1973 Decisions

The trend of Court decisions from 1957 was progressively permissive, with modification of the initial Roth test with the concept of national community standards and standards of "redeeming social values."

The Court reversed this trend with five 5 to 4 decisions on representative obscenity cases June 21, 1973.

In **Miller v. California** (No. 70-73), the Court ruled:

• Obscenity laws can be enforced against the publication and sale of works which "appeal to the prurient interest in sex, which portray (specifically defined) sexual conduct in a patently offensive way, and which, taken as a whole, do not have serious literary, artistic, political or scientific value."

• A jury of "average persons, applying contemporary community (rather than national) standards," can determine prurient appeal or patent offensiveness.

• "Some redeeming social value" is not available as a defense against prosecution for obscenity, as it had been since 1966.

In **Paris Adult Theater v. Slaton** (No. 71-1051), the Court ruled:

• States can assume, in the absence of clear proof to the contrary, that there is a causal connection between obscene material and crime and anti-social behavior.

• No constitutional doctrine of privacy protects the display of obscene material in public places.

At the time of the Court's decisions in 1973, at least 15 states had laws in line with the stated guidelines, 19 had statutes contain-ing the "utterly without redeeming social value" clause, and 12 or more had no legal definition of obscenity.

Subsequent decisions by the Supreme Court and other courts, along with related legislative actions, have failed, practically, to frame a definition of obscenity precise enough to be applied by law enforcement officials and lower courts with a minimum number of appeals. The status of laws regarding obscenity and pornography is considerably muddled, and prospects for future clarifications are uncertain.

ABBREVIATIONS

A.A.: Augustinianus Assumptionis; Augustinians of the Assumption (Assumptionists).

A.A.S.: "Acta Apostolicae Sedis"; Acts of the Apostolic See.

A.B.: Artium Baccalaureus; Bachelor of Arts.

Abb.: abbacy.

Abp.: Archbishop.

A.D.: Anno Domini; in the year of the Lord.

ad lib.: ad libitum; at your own choice.

A.M.: Artium Magister; Master of Arts.

A.M.D.G.: Ad majorem Dei gloriam; to the greater glory of God.

Ap.: Apostle.

A.U.C.: Ab Urbe Condita; from the founding of the city.

A.V.: Authorized Version (of the Bible).

b: born.

B.A.: Bachelor of Arts.

B.C.: Before Christ.

B.C.L.: Bachelor of Canon (Civil) Law.

Bl.: Blessed.

Bp.: Bishop.

Bro.: Brother.

B.S.: Bachelor of Science.

B.V.M: Blessed Virgin Mary.

c.: circa; about.

CARA: Center for Applied Research in the Apostolate.

C.E.: Common or Christian Era.

CCC: Canadian Catholic Conference.

CCD: Confraternity of Christian Doctrine.

CEF: Citizens for Educational Freedom.

C.F.A.: Congregatio Fratrum Cellitarum seu Alexianorum; Alexian Brothers.

CFM: Christian Family Movement.

C.F.X.: Congregatio Fratrum S. Francisci Xaverii; Xaverian Brothers.

C.I.C.: Codex Iuris Canonici; Code of Canon Law.

C.I.C.M: Congregatio Immaculati Cordis Mariae; Congregation of the Immaculate Heart of Mary (Scheut Fathers).

C.J.: Congregatio Josephitarum Gerardimontensium; Josephite Fathers (of Belgium).

C.J.M.: Congregation of Jesus and Mary (Eudists).

C.M.: Congregation of the Mission (Vincen-tians or Lazarists).

C.M.F.: Cordis Mariae Filius; Missionary Sons of the Immaculate Heart of Mary.

C.M.M.: Congregatio Missionariorum de Mariannhill; Missionaries of Mariannhill.

CMSM: Conference of Major Superiors of Men.

C.O.: Congregatio Oratorii; Oratorian Fathers.

COCU: Consultation on Church Union.

C.P.: Congregation of the Passion.

CPA: Catholic Press Association.

CPF: Catholic Press Features.

C.P.M.: Congregatio Presbyterorum a Misericordia; Congregation of the Fathers of Mercy.

C.PP.S.: Congregatio Missionariorum Pretiosissimi Sanguinis; Society of the Precious Blood.

C.R.: Congregation of the Resurrection.

C.R.M.: Clerics Regular Minor.

CRS: Catholic Relief Services.

C.R.S.P.: Clerics Regular of St. Paul (Barnabite Fathers).

C.S.: Missionaries of St. Charles.

C.S.B.: Congregation of St. Basil (Basilians).

C.S.C.: Congregatio Sanctae Crucis; Congregation of Holy Cross.

C.S.P.: Paulist Fathers.

C.S.S.: Congregation of the Sacred Stigmata: (Stigmatine Fathers and Brothers).

C.SS.R.: Congregatio Sanctissimi Redemptoris; Congregation of the Most Holy Redeemer (Redemptorists).

C.S.Sp.: Congregatio Sancti Spiritus; Congregation of the Holy Ghost.

C.S.V.: Clerks of St. Viator (Viatorians).

C.Y.O.: Catholic Youth Organization.

D.C.L.: Doctor Canonicae (Civilis) Legis; Doctor of Canon (Civil) Law.

Doctor Divinitatis; Doctor of Divinity.

D.N.J.C.: Dominus noster Jesus Christus; Our Lord Jesus Christ.

Doct.: Doctor.

D.O.M.: Deo Optimo Maximo; To God, the Best and Greatest.

D.V.: Deo volente; God willing.

e.g.: exempli gratia; for example.

ER: Eastern Rite News Service.

Er. Cam.: Congregatio Monachorum Eremitarum Camaldulensium; Monk Hermits of Camaldoli.

et al.: et alii or et aliae; and others.

exc.: except.

f., ff.: following.

F.D.P.: Filii Divini Providentiae; Sons of Divine Providence.

F.M.S.: Fratris Maristarum a Scholis; Marist Brothers.

F.M.S.I.: Filii Mariae Salutis Infirmorum; Sons of Mary, Health of the Sick.

Fr.: Father, or Friar.

F.S.C.: Fratres Scholarum Christianorum; Brothers of the Christian Schools (Christian Brothers).

F.S.C.J.: Congregatio Filiorum S. Cordis Jesu; Sons of the Sacred Heart (Verona Fathers).

I.C.: Institute of Charity (Rosminians).

ICEL: International Committee on English in the Liturgy.

i.e.: id est; that is.

IHS: Iesus Hominem Salvator; Jesus, the Savior of Men.

I.M.C.: Institutum Missionum a Consolata; Consolata Society for Foreign Missions.

I.N.R.I.: Iesus Nazarenus, Rex Iudaeorum; Jesus of Nazareth, King of the Jews.

J.C.D.: Juris Canonici Doctor; Doctor of Canon Law.

J.C.L.: Juris Canonici Licentiatus; Licentiate in Canon Law.

J.M.J.: Jesus, Mary, Joseph.

J.U.D.: Juris Utriusque Doctor; Doctor of Both Civil and Canon Laws.

K. of C.: Knights of Columbus.

K.H.S.: Knight of the Holy Sepulchre.

K.P.: Knight of Pius IX.

K.S.G.: Knight of St. Gregory.

K.S.S.: Knight of St. Sylvester.

LCWR: Leadership Conference of Women Religious.

LL.B.: Legum Baccalaureus; Bachelor of Laws.

LL.D.: Legum Doctor; Doctor of Laws.

LWF: Lutheran World Federation.

M.E.P.: Societe des Missions Etrangeres de Paris; Paris Foreign Missions Society.

M.H.M.: Mill Hill Missionaries.

M.I.C.: Congregatio Clericorum Regularium Marianorum sub titulo Immaculatae Conceptionis Beatae Mariae Virginis; Marian Fathers.

MM: Martyrs.

M.M.: Catholic Foreign Mission Society (Maryknoll Missioners).

M.S.: Missionaries of Our Lady of La Salette.

M.S.C.: Missionaries of the Sacred Heart.

M.S.F.: Congregatio Missionarorum a Sancta Familia; Missionaries of the Holy Family.

Msgr.: Monsignor.

NAB: New American Bible.

NAWR: National Association of Women Religious.

NC: National Catholic News Service.

NCC: National Council of Churches.

NCCB: National Conference of Catholic Bishops.

NCCL: National Catholic Council of the Laity.

NCCM: National Council of Catholic Men.

NCCS: National Catholic Community Service.

NCCW: National Council of Catholic Women.

NCEA: National Catholic Educational Association.

NCRLC: National Catholic Rural Life Conference.

NEB: New English Bible.

NFPC: National Federation of Priests' Councils.

NOBC: National Office for Black Catholics.

N.T.: New Testament.

O.A.R.: Order of Augustinian Recollects.

O.Carm.: Ordo Carmelitarum; Order of Calced Carmelites (Carmelites).

O.Cart.: Ordo Cartusiensis; Carthusian Order.

O.C.D.: Ordo Carmelitarum Discalceatorum; Order of Discalced Carmeelites.

O.C.S.O.: Order of Cistercians of the Strict Observance (Trappists). Other Cistercisions are of the Common Observance.

O. de M.: Ordo B. Mariae de Merced; Order of Mercy (Mercedarians).

O.F.M.: Order of Friars Minor (Franciscans).

O.F.M.Cap.: Order of Friars Minor Capuchin (Capuchins).

O.F.M. Conv.: Order of Friars Minor Conventual (Conventuals).

O.H.: Ordo Hospitalarius S. Joannis de Deo; Hospitaller Order of St. John of God.

O.M.I.: Oblates of Mary Immaculate.

O.P.: Order of Preachers (Dominicans).

O. Praem: Order of Premonstratensians (Norbertines).

O.S.A.: Order of Hermits of St. Augustine (Augustinians).

O.S.B.: Order of St. Benedict (Benedictines).

O.S.B.M.: Ordo Sancti Basilii Magni; Order of St. Basil the Great.

O.S.C: Ordo S. Crucis; Order of the Holy Cross (Crosier Fathers).

O.S.Cam: Order of St. Camillus (Camillians).

O.S.F.: Order of St. Francis; Franciscan Brothers; also various congregations of Franciscan Sisters.

O.S.F.S.: Oblates of St. Francis de Sales.

O.S.J.: Oblates of St. Joseph.

O.S.M.: Order of Servants of Mary (Servites).

O.S.P. Order of St. Paul the First Hermit (Pauline Fathers).

O.SS.T.: Ordo Sanctissimae Trinitatis Redemptionis Captivorum; Order of the Most Holy Trinity (Trinitarians).

O.T.: Old Testament.

P.A.: Protonotary Apostolic.

Ph.D.: Philosophiae Doctor; Doctor of Philosophy.

P.I.M.E.: Pontificium Institutum pro Missionibus Exteris; Pontifical Institute for Foreign Missions; Missionaries of Sts. Peter and Paul.

Pont. Max.: Pontifex Maximus; Supreme Pontiff.

PP., Pp.: Papa (Pope).

R.C.: Roman Catholic.

R.I.P.: Requiescat in pace; may he [she] rest in peace.

RNS: Religious News Service.

R.P.: Reverendus Pater (Reverend Father).

R.V.: Revised Version (of the Bible).

S.A.: Societas Adunationis (Franciscan Friars of the Atonement).

S.A.C.: Societatis Apostolatus Catholici; Society of the Catholic Apostolate (Pallottines).

Sch.P. or S.P.: Ordo Clericorum Regularum Pauperum Matris Dei Scholarum Piarum; Piarist Fathers.

S.C.J.: Congregatio Sacerdotum a Corde Jesu; Congregation of Priests of the Sacred Heart.

S.D.B.: Salesians of Don Bosco.

S.D.S.: Society of the Divine Savior (Salvatorians).

S.D.V.: Society of Divine Vocations.

S.F.: Congregatio Filiorum Sacrae Familiae; Sons of the Holy Family.

S.J.: Society of Jesus (Jesuits).

S.M.: Society of Mary (Marists); Society of Mary (Marianists).

S.M.A.: Societas Missionum ad Afros; Society of African Missions.

S.M.B.: Societas Missionaria de Bethlehem; Society of Bethlehem Missionaries.

S.M.M.: Societas Mariae Montfortana; Company of Mary (Montfort Fathers).

S.O.Cist: Sacer Ordo Cisterciensis; Cistercians of the Common Observance.

SODEPAX: Joint Commission for Society, Development and Peace.

S.P.: Piarist Fathers; Servants of the Holy Paraclete.

Sr.: Sister.

S.S.: Society of St. Sulpice (Sulpicians).

SS.CC.: Congregatio Sacrorum Cordium; Fathers of the Sacred Hearts.

S.S.E.: Society of St. Edmund.

S.S.J.: Societas Sancti Joseph SSmi Cordis; St. Joseph's Society of the Sacred Heart (Josephites).

S.S.L.: Sacrae Scripturae Licentiatus; Licentiate in Sacred Scripture.

S.S.P: Society of St. Paul.

S.S.S.: Sacerdoti del Sanctissimo Sacramento; Congregation of the Blessed Sacrament.

S., St.; SS., Sts.: Saint; Saints.

S.T.: Missionarii Servi Sanctissimae Trinitatis; Missionary Servants of the Most Holy Trinity.

S.T.B.: Sacrae Theologiae Baccalaureus; Bachelor of Sacred Theology.

S.T.D.: Sacrae Theologiae Doctor; Doctor of Sacred Theology.

S.T.L.: Sacrae Theologiae Licentiatus; Licentiate in Sacred Theology.

S.T.M.: Sacrae Theologiae Magister; Master of Sacred Theology.

S.V.D.: Societas Verbi Divini; Society of the Divine Word.

S.X.: Xaverian Missionary Fathers.

T.O.R.: Third Order Regular of St. Francis.

T.O.S.F.: Tertiary of Third Order of St. Francis.

UN: United Nations.

UNCTAD: United Nations Conference on Trade and Development.

UNESCO: United Nations Educational, Scientific and Cultural Organization.

UNICEF: United Nations Children's Fund.

USCC: United States Catholic Conference.

V.A.: Vicar Apostolic.

Ven.: Venerable.

V.F.: Vicar Forane.

V.G.: Vicar General.

V.T.: Vetus Testamentum; Old Testament.

WCC: World Council of Churches.

W.F.: White Fathers.

Y.C.M.: Young Christian Movement.

Zip Codes

These abbreviations have been approved for use with ZIP Code numbers.

Alabama, AL; Alaska, AK; Arizona, AZ; Arkansas, AR; California, CA; Colorado, CO; Connecticut, CT; Delaware, DE; District of Columbia, DC; Florida, FL;

Georgia, GA; Guam, GU; Hawaii, HI; Idaho, ID; Illinois, IL; Indiana, IN; Iowa, IA; Kansas, KS; Kentucky, KY; Louisiana, LA;

Maine, ME; Maryland, MD; Massachusetts, MA; Michigan, MI; Minnesota, MN; Mississippi, MS; Missouri, MO; Montana, MT; Nebraska, NB; Nevada, NV;

New Hampshire, NH; New Jersey, NJ; New Mexico, NM; New York, NY; North Carolina, NC; North Dakota, ND; Ohio, OH; Oklahoma, OK; Oregon, OR; Pennsylvania, PA;

Puerto Rico, PR; Rhode Island, RI; South Carolina, SC; South Dakota, SD; Tennessee, TN; Texas, TX; Utah, UT; Vermont, VT; Virginia, VA; Virgin Islands, VI;

Washington, WA; West Virginia, WV; Wisconsin, WI; Wyoming, WY.

TITLES AND FORMS OF ADDRESS IN LETTERS

For Churchmen

In general, it has been customary for Catholics to add the words "in Christ" to the appropriate conclusions of formal letters to ecclesiastical dignitaries, priests and religious. "Asking Your Excellency's blessing" and similar forms have also been customary.

Given below are forms of proper address, salutation and conclusion.

Patriarchs: His Beatitude (Christian Name and Surname), Patriarch of (See City); Your Beatitude; Asking the Apostolic Blessing of Your Beatitude, I am, Yours respectfully, (Name).

Cardinals: His Eminence (Christian Name) Cardinal (Surname); (if he is an archbishop or bishop, include Title of the See); Your Eminence; Asking the Blessing of Your Eminence, I am, Yours respectfully, (Name).

Archbishops and Bishops: The Most Rev. (Name), Archbishop or Bishop of (Name of See); Your Excellency; Asking Your Excellency's Blessing, I am, Yours respectfully, (Name).

Abbots: The Right Rev. (Name), Abbot of (Name of Abbey); Right Reverend and dear Abbot; I am, Yours respectfully, (Name).

Monsignors: The Rev. Monsignor or Monsignor (Name); Reverend and dear Monsignor; I am, Yours respectfully, (Name).

Rectors of Seminaries, Heads of Colleges: The Very Rev. (Name); Very Reverend and dear Father; I am, Yours respectfully, (Name).

Provincials of Religious Orders: The Very Rev. Father Provincial, (Name, Title of Order); Very Reverend and dear Father Provincial; I am, Yours respectfully, (Name).

Diocesan Clergy: The Rev. (Name); Reverend and dear Father; Respectfully yours, (Name).

Regular Clergy: The Rev. (Name); Reverend and dear Father (Religious Name); Respectfully yours, (Name). Benedictine and Cistercian Monks and Canons Regular are addressed as The Rev. Dom (Name).

Clerics in Major Orders below the Priesthood: The Reverend (Religious Name) or The Reverend Mr. (Name). Reverend Sir or Dear Mr. (Name); Respectfully yours, (Name).

Brothers and Sisters: Brother or Sister (Name); Dear Brother or Sister (Religious Name); Respectfully yours, (Name).

Protestant Minister: The Reverend (Name), Reverend Sir; Very truly yours, (Name).

Rabbi: Rabbi (Name): Reverend Sir; Very truly yours, (Name).

For Others

President: The President; Dear Mr. President; Yours very truly, (Name).
Vice-President: The Vice-President; Dear Mr. Vice-President; Yours very truly, (Name).

Member of Cabinet: The Honorable (Name), Secretary of (Name of Department); Dear Mr. (or Madam) Secretary; Yours very truly, (Name).

Ambassador: The Honorable, or His Excellency, for Ambassador of foreign country (Name), Ambassador to (Name of Country); Dear Mr. Ambassador (Your Excellency, for ambassador of foreign country); Yours very truly, (Name).

Senator: The Honorable (Name), United States Senate; My dear Senator, Dear Mr. (or Madam) Senator; Yours very truly, (Name).

Congressman: The Honorable (Name), United States House of Representatives, Dear Sir (Madam); Yours very truly, (Name).

Member of Supreme Court: The Honorable (Name), United States Supreme Court; Dear Mr. Justice; Yours very truly (Name).

Judge: TJHE Honorable (Name), Name of Court; Dear Sir, Dear Judge (Name); Yours very truly, (Name).

Governor: The Honorable (Name), Governor of (Name of State); Dear Sir; Yours very truly, (Name).

Mayor: The Honorable (Name), Mayor of (Name of City); Dear Sir; Yours very truly, (Name).

Military and Naval Officers: Rank, for general and commissioned officers, (Name); Dear Sir; Yours very truly, (Name). Warrant officers and flight officers are addressed as Mister; non-commissioned officers, by their titles.

King: His Majesty (Name); Sir, or May it please Your Majesty; Yours very truly, (Name).

Ecclesiastical Titles

According to instructions issued by Pope Paul Mar. 28, 1969, titles used by him with reference to cardinals, bishops and other church dignitaries are limited to: "Our Venerable Brother," "Venerable Brother," "Beloved Son."

Customary titles still stand for cardinals and bishops; e.g., "Eminence," "Excellency," "Most Reverend," "Lord Cardinal," "Monsignor," is used for prelates of honor and chaplains of the pope.

Recent changes in the life styles of religious have been accompanied by changes in titles of superiors. In some institutes, general superiors are known as presidents and the heads of convents as coordinators. Many superiors have relinquished the title of mother. Many institutes no longer require their members to adopt a religious name for use in place of a given name, and it has become customary for religious, sisters and brothers, to use family names.

MORE BOOKS FROM OUR SUNDAY VISITOR, INC.

THE WAY (Catholic edition) — THE LIVING BIBLE

The Catholic edition of *THE WAY* is perhaps the most meaningful version of the Bible you can own. Acclaimed by the Catholic community as communicating the message of Christ to our generation! Highlighted by Father Keith Clark's foreword, the text itself is a paraphrase of the Bible, done in contemporary American language and style. *THE WAY* features a durable "kivar" cover, 1,116 pages plus introduction and over 90 photographs and illustrations. No. 833 .... $5.95

TO SETTLE YOUR CONSCIENCE
by Reverend Cass Kucharek

The aftermath of "new morality" and the lack of proper religious instruction have created confusion for Catholics trying to solve everyday moral dilemmas. *TO SETTLE YOUR CONSCIENCE* erases those doubts by giving straight answers (based on solid Church principles) to hundreds of perplexing moral problems. It's an up-to-date guide to the proper formation of conscience, illustrated by down-to-earth examples. 262 pages, paperbound, No. 877 .... $3.95

THE FAITH OF MILLIONS
by Reverend John A. O'Brien, Ph.D.

The truths of our faith are as old as the Church itself, but they need to be restated for those who are seeking to find and understand the Church. To embody the numerous changes brought about by Vatican Council II and by the worldwide ecumenical movement, Fr. O'Brien sets forth Catholic teaching on all the moot questions on matters of religion. A splendid exposition of all the doctrines and practices of the Catholic religion. 438 pages, paperbound, No. 830 .... $4.95

If your bookseller does not have these titles, you may order them by sending listed price (we pay postage and handling) to the Book Department at the address below. Enclose check or money order — do not send cash.

Write for free book list.

Our Sunday Vistor, Inc. ● **Noll Plaza** ● **Huntington, IN 46750**

Please send me the CATHOLIC ALMANAC.

1975 "Holy Year" Edition
_____ copies clothbound, no. 871 @ $9.95
_____ copies paperbound, no. 818 @ $4.95

1976 Edition — Advance Order
_____ copies clothbound, no. 872
_____ copies paperbound, no. 820

( ) Payment enclosed $_____. We pay postage and handling.
( ) Bill me. Postage and 50¢ handling additional.
    Remittance must accompany orders under $5.00

( ) Yes. ( ) No. Do you wish to place a standing order for the CATHOLIC ALMANAC? You will automatically receive your copy each year as it is published. You will be billed annually.
    State number desired.
       _____ clothbound copies per year
       _____ paperbound copies per year

Name _____
                        (please print)

Address _____

City _____ **Prov. State** _____ **Zip** _____ CA75

Please send me the CATHOLIC ALMANAC.

1975 "Holy Year" Edition
_____ copies clothbound, no. 871 @ $9.95
_____ copies paperbound, no. 818 @ $4.95

1976 Edition — Advance Order
_____ copies clothbound, no. 872
_____ copies paperbound, no. 820

( ) Payment enclosed $_____. We pay postage and handling.
( ) Bill me. Postage and 50¢ handling additional.
    Remittance must accompany orders under $5.00

( ) Yes. ( ) No. Do you wish to place a standing order for the CATHOLIC ALMANAC? You will automatically receive your copy each year as it is published. You will be billed annually.
    State number desired.
       _____ clothbound copies per year
       _____ paperbound copies per year

Name _____
                        (please print)

Address _____

City _____ **Prov. State** _____ **Zip** _____ CA75

FIRST CLASS
PERMIT NO. 3
HUNTINGTON,
INDIANA

BUSINESS REPLY MAIL
NO POSTAGE STAMP NECESSARY IF MAILED IN THE U.S.A.

postage will be paid by:

Our Sunday Visitor, Inc.
SALES SERVICE DEPT.
NOLL PLAZA
HUNTINGTON, INDIANA 46750

FIRST CLASS
PERMIT NO. 3
HUNTINGTON,
INDIANA

BUSINESS REPLY MAIL
NO POSTAGE STAMP NECESSARY IF MAILED IN THE U.S.A.

postage will be paid by:

Our Sunday Visitor, Inc.
SALES SERVICE DEPT.
NOLL PLAZA
HUNTINGTON, INDIANA 46750